Nineteenth-Century Literature Criticism

Guide to Gale Literary Criticism Series

When you need to review criticism of literary works, these are the Gale series to use:

If the author's death date is:	You should turn to:

**After Dec. 31, 1959
(or author is still living)**

CONTEMPORARY LITERARY CRITICISM

for example: Jorge Luis Borges, Anthony Burgess,
William Faulkner, Mary Gordon,
Ernest Hemingway, Iris Murdoch

1900 through 1959

TWENTIETH-CENTURY LITERARY CRITICISM

for example: Willa Cather, F. Scott Fitzgerald,
Henry James, Mark Twain, Virginia Woolf

1800 through 1899

NINETEENTH-CENTURY LITERATURE CRITICISM

for example: Fyodor Dostoevsky, Nathaniel Hawthorne,
George Sand, William Wordsworth

1400 through 1799

LITERATURE CRITICISM FROM 1400 TO 1800
(excluding Shakespeare)

for example: Anne Bradstreet, Daniel Defoe,
Alexander Pope, François Rabelais,
Jonathan Swift, Phillis Wheatley

SHAKESPEAREAN CRITICISM

Shakespeare's plays and poetry

Antiquity through 1399

CLASSICAL AND MEDIEVAL LITERATURE CRITICISM

for example: Dante, Homer, Plato, Sophocles, Vergil,
the Beowulf Poet

Gale also publishes related criticism series:

BLACK LITERATURE CRITICISM

This three-volume series presents criticism of works by major black writers of the past two hundred years.

CHILDREN'S LITERATURE REVIEW

This series covers authors of all eras who have written for the preschool through high school audience.

DRAMA CRITICISM

This series covers playwrights of all nationalities and periods of literary history.

POETRY CRITICISM

This series covers poets of all nationalities and periods of literary history.

SHORT STORY CRITICISM

This series covers the major short fiction writers of all nationalities and periods of literary history.

ISSN 0732-1864

Volume 38

Nineteenth-Century Literature Criticism

*Excerpts from Criticism of the
Works of Novelists, Poets, Playwrights,
Short Story Writers, Philosophers, and Other
Creative Writers Who Died between 1800
and 1899, from the First Published Critical
Appraisals to Current Evaluations*

*Joann Cerrito
Editor*

*Judith Galens
Tina Grant
Alan Hedblad
Drew Kalasky
Elisabeth Morrison
Lawrence J. Trudeau
Associate Editors*

 Gale Research Inc. • *DETROIT* • *WASHINGTON, D.C.* • *LONDON*

STAFF

Joann Cerrito, *Editor*

Alan Hedblad, Judith Galens, Tina Grant, Drew Kalasky, Elisabeth Morrison, Lawrence J. Trudeau, *Associate Editors*

James A. Edwards, Christine Haydinger, Brian J. St. Germain, Christopher K. King, Anna J. Sheets, *Assistant Editors*

Jeanne A. Gough, *Permissions & Production Manager*
Linda M. Pugliese, *Production Supervisor*
Paul Lewon, Maureen Puhl, Camille Robinson, Jennifer VanSickle, *Editorial Associates*
Donna Craft, Rosita D'Souza, Sheila Walencewicz, *Editorial Assistants*

Sandra C. Davis, *Permissions Supervisor (Text)*
Maria L. Franklin, Josephine M. Keene, Michele Lonoconus, Denise Singleton, Kimberly F. Smilay, *Permissions Associates*
Brandy Johnson, Shalice Shah, *Permissions Assistants*

Margaret A. Chamberlain, *Permissions Supervisor (Pictures)*
Pamela A. Hayes, *Permissions Associate*
Karla Kulkis, Nancy M. Rattenbury, Keith Reed, *Permissions Assistants*

Victoria B. Cariappa, *Research Manager*
Maureen Richards, *Research Supervisor*
Mary Beth McElmeel, Robert S. Lazich, Tamara C. Nott, *Editorial Associates*
Daniel J. Jankowski, Julie K. Karmazin, Donna Melnychenko, *Editorial Assistants*

Mary Beth Trimper, *Production Manager*
Catherine Kemp, *Production Assistant*

Cynthia Baldwin, *Art Director*
Nicholas Jakubiak, C. J. Jonik, *Keyliners*

Contents

Preface   vii

Acknowledgments   xi

Preface

Since its inception in 1981, *Nineteenth-Century Literature Criticism* has been a valuable resource for students and librarians seeking critical commentary on writers of this transitional period in world history. Designated an "Outstanding Reference Source" by the American Library Association with the publication of its first volume, *NCLC* has since been purchased by over 6,000 school, public, and university libraries. The series has covered more than 300 authors representing 26 nationalities and over 15,000 titles. No other reference source has surveyed the critical reaction to nineteenth-century authors and literature as thoroughly as *NCLC*.

Scope of the Series

NCLC is designed to serve as an introduction for students and advanced readers to the authors of the nineteenth century, and to the most significant interpretations of these authors' works. The great poets, novelists, short story writers, dramatists, and philosophers of this period are frequently studied in high school and college literature courses. By organizing and reprinting the enormous amount of commentary written on these authors, *NCLC* helps students develop valuable insight into literary history, promotes a better understanding of the texts, and sparks ideas for papers and assignments. Each entry in *NCLC* presents a comprehensive survey of an author's career or an individual work of literature and provides the user with a multiplicity of interpretations and assessments. Such variety allows students to pursue their own interests; furthermore, it fosters an awareness that literature is dynamic and responsive to many different opinions.

Every fourth volume of *NCLC* is devoted to literary topics that cannot be covered under the author approach used in the rest of the series. Such topics include literary movements, prominent themes in nineteenth-century literature, literary reaction to political and historical events, significant eras in literary history, prominent literary anniversaries, and the literatures of cultures that are often overlooked by English-speaking readers.

NCLC continues the survey of criticism of world literature begun by Gale's *Contemporary Literary Criticism (CLC)* and *Twentieth-Century Literary Criticism (TCLC)*, both of which excerpt and reprint commentary on authors of the twentieth century. For additional information about *TCLC, CLC*, and Gale's other criticism series, users should consult the Guide to Gale Literary Criticism Series preceding the title page in this volume.

Coverage

Each volume of *NCLC* is carefully compiled to present:

- criticism of authors, or literary topics, representing a variety of genres and nationalities
- both major and lesser-known writers and literary works of the period
- 7-10 authors or 4-6 topics per volume
- individual entries that survey critical response to each author's work or each topic in literary history, including early criticism to reflect initial reactions; later criticism to represent any rise or decline in reputation; and current retrospective analyses.

Organization of This Book

An author entry consists of the following elements: author heading, biographical and critical introduction, list of principal works, excerpts of criticism (each preceded by an annotation and followed by a bibliographic citation), and a bibliography of further reading.

- The author heading consists of the name under which the author most commonly wrote, followed by birth and death dates. If an author wrote consistently under a pseudonym, the pseudonym will be listed in the author heading and the real name given in parentheses on the first line of the biographical and critical introduction. Also located at the beginning of the introduction to the author entry are any name variations under which an author wrote, including transliterated forms for authors whose languages use nonroman alphabets.

- The **biographical and critical introduction** outlines the author's life and career, as well as the critical issues surrounding his or her work.

- Most *NCLC* entries include **portraits** of the author. Many entries also contain reproductions of materials pertinent to an author's career, including manuscript pages, title pages, dust jackets, letters, and drawings, as well as photographs of important people, places, and events in an author's life.

- The list of **principal works** is chronological by date of first book publication and identifies the genre of each work. In the case of foreign authors with both foreign-language publications and English translations, the title and date of the first English-language edition are given in brackets. Unless otherwise indicated, dramas are dated by first performance, not first publication.

- **Criticism** is arranged chronologically in each author entry to provide a perspective on changes in critical evaluation over the years. All titles of works by the author featured in the entry are printed in boldface type to enable the user to easily locate discussion of particular works. Also for purposes of easier identification, the critic's name and the publication date of the essay are given at the beginning of each piece of criticism. Unsigned criticism is preceded by the title of the journal in which it appeared. Publication information (such as publisher names and book prices) and parenthetical numerical references (such as footnotes or page and line references to specific editions of works) have been deleted at the editors' discretion to provide smoother reading of the text.

- Critical excerpts are prefaced by **annotations** providing the reader with information about both the critic and the criticism that follows. Included are the critic's reputation, individual approach to literary criticism, and particular expertise in an author's works. Also noted are the relative importance of a work of criticism, the scope of the excerpt, and the growth of critical controversy or changes in critical trends regarding an author. In some cases, these annotations cross-reference excerpts by critics who discuss each other's commentary.

- A complete **bibliographic citation** designed to facilitate location of the original essay or book follows each piece of criticism.

- An annotated list of **further reading** appearing at the end of each author entry suggests secondary sources on the author. In some cases it includes essays for which the editors could not obtain reprint rights.

Cumulative Indexes

- Each volume of *NCLC* contains a cumulative **author index** listing all authors who have appeared in Gale's Literary Criticism Series, along with cross-references to such biographical series as *Contemporary Authors* and *Dictionary of Literary Biography*. Useful for locating authors within the various series, this index is particularly valuable for those authors who are identified with a certain period but who, because of their death dates, are placed in another, or for those authors whose careers span two periods. For example, Fyodor Dostoevsky is found in *NCLC*, yet Leo Tolstoy, another major nineteenth-century Russian novelist, is found in *TCLC* because he died after 1899.

- Each *NCLC* volume includes a cumulative **nationality index** which lists all authors who have appeared in *NCLC*, arranged alphabetically under their respective nationalities, as well as Topics volume entries devoted to particular national literatures.

- Each new volume in Gale's Literary Criticism Series includes a cumulative **topic index,** which lists all literary topics treated in *NCLC, TCLC, LC 1400-1800*, and the *CLC* Yearbook.

- Each new volume of *NCLC*, with the exception of the Topics volumes, contains a **title index** listing the titles of all literary works discussed in the volume. In response to numerous suggestions from librarians, Gale has also produced a **special paperbound edition** of the *NCLC* title index. This annual cumulation lists all titles discussed in the series since its inception and is issued with the first volume of *NCLC* published each year. Additional copies of the index are available on request. Librarians and patrons will welcome this separate index: it saves shelf space, is easy to use, and is recyclable upon receipt of the following year's cumulation. Titles discussed in the Topics volume entries are not included in the *NCLC* cumulative index.

A Note to the Reader

When writing papers, students who quote directly from any volume in Gale's Literary Criticism Series may use the following general forms to footnote reprinted criticism. The first example pertains to material drawn from periodicals, the second to material reprinted from books.

[1] T. S. Eliot, "John Donne," *The Nation and the Athenaeum,* 33 (9 June 1923), 321-32; excerpted and

reprinted in *Literature Criticism from 1400 to 1800,* Vol. 10, ed. James E. Person, Jr. (Detroit: Gale Research, 1989), pp. 28-9.

[2] Clara G. Stillman, *Samuel Butler: A Mid-Victorian Modern* (Viking Press, 1932); excerpted and reprinted in *Twentieth-Century Literary Criticism,* Vol. 33, ed. Paula Kepos (Detroit: Gale Research, 1989), pp. 43-5.

Suggestions Are Welcome

In response to suggestions, several features have been added to *NCLC* since the series began, including annotations to excerpted criticism, a cumulative index to authors in all Gale literary criticism series, entries devoted to criticism on a single work by a major author, more extensive illustrations, and a title index listing all literary works discussed in the series since its inception.

Readers who wish to suggest authors or topics to appear in future volumes, or who have other suggestions, are cordially invited to write the editors.

ACKNOWLEDGMENTS

The editors wish to thank the copyright holders of the excerpted criticism included in this volume, the permissions managers of many book and magazine publishing companies for assisting us in securing reprint rights, and Anthony Bogucki for assistance with copyright research. We are also grateful to the staffs of the Detroit Public Library, the Library of Congress, the University of Detroit Library, Wayne State University Purdy/Kresge Library Complex, and the University of Michigan Libraries for making their resources available to us. Following is a list of the copyright holders who have granted us permission to reprint material in this volume of *NCLC*. Every effort has been made to trace copyright, but if omissions have been made, please let us know.

COPYRIGHTED EXCERPTS IN *NCLC,* VOLUME 38, WERE REPRINTED FROM THE FOLLOWING PERIODICALS:

The Byron Journal, n. 9, 1981. Reprinted by permission of the publisher.—*Criticism,* v. 11, Fall, 1969. Copyright, 1969, Wayne State University Press. Reprinted by permission of the publisher.—*The Dublin Review,* v. 227, 1953. Reprinted by permission of the editor of *The Month* Magazine.—*ESQ: A Journal of the American Renaissance,* v. 34, 1988 for "The Radical Emerson: Politics in 'The American Scholar' " by Robert E. Burkholder. Reprinted by permission of the publisher and the author.—*Feminist Studies,* v. 2, 1975. Copyright © 1975 by Feminist Studies, Inc. Reprinted by permission of the publisher, c/o Women's Studies Program, University of Maryland, College Park, MD 20742.—*Germanic Notes and Reviews,* v. 16, 1985. Reprinted by permission of the publisher.—*Harvard Theological Review,* v. 79, October, 1986. © 1986 by the President and Fellows of Harvard College. Reprinted by permission of the publisher.—*The Hudson Review,* v. XII, Spring, 1959. Copyright © 1959, renewed 1987 by The Hudson Review, Inc. Reprinted by permission of the publisher.—*Irish University Review,* v. 10, Autumn, 1980. © *Irish University Review.*—*The Journal of Modern History,* v. 41, June, 1969 for "Bentham Scholarship and the Bentham 'Problem' " by Gertrude Himmelfarb. © 1969 by The University of Chicago. Reprinted by permission of The University of Chicago Press and the author.—*The Journal of the Rutgers University Libraries,* v. XLIII, June, 1981 for "Bentham's 'The Rationale of Reward' " by Richard F. Hixson. Reprinted by permission of the author.—*The University of Kansas City Review,* v. XXII, June, 1956 for " 'Glenarvon' Revisited" by Clarke Olney. Copyright University of Kansas City, 1956. Reprinted by permission of the publisher and the author.—*Michigan Germanic Studies,* v. XIII, Spring, 1987. Copyright © 1987 by Michigan Germanic Studies. All rights reserved. Reprinted by permission of the publisher.—*The New England Quarterly,* v. LIX, December, 1986 for "From Greenough to 'Nowhere': Emerson's 'English Traits' " by Richard Bridgman. Copyright 1986 by *The New England Quarterly.* Reprinted by permission of the publisher and the author.—*PMLA,* no. 100, 1985 for "Newman's 'Apologia pro vita sua' and the Tradition of The English Spiritual Autobiography" by Linda H. Peterson. Copyright © 1985 by the Modern Language Association of America. Reprinted by permission of the Modern Language Association of America.—*The Quarterly Journal of Speech,* v. LVIII, February, 1972 for "Reading Emerson for the Structures: The Coherence of the Essays" by Lawrence I. Buell. Copyright 1972 by the Speech Communication Association. Reprinted by permission of the publisher and the author.—*The Southern Humanities Review,* v. 11, Fall, 1977. Copyright 1977 by Auburn University. Reprinted by permission of the publisher.—*Studies in English Literature, 1500-1900,* v. XIII, Autumn, 1973 for "Wordsworth's 'The Prelude' and the Failure of Language" by Jim Springer Borck. © 1973 William Marsh Rice University. Reprinted by permission of the publisher and the author.—*The Wordsworth Circle,* v. VI, Autumn, 1975; v. X, April, 1979. © 1975, 1979 Marilyn Gaull. Both reprinted by permission of the editor.—*The Yearbook of English Studies,* v. 19, 1989. © Modern Humanities Research Association 1989. All rights reserved. Reprinted by permission of the Editor and the Modern Humanities Research Association.

COPYRIGHTED EXCERPTS IN *NCLC,* VOLUME 38, WERE REPRINTED FROM THE FOLLOWING BOOKS:

Abrams, M. H. From *Natural Supernaturalism: Tradition and Revolution in Romantic Literature.* Norton, 1971. Copyright © 1971 by W. W. Norton & Company, Inc. All rights reserved. Reprinted by permission of the publisher.—Baumgardt, David. From *Bentham and the Ethics of Today.* Princeton University Press, 1952. Copyright 1952, renewed 1980 by Princeton University Press. Reprinted by permission of the publisher.—Beatty, Arthur. From *William Wordsworth: His Doctrine and Art In Their Historical Relations.* The University of Wisconsin Press, 1922.—Bishop, Jonathan. From *Emerson on the Soul.* Cambridge, Mass.: Harvard University Press, 1964. Copyright © 1964 by the President and Fellows of Harvard College. All rights reserved. Excerpted by permission of the publishers and the author.—Cecil, David. From *The Young Melbourne and the Story of His Marriage with Caroline Lamb.* Constable & Co. Ltd., 1939. Renewed 1966 by David Cecil. Reprinted by permission of the publisher.—Craig, Gordon A. From *The End of Prussia.* The University of Wisconsin Press, 1984. Copyright © 1984 The Board of Regents of the University of Wisconsin System. All rights reserved. Reprinted by permission of the publisher.—Gelpi, Albert. From "Emerson: The Paradox of Organic Form," in *Emerson: Prophecy, Metamorphosis, and Influence.* Edited by David Levin. Columbia University Press, 1975. Copyright © 1975 Columbia University Press. Reprinted by permission of the author.—Gilmour, Robin. From "Dickens and the Self-Help Idea," in *The Victorians and Social Protest: A Symposium.* Edited by J. Butt and I. F. Clarke. David & Charles, 1973. © J. Butt and I. F. Clarke 1973. All rights reserved. Reprinted by permission of the publisher.—Gingerich, Solomon Francis. From *Essays in the Romantic Poets.* The Macmillan Company, 1924. Copyright, 1924 by Macmillan Company. Renewed 1952 by Solomon F. Gingerich. All rights reserved. Reprinted with the permission of the publisher.—Graham, Peter W. From *Don Juan and Regency England.* University Press of Virginia, 1990. Copyright © 1990 by the Rector and Visitors of the University of Virginia. Reprinted by permission of the publisher.—Harrold, Charles Frederick. From *John Henry Newman: An Expository and Critical Study of His Mind, Thought and Art.* Longmans, Green & Co., 1945. Copyright, 1945 by Charles Frederick Harrold. Renewed 1973 by Elizabeth H. Harrold. All rights reserved.—Havens, Raymond Dexter. From *The Mind of a Poet: The Study of Wordsworth's Thought with Particular Reference to "The Prelude."* Johns Hopkins Press, 1941. Copyright 1941, renewed 1969 by The Johns Hopkins Press. Reprinted by permission of the publisher.—Holloway, John. From *The Proud Knowledge: Poetry, Insight and the Self, 1620-1920.* Routledge & Kegan Paul, 1977. © John Holloway, 1977. Reprinted by permission of the author.—Houghton, Walter E. From *The Art of Newman's "Apologia."* Yale University Press, 1945. Copyright, 1945, renewed 1973 by Yale University Press. All rights reserved. Reprinted by permission of the publisher.—Jay, Paul. From *Being in the Text: Self-Representation from Wordworth to Roland Barthes.* Cornell University Press, 1984. Copyright © 1984 by Cornell University Press. All rights reserved. Used by permission of the publisher, Cornell University Press.—Lindenberger, Herbert. From *On Wordsworth's "Prelude."* Princeton University Press, 1963. Copyright © 1963, renewed 1991 by Princeton University Press. All rights reserved. Reprinted by permission of the publisher.—Lyons, David. From "Was Bentham a Utilitarian?" in *Reason and Reality.* The Macmillan Press Ltd., 1972. © The Royal Institute of Philosophy 1972. All rights reserved. Reprinted by permission of The Royal Institute of Philosophy.—Mitchell, Sally. From *Dinah Mulock Craik.* Twayne, 1983. Copyright © 1983 by G. K. Hall & Company. Reprinted by the permission of author.—Packer, B. L. From *Emerson's Fall: A New Interpretation of the Major Essays.* Continuum, 1982. Copyright © 1982 by B. L. Packer. All rights reserved. Reprinted by permission of the publisher.—Paul, Sherman. From *Emerson's Angle of Vision: Man and Nature in American Experience.* Cambridge, Mass.: Harvard University Press, 1952. Copyright 1952 by the President and Fellows of Harvard College. Renewed 1980 by Sherman Paul. Excerpted by permission of the publisher and the author.—Porte, Joe. From *Representative Man: Ralph Waldo Emerson in His Time.* Oxford University Press, 1979. Copyright © 1979 by Oxford University Press, Inc. Reprinted by permission of the publisher.—Porter, David. From *Emerson and Literary Change.* Cambridge, Mass.: Harvard University Press, 1978. Copyright © 1978 by the President and Fellows of Harvard College. All rights reserved. Excerpted by permission of the publishers and the author.—Rexroth, Kenneth. From *The Elastic Retort: Essays in Literature and Ideas.* The Continuum Publishing Company, 1973. Copyright © 1973 by Kenneth Rexroth. Used by permission of Bradford Morrow of The Kenneth Rexroth Trust.—Robinson, David M. From "Grace and Works: Emerson's Essays in Theological Perspective," in *American Unitarianism: 1805-1865.* Edited by Conrad Edick Wright. The Massachusetts Historical Society and Northeastern University Press, 1989. Copyright © 1989 by the Massachusetts Historical Society and Northeastern University Press. All rights reserved. Reprinted by permission of the publishers.—Sharrock, Roger. From "Newman's Poetry," in *Newman after a Hundred Years.* Edited by Ian Ker and Alan G. Hill. Oxford at the Clarendon Press, 1990. © Oxford University Press, 1990. All rights reserved. Reprinted by permission of the publisher.—Stebbins, Lucy Poate. From *A Victorian Album: Some Lady Novelists of the Period.* Columbia University Press, 1946. Copyright 1946, renewed 1974 by Columbia University Press, New York. Used by permission of the publisher.—Strickland, Margot. From *The Byron Women.* Peter Own Limited, London, 1974. © Margot Strickland 1974. All rights reserved. Reprinted by permission of the publisher.—Tanner, Tony. From *The Reign of Wonder: Naivety and Reality in American Literature.* Cambridge at the University Press, 1965. © Cambridge University Press 1965. Reprinted with the permission of the publisher and the author.—Tillotson, Geoffrey. From "Newman the Writer," in *Mid-Victorian Studies,* By Geoffrey Tillotson and Kathleen Tillotson. The Athlone Press, 1965. © G. and K. Tillotson, 1965. Reprinted by permission of the publisher.—Van Doren, Mark. From *The Noble Voice: A Study of Ten Great Poems.* Henry Holt and Company, 1946. Copyright, 1946, by Henry Holt and Company, Inc. Renewed 1973 by Dorothy G. Van Doren. Reprinted by permission of the Literary Estate of Mark Van Doren.—Warren, Joyce W. From *The American Narcissus: Individualism and Women in Nineteenth-Century American Fiction.* Rutgers University Press, 1984. Copyright © 1984 by Joyce W. Warren. All rights reserved. Reprinted by permission of Rutgers, The State University.—Wilkie, Brian. From *Romantic Poets and Epic Tradition.* The University of Wisconsin Press, 1965. Copyright © 1965 by the Regents of the University of Wisconsin. Reprinted by permission of the publisher.

PHOTOGRAPHS AND ILLUSTRATIONS APPEARING IN *NCLC,* VOLUME 38, WERE RECEIVED FROM THE FOLLOWING SOURCES:

By permission of F. DeWolfe Miller: **p. 147.**

Bettina von Arnim

1785-1859

(Born Catarina Elisabetha Ludovica Magdalena Brentano) German memoirist and essayist.

INTRODUCTION

Arnim is regarded as a distinguished author of the German Romantic era and a leading influence on the cultural and social revolutions of her day. An advocate of reform, she criticized the reign of King Friedrich Wilhelm IV and called for the humane treatment of the poor and oppressed in her acclaimed essays, *Dies Buch gehört dem König* and *Gespräche mit Dämonen*. Although respected for her political writings, she is best remembered for her unconventional relationship with the renowned German author Johann Wolfgang von Goethe. A fervent Goethe admirer, Arnim corresponded with the author over the course of several years, and after his death in 1831, she published a fictionalized account of their relationship incorporating versions of their actual letters. *Goethes Briefwechsel mit einem Kinde: Seinem Denkmal* (*Goethe's Correspondence with a Child: For His Monument*) established her literary fame, but shocked readers with its eroticism and, in the estimation of some, its irreverent treatment of a national hero.

Arnim was born in Frankfurt into a large and respected literary family. Her brother, Clemens Brentano, was an acclaimed Romantic poet, and her maternal grandmother, Sophie von La Roche, was an accomplished novelist and friend of Goethe. Arnim lost her mother at an early age and was sent to a convent school at Fritzlar. After her father's death in 1797, she lived with La Roche. Around 1804 Arnim befriended a young poet, Caroline von Günderode, whom she fondly called "The Günderode." Deeply impressed by her friend's spiritual integrity, Arnim was distraught when Günderode, disturbed over a failed relationship with a married man, committed suicide in 1806. Arnim's brother advised her to overcome her depression by reading Goethe's novel, *Wilhelm Meisters Lehrjahre* (1795-96; *Wilhelm Meister's Apprenticeship*); greatly affected by this work, Arnim began to conceive of herself as Goethe's spiritual child and as Mignon, a principal character in the novel. Arnim's affinity with Goethe was intensified by her discovery of letters from him to her grandmother which allude to his romantic feelings for Arnim's mother. Arnim soon became friends with Goethe's mother and passed many hours listening to recollections of Goethe's youth, eventually adopting Goethe's mother as her own. In 1807 Arnim arranged to meet the author himself, an encounter that proved to be an overwhelming experience for the impressionable young woman. Soon afterward she and Goethe began to correspond with one another, Arnim writing enthusiastic and

amorous letters to the much older and married Goethe. Although Goethe never returned her affection and eventually terminated the relationship following a dispute between Arnim and his wife, Arnim remained devoted to the author until his death in 1832. Nevertheless, in 1811 she married the poet and novelist Achim von Arnim. After her husband's death in 1831, she wrote and published *Goethes Briefwechsel* and *Die Günderode: Den Studenten* (*Correspondence of Fräulein Günderode and Bettina von Arnim*), tributes to the two most influential persons in her life.

In 1843 Arnim turned her attention to political and social issues. She considered herself an unofficial advisor to the king and in her writings such as *Dies Buch gehört dem König* and *Gespräche mit Dämonen* set forth a plan of social reform which included the abolition of capital punishment, the emancipation of women, and the dignified treatment of workers. Aware of the economic hardships of the weavers in the region of Silesia, Arnim also lashed out at the king for his insensitivity to their impoverished state. In 1846, the Silesian weavers revolted and Arnim's political writings were cited as the cause of the uprising. Arnim was viewed with suspicion by authorities, and her essays with their strong socialist leanings were eventually seized, but she continued to devote herself to the plight of the disadvantaged for the remainder of her life. After several years of illness following a stroke, Arnim died in 1859 at the age of seventy-four.

The first two sections of the *Briefwechsel* contain partly fictionalized versions of Arnim's correspondence with Goethe and his mother together with descriptions of her thoughts and dreams and the recounting of the occurrences of her daily life. The third part of the work, entitled "Tagebuch" ("Diary"), is an imaginary "continuation" of her epistolary interchange with Goethe after his death. Drawing upon the Romantic symbol of the child as representing the innocent relationship between God and humanity, the *Briefwechsel* is a contemplation of the ideal love between parent and offspring, God and his creation. Arnim, who lacked a parental figure in her own life, presents herself as an adoring child in awe of Goethe, who is cast in the role of both God and father in the work. In her recollection of her first meeting with Goethe in 1807, she raises Goethe to the level of the Divine by describing her relation to her idol as that of "a lost child turning like a sunflower to its God." Elsewhere, she compares Goethe's mother to the Virgin Mary, echoing the accolade from the Gospel of Saint Luke, "Blessed is the womb that bore you." Significantly, while much of the *Briefwechsel* is given a distinctly religious coloring, much is also presented in markedly sensuous terms, such as the erotically imagined scenes of Arnim as a child being fondled while seated on Goethe's lap and his request to have her unbutton her blouse in order to cool off. Arnim's use of documentary material to create a work of fiction caused much confusion for readers. In their attempt to distinguish the real from the imaginary, many dismissed the work as a series of offensively indiscreet revelations or fabricated lies. *Die Günderode* utilizes the same technique of incorporating actual letters and recollections in a novelistic account of a relationship. Like the *Briefwechsel, Die Günderode* is a meditation on love, but this time Arnim focuses on an idealized friendship. The work presents a fictionalized biography filled with Arnim's memories and dreams of her girlhood confidant. The correspondence discusses a wide variety of subjects, from descriptions of encounters with men to disputes over the merits of poetic verse. The biography, critics note, is not meant to be read as an historical portrait of the tragic young poet, but as a spiritualized story of the deep abiding love between friends, and—unlike the *Briefwechsel*—between equals.

Arnim's first political treatise, *Dies Buch gehört dem König*, is an attempt to awaken the "sleeping king," as she called him, to the needs of his people. Couched in poetic and visionary language, the work is a three-way conversation between Goethe's mother, a clergyman, and a town magistrate in which Frau Goethe blames the church and the political establishment for the impoverished state of the German people and implores the king to address the grievances of the poor. To the end of the work Arnim appends a sociological case study of the poverty of the Vogtland region and the effects of industrialism upon the Prussian territories. *Dies Buch* inspired many to write satiric addresses to the sovereign and raised the consciousness of

the German people to the need for a constitutional monarchy and a free press. In 1852 Arnim tried again to advise the king in her *Gespräche mit Dämonen*. Similar in style to *Dies Buch*, this address describes the horrors of prison life and the wretched living conditions of the poor. Although many applauded her efforts at reform, Arnim was often misunderstood and harshly criticized, labeled by many as a radical for her unceasing intercession on behalf of the politically disenfranchised.

Critical interest in Arnim outside of Germany has been minimal since most of her works have not been translated into other languages. However, she gained attention in America through the efforts of the Transcendentalists. In 1842 Margaret Fuller completed a partial translation of *Die Günderode* and introduced Arnim to the Transcendental community as "one whose only impulse was to *live.*" Although some found Arnim's adulation of Goethe and her intense subjectivity troublesome, many, including Ralph Waldo Emerson and Emily Dickinson, admired her passionate and youthful spirit and considered her truly in touch with the primitive and essential in nature. Similarly, in the early twentieth century Danish critic George Brandes characterized Arnim's animated literary style as having a "refined wildness, a rhythmic ring and flow, which astound and fascinate." In recent decades, some attention has been devoted to Arnim as a prototype of the emancipated woman. A close examination of her writings has led critics to stress that her works are not biographies but autobiographies, or psychological self-portraits. Others, however, maintain that the "Goethe," "Günderode," and "Bettina" found in Arnim's works are fictional characters created through literary dialogue and representing different aspects of the author's personality rather than historical persons. Although some critical debate persists regarding the merit of her works, Arnim's unique personality has continually fascinated commentators. As Arthur Helps and Elizabeth Jane Howard have observed, "She was a Liberal, a freak, an eccentric and a furious dilettante: her mind streaked with brilliance—her heart with affections, loyalties and adorations, although never, perhaps, with love—but above all she was a life-long, a militant romantic."

PRINCIPAL WORKS

Goethes Briefwechsel mit einem Kinde: Seinem Denkmal
(fiction) 1835 (*Goethe's Correspondence with a Child: For His Monument,* 1837-38)
Die Günderode: Den Studenten (fiction) 1840
[*Günderode* (partial translation), 1842; *Correspondence of Fräulein Günderode and Bettina von Arnim* (completed translation), 1861]
Dies Buch gehört dem König. 2 vols. (prose) 1843
Clemens Brentanos Frühlingskranz aus Jugendbriefen ihm geflochten, wie er selbst schriftlich verlangte (prose) 1844
Ilius Pamphilius und die Ambrosia. 2 vols. (prose) 1847-48
Gespräche mit Dämonen (prose) 1852
Bettina von Arnims Sämtliche Werke. 7 vols. [edited by Waldemar Oehlke] (prose and letters) 1920-22

Werke und Brief. 4 vols. [edited by Gustav Konrad and Joachim Müller] (prose and letters) 1959-63

Margaret Fuller (essay date 1842)

[*A distinguished critic and early feminist, Fuller played an important role in the developing cultural life of the United States during the first half of the nineteenth century. As a founding editor of the Transcendentalist journal* The Dial, *and later as a contributor to Horace Greeley's* New York Tribune, *she was influential in introducing European art and literature to the United States. She wrote social, art, and music criticism, but she is most acclaimed as a literary critic; many rank her with Edgar Allan Poe as the finest in her era. In the following excerpt, Fuller discusses Arnim's correspondence, questioning her objectivity and adoration of Goethe while delighting in the beauty of her friendship with Günderode.*]

Bettine Brentano's letters to Goethe, published under the title of **Goethe's Correspondence with a Child,** are already well known among us and met with a more cordial reception from readers in general than could have been expected. Even those who are accustomed to measure the free movements of art by the conventions that hedge the path of daily life, who, in great original creations, seek only intimations of the moral character borne by the author in his private circle, and who, had they been the contemporaries of Shakspeare, would have been shy of visiting the person who took pleasure in the delineation of a Falstaff;—even those whom Byron sneers at as "the garrison people," suffered themselves to be surprised in their intrenchments, by the exuberance and wild, youthful play of Bettine's genius, and gave themselves up to receive her thoughts and feelings in the spirit which led her to express them. They felt that here was one whose only impulse was to *live*,—to unfold and realize her nature, and they forgot to measure what she did by her position in society.

There have been a few exceptions of persons who judged the work unworthily, who showed entire insensibility to its fulness of original thought and inspired fidelity to nature, and vulgarized by their impure looks the innocent vagaries of youthful idolatry. But these have been so few that, this time, the vulgar is not the same with the mob, but the reverse.

If such was its reception from those long fettered by custom, and crusted over by artificial tastes, with what joy was it greeted by those of free intellect and youthful eager heart. So very few printed books are in any wise a faithful transcript of life, that the possession of one really sincere made an era in many minds, unlocking tongues that had long been silent as to what was dearest and most delicate in their experiences, or most desired for the future, and making the common day and common light rise again to their true value, since it was seen how fruitful they had been to this one person. The meteor playing in our sky diffused there an electricity and a light, which revealed unknown attractions in seemingly sluggish substances, and lured many secrets from the dim recesses in which they had been cowering for years, unproductive, cold, and silent.

Yet, while we enjoyed this picture of a mind tuned to its highest pitch by the desire of daily ministering to an idolized object; while we were enriched by the results of the Child's devotion to him, hooted at by the Philistines as the "Old Heathen," but to her poetic apprehension "Jupiter, Apollo, all in one," we must feel that the relation in which she stands to Goethe is not a beautiful one. Idolatries are natural to youthful hearts noble enough for a passion beyond the desire for sympathy or the instinct of dependence, and almost all aspiring natures can recall a period when some noble figure, whether in life or literature, stood for them at the gate of heaven, and represented all the possible glories of nature and art. This worship is, in most instances, a secret worship; the still, small voice constantly rising in the soul to bid them harmonize the discords of the world, and distill beauty from imperfection, for another of kindred nature has done so. This figure whose achievements they admire is their St. Peter, holding for them the keys of Paradise, their model, their excitement to fulness and purity of life, their external conscience. When this devotion is silent, or only spoken out through out private acts, it is most likely to make the stair to heaven, and lead men on till suddenly they find the golden gate will open at their own touch, and they heed neither mediator nor idol more. The same course is observable in the religion of nations, where the worship of Persons rises at last into free thought in the minds of Philosophers.

But when this worship is expressed, there must be singular purity and strength of character on the part both of Idol and Idolater, to prevent its degenerating into a mutual excitement of vanity, or mere infatuation.

"Thou art the only one worthy to inspire me;" cries one.

"Thou art the only one capable of understanding my inspiration," smiles back the other.

And clouds of incense rise to hide from both the free breath of heaven!

But if the idol stands there, grim and insensible, the poor votary will oftentimes redouble his sacrifices with passionate fervor, till the scene becomes as sad a farce as that of Juggernaut, and all that is dignified in human nature lies crushed and sullied by one superstitious folly.

An admiration restrained by self-respect; (I do not mean pride, but a sense that one's own soul is, after all, a regal power and a precious possession, which, if not now of as apparent magnificence, is of as high an ultimate destiny as that of another) honors the admirer no less than the admired. But humility is not groveling weakness, neither does bounty consist in prodigality; and the spendthrifts of the soul deserve to famish on husks for many days; for, if they had not wandered so far from the Father, he would have given them bread.

In short we are so admirably constituted, that excess anywhere must lead to poverty somewhere; and though he is mean and cold, who is incapable of free abandonment to a beautiful object, yet if there be not in the mind a counterpoising force, which draws us back to the centre in proportion as we have flown from it, we learn nothing from our experiment, and are not vivified but weakened by our love.

Something of this we feel with regard to Bettine and Goethe. The great poet of her nation, and representative of half a century of as high attainment as mind has ever made, was magnet strong enough to draw out the virtues of many beings as rich as she. His greatness was a household word, and the chief theme of pride in the city of her birth. To her own family he had personally been well known in all the brilliancy of his dawn. She had grown up in the atmosphere he had created. Seeing him up there on the mountain, he seemed to her all beautiful and majestic in the distant rosy light of its snow-peaks. Add a nature, like one of his own melodies, as subtle, as fluent, and as productive of minute flowers and mosses, we could not wonder if one so fitted to receive him, had made of her whole life a fair sculptured pedestal for this one figure.

All this would be well, or rather, not ill, if he were to her only an object of thought; but when the two figures are brought into open relation with one another; it is too unequal. Were Bettine, indeed, a child, she might bring her basket of flowers and strew them in his path without expecting even a smile in return. But to say nothing of the reckoning by years, which the curious have made, we constantly feel that she is not a child. She is so indeed when compared with him as to maturity of growth, but she is not so in their relation, and the degree of knowledge she shows of life and thought compels us to demand some conscious dignity of her as a woman. The great art where to stop is not evinced in all passages. Then Goethe is so cold, so repulsive, diplomatic, and courteously determined not to compromise himself. Had he assumed truly the paternal attitude, he might have been far more gentle and tender, he might have fostered all the beauteous blossoms of this young fancy, without ever giving us a feeling of pain and inequality. But he does not; there is an air as of an elderly guardian flirting cautiously with a giddy, inexperienced ward, or a Father Confessor, who, instead of through the holy office raising and purifying the thoughts of the devotee, uses it to gratify his curiosity. We cannot accuse him of playing with her feelings. He never leads her on. She goes herself, following the vision which gleams before her. "I will not," he says, "while the little bird from its nest," and he does not. But he is willing to make a tool of this fresh, fervent being; he is unrelenting as ever in this. What she offers from the soul the artist receives,—to use artistically. Indeed we see, that he enjoyed as we do the ceaseless bee-like hum of gathering from a thousand flowers, but only with the cold pleasure of an observer; there is no genuine movement of a greateful sensibility. We often feel that Bettine should perceive this, and that it should have modified the nature of her offerings. For now there is nothing kept sacred, and no balance of beauty maintained in her life. Impatiently she has approached where she was not called, and the truth and delicacy of spiritual affinities has been violated. She has followed like a slave where she might as a pupil. Observe this, young idolaters. Have you chosen a bright particular star for the object of your vespers? you will not see it best or revere it best by falling prostrate in the dust; but stand erect, though with upturned brow and face pale with devotion.

An ancient author says, "it is the punishment of those who have honored their kings as gods to be expelled from the gods," and we feel this about Bettine, that her boundless abandonment to one feeling must hinder for a time her progress and that her maturer years are likely to lag slowly after the fiery haste of her youth. She lived so long, not for truth, but for a human object, that the plant must have fallen into the dust when its prop was withdrawn, and lain there long before it could economize its juices enough to become a tree where it had been a vine.

We also feel as if she became too self-conscious in the course of this intimacy. There being no response from the other side to draw her out naturally, she hunts about for means to entertain a lordly guest, who brings nothing to the dinner, but a silver fork. Perhaps Goethe would say his questions and answers might be found in his books; that if she knew what he was, she knew what to bring. But the still human little maiden wanted to excite surprise at least if not sympathy by her gifts, and her simplicity was perverted in the effort. We see the fanciful about to degenerate into the fantastic, freedom into lawlessness, and are reminded of the fate of Euphorion in Goethe's great Rune.

Thus we follow the course of this intimacy with the same feelings as the love of Tasso, and, in the history of fiction, of Werther, and George Douglas, as also those of Sappho, Eloisa, and Mlle. de L'Espinasse. There is a hollowness in the very foundation, and we feel from the beginning,

> It will not, nor it cannot come to good.

Yet we cannot but be grateful to circumstances, even if not in strict harmony with our desires, to which we owe some of the most delicate productions of literature, those few pages it boasts which are genuine transcripts of private experience. They are mostly tear-stained;—by those tears have been kept living on the page those flowers, which the poets present to us only when distilled into essences. The few records in this kind that we possess remind us of the tapestries woven by prisoners and exiles, pathetic heirlooms, in noble families.

Of these letters to Goethe some have said they were so pure a product, so free from any air of literature, as to make the reader feel he had never seen a genuine book before.

Another, "She seems a spirit in a mask of flesh, to each man's heart revealing his secret wishes and the vast capacities of the narrowest life."

But the letters to Goethe are not my present subject; and those before me with the same merits give us no cause however trifling for regret. They are letters which passed between Bettine, and the Canoness Günderode, the friend to whom she was devoted several years previous to her acquaintance with Goethe.

The readers of the *Correspondence with a Child* will remember the history of this intimacy, and of the tragedy with which it closed, as one of the most exquisite passages in the volumes. The filling out of the picture is not unworthy the outline there given.

Günderode was a Canoness in one of the orders described

by Mrs. Jameson, living in the house of her order, but mixing freely in the world at her pleasure. But as she was eight or ten years older than her friend, and of a more delicate and reserved nature, her letters describe a narrower range of outward life. She seems to have been intimate with several men of genius and high cultivation, especially in philosophy, as well as with Bettine; these intimacies afforded stimulus to her life, which passed, at the period of writing, either in her little room with her books and her pen, or in occasional visits to her family and to beautiful country-places.

Bettine, belonging to a large and wealthy family of extensive commercial connexions, and seeing at the house of grandmother Me. La Roche, most of the distinguished literati of the time, as well as those noble and princely persons who were proud to do honor to letters, if they did not professedly cultivate them, brings before us a much wider circle. The letters would be of great interest, if only for the distinct pictures they present of the two modes of life; and the two beautiful figures which animate and portray these modes of life are in perfect harmony with them.

I have been accustomed to distinguish the two as Nature and Ideal. Bettine, hovering from object to object, drawing new tides of vital energy from all, living freshly alike in man and tree, loving the breath of the damp earth as well as that of the flower which springs from it, bounding over the fences of society as easily as over the fences of the field, intoxicated with the apprehension of each new mystery, never hushed into silence by the highest, flying and singing like the bird, sobbing with the hopelessness of an infant, prophetic, yet astonished at the fulfilment of each prophecy, restless, fearless, clinging to love, yet unwearied in experiment—is not this the pervasive vital force, cause of the effect which we call nature?

And Günderode, in the soft dignity of each look and gesture, whose lightest word has the silvery spiritual clearness of an angel's lyre, harmonizing all objects into their true relations, drawing from every form of life its eternal meaning, checking, reproving, and clarifying all that was unworthy by her sadness at the possibility of its existence. Does she not meet the wild, fearless bursts of the friendly genius, to measure, to purify, to interpret, and thereby to elevate? As each word of Bettine's calls to enjoy and behold, like a free breath of mountain air, so each of Günderode's comes like the moonbeam to transfigure the landscape, to hush the wild beatings of the heart and dissolve all the sultry vapors of day into the pure dewdrops of the solemn and sacred night.

The action of these two beings upon one another, as representing classes of thoughts, is thus of the highest poetical significance. As persons, their relation is not less beautiful. An intimacy between two young men is heroic. They call one another to combat with the wrongs of life; they buckler one another against the million; they encourage each other to ascend the steeps of knowledge; they hope to aid one another in the administration of justice, and the diffusion of prosperity. As the life of man is to be active, they have still more the air of brothers in arms than of fellow students. But the relation between two young girls is essentially poetic. What is more fair than to see little girls,

hand in hand, walking in some garden, laughing, singing, chatting in low tones of mystery, cheek to cheek and brow to brow. Hermia and Helena, the nymphs gathering flowers in the vale of Enna, sister Graces and sister Muses rise to thought, and we feel how naturally the forms of women are associated in the contemplation of beauty and the harmonies of affection. The correspondence between very common-place girls is interesting, if they are not foolish sentimentalists, but healthy natures with a common groundwork of real life. There is a fluent tenderness, a native elegance in the arrangement of trifling incidents, a sincere childlike sympathy in aspirations that mark the destiny of woman. She should be the poem, man the poet.

The relation before us presents all that is lovely between woman and woman, adorned by great genius and beauty on both sides. The advantage in years, the higher culture, and greater harmony of Günderode's nature is counterbalanced, by the ready springing impulse, richness, and melody of the other.

And not only are these letters interesting as presenting this view of the interior of German life, and of an ideal relation realized, but the high state of culture in Germany which presented to the thoughts of those women themes of poesy and philosophy as readily, as to the English or American girl come the choice of a dress, the last concert or assembly, has made them expressions of the noblest aspiration, filled them with thoughts and oftentimes deep thoughts on the great subjects. Many of the poetical fragments from the pen of Günderode are such as would not have been written, had she not been the contemporary of Schelling and Fichte, yet are they native and original, the atmosphere of thought reproduced in the brilliant and delicate hues of a peculiar plant. This transfusion of such energies as are manifested in Goethe, Kant, and Schelling into these private lives is a creation not less worthy our admiration, than the forms which the muse has given them to bestow on the world through their immediate working by their chosen means. These are not less the children of the genius than his statue or the exposition of his method. Truly, as regards the artist, the immortal offspring of the Muse,

> Loves where (art) has set its seal,

are objects of clearer confidence than the lives on which he has breathed; they are safe as the poet tells us death alone can make the beauty of the actual; they will ever bloom as sweet and fair as now, ever thus radiate pure light, nor degrade the prophecy of high moments, by compromise, fits of insanity, or folly, as the living poems do. But to the universe, which will give time and room to correct the bad lines in those living poems, it is given to wait as the artist with his human feelings cannot, though secure that a true thought never dies, but once gone forth must work and live forever.

We know that cant and imitation must always follow a bold expression of thought in any wise, and reconcile ourself as well as we can to those insects called by the very birth of the rose to prey upon its sweetness. But pleasure is unmingled, where thought has done its proper work and fertilized while it modified each being in its own kind. Let him who has seated himself beneath the great German oak, and gazed upon the growth of poesy, of philosophy, of criticism, of historic painting, of the drama, till the life of the last fifty years seems well worth man's living, pick up also these little acorns which are dropping gracefully on the earth, and carry them away to be planted in his own home, for in each fairy form may be read the story of the national tree, the promise of future growths as noble.

The talisman of this friendship may be found in Günderode's postscript to one of her letters, "If thou findest Muse, write soon again," I have hesitated whether this might not be, "if thou findest Musse (leisure) write soon again;" then had the letters wound up like one of our epistles here in America. But, in fine, I think there can be no mistake. They waited for the Muse. Here the pure products of public and private literature are on a par. That inspiration which the poet finds in the image of the ideal man, the man of the ages, of whom nations are but features, and Messiahs the voice, the friend finds in the thought of his friend, a nature in whose positive existence and illimitable tendencies he finds the mirror of his desire, and the spring of his conscious growth. For those who write in the spirit of sincerity, write neither to the public nor the individual, but to the soul made manifest in the flesh, and publication or correspondence only furnish them with the occasion for bringing their thoughts to a focus.

The day was made rich to Bettine and her friend by hoarding its treasures for one another. If we have no object of the sort, we cannot live at all in the day, but thoughts stretch out into eternity and find no home. We feel of these two that they were enough to one another to be led to indicate their best thoughts, their fairest visions, and therefore theirs was a true friendship. They needed not "descend to meet."

Sad are the catastrophes of friendships, for they are mostly unequal, and it is rare that more than one party keeps true to the original covenant. Happy the survivor if in losing his friend, he loses not the idea of friendship, nor can be made to believe, because those who were once to him the angels of his life, sustaining the aspiration of his nobler nature, and calming his soul by the gleams of pure beauty that for a time were seen in their deeds, in their desires, unexpectedly grieve the spirit, and baffle the trust which had singled them out as types of excellence amid a sullied race, by infirmity of purpose, shallowness of heart and mind, selfish absorption or worldly timidity, that there is no such thing as true intimacy, as harmonious development of mind by mind, two souls prophesying to one another, two minds feeding one another, two human hearts sustaining and pardoning one another! Be not faithless, thou whom I see wandering alone amid the tombs of thy buried loves. The relation thou hast thus far sought in vain is possible even on earth to calm, profound, tender, and unselfish natures; it is assured in heaven, where only chastened spirits can enter,—pilgrims dedicate to Perfection.

As there is no drawback upon the beauty of this intimacy—there being sufficient nearness of age to give Günderode just the advantage needful with so daring a child as Bettine, and a sufficient equality in every other respect—

so is every detail of their position attractive and picturesque. There is somewhat fantastic or even silly in some of the scenes with Goethe; there is a slight air of travestie and we feel sometimes as if we saw rather a masque aiming to express nature, than nature's self. Bettine's genius was excited to idealize life for Goethe, and gleams of the actual will steal in and give a taint of the grotesque to the groupes. The aim is to meet as nymph and Apollo, but with sudden change the elderly prime minister and the sentimental maiden are beheld instead. But in the intercourse with Günderode there is no effort; each mind being at equal expense of keeping up its fires. (pp. 313-23)

Margaret Fuller, in an originally unsigned essay, "Bettine Brentano and Her Friend Günderode," in The Dial: Magazine for Literature, Philosophy, and Religion, *Vol. II, No. III, January, 1842, pp. 313-56.*

Ralph Waldo Emerson on Arnim's genius, in a letter to Margaret Fuller (1839?):

The only thing in my mind to be said to you is to clear myself of my faint praise in some note lately concerning Bettina's book which now that I have read moves all my admiration. What can be richer and nobler than that woman's nature. What life more pure and poetic amid the prose and derision of our own time. So pure a love of nature I never found in prose or verse. What a lofty selection in character! What unerring instinct in action. If I went to Germany I should only desire to see her? Why do you not write to her? She must be worth all the Jamesons and Müllers on earth. It seems to me she is the only formidable test that was applied to Goethe's genius. He could well abide any other influence under which he came. Here was genius purer than his own, and if without the constructive talent on which he valued himself yet he could not have disguised from himself the fact that she scorned it on the whole—though I think he appears sometimes to great advantage under the sharp ordeal—he is too discreet and cowardly to be great and mainly does not make one adequate confession of the transcendant superiority of this woman's aims and affections in the presence of which all his Art must have struck sail.

Is it not wonderful what inspirations women have. I find Horace Walpole declaring every advantage to be on their side in his acquaintance with French society, &c They always add religion to talent, and so give our hope an infinite play until society gets possession of them and carries them captive to Babylon. If they would only hold themselves at their own price, if they would not subdue their sentiments, the age of heroes would come at once!

Ralph Waldo Emerson, in The Letters of Ralph Waldo Emerson, Vol. II, *edited by Ralph L. Rusk, Columbia University Press, 1939.*

Thomas Wentworth Higginson   (journal date 1878)

[*An American social reformer and writer, Higginson had a varied career that began with his association with the New England Transcendentalists during the 1830s and 1840s and lasted into the twentieth century. He was an active abolitionist and campaigner for women's rights as well as a prominent literary figure who wrote essays, criticism, history, biographies, and fiction. The following extracts from Higginson's diary for 1878 were taken from Mary Thacher Higginson's 1914 biography of her husband. They record the writer's travels in Germany to sites mentioned by Arnim and express his joy in evoking the mood and spirit of her works.*]

Just now I am reading *Günderode* with ever-new delight: I wish there were a million volumes. Really there is not an author in the world, save Emerson and Shakespeare, from whom I have had so much and so fresh enjoyment as from the perennial Child, Bettine. Her effervescence always intoxicates me with delight; though her life flowed prematurely away in it, like champagne left uncorked.

Bingen, Aug. 7. Hard at work on the castles with intervals of my dear Bettine Brentano on whose tracks I now am. . . . My main object just here is Bettine and I made a long dreamed of pilgrimage to her best loved haunt, whence many of her letters were written, the ruined chapel of St. Roch. . . . I found with dismay that the beautiful little ruin which Bettine describes as recently destroyed has been rebuilt but what was my delight to go round it and find a little ruin of two arches and a wall still remaining, with an altar and a stone crucifix, grim and battered, apparently the very one up which she climbed to stick a bunch of wild flowers in the top. I could have done the same in continuing her work for there were harebells like ours and heather in bloom all around, but just as I sprang down, a fair young priest such as she would have rejoiced in came reading his breviary round the corner and it was well to be discreet. He also cooled my ardor a little by saying that this little ruin was of a second chapel to St. Michael which also stood there—still I dare say it was the same crucifix. She used to write to Goethe there and kept his letters buried there and has an exquisite description of going to sleep there in the moonlight on the wall and having to sleep there all night. She planted grapevines and honeysuckle and lilies there and she says 'all sorts of plants,' but there were only some ivy roots of which I took one and shall try to make it grow.

Aug. 8. From Bingen to Frankfort. O, what a charming day! wandering along the Rhine with Bettine in my hand, studying out all the scenes of the letters I have always enjoyed so much. First I crossed by ferry to Rudesheim and tried to fix the spot where Günderode was found dead. . . . Bettine landed at Rudesheim that day and ran straight up Ostein, a mountain a mile high she says. . . . I went up the same hill. It is a steep paved vineyard path. The valley was utterly still and bathed in heat, it seemed, as B. writes elsewhere, as if the leagues of ripening grapes sent up an incense. Along the path grew yarrow, tanzy and succory, just as in New England; the present emperor loves succory flowers especially and they always bring him bunches of it on public days. . . . At two I went on by train to Winkel—Bettine's regular summer home. . . . I staid long on the shore [of the Rhine] and the nearly 70 years since 1809 seemed nothing—the two girls were still young to me. I think I found the place where Günderode died. . . . I walked back through the long villages again. It was very hot. I had an hour at the station and lay down

on a bench and slept as Bettine would have done. . . . It is such a delight to have an ideal object, especially in traveling alone.

Aug. 9. Frankfort. Here still was Bettine, but lost in the greater stream of Goethe. The Goethe house was my chief interest. . . . Below were his magnificent mother's rooms . . . portraits of her . . . in the very room where she used to sit and chat with Bettine and they were (as the latter says) the only two people *alive* in Frankfort or anywhere else. (pp. 343-46)

Thomas Wentworth Higginson, in a diary entry in 1878 in Thomas Wentworth Higginson: The Story of His Life *by Mary Thacher Higginson, Houghton Mifflin Company, 1914, pp. 343-46.*

George Brandes (essay date 1890)

[*Brandes, a Danish literary critic and biographer, was the principal leader of "Det modern gennbruch" ("the modern breaking-through"), the intellectual movement that helped bring an end to Scandinavian cultural isolation. He believed that literature reflects the spirit and problems of its time and that it must be understood within its social and aesthetic context. Often controversial, Brandes was a prolific and highly influential critic, admired for his ability to view literary movements within the broader context of virtually all of nineteenth-century literature. In the following excerpt from a study originally published in Danish in 1890, he lauds Arnim for her enthusiastic devotion to Goethe, her animated literary style, and her later interest in social reform.*]

Bettina von Arnim, a sister of Clemens Brentano, wife of Achim von Arnim, by family and marriage connected with the Romanticists, nevertheless belongs as an authoress to the Young German school. Rahel [Varnhagen von Ense] admired and worshipped Goethe timidly, with a beating heart, a quiet, dignified seriousness. Bettina's admiration showed itself in an insinuating, half-sensuous, half-intellectual devotion, a determined bur-like adhesiveness, and flights of the wildest enthusiasm.

In 1807, when she, as a native of the same town, made Goethe's acquaintance through his mother, she must have been twenty-three, but in her ways she was still a child, or rather a being midway between child and woman. She comes to Weimar, provides herself with a superfluous letter of introduction from Wieland, holds out both her hands to Goethe as soon as she sees him, and forgets herself altogether. He leads her to the sofa, seats himself beside her, talks about the Duchess Amalie's death, asks if she has read about it in the newspaper. "I never read newspapers," said I. "Indeed! I understood that you were interested in all that goes on at Weimar." "No, I am only interested in you, and I'm far too impatient to be a newspaper reader." "You are a kind, friendly girl." A long pause. She jumps up from the sofa and throws her arms round his neck.

This little anecdote suffices to show the difference between her position to Goethe and Rahel's. From her childhood she had been distinguished by a youthful daring more often met with in boys than girls. At Marburg they still show a tower to the top of which she climbed, drawing the ladder up after her, so that she might be alone. Along with the agility of a young acrobat, she had something of Mignon's childlike, innocent devotion. She is Mignon in real life, as charming as ever, and far less serious.

In 1835, when her *Goethe's Briefwechsel mit einem Kinde* came out, Bettina was fifty. Arnim had died in 1831, Goethe in 1832. She had got back the letters written by herself to Goethe between 1808 and 1811, when an end was put to their intercourse by an act of discourtesy on her part towards Frau Goethe, and had taken even greater liberties with these letters than Goethe took in *Dichtung und Wahrheit* with the experience of his past life. She expressed in them not only all that she had felt, but much that she now thought she ought to have felt; she gave to their intercourse a more passionate colouring than really belonged to it, and yet in the profoundest sense she was truthful. The letters were at first accepted as genuine. But strong suspicions were presently awakened by the fact of Bettina's having published poems, which were undoubtedly addressed to other women, as if they had been written to her; and there came a time when her letters lost all credit as historic documents, and everything in them was considered to be fictitious. In 1879, however, Loeper published the genuine letters written by Goethe to Bettina, and it was then seen that in them she had made almost no alteration; a few greetings were omitted and *thou* was substituted for *you*—nothing more. In only one of the original letters is she addressed as *thou,* but that letter is the only one which Goethe did not dictate, but wrote with his own hand, so Bettina's alteration was not altogether unjustifiable. Goethe was in the habit of enclosing in his letters any poem which he had just written. Bettina was conceited enough to imagine that poems addressed to Minna Herzlieb (even those which played upon the name Herzlieb, and were consequently incomprehensible to her) and to Marianne von Willemer, were meant for her. This was an absurd but excusable mistake. It was inexcusable of her to transpose these poems into prose and incorporate them in her earlier letters, thereby producing the impression that Goethe had simply put her thoughts and feelings into verse.

What she tells us of her intercourse with Goethe's mother, of her eagerness to gather from that mother's lips information about Goethe's childhood which might serve as an introduction to *Dichtung und Wahrheit,* and also what she tells about Beethoven and the relation in which she stood to him, is in all essentials absolutely true.

No one with any feeling for poetic enthusiasm who has read Bettina's book in his youth will ever forget the first impression produced by her style. There is a vitality about it, an animation, a refined wildness, a rhythmic ring and flow, which astound and fascinate. Turning from Rahel's dark hieroglyphs, which suggest a thousand secrets to us, but which we seldom really understand, because the living life which was the commentary is no more, it is refreshing to bathe in this clear spring of naïve and charming devotion. Rahel is more profound and more realistic. But talent is such a marvellous thing. The pleasure it gives is great. We can and must excuse much for its sake.

In these letters Bettina is twenty-three to twenty-five years old, Goethe fifty-eight to sixty. Hence her passion is not the ordinary human passion of a young woman for a young man. She has grown up with it; it is an inheritance from her mother, Maxe Brentano, who partly suggested Werther's Charlotte. She loves Goethe's mother, as a young woman always does love the mother of her beloved; she is grateful to her for having borne him—"how else should I have known him!" Her devotion to the son finds expression in letters to the mother, till she meets him; then she writes to himself.

After that first embrace she looks upon him as her own. She writes to his mother: "It is possible to acquire a kind of possession of a man which no one can dispute. This I have done with Wolfgang. And it is what no one ever did before, in spite of all these love affairs you have told me about. Love is the key of the universe; through it the spirit learns to comprehend and to feel everything. How else could it learn!"

These letters have been compared to ships laden with rich cargoes. Goethe is the guiding star on all their voyages.

All her thoughts of him are thoughts of enthusiastic devotion:

> I would I were sitting at his door like some poor beggar child, so that he might come out to give me a piece of bread. He would read in my eyes what I am, would take me into his arms and wrap his cloak round me to warm me. I know he would not tell me to go again; I should have

Bettina as Mignon.

my place in his house; years would pass, and no one would know where I was; years would pass and life would pass; I should see the whole world mirrored in his face, and more I should not need to learn.

Last May, when I saw him for the first time, he picked a young leaf from the vine at his window and held it against my cheek and said: "Which is softer, the leaf or your cheek?" I was sitting on a stool at his feet. How often I have thought of that leaf, and of how he stroked my forehead and my face with it, and played with my hair, and said: "I am a simple-minded man; it is easy to deceive me; there would be no glory in doing it." There was nothing brilliant in these words, but I have lived that scene over again a thousand times in my thoughts; I shall drink it in all my life, as the eye drinks light—it was not intellectual converse, no! but to me it surpasses all the wisdom of the world.

There is poetry in this exaltation and in the way in which she tells of his constant presence with her, of her longing for him, of her dumb jealousy of the famous women who came, as Madame de Staël did, to make his acquaintance; there is poetry in her distress at her inability to be of any use to him, and in her vivid appreciation of her own capacity.

I must tell you what I dreamt about you last night. I often have the same dream. I am going to dance for you. I have the feeling that my dance will be a success. A crowd has gathered round me. I look for you, and see you sitting alone, straight opposite to me; but you don't seem to see me. With golden shoes on my feet, my shining silver arms hanging listlessly by my side, I step forward in front of you, and wait. You lift your head, your eyes involuntarily rest upon me; with light steps I begin to trace magic circles, and you keep your eyes upon me. You follow me through all my bends and turns; I feel the triumph of success. All that you dimly feel I show you in my dance; you marvel at the wisdom it reveals. Presently I fling aside my airy mantle, and let you see my wings, and away I fly, up to the heights. It rejoices me that your eyes follow me, and I float down again and sink into your open arms.

This symbolic description is both graceful and felicitous. In Bettina's Goethe-worship there is something of the same love of mounting and climbing that she displayed in her childhood. She climbed up on to the shoulder of the great Olympian's statue—a statue she was perpetually modelling—drew the ladder up after her, and sat there alone, revelling in the pleasure of being so near him. But it was not her Goethe-worship merely as such which made Bettina an ideal character, a Valkyrie, in the eyes of Young Germany. What won their hearts was the political liberalism to which she gave expression in her letters, and with which she in vain tried to imbue the sage who sat aloof in Weimar, her ardent admiration for the brave resistance of the Tyrolese to the domination of France, her eager desire for the well-being of humanity, for the extermination of poverty and all the other ills of society. It made a powerful impression when she, a worshipper of

Goethe, but a more independent-minded one than Rahel, extolled Beethoven's republicanism as greater, worthier than Goethe's submissive loyalty. She tries to bring Goethe and Beethoven together; she wishes she could send Wilhelm Meister to the Tyrol, to Andreas Hofer, that he might learn to feel greater enthusiasm and to do manly deeds.

In the commencement of Frederick William's reign she was in favour at court. There was a frank, friendly intimacy between her and the king; she had almost as much influence upon him as Humboldt, when there was any question of assisting talent or alleviating misery. But before long her feelings led her openly to declare socialistic principles. In 1843 she published ***Dies Buch gehört dem König*** ("This Book belongs to the King"), a work in which she calls upon Frederick William to relieve the distress of his subjects. From her youth she had looked upon herself as the natural champion and advocate of the distressed. "The forsaken and unhappy possessed a magnetic attraction for her," says Hermann Grimm, who, as her son-in-law, knew her intimately. Her natural inclination to help others, and the early impressions made on her mind by the French Revolution, produced those political sympathies to which she unhesitatingly gave utterance, in the naïve expectation of receiving support from royalty.

In 1831, when the cholera raged in Berlin, she went fearlessly among the sick and suffering. Judging from the hard lot of the Berlin working classes, she came to the conclusion that the whole nation was in a bad way and in need of help. To her, liberty had always been a magic word. She believed that whenever the words "Let there be light!" resounded from the right quarter, liberty would manifest itself, and all the feelings and dreams of humanity would take shape in harmonious music, to the strains of which the peoples would march joyfully onwards.

Her book, which in a little introductory parable she dedicates to the king, is written in the form of conversations. Goethe's mother is the chief speaker. There is much warm feeling in the book, and a considerable amount of information on the subject of the distress among the lower classes, but too little political insight to make it readable nowadays.

The authoress reaches a climax with the words:

Our sign is the banner of liberty; its brightness lights up the black darkness of the times; its brilliancy dazzles and terrifies those who are on the shore, but we are glad and rejoice. . . . Dangers? Liberty knows no dangers! To it everything is possible. The storm itself, the wildest of all storms, is the captain of our ship."

Such sentiments were not likely to meet with a favourable reception at the Prussian court of that day. The book created a sensation, but put an end to the good understanding between Bettina and the king. It naturally only increased the political discontent of the masses, and a pretext was found for seizing her next book (on Clemens Brentano), because a repetition of the same sort of thing was feared.

Long before this, however, Bettina had received the unanimous homage of the younger generation. Those interested should read Gutzkow's account of his first visit to her, Mundt's description of her, Kühne's poetical appreciation. Even Robert Prutz, severe as he is on all the representatives and models of Young Germany, numbers himself among her admirers. "Bettina's letters are," he says, "the last bright blaze of Romanticism, the sparkling, crackling fireworks with which it closes its great festival; but they are at the same time the funeral pile upon which it consumes itself, the pillar of fire which rises from its ashes—and shows us the way." (pp. 290-96)

> George Brandes, "Rahel, Bettina, Charlotte
> Stieglitz," in his Main Currents in Nineteenth
> Century Literature: Young Germany, Vol.
> VI, *translated by Mary Morison, William
> Heinemann, 1905, pp. 277-304.*

Gordon A. Craig   (lecture date 1982)

[*Craig is an American critic, educator, and author of several works on Prussian history. In the following excerpt, taken from a lecture that was first delivered in 1982, Craig traces Arnim's career, particularly emphasizing her work as a political and social activist and her impact upon the future generation of reformers.*]

To call Bettina a realist would seem to be a willful denial of the extent to which she was herself a product of the romantic period. The granddaughter of Sophie de la Roche, the friend of Wieland, and herself the author of sentimental novels, she was the sixth of eight gifted and eccentric children of an Italian import dealer who lived in Frankfurt am Main and a German mother whose beauty had attracted the attention of the young Goethe. Bettina's older brother Clemens was a poet of considerable power, a collector of folk songs, and the author of fairy-tales (like "The Tale of Gockel and Hinkel") and some of the most influential stories of the romantic period, like the death-laden "History of True Kasperl and Beautiful Annerl." Clemens not only guided his sister's reading but introduced her to his friends and acquaintances in the arts, and she soon became spoiled, precocious, and self-centered, given to bizarre language and strange conceits. "My soul is a passionate dancer," she wrote to her brother. "She dances to hidden music which only I can hear. You may tell me to be calm and demure, but my soul does not listen and goes on dancing; if the dance were to stop, it would be the end of me. I trust the elements in myself that want to kick over the traces."

It was at Clemens's suggestion that, at the age of fifteen, she read Goethe's *Wilhelm Meister,* in consequence of which, and perhaps because of her knowledge of her mother's abortive affair with its author she became obsessed with the poet. She began to think of herself as Mignon, the mysterious child whom Goethe/Meister saves from the acrobats and who subsequently falls in love with him. Like Mignon, she began to strike exotic attitudes and to sleep with her hands folded on her breast. She made friends with Goethe's mother, who lived in Frankfurt, and could not rest until she had met the poet himself, which she succeeded in doing in 1807, thereafter bombarding him with a stream of letters filled with her dreams and enthusiasms and with demands and admonitions and decla-

rations of love that must have bewildered and perhaps exhausted the sage of Weimar, who was already fifty-eight years old when Bettina burst upon him. She had a similarly emotional correspondence with Karoline von Günderode, a poetess who finally committed suicide in a suitably romantic manner because she was disappointed in love, and with Ludwig van Beethoven, whose stature she, with her brother and E. T. A. Hoffmann, recognized sooner than most contemporaries and with whom, in long intimate letters, she discussed the electrical qualities of music and its power to dissolve the barriers between souls.

In a letter to Goethe's mother, Bettina wrote, "I really belong to the period of the extreme romantics, and I should have been a character in *Werther* and would have been turned out of doors by Lotte." But, if this was true, it was also true that, even when she was young, her emotional transports were always balanced by a strong satirical sense and the gift of self-mockery. Writing to her sister Gunda about a letter from Goethe, she could say:

> I have been so happy since I got this letter that
> the most terrible disaster might befall me and I
> would not notice it. Adieu, my friend and sharer
> of my joys, adieu, Gundel—[you want] 2 wursts,
> 3 lbs. noodles, ¼ cwt. candles, but what do you
> think? this very moment I have got a second let-
> ter from Goethe: it is incredible, a storm of
> blessed lightning strikes the house: the flames
> leap up over my head, and I do not move but
> burn with joy and enthusiasm: the ashes go with
> the wind, the spirit hies itself to Abraham's
> bosom or wherever it likes, but why does Gundel
> want such a quantity of noodles? I can't stand
> them.

The romantic was, in fact, quite capable of dealing with such mundane things as noodles and candles and, when she married Achim von Arnim, who had been her brother's collaborator in the collection of folk songs called *Des Knaben Wunderhorn,* she proved to be a loving wife and helpmate for twenty years, bearing seven children and managing Arnim's estate at Wiepersdorf and his house in Berlin with efficiency. Moreover, when her husband died in 1831, she did not hesitate to direct her old romanticism into practical channels, by writing two letter-novels, ***Goethe's Correspondence with a Child*** and ***The Günderode,*** that made her famous and left her reasonably well off.

In her youth, Bettina had once written, "What is the use of all my energy and enterprise if I have no means of applying it? I feel like a warrior who longs to do great deeds but who lies in prison laden with chains with no hope of rescue." This feeling of frustration had been relieved by her marriage, by her acquaintance with Goethe, and by her tribute to his memory, which was published, it should be remembered, at a time when his reputation was in decline and when it had become fashionable to denigrate his achievement. But what was she to do now that her debt to Goethe was discharged and her husband dead?

The answer was that she began to turn her attention to politics. Her house became a gathering place for the new political and cultural opposition to the government, a place where one might meet liberals of the 1813 generation like Varnhagen and Alexander von Humboldt, members of the reviving *Burschenschaft* movement (Bettina dedicated her Günderode book to the student generation), and radical writers of the Young German movement like Karl Gutzkow and Ludolf Wienbarg. Her salon was as famous as Rahel Levin's had once been and more oriented to contemporary political issues upon which Bettina did not hesitate to declare herself. She became, indeed, a force in liberal politics, and there was nothing adventitious about this. She had always been a free spirit and a believer in engagement, and even in her youth her brother had written a poem to her in which he said [in his *Gedichte,* edited by Wolfgang Frühwald, Bernhard Gajek, and Friedhelm Kemp, 1977] that everything that was touched by her creative spirit was awakened to a new life of freedom:

> Alles Bettine! dem liebend Dein schaffender
>   Geist sich genährt,
> Was Deine segnende Hand, was Dein Gedanke
>   berührt,
> Blühet schöner ein Freiheit verklärendes Leben.

An early instance of her new political engagement came in 1839. Two years earlier, seven professors of the University of Göttingen had been dismissed from their posts by the king of Hanover because they refused to break their oaths to a constitution that he had abrogated. Two of them, the philologists and folklorists Jakob and Wilhelm Grimm, who were members of the Prussian Academy, hoped to find posts in Prussia but received no support, either from the academy's president, Karl Lachmann, or from Karl Savigny, an intimate advisor of the king, both of whom justified their position with contrived political and legal arguments. This enraged Bettina, and she addressed a long letter to Savigny, who was her brother-in-law, with a copy to the king. She pointed out that the case of the Grimms might seem, as Savigny had intimated, too trivial to be brought to the government's attention, and yet the grand duke of Weimar had not hesitated to open his borders to the expelled professors. It was necessary, she wrote pointedly, for Prussia to do the same. "One can act greatly even in trivial things, but that which cries to heaven is never trivial."

Then in a passage that pointed to the future, Bettina wrote:

> I know you wouldn't say this to the king, for to tell a prince about the mistakes his government makes or to show him a more elevated point of view would be contrary to the politics of respect. . . . You treat princes like automata. . . . You make to them only the speeches they are able to answer without waking up, for the truth would waken them, and they wouldn't be automata any more, but independent rulers, and reason of state would no longer be bound up with baseness, but would be transformed into world wisdom, which comes from God's wisdom.

This passage helps to explain Bettina's attitude and behavior once Frederick William IV had become king. When the high hopes that had attended his accession began to fade, she became convinced that he was in the hands of evil counsellors. As she was to write later:

> Ah! the evil intrigues that encircle the lofty spirit of a prince, until the nobility of his soul is wounded to death and a woeful tragedy is performed . . . in which his retainers exude a fog of lies about him and no hero of the truth [*Wahrheitsheld*] is present to master this evil.

More than most princes, Frederick William needed a *Wahrheitsheld,* and Bettina nominated herself for that position.

This could be described as a quixotic and essentially romantic notion, and Werner Vordtriede has explained it [in his *Bettina von Arnims Armenbuch,* 1981] by saying that, in contrast to her brother Clemens, Bettina had foresworn Christianity but always needed a God on earth who could be father, friend, lover, and companion and that Frederick William was her substitute for Goethe, who had filled those roles. This wholly overlooks the fact that the king's chosen counsellors *were* bad counsellors, caught as they were in the romantic conservatism of the post-1815 period, and that Bettina's advice for the king was in no wise romantic but focused on some hard realities that were being generally overlooked. In her role as self-appointed royal advisor, she continued to call the king's attention to injustice to individuals, to breaches of civil liberties, to restrictions on thought and expression; but the center of her attention—and here she was certainly among the clearest-eyed of her generation—was the evils generated by the new industrialism.

As early as 1831, when she risked her life to bring relief to the victims of the cholera epidemic, Bettina had become aware of the misery and squalor of the area outside the Hamburger Gate in Berlin, an industry-created slum called the Vogtland. In the '40s, she often visited it with friends, and there is a story, doubtless apocryphal, that on one occasion her companion was a young man called Karl Marx. In 1842, when she published a curious work which she called "This Book Belongs to the King," she included at the end a collection of case studies of poverty in the Vogtland, an unprecedented little sociological study of the results of industrialism. The text of the King's Book, as it was called, was largely cast in the form of a series of discussions between Goethe's mother, a parson, and a *Bürgermeister,* in the course of which Goethe's mother, speaking for Bettina, placed the blame for these conditions upon the orthodox church and the bureaucracy.

The book might have had little effect. It was difficult to read; the king professed to be baffled by it; and after reading it a young poet named Theodor Fontane . . . wrote a poem to Bettina in which he said that her spirit was like a lark ascending to heaven but that, unfortunately, it often disappeared behind clouds that were impenetrable to ordinary humans:

> Dein Geist nimmt, wie auf Lerchenschwingen,
> Tief in den Himmel seinen Zug,
> Und freudig lausch' ich seinem Singen
> Und freudig folg' ich seinem Flug.
>
> Doch wie die Lerch' auf ihren Zügen
> Oftmals im Äther mir verschwimmt,
> So auch dein Geist auf seinen Flügen,
> Wenn er zu hoch ins Blaue klimmt.

But government heavy-handedness saved it. When a shortened version was prepared by Bettina's friend Adolf Stahr, it was seized by the authorities, which of course advertised it and inspired imitation. Adolf Glassbrenner wrote a poignant *Petition to the King* which purported to be from "ein janz armer Mann, der nicht weis, wo er Haupt hinkriechen soll" ("a very poor man who doesn't know where he can lay his head") and there were other experiments in this genre. Moreover, Bettina was herself encouraged to more systematic effort. She appealed to the press for information about poverty in other parts of Prussia, intending to publish it in an *Armenbuch* (Book of the Poor). In its original form, this plan had to be abandoned, again because of government intervention. Bettina was, indeed, getting on officialdom's nerves, and a widely publicized remark of hers to the effect that the king's enthusiasm for completing the long-delayed construction of Cologne Cathedral was misplaced and that it would do more good if he built it in Silesia and gave employment to the people of that distressed area led to furious charges from the ministry of the interior that she was inciting to riot. She was, in fact, held responsible for the subsequent rising of the Silesian weavers in 1846, an event that shocked the nation and seemed to portend the kind of collapse that came in 1848. During the revolution of that year, Bettina was under surveillance, and her pen was still. It was only after the revolution was over and reaction was setting in again that she returned stubbornly to her fixed idea and tried for the last time to talk with the king, this time in an even more turgid and largely unread book called *Conversation with Demons.*

It is clear, from sketches that Bettina made for the exordium of the unwritten *Armenbuch,* and from the strange dialogues between the author and the sleeping king in the new book, that Bettina did not know what caused poverty and, indeed, appeared at times to regard it as a form of damnation that had no rational cause and could be solved only by a general spiritual regeneration. What she was sure of was that the country could not survive this evil. She recognized, sooner than most, that the social problem was the real problem of the future and necessarily the government's first priority. And by the government, she meant the king. Between him and his people there was indeed—as Frederick William had sensed in his homage ceremonies—a mystical bond that made him the people's natural leader. If he refused to allow false counsellors to mislead him, if he was ever conscious of the problems of the poor, the fourth and most vulnerable estate of his realm, if he granted them their proper share in the nation's affairs, so that their voice was heard and their advice considered, the result could only be national integration and social peace. But first the king must awaken and seek his natural allies.

If all this seems too simple to be practical (Heinrich Heine, for one, thought it was and in one of his verses said that the very idea that Bettina might be taken seriously was a sign that the world was turned upside down), it should be remembered that, at a later time, when the nation was riven by class discord and political disorientation, a not unsophisticated man, Friedrich Naumann, returned to the essence of Bettina's idea in his *Demokratie und Kaisertum,* in which he saw a firm alliance between crown and people

as the alternative to social chaos. But we need not dwell upon the question of practicality. Bettina's realism lay in pointing out that the world had changed and no longer resembled the one that captivated the imagination of the king and his counsellors, and that the new industrialism and its social effects were the problem that had to be dealt with if Prussia was to become a sound and progressive state. As she once wrote:

> The poor should be able to have a share in public affairs, for the legislators would then acquire sounder views about citizenship and public welfare. Since the poor are a fourth, and indeed the greatest, estate, why are they not represented by deputies? . . . The interests of the other three estates must yield to that of this fourth estate. Cities have property; the land has property; rulers have property and thrive on it. Why has poverty no property? The poor, deprived of their rights, are citizens who are too weak to protect themselves. One can find protection for public freedom only where the true power is. We are not in a position to be free except with the people and through the people.

(pp. 30-9)

Gordon A. Craig, "Romance and Reality: Bettina von Arnim and Bismarck," in his The End of Prussia, *The University of Wisconsin Press, 1984, pp. 27-47.*

Charlotte M. Craig   (essay date 1985)

[*A native of Czechoslovakia, Craig is now a professor of German language and literature in the United States. In the following excerpt, she explores the influence of the women in Arnim's life and concludes that their example helped shape the memoirist into a great literary figure, social activist, and prototype of the emancipated woman.*]

"Jetzt rat Sie einmal, was der Schneider für mich macht," Bettina writes to Frau Rat Goethe on March 20, 1807 [in her *Werke und Briefe,* edited by Gustav Konrad, 1959], "Ein Paar Hosen . . . Ja!—Vivat jetzt kommen andre Zeiten angerückt . . . und dann werf ich mich in eine Chaise und reise Tag und Nacht Kourier durch die ganzen Armeen zwischen Feind und Freund hindurch; alle Festungen tun sich vor mir auf, und so geht's fort . . . wo einige Geschäfte abgemacht werden, die mich aber nichts angehn." The dawning of a new time, indeed. Brimming with enthusiasm, ebullient with the enterprising spirit which characterized her during most phases of her life, this autobiographical morsel sums up the quintessence of the young, venturesome girl ready to take on the world. Beyond capturing a charming pose of the trousered tomboy, this silhouette points to an evolving image—not a prototype—in an age of transition, while symbolically foreshadowing her future role as a pioneer feminist and advocate in social issues.

Paradoxical as it may seem, "wearing the pants" while casting herself as a child—really a mask for awakening womanhood—contributes to evoking the elusive property of the Eternal Feminine which made up a substantial ingredient of her enigmatic personality. Lacking a concrete definition, the quality has been perceived as a synthesis of various aspects ranging from pure and exalted to disparaging and, traditionally, the whole spectrum of meanings and misapprehensions between the two extremes, but always in the frame of reference of the "typically feminine." Defying evaluation by standard norms in this respect as well, Bettina emerges as atypical, and her mentors sensed it. Her volatility, her assertiveness—a veritable study in spontaneity—her ease in dealing with men and women in elevated strata, reflect her instinctive awareness of the equality between the sexes—an awareness which provided an essential, psychological balance in a young life which was dominated by women.

Half-orphaned at the age of eight, educated chiefly at the Ursuline Convent school in Fritzlar, Bettina came to feel drawn to two maternal figures who influenced her life at a highly impressionable stage, nurtured her intellect and her considerable artistic penchant, as well as sharpening her instincts along with her appetite for prominence.

Her maternal grandmother, Sophie La Roche, provided a home, as well as guidance and character molding to the now fully-orphaned Bettina and her sisters at the "Gril-

lenhütte" in Offenbach. The values which the surrogate mother sought to impart to her charges had been the values stressed in her literary products. Since her theories on the "modern education of women" had been enthusiastically accepted and subsequently forgotten, La Roche made no point of devising any rigorous curricular plans for Bettina of whose resistance to sustained concentration she was well aware. The experience of her own daughters' trauma had mellowed her tremendously.

In spite of the inevitable generation gap the relationship between Bettina and her grandmother is reported to have been tender, particularly because they were temperamentally suited to each other. To the surviving link with the past, to her heritage, then, Bettina owed her growing sense of mission: the anticipation of a maternal concern with what was, what is and will be, in short—the business of handing on a tradition while plotting her own course.

Surely, the lingering aura of the celebrated grandmother's earlier success and the idea of prominence left an indelible impression on Bettina. The title heroine of La Roche's best seller, *Geschichte des Fräuleins von Sternheim,* a paragon of the Eternal Feminine in all its positive aspects, had been Sophie La Roche's "paper maiden"—a surrogate daughter whom she proceeded to educate vicariously according to her practical ideals, for the benefit of her readers.

If the plot held limited appeal to a later generation, the epistolary genre certainly became the foremost instrument of Bettina's literary production and more: beyond the necessity as a means of communication, correspondence became a habit which she cultivated, a way of life. The grandmother's library, the discriminating circle of intellectuals and artists to which Bettina was exposed afforded her ample opportunity to develop her talents and, above all, her cult of celebrities, the satisfaction of being on familiar terms with the prominents, which is documented as a lifelong predilection, indeed a passion.

Among the most emotionally charged events of her life at the La Roche home is her discovery of Goethe's letters concerning his relationship with her mother, Maxe. At this point Bettina is twenty-one years of age and certainly no longer a child. While deeply moved at resurrecting the memory of her long-departed mother the find strikes her as a pre-ordained signal for her personal reapprochement to Goethe—a precious legacy which was to turn into an ambitious if problematic project more systematically pursued than any other in her career.

After Sophie La Roche's death, following the intimate friendship with Karoline von Günderode, which ended by the latter's initiative and suicide, Bettina, bereft again, chooses Frau Aja as her friend, confidante, and intermediary to Goethe. In spite of the age difference, this elective affinity soon turns into a mutually satisfying, close relationship. Bettina does not conceal the method behind her rapturous enthusiasm: ". . . es liegt was im Hintergrund dabei, was mich selig macht, die Jugend ihres Sohnes fließt wie Tau von ihren mütterlichen Lippen . . . und hierdurch lern' ich, daß, seine Jugend allein mich erfüllen sollte" [***Bettina von Arnims Sämtliche Werke,*** edited by Waldemar Oehlke, 1922]. Gaining access to Goethe, her ideal who was destined to become the central experience of her life, was her ambition.

Indeed, at Frau Aja's, Bettina felt truly as a child not only because she had found a spiritual home, but because, prompted by her urging, Goethe's mother took pride and pleasure in relating her son's youthful experiences to the spellbound Bettina. Apparently, the retrospect rejuvenated both the narrator and the eager listener who enjoyed steeping herself into the role of a youngster so as to gain the proper perspective of approach. Of these sessions Bettina reports, "Ich bin sehr glücklich mit dieser Frau, ich seh sie alle Tage, ich darf bei ihr gut und böse Launen äußern, wie ein verzogenes Kind bei der lieben Mutter" [*Bettinas Buefwechsel nut Goethe,* edited by Reinhold Steig, 1922]. The feeling was mutual. "Liebe—liebe Tochter!" Goethe's mother writes on June 13, 1807, "Nenne mich ins künftige mit dem mir so teuren Namen Mutter—und Du verdienst ihn so sehr, so ganz und gar—mein Sohn sei Dein inniggeliebter Bruder—Dein Freund, der Dich gewiß liebt und stolz auf deine Freundschaft ist"; and she signs the letter "Deine Dich liebende Mutter Goethe."

Bettina's sentiments are, to be sure, colored by different emotions. As she quotes his mother's lines in a letter to Goethe (June 15, 1807), she reaches for the telling rhetorical question to characterize her feelings: "Solche Worte schreibt mir Goethes Mutter; zu was berechtigen mich diese?—Auch brach es los wie ein Damm in meinem Herzen . . . Und was will ich denn? . . . Mutwilling und übermütig bin ich auch zuweilen. . . ."

In the manner of a practiced biographer, Bettina recorded reams of notes on Goethe while constructing an image in her mind before ever making his personal acquaintance. With motherly instinct and more than passing interest, Elisabeth Goethe followed Bettina's zealous queries. Responses, such as ". . . ich hab Dir's ja immer gesagt: wart nur bis einmal ein andrer kommt, so wirst du schon nicht mehr nach ihm seufzen," (March 14, 1807), or later, the hortative "Sei aber nicht zu toll mit meinem Sohn, alles muß in seiner Ordnung bleiben" (May 12, 1808), are not rare. When the pining Bettina vents her yearnings while trying to set Mother Goethe at ease, "da braucht Sie nicht zu fürchten, daß ich die Ordnung umstoße. Ich häng mich nicht wie Blei an meinen Schatz. Ich bin der Mond, der ihm ins Zimmer scheint . . ." (Schlangenbad, n.d. [May 1808]), Frau Rat chides her most resolutely:" . . . was bild'st Du Dir ein? . . . wer ist denn Dein Schatz, der an Dich denken soll bei Nacht im Mondschein?—Meinst Du, der hätt nichts Bessers zu tun?—Ja proste Mahlzeit. Ich sag Dir noch einmal: alles in der Ordnung, und schreib ordentliche Briefe, in denen was zu lesen ist" (May 25).

Of the meeting with Goethe in Weimar, Bettina reports (May 16, 1807) to have summoned all her courage for the first personal encounter. Yet, vacillating in an ambivalence of feelings, she chooses the route via an intermediary of influence: Wieland. Equipped with an introductory note from the puzzled Wieland, Bettina, teetering between inhibition and resolution, exhausted after three sleepless nights of travel, finally meets Goethe face to face on April 23, 1807. So monumental is the experience that impulse

overpowers her to revert to the apparatus of a child: right or wrong, disarming in her candor, she registers in rapid succession a spectrum of sentiments ranging from fright, curiosity, impatience, to the demonstrative gesture of an embrace and, spent from the tumultuous outbreak, she falls into a slumber held cradled to his chest.

The impact on her psyche and the subsequent summary to her elective "mother" seems to underscore the appellation "Kind": long accustomed to be so addresssed by Frau Aja, Bettina was now Goethe's "freundliches Kind"—a reference which exceeded the issue of the age difference, but provided a positive connotation of propriety, which ultimately found its way into the title of the published correspondence. Counting on Aja's intimate knowledge of her impetuousness, she makes a fleeting effort of excusing and legitimizing her behavior—a mingling of childlike and erotic manifestations: "Ach Mutter! . . . alles verging. Ich hatte so lange nicht geschlafen; Jahre waren vergangen in Sehnsucht nach ihm—ich schlief an seiner Brust ein; und da ich aufgewacht war, begann ein neues Leben."

There is no evidence of any reply to this ecstatic effusion. In September 1807, she resorts to Frau Aja as a "Mother Confessor," actually admitting pangs of jealousy over Goethe—a very feminine tailing, particularly where no legitimate claim exists: "Ich sag lhr, . . . daß ich ihr mein heimlichstes Herz vertraue;—ich muß wohl jemand haben, dem ich's mitteile." Her dependence on Aja as a psychological prop is documented in a letter of March 5 (1808): ". . . wenn die Mutter nicht wär, der Winter (in Frankfurt) wär unerträglich, so ganz ohne Hältnis . . . ."

If Bettina's passion for Goethe eventually moderated to an unaffected intimacy, if the mutual attraction had its fluctuation, their lives had been both enriched and complicated—aggravated and tempered by social convention. In Bettina's pathos, their relationship embodied the realization of her mother's inheritance to which she felt fully entitled, including the painful side effects and the consequences of resignation.

Upon his request, she handed over to Goethe her carefully compiled notes of his mother's memoirs for eventual use in his autobiography. A record of his past in the idiosyncratic style of the self-appointed transcriber—this contribution is probably the kindest—if not selfless—most defensible legacy among the assorted challenges Bettina had chosen to present to Goethe. Originally a personal indulgence, a wily girl's diversion, a means to a personal end, the exercise indeed became "Ereignis," i.e., it was ameliorated by the spirit of giving.

With characteristic capacity of creating Romantic chaos, Bettina managed to raise eyebrows, voices, suspicions. A high-strung intellectual with a low tolerance for average mentalities—especially in women—a discomfortingly inquiring mind, a contagiously undisciplined enthusiast, a flirt, a headache, a troublemaker—Bettina's endowment with the Eternal Feminine, inherited and acquired, emerges as a dominant factor. It is perpetuated in her marriage, her long widowhood, in her dealings with the influential and the high-minded. Accustomed from early youth to being surrounded by the prominent, she continues to seek out those who are mutually fascinating and, with advancing maturity, those who could be moved to act on her behalf for the support of others.

When Rahel Varnhagen von Ense quotes Schleiermacher describing Bettina as "lauter Sinnlichkeit, die sich aber niemals konzentriere" [in Ingeborg Drewitz's *Bettine von Arnim: Romantik—Revolution—Utopie,* 1969] K. A. Varnhagen cites her buoyancy, her magnanimity, her charity, along with her vanity and fixed ideas, Caroline Schlegel registers her aversion to Bettina's eccentricity plus dash of hysteria, of which she seems to have made a fetish, and Jacob Grimm defended her tendency toward exaggeration as typically feminine, the appraisals of these contemporaries contribute to the portrait of the aging Bettina.

Increasingly, she places her talents and powers selflessly in the service of those who, in her opinion, needed active support. In the face of adversity, sentiments and compassion galvanize her to sustained action. While her household and family duties had filled her time and drained her energies without providing sufficient challenges, she finds redeeming outlets for manifesting the Eternal Feminine within a societal context. Helping and advising young women, organizing others to raise funds and collect clothing during the cholera epidemic of 1831 are activities reminiscent of the motherly concerns and initiative of her grandmother's Lady Seymour, née von Sternheim, whose "reizende[r] Enthusiasmus von Wohltätigkeit, die lebende Empfindung des Edlen und Guten" are cited as an example to be emulated. But beyond that, the biographer and talented causeuse had become an activist and a polemicist—a role which, she felt, her time demanded of her. Theatrics have given way to serious pursuits. Agitation is inspired by the concern for the common good. More passionate than systematic in approach, she favored direct action over theorizing. The youthful image of her "wearing the pants," i.e., asserting herself and taking charge, extends into maturity and beyond. In her work with the guilds, the workers' locals, her intercession on behalf of women, support of poor minorities, her interest in the problems of students, her commitment to the fight for the rights of the defenseless and against the plight of the poor, by exposing a host of social shortcomings, she became an able advocate of the needs of the Prussian people. In her correspondence with her monarch, Frederick William IV she pleads the case of reform toward a constitution, a democratic society free from censorship—another big order and probably the most ambitious mission of her life. When she meets failure, the capacity for renunciation learned in earlier lessons stands her in good stead.

The extraordinary dedication to the principles of service helps channel her vitality, her inclination toward sensationalism, even her obtrusiveness and selfish interests, into the arena of humanitarian, social, and political thought and action. The truly ennobling aspects of the Eternal Feminine prevail. Bettina has given them a new dimension. (pp. 54-7)

> *Charlotte M. Craig, "Heritage and Elective Affinity: Bettina Arnim's Surrogate Mother and the Eternal Feminine," in* Germanic Notes and Reviews, *Vol. 16, No. 1, 1985, pp. 54-7.*

Marjanne E. Goozé   (essay date 1987)

[*In the following excerpt, Goozé analyzes Arnim's correspondence with Goethe as a distinctive literary creation in which the letters serve as the medium of a fantasy seduction of an absent lover.*]

Prominent German women of the late eighteenth and early nineteenth centuries such as Rahel Varnhagen, Henriette Herz, and Caroline Schlegel-Schelling are known primarily through their letters and diaries; and although Dorothea Schlegel, Sophie Mereau, and Bettine von Arnim also published literary works, they too have been remembered for their correspondences more than their published works. Recent interest in all of these women has led to new editions of their writings, biographies, and reassessments of letter-writing and diaries as literary genres. In the case of Bettine von Arnim, the issue of genre becomes particularly problematic. Not only was she a prolific letter-writer throughout her long life (1785-1859); she also revised, embellished, and expanded her original correspondence later in life, so that her letters produced both literary works and memoirs. Bettine von Arnim published four epistolary works: *Goethes Briefwechsel mit einem Kinde* (1835), *Die Günderode* (1840), *Clemens Brentanos Frühlingskranz* (1844), and *Iliùs Pamphilius und die Ambrosia* (1848). These books challenge the distinctions between fiction and non-fiction, document and autobiography. Christa Wolf [in her "Nun ja! Das nächste Leben geht aber heute an. Ein Brief über die Bettine." *Lesen und Schreiben. Neue Sammlung: Essays, Aufsätze, Reden,* 1980] points out how Bettine's writings simultaneously avoid and confront rigid categorizations, referring to Bettine's epistolary book form as "Brief-Buch." The hyphen both connects and divides the two concepts of letter and published work. Moreover, contemporary readers also need to remember that in the eighteenth and early nineteenth centuries letters were often public documents, shared and even stylistically evaluated among friends and family. Bettine's letters then are not just a bridge to her later work; they are in themselves aesthetic creations.

It was Bettine's first book, *Goethes Briefwechsel,* that made her famous and that has evoked the most questions regarding the authenticity of the correspondence. The problem of authenticity may be addressed by comparing the original correspondence with the published work. But whereas comparisons focus primarily on differences, we can come to understand how closely connected the concepts of "Brief" and "Buch" really are only through an examination of the literary aspects of the actual letters. A detailed analysis of one of Bettine's letters to Goethe may serve as a guide to further interpretations of letters and diaries in terms of their literary value for Bettine and other writers of the era, as well as shedding light on later literary productions. The close reading of one letter will demonstrate how letters contain many of the same elements as fictional texts. Bettine's letter exhibits an obvious artistic structure; it is a deliberately composed text and not a frivolously scribbled note.

I have selected Bettine von Arnim's letter to Goethe of March 7, 1809, because it reveals several important aspects of letter-writing. The powerful mixture of authority and adoration to be observed here in Bettine's letter dominates her writings. An analysis of her epistolary and dialogue tactics in this letter may serve then as an introduction to the narrative riches to be found in her other letters and books. Bettine's correspondences exhibit a complexity which challenge our view of writing and subjective expression. Her later epistolary and two dialogue books (***Dies Buch gehört dem König,*** 1843 and ***Gespräche mit Dämonen,*** 1852) contain many of the same complexities, for in them she exerts even greater mastery over her "characters" by writing and speaking for them.

The singularly most important aspect of letter-writting and epistolary fiction is their emphasis on multiple narrative perspectives. While correspondence is obviously a dialogue, even a single letter, such as the one to be discussed here, can also include multiple perspectives and voices. In this particular letter, Bettine speaks for her addressee Goethe by telling him what he will say and by inserting, through the many dashes in the text, a space for him to participate. The openness of the letter form is conducive to plurivocity and creative narration, but also can lead to negative evaluations of the form in terms of literary values. Women who, like Bettine and Rahel Varnhagen, expressed themselves in this form subjected themselves to accusations of dilettantism and unbridled subjectivity. For example: on the one hand Bettine's writings have been seen even by modern critics as the work of a dilettante, while others have accused her of failing due to her consuming narcissism. Both self-consciousness and lack of it are used to deny artistic achievement. Despite the plurivocal aspect of her writings, they have been described as being basically monologues, and all the speakers have been seen as reflections of Bettine herself, even though the epistolary books include actual letters by others. While in most instances Bettine, as the author, is actually writing all the parts, from a literary point of view the "character" Bettine may not be equated with the "author" Bettine. By perceiving of letters as literary texts, differentiations between authors, narrators, and characters can be made, and interpretations of letters in literary terms attempted. When we apply to letters such basic distinctions, standard for literary texts, we can view letters as more than the subjective expressions of their authors. The letter-writer then is an author much like any other; the letter itself is subject to textual analysis, and the addressee is a reader.

Bettine von Arnim's March 7 letter delineates the issues of presence and absence inherent in any epistolary situation, and it also raises the highly volatile question of women's subjectivity. Traditionally, women's letters and diaries were considered especially suited to the expression of women's subjective, rather than logical nature. This view implied, however, a concept of unified subjectivity that from our contemporary perspective has become somewhat spurious. My interpretation of Bettine's letter will serve to point out the necessity of accounting for the divided subjectivity present in written expression in general, and in letters in particular. Jacques Lacan's and feminist psychoanalytic theories assist in outlining the dynamics of the epistolary interplay between presence and absence and in exploring the nature of the writing and reading subject, as well as of the author and authorship.

Bettine's letter to Goethe goes beyond the usual problem of absence and presence by describing an erotic fantasy which is fulfilled by the actual sending of the letter. At the same time this fantasy expresses a desire for Goethe's presence that can never be absolutely realized. Because the letter was written down and sent to an absent Goethe, an explication of the fantasy requires an analysis of Bettine's discourse. The epistolary situation also assails the integrity of the subject, forcing Bettine as the writer to assume various roles; she speaks for Goethe and creates a narrating character for herself. In most cases the writing and sending of a letter may be interpreted as an acknowledgment of the physical distance between the writer and the addressee. An essential distinction needs to be made, however, regarding the nature of the terms "writer" and "addressee." J. Hillis Miller [in his "Thomas Hardy, Jacques Derrida, and the 'Dislocation of Souls',' in *Taking Chances: Derrida, Psychoanalysis, and Literature,* edited by Joseph H. Smith and William Kerrigan, 1984] has asserted that letter-writing "dispossesses both the writer and receiver of themselves." Writing creates phantoms who correspond. These "fantastic persons," as he calls them, he places beyond the writer and receiver. I fully concur with Hillis' distinction, but I would locate these phantoms within both the writer and receiver in Bettine's letter. It is precisely this distinction and location which make presence possible, even if it is only partial and predicated upon a split subject. The difficulties arising from the recitation of the fantasy itself even further serve to shatter the illusion of a unitary subject. In the fantasy described in Bettine's letter of March 7, 1809 absence is overcome through a complex splitting of the subjects, as the interpretation of the letter will show. For this reason the letter form, which seems to be an unequivocally subjective mode of expression that presumes a unified subject, assumes more complex dimensions.

In this letter the authority of the narrating subject tries to assert herself over the claims of other voices. By speaking for them she strives to maintain her authority, but is not always successful. Bettine can only invoke Goethe's presence by controlling the fantasy, and this also means controlling the narration of the fantasy. On the other hand, the dashes in the text, those moments where she loosens her control, allow that presence to manifest itself. Presence is dependent then upon a delicate balance between control and plurivocity. She creates presence through the act of writing by choosing precisely when to allow the other voices to emerge. Although they at times threaten to overwhelm her, the other voices never completely succeed, so that she retains her unauthorized authority to speak for them.

Her fantasy practices unauthorization—it breaks rules. She is unfaithful to the idyllic author, and this infidelity became even more pronounced as her career progressed, her book, ***Goethes Briefwechsel mit einem Kinde,*** becoming the epitome of "unauthorized," "illegitimate" writing. Bettine's habit of speaking for others, especially when she speaks for the godlike Goethe, undermines the patriarchal concept of the author as controller and owner of his texts. Her own texts are not closed off to other voices, but are open, and indeed, in their plurivocity deliberately include multiple voices. Through the open form, Bettine can not only express her desire to be with Goethe, she can also achieve her ultimate goal of presence by creating it herself. Her forthright erotic expression further contributes to the undermining of patriarchal authority, for her tone transgresses even the sentimental conventions of her time and transforms her letter-fantasy into a demand that he love her as well.

Letter-writing is a means of creating presence for Bettine; it was not a means of transmitting information, but of maintaining contact across distances. Goethe, on the other hand, merely wanted Bettine to provide him with information. On February 22, 1809 he wrote her asking her for "einige Nachricht" about her situation and the places she had visited, emphasizing, "meine Einbildungskraft folgt Dir mit Vergnügen . . . ." Bettine, who at the age of twenty-three was living alone in Munich, pursuing her music studies and often writing letters to fill lonely nights, replied on March 7, 1809. Shortly before the letter from Goethe arrived, she had received a note from his wife, Christiane, inviting her to visit. Goethe refers to this invitation in his own letter, albeit unenthusiastically. Although Bettine had already decided not to go even before the receipt of Goethe's letter because of her studies, she still stressed that Goethe remained "das Leben meines Lebens."

Because she chooses to remain physically distant from him, her March 7 letter is predicated upon her voluntary absence as well as Goethe's involuntary one. The letter itself, however, by means of the power of language, has the ability to reverse the physical reality produced by her decision and fulfill her desire for his presence. Language does not function in such a way as to represent a meeting between Bettine and Goethe. Instead, the acts of writing and sending the letter actually engender such an encounter for her, so that the fantasy elucidated in the letter invokes presence.

The structure of the letter written on March 7, which consists of six paragraphs, reflects the dynamics of Bettine's desire. This interpretation will focus on the fantasy which comprises the first two paragraphs, each only one sentence long. The fantasy operates as a replacement for a visit with Goethe by developing a scenario for such a meeting. Instead of going to him, Bettine orchestrates a situation where he visits her through the power of *his* imagination, not hers. Her desire is ostensibly displaced onto Goethe. She instructs and guides him, beginning her letter without salutation and with reference to his letter: "Wenn Deine Einbildungskraft geschmeidig genug ist, mir . . . zu folgen, so will ich's auch noch wagen / Dich zu mir zu führen." Bettine's further instructions are delivered in the imperative mood. But in addition to her commands, Bettine has allocated to Goethe his own space and time to act and respond to her demands by way of the many dashes inserted into the text. Her letters then are not only a part of a larger correspondence with Goethe; within individual

letters, and in this instance through the dashes, a space has been made for Goethe in the text. This space, however, is a place marked by a gap, by absence. The dashes, by opening up her text, indicate that the fantasy is not closed, but open. The openness of the fantasy, as we shall see, at times threatens to overwhelm the speaker in the letter and challenges her mastery of the situation, and her supposed control over Goethe's presence and absence.

Bettine, who names herself a child in the letter ("ein liebes treues Kind"), plays the child's game of *fort-da,* of disappearance and appearance, of presence and absence, that Sigmund Freud describes in *Jenseits des Lustprinzips.* The boy overcomes his passive situation vis-à-vis the mother, who comes and goes at will, through the manipulation of his string toy, which permits him to place himself in the active role. The game, incidentally, may also be played with oneself and a mirror. In the game it is first necessary to create the absence, which Bettine accomplishes by *not* visiting Goethe, in order to bring about presence. The child gains a feeling of mastery from her activity and derives pleasure from the second, the appearance, part of the game. Although the child's play appears to represent the absence of the desired other (in the child's case the desired other is the mother), the *fort-da* "is aimed at what essentially, is not there . . ." [Jacques Lacan, *The Four Fundamental Concepts of Psycho-Analysis,* translated by Alan Sheridan and edited by Jacques-Allain Miller, 1978]. The game, which in this instance is played out in her epistolary fantasy, "takes the place of representation." While the infant child needs the toy to express her game because she cannot speak, Bettine can and does speak, and through her letter as the means of the game, absence becomes present through language. The gap between presence and absence becomes the locus of what Lacan terms the Other, of the unconscious. The fantasy as a kind of game allows access to it, since fantasy belongs to both the conscious and the unconscious. In Bettine's fantasy, Goethe as presence comes to represent the object of desire, so that as he fills the gap between presence and absence he veils the Other. This is not to say that the game itself should be evaluated as representation, but that representation occurs within the fantasy created by the game. While Goethe as presence comes to represent her desire, the fantasy itself, and not the object, supports her desire. This is a crucial point for the analysis of the letter and of Bettine's relationship to Goethe, for Bettine's fantasy itself and not Goethe is the true object of her desire. The fantasy supports her desire and motivates her writing.

The dashes in the text allow her mastery over her projection of Goethe's imagination. The complexity of her creation manifests itself in the conflicting use of certain apparently opposing pairs: light and dark, hot and cold, rationality and passion, winter and spring. The dynamics of Bettine's creation of presence and of her expression of desire will be revealed by examining some of these pairs, as well as the dashes, and the structural and linguistic aspects. This will then lead to an exploration of the effect these dynamics exert on the epistolary process.

Bettine guides Goethe to her room and situates him: "sez Dich auf den blauen Sessel am grünen Tisch—mir gegenüber—ich will Dich—nicht küssen, nur ansehen—das Licht hier blendet mich—sez es bei seite—so;". The passage contains several important elements. The plethora of dashes are clearly gaps which mark action that cannot be spoken. How the dashes are interpreted, either as pauses in Bettine's narration, as Goethe's spoken responses, or as the traces of Goethe's actions, effects the reading of the letter. This ambiguity marks Bettine's ostensible displacement of her own desire onto Goethe. But Goethe not only meets her demands, he makes some of his own, as evidenced in the dash between the "ich will Dich" and "nicht küssen." Bettine then stresses that her demands are confined to the scopic. She wants only to gaze at him and therefore places him across from rather than next to her. The light, which should facilitate her gaze, instead blinds her. While her eyes are focused ahead, the light is put to the side. The seeming contradiction between blindness and sight has several ramifications. The light creates blindness because it invades her fantasy by too brightly illuminating the desired object—the aging Goethe. The adjustment in the arrangement of the situation is the first indication that, as the scenario develops, her desire intensifies and her goals change. On the other hand, this adjustment emphasizes that in spite of the imperatives she does not completely control the situation, because she does not exert total control over herself. Bettine then further appears to contradict her own interdiction against kissing, asking for his hand to kiss. The difference here is more than lexical—"küssen" versus "Mund drauf drücken". The issue resides in the aspect of mastery, which Bettine strives to maintain, since she believes that mastery is essential to the creation of presence.

Her object in the game lies in controlling Goethe's imagination, but she must first retain his attention—"Goethe?—folgt mir Deine Einbildungskraft immer noch?". The Goethe who is named here is therefore not the one who occupies the gaps marked by the dashes in the fantasy, but the one who is her addressee, the one who is far away. The dashes surrounding this aside indicate an exit from the fantasy. Like her Goethe, Bettine herself simultaneously plays several roles that are not always clearly distinguishable: she is fantasy participant and writer, character and author. In the very letter by which she inscribes a fantasy that includes both herself and Goethe, the subjects are divided through the epistolary process as such.

The remainder of the paragraph exhibits no imperatives and only one dash. Bettine's guidance does not cease; she merely alters her technique in the hope of insuring even greater control. Whereas the dashes left her vulnerable to Goethe's unspoken actions, she now phrases her fantasy in terms of what he must recognize, do, and say, and even provides him with a script. Her demands, phrased as they are through the modal verb *müssen,* have a less immediate impact and imply a kind of action yet to be performed. The absence of the many dashes further underscores the effect of directions not yet followed. This change in approach may reduce her vulnerability and appear to increase her control. But, by framing her demands through the verb *müssen,* the sense of immediacy—the reader's and writer's feeling that as she writes and reads the events

described occur simultaneously—is replaced with a sense of anticipation. This change in terms of demand, however, does not really provide her with greater mastery over the situation. Goethe's intrusions into the text come through the dashes and not through the use of the imperative mood. Bettine desires immediacy and not anticipation, therefore the *müssen* approach is quickly abandoned. Her tighter control over Goethe's actions leads to a reversal of the terms of physical contact as they were outlined in the first part of the paragraph. She does not take his hand; he is to take her into his arms. Yet this erotic move is almost countermanded by having him speak of her as a child. The sole dash in this part of the paragraph, however, permits Goethe to intrude into her fantasy so that Goethe is encouraged to move. The order of gazing and kissing has also been reversed from earlier—"siehst Du und must mich küssen". But this time the text unambiguously reveals that it is to be Goethe who is enamored of her and who will act. Since Bettine demands that he desire her, that he meet her desire, why should it matter who initiates contact? For her the question is once again one of control, of her ability through the fantasy to arouse and direct Goethe's desire.

My assumption regarding the obvious nature of Bettine's own desire is a critical point of contention. Bettine von Arnim's erotic feelings for Goethe are usually ignored, denied, or, when recognized, considered obscene by most critics, despite expressions such as this one from a letter to Max Prokop von Freyberg, which was written the day before her engagement to Achim von Arnim: "Die Schönheit seines [Goethe's] Leibes wie seiner Seele stehen wie zwei mächtige Grundpfeiler, die meines Lebens Gränzen bezeignen. . . ." Goethe, however, decided to ignore her erotic gestures, including the March 7 letter.

The second paragraph, which also consists of one sentence and appears at first glance to be merely a simple repetition of the opening paragraph, is both an intensification and continuation of it. The game of *fort-da* begins anew. He is not with her and is to join her, though not in her room, as before, but in "meines Herzens Kammer". Goethe's entrance thereby transcends the spatial dimension into the metaphorical and psychical. This intensification, however, does not reduce the physicality of the encounter; on the contrary, the description in different terms is conducive to more intimate contact. The splitting of the subject that takes place in this passage also encourages intimacy, although this splitting has traumatic consequences.

Goethe's entry into the actual chamber of the encounter requires him to act on his own. His guide, her "ich," does not enter with him. Instead, Bettine describes for him what he will discover. The description in future tense is directed beyond the present fantasy Goethe to the absent reader. Again the images of light and dark modulate and the pairing of hot and cold is added. The pronoun "es," which marks a further splitting of an already divided subject, refers to her heart as she tells him: "geh hin, poch an—es wird allein seyn, und wird Herein! Dir rufen, Du wirsts auf einem kühlen stillen Laager finden / ein freundlich Licht wird durch die Fenster scheinen und alles wird in Ruh und Ordnung seyn und Du willkommen."

While the opening imperatives echo those of the previous passage, they do not persist. The description, formulated in future tense, seems merely to reinforce the emphatic series of *müssen* projections, but there are significant differences. In the first paragraph the narrating, speaking subject within the fantasy had not yet further divided herself into an experiencing heart and an empathic but voyeuristic "ich." The speaking voice will not be able to experience the encounter directly but will visualize it. Unlike the simple subject fantasizing the scopic pleasure of gazing at Goethe (seen in the first paragraph), the split subject who now speaks derives no pleasure from her voyeurism. The future tense addresses itself to both the absent Goethe and the narrating "ich" within the fantasy. Both anticipate what will occur in the chamber. The anticipation here does not long remain unresolved as it does in the first paragraph; as the action heats up, the "ich" again formulates her description in the present tense.

The splitting into an experiencing "es" and a speaking "ich" allows the events in the chamber to be articulated. The "ich" must remain bound to what Jacques Lacan calls the Symbolic order, the order of discourse, to relate the experience to Goethe. While the fantasy may seem logically to belong to the Imaginary order, in this particular instance we are dealing not so much with the fantasy itself as with its articulation. And for this reason the speaker who describes the events in the fantasy does not enter the chamber, because the bedroom in the fantasy belongs to the realm of the Imaginary. In order to retain her linguistic powers, the "ich" must split herself, and thereby at least partially submit herself to her own illusions. As the speaker she defines her experience by explanatory and directive discourse. The "ich" who relies on her observation (which here appears to be telepathic) is dependent on the "es" who knowingly falls prey to the illusion.

The speaker ("ich") reflects what Jane Gallop calls [in her *The Daughter's Seduction: Feminism and Psychoanalysis,* 1982] "phallic desire." In traditional Freudian terms, the man who as a child viewed his mother as possessor of the phallus, now perceives of the woman—the object of his desire—as its possessor. It is important to remember that the term phallus is defined by Lacan as "the privileged signifier." Lacan further notes [in his "The Signification of the Phallus," *Écrits: A Selection,* translated by Alan Sheridan, 1977] that the "relation of the subject to the phallus . . . is established without regard to the anatomical difference of the sexes . . ." and yet "this very fact, makes any interpretation of this relation especially difficult in the case of women." When Lacan comes to actually using the term phallus, however, he clearly associates it with male anatomy, justifying his choice because "it is the most tangible element in the realm of sexual copulation," and "by virtue of its turgidity, it is the image of the vital flow as it is transmitted in generation." In fact, when the woman, in Lacanian terms, becomes the signifier of desire for the man, this desire can never be fulfilled, because the woman lacks the phallus. But for a woman the issue of fulfillment must be re-examined. Bettine's desire for the phallus, represented in the fantasy by Goethe, can be addressed, if not fulfilled, since "she finds the signifier of her own desire in the body of him to whom she addresses her demand for love."

And the speaking "ich" certainly demands love, although it should be remembered that it is the fantasy itself, rather than Goethe as the phallic signifier of desire, which sustains her desire.

What then of the "es" that experiences Goethe more directly? The experience of the "es" is not described; it lies beyond words. Its presence is marked by the dash as an absence. The reader's imagination must fill in the blank. The clue to its nature arises from the response of the speaker: "—Was ist das? Himmel! Das Zimmer ganz voll Dampf, die Flammen überm Bett zusammen schlagend; woher die Feuersbrunst? wer rettet hier?" The ensuing fire may be interpreted without controversy as the result of ignited passions. The description, provided for the reader Goethe, depicts the incendiary process as it occurs. The anticipatory future tense has realized itself in the present. The passionate flames raging over the bed threaten a part of the speaker to which she has no access. Indeed, in contrast to her heart, which is in danger of being consumed by heat, she elaborates on her own situation in opposing terms: "kalt und starr muß ich hier stehen, die Arme sinken lassen und kann nicht helfen, mitfühlend die Qual / und kann doch nicht helfen." Her consciousness has empathic powers, but cannot control her own imagination. By splitting herself she has succumbed to her own illusions and in part relinquished control in relation to them. The game of *fort-da* continued without the speaker and she has now assumed the passive position.

As a speaker she is bound through language to the Symbolic order. On the other hand, her heart—the "es"—experiences what the French call *jouissance.* Unlike phallic *jouissance,* there is a *jouissance* that goes beyond the phallus and which Lacan associates with women [in "God and the *Jouissance* of The Woman," *Feminine Sexuality: Jacques Lacan and the ècole freudienne,* translated by Jacqueline Rose and edited by Juliet Mitchell and Jacqueline Rose, 1982]. It is a *jouissance* of the entire body. Jane Gallop observes:

> Such *jouissance* would be sparks of pleasure ignited by *contact* at any point, any moment along the line, not waiting for closure, but enjoying the touching. As a result of such sparks, the impatient economy aimed at finished meaning products (theses, conclusions, definitive statements) might just go up in smoke.

Bettine's fantasy remains open, marked by a dash and a raging fire. The torment expressed by the speaker is interpreted through the matrices of signification as "die Qual," yet it is most probable that the articulated feeling belongs to the "ich" who has become alienated from her own fantasy. The creation of her own fantasy produces a splitting of the subject, and she is even further fragmented by her attempt to inscribe Goethe's desire. The fantasy ends in helplessness for all concerned—for the "es," the "ich," and the Bettine who writes knowing that through the fantasy she can make absence present. Even though Goethe's presence becomes more than merely represented, the splitting of the subject required to accomplish this dislocates her pleasure. She seduces while retaining her distance from Goethe and also from her own *jouissance.*

There are at least four individuals in the letter, even without considering the additional self-division that takes place in the second paragraph. As writer, Bettine is split, but by means of her writing she can make her own splittings into signifiers, so that each part—the writer, character, speaker—is individualized. Written expression of the fantasy, therefore, does not represent an encounter between Bettine and Goethe through simple signification. Instead each is split, and their presence is realized only by the splittings (the characters of Bettine and Goethe) and, in Bettine's case, only by a portion of each splitting, since she further divides herself into "ich" and "es."

She can consciously accept neither the split, nor the helplessness, nor her own *jouissance*. The fantasy has created presence but not fulfilled her desire. So, she assumes another discourse in order to persuade Goethe to desire her. The discourse of the following two and one-half paragraphs speaks from a distance. The writer Bettine takes over and tries to demonstrate her rationality, her recognition of the fantasy as illusion, and her sexual innocence.

The third paragraph is structured like the first two, containing one sentence. The subsequent ones each have three. But this paragraph begins from a different premise since the dominant power is not imagination but a cold rationality which denies feelings and passions. Bettine both acknowledges and disparages it. Rationality is a denial of the visual, the physical, and even the spoken elements of love and life. Bettine laments: "Zu, muß ich die Augen machen und darf nichts ansehen / was mir lieb ist . . . wenn ich die Hände ausstrecke, so ist es doch nur nach den lehren Wänden, wenn ich so spreche, so ists doch nur in den Wind." When the fantasy and the experience of the "es" are repressed, there remains only absence. Without the fantasy and its plurivocal structure, writing also becomes meaningless, so that only actual physical togetherness is conceivable. In this dimension she places herself passively at his feet, so that her most intimate act, later described as "Dein Knie an meine Brust zu drücken," is more idolatrous than erotic.

She then proceeds from the real to the metaphorical; her illustrations of Goethe's effect on her employ the same contrasting elements of light / dark and hot / cold, but they are enveloped in nature imagery so that desire is neutralized. Although the language of the passage is highly charged with passion, the use of conventional nature metaphors to express the relationship appears obviously contrived in the light of the direct language of the fantasy paragraphs, so that the expression of desire here lacks the erotic power of the fantasy. The word *begehren* is used three times here in the fourth paragraph. Her desire has been so repressed that she can state: "Du bist immer der einzige, der mir im unschuldigsten Begehren, unwissend was man nicht verlangen darf / doch völlig Gnüge leistete." Bettine often assumed the pretense of naiveté as a persuasive device in her letters, and here she is persuading herself as well. Her insistent denial of any knowledge of sexual propriety, formulated in the double negative, reveals precisely what she wishes to conceal.

Bettine then goes on to explain that in every letter she wants to profess and confess her love. Both the fantasy and the implied denial of its significance fall into the confessional mode which, according to Michel Foucault [in his *The History of Sexuality,* translated by Robert Hurley, 1980], has the infinite task of extracting a truth from the depths of self and language. In the final paragraph Bettine equates passion and truth. Through the confession she demands Goethe's recognition and pleads that he recognize no one but her. She enunciates this demand for exclusivity repeatedly through the word *einzig*. She proclaims his ultimate authority over her and her creation, because she makes him her reason for living and writing. Bettine, however, is only willing to acknowledge this as long as she believes him to agree with her completely. She has actually revoked his authority to speak. In creating her own Goethe character, Bettine has "unauthorized" her Goethe, taken away his power to speak for himself and to choose freely to love her.

Her unauthorized desire, however, also defeats her own aim of recognition and remains confined to the realm of the *fort-da* game to which she returns in the final paragraph. Goethe's presence cannot be engendered by demonstrated rationality or monologic confession, but only by the epistolary process which includes the sending of the letter as well as its plurivocal character. At the close of the letter the dashes and the imperatives reappear; the touching of hands, the embrace, and the demand that he declare his love—"sags;—jezt sags; daß Du mich lieb hast." Presence is achieved and desire expressed, but only among split subjects. Tomorrow in a continuation of the letter she will write of other things and refer to all of this as "dummes Zeug." She is compelled to repeat the cycle of desire, demand, and retraction as she prolongs her erotic correspondence.

Bettine von Arnim's fantasy letter is exemplary of her whole Goethe correspondence in its dynamics of dominance. The young Bettine is searching for her own voice and style as a writer. As we have seen, the voice she finds is never solo but always in dialogue with another, even if Bettine the writer must script all the parts herself. And later in life, when she edits and embellishes the correspondences, she even further empowers herself to speak for others. In this way she produces the unauthorized editions of her own life and others' that undermine the patriarchal authority of writing and, in particular, the authority of the ultimate German writer, Goethe. Her infidelity to her subject and her audacious presumption in writing for him create what may be termed a feminist writing that goes beyond the limits of representation and that challenges the conception of writing as absence, restoring to language its magical power to invoke presence. Through the epistolary process and the division of the subject necessitated by it, as well as by her self-inflicted fragmentation into "ich" and "es" in this particular letter, Bettine can create Goethe's presence and demand his love. The process, however, extracts a heavy toll: it is the presence and the love of fragments. (pp. 41-53)

Marjanne E. Goozé, "Desire and Presence: Bettina von Arnim's Erotic Fantasy Letter to Goethe," in Michigan Germanic Studies, *Vol. XIII, No. 1, Spring, 1987, pp. 41-57.*

FURTHER READING

Drewitz, Ingeborg. "Bettine von Arnim—A Portrait." Translated by Charles V. Miller. *New German Critique,* No. 27 (Fall 1982): 115-22.

Biographical sketch of Arnim highlighting her early career as a memoirist as well as her later years as a political essayist and activist.

Helps, Arthur and Howard, Elizabeth Jane. *Bettina: A Portrait.* New York: Reynal and Company, 1957, 223 p.

Biography of Arnim with extensive excerpts from her correspondence.

Kaiser, Nancy A. "A Dual Voice: Mary Shelley and Bettina von Arnim." In *Identity and Ethos: A Festschrift for Sol Liptzin on the Occasion of His 85th Birthday,* edited by Mark H. Gelber, pp. 211-33. New York: Peter Lang, 1986.

Explores the contradictions in the lives and writings of Shelley and Arnim. Kaiser concludes that though both writers asserted their independence as noted authors of the Romantic era, their works "implicitly recognized traditional modes of female self-expression."

Kittler, Friedrich. "Writing into the Wind, Bettina." In *Glyph: Textual Studies* 7, edited by Samuel Weber, pp. 32-69. Baltimore: The John Hopkins University Press, 1980.

Attempts to capture the "spirit" of Arnim. Kittler examines the memoirist's relationships with Günderode, Clemens Brentano, and Goethe, noting their impact upon her work.

Patterson, Rebecca. "Emily Dickinson's Debt to *Günderode." The Midwest Quarterly* VIII, No. 4 (July 1967): 331-54.

Investigates similarities between Dickinson and Arnim. Patterson hypothesizes that Dickinson was so greatly influenced by Arnim's *Günderode* that she deliberately incorporated many of Arnim's ideas and images into her own work.

Rolland, Romain. "Bettina." In his *Goethe and Beethoven,* translated by G. A. Pfister and E. S. Kemp, pp. 161-87. New York: Harper and Brothers, 1931.

Details the relationship between Arnim and Goethe with extracts from their correspondence.

St. Armand, Barton Levi. "Veiled Ladies: Dickinson, Bettine, and Transcendental Mediumship." In *Studies in the American Renaissance,* edited by Joel Myerson, pp. 1-51. Charlottesville: The University Press of Virginia, 1987.

Presents Arnim as the "most Transcendental of the German Romantics." St. Armand also analyzes Arnim's influence on the American Transcendentalist writer Thomas W. Higginson and poet Emily Dickinson.

Tatlock, Lynne. "The Young Germans in Praise of Famous Women: Ambivalent Advocates." *German Life and Letters* XXXIX, No. 3 (April 1986): 193-209.

An assessment of the "Young Germany," a liberal political movement of the nineteenth century. Tatlock contends that while the group's members supported the emancipation of women and enthusiastically accepted Arnim, their writings reveal that they fell prey to cultural stereotyping of women and regarded Arnim's genius as a mere accident of nature.

Additional coverage of Arnim's life and career is contained in the following source published by Gale Research: *Dictionary of Literary Biography,* Vol. 90.

Jeremy Bentham

1748-1832

(Also wrote under the pseudonym Gamaliel Smith) English philosopher and legal theorist.

INTRODUCTION

Noted for his bold challenge to conventional thinking about social theory, education, and jurisprudence, Bentham is widely regarded as the founder of Utilitarianism, an ethical movement prizing practical communal function—rather than intent, tradition, or perceived intrinsic value—in language, laws, public institutions, and actions. Extolling the "greatest happiness principle," the hypothesis of Scottish philosopher David Hume and others that society should maximize the happiness of the greatest number of people, Bentham systematically reformulated ethics and jurisprudence in an attempt to make these fields exact sciences that would enable objective calculation of the best interest of the public; toward this end, his famous works *A Fragment on Government* and *An Introduction to the Principles of Morals and Legislation* urge the reassessment of behavior and legal offenses based on the degree that their consequences diverge from the end of communal well-being. Bentham further introduced Utilitarianism into the public consciousness through his direct influence on prominent contemporary figures, notably economists Thomas Malthus and David Ricardo, law reformer Samuel Romilly, politician Francis Burdett, and philosophers James and John Stuart Mill.

Bentham was the son of a wealthy London attorney. His parents strictly supervised his childhood instruction, which precluded books written for the purpose of entertainment, and he earned the nickname "the philosopher" for his precocity, most notable in his early proficiency in Latin and Greek. He began his formal education in 1755 at Westminster School, attended Oxford from 1760 to 1763, and was called to the bar in 1766 upon completion of his legal studies at Lincoln's Inn. Bentham never practiced law, however, preferring instead to direct his attention to the physical sciences and to more theoretical applications of jurisprudence. In 1776 he wrote *A Fragment on Government,* in which he criticized jurist William Blackstone's traditional view of English common law and initially articulated the Utilitarian principle. In 1785 Bentham traveled to Russia, where his brother was employed as an estate manager, and remained there for three years. During this time he composed the *Defence of Usury,* which addresses the issues of taxation and government, and *Panopticon; or, The Inspection House,* a series of letters outlining a prison reform plan that would engross him for more than two decades. Returning to London, he was befriended by former prime minister William Petty, who

promoted Bentham and his theories among the aristocrats and politicians of English society.

Upon his father's death in 1792, Bentham inherited the family estate; now independently wealthy, he established his home as a center of English intellectual life. In that same year, Bentham, whose works were widely read in France, was proclaimed an honorary citizen of the newly formed French Republic. For the remainder of his life he devoted himself to writing about a vast array of social causes including the reform of the English Parliament and the Anglican Church, the improvement of education, and the humane treatment of women and homosexuals. To promote his causes, he cofounded a journal, *The Westminster Review,* in 1824 with James Mill. He also hoped to write a complete and comprehensive code of English law which would eliminate legal abuses and make adjudication more efficient and fair; in 1830 he published the first volume of his *Constitutional Code* and continued work on this project until his death.

Bentham's theory of morality and law was shaped by the thought of French philosopher Claude-Adrien Helvétius, who endorsed the primacy of sense perception as a source of knowledge, and the empiricism of thinkers such as Hume. Bentham was dissatisfied with the abstraction most evident in German philosophical Idealism of the late eighteenth and early nineteenth centuries. Furthermore, he abjured the subjectivity and disorder of the English legal system, the laws of which, he contended, were created and enforced according to the legislators' and jurists' personal sympathies. Bentham outrightly rejected intuitionism, which holds that absolute values are instinctively apprehended, and considered traditional philosophy to be nothing more than confused reasoning and empty speculations: "While Xenephon was writing history, and Euclid giving instruction in geometry, Socrates and Plato were talking nonsense under pretense of teaching wisdom and morality." He hoped to reshape society by rebuilding the moral order on an objective, measurable foundation, and defined human nature according to the principle of hedonism—the premise that the ultimate motives are the pursuit of pleasure and the avoidance of pain. Bentham held that each person seeks to fulfill needs and desires; the satisfaction of these is happiness, a term he used interchangeably with pleasure. Radically departing from Christian ethics, which consider the unrestrained pursuit of pleasure as immoral, he declared acts unethical if incompatible with the greater happiness of society.

In the attempt to establish a logical, standardized ethical framework, Bentham proposed the "felicific calculus"—an arithmetic method for quantifying the net amount of pleasure or pain resulting from a given action—as the means of assigning value to behavior. In his *Deontology* he also provided a table composed of fourteen basic pleasures (e.g., wealth, friendship) and twelve basic pains (e.g., enmity, deprivation), all of which he considered fundamentally comparable and subject to computation. In the interest of the community, his *Introduction to the Principles of Morals and Legislation* proposed legal reform based on the felicific calculus and the application of sanctions which, he maintained, should be preventive rather than vindictive. As he explained in his *Theory of Legislation* and *Rationale of Punishment and Reward,* the legislator's role is solely to measure the pain suffered by the general public against the pleasure enjoyed by the alleged offender. Bentham deemed an act unethical if the consequent pain outweighs the pleasure, in which case a sanction directly proportionate to the offense should be administered publicly and impartially. Hence, the purpose of incarceration, according to him, is not to cause unnecessary suffering but to inhibit, rehabilitate, and make examples of offenders so that others will be discouraged from committing crimes. Opposed to hard labor in prison, Bentham asserted in his penological work *Panopticon* that offenders must be taught to love work rather than loathe it if they are to become useful citizens.

The implementation of a new kind of educational curriculum and teaching methodology were key to Bentham's reform of morality. In his *Chrestomathia,* meaning "conducive to useful learning," he outlined his plan for melioration based on innovative monitorial systems employed by Scottish and English educators of the day. Bentham sought to supplant the liberal arts and the attendant emphasis on aesthetics, intuition, and feeling, with the pragmatic, rational knowledge of disciplines such as chemistry, engineering, and natural history. In addition, he advocated the use of visual aids and tables to hasten learning, the abolition of corporal punishment, and the exclusion of religious instruction.

Bentham's contemporaries, including William Hazlitt and John Stuart Mill, acknowledged him as a great critical thinker and reformer of philosophy, but found his intent difficult to discern, maintaining that his writing style was full of "philosophical jargon" and occasionally unintelligible. Charles Dickens, in his novel *Hard Times,* attacked the felicific calculus as a cold, mechanistic approach to human problems and took exception to Bentham's proposed educational reforms, characterizing Bentham's dismissal of the need for amusement and aesthetic enrichment as naive. Since the early twentieth century, critics have debated the role of pleasure in Bentham's thought. Questioning both the hegemony and homogeneity of this concept, moralists debate the interpretation of pleasure as a sovereign and qualitatively uniform experience. Further, detractors find hedonism, in which self-interest is implicit, inconsistent with the greatest happiness principle, which may require an individual to sacrifice for the benefit of others. Some scholars, such as Charles Warren Everett and C. K. Ogden, attempted to broaden understanding of Bentham by presenting him as an orthographist, linguistic theorist, and an intellectual in the vein of the prominent French Enlightenment rationalists known as *philosophes.* While many scholars consider Bentham's thought largely derivative and fault his application of the Utilitarian principle, arguing that his rigid program does not allow for the variety of human nature and the inconstancies and irregularities of the human will, they laud his effort to bring greater empiricism to the social sciences. As John Stuart Mill wrote: "He introduced into morals and politics those habits of thought and modes of investigation, which are essential to the idea of science. . . . It was not his *opinions,* in short, but his *method,* that constituted the novelty and the value of what he did; a value beyond all price. . . ." Moreover, few historians dispute his practical contributions to legislative reform and public administration, concurring that such advances as public health laws, universal suffrage, electoral districts, the secret ballot, and government intervention to ensure public safety, can all be attributed in part to Bentham.

PRINCIPAL WORKS

A Fragment on Government   (criticism)   1776
An Introduction to the Principles of Morals and Legislation
   (treatise)   1789
Panopticon; or, The Inspection House. 3 vols.   (letters)
   1791
Defence of Usury   (essay)   1796
Traités de législation civile et pénale. 3 vols.   (treatise)
   1802
   [*Theory of Legislation,* 1864]
Théorie des peines et des récompenses. 2 vols.   (treatise)
   1811
   [*The Rationale of Reward,* 1825; also published as *The Rationale of Punishment,* 1830]
A Table of the Springs of Action   (treatise)   1815
Chrestomathia   (essay)   1817

An Analysis of the Influence of Natural Religion on the Temporal Happiness of Mankind (essay) 1822

Codification Proposal Addressed . . . to All Nations Professing Liberal Opinions (essay) 1822

Not Paul, but Jesus [as Gamaliel Smith] (essay) 1823

Traité des preuves judiciares. 2 vols. (treatise) 1823 [*A Treatise on Juridical Evidence,* 1825]

The Book of Fallacies: From the Unfinished Papers of Jeremy Bentham (treatise) 1824

Rationale of Juridical Evidence. 5 vols. (essay) 1827

*Constitutional Code (treatise) 1830

Deontology; or, The Science of Morality. 2 vols. (treatise) 1834

The Works of Jeremy Bentham, Published under the Supervision of His Executor, John Bowring. 11 vols. (collected works) 1838-43

A Comment on the Commentaries: A Criticism of William Blackstone's Commentaries on the Laws of England (criticism) 1928

The Correspondence of Jeremy Bentham. 9 vols. (collected works) 1968-84

Of Laws in General (prose) 1970

*Volume one, only; first published in its entirety in *The Works of Jeremy Bentham.*

Francis Jeffrey   (essay date 1804)

[*A Scottish judge and literary critic, Jeffrey founded and, from 1803 to 1829, edited* The Edinburgh Review. *In the following excerpt from a review of Pierre-Etienne-Louis Dumont's edition of Bentham's* Traités de législation civile et pénale, *Jeffrey discusses Bentham's principles of legislation and declares Bentham's concept of the felicific calculus inferior to intuition as the foundation of an ethical system.*]

It is now about fifteen years since Mr. Bentham first announced to the world his design of composing a great work on the principles of morals and legislation. The specimen [*An Introduction to the Principles of Morals and Legislation*] which he then gave of his plan, of his abilities, was calculated, we think, to excite considerable expectation and considerable alarm in the reading part of the community. While the author displayed, in many places, great originality and accuracy of thinking, and gave proofs throughout of a very uncommon degree of acuteness and impartiality, it was easy to perceive that he was encumbered with the magnitude of his subject, and that his habits of discussion were but ill adapted to render it popular with the greater part of his readers. Though fully possessed of his subject, he scarcely ever appeared to be master of it, and seemed evidently to move in his new career with great anxiety and great exertion. In the subordinate details of his work, he is often extremely ingenious, clear, and satisfactory; but in the grouping and distribution of their parts, he is apparently irresolute or capricious; and he has multiplied and distinguished them by such a profusion of divisions and subdivisions, that the understanding is nearly as much bewildered from the excessive labour

and complexity of the arrangement, as it could have been from its absolute omission. In following out the discussions into which he is tempted by every incidental suggestion, he is so anxious to fix and to limit an ultimate principle of judgment, that he not only loses sight of the general scope of his performance, but pushes his metaphysical analysis to a degree of subtlety and minuteness that must prove repulsive to the greater part of his readers. In the extent and the fineness of these speculations, he sometimes appears to lose all recollection of his subject, and often seems to task his ingenuity to weave snares for his understanding.

The powers and the peculiarities which were thus indicated by the preliminary treatise, were certainly such as to justify some solicitude as to the execution of the principal work [*Traités de législation civile et pénale*]. While it was clear that it would be well worth reading, it was doubtful if it would be capable of being read: and while it was certain that it would contain many admirable remarks, and much profound and original reasoning, there was some room for apprehending that the author's propensity to artificial arrangement and metaphysical distinctions might place his discoveries beyond the reach of ordinary students, and repel the curiosity which the importance of the subject was so likely to excite. Actuated probably, in part, by the consciousness of those propensities (which nearly disqualified him from being the editor of his own speculations), and still too busily occupied with the prosecution of his great work, to attend to the nice finishing of its parts, Mr. Bentham, about six years ago, put into the hands of M. Dumont a large collection of manuscripts, containing the greater part of the reasonings and observations which he proposed to embody into his projected system. These materials, M. Dumont assures us, though neither arranged nor completed, were rather redundant than defective in quantity, and left nothing to the *redacteur,* but the occasional labour of selection, arrangement, and compression. This task he has performed as to a considerable part of the papers entrusted to him in [*Traités de législation civile et pénale*]; and has certainly given a very fair specimen both of the merit and the original speculations, and of his own powers of expression and distribution. There are some passages, perhaps, into which a degree of flippancy has been introduced, that does not harmonise with the general tone of the composition, and others in which we miss something of that richness of illustration and homely vigour of reasoning which delighted us in Mr Bentham's original publications; but in point of neatness and perspicuity, conciseness and precision, we have no sort of doubt that M. Dumont has been of the most essential service to his principal, and are inclined to suspect that, without this assistance, we should never have been able to give any account of his labours.

The plan which Mr Bentham has chalked out for himself in this undertaking, is more vast and comprehensive, we believe, than was ever ventured upon before by the ambition of any one individual. It embraces almost every thing that is important in the science of human nature, and not only touches upon all the higher questions of government and legislation; but includes most of the abstract principles of ethics and metaphysics, and professes to delineate those important rules by which the finest speculations of philosophy may be made to exert their influence on the actual condition of society. (pp. 1-3)

[*Traités de législation civile et pénale*] consists of four principal parts: 1. A general view of the principles of legislation, composed in a good degree, from the **Introduction** formerly published in English in 1789: 2. A general sketch of the complete system of laws which Mr Bentham proposes to erect upon those principles: 3. The application of those principles to the law in civil questions: and 4. The application of the same principles to the law with regard to crimes. To these are added, three detached treatises; one on the establishment of a new sort of house of correction, to be called the *Panoptique;* another on the method of promulgating the law; and the third on the influence of time and place in questions of legislation. From this short account of the contents of this publication, our readers will easily perceive that the merit of the whole system must depend upon the soundness of the principles upon which it is professedly founded, and that the character of the book must be determined, in a great degree, by the manner in which the first part of it is executed. As the subjects which are there treated of are of the greatest interest in themselves, and as they are discussed in a manner which the author at least conceives to be perfectly original, we shall endeavour to lay before our readers, a full view, both of the doctrines which he has delivered, and of the observations which have been suggested to us by their perusal.

M. Dumont, who has more than the common right of an editor to be partial to the work he has brought into the world, is persuaded that this publication must make an epoch and a revolution in the science of which it treats; and assures us, that the **Introduction,** upon the principles of which it is founded, though not hitherto distinguished by any great share of popular applause, is already considered in that light by the small numbers of competent judges by whom its merits have been appreciated. To this privilege, he says, Mr Bentham's speculations are entitled, because they have set the example of a new method of philosophising in politics and morality, and because they contain the elements of a new system of logic, by means of which ethics and legislation are for the first time advanced to the dignity of a *Science*. These pretensions, it cannot be denied, are sufficiently magnificent; and the confidence with which they are announced, naturally leads us to inquire into the facts by which they are supported.

The principle upon which the whole of Mr Bentham's system depends is, that *utility,* and utility alone, is the criterion of right and wrong, and ought to be the sole object of the legislator. This principle, he admits, has often been suggested, and is familiarly recurred to both in action and deliberation: but he maintains that it has never been pursued with sufficient steadiness and resolution, and that the necessity of assuming it as the exclusive test of our proceedings has never been sufficiently understood. There are two principles, he alleges, that have been admitted to a share of that moral authority which belongs of right to that of utility alone, and have exercised a controul over the conduct and opinions of society, by which legislators have been very frequently misled. The one of these he denominates the *ascetic principle,* or that which enjoins the mortification of the senses as a duty, and proscribes their gratification as a sin; and the other, which has had a much more extensive influence, he calls *the principle of sympathy or antipathy,* under which name he comprehends all those systems which place the basis of morality in the indications of a moral sense, or in the maxims of a rule of right, or which, under any other form of expression, decide upon the propriety of human actions by any internal, unaccountable feelings, without any view to their consequences. In this place he introduces, by way of parenthesis, a technical enumeration of the sources and causes of antipathy, of which he reckons six—the repugnance of the senses—mortified pride—disappointed endeavours, &c. &c.

He then sets himself to show that these principles have in many instances superseded the lawful authority of utility in the laws of most countries; and imputes to this cause the illusion which has led so many legislators to neglect the substantial happiness of their country, while they limited all their exertions to the promotion of its riches, its power, or its freedom.

In the next place he combats, with great ability, the arguments of those who have affected to consider the principle of utility as a dangerous guide for our conduct, and endeavours to show that such reasonings really amount to a contradiction in terms; since, to say of any action that it is hurtful, dangerous, or improper, is just to say that it cannot have been adopted upon the principle of utility.

As utility is thus assumed as the test and standard of action and approbation, and as it consists in procuring pleasure, and avoiding pain, Mr Bentham has thought it necessary, in this place, to introduce a catalogue of all the pleasures and pains of which man is susceptible, since these, he alleges, are the elements of that moral calculation in which the wisdom and the duty of legislators and individuals must ultimately be found to consist. The simple pleasures of which man is susceptible are fourteen in number, and are thus enumerated—1. pleasures of sense: 2. of wealth: 3. of dexterity: 4. of good character: 5. of friendship: 6. of power: 7. of piety: 8. of benevolence: 9. of malevolence: 10. of memory: 11. of imagination: 12. of hope: 13. of association: 14. of relief from pain. The pains, our readers will be happy to hear, are only eleven, and are almost exactly the counterpart of the pleasures that have now been enumerated. The construction of these catalogues M. Dumont considers as by far the greatest improvement that has yet been made in the philosophy of human nature.

It is chiefly by the fear of pain that men are regulated in the choice of their deliberate actions; and Mr Bentham finds that pain may be attached to particular actions in four different ways, 1. by nature: 2. by public opinion: 3. by positive enactment: and 4. by the doctrines of religion. Our institutions will be perfect when all these different functions are in harmony with each other.

The most difficult part of our author's task remains. In order to make any use of these 'elements of moral arithmetic,' which are constituted by the lists of our pleasures and pains, it was evidently necessary to ascertain their relative value, so as to enable him to proceed in his legislative calculations with some degree of assurance. Under this head, however, we are only told that the value of a pleasure or a pain, considered in itself, depends, 1. upon its intensity, 2. upon its proximity, 3. upon its duration, and 4. upon its certainty; and that, considered with a view to its consequences, its value is farther affected, 1. by its *secundity, i.e.* its tendency to produce other pleasures or pains; 2. by its *purity, i.e.* its being unmixed with other sensations; and 3. by the number of persons to whom it may extend. These considerations, however, the author justly considers as inadequate for his purpose; for by what means is the *intensity* of any pain or pleasure to be measured, and how, without this knowledge, are we to proportion punishments to temptations, or adjust the measures of recompense or indemnification? To solve this problem, Mr Bentham seems to have had recourse to his favourite system of enumeration, and to have thought nothing else necessary than to make out a fair catalogue of 'the circumstances by which the sensibility is affected.' These he divides into two branches—the primary and the secondary. The first he determines to be exactly fifteen, *viz.* temperament—health—strength—bodily imperfection—intelligence—strength of understanding—fortitude—perseverance—dispositions—notions of honour—notions of religion—sympathies—antipathies—folly or derangement—fortune. The secondary circumstances that determine the degree of sensibility to good and evil, are only nine, *viz.* sex—age—rank—education—profession—climate—creed—government—religious creed. By attending to these circumstances, Mr Bentham is of opinion that we may be able to estimate the value of any particular pleasure or pain to an individual, with sufficient exactness, to judge of the comparative magnitude of crimes, and of the proportionate amount of pains and compensations.

He now comes a little closer to his subject, and enters into an examination of the nature of those evils which it is the business of the legislator to prevent or alleviate. Evils are then arranged, with Mr Bentham's usual partiality for classification, under a great variety of divisions. Evils *of the first order,* are those which fall immediately upon one or a few specific individuals; *evils of the second order,* are those that fall upon entire classes of men under some particular description; and *evils of the third order,* are those that affect the condition of the whole community where they occur. Murder or theft is an instance of the first; persecution or cruelty to heretics, priests, rich men, parents, &c. &c. of the second; and all sorts of disorder and mismanagement, by which the security of the whole community is endangered, are instances of the third. Evils of the first order may be analysed into the *primitive,* or direct evil to the sufferer himself; and the *derivative,* or consequential evil that results to those connected with him, from the effects of his suffering. Evils of the second order consist, again, chiefly either in the *alarm* which is necessarily felt by all that description of persons upon whom it threatens to fall, or the *danger* which may actually exist in a degree either greater or smaller than the alarm. Evils of the third order are produced altogether by the alarm and apprehension of danger, which relaxes the exertions of industry, and gives a check to every sort of prosperity or improve-

ment. Evils are also distinguished by Mr Bentham into such as are either immediate or consequential—extensive or divisible—permanent or evanescent, &c.; but we do not observe that these distinctions, which indeed are capable of being multiplied to infinity, are made the basis of any part of his system.

Mr Bentham is now arrived at the proper object of his reasoning. Certain actions should be prevented, because they give rise to pains or evils; and to those under the name of crimes, the interests of society require certain punishments to be applied, in order to repress and prevent them effectually. But no action is deliberately performed by any reasonable creature, without the expectation of consequential good or pleasure to himself; and this pleasure is to be taken into account in fixing the measure of punishment, or bestowing the appellation of guilt. The construction of the criminal code comes then entirely to a matter of calculation. The gratification of the delinquent individual is to be taken into account on the one hand, and the suffering of the offended party on the other; and it is only where the latter evidently preponderates, that the act should be denominated a crime. In this comparison it will generally be found, that actions have been stigmatised as criminal, much more on account of the evil of *the second order* they produce, by the alarm and danger which they occasion to every one in a similar situation with the sufferer, than on account of the direct detriment that is sustained by the sufferer individually. In the case of offences against property, for instance, it may frequently happen that the gratification of the robber is fully greater than the mortification of the person whom he plunders; but the alarm and danger that would result from the impunity of such actions makes the whole mass of evil incomparably greater than that of good, and justifies the severe sanctions by which law has generally endeavoured to repress such acts of depredation.

In these particulars, Mr Bentham thinks that the principles of legislation and morality exactly coincide: the object of both is the same—the multiplication of human pleasures, and the diminution of pains. What then is the difference between the two codes, and how are their mutual limits to be ascertained? Legislation, Mr Bentham conceives, is merely morality invested with power; but this power it cannot exercise up to the very limits to which morality would carry its sanction of disapprobation. The reasons why law must always fall short of perfect justice, are, 1. Because law must operate chiefly by punishments which are evils in themselves; and that, to enact positive punishments for many noxious actions which are either easily concealed or of slight importance, would be to create a greater evil for the purpose of repressing a smaller one: and 2. Because many offences consisting in degree and continuance, such as unkindness, ingratitude, &c. are really incapable of being defined or established with precision, so that any law against them would either be ineffectual, or would produce more uneasiness by the general dread of prosecution, than it could cure by the example. Mr Bentham then goes on to show, that moral duties may be divided into prudence, probity, and benevolence. The first requires no sanction on the part of the legislature; the second is the proper sphere of law; and the third, though it may in general be left to the wisdom and the feeling of every individual, may yet be enforced by law in a greater number of cases than lawgivers have hitherto provided for. Instances of barbarous unkindness, and acts of cruelty to animals, ought, according to Mr Bentham, to be classed among offences cognisable by the law.

This properly completes Mr Bentham's general view of the principles of legislation. But in order to impress his readers more strongly with a sense of their importance and novelty, he proceeds, in a very long and a very able chapter, to exemplify and expose the various errors into which legislators have been led, by taking for their guide some other principle than that of utility. This chapter is divided into ten sections, under each of which he gives an instance of some false principle that has occasionally been permitted to interfere with those strict notions of utility by which the legislature ought to have been uniformly directed. Thus he says, 1. The antiquity of a law is no reason for adhering to it: 2. The pretended authority of religion is no sufficient ground for legislation: 3. The dread of innovation is no ground for withholding improvements: 4. An arbitrary definition can never be received as a reason for the authority of law: When Montesquieu defined the laws to be *'eternal* relations,' and when Rousseau called them 'the expression of the general will,' they both endeavoured to found, upon arbitrary assumptions, that authority which is only due to their acknowledged utility. 5. A metaphor is no reason for a law. In Mr Bentham's opinion, however, the proceedings of many wise legislatures have been governed by such slight analogies. In England a man's house is his *castle,* and therefore it is to protect him even against the officers of the law. In Italy a church is *the house of God,* in which criminals may therefore defy the justice of men. The ideas unluckily associated with such phrases as 'the balance of trade,'—'mother country,' &c. have given rise, according to Mr Bentham, to a great number of absurd regulations. 6. A law should never be supported by *fictions:* corruption of blood, the sovereign's ubiquity, immortality, &c. and the imaginary *contracts* upon which many writers have founded the whole fabric of society, are bad synonymes, or worse substitutes for utility. 7. A fantastic reason is no reason for a law. Why should a father have authority over his children, *because* they are born in his house, or *because* they are formed of his substance? The true reason is the utility. 8. Antipathies, or sympathies, are no reasons for an enactment: if they are founded in experience of utility, it is more satisfactory to go at once to the foundation: if they cannot be justified on that ground, they should have no authority whatsoever. 9. Assumption of the points in dispute, is no reason for a law. If luxury be defined a vicious or excessive indulgence in pleasure, then it certainly ought to be repressed; but before any law is made to repress it, it should be proved that it is really vicious; that is, that it is productive of evil. *Lastly,* A real law can never be justified by appealing to the authority of an imaginary one. It is saying nothing, to say that the *law of nature,* or the rule of right, requires such and such an enactment. These high-sounding words mean nothing more than the private opinion or inclination of the individual who uses them. Every reason, in short, that can be given for any enactment or institution, must either resolve itself into the assertion of its utility, or be rejected

as pernicious. The legislator has but one simple maxim to observe—to repress all those actions which tend to produce more pain than pleasure, and to promote all those which produce more pleasure than pain.

Having thus endeavoured to lay before our readers a very concise, but, we hope, a tolerably full and distinct account of Mr Bentham's principles of legislation, we shall now take the liberty of making a few of those observations, which could not have been stated before, without breaking the connexion of the subject, and obscuring the evidence upon which the system is founded. The first remark that suggests itself is, that if there is little that is false or pernicious in this system, there is little that is either new or important. That laws were made to promote the general welfare of society, and that nothing should be enacted which has a different tendency, are truths that can scarcely claim the merit of novelty, or mark an epoch by the date of their promulgation. The technical apparatus which Mr Bentham has employed to enforce these tenets upon his readers, appears to us to have been altogether unnecessary; and we have not yet been able to discover that it can be of any service in improving their practical application. There are many things, indeed, that seem to be very inaccurately laid down in the detail of these principles, and a still greater number that are assumed with too little limitation.

The basis of the whole system is the undivided sovereignty of the principle of utility, and the necessity which there is for recurring strictly to it in every question of legislation. Moral feelings, it is admitted, will frequently be found to coincide with it; but they are on no account to be trusted to, till this coincidence has been verified; they are no better than sympathies and antipathies, mere private and unaccountable feelings, that may vary in the case of every individual; and therefore can afford no fixed standard for general approbation or enjoyment. We cannot help thinking, that this fundamental proposition is very defective, both in logical consistency, and in substantial truth. In the first place, it seems very obvious to remark, that the principle of utility is liable to the same objections, on the force of which the authority of moral impressions has been so positively denied. How shall utility itself be recognised, but by a *feeling* similar to that which is stigmatised as capricious and unaccountable? How are pleasures and pains, and the degrees and relative magnitude of pleasures and pains to be distinguished, but by the feeling and experience of every individual? And what greater certainty can there be in the accuracy of such determinations, than in the results of other feelings no less general and distinguishable? If right and wrong be not precisely the same to every individual, neither are pleasure and pain; and if there be despotism and absurdity in imposing upon another, one's own impressions of wisdom and propriety, it cannot be just and reasonable to erect a standard of enjoyment, and a rule of conduct, upon the narrow basis of our own measure of sensibility. It is evident, therefore, that by assuming the principle of utility, we do not get rid of the risk or variable feeling; and that we are still liable to all the uncertainty that may be produced by this cause, under the influence of any other principle.

The truth is, however, that this uncertainty is in all cases of a very limited nature, and that the common impressions of morality, the vulgar distinctions of right and wrong, virtue and vice, are perfectly sufficient to direct the conduct of the individual and the judgement of the legislator, without any reference to the nature or origin of those distinctions. In many respects, indeed, we conceive them to be fitter for this purpose than Mr Bentham's oracles of utility. In the first place, it is necessary to observe, that it is a very gross and unpardonable mistake to represent those notions of right and wrong as depending altogether upon the private and capricious feelings of an individual. Certainly no man was ever so arrogant or so foolish, as to insist upon establishing his own individual persuasion as an infallible test of duty and wisdom to all the rest of the world. The moral feelings, of which Mr Bentham would make so small account, are the feelings which observation teaches us to impute to all men; those in which, under every variety of circumstances, they are found pretty constantly to agree, and as to which their uniformity may be reasoned and reckoned upon with almost as much security as in the case of their external perceptions. The existence of such feelings, and the uniformity with which they are excited in all men by the same occasions, are facts that admit of no dispute; and, in point of certainty and precision, we have seen already, that they are exactly on a footing with those perceptions of utility that can only be relied on after they have been verified by a similar process of observation. Now, we are inclined to think, in opposition to Mr Bentham, that a legislator will proceed more safely by following the indications of those moral distinctions as to which all men are agreed, than if he resolves to set them altogether at defiance, and to be guided by nothing but those perceptions of utility which he must collect from the same general agreement. It is now, we believe, universally admitted, that nothing can be generally the object of moral approbation, which does not tend, upon the whole, to the good of mankind; and we are not even disposed to dispute with Mr Bentham, that the true source of this moral approbation is in all cases a perception or experience of utility in the action or object which excites it. The difference between us, however, is considerable; and it is precisely this—Mr Bentham maintains, that in all cases we ought to disregard the presumptions arising from moral approbation, and, by resolute and scrupulous analysis, to get at the naked utility upon which it is founded; and then, by the application of his new moral arithmetic, to determine its quantity, its composition, and its value, and, according to the result of this investigation, to regulate our moral approbation for the future. We, on the other hand, are inclined to hold, that these feelings, where they are uniform and decided, are by far the surest tests of the quantity and value of the utility by which they are suggested; and that if we discredit their report, and attempt to ascertain this value by any formal process of calculation or analysis, we desert a safe and natural standard, in pursuit of one for the construction of which we have yet no rules nor materials. A very few observations, we trust, will set this in a clear light.

The amount, degree, or intensity of any pleasure or pain, is ascertained by feeling, and not determined by reason or reflection. These feelings are transitory in their own nature, and are not easily recalled with such precision as to enable us, upon recollection, to adjust their relative values. When they present themselves, however, in combinations, or in rapid succession, their relative magnitude or intensity is perceived by the mind without any exertion, and rather by a sort of immediate feeling, than in consequence of any intentional comparison. When a particular combination or succession of such feelings is repeatedly suggested to the memory, the relative value of all its parts is perceived with great readiness and rapidity, and the general result is fixed in the mind without our being conscious of any act of reflection. In this way, moral maxims and impressions arise in the minds of all men, from an instinctive and involuntary valuation of the good and the evil which they perceive to be connected with certain actions or habits; and those impressions may safely be taken for the just result of that valuation which we may afterwards attempt unsuccessfully with great labour to repeat. They may be compared, on this view of the matter, to those *acquired perceptions of sight* by which the eye is enabled to judge of distances; and by which we shall be much more safely and commodiously guided, within the range of our ordinary occupations, than by any formal scientific calculations, founded on the faintness of the colouring, and the magnitude of the angle of vision, compared with the average tangible bulk of the kind of object in question.

The comparative value of such good and evil, we have already observed, can be determined by feeling alone; so that the interference of technical and elaborate reasoning, though it may well be supposed to disturb those perceptions upon the accuracy of which the determination must depend, cannot in any case be of the smallest assistance. Where the preponderance of good or evil is distinctly felt by all persons to whom a certain combination of feelings has been suggested, we have all the evidence for the reality of this preponderance that the nature of the subject will admit, and must try in vain to traverse that judgement by any subsequent exertion of a faculty that has no jurisdiction in the cause. The established rules and impressions of morality, therefore, we consider as the grand recorded result of an infinite multitude of experiments upon human feeling under every variety of circumstances, and as affording by far the nearest approximation to a just standard of the good and the evil that human conduct is concerned with, which the nature of our faculties will allow. In endeavouring to correct or amend this general verdict of mankind in any particular instance, we not only substitute our own individual feelings for that large average which is implied in the prevalence of moral impressions, but we run the common risk of omitting or mistaking some of the most important elements of the calculation. Every one at all accustomed to reflect upon the operations of his mind, must be conscious how difficult it is to retrace exactly those trains of thought which pass through the understanding almost without giving us any intimation of their existence, and how impossible it frequently is to repeat any process of thought when we propose to make it the subject of observation. Our feelings are not in their natural state when we can study their aspects attentively; and their force and direction are better estimated from the traces which they leave in their spontaneous visitations, than from any forced revocation of them for the purpose of being measured or compared. When the object itself is inaccessible, it is wisest to compute its magnitude from its shadow; where the cause cannot be directly examined, its qualities are most securely inferred from its effects.

One of the most obvious consequences of disregarding the general impressions of morality, and determining every individual question upon a rigorous estimation of the utility it might appear to involve, would be, to give an additional force to the principles by which our judgments are apt to be perverted, and entirely to abrogate the authority of those *general rules* by which alone men are commonly enabled to judge of their own conduct with any tolerable degree of impartiality. If we were to dismiss altogether from our consideration those authoritative maxims which have been sanctioned by the general approbation of mankind, and to regulate our conduct entirely by a view of the good and the evil that promises to be the consequence of every particular action, there is reason to fear, not only that inclination might slip in a false weight into the scale, but that many of the most important consequences of our actions might be overlooked. Those actions are bad, according to Mr Bentham, that produce more evil than good: but actions are performed by individuals, and all the good may be to the individual and all the evil to the community. There are innumerable cases, in which the advantages to be gained by the commission of a crime are incalculably greater than the evils to which it may expose the criminal. This holds in almost every instance where unlawful passions may be gratified with very little risk of detection. A mere calculation of utilities would never prevent such actions, and the truth undoubtedly is, that the greater part of men are only withheld from committing them by those general impressions of morality, which it is the object of Mr Bentham's system to supersede. Even admitting, what might very easily be denied, that, in all cases, the utility of the individual is inseparably connected with that of society, it will not be disputed, at least, that this connexion is of a nature not very striking or obvious, and that it may frequently be overlooked by an individual deliberating on the consequences of his projected actions. It is in aid of this oversight, of this omission, of this partiality, that we refer to the *general rules* of morality; rules, which have been suggested by a larger observation, and a longer experience, than any individual can dream of pretending to, and which have been accommodated by the joint action of our sympathies with delinquents and sufferers to the actual condition of human fortitude and infirmity. If they be founded on utility, it is on a utility that cannot always be discovered, and that can never be correctly estimated in deliberating upon a particular measure, or with a view to a specific course of conduct; it is on a utility that does not discover itself till it is accumulated, and only becomes apparent after a large collection of examples have been embodied in proof of it. Such summaries of utility, such records of uniform observation, we conceive to be the *general rules of morality,* by which, and by which alone, legislators or individuals can be safely directed in determining on the propriety of any course of conduct. They are observations taken in the calm, by which we must be guided in the darkness and the terror of the tempest; they are beacons and strongholds erected in the day of peace, round which we must rally, and to which we must betake ourselves in the hour of contest and alarm.

For these reasons, and for others which our limits will not permit us to hint at, we are of opinion, that the old established morality of mankind ought upon no account to give place to a bold and rigid investigation into the *utility* of any course of action that may be made the subject of deliberation; and that the safest and the shortest way to the good which we all desire, is the beaten highway of morality, which was formed at first by the experience of good and of evil.

But our objections do not apply merely to the foundation of Mr Bentham's new system of morality: We think the plan and execution of the superstructure itself defective in many particulars. Even if we could be persuaded that it would be wiser in general to follow the dictates of utility than the impressions of moral duty, we should be fully at liberty to say that the system contained in these volumes does not enable us to adopt that substitute: it presents us with no means of measuring or comparing utilities. After perusing M. Dumont's eloquent observations on the incalculable benefits which his author's discoveries were to confer on the science of legislation, and on the genius and good fortune by which he had been enabled to reduce morality to the precision of a science, by fixing a precise standard for the good and evil of our lives, we proceeded with the perusal of Mr Bentham's endless tables and divisions, with a mixture of impatience, expectation and disappointment. Now that we have finished our task, the latter sentiment alone remains; for we perceive very clearly, that M. Dumont's zeal and partiality have imposed upon his natural sagacity, and that Mr Bentham has just left the science of morality in the same imperfect condition in which it was left by his predecessors. The whole of Mr Bentham's catalogues and distinctions tend merely to point out the *number* of the causes that produce our happiness or misery, but by no means to ascertain their relative magnitude or force; and the only effect of their introduction into the science of morality seems to be, to embarrass a popular subject with a technical nomenclature, and to perplex familiar truths with an unnecessary intricacy of arrangement. Of the justice of this remark, any one may satisfy himself, by turning back to the tables and classifications which we have exhibited in the former part of this analysis, and trying if he can find there any rules for estimating the comparative value of pleasures and pains, that are not perfectly familiar to the most uninstructed of the species. In the table of simple pleasures, for instance, what satisfaction can it afford, to find the pleasure of riches set down as a distinct genus from the pleasure of power and the pleasure of the senses, unless some scale were annexed by which the respective value of these pleasures might be ascertained? If a man is balancing between the pain of privation and the pain of shame, how is he relieved by finding these arranged under separate titles? Or, in either case, will it give him any information to be told, that the value of a pain or pleasure depends upon its intensity, its duration, or its certainty? If a legislator is desirous to know whether murder or forgery be the greatest crime, will he be contented to hear that the evil of every crime is either of the first, the second, or the third order, and that all crimes produce the two first, and have a tendency to produce the latter also, if they be not vigorously repressed? If he wish to learn what degree of punishment is suitable to a particular offence, will he be greatly edified to read that the same punishment may be more or less severe according to the temperament, the intelligence, the rank, or the fortune of the delinquent; and that the circumstances that influence sensibility, though commonly reckoned to be only nine, may fairly be set down at fifteen? Is there any thing, in short, in this whole book, that realises the trimphant Introduction of the editor, or that can enable us in any one instance to decide upon the relative magnitude of an evil, otherwise than by a reference to the common feelings of mankind? It is true, we are perfectly persuaded, that by the help of these feelings, we can form a pretty correct judgement in most cases that occur; but Mr Bentham is not persuaded of this; and insists upon our renouncing all faith in so incorrect a standard, while he promises to furnish us with another that is liable to no sort of inaccuracy. This promise we do not think he has fulfilled; because he has given us no rule by which the intensity of any pain or pleasure can be determined, and furnished us with no instrument by which we may take the altitude of enjoyment, or fathom the depths of sorrow. It is no apology for having made this promise, that its fulfilment was evidently impossible. (pp. 3-16)

> *Francis Jeffrey, "Bentham: 'Principles de Legislation, par Dumont',"* in The Edinburgh Review, *Vol. IV, No. VII, April, 1804, pp. 1-26.*

An excerpt from *An Introduction to the Principles of Morals and Legislation*

Nature has placed mankind under the governance of two sovereign masters, *pain* and *pleasure*. It is for them alone to point out what we ought to do, as well as to determine what we shall do. On the one hand the standard of right and wrong, on the other the chain of causes and effects, are fastened to their throne. They govern us in all we do, in all we say, in all we think: every effort we can make to throw off our subjection, will serve but to demonstrate and confirm it. In words a man may pretend to abjure their empire: but in reality he will remain subject to it all the while. The *principle of utility* recognises this subjection, and assumes it for the foundation of that system, the object of which is to rear the fabric of felicity by the hands of reason and of law. Systems which attempt to question it, deal in sounds instead of sense, in caprice instead of reason, in darkness instead of light.

Jeremy Bentham, in his Introduction to the Principles of Morals and Legislation, *T. Payne & Son, 1789.*

William Hazlitt (essay date 1825)

[*An English essayist, Hazlitt was one of the most important critics of the Romantic age. He was a deft stylist, a master of the prose essay, and a leader of what was later termed "impressionist criticism," a form of personal analysis directly opposed to the universal standards of critical judgment accepted by many eighteenth-century critics. In the following excerpt from an essay collection originally published in 1825, he scrutinizes Bentham's*

application of the principle of utility, judging it extreme and without regard for the inconstancy of the human will.]

Mr. Bentham is one of those persons who verify the old adage, that 'A prophet has most honour out of his own country.' His reputation lies at the circumference; and the lights of his understanding are reflected, with increasing lustre, on the other side of the globe. His name is little known in England, better in Europe, best of all in the plains of Chile and the mines of Mexico. He has offered constitutions for the New World, and legislated for future times. The people of Westminster, where he lives, hardly dream of such a person; but the Siberian savage has received cold comfort from his lunar aspect, and may say to him with Caliban—'I know thee, and thy dog and thy bush!' The tawny Indian may hold out the hand of fellowship to him across the GREAT PACIFIC. We believe that the Empress Catherine corresponded with him; and we know that the Emperor Alexander called upon him, and presented him with his miniature in a gold snuff-box, which the philosopher, to his eternal honour, returned. Mr. Hobhouse is a greater man at the hustings, Lord Rolle at Plymouth Dock; but Mr. Bentham would carry it hollow, on the score of popularity, at Paris or Pegu. The reason is, that our author's influence is purely intellectual. He has devoted his life to the pursuit of abstract and general truths, and to those studies

That waft a *thought* from Indus to the Pole.

and has never mixed himself up with personal intrigues or party politics. He once, indeed, stuck up a handbill to say that he (Jeremy Bentham) being of sound mind, was of opinion that Sir Samuel Romilly was the most proper person to represent Westminster; but this was the whim of the moment. Otherwise, his reasonings, if true at all, are true everywhere alike: his speculations concern humanity at large, and are not confined to the hundred or the bills of mortality. It is in moral as in physical magnitude. The little is seen best near: the great appears in its proper dimensions, only from a more commanding point of view, and gains strength with time, and elevation from distance!

Mr. Bentham is very much among philosophers what La Fontaine was among poets: in general habits and in all but his professional pursuits, he is a mere child. He has lived for the last forty years in a house in Westminster, overlooking the Park, like an anchoret in his cell, reducing law to a system, and the mind of man to a machine. He scarcely ever goes out, and sees very little company. The favoured few, who have the privilege of the *entrée,* are always admitted one by one. He does not like to have witnesses to his conversation. He talks a great deal, and listens to nothing but facts. When any one calls upon him, he invites them to take a turn round his garden with him.

Mr. Bentham is an economist of his time, and sets apart this portion of it to air and exercise; and there you may see the lively old man, his mind still buoyant with thought and with the prospect of futurity, in eager conversation with some Opposition Member, some expatriated Patriot, or Transatlantic Adventurer, urging the extinction of Close Boroughs, or planning a code of laws for some 'lone island in the watery waste,' his walk almost amounting to a run, his tongue keeping pace with it in shrill, cluttering accents, negligent of his person, his dress, and his manner, intent only on his grand theme of UTILITY—or pausing, perhaps, for want of breath and with lack-lustre eye, to point out to the stranger a stone in the wall at the end of his garden (overarched by two beautiful cotton-trees) *Inscribed to the Prince of Poets,* which marks the house where Milton formerly lived. To show how little the refinements of taste or fancy enter into our author's system, he proposed at one time to cut down these beautiful trees, to convert the garden where he had breathed the air of Truth and Heaven for near half a century into a paltry *Chrestomathic School,* and to make Milton's house (the cradle of *Paradise Lost*) a thoroughfare, like a three-stalled stable, for the idle rabble of Westminster to pass backwards and forwards to it with their cloven hoofs.

Let us not, however, be getting on too fast—Milton himself taught school! There is something not altogether dissimilar between Mr. Bentham's appearance and the portraits of Milton—the same silvery tone, a few dishevelled hairs, a peevish, yet puritanical expression, an irritable temperament corrected by habit and discipline. Or in modern times, he is something between Franklin and Charles Fox, with the comfortable double-chin and sleek thriving look of the one, and the quivering lip, the restless eye, and animated acuteness of the other. His eye is quick and lively; but it glances not from object to object, but from thought to thought. He is evidently a man occupied with some train of fine and inward association. He regards the people about him no more than the flies of a summer. He meditates the coming age. He hears and sees only what suits his purpose, or some 'foregone conclusion'; and looks out for facts and passing occurrences in order to put them into his logical machinery and grind them into the dust and powder of some subtle theory, as the miller looks out for grist to his mill! Add to this physiognomical sketch the minor points of costume, the open shirt-collar, the single-breasted coat, the old-fashioned half-boots and ribbed stockings; and you will find in Mr. Bentham's general appearance a singular mixture of boyish simplicity and of the venerableness of age.

In a word, our celebrated jurist presents a striking illustration of the difference between the *philosophical* and the *regal* look; that is, between the merely abstracted and the merely personal. There is a lackadaisical *bonhomie* about his whole aspect, none of the fierceness of pride or power; an unconscious neglect of his own person, instead of a stately assumption of superiority; a good-humoured, placid intelligence, instead of a lynx-eyed watchfulness, as if it wished to make others its prey, or was afraid they might turn and rend him; he is a beneficent spirit, prying into the universe, not lording it over it; a thoughtful spectator of the scenes of life, or ruminator on the fate of mankind, not a painted pageant, a stupid idol set up on its pedestal of pride for men to fall down and worship with idiot fear and wonder at the thing themselves have made, and which, without that fear and wonder, would in itself be nothing.

Mr. Bentham, perhaps, over-rates the importance of his own theories. He has been heard to say (without any appearance of pride or affectation) that 'he should like to live the remaining years of his life, a year at a time at the end of the next six or eight centuries, to see the effect which his writings would by that time have had upon the world.' Alas! his name will hardly live so long! Nor do we think, in point of fact, that Mr. Bentham has given any new or decided impulse to the human mind. He cannot be looked upon in the light of a discoverer in legislation or morals. He has not struck out any great leading principle or parent-truth, from which a number of others might be deduced, nor has he enriched the common and established stock of intelligence with original observations, like pearls thrown into wine. One truth discovered is immortal, and entitles its author to be so: for, like a new substance in nature, it cannot be destroyed. But Mr. Bentham's forte is arrangement; and the form of truth, though not its essence, varies with time and circumstance. He has methodised, collated, and condensed all the materials prepared to his hand on the subjects of which he treats, in a masterly and scientific manner; but we should find a difficulty in adducing from his different works (however elaborate or closely reasoned) any new element of thought, or even a new fact or illustration. His writings are, therefore, chiefly valuable as *books of reference,* as bringing down the account of intellectual inquiry to the present period, and disposing the results in a compendious, connected, and tangible shape; but books of reference are chiefly serviceable for facilitating the acquisition of knowledge, and are constantly liable to be superseded and to grow out of fashion with its progress, as the scaffolding is thrown down as soon as the building is completed.

Mr. Bentham is not the first writer (by a great many) who has assumed the principle of UTILITY as the foundation of just laws, and of all moral and political reasoning:—his merit is, that he has applied this principle more closely and literally; that he has brought all the objections and arguments, more distinctly labelled and ticketed, under this one head, and made a more constant and explicit reference to it at every step of his progress, than any other writer. Perhaps the weak side of his conclusions also is, that he has carried this single view of his subject too far, and not made sufficient allowance for the varieties of human nature, and the caprices and irregularities of the human will. 'He has not allowed for the *wind.*' It is not that you can be said to see his favourite doctrine of Utility glittering everywhere through his system, like a vein of rich, shining ore (that is not the nature of the material)—but it might be plausibly objected that he had struck the whole mass of fancy, prejudice, passion, sense, whim, with his petrific, leaden mace, that he had 'bound volatile Hermes,' and reduced the theory and practice of human life to a *caput mortuum* of reason, and dull, plodding, technical calculation. The gentleman is himself a capital logician; and he has been led by this circumstance to consider man as a logical animal. We fear this view of the matter will hardly hold water. If we attend to the *moral* man, the constitution of his mind will scarcely be found to be built up of pure reason and a regard to consequences: if we consider the *criminal* man (with whom the legislator has chiefly to do), it will be found to be still less so.

Every pleasure, says Mr. Bentham, is equally a good, and is to be taken into the account as such in a moral estimate, whether it be the pleasure of sense or of conscience, whether it arise from the exercise of virtue or the perpetration of crime. We are afraid the human mind does not readily come into this doctrine, this *ultima ratio philosophorum,* interpreted according to the letter. Our moral sentiments are made up of sympathies and antipathies, of sense and imagination, of understanding and prejudice. The soul, by reason of its weakness, is an aggregating and exclusive principle; it clings obstinately to some things, and violently rejects others. And it must do so, in a great measure, or it would act contrary to its own nature. It needs helps and stages in its progress, and 'all appliances and means to boot,' which can raise it to a partial conformity to truth and good (the utmost it is capable of) and bring it into a tolerable harmony with the universe. By aiming at too much, by dismissing collateral aids, by extending itself to the farthest verge of the conceivable and possible, it loses its elasticity and vigour, its impulse and its direction.

The moralist can no more do without the intermediate use of rules and principles, without the 'vantage-ground of habit, without the levers of the understanding, than the mechanist can discard the use of wheels and pulleys, and perform every thing by simple motion. If the mind of man were competent to comprehend the whole of truth and good, and act upon it at once, and independently of all other considerations, Mr. Bentham's plan would be a feasible one, and *the truth, the whole truth, and nothing but the truth,* would be the best possible ground to place morality upon. But it is not so. In ascertaining the rules of moral conduct, we must have regard not merely to the nature of the object, but to the capacity of the agent, and to his fitness for apprehending or attaining it. Pleasure is that which is so in itself: good is that which approves itself as such on reflection, or the idea of which is a source of satisfaction. All pleasure is not, therefore (morally speaking), equally a good: for all pleasure does not equally bear reflecting on. There are some tastes that are sweet in the mouth and bitter in the belly; and there is a similar contradiction and anomaly in the mind and heart of man.

Again, what would become of the *Hæc olim meminisse juvabit* of the poet, if a principle of fluctuation and reaction is not inherent in the very constitution of our nature, or if all moral truth is a mere literal truism? We are not, then, so much to inquire what certain things are abstractedly or in themselves, as how they affect the mind, and to approve or condemn them accordingly. The same object seen near strikes us more powerfully than at a distance: things thrown into masses give a greater blow to the imagination than when scattered and divided into their component parts. A number of mole-hills do not make a mountain, though a mountain is actually made up of atoms: so moral truth must present itself under a certain aspect and from a certain point of view, in order to produce its full and proper effect upon the mind. The laws of the affections are as necessary as those of optics. A calculation of consequences is no more equivalent to a sentiment than a *seriatim* enumeration of square yards or feet touches the fancy like the sight of the Alps or Andes.

To give an instance or two of what we mean. Those who on pure cosmopolite principles, or on the ground of abstract humanity, affect an extraordinary regard for the Turks and Tartars, have been accused of neglecting their duties to their friends and next-door neighbours. Well, then, what is the state of the question here? One human being is, no doubt, as much worth in himself, independently of the circumstances of time or place, as another; but he is not of so much value to us and our affections. Could our imagination take wing (with our speculative faculties) to the other side of the globe or to the ends of the universe, could our eyes behold whatever our reason teaches us to be possible, could our hands reach as far as our thoughts and wishes, we might then busy ourselves to advantage with the Hottentots, or hold intimate converse with the inhabitants of the Moon; but being as we are, our feelings evaporate in so large a space—we must draw the circle of our affections and duties somewhat closer—the heart hovers and fixes nearer home.

It is true, the bands of private, or of local and natural affection, are often, nay in general, too highly strained, so as frequently to do harm instead of good; but the present question is whether we can, with safety and effect, be wholly emancipated from them? Whether we should shake them off at pleasure and without mercy, as the only bar to the triumph of truth and justice? Or whether benevolence, constructed upon a logical scale, would not be merely *nominal*—whether duty, raised to too lofty a pitch of refinement, might not sink into callous indifference or hollow selfishness? Again, is it not to exact too high a strain from humanity, to ask us to qualify the degree of abhorrence we feel against a murderer by taking into our cool consideration the pleasure he may have in committing the deed, and in the prospect of gratifying his avarice or his revenge? We are hardly so formed as to sympathise at the same moment with the assassin and his victim. The degree of pleasure the former may feel, instead of extenuating, aggravates his guilt, and shows the depth of his malignity.

Now the mind revolts against this by mere natural antipathy, if it is itself well-disposed; or the slow progress of reason would afford but a feeble resistance to violence and wrong. The will, which is necessary to give consistency and promptness to our good intentions, cannot extend so much candour and courtesy to the antagonist principle of evil: virtue, to be sincere and practical, cannot be divested entirely of the blindness and impetuosity of passion! It has been made a plea (half jest, half earnest) for the horrors of war, that they promote trade and manufactures. It has been said, as a set-off for the atrocities practised upon the negro slaves in the West Indies, that without their blood and sweat, so many millions of people could not have sugar to sweeten their tea. Fires and murders have been argued to be beneficial, as they serve to fill the newspapers, and for a subject to talk of—this is a sort of sophistry that it might be difficult to disprove on the bare scheme of contingent utility; but on the ground that we have stated, it must pass for mere irony. What the proportion between the good and the evil will really be found in any of the supposed cases, may be a question to the understanding; but to the imagination and the heart, that is, to the natural feelings of mankind, it admits of none!

Mr. Bentham, in adjusting the provisions of a penal code, lays too little stress on the co-operation of the natural prejudices of mankind, and the habitual feelings of that class of persons for whom they are more particularly designed. Legislators (we mean writers on legislation) are philosophers, and governed by their reason: criminals, for whose control laws are made, are a set of desperadoes, governed only by their passions. What wonder that so little progress has been made towards a mutual understanding between the two parties! They are quite a different species, and speak a different language, and are sadly at a loss for a common interpreter between them. Perhaps the Ordinary of Newgate bids as fair for this office as any one. What should Mr. Bentham, sitting at ease in his armchair, composing his mind before he begins to write by a prelude on the organ, and looking out at a beautiful prospect when he is at a loss for an idea, know of the principles of action of rogues, outlaws, and vagabonds? No more than Montaigne of the motions of his cat! If sanguine and tender-hearted philanthropists have set on foot an inquiry into the barbarity and the defects of penal laws, the practical improvements have been mostly suggested by reformed cut-throats, turnkeys, and thief-takers. What even can the Honourable House who, when the Speaker has pronounced the well-known, wished-for sounds, 'That this House do now adjourn,' retire, after voting a royal crusade or a loan of millions, to lie on down, and feed on plate in spacious palaces, know of what passes in the hearts of wretches in garrets and nightcellars, petty pilferers and marauders, who cut throats and pick pockets with their own hands? The thing is impossible.

The laws of the country are therefore ineffectual and abortive, because they are made by the rich for the poor, by the wise for the ignorant, by the respectable and exalted in station for the very scum and refuse of the community. If Newgate would resolve itself into a committee of the whole Press-yard, with Jack Ketch at its head, aided by confidential persons from the county prison or the Hulks, and would make a clear breast, some *data* might be found out to proceed upon; but as it is, the *criminal mind* of the country is a book sealed, no one has been able to penetrate to the inside! Mr. Bentham, in his attempts to revise and amend our criminal jurisprudence, proceeds entirely on his favourite principle of Utility. Convince highwaymen and housebreakers that it will be for their interest to reform, and they will reform and lead honest lives; according to Mr. Bentham. He says, 'All men act from calculation: even madmen reason'; and, in our opinion, he might as well carry this maxim to Bedlam or St. Luke's, and apply it to the inhabitants, as think to coerce or overawe the inmates of a gaol, or those whose practices make them candidates for that distinction, by the mere dry, detailed convictions of the understanding. Criminals are not to be influenced by reason; for it is of the very essence of crime to disregard consequences both to ourselves and others.

You may as well preach philosophy to a drunken man, or to the dead, as to those who are under the instigation of any mischievous passion. A man is a drunkard, and you tell him he ought to be sober; he is debauched, and you ask him to reform; he is idle, and you recommend industry to him as his wisest course; he gambles, and you remind him that he may be ruined by this foible; he has lost his character, and you advise him to get into some reputable service or lucrative situation; vice becomes a habit with him, and you request him to rouse himself and shake it off; he is starving, and you warn him if he breaks the law, he will be hanged. None of this reasoning reaches the mark it aims at. The culprit, who violates and suffers the vengeance of the laws, is not the dupe of ignorance, but the slave of passion, the victim of habit or necessity. To argue with strong passion, with inveterate habit, with desperate circumstances, is to talk to the winds. Clownish ignorance may indeed be dispelled, and taught better; but it is seldom that a criminal is not aware of the consequences of his act, or has not made up his mind to the alternative. They are, in general, *too knowing by half.* You tell a person of this stamp what is his interest; he says he does not care about his interest, or the world and he differ on that particular. But there is one point on which he must agree with them, namely, what *they* think of his conduct, and that is the only hold you have of him. A man may be callous and indifferent to what happens to himself; but he is never indifferent to public opinion, or proof against open scorn and infamy.

Shame, then, not fear, is the sheet-anchor of the law. He who is not afraid of being pointed at as a *thief,* will not mind a month's hard labour. He who is prepared to take the life of another, is already reckless of his own. But every one makes a sorry figure in the pillory; and the being launched from the New Drop lowers a man in his own opinion. The lawless and violent spirit, who is hurried by headstrong self-will to break the laws, does not like to have the ground of pride and obstinacy struck from under his feet. This is what gives the *swells* of the metropolis such a dread of the *treadmill*—it makes them ridiculous. It must be confessed, that this very circumstance renders the reform of criminals nearly hopeless. It is the apprehension of being stigmatized by public opinion, the fear of what will be thought and said of them, that deters men from the violation of the laws, while their character remains unimpeached; but honour once lost, all is lost. The man can never be himself again! A citizen is like a soldier, a part of a machine, who submits to certain hardships, privations, and dangers, not for his own ease, pleasure, profit, or even conscience, but—*for shame.* What is it that keeps the machine together in either case? Not punishment or discipline, but sympathy. The soldier mounts the breach or stands in the trenches, the peasant hedges and ditches, or the mechanic plies his ceaseless task, because the one will not be called a *coward,* the other a *rogue:* but let the one turn deserter and the other vagabond, and there is an end of him. The grinding law of necessity, which is no other than a name, a breath, loses its force; he is no longer sustained by the good opinion of others, and he drops out of his place in society, a useless clog!

Mr. Bentham takes a culprit, and puts him into what he calls a *Panopticon,* that is, a sort of circular prison, with open cells, like a glass bee-hive. He sits in the middle, and sees all the other does. He gives him work to do, and lectures him if he does not do it. He takes liquor from him, and society and liberty; but he feeds and clothes him, and keeps him out of mischief; and when he has convinced him by force and reason together, that this life is for his good, he turns him out upon the world a reformed man, and as confident of the success of his handy-work as the shoemaker of that which he has just taken off the last, or the Parisian barber in Sterne, of the buckle of his wig. 'Dip it in the ocean,' said the perruquier, 'and it will stand!' But we doubt the durability of our projector's patchwork. Will our convert to the great principle of Utility work when he is from under Mr. Bentham's eye, because he was forced to work when under it? Will he keep sober, because he has been kept from liquor so long? Will he not return to loose company, because he has had the pleasure of sitting vis-à-vis with a philosopher of late? Will he not steal, now that his hands are untied? Will he not take the road, now that it is free to him? Will he not call his benefactor all the names he can set his tongue to, the moment his back is turned? All this is more than to be feared.

The charm of criminal life, like that of savage life, consists in liberty, in hardship, in danger, and in the contempt of death: in one word, in extraordinary excitement; and he who has tasted of it, will no more return to regular habits of life, than a man will take to water after drinking brandy, or than a wild beast will give over hunting its prey. Miracles never cease, to be sure; but they are not to be had wholesale, or *to order.* (pp. 1-13)

Mr. Bentham's method of reasoning, though comprehensive and exact, labours under the defect of most systems— it is too *topical.* It includes every thing; but it includes every thing alike. It is rather like an inventory, than a valuation of different arguments. Every possible suggestion finds a place, so that the mind is distracted as much as enlightened by this perplexing accuracy. The exceptions seem as important as the rule. By attending to the minute, we overlook the great; and in summing up an account, it will not do merely to insist on the number of items without considering their amount. Our author's page presents a very nicely dove-tailed mosaic pavement of legal commonplaces. We slip and slide over its even surface without being arrested anywhere. Or his view of the human mind resembles a map, rather than a picture: the outline, the disposition is correct, but it wants colouring and relief. There is a technicality of manner, which renders his writings of more value to the professional inquirer than to the general reader. Again, his style is unpopular, not to say intelligible. He writes a language of his own that *darkens knowledge.* His works have been translated into French— they ought to be translated into English. People wonder that Mr. Bentham has not been prosecuted for the boldness and severity of some of his invectives. He might wrap up high treason in one of his inextricable periods, and it would never find its way into Westminster Hall. He is a kind of Manuscript author—he writes a cypher-hand, which the vulgar have no key to. The construction of his sentences is a curious frame-work with pegs and hooks to hang his thoughts upon, for his own use and guidance, but almost out of the reach of everybody else. It is a barbarous philosophical jargon, with all the repetitions, parentheses, formalities, uncouth nomenclature and verbiage of law-Latin; and what makes it worse, it is not mere verbiage, but has a great deal of acuteness and meaning in it, which you would be glad to pick out if you could.

> [Bentham] writes a language of his own that *darkens knowledge.* His works have been translated into French—they ought to be translated into English. People wonder that Mr. Bentham has not been prosecuted for the boldness and severity of some of his invectives.
>
> —*William Hazlitt*

In short, Mr. Bentham writes as if he was allowed but a single sentence to express his whole view of a subject in, and as if, should he omit a single circumstance or step of the argument, it would be lost to the world for ever, like an estate by a flaw in the title-deeds. This is over-rating the importance of our own discoveries, and mistaking the nature and object of language altogether. Mr. Bentham has *acquired* this disability: it is not natural to him. His admirable little work *On Usury,* published forty years ago, is clear, easy, and vigorous. But Mr. Bentham has shut himself up since then 'in nook monastic,' conversing only with followers of his own or with 'men of Ind,' and has endeavoured to overlay his natural humour, sense, spirit, and style with the dust and cobwebs of an obscure solitude. The best of it is, he thinks his present mode of expressing himself perfect, and that whatever may be objected to his law or logic, no one can find the least fault with the purity, simplicity, and perspicuity of his style.

Mr. Bentham, in private life, is an amiable and exemplary character. He is a little romantic or so, and has dissipated part of a handsome fortune on impractical speculations. He lends an ear to plausible projectors, and, if he cannot prove them to be wrong in their premises or their conclusions, thinks himself bound *in reason* to stake his money on the venture. Strict logicians are licenced visionaries. Mr. Bentham is half-brother to the late Mr. Speaker Abbott. *Proh pudor!* He was educated at Eton, and still takes our novices to task about a passage in Homer or a metre in Virgil. He was afterwards at the University, and he has described the scruples of an ingenuous youthful mind about subscribing the Articles, in a passage in his *Church-of-Englandism,* which smacks of truth and honour both, and does one good to read it in an age, when 'to be honest' (or not to laugh at the very idea of honesty) 'is to be one man picked out of ten thousand!' Mr. Bentham relieves his mind sometimes, after the fatigue of study, by playing on a fine old organ, and has a relish for Hogarth's prints. He turns wooden utensils in a lathe for exercise, and fancies he can turn men in the same manner. He has no great fondness for poetry, and can hardly extract a moral out of Shakespear. His house is warmed and lighted by steam. He is one of those who prefer the artificial to the natural in most things, and think the mind of man omnipotent. He has a great contempt for out-of-door prospects, for green fields and trees, and is for referring every thing to Utility. There is a little narrowness in this; for if all the sources of satisfaction are taken away, what is to become of utility itself? It is, indeed, the great fault of this able and extraordinary man, that he has concentrated his faculties and feelings too entirely on one subject and pursuit, and has not 'looked enough abroad into universality [Bacon's *Advancement of Learning*]. (pp. 14-16)

> *William Hazlitt, "Jeremy Bentham," in his* The Spirit of the Age, or Contemporary Portraits, *Oxford University Press, 1947, pp. 1-16.*

John Stuart Mill   (essay date 1838)

[*Mill is regarded as one of the leading English philosophers and political economists of the nineteenth century. Initially an advocate of the Utilitarian philosophy of Bentham, he gradually diverged in an attempt to reconcile emotion and intuition with Utilitarian rationalism. In the following excerpt, Mill outlines Bentham's methodology and, while noting defects in his thought such as deficiency of imagination and overweening self-reliance, lauds Bentham as one of the most influential critical thinkers and philosophic reformers of his age.*]

There are two men recently deceased, to whom their country is indebted not only for the greater part of the important ideas which have been thrown into circulation among its thinking men in their time, but for a revolution in its general modes of thought and investigation. These men, dissimilar in almost all else, agreed in being closet-students—secluded in a peculiar degree, by circumstances

John Stuart Mill, English philosopher and disciple of Jeremy Bentham.

and character, from the business and intercourse of the world: and both were, through a large portion of their lives, regarded by those who took the lead in opinion (when they happened to hear of them) with feelings akin to contempt. But they were destined to renew a lesson given to mankind by every age, and always disregarded— to shew, that speculative philosophy, which to the superficial appears a thing so remote from the business of life and the outward interests of men, is in reality the thing on earth which most influences them, and in the long run overbears every other influence save those which if must itself obey. The writers of whom we speak have never been read by the multitude; except for the more slight of their works, their readers have been few: but they have been the teachers of the teachers; there is hardly to be found in England an individual of any importance in the world of mind, who (whatever opinions he may have afterwards adopted) did not first learn to think from one of these two; and though their influences have but begun to diffuse themselves through these intermediate channels over society at large, there is already scarcely a publication of any consequence, addressed to the educated classes, which, if these persons had not existed, would not have been very different from what it is. These men are, Jeremy Bentham, and Samuel Taylor Coleridge—the two great seminal minds of England in their age. (pp. 467-68)

A man of great knowledge of the world, and of the highest reputation for practical talent and sagacity among the official men of his time (himself no follower of Bentham, nor of any partial or exclusive school whatever) once said to us, as the result of his observation, that to Bentham more than to any other source might be traced the questioning spirit, the disposition to demand the *why* of everything, which had gained so much ground and was producing such important consequences in these later days. The more this assertion is examined the more true it will be found. Bentham has been in this age and country the great questioner of things established. It is by the influence of the modes of thought with which his writings inoculated a considerable number of thinking men, that the yoke of authority has been broken, and innumerable opinions, formerly received upon tradition as incontestable, are put upon their defence and required to give an account of themselves. Who, before Bentham, (whatever controversies might exist on points of detail), dared to speak disrespectfully, in express terms, of the British Constitution, or the English Law? He did so; and his arguments and his example together encouraged others. We do not mean that his writings caused the Reform Bill, or that the Appropriation Clause owns him as its parent: the changes which have been made, and the greater changes which will be made, in our institutions, are not the work of philosophers, but of the interests and instincts of large portions of society recently grown into strength. But Bentham gave voice to those interests and instincts: until he spoke out, those who found our institutions unsuited to them did not dare to say so, did not dare consciously to think so; they had never heard those institutions questioned by cultivated men, by men of acknowledged intellect; and it is not in the nature of uninstructed minds to resist the united authority of the instructed. Bentham broke the spell. It was not Bentham by his own writings; it was Bentham through the minds and pens which those writings fed—through the men in more direct contact with the world, into whom his spirit passed. If the superstition about ancestorial wisdom has fallen into decay: if the public are grown familiar with the idea that their laws and institutions are not the product of intellect and virtue, but of modern corruption grafted upon ancient barbarism; if the hardiest innovation is no longer scouted *because* it is an innovation—establishments no longer considered sacred because they are establishments—it will be found that those who have accustomed the public mind to these ideas have learnt them in Bentham's school, and that the assault on ancient institutions has been, and is, carried on for the most part with his weapons. It matters not although these thinkers, or indeed thinkers of any description, have been but scantily found among the persons prominently and ostensibly at the head of the Reform movement. All movements, except revolutionary ones, are headed, not by those who originate them, but by those who know best how to compromise between the old opinions and the new. The father of English innovation, both in doctrines and in institutions, is Bentham: he is the great *subversive,* or, in the language of continental philosophers, the great *critical,* thinker of his age and country.

The father of English innovation, both in doctrines and in institutions, is Bentham: he is the great *subversive,* or, in the language of continental philosophers, the great *critical,* thinker of his age and country.

—*John Stuart Mill*

We consider this, however, to be not his highest title to fame. Were this all, he were to be ranked among the lowest order of the potentates of mind—the negative, or destructive philosophers; those who can perceive what is false, but not what is true; who awaken the human mind to the inconsistencies and absurdities of time-sanctioned opinions and institutions, but substitute nothing in the place of what they take away. We have no desire to undervalue the services of such persons: mankind have been deeply indebted to them; nor will there ever be a lack of work for them, in a world in which so many false things are believed, in which so many which have been true are believed long after they have ceased to be true. The qualities, however, which fit men for perceiving anomalies, without perceiving the truths which would rectify them, are not among the rarest of endowments. Courage, verbal acuteness, command over the forms of argumentation, and a popular stile, will make, out of the shallowest man, with a sufficient lack of reverence, a first-rate negative philosopher. Such men have never been wanting in periods of culture; and the period in which Bentham formed his early impressions was emphatically their reign, in proportion to its barrenness in the more noble products of the human

mind. An age of formalism in the Church and corruption in the State, when the most valuable part of the meaning of spiritual truths had faded from the minds even of those who retained from habit a mechanical belief in them, was the time to raise up all kinds of sceptical philosophy. Accordingly, France had Voltaire, and his school of negative thinkers, and England had the profoundest negative thinker upon record, David Hume: a man, the peculiarities of whose mind qualified him to detect failure of proof, and want of logical consistency, at a depth which French sceptics, with their comparatively feeble powers of analysis and abstraction, stopt far short of: Hume, the prince of *dilettanti,* from whose writings one will hardly learn that there is such a thing as truth, far less that it is attainable; but only that the *pro* and *con* of everything may be argued with infinite ingenuity, and furnishes a fine intellectual excercise. This absolute scepticism in speculation very naturally brought him round to Toryism in practicc; for if no faith can be had in the operations of human intellect, and one side of every question is about as likely as another to be true, a man will commonly be inclined to prefer that order of things which, being no more wrong than every other, he has hitherto found compatible with his private comforts. Accordingly Hume's scepticism agreed very well with the comfortable classes, until it began to reach the uncomfortable: when the discovery was made that, although men could be content to be rich without a faith, men would not be content to be poor without it, and religion and morality came into fashion again as the cheap defence of rents and tithes.

If Bentham had merely continued the work of Hume, he would scarcely have been heard of in philosophy: for he was far inferior to Hume in Hume's qualities, and was in no respect fitted to excel as a metaphysician. We must not look for subtlety, or the power of recondite analysis, among his intellectual characteristics. In the former quality, few great thinkers have ever been so deficient; and to find the latter, in any considerable measure, in a mind acknowledging any kindred with his, we must have recourse to the late Mr Mill—a man who united all the great qualities of the metaphysicians of the eighteenth century, with others of a different complexion, admirably qualifying him to complete and correct their work. Bentham had not these peculiar gifts; but he possessed others, not inferior, which were not possessed by any of his precursors; which have made him a source of light to a generation which has far outgrown their influence, and, as we called him, the chief subversive thinker of an age which has long lost all that *they* could subvert.

To speak of him first as a merely negative philosopher—as one who refutes illogical arguments, exposes sophistry, detects contradiction and absurdity: even in that capacity there was a wide field left vacant for him by Hume, and which he has occupied to an unprecedented extent: the field of practical abuses. This was Bentham's peculiar province: to this he was called by the whole bent of his disposition: to carry the warfare against absurdity into things practical. His was an essentially practical mind. It was by practical abuses that his mind was first turned to speculation—by the abuses of the profession which was chosen for him, that of the law. He has himself stated what particular abuse first gave that shock to his mind, the recoil of which has made the whole mountain of abuse totter: it was the custom of making the client pay for three attendances in the office of a Master in Chancery, when only one was given. The law, he found, on examination, was full of such things. But were these discoveries of his? No: they were known to every lawyer who ever practised, to every judge who ever sat upon the bench, and neither before nor for long after did they cause any apparent uneasiness to the consciences of these learned persons, nor hinder them from asserting, whenever occasion offered, in books, in parliament, or on the bench, that the law was the perfection of reason. During so many generations, in each of which thousands of well educated young men were successively placed in Bentham's position and with Bentham's opportunities, he alone was found with sufficient moral sensibility and self-reliance to say in his heart that these things, however profitable they might be, were frauds, and that between them and himself there should be a gulph fixed. To this rare union of self-reliance and moral sensibility we are indebted for all that Bentham has done. Sent to Oxford by his father at the unusually early age of fifteen—required, on admission, to declare his belief in the thirty-nine articles—he felt it necessary to examine them; and the examination suggested scruples, which he sought to get removed, but instead of the satisfaction he expected, was told that it was not for boys like him to set up their judgment against the great men of the Church. After a struggle he signed; but the impression that he had done an immoral act, never left him; he considered himself to have signed a falsehood, and throughout life he never relaxed in his indignant denunciations of all laws which command such falsehoods, all institutions which attach rewards to the telling of them.

Bentham's method may be shortly described as the method of *detail;* of treating wholes by separating them into their parts, abstractions by resolving them into Things,—classes and generalities by distinguishing them into the individuals of which they are made up; and breaking every question into pieces before attempting to solve it.

—*John Stuart Mill*

By thus carrying the war of criticism and refutation, the conflict with falsehood and absurdity, into the field of practical evils, Bentham, even if he had done nothing else, would have earned an important place in the history of intellect. He carried on the warfare without intermission. To this, not only many of his most piquant chapters, but some of the most finished of his entire works, are entirely devoted: the **Defence of Usury;** the **Book of Fallacies;** and the onslaught upon Blackstone, published anonymously under the title of **A Fragment on Government,** which,

though a first production, and of a writer afterwards so much ridiculed for his style, excited the highest admiration no less for its composition than for its thoughts, and was attributed by turns to Lord Mansfield, to Lord Camden, and (by Dr Johnson) to Dunning, one of the greatest masters of style among the lawyers of his day. These writings are altogether original; though of the negative school, they resemble nothing previously produced by negative philosophers; and would have sufficed to create for Bentham, among the subversive thinkers of modern Europe, a place peculiarly his own. But it is not these writings that constitute the real distinction between him and them. There was a deeper difference. It was that they were purely negative thinkers, he was positive: they only assailed error, he made it a point of conscience not to do so until he thought he could plant instead the corresponding truth. Their character was exclusively analytic, his was synthetic. They took for their starting point the received opinion on any subject, dug round it with their logical implements, pronounced its foundations defective, and condemned it: he began *de novo,* laid his own foundations deeply and firmly, built up his own structure, and bid mankind compare the two: it was when he had solved the problem himself, or thought he had done so, that he declared all other solutions to be erroneous. Hence, what they did will not last; it must perish, much of it has already perished, with the errors which it exploded: what he did has its own value, by which it must outlast all errors to which it is opposed. Though we may reject, as we often must, his practical conclusions, yet his premises, the collections of facts and observations from which his conclusions were drawn, remain for ever, a part of the materials of philosophy.

A place, therefore, must be assigned to Bentham among the masters of wisdom, the great teachers and permanent intellectual ornaments of the human race. He is among those who have enriched mankind with imperishable gifts; and although these do not transcend all other gifts, nor entitle him to those honours "above all Greek, above all Roman fame," which by a natural reaction against the neglect and contempt of the world, some few of his admirers were once disposed to accumulate upon him, yet to refuse an admiring recognition of what he was, on account of what he was not, is a much worse error, and one which, pardonable in the vulgar, is no longer permitted to any cultivated and instructed mind.

If we were asked to say, in the fewest possible words; *what* we conceive to be Bentham's place among these great intellectual benefactors of humanity; what he was and what he was not; what kind of service he did and did not render to truth; we should say—he was not a great philosopher, but he was a great reformer in philosophy. He brought into philosophy something which it greatly needed, and for want of which it was at a stand. It was not his doctrines which did this, it was his mode of arriving at them. He introduced into morals and politics those habits of thought and modes of investigation, which are essential to the idea of science; and the absence of which made those departments of inquiry, as physics had been before Bacon, a field of interminable discussion, leading to no result. It was not his *opinions,* in short, but his *method,* that constituted the novelty and the value of what he did; a value beyond all price, even though we should reject the whole, as we unquestionably must a large part, of the opinions themselves.

Bentham's method may be shortly described as the method of *detail;* of treating wholes by separating them into their parts, abstractions by resolving them into Things—classes and generalities by distinguishing them into the individuals of which they are made up; and breaking every question into pieces before attempting to solve it. The precise amount of originality of this process, considered as a logical conception—its degree of connexion with the methods of physical science, or with the previous labours of Bacon, Hobbes, or Locke—is not an essential consideration in this place. Whatever originality there was in the method—in the subjects he applied it to, and in the rigidity with which he adhered to it, there was the greatest. Hence his interminable classifications. Hence his elaborate demonstrations of the most acknowledged truths. That murder, incendiarism, robbery, are mischievous actions, he will not take for granted without proof; let the thing appear ever so self-evident, he will know the why and the how of it with the last degree of precision; he will distinguish all the different mischiefs of a crime, whether of the *first,* the *second,* or the *third* order, namely, 1. the evil to the sufferer, and to his personal connexions; 2. the *danger* from example, and the *alarm,* or painful feeling of insecurity; and 3. the discouragement to industry and useful pursuits arising from the *alarm,* and the trouble and resources which must be expended in warding off the *danger.* After this enumeration, he will prove to you from the laws of human feeling, that even the first of these evils, the sufferings of the immediate victim, will on the average greatly outweigh the pleasure reaped by the offender; much more when all the other evils are taken into account. Unless this could be proved, he would account the infliction of punishment unwarrantable; and for taking the trouble to prove it formally, his defence is, "there are truths which it is necessary to prove, not for their own sakes, because they are acknowledged, but that an opening may be made for the reception of other truths which depend upon them. It is in this manner we provide for the reception of first principles, which, once received, prepare the way for admission of all other truths." To which may be added, that in this manner also do we discipline the mind for practising the same sort of dissection upon questions more complicated and of more doubtful issue.

It is a sound maxim, and one which all close thinkers have felt, but which no one before Bentham ever so consistently applied, that error lurks in generalities: that the human mind, is not capable of embracing a complex whole, until it has surveyed and catalogued the parts of which that whole is made up; that abstractions are not facts, but an abridged mode of expressing facts, and that the only practical mode of dealing with them is to trace them back to the facts (whether of experience or of consciousness) of which they are the expression. Proceeding upon this principle, Bentham makes short work with the ordinary modes of moral and political reasoning. These, it appeared to him, when hunted to their source, for the most part terminated in *phrases.* In politics, liberty, social order, constitution, law of nature, social compact, &c., were the catchwords: ethics had its analogous ones. Such were the arguments on which the gravest questions of morality and policy were made to turn; not reasons, but allusions to reasons; sacramental expressions, by which a summary appeal was made to some general sentiment of mankind, or to some maxim in familiar use, which might be true or not, but the limitations of which no one had ever critically examined. And this satisfied other people; but not Bentham. He required something more than opinion as a reason for opinion. Whenever he found a *phrase* used as an argument for or against anything, he insisted upon knowing what it meant; whether it appealed to any standard, or gave any intimation of any matter of fact relevant to the question; and if he could not find that it did either, he treated it as an attempt on the part of the disputant to impose his own individual sentiment on other people, without giving them a reason for it; a "contrivance for avoiding the obligation of appealing to any external standard, and for prevailing upon the reader to accept of the author's sentiment and opinion as a reason, and that a sufficient one, for itself." Bentham shall speak for himself on this subject: the passage is from his first systematic work, *Introduction to the Principles of Morals and Legislation,* and we could scarcely quote anything more strongly exemplifying both the strength and weakness of his system of philosophy.

> It is curious enough to observe the variety of inventions men have hit upon, and the variety of phrases they have brought forward, in order to conceal from the world, and, if possible, from themselves, this very general and therefore very pardonable self-sufficiency.
>
> 1. One man says, he has a thing made on purpose to tell him what is right and what is wrong; and that is called a 'moral sense:' and then he goes to work at his ease, and says, such a thing is right, and such a thing is wrong—why? 'Because my moral sense tells me it is.'
>
> 2. Another man comes and alters the phrase: leaving out *moral,* and putting in *common* in the room of it. He then tells you that his common sense tells him what is right and wrong, as surely as the other's moral sense did: meaning by common sense a sense of some kind or other, which, he says, is possessed by all mankind: the sense of those whose sense is not the same as the author's being struck out as not worth taking. This contrivance does better than the other; for a moral sense being a new thing, a man may feel about him a good while without being able to find it out: but common sense is as old as the creation; and there is no man but would be ashamed to be thought not to have as much of it as his neighbours. It has another great advantage: by appearing to share power, it lessens envy; for when a man gets up upon this ground, in order to anathematise those who differ from him, it is not by a *sic volo sic jubeo,* but by a *velitis jubeatis.*
>
> 3. Another man comes, and says, that as to a moral sense indeed, he cannot find that he has any such thing: that, however, he has an *understanding,* which will do quite as well. This understanding, he says, is the standard of right and wrong: it tells him so and so. All good and wise men understand as he does: if other men's un-

derstandings differ in any part from his, so much the worse for them: it is a sure sign they are either defective or corrupt.

4. Another man says, that there is an eternal and immutable Rule of Right: that that rule of right dictates so and so: and then he begins giving you his sentiments upon anything that comes uppermost: and these sentiments (you are to take for granted) are so many branches of the eternal rule of right.

5. Another man, or perhaps the same man (it is no matter), says that there are certain practices conformable, and others repugnant, to the Fitness of Things; and then he tells you, at his leisure, what practices are conformable, and what repugnant: just as he happens to like a practice or dislike it.

6. A great multitude of people are continually talking of the Law of Nature; and then they go on giving you their sentiments about what is right and what is wrong: and these sentiments, you are to understand, are so many chapters and sections of the Law of Nature.

7. Instead of the phrase, Law of Nature, you have sometimes Law of Reason, Right Reason, Natural Justice, Natural Equity, Good Order. Any of them will do equally well. This latter is most used in politics. The three last are much more tolerable than the others, because they do not very explicitly claim to be anything more than phrases: they insist but feebly upon the being looked upon as so many positive standards of themselves, and seem content to be taken, upon occasion, for phrases expressive of the conformity of the thing in question to the proper standard, whatever that may be. On most occasions, however, it will be better to say *utility:* *utility* is clearer, as referring more explicitly to pain and pleasure.

8. We have one philosopher, who says, there is no harm in anything in the world but in telling a lie; and that if, for example, you were to murder your own father, this would only be a particular way of saying, he was not your father. Of course when this philosopher sees anything that he does not like, he says, it is a particular way of telling a lie. It is saying, that the act ought to be done, or may be done, when *in truth,* it ought not to be done.

9. The fairest and openest of them all is that sort of man who speaks out, and says, I am of the number of the Elect: now God himself takes care to inform the Elect what is right: and that with so good effect, that let them strive ever so, they cannot help not only knowing it but practising it. If therefore a man wants to know what is right and what is wrong, he has nothing to do but to come to me.

Few, we believe, are now of opinion that these phrases and similar ones have nothing more in them than Bentham saw. But it will be as little pretended, now-a-days, by any person of authority as a thinker, that the phrases can pass as reasons, till after their meaning has been completely an-

alysed, and translated into more precise language: until the standard they appeal to is ascertained, and the *sense* in which, and the *limits* within which, they are admissible as arguments, accurately marked out.

It is the introduction into the philosophy of human conduct, of this method of detail—of this practice of never reasoning about wholes till they have been resolved into their parts, nor about abstractions till they have been translated into realities—that constitutes the originality of Bentham in philosophy, and makes him the great reformer of the moral and political branch of it. To what he terms the "exhaustive method of classification," which is but one branch of this more general method, he himself ascribes everything original in the systematic and elaborate work from which we have quoted. The generalities of his philosophy itself, have little or no novelty: to ascribe any to the doctrine that general utility is the foundation of morality, would imply great ignorance of the history of philosophy, of general literature, and of Bentham's own writings. He derived the idea, as he says himself, from Hume and Helvetius; and it was the doctrine no less, of the adversaries of those writers, the religious philosophers of that age, prior to Reid and Beattie. We never saw an abler defence of the doctrine of utility than in a book written in refutation of Shaftesbury, and now little read—Brown's 'Essays on the Characteristics;' and in Johnson's celebrated review of Soame Jenyns, the same doctrine is set forth as that both of the author and of the reviewer. In all ages of philosophy one of its schools has been utilitarian—not only from the time of Epicurus, but long before. It was by mere accident that this opinion became connected in Bentham with his peculiar method. The utilitarian philosophers antecedent to him had no more claims to the method than their antagonists. To refer, for instance, to the Epicurean philosophy, according to the most complete view we have of the moral part of it, by the most accomplished scholar of antiquity, Cicero; we ask any one who has read his philosophical writings, the 'De Finibus' for instance, whether the arguments of the Epicureans are not as perfect a specimen of σκιαμαχια as those of the Stoics or Platonists—vague phrases which different persons may understand in different senses, and no person in any definite sense; rhetorical appeals to common notions, to εικοτα and σημεια instead of τεκμηρια, notions never narrowly looked into, and seldom exactly true, or true at all in the sense necessary to support the conclusion. Of any systematic appeal to fact and experience, which might seem to be their peculiar province, the Epicurean moralists are as devoid as any of the other schools; they never take a question to pieces, and join issue on a definite point. Bentham certainly did not learn his sifting and anatomizing method from them.

This method Bentham has finally installed in philosophy; has made it henceforth imperative on philosophers of all schools. By it he has formed the intellects of many thinkers, who either never adopted, or have abandoned most of his peculiar opinions. He has taught the method to men of the most opposite schools to his; he has made them perceive that if they do not test their doctrines by the method of detail, their adversaries will. He has thus, it is not too much to say, for the first time introduced precision of thought into moral and political philosophy. Instead of taking up their opinions by intuition, or by ratiocination from premises adopted on a mere rough view, and couched in language so vague that it is impossible to say exactly whether they are true or false, philosophers are now forced to understand one another, to break down the generality of their propositions, and join a precise issue in every dispute. This is nothing less than a revolution in philosophy. Its effect is gradually becoming evident in the writings of English thinkers of every variety of opinion, and will be felt more and more in proportion as Bentham's writings are diffused, and as the number of minds to whose formation they contribute is multiplied:

It will naturally be presumed that of the fruits of this great philosophical improvement some portion at least will have been reaped by its author. Armed with such a potent instrument, and wielding it with such singleness of aim; cultivating the field of practical philosophy with such unwearied and such consistent use of a method right in itself, and not adopted by his predecessors; it cannot be but that Bentham by his own inquiries must have accomplished something considerable. And so, it will be found, he has; something not only considerable, but extraordinary; though but little compared with what he has left undone, and far short of what his sanguine and almost boyish fancy made him flatter himself that he had accomplished. His peculiar method, admirably calculated to make clear thinkers, and sure ones to the extent of their materials, has not equal efficacy for making those materials complete. It is a security for accuracy, but not for comprehensiveness; or, rather, it is a security for one sort of comprehensiveness, but not for another.

It is not to be denied that Bentham's method of laying out his subject is admirable as a preservative against one kind of narrow and partial views. He begins by placing before himself the whole of the field of inquiry to which the particular question belongs, and divides down till he arrives at the thing he is in search of; and thus by successively rejecting all which is *not* the thing, he gradually works out a definition of what it *is*. This, which he calls the exhaustive method, is as old as philosophy itself. Plato owes everything to it, and does everything by it; and the use made of it by that great man in his Dialogues, Bacon, in one of those pregnant logical hints scattered through his writings, and so much neglected by most of his pretended followers, pronounces to be the nearest approach to a true inductive method in the ancient philosophy. Bentham was little aware that Plato had anticipated him in the process to which he too declared that he owed everything. By the practice of it, his speculations are rendered eminently systematic and consistent; no question, with him, is ever an insulated one; he sees every subject in connection with all the other subjects with which in his view it is related, and from which it requires to be distinguished; and as all that he knows, in the least degree allied to the subject, has been marshalled in an orderly manner before him, he does not, like people who use a looser method, forget and overlook a thing on one occasion to remember it on another. Hence there is probably no philosopher of so wide a range, in whom there are so few inconsistencies. If any of the truths which he did not see, had come to be seen by him, he

would have remembered it everywhere and at all times, and would have adjusted his whole system to it. And this is another admirable quality which he has impressed upon the best of the minds trained in his habits of thought: when these minds do open to admit new truths, they digest them as fast as they receive them.

But this system, excellent for keeping before the mind of the thinker all that he knows, does not make him know enough; it does not make a knowledge of *some* of the properties of a thing suffice for the whole of it, nor render a rooted habit of surveying a complex object (though ever so carefully) in only one of its aspects, tantamount to the power of contemplating it in all. To give this last power, other qualities are required: whether Bentham possessed those other qualities we now have to see.

Bentham's mind, as we have already said, was eminently synthetical. He begins all his inquiries by supposing nothing to be known on the subject, and reconstructs all philosophy *ab initio*, without reference to the opinions of his predecessors. But to build either a philosophy or anything else, there must be materials. For the philosophy of matter, the materials are the properties of matter; for moral and political philosophy, the properties of man, and of man's position in the world. The knowledge which any inquirer possesses of these properties, constitutes a limit beyond which, as a moralist or a political philosopher, whatever be his powers of mind, he cannot go. Nobody's synthesis can be more complete than his analysis. If in his survey of human nature and of human life he has left any element out, then, wheresoever that element exerts any influence, his conclusions will fail, more or less, in their application. If he has left out many elements, and those very important, his labours may be highly valuable; he may have largely contributed to that body of partial truths which, when completed and corrected by one another, constitute practical truth; but the applicability of his system to practice in its own proper shape will be of an exceedingly limited range.

Human nature and human life are a wide subject, and whoever would embark in an enterprise requiring a thorough knowledge of them, has need both of large stores of his own, and of all aids and appliances from elsewhere. His qualifications for success will be proportional to two things: the degree in which his own nature and circumstances furnish him with a correct and complete picture of man's nature and circumstances; and his capacity of deriving light from other minds.

Bentham failed in deriving light from other minds. His writings contain few traces of the accurate knowledge of any school of thinking but his own; and many proofs of his entire conviction that they could teach him nothing worth knowing. For some of the most illustrious of previous thinkers, his contempt was unmeasured. In almost the only passage of Bowring's **Deontology** which, from its style, and from its having before appeared in print, may be known to be Bentham's, Socrates and Plato are spoken of in terms distressing to his greatest admirers; and the incapacity to appreciate such men, is a fact perfectly in unison with the general habits of Bentham's mind. He had a phrase, expressive of the view he took of all moral speculations to which his method had not been applied, or (which he considered as the same thing) not founded on a recognition of utility as the moral standard; this phrase was "vague generalities." Whatever presented itself to him in such a shape, he dismissed as unworthy of notice, or dwelt upon only to denounce as absurd. He did not heed, or rather the nature of his mind prevented it from occurring to him, that these generalities contained the whole unanalysed experience of the human race.

Unless it can be asserted that mankind did not know anything until logicians taught it them—that until the last hand has been put to a moral truth by giving it a metaphysically precise expression, all the previous rough-hewing which it has undergone by the common intellect at the suggestion of common wants and common experience is to go for nothing: it must be allowed, that even the originality which can and the courage which dares think for itself, is not a more necessary part of the philosophical character than reverence for previous thinkers, and for the collective mind of the human race. What has been the opinion of mankind, has been the opinion of persons of all tempers and dispositions, of all partialities and prepossessions, of all varieties in position, in education, in opportunities of observation and inquiry. No one inquirer is all this; every inquirer is either young or old, rich or poor, sickly or healthy, married or single, meditative or active, a poet or a logician, an ancient or a modern, a man or a woman; and if a thinking person, has, in addition, the accidental peculiarities of his individual modes of thought. Every circumstance which gives a character to the life of a human being, carries with it its peculiar biases; its peculiar facilities for perceiving some things, and for missing or forgetting others. But, from points of view different from his, different things are perceptible; and none are so likely to have seen what he does not see, as those who do not see what he sees. The general opinion of mankind is the average of the conclusions of all minds, stripped indeed of their choicest and most recondite thoughts, but freed from their twists and partialities: a net result, in which everybody's particular point of view is represented, nobody's predominant. The collective mind does not penetrate below the surface, but it sees all the surface; which profound thinkers, even by reason of their profundity, seldom do: their intenser view of a thing in some of its aspects diverting their attention from others.

The hardiest assertor, therefore, of the freedom of private judgment—the keenest detector of the errors of his predecessors, and of the inaccuracies of current modes of thought—is the very person who most needs to fortify the weak side of his own intellect, by a study of the opinions of mankind in all ages and nations, and of the speculations of philosophers of the modes of thought most opposite to his own. It is there that he will find the experiences denied to himself—the remainder of the truth of which he sees but half—the truths, of which the errors he detects are commonly but the exaggerations. If, like Bentham, he brings with him an improved instrument of investigation, the greater is the probability that he will find ready prepared a rich abundance of rough ore, which was merely waiting for that instrument. A man of clear ideas errs grievously if he imagines that whatever is seen confusedly

does not exist: it belongs to him when he meets with such a thing to dispel the mist, and fix the outlines of the dim vague form which is looming through it.

Bentham's contempt, then, of all other schools of thinkers; his determination to create a philosophy wholly out of the materials furnished by his own mind, and by minds like his own; was his first disqualification as a philosopher. His second, was the incompleteness of his own mind as a representative of universal human nature. In many of the most natural and strongest feelings of human nature he had no sympathy; from many of its graver experiences he was altogether cut off; and the faculty by which one mind understands a mind different from itself, and throws itself into the feelings of that other mind, was denied him, by his deficiency of Imagination.

With Imagination in the popular sense, command of imagery and metaphorical expression, Bentham was, to a certain degree, endowed. For want, indeed, of poetical culture, the images with which his fancy supplied him were seldom beautiful, but they were quaint and humorous, or bold, forcible, and intense: passages might be quoted from him both of playful irony, and of declamatory eloquence, seldom surpassed in the writings of philosophers. The Imagination which he had not, was that to which the name is generally appropriated by the best writers of the present day; that which enables us, by a voluntary effort, to conceive the absent as if it were present, the imaginary as if it were real, and to clothe it in the feelings which, if it were indeed real, it would bring along with it. This is the power by which one human being enters into the mind and circumstances of another. This power constitutes the poet, in so far as he does anything but melodiously utter his own actual feelings. It constitutes the dramatist entirely. It is one of the constituents of the historian; by it we understand other times; by it Guizot interprets to us the middle ages; Nisard, in his beautiful Studies on the later Latin poets, places us in the Rome of the Cæsars; Michelet disengages the distinctive characters of the different races and nations of mankind from the facts of their history. Without it nobody knows even his own nature, further than circumstances have actually tried it and called it out; nor the nature of his fellow-creatures, beyond such generalisations as he may have been enabled to make from his observation of their outward conduct.

By these limits, accordingly, Bentham's knowledge of human nature is bounded. It is wholly empirical; and the empiricism of one who has had little experience. He had neither internal experience nor external; the quiet, even tenor of his life, and his healthiness of mind, conspired to exclude him from both. He never knew prosperity and adversity, passion nor satiety: he never had even the experiences which sickness gives,—he lived from childhood to the age of eighty-five in boyish health. He knew no dejection, no heaviness of heart. He never felt life a sore and a weary burthen. He was a boy to the last. Self-consciousness, that dæmon of the men of genius of our time, from Wordsworth to Byron, from Goethe to Chateaubriand, and to which this age owes most both of its cheerful and its mournful wisdom, never was awakened in him. How much of human nature slumbered in him he knew not, neither can we know. He had never been made alive to the unseen influences which were acting on himself, nor consequently on his fellow-creatures. Other ages and other nations were a blank to him for purposes of instruction. He measured them but by one standard; their knowledge of facts, and their capability to take correct views of utility, and merge all other objects in it. His own lot was cast in a generation of the leanest and barrenest men whom Europe had yet produced, and he was an old man when a better race came in with the present century. He saw accordingly in man little but what the vulgarest eye can see; recognised no diversities of character but what he who runs may read. Knowing so little of human feelings, he knew still less of the influences by which those feelings are formed; all the more subtle workings both of the mind upon itself, and of external things upon the mind, escaped him; and no one, probably, who, in a highly instructed age, ever attempted to give a rule to all human conduct, set out with a more limited knowledge either of the things by which human conduct *is,* or of those by which it *should* be, influenced.

This, then, is our idea of Bentham. He was a man both of remarkable endowments for philosophy, and of remarkable deficiencies for it: fitted, beyond almost any man, for drawing from his premises, conclusions not only correct, but sufficiently precise and specific to be practical: but whose general conception of human nature and life, furnished him with an unusually slender stock of premises. It is obvious what would be likely to be achieved by such a man; what a thinker, thus gifted and thus disqualified, could be in philosophy. He could be a systematic and accurately logical half-man; hunting half-truths to their consequences and practical applications, on a scale both of greatness and of minuteness not previously exemplified: and this is the character which posterity will probably assign to Bentham. (pp. 468-84)

> *John Stuart Mill, in his review "The Works of Jeremy Bentham," in* The London and Westminster Review, *Vol. XXIX, April, 1838, pp. 467-506.*

John Hill Burton   (essay date 1843)

[*Burton was a Scottish historian. In the following excerpt taken from the introduction to his edition of Bentham's works, he discusses Bentham's literary style and method and their impact upon Bentham's critical reception.*]

It has been remarked by several of the critical writers of the day, whose opinions deserve and receive the highest respect, that among Bentham's writings there are numberless passages, of which the brilliant wit, the lively illustration, the spirited eloquence, and the expressive clearness, are not excelled in the works of any writer of the English language. It was conceived that, among those who support his opinions, as well as among those who are either indifferent or hostile to them, there might be many to whom a selection of those passages in Bentham's works which appear to be chiefly distinguished for merit of a simply rhetorical character, might be considered no unwelcome

contribution to the literature of the country. It is often in the midst of long and arduous processes of reasoning, or in the course of elaborate descriptions of minute practical arrangements, demanding from the reader severe thought and unflagging attention, that the most pleasing illustrations of playfulness, or pathos, or epigrammatic expression, are imbedded. He was himself singularly careless in the distribution of these portions of his intellectual riches. His mission he considered, especially in his later years, to be that of an instructor and improver; and the flowers which, equally with more substantial things, were the produce of his vigorous intellect he looked upon as scarcely worthy of passing attention, and deserving of no more notice than to be permitted to grow wherever the more valued objects of his labours left them a little room. (pp. viii-ix)

It is, moreover, generally in those of his works where there is the smallest proportion of ornamental writing, that the processes of reasoning are the most continuous and conclusive, and the most valuable to the Political and Philosophical student. In this respect, there is a great difference between the author's earlier and his later works. At an early period of his life, he had studied the formation of a pure style with great industry and success. He had a vivid and teeming fancy. He had enriched his mind with a multitudinous reading in every description of work which presented him with illustrations of the operations of the human mind in all ages, and in all parts of the world. He possessed, to an eminent degree, the faculty of arranging and adapting the knowledge thus acquired, to second and assist the operations of abstract reasoning, and to send forth his philosophy to the world, illustrated, and attractively adorned. As he advanced in life, he gradually changed his method; or perhaps it may be said, he allowed the most remarkable feature of his mind—his power of abstract reasoning—to master the others. It seemed to be a feeling which acquired greater force in his mind every day, that the time at his disposal was too valuable to be devoted to the art of pleasing; that there was a vast world of important subjects rising before him, which, even were he to live to the longest duration of the life of man, he could not with his utmost zeal and industry, exhaust; and that it was his duty to look to no other qualities in his style of composition, but those which were most eminently fitted to announce his reasoning with precision and accuracy. On this principle, he constructed a nomenclature for his own use, which has provoked no small amount of ridicule; but he was enabled to bear the laughter, when he remembered that, by always using the same word for the same thing, he not only abbreviated his own labours, but rendered his meaning more distinct. Much has been said of the intricacy and obscurity of the sentences in his later works. That they are complex is in many instances true; but that they are obscure and dubious, is so much the reverse of the fact, that their complexity arises, in a great measure, from the anxiety with which he guarded them against the possibility of their meaning being mistaken. So anxious is he that the mind should not, even for a passing moment, adopt a different understanding from that which he wishes to impress on it, that he introduces into the body of his sentences, all the limitations, restrictions, and exceptions, which he thinks may apply to the proposition broadly stated. It may be difficult for the mind to trace all the intricate windings of the sentence: still more difficult to have it in all its proportions clearly viewed at one moment; but when this *has* been accomplished, it is at once clear, that all the apparent prolixity arises from the skill with which the author has made provision, that no man shall have a doubt of what he means to say. . . . It will perhaps serve, in some measure, farther to account for the peculiar aspect of some of Bentham's later works, to explain, that he never prepared any of them for the press. This task he left to others, in the belief that the produce of his labours had intrinsic value, and would, through the assistance of editors, be adapted to the uses of society. Actuated by this feeling, when he had laid out his subject for the day, he laboured continuously on, filling page after page of MS. To the sheets thus filled he gave titles, marginal rubrics, and other facilities for reference: and then he set them aside in his repositories, never touching or seeing them again.

The present is not an occasion for inquiring whether this method fulfilled its author's wishes, and was, what he designed it to be, the most profitable occupation of his time and talents. It must be admitted, however, that whatever compensation it brought in other respects, it lost him readers, and impeded the promulgation of his doctrines. His early works had acquired a popularity with all classes of readers, which would have done much to propitiate favour for a few productions of a less attractive character. It happened, however, that works of the latter class crowded one upon another, until they became accumulated into a mass which overwhelmed and hid from the present generation the few early works which had given instruction and delight to the eighteenth century. Men gradually learned to

---

Henry Sidgwick on the antecedents of Bentham's literary style:

[It] seems to me that we get the right point of view for understanding [Bentham's] work in politics and ethics, if we conceive it as the central and most important realisation of a dominant and all-comprehensive desire for the amelioration of human life, or rather of sentient existence generally. . . . Thus, perhaps, we may partly account for the extreme unreadableness of his later writings, which are certainly "biblia abiblia." The best defence for them is that they are hardly meant to be criticised as books; they were written not so much to be read as to be used. Hence if, after they were written, he saw no prospect of their producing a practical effect, he kept them contentedly on his shelves for a more seasonable opportunity. In his earlier compositions he shows considerable literary faculty: his argument is keen and lucid, and his satirical humour often excellent, though liable to be too prolix. But the fashion in which he really liked to express his thoughts was the proper style of legal documents—a style, that is in which there are no logically superfluous words, but in which everything that is intended is fully expressed, and the most tedious iteration is not shunned if it is logically needed for completeness and precision.

Henry Sidgwick, in "Bentham and Benthamism in Politics and Ethics," Fortnightly Review, May 1877.

---

speak of Bentham as an unreadable author—a character which received countenance from writers who had, in their own persons, acknowledged the sterling value of his works, by plundering and adopting many of his precious thoughts. It is, indeed, in these less-adorned works, that the most valuable of Bentham's exposures of existing fallacies, and projects of practical amendment are to be found; and to the reader who is ambitious of mastering the great truths they contain, it can only be said, that there is no royal road to this department of knowledge, and that to acquire it, he must submit to the labour of steady and continuous study. (pp. ix-xi)

> *John Hill Burton, in an introduction to* Benthamiana: Or, Select Extracts from the Works of Jeremy Bentham, *edited by John Hill Burton, Simpkin, Marshall, & Co., 1843, pp. vii-xxiii.*

Thomas Garrigue Masaryk   (essay date 1898)

[*Masaryk was both the founder of the Czechoslovakian state and its first president. His thought was greatly influenced by his study of the American Revolution and the subsequent history of the United States under the Constitution. In the following excerpt taken from a lecture delivered in 1898, he cites shortcomings related to the reverence of pleasure in Bentham's philosophy of Utilitarianism.*]

Utilitarianism signifies the ethics of utility, of profit (from the Latin *utilis,* useful). The theory is that usefulness, advantage, ought to be the goal of every action. On the question what is it that determines usefulness, we obtain the answer: pleasure, well-being, happiness. Utilitarianism then is also hedonism, that is to say, the ethics of pleasure (from the Greek, *hedone,* pleasure). If we ask what type of satisfaction is specifically at issue, we are answered in two fashions. One group reply: my own advantage and only my advantage is the object of my efforts. Others rejoin: not merely my own gain, but that of the greatest possible number of people. It is in this sense that people speak in English philosophical jargon of a maximum, and a "maximation," of pleasure. Some go so far that they aspire to the greatest possible pleasure for all sentient creatures.

The classical land of this philosophy is England, where Bentham first elaborated it into a comprehensive system. Every man, said Bentham, naturally strives only for his own pleasure and for avoidance of suffering. I pause here to ask: is it accurate to state that man aspires only to pleasure? Those, for instance, who devote themselves to study and desire to learn something, do they seek pleasure solely, or knowledge? The utilitarian will say that they seek only their own pleasure, for all that men do is but a means to obtaining pleasure. That simply is not true. I do not deny that men do strive for pleasure, but they seek other things as well. The question is whether they strive *only* for pleasure.

A further question is whether it makes any difference what kind of pleasure people seek. Is it a matter of indifference, for example, whether one seeks satisfaction in beer or in a work of art? Bentham here makes no distinction; to him it does not matter what sort of pleasure may be sought. What is important only is that the pleasure be as great as possible, and the more intense it is the greater is its worth. Against this, John Stuart Mill objected that pleasures differ in quality. Mill, I think, is right. He who steals finds pleasure in his stealing. If we acknowledged that every pleasure was in itself good, the world would be in a sorry plight. It must be recognized that all pleasure is not good, but only that which is just and true.

We come here to the greatest difficulty. Bentham held that man is a thorough egoist by nature, that every man seeks pleasure for himself alone. How, though, can such an egoism lead to the utilitarian formula: that the pleasure, well-being, happiness of the greatest possible number of people should be the goal of every action? Whence the consideration for the greatest possible number, if man is a total egoist by nature? How can man come out of himself and enter socially into the interests of his neighbours? This is a difficult dilemma for those who maintain that man is nothing but an egoist, totally devoid of any love for his neighbour, and that what we call the love of our neighbour is but disguised egoism, subtle and refined. Some try to dispose of this difficulty by the assertion that when each finds his own happiness all will be happy. But can one identify "each" with "all"? This might be possible perhaps if each received his happiness direct from heaven and we had no need of others' help, and if it never happened that some men gained their profit through injuring others. How many are there, reputed to be happy, who have secured their happiness by the treading down of others? One cannot say that if each individual is well, all society is well too. If man did not possess at least a little disinterested love for his neighbours, there would be no such thing as society; at all events, society would not be healthy. The weak point of this philosophy—this ethics of pleasure, in brief—is that it denies the innate, disinterested kindliness of men towards each other. Ultra-egoism has rightly been rejected by the critical utilitarians. J. S. Mill went so far indeed as to demand self-sacrifice of the individual.

Utilitarianism spread in England and elsewhere because it appeared to be peculiarly practical. There is no need to reflect long when one is counselled to seek one's own advantage; everyone understands. And yet he only seems to understand. If each man really knew how to become happy, there would not be so much self-caused unhappiness. The motto: seek your own advantage, is not, then, so easy to carry into effect as people have believed. I do not deny, however, that it may be so to a certain extent.

Opponents of utilitarianism have reproached it with being moral trading which may be summed up in the formula: I give to you so that you may give to me. They have called it niggardly, vulgar, and unheroic. If we consider, though, the lives of the founders of this school, we must recognize that they were men of high moral worth. Bentham was consistent in his theoretic egoism. Yet, in spite of that, he worked constantly throughout his life for the common good, and his name is revered throughout the entire world, particularly in England. (pp. 52-6)

Thomas Garrigue Masaryk, "Utilitarianism,"
in The Ideals of Humanity, *translated by W.*

Preston Warren and How to Work: Lectures Delivered in 1898 at the University of Prague, *translated by Marie J. Kohn-Holocek, revised edition, George Allen & Unwin Ltd., 1938, pp. 52-9.*

Leslie Stephen   (essay date 1900)

[*Considered the most important English literary critic of the Victorian age after Matthew Arnold, Stephen has beeen praised by scholars for his judgment, moral insight, and academic vigor. Viewing all literature as an imaginary rendering in concrete terms of a writer's philosophy, he held that criticism should explicate characters, symbols, and events so that a reader may easily grasp an author's intent. In the following excerpt taken from his prominent study,* The English Utilitarians, *Stephen identifies the potential conflict in Bentham's writings between public happiness and individual well-being.*]

[Bentham's most important writing on economic theory] was the *Defence of Usury,* and in this . . . he was simply adding a corollary to [Scottish economist Adam Smith's] *Wealth of Nations.* The *Wealth of Nations* itself represented the spirit of business; the revolt of men who were building up a vast industrial system against the fetters imposed by traditional legislation and by rulers who regarded industry in general, as Telford is said to have regarded rivers. Rivers were meant to supply canals, and trade to supply tax-gatherers. With this revolt, of course, Bentham was in full sympathy, but here I shall only speak of one doctrine of great interest, which occurs both in his political treatises and his few economical remarks. Bentham objected . . . to the abstract theory of equality; yet it was to the mode of deduction rather than to the doctrine itself which he objected. He gave, in fact, his own defence [in his *Constitutional Code*]; and it is one worth notice. The principle of equality is derivative, not ultimate. Equality is good because equality increases the sum of happiness. Thus, as he says, if two men have £1000, and you transfer £500 from one to the other, you increase the recipient's wealth by one-third, and diminish the loser's wealth by one-half. You therefore add less pleasure than you subtract. The principle is given less mathematically by the more significant argument that 'felicity' depends not simply on the 'matter of felicity' or the stimulus, but also on the sensibility to felicity which is necessarily limited. Therefore by adding wealth—taking, for example, from a thousand labourers to give to one king—you are supersaturating a sensibility already glutted by taking away from others a great amount of real happiness. With this argument, which has of late years become conspicuous in economics, he connects another of primary importance. The first condition of happiness, he says, is not 'equality' but 'security.' Now you can only equalise at the expense of security. If I am to have my property taken away whenever it is greater than my neighbour's, I can have no security. Hence, if the two principles conflict, equality should give way. Security is the primary, which must override the secondary, aim. Must the two principles, then, always conflict? No; but 'time is the only mediator.' The law may help to accumulate inequalities; but in a prosperous state there is a 'continual progress towards equality.' The law has to stand aside; not to maintain monopolies; not to restrain trade; not to permit entails; and then property will diffuse itself by a natural process, already exemplified in the growth of Europe. The 'pyramids' heaped up in feudal times have been lowered, and their '*débris* spread abroad' among the industrious. Here again we see how Bentham virtually diverges from the *a priori* school. Their absolute tendencies would introduce 'equality' by force; he would leave it to the spontaneous progress of security. Hence Bentham is in the main an adherent of what he calls the '*laissez-nous faire*' principle. He advocates it most explicitly in the so-called ***Manual of Political Economy***—a short essay first printed in 1798. The tract, however, such as it is, is less upon political economy proper than upon economic legislation; and its chief conclusion is that almost all legislation is improper. His main principle is 'Be quiet' (the equivalent of the French phrase, which surely should have been excluded from so English a theory). Security and freedom are all that industry requires; and industry should say to government only what Diogenes said to Alexander, 'Stand out of my sunshine.'

Once more, however, Bentham will not lay down the 'let alone' principle absolutely. His adherence to the empirical method is too decided. The doctrine 'be quiet,' though generally true, rests upon utility, and may, therefore, always be qualified by proving that in a particular case the balance of utility is the other way. In fact, some of Bentham's favourite projects would be condemned by an absolute adherent of the doctrine. The Panopticon, for example, though a 'mill to grind rogues honest' could be applied to others than rogues, and Bentham hoped to make his machinery equally effective in the case of pauperism. A system of national education is also included in his ideal constitution. It is, in fact, important to remember that the 'individualism' of Benthamism does not necessarily coincide with an absolute restriction of government interference. The general tendency was in that direction; and in purely economical questions, scarcely any exception was admitted to the rule. Men are the best judges, it was said, of their own interest; and the interference of rulers in a commercial transaction is the interference of people inferior in knowledge of the facts, and whose interests are 'sinister' or inconsistent with those of the persons really concerned. Utility, therefore, will, as a rule, forbid the action of government: but, as utility is always the ultimate principle, and there may be cases in which it does not coincide with the 'let alone' principle, we must always admit the possibility that in special cases government can interfere usefully, and, in that case, approve the interference.

Hence we have the ethical application of these theories. The individualist position naturally tends to take the form of egoism. The moral sentiments, whatever they may be, are clearly an intrinsic part of the organic social instincts. They are intimately involved in the whole process of social evolution. But this view corresponds precisely to the conditions which Bentham overlooks. The individual is already there. The moral and the legal sanctions are 'external'; something imposed by the action of others; corresponding to 'coercion,' whether by physical force or the dread of public opinion; and, in any case, an accretion or

addition, not a profound modification of his whole nature. The Utilitarian 'man' therefore inclines to consider other people as merely parts of the necessary machinery. Their feelings are relevant only as influencing their outward conduct. If a man gives me a certain 'lot' of pain or pleasure, it does not matter what may be his motives. The 'motive' for all conduct corresponds in all cases to the pain or pleasure accruing to the agent. It is true that his happiness will be more or less affected by his relations to others. But as conduct is ruled by a calculation of the balance of pains or pleasures dependent upon any course of action, it simplifies matters materially, if each man regards his neighbour's feelings simply as instrumental, not intrinsically interesting. And thus the coincidence between that conduct which maximises my happiness and that conduct which maximises happiness in general, must be regarded as more or less accidental or liable in special cases to disappear. If I am made happier by action which makes others miserable, the rule of utility will lead to my preference of myself.

Here we have the question whether the Utilitarian system be essentially a selfish system. Bentham, with his vague psychology, does not lay down the doctrine absolutely. After giving this list of self-regarding 'springs of action,' he proceeds to add the pleasures and pains of 'sympathy' and 'antipathy' which, he says, are not self-regarding. Moreover, as we have seen, he has some difficulty in denying that 'benevolence' is a necessarily moral motive: it is only capable of prompting to bad conduct in so far as it is insufficiently enlightened; and it is clear that a moralist who makes the 'greatest happiness of the greatest number' his universal test, has some reason for admitting as an elementary pleasure the desire for the greatest happiness. This comes out curiously in the ***Constitutional Code.*** He there lays down the 'self-preference principle'—the principle, namely, that 'every human being' is determined in every action by his judgment of what will produce the greatest happiness to himself, 'whatsoever be the effect . . . in relation to the happiness of other similar beings, any or all of them taken together.' Afterwards, however, he observes that it is 'the constant and arduous task of every moralist' and of every legislator who deserves the name to 'increase the influence of sympathy at the expense of that of self-regard and of sympathy for the greater number at the expense of sympathy for the lesser number.' He tries to reconcile these views by the remark 'that even sympathy has its root in self-regard,' and he argues, as [English philosopher] Mr. Herbert Spencer has done more fully, that if Adam cared only for Eve and Eve only for Adam—neither caring at all for himself or herself—both would perish in less than a year. Self-regard, that is, is essential, and sympathy supposes its existence. Hence Bentham puts himself through a catechism. What is the 'best' government? That which causes the greatest happiness of the given community. What community? 'Any community, which is as much as to say, every community.' But *why* do you desire this happiness? Because the establishment of that happiness would contribute to *my* greatest happiness. And *how* do you prove that you desire this result? By my labours to obtain it, replies Bentham. This oddly omits the more obvious question, how can you be sure that your happiness will be promoted by the greatest happiness of all? What if the two criteria differ? I desire the general happiness, he might have replied, because my benevolence is an original or elementary instinct which can override my self-love; or I desire it, he would perhaps have said, because I know as a fact that the happiness of others will incidentally contribute to my own. The first answer would fall in with some of his statements; but the second is, as I think must be admitted, more in harmony with his system. Perhaps, indeed, the most characteristic thing is Bentham's failure to discuss explicitly the question whether human action is or is not necessarily 'selfish.' He tells us in regard to the 'springs of action' that all human action is always 'interested,' but explains that the word properly includes actions in which the motive is not 'self-regarding.' It merely means, in fact, that all conduct has motives. The statement which I have quoted about the 'self-preference' principle may only mean a doctrine which is perfectly compatible with a belief in 'altruism'—the doctrine, namely, that as a fact most people are chiefly interested by their own affairs. The legislator, he tells us, should try to increase sympathy, but the less he takes sympathy for the 'basis of his arrangements'—that is, the less call he makes upon purely unselfish motives—the greater will be his success. This is a shrewd and, I should say, a very sound remark, but it implies—not that all motives are selfish in the last analysis, but—that the legislation should not assume too exalted a level of ordinary morality. The utterances in the very unsatisfactory *Deontology* are of little value, and seem to imply a moral sentiment corresponding to a petty form of commonplace prudence.

Leaving this point, however, the problem necessarily presented itself to Bentham in a form in which selfishness is the predominating force, and any recognition of independent benevolence rather an incumbrance than a help. If we take the 'self-preference principle' absolutely, the question becomes how a multitude of individuals, each separately pursuing his own happiness, can so arrange matters that their joint action may secure the happiness of all. Clearly a man, however selfish, has an interest generally in putting down theft and murder. He is already provided with a number of interests to which security, at least, and therefore a regular administration of justice, is essential. His shop could not be carried on without the police; and he may agree to pay the expenses, even if others reap the benefit in greater proportion. A theory of legislation, therefore, which supposes ready formed all the instincts which make a decent commercial society possible can do without much reference to sympathy or altruism. Bentham's man is not the colourless unit of *a priori* writing, nor the noble savage of Rousseau, but the respectable citizen with a policeman round the corner. Such a man may well hold that honesty is the best policy; he has enough sympathy to be kind to his old mother, and help a friend in distress; but the need of romantic and elevated conduct rarely occurs to him; and the heroic, if he meets it, appears to him as an exception, not far removed from the silly. He does not reflect—especially if he cares nothing for history—how even the society in which he is a contented unit has been built up, and for much loyalty and heroism has been needed for the work; nor even, to do him justice, what unsuspected capacities may lurk in his own commonplace character. The really characteristic point is, however, that Bentham does not clearly face the problem. He is content

to take for granted as an ultimate fact that the self-interest principle in the long run coincides with the greatest 'happiness' principle, and leaves the problem to his successors. (pp. 307-15)

The limitations and defects of Bentham's doctrine have been made abundantly evident by later criticism. They were due partly to his personal character, and partly to the intellectual and special atmosphere in which he was brought up. But it is more important to recognise the immense real value of his doctrine. Briefly, I should say, that there is hardly an argument in Bentham's voluminous writings which is not to the purpose so far as it goes. Given his point of view, he is invariably cogent and relevant. And, moreover, that is a point of view which has to be taken. No ethical or political doctrine can, as I hold, be satisfactory which does not find a place for Bentham, though he was far, indeed, from giving a complete theory of his subject. . . . Bentham's whole life was spent in the attempt to create a science of legislation. Even where he is most tiresome, there is a certain interest in his unflagging working out of every argument, and its application to all conceivable cases. It is all genuine reasoning; and throughout it is dominated by a respect for good solid facts. His hatred of 'vague generalities' means that he will be content with no formula which cannot be interpreted in terms of definite facts. The resolution to insist upon this should really be characteristic of every writer upon similar subjects, and no one ever surpassed Bentham in attention to it. Classify and reclassify, to make sure that at every point your classes correspond to realities. In the effort to carry out these principles, Bentham at least brought innumerable questions to a sound test, and exploded many pestilent fallacies. If he did not succeed further, if whole spheres of thought remained outside of his vision, it was because in his day there was not only no science of 'sociology' or psychology—there are no such sciences now—but no adequate perception of the vast variety of investigation which would be necessary to lay a basis for them. But the effort to frame a science is itself valuable, indeed of surpassing value, so far as it is combined with a genuine respect for facts. It is common enough to attempt to create a science by inventing technical terminology. Bentham tried the far wider and far more fruitful method of a minute investigation of particular facts. His work, therefore, will stand, however different some of the results may appear when fitted into a different framework. And, therefore, however crudely and imperfectly, Bentham did, as I believe, help to turn speculation into a true and profitable channel. . . . if any one doubts Bentham's services, I will only suggest to him to compare Bentham with any of his British contemporaries, and to ask where he can find anything at all comparable to his resolute attempt to bring light and order into a chaotic infusion of compromise and prejudice. (pp. 316-18)

Leslie Stephen, "Bentham's Life," in his The English Utilitarians, Vol. I, *1900. Reprint by Peter Smith, 1950, pp. 169-326.*

Ernest Albee   (essay date 1902)

[*In the following excerpt, Albee discusses Bentham's*

A portrait of the adolescent Jeremy Bentham by Thomas Frye, 1761.

Utilitarianism within the context of the history of English moral philosophy.]

Though brought up a Tory, [Bentham] was by temperament 'of the opposition'—in all respects a Radical. He generally writes clearly, and not without force; but he constantly loses his temper, and even goes out of his way to vilify those whom he opposes by imputing to them interested motives. The result is that, however much the reader may happen to sympathise with the general tenor of his thought, he is almost sure to find his works irritating in style and method. Yet it was this very fervour of the reformer that commended Bentham so strongly to certain young men of radical tendencies in his own day. While [English theologian and Utilitarian philosopher William] Paley's *Moral and Political Philosophy* met with extraordinary success as a text-book, the author could not properly be said to have founded a 'school'. His work rather made explicit what had long been implicit in the ethical teaching of his own University. Bentham, on the other hand, was regarded, both by himself and by his immediate followers, as the inaugurator of a perfectly new régime. The statement of [English philosopher and mathematician William] Whewell [in his *Lectures on the History of Moral Philosophy in England,* Lecture xiii], that "The school of Bentham, for a time, afforded as near a resemblance as mod-

ern times can show, of the ancient schools of Philosophy, which were formed and held together by an almost unbounded veneration for their master, and in which the disciples were content to place their glory in understanding and extending the master's principles," is doubtless an exaggeration, but hardly so misleading as Mill would have us believe.

In considering Bentham's ethical system, it is important to decide, once for all, what works we should be prepared to recognise as authoritatively representing his doctrine. Three only need come under consideration: his *Fragment on Government* (1776), his *Principles of Morals and Legislation* (printed in 1780, but not published till 1789), and his posthumous work, *Deontology* (edited by his literary executor, [John] Bowring, and published in 1834). Of these, the *Fragment on Government,* which deals only very incidentally with ethical problems, is of importance for us only as indicating the author's attitude at the time when it was published. It is sufficient to note that, as early as 1776, he had adopted the general position with which his name later became identified, and also that the tendency toward violent polemics, which later became so disagreeable a feature of his works, was already clearly apparent. *The Principles of Morals and Legislation* is by far the best known of the three works mentioned, and it is upon this that expositions of Bentham's ethical system are commonly based. But, while one can clearly enough gather the author's general views on Ethics from the first few chapters of this book, one should always remember that it is primarily of Jurisprudence, and not of theoretical Ethics, that Bentham is here treating. In the case of a writer representing a really new principle in Ethics, or one more difficult to expound in comparatively summary fashion, this might lead to serious confusion, seeing that the relation between Ethics and Jurisprudence must itself be regarded as a vexed question.

The *Deontology,* then, is the only work which Bentham wrote on Ethics proper. But here we are confronted with a difficulty quite as serious as that just noted in the case of his *Principles of Morals and Legislation*; for the *Deontology,* which was a posthumous publication, was not merely 'edited,' in the ordinary sense, but (in part, at least) arranged from Bentham's papers by his enthusiastic friend and admirer, John Bowring, whom he had made his literary executor. The general impression seems to be, that Bowring took unwarranted liberties with the manuscripts, many of which had been handed over to him during Bentham's lifetime. But, while it would be rash to assert the contrary, I am not aware that any conclusive evidence to this effect has ever been produced. Indeed, most of the blemishes which are found in the book, and which would make one willing to believe that it had been changed here and there by another hand, can be almost exactly duplicated from those of Bentham's works which were published during his lifetime, and about whose authenticity there has never been the shadow of a doubt. Moreover, the style in many of the more important passages, including some of the most disagreeable, is unmistakably Bentham's. It should be further noted that, although there are two volumes of the *Deontology*—(1) "Theory of Virtue" and (2) "Practice of Virtue"—the first volume alone is of theoretical importance; and it is mainly with regard to the second volume, as it seems to the present writer, that the question of authenticity arises. (pp. 174-77)

[English poet and playwright John] Gay had remarked, at the beginning of the *Dissertation,* that the theoretical differences between moralists were less than might appear. Indeed, he suspects "that they only talk a different language, and that all of them have the same criterion in reality, only they have expressed it in different words". The suggestion doubtless is, that we must look for latent Utilitarianism in non-Utilitarian systems. Paley—apparently following the *Dissertation*—expresses himself in a similar way, but is more explicit. He says [in his *Elements of Moral and Political Philosophy,* 1785]: " 'The fitness of things,' means their fitness to produce happiness; 'the nature of things,' means that actual constitution of the world, by which some things, as such and such actions, for example, produce happiness, and others misery; 'reason' is the principle by which we discover or judge of this constitution; 'truth' is this judgment expressed or drawn out into propositions". And, again, Paley follows Gay in the doubtful thesis that "This is the reason that moralists, from whatever different principles they set out, commonly meet in their conclusions".

Bentham, on the other hand, never mentions non-hedonistic systems, except in terms of contempt. The following passages—taken almost at random from the ***Principles*** and the ***Deontology***—speak for themselves.

> The various systems that have been formed concerning the standard of right and wrong, may all be reduced to the principle of sympathy and antipathy. . . . They consist all of them in so many contrivances for avoiding the obligation of appealing to any external standard, and for prevailing upon the reader to accept of the author's sentiment or opinion as a reason for itself.

> . . . . .

> He who, on any other occasion, should say, "It is as I say, because I say it is so," would not be thought to have said any great matter: but on the question concerning the standard of morality, men have written great books, wherein from beginning to end they are employed in saying this and nothing else.

> . . . . .

> The *summum bonum*—the sovereign good—what is it? . . . It is this thing, and that thing, and the other thing—it is anything but pleasure—it is the Irishman's apple-pie made of nothing but quinces. . . . While Xenophon was writing history, and Euclid giving instruction in geometry, Socrates and Plato were talking nonsense under pretence of teaching wisdom and morality.

'Moral sense,' 'common sense,' 'understanding,' 'reason,' 'right reason,' 'nature,' and 'nature's law,' 'natural justice,' 'natural equity,' 'good order,' 'truth'—"all these are but the dogmas of men who insist on implicit obedience to their decrees".

Unlike his Utilitarian predecessors, then, Bentham becomes nervous, and often violent, at the mere mention of the term *'summum bonum';* but his own treatment of the question as to the fundamental ground of morality is in all essential respects identical with theirs. Not only does he, of course, regard happiness as the true Good, but his arguments to substantiate this view are those which had long been familiar before he wrote. Indeed, in the ***Principles of Morals and Legislation,*** he can hardly be said to argue the matter at all; but rather assumes dogmatically the Utilitarian criterion of morality. The Good is 'happiness' and 'happiness' is merely the 'sum of pleasures,' as Gay and [English moralist Abraham] Tucker had held. Moreover, there are no 'qualitative distinctions' between pleasures, as Tucker had explicitly taught—all concrete differences being reducible to differences of intensity and permanence. Not only does each seek his own happiness, but each is incomparably the best judge of what will make for his own happiness, as Tucker had been at pains to point out. Like Tucker, again, Bentham remarks that the words 'pleasure' and 'pain' are likely to prove misleading in ethical discussions, because they seem to imply too much, and suggests 'well-being' and its contrary as convenient substitutes, more general in meaning—just as Tucker had suggested the terms 'satisfaction' and 'dissatisfaction'.

Of course Bentham is not to be blamed for not developing the hedonistic conception of the Good beyond what had been done, *e.g.,* by Paley—for the simple reason that Paley and his predecessors had already stated Hedonism in perfectly unmistakable terms. But even in 1834, Bentham's ardent disciple, Bowring, was able to write: "It was in 1785 that Paley published his *Elements of Moral and Political Philosophy.* He mentions the principle of utility, but seems to have no idea of its bearing upon happiness. And if he had any such idea, he was the last man to give expression to it." (pp. 178-80)

But it might seem at first as if there were a difference between Bentham, on the one hand, and Gay, Tucker, and Paley, on the other, inasmuch as Bentham once for all adopted the formula, 'the greatest happiness of the greatest number,' as the corner-stone of his system. In other words, the previous Utilitarian systems—except [English philosopher and theologian Richard] Cumberland's, [Scottish philosopher and historian David] Hume's (in its later form), and [English psychologist and philosopher David] Hartley's—had assumed that all motives were ultimately selfish, while Bentham's, by virtue of its very formula, suggested devotion to one's fellow men. It cannot be too strongly insisted, however, that there is no theoretical difference between the four authors on this question regarding the motive of the moral agent. Bentham used the 'greatest happiness' formula because he was a reformer—obviously a fortuitous circumstance from the point of view of theoretical Ethics. Certainly none of the authors just mentioned had emphasised more strongly than Bentham does the necessary egoism of the individual. For instance, he says: "A man, a moralist, gets into an elbow-chair, and pours forth pompous dogmatisms about *duty*—and *duties.* Why is he not listened to? Because every man is thinking about *interests.*" And again: "To prove that the immoral action is a miscalculation of self-interest—to show how erroneous an estimate the vicious man makes of pains and pleasures, is the purpose of the intelligent moralist". Indeed, Bentham is at a disadvantage here, as compared with the others, because he is nowhere quite explicit with regard to the origin of sympathy and its place in his system. It may be well to note, in this connection, that he consistently holds that "the good produced by effective benevolence is small in proportion to that produced by the personal motives".

Not only, then, is the Good pleasure, according to Bentham's view; but the good immediately sought is not the pleasure of 'the greatest number,' but rather one's own. How may the good of each and the good of all be shown to coincide? For clearly they must coincide, if a multitude of self-seeking individuals are capable of working out a common good. This is a question which had been discussed, not only by the earlier Utilitarians, but by writers like [English philosopher Anthony Ashley Cooper, Third Earl of Shaftesbury] and [Scottish philosopher Francis] Hutcheson, who could not properly be classed with them. Indeed, up to this time, the non-Utilitarian writers seem to have had better success than the Utilitarians in their attempts to reconcile public and private interest. It is unnecessary to recapitulate here what has been discussed at length in the proper connection. For our present purpose, it is enough to notice that Bentham did not profit by the suggestions of those who, like Cumberland and Shaftesbury, had attempted to demonstrate the necessarily organic character of society. Though adopting the 'greatest happiness' formula, his logical position is distinctly that of eighteenth century Individualism.

From this point of view, rewards and (more particularly) punishments, or, as Bentham chooses to call them, 'sanctions,' must be looked to, in order to effect this reconciliation. Bentham's list of these 'sanctions' differs somewhat, as regards their number, in his various works bearing upon Ethics. In the *Fragment on Government,* three are mentioned: (1) the 'political,' (2) the 'religious,' and (3) the 'moral'. In the *Principles of Morals and Legislation,* four are recognised: (1) the 'physical,' (2) the 'political,' (3) the 'moral' or 'popular,' and (4) the 'religious'. In the *Deontology,* Bentham succeeds in distinguishing five 'sanctions': (1) the 'physical' (*i.e.,* natural consequences, abstracting from one's relations to other human beings); (2) the 'social' or 'sympathetic' (*i.e.,* consequences which result from one's personal or domestic relations); (3) the 'moral' or 'popular' (*i.e.,* public opinion); (4) the 'political' or 'legal'; and (5) the 'religious' or 'superhuman'. It is to be doubted if he improved matters by trying to distinguish sharply between (2) and (3); indeed, he himself hardly insists upon the separation. If we neglect this rather fine distinction, and regard the list of 'sanctions' in the *Principles of Morals and Legislation* as his complete list, an interesting comparison suggests itself. For this list of 'sanctions'— often regarded as particularly characteristic of Bentham— is identical with that given by Gay in the *Dissertation.*

It might be imagined by one who knew the early Utilitarians only at second hand, that Bentham's treatment of the particular virtues, as following from the Utilitarian principle, must be more definite and consistent than that of his predecessors; but, if anything, the contrary is true. Indeed, if we go so far as to rule out the *Deontology* altogether as unreliable—as I am not myself prepared to do—we must admit that Bentham never even attempted to give a systematic treatment of the particular virtues. The *Fragment on Government,* of course, contains nothing of the kind; and, in the *Principles of Morals and Legislation,* where he was writing mainly from the point of view of Jurisprudence, he very properly omitted any such treatment of the virtues. In the latter work, when writing of the distinction between Ethics and Jurisprudence, he merely remarks that the virtues may conveniently be divided into those of (1) 'prudence,' (2) 'probity' [justice], and (3) 'beneficence'.

In the *Deontology,* then, upon which we must here depend, Bentham begins by dividing virtue into two branches: (1) 'prudence,' and (2) 'effective benevolence'. Quite after the manner of Cumberland, 'prudence' is regarded as having its seat in the understanding; 'effective benevolence,' principally in the affections. 'Prudence,' in turn, is divided into (*a*) 'self-regarding,' and (*b*) 'extra-regarding'; while 'effective benevolence,' again is either (*a*) 'positive' (*i.e.,* productive of positive pleasure) or (*b*) 'negative' (*i.e.,* calculated to diminish pain). The latent confusion here, which Bentham might easily have avoided by retaining his earlier classification, hardly needs to be pointed out; indeed, the distinctions thus made are practically unmanageable. In his actual treatment of the virtues, he seems to use the term 'prudence' only in the first sense. This was, perhaps, almost inevitable; but the result is, that he is at a very serious disadvantage, not only as compared with Hume, but as compared with Tucker and Paley, in his treatment of what was for them all the fundamental virtue—Justice. In fact, Bentham's deduction of the particular virtues, so far as he considers them at all, is so manifestly weak, that one must charitably conclude that this part of the *Deontology* was—by him, at least—unfinished. If our knowledge of Ethics were confined to what is contained in the *Deontology,* we would have to agree most emphatically with Bentham, when he says: "Though the Linnæus of Natural History has appeared in the world, and restored its chaos into order and harmony, the Linnæus of Ethics is yet to come".

One important topic—Bentham's treatment of the hedonistic calculus—remains to be considered. Here, if anywhere, we must look for originality in Bentham's treatment of ethical problems. . . . [Both] Tucker and Paley taught, not only that we could not predict consequences in any particular case exactly enough thus to determine the rightness or wrongness of the proposed action; but also that there are obvious reasons, from the Utilitarian point of view, why we should not attempt to do anything of the kind. In other words, we must confine ourselves, in the main, to a consideration of the 'general' consequences of different classes of actions, and thus act upon a basis of 'general rules'. . . . [Both] authors were willing enough that, at the time of action, the agent should regard the moral law as an end in itself.

To Bentham, on the other hand, this probably would have seemed a pitiful subterfuge. He apparently holds that we not only may, but must compute in the particular case, and be largely determined by such computations. And, if there be virtue in terminology, he elaborated a formidable instrument for the hedonistic calculus. The value of pleasures and pains must be estimated in terms of their 'intensity,' 'duration,' 'certainty,' 'proximity,' and 'extent'. But this is not all. A pleasure or pain may be 'fruitful' or 'barren,' 'pure' or 'impure'. Of the distinctions thus made, the first five hardly require explanation. 'Extent' may properly be put by itself, as it refers merely to the number of individuals concerned. It is the multiplier, and not the multiplicand. 'Certainty' and 'proximity,' as the words would imply, refer only to the probability or improbability of the pleasures or pains being experienced, so that in the last resort 'intensity' and 'duration' are all that have to be considered. So far, Bentham's treatment of the hedonistic calculus in the **Deontology** corresponds exactly to his treatment in the **Principles of Morals and Legislation.** We have to be more careful, however, in the case of 'fecundity' and 'purity'. In the **Principles,** the 'fecundity' of a pleasure or pain is defined as "the chance it has of being followed by sensations of the *same* kind: that is, pleasures, if it be a pleasure: pains, if it be a pain". Its 'purity,' on the other hand, is defined as "the chance it has of *not* being followed by sensations of the *opposite* kind: that is, pains, if it be a pleasure: pleasures, if it be a pain". In the **Deontology,** the author says: "A pleasure or a pain may be fruitful or barren. A pleasure may be fruitful in pleasures, or fruitful in pains, or fruitful in both; and a pain, on the contrary, may be fruitful in pleasures or pains, or both." As regards 'purity,' he says in the same work: "A pleasure is considered pure, in the degree in which it is unaccompanied by counterbalancing pains—a pain is pure, in the proportion in which it is unaccompanied by counterbalancing pleasures".

It will readily be seen that, as used in the **Principles,** 'fecundity' and 'purity' both refer to the future. Given a pleasure or a pain, we call it 'fruitful,' if it is likely to be followed by other affections of the *same* kind; 'pure,' if it is *not* likely to be followed by other affections of the *opposite* kind. In the **Deontology,** as will be noted, the same terms are used, but with a somewhat different signification. The 'fruitfulness' or 'barrenness' of the particular pleasure or pain is here regarded as its productiveness or unproductiveness of future affections—whether of the same or of the opposite kind, or of both. 'Purity' and 'impurity,' on the other hand, apparently refer merely to the unmixed or mixed character of our affections, *i.e.,* pleasure without pain, or pain without pleasure. I do not understand that Bentham necessarily commits himself to the dubious position that we have states of consciousness which are at the same time pleasurable and painful. It is enough that, in some cases, circumstances are such that our consciousness vibrates back and forth between pleasure and pain with rapid alternation. Roughly speaking, we might say that pleasures and pains experienced under such conditions were 'impure,' in Bentham's sense. Perhaps it may seem finical to criticise Bentham's choice of technical terms; but it will be seen that the word 'fecundity,' as here applied, is rather misleading, as it almost inevitably suggests a causal relation between pleasures and pains themselves, which the author could not have intended.

After thus considering the general aspects of pleasure-pain, Bentham gives an elaborate classification of pleasures and pains in both the **Principles** and the **Deontology.** In the **Deontology,** the list is as follows: (1) pleasures and pains of sense, (2) pleasures of wealth, with the corresponding pains of privation, (3) pleasures of skill and pains of awkwardness, (4) pleasures of amity and pains of enmity, (5) pleasures of good reputation and pains of ill-repute, (6) pleasures of power, (7) pleasures of piety, with their contrasted pains, (8) pleasures and pains of sympathy or benevolence, (9) those of malevolence, (10) those of memory, (11) those of imagination, (12) those of expectation, and (13) those of association. The list given in the **Principles** is practically the same, except that still another class of pleasures is added, *i.e.,* those of relief. Such minor differences may be neglected; but Bentham himself pertinently points out that "Of the whole list of pains and pleasures, two classes only regard others—they are those of benevolence and malevolence. All the rest are self-regarding." It goes without saying that this list is a purely arbitrary one, having no warrant in Psychology, and that it is hardly, if at all, calculated to assist us in the actual computation of pleasures and pains. In fact, the list is mainly interesting, because it illustrates particularly well a limitation of Bentham's which has often been pointed out, *viz.,* his narrow and mechanical view of human nature.

Such, then, was Bentham's treatment of the hedonistic calculus. Without entering on any more general criticism of Bentham's Utilitarianism, we are now prepared to ask two questions: (1) Were the refinements which he introduced of practical importance? (2) Was he right in holding, as he at least seemed to do, that we should largely depend upon such computations as we can make in the individual case? The first question need not detain us long. The distinctions which we have just been examining seem, on the whole, to be helpful, though the particular words used to designate them do not always appear to be the best that might have been chosen. Any such related technical terms, which tend to abbreviate discussion, are likely to have considerable currency; and this has undeniably been true of those under consideration. At the same time, I fail to see that anything essentially new was contributed by Bentham even here, except the terms themselves; for all the distinctions are rather obvious, and apparently they had all been (at least, implicitly) recognised before.

The second question, *viz.,* whether Bentham was right in holding, as he at least seemed to do, that we may, and must, compute the probable consequences (including, of course, the remote consequences) in the particular case, and act accordingly—is in itself more important; but it hardly seems to admit of serious debate. For the question, of course, is not whether the moral agent is to take the probable consequences of his contemplated act into consideration—every sane man, whatever his ethical creed, is likely to do that—but whether such particular computations are to take precedence of general rules. Since we are not omniscient, we cannot predict with certainty the consequences of any action taken by itself. Moreover, it is important that we should not make the attempt: first, because we have not sufficient time for elaborate computations in a particular moral exigency; and secondly, because we are in no proper frame of mind to judge impartially in those cases where our own interests are to any important extent at stake.

In truth, all this is so evident that one might be tempted to believe that Bentham has commonly been misunderstood on the point in question; but to the present writer this seems hardly possible. There is no doubt, of course, that in the ***Principles of Morals and Legislation*** the hedonistic calculus is employed in the interest of 'general rules,' since the laws which the author has in mind would necessarily, *qua* laws, be general in their application. In the ***Deontology***, however, where the object is to guide the individual agent in his moral life, computations in the particular case seem, not merely often, but generally, to be suggested, while there is no single passage in the book which insists upon the importance of general rules, as opposed to such particular computations. The passages illustrating this general drift of the argument are far too numerous to quote. The following, which may fairly be regarded as typical, will probably suffice. Bentham says: "The province of Deontology is to teach him [the moral agent] a proper arithmetic, is to lay before him a fit estimate of pain and pleasure—a budget of receipt and disbursement, out of every operation of which he is to draw a balance of good". And again the author says:

> Vice may be defined to be a miscalculation of chances: a mistake in estimating the value of pleasures and pains. It is false moral arithmetic; and there is the consolation of knowing that, by the application of a right standard, there are few moral questions which may not be resolved with an accuracy and a certainty not far removed from mathematical demonstration.

It is evident, however, that Bentham's attempt to reduce our moral judgments to a series of problems in 'moral arithmetic' was not a success, and tended to put the Utilitarian doctrine itself in a false light. In fact, it would hardly be too much to say that Bentham blundered into an untenable position here, which his Utilitarian predecessors had had the good judgment to avoid. Of course, it is sometimes held that, since such particular computations are, on the one hand, impossible, and, on the other hand, dangerous to attempt, Utilitarianism as a system falls to the ground. The argument, however, does not seem at all conclusive. To say that we must act according to 'general rules,' is merely to recognise that we are finite beings; and surely this evident fact does not make for or against any particular form of ethical theory. Indeed, we must be very careful not to cite the concrete difficulties of our moral experience, as if they disproved the validity of ethical theories different from our own. No ethical theory can help us in such cases; we must rather depend upon what may fairly be called 'moral tact'. As [German philosopher Immanuel] Kant long ago pointed out in another connection, there can be no rules for the application of rules.

We have now examined with some care all that seems really essential in Bentham's ethical system. The results of our examination may be summed up in a few words. Bentham's conception of the Good was in all respects identical with that of his Utilitarian predecessors; and his adoption of the 'greatest happiness' formula did not imply a departure from what had become the traditional view of the Utilitarians, that the motive of the agent is uniformly egoistic. Moreover, he did not go beyond the others in showing how, in the natural order of things, public and private interest coincide; but depended wholly upon the four 'sanctions' which Gay had already distinguished. The 'theological sanction,' indeed, though named by him in each of his three lists, is practically disregarded in his treatment of Ethics. His actual procedure in this respect was doubtless an important influence in secularising Utilitarianism, but this was mainly due to his reputation as a writer on Jurisprudence. It is always to be remembered that, with his selfish theory of the moral motive, he was not himself in a position to explain complete obligation without reference to rewards and punishments after death. His deduction of the particular virtues, again, was clearly inferior to that which we find in the works of Tucker and Paley—not to mention Hume, whose work was, of course, on a very different and altogether higher plane. This, however, was at least partly due to the fact that he was treating primarily of Jurisprudence in his completed works. Indeed, the one important respect in which Bentham departs from his predecessors is in his dubious attempt to reduce Ethics to 'moral arithmetic,' in the grimly literal sense. This, however, cannot be regarded as a real advance in ethical theory, but quite the contrary. The inevitable conclusion, then, seems to be that Bentham contributed almost nothing of importance to Ethics, considered strictly as such, though he unquestionably did more than any of his contemporaries to bring the Utilitarian theory into popular ethical discussions. In fact, there were very special reasons why he was constitutionally unfitted to transform the older Utilitarianism, which, as a mere theory, had already been completely developed before he wrote, into anything like the modern form of the doctrine. These fatal limitations would have to be considered here, but for the fact that J. S. Mill has performed the task once for all in his classic essay on Bentham (1838), . . . which perhaps may itself, without exaggeration, be said to mark the transition from the eighteenth century Utilitarianism to that of the present time. (pp. 180-90)

Ernest Albee, "William Paley and Jeremy Bentham," in his A History of English Utilitarianism, *Swan Sonnenschein & Co., Ltd., 1902, pp. 165-90.*

Elie Halévy   (essay date 1904)

[*A French historian, Halévy is best known for his detailed and highly respected five-volume* Histoire du peuple anglais au XIX siècle *(1912-32;* A History of the English People in the Nineteenth Century, *1949-51). In his three-volume* La formation du radicalisme philosophique *(1901-04;* The Growth of Philosophic Radicalism*) Halévy chronicles the individuals and circumstances that contributed to the formation of Utilitarianism, or Philosophical Radicalism, focusing on the role of Bentham. In the following excerpt taken from the latter work, Halévy recounts Bentham's refutation of inherent and inalienable human rights as the basis of civil law.*]

Even as early as 1789 the theory of the Declaration of the Rights of Man and of the Citizen was repudiated by Bentham. At the beginning of this same year, he added to his *Introduction to the Principles of Morals and Legislation* a final note, in which he criticised the American 'declarations of rights', and in particular the 'declarations' of Virginia and Carolina. These two declarations lay down in their first article, 'that there are certain natural rights of which men, when they form a social compact, cannot deprive or divest their posterity, among which are the enjoyment of life and liberty, with the means of acquiring, possessing, and protecting property, and pursuing and obtaining happiness and safety'. This amounts to saying that 'every law, or other order, *divesting* a man *of the enjoyment of life or liberty,* is void'; in other words, that all penal laws without exception are void. Who can help lamenting that the American insurgents should rest so rational a cause upon such bad reasons? It is still the same scholasticism characteristic of all parties: 'with men who are unanimous and hearty about *measures,* nothing so weak but may pass in the character of a *reason:* nor is this the first instance in the world, where the conclusion has supported the premises, instead of the premises the conclusion' [Bentham].

But now France was following America's example, and Bentham deplored the fact. 'I am sorry', he wrote to [French journalist and Revolutionary leader Jacques-Pierre Brissot de Warville], 'that you have undertaken to publish a Declaration of Rights. It is a metaphysical work—the *ne plus ultra* of metaphysics. It may have been a necessary evil,—but it is nevertheless an evil. Political science is not far enough advanced for such a declaration. Let the articles be what they may, I will engage they must come under three heads—1. Unintelligible; 2. False; 3. A mixture of both. . . . You can never make a law against which it may not be averred, that by it you have abrogated the Declaration of Rights; and the argument will be unanswerable'. In 1795, Bentham collected his critical observations on this subject in some manuscripts which he entitled **'Anarchichal fallacies: being an examination of the Declaration of Rights issued during the French Revolution'.** Had not [English statesman Edmund] Burke, five years previously, called the Declaration of Rights the Digest of Anarchy? Any declaration of rights was useless; for what was its purpose? To set limits to the power of the crown? A constitutional code would fulfil this purpose. To set limits to the power of the various constituted bodies? When they were made dependent on the electoral body and on public opinion, their power was limited in the only way which could be effective. A people could not bind itself. The people's good pleasure was the only check to which no other check could add anything, and which no other check could annul. After these preliminary observations Bentham turned the force of his criticism against two points.

In the first place, the language of the Declaration of Rights is faulty. We are told that men *are* equal, that the law *cannot* alienate the liberty of the citizens. This is false, and the proof is that men make revolutions in order to re-establish the equality which has been suppressed, and to defend the liberty which has been threatened. What is stated in the indicative in the Declaration should be put into the imperative, and it should be said, if you like, that men *ought* to be equal, and that the law *ought* not to violate liberty. Herein lies the difference between the 'rational censor' of the laws and the anarchist, between the moderate man and the man of violence. The rational censor admits the existence of the law of which he disapproves, and demands its repeal; the anarchist denies its existence, and sets up his own desire and his own caprice as a law before which the whole of humanity is required to bow down. *That which is, is,* the maxim of the ontologist, is stupid and empty, but at least it is inoffensive. *That which is, is not,* is the dangerous maxim of the anarchist on every occasion when he comes across something in the form of a law which he does not like. France had just reformed the language of chemistry [with the system of chemical nomenclature devised by Lavoisier, Berthollet, Guyton de Morveau, and Fourcroy], but knew not how to reform the language of public law; the phraseology used by [Dutch politician Hugo] Grotius and [German jurist Samuel von] Puffendorf was preserved, and had become revolutionary and dangerous. A constitution which claimed to be the considered design of a whole nation, was less wise, and less productive of happiness, than the 'chance-medley' [Thomas Paine] of the British constitution.

In the second place, the Declaration of the Rights of Man admits the existence of four natural rights: liberty, property, security, and resistance to oppression. Now, these four 'natural rights' do not coincide with the four ends assigned to civil law in Bentham's philosophy. Liberty? Every law is a restriction of liberty, and consequently forms a restraint on this supposed inalienable right, unless liberty be arbitrarily defined as consisting in 'the power of doing every thing which does not hurt another.' . . . But is not the liberty of doing evil also liberty? Article II draws a distinction between the use and abuse of liberty of thought and opinion. But who is to make the distinction between them? The task of determining what must be considered an abuse of liberty is left to future legislators. 'What is the security worth which is thus given to the individual as against the encroachments of government?' What is the use of a protection dependent on good pleasure merely?—Property? But it is law which determines property. The clause would become clear if it were admitted that all the rights of property and all the property possessed by any individual, no matter how, were imprescriptible, and could not be removed from him by any law. But every tax and every fine is an attack on the right of property, and consequently justifies resistance and insurrection. Article 13 declares property to be inviolable, except in case of *necessity.* But is it necessity which orders the construction of new streets, new roads, new bridges, new canals? A nation could be satisfied with the natural means of communication received from nature, and still continue to exist: progress is not a necessity. In every change, there are disadvantages to be considered on the one hand and advantages on the other; but of what avail are all the advantages in the world when set against the rights of man, which are *sacred* and inviolable and derived from the laws of nature, which have never been promulgated and which cannot be annulled?—Security? Every law which imposes a constraint or threatens with punishment is an attack on security.—As to the fourth 'right', the right of resistance to oppression, this is not a fundamental right on the same ground as the others: it is a means pointed out to citizens whereby they can defend their rights whenever they consider them violated. The French, indeed, enlightened by six years' experience [of revolution], avoided mentioning this right in the 'Declaration of the Rights of Man and of the Citizen' of 1795. Nevertheless, the definition of it shows, with especial accuracy, the insurrectionalist and anti-social nature of the theory. The selfish and unsocial passions, which are useful and even necessary to the existence and the security of the individual, are none the less fatal to the public peace, when they are encouraged to the exclusion of the other passions. Yet this is the effect brought about by the Declaration of Rights, this is the morality of that celebrated manifesto, which acquired its notoriety by the same qualities which made the fame of the incendiary of the temple of Ephesus. (pp. 174-77)

> *Elie Halévy, "The Political Problem," in his* The Growth of Philosophic Radicalism, *translated by Mary Morris, The Beacon Press, 1955, pp. 155-80.*

Wesley C. Mitchell   (essay date 1918)

[*An educator and political economist who based his theories of economic activity on statistical findings, Mitchell served as an advisor to government agencies and co-founded the National Bureau of Economic Research. In the following excerpt, he applauds Bentham for introducing standards and methodological direction to the social sciences.*]

Jeremy Bentham has one service yet to perform for students of the social sciences. He can help them to work free from that misconception of human nature which he helped their predecessors to formulate. This rôle of emancipator he plays in the following [essay].

In the social sciences we are suffering from a curious mental derangement. We have become aware that the orthodox doctrines of economics, politics and law rest upon a tacit assumption that man's behavior is dominated by rational calculation. We have learned further that this is an assumption contrary to fact. But we find it hard to avoid the old mistake, not to speak of using the new knowledge. In our prefaces and introductory chapters some of us repudiate hedonism and profess volitional psychology or behaviorism. Others among us assert that economics at least can have no legitimate relations with psychology in any of its warring forms. In the body of our books, however, we relapse into reasonings about behavior that apply only to creatures essentially reasonable.

Bentham cannot help toward making the social sciences valid accounts of social behavior. But better than any one else he can help us to see the absurdity of the intellectualist fallacy we abjure and practise. For Bentham has no rival as an exponent of the delusions that haunt the backs of our heads, and gain control over our speculations when we are not thinking of psychology. The way to free ourselves from these delusions is to drag them into the light of full consciousness and make them face our other thoughts

about behavior. We can perform this psycho-analytic operation upon our own minds best by assembling in orderly sequence the pertinent passages scattered through Bentham's writings.

Bentham dealt not only with many branches of jurisprudence—criminal law, evidence, procedure, codification, international law, constitutional law—but also with economics, psychology, penology, pedagogy, ethics, religion, logic and metaphysics. Yet all his books read as one. They work out a single idea in diverse materials. They apply the sacred principle of utility whether the subject matter be colonies or Christianity, usury or the classification of the sciences, the crimes of judges or the reformation of criminals.

But utilitarianism as such is not the differentiating characteristic of Bentham. A line of English philosophers running back at least to Richard Cumberland in 1672 had expounded that doctrine before him. About these predecessors Bentham knew little; but "Utilitarianism had been so distinctly in the air for more than a generation before he published his *Principles of Morals and Legislation* that he could not possibly have failed very substantially to profit by the fact" [Ernest Albee, *A History of English Utilitarianism*]. Indeed, Bentham was conscious of doctrinal indebtedness to Hume, Hartley and Priestley in England, Helvetius in France, and Beccaria in Italy. Among his own contemporaries Utilitarianism prevailed widely outside the circle of professed philosophers. The regnant theologian of the day, William Paley, was as grim an exponent of the sacred principle as Bentham himself. In the English controversy about the French Revolution all parties agreed tacitly or explicitly in accepting utility as the final test of political institutions—Burke as well as Godwin, the respectable Whig Mackintosh as well as the agitator Tom Paine. And when Malthus, a clergyman, answered Godwin on the population issue he showed himself as good a utilitarian as his atheistical opponent. No one has studied currents of English thinking in these times so thoroughly as Elie Halévy, and he remarks [in his *La Formation du Radicalisme Philosophique*, vol. I]: "Towards the end of the eighteenth century, it is not only the thinkers, it is all the English who are speaking the language of utility." "It was plain," he adds in [volume II] "that the doctrine of utility was becoming the universal philosophy in England, and that the reformers must speak the language of utility if they wished their opinions to be understood—let alone accepted—by the public they were addressing." This view certainly accords with Bentham's own impression as recorded in his [*Works of Jeremy Bentham*]: "The opinion of the world (I am speaking of the people in this country) is commonly in favour of the principle of utility. . . ."

What did distinguish Bentham from other utilitarians, what made him the leader of a school, what keeps his work instructive to this day, was his effort to introduce exact method into all discussions of utility. He sought to make legislation, economics, ethics into genuine sciences. His contemporaries were content to talk about utility at large; Bentham insisted upon measuring particular utilities—or rather, the net pleasures on which utilities rest.

> **What did distinguish Bentham from other utilitarians, what made him the leader of a school, what keeps his work instructive to this day, was his effort to introduce exact method into all discussions of utility. He sought to make legislation, economics, ethics into genuine sciences.**
>
> *—Wesley C. Mitchell*

The ideal of science which men then held was represented by celestial mechanics; its hero was Newton, whose system had been popularized by Voltaire; its living exemplars were the great mathematicians of the French Academy. Bentham hoped to become "the Newton of the Moral World." Among the mass of his papers left to University College Halévy has found this passage:

> The present work as well as any other work of mine that has been or will be published on the subject of legislation or any other branch of moral science is an attempt to extend the experimental method of reasoning from the physical branch to the moral. What Bacon was to the physical world, Helvetius was to the moral. The moral world has therefore had its Bacon, but its Newton is yet to come.

Bentham's way of becoming the Newton of the moral world was to develop the "felicific calculus." There are several expositions of this calculus in his *Works;* but the first and most famous version remains the best to quote.

> Nature has placed mankind under the governance of two sovereign masters, *pain* and *pleasure.* It is for them alone to point out what we ought to do, as well as to determine what we shall do. On the one hand the standard of right and wrong, on the other the chain of causes and effects, are fastened to their throne.

Hence to know what men will do, to tell what they should do, or to value what they have done, one must be able to measure varying "lots" of pleasure or pain. How are such measurements to be made?

> To a person considered *by himself,* the value of a pleasure or pain considered *by itself,* will be greater or less, according to the four following circumstances: 1 Its *intensity.* 2 Its *duration.* 3 Its *certainty*. . . 4 Its *propinquity*. . . But when the value of any pleasure or pain is considered for the purpose of estimating the tendency of any *act* by which it is produced, there are two other circumstances to be taken into the account; these are, 5 Its *fecundity* . . . 6 Its *purity* . . . [When a community is considered, it is also necessary to take account of] 7 Its *extent;* that is, the number of persons to whom it *extends.* . . .

The unit of intensity is the faintest sensation that can be distinguished to be pleasure or pain; the unit of duration is a moment of time. Degrees of intensity and duration are to be counted in whole numbers, as multiples of these units. Certainty and propinquity are reckoned as fractions whose limit is immediate actual sensation; from this limit the fractions fall away. In applying the calculus, one begins with the first distinguishable pleasure or pain which appears to be produced by an act, multiplies the number of its intensity units by the number of duration units, and then multiplies this product by the two fractions expressing certainty and proximity. To bring in fecundity one computes by the preceding method the value of each pleasure or each pain which appears to be produced after the first one; the resulting values are to be added to the value previously obtained. To bring in purity one computes the values of all pains that attend a given series of pleasures, or of pleasures that attend a given series of pains: these values are to be subtracted from the preceding sums. That is, pleasure is a positive, pain a negative quantity. Since the unit of extent is an individual, one completes the computation by multiplying the net resultant pain or pleasure ascertained as above by the number of individuals affected. Usually however this last step is more complicated: not all the people affected are affected in the same way. In that case one does not multiply by the number of individuals, but makes a separate computation for each individual and then strikes the algebraic sum of the resultants.

If these technical directions for measuring "lots" of pleasure and pain be taken seriously, the felicific calculus is a complicated affair at best. In addition it is beset by subtler and graver difficulties, some that Bentham saw clearly, others that he barely glimpsed. Unfortunately the disciples who pieced his manuscripts together into books did not think fit to publish his sharpest bits of insight into the haze, so that later writers had to rediscover much that their master had descried. The type of social science on which Bentham worked might have been completed and superseded much sooner than it was had his difficulties been made known in his own lifetime.

(1) That all comparisons of the feelings of different men are questionable Bentham was perfectly aware. In his *Principles of Morals and Legislation,* indeed, he enlarged upon this topic by discussing thirty-two "circumstances influencing sensibility" to pleasure and pain. Since these thirty-two circumstances exist in an indefinite number of combinations, it would seem that the felicific calculus can scarcely be applied except individual by individual—a serious limitation. So long as he was thinking only of the problem of punishments Bentham accepted this conclusion. The legislator and the judge ought each to have before him a list of the several circumstances by which sensibility may be influenced: the legislator ought to consider those circumstances which apply uniformly to whole classes, for example, insanity, sex, rank, climate and religious profession; the judge ought to consider the circumstances which apply in varying degrees to each individual, for example, health, strength, habitual occupation, pecuniary circumstances etc.

But as Bentham's problems widened he concluded that his calculus must apply to men at large, if it was to yield scientific generalizations, although he still thought that this application rested upon an assumption contrary to fact. One manuscript found by Halévy runs:

Tis in vain to talk of adding quantities which after the addition will continue distinct as they were before, one man's happiness will never be another man's happiness: a gain to one man is no gain to another: you might as well pretend to add 20 apples to 20 pears . . . This addibility of the happiness of different subjects, however when considered rigorously it may appear fictitious, is a postulatum without the allowance of which all political reasoning is at a stand: nor is it more fictitious than that of the quality of chances to reality, on which that whole branch of the Mathematics which is called the doctrine of chances is established.

(2) Of course, this postulate of the "addibility" of the happiness of different men tacitly assumes that numerical values can be set on the feelings of each individual. But is that really true? Indeed, can any individual put a definite figure upon his own pleasures and pains, let alone compare them with the pleasures and pains of other men? The more Bentham dwelt upon this aspect of his calculus, the more difficulties he developed and the more assumptions he found necessary to his type of social science.

One fundamental doubt he sometimes overlooked, and sometimes admitted. Intensity is the first "element" in which feelings differ. Can any man count the intensity units in any one of his pleasures or pains, as he counts the duration units? Bentham usually assumes that he can, without telling how.

. . .the degree of intensity possessed by that pleasure which is the faintest of any that can be distinguished to be pleasure, may be represented by unity. Such a degree of intensity is in every day's experience: according as any pleasures are perceived to be more and more intense, they may be represented by higher and higher numbers. . . .

In his *Codification Proposal,* however, Bentham frankly grants that intensity is not "susceptible of measurement."

(3) With a closely-related problem, Bentham wrestled frequently: can a man make quantitative comparisons among his qualitatively-unlike pleasures or pains?

The difficulty here was aggravated by one of Bentham's favorite ideas. He held that most of our feelings are complexes made up of simple elements. One of the tasks which he essayed was to enumerate exhaustively the "simple" pleasures and the "simple" pains, which like the elements in chemistry cannot be decomposed themselves, but which can combine with each other in the most diverse ways. In his *Principles of Morals and Legislation* he listed fourteen simple pleasures (counting nine alleged pleasures of the senses as one) and twelve simple pains. In his *Table of the Springs of Action* he, or his editor, James Mill, modified the lists somewhat, but kept the general idea that in the last analysis our pleasures and pains are compounded of qualitatively unlike elements. Now, if that be literally true, how can one apply the felicific calculus even in the case of a single individual? Some common denominator seems needed for the two dozen or more elements; but if there exists a common denominator, are not the elements themselves homogeneous?

When he wrote his *Principles of Morals and Legislation* Bentham did not discuss, perhaps did not think of these questions. Despite all the trouble he took to describe "the several sorts of pains and pleasures," he referred to pain and pleasure as "names of homogeneous real entities." Throughout the book he assumed tacitly not only that different pains and different pleasures, but also that pains and pleasures are commensurable. Yet the one passage most to the present purpose shows that his method of comparing quantities was strictly limited. He says:

The only certain and universal means of making two lots of punishment perfectly commensurable, is by making the lesser an ingredient in the composition of the greater. This may be done in either of two ways. 1. By adding to the lesser punishment another quantity of punishment of the same kind. 2. By adding to it another quantity of a different kind.

Indeed in this whole treatise Bentham relies upon classification, and not upon calculation. He splits everything he discusses—pleasures, pains, motives, dispositions, offenses, "cases unmeet for punishment" etc.—into kinds, limits his quantitative comparisons to relations of greater and less, and makes even these comparisons chiefly among phenomena belonging to the same kind. He does indeed bid the authorities do things which imply bolder comparisons, as when he rules that "the value of the punishment must not be less in any case than . . . the profit of the offence;" but he does not make such comparisons himself.

And yet Bentham did find a way of reducing qualitatively unlike pleasures and pains to a common denominator, and so of putting figures on felicity. There are traces of this method in his published works, but much the best exposition remained in manuscript until Halévy's day. The following passages have peculiar interest as anticipations of [English economist Francis] Edgeworth's use of "indifference" and more definitely of [English economist Alfred] Marshall's "money measures."

If of two pleasures a man, knowing what they are, would as lief enjoy the one as the other, they must be reputed equal. . . . If of two pains a man had as lief escape the one as the other, such two pains must be reputed equal. If of two sensations, a pain and a pleasure, a man had as lief enjoy the pleasure and suffer the pain, as not enjoy the first and not suffer the latter, such pleasure and pain must be reputed *equal,* or, as we may say in this case, *equivalent.*

If then between two pleasures the one produced by the possession of money, the other not, a man had as lief enjoy the one as the other, such pleasures are to be reputed equal. But the pleasure produced by the possession of money, is *as* the quantity of money that produces it: money is therefore the measure of this pleasure. But the other pleasure is equal to this; the other pleasure therefore is as the money that produces this; therefore money is also the measure of that other pleasure. It is the same between pain and pain; as also between pain and pleasure.

. . . If then, speaking of the respective quantities of various pains and pleasures and agreeing in the same propositions concerning them, we would annex the same ideas to those propositions, that is, if we would understand one another, we must make use of some common measure. The only common measure the nature of things affords is money. . . .

I beg a truce here of our man of sentiment and feeling while from necessity, and it is only from necessity, I speak and prompt mankind to speak a mercenary language. . . . Money is the instrument for measuring the quantity of pain or pleasure. Those who are not satisfied with the accuracy of this instrument must find out some other that shall be more accurate, or bid adieu to Politics and Morals.

(4) That Bentham did not follow up this promising lead was due to a further difficulty. Every time he began thinking about money measures of feeling he was checked by the diminishing utility of wealth. The "quantity of happiness produced by a particle of wealth (each particle being of the same magnitude) will be less and less at every particle; the second will produce less than the first, the third than the second, and so on." " . . . For by high doses of the exciting matter applied to the organ, its sensibility is in a manner worn out." Consider the monarch with a million a year and the laborer with twenty pounds:

> The quantity of pleasure in the breast of the monarch will naturally be greater than the quantity in the breast of the labourer: . . . But . . . by how many times greater? Fifty thousand times? This is assuredly more than any man would take upon himself to say. A thousand times, then?—a hundred?—ten times?—five times?—twice?—which of all these shall be the number? . . . For the monarch's, taking all purposes together, *five times* the labourer's seems a very large, not to say an excessive allowance: even *twice,* a liberal one.

Quite apart from differences in the sensibility of different men to pleasure, then, equal sums of money can by no means be supposed to represent equal quantities of feeling.

Once, at least, Bentham thought he had found a solution of this difficulty. In the manuscript last quoted he argues:

> . . . money being the current instrument of pleasure, it is plain by uncontrovertible experience that the quantity of actual pleasure follows in every instance in some proportion or other the quantity of money. As to the law of that proportion nothing can be more indeterminate. . . . For all this it is true enough for practice with respect to such proportions as ordinarily occur (var.: small quantities), that *cateris paribus* the proportion between pleasure and pleasure is the same as that between sum and sum. So much is strictly true that the ratios between the two pairs of quantities are nearer to that of equality than to any other ratio that can be assigned. Men will therefore stand a better chance of being right by supposing them equal than by supposing them to be any otherwise than equal. . . .

> Speaking then in general, we may therefore truly say, that in small quantities the pleasures pro-

duced by two sums are *as* the sums producing them.

This passage lies on the frontier of Bentham's realm of thought. It shows that the idea of dealing with small increments of feeling occurred to him, as a method of avoiding the embarrassment caused by diminishing utility and still using money as a common denominator. But all this was rather dim: the idea did not develop vigorously in his mind. He missed, indeed, two notions that his disciples were to exploit later on: Bernoulli's suggestion that, after bare subsistence is provided, a man's pleasure increases by equal amounts with each equal successive percentage added to his income; and the plan of concentrating attention upon the increments of pleasure or pain at the margin.

The net resultant of all these reflections upon the felicific calculus collected from Bentham's books and papers might be put thus: (1) The intensity of feelings cannot be measured at all; (2) even in the case of a single subject, qualitatively unlike feelings cannot be compared except indirectly through their pecuniary equivalents; (3) the assumption that equal sums of money represent equal sums of pleasure is unsafe except in the case of small quantities; (4) all attempts to compare the feelings of different men involve an assumption contrary to fact. That is a critic's version of admissions wrung from Bentham's text; a disciple's version of his master's triumphs might run: (1) The felicific calculus attains a tolerable degree of precision since all the dimensions of feeling save one can be measured; (2) the calculus can handle the most dissimilar feelings by expressing them in terms of their monetary equivalents; (3) in the cases which are important by virtue of their frequency, the pleasures produced by two sums of money are as the sums producing them; (4) taken by and large for scientific purposes men are comparable in feeling as in other respects. . . . Heat these two versions in the fire of controversy and one has the substantial content of much polemic since Bentham's day.

The quintessence of Bentham's social science is the double rôle played by the felicific calculus. On the one hand this calculus shows how the legislator, judge and moralist ought to proceed in valuing conduct; on the other hand it shows how all men do proceed in guiding conduct. That is, Bentham blends utilitarian ethics with a definite theory of functional psychology. The ethical system has been more discussed, but the psychological notions are more important to students of the social sciences.

1. Human nature is hedonistic. It is for pain and pleasure alone "to determine what we shall do . . . They govern us in all we do, in all we say, in all we think: . . . " These words from the first paragraph of *Principles of Morals and Legislation* put simply the leading idea. "Nothing"—Bentham remarks in *A Table of the Springs of Action,* "nothing but the expectation of the eventual enjoyment of pleasure in some shape, or of exemption from pain in some shape, can operate in the character of a *motive.* . . . "

The psychological processes by which pleasure incites to action are more fully described in later passages. "Every operation of the mind, and thence every operation of the body," says the **"Essay on Logic,"** "is the result of an exercise of the will, or volitional faculty." The relations between will and intellect are explained by the *Table of the Springs of Action:*

> To the *will* it is that the idea of a pleasure or an exemption [from pain] applies itself in the *first* instance; in *that* stage its effect, if not conclusive, is *velleity:* by velleity, reference is made to the *understanding,* viz. 1. For striking a *balance* between the *value* of this *good,* and that of the *pain* or *loss,* if any, which present themselves as eventually about to stand associated with it: 2. Then, if the balance appear to be in its favour for the choice of *means:* thereupon, if *action* be the result, *velleity* is perfected into *volition,* of which the correspondent *action* is the immediate consequence. For the process that has place, this description may serve alike in *all* cases: *time* occupied by it may be of any length; from a minute fraction of *a second,* as in ordinary cases, to any number of years.

2. Human nature is rational. There is nothing in the felicific calculus "but what the practice of mankind, wheresoever they have a clear view of their own interest, is perfectly conformable to." This passage from Chapter IV of the *Principles* is supported in Chapter XVI by an answer to the objection that "passion does not calculate." But, says Bentham:

> When matters of such importance as pain and pleasure are at stake, and these in the highest degree (the only matters, in short, that can be of importance) who is there that does not calculate? Men calculate, some with less exactness, indeed, some with more: but all men calculate. I would not say, that even a madman does not calculate. Passion calculates, more or less, in every man: in different men, according to the warmth or coolness of their dispositions: according to the firmness or irritability of their minds: according to the nature of the motives by which they are acted upon. Happily, of all passions, that is the most given to calculation, from the excesses of which, by reason of its strength, constancy, and universality, society has most to apprehend: I mean that which corresponds to the motive of pecuniary interest: . . .

3. Human nature is essentially passive. Men do not have propensities to act, but are pushed and pulled about by the pleasure-pain forces of their environments.

> . . . on every occasion, *conduct*—the *course* taken by a man's conduct—is at the absolute command of—is the never failing result of—the *motives,*—and thence, in so far as the corresponding interests are perceived and understood, of the corresponding *interests,*—to the action of which, his mind—his *will*—has, on that same occasion, stood exposed.

Of course, this view of human nature as a passive element in the situation greatly simplifies the task of social science. Whenever one can make out what it is to men's interest to do, one can deduce what they will do. The only uncertainty arises from the actor's imperfect comprehension of his interest, of which more in a moment.

Human nature is also passive in the sense that men are averse to work. In his *Table of the Springs of Action,* Bentham includes both pleasures and pains of the palate, of sex, of wealth, of amity, of reputation, and so on through eleven heads until he comes to labor—under that head he recognizes nothing but pains. If any pleasure in activity is to be found in this table we must read it into the pleasures of power or of curiosity. Enlarging upon this point, Bentham says "*Aversion*—not *desire*—is the emotion—the only emotion—which *labour,* taken by itself, is qualified to produce: of any such emotion as *love* or *desire, ease,* which is the *negative* or *absence* of labour—*ease,* not *labour*—is the object."

4. Since men ought to follow the course which will secure them the greatest balance of pleasure, and since they do follow that course so far as they understand their own interests, the only defects in human nature must be defects of understanding.

> *Indigenous intellectual weakness—adoptive* intellectual weakness—or, in one word, *prejudice—sinister interest* (understand self-conscious sinister interest)—lastly, *interest-begotten* (though not self-conscious) *prejudice*—by one or other of these denominations, may be designated (it is believed) the cause of whatever is on any occasion amiss, in the opinions or conduct of mankind.

There is no such thing as a bad motive—or a disinterested action—but men may blunder.

Similarly, whatever lack of uniformity in human nature we find must be due to differences in men's intellectual machinery for calculating pleasures and pains. Such is the sole reason for the gulf that separates civilized men from savages. In "the variety and extent of the ideas with which they have been impressed . . . may be seen the only cause of whatsoever difference there is between the mind of a well educated youth under the existing systems of education, and the mind of the Esquimaux, or the New Zealand savage at the same age." Men do vary in sensibility, as we have seen; but the thirty-two "circumstances influencing sensibility" act by associating the motor ideas of pleasure and pain with the ideas of different objects or actions. So Bentham asserts, "Legislators who, having freed themselves from the shackles of authority, have learnt to soar above the mists of prejudice, know as well how to make laws for one country as for another." They must master the peculiar local circumstances affecting sensibility—that is all. In the *Codification Proposal addressed by Jeremy Bentham to all Nations professing Liberal Opinions* he even argues that a foreigner is in a better position to draft a general code of laws than a native.

The understanding, it will be noted, is conceived as a matter of associations among ideas. As hedonism explains the functioning of mind, so the "association principle" explains the structure of mind. Bentham derived this principle from [English psychologist David] Hartley, and left its working-out to James Mill.

5. Since whatever is amiss in the opinions or conduct of mankind is due to "intellectual weakness, indigenous or adoptive," education must be the one great agency of reform. And since the understanding is made up of associa-

tions among ideas, the forming and strengthening of proper associations must be the great aim of education.

In the possibility of establishing almost any desired associations in a child's mind, and even in the possibility of dissolving old and forming new associations in an adult mind Bentham had considerable faith. "As respects pleasures, the mind of man possesses a happy flexibility. One source of amusement being cut off, it endeavours to open up another, and always succeeds: a new habit is easily formed. . . ." Hence Bentham's interest in the educational experiments of the day, hence the time he spent in planning a "chrestomathic school . . . for the use of the middling and higher ranks in life," hence his financial support of [Welsh Socialist and philanthropist] Robert Owen's scheme of industrial education at New Lanark, hence his claims for the Panopticon Penitentiary as "a mill for grinding rogues honest, and idle men industrious."

In a larger sense, Bentham conceived all his work on law as part of an educational program. "The influence of government," says one of Dumont's treatises, "touches almost everything, or rather includes everything, except temperament, race, and climate. . . . The manner of directing education, of arranging employments, rewards, and punishments determines the physical and moral qualities of a people." A sharper point and a graver meaning were given to this task by Bentham's slow discovery that men do not all spontaneously desire "the greatest happiness of the greatest number." Thereafter the "self-preference principle" was a regular component of human nature as Bentham saw it, and the great task of statecraft was to contrive cunning devices by which necessarily selfish individuals must serve the pleasure of others to get pleasure for themselves. While [Scottish economist] Adam Smith and his disciples assumed that a natural identity of interests bound men together in economic affairs, Bentham thought it necessary to establish an artificial identity of interests in law and politics. The ruler himself was to be kept in tutelage his whole life long.

But robust as was Bentham's faith in the potency of schools and government to improve man's character and lot, it was modest in comparison with the expectations cherished by certain among his masters and his contemporaries. Helvetius and Priestley, Condorcet, William Godwin and Robert Owen believed in the "perfectability" of man. Bentham put his views in opposition to [English clergyman Joseph] Priestley's:

> Perfect happiness belongs to the imaginary regions of philosophy, and must be classed with the universal elixir and the philosopher's stone. In the age of greatest perfection, fire will burn, tempests will rage, man will be subject to infirmity, to accidents, and to death. It may be possible to diminish the influence of, but not to destroy, the sad and mischievous passions. The unequal gifts of nature and of fortune will always create jealousies: there will always be opposition of interests; and, consequently, rivalries and hatred. Pleasures will be purchased by pains; enjoyments by privations. Painful labour, daily subjection, a condition nearly allied to indigence, will always be the lot of numbers. Among

> the higher as well as the lower classes, there will be desires which cannot be satisfied; inclinations which must be subdued: reciprocal security can only be established by the forcible renunciation by each one, of every thing which might wound the legitimate rights of others.

Social science nowadays aims to give an intelligible account of social processes, to promote the understanding of social facts. While we may value such "science" mainly for its practical serviceability, we profess to distinguish sharply between our explanations of what is and our schemes of what ought to be.

In Bentham's world, on the contrary, the felicific calculus yields a social science that is both an account of what is and an account of what ought to be. For on the one hand "the chain of causes and effects" and on the other hand "the standard of right and wrong" are fastened to the throne of our two sovereign masters—whose books the felicific calculus keeps. Indeed, of the two aspects of the science the more reliable, and therefore the more scientific, is the account of what ought to be. The account of what is holds only in so far as men understand their own interests—that is, associate the ideas of pleasure and pain with the ideas of the proper objects and acts. Really to account for what is, on Bentham's basis, one would have either to observe with elaborate care what men do, or to work out their defects of understanding and deduce the consequences for conduct. Needless to say Bentham spent little time on such procedures.

Bentham plumed himself, indeed, upon assigning priority to normative science—in strict accordance with his philosophy. He writes:

> When I came out with the principle of utility, it was in the *Fragment,* I took it from Hume's *Essays,* Hume was in all his glory, the phrase was consequently familiar to every body. The difference between Hume and me is this: the use he made of it, was—to account for that which *is,* I to show what *ought to be.*

Practical conclusions regarding what ought to be done, then, were the chief product of Bentham's science. That, indeed, was what made Bentham the leader of the Utilitarians or philosophical radicals, who were first and foremost reformers. But it must be admitted that Bentham's attitude upon the crucial problem of reform was not derived strictly from his science. The felicific calculus turned out to be a singularly versatile instrument. Men could make it prove what they liked by choosing certain assumptions concerning the relative importance of various imponderable factors, or concerning the relative sensitiveness to pleasure of different classes of people. Some assumptions have to be made on these heads before the argument can proceed far, and the assumptions which seem natural to the utility theorist are those which yield the conclusions in which he happens to believe on other than scientific grounds. "All history proves" anything that a writer has at heart. The felicific calculus is equally obliging.

Now Bentham and his school believed firmly in the institution of private property. They might have proved that property, despite its resulting inequalities of wealth, is necessary to produce the greatest amount of happiness if they had been willing to assume that the propertied classes are more sensitive to pleasure than the poor. For, if some men are better pleasure machines than others, then to maximize happiness more wealth—the most important raw material of pleasure—should be fed to the better machines than to the poorer ones. Such is the course Professor Edgeworth was to take many years later. Bentham did not like that course: to make social science possible he felt obliged to assume that men are substantially alike in their capacity for turning commodities into pleasure. But he had another shift, just as effective, just as little needing proof to those who agreed with him, and just as unconvincing to a doubter.

Every code of laws that is to promote the greatest happiness he argues, must do so by promoting "the four most comprehensive particular and subordinate *ends, viz. subsistence, abundance, security,* and *equality.*" "Equality is not itself, as security, subsistence, and abundance are, an immediate instrument of felicity." It gets its claim upon us from the diminishing utility of wealth—other things being the same, a given quantity of wealth will produce more pleasure if distributed equally among a given population than if distributed unequally. But other things are not the same. Unless people had security in the possession of their wealth, they would not produce it, and so there would be nothing to distribute—equally or otherwise. Thus from the viewpoint of maximum happiness security is more important than equality. And granted security in enjoying the fruits of labor a certain inequality results. The conclusion is "that, so far as is consistent with security, the nearer to equality the distribution is, which the law makes of the matter of property among the members of the community, the greater is the happiness of the greatest number."

> Equality . . . finds . . . in security and subsistence, rivals and antagonists, of which the claims are of a superior order, and to which, on pain of universal destruction, in which itself will be involved, it must be obliged to yield. In a word, it is not equality itself, but only a tendency towards equality, after all the others are provided for, that, on the part of the ruling and other members of the community, is the proper object of endeavour.

We have seen that Bentham relied upon the felicific calculus to make himself the Newton of the moral world—the felicific calculus which was to treat the forces pain and pleasure as Newton's laws treated gravitation. But he did not really frame a quantitative science of the Newtonian type. His calculus, indeed, bore little resemblance to the mathematical conceptions by which in his own day chemistry and crystallography were being placed upon a secure foundation. No man could apply Bentham's calculus in sober earnest, because no man could tell how many intensity units were included in any one of his pleasures—to go no further. And indeed Bentham did not use the calculus as an instrument of calculation; he used it as a basis of classification. It pointed out to him what elements should be considered in a given situation, and among these elements *seriatim* he was often able to make comparisons in

terms of greater and less—comparisons that few men would challenge, though Bentham might not be able to prove them against a skeptic. So his science as he elaborated it turned out to be much more like the systematic botany than like the celestial mechanics of his day. Bentham himself was a classifier rather than a calculator; he came nearer being the Linnæus than the Newton of the moral world.

Far as he fell short of his dream, Bentham's line of attack upon social problems represented a marked advance upon the type of discussion common in his day—or in ours. Though he could not literally work out the value of any "lot" of pain or pleasure, he had a systematic plan for canvassing the problable effects of rival institutions upon the happiness of populations. By pinning debates conducted in "vague generalities" down to fairly definite issues he was often able to find a convincing solution for practical problems. The defects of the rival method if not the merits of his own stand sharply outlined in what Bentham says [in his Preface to *A Fragment on Government,* 2nd edition] about the dispute between England and her American colonies:

> I . . . placed the question . . . on the ground of the greatest happiness of the greatest number, meaning always in both countries taken together. With me it was a matter of calculation: pains and pleasures, the elements of it. . . . No party had any stomach for calculation: none, perhaps, would have known very well how to go about it, if they had. The battle was fought by assertion. *Right* was the weapon employed on both sides. "We have a *right* to be as we now choose to be," said people on the American side. "We have a right to continue to make you what we choose you should be," said rulers on the English side. "We have a right to legislate over them, but we have no *right* to tax them," said Lord Camden, by way of settling the matter. . . .

What he claimed for his results in his *Codification Proposal* may well be granted:

> How far short soever this degree of precision may be, of the conceivable point of perfection . . . at any rate, in every rational and candid eye, unspeakable will be the advantage it will have, over every form of argumentation, in which every idea is afloat, no degree of precision being ever attained, because none is ever so much as aimed at.

Probably every reader of this [essay] will share the impression that Bentham's conception of human behavior is artificial to an extreme degree. That impression is not due, I think, to any trick in my exposition. Nor is it due to any quirk in Bentham's mind. He can hardly be charged with doing violence to the commonsense notions of his day, unless it be violence to develop and accept their full consequences. The real reason why we find the conception artificial is that we have another stock of ideas about behavior with which Bentham's ideas are incompatible. Our business is to be consistent as he was, and to use the set of ideas in which we believe as fully as he used the set in which he believed. Then if our ideas prove wrong, as is not unlikely, we may at least give later comers the same kind of help that Bentham now gives us. (pp. 161-83)

Wesley C. Mitchell, "Bentham's Felicific Calculus," in Political Science Quarterly, *Vol. XXXIII, No. 2, June, 1918, pp. 161-83.*

C. K. Ogden   (essay date 1932)

[*An English linguist, psychologist, and founder of an intellectual weekly,* The Cambridge Magazine, *Ogden is best known for his works* The Meaning of Meaning, *in which he examined the psychological underpinnings of the word meaning, and* The System of Basic English, *in which he created a simplified version of the English language to be utilized as a standardized means of international communication. In the following excerpt taken from the introduction to his edition of Bentham's* Theory of Fictions, *he discusses the predicates of Bentham's intertwined philosophies of language and knowledge.*]

[Bentham's] Theory of Fictions was elaborated in order to cope with the symbolic factor [of language] in all its ramifications, legal, scientific, and metaphysical; and in the list of 'Instruments' by which his various discoveries were made possible, it appears as No. 1, epitomized as follows:—

Division of entities into real and fictitious; or say, division of noun-substantive into names of real entities, and names of fictitious entities:

By the division and distinction thus brought to view, great is the light thrown upon the whole field of logic, and thereby over the whole field of art and science, more especially the psychical and thence the ethical or moral branch of science.

It is for the want of a clear conception of this distinction that many an empty name is considered as the representative of a correspondent reality; in a word, that mere *fictions* are in abundance regarded as *realities.*

[French scientist and philosopher Jean Le Rond] D'Alembert is the author in whose [*Mélanges de littérature, d'histoire et de philosophie*] the notion of this distinction was first observed by me:— *être fictif* is the expression employed by him for the designation of the sort of object for the designation of which the appellation *fictitious entity* has ever since been employed.

In speaking of the faculties of the mind, the same distinction will also be found occasionally brought to view in the philosophical works of Voltaire.

By attention to this distinction it is that I was enabled to discover and bring to view, in the case of a numerous class of words, their incapacity of being expounded by a definition in the ordinary form, viz. the form *per genus et differentiam*, which form of definition it has, with how little success and benefit soever hitherto, perhaps universally been the practice to bestow upon them; and at the same time to bring to view the only instructive and useful exposition of which the

words of this class are susceptible, viz. the exposition by *paraphrasis*—the only form of exposition by which the import attached to them is capable of being fixed, and at the same time placed in a clear and determined point of view.

See, in particular, the class of political, including legal, fictitious entities, in respect of which, by indication of the relation which the import of the word in question bears in common to the fundamental ideas of pain and pleasure, a distinct and fixed meaning is thus given to a numerous tribe of words, of which, till that time, the meaning has been floating in the clouds and blown about by every blast of doctrine—words to the which, in the mind of many a writer, no assignable ideas, no fixed, no real import, had been annexed.

Instrument No. 2 is the division of entities, real and fictitious together, into physical and psychical; by means of which . . . he maintained that considerable light could be thrown both upon the origin and the formation of language, and on the connexion between the nomenclature of psychology on the one hand and that of physics and physiology on the other.

There is no name of a psychical entity which is not also the name of a physical entity, in which capacity alone it must have continued to have been employed, long before it was transferred to the field of psychical entities and made to serve in the character of a name of a psychical, and that most commonly a fictitious, entity.

(pp. xxvii-xxix)

It seems that philosophical and logical discussion has always consisted in the translation of common discourse into some technical analytic language which, it has been hoped, would provide proper devices for the efficient detection and correction of errors. Such translations have generally been vitiated by the introduction of irrelevant material into the analytic language. The simplicity and directness of the Benthamic translation is a welcome shock to minds familiar with the traditional irrelevances, because it is concerned from the outset with practical and linguistic issues. His analytic method throws into relief certain crucial turning-points in thought that have usually been dismissed as merely verbal. Perhaps his most important insistence is that words, no matter what their other developments in use may be, must, in so far as they are names used to refer beyond themselves, be interpreted as referring ultimately to something real and observed.

Language, according to Bentham—here anticipating the most striking feature of [French philosopher Henri] Bergson's presentation—is essentially a technological apparatus for dealing with the world of things in space. What is 'there' to be talked about is primarily a nexus of individual bodies, and when we seem to be talking about other sorts of entities our language is metaphorical—whatever the alleged status of its referents. All such fictional and metaphorical jargon is not only capable of translation but, for purposes of serious discussion or of technology, must be translated into something less deceptive.

> Perhaps [Bentham's] most important insistence is that words, no matter what their other developments in use may be, must, in so far as they are names used to refer beyond themselves, be interpreted as referring ultimately to something real and observed.
>
> —*C. K. Ogden*

The inevitable tendency is for logical translators to neglect this feature of language until it is too late to give it adequate attention. Makeshifts consequently mar the final results, or, as more often happens, entities are invented to correct distortions of reference and to populate the world with fictions. Bentham's powerful and original prophylactic device for such linguistic aberrations is the archetype which at the start fixes the reference of words to observed entities, and at the same time provides the foundation and framework for a verbal expansion to any degree of explicitness and exhaustiveness that we may need for accurate translation. In fact, the two processes of archetypation [the indication of "the *material image* of which the word, taken in its primeval sense, contains the expression"] and phraseoplerosis [word substitution intended to remove the oblique or elliptical element in a fictional statement] may carry translation beyond its primary function into what is usually called logical analysis; Bentham with characteristic vigour calls it the analysis of fictions. The expansion catches, analyses, and traces lines of reference for, those planetary adjectives and opaque metaphors that confuse the best minds even in the most familiar jargons. The archetypes, which are usually actual or pictured bodies in rest or in motion, act as symbolic and logical lenses and bring fictional terms to focus on a man's experience, or dissolve them into their original nothingness. This is more than even the most highly complicated logics have achieved. . . . (pp. xlvi-xlvii)

The endeavour to trace the principal relations between the fields of thought and language . . . led Bentham to develop the Theory of Fictions in relation to "the discoveries, half-concealed or left unperfected", of [English political radicalist and philologist] Horne Tooke; the upshot being that

> almost all names employed in speaking of the phenomena of the mind are names of fictitious entities. In speaking of any *pneumatic* (or say *immaterial* or *spiritual*) object, no name has ever been employed that had not first been employed as the name of some *material* (or say *corporeal*) one. Lamentable have been the confusion and darkness produced by taking the names of *fictitious* for the names of *real* entities.

In this misconception he traces

> the main if not the only source of the clouds in which, notwithstanding all their rivalry, Plato and Aristotle concurred in wrapping up the

whole field of *pneumatology.* In the phantoms generated in their own brains, it seemed to them and their followers that they beheld so many realities. Of these fictitious entities, many will be found of which, they being, each of them, a *genus generalissimum,* the names are consequently incapable of receiving what is commonly understood by a definition, viz. a definition *per genus et differentiam.* But, from their not being susceptible of *this* species of exposition, they do not the less stand in need of *that* species of exposition of which they are susceptible.

(pp. lxiii-lxiv)

We are concerned, in fact, with

> the entire field of human thought and action. In it is accordingly included the whole field of art and science; in it is moreover included the field of ordinary, *i.e.* unscientific *thought,* and ordinary, *i.e.* unartificial action—or say *practice,* including, together with the whole contents of these respective fields (viz. all the subjects, not only of human action but of human thought), all entities, not only real but fictitious; not only all real entities but all fictitious ones that have ever been feigned, or remain capable of being feigned: fictitious entities, those necessary *products of the imagination,* without which, unreal as they are, *discourse* could not, scarcely even could *thought,* be carried on, and which, by being *embodied, as it were, in names,* and thus put upon a footing with real ones, have been so apt to be mistaken for real ones.

(pp. lxv-lxvi)

Amongst the last entries in Bentham's Memorandum Book (1831, he being then in his eighty-fourth year) is the following:—

> Wherever there is a word, there is a thing; so says the common notion—the result of the association of ideas.

> Wherever there is a word, there is a thing; hence the almost universal practice of confounding *fictitious* entities with *real* ones—corresponding names of fictitious entities with *real* ones. Hence, common law, mind, soul, virtue, vice.

> Identity of nomenclature is certificate of identity of nature; diversity of diversity:—how absurd, how inconsistent, to make the certificate a false one!

(p. lxvii)

Bentham's own approach to the linguistic factors involved in all interpretation, in all symbolic analysis, is, as we have already indicated, essentially technological. There is the operator, the machine, the operation, the raw materials, the product, and so forth; there is the thinker or speaker with his ideas and emotions, there are the words and their ways, there are the entities real and fictional which the words through the thought which they symbolize may stand for.

Language, according to Bentham, must be regarded primarily as a system of *communication.* It has, of course, both solitary and social uses; it is used for designation as well as for discourse, for intransitive as well as transitive purposes; indeed "it is to its intransitive use that discourse", or transitive language, "is indebted for its existence". But whatever the importance of the intransitive use, for purposes of interpretation and analysis it is clearly secondary.

Though the operational or technological approach to language adopted in all Bentham's writings makes it necessary for him to stress its communicative (transitive) side, he was equally aware of the importance of the notational (intransitive) development:—

> By its transitive use, the collection of these signs is only the vehicle of thought; by its intransitive use, it is an instrument employed in the creation and fixation of thought itself. Unclothed as yet in words, or stripped of them, thoughts are but dreams: like the shifting clouds of the sky, they float in the mind one moment, and vanish out of it the next. But for these fixed and fixative signs, nothing that ever bore the name of *art* or *science* could ever have come into existence. Whatsoever may have been the more remote and recondite causes, it is to the superior amplitude to which, in respect of the use made of it in his own mind, man has been able to extend the mass of his language, that, as much as to anything else, man, it should seem, stands more immediately indebted for whatsoever superiority in the scale of perfection and intelligence he possesses, as compared with those animals who come nearest to him in this scale.

> Without language, not only would men have been incapable of communicating each man his thoughts to other men, but, compared with what he actually possesses, the stock of his own ideas would in point of number have been as nothing; while each of them, taken by itself, would have been as flitting and indeterminate as those of the animals which he deals with at his pleasure.

Of more interest, in view of its bearing on the technique of interpretation, is the distinction between the emotive and referential use of symbols. Words may be used either to refer ourselves and others to the things about which we are thinking, or to arouse emotions; to convey information, says Bentham, or for the purpose of excitation. The passage is one of considerable historical interest:—

> In respect of its transitive function, it is the medium of communication between one mind and another, or others.

> This communication may convey information purely, or information for the purpose of excitation, say—more simply, and, when as above explained, not less precisely—information or excitation; to one or other of these ends and purposes, or both, will language in every case be directed.

In so far as *information* is the end, the understanding is the faculty to which the appeal is made; in so far as *excitation* is the end, the will.

> [For] the purpose of simple communication, neither in act nor in wish need the philanthropist wish to apply any restriction to the powers of language. Of such communication, evil, it is true, may be the subject as well as good; but, in the mixed mass, good, upon the whole, predominates; and it cannot be rendered apt for the one purpose without being rendered proportionably apt for the other.

> Considered as applied to the purpose of excitation, the case may at first sight present itself as being, in some respects, different. In regard to passion, and thence in regard to affection, which is but passion in an inferior degree and always liable to be raised to higher degree, repression, not excitation, may appear to be the object to be wished for; passion being, in every part of the field, the everlasting enemy of reason, in other words, of sound judgment, *alias* correct and all-comprehensive judgment.

> But even to the lover of mankind, an acquaintance with the powers of language, even when applied to this dangerous purpose, is not without its use: for by the same insight by which the mode of increasing its powers in this line is learned, the mode of repressing them, when and in so far as applied to pernicious purposes, is learned along with it. In the case of moral, as in that of physical poison, an acquaintance with the nature and powers of the disease is commonly a necessary preliminary to an acquaintance with the proper nature and mode of applying the most efficient, and, upon the whole, the most benignant remedy.

For Rhetoric in general, and particularly political rhetoric, Bentham had little use. The logic of it is of a piece with its morality:

> a perpetual vein of nonsense, flowing from a perpetual abuse of words—words having a variety of meanings, where words with single meanings were equally at hand; the same words used in a variety of meanings in the same page; words used in meanings not their own, where proper words were equally at hand; words and propositions of the most unbounded signification, turned loose without any of those exceptions or modifications which are so necessary on every occasion to reduce their import within the compass, not only of right reason, but even of the design in hand, of whatever nature it may be: the same inaccuracy, the same inattention in the penning of this cluster of truths on which the fate of nations was to hang, as if it had been an oriental tale, or an allegory for a magazine; stale epigrams, instead of necessary distinctions; figurative expressions preferred to simple ones; sentimental conceits as trite as they are unmeaning, preferred to apt and precise expressions; frippery ornament preferred to the majestic simplicity of good sound sense; and the acts of the senate loaded and disfigured by the tinsel of the playhouse.

The criticism is verbal? "True, but what else can it be? Words—words without a meaning or with a meaning too flatly false to be maintained by anybody, are the stuff it is made of. Look to the letter, you find nonsense—look beyond the letter, you find nothing". (pp. lxx-lxxiii)

C. K. Ogden, in an introduction to his Bentham's Theory of Fictions, *Harcourt, Brace
and Company, 1932, pp. ix-clii.*

Michael Oakeshott   (essay date 1934)

[*Oakeshott was a conservative English political scholar
whose theories influenced British politics. In the following essay, he asserts that modern accounts of Bentham
indicate that he was intellectually zealous though not
philosophically gifted with the skills of discernment and
speculation.*]

Jeremy Bentham died on 6th June 1832. According to his
wish, his body was preserved for the obscure purposes of
science; but his ideas, quickly forgotten by his unapprecia-
tive countrymen, enjoyed a merely oblique, though extensive, survival in the views of the few men whom he influenced directly and in certain reforms and tendencies towards reform in the legal system of England. What was
mortal survived; what was immortal was buried and forgotten. But now, one hundred years later, though there is
no suggestion that this grotesque skeleton were better underground, there is more than one suggestion that what
was so thoughtlessly buried might be unearthed. Indeed,
this business of exhumation has already begun. It remains
to be seen, however, whether what comes to the surface
is merely a corpse—a spiritual corpse to be set beside the
still unburied skeleton—or a regenerate Bentham, a man
with a new life and a new meaning. Nobody gets out of

A portrait of Jeremy Bentham by H. W. Pickersgill, 1829.

his grave exactly as he was put in, but unless there is some
phoenix quality in the mind of Bentham, unless he was
buried alive by his contemporaries, mere exhumation will
do neither him nor us any good. My business is, then, to
consider this attempt to rehabilitate Jeremy Bentham, to
consider the skill with which it is being performed, and to
consider whether the result is something alive and with a
meaning for present consciousness, or just one more of
these embalmed corpses with too many of which the world
is already cumbered.

But first let us consider for a moment the Bentham who
was buried, the old, unregenerate Bentham. At his death,
to those who did not know him and to many who did, Bentham was, I suppose, little more than a figure of fun; an
eccentric old gentleman who wrote much and published
little. But to his intimates, to the 'School' which in later
years he gathered round himself, he was a master, 'the
great critical thinker of his age and country'. And by many
others he was recognized as a figure of importance in the
history of their time. Moreover, among those who have
left us their thoughts on the subject, there seems to have
been a considerable agreement with regard to the character of his genius. By his friends he was known as a man
of acute feeling; an affectionate man, extraordinarily sensitive to the pleasure and pain of others, 'passionately fond
of flowers', and with a peculiar sympathy for animals. He
was a man overflowing with benevolence towards the
human race; the hero of Fénelon come to life. Further, it
was recognized that, as far as his intellectual activity was
concerned, 'the field of practical abuses' was his field. His
genius, as he says himself, was for legislation. Bentham
'combined what had not yet been done, the spirit of the
Philanthropic with that of the Practical. He did not de-
claim about abuses; he went at once to their root; he did
not idly penetrate the sophistries of Corruption; he smote
Corruption herself. He was the very Theseus of legislative
reform—he not only pierced the Labyrinth—he destroyed
the Monster.' And the great benefit which he conferred
upon his age and country lay in 'the example which he set
of treating law as no peculiar mystery, but a simple piece
of practical business, wherein means were to be adapted
to ends, as in any other of the arts of life'. He was 'the man
who found jurisprudence a gibberish and left it a science'.
And he achieved this, because he combined with a considerable knowledge of English law a considerable contempt
for its precedents, its prejudices and its irrationality. But
Bentham was not, for some of his contemporaries, merely
a reformer of the law and of jurisprudence; he was 'the
great critical thinker of his age and country': and the lesson of his life was 'to show that speculative philosophy,
which to the superficial appears a thing so remote from the
business of life and the outward interests of men, is in reality the thing on earth which most influences them'. Bentham not only reformed the law so that (as Dicey says)
'the history of legal reform in England in the nineteenth
century is the story of the shadow cast by one man, Bentham', but he 'introduced for the first time precision of
thought into moral and political philosophy'. And finally,
according to the view which has been repeated by every
writer on Bentham since Mill's profound essay appeared
in 1838, 'it was not his *opinions* but his *method,* that constituted the novelty and the value of what he did'. Ben-

tham founded not a doctrine but a method; the 'method of detail', 'of testing wholes by separating them into their parts', the method of 'exhaustive classification'. He was primarily and predominantly a master of detailed analysis, the inventor of a method of thought destined to revolutionize every department of intellectual interest.

But the defects, no less than the merits, of Bentham's genius were recognized by his contemporaries. Mill, who at the age of fifteen 'embraced Benthamism as a religion', later conceived some doubts about the competence of his master's philosophy to explain all things in heaven and earth. And particularly, Bentham's genius appeared to suffer from the fact that his life was 'secluded in a peculiar degree, by circumstances and character, from the business and intercourse of the world'. In English philosophy it had become (and to some extent still remains) a tradition to separate experience from reflection, and Mill saw Bentham as a master of reflection whose experience was peculiarly and fatally restricted. 'He had neither internal experience, nor external; the quiet, even tenor of his life, and his healthiness of mind, conspired to exclude him from both.' And consequently 'he was not a great philosopher, but he was a great reformer in philosophy': (the contrast is, perhaps, illusory). And besides this defect, others saw in Bentham a man who 'did not appear to have entered very deeply into the metaphysical grounds of his opinions', a superficial thinker, a man 'who enumerates, classifies the facts, but does not account for them', a man whose thinking stops short of the satisfaction of thought. It is true that to Mill Bentham was a man who 'always knew his own premises'. But on this point Mill seems to have been misled by Bentham's contempt for established authorities, particularly the acknowledged authorities of jurisprudence, into thinking that his master was 'critical' in a more profound sense. A hundred men are contemptuous of all the obvious and established authorities for one man who really begins to think for himself, for one who is an independent thinker; and Bentham certainly was not that one.

This, then, is the old Bentham, the traditional Bentham to whom all the old books (including the eleven volumes of the 'Collected Works') introduce us. Other writers during the last thirty years have extended the picture. Some, like Leslie Stephen [in his *The English Utilitarians,* 1900] and M. Halévy [in his *The Growth of Philosophic Radicalism,* 1928], have shown us the connection between Bentham and his predecessors and contemporaries; others, like Professor Phillipson [in his *The Criminal Law Reformers,* 1923] and Mr Atkinson [*Jeremy Bentham: His Life and Work,* 1905], have given us a more detailed view of some special aspect of Bentham's work. Nevertheless, in the main, what they have had to say has not seriously modified, though it has considerably extended, the story told by Mill and other of Bentham's contemporaries. But the new, regenerate Bentham, revealed to us in half a dozen recently published books, appears to differ radically from the old. We are given a new view of Bentham's life and character, and we are given a new view of the range and significance of his ideas. The real Bentham, we are told, did not live the restricted life of the legendary Bentham; and the real Bentham was a man of a far more uni-

versal genius than his contemporaries ever supposed. It is, however, impossible here to discuss this rehabilitation in all its aspects, and I have chosen to consider it as it is attempted in the work of two writers: Mr C. W. Everett, of Columbia University, who, besides editing one of Bentham's hitherto unpublished works, has given us a new view of the life and character of Bentham [in his *Bentham's Comments on the Commentaries,* edited by Humphrey Milford, 1931]; and Mr C. K. Ogden, who has given us a new view of Bentham's ideas [in his *Bentham's Theory of Legislation,* 1931].

A new biography may be new because it is based upon new discoveries or because it ventures upon a new interpretation of material already well known. And it may be said at once that the novelty of Mr Everett's work on the early life of Bentham depends in the main (though not entirely) upon certain discoveries he has made during the last three years while examining the voluminous collection of Bentham MSS. in the British Museum and in University College, London. He has undertaken, on the strength of these discoveries, to refute biographically the traditional view (derived from Mill) that Bentham was incomplete 'as a representative of universal human nature', and to show us a Bentham less cut off from the world, less untouched by hope and fear, desire and disappointment, than the old Bentham appeared to be. Not one of Bentham's English school, he remarks, had known him before the age of sixty; and this incomplete acquaintance with the early life and fortunes of their master led them to misconceive his character, to think him less experienced than he actually was. His early love for Mary Dunkly was unknown to them, they were imperfectly acquainted with his strained relations with his father, and his intimate and affectionate relations with his younger brother Samuel. They knew only a Bentham passionately devoted to the reform of the law: they were ignorant of Bentham the lover, the man of the world, the man of moods, of gaiety and melancholy, the man who had a disappointment to forget, and the man who had difficult questions of personal conduct to settle. And Mr Everett has been able to show us this new Bentham directly and vividly in the hitherto unpublished letter to his brother Samuel. Henceforward, whatever defects may be found in Bentham's philosophy, it is no longer possible to account for them by referring to the 'secluded' character of his life.

But this fresh account of Bentham's early life does not stop there, with a mere amplification of our knowledge of the facts; it ventures upon a new interpretation of the old material, the biographical material to be found in the last two volumes of Bentham's collected works. This interpretation is sometimes a little uncertain and indefinite, but so far as it goes it is admirably performed. We are given a picture of Bentham's early life and activities less encumbered than is usually the case with the detail of his later theories, his ethical, legal and political opinions. Indeed, this is perhaps the first biography of Bentham written by a man whose interest lies in biography rather than in law or philosophy; and from this, I think, it derives its great merits. The book is short, boldly conceived, simply planned and executed in a manner at once thorough and unpretentious. As a biography its only defect is, I think, a tendency to over-simplification: certain events in Bentham's life are singled out and made to appear more 'decisive' than is the case in any man's life. Bentham's attendance at Blackstone's lectures, his friendship with Lord Shelburne, his meeting with Dumont at Lansdowne House—these no doubt were important events, but too much can be made of them as absolute 'turning-points'. In this, and in some other matters, Mr Everett seems to me to have been insufficiently critical, to have relied too much upon the appearance of things. And this relatively uncritical attitude has resulted in a partial failure to formulate clearly and unambiguously, and to place in the foreground, the real point of the biography. And it has resulted, also, I think, in an actual misunderstanding of certain aspects of Bentham's genius. For what, in effect, we are shown is not a Bentham who is a mere reformer of the law, a speculative thinker, a man whose work looks forward into the nineteenth century, an early democrat, but Bentham the *philosophe,* the creature of the eighteenth century, the native of France rather than of England, the companion in thought of Helvetius, Diderot, Voltaire and d'Alembert, one of the latest believers in Benevolent Despotism. And, when this view is grasped firmly, when its implications are fully appreciated, not only is a new Bentham revealed, but the two 'major problems' of Bentham's life (which Mr Everett states but solves only perfunctorily) are at once resolved: Why was Bentham's genius recognized more fully on the Continent, in North and South America and in Russia, than in England? And why did Bentham write so much and publish so little? Indeed, they disappear as problems because they become what we should expect, and not what puzzles us.

Now, the character of the *philosophe* is both peculiar and interesting; and, taken as a whole, it is so foreign to the English character that it does not surprise us that Bentham was so little regarded in his own country and so greatly respected outside it, wherever this *philosophe* civilization had developed and established itself. There are, I suppose, three prime elements in this character, and all were highly developed in Bentham. First, an age of *philosophisme* implies a peculiar confidence in knowledge, indiscriminate knowledge; it implies an hydroptic thirst for information about the present world, its composition and its laws, and about human nature, its needs and desires. The *philosophe* believes in knowledge in a way which we find difficult to understand—we who have long ago lost this confidence. And he can exist only when there is a certain rude copiousness about the supply of knowledge which permits no suggestion of a limit. His is an inventive, ingenious, mildly perplexed and easily satisfied mind; there is vitality but no discrimination. All knowledge appears equally significant; and there is so much to be learned that there is neither time nor inclination to stay and learn anything profoundly. One thing leads to another before it has itself been exhausted; and when every suggestion is followed, it is impossible to follow one suggestion far. It is true that the world of knowledge, after a visitation of *philosophisme,* somewhat resembles a September orchard after a plague of wasps, but to the *philosophe* himself his life appears an endless intellectual adventure; he is entirely ignorant of the senseless depredation his lack of discrimination involves, and he is unconscious of his vulgarity. And, if he is fortunate, the disenchantment which, it

would seem, must overtake such a way of living, can be avoided.

But secondly, besides this belief in encyclopaedic knowledge, the *philosophe* is remarkable for his general credulity. He does not know what it is to be perplexed; he only knows what it is to be ignorant. And he is protected from the dilemmas of doubt by a tough hide of self-confidence. Appearing to doubt everything and to be engaged upon the construction of a new world from the bottom up, he is really the most credulous of men. There is plenty of audacity and some courage in his thought, but little freedom and no candour. He does not, it is true, begin from the same place and with the same prejudices as his less enlightened contemporaries, nevertheless he begins with a whole miscellany of presuppositions which he has neither the time, the inclination nor the ability to examine. There is, in short, little or nothing in common between the *philosophe* and the philosopher. For the *philosophe* the world is divided between those who agree with him and 'fools'; 'science' is contrasted with superstition, and superstition is identified with whatever is established, generally believed or merely felt.

And thirdly, besides his thirst for knowledge and his naïve cast of mind, the *philosophe* is a rationalist, in the restricted sense that he believes that what is made is better than what merely grows, that neatness is better than profusion and vitality. The genius of the *philosophe* is a genius for rationalization, for *making* life and the business of life rational, for inculcating precise order, no matter at what expense.

There is, of course, much that is admirable in this type of mind; but it will be seen at once that its value lies solely in the present appreciation of life and the world which it achieves, and not in any contribution to knowledge it has to offer to later generations. If it gives no present enjoyment to those who possess it, it is idle to look for other achievements. It can make no serious contribution to our store of knowledge, it denies the traditions of the past and attempts to fasten no new traditions on the future. What was important to the eighteenth-century *philosophes* was not what they learned or discovered, not the knowledge they acquired, but merely the sense of life which the pursuit of knowledge engendered. And what is important to us is not the discoveries they made—these, for the most part, were negligible—but the general view of life by means of which they succeeded in making themselves at home in the world. The *philosophes* were the initiators of innumerable practical reforms, but in no direction did they achieve any real extension of knowledge; their minds were replete with half-conceived ideas. *Philosophisme,* that is, is a backwater so far as the main stream of European scholarship, philosophy and scientific research is concerned. The character of Voltaire's biblical criticism, for example, is entirely misconceived if it is considered as an attempt to make a serious contribution to the historical study of the Bible.

Now, the view I wish to suggest is that Bentham was, in all respects, a typical eighteenth-century *philosophe,* and that for this reason his reputation was greater on the Continent than in England. And for this view Mr Everett supplies much of the evidence we require. First, Bentham was moved by this peculiar, indiscriminate activity which belongs to *philosophisme,* and which accounts for his having completed so little of what he began. 'I am still persuaded, my dear Bentham,' writes George Wilson in 1787, 'that you have for some years been throwing away your time. . . . Your history, since I have known you, has been to be always running from a good scheme to a better. In the meantime, life passes away and nothing is completed.' Chemistry, the law, education, engineering, prison reform, psychology, economics—these were a few of the interests which served to supply material for his 'unnatural, unexampled appetite for innovation'. Never for a moment was his mind occupied with one thing to the exclusion of all others. And it is not surprising that, 'for the sake of expedition', Bentham should desire '5 or 6 pupils who were initiated in my principles to whom I could give as many parts of my plan to execute under my eyes'. In his undergraduate days at Oxford the study of chemistry had much engaged Bentham's attention; and along with chemistry, of course, went astronomy. But for Bentham, as for more than one of his brother *philosophes* on the Continent, the science which appeared more important than any other was the science of government, for by means of this the whole human race was to be rescued from superstition. To create a science of politics, to apply the scientific method to the field of law, to unite law and science, to discover some means for measuring accurately political satisfactions—these were his ambitions. And in pursuit of this end, two things appeared to Bentham's *philosophe* mind to be necessary: first, a clean start; secondly, a code, something made, organized and definite, as distinct from what had merely grown. The clean start he found, or he imagined, in Russia; though of course he did not stay there long enough to achieve anything significant. Russia was virgin soil for the legislator; it appeared to be in the condition which the eighteenth-century *philosophes* believed the human mind to be at birth, a *tabula rasa*. And secondly, the organization and rationalization of law implied in a code was what engaged Bentham's attention more nearly to the exclusion of other interests throughout the whole of his life. It was natural for a *philosophe* to hate the English common law and to be suspicious of judge-made law, for in both there is an element of uncertainty; on account of both, English law can never be an artistic whole. But, in his contempt of the first, Bentham seems to have forgotten that law must change, that law is an expression of what is and not of what ought to be; he forgot, in short, what many of the benevolent despots forgot. And his suspicion of the second was based upon a misconceived theory of knowledge. He appears to have believed that thought is always and expressly dominated by the circumstances of its generation, that there is nothing in thought independent of the psychological situation. The whole of every judgment, he believed, is *merely* the indication of the psychical state of the individual who judges. Such an opinion involves, of course, at once universal scepticism and self-contradiction; but Bentham was aware of neither of these implications. And in this matter, as in many others, he would have been on safer ground had he maintained his opinion as a mere prejudice instead of attempting to establish it as a principle. It is all very well to see Bentham's

influence everywhere in the legislation of the nineteenth century, but when we consider how extreme his views about English law actually were, what must be noticed is, not the number of his isolated suggestions which have been put into practice, but the total rejection which his fundamental principles have suffered.

My view is, then, that the value of Mr Everett's biography lies in what it suggests rather than in any specific interpretation of Bentham's life and mind which it offers. It suggests a Bentham different from the old, traditional Bentham, who was created by the liberal writers of the nineteenth century. In it Bentham is seen to belong to his century—the eighteenth century—and his environment. We are shown a living Bentham, a complete man, and not the mere thinker with which we have so long been obliged to content ourselves. And it remains to be seen whether, when this study is carried into Bentham's later life, yet another Bentham will appear. But, thus far, whatever his democratic sympathies, whatever specific modernity some of his suggestions show, what we have is Bentham the *philosophe*. And I venture to think that he remained a *philosophe* to the end.

It is now time to turn from this to the other side of the attempt to rehabilitate Bentham; from Mr Everett to Mr Ogden. This new edition of the ***Theory of Legislation*** is a reprint, with a few verbal alterations, of Hildreth's translation (originally published in 1864) of parts of the three volumes prepared by Dumont from Bentham's half-French and half-English manuscripts and published in Paris in 1802 under the title of ***Traités de législation civile et pénale,*** etc. Hildreth's was not the first translation; an earlier was published in 1830. And it is not the most recent; Mr C. M. Atkinson prepared a fresh, and on the whole better, translation with notes which was published in 1914. Setting aside, however, the need for this reprint, what are important for us now are Mr Ogden's "Introduction" and his "Notes." For it is in these that the attempt is made to give a new range and significance to Bentham's ideas.

The "Introduction" is divided into three parts. First there is a discussion of Bentham's genius and ideas generally, secondly a few pages on the ***Theory of Legislation*** itself, and thirdly, some consideration of the relations of Bentham and Dumont. And something of interest has been found to say on all these topics. I shall deal, however, only with the first. Nobody denies Bentham's importance in the history of English law and legislation and it would be difficult to exaggerate that importance; and the discussion of the Bentham-Dumont relationship is in the main of merely historical and biographical interest. What is important for us is the thesis which Mr Ogden undertakes to defend in the first part.

> It is that Bentham's merits, in spite of his great and deserved influence on the nineteenth century, are only now coming to be fully realized; that with every decade after the centenary of his death (1932) the significance of his achievement will become more obvious; and that fifty years from to-day he will stand out as one of the greatest figures in European thought, along with Ré-

aumur, Leibniz, Newton, Malthus and Helm-
holtz. . . .

The grounds for the view that the full recognition of Bentham's work is still to come are as follows:

1. His theory of Language and Linguistic Fictions.

2. His contribution to the problem of an International Language.

3. His insight into the Psychology of Value, in
conformity with the most recent tendency of
Criticism.

4. His proposals for the Codification of nearly
every legal system in the world, and particularly
the Constitutions of South America.

5. His services to International Law.

6. His work on the Foundations of Humanitari-
anism and Public Health.

Now, it cannot be denied that this estimate of Bentham's
genius and importance creates a considerable revolution
in the current view. And the question for us is, how far
can it be maintained?

With regard to Mr Ogden's thesis, three general observations may be made. First, he somewhat naïvely remarks
that 'of course any estimate of Bentham must depend to
a large extent upon our interests and our general approach'. Thus, if we are interested in what interested Bentham, he will be important; if not, not. And since Mr
Ogden is most interested in the theory of language, this is
the most important aspect of Bentham's work. Secondly,
the criterion of importance which Mr Ogden suggests is
this: wherever in a writer who died a hundred years ago
any ideas (however random, disconnected and undeveloped) appear which 'anticipate the modern view' of the
matter, that writer is important. What makes a long-dead
writer important are 'the echoes of modernity which reverberate through the fabric of his system'. And, whatever
we may think of this criterion, since Bentham was a *philosophe*, a man with an inventive mind, a man of innumerable 'ideas' none of which he worked out fully, it is not difficult, if we adopt it, to represent him as 'a giant in the history of English thought'. Indeed, if these are our 'interests',
and this our 'general approach', Bentham will have few
competitors for the place of first importance; though if
what we are after is modernity, I should have thought
that, so far from being modern, at least one half of the
grounds which are advanced to substantiate this claim on
behalf of Bentham belong to the last century. And thirdly,
Mr Ogden everywhere asserts Bentham's importance, provides us with numerous quotations from present-day writers who also assert his importance, but nowhere is this importance actually shown and brought home to us. We are
promised much, a bold thesis is proposed, but little or
nothing is fulfilled.

The view is, then, that Bentham's chief interest lay, not in
'the law as it ought to be' (as Bentham himself seems to
have thought) but in Orthology; and that his importance
in the history of thought lies in his contribution, not to

legal reform, but to the 'science of symbolism'. In this field
Bentham was 'a century ahead of his times', and he omitted to publish his writings on this subject merely because
'he had little hope of being understood'. But it must be
said at once that considerably more and better evidence
than Mr Ogden offers us must be produced before this
view can be established. That Bentham had this interest
has always been known, and it was an interest he had in
common with many of his contemporary *philosophes;* but
unless we are to consult merely our own preoccupations
as the criterion of what is important and of what interested
Bentham most, there seems no reason at all for not believing that the established view of Bentham as primarily interested in the law and as performing his most important
services in that field, is not merely established but also
true.

The notion of an International Language from which the
irrationalities and complexities (and subtleties) of all existing languages should have been removed, is one which
would naturally appeal to the *philosophe*. Whatever has
merely grown is for that reason abhorrent to him. And it
does not surprise us to find Bentham engaged, for a while,
with this notion. But whether, on this account, he is to be
considered 'one of the greatest figures in European
thought' appears to me doubtful, if not ridiculous.

And again, with regard to Bentham's psychology, all he
has to offer us is one or two half-formulated doctrines developed for the purpose of jurisprudence. And the fact
that there is to be found in Bentham's works a 'remarkable
anticipation of the modern account of appetency' will
scarcely persuade us that he was a great psychologist. The
mere fact that in Bentham there are to be found, disconnected and undeveloped, some of the ideas which for one
school or other of present-day psychologists appear, for
the moment, true, cannot be considered very significant or
important. And, in any case, although Mr Ogden loudly
announces Bentham the great innovator in psychology, no
evidence is produced to show that such a Bentham exists
outside his own fancy.

Bentham's services to International Law are neither extensive nor striking; and Mr Ogden says nothing to alter
this view. Indeed when we consider what Bentham might
have done, having regard to the state in which international law then was and to the real character of Bentham's genius, we are surprised that what he has to say is so commonplace and devoid of significance. Of the whole of Bentham's ***Principles of International Law*** (a very brief
work), only the last part, **"A Plan for an Universal Peace"**
(which has nothing to do with international law itself), is
of the least interest to-day. No amount of rehabilitation
will make Bentham rank as one of the great publicists of
international law. And what has Mr Ogden to say to the
contrary? Merely that 'the very term *international* was his
own creation'. But first, if it were, it would constitute no
very staggering contribution; and secondly, does he suppose that Bentham had never heard of *jus inter gentes*? We
shall be hearing next that Bentham is the greatest English
theologian, on the strength of a couple of Voltairian anti-
religious tracts.

Mr Ogden's "Notes" are designed, for the most part, neither to elucidate Bentham's meaning, nor (like the notes in Mr. Atkinson's edition of the *Theory of Legislation*) to elucidate points of law and legal history, but to drive home the thesis of the "Introduction," that is, 'to provide the student with references to the more important recent literature of the subject, partly in relation to psychology'. Thus, his first note is on the Principle of Utility, and the question proposed is, 'To what extent has the intervening century illuminated or invalidated (Bentham's) main position?' But the writer of the note seems unaware of the magnitude of the question he undertakes to dispose of in half a page, and unaware also of the destructive criticism of the last century which the utilitarian moral theory (as it appears in Bentham) has not managed to survive. He is satisfied with a reference to Sidgwick and to Dr Broad and the remark that 'there the matter rests'—which, of course, it does not. Other notes approach Bentham's most casual remarks with a pathetic seriousness, as if everything he wrote were full of 'echoes of modernity'. When Bentham, with a charming eighteenth-century carelessness, observes that 'the occupation of a savage after he has supplied himself with physical necessaries, the only ones he knows, are soon described', the note directs us to the latest works on anthropology for 'the modern treatment of these subjects'. Some of these "Notes," however, are more relevant, and the most useful are those which refer us to other passages in Bentham's works and those which elucidate some historical question.

In short, this attempt to represent Bentham as 'one of the greatest figures in European thought', as a greater orthographist than psychologist, and as a more significant figure in both of these fields than in the field of law and jurisprudence, must be considered to have failed. It has failed because there is no evidence to support it and because it rests upon a false criterion of significance and upon the mere excentricities of the writer who makes it. Bentham was an ingenious man, and if we look hard enough we shall certainly find in his works some 'remarkable anticipations' of fairly modern views. But what of it? Does that make him a giant? A thinker like Bentham does not trouble to discriminate or confine himself; he skims the cream. He is not listened to in his own day because he is ahead of his time; but, when it is all over, he has nothing to hand on to his successors save a few random suggestions, and a few inventions more ingenious than sound. This, I think, is the character of Bentham's genius whenever it applied itself outside the law; and it is a character which appears sometimes even in his legal writings.

Bentham as a thinker belonged essentially to the eighteenth century, and this fact has been obscured by writers on Bentham because they are determined to direct our attention away from what Bentham actually thought, towards the so-called after-effects or consequences of his thought. What has practical consequence is, almost always, the idea itself severed from the grounds and reasons which lie in the mind of the thinker, the mere *obiter dictum*. Cremation, contraception, co-education, this or that reform of the law, may be advocated for a hundred different reasons, and what is influential is, usually, the bare advocacy of the view. But when we come to consider what a man actually thought, it is not these bare ideas which are

important, but the grounds and reasons for them which he believed to be cogent, the *ratio decidendi*. And in the case of Bentham, these grounds and reasons were none of them original, were typical of eighteenth-century thought, and were nearly all fallacious. For Bentham, so far from having thought out his first principles, had never given them a moment's consideration. He had studied closely the work of Locke, Hume, Condillac and Helvetius. And while he was a thinker rather than a reader when it came to dealing with the law, he remained always a reader and not a thinker with regard to the philosophical first principles which lay behind. No man with so little interest in or aptitude for philosophy has ever taken so large a place in the history of philosophy as Bentham. It is safe to say that, so far as philosophy is concerned, there is nothing in the whole of Bentham's works which is original either in conception or exposition: his ideas and often the words and phrases in which he expresses them are derived almost entirely from the half-dozen philosophical writers whom he had studied. The principle of pleasure and pain came to Bentham from Helvetius, sympathy and antipathy from Hume, utility from any one of a dozen writers; his theory of knowledge is derived entirely from Locke and Hume; and wherever he ventures beyond what others had already thought out, he becomes at once confused and self-contradictory. Utilitarianism as Bentham left it is nothing more than a chaos of precise ideas. No man was ever more at the mercy of traditional doctrines in philosophy than Bentham, who is an example of that not uncommon character in England—a man revolutionary in almost all practical matters, but dependent, unoriginal and cluttered up with prejudice in matters of speculation.

No man was ever more at the mercy of traditional doctrines in philosophy than Bentham, who is an example of that not uncommon character in England—a man revolutionary in almost all practical matters, but dependent, unoriginal and cluttered up with prejudice in matters of speculation.

—*Michael Oakeshott*

The principle of utility performed wonders in the reform of the law, or rather wonders were performed in its name, but this was possible only because the inherent fallacies which lie at the root of this principle were unappreciated and neglected. The principle, for the purpose of reform, was a mere *obiter dictum;* its *ratio decidendi* was ignored or forgotten. But if we wish to discover Bentham's quality as a thinker, we shall turn from these *obiter dicta* to their *rationes decidendi,* and we shall find these, for the most part, pointing us back into the eighteenth century, and moreover disfigured with the most naïve blunders.

And when we turn from his doctrines to his method, we find something admirably suited to Bentham's schemes for reforming the law, but (as a serious contribution to thought) something so naïve and childish that it is difficult to understand how it could ever have been selected as the finest product of the genius of any man who achieved so much as Bentham achieved in the way of practical reform. Bentham's method is based, of course, upon his view that 'in the whole human race, considered at all periods of its history, the knowledge of particulars has preceded that of generals'. But it is not the mere fact that Bentham was one of the simplest and most unconstrained nominalists in the history of English thought which is fatal to his reputation as a philosopher, but the fact that he assumed nominalism to be the only possible theory of knowledge, and was neither interested nor troubled to think about the matter. His method is based throughout upon presuppositions which he had never so much as considered. Analysis and synthesis, data and generalization, materials and conclusions, the bricks and the building—this was Bentham's crude and unconsidered conception of the character of knowledge. Thought, for him, as for most of the English philosophers at that time, was merely decaying sensation; and reflection was replaced by 'analysis'.

It appears, then, that Mill's estimate of Bentham's genius is, with certain reservations, more accurate than the view with which we are now presented. Mr Everett has certainly proved to us that Bentham's life and character were somewhat different from what we had been led to suppose; thanks to him we are now in possession of a fuller knowledge of both than was at the disposal of Mill or any of the intimates of Bentham during his later years. But so far as the interpretation of his mind and genius goes, we have little advantage over Mill. And if it now appears that Mill was wrong in believing that this 'method' of Bentham's was so original and so significant, that he was wrong in thinking that Bentham's utilitarianism was good enough as a theory of law, though not sufficiently comprehensive as a theory of morals, his [1838] essay on Bentham still remains the best short account of the work and genius of his master. Bentham is a great and important figure in the history of English law, but there appears to me no doubt at all that if we follow the direction in which Mr Ogden points, and look in Bentham for a man whose main interest and most important work was in orthology, psychology, logic and philosophy, rather than in 'the law as it ought to be' and in jurisprudence, we shall end with an entirely false view of Bentham's excentric genius.

Bentham's life and work abound in remarkable contrasts: a man without any real interest in speculative thought for its own sake, and yet a 'hermit'; a man who shrank from the world, the practice of the law and the compromises of politics, and yet one whose beneficial influence was felt entirely in these practical matters; a man who by force, cunning and ridicule killed many of the fallacies which dominated legal and political theory, yet one whose arguments were, in most cases, misconceived, and whose own thought was riddled with the most naïve fallacies; a man who spent his life talking about first principles, but who never once got beyond a consideration of what is secondary and dependent. The lesson of his life is not, as Mill thought, to show how speculative philosophy enters into and influences practical life, but to show that what in spec-

ulation has always most influence upon practical life is something precise yet half-thought-out, something confused yet definite. It is not the philosopher, the victim of thought, who influences our practical conduct of life, but the philosophaster, the *philosophe*. 'It is the fashion of youth', wrote Hegel, 'to dash about in abstractions: but the man who has learnt to know life steers clear of the abstract "either-or", and adheres to the concrete.' And Bentham (says Mill) was 'a boy to the end'. (pp. 244-80)

> *Michael Oakeshott "The New Bentham," in* Determinations: Critical Essays, *edited by F. R. Leavis, Chatto & Windus, 1934, pp. 244-80.*

Jacob Viner   (essay date 1948)

[*Viner was an American educator, economist, and author of several books on international trade. In the following excerpt taken from a paper presented at the meetings of the American Economic Association in December 1948, he contends that Bentham intended Utilitarian principles to be instituted in the public rather than the private sphere—an important distinction, Viner claims, that eludes most detractors.*]

Bentham and the Benthamites . . . were never complacent about the condition of the people of England. They were "Radical Reformers," and they worked hard at their reforms: by working out detailed blueprints for them; by propaganda, agitation, intrigue, conspiracy; and, if truth be told, by encouragement to revolutionary movements up to—but not beyond—the point where resort to physical force would be the next step. Bentham, moreover, was a successful social reformer, more successful perhaps than anyone else in history except Karl Marx—I have in mind here only the realization and not the merits of programs of change—if he is given credit for those changes which came after his death as the result largely of the efforts of his disciples.

The list of reforms in England which derive largely from Bentham is a truly impressive one, and I present it here only in part: fundamental law reform in many of its branches; prison reform; adult popular suffrage, including woman suffrage; free trade; reform in colonial government; legalization of trade unions; general education at public expense; free speech and free press; the secret ballot; a civil service appointed and promoted on merit; repeal of the usury laws; general registration of titles to property; reform of local government; a safety code for merchant shipping; sanitary reform and preventive medicine at public expense; systematic collection of statistics; free justice for the poor. Bentham was the first person to propose birth-control as a measure of economic reform, and this *before* Malthus had published his first *Essay on the Principle of Population*. The Ministry of Health which he proposed would be made responsible not only for general sanitation and routine public health work, but also for smoke prevention, local health-museums, and the policing of the medical profession to prevent their formation of monopolies.

Related to the conditions of the time when these reforms

were proposed, Bentham's program was comprehensive, radical, and progressive without being visionary. The modern "democratic socialist" would find it wanting, since Bentham did not approve of tampering with the system of private property except through inheritance taxation and insisted on "compensation" where reform measures would involve violation of "reasonable expectations." He apparently never formulated any concrete proposals for social security on an insurance basis, but he approved in principle of government-administered and government-subsidized insurance against every conceivable type of social hazard for which individual prudence could not make adequate provision. It was too early for proposals to stabilize employment through monetary or fiscal measures, although Bentham did explore the possibility of increasing real investment and production through the "forced frugality" induced by the issue of paper money. Pronounced individualist though he was, his specific program of reforms in both the content and the processes of legislation, in governmental organization, and in public administration, made him a major source of inspiration for the Fabian socialists as well as for the laissez-faire liberals. (pp. 308-09)

Bentham's main concern with ethics was with the ethics which should be followed by moral leaders, not with the ethics of the ordinary man, not with private morals, except as they were data to be operated on by the elite. "The science," he said [in his *Theory of Legislation,* edited by C. M. Atkinson, 1914], "whose foundations we have explored can appeal only to lofty minds with whom the public welfare has become a passion." And by them, Bentham held, its lessons should be pressed on legislators, whether *their* minds were lofty ones or not. As Bentham acknowledged, he sometimes overlooked this, and wrote as if what he had to say was directed at private morals, and critics have made much of this oversight without treating it merely as a lapse from his fundamental purposes. It was Benthamism interpreted as a system of private ethics, didactic as well as descriptive, that has aroused the most violent and the most emotional antagonism. Even as private ethics, however, Benthamism has seemed so vulnerable a target to *odium theologicum* and *odium ethicum* only because the private ethics of the critics permitted them to attack Bentham's words without taking pains to ascertain what the thoughts were which these words were intended to communicate.

Bentham starts from the standard eighteenth-century proposition, common to theologians and to sceptical philosophers alike, that man operates "under the governance of two sovereign masters, pain and pleasure." Happiness is a net sum or aggregate of individually experienced pleasures and pains. Man, he claims, acts only in response to his "interests," by which he usually, and fundamentally, means whatever men are interested in, but, unfortunately, frequently allows to mean what men regard as in their self-interest. Men normally are interested to some extent in the happiness of others than themselves, and in exceptional cases are capable of "universal benevolence," or a dominating concern with the happiness of mankind at large, but generally, if they are left to themselves, there will be serious discrepancy between the actual behavior of individuals and the behavior which would conduce to "the greatest happiness of the greatest number." It is the function of legislation to coerce or bribe individuals to make their behavior coincide with that required by the greatest-happiness principle, and of education and moral leaders to mould men's desires so that they spontaneously associate the happiness of others with their own happiness.

Bentham nowhere attempts or asserts the possibility of a positive demonstration that greatest happiness, whether as hedonism or as eudaemonism, is the proper moral objective for the common man, the moral leader, or the legislator, and his only argument in support of the greatest-happiness principle is the negative one that the rival principles proposed by other ethical systems are either resolvable upon scrutiny to verbal variants of the utility principle, or are sheer *ipse dixitism,* or are meaningless patterns of words.

"Pleasure" and "happiness" were to Bentham widely inclusive terms, involving not only the pleasures of the senses but also those of the heart and the mind. Pleasures, moreover, which in their "simple" or primary form, genetically speaking, were pleasures of self could by "association of ideas" become associated with the pleasures of others. Man, by living in society, by education, and by acts of parliament, could be made good. The eighteenth-century utilitarians may have traded, as a German philosopher has put it, "in the small wares of usefulness (*Nutzlichkeitskrämerei*)." Or it may be that to accept the pursuit of pleasure as a proper end of man is "swinish doctrine," if it be proper to assume that man pursues swinish pleasures. But a utilitarian does not have to be a Philistine. If in Bentham's exposition of his psychology there was often undue stress on the selfish sentiments, this fault—which was much more evident in [Scottish philosopher and Bentham apologist] James Mill than in Bentham—was the result of lack of imagination and of feeling, or of faulty observation—itself the consequence of these lacks—rather than any inherent incompatibility of broader views with the logic of his system. One important manifestation of this—systematic on the part of James Mill but only occasional and incidental on the part of Bentham—was the assumption that even when one's own pleasure had through association of ideas become involved in the pleasure of other persons, the affectionate sentiments toward others still contained an element of conscious reference back to one's own pleasures. This, by implication at least, was a proclamation of the universal prevalence of psychological hedonism.

The eighteenth century is often termed the "Age of Reason," and it is correctly so termed if by the phrase is meant that it was the age in which philosophers held that the credibility of all things should be tested by reason. But from the point of view of its prevailing psychological doctrines, it could more properly be called the "Age of the Passions" because of its stress on the emotions and the instincts, the affections and aversions, and its playing down of the role of reason in the behavior of the ordinary man. [Scottish philosopher and historian] David Hume was writing in the spirit of his times when he declared that: "Reason is and ought only to be the slave of the passions, and can never pretend to any other office than to serve and obey them." The normal role of reason was that of an obedient servant of the passions, a passive agent for the comparison of their relative intensities and for the justification of the choices made between them. "So convenient a thing," said [American statesman, scientist, and philosopher] Benjamin Franklin, in his *Autobiography,* "it is to be a reasonable creature, since it enables one to find or make a reason for everything one has a mind to do."

For the moral philosopher and the properly conditioned legislator, however, Bentham assigned more important roles to reason, first, that of moulding the passions of individuals so that they would contribute more to the augmentation of general happiness, and second, that of providing a technique for the comparison of passions of individuals with a view to making a socially oriented choice between them where choice had to be or could be made. It was for this social purpose, and not for the routine behavior of routine individuals, that Bentham endeavored to construct what he at different times labelled as a "moral thermometer," a "moral arithmetic," a "felicific calculus."

Much amusement has been derived from Bentham's attempt to develop a technique by which the quantities of pleasure and pain could be measured by the legislator or the benevolent philosopher. Wesley Mitchell's well-known essay on "Bentham's Felicific Calculus," is the fullest and the least unsympathetic account I am acquainted with of Bentham's position on this question. Mitchell points out the excessive degree of hedonism attributed by Bentham to mankind, and comments penetratingly on Bentham's attempt to find a common denominator through money for the pleasures of different persons. Mitchell says that in fact Bentham used the calculus not as an instrument of calculation, but as a basis of ordinal classification. "It pointed out to him what elements should be considered in a given situation, and among these elements *seriatim* he was often able to make comparisons in terms of greater and less." I think this is a somewhat misleading description of Bentham's method. The "classification" was not *seriatim,* was not in terms of higher and lower, but merely of pro and con, of pleasure and pain, and was wholly preliminary to rather than part of the calculus. The "calculus" as he actually used it was merely a mental comparison of the comparative weights of the pros and cons, a technique which neither calls for fancy labels nor is properly conducive either to merriment or to measurement.

Bentham did not invent the concept or the terminology of "moral arithmetic." Play with the idea of measuring the unmeasurable and resort to the language of measurement where it was silly to attempt to apply it goes back to at least the seventeenth century, when the prestige of geometry and later of algebra tended to trap all philosophers with scientific pretensions into casting their analysis into pseudo-mathematical form. Mandeville [in his *A Treatise of the Hypochondriack and Hysterick Diseases*], as early as 1730, laughed at physicians who studied mathematics because it was fashionable, and cited one who had advised that for certain diseases "the doses of the medicines are to be as the Squares of the Constitutions." Thomas Reid, in his *Essay on Quantity* of 1748, questioned the possibility of reducing to measurement such things as sensations, beauty, pleasure, and the affections and appetities of the mind, even though they "are capable of more and less," and he warned that to apply mathematical language to non-measurable things is "to make a show of mathematical reasoning, without advancing one step in real knowledge."

Bentham never went far afield for the sources of his ideas, and I suspect that Benjamin Franklin was his source, direct or indirect, for this idea of classification by "bipartition" plus "measurement" of the relative weight of the two classes. Franklin a few years earlier, in 1772, had been expounding it in private correspondence with Joseph Priestley and Richard Price—with all three of whom Bentham had personal contacts—in very much the same terms as Bentham was later to use, and under the similar, and already old, label of "moral or prudential algebra."

None of Bentham's immediate disciples showed any interest in this aspect of Bentham's thought, and it was not until Jevons drew attention to it and made it the basis of his subjective theory of economic value that it had any influence, for good or bad. I like to think, more so probably than Wesley Mitchell would have appreciated, that Bentham's felicific calculus was merely one more manifestation of the inferiority complex which practitioners of the social "sciences" had in the eighteenth century, and have reacquired in the twentieth, towards mathematics, towards the exact sciences, and towards quantification as one of the higher virtues. Since with the application of "political arithmetic" to "moral arithmetic" we now all accept without protest the derivation of measured "propensities" from correlations between psychological and otherwise promiscuous statistical aggregates compiled catch-as-catch-can on anything up to global scale, our readiness to laugh at Bentham's modest and wholly platonic gestures in this direction excites my propensity for amazement.

There remains one question, specially important for economics, where the influence of Bentham on J. S. Mill is obvious, the question of laissez-faire, or the economic role of government. Élie Halévy, in his great but tendentious work on the Benthamites [*La Formation du Radicalisme Philosophique,* 3 vols., 1901-04], has made much of the existence in Bentham's system of a conflict between his juristic and his economic doctrines. According to Halévy, Bentham in his juristic theory makes it the primary function of government to create an *artificial* harmony between the interests of individuals and the public interest, whereas in his economic theory he reaches laissez-faire conclusions on the basis of an implied natural or spontaneous harmony of interests. This has become a stereotype of present-day comments on Bentham, and although there may be exceptions to the natural law which proclaims that stereotypes in the field of the history of ideas provide a light which blinds rather than guides, this is not one of them.

Bentham did interpret the function of government, under the influence largely of Helvétius, as that of creating, through the application of rewards and punishments, an approach to harmony between the interests of individuals and the social interests. He did prescribe limits for the field for governmental intervention in economic matters, but these limits were not, as we shall see, very narrow ones, and in any case were not so narrow as to give scope for a doctrine of natural harmony of interests, in the sense of a harmony preordained or inherent in the nature of man living in a society unregulated by government. Of explicit formulation by Bentham of a doctrine of natural harmony I can find not the slightest trace in his writings, and such a doctrine would be in basic conflict not only with his juristic theories but with his whole cosmological outlook. Faith in natural harmony always stems from either faith in the continuous intervention of a beneficent Author of Nature or faith in the workings of a natural evolutionary process, and the Benthamites rejected the former and had not yet heard of the latter.

It has been common since Adam Smith's day to take for granted *in economics* the role of the state with reference to the protection of legal property rights and the enforcement of contracts, leaving it to juristic inquiry to explore the problems of theory and of practice in this field. Such was also the procedure of Bentham, and in his juristic writings he keeps very much in mind that "passion . . . from the excesses of which, by reason of its strength, constancy, and universality, society has most to apprehend; I mean that which corresponds to the motive of pecuniary interest." Here he deals with the problem of "repression" of harmful economic activity by means of civil and penal law. If Bentham believed that there was a natural harmony of private and public interests in the economic field, it was one, therefore, which would prevail only after the magistrate and the constable had performed their duties.

But Bentham does not advocate anything like "anarchy plus the constable." His most general proposition of a laissez-faire character is as follows:

> With the view of causing an increase to take place in the mass of national wealth, or with a view to increase of the means either of subsistence or enjoyment, without some special reasons, the general rule is, that nothing ought to be done or attempted by government. The motto, or watchword of government, on these occasions, ought to be—*Be Quiet.*

This may sound like a sweeping enough support of laissez-faire, if, as is common though rarely desirable practice in such matters, it be read carelessly and out of its context. There are important qualifications, explicit or implied, within this apparently emphatic text. First, the text deals with "encouragement" and not with "repression" of economic activity. As I have already pointed out, Bentham deals with the problem of repression of harmful economic activity as a problem in law and not in economics. Second, the general rule of doing nothing positive is applicable only if there is no special reason to the contrary. A rule is not equivalent for him to a principle, nor a "motto" to a dogma.

Bentham presents three grounds for the general rule against governmental activity of a positive kind in the economic field: (1) in this field, individuals know their own interest better than government can; (2) individuals operate more ardently and more skillfully in pursuit of their own interests than government can or will operate on their behalf; (3) governmental intervention means coercion, either directly or indirectly through taxation, and coercion involves "pain" and therefore is an evil.

Bentham is ready to approve of any departure from the general rule, however, if a case can be made for such departure on utility grounds. "Indiscriminate generalizations" are an error, he says, and "In laying down general rules, [even] fortuitous and transient cases ought not to be forgotten." And he lives up to his doctrine as, for instance, when he says that "what ought not to be done with the intention of supporting an unprofitable branch of trade, may yet be proper for preventing the ruin of the workmen employed in such business," or, when opposing in general any restrictions on the introduction of labor-saving machinery, he approves, however, of transitory aid to workmen injured economically by such introduction.

Bentham does not, moreover, limit his exceptions from the non-intervention rule to fortuitous and transient cases, but presents an elaborate analysis of the circumstances under which government should not ("non-agenda") and those under which it should ("agenda") intervene. The argument may, to some tastes, be weighted too heavily on the side of *non-agenda,* but it is free from any dogma except the utilitarian one with which it is supposed by Halévy to clash.

Whether government should intervene, says Bentham, should depend on the extent of the power, intelligence, and inclination, and therefore the spontaneous initiative, possessed by the public, and this will vary as between countries. "In Russia, under Peter the Great, the list of *sponte acta* being a blank, that of *agenda* was proportionally abundant." Government has special responsibilities for providing security against food shortages as well as military security. He approves of government aid in the construction of roads, canals, iron railways, of public hospitals for the sick, hurt and helpless, of public establishments for the "occasional maintenance and employment of able-bodied poor," and, as we have seen, of public health activities on a scale still unknown. He was an ardent advocate of general education at public expense and he urged the extension of governmental registration services to make fraud more hazardous—and also of the systematic collection of economic statistics, but with a proviso which I suspect saps his concession of most of its virtue for modern statisticians, namely, that "no institution should be set on foot for the furnishing any such articles, without a previous indication of the benefit derivable from such knowledge, and a conviction that it will pay for the expense."

Whatever its merits or defects, this treatment of the economic role of government is not in manner or substance doctrinaire, is not in any detail, as far as I can see, inconsistent with his general "principle of utility," and does not have in it, explicitly or implicitly, any trace of a doctrine of natural harmony of interests. It is to be borne in mind, moreover, that the best Bentham hopes for after all that can be done artificially to harmonize private interests with the public interest will still be far from perfect harmony.

This has, indeed, been made the basis from another point of view of attack by moral philosophers of other faiths against utilitarianism: it is taken to task for failing to build a bridge between individual and general happiness. But this would be a valid criticism only if either it had professed to have succeeded in doing so and failed, or if it were a proper demand of *any* moral philosophy that it should provide a *practicable* scheme of perfect harmony of interests. Bentham did not completely bridge the gulf between private interests and the general interest, but neither did he deny the existence of such a gulf, and he did propose two ways, education and government, by which the gulf could be somewhat narrowed—with religion, though grudgingly, accepted as a useful part of education in so far as it educates for virtue. Does anyone know of a third way? (pp. 311-19)

> *Jacob Viner, "Bentham and J. S. Mill: The Utilitarian Background," in his* The Long View and the Short: Studies in Economic Theory and Policy, *The Free Press, 1958, pp. 306-31.*

David Baumgardt   (essay date 1952)

[*A German critic and educator, Baumgardt wrote numerous works about philosophy, including studies about Franz von Baader, Spinoza, Maimonides, and Western mystics. In the following excerpt from his* Bentham and the Ethics of Today, *he argues that Bentham's hedonistic philosophy is founded on a single, positivistic principle that describes human behavior more accurately than modern ethical theories.*]

If the only task of the moralist can be, and should be, the description of what the plain man thinks to be moral then, it is true, Bentham's utilitarianism is the most inappropriate theory which could be offered. If there is anything to which all plain men of different ages and societies will agree, it is that they do not conceive of morality in terms of happiness.

They all refuse to identify moral behavior, *per definitionem,* with the production of happiness. They refuse to commit this "naturalistic fallacy"; and up to this point they are even in agreement with Bentham. The point on which all plain men contradict Bentham is his thesis that the maximizing of happiness is the proper criterion of morality.

If, therefore, the epistemological dogmatism of the plain man were the only proper basis for ethical argument, then it would be indeed "an easy game" [according to Sir W. David Ross in his *The Foundations of Ethics*] to expose the alleged fallacies of Bentham's hedonism. But that the epistemological wisdom of the plain man is sacrosanct in ethics represents such a misleading "conventional fallacy" that even the most elaborate criticism of Benthamism built up on this uncertain ground is valueless.

For the plain man, and the most sophisticated interpreters of his morals, live in an atmosphere of completely *false security* in believing that the different *prima facie* duties and values of their different environments are universally valid and even "more evident" than the axioms of geometry. It

may be true that the plain man thinks e.g. an "intense malevolence" always worse than a "tepid" malevolence. But is this belief of the plain man a self-evident axiom? The New Testament certainly does not share this opinion of Sir David Ross; for it prefers the wicked to the tepid.

By starting with completely unwarranted axioms, the plain man's ethics must, of necessity, end in relativism of judgment, and not only in that relativity which Bentham teaches. The ethics of the plain man, in different times and communities, must end in real subjectivism of judgment, while the subjective feelings on which Bentham's hedonism is based are neutral, objective, and not arbitrarily changeable facts.

From the point of view of all plain men, the rejection of Bentham's hedonism stands as much to reason and is as natural as their rejection of the concepts of modern chemistry, of physics, and astronomy. What a plain man still means by salt is not a compound of Na and Cl, but the "indefinable" quality salt. What he means by traveling is that he passes towns and villages in his car, not the "absurd, sophisticated" teaching that perhaps towns and villages pass by while his car remains unmoved. What he means by a sunset is that the sun sets, not that the earth moves and we on its surface temporarily lose sight of the sun during our movement. If these plausible ideas of the plain man are deemed the ultimate standard of truth, then Aristotelian physics, medieval alchemy, Ptolemaic astronomy are certainly far "superior" to later scientific theories in these fields.

As does the conscience of the common man so do alchemy, Aristotelian physics, anti-Copernican astronomy, and anti-Benthamism set out confidently, with an evident insight into the true "essence" of a great number of "indefinable" qualities, complicated relations between celestial bodies, chemical elements, *prima facie* duties or absolute values. But in the end, in the concrete cases of reality, all such evident insight into the "good in itself," the "good through and through," the indefinable absolute rightness, and the intrinsic values melts down to something distressingly unrevealing; or, as the most mature anti-hedonistic teaching admits, this evident knowledge of ethical principles turns out to be "highly fallible" [Ross], if applied to ethical particulars. Moreover, even the principal "infallible" insights in all these branches of knowledge must, to every critical mind, finally appear as a mere agreement in words, and not an agreement with regard to real issues.

The same movement of the sun over the sky seems, on the same day, at one point of the unmoved, flat earth, an evident movement of many more hours than at another point of the same flat planet. The common evident characteristics of gold, immediately given, apply to shiny brass as well as to gold. The plain believer in a purely "natural" ethics of egoism and force can rely on an immediate ethical insight with as much right as the plain believer in the contradictory ethics of unselfishness and absolute love. The defender of Christian values may disparage the virtues of vitality and force a thousand times, as private and public vices; as far as immediate ethical insight is concerned, he is no better off than those who equate virtue with sheer power. The fascist, too, possesses immediate insight into a whole system of absolute values and *prima facie* obligations, all of which are completely contradictory to those of the Christian pacifist. Both are able to believe with equal honesty in the universal validity of their contradictory experiences. Bentham avoided this uncritical generalization of alleged evident insight in ethics.

It is true that anti-hedonism, even in its most subtle types, keeps nearer the language of the plain man than Benthamism. But so long as, even in our Western civilization, pacifism, for instance, is considered by the Quaker as a high virtue, and by the fascist as evidence of a morally most detestable degeneration, there seems to me no reason for thinking slightingly of Bentham's ethics. For Bentham tries to bridge over these far too much ignored contradictions between the "evident insights" of different plain men or geniuses of opposite strain.

This bridging of opposite ethical beliefs is not to be regarded as just another dogmatic teaching, but should be taken . . . as a critical "hypothesis" in ethics. The utility principle must be considered a hypothetical supposition, whose value as a neutral ethical criterion has been elucidated in detail by Bentham, particularly by a minute analysis of the ethical relevance of the different elements of acts and of ethical judgment.

If, according to Bentham's best advice, the hypothetical character of the utility principle is duly taken into account, full justice can be done to one of Henry Sidgwick's most important remarks on hedonistic empiricism. As Sidgwick rightly saw, such a principle as that of maximizing felicity cannot pass as an insight won by purely empirical observation and induction. The fundamental principle of empirical hedonism can by no means be empirically given; it has to be intuitively presupposed as merely hypothetical truth. However, the preferableness of the utility principle to other hypothetical tenets can be demonstrated, if it can be critically shown that the hypothetical utility principle is less capricious and gives a more coherent explanation of ethical phenomena than its rivals. (pp. 527-30)

[Hence, critics should] judge Bentham's hedonism from this "censorial" epistemological standpoint—a point of view whose consideration he so often, but vainly, recommended to his followers as well as to his opponents.

Of the numerous charges brought against Bentham's general methodology, a good many contradict each other and each of these contradictory statements seems to me to miss the mark. Bentham has been accused of oversimplification as well as over-complication even by half-utilitarians.

Many attempts have been made to supplement the "oversimplifying monism" of the utility principle by the principles of moral fitness or rightness, or by a multitude of value principles. . . . [Modern] ethicists have been too eager to put their faith in greater and greater specialization of independent moral principles. But they have been less successful in discovering the degree of homogeneousness between seemingly diverse moral characteristics. Doubtless, it is more important that a theory be true than that it be simple; but equally, the fact that Ptolemaic astronomy or Paracelsian alchemy leads, in its results, to more complications than Kepler's or Lavoisier's theories, is no evidence of the superiority of the former. It does not seem justifiable to me that contemporary anti-hedonists should dismiss Bentham's utilitarianism as "child's play" [C. D. Broad, *Five Types of Ethical Theory*], as "a product of the craving for a simple creed," for a simple, "readily applicable criterion" [Ross]. For at the very roots of their own theories these anti-hedonists make use of far too simple ethical intuitions and fall prey to a rather conventional craving for over-simplified absoluteness.

On the other hand, particularly in the nineteenth century, Bentham's critics frequently condemned his overcomplicated calculations in matters of morality. These complications, it was maintained, compared ill with the straightforwardness and simple lucidity of anti-hedonistic intuitivism. Yet again this criticism failed to realize that the seemingly evident principles of moral intuitivism possess only a mock simplicity, a sham evidence, such as the "laws of raininess and the supplementary laws of sunshine" of which F. H. Bradley spoke ironically. Or even more frequently the criticism of Bentham's overcomplications was simply due to the fact that his critics confounded a criterion of morality with explicit reflections accompanying all moral action; and, of course, these objections against hedonism are of no higher value than certain objections which could be made against the value of grammatical rules.

Unquestionably, grammatical rules need not be consulted during a speech, any more than the utility principle during a moral act. A continuous consultation of grammar may even impede any fluent speech, as much as an express detailed calculation along the line of the utility principle may prevent moral action when swift decision is vital; but this is certainly no conclusive objection against either the value of grammar, or the ethical importance of the utility principle.

The hedonic calculus has also been criticized for rather opposite reasons. Earlier critics took exception to it as an attempt to overrationalize human action. Especially the higher types of human behavior, it was felt, cannot and should not be subjected to an analysis in merely rationalistic mathematical terms. More recent critics agree with Bentham as to the high desirability of a felicific calculus. But, according to them, the whole project must of necessity remain utopian, much as Bentham's tendency to precision and rationalization is to be welcomed.

I do not wish to re-open here the historic question of the details of Bentham's algedonic calculus and wish to refrain from any discussion of its systematic value or disvalue independently of Bentham's analyses. But, broadly speaking, is it not strange that when psychologists report the most complicated intelligence test in one precise quotient, when educators do not hesitate to use exact figures in judging examination papers, even the hope of a future more correct estimate of pleasure feelings should be declared chimeric?

With reference to a number of misapprehensions which traditionally occur at this point, it has to be remembered that the hedonic calculus by no means denies the existence of qualitative differences between different pleasures. But it tries to compare these different qualities by reducing them—or at least their causes or their intended and actual effects—to a common denominator, just as Newton carried out a reduction of color and tone qualities to quantitatively determinable characteristics, without denying that we always experience qualitative differences. And why should what is possible in an analysis of color phenomena be a priori impossible in an analysis of emotions? In this case, too, the task is to make out, in positive and negative quantities of "affective tones," a neutral common denominator which makes possible the comparison of seemingly incomparable qualities of emotion.

Though opposed to Bentham's utilitarianism in general, René Le Senne in principle has given an appropriate interpretation of the tendencies of Bentham's felicific calculus by stating [in his *Traité de morale générale*]: "Les événements physiques sont aussi des qualités: pourtant les physiciens ont trouvé les moyens de les faire tomber sous la mesure. Le moraliste n'a qu'à s'inspirer de leur exemple." Professor William P. Montague also sees "the missing link in the case of Utilitarianism" in "the inconsistency which resulted from Mill's appeal to a quality other than pleasure for evaluating pleasures" ["The Missing Link in the Case of Utilitarianism," *Studies in the History of Ideas,* ed. by the Department of Philosophy of Columbia University, vol. II]. But he, too, thinks that this "gap in the logic of Utilitarianism" can be filled by conceiving that spiritual satisfactions are in the end "not qualitatively alien to sensory desires, though infinitely . . . greater in magnitude."

To Benedetto Croce, it is true, quantitative utilitarianism is, to say nothing worse, an indulging in an "ingegnosa fraseologia. . . . Ma la medisimezza o la simiglianza delle parole non basta a cancellare la profonda distinzione delle cose" [*Filosofia della practica economica ed etica*]. To this, I think however, consistent utilitarianism can reply with at least as much reason that the deep contrast existing between mere ethical *terms* is not sufficient to extinguish the similarity existing between the *realities* which these terms should properly express. But be this as it may, and even if one thinks that W. Whately Smith's Cambridge experiments [attempting to measure feelings], B. B. Friedman's and other types of measurement of "affective tones" are so far by no means conclusive, there is another objective viewpoint at our disposal.

In the analysis of our own feelings and those of others, not only our own and others' satisfactions and dissatisfactions should be taken into account. To the exploration of the quanta and the intensities of feelings still another objective approach is open. Primarily, in crucial cases or experiments, the degree of a feeling is best revealed by the trend of behavior which is determined by the pleasure or displeasure in question. We ourselves, and others, may frequently misjudge the degree of a certain emotion if we examine it only by introspection or measure nothing but its physiological concomitant. However, if we closely scrutinize the kind of behavior which has been caused, or prevented, by our emotions, then another unbiased criterion of the strength of those feelings is secured. There is no reason for giving up this criterion as long as we maintain the well-founded hypothesis that every action is determined by a desire which impels the agent, consciously or unconsciously, to perform that particular action more than any other in his power.

In any case, rough comparisons of degrees of pleasure take place daily, as often as the difference between a cold and hot day is detected even without a precise thermometer; and even such rough calculations are, at least, no less exact than the vague and highly disputable utterances on higher and lower degrees of values in contemporary ethics. Further, I think it is by no means a fatal objection against the hedonic calculus if we admit that the moral arithmetic cannot lead in every case to a final positive or negative judgment about the morality of an act. As Professor R. B. Perry justly points out [in his *General Theory of Value*]: "That better means more intense and durable pleasure is not disproved by showing that it is extremely difficult to determine which of two pleasures is the more intense and durable, for it may well be that it is extremely difficult to discover which of two objects is the better."

It is only too common an objection to hedonism that it cannot answer the question: What should be done if one course of action promises the same amount of happiness as another, but the one can secure only less happiness for more people and the other more intense happiness for fewer? The simple answer to this is that if ever such a case arose neither of these two alternative lines of conduct could be said to be less or more moral. Provided that the more intense happiness of a few is not outweighed by misery and hardships of the many, the more even distribution of the same amount of happiness is—contrary to some common pseudo-democratic belief—not in itself a higher value.

G. E. Moore, A. J. Ayer and—probably more than any other moralist—Georg Simmel have gone into comparatively greater detail on these questions. But none of them—including Bentham—has done sufficient justice to these details. Primarily it has not been sufficiently emphasized that the decisive problem of critical ethics cannot concern the question of absolute morality but only the question: is one of several possible acts relatively more moral than the others or not?

In this connection it is certainly one of the greatest merits of consistent hedonism that it forces the moralist, far more than any other moral teaching, to go into the most conscientious and impartial weighing of complicated emotional details. The main problems of hedonism do not end with the proclamation of the hedonistic principle, as is almost universally believed, but they start with this proclamation.

As to the fallibility of exact estimates of degrees of feeling, however, we may add: it is no reason for rejecting meteorology altogether, if certain meteorological predictions fail in very complicated climates and weather conditions. Meteorology remains, nonetheless, superior to all attempts to explain the rainfall by a command of Jupiter Pluvius—or by a prima facie obligation to work in the fields after rain. Moreover, there are certainly cases of behavior which are equally good or equally bad; and, therefore, it is not the fault of an algedonic estimate if, in these cases, it does not lead to an indictment or a recommendation. In marked cases of morality or immorality, however, a felicific estimate provides a clear justification for the moral standard of the great world religions while consistent anti-hedonism and eclectic, inconsistent eudaemonism completely fail to do so.

Of the many objections which have been raised against a consistent ethical use of the greatest-happiness principle only two may be considered briefly. They seem to supplement each other effectively: the reference to the criminal's pleasure and the martyr's suffering.

Again and again, it has been called an outright absurdity to term the happiness of the evil-doer ethically good and the suffering of the martyr morally evil; and by these two examples alone any universal use of the utility principle, even its hypothetical employment, seemed to be sufficiently invalidated. For certainly Bentham's and any consistent use of the greatest-happiness principle must count every suffering *qua* suffering as evil and every pleasure *qua* pleasure as good.

Of course, the consistent hedonist will have no difficulty in correcting the widespread error that pleasure must always be the common type of gaiety, and melancholy or even religious despair must always be painful. Miguel de Unamuno, for instance, has sufficiently elucidated [in his "Sobre la europeización (Arbitrariedades)" in his *Ensayos,* vol. VII] what a "most disagreeable effect" and "profound disgust" the "joie de vivre" of a Parisian boulevard produced on him and how happy he felt "in the midst of anguished multitudes clamoring to heaven for mercy." And he is certainly right in denying that this is "a paradox." Consistent hedonism, too, can confirm that this seemingly paradoxical use of the terms *gay* and *disagreeable* does not contradict the hedonistic principle that every kind of pain caused by hilarity is bad and every spiritual enjoyment of "muchedumbres acongojadas . . . que entonen un *de profundis*" is good.

But critical hedonism can and must go even further. There is no doubt that on the ground of common morality the criminal's pleasure appears a priori as ethically bad and the saint's suffering a priori as morally valuable. From the point of a critical ethics, however, this seems to me in no way conclusive. First, who is a criminal or which act is evil is by no means self-evident. Before any such ethical judgment can be passed, this judgment has to be justified by a general criterion of good and evil. For whoever is a criminal on the ground of a consistent "master" morality is generally a saint, if judged by the standard of a morality of altruism and vice versa. Therefore no judgment which itself presupposes ethically controversial judgments can invalidate a hypothetical principle of ethics which, at least, attempts to base moral judgment on morally neutral data. If worst comes to worst the hypothetical principle may be termed ethically as much biased as the opposite particular moral judgments on criminals and saints, but not more biased.

Second, the motives which make the condemnation of the criminal's pleasure seemingly justified can be taken into consideration in a far more consistent and critical way if the pains caused or suffered by the criminal or the martyr are methodologically separated from the pleasures acquired or produced by them. There is no cogent reason left for calling the evil-doer's happiness in itself bad, if all pains of others which his acts bring about are clearly marked as ethically bad. And on the other hand no martyr's pain is ethically valuable in itself, unless it is coupled with spiritual or even material blessings for him and others.

If this seems to be too much ethical generosity, too much liberalism or libertinism, it may be asked whether it is in any respect a sign of higher Christian or Jewish morality to insist on the a priori badness of the criminal's pleasure. Is it really evidence of greater morality to prefer a world in which none of the pains caused by the evil-doers were removed and only the pleasure of the criminal had gone? Would it be an ethically worse world in which all the martyr's spiritual and material happiness bought by his pain were preserved but his suffering were removed? Are they self-evident axioms, these statements about the moral badness of the criminal's pleasure and the moral goodness of saintly suffering? Or are these "self-evident" insights perhaps no more than manifestations of certain Puritan prejudices? Anti-hedonists, such as H. W. B. Joseph and W. D. Ross, have certainly done no justice to the critical presuppositions and implications of consistent hedonism at which I just tried to hint.

If we turn now—in a similarly incomplete and, unfortunately, most sketchy fashion—from methodological to psychological questions, it certainly must be granted that Bentham's psychology shows nothing of the refinement of psychological studies of the twentieth century. Even compared with that of his contemporaries, his psychology was that of a jurist and a political observer, not that of a professional laboratory psychometrist or of a sensitive poet. Regrettably, his illustrations of happiness-sentiments are usually too redolent of the bench or the stock exchange.

In this respect, Bentham's ethics certainly cannot be taken as a model. Aside from this point, what he termed pleasure ought to be termed the hedonic tone or the hedonic color of preconceived or actually experienced states of mind. In this way pleasure, as a concomitant quality of mental experiences, would be protected from being misunderstood as a special kind of mental event, separate from other data of consciousness. If, however, such precautions are explicitly taken, in line with Bentham's implicit statements, I think that all the numberless refutations of hedonistic psychology piled up in ethical textbooks can be shown to fall to the ground.

Friedrich Nietzsche, in agreement with other anti-hedonists, has objected to hedonistic psychology by remarking that "it is not man who seeks pleasure, it's only the Englishman." This criticism does certainly not strike either at the root or at any vital point of Bentham's hedonism. First, in speaking of pleasure as an end, or the end, of human action, Bentham evidently does not have in mind pleasure in general, distinguished from all concrete pleasant or happy or extremely joyful experiences. He thinks only of the hedonic tone of concrete human aims and ends, which alone makes these ends attractive to the human will, just as we mean concrete beef, pork, or mutton when we speak of eating meat, and do not think of meat in the abstract.

Second, if F. H. Bradley or Nietzsche emphasizes that man never strives for ηδονη ["pleasure"], but at best for ηδεα ["insight"], Bentham's hedonism is by no means at issue on this point; he cannot be confuted by the statement that every pleasant feeling must have still another "content than its pleasantness" [Bradley, *Ethical Studies*]. Wherever Bentham speaks of pleasure, he certainly thinks of concrete pleasant activities or states of mind, and not of a special mental event isolated from all others, a separate entity ηδονη.

Since Henry Sidgwick coined the phrase, much has been made of the so-called hedonistic paradox; and it is paradoxically true that the more we strive explicitly for pleasure, the less we obtain it. Or, as Max Scheler said [in his *Der Formalismus in der Ethik und die materiale Wertethik*], in extending this argument, the value of the agreeable, like all the other values we aim at, appears only on the "back of our deeds" and ought not to appear in our intentions. Whoever attempts to realize the value of the pleasant directly in itself, turns out to be a decadent *bonvivant;* whoever attempts to realize other values directly, with the sole aim of demonstrating his righteousness, is a sanctimonious pharisee. There is not a special kind of mental events called pleasures, actually detachable from other psychological events; and there are no experiences of values in our intellectual life which could actually be severed from the flow of other experiences.

I should even say that anyone who would believe in the existence of pleasure or values actually, and not only methodologically, separable from concrete pleasant or valuable experiences, would be more than a degenerate *bon-vivant* or a bigoted pharisee: he would be a hopeless Don Quixote.

Such criticism however, it should be clear, does not concern any essential point of Bentham's psychology. He presupposes nothing but the existence of a hedonic tone, or better to say, an algedonic, a "positive or negative affective tone," an affective coloring of our concrete experiences. In this shape, as a "positive affective tone" of mental experiences, pleasure can indeed be verified as the determining factor of human action. Even the voluntary martyr ultimately finds, in the torture he has to undergo, more hedonic attraction than in the desertion of his cause. Nor would malice or revenge take any interest in the suffering of others, unless the idea of this suffering were pleasant to the maligner and the avenger. And if, from the standpoint of an unbiased psychological observer, the pleasantness of these feelings were not outweighed by the sufferings of others which are connected with it, malice and revenge would not be ethically condemnable according to the impartial, critical moralist Bentham.

Finally, H. Rashdall finds a mistaken *hysteron proteron* in hedonistic psychology. For, as he maintains [in his *The Theory of Good and Evil*], hedonism "puts the cart before the horse"; in reality the imagined pleasantness is created by the desire, and not, as hedonism assumes, the desire by

the imagined pleasantness. Certainly, if Bentham had assumed that we have first to sit down and to think of a certain pleasantness before desiring it, he would have been wrong. It has readily to be granted that, in the complicated intermixture of imagination, desire and action, no strict line of demarcation can be drawn between a distinct idea of pleasantness and desire, between a hedonic tone as a "causa finalis" and one as a "causa efficiens." Pleasantness may be given as an integral part of desire itself.

All this does not interfere with any essential thesis of Bentham's psychology. All he presupposes is that, in judging actions ethically, we are allowed to discuss and compare the hedonic tones of the different ends of acts in methodological abstraction. This, however, in no way implies that, in reality, in the actions themselves, the hedonic tone is psychologically given in disjunction from the act, either before or after the act. Therefore the alleged paralogism, the *hysteron proteron* mentioned above, is by no means an indispensable premise of Bentham's psychology.

Neither the so-called hedonistic paradox, nor the hedonistic *hysteron proteron,* nor the experiences of martyrdom, revenge, and malice are in contradiction with the essential presuppositions of Bentham's hedonism. Even in the field of psychological fundamentals, the objections of oversimplification raised against Bentham's main theses are commonly due to oversimplifications on the part of his critics.

In the nineteenth century Bentham's psychology was perhaps more accused of overcomplication than of oversimplification. The hedonist was especially often ridiculed because he was supposed to carry out so many complicated calculations previous to his acts that he would miss every chance of acting. In truth, Bentham never assumed that every human action must be accompanied by a circumstantial, conscious, rational calculation of consequences. He explicitly granted that, more often than not in our actions, only an intuitive, unperceived calculation of consequences takes place and psychologically no more than this is required by his doctrine. The detailed, rational estimate of all the hedonic effects of our actions is only needed for judging the ethical value of these acts: it is by no means essential for their performance.

From the viewpoint of pedagogy, of education and religion, perhaps even more objections have been raised against Bentham's ethics than from any other quarter; and again rather opposite arguments have been advanced for this purpose.

Coleridge and Carlyle thought the anti-idealistic, immoral character of Bentham's teaching and personality quite evident. They therefore contented themselves with abusing Bentham and his followers as "paralytic radicals," and believed it "God's mercy . . . that our (philosophic) Jacobins were infidels and a scandal to all sober Christians; had they been like the old Puritans, they would have trodden Church and King to dust—at least for a time." That Bentham and practically all his followers could easily rival the Carlyles and Coleridges *qua* moral characters obviously escaped the attention of these champions of idealistic ethics. Bradley even spoke of a "degradation," a "prostitution" and "bastardisation" of ethics by utilitarianism.

Fiery tongues of this brand are fortunately no longer heard today.

On the contrary, more academically minded moralists such as Henry Sidgwick and C. D. Broad see too much "reforming fire," too white a "heat of moral enthusiasm" in Bentham and his successors. But all these *dicta,* which keep hedonism so severely in leading strings, are certainly more representative of the critics' own sentiments than they are of Bentham's teaching. Nevertheless these sentiments too are, in all probability, responsible for the lack of a sufficiently impartial analysis of Bentham's moral theory.

In scores of stock objections to Bentham's hedonism, similar pedagogical or religious scruples are tacitly involved. Preoccupied with the more conspicuous and seemingly more urgent problems of pedagogy, with the contrasts between duty and inclination, between altruistic and egoistic behavior, anti-hedonism generally not only slurs over Bentham's more fundamental methodological inquiries but also fails to note his full recognition of the ethical problem of unselfishness.

It is true that the problem of altruism and that of subduing selfish inclinations has no such central place in Bentham as it does in practically all anti-hedonistic theories. But Bentham himself never taught that personal sacrifices in favor of the greatest happiness of the greatest number are avoidable. Bentham's hedonism is in no way essentially bound up with the assumption of a utopian harmony between all individual and general interests of mankind. It is J. S. Mill and not Bentham who drew very near this illusion and the fallacy of identifying "valuable" with "actually desired."

In textbooks just published Bentham's hedonism is still reproached because it "can produce submission, but not loyalty, conformity, but not devotion; . . . In all the higher motives there is something more than a balancing of pleasures and pains" [William Henry Roberts, *The Problem of Choice*]. Certainly, at first glance, Bentham's ethics of consequences seems to pervert and to paralyze the main emphasis which, pedagogically, has to be laid on the motives and not the results of human acts. In the eyes of many anti-hedonists, Bentham's utilitarianism, by a superficial reversion of all progressive educational insight, leads back to a primitive and gross "by their fruits ye shall know them."

Utilitarianism seems to throw to the wolves the greatest educational achievements of a moral "trial of the hearts and reins" brought about by the teaching of the Jewish prophets, of Abelard, Kant, and John Ruskin who taught us to examine above all man's motives, his heart and spirit. But, in truth, Bentham did not underrate the pedagogical importance of a primary appeal to human motives.

What he did was to show why in ethics even motives cannot be judged impartially without references to the consequences of acts, i.e. why in ethics even motives can be judged objectively only as indications of prevalently beneficial or mischievous consequences. The basic importance of this doctrine of motives can, perhaps, best be demonstrated by a thought-experiment supplementing Bentham's teaching. Certainly, for argument's sake, it is entirely within the realm of *logical* possibility to suppose that hatred would prevalently produce more happiness than love. But under these presuppositions it would be evident that, then, hatred could no longer be considered as an "intrinsically" bad motive. Under these circumstances, hatred allegedly bad under all circumstances, bad independent of all its consequences, would have to be thought prevalently good. And by a similar thought experiment it becomes manifest that kindness and generosity would have to be deemed bad if prevalently they were to bring about misery.

That is, under all these circumstances the moral value of the motive fully reveals itself as dependent on the consequences of the act whereas the moral value of the consequences is not in the same sense dependent on the motive. It is in vain, therefore, to proclaim on behalf of the ethics of motives that hatred is a priori bad, bad in itself, and love is good by its very essence.

It would be utterly absurd to base the critical moral judgment on any of those "mysteriously evident" characteristics of motives—characteristics which would flagrantly give the lie to the deepest, fundamental, evident experiences concerning happiness and pain. Vice versa, however, it remains entirely consistent to insist that love is good because and in so far as it leads to greater happiness and that hatred is bad only because and in so far as it leads to greater pain.

The educator can stress the moral value of love and disvalue of hatred only *after* the moralist has ascertained that hatred produces on the whole (though not always) far more suffering than happiness and love more joy than pain. Any impatience, however, any short cut taken by pedagogy in the answers to these questions would be disastrous and completely confusing. These impatient answers are disastrous even when extolling blind love which ignores all the demands of justice and undermines, thus, the foundations on which true love can alone thrive; and these direct moral appeals to motives are, of course, even more pernicious when they preach hatred as the only evidence of manliness and virtue and denounce even the understanding of an opponent as a sign of degeneration.

The educator is fully entitled to appeal, first of all, to the motives of men. Without vigorous good motives every individual and every society is in a state of decay. Good motives demand the utmost cultivation by every moral leader of every group of men. But before this cultivation can take place, the epistemology of ethics must have ascertained what the good motives are and why they are good.

Only on the basis of these critical reflections can it be shown why our Judaeo-Christian motives are good and not the motives of sheer power or any type of ethical relativism and nihilism. Our common theories of morals, however, yield far too much to the pressure and the exigencies of uncritical pedagogy. They are but made to order for these educational needs and lack, therefore, any sufficiently firm basis, as this can be provided only by the impartial, critical moralist. Bentham, however, insisted, I think with reason, that ethical inquiry should logically never be made subsequent and subservient to educational practice.

As practical application of any knowledge is always based and must be based on some type of theory, this is no less the case in morals. Only ethics can tell us which educational practice is morally valuable and which is morally valueless.

Certainly it must be granted that the truly "edifying" character of Bentham's ethics is often hidden under cool, sober reasoning of a prevailingly juristic character. But I think it should be no less readily granted that, what Bentham's hedonism lost by its juristic diction, it gained in precision and in a closer approach to the hard realities of life. It was never his intention to degrade moral behavior to the lower level of mere legalism; he endeavored to elevate the theory of morals, so far as possible, to the higher level of juristic exactness.

Last, but not least, Puritanism and the majority of religious beliefs seem to be irreconcilably antagonistic to Bentham's hedonism; and, on the other hand, Bentham's failure to understand the vital, genuine importance of religious life cannot be explained away. But if religion ever had and continues to have meaning, it centers around the "Urerlebnisse," the fundamental experiences of human blessedness and human despair; and, on principle, a consistent hedonism finds it certainly less difficult to include the highest types of pleasure and pain than to exclude them. Too often it has been said that hedonism deals only with "materialistic" feelings and, therefore, degrades ethics. Yet hedonism in itself does not only allow but even demands any possible elevation in this respect. Consistent hedonism does not only permit but even insists on the inclusion of all types of feeling: the whole world of artistic emotion and the truest religious sentiments. If there is, in Bentham's moral philosophy, almost nothing of the religious spirit in the common sense of the word, the gist of his teaching certainly rather invites than forbids its extension toward liberal modern religion.

It has been said by a leading English moralist of the day that, "in the long run," we "will have to choose between Bentham and Kant" in ethics. Be this as it may, there seems to me no doubt that an analysis of Bentham's ethics, far more detailed than any I could give [here], can be of decisive consequence not only for writing the history of modern ethics, but also for any systematic ethical reasoning.

Bentham's mummy, preserved at University College, London, suffered in World War II at the onslaught of contemporary barbarians who might have belonged to a pre-Egyptian civilization. Wisely, therefore, the mummy was withdrawn for repair into the Egyptian department of the College's collections, as we were informed in a bulletin of London University of 1940. Bentham himself, in contrast to this withdrawal, once humorously said to Philarète Chasles that he would like to return to life each century for a short time, in order to instruct himself as to the fate of his moral theories. I am by no means sure that Bentham would not regard me as far too critical of his philosophy of morals. But I hope, at least, that both he and my sever-

est critics will grant that I offer a fairer and more patient presentation of his ethical teaching than he has been accorded hitherto. (pp. 530-45)

> *David Baumgardt, in his* Bentham and the Ethics of Today, *Princeton University Press, 1952, 584 p.*

Gertrude Himmelfarb   (essay date 1969)

[*Himmelfarb is a prominent American historian who specializes in studies of English Victorian society. In the following excerpt, she discerns the difficulty in discriminating between the authentic Bentham and editorial interpretations of his person and thought.*]

Bentham has finally, indubitably, "made it." Not as he had hoped to make it in his own time, as the reformer, indeed transformer, of society, law, and philosophy . . . but rather as historical reputations are made—by becoming the focus of controversy. The controversy has already attracted the attention of bibliographers and commentators, and one may be confident that before long it, and thus Bentham himself, will [acquire] . . . the title and status of a historical "problem." (p. 189)

Or rather problems. . . . The first and most obvious problem is ideological: What were Bentham's philosophical, political, and social ideas? How can Benthamism be defined in relation to such issues as laissez-faireism and collectivism, individualism and government interventionism? (The advantage of putting these questions so baldly is that one can see immediately a host of others lurking behind each of these. E.g., what was the connection between Bentham's philosophy and politics? Between his political and social views? Between Bentham and Benthamism? Between collectivism and government interventionism?) The second problem is historical: What was the actual, practical influence of Bentham and / or Benthamism on English history—the "nineteenth-century revolution in government," the development of the welfare state, the emergence of a planned society, or whatever it is that is presumed to have happened? The third problem (which has been injected into the controversy only recently) may be described as historiographical: Have some historians, in addressing themselves to the first two problems, been guilty of a political bias, notably a "Tory interpretation of history"? Have they "denigrated" Bentham's ideas and "belittled" his influence out of a distaste for social planning, a suspicion of ideology, and a belief that the "historical process" operates independently of men and ideas?

If these problems are complicated in themselves, they are still more complicated as they relate to each other, for they lend themselves to a variety of permutations and combinations. There are those who, interpreting Bentham as a laissez-faireist, have ascribed to him the largest influence in determining the laissez-faire character of mid-Victorian society. Others, interpreting him as a collectivist, have ascribed to him the largest influence in introducing collectivism into mid-Victorian society. Still others have interpreted him as a laissez-faireist who could not, for that reason, have had any influence on the growing collectivism of the century. And still others have interpreted him as a collectivist whose particular ideology had little influence on the emerging institutions, agencies, administrative techniques, and structures.

The historiographical problem is also complicated by the confusion between the "Tory interpretation," in the above sense, and the more conventional idea of a "conservative interpretation"—the latter being the familiar theory that conservatives (or Tories; the name is of no significance in this context) played a crucial part in the passage of social legislation. The "conservative interpretation," in this second sense, generally (although not necessarily) presupposes some notion of Tory democracy, paternalism, or similar ideology, in which case it may be presumed to be as unpalatable to the anti-ideological "Tory interpretation" as the Benthamite or any other ideology. But a more fundamental confusion inherent in the idea of the Tory interpretation is so obvious one is embarrassed to dwell on it: the confusion between description and prescription, between the historian's analysis of the past and what he is presumed to favor in the present—a confusion compounded by the fact that at least some of the putative Tory interpreters are, as it happens, not present-day Tories.

I have pointedly refrained from identifying the historians who may be associated with the various theories or interpretations because the present summary is so bare and schematic as to be almost a travesty of what in some cases are works of exemplary scholarship, thoughtfulness, and subtlety. Yet the summary may suffice to suggest some of the dimensions of the "Bentham problem." One commentator, reflecting on the fact that this has become the warmest debate in nineteenth-century English history, confessed that he could not understand why the participants were so exercised, what it was that was "bugging them." What is bugging them, evidently, is nothing less than the character of nineteenth-century English history, and perhaps of the twentieth century as well. Ideas, ideologies, and institutions; political and social reforms; legal and administrative developments; the role and relationship of social classes and economic interests; the peculiar conjunction of revolution, reform, and permanence; the part played by individuals, factions, parties, and "historical processes"; questions of motive, impulse, inspiration, causation—all this and more is at stake in this debate. (pp. 190-91)

The attribution of historical bias must depend to some extent upon a conception of the "real" Bentham, bias being largely (although not entirely) a measure of the departure from reality.

It is at this point, the determination of the "real" Bentham, that any study or edition of Bentham runs into difficulty. For what is the "real" Bentham? On the most obvious level, there is the difficulty of making sense of the manuscripts, or, rather, of making them coherent as works. If Bentham himself could not do this, who are we to attempt it? It was in his lifetime, with his approval, and presumably under his supervision that Etienne Dumont, James Mill, John Stuart Mill, Francis Place, George Grote, Samuel Romilly, Edwin Chadwick, Southwood Smith, Peregrine Bingham, and others labored to produce the works that bear Bentham's name. At one time or an-

other Bentham quarreled with some of these and accused them of misinterpreting him, but since he did not particularize his grievances and since his acrimony seems to have been more often personal than intellectual, it is not easy now to say when or if they did depart from his meaning. Moreover, the charges of misinterpretation often come from Bowring, whose testimony is itself suspect.

Of all the editors Bowring is probably the least trustworthy: his edition of *The Works of Jeremy Bentham* (1843) was issued after Bentham's death and gives signs not only of animus against Bentham's earlier disciples, editors, and friends, but also of a point of view significantly different from Bentham's on at least one important subject. A Unitarian in good standing, Bowring did what he could to minimize or omit evidence of Bentham's irreligion; Bowring's edition of the *Deontology* (not included in the *Works*) is for this reason particularly questionable. But most of the writings included in the *Works* were reprinted from editions published in Bentham's lifetime. And in the case of those published for the first time by Bowring, it is by no means clear . . . shall see, whether his version is more or less trustworthy than any we can presume to put in its place. And if Bowring cannot be easily superseded, still less can Bentham's other editors.

But there are other, more serious difficulties involved in discovering the "real" Bentham. Even if one knew where a previous editor erred, if one had a single, straightforward, definitive manuscript to transcribe, one would still have the problem of establishing Bentham's real identity. And even if one could establish Bentham's ideological identity, it would be rash to assume that this constituted a total identification. For, in fact, it might turn out to be a serious distortion of his historical identity. Historically, the "real" Bentham is not the pristine, unadulterated, aboriginal writer revealed in the manuscripts, but precisely the edited, possibly corrupted, almost certainly simplified Bentham that we have always known. It is this Bentham—Bentham à la Bowring, Dumont, *et al.*—who alone could have exercised the influence claimed for or denied to him. And not only the political or social influence but the intellectual one as well. For even ideologically, this was the Bentham known to his contemporaries and to later generations. His were the ideas to which they responded, and his were the ideas transmitted under the label of Benthamism. (pp. 192-93)

Gertrude Himmelfarb, "Bentham Scholarship and the Bentham 'Problem',' in The Journal of Modern History, *Vol. 41, No. 2, June, 1969, pp. 189-206.*

David Lyons   (essay date 1972)

[*Lyons is an American educator in the field of political and legal philosophy and the author of* In the Interest of the Governed: A Study in Bentham's Philosophy of Utility and Law *(1973). In the following essay, he provides an interpretation of Bentham's Utilitarianism that accounts for the interests of the individual as well as society.*]

The principle of utility is Bentham's basic test for morals

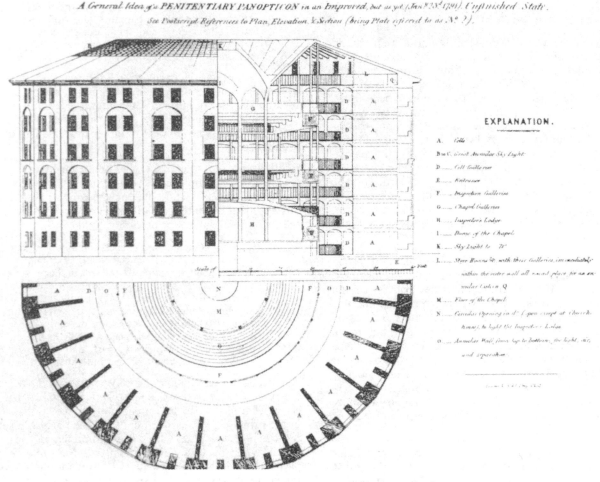

The Penitentiary Panopticon as envisioned by Jeremy Bentham.

and legislation. But there is room for doubting what that principle is supposed to say. I shall argue that one important element of modern utilitarian doctrines cannot be found in Bentham's.

Some aspects of his views will not be questioned here. He holds, for example, that acts should be appraised by their consequences alone. The effects that count are 'pleasures' and 'pains', that is, the effects upon human happiness, interest or welfare.

The utilitarian wants happiness promoted, of course, and his benevolence is usually thought to have no limits. He is accordingly called a 'universalist'. Now, in some relevant senses that might be given the term, Bentham is a universalist. He holds that every pleasure in itself is good and every pain an evil. He also holds that every relevant interest must be given due consideration. Even the pain we cause a malefactor by punishing him must be taken into account. His punishment cannot be justified unless his pain is small enough to make the punishment 'profitable'. In the same way, the pleasure to be got from deliberately malicious action may not be discounted.

But this does not imply the view that every affected interest is relevant. On the contrary, the 'benevolence' of Bentham's utilitarianism extends no further than the borders of one's political community. It is not universalistic but parochial.

The restriction is significant. For the interest of a powerful nation might conflict with that of mankind at large. One committed to testing acts by the interest of the agent's community, therefore, could find himself endorsing conduct detrimental to mankind as a whole.

Bentham's basic principle is not, however, simply parochial. I shall argue that he embraces a dual standard—one for the public (or political) sphere, another for the private. But these are conceived by him as resting upon a more fundamental principle of utility. Direct support for this interpretation comes chiefly from his ***Introduction.*** The position I shall reconstruct may not be Bentham's constant view. It seems consistent with his early writings, notably his most important ***Introduction,*** but is divergent in some ways from his later works. However, more than fifty years elapsed between the writing of the ***Introduction*** and Bentham's death in 1832, when he was still producing manuscripts that would be used by editors in his posthumous publications. This span of time alone should make us hesitate to assume that Bentham's later works are consistent with and can always be used to interpret his early ones.

There is good evidence for supposing that Bentham's views changed by the end of this period.

If we consider the whole of Bentham's works, we find that, in the majority of cases, when he gives a prominent statement of his standard he explicitly limits the interests to be considered to those within the political community in question. He states that the 'end' that ought to be adopted is, say, the 'greatest happiness' of the community or of its members. Now, there is no other kind of evidence to suggest that Bentham vacillates between parochialism and universalism. It is possible, therefore, to regard the majority of cases, in which the parochial restriction is imposed, as fuller statements of the appropriate standard, and the minority of cases, in which it is left out, as elliptical or shortened statements. Since he states his position so often, in so many works, he may well assume it amply clear without complete elaboration every time.

In any case, the parochial restriction is explicitly imposed throughout the *Introduction,* which contains his most complete elaboration of these doctrines and is, unlike many of his later works, entirely his own production, not having passed through the hands of rewriters, editors or translators. The restriction is found in the first chapter, as we shall see, and also in the opening paragraphs of Chapters iii, vii, xiii, xvi—wherever, in fact, occasion arises to state the appropriate general standard. This evidence makes it extremely difficult to regard Bentham as a universalist. It cannot be explained away, and I shall try to show how apparent counter-evidence dissolves on careful scrutiny.

The parochial restriction is there, in black and white, and one who persists in calling Bentham a universalist must tell us why. He might try this. Since the restriction is sometimes omitted, perhaps Bentham adds it when he thinks that the only interests likely to be affected by the acts under consideration are within the agent's community. This hypothesis of course does not explain why Bentham bothers to add the qualification, but some account is needed, this one seems as good as any, and it is perfectly intelligible. But I believe that there is not a shred of evidence to support it. If we look at the various works cited, we shall find no relevant feature linking those in which the restriction is omitted that is absent when it is imposed.

Someone might alternatively conclude that Bentham subscribes to a parochial form of utilitarianism. The evidence does not support the standard universalistic account, that one ought to promote the happiness of *everyone* affected; but so far it seems to yield the narrow principle which says one ought to promote the happiness of one's *community.* But this would not account for further evidence, to which we now turn.

At the beginning of the *Introduction,* Bentham offers an 'explicit and determinate account', and his most elaborate explication of the principle of utility, as follows:

> By the principle of utility is meant that principle which approves or disapproves of every action whatsoever, according to the tendency which it appears to have to augment or diminish the happiness of the party whose interest is in question:

or, what is the same thing in other words, to promote or to oppose that happiness. I say of every action whatsoever; and therefore not only of every action of a private individual, but of every measure of government.

But whose interest is 'in question'? Bentham does not say everyone's; nor does he say the community's or its several members'. His 'explicit and determinate account' is, so far, compatible with indefinitely many variations of utilitarianism, and offers no support to either universalism or parochialism.

Bentham goes on to explain what he means by utility. He is concerned to emphasise that he does not mean conduciveness to just any end whatsoever, which need not involve human happiness. In making this point he seems to tell us more about his principle:

> By utility is meant that property in any object, whereby it tends to produce benefit, advantage, pleasure, good, or happiness (all this in the present case comes to the same thing) or (what comes again to the same thing) to prevent the happening of mischief, pain, evil, or unhappiness to the party whose interest is considered: if that party be the community in general, then the happiness of the community: if a particular individual, then the happiness of that individual.

This argues clearly against the universalistic and parochial interpretations. For it seems reasonable to combine the account of utility with the immediately preceding account of the principle. We can assume that 'the party whose interest is in question', to whom Bentham refers in one paragraph, when he states his principle, is the same as 'the party whose interest is considered', to whom he refers in the next paragraph, when explaining his notion of utility. But this 'party' can be either 'the community' or some 'particular individual'. Consequently, his principle never seems to require that everyone's interests be considered—which rules out universalism. But neither does it say that the interests of the entire community must always be considered—which means that Bentham has no simply parochial form of utilitarianism. The community must be considered in some cases, but a particular individual need only be considered in others.

Can this evidence be explained away? By now, no plausible case can be made for the universalistic interpretation, but one might try to defend the parochial account as the former was defended before: Bentham always wants one to consider *all* the members of one's community; but he believes that sometimes only the interests of a particular individual can be affected by an action, and then, of course, it is necessary to consider only the happiness of that person. The trouble here, however, is the same as before: no evidence can be found to support this otherwise unconvincing explanation.

But we can go further. We may ask *why* Bentham says that the community must be considered in some cases while only an individual need be considered in the others. An answer may be found in the last chapter of the book.

Bentham explains and defends his principle of utility in the first two chapters of the *Introduction* and devotes the next fourteen chapters to his analysis of motivation and action and to applications of his principle to the law. In the final chapter he returns to more general topics of 'morals and legislation'. In the first section he discusses the 'Limits between private ethics and the art of legislation', which begins with a definition of ethics from a utilitarian point of view: 'Ethics at large may be defined, the art of directing men's actions to the production of the greatest possible quantity of happiness, on the part of those whose interest is in view.' *That* sort of phrase again: 'whose interest *is in view*'. Bentham defines ethics in the same kind of terms he uses in his 'explicit and determinate account' of the principle of utility. This seems promising.

Bentham then *divides* ethics by reference to the person or persons whose actions are so 'directed'. This seems important, for he does *not* effect the partition in terms of those whose interests are *affected,* as the universalistic account would lead us to expect:

> What then are the actions which it can be in a man's power to direct? They must be either his own actions, or those of other agents. Ethics, in as far as it is the art of directing a man's own actions, may be styled *the art of self-government,* or *private ethics.*
>
> What other agents then are there, which, at the same time that they are under the influence of man's direction, are susceptible of happiness? They are of two sorts: 1. Other human beings who are styled persons. 2. Other animals, which on account of their interests having been neglected by the insensibility of the ancient jurists, stand degraded into the class of *things.* As to other human beings, the art of directing their actions to the above end [that is, their *own* happiness] is what we mean, or at least the only thing which, upon the principle of utility, we *ought* to mean, by the art of government: which, in as far as the measures it displays itself in are of a permanent nature, is generally distinguished by the name of *legislation:* as it is by that of *administration,* when they are of a temporary nature, determined by the occurrences of the day.

Thus, Bentham divides ethics into 'the art of *self-*government', or 'private ethics', on the one hand, and 'the art of government' (in the ordinary, political sense), on the other. (As he suggests elsewhere, we might call the latter 'public ethics'.) Ethics from a utilitarian standpoint then has a dual character. But so does utility itself, since it concerns either an individual or a community.

It seems reasonable to suppose that the respective parts correspond. We are told pretty clearly that the art of government is the art of 'directing' persons towards their own happiness. And government (in the ordinary sense) may be thought to 'direct' all the members of the community. This correlates the public part of ethics with that kind of utility that concerns the happiness of the community. For as Bentham has told us, the 'interest of the community' is just 'the sum of the interests of the several members who compose it', and they could be the ones 'directed' by the government. The other correlation is then obvious: one must identify the 'particular individual' that the other kind of utility concerns as the *self*-directing (or self-

governing) agent of private ethics. Under the art of government, or government according to the dictates of utility, the interests of the entire community, that is, of all its members, are promoted. Under the art of self-government, the interests of the single, self-directing agent concerned are served.

The simplest way of accounting for all this is roughly as follows. Bentham's *basic* principle of utility says that one ought to promote the happiness of those under one's 'direction', that is, subject to one's direction, influence or control. The relevant interest for applying the principle—the interest 'in question', to be 'considered' or 'in view'—is always that of the person or persons under one's governance. We may call this a *differential* principle since the range of relevant interests is not fixed in the usual way. (It is neither everyone's, nor all those affected, nor all within the agent's community.) Bentham conceives his principle as applying in two different contexts, private and public. Ethics is private when a man 'directs' his own behaviour and no one else is subject to his control. He decides what he himself shall do; he does not direct others. The standard that accordingly applies is that of self-interest. Ethics is public in the context of government in the ordinary sense. It should be emphasised now that government, for Bentham, is concerned not merely with determining what people *ought* to do, but also with controlling, or at least influencing, behaviour. The law must provide (or at least make use of) motivation to comply with its directives—by the threat of punishment if necessary (and Bentham thinks it always is). The government as a whole—personified in Bentham's 'sovereign'—'directs' all the members of the community. All 'measures of government' therefore must serve the interests of the entire community. But (Bentham seems to reason), this can only be accomplished if each 'government functionary' tries, in every one of his official actions, to serve the interests of all its members. Bentham therefore embraces a *dual standard:* in political affairs the happiness of all members of the community should be served, while in private matters one should serve his own best interests.

The evidence for this account of Bentham's basic normative position is much stronger than one might at first expect, for the universalistic interpretation is quite generally accepted without question. It is not uniformly strong—parts are determined by explicit textual evidence, but other parts result from an attempt to forge a coherent whole that fits the tenor of Bentham's thought as well as the texts. In the remainder of this essay I shall consider further evidence and ramifications of my reconstruction, arguing that it is far more defensible than any of the alternatives.

Though not much more extensive than we have already seen, the evidence that Bentham has a dual standard is quite strong. Consider, for example, Bentham's summary at the end of the first section of the last chapter of the *Introduction,* where he has defined and partitioned ethics:

> To conclude this section, let us recapitulate and bring to a point the difference between private ethics, considered as an art or science, on the one hand, and that branch of jurisprudence which

contains the art or science of legislation, on the other. Private ethics teaches how each man may dispose himself to pursue the course most conducive to his own happiness, by means of such motives as offer of themselves: the art of legislation (which may be considered as one branch of the science of jurisprudence) teaches how a multitude of men, composing a community, may be disposed to pursue that course which upon the whole is the most conducive to the happiness of the whole community, by means of motives to be applied by the legislator.

Such evidence cannot be ignored.

It must be emphasized that the passages quoted so far, while brief, are quite prominent and explicitly definitive. They place severe constraints on any acceptable interpretation of Bentham's utilitarianism. Beyond this point, however, positive supporting evidence for my reconstruction is quite rare. What can be shown is that apparent counter-evidence is at best weak or inconclusive.

Consider the parochial restriction itself, which we found sprinkled liberally throughout Bentham's writings, in most of the places in which he offers statements of his general position. Now we are in a position to understand his use of the qualification. In accordance with my earlier suggestion, let us assume that Bentham has a parochial standard not only where he explicitly imposes it, but also in the fewer cases where he does not explicitly state it. Then we can note an interesting fact. Whenever Bentham says or (as we are assuming) implies that his principle requires us to promote the happiness *of the community,* he is concerned with what he would classify as *political* issues. The topics with which he deals vary widely, from the character of law, through government structure and legal codification, to legal punishments and rewards, judicial procedure and evidence, political economy and tactics. But each subject falls under the art of government. Bentham's use of the parochial restriction thus appears consistent with the dual standard. For in political contexts, his principle says that we must serve the happiness of the members of the community. In particular, wherever Bentham formulates his general position in the ***Introduction*** it has the parochial qualification added, and in each case it is clear that he conceives his main concern to be with matters of legislation. There is considerable evidence, then, that Bentham employs the standard of community interest in the appropriate places. This is true throughout his works if we discount the smaller number of cases in which the parochial restriction is omitted—or rather regard those formulations as elliptical. But in the ***Introduction*** no such added conjectures are required. In this respect, this text fits the dual standard perfectly.

But is there comparable evidence that Bentham correspondingly employs the standard of *self-*interest in what he regards as private matters? There is not much evidence to consider, for Bentham is rarely concerned with strictly private ethics, even in the ***Introduction.*** His philosophical as well as personal interests are always concentrated on political issues. The most directly relevant evidence outside the ***Introduction*** may be summarised as follows. (1) Bentham offers a similar division of ethics in ***A Table of***

the Springs of Action and the ***Chrestomathia.*** But neither is used to generate results like those found in the final chapter of the ***Introduction.*** (2) One passage of the ***Fragment on Government*** dealing with the difficult question of justified resistance, while somewhat ambiguous, nevertheless seems to challenge my reconstruction. (3) So does Bentham's ***Deontology,*** which suggests that private ethics should be tested by 'public happiness'. The ***Fragment***'s evidence might be discounted since by the time of its writing Bentham's fully developed position (of his later ***Introduction***) was probably not yet developed. There is even more reason to discount the ***Deontology:*** it is a late production not necessarily reflecting Bentham's views through most of his career, and it was published posthumously after passing through Bowring's editorial hands, which throws considerable doubt upon the text's authenticity. In any case, that seems to be all there is. There is little if any further evidence to test the private prong of Bentham's dual standard. And no similarly unfavourable evidence may be found within the ***Introduction*** itself.

The evidence further afforded by the ***Introduction*** requires and warrants more careful consideration. Some items are, of course, relatively trivial. For example, in one place Bentham suggests that only the 'most extensive' benevolence coincides with the dictates of utility. This may be taken as implying universalism. But even this, the most universalistic-sounding passage in the book, can be understood, in context, as expressing opposition only to that 'partial' kind of goodwill that does not extend to all the members of one's community and that therefore fails to harmonise with the parochial standard. Similarly, Bentham's calculus of pleasures and pains in Chapter iv includes the factor of 'extent': 'that is, the number of persons to whom it [a pleasure or pain, or rather the class of pleasures and pains caused by the same act] *extends;* or (in other words) who are affected by it'. This may make it appear as if Bentham always wants us to consider whoever is affected by an act. But this does not follow, for so long as the method is to be used for political affairs, it must take account of extent—at least within the bounds of one's community. The same accounting procedure would be used in private matters, except that extent need not be considered. Bentham seems to say as much, in fact, at the end of the chapter, when he claims that his method 'is nothing but what the practice of mankind, wheresoever they have a clear view of their own interest, is perfectly conformable to', and then proceeds to illustrate this claim, mentioning all factors save extent, not because others' interests cannot be affected in his example, but because it falls within the sphere of private ethics. No other passages requiring direct comment may be found outside the first and last chapters of the book, to which we now turn.

The first threat to my reading of Bentham appears shortly after the two paragraphs in Chapter i on which it is partly based. In paragraph 6, for example, Bentham says:

> An action then may be said to be conformable to the principle of utility, or, for shortness sake, to utility (meaning with respect to the community at large), when the tendency it has to augment the happiness of the community is greater than any it has to diminish it.

This seems to say that the happiness of the community is the *single* standard of utility. It suggests that Bentham has a parochial principle and no dual standard. Similar suggestions may be found in paragraphs 7 and 9.

But let us look at the context, the first part of Chapter i. After an introductory paragraph, Bentham states his principle and defines utility (in paragraphs 2 and 3, already quoted in full). He then (paragraph 4) explains what he means by 'the interest of the community', for he believes the expression can be misleading. Since his analysis is in terms of the interest of individuals, he explains that notion too (paragraph 5). The troublesome passages then follow. Now, if Bentham has returned to his *general* discussion of utility in paragraph 6, the new account is threatened. But it is possible that, instead of continuing the discussion left with paragraph 3, about utility in general, Bentham continues the one left with paragraph 4, about the *particular kind* of utility that concerns the entire community. The present problem would then dissolve. Paragraphs 6-9 themselves can be read in either way. For example, the parenthetical remark in paragraph 6 (where 'meaning with respect to the community at large' qualifies 'utility') could *either* mean that utility always concerns the entire community *or else* that the immediate point is limited to that kind of utility. But the definition of utility offered just before, in paragraph 3, makes the former reading quite implausible, since Bentham explicitly says there that it sometimes concerns only a particular individual. So this objection seems to fail.

But that is not the end of troubles suggested by this passage. If paragraphs 6-9 are to harmonise with my reading, then, since the standard mentioned is the happiness of the community, the acts 'conformable to utility' by this standard must be political. But in the very next paragraph (7), Bentham makes the same point, in the same terms, about 'measures of government', which he explains are 'but a particular kind of action, performed by a particular person or persons'. My reading of paragraphs 6-7 would then seem to have Bentham inexplicably repeating the same point about political actions in two successive paragraphs. Or, does Bentham have an as yet unexplained distinction between political acts in general (the subject of paragraph 6) and measures of government in particular (the subject of paragraph 7), both of which fall under the art of government? I think he might. Let us assume that Bentham has the political standard of community interest which he derives from a more basic principle of utility. The standard can be derived from the principle only by applying the principle to government *as a whole,* as my account above assumed. He cannot apply it first to real public officials since (as he must be well aware) most 'government functionaries' do not 'direct' their entire community but only, at best, some segment of it. Only the government as a whole could be thought to have *all* the members of the community subject to its governance. There is therefore room for a distinction between the official acts of government functionaries (the subject of paragraph 6) and measures of government in particular (the subject of paragraph 7). The latter are attributable to the government as a whole but are none the less identical with some acts of individual officials (such as kings and ministers) or of several collectively (such as legislators). The possibility and, on my account, the need for such a distinction may be used to explain the superficial similarities between paragraphs 6 and 7.

Larger issues emerge when we consider the final chapter of the **Introduction,** specifically the first section, which supplies the other passages on which my new interpretation is based. It will suffice to consider paragraph 8, where Bentham begins the main part of his discussion of the 'Limits between private ethics and the art of legislation'. The first part of this paragraph reads as follows:

> Now private ethics has happiness for its end: and legislation can have no other. Private ethics concerns every member, that is, the happiness and the actions of every member of any community that can be proposed; and legislation can concern no more. Thus far, then, private ethics and the art of legislation go hand in hand. The end they have, or ought to have, in view, is of the same nature. The persons whose happiness they ought to have in view, as also the persons whose conduct they ought to be occupied in directing, are precisely the same.

This part may look at first more troublesome than it actually is. Bentham says, for example, that private ethics and the art of legislation both have 'happiness' as their proper end. But this does not preclude a dual standard, for the end is specified ambiguously as 'happiness'. Bentham explicitly leaves room for the different ends of private ethics and the art of legislation when he says that they are, not identical, but 'of the same nature'. Similarly, in their *different* ways, both private ethics and the art of legislation are concerned with the happiness and the direction of everyone. (The differences are reviewed at the end of this section of the chapter, in Bentham's recapitulation, quoted above.) Bentham continues:

> The very acts they ought to be conversant about, are even in a *great measure* the same. Where then lies the difference? In that the acts which they ought to be conversant about, though in a great measure, are not perfectly and throughout the same. There is no case in which a private man ought not to direct his own conduct to the production of his own happiness, and of that of his fellow-creatures: but there are cases in which the legislator ought not (in a direct way at least, and by means of punishment applied immediately to particular individual acts) to attempt to direct the conduct of the several other members of the community. Every act which promises to be beneficial upon the whole to the community (himself included) each individual ought to perform of himself: but it is not every such act that the legislator ought to compel him to perform. Every act which promises to be pernicious upon the whole to the community (himself included) each individual ought to abstain from of himself: but it is not every such act that the legislator ought to compel him to abstain from.

Now, if one is seeking arguments against my new interpretation, he might grasp upon the last sentences of this paragraph. Bentham says that a 'private man' should always do what is beneficial to the community and abstain from what is pernicious to it. But how could private ethics based on the standard of *self*-interest lead in this direction? The answer may seem to be that it could not, and the upshot would again be that Bentham has a single standard, of community interest, in both private and political affairs.

But this conclusion is pretty well blocked by what Bentham says as well as by what his statements imply. One might look at the same passage from the other side, and ask why Bentham says that a man ought *always* to serve his *own* interests *as well as* his community's. A single-standard interpretation of Bentham could be compatible with this—but *only* if Bentham believes that personal and community interests harmonise, so that one does not conflict with the other in the long run. But if Bentham believes that, then the passage is also compatible with the dual-standard reading. I shall argue that Bentham assumes that interests so converge. But first let us consider another important objection that might be based upon this passage.

Bentham is concerned with the relations between private ethics and the art of legislation, which he develops in terms of (roughly) the acts they require or allow. It will simplify matters considerably if we restrict our attention to acts opposed by a utilitarian private ethics—which we shall call 'wrong'—and acts that utility says ought to be prohibited by law—which we shall call 'crimes'. (What is said about these holds, *mutatis mutandis,* for acts approved by private ethics and that ought to be required by law.) Now, Bentham says that private ethics opposes acts that legislation ought not to forbid, and this may suggest that 'crimes' are a proper sub-class of 'wrong' actions. Furthermore, he also suggests, and in the subsequent paragraphs confirms the suggestion, that legal punishment makes the difference. Private ethics may oppose acts with which legislation ought not to interfere because in such cases punishment would be 'unprofitable' or 'needless'. If we consider Bentham's views about the law and legal punishment, these claims can be readily explained. When private ethics approves or disapproves an act no costs or risks are essentially involved, for here 'private ethics' merely represents the dictates of utility within the sphere of private conduct. It has nothing necessarily to do with, say, the 'moral' or 'popular sanction', those social pressures that manifest and partly constitute conventional morality. For the latter need not conform to utility's dictates. But Bentham believes that punishment must be part of legal interference, added to commands and prohibitions. Once punishments are introduced, however, costs and risks are *necessarily* involved, and these cannot be justified unless they are outweighed by a greater 'mischief' thereby prevented by the law. It may appear, therefore, that utilitarian 'crimes' are a sub-class of utilitarian 'wrong' actions. For an act need only be 'mischievous' on the whole for private ethics to oppose it, but, in view of the inevitable costs and risks of legal interference, as act must be more than merely mischievous for legal prohibition to be warranted. The mischief prevented by legally forbidding the act must be greater than the mischief resulting from the introduction of legal sanctions. But, if punishment explains in such a simple way why 'crimes' are a sub-class of 'wrong' actions, then it would seem that the very same standard is applicable to both private ethics and the art of legislation.

For if different standards were employed—self-interest in private affairs, say, and community interest in public matters—then the relations between these two classes of acts would be far more complex than the passage seems to imply.

I have already shown how this objection can be met, even on its own terms. If, as the passage indicates, Bentham believes that personal and community interest converge, then a dual-standard interpretation could be used to develop the same account of the relationship between private ethics and the art of legislation. But we cannot leave matters there, for we should not accept the objection on its own terms. It offers a plausible picture of utilitarian reckoning—one that J. S. Mill, for example, may assume in his essay *On Liberty*. But it is too simple, it is not Bentham's, and it does violence to the text.

Bentham's marginal note for the paragraph says only that 'Every act which is a proper object of ethics is not of legislation'. This seems to mean that some acts that private ethics opposes should not be prohibited by law. But it does not say, nor does the passage imply, that every act that ought to be prohibited by law would independently be opposed by private ethics. In fact, he denies this a few paragraphs later, when he observes that laws must define property before private ethics can oppose infringements of legal property rights. Similarly, Bentham does not say that punishment is the only factor determining the relations between private ethics and the art of legislation. Another factor soon to be discussed by him is the legislator's ignorance of individuals and their particular circumstances.

Now it may be thought that Bentham's theory of punishment (in the *Introduction* and elsewhere) is based on the belief required for the original objection, namely, that the interests of different persons do not necessarily harmonise. What need could Bentham see for punishment if he did not suppose that a man's interest would often conflict with his community's? After all, he believes that men seek their own happiness first, that they calculate, and that they know their own interests best. So, he could not think that men would need much help from legal sanctions to do what a utilitarian legislator would require of them unless he also thinks that self-interest often diverges from community interest. Bentham must think that punishment is needed to *change* and *adjust* the interests of individuals, in order to effect an *artificial* harmony. Bentham's rationale of punishment denies a natural harmony of interests.

Most of the premises of this argument are false, as well as its conclusion. Bentham says that 'all men calculate', but he does not mean that they always reach the right conclusions, even about their own interests. He says that a man needs no assistance from legislation to discharge his 'duty to himself', but his point is that, while 'a man knows too little of himself', a legislator knows even less. His theory of punishment is based on the idea of adjusting men's 'motives' and thus affecting their inclinations to behave one way rather than another, but this does not entail *reversing* their interests in the long run. Nor does he argue that way in the *Introduction* or, in general, elsewhere. Finally, the argument assumes that Bentham is a 'psychological egoist' who believes that men are essentially self-centered. Now this is perhaps understandable, for Bentham's theory of motivation is a kind of 'psychological hedonism', which is usually assumed to be a special form of egoism. But Bentham's hedonism is not like that. In the *Introduction* and elsewhere, Bentham quite clearly believes that we have *non*-egoistic interests in the welfare of others, of the 'sympathetic' as well as the 'antipathetic' varieties. He never suggests that these interests are 'reducible' to or grounded upon beliefs about self-interest. In fact, in the two paragraphs immediately preceeding the one at issue, this point is confirmed. His argument seems designed to show that private ethics, like legislation, supports the general requirements of 'probity' and 'beneficence' as well as those of 'prudence'. Now, his simply undertaking to establish the point supports the dual-standard interpretation; and his form of argument does the same. He does not argue there (as Bowring has him argue in the *Deontology*) that one ought to help others and not hurt them because they will reciprocate one's good or bad treatment of them. He claims, rather, that all men *are* moved to some degree by 'social' motives such as 'sympathy' and are naturally concerned about the happiness of others. Others' interests are, or tend to become, one's own. And thus prudence in a subtle way requires that we discharge our 'duties' of probity and beneficence towards others. For we stand to suffer if we hurt others or fail to help them because we have interests in their welfare that are antecedent to and independent of our fear of their retaliation and our hope of their goodwill. Less wonder, then, that Bentham should be found assuming in the very next paragraph that different individuals' interests converge in the long run.

If we did assume that Bentham is a psychological egoist, another objection might occur to us. Private ethics based on self-interest might be said to have no point, since it would only tell us all to do what we will try to do anyway, that is, pursue our own happiness. And the requirement of public ethics, that legislators promote the general happiness, would suffer the opposite fate: it could not be followed except coincidentally, since legislators, like all men, are preoccupied with their own interests. But, as to the former point, Bentham seems to make clear that he is not proposing any change in the basic standard of men's private deliberations. 'In all this', he says, 'there is nothing but what the practice of mankind, wheresoever they have a clear view of their own interest, is perfectly conformable to'. In this regard, he is chiefly trying to show us what our most enlightened deliberations demand and how to make our calculations as knowledgeable and rational as possible. Bentham's main interest in the *Introduction* and elsewhere, however, is not private ethics but legislation. So let us see how legislation fares against this objection. It is clear that psychological egoism presents a problem for the new interpretation if, and only if, it causes difficulties for the competing views of Bentham's principle too. For the other interpretations have Bentham requiring legislators to promote the interests of others, and not just their own. This coexists happily with psychological egoism only if Bentham assumes that interests converge. But, if we are willing to grant that, then once again the threat to my interpretation disappears. This objection cannot serve to make it less plausible than the others.

My defence of the claim that Bentham has a differential principle of utility from which he derives a dual standard has turned in part upon two further claims that may be controversial. I have asserted that in the *Introduction,* and generally elsewhere, Bentham does not embrace an egoistic view of human nature. I have also argued that he assumes a real convergence of interests among different individuals. A full defence of these two claims cannot be given here. But some additional light on the state of Bentham's views at the time of writing his *Introduction* may be got by considering one of his last and major works, the *Constitutional Code.*

This is one of the few places in which Bentham makes an explicit general statement that might be construed as endorsing psychological egoism. It arises when he presents the basic principles of the work. The first is introduced as follows: 'The right and proper end of government in every political community, is the greatest happiness of all the individuals of which it is composed, say, in other words, the greatest happiness of the greatest number.' But, Bentham notes: 'The *actual* end of government is, in every political community, the greatest happiness of those, whether one, or many, by whom the powers of government are exercised.' The reason for this fact, and for the consequent divergence possible between the right and proper end and the actual end of government, is the predominance of 'self-preference'. Bentham writes:

> By the principle of self-preference, understand that propensity in human nature, by which, on the occasion of every act that he exercises, every human being is led to pursue that line of conduct which, according to his view of the case, taken by him at the moment, will be in the highest degree contributory to his own greatest happiness, whatsoever be the effect of it, in relation to the happiness of other similar beings, any or all of them taken together.

One who believes that men are so constituted would surely qualify as a 'psychological egoist'. But Bentham refrains from endorsing so strong a view. The evidence for self-preference is empirical, he tells us, the history of nations and the survival of the race. The egoistic thesis could be taken as an incontrovertible 'axiom', but Bentham says it need not be so understood. And Bentham does not need so strong a premiss in order to make his point. He wants to lay down guidelines for the structure of government, and for this purpose, and for legislation generally, he says, it makes no difference whether we suppose that men are always selfish or that they are selfish only in the 'bare majority' of instances. Self-preference is, in any case, 'predominant'. And so, he thinks, our institutions should be designed from the ground up on the assumption that self-preference is unavoidable and universal. The argument may be questioned, but hardly the fact that Bentham employs it.

It appears, therefore, that Bentham is willing to commit himself to a view no stronger than this: 'In the general tenor of life, in every human breast, self-regarding interest is predominant over all other interests put together'. Where Bentham finally comes to state a clear, general position on the matter, then, he does not adopt a strictly egoistic conception of human nature.

And even this guarded view appears to represent a conscious, acknowledged departure from his earlier one—or rather his earlier lack of any clearly thought out position on the matter. According to Bowring, Bentham wrote that it took him sixty years to comprehend the great antipathy to his utilitarian doctrines in *A Fragment on Government.* The cause was finally perceived to be the principle of self-preference, of which he disclaimed any 'clear perception' until late in his career.

The emergence of this conscious, if qualified, belief in human egoism appears to have accompanied his recognition that interests might conflict and that the interests of some, at least, might diverge from the predominant interest in his community. That fact, he explains in the *Constitutional Code,* is why he needs to say 'the greatest happiness of all' if his formula is 'to serve for all occasions'. The possibility of what Bentham here calls 'competition' provides occasion for self-preference to operate. Without the recognition of this possibility, self-preference might not be recognised, and so it could not awaken an awareness of the problem that Bentham now regards as so serious—misrule caused by 'sinister interest'.

Given the greatest-happiness principle and a principle of self-preference, Bentham deduces a third 'principle': 'Call it, the *means-prescribing,* or *junction-of-interests-prescribing,* principle', which tells us 'the *means* of bringing what is into accordance with what ought to be', namely, bringing 'the particular interest of rulers into accordance with the universal interest', either by punishment and reward or by limiting their powers. The *Constitutional Code* is one of the few places in which Bentham mentions or makes apparent use of such a principle. In these places, his applications are mainly limited to 'security against misrule', that is, control of legislators and administrators, not private citizens. So on the one hand it does not appear as if Bentham views legal sanctions in general as warranted by such a 'principle', that, is, required because of a substantial disharmony of interests. But on the other hand, it would seem that the *Constitutional Code* is where Bentham finally states principles that are erroneously associated with the *Introduction.* And this late work represents a striking departure from such earlier writings.

I wish to consider now a different sort of difficulty. It often happens that competing interpretations are all more or less compatible with a single text and that some are ruled out because they seem philosophically objectionable. A consideration like this might be thought to apply here. For the dual standard I am imputing to Bentham is much like a pair of non-equivalent principles, and it is possible for such principles to conflict in practice. The dual standard might accordingly be characterised as internally 'inconsistent', and this provides a *prima facie* case against my reading. For example, a legislator is supposed to 'direct' others so that they will realise *their* own happiness. But in legislating, as in everything else that he does, a lawmaker is deciding what he himself shall do as well as acting officially. He is deciding, say, whether to vote for a certain piece of legislation. But in deciding what to do, and thus 'directing'

his *own* behaviour he is presumably advised by the standard of private ethics to seek his own happiness. But these two ends might be incompatible, in the sense that an occasion can arise in which, if he serves the community best he fails to serve himself as well as possible, and vice versa. The dual standard would then prescribe incompatible courses of action for him, and its prescriptions might then be considered 'inconsistent'.

Several replies are possible, one of which should be obvious. While the dual standard as sketched out so far may be 'inconsistent' in the sense specified, it does not seem that such a problem would have occurred to the Bentham who is oblivious to conflicts between different individuals' interests and assumes that they harmonise. So, the philosophical objection to a dual standard cannot discredit the *interpretation.* Furthermore, Bentham does not embrace the dual standard as if it consists of two distinct, independent and mutually exclusive 'first principles'. He conceives the dual standard as deriving from his more basic principle of utility. And thus it would be reasonable for him to assume that the dual standard is not internally inconsistent—or rather to construe it so that it is as self-consistent as the principle from which it is supposedly derived. Finally, there are independent grounds for claiming that the dual standard would not yield such incompatible prescriptions.

The difficulty we have been considering arose because we assumed in effect that public ethics falls within or at least overlaps private ethics. In view of Bentham's unqualified reference to 'self-government', it seemed reasonable to suppose that private ethics concerns whatever a person may be said to do of his own accord. If the art of government then covers all acts of 'governmental functionaries' and all 'measures of government', it would seem that the two areas overlap. But, alternatively, the public sector could be delimited first, with private ethics covering only what remains. This is the approach implied by Bentham in the *Chrestomathia,* where he calls the sectors 'state-regarding' and 'not-state-regarding ethics' respectively. This way of drawing it makes the branches mutually exclusive as well as exhaustive. Now, we have no direct evidence that Bentham assumes this qualification when he makes the same distinction in his earlier *Introduction,* but it does not seem unreasonable to apply it there. For its style conforms to Bentham's usual method of division, it would not alter Bentham's essential commitments, and it is the sort of qualification one would expect made once it is found lacking. Given this division, 'inconsistency' cannot be a problem, for the two parts of ethics would not overlap at all and the two standards would have no applications in common.

I do not mean to suggest that there are no philosophical objections to the resulting theory. We may of course ignore those that could accrue to any form of utilitarianism which Bentham might be thought to hold, since these could not discredit my interpretation. The main troubles for this particular theory would seem to concern Bentham's derivation of the dual standard from the differential principle. Now, in speaking of this derivation I am admittedly extrapolating well beyond the surface of the text.

But I believe that the evidence already displayed shows that some such derivation is implicit and is mediated by the division of ethics found in the ***Introduction,*** Chapter xvii. My account is claimed to fit the textual facts as simply as possible, and to conform to the spirit of Bentham's philosophy as well. Since Bentham's derivation is not explicitly developed, it is possible that my account does not do justice to his intentions. But as far as I can see, Bentham's division of ethics obscures some implications of his basic principle, which says that one ought to promote the happiness of those subject to one's direction, influence or control. For, apparently without reason, it excludes other forms of 'direction' besides government in the ordinary sense (in which an entire community is supposed to be 'directed') and self-government (in which a particular individual 'directs' himself). Outside the realm of official behaviour there are comparable ways in which one individual can influence and indeed control the behaviour of other agents. In view of these possibilities, it would seem that the Benthamic principle is capable of generating not two but indefinitely many standards.

How could Bentham overlook such possibilities? Perhaps through a combination of satisfaction and distraction. In writing the ***Fragment on Government*** several years before completing the ***Introduction,*** Bentham had endorsed a 'principle of utility'. But that seems to have been an early stage in the development of his thought. The general idea of a 'greatest happiness' principle was admittedly not original and seems to have been current at the time. Moreover, the principle's character in the ***Fragment*** may appear to us to be ambiguous—since it is there applied only to politics (with one possible exception noted)—and it is never formulated very fully. It is not implausible to suppose that while writing the ***Introduction*** Bentham discovers what seems to him a more powerful and complex principle, which could yield not only the appropriate standard for judging the affairs of government (which had been and always would remain his central concern) but generates the principle of prudence as a bonus. How tempting such a principle and derivation must be! But just at that time Bentham's attention is drawn away from his inadequately developed derivation and thus he fails to give it the critical examination that it warrants. In writing the final chapter of the ***Introduction*** (where the implicit derivation may be perceived) Bentham is preoccupied at first with the very different topics that he announces for the chapter, such as the distinction between civil and criminal law, and then with much more general and difficult questions to which he is led. His continued research delays final completion of the work, persuades him to put off its publication even after it has been printed, and drives him to devote a year or two to developing what becomes his fullest work on the nature of law. Finally, we must also recall that Bentham could not yet be sensitive to many problems of his dual standard. He does not acknowledge that different individuals' interests can really conflict; that recognition comes only much later. And so, we find in the first and last chapters of the ***Introduction*** some of the limits of Bentham's moral reflections for many years to come.

If my account is even a plausible competitor against the standard, universalistic interpretation of Bentham's principle, how is it possible that the relevant evidence has been so widely overlooked by commentators, critics and followers? I believe, in fact, that the evidence *against* the universalistic account is so clear that my interpretation so far does not depend on explanations of others' misunderstandings. But one may speculate, and a number of factors would seem relevant. First of all, Bentham's specific conclusions are probably not much different from those a universalist might have been led to draw, since they mainly concern domestic political arrangements. His parochialism in politics would therefore be obscured. Secondly, some of his best-known formulations of the principle of utility (such as the informal statement of it in the ***Fragment***) are not overtly qualified with the parochial restriction. Third, his 'explicit and determinate account' in the ***Introduction*** is, by itself, obscure and might well appear to be a clumsy universalism—at least if that is what the reader expects to find. One must dig deeper into the book to discover a clear alternative, and then one finds it only in predictably neglected places. The discussion of ethics, for example, is found only in the final chapter of the book, the announced topics of which would not attract attention to these questions. It is not surprising, therefore, to find at least one writer quoting Bentham's 'explicit and determinate account' of the principle of utility, contained in Chapter i, without commenting on the division of ethics in Chapter xvii—still less combining the two and drawing the appropriate conclusions. But even this most prominent and explicit account would seem to be neglected: it is rarely quoted, and commentators raise no relevant questions about it, despite its singularity.

The subsequent direction of 'utilitarianism' may be partly responsible. Mill, Sidgwick, Moore and others seem to have been universalists—and never to have conceived utilitarianism in any other way. Or perhaps it should be said that they viewed the alternatives as more limited: egoism against universalism, on the one hand, and hedonism against 'ideal' utilitarianism on the other. Mill does not comment on this aspect of Bentham's views. He was preoccupied with different alleged errors of Bentham's and may have overlooked the issues here or underestimated them. Sidgwick, apparently alone among philosophers, does acknowledge the existence of some evidence that Bentham had a dual standard—though he does not indicate the evidence. But even so, he fails to note the difference between Bentham's supposed universalism and the parochialism explicitly expressed in the statement of Bentham's that Sidgwick quotes in this discussion [in his *The Methods of Ethics,* 1907]. What needs explaining, I think, is how these issues get obscured—how one as acute as Sidgwick, for example, fails to ask what now may seem some obvious questions.

Other factors may have contributed as well. Bentham's dual standard could easily be obscured because his preoccupation with political affairs leaves him few occasions for applying the standard of his private ethics. As we have seen, some of his related views have been misconstrued; he has been taken as a psychological egoist, for example, and, as his eighteenth-century faith in the natural harmony of human interests grew out of fashion, readers may have come to think it less than plausible that Bentham held so naïve a view. Finally, since J. S. Mill, Bentham's philosophical contributions have not been very highly regarded; they are probably caricatured more often for use in examples than studied seriously. Add to all this the burial of Bentham's work in the unfortunate and confused Bowring edition of his *Works* (or else in unpublished manuscripts) and the distorting effect of an otherwise chaotic publishing history, and one may understand how gross misconceptions could persist, especially as they obscure possible change and development in Bentham's thought. (pp. 196-221)

> *David Lyons, "Was Bentham a Utilitarian?"* in Reason and Reality, *The Macmillan Press Ltd., 1972, pp. 196-221.*

An excerpt from *A Table of the Springs of Action*

The law is every man's best friend: to her under God he is indebted for every thing that is dear to him. To her he owes every thing which he enjoys: whatever protection he has for his peace of mind, his person, or his honour. To her the rich man owes his wealth; the poor man his subsistence; every man who is free, his freedom.

Jeremy Bentham, A Table of the Springs of Action, *R. & A. Taylor, 1815.*

Richard F. Hixson   (essay date 1981)

[*Hixson is an American educator specializing in the field of journalism. In the following excerpt, Hixson explicates Bentham's* Rationale of Reward, *noting the application therein of the hedonistic principle to social governance.*]

[*The Rationale of Reward*] is but one of Bentham's many treatises that suggest that society should—"ought," as compared to "is," as Bentham frequently prefers—contrive by its laws and its systems of punishments and rewards to see that serving society is pleasant and that serving one's own interests at the expense of society's is painful. If it is indeed possible to reduce his vast works to such a phrase, it is this one, for Bentham struggled thematically throughout his life between what is and what ought to be, and learned early on that what men say is one thing, what they do is another, and what they ought to do is sometimes still a third. Bentham is of course fascinating to read and to try to understand, because his theories are often supported by observation or applied to situations in government and jurisprudence, as well as to criminology and arts and letters in general. *Reward* is no exception. (p. 18)

Bentham, in his **"Preliminary Observations,"** writes that the greatest happiness of the greatest number ought to be the object of every legislator, and for accomplishing his purposes towards this objective, he possesses two instruments—punishment and reward. "The theories of these two forces divide between them, although in unequal shares, the whole field of legislation." Reward, meanwhile, is defined as "a portion of the matter of good."

Cause must be distinguished from effect, and the means of obtaining pleasures or exemptions from pains, as well as the pleasures or exemptions from the pains themselves. What a legislator must bestow is the former, or the *means,* not the pains themselves.

The avoidance of pain, or, conversely, the attraction of pleasure, is but a *portion* of the matter of good, " . . . in consideration of some service supposed or expected to be done, [it] is bestowed on some one, in the intent that he may be benefited thereby." This pain-less ingredient, so central to Bentham's utilitarianism, is supposed to operate as *the* motive for the performance of socially useful actions. Bentham prefers extraordinary services to those of an ordinary or routine and occasional nature, for the former are rendered on behalf of the whole community, i.e., inventions, services in time of war, great discoveries in national welfare and science. "Reward is to good, what punishment is to evil," thus the absence of good is comparatively an evil and the absence of evil is comparatively a good.

The notion of evil—"all sorts of evil"—is included in Bentham's notion of reward, which is to say that punishment is useful; Bentham insists that the opposite of reward—pain or punishment—produces a positive effect that sustains the real value of reward. Presumably, the threat of punishment encourages the pursuit of reward. (I am reminded here of John Milton's theme in *Paradise Lost,* which, oversimplified, suggests that only through the knowledge of evil is man able to discern good.) When it comes to the enactment of laws, Bentham argues that the most favorable opportunities for legislation are those in which both punishment and reward are intertwined, especially if punishment immediately follows the omission of dutiful service and if reward follows its performance. Immediacy is the key.

Before going on with the text of *Reward,* it is significant to point out that central to Bentham's utilitarian sociology is mankind's need for security. As he writes in *The Book of Fallacies* (1824): "True it is, that all laws, all political institutions, are essentially dispositions for the future; and the professed object of them is to afford a steady and permanent security to the interests of mankind." To Bentham, laws provide predictability and, thus, security in life. Law is the difference between animals and man, or as [Mary Peter Mack states in her *Jeremy Bentham: An Odyssey of Ideas*]: "Law is the specifically human way of recognizing, using, and subduing time. Its victory is security." Throughout his life, from Westminister to Oxford to Lincoln's Inn, Bentham sought to work out a utilitarian rationale of law that required legislators whose business it would be to increase happiness.

Bentham returned to that theme in *Reward.* He insisted, further, that the legislator should enact laws which would execute themselves. "The law's provisions are so arranged the punishment immediately follows its violation, unaided by any form of procedure: that to one offence another more easily susceptible of proof, or more severely punished, is substituted." Just as reward diminishes not only punishment but the very need for pain, it is by the taking away of liberty or security that power is conferred. "Fortunate America! fortunate on so many accounts, if to possess happiness it were sufficient to possess every thing by which it is constituted, this advantage is still yours: preserve it for ever, bestow rewards, erect statues, confer even titles, so that they be personal alone; but never bind the crown of merit upon the brow of sloth."

In accordance with Bentham's principle of utility, the costly matter of reward ought only to be employed in the production of service to the community at large, that a reward can only consist of a *portion* of the matter of reward and be employed as a *motive* for the production of service. Rewards, however, do not have to be promised to be effective, though they may be expected. "A promised reward, bestowed upon one who has not deserved it, is entirely lost. An unpromised reward, thus improperly bestowed, is not necessarily lost." Bentham argues that reward should be substituted for punishment throughout the whole field of legislation. For, if people are motivated by the fear of punishment, they will exert themselves just enough to avoid punishment and no more. Although personal motivation may be conditioned by fear, the individual ought to be motivated by reward, not punishment.

Punishment is best used for restraint or prevention, reward for excitement and production—the one a bridle, the other a spur! Punishment relates more directly to crimes, especially where, in Bentham's words, "very extensive mischief may be produced by a single act." Punishment is the only eligible means of regulating conduct of people in general; reward ought to be reserved for directing actions of particular individuals. And, finally, necessity compels the employment of punishment, whereas reward is a luxury. "Discard the first, and society is dissolved: discard the other, and it still continues to subsist, though deprived of a portion of its amenity and elegance."

Bentham urges avoidance of "anything in the shape of reward" which may tend to interfere with the performance of duty. He says that factitious reward is superfluous, preferring instead natural reward governed by several rules: 1) the aggregate value of the natural and factitious reward ought not to be less than is sufficient to outweigh the burden of the service; 2) factitious rewards may be diminished in proportion as natural ones are increased; 3) reward should be adjusted in such a manner to each particular service, "that for every part of the benefit there may be a motive to induce a man to give birth to it" (in other words, the value of reward should advance with the value of service); and 4) when two services are in competition and a person cannot be induced to perform both, the reward for the greater service ought to be enough to induce him to prefer it to the lesser. "If punishment ought not to be inflicted without formal proof of the commission of crime, neither ought reward to be conferred without equally formal proof of desert." In response to the adage "virtue is its own reward," Bentham argues for reward, if applicable, to virtuous and striking actions, "readily susceptible of proof, which arise out of extraordinary circumstances." Rewards cannot be instituted for parental kindness, conjugal fidelity, adherence to promises, veracity, gratitude, and pity, for these rewards would indeed be contrived for behavior normally expected.

In Book II, Bentham turns to the pragmatic issue of salary—"emolument of a determined amount paid at regularly recurring periods." The greater the service, the greater the reward, and the greater is the motive it constitutes. Moreover, the greater the motive, the more strenuous the exertion it has a tendency to produce; and the more strenuous the exertion, the greater will be the value of the service. Good service begets good money and good money begets good service. "Hence it follows that, if salary be reward, as far as funds can be found, salaries cannot be too large." There must be other motives, because salaries are frequently out of proportion to service—large salaries for small service, small salaries for admirable service. Among "other motives," Bentham suggests the pleasures of power (to balance the pains), the fear of shame (to keep from sinking below mediocrity), and, of course, the hope of fame and celebrity, all being rewards beyond mere (but necessary) emolument. However, salaries and other emoluments are not minimized; they ought to be the least that the individuals qualified are willing to accept for their performance. Such minimal rewards are likely to produce good service in the future. But, to place individuals above want, salaries must be sufficient to avoid corruption. Finally, a "pension of retreat" is recommended as a debt of humanity paid by the public to its retired servants.

Book III is an attempt to apply the rationale of reward to art and science, which, contrary to popular opinion at the time, are inseparable. Bentham arranges the arts and sciences into two divisions—those of amusement and curiosity and those of utility, both immediate and remote—but these two branches of human knowledge and endeavor require different methods of treatment by governments. The arts and sciences of amusement are ordinarily called fine arts and those of curiosity the sciences of heraldry, of medals, of pure chronology, of knowledge of ancient and barbarous languages, and of the study of antiquities. "The utility of all is exactly in proportion to the pleasure they yield." Of significance to our own time as well as to Bentham's is the philosopher's perceived role of governments vis-à-vis the arts and sciences. Governments are to remove the discouraging circumstances under which artists and scientists labor, and they must favor their advancement and contribute to their diffusion. But, such support and funding ought to be bestowed in the shape of reward: "Talents are rewarded by giving new means of increasing them."

Since governments are supposed to be representative of the governed, it follows that Bentham would support the value of public opinion. In fact, we have Bentham to thank for providing us with the first detailed discussion of public opinion in English. He saw public opinion as integral to the democratic state. As posited by Bentham and confirmed much later by Raymond Williams and others, democracy is no longer a cliché for "mob rule," but instead is at the pinnacle of the grammar of political virtue. In the second chapter of his ***Essay on Political Tactics*** (1791), entitled "Of Publicity," Bentham identified the "fittest law for securing the public confidence . . . that of publicity." To the question, "Where are the best men?" he answers that they may not be in the legislature; he is, thus, arguing on behalf of the need for informed public opinion. He gives but passing reference to public opinion in **Reward,** noting only that a single individual is seldom able to withstand or change the laws established by public opinion: "As the public mind becomes enlightened, these laws will change of themselves."

In Book IV, which Dumont extracted from **A Manual of Political Economy,** Bentham applies his rationale to production and trade. His application is based on one principle—the limitation of production and trade by the limitation of capital. Competition is encouraged, but loans are seen as false encouragement. "Taxes ought to have no other end than the production of revenue, with as light a burthen as possible." Bentham excludes "intoxicating liquors" from unburdensome taxation, however, reasoning that a high tax may diminish their consumption by increasing their price. The theory may be reasonable on the face of it, but it is fallacious, if not contradictory. It is fallacious for obvious reasons and it contradicts Bentham's earlier point that cause must be distinguished from effect when considering the value of reward and punishment. Besides, there seems to be no contemporary evidence that price affects the sale of alcoholic beverages. Colonization, too, bears on production and trade. "When an excess of population, in relation to territory, exists or is foreseen, colonization is a very proper measure. As a means of increasing the revenue of the mother country, it is a very improper measure."

In summary, **The Rationale of Reward** encompasses a number of Bentham's theories and observations. It is based on the legislator's obligation to promote the greatest happiness of the greatest number. It sees the avoidance of pain as the primary motive for community service, but recognizes that reward and punishment are intertwined as methods for inducing pleasure and service. The immediate application of reward and punishment is critical. Statutory law insures predictability and security. Salary, commensurate with performance, is an important form of reward. Governments, susceptible to enlightened public opinion, are responsible for encouraging and supporting art and science. Taxation and colonization are viable when used fairly and judiciously.

With **Reward,** Bentham provides us with an overview, or guide, to his works in general. His overriding position is that mankind is governed by two sovereign motives—pain and pleasure. Throughout his life Bentham sought to apply this basic notion to most of society's institutions. He was much less a pure philosopher than a critic of law and of judicial and political institutions. He tried to define the basic concepts of ethics and then to apply them to the world in which he lived. For this reason his works will always find an audience. (pp. 19-24)

> *Richard F. Hixson, "Bentham's 'The Rationale of Reward',"* in The Journal of the Rutgers University Libraries, *Vol. XLIII, No. 1, June, 1981, pp. 18-24.*

James E. Crimmins   (essay date 1986)

[*Crimmins is the author of* Secular Utilitarianism: Social Science and the Critique of Religion in the Thought of Jeremy Bentham *(1990). In the following excerpt focusing on Bentham's critique of religion, Crimmins examines the metaphysical presuppositions in Bentham's theory of language.*]

The utilitarian philosopher Jeremy Bentham (1748-1832) has long been recognized as an exponent of a new science of society. However, scholars of his thought have given scant attention to at least one important aspect of that science: the relationship between the metaphysical presuppositions of his social science and his view on religion. Rarely is it considered that Bentham's aspiration to create a science of society in emulation of physical science was fundamental to his critique of religion just as it was to all other areas of his thought. This critique of religion was set out principally in a series of works written between the years 1809 and 1823. **Swear Not at All** was published in 1817, and followed a year later, after earlier efforts were aborted in 1809 and 1813, by **Church-of-Englandism and its Catechism Examined.** The **Analysis of the Influence of Natural Religion on the Temporal Happiness of Mankind** appeared in 1822 and **Not Paul, but Jesus** in 1823. It was not merely a coincidence that in the very period when Bentham devoted so much of his time to religion his work on metaphysics and logic substantially reached fruition. The **"Book on Logic,"** on which Bentham worked at intervals between 1811 and 1821, was intended to give a full description of his "method." The work was never completed but was eventually edited and included in several fragments in John Bowring's edition of **The Works of Jeremy Bentham.** The essay on **"Nomography"** with an appendix on **"Logical Arrangements, or Instruments of Invention and Discovery Employed by Jeremy Bentham"** is included in the third volume, and in the eighth volume is to be found the **"Essay on Logic," "A Fragment on Ontology,"** the **"Essay on Language,"** and the **"Fragments on Universal Grammar."** The metaphysics described in these essays by Bentham was initially developed by him during the formative years of his intellectual life in the early 1770s, and he was always aware of its particular consequences in the field of religion.

Almost from the first time he put pen to paper he made known his distaste for the common notion of "metaphysics," understood as abstract thinking or the science of things transcending what is physical or belonging to Nature, though he was later to employ the term to describe his own speculations in the field of linguistics. These speculations fostered a descriptive view of language and a nominalist understanding of the world, both of which were central features of his approach in all fields of knowledge. For Bentham words, ideas, and propositions must represent, be signs for, or describe perceptible discrete physical entities. If they do not then they are abstractions or general terms which must be reduced to "real entities" before they can be correctly understood. Where ontological analysis fails to establish physical referents for a "fiction," to use Bentham's term, it can be assumed that it does not exist in any tangible form and so cannot be "known" in any certain or scientific sense of that term. These, in brief, are the presuppositions upon which he based his theory of knowledge. The ramifications of this theory for a religion which assumes that man's nature has its spiritual as well as its physiological side, and that there exists a reality beyond the perceptible material world, are perhaps not difficult to discover, but the peculiar nature of Bentham's critique of religion has been consistently overlooked by scholars of his thought and by those interested in secular trends in the nineteenth century.

Drawing upon his early unpublished manuscripts as well as his later published work, it is my intention in this essay to trace the intimate relationship that exists between Bentham's metaphysics and his critique of religion. Though it is true, as many have pointed out, that he harbored doubts regarding the manner in which official religion was administered even as a youth at Oxford, my interest here is with the systematic presentation of these and other doubts about religious beliefs. In short, I am concerned with the specific terms in which he came to express his unbelief. It was not his "religious upbringing" or "the religious training he suffered as a boy" which lay at the root of his utilitarianism, as Mary Mack has argued [in her *Jeremy Bentham: An Odyssey of Ideas*]. The history of his disaffection, first with the Church and later with religion itself, is one of a gradual process, and it is difficult to say with precision when it took the form of a definitive stance in his mind. What can be said, however, is that the emergence of the metaphysical principles upon which his theory of knowledge is grounded were crucial to this development and are, therefore, a necessary component of the attempt to explain it.

An unpublished manuscript from the year 1773 speaks characteristically of Bentham's aspiration to follow in the footsteps of Newton and Locke, but is also indicative of the subsequent direction of his thoughts on religion. In the process of eulogizing the achievements of "those heroes of the intellectual world, whose mortal works have placed their country on the summit of the scale of nations," he pauses to reflect that both men were religious heretics: "Fire is not more at variance with water, than was Locke with orthodoxy. . . . Newton was an heretic: the few lost hours which that great man stole from the region of certainty to waste upon the region of unintelligibles led him into Heresy". But neither Newton nor Locke is to be lauded for their religious opinions, heretical or otherwise, since it is in this respect that they left "the region of certainty" to inhabit "the region of unintelligibles." Even from this early date, then, science as Bentham understood it was deemed to be antithetical to religion, and the manner in which he rigidly applied the presuppositions of his own theory of knowledge to the examination of religious beliefs over the course of his life stands as a compelling testimony to the foundations of his unbelief.

Bentham's faith in the value of science to social analysis was vividly stated at the onset of his philosophical career. In *A Fragment on Government* (1776), his first major publication, he wrote that he inhabited "a busy age; in which knowledge is rapidly advancing towards perfection," and if this was so in "the natural world" where "everything teems with discovery and with improvement" there was surely considerable room for making discoveries and improvements in the moral world. As Newton had banished the vocabulary of mysticism and superstition from natural science, so Bentham made it his aim to rid the moral or social sciences of verbal and philosophical superstitions.

It is likely that the empirical character of this philosophy was also influenced by the work of David Hume, among others. As we know, the young Bentham was familiar with the *Treatise of Human Nature* and cited it as one of the major influences in bringing him to the doctrine of utility. He would no doubt also have been impressed by Hume's subtitle to the work: "Being an ATTEMPT to Introduce the Experimental Method of Reasoning into MORAL SUBJECTS." This was the goal Hume set for himself and for his age: it was a goal founded on the belief that scientific inquiry was of the utmost social relevance but, more particularly, it was an approach based on the strictest separation of facts and values. In manuscripts dating from *ca.* 1774 under the title **"What Things Exist?"** Bentham proclaimed his own belief in the material world as the essence of an objective reality: "I assume and take it for granted, that among the objects that offer or are supposed to offer themselves to our senses, are some that actually exist. I assume in a word the existence of what is called the material world." Later on in the **"Fragment on Ontology"** Bentham was to echo the sentiment in more specific terms: "No substance can exist but it must be itself matter; be of a certain determinate form; be or exist in a certain determinate quantity".

The central feature of Bentham's social science, however, was his conception of a neutral discipline of linguistic analysis, an "invention" or "discovery" fundamental to the manner in which he conceived the world. Around the same time that he first addressed himself to specifically religious matters in 1773, we also find him speculating upon a utopian future when academies might be established not only for ethics and politics (and possibly theology), but also for English language, under the auspices of which research would be undertaken into "language in general, Grammar, Logic, particularly Metaphysics." At the same time Bentham was moving toward a synthesis between his materialism and a theory of language in which there existed a precise correlation between things, on the one hand, and words, ideas, and propositions, on the other. The following observation on the nature of metaphysics, in connection with a barely disguised hit at certain religious beliefs, is a fairly typical one of the time (*ca.* 1776):

> To be skilled in Metaphysics is neither to hold for Atheism nor for Theism. Metaphysics is neither infidelity nor credulity. It is not to know that there are neither God nor Angels. It is not to hold the soul to be mortal, nor to hold it to be immortal. But it is this: in talking whether of God or of Angels or of the immortality of the soul or of its mortality . . . to know and to be able to make others know what it is we mean.

For Bentham, then, "metaphysics" meant linguistic analysis. In another early manuscript he credited Locke with the invention of "modern Metaphysics" and described it as

> that science which teacheth the signification of words, and the ideas which they signify: which it does . . . [by] shewing how all the ideas we

have that are complex, arise from, and are made up of simple ones. Thus it is that . . . every science has its metaphysics: there is no science that has not a set of terms that are more particularly its own. (*ca.* 1773)

A good neutral dictionary is essential to the possibility of a science of morals and politics, just like any other science, and in religion, as elsewhere, Bentham professed to keep personal prejudices out of the matter. In words strikingly reminiscent of those of D'Alembert's *Encyclopedie* article "Elements des sciences," he asserts that "the heights of science" are only to be scaled via an "orderly, unbroken, well compacted chain of definitions" (*ca.* 1776). If scientific method demanded precision in terminology, this he was prepared to provide:

> Define your words says Locke: Define your words says Helvetius. Define your words says Voltaire. Define your words says every man who knows the value of them, who knows the use of them, who understands the things they are wanted to express. . . . Philosophers I have obeyed you. I *have* defined my words. (1778)

Definition, central to any theory of linguistics, was for Bentham the "sole and sovereign specific against the maladies of confusion and debate" (*ca.* 1776). It was in the same year as this last quotation that he initiated his intended *magnum opus,* tentatively entitled **"Elements of Critical Jurisprudence,"** by analyzing key terms in political and legal theory. Ambiguities in legal terminology Bentham found especially monstrous and ruminated upon them at great length. He pursued the tasks of terminological invention and clarification unremittingly in his legal studies, convinced that "the import of . . . fundamental words, is the hinge on which the main body of the science turns," and that "it is not uncommon for questions of the first practical importance to depend for their decision upon questions concerning the import of these words."

Amid the barrage of criticisms of imprecise and archaic language usage in these early manuscripts Bentham introduced his theory of "real" and "fictitious" entities. Here he foreshadowed what in the later work he carefully and systematically developed. "The substances that are capable of being defined," he tells us, "are such only as are significant of themselves." But there are also words like "right," "power," "motion," and "gratitude" that "are not in truth significant of themselves, but only by fiction. . . . Such are all those terms though substantives in point of grammatical form." And in a tempered attack on religionists he writes:

> To maintain that there is a command from God to such an[d] such an effect, and at the same time allow that no signs of it can be produced, is to say that—to make no differences between expression and non-expression, between signs and no signs, between speaking and non-speaking, between writing and non-writing.

In manuscripts of later date (*ca.* 1790) we find Bentham proposing to give to abstractions the new name of "fictions" and emphasizing that, while sometimes useful and even essential to discourse, abstractions are not "real" en-

tities. By labeling abstractions "fictions" Bentham felt able to use them without sacrificing the conviction that they often functioned as an aid to discourse, and more importantly that they could be reduced (though not in every case) to particulars—in many cases fictions were a convenience of discourse which could, if required, be reduced to real entities. Hence in *Of Laws in General* (written 1776-80) we find Bentham referring to incorporeal objects as "nothing but so many fictitious entities" which must be "either one or several corporeal objects considered in some particular point of view."

Naturally, Bentham had not fully formulated his ontological ideas in the early writings. The culmination of his thoughts in this area of investigation came about in the years 1813-15 when he prepared the manuscripts later used for **"A Fragment on Ontology."** The dichotomy between real and fictitious entities was at the heart of Bentham's work on language at this time. In the **"Essay on Logic"** he informs us that the subjects of linguistic analysis are real and fictitious entities, and the task of this analysis is to be understood as "psychical arrangement," that is to say, the distinction and arrangement of "the *names,* and, through the names the *ideas*" of the discourse of such subjects as come to view. In **"A Fragment on Ontology"** he described the field of ontology as "the field of supremely abstract entities." Entities, he writes, may be "perceptible" (made known by the immediate testimony of our senses) or "inferential" (the product of a chain of reasoning). A real entity is an entity "belonging to the essence of reality"; its qualities are "solidity" and "permanence." Those real entities which are perceptible are corporeal substances; those which are inferential are incorporeal and belong to the world of ideas. Fictitious entities, the primary focus of Bentham's analysis, are entities to which existence is ascribed by the grammatical form of expression, but to which "in truth and reality existence is not meant to be ascribed."

But fictitious entities are not to be condemned because of their translucent character, since they are necessary to the possibility of discourse, at least at a refined level, taking place. We speak of them and use them (words like "motion," "relation," "faculty," and "power") as if they really exist without meaning that they do, but we do it to facilitate conversation and to exchange ideas. Nevertheless, implicit in what Bentham says here is an outright denial of the notion of an incorporeal reality; it is an impossibility, since incorporeal substances belong only to the world of ideas and cannot be reduced to real entities. The main aim of Bentham's analysis, however, is to point out that linguistic confusions are often caused by taking a fictitious entity to have a real existence. Nor is this a difficult mistake to make, since every fictitious entity is spoken of as if it were real:

> Of nothing that has place, or passes, in our minds can we give any account, any otherwise than by speaking of it as if it were a portion of space, with portions of matter, some of them at rest, others moving in it. Of nothing, therefore, that has place or passes in our mind, can we speak, or so much as think, otherwise than in the way of a fiction.

The purpose of distinguishing between real and fictitious entities is to limit the confusion that can be caused by the use of fictions by attaching clear ideas to terms in general use, and thereby to obviate errors and disputes which arise from want of clarity. Bentham had no doubts about the consequences which arise from the lack of clarity in the language of religion. In a manuscript dating from 1773 he wrote of the pernicious effects on the human character of inculcating incomprehensible tenets of belief:

> That state of prepared imbecility which is necessary to a mind for the tranquil reception of one parcel of Nonsense, fits it for another. . . . A man who after reading the scriptures can bring himself to fancy the doctrines of the Athanasian Creed . . . his mind if not already blotted over with hieroglyphical chimeras is a sheet of blank paper, on which any one who will press hard enough may write what scrawls he pleases.

Bentham was to return to this theme on many occasions in the future, but it was clear from the outset that his theory of knowledge entailed an obvious bias against the claims of religion. The only objects which have a real existence are those which are corporeal, single and entire of themselves. Sense impressions provide us with the data of the external world and these are translated into mental images and abstractions for the purpose of discourse. Convinced that the reality of the world of appearances is a matter of sense experience, Bentham argued that when all the characteristics of the evidence observed by a man are noted, belief and disbelief are no longer at his descretion; one or the other is the necessary consequence of the preponderance of evidence on the one side or the other. The business of knowing, he writes in the **"Essay on Logic,"** is simply a matter of observation, inference, and verification: "Experience, Observation, Experiment, Reflection, or the results of each and all together; these are the means, these are the instruments by which knowledge—such as is within the power of man—is picked up, put together, and treasured up." It is evident that on these terms the belief in a transcendent order is an illusion, and religious beliefs generally cannot be anything other than the consequence of man's appalling ignorance of the world he lives in, of its matter and its principles of motion.

Given this analysis of the use and meaning of words and of the confusion they may produce, it is not such a curious phenomenon as might first appear that we should find Bentham's definitive statements about the nature of the soul and the supposed existence of God, not in any of his writings on religion but in one of his essays on metaphysics—**A Fragment on Ontology.**" The belief in the soul's immortal nature and in the existence of an all-powerful and omnipresent God must have appeared to Bentham as obvious and attractive subjects for linguistic analysis. Not surprisingly he found that the soul could not be classified as anything other than an inferential entity. Lest there be any doubt as to his meaning Bentham adds in a footnote that those who do not believe in the reality of the soul as an independently existing phenomenon, must conclude that it is a fictitious entity, in which case it might be considered as "that whole, of which so many other psychical entities, none of which have ever been considered any oth-

erwise than fictitious, such as the understanding, and the will, the perceptive faculty, the memory, and the imagination, are so many parts." That this is his own conception of the soul, stripped of all mysticism and superstition, there is no question. With reference to the existence of God his position is no less clear:

> Should there be a person who, incapable of drawing those inferences by which the Creator and Preserver of all other entities, is referred to the class of real ones, . . . the class to which such person would find himself in a manner, compelled to refer that invisible and mysterious being would be, not as in the case of the human soul to that of fictitious entities, but that of non-entities.

Whereas Bentham can envisage that the soul may exist as the sum of the human psyche, he cannot transform "God" into anything reminiscent of the common understanding of that term. The mysticism that is stripped from the idea of the soul cannot be banished from the idea of God to leave anything remotely acceptable in its place. That the notion of God is a source of fictions and that God is a non-entity are conclusions to which Bentham's metaphysics inevitably leads, and it was these principal ideas which lay at the heart of all his thoughts on religious beliefs. If you do not have good, that is to say "scientific," grounds to suppose or infer the existence of God, what is there left to say for a religion which merely assumes his reality? Over forty years earlier Bentham had intimated that the Science of Divinity might be a barren field of inquiry: "Either Divinity is an important science," he wrote, "or it is important to know that it is not: It is of importance, and of the last importance to know whether any of it is of importance, and how much and what, if any" (1773). The fruit of the metaphysical investigations he began in the early 1770s and continued into his later years, was to show that Divinity served the entirely negative function of revealing the absurdities fostered by the superstitions which have their source in religious beliefs.

Yet if Bentham did not always conduct his investigations with the same kind of scientific open-mindedness that he preached, the supposed infallibility of science made it more than merely a useful propaganda weapon in his attack on religion. Disaffected with the overbearing authority of organized religion while still a youth at Oxford, his animosity increased throughout his middle years as the Bishops in the House of Lords vetoed one progressive reform after another (or so it seemed to Bentham), until in later life he became openly and vehemently hostile to the political influence of the Church of England. The original source of Bentham's distaste for established religion, therefore, could not be said to derive from the presuppositions of his social science. In the **"Essay on Logic,"** however, he presents us with a calm but pointed conjectural history of the term "church" and its signification, applying in masterly fashion the lessons of logic and linguistic analysis which together form the theoretical principles of his social science. The hyperbole and vitriolic language which all too frequently mar Bentham's criticisms in the works on religion of the same period are not to be found here. Instead his exposition is both instructive and thoughtfully crafted.

The genesis of the term "church" from its Greek form *ecclesia,* signifying an assembly of persons for any purpose, to its early Christian usage, intended to refer to an assembly of those of a particular faith, was accompanied, Bentham claims, by the evolution of the role of the instructor or teacher of that faith. Instead of the Latin *servus,* meaning "servant," the English noun "minister" came to be employed to designate these instructors, and later *episcopi,* signifying "overseers of the behavior of the faithful," was replaced by the epithet "bishop." This gradual transformation in terminology was accompanied by a transformation in the role of the officials of the faithful: instead of being their servants they were now their rulers. Largely as a result of this transformation the term "church" came to mean different things to different people: "viz. 1. The whole body of the persons thus governed; 2. The whole body of the persons thus employed in the government of the rest; and, 3. The all-comprehensive body, or grand total, composed of governed and governors taken together." Added to this a fourth meaning soon emerged indicating the place of assembly itself, and God, "although present at all times in all places, was regarded as being in a more particular manner present at and in all places of this sort." These places of worship soon became objects of veneration themselves. In one word, says Bentham, they became "holy." At this point an "insensible transition" took place by which the terror and respect that the members of the congregation held for their holy place of worship "came to extend itself to, upon, and to the benefit of, the class of persons in whose hands reposed the management of whatsoever was done in these holy places: holy functions, made holy places, holy places and holy functions made holy persons." Bentham's anticlericalism is introduced with a certain irony: "contemplating themselves altogether in the mirror of rhetoric, it was found that all these males put together . . . composed one beautiful female, and worthy objects of the associated affections of admiration, love, and respect—the Holy Mother Church." But the important consideration here is that Bentham's nominalist view of the world dictated that the whole could never be greater than the sum of its components. Here, however, the Church was laying claim to a holiness which far outstripped "the aggregate mass of holiness" of the several "holy males" of which it was composed. The consequence was the elevation of the Church to infallibility even though its holy men remain fallible: "Her title to implicit confidence, and . . . implicit obedience, became at once placed upon the firmest ground, and raised to the highest pitch." It was but a short step to the opinion that an infallible Church could not suffer disobedience and the demand that her enemies be punished; it came to be feared that a Church capable of being disobeyed was capable of violation and destruction. The willingness of the "servants" of the Church to sanction the punishment of heretics and recalcitrant members, further secured the position and advantage of their rulers.

One assumes at this point that Bentham has brought the history of the Church up to its present condition. It is clear that any linguistic analysis based on the potted history he presents here will throw up problems of an insuperable nature. The attempt categorically to define "church" is doomed to fail; no one exposition, complete and correct, can be given of it. For the same reason that he denied any real existence to groups or collectivities beyond the existence of their individual parts, and any real existence to universals or abstract terms, Bentham's favorite analytical tool, for which he claimed to be indebted to D'Alembert, was the decomposition or breaking up of the complex into the simple. This exhaustive analytic method entailed the classifying of phenomena by a dichotomous or bipartite divisions of generic terms. By repeating the operation indefinitely, the aim is to ensure that each class is genuinely exclusive and that nothing is left out of the account or ever counted twice. "God," of course, is uniquely resistant to such an analytic procedure, but "church" provided Bentham with a suitable subject. In the attempt to define "church" he had recourse to logical or bipartite division as the necessary preliminary or accompaniment to definition, but this division made any further exposition in the shape of definition redundant. Linguistic analysis shows that its several senses are easily mistaken for each other such that the word invariably produces confusion. "In all matters relative to the Church," writes Bentham,

> in so far as concerns the interests of the members of the Church, the good of the Church ought to be the object pursued in preference to any other. By each of two persons this proposition may, with perfect sincerity, have been subscribed. But according as to the word Church, the one or other of two very different, and in respect of practical consequences, opposite imports, has been annexed, their conduct may, on every occasion, be with perfect consistency exactly opposite; one meaning by the word church *the subject many,*—the other, by the same word, *the ruling few.*

The snipe at the clerics is again barely disguised, but the linguistic analysis can hardly be faulted. What is meant by "church" by one man may not be what is meant by another, and thus what is meant by "the good of the Church" becomes a contentious issue. The consequence is confusion, and the confused mind is a mind easily deceived and manipulated. It is Bentham's claim that the clergy very often employ ambiguous terminology to serve precisely this purpose. In ***Church-of-Englandism*** the manner of such deception is not left for the reader to infer but is plainly stated. However, to read this work without an understanding of Bentham's logic, nominalism, and theory of language is to view it in an incomplete fashion. Often what looks to be petty carping and trivial criticism (though Bentham was prone to this too) in the writings on religion, is really the outcome of a process of thought, the detail of which does not appear in these texts. For Bentham's approach is all-encompassing, developed and employed by him throughout his long life, and was brought to bear on religious questions with as much precision as it ever was in the fields of ethics and jurisprudence.

Throughout Bentham's later speculations on religious matters the metaphysical principles he had developed in earlier life are clearly in evidence. Religious beliefs, he argued, are the consequences of a fundamental misunderstanding of the nature of the world by men, a misunder-standing exacerbated by the usage of language unavoidably fraught with the terminology of fictions. Yet throughout his life Bentham advocated the universal toleration of all religions. His first unpublished work on religion in 1773 was upon this theme. Even at this early date Bentham was certain that subscription to articles of faith and the imposition of compulsory oaths (the traditional methods employed by the ecclesiastical establishment to exclude non-Anglicans from positions in public life) entailed a perversion of both a man's moral understanding and his intellect. They lead us, he argued, to mistrust our own reason and to assert belief in that which we plainly cannot comprehend and even that which under other circumstances we would deny outright. The confusions caused by the linguistic vagaries in which religious beliefs are couched by the Church lend themselves well to that obsequiousness to authority, secular as well as ecclesiastical, which has ever proved an impediment to social and political improvement. Bentham's message in these early manuscripts is clear: what religious truth, like all other truths, needs is "the liberty of making itself heard" (*ca.* 1774).

Returning to the same theme forty years later in *Swear Not at All* Bentham, in a more deliberate manner than hitherto, sought to expose the tenuous foundations upon which such practices as subscription and compulsory oaths were founded. The text for this tract is taken from Matt 5:34. Ten years after its publication Bentham remarked to his constant companion and literary executor John Bowring: "Was ever text more clear than that, 'Swear not at all,'—but it has been cavilled away by glosses and meanings which in no other case would be listened to for a minute" (1827-28). In writing *Swear Not at All* Bentham set out to strike a blow at the system of oath-taking by stripping the biblical text of all its "glosses and meanings." His principal line of argument is that the divine punishment threatened for the breaking of an oath is of such an uncertain nature that the mere taking of an oath cannot be relied upon as testimony to the honesty of the swearer. In his early work on ethics and legislation Bentham had mounted a forceful case to prove the uncertain nature of the belief in a future state of rewards and punishments; the experiential and linguistic considerations which characterized the earlier analysis produced similar results in the pages of *Swear Not at All*.

The practice of administering oaths was for Bentham an example of the deliberate deception practiced by the Church. The supposition upon which the efficacy of oaths depended was the certainty of punishment for disobedience, yet the penalty for the violation of an oath is never experienced by anyone. No man can say with certainty that there has ever been an instance when God has punished a man for breaking an oath; there are no empirical grounds upon which to base the belief that He will punish or ever has punished an oath-breaker. What knowledge we have of God's wrath is necessarily of an uncertain nature. Any supposition of certainty made by the Church, therefore, is the purposeful exploitation of a fiction—a method of deception and control. To the extent that this is admitted the ceremony of oath-taking is divested of its binding

force and of any useful influence ascribed to or expected of it.

Bentham developed the criticism in greater detail in the *Analysis of the Influence of Natural Religion on the Temporal Happiness of Mankind.* Here he contends that the man of science must be opposed to the belief in an "inscrutable agent of boundless power," interfering in worldly affairs at will, a product of fancy instead of reason. In so far as such a conception is generally accepted or believed, it gives rise to untold delusions and makes all theory of human conduct impossible. Like Hume, Bentham met the argument from design on its own ground—the world of experience. He finds it to be "completely extraexperiential"; it describes a transition from confusion to order but no one has ever had experience of this "preliminary chaos." Nor is the original creative power of God certified by experience, hence to introduce the notion of an "omnipotent will" in order to explain the facts is really no explanation at all, only a collection of meaningless words. Men "should not attempt to account for the original commencement of things—because it is obvious that experience must be entirely silent upon the subject." When we infer that the world was created by an intelligent being we infer the action of an unknown being performing an inconceivable operation upon inconceivable materials, and as such the inference is illusory. The disjunction between the belief that the world was created by an intelligent agent and man's experience of the world required no further elaboration for Bentham. His positive belief in the physical facts afforded man by sensory perception, to the exclusion of all other forms of knowledge, was unshakable. Unlike Hume he stopped short of philosophical skepticism: either there is undeniable evidence to support a proposition or there is not—if there is not, then it is a belief which has nothing to do with the world of experience and is, therefore, irrelevant to any discussion of the relationship between man and his world. Even if it were granted (which Bentham does not) that the world was created by a designing intelligence, he argues that we would still not be justified in ascribing any intentions to its creator other than what are actually realized in the visible constitution of things. If on examination we perceive in the world inequalities of fortune irreconcilable with our notions of morality we have no grounds for inferring that God's intentions have been thwarted. To the extent that men use nature and experience as a guide in their speculations about the Supreme Being, should he exist, must surely be seen as more likely to impose pain than grant pleasure. Nor can we assume that the injustices of this life will be rectified in a life to come. The attempt to visualize futurity is "to exalt the conceptions of fancy to a level with real and actual experience, so that the former shall affect the mind as vividly as the latter," which, adds Bentham tersely, "is the sole characteristic of insanity, and the single warrant for depriving the unhappy madman of his liberty."

Experience of the perceptible physical world is the touchstone of this account. On such terms it is inconceivable to Bentham that religion should exercise the least influence upon human conduct. The pleasures and pains of this life unavoidably affect our conduct and experience teaches us the actions to which they are attached. Such knowledge is not available to us in respect of a posthumous existence. The views men hold of the character of this future world can only be based upon the conceptions they entertain of the character of the Deity, but these conceptions are notoriously distinguished by their failure to account for all the evidence. The only conclusion to be drawn from the "fundamental data," according to Bentham, is no more or less than the idea of God as a capricious and tyrannical being impressing upon us "extreme and unmixed fear." To assume that the Deity treats man with favor and kindness is a presumption entirely inconsistent with reality. The actual conception of the Deity should be one which fluctuates between good and evil, "but infinitely more as an object of terror than of hope."

For Bentham, then, knowledge is derived from experience and consists in "certain facts," or "in believing facts conformable to experience," and to attribute events to the interference of the Deity is to "dethrone and cancel the authority of experience." He could not accept the "noble lie" or "double truth" view of the social utility of religion held by Voltaire and others, insisting that all human errors are just so many consequences of such "unsanctioned belief," belief, that is, in "uncertified experience." Belief in anything other than verifiable real entities, he argued, only serves to derange the mental system and prepare the intellect to receive unspecified quantities of other useless and

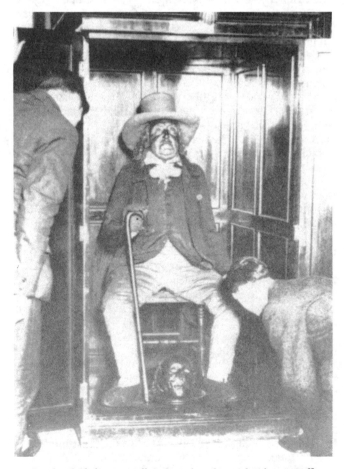

Bentham's skeleton—stuffed, dressed, and topped with a wax effigy of his head—on display at University College, London.

uncertified beliefs. Moreover, the disjunction between belief and experience impairs a man's power to make sound judgments concerning his temporal well-being.

Bentham freely admits the inviolability of the course of nature to be a gratuitous assumption, but he argued that it is one which is essential to our understanding of truth— it is "the root from which all incompatibility between two assertions, and therefore all proof of the falsehood of either, is derived." That he was more interested in the polemical point than in the internal logic of these remarks, however, is evident, for he adds, in characteristic utilitarian fashion, that if a man did not assume the uniformity of nature he would never have "the power of distinguishing the true methods of procuring enjoyment or avoiding pain, from the false ones; . . . qualifying us indeed for the kingdom of heaven, but leaving us wholly defenceless against the wants and sufferings of earth." The preference for reason and science over divinity is, therefore, a rational choice for Bentham. The whole fabric of human happiness depends on the conformity of belief with experience; in posing a threat to this conformity the extra-experiential beliefs of religion pose a threat to human happiness.

This attack on natural religion in the *Analysis* was later to be supplemented by Bentham's critique of revealed religion in *Not Paul, but Jesus.* But it was in *Church-of-Englandism* that he first concerned himself specifically with the teachings of organized religion in a systematic fashion. Those articles of belief which Bentham particularly singled out as absurd or lacking in sense included the notion of the devil as God's protagonist, the idea that God was conceived of the Holy Ghost, the claims that Christ was born of a virgin mother and that the son of God died a mortal death, and the doctrines of the Trinity and the Communion of Saints. In treating of these propositions he turned his irony to good effect, but it is his theory of language that dictated the terms of his analysis. Never could there have been a subject so open to an attack founded on the demand for definitions and unambiguous language as the Church of England Catechism, and Bentham clearly relished the prospect of its examination. We need not follow him through his entire critique; its character is readily conveyed by a few brief examples.

Bentham found the doctrine of the Trinity to be a glaring example of a proposition lacking any obvious sense, but in which children are expected to avow belief. Such an avowal is to utter "sounds without sense; mere words without meaning." If the Holy Ghost is the Holy Spirit of God, why do we need to profess belief in both God and His spirit? "Believing in a man, what more do you do, by believing in his spirit likewise?" It is only to "string words upon words,—and then, for every word, believe or pretend to believe, that a correspondent really existing object is brought into existence." Words must correspond to objects, to real entities, or they must be capable of reduction by paraphrasis to real entities. If neither is possible then the word is a fiction generating confusion and capable of misapplication in unscrupulous hands. The article of belief in "the Holy Catholic Church" is another case in point. Is it the Church of England that is meant here, asks Bentham, or is it the Roman Catholic Church, the Church of the Papists who once persecuted English Protestants? What is it that makes the Church holy? The article is a confused proposition to which no explanation is so much as hazarded. If the "poor child" were to think upon the subject "how distressing must be the perplexity, into which he here finds himself plunged." For the presuppositions of the sacrament of communion Bentham has even harsher words: the transubstantiation or metamorphosis of bread and wine into body and blood "is the *pure* grim-gribber of modern *technical* theology." In Luther's reform of Roman Catholic theology the body and blood of Christ are said to accompany the bread and wine. This theory of consubstantiation Bentham calls "the *adulterated* grim-gribber," and finds in it a greater source of confusion than in the theory of transubstantiation: "On the *con* plan the mess has more matter in it than in the *trans:* and the more the worse." The whole idea of communion is for Bentham "cannibalism." The trick in the explanation, he says, is to refer to the "spiritual sense" of the proposition; this is an appeal to a "purer" and "superior" sense than that of the "carnal" or "temporal" sense. It is by this means that the Church transforms something false or absurd into something true or reasonable. If there is a mind to subdue this is the way to do it, by introducing "the *spiritual* sense—alias the nonsensical sense."

The Catechism to Bentham, it seems, was nothing but a mass of confusing propositions to which the child is made to give his assent without any understanding of what it is he has assented to. He is made to declare "that he believes whatever is thus forced into his mouth, without knowing so much as *who* it is that put it where it is, much less *what* it is." The only thing learnt from this mode of instruction is "the art of *gratuitous assertion*—the art of speaking and writing without thinking—and the art of making *groundless inferences.*" Such are the pernicious consequences of "catechetical instruction."

The attack on religious beliefs was extended by Bentham in *Not Paul, but Jesus* to include the belief in miracles. Here again the metaphysical principles of his social science are in evidence, though on this occasion the discussion is carried on in terms more appropriate to a courtroom than a philosophical or theological controversy. Miracles, he had written in the *Analysis,* are founded upon the extra-experiential belief that God interferes in earthly affairs, or to put it in a cutting fashion, they are "fictions by which the human intellect has . . . been cheated and overrun." Given this view of affairs it is hardly surprising that Bentham finds little in the way of evidence to support the belief in Paul's miracles. He was unwilling to afford the Scriptures a special status in this regard: they were to be treated as any other historical writings, that is, according to methods applied in all other areas of human history. If miracles, being events which transcend or violate the laws of nature, do occur then we cannot draw a line and admit the truth only of a special class of reports of miracles, denying on general historical grounds that any other reports down through the ages could possibly be true—since if we were to do this we would be giving up the possibility of writing history altogether. On the other hand, if we accept the historian's assumption of a connection between natural causes and nat-

ural events, then we must deal not with miracles but with stories of miracles. This, in brief, was Bentham's position, and he encountered few difficulties in supplying accounts of the "stories" of Paul's miracles. Some he explained in terms of natural events, some he dismissed because of the lack of corroborative evidence, while others he condemned as frauds perpetrated by Paul and explained in terms of subterfuge. Bentham's strong case, however, is much like that given by Hume in his essay "On Miracles." If a miracle were reported today the response of persons who heard of it would certainly be skeptical. Who can doubt, says Bentham, that if Paul's exorcism of Lydia (Acts 16:16-18) were reported in some newspaper, as having happened at the present time, that it would "by its disconformity to the manifest state of things, and the whole course of nature, be regarded as too absurd and flagrantly incredible to deserve to be entitled to a moments notice." What is believed to have happened at so many centuries distance, however, is accepted on the authority of the testimony of witnesses. Yet for the most part such evidence is at best of a circumstantial kind. The legal bent of Bentham's critique is evident: Paul's revelation and miracles are based on flimsy and often conflicting evidence. "On such evidence," he asks, "would any judge fine a man a shilling?" And in an extraordinary outburst he censured Locke and Newton for believing when the evidence was so slight: "O Locke! O Newton! where was your discernment!"

The metaphysical speculations upon which Bentham's critique of religion, natural and revealed, is founded have now been explained, and its consequences for ecclesiastical doctrines and religious beliefs brought to light. However, that this mode of analysis should fail in certain crucial instances is a testimony to its limitations and, indeed, to the inappropriateness of its application to the religious life of man. It is to the flaws in Bentham's critique that I now turn in the concluding section of this essay.

It is evident that Bentham held a narrow, wholly materialistic, conception of what constitutes knowledge, and this can be traced, in part at least, to a metamorphosis that takes place in his speculations on language. The terms "theory," "logic," "classification," "definition," and "nomenclature" are frequently very nearly synonymous in his vocabulary. In the **"Essay on Logic"** he came close to admitting as much: "In the whole field of the art of logic, so large is the portion occupied by the art of methodization . . . that the task of showing what it . . . can do, is scarcely distinguishable from the task of showing what . . . Logic can . . . do." The crucial step in this metamorphosis, however, is not expressly acknowledged by Bentham but took place very early on in his thought. It is the reduction of science and philosophy to "metaphysics," defined in terms of a theory of language which insists upon the correspondence between words, ideas, and propositions, on the one hand, and perceptible physical objects, on the other. But it is not merely that for Bentham metaphysics becomes linguistic analysis; more importantly this step means that the structure of reality itself is now seen, can only be seen, in terms of the structure of language. This metamorphosis lies at the heart of his narrow understanding of what constitutes knowledge and is therefore central to his understanding of religion. The irrational and the metaphysical (in the conventional sense meant by Bentham to refer to all spurious reasoning upon the principles of nature and thought) had to be expunged from discourse; language which has no bearing on the facts of experience is useless, frequently pernicious in its consequences, and certainly opposed to truth. Ultimately this was to mean the imposition on religious ideas of an alien, human-centered conception of language, an imposition which effectively stripped religious beliefs of their spiritual content. On such terms theology is necessarily pre-judged as irrelevant, since it deals not with the facts of ordinary experience but with a reality which transcends the materialism of the physical world. Just as the language of opinion can have no place in the discourse of the sciences, natural or moral, so, for Bentham at least, neither can the untestable and unverifiable tenets of theology.

Though it claims to be extra-religious, the anti-religious tendency of this approach is readily apparent, as is that of any approach to religion that refuses to treat religious knowledge as if it were not qualitatively different from the verifiable knowledge we possess of the physical universe. In Bentham's thought, however, the problems caused by materialism are compounded by the metaphysical presuppositions of his theory of knowledge. According to this theory, reality is first "known" and then represented by language. Northrop Frye has observed [in his *The Great Code: The Bible and Literature*] (without referring to Bentham) that within this conception of the function of language "a true verbal structure is one that is *like* what it describes." As there is no reality beyond sense experience so there is no reality beyond the language that describes that reality, and all propositions can be tested, disproved, or verified against this objective order. Frye shrewdly rationalizes the consequences of this view of language for religion thus:

> In a conception of language where no premises are beyond scrutiny, there is nothing to stop anyone from returning to square one and the question: Is there a God? What is significant about this is that the answer . . . can only be no, because any question beginning with "is there" is, so to speak, already an ungodly question, and "a god" is for all practical purposes no God.

Not amenable to sense perception and therefore unknowable, "God" is linguistically unfunctional, except when employed in a historical sense or when used to describe other, presumably pre-scientific, belief systems. By extension, when rigidly adhered to, all questions of a spiritual or transcendental nature are unmeaning within this theory of language: for all intents and purposes, God, the soul, faith, grace, and all other such features of man's spiritual life, are illusions. This is how matters stood for Bentham. The obvious flaw in his reasoning, however, is that the inability of a language to apprehend certain human experiences does not thereby testify to the unreality or nonexistence of those experiences. Frye refers to this fallacy as one of "misplaced concreteness," and there is a certain satisfaction in being able to charge the arch-exposer of fallacies with the perpetration of one of his own.

If Bentham expected any popular success for his criticisms of religion, he was to be sadly disappointed. The character of his attack was manifestly inappropriate to his subject. Though he explicitly rejected the notion that exaggeration is useful in attempting to persuade men to embrace the utilitarian doctrine, to accept utilitarian legislation, and to influence them to perform socially desirable actions, if vitriolic language was called for in order to move the reader to an emotional response on questions of religion, Bentham had no qualms about employing it. Ridicule and passages of scurrilous irony were all introduced to bolster the indictment of religion and references to the Church as "the Whore of Babylon," to the clergy as "plunderers," to the Catechism as a "poison," and the like, are frequent. For all his vaunted reverence for precision in language and for all his warnings about the dangers implicit in the very nature of language, his critique was frequently conducted in terms reminiscent of the rabid anticlerical literature one usually associates with the French *philosophes.* Moreover, Bentham surely expected linguistic clarification in religion to accomplish more than it really could. The committed Christian, irrational as it may seem to Bentham, is not likely to be moved to disbelief because the ideas of the soul, spirit, or grace are exposed as fictions irreducible to any physical properties or real entities. Indeed, it is just as likely that such an analysis will serve to confirm the believer in his faith by reinforcing the notion that such conceptions must have their source in something that cannot be fully comprehended by mere mortals. This seems to have been very much the argument of Bentham's friend, the anti-slave trader, William Wilberforce. Christianity, he argued [in his *A Practical View of the Prevailing Religious System of Professed Christians . . . Contrasted with Real Christianity*], cannot be reduced to "a mere system of ethics," for "this is to separate the practical precepts from the peculiar doctrines it enjoins." Men must not "confound the Gospel of Christ with the systems of philosophers," but be "impressed with the weighty truth, so much forgotten in the present day, that Christianity calls on us, as we value our immortal souls, not merely in *general,* to be *religious* and *moral,* but specially to believe the doctrines, imbibe the principles, and practise the precepts of Christ." To Bentham, of course, this is an irrational response, but in so far as he relied on plain descriptive language to overcome it he surely underestimated the conviction with which believers hold to their faith, and overestimated the power of his metaphysics to have an impact on it. Yet Bentham remained convinced throughout his life that if men ignored reason and continued to place their trust in the doctrines of religion there could be little hope that they might improve their stock of happiness:

> When a man has once got into the way of making Revelation serve him instead of Reason, and the opinions in which men in authority hold instead of Revelation, and the opinions which men in authority avow instead of what they hold, he is prepared for the embracement of every absurd and mischievous error, and for the rejection of every salutary truth. (1781-85)

His mind "enfeebled," the only support a man can find for such a system, says Bentham, is "blind credulity," and he will resist all objects and defend that system not because it is true, but simply because he has resolved to defend it.

The alternative is that men should make use of their own reason. But Bentham's reliance on reason or the authority of science is conspicuous by his complete failure to attempt, in his religious or other writings, to come to terms with the spiritual aspect of religion. The peculiarly narrow focus of his thoughts is directly related to the presuppositions of his metaphysics. He simply ignored the fact that religious knowledge ultimately depends on faith. In an early manuscript of 1773, it is true, Bentham endeavored to define "faith," but it is a facile and hopelessly inadequate attempt in which he reduced it to the "merit" of believing the incredible: "The greater the difficulty of doing any thing the greater the merit. The greater the difficulty in believing a thing the greater the merit in believing it." Such a train of reasoning taken to its limits, he declared, was "calculated to produce the greatest extravagances of credulity." On these terms faith is reduced to the outcome of stupidity or of ignorance of the "real" world, and this was the conclusion embraced by Bentham. The critical mind which begins by thinking and not believing and requires that there be empirical evidence that can be tested and verified before anything be accepted as final, is clearly not one that feels comfortable with "faith." Certainly the critical method will dissolve any false certainty upon which a man rests his religion, but rarely does logic or reason affect the quality or power of religious feelings. In this dilemma lies both Bentham's failure to come fully to terms with the subject matter of his religious writings, and the failure of these writings to make their mark as serious contributions to the literature on theological matters. Not that he thought of himself as writing theology; he would undoubtedly have been appalled if his religious works were accepted as such. But this cannot excuse the fact that whenever he touched on religion in its more sublime and subtle aspects his criticisms are unsatisfactory. Characteristically, Bentham could only admit that religious beliefs such as that in the "fall of man" were incomprehensible to him. He was singularly incapable of understanding that such religious teachings can be and are held by many persons regardless of the conclusions of rational science, that they are beyond the realm of, and thus not open to, the criticisms of scientific reasoning. He thought of theology as the mere ignorance of natural causes reduced to a system, and believed that knowledge of nature would eventually destroy religion. Convinced that scientific knowledge was the one thing needed for the happiness or well-being of man, he sought to remove religion from its privileged position not only in public life but also in the hearts of men. It is needless for us to dwell upon the too evident fact that Bentham ultimately failed in his mission, but this is not to say that his religious views had no impact upon his contemporaries. His crusade to secularize English social and political life called many to the utilitarian colors, and the subsequent retreat of religion in the nineteenth century cannot be entirely explained without reference to those who set themselves up as its implacable opponents. (pp. 387-411)

James E. Crimmins, "Bentham's Metaphysics and the Science of Divinity," in Harvard Theological Review, *Vol. 79, No. 4, October, 1986, pp. 387-411.*

FURTHER READING

Altick, Richard D. "The Utilitarian Spirit." In his *Victorian People and Ideas,* pp. 114-45. New York: W. W. Norton and Co., 1973.
    Explores the social, economic, and political influence of Bentham and his associates on Victorian England.

Atkinson, Charles Milner. *Jeremy Bentham: His Life and Work.* New York: Augustus M. Kelley, 1969, 247 p.
    Critical and biographical study of Bentham.

Brinton, Crane. "Bentham." In his *English Political Thought in the Nineteenth Century,* pp. 14-30. London: Ernest Benn, 1933.
    Examines Bentham's political philosophy and his influence upon the nineteenth-century reform of English law.

Brockriede, Wayne E. "Bentham's Philosophy of Rhetoric." *Speech Monographs* XXIII, No. 4 (November 1956): 235-46.
    Sketches a linguistic theory rooted in reason and empirical verification that, according to Brockriede, derives from Bentham's utilitarian philosophy and statements regarding rhetoric.

Bronowski, J., and Mazlish, Bruce. "Jeremy Bentham." In their *The Western Intellectual Tradition from Leonardo to Hegel,* pp. 430-49. New York: Harper and Brothers, 1960.
    Analyzes the philosophical groundwork laid by Bentham which gave rise to the nineteenth-century legislative revolution in England.

Catlin, George. "The Early Utilitarians: Jeremy Bentham." In his *The Story of the Political Philosophers,* pp. 342-80. New York: McGraw-Hill Book Co., 1939.
    Introductory study of the principal ideas and persons associated with the early development of Utilitarianism.

Crimmins, James E. *Secular Utilitarianism: Social Science and the Critique of Religion in the Thought of Jeremy Bentham.* Oxford, Eng.: Clarendon Press, 1990, 348 p.
    Probes Bentham's views on religion and the significance of atheism within the context of his political theory and his desire to create a utilitarian society. Crimmins maintains that though Bentham's religious writings were composed towards the end of his life, his early works also demonstrate an interest in issues of a religious nature.

Eisenach, Eldon J. "The Dimension of History in Bentham's Theory of Law." *Eighteenth-Century Studies* 16, No. 3 (Spring 1983): 290-316.
    Examines Bentham's conception of natural—or hypothetical—history, which Eisenach perceives as the course of a society governed by the utility and logic of civil law rather than by the customs and tradition of political rule.

Empson, W. "Jeremy Bentham." *The Edinburgh Review* LXXVIII, No. clviii (October 1843): 460-516.
    A review of John Bowring's *Memoirs of Jeremy Bentham* with a sketch of Bentham's life and career.

Everett, Charles Warren. "Introduction." *A Comment on the Commentaries: A Criticism of William Blackstone's Commen-*

taries on the Laws of England by Jeremy Bentham, edited by Charles Warren Everett, pp. 1-28. Oxford, Eng.: Clarendon Press, 1928.

Probes the philosophical groundwork of Bentham's *Comment on the Commentaries.* Begun in 1774, the work, Everett claims, is the seminal piece in which Bentham first set forth the utilitarian basis of law.

Himmelfarb, Gertrude. "The Haunted House of Jeremy Bentham." In her *Victorian Minds,* pp. 32-81. New York: Alfred A. Knopf, 1968.

Synopsizes Bentham's penal reform plan. Himmelfarb argues that the real motive for the *Panopticon* was personal rather than humanitarian, an attempt to actualize Bentham's Greatest Happiness Principle and his theory of reward and sanction.

Jennings, W. Ivor. "Jeremy Bentham." In *Some Makers of the Modern Spirit: A Symposium,* edited by John Macmurray, pp. 125-37. 1933. Reprint. Freeport, N.Y.: Books for Libraries Press, 1968.

An overview of Bentham's life, ideas, and works.

Letwin, Shirley Robin. "Jeremy Bentham: Liberty and Logic." In her *The Pursuit of Certainty,* pp. 127-88. Cambridge, Eng.: Cambridge University Press, 1965.

Argues that Bentham embraced the spirit of the eighteenth-century French philosophes in his attempt to remake the world according to a rational pattern.

Lieberman, David. "Historiographical Review from Bentham to Benthamism." *The Historical Journal* XXVIII, No. 1 (March 1985): 199-224.

Traces the historical interest in Bentham's career and works while reviewing both recent works about Bentham and new editions of his work.

Lyons, David. *In the Interest of the Governed: A Study in Bentham's Philosophy of Utility and Law.* Oxford, Eng.: Clarendon Press, 1973, 150 p.

Elucidates the nucleus of Bentham's philosophy with particular focus on the principle of utility and the nature of law as found in his *An Introduction to the Principles of Morals and Legislation* and *Of Laws in General.*

Mack, M. P. *Jeremy Bentham: An Odyssey of Ideas.* New York: Columbia University Press, 1963, 482 p.

In-depth presentation of Bentham's life and thought.

Neill, Thomas P. "Bentham: The Human Calculating Machine." In his *Makers of the Modern Mind,* pp. 223-52. Milwaukee: The Bruce Publishing Company, 1949.

Discusses the significance of the "Philosophical Radicals," the intellectual coterie associated with Bentham. Neill emphasizes the influence of Bentham on this group of "men who put all their chips on cold, calculating reason."

Parekh, Bhikhu, ed. *Jeremy Bentham: Ten Critical Essays.* London: Frank Cass and Co., 1974, 204 p.

Collection of essays by such critics as J. S. Mill, William Whewell, and Wesley C. Mitchell dealing with Bentham's influence on the administrative and political reforms of the nineteenth century.

Pollock, Frederick. "Modern Theories of Sovereignty and Legislation." In his *An Introduction to the History of the Science of Politics,* pp. 98-136. 1890. Reprint. London: Macmillan and Co., 1935.

Probes Bentham's political definition of society.

Secor, Marie J. "Bentham's *Book of Fallacies:* Rhetorician in Spite of Himself." *Philosophy and Rhetoric* 22, No. 2 (1989): 83-94.

Argues that Bentham's treatment of fallacy in his *Book of Fallacies* should be studied from the point of view of rhetoric rather than logic because, according to Secor, the work explores the nature of argumentation.

Sidgwick, Henry. "Bentham and Benthamism in Politics and Ethics." In his *Miscellaneous Essays and Addresses,* pp. 135-69. London: Macmillan and Co., 1904.

Excogitation of Bentham's moral philosophy and political theory.

Sil, N. P. "Bentham's Jurisprudence Revisited: The Principle of Utility Versus Utilitarianism." *Modern Age* 30, Nos. 3-4 (Summer / Fall 1986): 245-50.

Challenges charges of ambiguity and contradiction directed at Bentham's effort to base Utilitarianism on egoistic hedonism.

Thompson, T. P. "Bentham's *Science of Morality.*" *The Edinburgh Review* LXI, No. cxxiv (July 1835): 365-79.

Negatively reviews Bentham's *Deontology,* notably objecting to Bentham's apparent denial of innate moral conscience.

Vaughan, Frederick. "Political Hedonism Entrenched." In his *The Tradition of Political Hedonism from Hobbes to J. S. Mill,* pp. 196-240. New York: Fordham University Press, 1982.

Discusses Bentham's political hedonism as an outgrowth of his Greatest Happiness Principle and his felicific calculus. Vaughan judges that Bentham was unsuccessful in his attempt to reconcile individual desires with collective pleasure.

Wallas, Graham. "Jeremy Bentham." *Political Science Quarterly* XXXVIII, No. 1 (March 1923): 45-56.

Biographical sketch of Bentham's life and career.

Welsh, Alexander. "Burke and Bentham on the Narrative Potential of Circumstantial Evidence." *New Literary History* 21, No. 3 (Spring 1990): 607-27.

Discerns Bentham's contribution to the legal distinction between circumstantial evidence and direct testimony of events.

Zimmer, Louis B. "J. S. Mill and Bentham on Liberty: The Case of the Unacknowledged Mentor." *The Historian* LII, No. 3 (May 1990): 375-93.

Analyzes the philosophical dependence of Mill on Bentham with attention to Mill's eventual departure from the Benthamite utilitarianism which he had originally espoused. Zimmer states that Mill claimed to have developed his own strain of Utilitarianism though "the curious and inescapable fact remains that much of Ben-

thamite utilitarianism is to be found in Mill's famous
essay [*On Liberty*]."

Additional coverage of Bentham's life and career is contained in the following source published by Gale Research: *Dictionary of Literary Biography*, Vol. 107.

Dinah Mulock Craik

1826-1887

(Born Dinah Maria Mulock) English novelist, essayist, short story writer, and poet.

INTRODUCTION

Craik was a popular and prolific novelist who also wrote essays, short stories, fairy tales, and poetry for both children and adults. She is best known for the novel *John Halifax, Gentleman,* a rags-to-riches story featuring an orphan hero who embodies Christian virtue and exemplifies the rise of the British middle class. The work's tremendous popularity made Craik famous, and critics and scholars view *John Halifax* and Craik's other sentimental novels as reflections of the values of the Victorian age and as barometers of the tastes of late nineteenth-century audiences.

Born in Stoke-on-Trent, Staffordshire, Craik was the eldest child and only daughter of a Protestant minister. Her father, Thomas Mulock, fell out of favor with his congregation and lost his ministry in 1831; he then relocated his family to nearby Newcastle-under-Lyme. Life there was uncertain for Craik and her two brothers, Tom and Ben. Their eccentric and unstable father was often absent for long periods—including stays in both prison and a lunatic asylum—and their mother supported them by operating a small school in the family's home. Craik, a precocious scholar, dropped out of school to assist her mother with the teaching duties and was instructing students in elementary Latin by the time she was thirteen. Craik's mother received a small inheritance in 1839, and soon thereafter Thomas Mulock rejoined his family, but only after consenting to place the money in a trust for his wife and children. About 1840 the family moved to London, where Craik and her brothers studied language, art, and music. However, domestic life soon deteriorated, and Craik returned with her ailing mother to Staffordshire in 1844, hoping to open another school. Her mother died the next year, and Thomas Mulock, after unsuccessfully attempting to secure the principal from the trust for himself, completely abandoned his children. Craik, then nineteen, was unable to inherit her portion of her grandmother's estate for two more years; she returned to London, proposing to support herself and her brothers through her literary efforts.

Craik had first published a poem in the *Staffordshire Advertiser* in 1841, and, with the aid of some friends, she was able to place several poems and stories in *Chambers's Edinburgh Journal* and *Chambers's Magazine* in 1845 and 1846. Yet the family was still nearly destitute, and Craik's brother Tom gave up his study of painting to apprentice himself on a merchant ship; he died in an accident in 1847. Later that same year, Craik received her inheritance, and the financial freedom allowed her to both support Ben and

complete her first full-length novel, *The Ogilvies,* which was published in 1849. With the appearance of *Olive* a year later, Craik gained a foothold in London literary society. When Ben left for Australia to embark on a career as a civil engineer, Craik took lodgings with a female friend and defied convention by independently pursuing her writing career and living without a male chaperon. She continued to work ceaselessly, placing stories with a variety of periodicals and completing *The Head of the Family* in 1852 and *Agatha's Husband* in 1853. Craik's 1856 novel, *John Halifax, Gentleman,* quickly went through multiple editions, earning Craik financial security and literary fame. Her stature as a best-selling novelist ensured her success as a journalist, and periodicals sought her out not only for her fiction but for essays on social issues of the day; the most famous of these was *A Woman's Thoughts about Women,* an 1857 essay that championed better educational and occupational opportunities for women in an era when "the woman problem"—the question of which roles were acceptable for unmarried women—was at the center of public debate in England.

Craik was in her late thirties and resigned to living alone when George Lillie Craik, a partner in the publishing firm of Macmillan and Co., was injured in a railway accident near her home and taken there to convalesce. Although he was eleven years her junior, the two soon fell in love and their romance culminated in marriage in 1865. The couple built a house in Kent financed from the proceeds of *John Halifax, Gentleman* and adopted an abandoned baby girl, Dorothy, in 1869. Craik continued to publish steadily for the remainder of her life, composing several children's books inspired by her daughter, among them *The Adventures of a Brownie* and *The Little Lame Prince and His Travelling Cloak*. She died suddenly of heart failure in 1887.

Despite a vast literary output encompassing some twenty novels, twelve children's books, four volumes of poetry, and over one hundred and fifty short stories and essays, Craik is remembered chiefly for *John Halifax, Gentleman*. While representative of Craik's fiction in its reliance on conventional romantic formulas and its depiction of ordinary people in a domestic setting, *John Halifax* is unique in its focus on a male, rather than a female, protagonist. John Halifax emerges as both the hero of an adventure story and a model of virtuous conduct as he teaches himself to read, fights fires, prevents floods, and quells riots. His rise from penniless urchin to business owner to magistrate and community leader is narrated by his lifelong friend, the crippled Phineas Fletcher, whose tone of open admiration lends an almost mythic stature to the middle-class values of self-reliance, self-control, industry, and initiative. Written in the confident mood following Engand's Great Exhibition of 1851, *John Halifax* is a celebration of British technology and progress, underscored by Halifax's use of recent advances such as steam power to run his mill and inoculations to immunize his family against smallpox. The novel confirms the Protestant ethic, demonstrating that hard work and benevolent acts lead to worldly as well as heavenly reward. The work also functions as an historical allegory documenting the rise of the middle class, with Halifax's business success and subsequent appointment to magistrate representing the passage of economic and political power from an aristocracy based on the ownership of land to an industrious middle class based on the production of goods. The democratic ideals of the novel are symbolized by Halifax's only possession: his father's Greek Testament, inscribed "Guy Halifax, Gentleman"—which Craik asserted stood for the inherent worth of all men, regardless of economic or social status.

Craik's largely middle-class audience swept up copies of a book that contemporary reviewers found both instructional and entertaining; *John Halifax* was hailed as a practical guide to virtue and prosperity as well as an exciting story. Literary critics, however, found the novel overly sentimental and didactic, and objected to Craik's frequent sermonizing. They also maintained that the plot was contrived and farfetched, and that the character of Halifax was unrealistic in its absolute goodness. Commentators also pointed out what they viewed as major inconsistencies in the work, positing that the novel betrayed a basic economic hypocrisy by implying that material riches were an integral part of Halifax's success while the character himself continually denied their value. Furthermore, these critics found fault with the symbol of the Greek Testa-

ment, asserting that it begged the question of democracy and equality by leaving open the possibility that Halifax was predisposed to his rise by heredity. The novel's very popularity militated against a favorable critical reaction, and critics contended that it proved Craik was not a literary artist but a writer for the masses. After the publication of *John Halifax* Craik was dismissed as "a women's novelist"; her works were seldom seriously considered, and when they were, commentators praised them primarily for their purity and high moral tone. With their virginal heroines, sentimental plots, and intrusive sermonizing, Craik's later novels were often cited for evincing the worst elements of the Victorian stereotype. As the nineteenth century passed, interest in Craik faded almost completely, and *John Halifax*—though it continued to be reprinted—became characterized as an artifact of smug, middle-class complacency.

However, recent reexaminations of Craik's oeuvre, conducted principally by feminist critics, have noted subversive elements in her fiction. These commentators assert that Craik strove to present a veiled critique of Victorian society, portraying the conflicts facing women in the late nineteenth century in a disguised form. The virtuous John Halifax, they maintain, is an idealized version of how a woman would act given the same rights and opportunities as a man, while the alert but incapacitated Phineas Fletcher—one in a long line of crippled characters in Craik's stories, from *Olive* to *The Little Lame Prince*—symbolizes the powerless state of women. Central to these arguments is Craik's *A Woman's Thoughts about Women*, which addresses the plight of unmarried women and affirms their right to be self-dependent, even while upholding marriage and motherhood as women's highest goals. From this perspective, the heroines of Craik's sentimental novels can be seen as unconventional in many ways, feminist critics argue, and the turmoil experienced before and even after marriage by the protagonists in novels such as *Olive, Agatha's Husband*, and *A Life for A Life* elucidates Craik's conviction that even the role of wife and mother could be extremely difficult at times. Such criticism inevitably reconsiders Craik's own biography. Commentators observe that the tension in Craik's personal life between the demands of her literary career and the feminine ideal of wife and mother found expression in her delineation of the complexities of Victorian society, even in such seemingly unambiguous tales as *John Halifax, Gentleman*.

PRINCIPAL WORKS

Michael the Miner (juvenilia) 1846
How to Win Love; or, Rhoda's Lesson (juvenilia) 1848
Cola Monti; or, the Story of a Genius (juvenilia) 1849
The Ogilvies (novel) 1849
Olive (novel) 1850
The Half-Caste: An Old Governess's Tale (novel) 1851
Alice Learmont (fairy tale) 1852
Bread upon the Waters; A Governess's Life (novel) 1852
The Head of the Family (novel) 1852
Agatha's Husband (novel) 1853
Avillion and Other Tales (short stories) 1853

A Hero: Philip's Book   (short stories)   1853
The Little Lychetts   (juvenilia)   1855
John Halifax, Gentleman   (novel)   1856
Nothing New   (short stories)   1857
A Woman's Thoughts about Women   (essay)   1857
Domestic Stories   (short stories)   1859
A Life for a Life   (novel)   1859; also published as *A Life for a Life* [revised edition], 1860
Poems   (poetry)   1859
Romantic Tales   (short stories)   1859
Studies from Life   (essays)   1861
Mistress and Maid   (novel)   1862
The Fairy Book   (fairy tales)   1863
Christian's Mistake   (novel)   1865
A Noble Life   (novel)   1866
Two Marriages   (novel)   1867
The Woman's Kingdom   (novel)   1868
A Brave Lady   (novel)   1870
The Unkind Word and Other Stories   (essays, short stories)   1870
Fair France: Impressions of a Traveller   (travel essay)   1871
Hannah   (novel)   1871
The Adventures of a Brownie, as Told to My Child   (fairy tale)   1872
My Mother and I: A Girl's Love Story   (novel)   1874
The Little Lame Prince and His Travelling Cloak   (fairy tale)   1875
Sermons out of Church   (essays)   1875
The Laurel Bush: An Old-Fashioned Love Story   (novel)   1876
Young Mrs. Jardine   (novel)   1879
Thirty Years: Being Poems New and Old   (poetry)   1880; also published as *Poems,* 1888
Children's Poetry   (poetry)   1881
His Little Mother and Other Sketches   (short stories)   1881
Plain Speaking   (essays and short stories)   1882
Miss Tommy: A Medieval Romance   (novel)   1884
About Money and Other Things   (essays and short stories)   1886
King Arthur: Not a Love Story   (novel)   1886
Concerning Men and Other Papers   (essays)   1888

Henry James   (essay date 1866)

[*James was an American-born English novelist, short story writer, critic, and essayist of the late nineteenth and early twentieth centuries. He is regarded as one of the greatest novelists of the English language and is also admired as a lucid and insightful critic. As a young man, he travelled extensively throughout Great Britain and Europe and benefited from the friendship and influence of many of the leading figures of nineteenth-century art and literature: in England, he met John Ruskin, Dante Gabriel Rosetti, William Morris, and Leslie Stephen; in France, where he lived for several years, he was part of the literary circle that included Gustave Flaubert, Émile Zola, Edmond de Goncourt,*

Guy de Maupassant, and Ivan Turgenev. Thus, his criticism is informed by his sensitivity to European culture, particularly English and French literature of the late nineteenth century. James was a frequent contributor to several prominent American journals, including the North American Review, *the* Nation, *and the* Atlantic Monthly. *In the following review, originally published in 1866, James compares characters and incidents in* A Noble Life *to those in* John Halifax, Gentleman, *describing Craik as a "fairly successful novelist" whose work suffers from "excessive sentimentality."*]

Noble lives have always been a sort of specialty with the author of **John Halifax.** Few novelists, in this age of sympathy with picturesque turpitude, have given us such flattering accounts of human nature, or have paid such glowing tributes to virtue. **John Halifax** was an attempt to tell the story of a life perfect in every particular; and to relate, moreover, every particular of it. The hero was a sort of Sir Charles Grandison of the democracy, faultless in manner and in morals. There is something almost awful in the thought of a writer undertaking to give a detailed picture of the actions of a perfectly virtuous being. Sir Charles Grandison, with his wig and his sword, his high heels, his bows, his smiles, his Johnsonian compliments, his irreproachable tone, his moderation, his reverence, his piety, his decency in all the relations of life, was possible to the author, and is tolerable to the reader, only as the product of an age in which nature was represented by majestic generalizations. But to create a model gentleman in an age when, to be satisfactory to the general public, art has to specify every individual fact of nature; when, in order to believe what we are desired to believe of such a person, we need to see him photographed at each successive stage of his proceedings, argues either great courage or great temerity on the part of a writer, and certainly involves a system of bold co-operation on the reader's side. We cannot but think that, if Miss Mulock had weighed her task more fairly, she would have shrunk from it in dismay. But neither before nor after his successful incarnation was John Halifax to be weighed or measured. We know of no scales that will hold him, and of no unit of length with which to compare him. He is infinite; he outlasts time; he is enshrined in a million innocent breasts; and before his awful perfection and his eternal durability we respectfully lower our lance. We have, indeed, not the least inclination to laugh at him; nor do we desire to speak with anything but respect of the spirit in which he and his numerous brothers and sisters have been conceived; for we believe it to have been, at bottom, a serious one. That is, Miss Mulock is manifestly a serious lover of human nature, and a passionate admirer of a fine man and a fine woman. Here, surely, is a good solid basis to work upon; and we are certain that on this point Miss Mulock yields to none in the force of her inspiration. But she gives us the impression of having always looked at men and women through a curtain of rose-colored gauze. This impediment to a clear and natural vision is nothing more, we conceive, than her excessive sentimentality. Such a defect may be but the exaggeration of a virtue, but it makes sad work in Miss Mulock's tales. It destroys their most vital property—their appearance of reality; it falsifies every fact and every truth it touches;

and, by reaction, it inevitably impugns the writer's sincerity.

The volume before us [*A Noble Life*] contains the story of an unfortunate man who, born to wealth and honors, is rendered incompetent, by ill-health and deformity, to the simplest offices of life, but whose soul shines the brighter for this eclipse of his body. Orphaned, dwarfed, crippled, unable to walk, to hold a fork, a book, or a pen, with body enough to suffer acutely, and yet with so little that he can act only through servants upon the objects nearest to him, he contrives, nevertheless, to maintain a noble equanimity, to practise a boundless charity, and to achieve a wide intellectual culture. Such is Miss Mulock's noble life, and this time, at least, we do not contest her epithet. We might cite several examples to illustrate that lively predilection for cripples and invalids by which she has always been distinguished; but we defer to this generous idiosyncrasy. It is no more than right that the sickly half of humanity should have its chronicler; and as far as the Earl of Cairnforth is concerned, it were a real loss to the robust half that he should lack his poet. For we cannot help thinking that, admirable as the subject is, the author has done it fair justice, and that she has appreciated its great opportunities. She has handled it delicately and wisely, both as judged by its intrinsic merits and, still more, as judged by her own hitherto revealed abilities. She has told her story simply, directly, and forcibly, with but a moderate tendency to moralize, and quite an artistic perception of the inherent value of her facts. A profound sense of the beauty of the theme impels us to say that of course there are many points in which she might have done better, and to express our regret that, since the story was destined to be written, an essentially stronger pen should not have anticipated the task; since, indeed, the history of a wise man's soul was in question, a wise man, and not a woman something less than wise, should have undertaken to relate it. In such a case certain faulty-sketched episodes would have been more satisfactory. That of Helen Cardross's intimacy with the earl, for instance, would probably have gained largely in dramatic interest by the suggestion of a more delicate sentiment on the earl's part—sensitive, imaginative, manly-souled as he is represented as being—than that of a grateful nursling. Such a feat was doubtless beyond Miss Mulock's powers—as it would indeed have been beyond any woman's; and it was, therefore, the part of prudence not to attempt it. Another weak point is the very undeveloped state of the whole incident of the visit of the earl's insidious kinsman. If this had been drawn out more artistically, it would have given a very interesting picture of the moves and counter-moves about the helpless nobleman's chair, of his simple friends and servants, and his subtle cousin.

Good story-tellers, however, are not so plentiful as that we should throw aside a story because it is told with only partial success. When was more than approximate justice ever done a great subject? In view of this general truth, we gladly commend Miss Mulock as fairly successful. Assuredly, she has her own peculiar merits. If she has not much philosophy nor much style, she has at least feeling and taste. If she does not savor of the classics, neither does she savor of the newspapers. If, in short, she is not George Eliot on

the one hand, neither is she Miss Braddon on the other. Where a writer is so transparently a woman as she and the last-named lady betray themselves to be, it matters more than a little what kind of woman she is. In the face of this circumstance, the simplicity, the ignorance, the want of experience, the innocent false guesses and inferences, which, in severely critical moods, are almost ridiculous, resolve themselves into facts charming and even sacred, while the masculine cleverness, the social omniscience, which satisfy the merely intellectual exactions, become an almost revolting spectacle. Miss Mulock is kindly, somewhat dull, pious, and very sentimental—she has both the virtues and defects which are covered by the untranslatable French word *honnête*. Miss Braddon is brilliant, lively, ingenious, and destitute of a ray of sentiment; and we should never dream of calling her *honnête*. And, as matters stand at present, to say that we prefer the sentimental school to the other, is simply to say that we prefer virtue to vice. (pp. 167-72)

> *Henry James, "'A Noble Life',"* in his Notes
> and Reviews, *1921. Reprint by Dunster House,*
> *1968, pp. 167-72.*

The British Quarterly Review   (essay date 1866)

[*In the following excerpt, the* British Quarterly Review *critic examines Craik's novels to characterize her writing style as simple and direct but lacking in "poetic richness." The critic also laments Craik's lack of insight into character, but posits that the strength of her writing consists in the "pure moral tone" of her message.*]

It is in general the duty of a critic to respect absolutely the incognito of a writer, but the 'Author of *John Halifax*' is so well known as the lady who was Miss Mulock, and is Mrs. Craik, that we commit no breach of confidence, and cannot be considered impertinent in speaking openly of her. She takes the title of 'Author of *John Halifax*,' so it seems, rather to identify her with that particular book than as a veil behind which she may conceal her own personality. It is the work which she offers, and which the public is willing to receive, as representative both of her style and character.

In the world of letters few authors have so distinct, and at the same time so eminent a position as this lady. Other writers are cleverer, more impassioned, more brilliant, but we turn from their eloquent words to her tales of simple goodness with a sense of rest and relief. Her records do not tell of strong mental conflict, of great wrong or crime; there are no bright lights and no dark shadows in her life scenes; and thus living in stormy and troubled times, rife with conflict and crime, those who are climbing the weary upward road can 'rest and be thankful,' when she speaks. And for this reason her most ardent admirers are found, not chiefly among those who lead a quiet, uneventful life, and seek in a novel for some relief from the monotony of it, but among the earnest workers and able thinkers of the time, those who are familiar with

> The power of the night, the press of the storm,
>   The post of the foe;

for Mrs. Craik's great charm is a repose of manner, a quiet dignity of style, which, while it impresses all readers by its calm purity, appeals more especially to the cultivated and refined. *Restful* is, perhaps, the term that can best be applied to her writings. She does not look deep down into the inner conflicts, the great moral struggles of our nature from which George Eliot draws back the veil; nor can she reach the pure and lofty air of poetic inspiration in which George MacDonald soars; she does not even give us the broad, pleasant, infinite variety of human character and life which Anthony Trollope depicts, but she takes some quiet corner of the earth, which is planted with roses perhaps, or perhaps brings forth thorns and briars chiefly, and she says, 'See, men and women have lived and suffered here. Be patient and steadfast, you who live and suffer; endure as they endured, and you also will find rest and peace. Do right, do your duty, and be patient: all must be well, for God is over all.'

Very pathetic is this teaching, very powerful too in its earnest, absolute purity and goodness; for this is an author whose pages are unsullied by any taint. Good is good, and evil is evil; she believes in no doubtful border-land, no debateable ground between the two, and thinks that evil is not to be palliated or extenuated. It is impossible to exaggerate the importance of a pure moral tone in the literature of fiction; for the influence of fiction on the manners and morals of a nation is almost incalculable, it acts most powerfully either for good or evil. A writer of fiction having first excited the imagination or kindled the enthusiasm of readers, who are for the most part young and susceptible, can present them with an image of exalted virtue or of vice made attractive, which shall be all-powerful in its after-effects. It is no mean task to make the timid trust in God, and to help the trustful to hope; to make those who hope strong in faith, and the faithful victorious. (pp. 32-4)

Mrs. Craik, as we have said, stands invariably on the side of truth and goodness. These we never miss, but her books somewhat lack the great charm of beauty, of poetic richness of style. It is one of the chief misfortunes of almost every female novelist that her own education, as a woman, has been wretchedly defective. Her first novel stands ordinarily as an exercise in composition, and enables her to write English grammatically. Perhaps we ought rather to say, that it helps her to understand her own language. We find, for example, all Mrs. Oliphant's earlier novels disfigured by grammatical errors and verbal inaccuracies, of which the more careful of her later books show few traces. She has, after some twenty years of practice, reached what should have been the starting-point; her early novels were exercises in composition which the public was called on to criticise and correct. In addition to this, that which is called the *education* of the majority of women leaves them not only without information, but without intelligent interest in any subject that does not immediately concern them. The past, with all its wealth of words and deeds, does not exist for them. They are shut in to the present, or rather, to some small fragment of the present. They are, as women, keenly alive to moral excellence; they have an instinctive perception of, and appreciation for it, they never lose their faith in it; no woman could write such a book as [Wilkie Collins's] *Armadale;* no woman could ei-

ther believe in or delineate Miss Gwilt. At the same time, their intellectual insight is limited, and this must be the case whilst the intellect is dwarfed as it has been hitherto. It seems impossible for a woman to realize what an intellectual man is, what he does and says. Clever female novelists never let such a man speak at all; they know that they can see only the outside, and that they are ignorant of the machinery which sets the thing going, and the principle of the machinery; and so they discreetly tell you what kind of case it has, but nothing more.

Christian's Mistake is one of the most perfect of Mrs. Craik's stories, but the '**Master of St. Bede's**' is a shadow. If he were not a shadow, the reader would find out that he was very unlike the master of a college, and that although a good, kind, quiet man, his mind is a blank. Mrs. Gaskell . . . has always put women in the foreground of her stories, very exquisitely and delicately painted; and with consummate skill she has left the men distant and shadowy like the mountains. The 'Author of *John Halifax*' shows equal discretion in her later and more perfect stories.

We have said that this lady lacks some of the higher beauties of style, but she possesses the great charm of simplicity and directness. She tells you a simple story, and she wishes you to know and feel that it is simple, and to receive it in all simplicity. The brook winds on, clear and fresh, through the meadows. You can see the pebbles and moss in its bed, and here and there a quiet trout beside a stone; it is all so simple and still that sometimes you are surprised at the life—that is the thought—there is in it.

Any reader who has failed to realize the excellence of a simple style should read a chapter of *Cradock Nowell;* under other circumstances such a penance need not be imposed upon him. Mr. Blackmore's aim appears to be to make his stream of thought and talk so turbid that it shall be impossible to ascertain if it is deep or shallow; to write a garble of Greek and Latin and unintelligible English, which is alike hateful and foreign to all three languages. For example,—

> But John, though fully alive to the stigmotype of his position, allowed his epidermis to quill toward the operator, and abstracted all his too sensitive parts into a sophistic apory.

He would be a bold man who should venture to predict either that there was or was not anything under this film of pedantic conceit. Mr. Blackmore should either have put the story into English or into the fire. If we turn from such a writer to the 'Author of *John Halifax,*' we feel that she is not trying to impose upon us, and to make us believe that there is more than meets the eye in what she writes. We repay her by looking carefully for delicate shades of meaning and subtle thoughts, and are rewarded by finding them. In her later works her aim has become very obvious. She tries, as we have said, to tell a simple story simply. She acknowledges that there are great crimes and great criminals in society, many in every age who are overtaken by some extraordinary fate; but she sees that the greater part of mankind lead externally quiet and unexciting lives, and yet these are also life-dramas. They have their great apotheosis, and are consecrated by grief and pain. The child brings his share of joy and love and hope, and the man must see it perish on the cold earth, fade away amidst the daily cares and in the trivial routines of life; must see his hope grow wan and pale and then die. But joy and love and hope shall rise again, glorified even here upon earth; and he, too, shall rise with them, glorified, and able to look beyond the grave to the everlasting in the heavens. It is appointed to each one of us thus to learn to believe in the resurrection of the dead and the life of the world to come. We have to find each one of us that the world—the temporal and visible—is not enough for an immortal soul, and that the invisible and spiritual can alone satisfy its longings. We learn this lesson, each in a different manner, but sorrow and suffering are the ministers appointed to proclaim it. Taking this view, the lady of whom we write does not seek for any extraordinary incidents to excite and awaken the interest of her readers, for with such a faith she can dare to take a simple, healthy good nature, and show how it is purified and refined by the fire of affliction.

It is interesting to compare the first novel of a writer like Mrs. Craik with the work of her later and maturer years. *The Ogilvies* was published seventeen years ago. It is a story of wilful passionate first-love, and is written with a fire and enthusiasm wanting in later works; it gives also a promise of dramatic power which has never been fulfilled. We miss, however, the high moral tone of *John Halifax, Mistress and Maid,* and *Christian's Mistake.* It is not that Eleanor Ogilvie and Philip Wychnor are not as good and true as any of Mrs. Craik's later heroes and heroines, but that her sympathy and that of the reader is centred on Katherine Ogilvie and Paul Lynedon, who are not so good. Katherine Ogilvie is a girl of sixteen, who falls in love,—*falls* is scarcely the right word,—she shuts her eyes and plunges headlong into love: Neither can we say that she falls in love *with* Paul Lynedon, for Paul Lynedon is unconscious of the state of this young lady's affections, being at the time in love with her cousin Eleanor. There is an overwhelming amount of sentimentalism in the first volume, and an evident conviction in the author's mind that fascinating men like Paul Lynedon ought to marry girls who passionately admire their fine eyes and wavy hair. But there are occasional scenes of remarkable power, and an indication from the first, of the struggle in the author's mind between her sympathy with Katherine's passionate love and the conviction that there is something higher and nobler than passion: Paul Lynedon is intended to be strong and dark, a lady's hero of the Byronic school, but he and all the other men in the book stand too prominently forward; so that the reader not only sees them, but sees *through* them, discovers that they are gauze and pasteboard. Paul Lynedon is rejected by Eleanor Ogilvie, and then takes the natural course of such men—he goes to Italy. Meanwhile Katherine marries her cousin Hugh, but does not promote, by this step, either his happiness or her own. After a few years, Paul Lynedon returns to England. He had forgotten the plain, dark, affectionate Katherine, but in a novel, he naturally loves at first sight the young and beautiful Mrs. Ogilvie. Just at the right moment the husband, poor Hugh, breaks his neck, and, after a short widowhood, Katherine Ogilvie consents to become Mrs. Lynedon.

Up to this point *The Ogilvies* might have been the first work of any sensational writer, but at this point we find an indication of character which is well worthy of notice. The author feels that this story of passion and wrong-doing cannot end to Katherine Ogilvie either happily or peacefully—that it ought not to do so. Perhaps in real life Katherine's Nemesis might not have come as heart-disease, but it must have come in some form, and the scene here described has great dramatic force.

> Paul made her sit by the open window, while he leaned over her, pulling the roses from outside the casement and throwing them leaf by leaf into her lap. While he did so, she took courage to tell him of the letter to her mother. He murmured a little at the full confession, but when he read it he only blessed her the more for her tenderness towards himself.

> "May I grow worthy of such love, my Katherine," he said, for the moment deeply touched; "but we must not be sad, dearest. Come, sign your name—your new name. Are you content to bear it?" continued he, with a smile.

> Her answer was another, radiant with intense love and perfect joy. Paul looked over her while she laid the paper on the rose-strewed windowsill, and wrote the words, "Katherine *Lynedon.*"

> She said them over to herself once or twice with a loving intonation, and then turned her face on her bridegroom's arm, weeping.

> "Do not chide me, Paul; I am so happy, so happy. Now I begin to hope the past may be forgotten us—that we may have a future yet."

> "We may? We *will!*" was Lynedon's answer.

> While he spoke, through the hush of that glad May-noon came a sound—dull, solemn! Another, and yet another! It was the funeral bell tolling from the near church tower.

> Katherine lifted up her face, white and ghastly. "Paul, do you hear that?" and her voice was shrill with terror. "It is our marriage-peal—we have no other; we ought not to have. I knew it was too late!"

> "Nay, my own love," answered Paul, becoming alarmed at her look. He drew her nearer to him, but she seemed neither to hear his voice nor feel his clasp. The bell sounded again. "Hark! hark!" Katherine cried. "Paul, do you remember the room where we knelt, you and I; and *he* joined our hands, and said the words—'Earth to earth—ashes to ashes? It will come true; I know it will, and it is right it should."

> Lynedon took his bride in his arms, and endeavoured to calm her. He half succeeded, for she looked up in his face with a faint smile. "Thank you! I know you love me, my own Paul, my—"

> Suddenly her voice ceased. With a convulsive movement she put her hand to her heart, and her head sank on her husband's breast.

That instant the awful summons came. Without
a word, or sigh, or moan, the spirit passed!

We have scarcely alluded to Eleanor Ogilvie and Philip
Wychnor, the good people of the book. They are, in fact,
very uninteresting. No doubt, from the first, Mrs. Craik
has desired to show that there is something nobler than
high birth, more attractive than beauty, more powerful
than intellect; she has always felt this, but has not always
possessed the power of depicting moral worth in a pleasing
form. There is a want of artistic power and insight in many
of her books. She chooses in **Olive** a deformed girl for a
heroine, finding great difficulty in making this a pleasing
or even a prominent figure in a work of art, she has to soft-
en down the deformity; and so she gives you to understand
that though Olive was deformed, no one noticed it. This
is a mistake: the introduction of deformity in a work of art
can only be justified if it teaches a higher lesson than beauty; it may do so; but clearly we must recognise it for what
it is; and it must not deceive us by trying to *appear* beauty
while it *is* deformity.

Again, in **A Life for a Life,** we have the story of a man
who is a prey to remorse on account of a murder which
he had committed, and who feels that his crime must be
expiated by punishment. But Mrs. Craik shrinks from the
murderer, and cannot make him a hero; and therefore she
is careful to inform you that this was not a premeditated
murder, but a mere accidental blow. Now a man may regret an accident his whole life long; but, so long as he is
sane, he cannot feel remorse for it, however disastrous its
consequences; and the expiation of imprisonment would
be a work of supererogation.

Even in the story of **John Halifax** we have the same artistic and intellectual blunder—the characteristic irresolution of this writer. If we could erase half a dozen sentences
from this book, it would stand as one of the most beautiful
stories in the English language, conveying one of the highest moral truths. If it teaches anything it is the nobility of
man as man. The ragged body, with his open, honest face,
as he asks the respectable Quaker for work, is no beggar;
the lad who drives the cart of dangling skins is not inferior
to Phineas Fletcher, who watches for him from his father's
windows, and longs for his companionship in the garden
and the fields; and the tanner—the honest and good man
who marries Ursula March, a lady born—is her equal.
Mrs. Craik might have shown that men, in the sight of
God, are equal, and that therefore all good men must be
equals upon earth. But no, she shrinks from the full expression of so startling a theory, and therefore gives John
Halifax a little Greek Testament, in which is written 'Guy
Halifax, Gentleman,' and we must conclude that all his
moral excellence and intellectual worth were derived from
ladies and *gentlemen* who had been his remote ancestors,
but with whom he had never been in personal contact at
all, since at twelve years old he was a ragged orphan, unable to read and write. It is impossible to answer the question, 'What does the author mean by gentleman?' since
this shadowy word in a book is a loophole through which
she escapes from the charge of holding the very democratic view that a gentleman is a man of noble nature who
leads an unselfish life. She does depict a noble nature and
an unselfish life; but seeing that John Halifax did begin the

world as a poor friendless boy, she might have allowed us
to think that such a development was possible to man as
man. We can't all of us find little Greek Testaments with
the inscription 'Gentleman' after the names of our ancestors. Still this book is in many ways remarkable. We find
a gradual development in **Olive, Agatha's Husband,** and
The Head of the Family, but not until **John Halifax** does
the author throw her whole weight into the scale of goodness. She finds that her power as well as her inclination is
in that direction, and henceforth she strips off all outer
amenities as of plot and circumstance, and aims at depicting good, but ordinary men and women, leading good and
honest lives. Other novelists acquire the art of adding effect to effect, and horror to horror. This one gradually
strips off all adventitious circumstances of interest, and
tries to make her stories not rich and full but pure and
high.

JOHN HALIFAX, GENTLEMAN.

BY

THE AUTHOR OF

"THE HEAD OF THE FAMILY," "OLIVE,"

&c. &c.

" And thus he bore, without abuse,
The grand old name of Gentleman."
TENNYSON'S "IN MEMORIAM."

IN THREE VOLUMES.

VOL. I.

LONDON:
HURST AND BLACKETT, PUBLISHERS,
SUCCESSORS TO HENRY COLBURN,
13, GREAT MARLBOROUGH STREET.
1856.

The title page of John Halifax, Gentleman, *Craik's most famous
novel.*

John Halifax is the culmination of her power; and this the author recognises by invariably styling herself the 'Author of *John Halifax*.' In this book she retains something of the fulness and freshness of her youth. There is more vital energy and a greater variety of character than we find in her more recent novels, and then the story is told in such a way that the very deficiencies become merits and virtues. This lady's conception of the masculine character and nature is shadowy, and her children are mere rag dollies. Now the story of John Halifax is told by his friend Phineas Fletcher. Phineas is the son of a Quaker, and has been from his youth a great sufferer and confirmed invalid. His nature is delicate, susceptible, tender, and feminine. Indeed, for all practical purposes a woman might as well have told the story, but then no woman except a wife or sister could have had the necessary intimate relation to the hero. A wife would not have had it long enough, and a sister with another Greek Testament would have been very embarrassing. The author discovered, as we have said, the very best method of telling her story. What should Phineas Fletcher know of mankind and the world! He looks at his hero and his friend as a woman would do—simply believes in him and loves him. How can the lonely man understand children! He is scarcely familiar with the outside of them and you don't feel sure that he knows they run upon two legs.

It is essential to the truth and unity of the story that it should be told in this manner, and the author could not have told it at all from another point of view. At the same time the reader knows that he sees the life of John Halifax through the mind of Phineas Fletcher, and therefore pictures it as fuller and stronger and more manly than it is; and yet can admire the exceeding delicacy of the delineation, and the beauty of the touches which a stronger man would neither have needed nor desired to give. The friendship of these two men—a friendship like that of Jonathan and David—is told without words; neither of them needs to protest, for we feel its truth and loyalty from the first meeting of the two boys to the last farewell that Phineas takes of his friend. The story of such a friendship would alone be a noble lesson, but with it is the story of a no less noble life. The friendless boy becomes the prosperous man, the struggles of his youth are succeeded by the sorrows of maturer age, but throughout we see the same resolute figure, bold and honest—the boy who could not tell a lie or deceive his master—the man who could not stoop to a mean or unworthy action. The story of his love is exquisitely told, with the kind of half-wistful comprehension which we should expect from Phineas Fletcher. Poor John thinks his love for the lady and the heiress hopeless, and intends to leave England as soon as he has recovered from a severe illness. Phineas contrives to bring Ursula March to see him.

> And now the room darkened so fast, that I could not see them; but their voices seemed a great way off, as the children's voices playing at the old well-head used to sound to me when I lay under the brow of the Flat in the dim twilights at Enderley.
>
> "I intend," John said, "as soon as I am able, to leave Norton Bury, and go abroad for some time."
>
> "Where?"
>
> "To America. It is the best country for a young man who has neither money, nor kindred, nor position—nothing, in fact, but his own right hand with which to carve out his own fortune—as I will, if I can."
>
> She murmured something about this being quite right.
>
> "I am glad you think so." But his voice had resumed that formal tone which ever and anon mingled strangely with its low, deep tenderness. "In any case, I must quit England. I have reasons for so doing."
>
> "What reasons?"
>
> The question seemed to startle John—he did not reply at once.
>
> "If you wish, I will tell you; in order that, should I ever come back—or if I should not come back at all, you who were kind enough to be my friend, will know I did not go away from mere youthful recklessness, or love of change."
>
> He waited, apparently for some answer—but it came not, and he continued:
>
> "I am going, because there has befallen me a great trouble, which, while I stay here, I cannot get free from or overcome. I do not wish to sink under it—I had rather, as you said, 'do my work in the world,' as a man ought. No man has a right to say unto his Maker, 'My burthen is heavier than I can bear.' Do you not think so?"
>
> "I do."
>
> "Do you not think I am right in thus meeting, and trying to conquer, an inevitable ill?"
>
> "*Is* it inevitable?"
>
> "Hush!" John answered, wildly. "Don't reason with me—you cannot judge—you do not know. It is enough that I must go. If I stay I shall become unworthy of myself, unworthy of—Forgive me, I have no right to talk thus; but you called me 'friend,' and I would like you to think kindly of me always. Because—because—" And his voice shook—broke down utterly. "God love thee and take care of thee, wherever I may go!"
>
> "John, stay!"
>
> It was but a low, faint cry, like that of a little bird. But he heard it—felt it. In the silence of the dark she crept up to him, like a young bird to its mate, and he took her into the shelter of his love for evermore. At once, all was made clear between them; for whatever the world might say, they were in the sight of heaven equal, and she received as much as she gave.

Ursula March—afterwards Ursula Halifax—stands quite apart from ordinary heroines. She is not beautiful, but she is young, bright, and resolute. She has decidedly a will of her own, and one suspects a temper also; but it never interferes with the comfort of husband, children, or friends, and only gives that spice of determination which no woman who has not a temper can acquire. She is a good wife and mother, and bears the sorrows which befall her very nobly and patiently: but her first attitude is always one of resistance. This we see not only in the following extract, but in her conduct at a later period, when a woman whose child has the small-pox is in the house, and her own children are exposed to danger:—

> They were bonny eyes! lovely in shape and colour, delicately fringed; but there was something strange in their expression, or rather, in their want of it. Many babies have a round, vacant stare—but this was no stare, only a wide, full look, a look of quiet blankness, an *unseeing* look.
>
> It caught Dr. Jessop's notice. I saw his air of vexed dignity change into a certain anxiety.
>
> "Well, whose are they like, her father's or mine? His, I hope—it will be the better for her beauty. Nay, we'll excuse all compliments."
>
> "I—I can't exactly tell. I could judge better by candle-light."
>
> "We'll have candles."
>
> "No, no! Had we not better put it off altogether till another day! I'll call in to-morrow and look at her eyes."
>
> His manner was hesitating and troubled, John noticed it.
>
> "Love, give her to me. Go and get us lights, will you?"
>
> When she was gone, John took his baby to the window, gazed long and intently into her little face, then at Dr. Jessop. "Do you think—no—it's not possible—that there can be anything the matter with the child's eyes?"
>
> Ursula coming in, heard the last words.
>
> "What was that you said about baby's eyes?"
>
> No one answered her. All were gathered in a group at the window, the child being held on her father's lap, while Dr. Jessop was trying to open the small white lids, kept so continually closed. At last the baby uttered a little cry of pain—the mother darted forward, and clasped it almost savagely to her breast.
>
> "I will not have my baby hurt! There is nothing wrong with her sweet eyes. Go away; you shall not touch her, John."
>
> "Love!"
>
> She melted at that low, fond word; leaned against his shoulder, trying to control her tears.
>
> "It shocked me so, the bare thought of such a thing. O! husband, don't let her be looked at again."
>
> "Only once again, my darling. It is best. Then

> we shall be quite satisfied. Phineas, give me the candle."
>
> The words—caressing, and by strong constraint, made calm and soothing—were yet firm. Ursula resisted no more, but let him take Muriel—little, unconscious, cooing dove! Lulled by her father's voice, she once more opened her eyes, wide.
>
> Dr. Jessop passed the candle before them many times, once so close that it almost touched her face; but the full, quiet eyes never blenched nor closed.
>
> He set the light down.
>
> "Doctor!" whispered the father, in a wild appeal against—ay, it was against certainty. He snatched the candle, and tried the experiment himself.
>
> "She does not see at all. Can she be blind?"
>
> "Born blind!"
>
> Yes, those pretty baby-eyes were dark—quite dark.
>
> There was nothing painful nor unnatural in their look, save, perhaps, the blankness of gaze which I have before noticed. Outwardly, their organization was perfect; but in the fine inner mechanism was something wrong—something wanting. She never had seen—never would see—in this world.
>
> *"Blind!"* The word was uttered softly, hardly above a breath, yet the mother heard it. She pushed every one aside, and took the child herself. Herself, with a desperate incredulity, she looked into those eyes, which never could look back either her agony or her love. Poor mother!
>
> "John! John! oh, John!"—the name rising into a cry, as if he could surely help her. He came, and took her in his arms, took both wife and babe. She laid her head on his shoulder in bitter weeping. "Oh, John! it is so hard. Our pretty one, our own little child!"
>
> John did not speak, but only held her to him—close and fast. When she was a little calmer, he whispered to her the comfort—the sole comfort even her husband could give her—through whose will it was that this affliction came.
>
> "And it is more an affliction to you than it will be to her, poor pet!" said Mrs. Jessop, as she wiped her friendly eyes. "She will not miss what she never knew. She may be a happy child. Look, how she lies and smiles."
>
> But the mother could not take that consolation yet. She walked to and fro, and stood rocking her baby, mute indeed, but with tears falling in showers. Gradually her anguish wept itself away, or was smothered down, lest it should disturb the little creature asleep on her breast.
>
> Some one came behind her, and placed her in the arm-chair, gently. It was my father. He sat down by her, taking her hand.

"Grieve not, Ursula. I had a little brother who was blind. He was the happiest creature I ever knew."

My father sighed. We all marvelled to see the wonderful softness, even tenderness, which had come into him.

"Give me thy child for a minute." Ursula laid it across his knees; he put his hand solemnly on the baby-breast. "God bless this little one! Ay, and she shall be blessed."

These words, spoken with as full assurance as the prophetic benediction of the departing patriarchs of old, struck us all. We looked at little Muriel as if the blessing were already upon her; as if the mysterious touch which had sealed up her eyes for ever, had left on her a sanctity like as of one who has been touched by the finger of God.

The blind child Muriel moves for a short time in a soft dreamy way through the story, with an influence felt by all. The relation to her father is very beautifully described:—

To see her now, leaning her cheek against his— the small soft face almost a miniature of his own, the hair, a paler shade of the same bright colour, curling in the same elastic rings—they looked less like ordinary father and daughter than like *a man and his good angel:* the visible embodiment of the best half of his youth.

The influence of Muriel is indeed an abiding influence, and in this again we see the writer's earnest truth, and her truthfulness to nature. The child is not introduced for the sake of two or three pathetic scenes, her death does not remove her from our view any more than it takes a child from the home and the heart of parents who have once realised the true and abiding tie between parent and child. Ursula can look down upon the face of her dead husband and say, 'How glad her father will be to have her again— his own little Muriel!' for she knows that death has been absence but not loss.

Mrs. Craik has, indeed, the rare power of indicating the ideal of every relationship; she cannot always show it, but she can, as we said, indicate it. How beautifully, in the following passage, she points out the very truth of one side of parental duty.

"But if things had been otherwise—if you had not been so sure of Maud's feelings—"

He started, painfully; then answered—"I think I should have done it still."

I was silent. The paramount right, the high prerogative of love, which he held as strongly as I did, seemed attacked in its liberty divine. For the moment, it was as if he too had in his middle-age gone over to the cold-blooded ranks of harsh parental prudence, despotic paternal rule; as if Ursula March's lover and Maud's father were two distinct beings. One finds it so, often enough with men:

"John," I said, "could you have done it? could you have broken the child's heart?"

"Yes, if it was to save her peace—perhaps her soul, I *could* have broken my child's heart."

He spoke solemnly, with an accent of inexpressible pain, as if this were not the first time by many that he had pondered over such a possibility.

"I wish, Phineas, to make clear to you, in case of—of any future misconceptions—my mind on this matter. One right alone I hold superior to the right of love—duty. It is a father's duty, at all risks, at all costs, to save his child from anything which he believes would peril her duty—so long as she is too young to understand fully how beyond the claim of any human being, be it father or lover, is God's claim to herself and her immortal soul. Anything which would endanger that, should be cut off—though it be the right hand—the right eye. But thank God, it is not thus with my little Maud."

John Halifax is, as we have said, up to the present time, the culminating effort of the author. She seems to stand, as it were, above herself, and to direct her own powers. She has thrown her whole strength into it, so that it is full and rich in incident beyond any other of her works. The simplicity of her style and the beauty of her pure nature have nowhere so full a grace, and we feel that it is a life-long acquisition to have known such people as John and Ursula Halifax and Phineas Fletcher. Finding, however, that her power lay in the delineation of good men and women and of home scenes, she has, in her later works, abandoned still more the interest of plot and the delineation of varied character. Not one of her later works is in any respect so rich or so complete as *John Halifax,* not one, with the exception of *Christian's Mistake,* so healthy.

'Lord Erlistoun' is a story told also by a man, but then Mark Brown is strong and common-place, and so we cannot see why he should write a sentimental story. *A Life for a Life* is not so much sentimental as morbid. Besides, the story is told twice over; and as there is very little of it, we don't care to read it once in a man's diary and once in a woman's. And a diary, as the novelist uses it, is such an incredible thing. It contains every incident which can at any time be available in the development of the story, and shows that the diarist was always in the right place at the right time, so as to hear and see every thing that it was essential he should hear and see. Now a diary out of a novel shows, curiously enough, that the diarist very rarely noticed, at the time they occurred, words and actions which proved afterwards to be of great importance, and the omissions of such a diary are far more remarkable than the entries. For this reason, the use of a diary is the only utterly improbable way of getting a story told, and to use two diaries instead of one, is to convert the improbable into a direct impossible. These faults, however, lie on the surface; whereas, if we look beneath the surface, we see the abiding excellence of the author. There is a noble self-renunciation in Jean Dowglas, and an earnest endeavour to depict true Christian repentance in *A Life for a Life.*

Mistress and Maid is again a very good book. With characteristic indecision, the writer seems to have changed her plan, and her first intention is not carried out. Mistress and maid are separated whilst the character of the latter is still unformed, so that we do not see the life-long influence of the mistress on her maid. We see just enough to make us wish to know more. The uncouth girl is gradually tamed by two of her mistresses, and undergoes a very salutary discipline at the hands of a third, whose tongue and temper are a scourge. We want to know more about her, and to trace the development of her mind and character. This we cannot do, but we get occasional hints and glimpses, and at length the character of Elizabeth Hand stands out clear and strong. We recognise its truth and fidelity and beauty, and acknowledge this to be an accurate delineation of a class of women whom we are proud to call English servants. The sympathy of the writer gives her a true insight into the nature of any good woman, and the parting between Elizabeth and her faithless lover is quite perfect in its way.

> Tom stood there alone. He looked so exactly his own old self; he came forward to meet her so completely in his old familiar way, that for the instant she thought she must be under some dreadful delusion; that the moonlight night in the square must have been all a dream—Esther, still the silly little Esther, whom Tom had often heard of and laughed at; and Tom, her own Tom, who loved nobody but herself.
>
> "Elizabeth, what an age it is since I've had a sight of you!"
>
> But though the manner was warm as ever—
>
> > In his tone
> > A something smote her, as if Duty tried
> > To mock the voice of Love, now long since flown,
>
> and quiet as she stood, Elizabeth shivered in his arms.
>
> "Why, what's the matter? Aren't you glad to see me? Give me another kiss, my girl, do!"
>
> He took it; and she crept away from him and sat down.
>
> "Tom, I've something to say to you, and I'd better say it at once."
>
> "To be sure. 'Tisn't any bad news from home, is it?" Or looking uneasily at her—"I haven't vexed you, have I?"
>
> "*Vexed* me," she repeated, thinking what a small foolish word it was to express what had happened, and what she had been suffering.
>
> "No, Tom, not vexed me, exactly. But I want to ask you a question. Who was it that you stood talking with, under our tree in the square, between nine and ten o'clock, this night three weeks ago?"
>
> Though there was no anger in the voice, it was so serious and deliberate that it made Tom start:
>
> "Three weeks ago! how can I possibly tell?"

> "Yes, you can; for it was a fine moonlight night, and you stood there a long time."
>
> "Under the tree, talking to somebody? What nonsense. Perhaps it wasn't me at all."
>
> "It was, for I saw you."
>
> "The devil you did!" mumbled Tom.
>
> "Don't be angry—only tell me the plain truth. The young woman that was with you was our Esther here, wasn't she?"
>
> For the moment Tom looked altogether confounded. Then he tried to recover himself, and said, crossly, "Well, and if it was, where's the harm? Can't a man be civil to a pretty girl without being called over the coals in this way?"
>
> Elizabeth made no answer, at least, not immediately. At last she said, in a very gentle, subdued voice—
>
> "Tom, are you fond of Esther? You would not kiss her if you were not fond of her. Do you like her as—as you used to like me?"
>
> And she looked right up into his eyes. Hers had no reproach in them, only a piteous entreaty, the last clinging to a hope she knew to be false.
>
> "Like Esther? of course I do. She's a nice girl, and we are very good friends."
>
> "Tom, a man can't be 'friends,' in that sort of way, with a pretty girl of eighteen, when he is going to be married to somebody else. At least, in my mind, he ought not."
>
> Tom laughed, in a confused manner. "I say, you're jealous, and you'd better get over it."
>
> Was she jealous? Was it all fancy, folly? Did Tom stand there, true as steel, without a feeling in his heart that she did not share, without a hope in which she was not united, holding her, and preferring her, with that individuality and unity of love, which true love ever gives and exacts, as it has a right to exact?
>
> Not that poor Elizabeth reasoned in this way, but she felt the thing by instinct without reasoning.
>
> "Tom," she said, "tell me outright, just as if I was somebody else, and had never belonged to you at all, Do you love Esther Martin?"
>
> Truthful people enforce truth. Tom might be fickle, but he was not deceitful; he could not look into Elizabeth's eyes and tell her a deliberate lie; somehow, he dared not.
>
> "Well then—since you will have it out of me—I think I do."
>
> So Elizabeth's "ship went down." It might have been a very frail vessel, that nobody in their right senses would have trusted any treasure with, still she did; and it was all she had, and it went down to the bottom like a stone.
>
> It is astonishing how soon the sea closes over this

sort of wreck; and how quietly people take—when they must take, and there is no more disbelieving it—the truth which they would have given their lives to prove was an impossible lie.

For some minutes Tom stood facing the fire, and Elizabeth sat on her chair opposite, without speaking. Then she took off her brooch, the only love-token he had given her, and put it into his hand.

"What's this for?" asked he, suddenly.

"You know. You'd better give it to Esther. It's Esther, not me, you must marry now."

And the thought of Esther—giddy, flirting, useless Esther—as Tom's wife, was almost more than she could bear. The sting of it put even into her crushed humility a certain honest self-assertion.

"I'm not going to blame you, Tom; but I think I'm as good as she. I'm not pretty, I know, nor lively, nor young; at least, I'm old for my age; but I was worth something. You should not have served me so."

Tom said the usual excuse, that he "couldn't help it." And suddenly turning round, he begged her to forgive him, and not forsake him.

She forsake Tom! Elizabeth almost smiled.

"I do forgive you; I'm not a bit angry with you. If I ever was, I have got over it."

"That's right. You're a dear soul. Do you think I don't like you, Elizabeth?"

"Oh yes," she said, sadly, "I daresay you do, a little, in spite of Esther Martin. But that's not my way of liking, and I couldn't stand it."

"What couldn't you stand?"

"Your kissing me to-day, and another girl to-morrow. Your telling me I was everything to you one week, and saying exactly the same thing to another girl the next. It would be hard enough to bear if we were only friends, but as sweethearts, as husband and wife, it would be impossible. No, Tom, I tell you the truth, I could not stand it."

She spoke strongly, unhesitatingly, and for an instant there flowed out of her soft eyes that wild, fierce spark, latent even in these quiet, humble natures, which is dangerous to meddle with.

Tom did not attempt it. He felt all was over. Whether he had lost or gained, whether he was glad or sorry, he hardly knew.

"I'm not going to take this back, anyhow," he said, "fiddling" with the brooch; and then going up to her, he attempted, with trembling hands, to re-fasten it in her collar.

The familiar action, his contrite look, were too much. People who have once loved one another, though the love is dead (for love *can* die), are not able to bury it all at once, or if they do, its pale

ghost will still come knocking at the door of their hearts, "Let me in, let me in."

Elizabeth ought, I know, in proper feminine dignity, to have bade Tom farewell, without a glance or a touch. But she did not. When he had fastened her brooch, she looked up in his familiar face, a sorrowful, wistful, lingering look, and then clung about his neck.

"O Tom, Tom, I was so fond of you!"

And Tom mingled his tears with hers, and kissed her many times, and even felt his old affection returning, making him half oblivious of Esther; but mercifully—for love rebuilt upon lost faith is like a house founded upon sands—the door opened, and Esther herself came in.

The heroine of the story, however, is the Mistress—not the Maid. And we turn from Elizabeth to the bright and resolute Hilary Leaf, who, of the three sisters, is, we conclude, *the* mistress. Hilary Leaf is a self-reliant, energetic little woman, who tries to keep school unsuccessfully, and then—a lesson to many other women under similar circumstances—keeps a shop successfully. She is really a very good little thing, and deserves a better fate than to marry the reticent Scotchman to whose lot she falls.

Robert Lyon and Hilary Leaf have been intimately acquainted, and have loved each other for some years. At length he leaves England for India, having first begged Hilary "to trust him" in his absence. No one can be surprised that in an absence of ten years, during which he corresponds with her sister, but—in accordance, we presume, with Scottish notions of propriety—never writes one line to Hilary, she has many doubts as to whether she is to *trust him* as a friend or as a lover. The man who really loves a woman, and intends to marry her, and yet leaves her *free,* that is, imagines the possibility of her loving and marrying some one else, must lack either self-respect or true love, and most probably both. Robert Lyon could only have refrained from telling Hilary that he loved her and asking her to marry him when he returned to England, for her sake or his own. Now, Hilary would have gone down on her knees and thanked God for the assurance of Robert's love any and every day of his absence; it would have helped her in every trial that she had to endure. If he had loved her unselfishly he would have known this. Is it not probable that he actually did marry in India, and that he returned a widower, having left his children to the care of his wife's relatives in India? If not, his silence was neither true nor honest, nor creditable to him as a man. In fact, he has no more heart than a tailor's dummy. He is no more than a carved wooden head on an oak stick, and he has to be kept carefully out of the way that the reader may not see he is a stick. He comes home, however, and then there can no longer be any doubt. The good little woman will marry him after all, but she cannot go to India and leave the lonely sister—her only friend—now old and feeble. She tells him so, but the masculine element in his nature, which had apparently been dormant for fifteen years, revolts, and Hilary has every right to the sympathy of the reader.

"Robert, I want to talk to you about Johanna."

"I guess what it is," said he, smiling; "you would like her to go out to India with us. Certainly, if she chooses. I hope you did not suppose I should object?"

"No; but it is not that. She could not go; she would not live six months in a hot climate; the doctor tells me so."

"You have consulted him?"

"Yes, last week; confidentially, without her knowing it. But I thought it right. I wanted to make quite sure before—before. Oh, Robert—"

The grief of her tone caused him to suspect what was coming. He started.

"You don't mean that! Oh, no, you cannot! My little woman—my own little woman—she could not be so unkind."

Hilary turned sick at heart. The dim landscape, the bright sky, seemed to mingle and dance before her, and Venus to stare at her with a piercing, threatening, baleful lustre.

"Robert, let me sit down on the bench, and sit you beside me. It is too dark for people to notice us, and we shall not be very cold."

"No, my darling;" and he slipped his plaid round her shoulders, and his arm with it.

She looked up pitifully. "Don't be vexed with me, Robert, dear; I have thought it all over; weighed it on every side: nights and nights I have lain awake, pondering what was right for me to do. And it always comes to the same thing."

"What?"

"It's the old story," she answered, with a feeble smile. " 'I canna' leave my minnie.' There is nobody in the world to take care of Johanna but me, not even Elizabeth, who is engrossed in little Henry. If I left her, I am sure it would kill her. And she cannot come with me, dear!" (the only fond name she ever called him) "for these three years—you say it need only be three years—you will have to go back to India alone!"

Robert Lyon was a very good man; but he was only a man, not an angel; and though he made comparatively little show of it, he was a man very deeply in love. With that jealous tenacity over his treasure, hardly blameable, since the love is worth little which does not wish to have its object all to itself, he had, I am afraid, contemplated, not without pleasure, the carrying off of Hilary to his Indian home; and it had cost him something to propose that Johanna should go too. He was very fond of Johanna; still—

If I tell what followed, will it for ever lower Robert Lyon in the estimation of all readers? He said coldly, "As you please, Hilary," rose up, and never spoke another word till they reached home.

Mrs. Craik's last novel, *A Noble Life,* is by no means a happy effort. It has neither the interest nor the merit of an authorized biography. The original of the 'Earl of Cairnforth' is carefully photographed, and is accurate in every painful detail: this was unnecessary, and ought to have been impossible. The story, as a story, is too shadowy for analysis, and does not deserve the dignity of its two volumes, its broad margins, and large type. But *Christian's Mistake,* which preceded this, is a very beautiful story. The title is rather puzzling, and the *mistake* not very obvious. Christian is a young governess, the orphan child of an unworthy father, and she marries an elderly and respectable college don, a widower with two children, whom she does not love. Of course *this* is not the *mistake,* if it is anything it must be called by a stronger name. But the Master of St. Bede's not only knows that Christian does not love him, but knows from letters which have fallen into his hands before they were married, that she has felt a transient girlish affection for a worthless undergraduate. Again, that the Master did not return these letters was something much graver than a *mistake.* Ultimately, however, the sister of the Master's first wife suspects a previous intimacy with the undergraduate, and Christian has the satisfaction of an explanation with her husband. There must have been a *mistake* somewhere, but as we have said it is not obvious.

The author of *John Halifax* takes the unpromising material of this story, and it is pliant in her hands. She does not say that young girls should marry elderly men whom they do not love, but she sees this as a fact, and shows how a good man and a good woman would act, supposing they stood in this relation to each other. Dr. Grey does love his young wife, therefore he meets with no trials and no difficulties, and occupies a very subordinate place in the story. It is Christian whose life we follow with the keenest interest. She has great respect for her husband, and is very grateful for his kindness to her, but neither respect nor gratitude guides her; it is *duty* which is her watchword. She has undertaken the duties of wife and step-mother, and resolves to fulfil them righteously. We follow with increasing interest the still calm figure of the young wife, who bears so patiently all the discomforts of her new home. She has to suffer insolence from servants, insolence from the children, insolence from the sister of her husband's first wife, and to bear with a very exasperating habit of the Master's, that of reading at meals. But she endures to the end, and so finds with duty love, love awakened in herself, and called forth towards her from those whom she serves so faithfully. It would seem impossible to love the children—who are only interesting in so far as they are disagreeable, and yet they are gradually brought under the sweet influence of the young mother-in-law. The following extracts show some of the difficulties which she had to encounter:—

> She took no notice of what was said, but merely desired the little girl to bring pillows and a footstool, so that she could hold Arthur as easily as possible till the doctor came. And then she bade her take off the diamond bracelets and the hanging laces, and told her where to put all this finery away; which Letitia accomplished with aptitude and neatness.
>
> "There, that will do. Thank you, my dear. You

are a tidy little girl. Will you come and give me a kiss?"

Letitia obeyed, though with some hesitation, and then came and stood by her step-mother, watching her intently. At last she said,

"You are crumpling your pretty white silk dress. Won't that vex you very much?"

"Not very much, if it cannot be helped."

"That is odd. I thought you liked fine clothes, and married papa that he might give you them. Phillis said so."

"Phillis was mistaken."

More than that Christian did not answer; indeed, she hardly took in what the child said, being fully engrossed with her charge.

Letitia spoke again.

"Are you really sorry for Atty? Aunt Henrietta said you did not care for any of us."

"Not care for any of you!" And almost as if it were a real mother's heart, Christian felt hers yearn over the poor pale face, growing every minute more ghastly.

"I wonder where papa can be, Letitia! Go and look for him. Tell him to send Barker for the doctor at once."

And then she gave her whole attention to Arthur, forgetting everything except that she had taken upon herself towards these children, all the duties and anxieties of motherhood. How many—perhaps none—would she ever win of its joys? But to women like her, duty alone constitutes happiness.

. . . . .

"Titia," said Dr. Grey, with sudden energy, as if the thought had been brewing in his mind for many minutes, "is there not a piano in the drawing-room? There used to be."

"Yes, and I practise upon it two hours every day," answered Letitia, with dignity. "But afterwards Aunt Henrietta locks it up and takes the key. She says it is poor mamma's piano, and nobody is to play upon it but me."

As the child said this in a tone so like Aunt Henrietta's, her father looked—as Christian had only seen him look once or twice before, and thought there might be circumstances under which anybody displeasing him would be considerably afraid of Dr. Arnold Grey.

"Did you know of this, Christian?"

"Yes," she answered, very softly, with a glance, half warning, half entreating, round upon the children. "But we will not say anything about it; I never did, and I had rather not do so now."

"I understand. We will speak of it another time."

But he did not; neither that night, nor for several days; and Christian felt only too thankful for his silence.

Sometimes, when after ringing at intervals of five minutes for some trifling thing, Barker had sent up "Miss Gascoigne's compliments, and the servants couldn't be spared to wait up-stairs;" or the cook had apologised for deficiencies in Arthur's dinners, by "Miss Gascoigne wanted it for lunch," and especially, when to her various messages to the nursery no answer was ever returned—sometimes, it had occurred to Christian—gentle as she was, and too fully engrossed to notice small things—that this was not exactly the position Dr. Grey's wife ought to hold in his—and her—own house. Still she said nothing. She trusted to time and patience. And she had such a dread of domestic war, of a family divided against itself.

Great care has been bestowed on the three women who are alone prominent in this story, Miss Grey, Miss Gascoigne, and Christian. Miss Gascoigne, sister of the first wife, is second only in interest to Christian, and is cleverly but very imperfectly sketched. Like the children, she is excessively disagreeable; still, the author assures us that—

> It may seem an odd thing to assert, and a more difficult thing still to prove, but Miss Gascoigne was not at heart a bad woman. She had a fierce temper and an enormous egotism, yet these two qualities, in the strangely composite characters that one meets with in life, are not incompatible with many good qualities.

. . . . .

Miss Gascoigne was not a bad woman, only an utterly mistaken and misguided one. She meant no harm—very few people do deliberately mean harm—they only do it. She had set herself against her brother-in-law's marriage—not in the abstract, she was scarcely so wicked and foolish as that; but against his marrying this particular woman. Partly because Christian was only a governess, with somewhat painful antecedents, one who could neither bring money, rank, nor position to Dr. Grey and his family, but chiefly because it had wounded her self-love that she, Miss Gascoigne, had not been consulted, and had had no hand in bringing about the marriage.

Therefore she had determined to see it, and all concerning it, in the very worst light; to modify nothing, to excuse nothing. She had made up her mind that things were to be so-and-so, and so-and-so they must of necessity turn out. *Audi alteram partem* was an idea that never occurred, never had occurred, in all her life, to Henrietta Gascoigne. In fact, she would never have believed there could be "another side," since she herself was not able to behold it.

We must add the last sentences of this book, because they are the key, not only to this story, but to every story by the author of **John Halifax.** 'At last this hope had quite to be let go, and its substitute accepted—as we most of us have, more or less, to accept the will of Heaven, instead of our will, and go on our way resignedly, nay cheerfully, knowing that, whether we see it or not, all is well.'

Looking back, as we are now able to do, we find that this author has insight only through her sympathy, and that this fact accounts at once for her strength and weakness. She cannot paint enthusiasm, she does not seek strength or height of character, but she looks for goodness. She knows a good woman through and through, but other women from the outside only. It is not that she understands all women and no men, for she cannot delineate the internal life of all women. Lady Caroline Brithwood in *John Halifax,* is a complete failure. Miss Gascoigne is rather a clever sketch than a finished picture. At the same time her sympathy with a good man is complete on the moral, but defective on the intellectual side, and this deficiency is felt more in men than in women, because we need to feel the intellect of a man in whom we take any sustained interest. An accurate delineation of children needs also intellectual insight as well as sympathy; they are in a stage of growth and transition, and the physical and intellectual preponderate. Aaron and Eppie in *Silas Marner,* Ninna and Lillo in *Romola,* are the perfection of children, round, soft, loveable realities. Goodness in a loveable child is latent rather than developed, and it is certainly not the only attraction of childhood. But Mrs. Craik must find that or nothing in children. The disagreeable Atty and Titia are, therefore, spiteful, ill-natured grown people on a small scale, and the children whom she depicts are such in virtue only of their using baby-talk.

An excerpt from *John Halifax, Gentleman*

Jael brought him in; Jael, the only womankind we ever had about us, and who, save to me when I happened to be very ill, certainly gave no indication of her sex in its softness and tenderness. There had evidently been wrath in the kitchen. "Phineas, the lad ha' got his dinner, and you mustn't keep 'un long. I bean't going to let you knock yourself up with looking after a beggar-boy."

A beggar-boy! the idea seemed so ludicrous that I could not help smiling at it as I regarded him. He had washed his face and combed out his fair curls; though his clothes were threadbare, all but ragged, they were not unclean; and there was a rosy, healthy freshness in his tanned skin, which showed he loved and delighted in what poor folks generally abominate—water. And, now the sickness of hunger had gone from his face, the lad, if not actually what our scriptural Saxon terms "well-favored," was certainly "well-liking." A beggar-boy, indeed! I hoped he had not heard Jael's remark. But he had.

"Madam," said he, with a bow of perfect good-humor, and even some sly drollery, "you mistake; I never begged in my life. I am a person of independent property, which consists of my head and my two hands, out of which I hope to realize a large capital some day."

Dinah Mulock Craik, in her John Halifax, Gentleman, *A. L. Burt Co., 1856.*

This lady lacks the deep and full insight of George Eliot; lacks even the knowledge of the outside look of all ordinary characters, which distinguishes so many novelists of only average ability. In language she has no wealth of poetical imagery; her views are neither broad nor profound, she has no wide field of vision, and the depths of spiritual struggle are unknown to her; but she looks high into the pure heavens, and points always upwards and onwards. All her charm and all her power lie in this marvellous purity of moral tone. There is no trifling with sin, no extenuating or making light of it. Right may be painful, it may entail suffering and self-denial, but it must be done. Wrong must be avoided. The petty meannesses and falsehoods of society, and its general insincerity, she never for a moment tolerates or condones. Her good men and women are absolutely honest and truthful to their superiors, their equals, and their inferiors. Surely we have a right to say that such teaching has at the present time an almost inestimable value, and that the 'Author of *John Halifax*' is doing good service both in her generation and for all time. (pp. 37-58)

> *"The Author of* John Halifax," *in* The British Quarterly Review, *Vol. XLIV, No. 77, July, 1866, pp. 32-58.*

S. M. Ellis (essay date 1926)

[*Below, Ellis provides an overview of Craik's life and literary career, centering on her most famous novel,* John Halifax, Gentleman.]

The birth centenaries of the notable Victorians arrive frequently now. That of Dinah Mulock occurs this month. She, like R. D. Blackmore, is remembered as the writer of one book, though the author of many others of varying merit. It is a matter of opinion whether *Lorna Doone* is really Blackmore's best work; certainly *Springhaven* and *The Maid of Sker* are on the same plane of excellence. But *John Halifax, Gentleman* far surpasses the twenty or so other novels written by Miss Mulock. That book won, and holds deservedly, a special place for its author in the vast gallery of Victorian literature, a place just below the line of her great female contemporaries, Charlotte and Emily Brontë, George Eliot, and Mrs. Gaskell. To the last-named she most nearly approximates—the Mrs. Gaskell of *Mary Barton* and *North and South;* for that writer soared higher with *Cranford* and *Sylvia's Lovers*—the exquisite story which has given to Whitby for all time an association of sorrowful romance.

Dinah Maria Mulock was a native of the Pottery district in Staffordshire, though she was of Irish descent on the paternal side—a member of the Mulock family of Kilnagarna, Co. West Meath. Her father, Thomas Samuel Mulock, was born near Killiney Bay, Co. Dublin, in 1789.

Thomas Mulock was an extraordinary person, a shiftless, irascible and talented Irishman of stage type, a figure that might have been limned in the pages of Charles Lever. As a young man of twenty-three, about 1812, he started in business at Liverpool with a partner named Blood. Four years later he was well known as a frequent writer to the press, a vigorous public speaker, a violent Tory and supporter of Canning, and as a distinctly eccentric character.

His attacks in *The Courier* upon the Liberals caused his opponents to term him "Bloody Moloch" in pleasing allusion to the joint name of his commercial firm. In 1817 he retired from business in order to devote himself to literary pursuits of a serious nature, for religious mania had already taken possession of his mind. He went to Oxford and matriculated at Magdalen Hall. In 1819 he issued a pamphlet entitled "An Answer given by the Gospel to the Atheism of All the Ages," in which there was some praise of Byron's poetry. He later wrote to Byron, who mentions him as "Muley Moloch" in letters to John Murray and Thomas Moore (March 1st and December 9th, 1820): "He wrote to me several letters upon Christianity to convert me. . . . I thought there was something of wild talent in him, mixed with a due leaven of absurdity." Thomas Moore came across Mulock personally this same year (1820) at Paris, and attended a series of lectures on English literature given there by him.

A year or two later Mulock is found at Stoke-upon-Trent, Staffordshire, where he preached at a chapel (still existing) in Thomas Street. He resided in one of two cottages called Longfield at Hartshill, midway between Newcastle-under-Lyme and Stoke-upon-Trent. At the adjoining and larger cottage lived Mrs. Mellard (widow of Thomas Mellard, a prosperous tanner of Newcastle) and her two daughters, Mary and Dinah. So it came about that Thomas Mulock married his neighbour, Miss Dinah Mellard (a young woman of thirty-one), in June, 1825; and as they continued to reside in this Hartshill cottage, Longfield, here was born their eldest child and only daughter, Dinah Maria Mulock, on April 20th, 1826. Two sons, Thomas Mellard Mulock and Benjamin Robert Mulock, followed respectively in 1827 and 1829.

In 1831 the Mulocks removed to Newcastle-under-Lyme, living first in Lower Street and later at a house now known as No. 7, Mount Pleasant. The daughter Dinah was educated at Brampton House Academy, one of the first buildings to be erected on the large public field of Newcastle called The Marsh. Dinah Mulock was a clever child and soon mastered the curriculum of what was in those days considered sufficient knowledge for a girl in a provincial town. At the age of ten she wrote some verses entitled **"The Party of Cats"**; and by the time she was thirteen she was helping her mother in the management of a small school, where Dinah taught a class of junior boys. A leading solicitor in Hanley, in later years, used to recall how as a boy he received his elementary Latin lessons from the little girl who was in the future to be famous as the author of *John Halifax, Gentleman.*

Memories of Miss Mulock's early life in the Potteries can be found in several of her books. Her birthplace, Hartshill, is the scene of **"The Italian's Daughter"**—a story in the volume entitled *Avillion and other Tales* (1853)—and here is pictured the region of the Five Towns when there were still intervening rural spaces as yet undevoured by the octopus of commerce. In *Stories from Life* (1861) there are interesting pictures of Newcastle-under-Lyme as it was in the author's girlhood, including an account of the old custom of Clouting-Out Day on November 9th; and in *Olive* (1850) Newcastle is described as Oldchurch:

There was a curious fascination about Oldchurch. She never forgot it. The two great wide streets, High Street and Butcher Row, intersecting one another in the form of a cross; the two churches—the Old Church, gloomy and Norman, with its ghostly graveyard. . . . Those strange furnace fires, which rose up at dusk from the earth and gleamed all around the horizon, like red, fiery eyes open all night long, how mysteriously did they haunt the imaginative child.

The great joy of the Mulock children was to visit their maternal grandmother, Mrs. Mellard, who had removed from Hartshill to "The Big Haise" (house) at Bucknall, whither they used to drive from Newcastle in a quaint sort of carriage or jaunting-car, which was covered in by curtains drawn over a brass frame. The fruit orchard at "The Big Haise" was naturally an attraction to the children, and years later Dinah pictured these early scenes in her poem, **"The Shaking of the Pear Tree,"** which also again expressed the fascination of the furnace fires of the Potteries glowering luridly at night:

The children's homeward silence,
The furnace fires that glowed,
Each mile or so, out-streaming
Across the lonely road.

In 1839 old Mrs. Mellard died at Bucknall, and some share of her money naturally passed to her daughter, Mrs. Mulock. The egregious Thomas Mulock, who was never reluctant to avail himself of the hospitality of other people's banking accounts, accordingly resolved to remove himself and his family to London where, Micawber-like, they roved from one set of apartments to another. In the autumn of 1840 Dinah Mulock writes from 14, Earl's Court Terrace, Brompton; in February, 1843, they were at 14, Chatham Place, near Blackfriars Bridge, the very same house, it is interesting to note, which was later occupied by Dante Gabriel Rossetti from 1852 to 1862, and where his wife came by her tragic death. After a visit to Ramsgate in September, 1843, the Mulocks took up their abode at 8, Southampton Row, where Thomas Mulock deigned to carry on for a time the work of resident manager and secretary of "The Institution for Assisting Heirs-at-Law."

In the meanwhile Dinah Mulock had her first publication in the form of a poem on the birth of the Princess Royal, which appeared in *The Staffordshire Advertiser* on January 16th, 1841. She studied French, Latin, Italian, and Greek, and learned Irish from her father's friend, Thaddeus Connellan. She had drawing lessons at the Government School of Design at Somerset House, and she enjoyed hearing Adelaide Kemble sing in "Norma" at Covent Garden. "The music haunted me," she wrote, "for days and days, until I had some of the duets, and then I go and sing them with Maria Knowles (Sheridan Knowles's daughter)." But this was a trying time for the young girl of sixteen. Both her mother and her brother Thomas were in very delicate health. At last Dinah decided to part company with the impossible father. She took her mother back to Staffordshire in 1844, where they stayed at Barton and Lysways Hall. She stated: "We had a delightful country visit; the neighbourhood about Lichfield is certainly the prettiest part of Staffordshire, and very proud I was of my own dear county, which I never saw in its full beauty before." Mrs. Mulock died in 1845 and her elder son Thomas was accidentally killed in 1847. Dinah henceforth looked after her only surviving younger brother, Benjamin, and the father passed out of their lives, caring nothing what became of them. Thomas Mulock made no provision at all for his children, and they were dependent on the small income accruing from their grandmother's estate and what they would be able to earn.

Old Thomas Mulock went off to Scotland, where in 1850 he seems to have been editor of *The Inverness Advertiser.* In 1855 he was back at Newcastle-under-Lyme, participating in all kinds of disputes and quarrels, including an indictment, in his best Micawber style, of his former protégé, the Emperor Napoleon the Third. He was twice imprisoned for contempt of court, and finally and mercifully died, at Gothic House, Stafford, in 1869, at the age of eighty. In his last years his now celebrated daughter had contributed to his support, and she attended his funeral. Miss Mulock's forbearance towards an unsatisfactory father is almost comparable with the self-sacrifice and forgiveness Miss Mitford exercised in favour of her abominable old father.

We must return to 1848, and observe Dinah Mulock living with her young brother in an obscure street off Tottenham Court Road, and writing her first novel, *The Ogilvies,* published in 1849. This sad and tragic story was dedicated to the mother she had loved so well and lost. A portion of the book describes Lichfield. Mr. Hyde, the printer at Newcastle, stated: "Miss Mulock got a pretty good sum for a novel she wrote and which was very successful for a first work." *Olive,* which followed in 1850, was a distinct improvement in style, for it was not so exclamatory as *The Ogilvies.* Part of the scene of *Olive* is laid at Brompton, as Miss Mulock had known it in 1840, when it was mainly a district of market gardens and a few scattered houses occupied by artistic and theatrical people. Farther on there were open fields on the land now covered by the houses and squares of Earl's Court. *The Head of the Family, Agatha's Husband,* and some volumes of fairy and other tales, appeared between 1852 and 1857, though during these years Dinah Mulock was also writing her masterpiece, *John Halifax, Gentleman.*

Miss Mulock had by now made acquaintance with a circle of literary people. Clarence Dobell, brother of Sydney Dobell, the poet, first met her about 1851, and he said she was then well known as the author of *Olive,* though the book had appeared anonymously. Her friends included Alexander Macmillan, Mrs. Oliphant, Charles Edward Mudie (founder of the Select Library), Camilla Toulmin (Mrs. Newton Crosland), and John Westland Marston, the dramatist. To Marston's son, Philip Bourke Marston, the poet, born in 1850, Miss Mulock stood godmother, and her poem **"Philip, my King"** was addressed to him as a child:

> Look at me with thy large brown eyes, Philip my
>   King,
> Round whom the enshadowing purple lies
> Of babyhood's royal dignities; . . .

> A wreath not of gold, but palm: one day, Philip
>   my King,
> Thou too must tread, as we trod, a way
> Thorny and cruel and cold and grey. . . .

Philip Marston lost his sight at an early age, which probably suggested the idea of the blind child Muriel in *John Halifax, Gentleman.*

With increasing literary success Miss Mulock was able to take a little house in the north of London—12, Melville Terrace, Torriano Avenue, Camden Town. Mrs. Oliphant has described her in these years as a tall, slim girl, a writer with a recognised position, and generally surrounded by a bevy of admiring and ambitious young women. At Camden Town, she relates:

> Miss Mulock had a little house in a little street full of pretty things, with all her little court about her. . . . She was always the centre of an attached group, to which her kind eyes, full of the glamour of affection, attributed the highest gifts. They were all a little literary—artists, musicians, full of intellectual interests and aspirations, and taking a share in all the pleasant follies, as well as wisdom, of their day. . . . She sang sweetly, with great taste and feeling, knew a great many nice people, and fully enjoyed her modest youthful fame. [*Macmillan's Magazine,* December, 1887].

The "pleasant follies" included the fashionable interest in Spiritualism, and mild séances were held at 12, Melville Terrace.

In 1853 Dinah Mulock went on what proved to be a momentous visit to Detmore, the home of the Dobells at Charlton Kings, near Cheltenham. She was then about to commence writing *John Halifax, Gentleman,* and a chance expedition to Tewkesbury gave her the initial scenes for her great story. Mr. Clarence Dobell has related:

> In the summer of 1853 she one day drove over with me to see the quaint old town of Tewkesbury. Directly she saw the grand old Abbey and the mediæval houses of the High Street, she decided that this should form the background of her story, and, like a true artist, fell to work making mental sketches on the spot. A sudden shower drove us into one of the old covered alleys opposite the house, I believe, of the then Town Clerk of Tewkesbury, and while we stood there a bright-looking but ragged boy also took refuge at the mouth of the alley, and from the Town Clerk's window a little girl gazed with looks of sympathy at the ragged boy opposite. Presently the door opened, and the girl appeared on the steps and beckoned to the boy to take a piece of bread, exactly as the scene is described in the opening chapter of *John Halifax.* We had lunch at the Bell Inn, and explored the bowling-green, which also is minutely and accurately described, and the landlord's statement that the house had once been used by a tanner, and the smell of tan which filled the streets from a tanyard not far off, decided the trade which her hero was to follow.

In the book Tewkesbury is called "Norton Bury," and Cheltenham is "Coltham." The house which, in memory of her birthplace, Miss Mulock named "Longfield," in reality pictures very exactly the green, lush setting of Detmore, the Dobells' house, which stands above a wooded slope rising from meadow and stream. Miss Mulock also described Sydney Dobell's cottage (where he was then finishing *Balder*) at Amberley Hill, beyond Painswick and Stroud, for Amberley and its high Common is the "Enderley" of her story. Over thirty years later, when accepting a photograph of "Rose Cottage" from a local workman, Miss Mulock wrote: "It is strange, yet sweet, to me in my old age to think I have done some little good in any quarter."

So it came about that the setting of *John Halifax, Gentleman* was placed in one of the loveliest districts of England—that happy, richly coloured vale which lies protected, as in a vast amphitheatre, by the Cotswold and the Malvern Hills. Thirty-four years later, and a week or two before her sudden death, Miss Mulock (now Mrs. Craik) saw the fair scene again. In September, 1887, she once more visited Charlton Kings, and again she and Clarence Dobell went over to Tewkesbury and repeated their programme of that eventful day so long ago. They inspected the Abbey and lunched at the Bell Inn, where the landlady told them how hundreds of visitors, especially Americans, came to Tewkesbury to see the scenery of *John Halifax, Gentleman.* After her return home, Miss Mulock wrote to Clarence Dobell: "Our visit was truly happy, especially the bright day of Tewkesbury, where my heart was very full. . . . It wasn't *the book:* that I cared little about. It was the feeling of 34 years of faithful friendship through thick and thin."

John Halifax, Gentleman (1856) is undoubtedly a great and vivid story, with touches of genius here and there. The first twenty chapters are perhaps the best, for after John Halifax's marriage the domestic sentiment and pathos are rather over-stressed in the conventional way of that period of novel writing. The death of the child Muriel too much resembles that of Paul Dombey, who had died some nine years before. There are also some *bétises* in the story. The behaviour of Mr. Brithwood to John Halifax, and the unheroic way Halifax took his blow, are quite impossible. Both Brithwood and Lady Caroline are unreal puppets, like Miss Ingram and the rest of the amazingly insolent "aristocrats" who visit Thornfield Hall in *Jane Eyre*. It is clear that both Charlotte Brontë and Dinah Mulock drew this class of society from their imagination and not from actual knowledge or observation. But the earlier scenes of *John Halifax, Gentleman* in Tewkesbury are admirable, and seldom before or since has the spirit of a great friendship been so ably presented. Best of all is the chapter describing how the two boys go secretly to Cheltenham to see Mrs. Siddons act. The whole episode lives, and Miss Mulock was correct in her facts here, for Mrs. Siddons did appear at Cheltenham in the summer of 1798, the year of this part of the story.

John Halifax, Gentleman has gone through countless editions, and no doubt it brought a substantial sum to its author. In February, 1859, Dinah Mulock and her brother were able to move to a charming, old-fashioned house, surrounded by trees and with a large garden behind, called Wildwood, at North End, on the Golder's Hill side of Hampstead Heath. Here Miss Mulock entertained a good deal, and on one occasion Sydney Dobell and W. J. Linton met there. Miss Mulock was renowned locally for her good works. She had some covered-in shelves erected, outside her house, wherein loaves of bread were placed daily, with a notice requesting anyone in want to help himself. But of course the charity was soon abused and it had to be discontinued.

Dinah Mulock had hoped to "settle" at Wildwood for good, but sorrow still pursued her, and after the tragic death of her only surviving brother, who was killed by an accident in 1863, she no doubt found the situation lonely; in the summer of 1864 she disposed of the house to her fellow county-woman, Eliza Meteyard, who here wrote her *Life of Josiah Wedgwood* (1865).

At the age of thirty-nine Dinah Mulock was married, at Bath, on April 29th, 1865, to George Lillie Craik, a partner in the publishing firm of Macmillan. Her husband was eleven years her junior, but probably the mothering instinct was strong in her, for she had all her life been accustomed to look after her young brothers. She had no children of her own, but in 1872 she adopted a little girl, whom she named Dorothy, and the child accompanied Mrs. Craik when she revisited, in 1878, after an absence of thirty-three years, her birthplace, and Stoke-upon-Trent, Newcastle-under-Lyme, and Bucknall.

After their marriage Mr. and Mrs. Craik resided for a time at Chilchester Lodge, Beckenham, while their future home was being built. This was The Corner House, Shortlands, Bromley, and here Mrs. Craik lived from 1869 for the last eighteen years of her life. They were peaceful, happy years, with the society of many friends. Nearly every year she produced a new book, but she was never destined to touch again the high mark of *John Halifax, Gentleman.*

Mrs. Craik died very suddenly from heart disease on October 12th, 1887, the end she had long been prepared for and expected. All through her life she had been sensitive to the horror of death. It early found expression, in its particular terror to the mind of a child, in *Olive,* written when she herself was still quite young; and in several of her stories can be found a detailed description of a sudden death such as her own proved to be. Mrs. Craik was buried at Keston, in Kent, and Holman Hunt and John Morley were among the mourners. Mrs. Oliphant, who knew her well, pronounced Mrs. Craik to be "a good and pure woman, full of all tenderness and kindness, very loving and much beloved." There could be no finer epitaph. (pp. 1-5)

S. M. Ellis, "Dinah Maria Mulock (Mrs. Craik)," in The Bookman, *London, Vol. LXX, No. 415, April, 1926, pp. 1-5.*

Lucy Poate Stebbins (essay date 1946)

[*In the excerpt below, Stebbins assesses Craik's literary achievement, ranking her as the preeminent Victorian sentimentalist. The critic praises* John Halifax, Gentleman *as a historical chronicle, but dismisses the rest of her novels as puerile.*]

Sentimental novels are confined to no period and differ surprisingly little in treatment, subject, and style from one generation to another. They are properly domestic, although the marriage finale was less common in the last century than today, when the Sweet and Simple chronicles almost invariably close just this side of the altar. Among Victorian sentimentalists Dinah Maria Mulock Craik was preëminent in talent.

Her simple history accounts for the quality of her work. Her father was a handsome, eccentric Irishman who became a Baptist preacher and removed from one small charge to another, sometimes to none, so that her girlhood was insecure and she received little schooling but was herself a teacher at thirteen in a class managed by her mother. She grew up tall, slender—what the Victorians called "willowy"—a very pretty girl with a soulful gaze and the friendly manner appropriate to a minister's daughter. Like Eliza Lynn Linton, she yearned for London as the promised land. In 1840 the family moved to the metropolis and a few years later, Dinah, in her early twenties, had become the center of a literary and artistic group. To have an English version of the *salon* was every writing woman's ambition; the gatherings in Dinah Mulock's Hampstead cottage were as cheerful as they were second-rate. She was an excellent business woman and knew how to get the most money from her books; Mrs. Oliphant reported that Hurst the publisher used to turn pale when he spoke of Miss Mulock's bargaining powers. When she married it was into the business; her husband, the crippled Mr. Craik, ten years her junior, was a partner of her friend, Alexander Macmillan.

She loved children and adopted a little daughter, whom she named Dorothy—the gift of God. Mrs. Craik wrote touchingly sentimental poems on childhood as well as those two excellent and still much read juveniles, *The Adventures of a Brownie* (1872) and *The Little Lame Prince* (1875). As she grew older and her interest in her characters faded, she tried to replace her lost freshness by pious admonitions. In many ways the busy, kindly, saving woman remained a little girl; she had neither time nor inclination to study; Renan's *Life of Christ* horrified her into a decision that all she could do was blindly trust and hold fast the beliefs of childhood. Her trade was the writing of love stories, and she enjoyed the position she held in the respect of Evangelical wives and mothers. She built a fine house on the proceeds of her books, and, in spite of criticism, accepted a pension from the crown which she did not in the least need.

Her only important novel, *John Halifax, Gentleman* (1856), is the life story of a good man, to whom integrity, intelligence, and industry bring success. A certain breadth of view is shown in the realistic treatment of the second generation, who develop in opposition to the wishes of the parents but tend in maturity to return to the family pattern. Mrs. Craik liked the first-person narrative, a device which is successful only with the most skillful writers. The narrator of *John Halifax, Gentleman* is a crippled Quaker,

Dinah Mulock Craik in 1858.

Jonathan to the David of the knightly hero. John Halifax's innocent snobbery arises from his sole inheritance, a little New Testament inscribed with his father's name followed by the word *Gentleman.* This relic not unnaturally inspires him to shape his life after the Victorian ideal and become a Gentleman himself. The book is uncommonly interesting as a chronicle of the first half of the century. John Halifax is a tanner, a millowner, master of men, an innovator with machinery; he has vaccinated his children, stopped a run on the bank, ousted the wicked lord's candidate in a parliamentary election. He may seem too pious, too uxorious for modern taste; his virtues are Arthurian; he may be a British replica of the Prince Consort, but he deserves respect, even applause.

Mrs. Craik wrote many other novels, all of them very bad. Her first, *The Ogilvies* (1849) was a silly book; Mrs. Carlyle called it "full of love as an egg is of meat—old, high-flown romantic Circulating Library sort of Love." Yet Miss Mitford could be convinced that the author of this foolish tale was her adored Mrs. Browning. Twenty years later, *The Woman's Kingdom,* and thirty years later, *Young Mrs. Jardine,* were no less puerile. Mrs. Craik's own favorite, *A Life for a Life* (1859), was a preposterous hodgepodge of slaying, coincidence, fidelity, persecution, with an old Oedipus in the background, a ministerial father, apparently modeled on Mr. Brontë as he had been portrayed in the recently published biography of Charlotte Brontë. Mrs. Craik was also indebted to Charlotte Brontë for her small, plain, pale heroines and for her bold assertion that a woman might decently love before she knew her love returned, although she did not go to the Brontë length of permitting her heroine to confess her passion. Indeed her novels of contemporary life were hedged about with propriety; two brothers who had spent a summer in the same lodginghouse with twin sisters could not, without impertinence, inquire the girls' London address; even under harrowing anxiety a young man might not enter a young lady's sitting room without first summoning the landlady to chaperon him. Yet this wearisome etiquette is less annoying than Mrs. Craik's personal piety. We might forgive her characters their spiritual soliloquies and prayers, but we cannot forgive her own interpolations, her frequent reminders of "One" who sits above, her growing dependence on exhortation. In spite of her humbug, her effervescence and shallowness, *John Halifax, Gentleman* entitles her to fifth place among women novelists of the century, directly after the four great writers, Charlotte Brontë, Elizabeth Gaskell, George Eliot, and Mrs. Oliphant. (pp. 29-32)

> Lucy Poate Stebbins, *"A Ladies' Miscellany,"* in her A Victorian Album: Some Lady Novelists of the Period, *Columbia University Press, 1946, pp. 3-45.*

Robin Gilmour   (essay date 1973)

[*In the following excerpt, Gilmour examines* John Halifax, Gentleman *in the context of the self-help novel, a work championing "the values of achievement over those of birth and station," as exemplified by Samuel Smiles's* Self-Help *(1859). The critic contrasts Craik's uncritical celebration of John Halifax's success story with Charles Dickens's ironic portrayal of Pip's rise in* Great Expectations *(1861).*]

Self-help is one of the mainstream Victorian notions that has travelled least well into the twentieth century, and it is still associated in the popular mind with the more unpleasant aspects of Victorian life—with *laissez-faire* economics, with the cult of success and the worship of respectability, with hypocritical attempts on the part of middle-class propagandists to inculcate their own values and goals in the working population. There is of course some truth in the popular view, but I believe self-help deserves more sympathetic consideration than it sometimes gets, especially from those interested—as the student of the Victorian novel inevitably is—in the crucial and highly complex question of class in the Victorian Age.

The period (as everyone knows) saw the rise of the middle classes into political and social influence, and self-help was an essential part of their creed: it championed the values of achievement over those of birth and station, and as such was a weapon in their quarrel with the established order. (p. 71)

Self-help is usually associated with Samuel Smiles. He was not the earliest nor the only writer in the field, but he is certainly the most representative. His *Self-Help* (1859) was as popular and influential as it was, not because it said anything essentially new, but because it gave succinct and memorable expression to ideas already widely current in the mid-Victorian period. It has to be said at once that

Smiles is a repetitive and not very subtle thinker, and his works will never merit more than a footnote in the official histories of ideas; yet there is a sense in which he and others like him are valuable to us for that very reason. We catch in their more ephemeral writings a note which is sometimes missing from the enduring masterpieces—an echo from that evanescent context of social and moral assumptions which Lionel Trilling has called, in an apt phrase, 'a culture's hum and buzz of implication' [in his *The Liberal Imagination*]. In Smiles' case the hum comes from the engine-room of the Victorian period. His purpose in writing *Self-Help,* so he wrote in his *Autobiography,* was 'principally to illustrate and enforce the power of George Stephenson's great word—PERSEVERANCE'. (p. 72)

John Halifax, Gentleman can be seen as the classic self-help novel. It was written by Dinah Mulock, who later married George Lillie Craik. . . . *John Halifax, Gentleman* is an uncritical fictional celebration of a poor boy's rise in the world and, being fiction, it reveals many of the unconscious assumptions involved in such a rise. It was published in 1856, and although the action is set at the end of the eighteenth and beginning of the nineteenth century, it is a characteristically mid-Victorian work. This story of the orphan boy who rises from tanner's lad to prosperous mill-owner could only have been written, one feels, in the years after the Great Exhibition, the high noon of Victorian prosperity. The aggressive ring of the title, with its emphasis on the word 'Gentleman', suggests the self-assertive insecurity of the new Victorian middle class, conscious of their emergence into commercial prominence but uncertain of their precise place in the traditional hierarchy. Mrs Craik's treatment of this emergent type is entirely uncritical: there is no suggestion of irony in the quasi-religious solemnity with which she celebrates the moral and domestic pieties of the new middle class. In *John Halifax, Gentleman* we are unashamedly offered the hero as Victorian businessman and paterfamilias:

> . . . my eyes naturally sought the father as he stood among his boys, taller than any of them, and possessing far more than they that quality for which John Halifax had always been remarkable—dignity. True, Nature had favoured him beyond most men, giving him the stately, handsome presence, befitting middle age, throwing a kind of apostolic grace over the high, half-bald crown, and touching with a softened gray the still curly locks behind. But these were mere accidents; the true dignity lay in himself and his own personal character, independent of any exterior.

If John Halifax ends up as a commercial patriarch, he starts out as the archetypal self-help hero. Although he believes his father to have been 'a scholar and a gentleman' (ch 1), this hint of genteel birth is never proved and we learn that 'his pedigree began and ended with his own honest name' (ch 2). He is an orphan, alone in the world and uneducated—he is in his teens before he learns to write his own name. But he is the possessor of a 'firm, indomitable will' (ch 8), and he is quite prepared to pursue knowledge under difficulties. He educates himself and, like Smiles' great hero George Stephenson, spends his leisure time constructing models of the machines he is later to employ in his factory. He prospers in the tanner's yard, marries a 'lady'—Ursula March—and using her capital sets himself up as a mill-owner. When his landlord, Lord Luxmore, diverts the stream which powers the mill, John proves his independence and resourcefulness by installing steam machinery in his factory, and his prosperity steadily increases—even in the lean years, for John Halifax is too prudent to invest his capital in risky foreign speculations. In short, we are in the world of *Self-Help,* where character is destiny and God helps those who help themselves. 'I am what God made me,' John Halifax declares at the outset of his career, 'and what, with His blessing, I will make myself' (ch 14).

There are some interesting parallels between Mrs Craik's novel and *Great Expectations,* and . . . Pip's efforts to become a gentleman should be seen in the light of the Smilesian concept of 'self-culture' which is common to both novels. Like Pip, John Halifax feels ashamed of his 'ugly hands' and of his employment in manual labour, and his ambitions are similarly confused with a sexual motive: he wants to marry Ursula, although he knows that she is a 'gentlewoman' and he only a 'tradesman' (ch 15). His friends advise him to respect his station—as Joe and Biddy advise Pip—but he perseveres, marries Ursula, and becomes in time a landed proprietor; unlike Pip, he becomes a 'prosperous man' who 'drove daily to and from his mills, in as tasteful an equipage as any of the country gentry . . . ' (ch 29). The difference between the two novels lies in the attitude to success: whereas **John Halifax, Gentleman** is a laudatory celebration of a successful self-help career, Dickens sets out to explore the inner assumptions and contradictions which such a career of 'great expectations' involves, and there is a whole dimension of irony in his novel which is quite absent from Mrs Craik's.

Yet it is precisely this lack of irony in **John Halifax, Gentleman** which makes it interesting. Mrs Craik's very closeness to her subject, her uncritical relationship to the self-help idea, makes her novel a revealing document. When, towards the end, John Halifax starts to rehearse the story of his rise from humble origins, his son interrupts him with the comment, 'We are gentlefolks now' (ch 29); the hero's reply, 'We always were, my son', is quoted by Taine in his essay on 'Landed Proprietors and English Gentlemen' [in his *Notes on England,* 1872], and it illustrates perfectly the ambiguity surrounding the idea of the gentleman in self-help literature. For although Mrs Craik is here saying, with Smiles, that the poor man can become a gentleman, that what matters is independence and integrity and dignity, at the same time John Halifax is only secure in social status when he has *justified* himself by acquiring the symbols of hereditary class—the large estate, the county acquaintance, an aristocratic son-in-law, a carriage that is as 'tasteful . . . as any of the country gentry'. Moreover, these achievements figure in the novel as themselves the *reward* of a lifetime's self-help: success is measured in terms of a breakthrough into a rigid social hierarchy. The whole drift of the novel bears out the truth of Asa Briggs' observation that 'in the battle between the self-made man and the gentleman, the self-made man won in England only if he became a gentleman himself, or tried to turn his son into one' [*Victorian People,* 1965].

This battle was not only fought out on the Victorian social front; it also took place in the minds and hearts of the Victorians themselves. The ambivalence in the self-help idea which I have examined in **John Halifax, Gentleman** was shared by Dickens for much of his creative life, and was only finally resolved in *Great Expectations.* The depth of perception and honesty of feeling in that late novel are the product of Dickens' imaginative mastery of the ambiguities involved in becoming a 'gentleman', and represent the culmination of a long process of debate in his art between the idea of the gentleman and the values of self-help and the self-made man. (pp. 77-80)

> *Robin Gilmour, "Dickens and the Self-Help Idea," in* The Victorians and Social Protest: A Symposium, *edited by J. Butt and I. F. Clarke, David & Charles, 1973, pp. 71-101.*

An excerpt from *John Halifax, Gentleman*

In front of the mill we found a considerable crowd; for the time being ripe, Mr. Halifax had made public the fact that he meant to work his looms by steam, the only way in which he could carry on the mill at all. The announcement had been received with great surprise and remarkable quietness, both by his own work-people and all along the Enderley valley. Still there was the usual amount of contemptuous scepticism, incident on any new experiment. Men were peering about the locked door of the engine-room with a surly curiosity; and one village oracle, to prove how impossible it was that such a thing as steam could work anything, had taken the trouble to light a fire in the yard and set thereon his wife's best tea-kettle, which, as she snatched angrily away, scalded him slightly, and caused him to limp away swearing, a painful illustration of the adage, that "a little knowledge is a dangerous thing."

"Make way, my good people," said Mr. Halifax; and he crossed the mill-yard, his wife on his arm, followed by an involuntary murmur of respect.

"He be a fine fellow, the master; he sticks at nothing," was the comment heard made upon him by one of his people, and probably it expressed the feeling of the rest. There are few things which give a man more power over his fellows than the thoroughly English quality of daring.

> *Dinah Mulock Craik, in her* John Halifax, Gentleman, *A. L. Burt Co., 1856.*

Elaine Showalter   (essay date 1975)

[*In the essay below, Showalter suggests that Craik's novels transcend sentimental conventions to present a veiled critique of the plight of Victorian women, a topic more directly faced by Craik in essays such as* A Woman's Thoughts about Women.]

The second wave of Victorian women novelists—Margaret Oliphant, Charlotte Yonge, Mrs. Henry Wood, Dinah M. Craik, et al.—is seldom taken seriously by literary scholars. Born between 1820 and 1840, these women consolidated the professional gains achieved by the first great generation of women novelists, the Brontës, Mrs. Gaskell, and George Eliot. These were the novelists with a purpose—self-disciplined and steadily productive over many years, active in journalism as well as literature. Feminists have scorned them, too, for despite their conspicuous achievements in the literary marketplace, these novelists generally opposed organized movements for women's rights and stressed an individualistic need for personal strength. Once the onus of authorship was overlooked, their lives were exemplary; and even when their life experience fell short of the Victorian feminine ideal, their novels celebrated the domestic, the bourgeois, and the conventional.

Yet modern literary criticism, with the aid of psychoanalysis and sociology, has uncovered a dark complexity in many Victorian classics once thought to be just as conventional, innocent, and artless. Perhaps the disguises these women novelists assumed in order to conciliate as well as to conceal have worked too well. The ideal of the Victorian woman, with regard to her sexual anesthesia, her religiosity, her passivity, and her domesticity, was patently dysfunctional, and the Victorians knew it. Women were forced to devise strategies of adjustment to a role that everyone, including themselves, tacitly acknowledged to be unreal. The woman's domestic novel was one element of this strategy. Both an expression of the conflicts in the female role and an escape valve for the emotions it left unresolved, the novel written by women and for women had a special, extraliterary function. Misled by the public antifeminism of many female novelists, scholars have ignored the deeper content of the books, and the devices by which sentimental narratives articulated female conflict about achievement and affiliation.

Ann Douglas Wood's analysis of this paradox among American sentimental novelists applies with equal accuracy to their English counterparts:

> The Sentimentalists were out to exploit the world in which they lived. On the one hand, they spouted, and probably consciously subscribed to, the trite messages and themes society dictated as their portion, but, more importantly, because they genuinely wanted places in their society, no matter how critical of it outwardly or inwardly they might be. Yet, on the other hand, since their society was significantly less eager to have them, as women, in positions of power than they were to be there, in order to obtain their goals they were forced into the ways of subversion and into a position, no matter how camouflaged, of opposition ["The Literature of Impoverishment: The Women Local Colorists in America, 1865-1914," *Women's Studies* 1, 1972].

Women writers expected their readers to understand these covert messages, but not to betray them; in a telling analogy in *The Daughters of England,* Mrs. Ellis, an arch conservative, insisted on a basic trust between women which amounted to sexual solidarity:

> What should we think of a community of slaves, who betrayed each other's interest? of a little band of shipwrecked mariners upon a friendless shore who were false to each other? of the inhabitants of a defenceless nation, who would not unite together in earnestness and good faith, against a common enemy?

Undoubtedly Mrs. Ellis would have been shocked if a reader had pursued these comparisons to their logical ends and inquired whether women were slaves, and whether their common enemy was patriarchy; but the sense of defenseless unity created a special relationship between the female novelists and their female readers. In looking at the career and works of one of these novelists, Dinah Mulock Craik (1826-1887), we can see how her personal struggles as a professional woman were transformed into a literature that created a bond, even a kind of genteel conspiracy, between novelist and audience.

A hard truth that Victorian women writers learned was that "authoress" was a term and a category capacious enough to accommodate them all, whether they were artists or hacks, evangelicals or sensationalists. Inevitably even the most flattering critics would disclose that they had special standards for women writers, standards which the most exacting and gifted found exasperatingly low. When a French critic in 1860 compared George Eliot to Dinah Mulock, Eliot was not amused, and complained indignantly to a friend that "the most ignorant journalist in England would hardly think of calling me a rival of Miss Mulock—a writer who is read only by novel-readers, pure and simple, never by people of high culture. A very excellent woman she is, I believe, but we belong to an entirely different order of writers" [*The George Eliot Letters,* edited by Gordon Haight, 1954].

Eliot's annoyance came, very naturally, from the reminder that in the eyes of male critics the intellectual differences between her books and those of lesser talents were canceled out by the fact of their shared womanhood. In her efforts to meet, and to set, a high standard of female literary professionalism, Eliot scorned less learned and weighty novelists who spoke to an audience that would not read German philosophy or Greek tragedy. In fact, Dinah Mulock Craik excelled at the peculiar combination of didacticism and subversive feminism, which at much more developed levels of intellect, characterized the novels of Charlotte Brontë and George Eliot. A literary celebrity of her day, she was a prolific writer who published fifty-two books. The most celebrated of these, ***John Halifax, Gentleman,*** is still in print in England. Despite Eliot's condescension, and despite posterity's indifference, Craik was both influential and representative; and it is chiefly because she wrote for "novel-readers, pure and simple," the mass middle-class audience, that she makes an appropriate case study in Victorian female authorship.

While she received praise from "people of high culture," including R. H. Hutton and Henry James, the male literary establishment was neither the audience Craik intended to reach nor the audience that supported her. Much of her popularity with women readers came from her understanding and expression of the Victorian female dilemma: the plight of the unmarried woman. Unmarried herself until her thirty-eighth year, she experienced the struggles of the single, working woman in a society designed for married idle women, and she made this experience the emotional center of a series of novels and stories dealing with female vocational energies, alternative life styles, and even, in Victorian guise, sexual frustration. Sore maiden hearts, troubled by stern advice of "compulsory wifehood in Australia" or "voluntary watchmaking at home" [*A Woman's Thoughts About Women*], were sustained by her fantasies of earthly or heavenly rewards and cheered by practical advice; while matrons and debutantes were alternately flattered and challenged by her idealization of the domestic role. After her marriage in 1864, she changed the emphasis of her fiction to more conventional subjects: the satisfactions of matrimony, power struggles in the family, and the reform of puritan laws like the one forbidding marriage to a deceased wife's sister.

Throughout her career, Craik specialized in tales of women's suffering and endurance. In her novels a typical plot features a plain, intense heroine locked in adoring bondage to a benevolently despotic father, whose morbid scruples somehow interfere with her marriage to even a suitably paternal prospect. If the father gives his consent, the fiance has scruples. In *The Head of the Family,* Hope Ansted's lover must give her up because of his duty to support and educate his brothers and sisters. In the more sensational *A Life for a Life,* Dora Johnston's fiance imagines he has accidentally killed her brother. In *Agatha's Husband* and *Christian's Mistake,* Agatha and Christian manage to get married, but then must cope with the inexplicable coldness of their husbands, both of whom, it turns out, are worrying that their wives really love other men. It is not easy to get married in Craik's world; the psychic stress her heroines sustain before they are rewarded with matrimony seems disproportionate to the gain. As one contemporary reader noted:

> *The Head of the Family,* by Miss Mulock, has some merits, but there is too much affliction and misery and frenzy. The heroine is one of those creatures now so common (in novels) who remind me of a poor bird that is tied to a stake (as was once the cruel sport of boys) to be shied at till it died. Only our gentle lady writers at the end of all untie the poor battered bird, and assure us that it is never the worse for all the blows it has had—nay, the better—and that now, with its broken wings and torn feathers and bruised body, it is going to be quite happy [Mrs. Austin, in a letter quoted in Amy Cruse's *The Victorians and Their Books,* 1935].

Today Craik is best known in the United States for a children's book, *The Little Lame Prince,* a melancholy fable that reflects many of her characteristic themes and images. The orphaned and crippled Prince Dolor is sent into exile by his wicked uncle, who pretends the child has died and takes over the kingdom of Nomansland. Imprisoned in a tower, cared for by a female convict, Prince Dolor nonetheless grows up remarkably sane, stoical, and kind. As with many of Craik's heroes, his dilemma seems feminine. Deprived of physical power, education, companionship, mobility, and a future, he accepts all these conditions as natural, and becomes gentle instead of bitter. His imprisonment is lightened by a fairy godmother, who gives him a "travelling cloak"—imagination. At last he is rescued

and restored to his kingdom, which by then he does not want but accepts with the same tranquil sweetness he has developed in exile. It does not seem too far-fetched to see this as an allegory of Craik herself—cast out of the happy kingdom of the family by her father's desertion, crippled by her female role, and finally redeemed through self-discipline and imagination. At the end of the story Craik interrupts the narrative to complain of her own tiredness, and to remind the reader that she has family responsibilities pulling her from her work.

It was well-known to her contemporaries that Craik, as one critic respectfully observed, had "been necessitated by circumstances to choose a vocation"; but few seem to have known the details of her alleged misfortune. According to the obituary notice by Margaret Oliphant in 1887, Craik, as a teenager, ran away with her sick mother and two younger brothers to escape the mistreatment of her father, and then labored to support them all by her pen. Only this tragic responsibility, according to Oliphant, had impelled her to seek publication, and, even so, her mother, "broken in spirit and in health," had died, and one of her brothers as well. The obituary calls up tender and inspiring pictures of the young Dinah "writing her pretty juvenile nonsense of love and lovers . . . to get bread for the boys and a little soup and wine for the invalid over whose deathbed she watched with impassioned love and care . . . " ["Mrs. Craik," *Macmillan's* 57, December 1887].

It was quite a story, but it was not exactly the truth. The truth was that Craik's father, an Irish evangelist whose eccentricities had been demonstrated by many domestic and professional peculiarities, culminating in several terms in the Newcastle County Asylum, moved his family from the Potteries to London in 1840, and then deserted the children when their mother died in 1845. Craik's life, and the lives of her younger brothers Tom and Ben, were suddenly and spectacularly changed by this demonstration of paternal irresponsibility. Despite Thomas Mulock's odd and marginally respectable career, the children had been raised as "ladies and gentlemen": the oldest son planned to become a painter, and had studied at the British Museum; Craik studied foreign languages, and went to balls. None of them was prepared for the change their father's desertion brought upon them. Although they had been left some money through their mother's estate, they could not inherit until they came of age, and Craik was only nineteen. Their trustee, Mr. Hyde, wrote that "after Mrs. Mulock's death in 1845, the children were left entirely destitute for a time until they could get into employment, as Mr. Mulock would have nothing to do with them, and refused to assist them in any way" [quoted in Aleyn Lyell Reade's *The Mellards and Their Descendants,* 1915].

Educated to believe in male superiority and male protection, Craik found herself the head of the family, forced to become financially independent. Her response to her new role demonstrated her essential strength; she survived the crisis, although it destroyed her brothers. Tom, who had planned to become a painter, enlisted in the navy and was killed in a fall from the mast his very first day at sea. (The father returned briefly, to claim the money that passed to him at his son's death.) The second brother, Ben, was permanently disoriented by the abrupt shift in roles and ex-pectations. He wandered aimlessly for years, trying one career after the next. Eventually he was committed to a lunatic asylum; he died in an escape attempt in 1863.

It is difficult to know why this story was suppressed in favor of the more flowery version. Perhaps it was simply the last triumph of sentimentalism over hard reality. Many female writers of the earlier generations needed ex-ternal events, usually financial or emotional disasters, to push them into print. Writing for money then became a heroic necessity, not merely an assertion of ego. As the century wore on, the stories of entering the profession be-came a genre in themselves. Perhaps, too, Craik wished to protect her own ego, feeling that her father's desertion might look like a judgment of her. Painfully insecure as an adolescent, she had felt unattractive and lonely; later she told young neighbors in Kent that she remembered evenings of weeping after dances where she had been a wallflower. Brought up to regard men as her superiors, the ambiguities of her new relationship to her brothers and her father were difficult for her to reconcile. On the one hand, there is some evidence that she blamed Mulock for her brother's death, and for her mother's death as well; in **Christian's Mistake,** to take one example, there is a refer-ence to a father whose life was so destructive that "the greatest blessing which could have happened to his daugh-ter was his death." Mrs. Oliphant's story, which makes Mulock's behavior sound even more melodramatically wicked than it was, is apparently the version Craik told her friends. But we need also to take note of the fact that as soon as she was making money, she contributed to her father's support. He came around for his handouts until his death in 1869.

This family situation, which would have provided rich material for Dickens or Gaskell, functioned primarily as a catalyst for Craik. It released and excused her creative drives, propelling her forcefully into a life and career for which her intellectual interests, her introspectiveness, and her discomforts with the female role had prepared her. While the beginning of her career was full of conflict, years of successful effort as a writer changed her; she came to accept the need to write as essential and primary, and when she married, in middle life, she continued to work in spite of her husband's objections.

Although she alternated between despair and exhilaration over her new independence, Craik slowly began to discov-er the satisfactions of self-reliance. In 1847 she came into her inheritance of £400. Her brother Ben went off to train as a civil engineer; and she boldly took lodgings by herself in Camden Town, then one of the poorer and less respect-able sections of London. (It is where Bob Crachit, in Dick-ens' *A Christmas Carol,* lives.) Writing poetry for *Cham-bers Journal,* and working on a novel, she began to make friends among the smaller fry of the London literary scene. Mrs. Oliphant met her at this time and remembered her as

> a tall young woman, with a slim pliant figure, and eyes that had a way of fixing the eye of her interlocutor in a manner which did not please my shy fastidiousness. It was embarrassing, as

if she meant to rend the other upon whom she gazed—a pretension which one resented. It was merely, no doubt, a fashion of what was the in-tense school of the time. But Dinah was always kind, enthusiastic, somewhat didactic and apt to teach, and much looked up to by her little band of young women [*Autobiography and Letters of Mrs. M. O. W. Oliphant,* edited by Mrs. Harry Coghill, 1899].

Although this account is colored by Mrs. Oliphant's envy and self-righteousness, it suggests that success gave Dinah confidence in her new role, and that she soon wished to instruct other women in the lessons she had learned. In her writings, she always stressed the need for practical training and self-discipline for girls: punctuality, accura-cy, account-keeping. "To be able to earn money, or failing that, to know how to keep it, and to use it wisely and well," she wrote in **About Money,** "is one of the greatest blessings that can happen to any woman." By 1850 she had earned £300 for the copyrights of her first two novels; and had begun to write a third. Some people thought she was writing too fast. " . . . Our nice little friend Miss Mulock is advertising another," Mrs. Gaskell wrote to Maria James in 1851. "I wish she had some other means of support besides writing. I think it bad in its effect upon her writing, which must be pumped up instead of bubbling out, and very bad for her health, poor girl. I heard of your kind way of occasionally taking her for a drive, and I si-lently thanked you for it" [*The Letters of Mrs. Gaskell,* ed-ited by J. A. V. Chapple and Arthur Pollard, 1966].

It was true that the pressures of maintaining steady pro-duction, under the system of outright sale of copyright, gave the woman novelist whose sole income came from her writing little time for art. Craik kept busy at the pump, turning to homeopathic doctors for remedies to keep her going. With her third novel, **The Head of the Family,** she had a popular success; the book went through six editions, and she began to pressure her publisher, Edward Chap-man, for better terms. When he resisted, she applied to Macmillan's for a regular job as a reader, which would have gotten her off the treadmill of steady production. But before taking the job she met a new publisher, Henry Blackett, at a party given by Mrs. Oliphant, and he made her a good offer for the novel which was to make her for-tune, **John Halifax, Gentleman.** Mrs. Oliphant never for-gave herself for having thus helped a rival to "make a spring . . . quite over my head;" the competition between women writers of this generation was as intense and ritual-ized as was their avoidance of competition with men.

After the publication of **John Halifax,** Craik's financial worries were over; she could afford to pick and choose among offers. Henry Blackett came to dread her business acumen. But in her letters, her essays, and especially in her novels, the pleasures of success and its lessons are counter-balanced, and often outweighed, by a recurrent lament for the life that might have been: the dependent life, the life of the angel in the house, the "safe negativeness," the "de-licious retirement," "the exquisite absorption of home" [**A Woman's Thoughts About Women**].

Paying lip service to the "safe negativeness" of domestic anonymity might be taken simply as a sign of shrewd flattery of one's readers, but in Dinah Mulock Craik's case it represented a genuine ambivalence. While we may not be surprised to discover that the novels she wrote in the fifteen years of her career preceding her marriage are all concerned with the role of the unmarried woman in society, we can wonder why this obsession was never noted by her contemporaries. She may have concealed her purpose so effectively behind a thick veil of Victorian morality that it went undetected; or perhaps her female readers sympathetically refrained from comment. She was not, of course, a crusader. She repeated the conventional theories that women were inferior to men in terms of power but had been given a great capability for exercising influence.

Many sophisticated male critics mocked her sentimental formulas for demonstrating female influence, formulas that depended on graphic and prolonged displays of stoical womanly suffering. The pre-Raphaelite artists Edward Burne-Jones and William de Morgan amused themselves by lampooning her popular martyred heroines, especially a blind girl named Muriel in *John Halifax, Gentleman:*

> "Yea, I
> Was 'Agatha's Husband's Wife,' an awful bore,
> A woeful and abominable bore."
> "And I was 'Mrs. Halifax, Lady!" cried another.
> And then a third and smaller one,
> "And I was Muriel in the self-same novel
> As she who last addressed thee." Then they all
> With one accord set up a mournful song,
> "Go tell Miss Mulock to ha' done, and make
> Night hideous with her bores no more."

Craik's female martyrs were overdone to the point of morbidity, as R. H. Hutton observed in a contemporary essay about her novels. The "suffering women live only for others," he objected; "the 'beautiful light' is always on their faces; their hands 'work spasmodically' at least once in every two or three chapters" ["Novels by the Authoress of *John Halifax,*" *North British Review* 29, 1858]. Henry James, too, laughed at the long line of crippled heroes and heroines in her books. "We might cite several examples," he wrote in 1866, "to illustrate that lively predilection for cripples and invalids by which she has always been distinguished; but we defer to this generous idiosyncrasy. It is no more than right that the sickly half of humanity should have its chronicler" [*A Noble Life, Notes and Reviews,* 1921]. But what was the sickly half of humanity? To Dinah Mulock Craik, it meant women—invalids, as doctors confidently claimed, by nature of their sex alone. Unmarried women were the cripples—thwarted in the only role which endowed their lives with meaning and weight; freaks in a society that had no use for them. In Craik's fiction unmarried women and their struggles are represented by afflicted characters of both sexes.

These terms may sound extreme, and so it may be helpful to look for a moment at the views of Craik's contemporaries. In an early essay on marriage and divorce, John Stuart Mill described the relentless single-mindedness with which society shaped its women for the marriage market, using the same physical imagery of disease that typifies Craik's writing about unmarried women: "A single woman therefore is felt both by herself and others as a kind of excrescence on the surface of society, having no function or office there" ["Early Essays on Marriage and Divorce," in *Essays on Sex Equality,* edited by Alice Rossi, 1970]. In addition to society's perception of them, single middle-class women internalized their role conflict and expressed it through a variety of forms of invalidism: either the adolescent crisis which constituted a refusal to accept adult womanhood and its limitations, or the passive resistance of total collapse and helplessness, or the chronic fatigue and lassitude of deep depression and frustration. In her essay "Cassandra," written in 1852, but suppressed at the advice of friends at Oxford, Florence Nightingale described the psychosomatic results of enforced passivity:

> What these suffer—even physically—from the want of such work no one can tell. The accumulation of nervous energy, which has had nothing to do during the day, makes them feel every night when they go to bed, as if they were going mad; and they are obliged to lie long in bed in the morning to let it evaporate and keep it down ["Cassandra," in Ray Strachey's *The Cause*].

After the census of 1851, England seemed indeed to be suffering a serious outbreak of spinsterdom. According to the population return, a full 30 percent of women over the age of twenty were unmarried, and another 13 percent were widowed. This meant a surplus in the population of 750,000 adult women without male protection, support, and guidance. The reasons for this sudden surplus—according to the excess of female infants surviving, the surplus doomed to "natural celibacy" should have been only 1 to 5 percent—were investigated by such social philosophers as W. R. Greg, who found the census figures deeply alarming, signifying a state of social devolution: "There is an enormous and increasing number of single women in the nation, a number quite disproportionate and quite abnormal; a number which, positively and relatively, is indicative of an unwholesome social state" [*Literary and Social Judgments,* 1873]. He surmised that emigration, the rising costs of a middle-class genteel "establishment," and male profligacy were chiefly to blame; men were evading their responsibilities to women and to England in a most outrageous way, patronizing prostitutes rather than settling down to virtuous (and expensive) monogamy; and at a last ditch, sailing for Australia or America unencumbered.

Much as he deplored such behavior, Greg had realistically to acknowledge the futility of preaching to men. Instead, he thought it sensible for women to take matters into their own hands—not by any unseemly or unwomanly independence, but by a more vigorous pursuit of husbands. To this end, Greg proposed that women should be shipped out to the colonies where they would be scarce and desirable commodities. His vision of the great spinster debarcation is unintentionally hilarious, and worked out with Swiftian logic. For not only must the women be deployed in modest numbers to ensure a perfectly ladylike accommodation; they must be chaperoned in the proportion of one to ten, so that they would arrive at Boston or Van Dieman's Land with unblemished characters. Therefore, much like the man going to Saint Ives in the nursery rhyme, Greg finally estimated that ten thousand vessels would be required to transport all the wives. There was, in fact, a Female Emigration Society, directed by Mrs. Caroline Chisholm, that functioned in much the way Greg described.

Mill was sympathetic, Greg benevolently indifferent to the feelings of the woman thus cavalierly to be packed for export. But the situation was real enough and, for a woman trying to define her life and make choices about her future, it was exceedingly painful. The term Greg uses for unmarried women—"redundant"—expressed all too accurately society's view of the spinster. What is less often understood is the way in which these women experienced themselves, and internalized or rejected society's view of them, and in this respect Dinah Craik was to excel.

If we want to discover the kind of solace the unmarried might expect from their married sisters, we can look at *The Afternoon of Unmarried Life,* a well-meaning handbook written by Mrs. A. J. Penny, and, wisely, published anonymously. Penny, who was in fact writing her book in indignant response to Craik's more radical text, *A Woman's Thoughts About Women* (which appeared the same year, but had been serialized first in *Chambers Magazine*) was a real Job's comforter. Smugly married herself, she threw up her hands at the spectacle of women writers' daring: "The old barriers of womanly reserve have been demolished more and more every year by works of fiction which owe at least the greater portion of their popularity to the amazing want of shade that distinguishes them; in these the feelings of women have been exposed, analyzed, and as I think, degraded, by the pens of women." Penny excuses herself for venturing out of the shade by pointing out the need to censure her unmarried countrywomen, and persuade them to "withdraw from public inspection those feelings which can only be directed happily in channels of private beneficence and quiet zeal."

Throughout her book, Penny tacitly assumes that singleness means misery, and advocates Christian resignation to "the dumb griefs of single life." Sublimation can be achieved through a determined effort at self-mortification; exploring the work options within the home in which she envisages her reader, a hapless dependent, Penny writes encouragingly, "There is always some unrelished occupation that may devolve upon a willing coadjutor; in default of every other, the dullest branch of family correspondence will often be gladly conceded." At best, there is heaven to look forward to, a celestial spa in which, Penny hints, God may relent and provide seraphic male companionship.

Dinah Mulock Craik allowed herself no such fantasies. Her program for single women was tidy, efficient, and practical. Through her fiction, like George Eliot, she tried to put women back in touch with their suffering, with their everyday tragedies. Through her essays, moreover, she presented them with a program of self-reliance and self-development, rational and thoroughly British. Eliot's heroine was Antigone; Craik worshipped Dick Whittington.

Craik's most thorough discussion of the redundant woman was *A Woman's Thoughts About Women.* With Charlotte Yonge's *Womankind,* this collection of essays

is the Holy Living and Holy Dying of Victorian Anglican Spinsterhood. On the very first page Craik made clear that she was not concerned with married women, who "have realized in greater or less degree the natural destiny of our sex," but with "the single women, belonging to those supernumerary ranks, which, political economists tell us, are yearly increasing." The book is a curious mixture of bitter personal experience, homely piety, and devotion to what Anna Jameson called "the communion of labour," as well as hard-headed advice, genuflection to the idols of male superiority, and democratic concern for women. The author was thirty-two years old; it seemed to her that she had been a "working woman all her life"; and in part the book gave her a chance to test her own theories on the consolations of that role.

Above all things, she recommended self-dependence. It did not come easily to women; ". . . from babyhood they are given to understand that helplessness is feminine and beautiful; helpfulness . . . unwomanly and ugly." Women's energies, she thought, were not concentrated on useful work, but were "devoted to the massacre of old Time." Her advice was brisk and bolstering: avoid false pride, get yourself educated and trained, don't worry about what men will say. She cited case histories of women who took over businesses, or started them. Since she was writing mainly for the middle class, Craik emphasized the professions; but she also discussed handicrafts, trades, and the plight of domestic servants and prostitutes. Her belief that "persistent, consecutive work" was the duty and the fulfillment of men and women alike, led her to develop embryonic theories of equal education for boys and girls and to advocate women's entrance into all the professions. "The exercise of every faculty, physical, moral and intellectual" was the guarantee of a full life for man or woman; *not* the possibility of marriage, delightful a prospect though that might appear.

Craik's views were neither radical nor particularly rosy. Her advice was heavily bolstered by a sense of Christian resignation, rather grim in its insistence that happiness was not really important. It revealed many polite prejudices (for example, warning respectable women against acting or singing careers), and it made heavy-handed jokes about the nonsense of women's rights. For these reasons, American feminists reading the book classed it with Mrs. Ellis's interminable prosings on the duties of the woman in all the roles of her life.

Yet Craik had enough imagination to see that while women could not depend on men to give them homes and to support them, they could, if they wished, depend on each other. When she thought of the single woman, she thought not only of the orphaned young lady, or the governess, or the authoress, but also of the cook, the housemaid, the seamstress—and the prostitute. In her chapter on "Female Servants," she insisted that the moral bonds of sisterhood should govern the relationship between employers and domestics:

> To say to these "ladies" that the "women" they
> employ are of the same feminine flesh and blood,
> would of course meet nominal assent. But to attempt to get them to carry out that truth practi-

cally—to own that they and their servants are of like passions and feelings, capable of similar elevation or deterioration of character, and amenable to the same moral laws—in fact, all "sisters" together, accountable both to themselves and to the other sex for the influence they mutually exercise over one another, would, I feel be held simply ridiculous.

Sisterhood meant that women should not send their maids on errands at night, nor forbid them to entertain "followers," nor dismiss them without a character reference if they became pregnant. Robed "in that strong inner purity which alone can make a woman brave" they could even venture forth to help the lost and fallen, indeed, they must. With her customary practicality, Craik suggests that respectable women could begin by finding jobs for the unchaste.

While *A Woman's Thoughts About Women* does not cater to the self-pity of the unmarried woman, neither does it avoid confronting the emotional issues of her life. Depression, anxiety, hypochondria, the realization of aging—Craik writes about them all. "It is a condition to which a single woman must make up her mind, that the close of her days will be more or less solitary." Yet the final chapter, "Growing Old," in which these melancholy subjects are most considered, is also the most optimistic and advanced part of the book. In middle age, Craik wrote, a woman is both less vulnerable and more independent. She presents fewer sharp angles "for the rough attrition of the world"; and she will "have learned to understand herself, mentally and bodily." Thus at peace with her regrets, she can begin to make full use of her abilities and define her role. Here Craik begins to reveal for the first time something of her pride, her suffering, and her peace, ending, perhaps, on a stronger note than she intended:

> Would that, instead of educating our young girls with the notion that they are to be wives or nothing— . . . we could instil into them the principle that, above and before all, they are to be *women,*—women, whose character is of their own making, and whose lot lies in their own hands. . . . Marriage ought always to be a question not of necessity, but choice. Every girl ought to be taught that a loveless union stamps upon her as foul dishonour as one of those connexions which omit the legal ceremony altogether; and that however pale, dreary, and toilsome a single life may be, unhappy married life must be tenfold worse—an ever-haunting temptation, an incurable regret, a torment from which there is no escape but death. There is many a bridal-chamber over which ought to be placed no other inscription than that well-known one over the gate of Dante's hell: "lasciate ogni speranza voi chi entrate." ["Abandon all hope ye who enter here."]

Chapman and Hall published the early novels in which she expressed these ideas and concepts more obliquely. "I have tried so hard to perfect the novel in every way," she wrote to Edward Chapman of *Olive.* "And now I can only say that there is not a sentence or line, which I thought could be improved—that I have not done to the best of my power" [in an unpublished letter dated 4 November 1850,

AM 17356, Morris L. Parrish Collection of Victorian Novelists, Princeton University Library]. She dedicated the novel to her mother—and in it we can see her conflicts as a female writer dramatized.

Olive Rothesay, the heroine of the book, is the first of Mulock's cripples. She suffers, we are told, from a spinal curvature so serious that she is a source of anguish and self-recrimination to her parents; yet the curvature is so slight that it can apparently be concealed by her flowing hair. From birth Olive brings sorrow to her family; her father rejects her mother and eventually her father's death leaves them penniless.

We are given to understand that Olive cannot hold any hopes of marriage; and thus she begins to consider painting as a profession. Craik is careful to give her heroine the most heart-rending and humble motives. First of all, she is not *ambitious,* for ambition implies self-love and egocentrism: "It was from no yearning after fame, no genius-led ambition, but from the mere desire of earning money, that Olive Rothesay first conceived the thought of becoming an artist." Then, Olive does not challenge male superiority, but accepts her sphere, the domination of the heart and affections. How she is to express these in her paintings is never made clear; but she is most appropriately led to a teacher whose contempt for women and whose wish to debase them coincides with her own self-hatred.

The teacher, Michael Van Brugh, is one of the many spokesmen in Craik's novels for patriarchal rule and female submission. With regard to Olive's artistic potential, he argues that "genius, the mighty one, scorns to exist in weak female nature; and even if it did, custom and education would certainly stunt its growth." Though he condescends to teach her, and even comes to regard her as "his cherished pupil—the child of his soul," her femaleness never ceases to be a source of regret to him. Meanwhile Olive drudges away. Because she is crippled, and thus unfit for marriage, she has a certain freedom to inflict further damage on herself; no one can really object to another spot on the garment already spoiled. This is Craik's justification for Olive's studies in anatomy, an area of study that she generally regarded as unwomanly. It is Olive's despair over her body that liberates her mind; "that sense of personal imperfection . . . gave her freedom." Add to this sense of being maimed her concept of her "sex's weakness and want of perseverance" and her artist's struggle against "a sense of utter unworthiness and self-contempt" and one must ask how such a destructive self-image could ever generate anything.

Yet there is a subcurrent of rebellion and anger in this novel. One notices first of all that the epigraphs and quotations scattered throughout are from Romantic poetry, *The Princess,* and even *The Revolt of Islam.* Olive's sense of inferiority is immense, but on the other hand she identifies through her lameness with the Romantic hero, the alien, the artist. If she is cut off from the satisfactions of the family, the plump comforts of an establishment, yet in her own domain—the heart and the affections—she can create an interior of magnificent richness. So, as she reads Shelley and Byron, she can cry out "I, too, am one of those outcasts; give me this inner life which atones for all! . . .

Woman as I am, I will dare all things—endure all things! Let me be an artist!"

Art is both the disease and the cure. In Olive Rothesay's world, art is unwomanly, but she sees around her everywhere women more helpless than herself, the victims of their husbands, fathers, and brothers. To be womanly—but unmarried—is to suffer. Van Brugh, her teacher, "from mere carelessness," Craik writes ironically, "had reduced the womankind about him to the condition of perfect slaves." His sister, Meliora, spends her whole life waiting on him. The other women fare no better. Olive's father, besides tormenting her mother (who eventually also goes blind), has a quadroon mistress, whose degraded life as "the white man's passing toy—cherished, wearied of, and spurned," fills Olive with gratitude for her own pure state. In contrast to such wasted lives, sacrificed to male selfishness, the Anglican sisterhoods seem tempting, and Craik explores the option of the convent with some enthusiasm.

Characteristically, the novel ends with Olive's marriage: "her clinging sweetness, her upward gaze" find an object, and she lays down her brushes with a grateful heart. Art gets short shrift when a more substantial means of support appears. Craik herself was not so changeable. Yet even in the ending the book reveals both her personal preoccupations and the tense ambiguities in the lives of female writers. The figure of the selfish and rejecting father is obvious enough; what is curious is that the teacher and the prospective husband are also selfish and stern. The male approval so inexplicably withheld by the father must be re-earned from father surrogates.

Olive is crippled first because she is a woman. (In later novels Craik did not reveal herself so crudely, and usually made the crippled character male, but the behavior and emotion of her invalids are always feminine.) Olive is further stigmatized because she is unmarried; and finally she is handicapped because she is an artist. The novel has similarities to *Aurora Leigh;* and the life of Elizabeth Barrett Browning affords one vivid proof of the psychosomatic power of the female artist's self-mistrust. Craik cared enough about writing to defy her husband when he made his long dreamed-of appearance; she worked until her death. Yet to be chosen by a man, to be publicly labeled as desirable, as normal, lovable, was as intense a wish for her as the wish to write.

This split consciousness was further explored in her most successful novel, *John Halifax, Gentleman.* There are two heroes in this novel: John, the orphaned tannery apprentice, who eventually rises through hard work and innate gentlemanliness to become an M.P., and the crippled narrator, Phineas Fletcher. Critics immediately declared that Phineas (like some of Charlotte Brontë's heroes) was a woman in disguise. "During the early part of the tale," R. M. Hutton chided, "it is difficult to suppress a fear that Phineas Finn will fall hopelessly in love with John Halifax, so hard is it to remember that Phineas is of the male sex. Afterwards, when he professes to be an uncle, the reader is aware constantly that he is really an aunt, and a curious perplexity is apt to arise in the mind on the subject." While Phineas—crippled, gentle, domestic—clearly had the at-

tributes of one kind of Victorian woman, critics did not notice that Halifax was also a projection of a different kind of female experience, much closer to Craik's own.

John Halifax occupies a peculiar place in the history of heroes of English fiction. Like Charlotte Yonge's Oxford Movement heroes, he represented to a generation the epitome of Christian gentlemanliness, a manliness stripped of all virility. Passion is depicted in this novel as violent action; male sexuality is symbolically represented through the energy with which Halifax fights floods, fires, and rioters. A later novel, Mrs. G. Linneaus Banks' *The Manchester Man,* copied the plot of *John Halifax* in precise detail, even to making the apprentice work for a tanner and setting the story in the days of the Peterloo Riots, and it too was successful. There were many to admire tales of such noble lives. Even Henry James, while deploring the awfulness of noble lives in general, smilingly declined to attack John Halifax; "He is infinite; he outlasts time; he is enshrined in a million innocent breasts; and before his awful perfection and his eternal durability we respectfully lower our lance."

But Craik's female contemporaries were more critical and detected in the novel both external pressures and inner hypocrisy. Mrs. Oliphant found the novel flimsy. George Eliot may have intended the relationship of Phillip Wakem and Tom Tulliver in *The Mill on the Floss* to repudiate Craik's sentimental portraits of Halifax and Fletcher; Robert Colby [in his *Fiction With a Purpose,* 1967] has suggested that Eliot's insistence that Tulliver was not "moulded on the spoony type of the Industrious Apprentice" refers to the pious Halifax. Whether Craik agreed, we cannot tell, but she disliked *Mill on the Floss,* and in a long (and anonymous) essay, she attacked its morality, claiming that Tulliver was a much nobler character than his sister Maggie.

The most perceptive comment came from Madame Mohl, the feminist friend of many female writers. She saw in the novel a basic economic hypocrisy; it is a success story in which the hero always insists he cares nothing about money. "The author wants to show her blame of the love of money and finery," she wrote, "and shows all the time the importance she attaches to it" [quoted in Cruse]. As I have shown, Dinah Mulock Craik needed money; more than anything she prided herself on her ability to earn a living, to be independent, and to support her brother. On the other hand, she was painfully aware of the unwomanly and aggressive aspects of her financial acumen. In her novel, Fletcher and Halifax represent the two sides of her self-image: the crippled looker-on at other people's happy marriages and lives, permanently disbarred from such joy; and the energetic, successful, and admired leader. In the creation of characters like John Halifax, Craik projected her own ambitions and struggles onto male heroes who could more appropriately embody her ideals. Like Halifax, Craik had to make her own way in the world. But unlike the upwardly mobile culture hero of Victorian fiction, the successful professional woman could never express open satisfaction with her achievements. It is interesting to see how the early Victorian women novelists project their wishes to be included in the establishment upon male figures. In Charlotte Brontë's first novel, *The Professor* (published posthumously in 1857), the male narrator, who has left England because of the humiliation inflicted upon him by the systems of class and patriarchy, can hardly wait to make enough money to return and send his son to Eton. Just as the Brontë girls instinctively chose to play male roles in their childhood fantasy games, so the Victorian women novelists expressed through their portraits of men the qualities within them which were beyond the boundaries of the feminine ideal.

At the same time, through the crippled Fletcher and other maimed male characters in her fiction, Craik expressed her sense of freakishness and abnormality. "Stricken with hereditary disease," Phineas says, "I ought never to seek to perpetuate it by marriage." Perhaps, too, the example of her father and brother made Craik fear for the stability of her own mind, and dread hereditary madness. But marriage and motherhood came to her in ways so sensational she would never have dared to use them in a novel. In 1864 the Midland Railway had an accident near her home in Hampstead, and George Lillie Craik, an editor of Macmillan's who had been injured in the accident, was taken to her home to recover. Proximity and mutual dependence led to love, and they were married in 1865. Their marriage seemed miraculous to her; her letters struggled to express rapture while maintaining decorum. Safe in the shelter of matrimony, she could even afford to make light of her long singleness:

> When people are happily married—they are so very happy! thank God—but I never alter my creed that a single woman may be perfectly happy in herself—if she chooses—and that the single life is far better than any but the very happiest married life. . . . It is an old joke against me that I never did properly appreciate the nobler sex!—I always like women best.—How lucky I was to find such an exceptional character as my own husband. One does not like to talk of such things—but oh—we are *so* happy! [in an unpublished letter, AM 17229, Morris L. Parrish Collection of Victorian Novelists, Princeton University Library]

The very fortuitiousness of the match made it especially blessed and seemly to her, for in all true marriages, she thought, now as in Eden, the man and the woman do not deliberately seek—but are brought to—each other.

Like other Victorian husbands, Mr. Craik wished his wife to give up her writing; but according to her biographer, "a childless wife could hardly agree for long to such a condition" [Reade]. In fact, her career provided them with the luxury of a house in Kent: "I build the house with *books,*" she wrote [quoted in W. M. Parker's introduction to the 1869 edition of *John Halifax, Gentleman*]. The stream of novels was uninterrupted, although the subject matter shifted, first to love stories, then to domestic-problem novels. Only motherhood was lacking—whether because of her age, or because of the extent of her husband's injuries, or their fears of hereditary insanity, is not known. But in January 1869, a baby girl was discovered lying half-frozen in the Hampstead snow. Mrs. Craik adopted her. Motherhood, she wrote soon after, "is twenty thousand times bet-

ter than writing novels." [quoted in Reade]. But she continued to write, and she also kept her Civil List pension—awarded to her in 1864 when, for the first time in her life, she did not need it. As Mrs. Oliphant tactfully argued in her obituary of Craik, the pension was the only public recognition given to English writers.

In the second half of her career, Mrs. Craik wrote several children's books. The novels concentrated on the joys of family life and the need for women to submit to their husbands. In *The Woman's Kingdom,* for example, she told how Edna, a plain, hardworking heroine, almost succumbed to despair before she married a kindly doctor. Memories of her own past are vivid in the description of "that morbid dread of the future—that bitter sense of helplessness and forlornness which all working women have at times" which fills Edna with "a strange momentary envy of the women who did not work, who had brothers and fathers to work for them, or at least to help them with the help that a man, and only a man, can give."

Craik's father had abandoned her. Her surviving brother, Ben, went mad, and died escaping from his asylum. Yet it never occurred to her to wonder at male weakness. Now that she had a man's help she was not about to see it mocked or threatened by a new generation of women less reverent of male authority and conjugal bliss. Like other women writers of her generation who had struggled along without male assistance—such as Margaret Oliphant, Elizabeth Lynn Linton—she believed in individual strength rather than group action. If women were weak, they could toughen themselves as she had done; if they suffered, they could steel their wills to endure. And if they wished, they could prevail and perhaps be rewarded in the end. Women had a duty to help each other; but they must never let loyalty to their own sex supersede obeisance to men. Just before her death Craik wrote to Oscar Wilde who, with his mother, was editing a woman's magazine:

> For myself, whatever influence I have is, I believe, because I have always kept aloof from any clique. I care little for Female Suffrage. I have given the widest berth to that set of women who are called, not unfairly, the Shrieking Sisterhood. Yet, I like women to be strong and brave—both for themselves, and as the helpers, not the slaves or foes, of men [in an unpublished letter, AM 17690, Morris L. Parrish Collection of Victorian Novelists, Princeton University Library].

This stubborn individualism, and refusal to understand women's suffering—her major theme—as a collective problem, did not take Dinah Craik far in analyzing the forces operating in her own life. Nonetheless, if we are to understand the women of the past, we must approach them within the framework of their own experience, and within the limits of their own psychological and political vocabularies. Craik's insistence that each woman was responsible for her own happiness or distress had affinities to the elitist ideology of will and self-discipline that characterized the careers of the pioneer female writers and reformers. But in many ways this ideology was the precondition of their success, the fuel which gave them the energy to compete in the face of educational disadvantage, parental discouragement, and institutional discrimination. Like religious heretics who challenged every particular of orthodoxy while clinging to membership in the church until the moment of excommunication, Victorian women often chopped away at all the branches of the patriarchal myth without questioning its basic truth. Faith in the general principle of male superiority and female inferiority might not have stood up to a severe questioning; but they did not question. As Caroline Norton wrote, in the midst of her fierce battles to get custody of her children away from her brutal and malicious husband, "I believe in the natural superiority of man, as I do in the existence of God." Perhaps such a statement of faith gave professional women a basic sense of security, of oneness with public opinion, which quieted some of the anxiety about their role and allowed them to work productively.

Harriet Taylor put this tendency in its harshest light when she attacked the female novelists of 1851 for hypocrisy in "disdaining the desire for equality or citizenship, and proclaiming their complete satisfaction with the place society assigns to them" ["The Enfranchisement of Women," in Rossi]. Taylor thought this was a case of "studied display of submission," designed to win "pardon and toleration" from men. I think it is unlikely that women consciously made the effort to appease, but obviously the pressures of the situation were intense. Even rebels like Charlotte Brontë were outraged at Taylor's accusations and felt that their mutual obligations as women had been violated by her crude outburst.

It is difficult to say how consciously Craik intended her oppressed heroines, her ambitious heroes, her cripples and invalids, to speak for the secret conflicts of her readers; but she did feel that women could both read between the lines of each other's books and refrain from betraying the messages that they deciphered. "The intricacies of female nature," she wrote, "are incomprehensible except to a woman; and any biographer of real womanly feeling, if even she discovered, would never dream of publishing them" ["Literary Ghouls: A Protest from the Other World," *Chamber's Journal,* 21 August 1858]. In looking at Victorian fiction, and the careers of the sentimentalists,

we should remember that the intricacies of female nature are often waiting there for our less reticent age to reveal. (pp. 5-21)

Elaine Showalter, "Dinah Mulock Craik and the Tactics of Sentiment: A Case Study in Victorian Female Authorship," in Feminist Studies, *Vol. 2, Nos. 2 & 3, 1975, pp. 5-23.*

Sally Mitchell   (essay date 1983)

[*Below, Mitchell describes the plot, characterization, and major themes of* John Halifax, Gentleman, *a work she asserts was intended as both a "celebration of British technology, industry, and commerce" and "a practical guide to virtue and prosperity." Mitchell maintains that the character of John Halifax serves as a model of exemplary behavior as well as a representative of the ascendance of England's middle class.*]

Craik distilled the ideals of the new commercial and industrial middle class in *John Halifax, Gentleman* (1856), the archetypal story of a poor boy who makes good through honesty, initiative, and hard work. The book echoed the mood of the 1851 Great Exhibition with its celebration of British technology, industry, and commerce. It was one of the first novels to have a tradesman as hero. It confirms the Protestant ethic by showing that the virtues that lead to heaven also bring success on earth. The book helped to overcome the resistance to fiction among nonconformists, who were in a majority among the artisans, shopkeepers, clerks, and small manufacturers of the expanding middle class. The exemplary life of John Halifax could be read both as a story and as a practical guide to virtue and prosperity.

When the book opens in 1794 John Halifax is a fourteen-year-old orphan who has been supporting himself as a farm laborer. The first words that he speaks are, "Sir, I want work; may I earn a penny?" Abel Fletcher, a Quaker tanner, pays John to help his invalid son Phineas back to the house. Phineas Fletcher, who is the book's narrator, immediately adores John's independence, gentleness, and good spirits.

John goes to work for Abel Fletcher in the least desirable tanyard job, driving a cart around to collect stinking animal hides. He lives in an attic, teaches himself to write and figure (Phineas supplies books, including *Robinson Crusoe* and *The Pilgrim's Progress*), and in his spare time makes models of machinery. Once he is literate, John is promoted to a more responsible position as clerk. He has enough initiative and forethought to keep watch on the tanyard one night during a flood; afterwards, since his action shows that he identifies with propertied interests, he is allowed to be Phineas Fletcher's friend as well as Abel Fletcher's employee. When there are food riots during the Napoleonic Wars, John Halifax saves his master's life from a hungry mob. Fletcher takes John as apprentice and promises to make him a partner when he turns twenty-one.

In the following summer John goes with Phineas to spend a month in the countryside near Enderley. Another invalid—a gentleman, Mr. March, a former governor in the West Indies—lodges in the other half of the cottage. John

---

falls in love with March's daughter Ursula. He also sees an old cloth mill and starts thinking about the machines he could devise to make the mill productive. Mr. March dies. John makes himself tactfully useful and earns Ursula's respect, but it is impossible for a tradesman's apprentice to court a gentleman's heiress. John falls ill and thinks about emigrating. However, Phineas goes to Ursula, who proves that she is self-sufficient enough to ignore convention and ask John Halifax to stay in England.

Ursula's trustee, Squire Brithwood, disapproves of the marriage and withholds the money that Ursula had inherited from her father. Ursula and John live in domestic content on rather narrow means. They have some sorrows: their eldest child is born blind, the tanyard's prosperity declines, the dream of mechanizing the cloth mill remains unrealized. Then Lord Luxmore, owner of the Enderley property, offers John the lease on the mill and forces Brithwood to pay Ursula's inheritance so that John has the capital he needs. Luxmore expects in return to be sure of the voters in Kingswell. But honest John Halifax encourages his tenants to vote freely, and thus he keeps Luxmore's corrupt nominee out of Parliament.

Luxmore retaliates by diverting a stream that crosses his estate so there is no longer water enough to turn the mill-wheel. Faced by financial ruin, John Halifax turns adversity into golden opportunity. He devises a way to run his machinery with steam, calls in mechanics from Manchester to build the engines, wins the trust of the workers, and peacefully brings the Industrial Revolution to Enderley.

The last quarter of the book shows John Halifax accepting the responsibilities that come with wealth. The mill prospers in the expanding postwar economy. John and Ursula are reluctant to leave the modest house where their children grew up and their private life was restricted to their family. John, however, decides that duty requires him to move to an imposing gentleman's residence. Beechwood Hall signifies his position and allows him to exercise power and influence in his community. He becomes a magistrate; he props up the local bank during a financial panic; he decreases unrest among the lower orders; he refuses nomination to Parliament only because of declining health. On the last pages John Halifax makes a good end: he and Ursula both die quietly in the fullness of life within hours of each other and without any fear or pain.

John Halifax, Gentleman is precisely dated. The hero is born in 1780, when enclosure was erasing the last traces of medieval agriculture and Boulton and Watt were working on the rotary drive that would make steam engines useful for something besides pumping out mines. The book begins in 1794, when English aristocrats watched their counterparts across the Channel vanish amid the Reign of Terror. It ends in 1834, two years after the Reform Bill abolished pocket boroughs and gave the vote to most middle-class men. The achievements and experiences of John Halifax correspond allegorically to the events that transferred power from the aristocracy to the middle class.

The foundation stones are literacy, technology, and what Samuel Smiles, author of the 1859 best seller *Self-Help,* would call the "art of seizing opportunities." John Halifax, like the class that he symbolizes, rises from a subordinate position by learning to read, by tinkering with machinery, and by taking the risks needed to introduce the factory system and the steam engine. His life encompasses the origins of the industrial middle class; he evolves from farm laborer to manual laborer to clerk to apprentice to tradesman to inventor-capitalist-manufacturer. The stages of his rise relative to the old class hierarchy are indicated by two marriages: John Halifax marries the daughter of a gentleman; thirty-three years later their daughter Maud is united to an aristocrat.

The aristocracy's conservative intransigence, however, creates the conditions that make it necessary and possible for the middle class to seize power. After the Kingswell election the Earl of Luxmore realizes that his way of life is endangered; the manufacturer has enough influence to keep the aristocrat from controlling parliamentary representation. Luxmore tries to turn back the clock by diverting the stream and thereby abolishing the factory and its machines. At that point, John Halifax is able to tip the balance in favor of the new class. Introducing steam to run the machines does not merely supply a more efficient means of production; it alters the source of economic power. For centuries landowners had controlled natural resources and the supply of energy. But with the coming of steam, manufacturers no longer depended on the land and its streams. Economic power passed from the owners of land to the makers of goods.

The book's political events show the new power at work. John Halifax not only keeps the aristocrat from controlling elections, he also becomes a magistrate, and he has enough money to prop up the economy and prevent a bank failure. In other words, John Halifax exercises political power even before he and his class have a formal role in government. The invitation to run for a seat in Commons after 1832 shows that the Reform Bill simply ratified the transfer of real power which had already taken place.

The story's minor details reflect other transformations within the half-century. John Halifax vaccinates his children against smallpox. The status of the old trades (like tanning) declines. Religious disabilities are removed: early in the story the militia will not protect Abel Fletcher's property because he is a Quaker, and Luxmore's Catholic son is not eligible to sit in Parliament. The railroad links London to the provinces as the Halifax children reach adulthood. Intemperance declines. Social control is transferred from the hands of careless justices of the peace like Squire Brithwood to responsible magistrates like John Halifax. Public order is established—by the end of the book John Halifax no longer goes about armed when he has to carry large sums of money, although in the last years of the eighteenth century even the Quaker Abel Fletcher kept a pistol by his cash box.

The social values are reinforced by emblematic characters. Squire Brithwood and the Earl of Luxmore represent the failings of the upper classes. Luxmore is a caricature dissolute aristocrat; he is more at home in France than England and is symbolically destroying his own country by cutting down the trees on his estate to pay his debts. Brithwood is an eighteenth-century survival: the coarse, corpulent, drinking, fox-hunting squire. He allies himself with aristocratic decay by marrying Luxmore's Frenchified daughter Lady Caroline.

Sir Ralph Oldtower stands for the good old English values. He is identified with knightliness, public duty, and plain living. He resides on his property, has an exemplary family life, and looks after his tenants' welfare. He is also democratic enough to offer friendship to John Halifax.

Other admirable characters represent traditional middle-class professions: the banker, the doctor and his wife the governess. These characters function as a bridge; they value John Halifax for his hard work and his moral worth, and their social recognition helps integrate the rising tradesman into the middle class. The wrong kind of class interaction is seen in the thoughtless (and French) *egalité* of Lady Caroline, who patronizes John Halifax as a romantically idealized "man of the people." The xenophobic reference indicates that her attitude is wrong because it destroys the established order instead of changing it gradually, and because mindless equalitarianism fails to measure the difference in worth between one man and another.

Lady Caroline Brithwood's appearances in the novel graph the decline of the aristocracy and the ascent of middle-class moral values. Early in the story she is a focus of attention and admiration; her marriage from Lady Hamilton's house links Norton Bury to stirring national events. At this point John Halifax is a tanyard laborer and is too low even to be recognized; when he saves Squire Brithwood from drowning, the Squire tosses him half a crown instead of thanking him.

By mid-book Admiral Nelson's death has revealed the details of his extramarital liaison with Lady Hamilton and given dubious overtones to Caroline Brithwood's connection with the Hamilton circle. Both John and Ursula Halifax are morally uncomfortable when Lady Caroline—who now treats them as equals—pays a social visit. At the book's end she is a crazy over-rouged adulteress wandering the streets of Norton Bury. Ursula Halifax exercises admirable charity by taking her in and nursing her until she dies.

The story of Luxmore's son indicates the aristocracy's adaptation to middle-class values. John Halifax at first refuses to allow Lord Ravenel to court his daughter Maud, not because of the difference in station but because Ravenel has been idle. He redeems himself by going off to America and working as a clerk. When he inherits the estate, he sells it to pay his father's debts and becomes plain William Ravenel, a partner in the Halifax family firm and a good bourgeois husband for Maud. Thus although the marriages of John Halifax and his daughter Maud lend the sanction of aristocratic legitimacy to the new middle class, they do not simply absorb newcomers into the old class structure, but rather incorporate the aristocracy into a middle-class value system.

Yet clearly it is important that John Halifax be shown achieving the marriages and the big house and the social acceptance. For many readers, the democratic idealism of the book is further marred by another inconsistency. The

British Quarterly Review called it an "artistic and intellectual blunder—the characteristic irresolution of this writer" ["The Author of *John Halifax,*" *British Quarterly Review* 44, 1866]. John Halifax has one possession inherited from his father—a Greek Testament inscribed "Guy Halifax, Gentleman." The inscription and the language indicate that although John did not have the social and material advantages gentlemen could give to their sons, he was in fact, by blood, a representative of the class born to property and education and, furthermore, that he was aware of it. Did that advantage—which, perhaps, predisposed him to intelligence and gave him self-confidence—account for his rise? If so, the premise of the book is virtually negated, and Craik (like many other presumably democratic Victorians, including Dickens) is seen to be unwilling to accept social mobility unless it can be accounted for by a history of "good blood." On the other hand, Frances Martin, who was close to Craik and helped read proof for the book, insisted that the Greek Testament was a symbol, and that the inscription "Gentleman" was "the inalienable possession of every human being" [in her "Mrs. Craik," *Athenaeum,* 22 October 1887].

Gentlemanliness, Craik believed, was a sense of honor, fidelity, and obligation. The strength of the middle class came from its inclusiveness and its position in the middle—or at the center—of society. John Halifax preserves the nation by standing between an aristocracy that has abandoned social responsibility and the poor who are too shortsighted to rule. The book shares the Dickensian mood of humanitarian benevolence. Craik's mobs do not have the political sophistication to identify the source of their discomfort nor are they well organized enough to be really threatening. The middle-class solution to social problems is meliorist. The poor cause troubles because they are hungry, and John Halifax offers the immediate domestic solution of a good dinner instead of stopping to analyze the cause of their hunger. During the food riots the authoritarian Abel Fletcher throws his grain in the river rather than give in to the force of the mob. They respond—naturally enough—by threatening to burn his house. Because John Halifax stands in the middle he understands both hunger and property; he saves the house by giving all the food in it to the rioters. This approach to social problems seems—even for the mid-nineteenth century—extraordinarily shallow. Nevertheless, it reflects a confident assumption of moral inclusiveness. The middle class—as Craik and her readers believed—could understand the feelings and needs of both upper and lower classes, and were thus the best rulers in an age of progress and change.

John Halifax, Gentleman is unusual because it so thoroughly celebrates its central character and its society. Novelists who write with a social purpose in mind almost invariably do so by showing examples of the evils that need to be corrected. Craik, instead, provided a model to emulate, a vision of the world that should be. She made the book appeal to the reading public by reinforcing their own values, by making an ordinary man into a hero of epic proportions, and by using literary techniques that shape and guide the reader's emotional response.

John Halifax himself is a compendium of middle-class virtues. He embodies the holy trinity of economic individualism: self-help, self-denial, and self-control. He is so patently honest that occasions that might put him to the test need not arise. Drink never appears in his presence. He is thrifty enough to go on living in an attic even after he is manager of the tanyard. Cleanliness sets him apart from the mass of poor boys when he first appears. Study allows him to rise above manual labor. He uses leisure constructively by making models; much later, he plans to give a course of public lectures after he retires from the mill. Initiative and duty lead him always to do more than is required. Economic prudence keeps him from risking his money in speculation after he is rich, and thus gives him the bags of gold to save the bank. Sexual morality exists without effort; he never thinks about women until he sees Ursula. He wastes no time on superficial society; his private life is entirely family-centered. He has enough courage to rescue March and Brithwood from a river and face a mob unarmed, but he does not take unnecessary risks; introducing steam to the mill is the chief indication of his "thoroughly English quality of daring."

The hero's struggles and failings—if any—have almost no place in the book. The story, however, is not told by an omniscient author—it is narrated by a man who admires John Halifax. Only the barest hints of internal conflict indicate that John exercises willpower in order to become such an admirable person. Once at twenty he confesses to Phineas that

> many wrong things are pleasant—just now, instead of rising to-morrow, and going into the little dark counting-house, and scratching paper from eight to six, shouldn't I like to break away!—dash out into the world, take to all sorts of wild freaks, do all sorts of grand things, and perhaps never come back to the tanning any more.

John's one very small patch of wild oats—a trip to the theater—is immediately and drastically punished. Craik's general plan, however, was to encourage rather than frighten. She assumed that people were basically good and that they would admire the same traits she admired. Thus she wrote scenes that show John Halifax earning respect and love from people in all ranks of society.

The character of Ursula Halifax is constructed on the same principle: a model woman to match a model man. She is, however, not so central nor so richly detailed. By mid-book she becomes a stereotype; she is generally called simply "the mother," and the limitations in her character reveal that Craik could not so wholeheartedly accept the role as an encompassing expression of ideal womanhood.

Ursula March, unmarried, is an attractive heroine. In the opening scene she struggles to exercise charity and heroically suffers a wound for her cause; she is cut by the bread-knife when a servant tries to keep her from giving a slice from the loaf to a hungry working boy. She is well educated, devoted to her father, energetic, fresh, healthy, and not at all ethereal. She is self-sufficient enough to move out of her trustee's house when she begins to suspect

that Lady Caroline Brithwood is an unsuitable companion. And she disregards conventions to love John Halifax.

Ursula Halifax retains some of these virtues. She startles the neighbors when she offers refuge to Lady Caroline. After John becomes master of the Enderley mill Ursula is said to have " 'half-a-dozen plans on foot' " for doing good to the men and women who work for her husband.

The public duties of Ursula Halifax, however, remain merely words—we never see her exercising them. Her life in the novel is enclosed by her role, and total absorption in motherhood has some negative reverberations. Worry about her children makes Ursula angry when Mary Baines brings smallpox into the house; John has to remind her that the golden rule forbids her to force a sick baby out into the cold. The intellectual abilities she had as a girl are trivialized; Phineas tells us that Ursula Halifax is an invaluable moral influence for her daughters but an inadequate teacher of ordinary lessons. She is jealous and petty when a governess comes into the household. In fact, she is too much "the mother"; she loves her children too utterly and cannot survive beyond the end of the role. When her eldest son Guy leaves home, Ursula Halifax slips into the physical decline that leads to her death.

The haze of sentiment draped around "the mother" fails to cloak the ways that Ursula Halifax dwindles inside the confinement of the role. "The mother," however, is only one aspect of the woman. The book explores others in disguised fashion. As one early reviewer remarked, "it is difficult to suppress a fear that Phineas Fletcher will fall hopelessly in love with John Halifax, so hard is it to remember that Phineas is of the male sex" [R. H. Hutton, "Novels by the Authoress of *John Halifax, British Quarterly* Review 29, 1858]. Phineas is passive, helpless, admiring, a disappointment to his father because he will never be able to take over the business and carry on the name, a listener to others' schemes, a writer of notes, hearer of lessons, and avid spectator to events in which he can take no part. These traits might well be admirable in a woman; the man who has them is crippled.

Finally, critics have often called John Halifax himself a "woman's man." In context, the words imply that Craik, like other Victorian female writers, did not have enough experience and intelligence to create a whole man from the inside out, and therefore generalized the surface features that she could observe. Modern criticism gives the phrase another dimension. Elaine Showalter's "Dinah Mulock Craik and the Tactics of Sentiment: A Case Study in Victorian Female Authorship" suggests that characters like John Halifax allowed Craik to project "her own ambitions and struggles onto male heroes who could more appropriately embody her ideals" [*Feminist Studies* 2, 1975]. John Halifax can be honest about his ambition and be praised for his achievements; a woman, even a competitive professional writer, could not do so without being suspected of unwomanliness.

John Halifax struggles to make his own way in the world and yet do no harm to those he encounters. He may indeed be "a woman in trousers"—that is, an idealization of Craik's beliefs about how women would behave and what

The Corner House in Kent, designed for Craik by William Morris and built with the proceeds from John Halifax, Gentleman.

women could achieve if they had the freedom and independence that were granted to a male, even a male outsider. Some of John Halifax's virtues raise traditional feminine traits to heroic stature: he meets the rioters with persuasion instead of force; he quells anger with food. He avoids going to law for the money Brithwood owes, just as a woman could not go to law for justice in her own name. Even the gentleness, the nurturing, the deep love for the blind, most helpless of his children seem more admirable in a man because voluntary.

The narrative tactics of *John Halifax, Gentleman* enlist the reader's emotional response by tapping sources of sentiment and encouraging identification. The invalid narrator bridges the separate spheres of woman and man; he has a feminine viewpoint yet he can share a man's life and thoughts. Craik makes him a namesake and descendant of the historical Phineas Fletcher, a Jacobean scholar, clergyman, and pastoral poet. The pastoral tradition supplies a model for the paradoxical mix of pretended distance and actual subjectivity created by the narrator; the pastoral poet, wearing his shepherd's mask, could introduce personal emotion into his verse while pretending to write objectively about an invented world. Fletcher's major work, *The Purple Island* (which is mentioned several times in the novel) is, like *John Halifax, Gentleman,* a Christian epic with the ordinary citizen as hero.

Phineas Fletcher's primary function, however, is to admire John Halifax. He unabashedly loves his friend; he can dwell on John's character, praise his strengths, and approve of his actions in a way that would be impossible for an omniscient author. Thus he controls the emotional response; his personal mediation gives the reader permission to feel and supplies the emotions that Craik wants to elicit about her central character.

Phineas's narration also provides a recursive tension that makes the part of the story devoted to John Halifax's success more interesting than it might otherwise be. For example, late in the book, while John Halifax is winning the gratitude of both high and low by depositing his bags of gold in the bank, Phineas Fletcher walks outside the banker's house remembering how he once came to Ursula in the same garden when the tanner's apprentice was too poor to declare his love. The emotional overlay not only allows us to reexperience the earlier pleasure of tension aroused and satisfied but also re-creates the original tension in order to heighten the effect of the later scene.

The book's essential anachronism supplies a similar emotional reward. The central character appears threatened by the opinions and behavior of the world he lives in. John Halifax, however, is simply ahead of his time. By the time Craik wrote, most people approved of the things John Halifax espoused. Thus the tension aroused when the hero comes in conflict with social norms creates a pleasurable irony; the readers' own opinions appear to be under attack and the emotional identification leads to a delicious satisfaction when—as history makes inevitable—John Halifax and the reader are vindicated.

Not all readers, however, could be involved in events of

the wide world. Despite the broad canvas of the historical allegory, Craik ensured the widest degree of reader identification by confining the scenes primarily to the domestic circle. Because the invalid narrator controls the story by reporting only what he knows, the woman novelist need not follow John Halifax into the tanyard or factory nor understand the details of his inventions. In fact, domestic virtues impinge even on the factory world; one reason the workers accept the steam engine so easily is that the mill women are touched by the master's love for his blind daughter. The only real threats to the novel's perfect world are threats that strike at the family: the illness and death of children, the hurt and dissention when two bothers fall in love with the same woman.

The problem of the next generation is one implicit irony in the self-help story. Guy Halifax is briefly tainted by his father's wealth; he yearns for ballrooms and fox hunts and gets into a fight when he has too much to drink. Guy is redeemed by shipwreck, privation, and hard work in America where he too is classless and fatherless, thus comforting every reader with the demonstration that the only advantages worth having are the ones earned by individual effort.

Incidental material reflects other prejudices of the mass audience: anti-French feeling, rural nostalgia, wholehearted provincialism, a mild pacifism, and distrust of the military. Craik manages not to offend any reader's religious sentiments. Lord Ravenel's fall into temporary skepticism may reflect the fear of Roman influence aroused by Newman's conversion in 1845, but old Catholics are treated sympathetically. The hero's faith is carefully nonspecific. There is no clergyman among the characters. A last-minute crisis forces Phineas to stay home from the book's featured wedding, so we have no description of the church or the ceremony. The only religious observance that we see is family Bible-reading, which both Anglicans and dissenters could approve.

John Halifax, Gentleman was an enormously successful book. Hurst and Blackett were kept busy resetting the type; four sets of plates had been used by 1858. The first cheap edition was illustrated with a steel engraving by Pre-Raphaelite painter J. E. Millais. An 1863 listing of the era's most popular books put *John Halifax, Gentleman* just behind *Uncle Tom's Cabin.* And the sales continued for the next fifty years. There were copies from eleven separate English publishers in 1898; American pirates (ranging from the big New York and Philadelphia houses to the Chicago Union School Furnishing Company) produced at least forty-five different editions before 1900. In the twentieth century the book has been abridged, retold, published as a supplemental reader, included in sets of mail-order imitation-leather-bound classics, and offered on thin paper to go into soldiers' pockets. It has also been a television serial.

Craik sometimes introduced her essays with the modest disclaimer that she did not strive for original thought, but only hoped she might be able to put into words ideas that had occurred, perhaps half-consciously, to a great many people. *John Halifax,* clearly, hit exactly the right note. It gave a dramatic form to the heroic myth of the middle class, made it accessible with the domestic setting, and added the emotional attractions of love and pathos. The book satisfied readers' needs and desires, reflected their own beliefs, and gave them the dignity of literary significance. It expressed faith in continued progress, offered respect to business, said that poverty was not a disgrace but rather a necessary spur to industry and that economic success was a laudable goal. It showed the rewards of hard work and self-help and proclaimed that any practical occupation was valuable.

Besides expressing the reader's sentiments, the book supplied the psychic reward of identification with the major characters. The glow of approving admiration surrounded not only the successful John Halifax but also the domestic Ursula and the onlooker Phineas. Readers were personally involved. The characters took on the independent existence that blurs the distinction between life and literature; tourists flocked to Tewkesbury to see the places where John Halifax had lived. For some readers the book became a kind of testament, a personal gospel to be compared with *The Pilgrim's Progress* and the *Imitation of Christ.*

The literary establishment did not provide quite the same approval. The first reviewers said the book was Craik's best to date, but they did not foresee its enormous success. They found things to criticize: the story was too idealized; an industrious lad might get rich but he was not likely to become polished enough to enter good society. Some reviewers found the friendship between Phineas and John absurd, though others were touched, and wondered why novels did not more often describe the emotions of masculine friendship. Intellectuals had a tendency to scoff. William de Morgan and Edward Burne-Jones did a lampoon of Ursula and Muriel Halifax; George Eliot may have been thinking of John Halifax when she insisted that Tom Tulliver in *The Mill on the Floss* was not "moulded on the spoony type of the Industrious Apprentice" [quoted in Robert A. Colby's *Fiction with a Purpose,* 1967].

To an extent, the book's very popularity put it beyond the reach of literary criticism and harmed Craik's reputation among serious writers. "There is something almost awful," wrote Henry James,

> in the thought of a writer undertaking to give a detailed picture of the actions of a perfectly virtuous being. . . . We cannot but think that, if Miss Muloch [*sic*] had weighed her task more fairly, she would have shrunk from it in dismay. But neither before nor after his successful incarnation was John Halifax to be weighed or measured. We know of no scales that will hold him, and of no unit of length with which to compare him. He is infinite; he outlasts time; he is enshrined in a million innocent breasts; and before his awful perfection and his eternal durability we respectfully lower our lance [*Notes and Reviews,* 1921].

By the end of the century critics found it hard to consider the book literature at all. Those who believed in it elevated it to the status of a social force, which had helped to change the nation by sweeping away old habits and conventions and creating a climate of respect for democratic equality and the dignity of work. Those who were not affected described it as a tract. As the pendulum swung against Victorianism and Victorian values, the book was rather typically labeled "altogether harmless, and faultlessly proper, and irredeemably commonplace" [Hugh Walker, *The Literature of the Victorian Era,* 1910].

John Halifax, Gentleman remains the best known of Craik's novels. Modern literary scholars appreciate—though they may not approve—the author's celebration of middle-class values and find the book useful as an artifact of social history. Craik's knowledge of the reading public, her own experience as a self-made professional, and her emotional involvement with the characters give the book authority and conviction. (pp. 39-52)

> *Sally Mitchell, in her* Dinah Mulock Craik, *Twayne Publishers, 1983, 146 p.*

FURTHER READING

"Mrs. G. L. Craik (Miss D. M. Mulock)." *The Academy* 32, No. 807 (22 October 1887): 269-70.
　　Obituary notice eulogizing Craik's literary efforts.

"A Novel of the Season." *Chambers's Edinburgh Journal* XV, No. 366 (4 January 1851): 4-7.
　　Highly favorable review of *Olive,* outlining the plot and characterization and asserting that the novel depicts "the story of a Model Woman."

"Our Female Novelists." *The Christian Remembrancer* XXXVIII, No. CVI (October 1859): 305-39.
　　Analyzes character and plot in *A Life for a Life* from a Christian perspective, focusing on Craik's themes of penitent criminals and equality in marriage.

"Recent Novels: *Agatha's Husband.*" *The Edinburgh Review* XCVII, No. CXCVIII (April 1853): 380-90.
　　Mixed review of *Agatha's Husband* and *The Head of the Family.* The critic praises Craik's psychological insight and moral tone but objects that her protagonists are unrealistically virtuous and that her plots are often repetitive.

Foster, Shirley. "Dinah Mulock Craik: Ambivalent Romanticism." In her *Victorian Women's Fiction: Marriage, Freedom and the Individual,* pp. 40-70. London: Croom Helm, 1985.
　　Comprehensive analysis of Craik's attitude toward women and marriage as reflected in her life, her fiction, and her essays.

[Harrison, A. B.]. "Miss Mulock (Mrs. Craik)." *Littell's Living Age* CXXXIII, No. 1717 (12 May 1877): 371-73.
　　Assesses Craik's literary accomplishments, asserting that despite flaws in her prose, Craik "conduces to the moral elevation, as well as to the delight of her readers."

[Hutton, R. H.] "Novels by the Authoress of *John Halifax.*" *The North British Review* XXIX, No. LVII (November 1858): 466-87.

Focuses on Craik's works in an exploration of the differences between female and male writers of the day.

Martin, Frances. "Mrs. Craik." *Athenaeum,* No. 3130 (22 October 1887): 539.
　　Obituary notice by Craik's longtime friend, educator Frances Martin. Martin focuses on *John Halifax, Gentleman,* praising Craik's prose style and examining the symbolism of Halifax's Greek Testament.

Mitchell, Sally. *Dinah Mulock Craik.* Boston: Twayne, 1983, 146 p.
　　Definitive study of Craik's life and career, centering on Craik's concern with women's issues and the popular and critical responses to her works.

Nourse, Robert. "An Old Book for New Readers." *The Dial* IV, No. 38 (June 1883): 36-7.
　　Commends *John Halifax, Gentleman* to American readers as "an impetus to an industrious and happy life."

[Oliphant, Margaret.] "Mrs. Craik." *Macmillan's Magazine* 57 (December 1887): 81-5.
　　Obituary of Craik by novelist and contemporary Margaret Oliphant.

"The Author of *John Halifax.*" *The Overland Monthly* XI, No. 6 (December 1873): 537-38.
　　Recounts an 1873 meeting with Craik.

Rollins, Alice Wellington. "The Author of *John Halifax.*" *The Critic* 11, No. 200 (29 October 1887): 214.
　　Retrospective account of Craik's literary career.

"Mrs. Craik's Poems." *The Spectator* 61, No. 3140 (1 September 1888): 1198-99.
　　Praises the high moral tone of Craik's 1888 volume of collected poetry, while averring that her poems "abound in sentiment, but have too little force and substance."

Spilka, Mark. "Victorian Keys to the Early Hemingway: Part 1—*John Halifax, Gentleman.*" *Journal of Modern Literature* 10, No. 1 (March 1983): 125-50.
　　Examines the impact of *John Halifax, Gentleman* on Ernest Hemingway's early development.

Showalter, Elaine. *A Literature of Their Own: British Women Novelists from Brontë to Lessing.* Princeton, N. J.: Princeton University Press, 1977, 378 p.
　　Contains scattered references to Craik, including an examination of her relationships with her various publishers throughout her career.

Thomson, Patricia. *The Victorian Heroine: A Changing Ideal 1837-1873*. London: Oxford University Press, 1956, 178 p.
    Discusses Craik's treatment of women and various social issues in her fiction and essays.

Additional coverage of Craik's life and career is contained in the following sources published by Gale Research: *Dictionary of Literary Biography: Victorian Poets After 1850*, Vol. 35 and *Something about the Author*, Vol. 34.

Ralph Waldo Emerson

1803-1882

American essayist and poet.

For further discussion of Emerson's career, see *NCLC,* Volume 1.

INTRODUCTION

Emerson was one of the most influential American writers of the nineteenth century and a leader of the Transcendentalists, a group of New England literary figures who were drawn together by their belief in the presence of the divine in human beings and nature and their assertion that each individual must determine what is morally correct regardless of religious dogma. Emerson is best known for his essays, which are regarded as important literary expressions of Transcendentalism, and his work is noted for having influenced such acclaimed writers as Herman Melville, Nathaniel Hawthorne, Walt Whitman, Henry David Thoreau, and Emily Dickinson.

Born in Boston, Emerson was descended from a long line of Unitarian ministers. After graduating from Harvard in 1821, he taught school in Boston for four years and attended Harvard Divinity School in 1825. The following year he was approved to preach as a Unitarian minister, and he was ordained pastor of Boston's Second Church in 1829. That year Emerson married Ellen Tucker, whose death in 1831 left him an inheritance that ensured his financial independence. In 1832, after expressing objections to the traditional meaning and function of the Communion ritual, Emerson announced to his congregation that he could no longer perform the ceremony in good conscience, and he resigned from his position as pastor. He spent the next year traveling in Europe, where he met such influential writers as William Wordsworth, Samuel Taylor Coleridge, and Thomas Carlyle, and visited the botanical gardens of the Jardin des Plantes in Paris, an experience he claimed inspired his interest in the mystical significance of nature.

Returning to America in 1833, Emerson settled in Concord, Massachusetts. He returned to the pulpit as a guest speaker in various churches but soon turned to public lecturing, establishing himself as one of the most successful speakers on the popular lyceum lecture circuit. In 1836 he published his first work, an essay entitled *Nature,* and helped found what became known as the Transcendental Club, a group that included Thoreau, Hawthorne, and Margaret Fuller. Emerson frequently contributed poetry to the group's journal, the *Dial,* and later served as its editor. Also during this time, Emerson delivered two important orations. His "American Scholar," addressed to Harvard's Phi Beta Kappa Society, was widely regarded as a call for distinctly American arts and literature and was

hailed by Oliver Wendell Holmes as "our intellectual Declaration of Independence." His "Divinity School Address" to the graduating class of Harvard's Divinity School created controversy by challenging the authority of the church and the divinity of Jesus. Emerson's second trip to Europe in 1847-48 included a lecture tour in Britain and served as the inspiration for his *English Traits,* an evaluation of English society and culture which he published in 1856. For the next two decades, Emerson continued to write and lecture, and he came to be regarded as "the Sage of Concord." However, his later years were characterized by a gradually advancing senility, and he died in Concord in 1882.

Critics trace the philosophical and religious outlook of Emerson's works to many sources, among them the Unitarian religion, German philosophical Idealism, the work of Swedish scientist and mystic Emmanuel Swedenborg, the poetry of Wordsworth and Coleridge, and the Hindu scriptures, all of which emphasize the unity of nature, humanity, and God. Many commentators have described the contents of *Nature* as embodying the essence of his Transcendental philosophy. In this work, Emerson called upon humanity to "enjoy an original relation to the universe."

Maintaining that each law of nature has a counterpart in the spiritual realm, Emerson argued that nature is a symbolic language that can reveal the mind of God, and through the experience of oneness with nature, direct communion with God is possible for every individual. Emerson's description of this phenomenon is contained in a well-known passage in *Nature* in which he compares himself to a "transparent eyeball" through which flows the unity of God and nature. Many of Emerson's essays are regarded as an elaboration of the philosophical foundation established in *Nature*. Among the best known are "Self-Reliance," "The Over-Soul," and "Compensation."

Well received by most nineteenth-century scholars, Emerson's prose works fell out of favor with critics in the 1920s and 1930s. While many acknowledged Emerson's ability to encapsulate his point of view in brilliant aphorisms, some charged that his work lacks unity and a logical structure; his paragraphs, it was alleged, comprise strings of unrelated sentences, and some claimed that his essays make as much sense when read from end to beginning as when read from beginning to end. Critics found support for these charges in details of Emerson's life: as a speaker, he was known to spontaneously shuffle his lecture notes to reorganize his presentation, and he once described his paragraphs as consisting of "infinitely repellent particles." Many recent scholars, however, have reevaluated Emerson's work, commonly identifying a dialectical structure in Emerson's philosophy unifying his otherwise disparate statements. Furthermore, once faulted for its "optimism" or denial of the existence of evil and suffering, Emerson's philosophical position on the problem of evil has been reexamined by several critics, notably Newton Arvin, who viewed it as part of a religious tradition that defines evil as the absence of good.

Emerson's poetry, emphasizing nature as symbolic of the divine and focusing on the commonplace and everyday experience, has often been cited as having made possible the work of Thoreau and as an important influence on generations of subsequent American poets. While it is generally acknowledged to be stylistically flawed, some have argued that meter and diction are subordinate to thematic concerns in Emerson's poetry. Albert Gelpi has asserted that Emerson intended his poems to convey the same moral messages he expounded in his essays and lectures and that he used poetic forms that would best convey the experience of inspiration.

The publication of an exhaustive sixteen-volume edition of Emerson's journal writings has given scholars ample material for new insights into his work. With the resulting increase in critical attention has come renewed recognition of Emerson's importance and influence—a phenomenon anticipated by William James, who, speaking on the hundredth anniversary of Emerson's birth, predicted that "his words . . . are certain to be quoted and extracted more and more as time goes on, and to take their place among the Scriptures of humanity."

PRINCIPAL WORKS

Nature   (essay)   1836

An Oration, Delivered Before the Phi Beta Kappa Society at Cambridge   (essay)   1837; also published as *The American Scholar,* 1901
An Address Delivered Before the Senior Class in Divinity College, Cambridge   (essay)   1838
Essays   (essays)   1841; also published as *Essays: First Series,* 1854
Essays: Second Series   (essays)   1844
Poems   (poetry)   1847
Nature, Addresses, and Lectures   (essays)   1849
Representative Men: Seven Lectures   (essays)   1850
English Traits   (essays)   1856
The Conduct of Life   (essays)   1860
May-Day and Other Pieces   (poetry)   1867
Society and Solitude   (essays)   1870
Letters and Social Aims   (essays)   1876
Natural History of Intellect, and Other Papers   (essays) 1893
The Complete Works of Ralph Waldo Emerson.   12 vols. (essays and poetry)   1903-21
The Letters of Ralph Waldo Emerson.   6 vols.   (letters) 1939
Journals and Miscellaneous Notebooks.   16 vols.   (journals and notebooks)   1960-82

Sherman Paul   (essay date 1952)

[*Paul is an American educator and critic. In the following excerpt, he discusses Emerson's theory regarding the nature of inspiration and insight, focusing on Emerson's belief that a change in intellectual perception, similar to a shift from proximate to distant vision, is essential to apprehending moral truth.*]

> *What is life but the angle of vision? A man is measured by the angle at which he looks at objects.*
> EMERSON, **"Natural History of Intellect."**

> *For the whole world converts itself into that man and through him as through a lens, the rays of the universe shall converge, withersoever he turns, on a point.*
> EMERSON, *Journals.*

For the Emerson who defined the problem of insight in terms of the alignment of the axis of vision and the axis of things—"The ruin or the blank, that we see when we look at nature, is in our own eye. The axis of vision is not coincident with the axis of things, and so they appear not transparent, but opaque"—the passage on the transparent eyeball is justly the representative anecdote of his experience of inspiration. "In the woods," he wrote,

> we return to reason and faith. There I feel that nothing can befall me in life—no disgrace, no calamity (leaving me my eyes) which nature cannot repair. Standing on the bare ground—my head bathed by the blithe air, and uplifted into infinite space—all mean egotism vanishes. I become a transparent eyeball; I am nothing; I see all; the currents of the Universal Being circulate through me; I am part or particle of God.

The original *Journal* record is less compact, and except for an afterthought, less significant. The transparent eyeball is omitted, but its characteristic power is added: "There the mind integrates itself again. The attention, which had been distracted into parts, is reunited, reinsphered. The whole of nature addresses itself to the whole man. . . . It is more than a medicine. It is health." In terms of Emerson's visual experience, the transparent eyeball was more than a lucky image. Twenty-five years later he noted that Plotinus had said of the heavens, "There . . . every body is pure (transparent), and each inhabitant is as it were an eye." And throughout his many observations of the inspirational process, Emerson often converted thought into its visual counterpart, light: "Thought is nothing but the circulations made luminous." As a representative experience of inspiration, then, the famous passage in *Nature* indicates that for Emerson the primary agency of insight was seeing.

The eye was Emerson's most precious endowment. Everywhere in his writing it was a symbol of all the stages of inspiration, and still he could not resist the extended tribute he gave it in **"Behavior."** He confessed his own poor ear, knowing that he had compensation in his eye: "My lack of musical ear is made good to me through my eyes. That which others hear, I *see*." What his ear brought him, he often described visually; he compared the "thread of sound" in a singer's voice to "a ray of light," and the rippling pond struck his eye with a delight as great as that of an aeolian harp to the ear. Light and music were analogous in their law, and he felt that in "the splendid function of seeing" he had the power of "recurring to the Sublime at pleasure."

The eye, then, was his prominent faculty. (Christopher Cranch, perhaps unwittingly, caricatured Emerson as an eye mounted on two spindly legs.) Seeing, for him, was constitutional: by bringing his total sensual response to nature, it was tantamount to spiritual health. He was aware of this in his youth because his eyesight wavered with his indecisions. The Emerson heritage (more dramatically revealed in the mental collapse of Edward) was transmitted, perhaps, in his weak eyes. When his eyesight failed him early in his striving for greatness, he wrote of his convalescence, "I rejoice in the prospect of better sight and better health . . . Loss of eyes is not exactly one of Socrates's superfluities." How intimately his sight and health were connected, he was far from realizing here; but by the time of *Nature,* he could think of no greater calamity than the loss of his eyes.

For Emerson, the eye, in its own functions, focused the problem of his double consciousness of nature-as-sensation and nature-as-projection. Without the awakening stimulus of light, he was spiritually blind: "The light of the body is the eye." He would have agreed with Sampson Reed's attribution of the powers of Reason and Understanding to the eye, and especially with its unifying role in bringing the two awarenesses of nature into controlled equilibrium. "The eye," Reed wrote [in his *Growth of the Mind,* 1829] "appears to be the point at which the united rays of the sun within and the sun without, converge to an expression of unity."

Emerson found this true of his own experience. The eye brought him two perceptions of nature—nature ensphered and nature atomized—which corresponded to the distant and proximate visual powers of the eye. These powers, in turn, he could have called the reasoning and understanding modes of the eye. And to each he could have assigned its appropriate field of performance: the country and the city. The sympathy with nature he hoped to attain by seeing, he found in cultivating the distant powers of vision of the eye; for in distant vision he discovered a state of perception in which he felt a heightened intimacy with the natural process itself. Dorothy Emmet [in her *The Nature of Metaphysical Thinking,* 1945], has called this *feeling* of organic intimacy "the adverbial mode of perception." As a qualitative feeling of the total presence of nature, it might be compared to William James's pure experience or stream of consciousness. For from this undifferentiated total awareness, by focusing the attention, one selected or differentiated objects. Emerson, especially after he wrote **"Experience,"** was aware of the selecting or accusative mode of perception. But before he saw nature as *flux,* he found one of the difficulties of attaining insight by seeing, in the almost inescapable accusative perception of the natural eye. As Dorothy Emmet has pointed out, of the senses sight is the most highly developed, seldom perceiving in the "primitive" adverbial mode. In seeing, one is usually aware of specific objects, unless one rises to the higher level of "aesthetic seeing" in which one again consciously attempts to enjoy the whole as well as to differentiate its parts.

As the agency of correspondence with nature and of inspiration, sight demanded a consciousness of its behavior that in itself might prohibit influx. It demanded, as well, scope of activity—the wide panorama—or the widening of Emerson's literal angle of vision, that is to say, the diffusion of his focus into a blur of relatedness. Before "strained vision" reconstructed his experience in nature, he had to achieve the "indolent vision" of reception. In this way, Emerson's sensory equipment provided initial difficulties that Thoreau, for example, did not have. Thoreau was fortunate in his exceptional hearing—the sense that discriminates least—and held easier converse (sympathetic correspondence) with nature. But in other ways, Emerson found sight rewarding: chiefly, by converting his inspirational experiences with the stars and heavens into an astronomy of the imagination, he had the formal means for intellectualizing his experience that Thoreau never acquired.

The blur of relatedness of adverbial perception was achieved by Emerson in distant vision. When he began his essay, **"Circles,"** he diagramed the need for this mode of vision: "The eye is the first circle," he wrote, "the horizon which it forms is the second." The distance between the eye and its horizon, however, could be progressively extended, and for Emerson, had to be extended. For one could view trifles as well as the stars: "Our little circles absorb us and occupy us as fully as the heavens; we can minimize as infinitely as maximize, and the only way out of it is (to use a country phrase) to kick the pail over, and accept the horizon instead of the pail, with celestial attractions and influences, instead of worms and mud pies." And what (or how much) one viewed made the difference between Reason and Understanding. With this in mind, he would have welcomed Ortega y Gasset's comment that

" 'Near' and 'far' are relative, metrically . . . to the eye they have a kind of absolute value. Indeed, the *proximate vision* and the *distant vision* of which physiology speaks are not notions that depend chiefly on measurable factors, but are rather two distinct ways of seeing" [*Partisan Review,* August 1949]. Bearing out Emerson's own experience, Ortega explains that in proximate vision the eye converges on a central object, thereby limiting its horizon or field of vision. The object closely seen *is taken possession* of by the eye: it takes on "corporeality and solidity." In this respect, proximate vision is atomic—dissociating, analyzing, distinguishing—and, for Ortega, a feudal mode of seeing. To the political implications of proximate vision, especially in the identification of a similar atomism in Lockean perception with the commercial but spiritually sterile England of the 1840's, Emerson might have assented. He knew that "there is nothing of the true democratic element in what is called Democracy." True democracy had to transcend a commercialism that possessed trifles.

Democratic vision, for him as well as for Ortega (and Whitman should be recalled throughout), was the distant vision in which synthesis and relatedness were achieved. It was the wider look in which all things were alike or equalized. In distant vision, as in Emerson's angle of vision, "the point of view becomes the synopsis" [in Ortega's words]. In the "optical democracy" of distant vision, if "nothing possesses a sharp profile; [if] everything is background, confused, almost formless," still "the duality of proximate vision is succeeded by a perfect unity of the whole visual field." Democratic vision was a mode of sympathy, the result of the love that blends and fuses. Describing this change from proximate to distant vision, from feudal to democratic vistas, in respect to the almost tactile sense of objects or "trifles" that one has in the former, Ortega corroborates Emerson's own experience of the dislimning of objects:

> As the object is withdrawn, sight loses its tactile power and gradually becomes pure vision. In the same way, things, as they recede, cease to be filled volumes, hard and compact, and become mere chromatic entities, without resistance, mass or convexity. An age-old habit, founded in vital necessity, causes men to consider as 'things,' in the strict sense, only such objects solid enough to offer resistance to their hands. The rest is more or less illusion. So in passing from proximate to distant vision an object becomes illusory. When the distance is great, there on the confines of a remote horizon—a tree, a castle, a mountain range—all acquire the half-unreal aspect of ghostly apparitions.

Emerson made the same distinction in the reality of objects by distinguishing the masculine and feminine traits of the eye. "Women," he wrote, "see quite without any wish to act." And so with men of genius: "They have this feminine eye, a function so rich that it contents itself without asking any aid of the hand. Trifles may well be studied by him; for he sees nothing insulated." When he wrote that he was easily untuned by necessary domestic concerns and needed "solitude of habit" for inspiration, he confessed his "more womanly eyes." For the same reason he had to distance an object to see it: "If you go near to

the White Mountains, you cannot see them; you must go off thirty or forty miles to get a good view." Freed from the object, "the eye," he discovered, "possesses the faculty of rounding and integrating the most disagreeable parts into a pleasing whole."

This power to dislimn and integrate objects, an original endowment of the youthful eye, Emerson found hampered by culture or education: Even the first shock of Reason, by destroying one's faith or instinctive belief in the indissoluble union of man and nature, interrupted its functioning. After this momentary skepticism, however, the eye of Reason helped the natural eye renew its distant powers. "Until this higher agency intervened," he wrote,

> the animal eye sees with wonderful accuracy, sharp outlines and colored surfaces. When the eye of Reason opens, to outline and surface are at once added grace and expression. These proceed from imagination and affection, and abate somewhat of the angular distinctness of objects. If the Reason be stimulated to more earnest vision, the outlines and surfaces become transparent, and are no longer seen; causes and spirits are seen through them.

And just as Emerson restores the distant powers with the eye of Reason, so Ortega connects the need for the integration of distant vision with the post-Renaissance trend toward subjectivism in epistemology. For when one tries to diffuse the focus of the eye and thereby "to embrace the whole field," objects lose their solid-convexity and the whole field becomes concave: the horizon literally becomes circular, as Emerson felt when he viewed "the bended horizon." The "limit," Ortega says, "is a surface that tends to take the form of a hemisphere viewed from within." And this concavity begins, as Emerson also noted, at the eye. The result was the exhilaration of feeling one's centrality and penetration of space, and Emerson felt this in viewing the landscape and the heavens. He noted Aristotle's notion of space as container and pictured the world as "a hollow temple," the beauty and symmetry of which depended on the eye. Ortega confirms this sense of space in distant vision: "What we see at a distance is hollow space as such. The content of perception is not strictly the surface in which the hollow space terminates, but rather the whole hollow space itself, from the eyeball to the . . . horizon." In this way the eye can be said to form the first circle, because, paradoxically, in distant vision the object "begins at our cornea." "In pure distant vision," Ortega explains, "our attention, instead of being directed farther away, has drawn back to the absolutely proximate, and the eye-beam, instead of striking the convexity of a solid body and staying fixed on it, penetrates a concave object, glides into a hollow." Emerson recognized this *nearness:* "Really the soul is *near* things, because it is the centre of the universe, so that astronomy and Nature and theology date from where the observer stands." The eye (or soul), then, becomes the center of the angle of vision. Or, as Ortega says, "in fixing upon the object nearest the cornea, the point of view is as close as possible to the subject and as far as possible from things." The eye no longer revolves "ptolemaically" about each object, "following a servile orbit." In the Copernican change to distant-subjective vision—in the visual revolution of the episte-mologies of Descartes, Hume, and Kant—"the eye . . . is established as the center of the plastic Cosmos, around which revolve the forms of objects." Emerson realized this change as early as 1831, when he wrote, "The point of view is of more importance than the sharpness of sight."

The requirements of distant vision compelled Emerson to arm the natural eye. Extremely "sensible . . . to circum-stances"—he felt mean in the city streets—he needed as a condition of inspiration the wide, panoramic view. When only seventeen years old, he remarked on the scope of vi-sion: "It is a singular fact that we cannot present to the imagination a longer space than just so much of the world as is bounded by the visible horizon." For the higher see-ing he needed to go beyond this horizon; but, at least for the dislimning of objects by which inspiration was achieved, he needed to see *to* the horizon. The horizon, he would have admitted, was essential to his best working at-titude: it was what the German Romanticists called the *Idealeferne.* He complained to his brother Edward, "I am trying to learn to find my own latitude but there is no hori-zon in C[hardon] St." And after he left the church, free to follow a literary life, he wrote to Lydia Jackson that in Concord he could possess his soul but that to go to Plym-outh "would be to cripple me of some important re-sources." He felt that he must have "a scope like nature itself, a susceptibility to all impressions . . . the heart as well as . . . the logic of creation." For this, Concord was preferable.

One important resource was nature: in the rural landscape he found an attractive release from the visual confines of city life. "We need nature," he wrote, "and cities give the human senses not room enough. I go out daily and nightly to feed my eyes on the horizon and the sky, and come to feel the want of this scope as I do of water for my wash-ing." But even in the woods, unless he could fuse the detail by walking rapidly, he felt annoyed. Of what use was his genius, he wrote, "if the organ . . . cannot find a focal dis-tance?"

His best focal distance was the unlimited extent: the heav-ens, the sea, the fields, and preferably the line of the hori-zon in which heavens and earth, sea and sky met. "The imaginative faculty of the soul," he wrote, "must be fed with objects immense and eternal." In the horizon he felt "the true outline of the world," and the "astonishment" of landscape was "the meeting of the sky and the earth." Here was the mystic line, the visible symbol in nature itself of the dualism of the universe. And if the finite limit of the horizon suggested the illimitable, its hazy fading in the distance promised the bipolar unity of the moment of in-spiration. For Emerson, the far was "holy," especially when the world itself began to dislimn; and haze, by dou-bling the distance, seemed to double the quantity of nature one grasped in his angle of vision. "From your centre," Emerson recorded, "Nature carries every integral part out to the horizon, and mirrors yourself to you in the uni-verse." In this way the hazy distance tempted his eye and compensated for "the cramp and pettiness of human per-formances." By providing intimations of spiritual release, a landscape—"a long vista in woods, trees on the shore of

a lake coming quite down to the water, a long reach in a river, a double or triple row of uplands or mountains seen one over the other"—rewarded Emerson not only with first sight, but with second sight and insight. With only the horizon before him, he could launch himself into the sea of being, certain that he was able

> to possess entire nature, to fill the horizon, to fill the infinite amplitude of being with great life, to be in sympathy and relation with all creatures, to lose all privateness by sharing all natural ac-tion, shining with the Day, undulating with the sea, growing with the tree, instinctive with the animals, entranced in beatific vision with the human reason.

This sympathetic correspondence with nature, the harmo-ny of man and the vegetable, followed from breaking the artificial bonds of city life and expanding with the horizon of the "medicinal" fields. Coming into nature, Emerson wrote, "We come into our own and make friends with matter." This sympathy with matter, in a sense opening up the circulations of being, was the ground of the mo-ment of ecstasy. Following the rapture of the transparent eyeball, Emerson immediately and significantly added:

> I am the lover of uncontained and immortal beauty. In the wilderness, I find something more dear and connate than in streets or villages. In the tranquil landscape, and especially in the dis-tant line of the horizon, man beholds somewhat as beautiful as his own nature.

> The greatest delight which the fields and woods minister, is the suggestion of an occult relation between man and the vegetable . . . [and] the power to produce this delight does not reside in nature, but in man, or in a harmony of both.

Emerson's retreat to nature, then, having the precipitancy of constitutional need, was an advance on Reason. In the city he found more to be discontented with than the com-munion service. And, as we will see, he was much too gre-garious (and ambitious) to seek forgetful solitudes for "ro-mantic" reasons or for the picturesque alone. [the critic adds in a footnote that Emerson, however, "knew 'that our hunting of the picturesque is inseparable from our protest against false society'."]. In an early sermon on **"Trifles"** (1829), he illustrated the wide range of the mind by comparing it with the distant and proximate powers of the eye: "It is like the range of vision of the eye that ex-plores the atmosphere and catches the dim outline of a mountain a hundred miles distant and examines the anato-my of the smallest insect." But then he pointed out the dangers of close vision with which he himself was familiar. "If you bury the natural eye too exclusively on minute ob-jects," he said, "it gradually loses its powers of distant vi-sion." And this tendency to magnify things, to lose the sense of relationship in an obsession with trifles, distin-guished society. In the perspectives of nature he tried to escape this tyranny of things.

For the city (and society) dissipated his energy and con-centration, and waylaid his senses. He said the age was oc-ular, but he diagnosed its difficulties as ophthalmia. The city was shortsighted business. In America, he wrote Margaret Fuller, "We cannot see where we are going, preternaturally sharp as our eyes are at short distances . . . strange malady, is it not?" And the reason for the disease was that

> the City delights the Understanding. It is made up of finites; short, sharp, mathematical lines, all calculable. It is full of varieties, of successions, of contrivances. The Country, on the contrary, offers an *unbroken horizon,* the monotony of an *endless* road, or *vast* uniform plains, of *distant* mountains, the melancholy of uniform and infinite vegetation; the objects on the road are few and worthless, the eye is invited ever to the horizon and the clouds. It is the school of Reason (italics supplied).

One of the serious needs of America, he noted, was a " 'general education of the eye'."

For the same reason, he would have put telescopes on every street corner! There they could remind the shortsighted—men with "microscopic optics"—that "they were born heirs of the dome of God" and that the stars were the last outpost of God's providence. "God be thanked," Emerson wrote of his own need for the heavens, "who set stars in the sky! planted their bright watch along the infinite deep and ordained such fine intelligence betwixt us and them." The stars seemed to him to take him beyond the horizon: "The blue zenith," he wrote, "is the point in which romance and reality meet." And in astronomy he felt the visual promise of "everything"; the lawful heavens promised him successful moral navigation, and he took nightly walks under the stars to take his spiritual bearings. Obsessed with astronomy throughout his life, he even symbolized the mind as a quadrant. By sighting the sun and stars, he hoped to find his latitude. In the contemplation of the stars he participated in their animating law: "I please myself rather with contemplating the penumbra of the thing than the thing itself." And he found that this referred him "to a higher state than I now occupy."

When Emerson suggested that the American scholar—"the world's eye"—become an astronomer, he was speaking from this experience, and he was contrasting observation and vision. He wanted the scholar to feel "the grandeur of the impression the stars and heavenly bodies make on us." Then they would value their gleams more than an "exact perception of a tub or a table on the ground." They would literally have a wide horizon for every fact and discover "the inextinguishableness of the imagination." In their penetration of space they would realize the "immense elasticity" of the mind, and would be startled into wonder—and wonder reborn was the first affirmation of transcendental experience.

Even more than the distant vision it satisfied, astronomy gave Emerson a chance to speak for "the sovereignty of Ideas." As a student of thirteen, he chose astronomy for the subject of a free theme, and astronomy—imaginatively interpreted—excited him during the long remainder of his life. Herschel's great astronomy was his source book, and his "The General Nature and Advantages of the Study of the Physical Sciences," as much as Emerson's own delight in the Jardin des Plantes, directed him to the natural sciences. In them, he was searching for the moral law, and astronomy—"thought and harmony in masses of matter"—seemed to Emerson its most grandiloquent expression. Calvinism and Ptolemaic astronomy lacked this moral grandeur for Emerson: they had yet to grasp the moral beauty of the Newtonian universe. They did not know "the extent or the harmony or the depth of their moral nature." Like the Unitarians, "they are clinging to little, positive, verbal versions of the moral law, and very imperfect versions too, while the infinite laws, the laws of the Law, the great circling truths whose only adequate symbol is the material laws, the astronomy, etc., are all unobserved." For to observe the stars was, for Emerson, to "come back to our real, initial state and see and own that we have yet beheld but the first ray of Being." It was in the search for this experience that he began *Nature,* and it was the end of all he said in *Nature* to bring men "to look at the world with new eyes." In viewing the stars he escaped into loneliness and health, because alone in an atmosphere "transparent with this design" he felt "a perpetual admonition of God and superior destiny." Again he undulated with the sea of being, rested his immortality in the immortal stars, and found in their great circles the laws that merger transformed into ideas. Properly *distant,* the natural unarmed eye achieved an angle of vision in which perception had a destiny. Properly distant, restored to its natural scope, the eye was no longer retrospective, but prospective.

Emerson's critics, understandably, seized the central and striking image of the eyeball. Cranch has left us nothing that will give him as much fame, perhaps, as his good-natured sketch of this passage. But the Very Rev. Henry A. Braun, reviewing *Nature* in *The Catholic World,* cited the passage as evidence of insanity: "We wonder, when he wrote that, whether he was not bilious and his 'eyeball' bloodshot as he looked at it in the glass?" He was using this "critical" bludgeon to prove that "Nature is not the correlative of the mind." *The Westminster Review* of London also singled it out as full of familiar truths, but here too much relied on and simplified: "They are propounded as if they lay on the surface of truth and within the grasp of all men, and contained not problems . . . in the solution of which the lives of thoughtful men have gone by, leaving the giant contradictions of our moral being just as they were, standing face to face, irreconcilable."

What these and other critics have often failed to see is that the transparent eyeball is only representative for Emerson of one aspect of the mind, and that the angle of vision as a metaphor of inspiration has its origins in Emerson's thought in the religious affirmation of compensation. For the problem of the mind, as it presented itself to Emerson, was that of a twofold process. Structurally, this process was represented by the two poles or termini of the mind: Intellect Receptive and Intellect Constructive. They recreated in man-the-microcosm the cosmological dualism of the universe. Functionally, they presented the problems of inspiration and its control, of passivity or "pious reception" and concentration or form. Between these poles the life of the mind played like a sputtering spark, and Emerson's creative task was to prohibit a surplus of energy to store itself at either pole and thus intermit the circuit.

"Standing on the bare ground, — my head bathed by the blithe air, & uplifted into infinite space, — all mean egotism vanishes. I become a transparent Eyeball."   *Nature, p. 13.*

Christopher Cranch's caricature of Emerson as a "transparent eyeball."

"Human life," he wrote, "is made up of two elements, power and form, and the proportions must be invariably kept, if we would have it sweet and sound." Seen in another way, this mental equilibrium required innocence and sophistication, that is, the openness of response and mature judgment that modern critics of the arts often remark on as impossible: "The lover of nature is he whose inward and outward senses are still truly adjusted to each other; who has retained the spirit of infancy even into the era of manhood." Although the receptive aspect of this process—certainly the more primary in Emerson's experience—was mystical merger, Emerson was not a mystic in the usual "visionary" sense of the word. He was not seeking in the angle of vision an escape from the world; as it formed, the angle of vision was to make *use* of the world. But mystical union, for him, was an epistemological necessity. Vision, he said of the inner seeing of the mind, "is not like the vision of the eye, but is union with the things known." The knowledge of merger, however, had its use only in the prudential world; if knowledge *began* in reception, it ended in action. Mysticism ended in rest. And "Man," he wrote, "was made for conflict, not for rest. In

action is his power; not in his goals but in his transitions man is great."

The transitions, or better, the transmutation of mystical power into form was his best description of the life of the mind. In this process the mind was a transmitter, a conduit through which the infinite was funneled from the spiritual reservoir to the prudential tap. Or again, to switch the metaphor, mind was the lens converging the rays of spirit on the daily affairs of man. Standing between the worlds of spiritual laws and prudential affairs, man's "health and erectness," Emerson wrote, "consist in the fidelity with which he transmits influences from the vast and universal to the point on which his genius can act." The point of action was found in everyday life, just as the only way of making the mystical power of insight available was by conveying it to men in the "language of facts." The ray of spiritual light, he pointed out in illustration, "passes invisible through space, and only when it falls on an object is it seen." Similarly, "when the spiritual energy is directed on something outward, then it is a thought." Speaking of his own experience of transition as ebb and flow, Emerson described the same process more "psychologically":

> The daily history of the Intellect is this alternating of expansions and concentrations. The expansions are the invitations from heaven to try a larger sweep, a higher pitch than we have yet climbed, and to leave all our past for this enlarged scope. Present power, on the other hand, requires concentration on the moment and the thing to be done.

In this twofold process of expansion and concentration, nature was instrumental both as the activator of insight and as the object of focus. Correspondence, therefore, as an inspirational means, was sympathy with nature, as well as the doctrine of its expression. And Emerson had in mind the natural history of its agency in inspiration when he gave his course in philosophy at Harvard in 1870-1871. He proposed early in **"Natural History of Intellect"** an aim that had absorbed the full span of his life. "My belief in the use of a course on philosophy," he explained,

> is that the student shall learn to appreciate *the miracle of the mind;* shall learn its subtle but immense power, or shall begin to learn it; shall come to know that in *seeing* and in no tradition he must find what truth is; that he shall see in it the source of all traditions, and shall see each one of them as better or worse statement of its revelations; shall come to trust it entirely, as the only true; to cleave to God against the name of God. When he has once known the oracle he will need no priest. And if he finds at first with some alarm how impossible it is to accept many things which the hot or the mild sectarian may insist on his believing, he will be armed by his insight and brave to meet all inconvenience and all resistance it may cost him. He from whose hand it came will guide and direct it (italics supplied).

How biographical this passage was, only those students knew whose fathers or grandfathers had witnessed and told them of the storm following **"The Divinity School Address"** (1838). To appreciate the miracle of the mind then had been to challenge the reigning miracle of tradition. Emerson had taken the word "miracle" in its traditional, linear sense and had reinterpreted it in terms of the vertical dimension of human consciousness. He said that "the word Miracle as pronounced by Christian churches gives a false impression . . . It is not one with the blowing clover and the falling rain." By divorcing the miracle from an immediate sense of the presence of God in the process of nature, only known by man by sharing that process, the miracle that remained applied only to past events credited by historical testimony. "By withdrawing it [the preaching of the miracle] from the exploration of the moral nature of man, where the sublime is, where are the resources of astonishment and power . . . " the miracle as a support of faith became a dead word, not a living thing. In its sterility was the history of fifty years of America's waning spiritual life. And because of this, for Emerson, redemption was no longer to be sought in the Church but in the soul—in man's own experience of self-reflection. To his generation, long given to thinking of miracles as events of the past, his reaffirmation of their immediacy in consciousness was revolutionary. But as a result of this tremendous semantic shift, a generation later he could quietly say that truth was more likely to be revealed in psychology than in history.

In the early sermons one can trace Emerson's growing awareness of the fact that the revitalization of faith had to come not from **"Miracles"** (1831) but from **"The Miracle of Our Being"** (1834). Miracles were important to faith, because, as Emerson said, "a miracle is the only means by which God can make a communication to men, that shall be known to be from God." For this reason Emerson retained it as historical fact (although he modified the usual interpretation by making the miracle accord with the moral expectations of man). To deny the miracle would have been to deny that God can communicate with man, and this was sufficient reason for him to keep it, in the face of a mechanistic universe that seemed to dull men's senses to the need for miracles. "There are thousands of men who, if there were no histories and if the order of natural events had never been broken, would," he explained the miracle as a departure from the order of nature, "never ask in the course of their lives for anything beyond a secondary cause and never ask for the first." Never shocked into wonder, unless by a breach in nature itself, these "secondary" men found sufficient the explanation afforded by secondary causes. But for Emerson, primary man himself must startle nature with "an instructed eye." He must discover the genuine miracle in his own life, that is, in his relation to the laws of nature—in the fact, for example, that he can will the raising of his arm, communicate his thoughts, and conduct his life, certain that the law of compensation will not fail him. Then he will realize that he can believe in miracles because he is "such a manifestation," because "all our life is a miracle. Ourselves are the greatest wonder of all." Once he has recognized the informing law of his life and of nature, he will no longer find the miracle in departures from natural order, but in the moral bond uniting his constitution and that of the universe. Miracle at this stage in Emerson's sermon has been transformed into the awareness of a higher source of law operating in both nature and man: in the fact that man's sympathy with nature is the basic correspon-

dence revealing God. What he omitted here, but emphasized in the later sermon, was the fact that only in self-reflection (as opposed to the observation of nature) man became aware of the need for a higher law as explanation of his sympathy with nature. For to reflect, he wrote, "is to receive truth immediately from God without any medium." And the noblest fact was that of "being addressed on moral grounds": "This fact is so close to the first fact of our *being,* that, like the circulation of the blood, or the gravity of bodies, it passes long unnoticed from the circumstance of its omnipresence."

When Emerson asked men to reflect on the miracle of their being he first pointed out the wonderful sympathy between nature and man, the way the universe was made to serve man and unfold his faculties. He distinguished, however, between superficial wonder in the external fitness of things and ecstatic wonder of man in the "bare fact" of his existence as a man. He significantly added,

> This external fitness is wonderful, but I doubt if to those who saw this only, it would ever have occurred to remark upon the marvel . . . [because] it may be said of the things apprehended by the senses, that they are so nicely grooved into one another that the sight of one suggests the next preceding, and this the next before, so that the understanding in the study of the things themselves would run forever in the round of second causes, did not the soul at its own instance sometimes demand tidings of the First Cause.

The recognition of the *moral* fitness of the universe to man's needs, therefore, required one to get above the round of secondary causes, to get free from the enslavement to trifles, and to view the spectacle from the soul's vantage in the wonder of direct union with the First Cause. This was the supreme moment in the spiritual life of man, and it was toward this moment that Emerson had been groping in his need to destroy "the Chaos of Thought" of a morally unredeemed universe. "Rend away the darkness," he journalized when he was twenty, "and restore to man the knowledge of this principle [a moral universe], and you have lit the sun over the world and solved the riddle of life." And it was in "the exercise of reason, the act of reflexion" that man lit the sun: "the chief distinctions of his condition begin with that act." Echoing Coleridge, he glorified man's release from "brutishness": "Awakened to truth and virtue—which is the twofold office of Reason, he passes out of the local and finite, he inspires and expires immortal breath."

When the inspired primary man now *contemplates* the world about him, he discovers in himself "a point or focus upon which all objects, all ages concentrate their influence." He is now at "the heart of the world," at "the centre of the Creation." From this angle of vision the universe seems to exist only for his benefit. Life is no longer "an insupportable curse." Now "man lives for a purpose. Hitherto was no object upon which to concentrate his various powers. Now happiness is his being's end and aim." Now, like the "lowest natures"—a leaf, a grain of sand—he is intimately allied to the organic process. Emerson best described this intimacy—and he was a naturalist only to reveal it—when he wrote:

> Look at the summer blackberry lifting its polished surface a few inches from the ground. How did that little chemist extract from the sandbank the spices and sweetness it has concocted in its cells? By any cheap or accidental means? Not so; but the whole creation has been at the cost of its birth and nurture. A globe of fire near a hundred millions of miles distant in the great space, has been flooding it with light and heat as if it shone for no other. It is six or seven months that the sun has made the tour of the heavens every day over this tiny sprout, before it could bear its fruit. The sea has evaporated its countless tons of water that the rain of heaven might wet the roots of this little vine. The elastic air exhaled from all live creatures and all minerals, yield this small pensioner the gaseous aliment it required. The earth by the attraction of its mass determined its form and size; and when we consider how the earth's attraction is fixed at this moment on equilibrium by innumerable attractions, on every side, of distant bodies,—we shall see that the berry's form and history is determined by causes and agents the most prodigious and remote.

By recognizing in the humble blackberry one instance of the focusing of the beneficence of the universe, man himself could see that he, too, was a "center round which all things roll, and upon which all things scatter gifts." Knowing the benefits of his implication in nature, he no longer felt caught in the web of circumstances; instead, in his new freedom, "he stands upon the top of the world; he is the centre of the horizon." Emerson found this a favorite way of expressing the new release from events man discovered in viewing the activity of his mind as an angle of vision. When he looked at the rainbow, he believed himself "the center of its arch," and this feeling of centrality he found in viewing a landscape between his legs or in the rapid movement of a train. But he realized that these experiences were true of all men, that the angle of vision equalized, by making available to any man as much of the universe as his vision could contain. In this way, although dependent on nature, man was "absolutely, imperially free."

But the freedom of perception went beyond this awareness of the benefit of nature. Man, Emerson added, "is not designed to be an idle eye before which nature passes in review, but by his action is enabled to learn the irresistible properties of moral nature, perceived dimly by the mind as laws difficult to be grasped or defined, yet everywhere working out their inevitable results in human affairs." Freedom was only to be found in the perception of the correspondence of the physical and moral laws. The whole message of compensation—the animating force in Emerson's vision—depended on perceiving this, that "the Creation is so magically woven that nothing can do him [man] any mischief but himself." The secondary man (the unregenerate), with his idle eye, will be ground to powder by the laws, will find in nature as much obstacle as benefit. But the primary man, armed by his perception of the moral necessity of law, will be defended "from all harm he wills to resist; the whole creation cannot bend him

whilst he stands upright." The only freedom, like perception, was of this moral order.

The awakening of Reason was, for Emerson, this moral awakening: inspiration *was* moral regeneration. The moral sentiment (or Reason) was the "tie of faith" made alive by the human mind. The law it revealed as the basis of the human mind was the content of inspiration; when seen in nature it was "fatal strength." And, as he repeated in his Harvard lectures, what was of greater worth than the dangerous knowledge of this power of the mind?

> To open to ourselves—to open to others these laws—is it not worth living for? to make the soul, aforetime the servant of the senses, acquainted with the secret of its own power; to teach man that by self-renouncement a heaven of which he had no conception, begins at once in his heart;—by the high act of yielding his will, that little individual heart becomes dilated as with the presence and inhabitation of the Spirit of God.

Not only is this the religious burden of this sermon (as of the more secular essays on **"Worship," "Inspiration,"** and **"Spiritual Laws"**), it is the religious context in which Emerson always thought of the experience of inspiration. When he enjoins men to see in the exaltation of Reason the transcendence of evil and the hidden spiritual good of their worldly failings, he is not mistaking the sense of power in inspiration for an irresponsible release of energies. "What is it," he says of the insight of inspiration, "but a perception of man's true position in the universe and his consequent obligations. This is the whole moral and end of such views as I present." The power to overcome trifles resided in *this insight* and in no other, because, for Emerson, inspiration had no other "meaning" than that of compensation. If vision was to release him from the bondage of the senses, its message had to be a response to his most deeply felt need, had to answer his "metaphysical pathos." And in his moments of vision he found this assurance,

> that the Father who thus vouchsafes to reveal himself . . . will not forsake the child for whom he provideth such costly instruction—whom every hour and every event of memory and hope educate. What does it intimate but presages of an infinite and perfect life? What but an assured trust through all evil and danger and death?

Inspiration experienced only as the ecstatic moment of heightened power was irresponsible, as one suspects from the passage on the transparent eyeball. But bringing with it the obligation (as well as the power) to communicate this insight to others, it made expression, either in act or word, its moral end. Men might feel at the receptive pole the spontaneous, instinctive flood of inspiration; they might balance it by reflecting on it, that is, by standing above it watch its operation and grasp its law. But at the constructive pole, this thought—"always a miracle"— demanded for its publication the control of the spontaneous flow. For in the very way he described the mind, for Emerson inspiration was always saddled with a moral rider; intuition was always coupled with duty. "The poet," he instructed, "who shall use nature as his hieroglyph must have an adequate message to convey thereby." And because insight had to end in a message, the freedom of intuition demanded the necessity of precise form; and once Emerson became aware of this condition, he found, as all conscious artists have; that the reception of inspiration became even more difficult. He found that he needed *two* inspirations, one by which to see, the other by which to write; and by intellectualizing his vision of the laws, he saved himself from the decay of the first, and had more and more only to consider the ebb and flow of the second.

Emerson intellectualized his vision by constructing an astronomy of the imagination. His constitutional need for *seeing* determined the spatial character of his thought; and his devotion to astronomy, especially the Newtonian revelation of gravitational attraction beyond the surface of the earth, provided him his symbols for expressing the fundamental correspondence of physical and moral laws. In the circle he not only found an equivalent for the Coleridgean Idea, but in its compensatory action he saw the moral law of compensation. The daily life of the mind, its ebbing and flowing, he found he could express in the solar cycle of day and night; and this almost "primitive" dependence on the sun and stars, he made the visual metaphor of the process of inspiration. He believed that the most ordinary symbols were adequate to the fullest expression, and day and night were, indeed, the common pulse of the universe.

Men were literally born in darkness, he wrote: "Out of darkness and out of the awful Cause they come to be caught up in this vision of a seeing, partaking, acting and suffering life." As in the womb, they rested in the "circumambient" unconsciousness of God, becalmed on the ebbless sea of the Over-Soul. And so when Emerson took his nightly walk, he felt that "nothing in nature has the softness of darkness . . . or the unutterable gentleness to the sense." In darkness, as in sleep, he felt that he was falling back on God. "If I have weak . . . eyes," he wrote, "no looking at green curtains, no shutting them . . . are of certain virtue . . . but when at last I wake up from a sound sleep, then I know that he that made the eye has dealt with it for the time and the wisest physician is He." In sleep and night were the restorative virtues of a return to the source of life; one ebbed or returned in the night only to flow with insight in the day. He copied from Sophocles

> Dost thou behold the vast and azure sky
> How in its liquid arms the earth doth lie?

and saw in the protective maternity of Lidian for little Waldo a similar image of God's providential care of man. Darkness, then, far more than its usual associations with skepticism and atheism, represented for Emerson a preparation—a night journey of sorts—for the day.

In Emerson's analogy, night was the creator of day, just as in Thoreau's, silence was the *background* of sound. For Emerson, day was the course of living the problems of life from their "uttermost darkness into light." Knowledge of God, he found in Scholastic philosophy, was *matutina cognitio,* morning knowledge; and the self-recovery by which man regained insight and expanded beyond his previous limits he spoke of as *Easting.* Man's mind, he wrote, by "his efforts at self-knowledge . . . will revolve so far that the increasing twilight will give place to the Sun, and

God will appear as he is to his soul." He likened conversion to "day after twilight," and the self-evidency of its truth was its sun-like light. In **"Threnody"** he called it the "super-solar blaze." If this ecstasy of inspiration was a "new morn risen on noon," immortality was the "Day" following the long life of morning.

But any change in the hodiernal cycle, suggesting the transitions of mind, represented the moment of inspiration. Sunset as well as the dawn expressed for Emerson the qualitative feeling of influx. He believed "that no hour, no state of the atmosphere but corresponded to some state of the mind." But even in the bright day of inspiration he felt that the sun needed shadow. Realizing this polarity, he could accept the darkness and opacity of man and nature as the ground of light. He could extend the analogy by saying that sin was opaque and innocence transparent, that society mistook darkness for light, and that the problem of inspiration in writing was to make daylight shine through the word. And in **"Works and Days"** he could contrast works and faith, "huckstering Trade" and the "deep to-day." His whole philosophy of the moment—of the time-transcending of the total response to nature—was expressed in this comparison: "Works and days were offered us, and we took works . . . [But] he is only rich who owns the day."

Emerson experienced the day in his adverbial perception of nature, in his feeling of intimate union with the law in and behind the natural process. His awareness of law, of natural order and harmony, was expressed in its mental correlative, the Idea. And the possibility of representing a total feeling in a thought derived from the basic correspondence of the mental and physical spheres. "The crystal sphere of thought," he wrote, "is as concentrical as the geological globe we inhabit." This correspondence made possible a method of expression that seemed to him to unfold thought according to the method of nature.

He liked Plato's expression "that God geometrizes." Plato, too, he found, geometrized, and this made him both a poet and a man who "at the same time [is] acquainted with the geometrical foundations of things, and with their moral purposes, and sees the festal splendor of the day." Plato was the "great-eyed," and his second sight explained his stress on geometry. His geometry of Ideas made possible the communication of inspiration and somehow preserved its splendor: "In his broad daylight things reappear as they stood in the sunlight, hardly shorn of a ray, yet now portable and reportable." A similar "geometric, astronomic morals" Emerson wanted for himself, and demanded earlier of the teacher he would become: "The Teacher that I look for and await shall enunciate with more precision and universality, with piercing poetic insight those beautiful yet severe compensations that give to nature an aspect of mathematical science."

In Emerson's geometry of morals, the circle was the basic figure. He derived it, perhaps from his own sense of the bending horizon, from his own experience of the eye as the first circle and the horizon as the second; and like the horizon, it symbolized the Unattainable and the progressive ascent by which one advanced on the chaos and the dark. As the "primary figure," the "highest emblem in the cipher of the world," the circle represented as well the unifying Idea (as he adapted it from Coleridge), and its concentric expansion represented the process of ascending generalization, each step of which, in man's moral progress, was his highest knowledge of God. For God's creation of nature was also circular: "Nature can only be conceived of as existing to a universal and not to a particular end," he wrote, "to a universe of ends, and not to one,—a work of *ecstasy,* to be represented by a circular movement, as intention might be signified by a straight line of definite length." By similar ecstasies and self-recoveries man retraced in his own advancing circles of thought, the advancing circles of God in nature. And by taking up the angle of vision, every man could become the center of the circle, at one with God; for in Emerson's astronomy, as in St. Augustine's, God was "a circle whose center was everywhere, and its circumference nowhere." God was the "centripetal force" in "the depths of the soul," saving man, in the unending antagonism of centripetal and centrifugal forces, from the circumferential ignorance. Man's life in God began from the moment of ecstasy, and from "there the Universe evolves itself as from a centre to its boundless irradiation." Again the circular growth of the self described this idea and god-seeking: "The life of man is a self-evolving circle, which, from a ring imperceptibly small, rushes on all sides outwards to new and larger circles, and that without End." And if God was the greatest circle, and the circle in its nature compensatory, Emerson could find in his notion of God as "the Great Compensation" a symbol of the Over-Soul as container and resolution of all antagonism; and the Over-Soul, as the circumambient atmosphere he felt overhanging him like the sky—a "heaven within heaven"—filled the intellectual circle with the content of his living experience.

Like the Ideas they represented, circles were compensatory. In the dialectic of inspiration (and thought) they represented the limit of each expanding ebb and flow. Each Idea, by compensating for a multitude of observations, was an ascent; each Idea became a higher platform from which to survey the prospect for a still higher generalization looming on a still more distant horizon. Ascending to thought in this way was the intellectual equivalent of distant visioning; the synthesis was in the focus of ever widening vistas—and one's visual reach was best achieved in ascent. Emerson described this intellectual visioning:

> But now and then the lawless imagination flies out and asserts her habit. I revisit the verge of my intellectual domain. How the restless soul runs round the out-most orbit and builds her bold conclusion as a tower of observation from whence her eyes wander incessantly in the unfathomable abyss. I dimly scrutinize the vast constitution of being.

This intellectual restlessness was the true compensation. Emerson said that his cardinal faith was "that all secrets of the less [the prudential] are commanded by the larger generalization [the spiritual]." And "ascent" was the proper word, because he always felt that the spiritual laws were *above* prudential concerns. The compensation of insight or self-recovery, then, lay in the power to press beyond the limits of a previous thought. When his center

proved to be merely another circumference, he felt his powers decay. He felt the heart's refusal to be imprisoned in an Idea, and he expressed this by saying "that around every circle another can be drawn . . . there is no end in nature." Or to return to the analogy of night and day, "There is always another dawn risen on mid-noon," and " 'He who contemplates hath a day without night.' "

The possibility that with the returning life of influx he would regain a wider angle of vision seemed to him evidence in itself of God's presence in the universe. Unable to state the truth once and for all, unable to rest in an idea—these were signs to Emerson that in the harmony of man and the universe it was with man as it was with God: "There is no outside, no enclosing wall, no circumference to us." But the spasms of inspiration also showed him how humanly dependent he was, how fragmentary was the view from his angle of vision. He wrote that "a glimpse, a point of view that by its brightness excludes the purview, is granted, but no panorama. A fuller inspiration should cause the point to flow and become a line, should bend the line and complete the circle."

He could avoid the parallax of insight by a sympathetic correspondence with nature; in his own experience of distant vision and reflection he found that he could align himself with the axis of things. Whatever the magnetism of the universe was, for him, it directed his eye to the horizon and beyond to the "aboriginal self," to the "science-baffling star, without parallax." The deep force of "Spontaneity or Instinct" directed him, opened his eye in reflection to the source of being and light which he realized as Intuition. Beyond this his metaphysics of inspiration and self-reliance could not go. For he knew that he could not willfully make his inspiration consecutive; it was like the coming of day, dependent on the law, and therefore to be awaited with assurance. But its coming always predicted night. An idea might at the moment of its conception bind a fragmentary nature within its circle, but in the total demands of an angle of vision come full circle, it could only serve as an arc. Emerson learned this more and more from the infrequency of his inspirational experiences; and when his early static conception of nature gave way to one of illusion and flux, he found that the arc again provided the only way in which his angle of vision could accommodate the ceaseless flow.

By joining the static and mechanistic circle of Newtonian astronomy (his debt to eighteenth-century science) with the dynamic science of Ideas or dialectic of Coleridge, Emerson made his circle an organic symbol capable of representing both the unfolding mind and the ascending natural chain of being. His circle united his two desires: the desire for fixity or centrality in the universe of the spirit, and the desire for change and growth and freedom in the organic universe of prudence. He wanted it to show both the "evanescence and centrality of things." He wanted a symbol for what the ancient myths taught him was still true in human experience, that "things are in a flood and fixed as adamant: the *Bhagavat Geeta* adduces the illustration of the sphered, mutable, yet centered air or ether." The circle symbolized this sphered mutability, the growth that depended on a fixed center in being. As the center of the circle, God (through his sympathetic correspondence with Him) provided him the fixity and centrality he needed when nature became an ever-changing screen of "slippery sliding surfaces"; the circumference of the circle, the human and natural limitations, receded in the ecstatic use of nature as the representative of law, whether that law was perceived directly in nature, or, later, through nature. That the perpetual *transformations* witnessed in the natural process expressed in their tendency the circular ascent of spirit were as much a miracle to Emerson as the mind's self-expansions. For both were affirmations of the infinite, of the compensation of ascent, of the power of new prospects. Limited by his human angle of vision and the fitful light of self-reflection or intuition, Emerson still had for his own the arc of nature, and the arc perceived in the fullness of his ecstatic insight promised a corresponding circle and represented for him its portable and reportable truth. (pp. 71-102)

> *Sherman Paul, in his* Emerson's Angle of Vision: Man and Nature in American Experience, *Cambridge, Mass.: Harvard University Press, 1952, 268 p.*

Newton Arvin   (essay date 1959)

[*Arvin was an American educator and critic whose works include biographies of Hawthorne, Whitman, and Melville. In the following essay, he counters the criticism that Emerson did not acknowledge the existence of evil, placing Emerson's views in a context of philosophical and religious tradition.*]

No one knew better than Emerson that every generation goes through a necessary and proper ritual-slaying of its parents; that Zeus, as he would say, is forever destroying his father Cronos; and that, if the writers of one age reject, with a kind of sacrificial solemnity, the writers who have just preceded them, this is quite as it ought to be—is the Method of Nature herself. "Our life," he said, "is an apprenticeship to the truth that around every circle another can be drawn; that there is no end in nature, but every end is a beginning; that there is always another dawn risen on mid-noon, and under every deep a lower deep opens." He could not have been surprised, therefore, and probably he would not even have been much disturbed, if his sons, or his son's sons, turned upon him, metaphorically speaking, and put him to the knife on the reeking altar of literary and intellectual change. Certainly this is what happened. Emerson had been the Socrates and even the Zoroaster of the generation of young men and women for whom he first spoke, and to tell the truth, it was not until a third age had arrived that the Imitation of Emerson was followed by his Immolation.

This rite was performed by the literary leaders of the period of the First World War. Almost forty years ago Mr. T. S. Eliot, whose voice was rightly to carry so far, remarked that "the essays of Emerson are already an encumbrance." Three or four years later D. H. Lawrence expressed a somewhat less drastic but in its implications almost equally repudiative view: "I like Emerson's real courage," he said. "I like his wild and genuine belief in the

Over-soul and the inrushes he got from it. But it is a museum-interest. Or else it is a taste of the old drug to the old spiritual dope-fiend in me." Emerson, not as a tonic, but as a narcotic—this is the Emerson who came more and more to serve as an image of the man for the new era. The greatest poet of that generation put the case against him with almost filial finality. Speaking, in his autobiography, of his friend, the Irish poet AE, William Butler Yeats observed that he sometimes wondered what AE "would have been had he not met in early life the poetry of Emerson and Walt Whitman, writers who have begun to seem superficial," said Yeats, "because they lack the Vision of Evil."

There was much in Emerson's writings, Heaven knows, to account for these rejections; but the ground on which Yeats put *his* was the most serious and the most fundamental—the deficiency in Emerson of what a Spanish writer of that period called famously the Tragic Sense of Life. And indeed it did not have to be left to the age of Eliot and Yeats to express a dissatisfaction with this blindness of Emerson's. There were writers, as there were doubtless readers, of his own time who found him terribly wanting in any true awareness of what one of them called the Power of Blackness. Hawthorne, who was his neighbor in Concord, had a due respect for Emerson as a man; but Emerson the transcendental optimist addressed no word of authority to the ear of Hawthorne—who described him as "Mr. Emerson—the mystic, stretching his hand out of cloudland, in vain search for something real." And Hawthorne's younger contemporary Melville could be even more severe; in the margin of his copy of Emerson's essays, adjoining a particularly cheerful passage in the essay on **"Prudence,"** Melville wrote: "To one who has weathered Cape Horn as a common sailor, what stuff all this is." A much younger man than either Hawthorne or Melville, Henry James, would not have spoken of Mr. Emerson, his father's friend, in just this vein of disrespectful impatience, but he too could not refrain from remarking that there was a side of life as to which Emerson's eyes were thickly bandaged. "He had no great sense of wrong," said James—"a strangely limited one, indeed, for a moralist—no sense of the dark, the foul, the base."

They all mount up—judgments like these, and there are a hundred of them—to what sometimes seems like not only a damaging but a fatal indictment of Emerson as a writer whom we can ever again listen to with the old reverential attention. A writer who lacks the Vision of Evil, who has no great sense of wrong—how can he be read with respect, or perhaps read at all, in a time when we all seem agreed that anguish, inquietude, the experience of guilt, and the knowledge of the Abyss are the essential substance of which admissible literature is made? It is a painful question to any reader who cannot suppress his sense of a deep debt to Emerson. But it is a question that must be asked, and one has to confess that, as one turns the pages of his essays, the reasons stare one in the face why Hawthorne and Melville, Eliot and Yeats, should have answered it so negatively.

Certainly it is hard to understand how a writer of even the least seriousness could dispose so jauntily as Emerson sometimes does of the problem of moral evil—genially denying, in fact, or seeming to, that it is a problem at all. Are we really listening to a moralist who expects to be heard respectfully when we find Emerson saying, à propos of young people who are troubled by the problems of original sin, the origin of evil, and the like: "These never presented a practical difficulty to any man,—never darkened across any man's road who did not go out of his way to seek them. These are the soul's mumps and measles and whooping-coughs. . . . A simple mind will not know these enemies"? We rub our eyes as we read, and then open another volume and find the same sage and seer reassuring us even more blandly that "The less we have to do with our sins the better. No man can afford to waste his moments in compuctions."

Did any writer on morals, we are tempted to ask at such moments, ever go farther than this toward inculcating a hard complacency, a shallow self-righteousness, in his readers? The feeling of unreality that rises in us at these times is almost dreamlike, and so it is on at least some of the occasions when Emerson turns his gaze reluctantly to what used to be called natural evil—to the facts of human misery and suffering—to the Tragic. Is it possible to recognize, in the sun-warmed landscape of the Emersonian center, the terribly familiar world of primordial human experience—that world in which sunshine and warmth have alternated, for most men, with bitter cold and darkness? It is easy to get the mistaken impression that, for Emerson, there were indeed no Cape Horns in experience, no jungles, no Arctic nights, no shark-infested seas; only the amiable rustic landscape of the Concord fields and woodlots. "I could never give much reality to evil and pain," he wrote in his late fifties, and though he had also said quite different things from this, it is true that at the *center* of his mind the space was wholly free from either pain or evil. His thought may be in some sense on the hither side of the tragic; it may be in another sense beyond the tragic; *non*-tragic it undeniably is. He himself was quite clear about this. "And yet," he writes in a characteristic poem,

> And yet it seemeth not to me
> That the high gods love tragedy.

Nor did he love it himself. I am speaking now not of the literary form but of tragedy as an aspect of experience—a subject to which only once in his mature career did Emerson give sustained attention. This was in a short essay he contributed to the *Dial,* an essay called **"The Tragic"** that was based in part on a lecture he had given a little earlier. It is true that Emerson published this essay in a magazine, but characteristically he never reprinted it, and it was left for his literary executors to include it in a posthumous volume. The theme of this piece is that, after everything has been said that may be said on the topic of human misery, in the end one returns to the knowledge that suffering is a kind of illusion, that it has no absolute or ultimate reality. All sorrow, says Emerson, "is superficial; for the most part fantastic, or in the appearance and not in things . . . For all melancholy, as all passion, belongs to the exterior life. . . . Most suffering is only apparent." And he goes on to speak of the self-operating compensations for suffering in a passage about the horrors of the slave-trade that

tempts one, for a moment, to throw his book into the fire, as Whittier is said to have thrown *Leaves of Grass.*

To fix one's attention on passages such as this is to wonder how it is humanly possible for a man to have so weak a memory of his own sorrows or so little compassion for those of other men. Along with this there is that other strain in Emerson that has driven so many readers away from him—the strain in which he seems to be saying that progress, amelioration, an upward movement of things is a law of nature, like gravitation or natural selection, and that the painful human will is very little engaged in it. "Gentlemen," he said to one audience, "there is a sublime and friendly Destiny by which the human race is guided . . . to results affecting masses and ages. Men are narrow and selfish, but the Genius or Destiny is not narrow, but beneficent. . . . Only what is inevitable interests us, and it turns out that love and good are inevitable, and in the course of things." This is the very lotus-dream of progress, you will say, and so is that Emersonian conviction that good ends are always served whether by good men or bad; that rogues and savages are as effectual in the process as prophets and saints. "The barbarians who broke up the Roman Empire," he says, "did not arrive a day too soon." This apparently effortless emergence of good from evil, we are told, is a law not only of nature but of history. "Through the years and the centuries," says Emerson, "through evil agents, through toys and atoms, a great and beneficent tendency irresistibly streams."

"Irresistibly," did you say? Did you say that "love and good are *inevitable*"? Are we to understand that the Destiny that guides human history is simply "friendly" and "beneficent"? To the ears of contemporary men there is a mockery of unreality in such language that makes the language of the Arabian Nights seem to ring with the strong accents of realism. In the fearful light of what has happened in history since Emerson said these things—not to speak of what happened before—can one be merely indignant if some thoughtful men have long since settled it that Emerson is not for them? Can one even be wholly surprised if he has sometimes been relegated to the shabby company of faddists and faith-healers, or the equally questionable company of those who have preached the gospel of success, the strenuous life, or the power of positive thinking? The truth is, these charlatans have often drawn, either directly or indirectly, on Emerson himself, and, alas, one can only too easily see why. Let us face it. If Emerson has been coarsened and vulgarized by these people, it is because there are aspects of his thought that have lent themselves to this process. And it is as certain as any human forecast can be that no writer of comparable scope and authority will ever again tell us *in just those tones* that moral evil is negligible and that suffering is a mere illusion.

Yet no one in his sense supposes for a moment that Emerson really belongs in the company of Bruce Barton or Dale Carnegie any more than Plato belongs in the company of Norman Vincent Peale. A powerful instinct tells us that, as he himself remarked of Channing, Emerson is still in some sense our bishop, and that we have not done with him yet. There is no danger of our ever having too many guides or fortifiers, and we know perfectly well that, though we are determined to hold on to Hawthorne and Melville, we cannot afford to dispense with Emerson either. We can afford to dispense with him so little that I suppose most of us are willing now to look at the whole of his work dispassionately and raise for ourselves the question whether his essays are really, after all, a mere encumbrance—or drug. If there proves to be more than this to say, we can hardly be losers. And the more critically one looks at his work, the more it becomes clear that there is a a good deal more to be said. No great writer is ever rectilinear—is ever unequivocal or free from contradictions—and Emerson, who consciously disbelieved in straight lines and single poles, is at least as resistant to simple formulas as most. Not only so, but, after all, the problem of evil—the tragic question—is hardly a simple one itself, and the truth is that men have given more than one answer to it. It is a matter of elementary critical justice, surely, to try to arrive at a view of Emerson not only in the flat but in depth.

To tell the truth, there is a greater willingness nowadays to work toward such a view than there was thirty or forty years ago. It has become more usual than it once was to recognize that that celebrated optimism of Emerson's was somewhat less the product of good fortune or of a natively happy temper than it was an achievement both of intellectual and emotional discipline. It was a conviction he had arrived at after youthful years during which he had as good reasons as most men—poverty, ill health, bereavement, anxiety—for questioning the absolute rightness of things. No one who has read his early letters and journals can fail to be conscious of the minor strain that runs through them—the strain of sadness, apprehension, and doubtfulness of the goods of existence. The young Emerson can sound strangely like the mature Melville. He was only twenty, and a year or two out of college, when he wrote in his journal: "There *is* a huge and disproportionate abundance of *evil* on earth. Indeed the good that is here is but a little island of light amidst the unbounded ocean." Three or four years after this, forced by his alarming physical weakness, he gave up preaching temporarily and went South in search of recovery. It was a period of dire low spirits and anxiety for him, and one can understand his writing from St. Augustine to his aunt, Mary Moody Emerson: "He has seen but half the Universe who never has been shown the house of Pain. Pleasure and Peace are but indifferent teachers of what it is life to know." One might suppose that this outcry was only the bitter expression of a passing state of physical and emotional misery; but it was more than that. A dozen years had elapsed after his stay in the South when he contributed to the *Dial* the essay on **"The Tragic"** I have already alluded to. That essay, oddly enough, begins with one of the sentences from the old letter to his aunt; let me quote it again: "He has seen but half the universe who never has been shown the house of Pain." And he goes on at once, in the essay, to say: "As the salt sea covers more than two thirds of the surface of the globe, so sorrow encroaches in man on felicity."

Whatever his theory of suffering may have come to be, Emerson cannot be accused, at least in his earlier years, of having denied to it a kind of reality. On the contrary, there are passages in the sermons he preached as a young minister that remind one much more of the sombre Calvinist homilies of his forebears than of the characteristically hopeful and cheerful Unitarians in whose ranks he was for a time enlisted. A few weeks after he returned from St. Augustine, in 1827, he preached a sermon on the theme of change and mortality that strikes an even Biblical note of sorrow and affliction. "Have we brought in our hands," he asks, like a kind of Unitarian Job—"Have we brought in our hands any safe conduct to show to our ghastly enemies, Pain and Death? Shall we not, my brethren, be sufferers as all our fathers were? Shall we not be sick? Shall we not die?" And a little later in the same sermon he alludes, in a phrase that suggests Hawthorne rather than the familiar Emerson, to "the dark parable of human existence."

It is quite true that these Old Testament accents become less and less characteristic of him as he approaches the maturity of his powers, and that the Emerson of the great middle period—of the famous addresses at Harvard, Dartmouth, and Waterville, and of all the best-known essays—is the Emerson whom we have to think of as the Orpheus of Optimism. But, even in this period, and certainly later, there is another tone, an undertone, in his writings which we should listen to if we wish to sensitize ourselves to the complex harmony of his total thought. That thought, to change the image, is a polarized thought, and if at one pole we find a celebration of the powers of the human will, at the other pole we find an insistence on its limitations—on the forces in nature that are not friendly but hostile and even destructive to human wishes, and on the discrepancy between what a man aspires to do and what nature and circumstance allow him to do. "The word Fate, or Destiny," he says in the essay on Montaigne, "expresses the sense of mankind, in all ages, that the laws of the world do not always befriend, but often hurt and crush us. Fate, in the shape of . . . nature, grows over us like grass. . . . What front can we make against these unavoidable, victorious, maleficent forces?"

Are there, then, along with, or running counter to, the "great and beneficent tendency," forces of immense potency in nature which are not amiable but fierce and ruinous? Yes, so Emerson tells us—not only in this essay of the forties but in a lecture he delivered several times in the fifties and at last published as the essay on **"Fate"** in *The Conduct of Life.* It is an essay that should be read by everyone who imagines that for Emerson there were not really any Cape Horns in experience. "No picture of life," he says, "can have any veracity that does not admit the odious facts." And he lays himself out to suggest what those facts are—the facts of nature's ferocity—with a grim thoroughness that suggests the authors of *Candide* or *Rasselas* or *Moby Dick* much more vividly than the author of **"The Over-Soul."** Here is all the familiar imagery of naturalistic pessimism—the imagery of earthquakes and volcanic eruptions, of plagues and famine, of tooth and claw. "The habit of the snake and spider, the snap of the tiger and other leapers and bloody jumpers, the crackle of the bones of his prey in the coil of the anaconda"—these are all in nature, he insists, and so are "the forms of the shark . . . the jaw of the sea-wolf paved with crushing teeth, the weapons of the grampus, and other warriors hidden in the sea." Could Voltaire or Melville or Zola say more?

Yet the savagery of nature—nature's Darwinism, to call it so—furnishes less of the stuff of the essay on **"Fate"** than what I spoke of a moment ago, the restrictiveness of nature; the tight limits set about the human will, human aspiration, human effort, by all the forces of heredity and circumstance that Emerson dramatizes by the old word Fate. "The Circumstance is Nature," says he. "Nature is what you may do. There is much you may not . . . The book of Nature is the book of Fate." Within these merely natural and material boundaries men are the creatures of their conditioning. "How shall a man," asks Emerson, "escape from his ancestors, or draw off from his veins the black drop which he drew from his father's or his mother's life?" A demonstration of these painful truths that fascinated Emerson for a time, a few years earlier, had been the new science of statistics—the science that seemed to settle it that human behavior can be reduced to mathematical terms and predicted as confidently as the precession of the equinoxes. Perhaps it can, says Emerson, with a quiet smile, in the essay on Swedenborg: "If one man in twenty thousand, or in thirty thousand," he says, "eats shoes or marries his grandmother, then in every twenty thousand or thirty thousand is found one man who eats shoes or marries his grandmother." At any rate, viewed from the outside, as objects, as mere creatures of nature and society, men live and work within lines that are for the most part drawn not by them but for them. We must learn what not to expect.

In short it is not true that Emerson's optimism is quite so unmodulated as it has often been represented as being, or that he was so incapable as Yeats thought him to be of the Vision of Evil. I have been speaking of Evil just now in the sense of suffering and frustration, but even if it is a question of moral evil, of human malignancy, depravity, and vice, it is not true that Emerson averted his gaze from it quite so steadily as his detractors have said. Neither suffering nor wickedness is his primary theme; they are not even secondary; in his work as a whole they are tiny patches of grayness or blackness in a composition that is flooded with light and high color. But, even if we ignore the sermons of his youth, in which the New England sense of guilt and sinfulness sometimes throbs and shoots as painfully as it ever does in Hawthorne—even if we ignore these early writings, it is not true that Emerson's view of human nature was a merely smiling and sanguine one. To be sure, it was the feebleness of men, their incompetence, their imbecility, that he castigated, when he was in this vein, more often than their depravity. But, when he chose, he could express himself as unsentimentally as any moral realist on the brutishness of which men are capable. It was no mere idealist who said, with some humor indeed, in speaking of the Norman Conquest: "Twenty thousand thieves landed at Hastings."

This bluntness is very characteristic of him, and when he was really deeply stirred by the spectacle of systematic cruelty and injustice, as he was during the long anguish of the anti-slavery struggle, he could wrench off certain specious masks and disguises as unsparingly, as realistical-

ly, as any of his Calvinist ancestors could have done. Read the **"Address"** he delivered at Concord on the anniversary of the emancipation of slaves in the West Indies if you wish to have a glimpse of Emerson the moral realist. They tell us, he says in his speech, that the slave-holder does not wish to own slaves for the love of owning them, but only because of the material advantages his ownership brings. Experience, however, he goes on to say, does not bear out this comfortable evasion, but shows "the existence, beside the covetousness, of a bitterer element, the love of power, the voluptuousness of holding a human being in his absolute control." Men are capable, says Emerson, of liking to inflict pain, and the slave-holder "has contracted in his indolent and luxurious climate the need of excitement by irritating and tormenting his slave."

It is hard to see how the Vision of Evil, at least for a moment, could be much keener or more terrible than this; and in the whole slavery connection Emerson said a good many things almost equally piercing. But it remains true that his animadversions on human wickedness, like his allusions to human suffering, are closer to the circumference than to the center of Emerson's thought; they give his writings their moral chiaroscuro, but they are not dominant, and I have perhaps dwelt too long on them. His controlling mode of thought, even in his later and more skeptical years, is a certain form of Optimism and *not* a form of the Tragic Sense, and what I should like to say now is that, however we may ourselves feel about this philosophy, it was one that rested not only on a deep personal experience but on a considered theory of Evil, and moreover that this was a theory by no means peculiar to Emerson, or original with him: on the contrary, it had a long and august tradition behind it in Western thought and analogies with the thought not only of Europe but of the East. To put it very briefly, it is the theory that identifies Evil with non-existence, with negation, with the absence of positive Being. In his own writings Emerson expressed this doctrine first in the famous **"Address"** at the Divinity School at Harvard in 1838, the manifesto of his heterodoxy. "Good is positive," he said to the graduating class that day. "Evil is merely privative, not absolute: it is like cold, which is the privation of heat. All evil is so much death or nonentity. Benevolence is absolute and real."

Such language as this has become terribly unfamiliar to us, and Heaven knows for what good reasons, in our own guilt-ridden and anxious time; some of us may find it hard to believe that reasonable men ever entertained such a view. The truth is, however, that it is not only a philosophical but an essentially religious view, and that its sources, to speak only of the West, are in the Platonic and Neo-Platonic tradition and in Christian theology on the side on which it derives from that tradition. It was from these sources, indeed, that Emerson drew his theoretical Optimism. When Plato identified the Good with absolute reality, and Evil with the imperfectly real or the unreal, he was speaking a language beyond Tragedy; and let us not forget that he proposed to banish tragic poetry from his ideal Republic—to banish it on the ground that the wise and virtuous man will wish to control the emotions of grief and sorrow rather than to stimulate them. As for Plotinus, the greatest of the Neo-Platonists, whom Emerson read with such excitement in the few years before the **"Address"** at the Divinity School, he too denied that Evil can have a part in real existence, since this—real existence—is by definition good. "If then evil exists," says Plotinus, "there remains for it the sphere of not-being, and it is, as it were, a certain form of not-being." The sentence reads very much like Emerson's own.

At any rate it was this Neo-Platonic denial of any absolute or ultimate reality to Evil that seems to have found its way into Christian orthodoxy in the writings of St. Augustine—"a man," as Emerson says, "of as clear a sight as almost any other." The Manicheans had attributed to Evil a positive and independent existence, and Augustine as a young man had fallen under their spell; but he had broken away from them at the time of his conversion, and steeped as he was in the thought of the Neo-Platonists, he arrived at a theory of Evil that, on one level, seems indistinguishable from theirs. "Evil has no positive nature," he says in *The City of God;* "but the loss of good has received the name 'evil.' " In itself it is purely negative, a diminishment or corruption of the good, for, as he says, "no nature at all is evil, and this is a name for nothing but the want of good." Of course, as one need not say, Augustine does not deny that *sin* has a kind of reality, but he conceives of it as an essentially negative reality—as a rejection or refusal of the Good, not as an ultimate and independent essence in itself.

No sane man, of course, whatever his metaphysics, can refuse to recognize that wrong-doing is in some sense a *fact;* and Emerson was much too clear-sighted a moralist not to find a place in his thought, as Augustine had done, for what his ancestors had called "sin," though his account of it is not quite the same as Augustine's. He accounts for it, in a more purely transcendental way, by distinguishing between what is real to the intellect and what is real to the conscience—real, that is, in the conduct of life itself. "Sin, seen from the thought," he says, "is a diminution, or *less;* seen from the conscience or will, it is pravity or *bad.* The intellect names it shade, absence of light, and no essence. The conscience must feel it as essence, essential evil. This it is not; it has an objective existence, but no subjective." Objectively, that is, and when the conscience speaks, the savagery of the slave-holder is real enough; subjectively, and when the voice of the mind is heard, that savagery is seen for the "absence of light," the essential unreality, it is. Despite their differences, Augustine and Emerson are saying at least not dissimilar things.

Convictions such as this, at any rate, are at the heart and core of his philosophic optimism. Both sin and suffering, moral and natural evil, *appear* in experience; but they are indeed appearances, not ultimate realities; what reality they have is relative, external, transitory; absolutely speaking, they are shadows, phenomena, illusions. We may, in our time, find such convictions as these mistaken, but let us recognize them for what they are. They are convictions of an essentially religious sort, and like Plato's, or Plotinus's, or Augustine's, they are in themselves inconsistent with the Tragic Sense. We are in the habit of assuming that the most serious and profound apprehension of reality is the Sense of Tragedy; but it may be that, in assuming

this, we ourselves are mistaken. It may be that there are points of view from which the Tragic Sense must be seen as serious and profound indeed, but limited and imperfectly philosophical. It may even be that there can exist a kind of complacency of pessimism, as there is certainly a complacency of optimism; and that many of us in this age are guilty of it. We hug our negations, our doubts, our disbeliefs, to our chests, as if our moral and intellectual dignity depended on them. And indeed it does—so far as the alternative is to remain *this side* of Tragedy, and to shut our ears and eyes to the horrors of experience. Our impatience with Emerson is by no means wholly baseless. We feel, and we have a right to feel, that, if we take his work as a whole, there is a certain distortion in the way it reflects the real world; a certain imbalance and deformation in the way in which the lights and shadows are distributed. The shadows are too meager, and sometimes they are too easily conjured away. We have a right to feel that, too much of the time, Emerson is speaking with a lightheartedness that seems to keep him on this side of Tragedy.

What I have been trying to suggest, however, is that we cannot justly leave him there—that the time has come to remind ourselves that it is possible to reach beyond Tragedy, as well as to remain on the hither side of it; that this is what the religious sense has always done; that Tragedy, as a poetic form, has flourished only rarely, in periods of disbelief and denial; and that, for Emerson, disbelief and denial were simply impossible, ultimately, in the light of his transcendental faith. We may well dislike the tone he often takes, but if we wait patiently enough, we shall find him taking other tones; and in the end we must recognize that, whatever our own convictions are, the best of Emerson is on the other side of Tragedy. I have tried to show that he did not simply *find* himself there; if he had got beyond Tragedy, it was because he had *moved* beyond it. "It requires moral courage to grieve," says Kierkegaard; "it requires religious courage to rejoice." We would be less than just, I think, if we denied that Emerson's courage was both moral and religious.

His acquaintance with the religious literature of the world was very wide; it was by no means confined to the Christian or even the Western tradition; and perhaps we might concede that his perspective was wider and deeper than that which most of us can command. While he was still in his thirties he began to read some of the Hindu scriptures as they appeared in translation; and he quickly recognized in them philosophical and religious insights that seemed at times to be mere anticipations of his own. When he read the Upanishads, or the *Bhagavad-Gita,* or the *Vishnu Purana,* what he found in them was a conception of the ultimate and impersonal Ground of Being—of Brahma—that had much in common with the Absolute of the Neo-Platonists and with his own God or Over-Soul. He found more than that. He had already arrived at the conviction that, as he said, "Within and Above are synonyms"; that the Over-Soul and the individual soul are one; that the kingdom of God, as the gospel says, is within you. The Upanishads only confirmed him in this conviction—confirmed him by their expression of the doctrine that the Absolute Self and the individual self are identical; that Brahma and Atman, as they say, are one; that, as they also say, "*That* art *Thou.*" This too was a doctrine that left the Tragic Sense behind it. According to the Upanishads, the man who, as a result of intense discipline and concentrated meditation, attains to a knowledge of the Self—call it either Brahma or Atman, for they are the same—has transcended the illusory realm of human wretchedness and wickedness, and is beyond either. "He who knows the Self," says the *Brihadaranyaka Upanishad,* "is honored of all men and attains to blessedness. He who meditates upon Brahma as such lacks nothing and is forever happy. He who meditates upon Brahma as such becomes himself invincible and unconquerable. . . . Indeed, the Self, in his true nature, is free from craving, free from evil, free from fear."

When one reads passages like this, and there are many of them, one finds it easy to understand why the literary form of Tragedy—the tragic drama—is unknown in Sanskrit literature. In any case, I do not wish to imply that there are no important differences, even in this connection, among the thinkers I have spoken of; that the Neo-Platonist Plotinus, the orthodox Christian Augustine, and the authors of the Upanishads were perfectly at one in their view of Good and Evil; and that Emerson is indistinguishable from any of them. The differences are vital, some of them, and certainly there is much in Emerson, especially in his tone, that would have struck his great predecessors as very dubious indeed. I have intended only to suggest that it is superficial to rule out the whole of him, once for all, on the ground that he lacked the Vision of Evil; to see him as nothing but a transcendental American optimist of the mid-nineteenth century; to fail to see that his view of these things was in a great philosophic and religious tradition; and that he rejected Tragedy not because he was by temperament wholly incapable of tragic insight but because it seemed to him that, as Karl Jaspers has said, "tragedy is not absolute but belongs in the foreground"; it belongs, as he says, "in the world of sense and time," but not in the realm of transcendence. It belongs, let us say, in the world of appearance, of the relative, of illusion; not in the realm of transcendent reality and truth in which Emerson's faith was complete. And perhaps it is only readers who have a comparable faith, who will now accept him as master and guide; accept him as Dante accepted Vergil: "tu duca, tu segnore, e tu maestro."

Yet this is not quite true either, and I suppose has never been. There seem always to have been readers, there seem to be readers still, who have not been able to share Emerson's idealistic religious beliefs, and who nevertheless have found him, in spite of everything, an intellectual and moral stimulant—a cup-bearer, not an anaesthetist. Certainly Baudelaire did not share Emerson's optimism, yet Baudelaire pored over **The Conduct of Life,** and said that Emerson had "a certain flavor of Seneca about him, which effectively stimulates meditation." Certainly André Gide did not share Emerson's transcendentalism, yet Gide describes Emerson's essays as "reading for the morning," and clearly he found in them that *matutina cognitio* or "morning knowledge" which Emerson himself, borrowing a phrase from Thomas Aquinas, had described as the knowledge of God. Certainly Nietzsche did not share Emerson's other-worldliness, yet Emerson was one of his two

or three great teachers and models. He is said to have carried copies of the essays, heavily annotated, with him whenever he travelled; and it was precisely Emerson's capacity for joy that Nietzsche seems most to have cherished in him. There is a paragraph in *The Twilight of Idols* in which he compares Emerson with Carlyle, to the disadvantage of the latter: Emerson, says he, "is much more enlightened, much broader, more versatile, and more subtle than Carlyle; but above all, he is happier . . . His mind is always finding reasons for being contented and even thankful." For the author of *Zarathustra* this could only have been a token of Emerson's greatness.

Why is it that men of this sort, so little given to easy solutions and facile reassurances, have again and again found Emerson so bracing? Not, surely, because they have been willing to accept his transcendental theory of Evil, but because that theory, in Emerson as in some other thinkers, proved to be wholly consistent with a moral strenuousness seldom encountered in modern writers one can respect. For the truth is that, in this connection as in others, Emerson is a polarized, a contradictory, writer; and if, at the one extreme, you find the peculiar moral passiveness that contents itself with a "beneficent" and "irresistible" tendency toward the Good, at the other extreme you find the equally if not more characteristic celebration of the active and energetic will. It is what Emerson often calls Power, and in the essay on **"Fate"** from which I have quoted, after giving the devil his due, and making every concession to the determinists that seems to him possible, he goes on to insist that, among the forces operating in the universe, the human will is one—and that, ideally speaking, it counterweighs all the others. "For though Fate is immense," he says, "so is Power, which is the other fact in the dual world, immense. If Fate follows and limits Power, Power attends and antagonizes Fate. We must respect Fate as natural history, but there is more than natural history." This "more" includes the freedom of the human will, and it has to be reckoned with just as seriously as the laws of physics and chemistry; indeed, it is itself a law just as truly as they are, and more truly. "A part of Fate," as he says, "is the freedom of man." And what this should teach us, he goes on to say, is not a fatalistic acceptance, but an exhilarated and courageous activism. " 'Tis weak and vicious people," he says, "who cast the blame on Fate. The right use of Fate is to bring up our conduct to the loftiness of nature. Rude and invincible except by themselves are the elements. So let man be. Let him empty his breast of his windy conceits, and show his lordship by manners and deeds on the scale of nature. Let him hold his purpose as with the tug of gravitation." The true lesson to be learned from the facts of determinism is that we can afford to be brave. " 'Tis the best use of Fate," as he says, "to teach a fatal courage . . . If you believe in Fate to your harm, believe it at least for your good." The one is quite as philosophical as the other.

It would be very unjust, in short, not to recognize the strenuous strain in Emerson's optimism; not to keep reminding ourselves of such injunctions as the one with which he approached the conclusion of his essay on **"New England Reformers"**: "That which befits us, embosomed in beauty and wonder as we are, is cheerfulness and courage, and the endeavor to realize our aspirations." The word "endeavor," like the word "work," is a thematic word in Emerson. And yet I suppose that, even in saying this, we are not quite at the center of the Emersonian vision. I have said that his thought—or better his feeling—moves back and forth between a trusting passiveness and an energetic activism; and for the most part this is true. But there are moments in his work when the dichotomy between the passive and the active is transcended, and what he express-es is a spiritual experience that partakes of both—an expe-rience of such intensity, yet of such calm, that neither of the words, "active" or "passive," quite does justice to it. In recording such moments he expresses most perfectly that joy which according to Kierkegaard, demands reli-gious courage. One of the most eloquent of these passages occurs in the great address on **"The Method of Nature"** which he read at Waterville College, now Colby, in 1841:

> We ought to celebrate this hour by expressions of manly joy. Not thanks, not prayer seem quite the highest or truest name for our communica-tion with the infinite,—but glad and conspiring reception,—reception that becomes giving in its turn, as the receiver is only the All-Giver in part and in infancy. I cannot,—nor can any man,—speak precisely of things so sublime, but it seems to me the wit of man, his strength, his grace, his tendency, his art, is the grace and the presence of God. It is beyond explanation. When all is said and done, the rapt saint is found the only logician. Not exhortation, not argument be-comes our lips, but paeans of joy and praise.

If I had to say where we are most likely to find the quintes-sential Emerson, I should point to passages like this. Cer-tainly there are other Emersons, and they are not to be made light of; there is the trumpeter of non-conformity; there is the attorney for the American intellectual; there is the New England humorist. But none of these, it seems to me, speaks in quite so special and incomparable tones as the Emerson whom one would like to call, not after all a moralist, nor a prophet, nor even a teacher, but a hymn-ist or psalmist—one who, at his most characteristic, utters psalms of thanksgiving, or, as he says, "paeans of joy and praise"; whose most intimate mode of expression is always a *Te Deum*. This is the Emerson who is bound to disap-point us if we look in his work for a steady confrontation of Tragedy or a sustained and unswerving gaze at the face of Evil. They are not there, and we shall lose our labor if we look for them. But there is no writer in the world, how-ever comprehensive, in whose work we are not conscious of missing *something* that belongs to experience; and now that critical justice has been done to what is wanting in Emerson, we can surely afford very well to avail ourselves of all that is positively there. What is there, as we have to recognize when we have cleared our minds of the cant of pessimism, is perhaps the fullest and most authentic ex-pression in modern literature of the more-than-tragic emotion of thankfulness. A member of his family tells us that almost his last word was "praise." Unless we have deafened ourselves to any other tones than those of an-guish and despair, we should still know how to be inspirit-ed by everything in his writings that this word symboliz-ed by everything in his writings that this word symboliz-es. (pp. 37-53)

Newton Arvin, "The House of Pain: Emerson and the Tragic Sense," in The Hudson Re-view, *Vol. XII, No. 1, Spring, 1959, pp. 37-53.*

Alfred Kazin on Emerson:

Emerson in his great early period was exalted, perfectly confident, as he confronted every difficulty under the Amer-ican sun. To this day his readers cannot find the right name for his composite role. He was indifferent to labels and in 1850 shrugged them off—"Call yourself preacher, pedlar, lecturer, tinman, grocer, scrivener, jobber, or whatever low-est name your business admits, and leave your lovers to find the fine name."

Emerson was not just an "essayist," and his ideas were not original enough to make him a "philosopher." The literary categories that Emerson derided are now so fixed that Em-erson's role as a thinker-at-large (who became a presiding influence) seems more complex than in fact it was. America does not have names for literary men like Diderot who are fomenters of a new consciousness; Victorian "prophets" like Arnold, Ruskin, Mill, Carlyle; rebels of thought like Nietzsche, William James, Shaw, Sartre.

Emerson as much as anyone in his time—and perhaps a lit-tle more—remains one of them. His whole effort as writer and speaker was to persuade "the American this new man" to *be* a new man. He could not imagine literature's *not* seek-ing to uproot society by changing the individual. He could not imagine a new world of thought without literature as its medium. Literature was central, and literature was transfor-mation. The writer was a sacred figure through whom new life passed to the people. Without Carlyle's storminess at the degradation of modern man, but with just as much au-thority, Emerson tacitly considered himself as much of a hero as his country needed.

Alfred Kazin, in his An American Procession, *Alfred A. Knopf, 1984.*

Jonathan Bishop   (essay date 1964)

[*In the following excerpt, Bishop discusses Emerson's concept of the soul, deeming it essential to an under-standing of his work.*]

The epigraph of the late Stephen Whicher's fine anthology of *Selections* from Emerson is a sentence from **"The Amer-ican Scholar"**: "The one thing in the world, of value, is the active soul." The motto is well chosen. For the Soul in En-tire Action is the central drama of all Emerson's work. Whatever else may be the immediate topic, this is his real subject. Every sentence, every paragraph, every essay, poem, lecture, or journal note attracts our best attention to the degree that it manifests and promulgates the victory of the Soul. We cannot understand what Emerson is get-ting at until we have made the connection between the particular piece of wit we appreciate and an ideal of com-plete human activity.

Such a summary statement is not hard to make and has been made—more often, perhaps, in classrooms than in published studies, which are apt to strike into the problem of Emerson at some less obvious, less important point. But what does this conception of the active Soul mean? How are we to explain it? By an explanation of any idea or action we ought to understand such a representation of it as will render it possible for our own minds, a formulation that will bring forward anew its living truth. It may be presumed that Emerson hoped he was saying truths himself. We are not then approaching him on the right path until our critical progress makes his beliefs and demonstrations more obviously *so*. Otherwise we will find to our chagrin that we have only been learning that someone once said something under the illusion that it made sense.

Suppose, though, we do not slide away, but face the problem. How can we understand what Emerson meant when he so variously argued over a lifetime that the only thing of value was the active Soul? One had best start with the word "soul" itself. Any sentence worked out to concentrate in little the whole of Emerson's doctrine about human possibilities would need the word for a grammatical subject. But its contemporary connotations are all wrong—religiosity, gentility, hypocrisy—"soul" has a whole set of unhappy associations. Yet in the midst of prejudice a second thought can remind us that we have lost something by the modern degradation of this word. There is nothing that will really replace its useful chord of meanings.

For Emerson the word had not lost to the attritions of irony its noble Christian denotation, or the overtones accumulated by a long generation of romantic poetry and philosophy. The historian of the ideas to which Emerson owed his spiritual vocabulary can trace this inheritance. None of the definitions cast up in a modern dictionary is entirely irrelevant. We can learn there that "soul" means that by virtue of which a living creature is alive, or the essentializing quality of any object, idea, or institution. This is the root meaning. It can mean also the self, or that portion of a man distinct from the body and its urges, especially that portion of the portion that relates to God. This can be either the mind or the conscience. Finally, it is this further portion, considered as something immortal, which survives the death of the body. All these meanings influence each other, and all are involved in Emerson's specialization of the term. If one dips at random into the body of Emersonian prose, taking note of the sentences that contain the word, it is easy to arrive at a rough list of modern synonyms for parts of its meaning: life, energy, sensibility, creativity, courage, emotional reality, love, sentiment, confidence, conscience, essence, authenticity, integrity, identity, intellect, genius, the spirit of an age. In general (that is, in most contexts to some degree) it means the principle of initiative in life, morals, and mind—the imaginable subject of admirable action. It is interesting that we have no such word ourselves, a fact that says something about our cultural condition. Modern terms for desirable subjectivities—my list of synonyms above includes some of them—are perhaps more exact but too specialized, and their meanings seem to have no necessary connection with each other. The one popular general word, "psyche," means the space in which experience occurs, not the re-

sponsible initiator of that experience. Apparently we do not believe there is such a thing.

Here and there, through the lectures especially (he feels his formal philosophic obligations far less in the essays), one can find Emerson attempting to schematize the relation of the different submeanings gathered under the term. He will say, for instance, that God enters the sphere of terrestial life as Reason, the agent that perceives absolute truth and good; and Reason descends into unphilosophic affairs as Common Sense, which may in turn be contrasted to the Private Will. Or Instinct and the Understanding (elsewhere the opposite of Reason) combine as Reason to face Nature. The Soul as a whole would then be so much of instinct as would go through the mind to nature or through conscience to moral action. These attempts at abstract formulation, however, are secondhand, occasionally inconsistent with each other, and not terribly important. Emerson could be as baffled by Coleridge as any of that seminal thinker's latter-day adherents. The important aspect of the term to keep in mind is its persistent ambiguous inclusiveness.

Within the circle drawn by its power of reference there seem to be three main realms: intellectual perception, moral individuality, and organic instinct. The Coleridgean "understanding" seems to work for Emerson as a name for consciousness isolated both from impulse and from evaluated feeling. A modern term with approximately the same pejorative weight would be "rationality." Similarly, the spirit of individuality, isolated, becomes "personality," the mundane defensive self—never, for Emerson, an agent of good action on its own. "Instinct" isolated is physical power, about which Emerson had divided feelings, but of which he usually disapproved for the same kind of reason. His appreciation for the proper congruence of all three faculties when they work together as Soul, and his complementary disapproval of any one of them setting up for itself, leads him to a generalized distrust of technical intellect, of traditional social influence, and of the body. It helps to support a corresponding trust in democracy (which is based on the common sense of men in general) and science (which assumes a common nature for common reason to know).

Emerson is interested, then, in the motions of life as actions originating in some actor, or in a faculty of some actor. The ambiguity of the term "soul" allows him to subsume under the term a great variety of such motions and to make each a potential model of any one of the others or of the whole. Thus when animal force, or conscience, or intellect, or even some natural principle like magnetism appears as the cause for an event in the world, he can use that event as a relevant illustration of a major pattern of experience for which Soul is the master term. This freedom of illustration is at the root of his interest in heroes; an extraordinary man, even though immoral, is at least a striking instance of subjective power in action. Such men are not acted upon but act. So they exhibit at least part of the Soul and stand as metaphors for the full resources of the unheroic who identify with them.

At the same time, the general notion of the Soul gives Emerson a criterion by which to judge the inadequacy of ways of life in which the full powers implied by the term are not used. Judgments can be made against the inhibition of "lower" as well as "higher" faculties. The Soul incorporates energy as well as character. The large ambiguity of Emerson's key term implies a putative whole experience which would engage all the faculties of the subject together. His theory of the Soul can do implicit justice to initiatives with which his inherited unconscious habits kept him out of official sympathy.

The rigors of New England culture hindered Emerson from doing personal justice to every action his term would theoretically give him a chance to praise. Analogous influences can inhibit a modern reader from understanding all that Emerson was able to admire explicitly. The general ideal is close enough to appreciate without difficulty; "the whole man" is one of our cant phrases. But a modern reader would have more difficulty than Emerson in believing, for one thing, that the prototypical experience of the whole man begins with communion with nature. The very notion seems as antique as the pastoral genre in which it was traditionally expressed. And pastoral, in life as in letters, seems not merely old-fashioned, but debilitating, immature, a matter for vacations, not a foundation for grown-up experience. Maturity, it is easy to assume, starts with an abandonment of the old infantile pretension to an intimate relation with nature in favor of commitment to the social mode. Yet Emerson believed that the laudable motions of good experience included as their ground-note a conscious sense of union between the subject of action and aspects of external nature. Why? The simple question requires a plain answer, before one can trust oneself to feel in touch with the meaning of his idea of the Soul. This, the very foundation of Emerson's theory of the Soul, is a hard place to get over.

Another hard part of this putative Emersonian Whole is the moral dimension, what Emerson calls the "moral sentiment." He meant by this phrase something that for him was an essential constituent of an entire subjectivity. Therefore the term must mean, not an outward norm (the automatic definition a modern reader would give it) or even an "inner check" (the internalization of such an outward norm), but an initiating inward force. The conventional wisdom of Emerson's age made it easy to accept the natural inwardness of the conscience; the conventional wisdom of ours makes it next to impossible. A modern reader would be inclined to start by assuming that moral experience is learned from without, not generated from an inborn faculty. But to Emerson the "moral law" is quite a separate matter from the conventions of the social world. It is a part of the Soul, something native and outmoving, which runs parallel to instinct and mind. Called upon to define the word Soul formally, he would doubtless have spoken first of this ethical initiative. The difficulty is crucial to a sympathetic understanding of Emerson's message. . . . (pp. 19-23)

The Soul's action for Emerson, then, starts in an instinctive relation to nature and includes (in a way to puzzle about) virtue; it ends as mind. The metamorphosis of circumstances into consciousness is the consummation of the Soul's great act. The trajectory of that act is sketched in a hundred remarks. For Emerson, events, things, and institutions are all finally dissolved in intellect, which finds itself by its own act the re-creator of all it sees. "In some contemplative hour" experience "detaches itself from the life like a ripe fruit, to become a thought of the mind. Instantly it is raised, transfigured; the corruptible has put on incorruption." Or again: "I notice that all poetry comes or all becomes poetry when we look from within & are using all as if the mind made it."

"Using all as if the mind made it"—there is a kind of danger in the relief such succinct formulations of intellectual action can stimulate. For if the more primary relation to nature is forgotten, and the moral element in the action of the Soul neglected, its intellectual dimension may become too obvious. We can find it even too easy to accept Emerson's definition of the Soul on this side. It would be right to think that Emerson meant intellectual action as the verge or limit of all actions of the Soul. He did not, though, think that the acts of the mind were all he had the privilege of celebrating. "Thinkers," as he knew well, tend to overestimate the independence of the mind (when they are not denigrating it) and are easily tempted by arguments that apparently sanction their caste bias. They like to feel free of the world, of their own personal and physical faculties, and rush into the real freedom of rational action as if it were absolute. But, in Emerson's terms, this is to interpret the acts of the reason as instances of understanding merely, or mind separate from the other agencies of life. Still, probably no inquiry into Emerson's idea of the Soul (including this one) could avoid overemphasizing the intellectual dimension of his doctrine, either directly by partial paraphrasing or indirectly by assuming that his work is wholly explainable in philosophic terms.

There is another reason for the tendency to intellectualize Emerson's message. Emerson is dead; only "Emerson" lives. And this second figure lives only in words. One knows what he says by reading those words: "he" is my inference, and inferences are made by the mind. Here indeed is an ultimate meaning for the word Soul. It must mean the mind of the reader understanding what is before it, following some verbal action upon the page. This literary action is all that an author can be sure he will share with his reader. It will be as a mind that the reader's Soul performs. A reader's other faculties are not entirely asleep—how could they be? Life continues around him and within him; he cannot help experiencing admirations and repugnances. But when these faculties act for him as he comprehends the text before his eyes, they act in subordination to the mind. There is much in Emerson that comments upon this terminal condition of all literary action: to announce it, even to exploit it, is one of his purposes. But its very obviousness can fortify a tendency to overintellectualize the idea of the Soul. Emerson preaches against bookishness—but we ourselves read his preachment in a book. (pp. 23-5)

Jonathan Bishop, in his Emerson on the Soul, *Cambridge, Mass.: Harvard University Press, 1964, 248 p.*

Tony Tanner   (essay date 1965)

[*Tanner is an English educator and critic. In the following excerpt, he explores the sense of wonder in Emerson's works, suggesting that Emerson's promotion of a childlike attention to the commonplace was an important influence on subsequent American literature.*]

Emerson unquestionably played a key role in the shaping of the American imagination, and yet he seems to have had some trouble in defining his own role in his own times. Once he ceased to be a minister he did not start to become an artist; his work has neither the intense passion or still serenity of the true mystic nor the intellectual rigour of the philosopher. He experimented with various characters or projections of parts of his own uncommitted imagination—the Scholar, the Seer, the Man of Genius, the Contemplative Man, the Student, the Transcendentalist, even the Reformer and the Hero. Professor Henry Nash Smith is surely correct in referring to these [in *The New England Quarterly,* March-December 1939] as 'a collection of embryos' and in going on to suggest that we should understand the essays and addresses in which Emerson deploys these characters as 'rudimentary narratives rather than as structures of discursive reasoning'. In his work, therefore, it is wiser to seek the suggestive drift of the whole than to attempt to establish a consistently developed system of thought. In his many characters he canvassed many problems, but recurringly, insistently, he returned to the discussion of the relationship between man and nature, 'the marriage of thought and things'. He saw no basic hostilities in nature and no radical evil in man. When he does turn his attention to the problem of pain and suffering his tone remains suspiciously bland. It is hard to feel that he has deeply registered some of the more rigorous paradoxes of existence; hard to feel that he ever experienced the chaos within. Evil was neither lasting nor real to Emerson. Thus the problem he addresses himself to is not how to restrain what is dark in man, but rather how to maintain a sense of the enveloping, involving divinity of the world. 'What is life but the angle of vision' he asserts, and much of his work is occupied with attempts to define the appropriate angle of vision. He felt that one of America's deepest needs was a 'general education of the eye' and it was just such an education that many of his essays and addresses attempted to give. I want to suggest that in the course of his 'education' he procured special prestige for the angle of vision of the child.

In his diagnosis of what was wrong with contemporary attitudes towards the world, Emerson insisted that the fault was not in the world itself so much as in man's manner of regarding it. 'The ruin or the blank that we see when we look at nature, is in our own eye. The axis of vision is not coincident with the axis of things, and so they appear not transparent but opaque. The reason why the world lacks unity, and lies broken and in heaps, is because man is disunited with himself.' If things appeared to lack unity that was because of some disorder in the eye: a new eye would unify the world in a new way—salvation is visual. Emerson shifts attention from environment to spectator. In one way he was merely continuing the tradition of neoplatonic thought among the romantics. When he writes: 'Not in nature but in man is all the beauty and worth he

sees' we hear echoes of Blake and Goethe, and Coleridge. But in emphasizing the responsibilities and creative powers of 'the eye of the beholder' he had a motive which the European romantics could not have had. For, as long as the interest of a locale was considered to be inherent in the place rather than the viewer, then Americans would be forever looking to Europe. By denying a hierarchy of significance among external objects he not only eliminated the special prestige of Europe (since everywhere is equally significant), he confronts the eye with an enormous, if exciting, task.

In the introduction to his earliest work he had written: 'Why should not we also enjoy an original relation to the universe?' and he had started out with the resolution: 'Let us interrogate the great apparition that shines so peacefully around us.' Emerson wanted the eye to see the world from scratch, wanted to inculcate 'the habit of fronting the fact, and not dealing with it at second hand, through the perceptions of somebody else'. But from the start we should alert ourselves to a doubleness which is inherent in almost everything Emerson says about man's visual relationship with nature. Briefly this doubleness consists of an emphasis which points both to the importance of particulars *and* the unmistakable presence of general truths. The world is full of isolated details which should command our equal attention and reverence, and yet ultimately it is all one vast simple truth: the world is both a mosaic *and* a unified picture which admits of no fragmentation. To pick up his own words the world is both opaque and transparent—it both resists and invites visual penetration. His complaint is that 'as the high ends of being fade out of sight, man becomes near-sighted, and can only attend to what addresses the senses'. The senses bring us indispensable particulars but to limit knowledge to the 'sensuous fact' is to be a Materialist: the Idealist, by a deliberate 'retirement from the senses', will discern truths of which material things are mere representations, truths of 'the high ends of being'.

> We live in succession, in division, in parts, in particles. Meantime within man is the soul of the whole; the wise silence, the universal beauty, to which every part and particle is equally related; the eternal ONE. . . . We see the world piece by piece, as the sun, the moon, the animal, the tree; but the whole, of which these are the shining parts, is the soul.

Man must see all the shining parts of the world anew, as for the first time with his own uninstructed eye: but this is merely the prelude to his discerning 'the ONE.' Emerson's work would seem to prescribe an ascent from materialism to idealism and thence to mysticism—a passionate scrutiny of the minute particulars of a world which suddenly turns transparent and gives us an insight into 'the background of being', 'the Over-Soul', 'the ONE'. This duality of vision Emerson himself recognized, noting in his journal: 'Our little circles absorb us and occupy us as fully as the heavens; we can minimize as infinitely as maximize, and the only way out of it is (to use a country phrase) to kick the pail over, and accept the horizon instead of the pail, with celestial attractions and influences, instead of worms and mud pies.' Emerson is not consistent in his advice for he is quite as likely to recommend that a man should scrutinize the pail rather than kick it over. But the passage describes very graphically one of his own habitual practices; for both visually and stylistically he moves from the pail (the discrete detail) to the horizon (the embracing generalization). Sherman Paul, who has written so well on Emerson, shrewdly adopts an idea from the work of Ortega y Gasset, and makes a similar point about Emerson [in his *Emerson's Angle of Vision*, 1952]. 'The eye brought him two perceptions of nature—nature ensphered and nature atomized—which corresponded to the distant and proximate visual powers of the eye.' Emerson, seeking a sense of the unity and inter-involvement of all things, felt there was a great value in focusing the eye on 'an unbroken horizon': not only because the unbroken horizon offers an image of an unbroken circle, not only because at the horizon different elements meet and marry, but also because when the eye pitches its focus thus far, all things between it and the horizon fall into what Paul calls 'a blur of relatedness'. Seen thus, individual things seem not to be discrete and unrelated but rather a part of one vast unifying process. The world appears as a concave container. On the other hand, when the eye fastens on to one single detail the rest of the world falls away and one is only conscious of the separateness and isolation of the thing: there is no hazy unity but only the encroaching fragment. The world becomes convex, thrusting out its differentiated particulars. The dangers of the close scrutinizing vision were clear to Emerson: 'If you bury the natural eye too exclusively on minute objects it gradually loses its powers of distant vision.' The paradox is, I think, that Emerson himself effectively, if unintentionally, stressed the value of the close scrutinizing vision. In his case, of course, the detail seldom failed to reveal the divine spirit which rolls through all things. But Thoreau developed a habit of close scrutiny, a reverence for details, which occupied itself with 'minute objects' to a degree never intended by Emerson. Thoreau was convinced that every fact, no matter how small, would flower into a truth, conveying to him a sense of the whole, the unity which maintained the details. Yet he seems to bear out Emerson's warning in a late melancholy complaint: 'I see details, not wholes nor the shadow of the whole.' In such a phrase he seems to anticipate what could, and I think did, happen to subsequent writers.

For many of them the eye got stuck at the surface, it was arrested among particulars. The mosaic stayed illegible with no overall, or underall, pattern discernible. Emerson himself gives intimations of such a possibility. 'Nature hates peeping' and, more forcefully, 'Nature will not be a Buddhist: she resents generalizing, and insults the philosopher in every moment with a million of fresh particulars'. One of Emerson's natures is one divine unbroken process wherein all the teeming, tumbling details are seen as part of a flowing Unity, a Unity not described so much as felt, passionately, ubiquitously, empathetically. This is the nature that Whitman was to celebrate. But the other nature described by Emerson is a mass of discrete, clearly defined objects, a recession of endless amazing particulars—particulars which seem to quiver with hidden meanings but which never afford us the revealing transparency. This nature of clear contours and suggestive details is the nature of Anderson, Stein, Hemingway and many others.

Emerson as a young man.

As we noticed, the threat to the Transcendentalist lay precisely in the extreme generality of his assertions, his reliance on the all-explaining presence. For without a final mystical concept of nature Emerson confesses that he is left 'in the splendid labyrinth of my perceptions, to wander without end'. Without the affirmed presence of the Over-Soul the world becomes a labyrinthine maze of perceptions which do not add up. The only way out of the maze was to look at it in a different way: this is why Emerson continually raises the question of how man should look at the world.

'Make the aged eye sun-clear'—so Emerson appeals to Spring in one of his poems: it is an appeal which follows logically from his constant complaint that 'we are immersed in beauty, but our eyes have no clear vision'. The age of an eye is presumably its sum of acquired habits, its interpretative predispositions, its chosen filter through which it sieves the world even while regarding it. Emerson thought that a person could become fixed in his ways of looking just as we talk of people getting fixed in their ways of thinking. Consequently he wants the eye to be washed clear of those selective and interpretative schemata which prevent us from 'an original relation to the universe'. As we now think, without these acquired schemata vision would be impossible: we have to learn to see and a 'washed' eye would be an eye blinded by undifferentiated confusion. But the important thing is not that Emerson did not understand the mechanics of sight but that he thought it possible and desirable to start looking at the world as though one had never seen or heard of it before. What Emerson wanted from man was a renewed faculty of wonder. 'All around us what powers are wrapped up under the coarse mattings of custom, and all wonder prevented . . . the wise man wonders at the usual.' 'The invariable mark of wisdom is to see the miraculous in the common.' In this kind of visual relationship between the eye and the world, the eye stands completely passive and unselective while the surrounding world flows unbroken into it. Something like this was envisaged by Emerson when he described himself in the following way:

> Standing on the bare ground—my head bathed by the blithe air and uplifted into infinite space—all mean egotism vanishes. I am become a transparent eyeball; I am nothing; I see all; the currents of the Universal Being circulate through me; I am part or parcel of God.

The notable aspect of this visual stance is its complete passivity, its mood of pious receptivity. Unfocusing, unselecting, the eye is porous to the 'currents of the Universal Being'. Rather similar is Emerson's description of the delight he receives from a fine day which 'draws the cords of will out of my thought and leaves me nothing but perpetual observation, perpetual acquiescence, and perpetual thankfulness'. Thus relieved of the active will and conscious thought, Emerson could feel himself reabsorbed into the flowing continuum of unselfconscious nature.

Of course it was because of his optimistic mysticism that Emerson endorsed this mode of seeing, for he was convinced that if man could reattain a primitive simplicity of vision the ubiquitous divinity of the world would suddenly become clear to him. The wonder he advises is a form of visual piety: to see naively is to see religiously. This explains his interest in the animal eye and the child's eye—neither of which have been overlaid with the dust and dirt of custom and second-hand perception, both of which are free from the myopic interference of reason. The child sees better than the man. 'To speak truly, few adult persons can see nature. Most persons do not see the sun. At least they have a very superficial seeing. The sun illuminates only the eye of the man, but shines into the eye and the heart of the child.'

The desired point of view is one which allows nature unhindered, uninterrupted access to the eye, thence to the heart. Because for Emerson this meant capitulation to a superior source of virtue. 'Man is fallen; nature is erect' and 'all things are moral'. It follows we must not try and impose our will on nature but rather 'suffer nature to intrance us' for our own good. Man's fall is not into knowledge of evil—but into consciousness: for Emerson, as Yeats noted, has no 'vision of evil' and maintains, rather incredibly, that what we call evil would disappear if we acquired a new way of looking at things: 'the evils of the world are such only to the evil eye.' How such evil finds its way into an intrinsically benign and moral universe is not clear—but the extremity of Emerson's position is. To be conscious is the curse, for to be conscious is to be alienated from our original home or womb (and Emerson often uses words like 'cradle' and 'nestle' and 'embosomed' to describe the proper quasi-infantile relationship with nature), it is to have lost the comfort of our primary ties. The unselfconsciousness of animals is enviable. 'The squirrel hoards nuts and the bee gathers honey, without knowing what they do, and they are thus provided for without selfishness or disgrace.' Man's dilemma is based solely on his consciousness. 'Man owns the dignity of the life which throbs around him, in chemistry, and tree, and animal, and in the involuntary functions of his own body; yet he is balked when he tries to fling himself into this enchanted circle, where all is done without degradation.' Only the *involuntary* actions of man have any dignity: we hear nothing of 'the dignity of judgment' in James's phrase, nothing of the enlightened will, of considered intent, of the disciplined pursuit of noble ends. Consciousness is seen only as an inhibitor—for what Emerson really wants is to get back into the enchanted circle, to regain what he calls 'the forfeit paradise'.

> And so, perchance, in Adam's race,
> Of Eden's bower some dream-like trace
> Survived the Flight and swam the Flood,
> And wakes the wish in youngest blood
> To tread the forfeit Paradise,
> And feed once more the exile's eyes:

And he makes the point as strongly in prose: 'Infancy is the perpetual Messiah, which comes into the arms of fallen men, and pleads with them to return to paradise.' Not a change of heart but a change of eye, a new mode of access into nature, is the burden of Emerson's lay sermons. As exemplars he cites 'children, babes, and even brutes' because 'their mind being whole, their eye is as yet unconquered; and when we look in their faces we are disconcerted'. Man's eye has been conquered—that was the fall: man has been 'clapped into jail by his consciousness'. This is why the child sees the sun properly and the adult does not. 'Infancy, youth, receptive, aspiring, with religious eye looking upward, counts itself nothing and abandons itself to the instruction flowing from all sides.' This is the child's genius: the openness to sensations, the visual abandon he is capable of. We are at our best when we too can 'gaze like children'. 'It is very unhappy, but too late to be helped, the discovery we have made that we exist. That discovery is called the Fall of Man. Ever afterwards we suspect our instruments. . . . Once we lived in what we saw; now the rapaciousness of this new power, which threatens to absorb all things, engages us.' 'We suspect our instruments'—Emerson diagnoses a crisis of vision: we see, but we are not sure what we see and how correct is our seeing. There is perhaps something greedy and predatory about the conscious eye, which scans the panorama of creation with utilitarian intention, every glance of which is an act of visual spoliation. But the eye which seeks passively and humbly for true connection and orientation lacks confidence. However the child and the animal still seem to live in what they see with no subject—object dichotomy to haunt them, with none of the sense of severance which assaults the conscious eye. If the adult eye is glazed and dull and blind to the lessons of nature, still the naive eye—idiot, Indian, infant—seems to pay the most profitable kind of attention to things, to enjoy a lost intimacy with the world, to have the freshest, clearest perceptions. Thus Emerson seems to have seen the problem and located the salvation.

Whether or not Emerson felt he had any medical and anthropological evidence for his description of the naive eye of the child and native is not important: for ultimately he was using the notion as a metaphor. His conception of the naive eye is not scientific so much as religious. It was a prelude to worship rather than a preparation for action. It is in this light that such curious passages as the following should be read:

> The child with his sweet pranks, the fool of his senses, commanded by every sight and sound, without any power to compare and rank his sensations, abandoned to a whistle or a painted chip, to a lead dragoon or a ginger-bread dog, *individualising everything, generalising nothing*, delighted with every new thing, lies down at night overpowered by the fatigue which this day of continual pretty madness has incurred. *But nature has answered her purpose with the curly dimpled lunatic. . . .* This glitter, this opaline lustre plays around the top of every toy to his eye to insure his fidelity, and he is deceived to his good. *We are made alive and kept alive by the same arts.* [my italics]

It is the intellectual (not the mystical) generalization, so detrimental to a proper habit of awe, which Emerson is writing against; it is a new sort of naive wondering individualizing he is anxious to inculcate. And although he indulgently calls the child a 'dimpled lunatic' he elsewhere talks more seriously of 'the wisdom of children'. Although he sometimes asserts a superior mode of vision which sees through all particulars to the Over-Soul, although he sometimes warns against the rapt attention to detail with which he credited the child, the savage and the animal; nevertheless he often returns to the superiority of the naive eye precisely because of the generous attentive wonder it displays in front of nature's multiple particulars.

Perhaps the child was ultimately Emerson's image for his own best intentions. 'The first questions are always to be asked, and the wisest doctor is gravelled by the inquisitiveness of the child.' Adult maturity is no real maturity since we have lost the right approach to nature, the knack of correct penetration: in fact we no longer ask the right questions. The child in his unencrusted innocence does. There is a dangerous form of extremism here: Emerson's rejection of the past includes not only a denial of the accumulated wisdom of the race but also the lessons of experience. The inquiry ideally should commence afresh each day. Nothing accrues, everything is always to be asked: such is the extreme implication of the Emersonian stance. And certainly since his time the habit of renewed wonder, the ever-novel interrogation of experience has become a recurring theme in American literature, a temperamental predisposition and a literary strategy. Naivety has become an important form of wisdom.

. . . . .

> If we cannot make voluntary and conscious steps in the admirable science of universals, let us see the parts wisely, and infer the genius of nature from the best particulars with a becoming charity.
>
> (Emerson)

I have already suggested that although Emerson's vision alternated between detail and generalization, the 'mud pies' and the 'celestial influences', the overall effect of his work is to secure a new respect for close vision. What I want to point out in this section is how Emerson, despite his own preference for 'the admirable science of universals', focused unusual and exciting attention on 'the best particulars'. More remarkably he often equated the best particulars with low and commonplace objects and continually suggested that the need for 'a language of facts' could best be answered by turning to the vernacular. These emphases alone make him a major figure in American literature and they merit special attention here. Only rarely does Emerson give the impression that it might be disconcerting if one could not make the pieces of the mosaic add up to one flowing, binding picture. We just have some hints. 'But all is sour if seen as experience. Details are melancholy; the plan is seemly and noble.' Having lost all sense of the 'seemly and noble' plan Henry Adams, for one, found the remaining heaps of particulars not only sour and melancholy but terrifying. Emerson, to whom mystical generalizations came all too easily, could tie up the world in a sentence. 'Our globe seen by God is a transparent law, not a mass of facts.' Facts on their own were indeed 'heavy, prosaic' and 'dull strange despised things': but Emerson maintained that simply by wondering at them man would find 'that the day of facts is a rock of diamonds; that a fact is an epiphany of God'. With such experience open to him Emerson could well afford to stress the value of a close regard for facts.

If you believe that the universe is *basically* such a perfect continuous whole then certain things follow. For a start every detail will be equally significant. 'A leaf, a drop, a crystal, a moment of time, is related to the whole, and partakes of the perfection of the whole. Each particle is a microcosm, and faithfully renders the likeness of the world.' 'There is no fact in nature which does not carry the whole sense of nature.' 'The world globes itself in a drop of dew. The microscope cannot find the animalcule which is less perfect for being little.'

Now the interesting aspect of this belief that 'the universe is represented in every one of its particles' is that it can easily lead, not to the mystical generalization, but to an extreme of particularization, a devoted preoccupation with the minutiae of existence. It can encourage a prose devoted to ensnaring the crystalline fragments of momentary experience. Emerson works against his own intentions here by giving a tremendous prestige to the smallest details of the material world: his mystical enthusiasm is, as it were, diffused among all the details he sees. There is no hierarchy of value or significance operative: *all* details are worthy of the most reverent attention because all are equally perfect and equally meaningful. If Thoreau, as Emerson said, was 'equally interested in every natural fact', then he was only putting into practice an Emersonian prescription. The implications of this attitude are worth pondering. If every fact is equally interesting where does one find a criteria of exclusion, a principle of abridgement without which art cannot start to be art for it cannot leave off being nature? Emerson is endorsing an eye which refuses to distinguish and classify, which denies priorities of importance and significance, which refuses to admit of any sort of difference in import and value. From one point of view one could call this the egalitarian eye: an eye which affirms the equality of all facts. All facts are born equal and have an equal claim on man's attention. Yet in most art there is what we might call an aristocratic tendency: a claimed prerogative to exercise a lordly right of selection, omission, evaluation, and rearrangement. The aristocratic eye tyrannizes its facts: the egalitarian eye is tyrannized by them. This is not to say that the egalitarian or naive eye cannot discover things to which the aristocratic eye remains blind: it can, for it has that humility which makes new insights possible. It needed the naive eye as described by Emerson and adopted by Thoreau and Whitman, for America to be seen at all in its own right. But it is worth pointing out at this stage that there are distinct problems of organization and evaluation inherent in Emerson's concept of vision. What is completely absent is any sense of a scale of relative complexity, any feeling that small clusters of selected facts can yield a restricted amount of wisdom, any notion of a gradual increase of intelligence, any awareness of various modes of classification, any reference to the accumulating density of experience. There is the leaf—and there are the hidden laws of the universe: and nothing in between. Certainly not society, the notable omission in Emerson. For Emerson is a man talking metaphysics with his eye glued to the microscope, and plenty of American writers have taken their turn at the microscope after Emerson and his disciple Thoreau. This notion of Emerson's had far-reaching repercussions. For if the meaning of the world is to be found in a drop of dew, then the meaning of a given situation may be contained in the contingent objects which surround the participants. The lesson could be drawn from Emerson's thought that if the writer looks after the details the significances will look after themselves. A writer might construe his task to be a scrupulous itemizing of particulars, from the smallest to the largest with no accompanying distribution of significance, no perspective with its recession of priorities, no 'comparison and ranking of sensations'. Indeed he gives a clear warrant for such an attitude. Thus: 'the truth-speaker may dismiss all solicitude as to the proportion and congruency of the aggregate of his thoughts, so long as he is a faithful reporter of particular impressions.' This means that a work of art depends for its form on the individual notation; no larger unit of meaning need be constructed. As he very revealingly wrote— 'ask the fact for the form': an attitude far removed from that which relies on the form to assign meaning to the fact. Although Emerson talked of the importance of the 'Intellect Constructive', the major emphasis of his work falls on the 'Intellect Receptive'.

Emerson's belief that the part contained the whole—by implication, or in shorthand as it were—leads quite naturally to his mystique of facts. We remember his instructions to 'see the miraculous in the common': he goes on to arraign our blindness to the worth and significance of small everyday facts. 'To the wise, therefore, a fact is true poetry, and the most beautiful of fables.' Facts contain their own story if we will simply look at them afresh. 'Pleads for itself the fact' he says in one of his poems and he means just that: things will 'sing themselves' if we learn to listen in the right way. Again we note that the prescribed attitude is passive. We do not impose a meaning

on facts, rather we try and make 'facts yield their secret sense'. 'Every moment instructs and every object; for wisdom is infused into every form.' Genius, then, will consist of 'the habit of fronting the fact'; the intellect is ravished 'by coming nearer to the fact'.

Emerson's emphasis was most important for American writers of the time: because among other things he was continually dragging eyes back to the worth and status of American facts. He scorned artists who could only discern beauty through the conventions of the old 'sublime'. 'They reject life as prosaic, and create a death which they call poetic.' Emerson was constantly canvassing for an artistic acceptance of prosaic everyday life. It is the instinct of genius, he affirmed,

> to find beauty and holiness in new and necessary facts, in the field and road-side, in the shop and mill. Proceeding from a religious heart it will raise to a divine use the railroad, the insurance office, the joint-stock company; our law, our primary assemblies, our commerce, the galvanic battery, the electric jar, the prism, and the chemist's retort; in which we seek now only an economical use. . . . The boat at St Petersburg which plies along the Lena by magnetism, needs little to make it sublime.

We can hear prophetic echoes of Whitman's enthusiastic listing of things here. It may sound naive to us but at the time this opinion of Emerson's rendered American literature a real service: his influence helped to make available whole areas of contemporary American life which had hitherto been considered all but ineligible for serious treatment. It was Emerson's insistence on 'the worth of the vulgar' which made Whitman's work possible. He himself chooses the simplest of objects as carriers of sublime revelations. His prose often seems to create a still-life of separately attended-to particulars. It conveys a sense of the radiance of things seen. Emerson succeeded in vivifying the 'common, the familiar, the low': he dignified the details of 'the earnest experience of the common day'. He invokes a new respect for contingent, mundane particulars.

But in order to see details properly man has to separate one thing from another. So although Emerson believes that there are no walls or separating barriers in the flowing tide of nature he yet talks of 'the cool disengaged air of natural objects' and affirms that 'things are not huddled and lumped, but sundered and individual'. Emerson the mystic talked on and on about the fluid inter-relatedness of all things, the transparency of nature to the ONE: but the Emerson whose influence is most marked in American literature was the man who asserted that 'the virtue of art lies in detachment, in sequestering one object from the embarrassing variety', who approved 'the power to fix the momentary eminency of an object'. And if it be asked what connection this particular virtue has with the naive eye we should recall that Emerson said: 'To the young mind everything is individual, stands by itself'. The naive eye, as he depicted it, was likely above all others to be alert to the unique significance of the isolated random details of the material world.

In encouraging a new way of 'seeing' Emerson also made

some comments on 'saying', on 'the language of facts' which we must now examine.

First, the indictment: 'The corruption of man is followed by the corruption of language . . . new imagery ceases to be created, and old words are perverted to stand for things which are not; a paper currency is employed, when there is no bullion in the vaults . . . But wise men pierce this rotten diction and fasten words again to visible things.' Secondly, the precedent from which we should learn. 'Children and savages use only nouns or names of things, which they convert into verbs, and apply to analogous acts.' As well as the child and the savage, Emerson cites the 'strong-natured farmer or backwoodsman' as exemplifying the proper use of language. This equating of the child, the savage, and the vernacular type is questionable if a serious attempt to analyse speech-habits is being offered. But they occur more as exemplars in a sermon. Emerson wants to communicate the notion of some sort of verbal intimacy with the stuff of nature, a state in which words and things are at their closest. We should see like children: we should also speak like children and vernacular types, or at least with the simple, specifying concreteness that Emerson imputes to them. Just as Emerson wanted the eye to concentrate on concrete facts, so he wishes language to be full of concrete factualness, and for the same reasons: a new or renewed intimacy with these facts affords us our quickest means of contact with the unifying sublime presence which runs through all things. So the concentration is always on the simplest forms of speech, on the speech which arises from physical involvement with nature rather than the subtle refined concepts used by those who meditate on life through the mind's eye. 'Life lies behind us as the quarry from whence we get tiles and copestones for the masonry of to-day. This is the way to learn grammar. Colleges and books only copy the language which the field and work-yard made.'

An important by-product of this contention of Emerson's is his complete rejection of the classification of facts, things, and words into 'high' and 'low', a classification based on the dualism of spirit and body which was then still a major influence on New England thought. 'The vocabulary of an omniscient man would embrace words and images excluded from polite conversation. What would be base, or even obscene, to the obscene, becomes illustrious, spoken in a new connection of thought.' The effect of this enlightened passage is to offer a card of eligibility to a whole range of experience and vocabulary which had hitherto been considered inherently unfit for literature.

More central to Emerson's theory of language is his assertion that 'It does not need that a poem should be long. Every word was once a poem', and the related idea that 'bare lists of words are found suggestive to an imaginative and excited mind'. Every word was once a poem because every word was once a thing, or at least a 'brilliant picture' of a thing. ('Language is fossil poetry' wrote Emerson, thus anticipating Fenellosa's notion of language as a pyramid with an apex of generality and a base composed of 'stunned' things.) Since every thing equally displays or hints at the divine plan of the universe, a list of words becomes a list of revelations, each noted fact an encountered epiphany. The influence of this belief on Emerson's own style can be discerned. His style, most characteristically, is composed of an effortless shifting from the suggestive list of facts and things to what he revealingly calls 'casual' abstraction and generalization. In his own words: 'There is the bucket of cold water from the spring, the wood-fire to which the chilled traveller rushes for safety—and there is the sublime moral of autumn and noon.' The philosophy is revealed in the style: he ascends direct from 'a crystal' to the 'Universal Spirit'. Clusters of unrelated facts occur continually, embedded in his discursive sentences, pegging them to the ground. Examples can be proliferated. 'There is nothing but is related to us, nothing that does not interest us—kingdom, college, tree, horse, or iron shoe—the roots of all things are in man.' His prose asserts but never analyses these relationships. We could recall the famous passage on the 'worth of the vulgar' which employs a similar method of assembling 'things', but things left separate and static: 'The meal in the firkin; the milk in the pan; the ballad in the street; the news of the boat; the glance of the eye; the form and gait of the body;'—details which reveal not any one man's world but God's world. Such passages in Emerson serve as the springboards for his sublime leaps: and obviously even as he is enumerating these 'things', telling his beads of facts as we might say, they seem to reveal universal laws to him. As in Whitman, they 'sing' to him. The more successful passages in Emerson are weighed down with concrete facts, laced with particulars which alert the mental eye. What has gone from his writing is almost all purposive complexity of syntax: his style is extremely paratactic and his sentences often start with an unintroduced enumeration of things, things held up for our beholding in the belief that they will 'plead for themselves'. One final example must suffice:

> The fall of snowflakes in a still air, preserving to each crystal its perfect form; the blowing of sleet over a wide sheet of water, and over plains; the waving rye field; the mimic waving of acres of houstonia, whose innumerable florets whiten and ripple before the eye; the reflections of trees and flowers in glassy lakes; the musical, steaming, odorous south wind, which converts all trees to wind-harps; the crackling and spurting of hemlock in the flames, or of pine logs, which yield glory to the walls and faces in the sitting-room—these are the music and pictures of the most ancient religion.

This is writing of considerable visual sensitivity but which has no sense whatever of the relation and inter-relation of things and things, things and people, people and other people. It is a prose that stops before society and the problems of human behaviour start. His idea that 'bare lists of words are suggestive' is crucial here. They are suggestive if the words are what he thought words should be—concrete facts, pictures of things—but even so such bare lists help us not at all in the problems of living among those facts and things. Emerson's prose feels its way over the surfaces and round the contours of parts of the empirical world but has no means of discussing the problems of action and interruption in that world. By way of meaning he can only produce the mystical generalization, but as faith in such generalizations has diminished it is the former aspect of his prose, the respect for details, which seems to have had most influence in American literature.

Of the duality of his own vision he writes very clearly. 'We are amphibious creatures, weaponed for two elements, having two sets of faculties, the particular and the catholic. We adjust our instruments for general observation, and sweep the heavens as easily as we pick out a single figure in the terrestrial landscape.' Emerson found it easy to 'sweep the heavens' but subsequent writers have found it less so. The heavens have changed for one thing—or rather man's relationship with them has. They now seem to mock, whereas to Emerson they seemed to smile on, the 'casual' all-explaining generalization. But there remains the 'faculty' for particulars, and the ability to isolate 'single figures in the terrestrial landscape' and this faculty has perhaps been cultivated as the other faculty has increasingly come under suspicion—though it has by no means disappeared. Not surprisingly Emerson admired Plato above all others, and in his essay on him he manages to tell us a good deal about himself. This is Emerson's Plato: 'If he made transcendental distinctions, he fortified himself by drawing all his illustrations from sources disdained by orators and polite conversers; from mares and puppies; from pitchers and soup-ladles; from cooks and criers; the shops of potters, horse-doctors, butchers and fishmongers.' Plato, that is, obeyed Emerson and 'embraced the common, explored and sat at the feet of the familiar, the low'. Perhaps the most revealing thing that Emerson says about Plato is this: 'Plato keeps the two vases, one of ether and one of pigment, at his side, and invariably uses both.' The pigment of low concrete facts and the either of mystical generalization—they are both to be found in Emerson. And it is worth repeating that for him peculiar prestige attaches itself to the 'low' in language and in facts and in people. 'The poor and the low have their way of expressing the last facts of philosophy as well as you.' As well as, and by veiled implication, perhaps better. There is actually a preference for those minds which 'have not been subdued by the drill of school education'. 'Do you think the porter and the cook have no anecdotes, no experiences, no wonders for you? Everybody knows as much as the savant. The walls of crude minds are scrawled over with facts, with thoughts.' This is an attitude which could endorse the vernacular as a literary mode; which could encourage the belief in the superior wisdom of the backwoodsman, the rural inhabitant, the person living outside any urban-civilized field of force. It is difficult to assess the influence of one writer. Emerson is perhaps as much symptom as cause. The point is that certain novel attitudes and predilections which recur in many American writers seem to emerge articulated in Emerson's work for the first time. Some of these might be summed up as follows: the emphasis on 'seeing' things freshly; the prescription for the innocent non-generalizing eye; the concomitant preference for simple people and simple speech, whether that of the uneducated labourer, the savage or the child; the exhortation to accept *all* facts, the vulgar trivia of the world, as being potential harbingers of meaning; the celebration of the details of the concrete world and the (more than intended, perhaps) prestige accorded to the particularizing faculty, that faculty which develops the closest relationships between man and the natural world. 'We penetrate bodily

this incredible beauty; we dip our hands in this painted element; our eyes are bathed in these lights and forms.' Mysticism, yes: but a mysticism which encouraged a scrupulous yet wondering rediscovery of material appearances, which attached maximum importance to a new intimacy with the basic undistorted 'pigment' of 'this painted element', the world. In encouraging men to 'wonder at the usual' Emerson bestowed perhaps his greatest benefit on American literature. (pp. 26-45)

Tony Tanner, "Emerson: The Unconquered Eye and the Enchanted Circle," in his The Reign of Wonder: Naivety and Reality in American Literature, *Cambridge at the University Press, 1965, pp. 26-45.*

R. A. Yoder (essay date 1969)

[*In the following essay, Yoder examines the dialectical structure of Emerson's essays, showing ways in which this structure changed over the course of Emerson's career.*]

We have put aside Emerson the figurehead and Emerson the philosopher, and we look now at the man—a "man thinking," admired most of all for the absorbing process of his inner life. To see this process is of course to emphasize the conflicts and changes in his thinking; we are forced to take at face value Emerson's own statement, "I have no System," and we are more than ever conscious of a second crisis in his life or a later Emerson who shows us, much like Wordsworth in England, how quickly the Romantic lamp is dimmed.

The inner process tells something important about the outward product, the works Emerson published during his life. It is easier, now, to understand why the essays do not submit to paraphrase or summary: the vitality of the inner life shows more clearly that ordinary logic would not serve Emerson's purpose; that purpose and the method it implies have been defined by John Holloway, who was writing about Carlyle, Newman, and Arnold but knew that Emerson belongs to the company of these Victorian sages:

> . . . the sage has a special problem in expounding or in proving what he wants to say. He does not and probably cannot rely on logical and formal argument alone or even much at all. His main task is to quicken his reader's perceptiveness; and he does this by making a far wider appeal than the exclusively rational appeal. He draws upon resources cognate, at least, with those of the artist in words. He gives expression to his outlook imaginatively. What he has to say is not a matter of 'content' or narrow paraphrasable meaning, but is transfused by the whole texture of his writing as it constitutes an experience for the reader.

So we must attend, not to the logical argument, but to the rhetoric of the work if we are to understand fully the experience of Emerson's essays. By "rhetoric" I mean the chiefly literary effects—the telling ways of using phrases or images, or conveying a tone or personality, or organizing one's subject—insofar as they can be distinguished from subject, argument, and conclusion.

These two insights, then, direct our contemporary approach to Emerson: first, that he experienced a second crisis and change of view in the 1840s; and second, that his work must be analyzed as the special art of the sage. Putting them together, I want to consider just how the inward change in Emerson's life and thought is revealed in the outward product, and to do this I will examine one aspect of the sage's rhetoric, the shape or structure of his essays.

Most interpreters of Emerson have agreed that dialectic, in one sense or another, describes the structure of his essays; they have not agreed on the sense. They claim too much, I believe, when they insist that Emerson employed a dialectical logic. True, Emerson did set apart "Dialectic" as "the science of sciences . . . the Intellect discriminating the false and the true. It rests on the observation of identity and diversity." And an earlier statement from this same essay on Plato suggests that for Emerson dialectic and philosophy were practically synonymous:

> Philosophy is the account which the human mind gives to itself of the constitution of the world. Two cardinal facts lie forever at the base; the one, and the two.—1. Unity, or Identity; and, 2. Variety. We unite all things by perceiving the law which pervades them; by perceiving the superficial differences and the profound resemblances. But every mental act,—this very perception of identity or oneness, recognizes the difference of things. Oneness and otherness. It is impossible to speak or to think without embracing both.

But Emerson never defined more precisely this philosophy or its method, and none of the intricate explanations of his dialectical logic has been persuasive enough to gain general assent—for good reason, it seems to me, because if they fit one essay they irreparably strain another. Take, for example, one version of Emerson's method, the "twice-bisected line" proposed by Walter Blair and Clarence Faust some twenty years ago [in *Modern Philology*, November 1944]. Although Emerson called the twice-bisected line "a key to the method and completeness of Plato," he would have been the first to agree that completeness is not necessarily the mark of greatness. In fact, what made Plato great, according to Emerson, was that he "apprehended the cardinal facts." "No man ever more fully acknowledged the Ineffable," but at the same time Plato could affirm, "And yet things are knowable." To see the world as knowable and yet a mystery, to see both identity and diversity, this "double consciousness" is both the art and the achievement of the sage. An awareness of the "two sides" reaches to the heart of every philosophical problem, Emerson wrote in his journal for the autumn of 1841:

> The whole game at which the philosopher busies himself every day, year in, year out, is to find the upper and the under side of every block in his way. Nothing so large and nothing so thin but it has two sides, and when he has seen the outside, he turns it over to see the other face. We never tire of this game, because ever a slight

shudder of astonishment pervades us at the exhibition of the other side of the button,—at the contrast of the two sides. The head and the tail are called in the language of philosophy *Finite* and *Infinite*, Visible and Spiritual, Relative and Absolute, Apparent and Eternal, and many more fine names.

This idea, that everything is two-sided, and that its polarity can be defined by a string of analogies based on the antithesis of identity and diversity, is the essence of Emerson's method. It is simple, but it fits most of the essays.

What Emerson practiced, then, was no rigorous and schematic organization but a mere habit of mind. His habit from youth was to divide any subject into two opposite or contrary sides and to examine the subject from each side, much as a formal debater is required to argue both sides of the question. And it is constantly his technique to dichotomize within an essay, and even to arrange his essays in antithetical pairs. In this loose sense of setting opposing concepts against each other, dialectic was Emerson's device for organizing what he had to say, and he used it at every stage of his career. There is an important difference, however, between the way Emerson's dialectic shapes an early essay like **"The Over-Soul"** and the structure it gives to the essays he wrote during the 1840s. The difference, briefly, is that in **"The Over-Soul"** the opposed pairs are arranged in a series of parallel paragraphs; in later essays the paragraphs themselves become units dialectically opposed and thus form contrastive, not parallel, series.

"The Over-Soul" is representative of Emerson's unwavering Romanticism during the 1830s. In it, as Holloway said of Carlyle, "the nerve of proof simply cannot be traced." Emerson summons not argument or proof, but rather wave after wave of assertion, all striking from the same direction so that a tremendous cumulative force is built up and the rock of opposition finally shattered—the metaphor is Emerson's favorite, of course, and one of his finer quatrains epitomizes the rhetorical strategy and effect of **"The Over-Soul"**:

> All day the waves assailed the rock,
>   I heard no church-bell chime,
> The sea-beat scorns the minister clock
>   And breaks the glass of Time.

Scorning the clock-logic of systematic thought, Emerson assails doubt with all the repeated power of a central, oceanic awareness, for which every paragraph of **"The Over-Soul"** is an analogy or variation.

That central awareness is the experience of revelation. Cast in dialectical or polar terms, it is the awareness of identity in the midst of diversity, or it is using Reason in place of the Understanding. These generalized polarities, identity and diversity, Reason and Understanding, are in fact never mentioned in the essay, but the key terms in every paragraph are surrogates for them, and most important the dialectical relationship between the terms is always the same. In the first paragraph, for example, the "reality" we experience in "brief moments" is set against our "habitual" awareness. Then the "incalculable" balks the "calculator". We live in "parts" for the sake of calculation, but in reality we are "ONE," integral with the single spiritual principle of the universe. The soul is "indefinable, unmeasurable," triumphant over things bound in time and space. The "soul's advances" can be represented only by "metamorphosis" as distinct from linear or arithmetic gradations. And this growth involves a detachment from persons. The soul, because it is general and linked to the Over-Soul, can never cross another man's soul the way one man's will can set itself against another's. Thus we have still another set of opposed terms, impersonal soul against personal will. Moreover, the expression of one's soul is not a matter of personal or voluntary control. We are told not to "interfere with our thought" but to accept the "tide of being which floats us into the secret of nature." When "private will is overpowered," its limited and partial effects may be replaced by involuntary genius. Thus, in another dichotomy, revelation is distinguished from "low curiosity."

The next variation distinguishes those who speak from within from those who speak from without, and this is illustrated by such opposites as the poets Herbert and Pope and the common Romantic antithesis of Kant and Locke. From these specific illustrations Emerson generalizes again to separate the Coleridgean terms genius and talent. Talent is merely the "knack and skill" by which the scholar turns his morbid, monomaniac tendencies into some kind of virtue; talent lessens the man, while genius is the quality of intellect that broadens and makes him more humane. The last polarity sets off the "lowly and simple" from the vain, ambitious, and cultivated; since revelation demands "entire possession," it excludes sophisticated men, who are so intent upon dividing and refining distinctions that they can never give themselves to a momentary enthusiasm.

Pair after pair, this dialectical momentum continues through Emerson's summary and peroration where the key terms and images of the essay reappear. The central theme of unity is neatly recapitualted in a characteristic metaphor of flowing: The Over-Soul works like blood circulating, and that blood is indivisible like the sea.

> . . . the heart in thee is the heart of all; not a valve, not a wall, not an intersection is there anywhere in nature, but one blood rolls uninterruptedly an endless circulation through all men, as the water of the globe is all one sea, and, truly seen, its tide is one.

And the peroration recalls how a man awakens to ONEness and lives no longer in parts: "He will weave no longer a spotted life of shreds and patches, but he will live with a divine unity."

There should be no doubt that the rhetorical structure of this essay is a series of parallel dichotomies. The point can best be summarized graphically:

IDENTITY	DIVERSITY
REASON	UNDERSTANDING
brief	habitual
incalculable	calculable
ONE	parts
unmeasurable	bounded
metamorphosis	linear gradation

impersonal	personal
spontaneous	voluntary
soul	will
Revelation	low curiosity
speakers from within	speakers from without
Herbert	Pope
Kant	Locke
genius	talent
simple	sophisticated
unity	"shreds and patches"

There is no let-up in this series; its steady flow is never broken by a turn or counter-assertion, and there is hardly a contrastive transition in the whole essay. The only one, in fact, begins a brief paragraph in the middle ("But beyond this recognition . . . ") where Emerson seems to distinguish between the self-trust inspired by the soul (a theme closer to **"Self-Reliance"**) and the soul's revelation of truth. This point might have been an important turn or bisection in the essay, but actually it is subdued and hardly affects the tide that sweeps through the whole. The harmony and unity implied by Emerson's use of parallel series in **"The Over-Soul"** reinforces not only the theme of this essay but also the broad assumption of his early faith—the assumption of a correspondence between nature and the mind, and its corollary that "there are no questions to ask which are unanswerable."

In 1836 Emerson had been positive and assured, speaking almost *ex cathedra* about nature. His Orphic poet had pierced easily through appearances to the central law, and the questions were all answered. How different things are five years later. When Emerson delivered **"The Method of Nature"** in the summer of 1841, the poet was unable to pierce an inch: "the method of nature: who could ever analyze it? That rushing stream will not stop to be observed." The old question of 1836, "To what end is Nature?" can no longer even be posed—Nature "does not exist to any one or any number of particular ends, but to numberless and endless benefit." At this point the relationship between man and Nature ceases to be straightforward:

> I conceive a man as always spoken to from behind, and unable to turn his head and see the speaker. In all the millions who have heard the voice, none ever saw the face. . . . That well known voice speaks in all languages, governs all men, and none ever caught a glimpse of its form.

In **"The Sphinx," "To Rhea," "Woodnotes,"** and **"Monadnoc,"** all poems of this period, a remote, unembodied voice speaks for nature as a whole, lecturing the poet from nearby rocks, trees, and mountains.

Thus for Emerson in the early 1840s Nature has changed her personality, if not her principles. If the conclusions of his essays represent her principles, they are substantially what they were in the first *Nature* or in **"The Over-Soul."** But in emphasis, in tone and imagery, and above all in their rhetorical shape, essays like **"Circles," "Nature"** (in *Essays: Second Series*), **"Experience,"** or **"Montaigne"** differ markedly from the earlier ones. The old ideas are like unanalyzable counters arranged in a new way—before they overwhelmed the reader with nature's unity, now they dazzle him with nature's unpredictability. In 1839

Emerson decided that the philosopher must become a poet in order to express "fluxional quantities and values," and the keynote of these later essays comes appropriately from one of the poet's gnomic utterances: "Mount to paradise / By the stairway of surprise" (**"Merlin"**). The shape of art imitates the shape of life, and (Emerson repeats in **"Circles"** and **"Experience"**) "Life is a series of surprises." It is our continual "astonishment" that makes the game interesting. Thus the later essays astonish us with an assortment of surprises, ambiguities, conclusions pulled out of a hat. To this end, the parallelisms of **"The Over-Soul"** offer no advantage, since change and contrast are the essentials of surprise.

A structure of contrastive divisions characterizes the essays written by Emerson after 1840. In fact, it can be seen already in **"Compensation,"** probably written a short time after **"The Over-Soul."** **"Compensation"** is perhaps Emersons's classic statement of polarity or a dialectic process operating in nature. At the same time, there is a real dialectical conflict, unobtrusive at first but erupting in the end, that gives **"Compensation"** a more dramatic structure than its major theme suggests. The essay begins with a series of assertions about polarity, or the balance of opposites, in nature—here are the lead sentences that link a group of paragraphs: "Polarity, or action and reaction, we meet in every part of nature . . ." ; "The same dualism underlies the nature and condition of man. Every excess causes a defect; every defect an excess"; "Every act rewards itself, or in other words integrates itself, in a twofold manner . . . "; "All things are double, one against another . . ."; What Emerson seems to be saying, what is implied or hinted at by this doctrine of compensation, is that Nature is a sort of Manichean balance where good and evil cancel each other out. If he does not say this precisely, he comes very close—for example, the maxim "Every sweet hath its sour; every evil its good" strongly suggests that every good has its evil, too. And Emerson depends on the reader's assimilating this implied amorality of nature, so that in the middle of the essay he can suddenly turn on the idea apparently established and end the essay on compensation with a counter-assertion. Here is the major turning point:

THESIS: Thus do all things preach the indifferency of circumstances. The man is all. Everything has two sides, a good and an evil. Every advantage has its tax. I learn to be content.

ANTITHESIS: But the doctrine of compensation is not the doctrine of indifferency.

THESIS: The thoughtless say, on hearing these representations,—What boots it to do well? there is one event to good and evil; if I gain any good I must pay for it; if I lose any good I gain some other; all actions are indifferent.

ANTITHESIS: There is a deeper fact in the soul than compensation, to wit, its own nature. The soul is not a compensation, but a life.

The balance in nature with its corollary of moral indiffer-

ence is a fact of appearance only, and we must understand that beyond appearance is the reality of the soul. Thus the concept of the soul, the same idea as in **"The Over-Soul,"** becomes the antithesis of this essay and the means by which apparent evil and "calamity" can be understood as ultimate good.

"Circles," which immediately follows **"The Over-Soul"** in *Essays: First Series,* must have been written in the fall of 1840. Its rhetorical structure is exactly that of **"Compensation,"** as an allusion in the opening paragraph suggests: "One moral we have already deduced in considering the circular or compensatory character of every human action." The action and reaction of compensation are represented here by two 180-degree arcs of a circle, "this first of forms" that returns upon itself. But if the figure of a circle symbolizes the compensation that works in every human action, it also symbolizes the deeper fact that no action is ever fixed or completed, that no single viewpoint or summary of events is ever final: "The life of a man is a self-evolving circle, which, from a ring imperceptibly small, rushes on all sides outwards to new and larger circles, and that without end." "There are no fixtures in nature," that is the dominant theme of the essay. With it Emerson is able to work the same effect as in **"Compensation"**: he plays upon the moral ambiguity that inheres in this idea—is the change in nature and man a change for better or for worse? Or is it simply indifferent, and the world mere change? Some paragraphs in **"Circles"** imply mere flux: "Our moods do not believe in each other"; "There is no virtue which is final . . .." Others suggest progress through a synthesis of opposites, as in this passage that calls to mind the dialectical method of the Socratic dialogues and then the doctrine of the Over-Soul: "By going one step farther back in thought, discordant opinions are reconciled by being seen to be two extremes of one principle, and we can never go so far back as to preclude a still higher vision. . . . Generalization is always a new influx of the divinity into the mind." Toward the end of the essay, however, Emerson assumes that the reader, as in **"Compensation,"** has been led to view the process as merely flux and indifference:

> And thus, O circular philosopher, I hear some reader exclaim, you have arrived at a fine Pyrrhonism, at an equivalence and indifference of all actions, . . .
>
> . . . But lest I should mislead any when I have my own head and obey my whims, let me remind the reader that I am only an experimenter. Do not set the least value on what I do, or the least discredit on what I do not, as if I pretended to settle any thing as true or false. I unsettle all things. No facts are to me sacred; none are profane; I simply experiment, an endless seeker with no past at my back.

And this leads him into the last and crucial turn of the essay where the whole thesis of fluidity and impermanence is countered by the antithesis of the soul:

> Yet this incessant movement and progression which all things partake could never become sensible to us but by contrast to some principle of fixture or stability in the soul. Whilst the eter-

nal generation of circles proceeds, the eternal generator abides. That central life is somewhat superior to creation, superior to knowledge and thought, and contains all its circles.

Actually, these ideas of unity and the soul, which usually dominate Emerson's perorations, are overshadowed in the conclusion of **"Circles"** by themes of newness and change. Yet the turn of thought is placed and introduced so as to receive emphasis; Emerson gives it prominence, even if it is not required for his conclusion.

When Emerson came to write his "new chapter on Nature," he abandoned the form of the old. *Nature* of 1836 moved serenely from the level of material and practical apprehension to spiritual insight; its transitions are smooth, as in **"The Over-Soul,"** without turns or hesitations. In contrast to such uninterrupted ascension, **"Nature"** as it appears in *Essays: Second Series* is organized, not from bottom to top, so to speak, but from side to side, in terms of polarities. First Emerson distinguishes *natura naturata* and *natura naturans,* the passive landscape on the one hand and the active or creative principle on the other. Both of these he treats with a slight indirectness or ambiguity, the same quality we observed in **"Compensation"** and **"Circles."** Nature as landscape "must always seem unreal and mocking," and there is something untrustworthy or exaggerated in men's descriptions of nature. Nature as principle or cause is secret—an unfathomable, slippery Proteus who can never be pinned down. Then, quite out of the air, Emerson proposes a second dichotomy: "Motion or change and identity or rest are the first and second secrets of nature: Motion and Rest." Identity, which under the doctrine of correspondence was the guiding principle of *Nature* (1836), is briefly explained, and then Emerson turns to the opposite principle of motion ("If the identity expresses organized rest, the counter action also runs into organization"). At this stage, motion is more important to him because it is motion and change that give nature its dominant personality in this essay— nature is Proteus who constantly changes shape, or the Sphinx who befuddles mankind. The theme of mockery and deceit, muted in its introduction, now returns with full force: the "overfaith" of man in himself is mirrored in nature where there is "something mocking, something that leads us on and on, but arrives nowhere." If this sense of nature that urges us toward vague goals is the active principle or *natura naturans,* the same deceitfulness is evidenced in the *natura naturata.*

> Quite analogous to the deceits in life, there is, as might be expected, a similar effect on the eye from the face of external nature. There is in woods and waters a certain enticement and flattery, together with a failure to yield a present satisfaction. This disappointment is felt in every landscape. . . . The pinetree, the river, the bank of flowers before him [the poet] does not seem to be nature. Nature is still elsewhere. . . . It is the same among the men and women as among the silent trees; always a referred existence, an absence, never a presence and satisfaction.

At this point, clearly, the deceitfulness of nature has become Emerson's dominant theme or thesis, and the reader

should be feeling appropriately uncomfortable, "encamped" but "not domesticated" in this alien world. To assure that he does, Emerson adds one last rhetorical question—"Must we not suppose somewhere in the universe a slight treachery and derision?" And then Emerson reverses himself in a now familiar final turn to the essay:

THESIS: We cannot bandy words with Nature, or deal with her as we deal with persons. If we measure our individual forces against hers we may easily feel as if we were the sport of an insuperable destiny.

ANTITHESIS: But if, instead of identifying ourselves with the work, we feel that the soul of the Workman streams through us, we shall find the peace of the morning dwelling first in our hearts, and the fathomless powers of gravity and chemistry, and over them, of life, pre-existing within us in their highest form.

The uneasiness which the thought of our helplessness in the chain of causes occasions us, results from looking too much at one condition of nature, namely, Motion. But the drag is never taken from the wheel. Wherever the impulse exceeds, the Rest OR Identity insinuates its compensation.

The thesis that rose out of a consideration of motion is thwarted by the antithesis of rest—Emerson is into his last paragraph, into the peroration that urges us to heed universal law, to forget "our servitude to particulars"; and thus our uneasiness is dispelled.

I think now we can summarize the rhetorical structure or strategy that these essays have in common. They all assert a basic dichotomy and develop a balance between its opposite or extreme terms. This equilibrium gradually disintegrates, and a single theme or thesis emerges, often indirectly by image and suggestion rather than by direct statement. The theme or thesis expresses doubt or moral ambiguity in nature. It builds up assertive power until suddenly it is dashed away by a climactic turn in the essay, almost always indicated by a contrastive conjunction ("But," "yet," "whilst"). The antithesis introduced by the turn is an expression of unity and hope, and leads into Emerson's peroration.

A glance at several other essays of the same decade, the 1840s, should show that this structure is more than accidental. **"Experience,"** for example, is a set of variations based on the idea that "life is a train of moods like a string of beads." The crucial turn comes in a long paragraph about two-thirds through the essay, the gist of which is that the seeming unrelatedness of the parts or moods of our lives is no proof that they are not or will not be related. And it moves to this sentence, which should be compared with the turning sentences of **"Compensation"** and **"Circles":**

> If I have described life as a flux of moods, I must now add that there is that in us which changes not and which ranks all sensations and states of mind.

Or to take another example, the essay **"Montaige; Or,**

the Skeptic" from *Representative Men.* The dualism by which it is constructed is obvious in the first paragraph, and out of the opposition between abstractionist and materialist arises the third party, the skeptic, who represents the thesis of the essay and is the type for whom Montaigne is representative. In the course of the essay, however, the concept of a skeptic is stipulatively limited until skepticism is identified with self-reliance, hence with "belief " (in the "affirmations of the soul") and "faith" (presumably faith in oneself). The thesis is modified so that skepticism with regard to custom or dogma is approved, while skepticism or disbelief in man's power to apprehend the ultimate unity of nature is impossible. Thus Emerson can bring off this surprising climax, in which the apparent thesis of the essay is overturned.

> The final solution in which skepticism is lost, is in the moral sentiment, which never forfeits its supremacy. All moods may be safely tried, and their weight allowed to all objections: the moral sentiment as easily outweighs them all, as any one. This is the drop which balances the sea. I play with the miscellany of facts, and take those superficial views which we call skepticism; but I know that they will presently appear to me in that order which makes skepticism impossible. A man of thought must feel the thought that is parent of the universe; that the masses of nature do undulate and flow.

In still later essays, the conflict and surprise generated by Emerson's dialectic is discernible though muted. More than ever he would depend on an antithesis, usually some version of Motion and Rest, to establish a working balance. But, as if he now began to accept a universe of flux and ambiguity as a commonplace unworthy of emphasis, he does not build rhetorically in that direction—that thesis is underplayed; and nor then does he give so much prominence to a surprising reversal of direction in the end. "Fate," despite the limitations it places on man, never overwhelms us. Balance returns again and again as power and fate, or intellect and fate, or thought and nature, terms that stand roughly for the individual consciousness and the external world—so we are back where Emerson began twenty years before, pondering the relation between ME and NOT-ME. And the only answer, now, to this mystery is to trust compensation, "the cunning co-presence" of limit and liberty in nature that assures us damages will be paid when nature is liable. Given a balance maintained throughout, there is little surprise in Emerson's peroration, despite its suddenness; there is no transition, no emphatic change of direction, but only the simple, hortative beginning—"Let us build altars . . . "—that signifies Emerson's final movement.

Emerson always experienced difficulty in organizing his fine phrases, more than ever as years went by. Lecturing at Harvard in 1870, he seemed indifferent to the problems of organizing and dramatizing his thoughts: "What I am now to attempt is simply some sketches or studies . . . ," he said in the introduction to *Natural History of Intellect.* The series of dichotomies that follows is loose and casually related, even for Emerson (one paragraph begins: "Well, having accepted this law of identity pervading the universe, we must next perceive that whilst every creature

represents and obeys it, there is diversity, there is more or less of power." At the end, Emerson makes no attempt at his former rhetorical magic by which the whole thrust of the essay is reversed or contraries are suddenly reconciled. There is only a humble conclusion, pathetic almost, for a once great master of the dramatic peroration:

> We wish to sum up the conflicting impressions by saying that all point at last to a unity which inspires all. . . .

Thin and transparent this sentence is, and it should remind us that if logic or argument counted for everything, then all of Emerson's conclusions could be adequately summarized this way. It should remind us that Emerson at his best is Merlin weaving a spell upon us—whether the spell is magic or rhetorical sleight-of-hand makes no difference, the point is we are caught up in a dramatic presentation the way we are not in a philosophical argument.

Dialectic is an essential element in Emerson's dramatic presentation, as I have tried to show. Emerson fashions it into a device or structure that reflects his view of life, and it changes as he changes. In the essays of the early 1840s he adopts a strategy of dramatic reversal that can surprise and awaken and finally relieve his audience, both listeners and readers. This strategy enables him to keep his early ideal of a knowable nature and yet to take full account of the unknowable that lurks beyond reason and faith.

To acknowledge the ineffable and yet affirm that things are knowable is a greatness beyond consistency. The ability, temperamentally and then artistically, to face this paradox

---

Hyatt H. Waggoner on Emerson's poetry:

One of the very few judgments on which there has been widespread agreement among readers of Emerson's poems is that they are exceptionally uneven in quality. Admirers and detractors alike tend to agree on this judgment even while they interpret it differently. My own experience of reading straight through the volume of collected poems several times has shown me no reason to challenge the general opinion. There are more than a dozen poems I find myself wishing to return to frequently and think it might be possible to defend as classics of their kind, perhaps twice as many more that seem to me well worth remembering and now and then rereading despite their flaws, a larger number that I value only for a passage or two or even a line, and then the rest, the ones that do not speak to me at all, that I find boring or even irritating to read. Emerson's collected poetry is a volume to skip around in, make one's own anthology out of. Though something like this is no doubt true of the collected works of all poets except perhaps the very greatest, it seems more true of Emerson's work than it does generally of poets who put more emphasis on craft and relied less on inspiration. Distinguished poetic reputations have often rested on a smaller number of memorable poems, but perhaps few if any classic poets have published so much verse that strikes one as skirting the edge of doggerel.

Hyatt H. Waggoner, in his Emerson as Poet, *Princeton University Press, 1974.*

is what I take Emerson to mean by a "double consciousness." Facing it and making it central to his art in the 1840s brings Emerson closer to Hawthorne and Melville, who are often at odds with Romantic enthusiasm and the Transcendental mysteries. But Emerson's Romanticism is complex and dynamic, and this rhetoric of contrast leads his art toward the ambiguity of Hawthorne—Saadi can be just as inscrutable as Hawthorne telling what had been witnessed on the scaffold or as Miles Coverdale. Moreover, if Melville shields Ishmael from the fate of the arch-Transcendentalist Ahab, it is because Ishmael has learned a lesson along the way:

> Doubts of all things earthly, and intuitions of some things heavenly; this combination makes neither believer nor infidel, but makes a man who regards them both with equal eye.

This "equal eye" is the fine-tempered balance yielded by Emerson's dialectic and the wisdom in his later essays. (pp. 313-28)

R. A. Yoder, "Emerson's Dialectic," in Criticism, *Vol. 11, No. 3, Fall, 1969, pp. 313-28.*

Lawrence I. Buell (essay date 1972)

[*Buell is an American educator and critic. In the following essay, he argues that Emerson's essays are characterized by sophisticated structure and careful organization.*]

Emerson has never been taken very seriously as an artist of wholes. Even some of his best friends, like Alcott, claimed that he could be read as well backwards as forwards, and the best recent critic of his style [Jonathan Bishop, in his *Emerson on the Soul,* 1964] agrees that he was primarily "a worker in sentences and single verses." Indeed, Emerson himself admitted that his essays lacked continuity. Nor did this disturb him greatly, for in his study of other authors he himself "read for the lustres"; and in his critical theory he made much of the importance of symbolism and analogy but had little to say about form. Likewise, as a lecturer he was apt to make up his discourse as he went along, shuffling and reshuffling his papers as he spoke. Even if he had wanted to compose an orderly lecture, his method of composition by patching together passages from his journals would seem to have been an almost insuperable handicap.

This weight of evidence, however, has not kept a growing minority of Emerson's readers from insisting that there is an authentic and sophisticated unity to at least some of his prose. **"The Poet," "Self-Reliance," "Art,"** and especially *Nature* and **"Experience"** have all been defended as intricately structured wholes. Unfortunately, these defenses have labored under two sorts of disadvantages, which have kept their conclusions from carrying the weight they deserve. First, they have usually emphasized very general and abstract patterns in the essays: "dialectical unity," Plato's twice-bisected line, "upward" movement, and the like. *Nature* treats its topics on an ascending order in the scale of being; the chapters in *Essays, First Series* are organized on the principle of complimentary pairs—few would dispute such claims as these. What is at issue, rath-

er, is Emerson's control over his subject from section to section, paragraph to paragraph, especially after *Nature,* which is much more explicitly blocked out and argued than the essays. A student of mine put the problem exactly when he said that it's easy enough to see Emerson clearly from a distance but as you get close everything becomes foggy.

Secondly, previous studies of Emersonian structure have not taken into account the process of composition from journal to lecture to essay. Therefore they have not been able to speak directly to the assumption that Emerson failed to synthesize his raw materials where Thoreau, in *Walden,* succeeded. To know where Emerson succeeds and fails in composition, one has to catch him in the act.

This paper, accordingly, will attempt to pin down the extent to which Emerson's essays have continuity, taking their genesis into account when it is useful, and disregarding for the moment the metaphysical implications of Emersonian structure (*Nature* as scale of being, *"Nominalist and Realist"* as bi-polar unity, etc.), important as these implications are. I do not mean to argue that Emerson mastered form as he did the aphorism; but I would contend that he was far more in control than at first appears, and that the appearance of formlessness is to a large extent a strategy on Emerson's part calculated to render his thoughts more faithfully and forcefully than direct statement would permit. The same holds true, I suspect, for a number of other literary artists who also seem positively to cultivate haphazardness as a stylistic attribute: e.g., Montaigne, Hazlitt, and Robert Burton.

In Emerson's case it is certainly clear that the dense, obscure style for which he is best known was a deliberate choice. Most of his early sermons are plain and lucid, sometimes to the point of formula, and in later life he was quite capable of the same style when he pleased, as in the **"Historical Discourse at Concord,"** a number of his printed lectures, and most of *English Traits.* Whereas there is a real doubt whether Walt Whitman could have written a decent poem in conventional metre, there is no question that Emerson knew, and could use, all the techniques of conventional prose style.

As to the organization of Emerson's mature essays, it is likewise fair to say: (1) that there is usually more order than we at first notice, and (2) that Emerson provides enough clues to ensure continuity, though in a studiously offhand, and sometimes downright misleading manner. We read the first nine pages of **"Intellect"** with a sense of wandering, when all at once appears the general proposition which snaps the essay into a degree of focus: "In the intellect constructivestructive . . . we observe the same balance of two elements as in intellect receptive," and we see that Emerson has been developing this general distinction all the while. Or in **"Self-Reliance"** we come upon: "The other terror that scares us from self-trust is our consistency." The *other* terror? Oh yes—conformity. But it was introduced, six pages before, in simple antithesis to self-reliance, with no indication to the effect "now, reader, we shall discuss the two threats to self-reliance." But presently comes the conclusion: "I hope in these days we have heard the last of conformity and consistency," and the ten pages spring together as a unit—not clarifying all the vagaries therein, but reassuring us that the Ariadne's thread is still in hand. Emerson could easily have guided his reader somewhat more, but of course he could not spend the day in explanation.

These intimations of order, which are continually turning up in the essays, encourage us to search for more. "If you desire to arrest attention," Emerson writes in his journal, "do not give me facts in the order of cause & effect, but drop one or two links in the chain, & give me with a cause, an effect two or three times removed." This is a far better description of his method, overall, than "infinitely repellent particles," for upon close examination of the essays one can find a number of recurring devices used by Emerson both to supply and to conceal continuity.

The one just illustrated might be called the "buried outline." The key is either withhelld for several pages, as in the two essays above, or thrown out so offhandedly that one is likely to miss it, as in **"The Poet,"** where the plan for the essay is tucked into a part of the last sentence in the long exordium. **"Experience"** is an especially provoking case. "Where do we find ourselves?" the essay begins. Where indeed? Not until the beginning of the second section do we learn that the first has been about "Illusion"; indeed, a previous hint suggests that "Surface" is the subject. And the final organization of the essay is not clarified until near the end, when Emerson draws up a list of the seven topics he has covered.

Actually, the reader is most fortunate to get such an exact list from Emerson; not only do all the items apply, they are even given in the right order. Possibly he is atoning for the prefatory motto, which also contains a sevenfold list, but one which corresponds only in part to the essay's structure. The reader who approaches the essay with it as a guide is bound to be misled. This is a second typical Emersonian tactic for "providing" structure—the careless list. Along with his passion for drawing up rosters of great men, immortal books, natural facts, and the like, seems to have gone an abhorrence for following them up. **"Self-Reliance,"** he predicts, will work revolutions in men's "religion," "education," "pursuits," "modes of living," "association," "property," and "speculative views," and he starts to go down the list. But he gets through only four items, of which the last three turn out to be "travel," "art," and "society." In **"Culture"** Emerson is a little more accurate: he lists four antidotes to "egotism" ("books," "travel," "society," "solitude") and covers all of them. But they might just as well have been called "education," "travel," "city," and "country."

Even if one concedes the worst to Emerson's detractors, it is inconceivable that the sloppy way he uses lists could be accidental. The device is too simple. He could have done better as a schoolboy. Surely Emerson is inexact on purpose, either to suggest that demonstration of his principle is endless (as in the long list in **"Self-Reliance,"** which is only half followed up), or, more commonly, to give a tentativeness to his subject. "I dare not assume to give their order, but I name them as I find them in my way," he says of the lords of life in **"Experience"**. The motto proves his point—there they simply occur to him in a dif-

ferent way. The inaccurate list gives Emerson the fluid framework he needs to suggest both that his ideas have a coherence and that they are in a state of flux. Even when he categories precisely, as in *Nature,* he likes to add a disclaimer. Nature's "multitude of uses," he says, "all admit of being thrown into one of the following classes. . . . " As if the act of classification, though necessary, were distasteful to him.

A third way in which Emerson uses and conceals structure is to develop a point without ever stating it. Consider this progression from **"Spiritual Laws."** (Brackets indicate material adapted from lectures and journals.)

> [. . . 'A few strong instincts and a few plain rules' suffice us.]
>
> [My will never gave the images in my mind the rank they now take. The regular course of studies, the years of academical and professional education have not yielded me better facts than some idle books under the bench at the Latin School. What we do not call education is more precious than that which we call so. We form no guess, at the time of receiving a thought, of its comparative value. And education often wastes its effort in attempts to thwart and balk this natural magnetism, which is sure to select what belongs to it.]
>
> In like manner our moral nature is vitiated by any interference of our will. People represent virtue as a struggle, and take to themselves great airs upon their attainments, and the question is everywhere vexed when a noble nature is commended, whether the man is not better who strives with temptation. But there is no merit in the matter. [Either God is there or He is not there.] [We love characters in proportion as they are impulsive and spontaneous. The less a man thinks or knows about his virtues the better we like him. Timoleon's victories are the best victories, which ran and flowed like Homer's verses, Plutarch said. When we see a soul whose acts are all regal, graceful and pleasant as roses, we must thank God that such things can be and are, and not turn sourly on the angel and say 'Crump is a better man with his grunting resistance to all his native devils.']
>
> [Not less conspicuous is the preponderance of nature over will in all practical life.]

Not until the end of this sequence, if at all, do we begin to see how well-controlled it is. At first the initial paragraph transition comes as a shock—seemingly one of those instances in which Emerson was unable to dovetail two blocs of thought taken from lectures. His argument, a defense of total spontaneity, reinforces this suspicion. So may the next transition ("In like manner . . . "), which is almost as baffling as the one before. It is not clear to what "moral nature" is being compared. Like what? Like education? Like the Latin School? But eventually one sees that Emerson is developing a familiar threefold sequence: never explicitly stated, as, e.g., "The mind grows by nature, not by will." Had Emerson written this, he would have been almost pendantically straightforward—which is probably why he didn't.

As it is, the clues in the opening sentence of the next paragraph probably will not suffice to enlighten the reader as to what Emerson is about, because he immediately goes off on another tack. Rather than develop his second point at once, he turns back to dispense with the popular view ("People represent . . . "), and his attack takes the form of a battery of aphorisms which are sufficiently oblique to the opening sentence and to each other as to force the reader to strain for the connection. The statement, "Our moral nature is vitiated by any interference of our will," is vague and self-contradictory, and the vatic pronouncement, "Either God is there or he is not there," hardly clarifies matters. Both the tactic of veering away from an initial statement and then working back to it, and the tactic of fanning out from a statement with a barrage of apothegms (to be brought back abruptly, oftentimes, at the start of a new paragraph) are also typical of Emerson. Since the first three sentences of the paragraph have no apparent antecedent in journal or lecture, it would seem that the former strategy was deliberately manufactured for the occasion.

But is the rest of the paragraph under control? To be sure, some of it is memorable, but is it any more than a bag of duckshot? Even where a connection may be traced from point to point there may be no real development. In much of the passage Emerson seems to repeat himself rather than move forward. But again a close look shows more sophistication than at first appears. Though the last five sentences *could* be rearranged, there is a logic to their order: from the divine to the homely and back again, from "God" to "characters" in general, to a representative man, to a specific historical example, to a contemporary example which is more earthy and concrete and yet at the same time, by contrasting Crump with a great "soul" or "angel," brings us back to God and clinches Emerson's point about the divine quality of spontaneity. The previous paragraph unfolds with equal delicacy in a reverse fashion. A sudden and particular perception of the speaker's is given perspective by a parallel from his schooldays, which in turn suggests a general theory of education.

Not all passages in the essays will serve my case as well as the one just discussed. On the other hand, there are passages far more intricately designed. Here is one from **"Self-Reliance."**

[I suppose no man can violate his nature. All the sallies of his will are rounded in by the law of his being, as the inequalities of Andes and Himmaleh are insignificant in the curve of the sphere. Nor does it matter how you gauge and try him. A character is like an acrostic or Alexandrian stanza;—read it forward, backward, or across, it still spells the same thing.] In this pleasing contrite wood-life which God allows me, [let me record day by day my honest thought without prospect or retrospect, and, I cannot doubt, it will be found symmetrical, though I mean it not and see it not.] My book should smell of pines and resound with the hum of insects. [The swallow over my window should interweave that thread or straw he carries in his bill into my web also.] We pass for what we are. [Character teaches above our wills.] Men imag-

ine that they communicate their virtue or vice only by overt actions, and do not see that virtue or vice emit a breath every moment.

Upon first reading, this paragraph seems to consist simply of variations on the theme of the topic sentence. What it says about achieving formal unity without conscious intent sounds like wishful thinking; the speaker seems to be hoping that he built better than he knew. One is tempted to substitute "paragraph" for "character" and take Emerson as encouraging the reader to read him as Alcott suggested. And yet the passage will indeed "be found symmetrical," if we look closely, and the way to see this is by making that very substitution, by seeing a double meaning in "character." The paragraph turns on the pun "character" equals "writing." Every man is defined by his nature, as a landscape in nature is limited by the horizon; and that nature can be read in his "character," as a poem is read. The poet, too, is defined by his landscape (and here Emerson brings the senses of nature as character and nature as countryside together), which if he is true to himself will be found, down to the last straw, in what he writes. For "character," whatever our conscious intention, "communicates" itself in our every "breath" or utterance.

In order to create this impressive piece of double-entendre, Emerson . . . drew on two and perhaps three lectures, and two journal passages, adding several new aphorisms. And in none of those individual passages is the eventual design more than adumbrated. But surely in synthesizing them Emerson must have known what he was about, judging not only from the effect of the ensemble but the fact that he added the sentence about "my book" and went back to [his journals], after using the same passage in abbreviated form twice previously, to retrieve the metaphor of character as poem.

I hope that by now I have succeeded in showing that at his best Emerson was capable of full control over his materials, even when they were very diverse. How consistent that control was throughout a given essay remains to be seen, however. Undoubtedly Emerson had some clear-cut failures, especially in his old age, when like Thoreau he lost the power to synthesize. **"Books"** is an obvious example; it is little more than a catalogue. Another instance is **"Poetry and Imagination,"** for which manuscripts also survive. These suggest that except for the introductory section, no part of the essay has a fixed and authentic order. The "essay" cannot, for the most part, be considered as much more than a collection of sayings. The last ten pages especially seem to have undergone a last-minute re-shuffle before publication, involving a dozen or so thought-units.

But it is unfair to pick on Emerson in his old age, when Cabot was beginning to take over his editorial work. All the texts arranged by Cabot and Edward Emerson are more or less corrupt anyway, and more than the footnotes of the Centenary Edition indicate, because of the amount of silent cutting and patching that was done to prepare Emerson's lecture notes for publication. Of course, the fact that the unusual desultoriness of **"Poetry and Imagination"** and other late works does not seem to have bothered critics is a sign that this is what one expects from Emerson.

Nevertheless, close scrutiny of his earlier prose reveals that he did pay a considerable attention to organization, even in some essays which are usually assumed to be formless. A discussion of two such hard cases, **"History"** and **"The Over-Soul,"** should support this statement.

"History" is Emerson's most ambitious essay. Its scope is wider even than *Nature,* inasmuch as it traces the operation of cosmic unity-in-diversity in man's past as well as in his present environment. The vastness of this subject leads Emerson to a diffuseness of illustration extraordinary even for him, and practically overwhelming for the reader. The first page or so is highly explicit; the rest seems a maze of redundancy. Still, it has a plan, though with characteristic nonchalance Emerson puts off a direct statement of it until near the close, and even then is misleadingly vague: ". . . in the light of these two facts, namely, that the mind is One, and that nature is its correlative, history is to be read and written." This indicates hazily, the essay's structure. After a long prologue which treats his themes in miniature (paragraphs 1-6), Emerson shows first that to the perceiving mind, the diverse manifestations of nature and history are governed by the same laws as itself (pars. 7-18) and then the converse proposition, that everything in individual experience is writ large in history and nature (pars. 19-44). In somewhat more detail, the essay can be summarized as follows:

> *Prologue.* The individual mind partakes of the universal mind common to all men (par. 1). Therefore, while in order to understand the mind one must know all of history, which is the record of the mind, the whole of history can be explained from individual experience (2-3). Every experience of ours is duplicated in history; every fact in history is applicable to us (3). This principle of universality in the particular explains our reverence for human life and the laws of property, our identification with what we read (4) and with the "condition" of the great and the "character" of the wise (5); let us then apply this principle to the theory of history as well and take it as a commentary on us, rather than the reverse (6).

> *First Proposition* (Unity-in-Diversity). All history has its counterpart in individual experience (7). We must therefore go over the whole ground of history and internalize it to learn its lesson (8-9). All study of antiquity—e.g., ancient and medieval architecture—is the attempt to reduce "then" to "now" (11-12). Just as man (12) and external nature (13) manifest a unity amid diversity of temperaments and forms, so with history, as in the diversity of Greek culture (14). Further instances of the cosmic principle of unity-in-diversity are the resemblance between human and natural forms (15-16), the similarity of the creative process in diverse areas (17), and the similarity with which great souls and great art affect us (18).

> *Second Proposition* (Diversity-in-Unity). Everything in and of us has its counterpart in the not-

me (19). For instance, common experience sometimes takes on cosmic significance (20); everyday objects supply civilization with models for its great architecture (21-24); the conflict in human nature between love of adventure vs. repose has caused the dispute throughout history between nomads and settlers (25). Each individual experiences in himself the primeval world (27), a Grecian period—i.e., a state of natural innocence (28-29), an age of chivalry and an age of exploration (30). Likewise with religious history (30-31): Christianity (32), ancient religion (33), monasticism (34-35), the reformation and its aftermath (36) all express various intuitions and moods in the individual. The same is also true of literature from Greek fable (38) to Goethe (39), from medieval romance (40-41) to Sir Walter Scott (42). Finally, man has affinities with all of nature as well as history. Men like Napoleon need the whole of nature in which to operate (43); and the endeavors of geniuses, and even ordinary people as well, have universal implications (44).

> *Conclusion* (45)—quoted above.

> *Peroration* (46-48).

This précis hardly captures the greatness of Emerson, but it may be argued that an awareness of what it does convey is essential to a just appreciation of that greatness. Otherwise one must picture Emerson simply as a talented aphorist who ran wild for forty pages.

As the summary shows, Emerson did not have total control over his subject. Paragraphs 16-18 are anti-climactic. The peroration is too diffuse. More seriously, Emerson feels obliged to go over his whole ground twice; that at least is the impression created by the preface, whose first three paragraphs splice together the pivotal passages of his 1838 lecture on history, which contains all his essential thoughts on the subject. The sense of redundancy is increased by Emerson's nonchalance in distinguishing between his two propositions (cf. pars. 7, 19, 24, 26), nor is it clear whether some parts of the essay are "about" history, or nature, or the principle of unity-in-diversity underlying both. Finally, need it be said that Emerson never really confronts the question of history's importance? On the one hand, it is all-important, as a clue to our nature; on the other, it is superfluous, since we contain all history within ourselves. One should be prepared for ambivalence on so abstract a point, but he may justly expect at least an explicit statement of the problem.

When all this is deducted, though, it remains that the essay has method. After the first three paragraphs of lecture-in-miniature, Emerson prepares for his first proposition, as he often does, by appeals to common sense experience: the way we regard property, reading, etc., should prepare us for the philosophical view which he is about to outline. He begins proposition two in the same manner, with four personal anecdotes which bear witness to his point. The "argument" in both sections moves, roughly speaking, from this existential level to a variety of limited examples (e.g., Gothic architecture) to something like a comprehensive statement (12-14; 27-44). The nature of that statement differs according to the point. Proposition one, unity-in-diversity, can be stated more simply than proposition two, diversity-in-unity, which necessitates short sketches of the history of society, religion, literature, and science. If this portion of the essay seems prolix it is because as in *Nature* Emerson is trying to apply his principle to all main branches of his subject. Altogether, then, while structure is not Emerson's strongest point in **"History,"** the essay does have a form distinct enough for the careful reader to perceive.

So too, I think, does **"The Over-Soul,"** despite the fact that it has been singled out as an arch-example of discombobulated afflatus. As I shall explain later, I think that the essay does fall apart about three-quarters of the way through, but until then Emerson has his materials well in hand.

The essay begins with a long and stately exordium (pars. 1-2), stitched together mainly from two passages from lecturers and one directly from the journals, which supply its three stages of movement: the initial paradox, "our vice is habitual," yet we hope; the question, what is the ground of this hope?; and the preliminary answer, "man is a stream whose source is hidden." The way in which the passage converges to a focus on this metaphor is emphasized by the switch from the general "we" and "man" to the personal "I": "*Man* is a stream whose source is hidden. *Our* being is descending into us from *we* know not whence. The most exact *calculator* has no prescience that somewhat incalculable may not balk the very next moment. *I* am constrained every moment to acknowledge a higher origin for events than the will *I* call *mine*" (italics mine). Emerson's supposed reticence and Thoreau's greater self-assertiveness have distracted us from the fact that Emerson too was adept at the subjective mood, and this is a good instance. The device of funneling in from the abstract to the personal, used now and again in other essays too, makes the passage fall somewhat as a leaf falls, circling, zigzag, into one's hand. Then, as the first-person mood continues for another paragraph, along with the metaphor, it adds a sense of urgency to the previous questions, the urgency of a personal witness.

The essay now proceeds to identify the mysterious source of power (par. 3). It is the Over-Soul, which inheres in everyone and everything and is always accessible to us whether we sense it or not. Again the speaker ends his definition on a personal note: "I dare not speak for it"; but he will try to give some hints.

In the next section, as I see it (pars. 4-13), Emerson tries to indicate the signs of the Soul's operation—how it feels, some of the ways we can identify it, and so forth. The orientation here is mainly empirical ("If we consider what happens in conversation . . . "; "Of this pure nature every man is at some time sensible," etc.) At first the discussion is carried on in very general terms: the Soul animates all the faculties (par. 4); it is ineffable but everyone has felt it (5). Then Emerson attempts to particularize: its onset is marked by a suspension of the sense of limitations of time, space, and nature (6-7); it comes not by gradation but in a sudden access of power (8), both in virtue (9) and in intellect (10); it reveals itself through other people, humble as well as lofty (11-12), young as well as old (13).

Though Emerson's handling of continuity is not unexceptionable, altogether he manages successfully to coordinate the large blocs from three different lectures which furnished him with most of his text for this section. For instance, the paragraph sequences 4-5 and 12-13, each of which involves a juxtaposition of passages from different lectures, sustain the motif of affirmation followed by pietistic diffidence.

After the second of these semi-withdrawls Emerson strikes out in a different direction: "The soul is the perceiver and revealer of truth." Here is another case of the buried outline (even more elusive than in **"History,"** since it is defective as well as soft-pedaled—more of which in a moment). The statement announces a shift of emphasis in the next section (14-24) from the experience of the holy to analysis of the Soul's powers. The shift is by no means total, for at one point Emerson gives a glowing account of the emotion of the sublime (16) and later he describes how to identify the tone of an inspired person (22-23); still, the basic framework of discussion is an anatomy of the Soul's attributes. Emerson distinguishes four. The Soul enables us to perceive truth beneath appearance (14); it reveals Absolute Truth (15-19); it reveals our character to others and vice-versa (20-23); it inspires the acts of genius and, potentially, those of all other men as well (24).

Only the first two of these points, we note, are prefigured in the outline. It is hard to know whether to ascribe this to subtlety or incompetence. That Emerson held them distinctly in his own mind is suggested by the fact that points corresponding to one, three, and four are explicitly distinguished and spelled out in his lecture, **"The Doctrine of the Soul"** (1838), which is the chief source for this section, while the bulk of point two comes from one short sequence in **"Religion"** (1840). On the other hand, some of the material from the former work appears in support of a different point in the essay, and the last category in the lecture version, "action," bears but a partial resemblance to "genius." Other features of this section of the essay also suggest a loss of direction: the paragraphs are longer than before, the transitions are weaker (cf. 17-18, 21-22, 23-24), the lecture passages are less spliced. And yet a distinguishable framework *is* still maintained, as is the former tactic of qualifying the grand claims for the Soul with the enjoinment of personal humility (19, 23).

Until the section's end, that is. At this point, in conclusion to his discussion on genius, Emerson rises to an unexpectedly insistent note: "Why then should I make account of Hamlet and Lear, as if we had not the soul from which they fell as syllables from the tongue?" As usual, pride goes before a fall, for at this point the essay definitely does fall apart, at least temporarily (25-28), under the rising tide of feeling. Beginning with the passage on enthusiasm (16), Emerson's prose has taken on an intoxication which now seems to carry it away. Perhaps this is inevitable, since the subject is now precisely the imperativeness of abandonment: "This energy does not descend into individual life on any other condition than entire possession." The soul must cast off all pretense and open itself humbly and totally to God. For several pages Emerson celebrates this point, reaching a crescendo in paragraph 28:

Ineffable is the union of man and God in every act of the soul. The simplest person who in his integrity worships God, becomes God; yet for ever and ever the influx of this better and universal self is new and unsearchable. It inspires awe and astonishment. How dear, how soothing to man, arises the idea of God, peopling the lonely place, effacing the scars of our mistakes and disappointments! When we have broken our god of tradition and ceased from our god of rhetoric, then may God fire the heart with his presence. It is the doubling of the heart itself, nay, the infinite enlargement of the heart. . . .

And so on, for another page and a half. Much of the writing here is very fine, notably the next-to-last sentence, but the effect of the whole is chaotic: hyperbolic affirmation ("The simplest person . . . becomes God"), heightened by the sense of awe and ineffableness, but shot through also with a sense of longing ("How dear, how soothing . . . "; "may God fire the heart with his presence"), so that finally one is conscious both of an exuberance and a desperation in the passage. It is a doxology, but also a *de profundis,* a passionate prayer for the fulfillment of the soul's need. In suggesting, then, that pride led the speaker to a lapse of coherence, I was not being entirely facetious. Once he has swelled to the thought "Why shouldn't *I* come into my own?", "In what way am *I* inferior to Shakespeare?" it is quite understandable that he should fall victim to the dualism which he has been holding in check by the affirmation-resignation device previously described. To put the matter in the language of New England theology, Emerson wants to assert, in the Arminian tradition, that preparation (in this case, simplicity and sincerity) will ensure grace; but secretly he senses as well as Jonathan Edwards did that grace is of God and man has no control over its workings. And so the rhetoric of Emerson's hymn to the "entire possession" of the soul by the soul becomes turbid with undercurrents of frustration.

In the conclusion, however, and the peroration which follows, the essay regains its composure (29-30). "Let man then learn the revelation of all nature and all thought to his heart; this, namely; that the Highest dwells with him"—the tone here is calm, and the problem of dualism is resolved by two sorts of backings-off. First, primary emphasis is placed on an uncontroversial (for Emerson) point: faith is to be determined by experience and not by authority. And second, the very real problem of how inspiration is to come to the soul is circumvented by resorting to generalizations about the process of spiritual growth. "I, the imperfect, adore my own Perfect. . . . More and more the surges of everlasting nature enter into me. . . . So come I to live in thoughts and act with energies which are immortal," etc. Logically this is inconsistent with what was said about the soul's onsets being sudden and unpredictable, but emotionally and structurally it provides a graceful conclusion to the essay, which in retrospect is seen to flow like this: exordium; statement of subject; signs of the Soul; attributes of the Soul; preparation for grace; prospects.

We have seen that Emerson's prose preserves at least the semblance of order even in many places where it seems aimless. But how much importance should we attach to this fact? After all, it is no compliment to regard the two essays just discussed as attempts at systematic thought, inasmuch as Emerson obscures the central issues of the relation of self to history and soul to Soul. Emerson's vitality, especially for the modern reader, lies in the provocativeness of his *obiter dicta,* not in his powers of reasoning. Yet the impact of his orphic sayings, as I have already suggested, depends partly upon the structure which loosely sustains them. For one thing, the sense of totality enhances one's pleasure in the individual detail, as Emerson himself well knew. "Nothing is quite beautiful alone; nothing but is beautiful in the whole." Furthermore, the way in which structure appears in Emerson—faintly adumbrated, often concealed, rarely very explicit—happens to be an excellent representation of the peculiar sort of ambivalence Emerson maintained, all his life, toward the idea of totality. Mainly he held to the simple principle of the microcosm, which underlies his theory of symbolism and which is often blamed for aggravating his tendency toward formlessness. But he also entertained at least three other models of universal order, all of which are more specific than the microcosmic principle: 1) nature as operating on a principle of polarity (**"Compensation"**); 2) nature as an upward flowing through "spires of form" (**"Woodnotes," "Nature"**); and 3) nature as a book of meanings ("Language"). In short, Emerson's thought ran the whole gamut from complete open-endedness ("In the transmission of the heavenly waters, every hose fits every hydrant") to complete schematicism ("Natural objects . . . are really parts of a symmetrical universe, like words of a sentence; and if their true order is found, the poet can read their divine significance orderly as in a Bible"). He desires to claim the utmost liberty for the imagination, on the one hand, and to preserve the prospect of a coherent worldorder on the other. Against this background, his use of structure is most significant and appropriate. It furnishes the essays with the same combination of abandonment and unity that he observed in nature.

Indeed many of the essays derive their structures from one or another of Emerson's models of universal order, such as the principle of polarity or the principle of upward flowing, as those who have defended his coherence have pointed out. The two propositions in **"History,"** for instance, are in a sense polar, being opposite ways of viewing the same thing. But I would not want to claim that this pale abstraction is the "subject" of **"History,"** nor, again, that the subject of *Nature* is the six-fold hierarchy of nature from commodity to spirit. Rather I take it that the subject is the process of discovering the method of history or nature as Emerson sees it. In reading him, one seems meant to feel as he himself felt in reading nature, that

> every one of those remarkable effects in landscape which occasionally catch & delight the eye, as, for example, a long vista in woods, trees on the shore of a lake coming quite down to the water, a long reach in a river, a double or triple row of uplands or mountains seen one over the other . . . must be the rhetoric of some thought not yet detached for the conscious intellect.

Emerson's rhetoric gives off intimations of order, which

the reader seeks to follow up without withering them into formulae.

Though it may be praising Emerson overmuch to compare his structures to those of nature, it remains that his achievement in the area of form has been underrated. In particular, more attention needs to be paid to his habits of composition. Thoreau scholarship is ahead in this respect, doubtless because of the currency of the half-truth that he was the more dedicated artist. As the volumes of Emerson's journals, miscellaneous notebooks, and lectures continue to appear, making the record of his revisions more available than it has been, we may expect a general reappraisal of Emerson as an artist of wholes as well as parts.

Such a reappraisal, however, should not be apologetic, should not make the mistake of seizing upon the ordering elements in Emerson's prose as if they were the sole thing which saves his essays from disaster. We must also accept the validity, at least for him, of the openended kind of discourse Emerson was attempting. It was his temperamental preference to be suggestive, rather than definitive; this was also what was expected in the lyceum; and the empirical fact is that his mode of communication succeeded. In retrospect it may seem a bit amazing that a man of such intellectual sophistication, speaking in such an elusive style, with virtually no attempt at crowdplay, should have been regularly received with "something close to veneration" [in the words of Carl Bode in his *American Lyceum,* 1956] in a forum where popular entertainment was the norm. The paradox largely resolves itself when one realizes that Emerson's admirers were looking for stimulation and elevation rather than rigorous thought or hard data. The same spiritual malaise which led Emerson into skepticism and out of the church, in search of alternative ways to express religious sentiment, was widely shared by his audiences; indeed it was one of the main reasons for the rise of the whole lyceum movement. In such a spiritual climate, vague moral uplift seemed much more appropriate than rational precision, which was fast becoming discredited in matters of belief.

No man is totally a product of his times, least of all a genius. The prevailing reverence for Emerson did not mean universal understanding or approval, as this record of an 1857 lecture in Emerson's home town suggest: "Friday Eve Jany 2, 1857 R. W. Emerson lectured. Subject, *The Times: politics, preaching, bad boys, clean shirts &c &c.*" But the important point is that after some initial hesitation over Emerson's heresies, most of New England did accept him on his own terms, as a poet, whose proper role was not to explain but to inspire. Had Emerson descended more often to the former, much of the sense of the poetic and the mysterious which was responsible for his charisma would have been lost. (pp. 58-69)

Lawrence I. Buell, "Reading Emerson for the Structures: The Coherence of the Essays," in The Quarterly Journal of Speech, *Vol. LVIII, No. 1, February, 1972, pp. 58-69.*

Second Church of Boston, where Emerson served as pastor from 1829-1832.

Albert Gelpi (essay date 1975)

[*Gelpi is an American educator and critic. In the following essay, he examines Emerson's theory of poetics, focusing particularly on the relationship between inspiration and poetic form.*]

Although Emerson published only two volumes of verse, he insisted that in all his thinking and writing he was a poet; such was his encompassing activity and purpose in prose and verse. But while Emerson's prose has received extended critical attention, his verse needs and deserves more study than it has received so far, and needs more perceptive study than the assumptions of the New Criticism and other schools of normative and formalist criticism have allowed in the academy until quite recently. The reason is simple: formalist criticism makes assumptions—about the sources of poetry, the relation of the poem to experience, the function of language and form, in short about the entire activity of the poet—which run counter to all of Emerson's assumptions. By formalist norms Emerson's poems seem flawed by loose ends, careless structure and slack diction, but those norms are largely irrelevant to what Emerson is doing, or at any rate attempting. We now see more clearly that we must develop a criticism whose axioms and procedures are consonant with Emerson's poetry (and that of the American poets who follow in his wake); in fact, we need a criticism which springs from those poems and so can open them up for us and allow us to enter them and participate in them on their own terms.

This essay, therefore, is not about Emerson's poems but about the underlying principles of his poetics, so that we can begin to attune ourselves more acutely to the poems than the training of most of us would permit. It is important to understand Emerson's poetics, with all its ambivalences and paradoxes, not just for what it accomplished in Emerson's work but also for what it engendered in the dynamics of language and form in the American tradition thereafter. Emerson's theory itself is part of the Romantic rejection of neoclassical formalism, but its radical and revolutionary character stems from the fact that Emerson brought to certain Romantic notions a Yankee earnestness and literalness that carried them much further in theory and practice than English and continental Romantics had dared. His notion of the aim and activity of the poet so splendidly epitomized the idealistic strain in the New England (and American) character that his words blazed a path for others to explore, extend, and depart from on their own excursions, and that path is the main line of the American tradition.

At the beginning of *Nature* a simple statement carries momentous psychological, moral, and aesthetic implications: the poet is "he whose eye can integrate all the parts." The poet as "eye" is far more than a naturalist observing phenomena in minute detail like Frederick Goddard Tuckerman out in Greenfield or even Emerson's friend Thoreau camping out on Emerson's ground at Walden Pond. For all of Emerson's love of the woods and lakes around Concord, Emerson would write an essay on the **"Natural History of Intellect"** while Thoreau was to write the "Natural History of Massachusetts." Emerson would continue to complain that naturalists, with their labels and discriminations, were always pointing to the particular instead of the universal: "Our botany is all names, not powers. . . . " In old age Emerson cited Blake's goal of seeing through the eye, not with it, but already in *Nature* in 1836 he had recognized that "the eye is the best of artists" because it reveals to the imagination—not just to the intellective understanding—"the integrity of impression made by manifold natural objects." There are two kinds of seeing: with the eye and through the eye, sensory and spiritual; the second proceeds from the first but cannot be accounted for or bound by mere visual impressions:

> To speak truly, few adult persons can see nature. Most persons do not see the sun. At least they have a very superficial seeing. The sun illuminates only the eye of the man, but shines into the eye and heart of the child. The lover of nature is he whose inward and outward senses are still truly adjusted to each other. . . .

The eye is not just the ocular sense; the "eye" orders all the senses and faculties in a single experiential perception of the interpenetration of all things. Again and again the essays specify the eye as the poetic organ: the "cultivated eye"; "the wise eye"; "the world's eye"; "the comprehensive eye"; "the plastic power of the human eye"; "the supernatural eye."

The miracle of incarnation transpires not just in church sacraments but in all life, which is sacramental; Emerson used a theological term to make his point: "this contemporary insight is transubstantiation, the conversion of daily bread into the holiest symbols. . . . " In *Nature* Emerson tried to describe this conversion. It is a famous and familiar passage, but it deserves quotation here because, like the fifth section of Whitman's "Song of Myself," it presents the generative experience from which the whole work and the whole vision proceed. The statements are at once declarative and open-ended; they set down an experience of vision beyond analysis.

> In the woods, too, a man casts off his years, as the snake his slough, and at what period soever of life, is always a child. . . . There I feel that nothing can befall me in life,—no disgrace, no calamity (leaving me my eyes), which nature cannot repair. Standing on the bare ground,— my head bathed by the blithe air, and uplifted into infinite space,—all mean egotism vanishes. I become a transparent eye-ball; I am nothing; I see all; the currents of the Universal Being circulate through me; I am part or parcel of God.

The punning identity of the pronoun "I" and the "eye" as its central and coordinating organ punctuates the stages of the process: I expand into the cosmos until my immensity coincides with cosmic Unity. The imaginative process, then, is a penetration into the divine mystery of life and living, an inseeing and not just a seeing; and this insight operates simultaneously as expansion and integration.

In *Representative Men* Emerson said: "Two cardinal facts lie forever at the base; the one and the two.—1. Unity, or Identity; and 2. Variety . . . Oneness and Otherness. It is impossible to speak or think without embracing both." The perception of Variety and Unity is the function respectively of the different cognitive faculties of Understanding and Reason. Understanding is the logical-rational faculty which operates deductively and inductively on the data supplied by the senses; Reason is the transcendental faculty which sees intuitively universal truths in Nature. This distinction became standard as the German transcendentalist philosophers came into England and America through people like Coleridge and Carlyle. In the "Discipline" chapter of *Nature* Emerson stated it in these words: "The understanding adds, divides, combines, measures, and finds nutriment and room for its activity in this worthy scene. Meantime, Reason transfers all these lessons into its own world of thought, by perceiving the analogy that marries Matter and Mind." Experience, therefore, brings the mind to unriddle itself and embrace the two in the one; the data which the Understanding gathers concerning natural and psychological phenomena constellate in the Unity which Transcendental Reason intuits. For Emerson, Understanding and Reason are only the philosophical terms for the poet's seeing with the eye and seeing through the eye. The very recognition that "the world I converse with in the city and in the farms, is not the world I *think*," begins the process of reintegration, and further acts of perception begin to bind the perceiver to the perceived both naturally and transcendentally, concentric with "the eye of Reason." The Imagination is a function of Reason.

Thus in the essay on **"The Poet,"** Emerson summed up the power of insight and extended it into the more problematical area of articulation and expression:

> The poet is the person in whom those powers are

in balance, the man without impediment, who sees and handles that which others dream of, traverses the whole scale of experience, and is representative of man, in virtue of being the largest power to receive and to impart.

The poet's "power to receive and to impart"—a double power; vision alone is insufficient, even for the seer. "Always the seer is a sayer" as well; his secondary but essential role is "the Namer or Language-maker." The poet must write poems, for "the man is only half himself, the other half is his expression." Even with the insight of Imagination only the poet's doubling back on himself to formulate and issue his own statement can bring experience to fuller consciousness; the wordless Reason incarnates itself in natural forms, in human experience, and so in human speech.

The three axioms posited at the beginning of the "Language" chapter of **Nature** make the same point by moving in the other direction, from words to things to spirit, in a chain of correspondences. Again these familiar sentences are crucial to Emerson's poetic theory:

1. Words are signs of natural facts.

2. Particular natural facts are symbols of particular spiritual facts.

3. Nature is the symbol of spirit.

The tongue moves with the eye and with "the eye of Reason." Emerson's theory of language assumes that words are at root so connected with objects that the primitive meaning of all words, even abstractions, designates an object. He gave examples in the "Language" chapter and returned to the subject often, as here in **"The Poet"**:

> For though the origin of most of our words is forgotten, each word was at first a stroke of genius, and obtained currency because for the moment it symbolized the world to the first speaker and to the hearer. . . . Language is fossil poetry.

The poet's task is to save language from dead forms—fossilization and abstraction—by constantly making it new (as Pound's phrase goes): "Every word was once a poem. Every new relation is a new word." Or should ideally be. Emerson's linguistic assumptions may be scientifically questionable, but they link his metaphysics and his aesthetics. The "natural sayer" will in theory make language correspond immediately to experience by attaching words as much as possible to the objects they signify. From the same premises Thoreau says in "Walking": "he would be a poet . . . who nailed words to their primitive senses, as farmers drive down stakes in the spring, which the frost has heaved; who derived his words as often as he used them,—transplanted them to the page with earth adhering to their roots. . . . "

So organic is the finding of words that the "natural sayer" cannot rely primarily on training and discipline and practice to perfect his technique and sharpen his tools. In fact, he must be wary of the danger inherent in a mistaken trust in external arrangements. No craftsman applying his developed skills to inchoate materials, Emerson's

"Language-maker" would, to the contrary, be the "receiver," the "instrument," the "bard of the Holy Ghost" "passive to the superincumbent spirit." In the open moments between the "incoming" and "receding of God," he is "nothing else than a good, free, vascular organization, whereinto the universal spirit freely flows." The poet is not the cool catalyst, as T. S. Eliot came to claim in his argument for impersonality, but the vascular tissue and living membrane; Emerson's analogy is not chemistry but biology. After the inspiration the bard's words imitate the workings of Spirit in Nature, or such is that aim:

> For poetry was all written before time was, and whenever we are so finely organized that we can penetrate into that region where the air is music, we hear those primal warblings and attempt to write them down, but we lose ever and anon a word or a verse and substitute something of our own, and thus miswrite the poem. The men of more delicate ear write down these cadences more faithfully, and these transcripts, though imperfect, become the songs of the nations.

On the highest level the poet's ingenuity and technical skill can even be an inhibitive intrusion on the creative process; to the extent that he concentrates on making language he may be interfering with the flow of inspiration to and through the medium. Paradise, Pound would repeat in *The Pisan Cantos* against Baudelaire's aestheticism, is not artificial but is the *tao,* or the divine process of nature.

Consequently Emerson's theory had to be of two minds about the efficacy of language. All words must be nailed to things, and yet "all the facts in Nature are nouns of the intellect, and make the grammar of the eternal language." The poet must speak, but as the essential poetry moves into language, it will be at once exalted as the "word" of God and halting as human speech. To the extent that the poet is the instrument through which Reason expresses itself, language is invaluable; to the extent to which the poet speaks his own associations, language is a noisy distraction. On the one side lies Silence, on the other gibberish; and in the middle the situation is complicated by the fact that Silence can only express itself on the poet's tongue and by the fact that as the poet's tongue strives to express Silence it concentrates its many, noisy words towards a single, indiscriminate, primitive syllable, like the Hindu mystic repeating "Om" till he returns to unconsciousness or pure consciousness. Is that "Om" wisdom or gibberish? The mystic says that it conveys All *and* Nothing, a false distinction which exists only in human speech.

But by its very nature language must negotiate that middle ground without lapsing into All or Nothing, into Silence or gibberish. For, to someone like Emerson, words are (or can be) the irreplaceable translations from the wordless sublime moving through time and space: the oracle "has only to open his mouth, and it [universal nature] speaks." Yet even the oracle's words, not to mention those of less inspired mortals, will necessarily convey only a "corrupt version" of his unspeakable meaning. Lao Tsu begins *Tao Te Ching* with: "The Tao that can be told is not the eternal Tao. The name that can be named is not the eternal name." Emerson said that words "cannot cover the dimensions of what is in truth. They break, chop, and impoverish it." Even words rooted in things are only a gesture toward the meaning of things. Since the paradox of language is that "words are finite organs of the infinite mind," even the successful poem will be an incomplete articulation. Language has form, and so limits, but meaning does not; or, in the words of a couplet whose halting inadequacy is most imitative, "The great Idea baffles wit, / Language falters under it." At best, effort and subtle discriminations and the filing of lines and cadences can clarify a poem up to a certain point, and at worst they can break the circuit of inspiration. The "true poet" learns to acknowledge humbly that "there is a higher work for Art than the arts."

Emerson's ambivalence about language seemed to lead him into contradiction. If words are literally the organs of the infinite mind, the poet can do no better than merely submit, but if they are his words, the poet is to some extent and at some level responsible for what he says. At times Emerson spoke as though inspiration were a matter of unconscious receptivity, almost of automatic writing. Yeats claimed that *A Vision* derived from his wife's automatic writing and generated images and metaphors for his poems, but he made no claim of automatic writing for himself as composer either of *A Vision* or of his poems. There have been Romantic claims of more or less spontaneous creation—most notably perhaps Coleridge's account of the writing of "Kubla Khan." Even more extremely, closer to home and farther down the line, Jack Kerouac said that he tried to open his mouth and let the Holy Ghost speak, as Jesus had urged His disciples; Ginsberg usually prepares an audience for his incantatory poems by long repetitions of "Om" and other chanted prayers. Can Emerson really believe that a poet is a simple medium? For that matter is it simple to be a medium? Consciousness cannot be excluded by fiat, especially not in the act of writing. The inspiration may be spontaneous and unconscious, but the composition cannot be. As a practicing poet, Emerson knew this. Ginsberg submits to revision the poems which he later reads after those incantations. Even something as close to automatic writing as Kerouac's "spontaneous prose" and verse appears to be is not always unrevised; *On the Road,* his most widely admired book, went through several versions.

Emerson's ambivalence is part of the larger Romantic dilemma. For all his vaunting claims, Shelley too acknowledged, in his *Defence of Poetry,* that the inspired poet comes to words only as the wordless inspiration is fading; the challenge to the Romantic poet is somehow to validate his inspiration. Emerson's essays and poems took a deliberately extreme position in enunciating the notion of a poetry whose source lies outside the poet but whose realization in language and form is through the agency of the poet. Coleridge had also distinguished between poetry and the made poem. The activity begins in the encounter of the poet and nature through an impulse, presumed to come from above, which emerges from the poet's psychic unconscious. He must submit to these energies breaking into consciousness as words and attend that their expression corresponds to the experience. The poem is made from the poetry as nonverbal or preverbal instinctual impulses find

articulation, take direction and cohere. "Hence," declared Emerson, "the necessity of speech and song; hence these throbs and heart-beatings in the orator, at the door of the assembly, to the end namely that thought may be ejaculated as Logos, or Word." The paradox for the prophet, whether poet or orator (and the prophetic call links the two) is that, unlike the talkers who speak *"from without,* as spectators merely," he must "speak *from within,* or from experience," making sure that the utterance published under his name coheres to tally the ejaculative, eruptive experience inside.

Finally, therefore, Emerson's contradictory statements can be seen as related in the attempt to describe the gestation and birth of the poem: a process so subtle that the poet cannot sort out, in the matrix of his psyche where it all grows, unconscious intuition from deliberated choice. Ex post facto theory dissects what is fused in the act. The seeming contradictions are two ways of accounting for organic poetry: the paradox of its inspiration and execution. We think of the poet's Muse: a transpersonal inspiration. But since he encounters the Muse and expresses the Muse only in the forms of Nature and since the poem gestates in his mind, not hers, the process is mutually procreative. Does she shape the poem out of him, or does he shape her in the poem? Both; the father and the mother of the poem are one, the poet is Eros and Psyche.

Emerson felt impelled to take an extreme position in arguing for the mysterious sources and resources of poetry in part because of the literary situation in mid-nineteenth-century America. There were many—and Emerson probably had Edgar Allan Poe and Alfred Tennyson in mind—who called themselves poets but who, he believed, had only technical virtuosity:

> For we do not speak now of men of poetical talents, or of industry and skill in metre, but of the true poet. I took part in a conversation the other day concerning a recent writer of lyrics, a man of subtle mind, whose head appeared to be a music-box of delicate tunes and rhythms, and whose skill and command of language we could not sufficiently praise. But when the question arose whether he was not only a lyrist but a poet, we were obliged to confess that he is plainly a contemporary, not an eternal man.

"The finish of the verses" is a consequence of poetry rather than an originating constituent. Poetry does not arise from or reside in the poem, but vice versa; the experience is not verbal, and language is no substitute for vision. In Emerson's mind Poe's fatal mistake lay in not understanding that "it is not metres but a metre-making argument that makes a poem." The intricacy of Poe's forms and the musicality of his language only confirmed him a victim of his "poetical talents." By contrast Emerson said of Thoreau that "his genius was better than his talent." He lacked "lyric facility and technical skill" and his verses were often unfinished. But even when he wrote inferior poems, "he had the source of poetry" so surely that "he held all actual written poems in very light esteem." The difference, Emerson says elsewhere, is the difference between the poet who speaks from character and the poet who speaks from language. So basic is the distinction between poetry and the poem that for Emerson Poe is a bad poet who often wrote good poems while Thoreau is a good poet who often wrote clumsy poems.

All of this is not to say that Emerson had no regard for poetic form, but rather that he regarded poetic form with the same ambivalence that he felt toward language, and for the same reasons; form, like the words which comprise it, is both the received and the achieved. The poet cannot dictate the form arbitrarily but he has to help it define itself from within. For all his inveighing against artifice, Emerson was by no means oblivious to craft and structure; he was challenging Poe's notion of form with his own. If the poem was to incarnate the experience, then the whole poem would have to imitate the dimensions and shape of reality. Emerson said, after all, that a metre-*making* argument *makes* the poem. If a rigid and preconceived form— *forma ab extra,* Coleridge had called it—distorts words to its own shape, then organic form, at least ideally, grows out of the unique experience: "a thought so passionate and alive that like the spirit of a plant or an animal it has an architecture of its own, and adorns nature with a new thing."

The idea of form as internal exfoliation parallels Blake's maxim in *The Marriage of Heaven and Hell:* "Reason is the bound or outward circumference of Energy," the bounded limits being merely the demarcation which measures for consciousness the particular moment's explosive dimensions. Like each symbolic word, the "new thing" which evolves as the poet "resigns himself to his mood . . . is organic, or the new type which things themselves take when liberated." Thus while in the achieved poem "the thought and form are equal in the order of time," "in the order of genesis the thought is prior to the form." Translating a sonnet of Michelangelo's, Emerson saw the artist's hand instinctively drawing out the form hidden but inherent in the material:

> Never did sculptor's dream unfold
> A form which marble doth not hold
> In its white block; yet it therein shall find
> Only the hand secure and bold
> Which still obeys the mind.

To the end of his life Emerson argued that "rightly, poetry is organic. We cannot know things by words and writing, but only by taking a central position in the universe and living in its forms." Words are not *about* things; they are directly related to things and so become things in their own right. But like other things words contain and do not contain, express and do not express their meaning. If language incarnates spirit, as the axiom in the "Language" chapter of **Nature** says, it does so only pursuant to the Spirit. Words and the form that words assume are consequent upon the seeing:

> This insight, which expresses itself by what is called Imagination, is a very high sort of seeing, which does not come by study, but by the intellect being where and what it sees; by sharing the path or circuit of things through forms, and so making them translucid to others. . . . The condition of true naming, on the poet's part, is his resigning himself to the divine *aura* which

breathes through forms, and accompanying that.

The present participles which stitch together all of Emerson's discussions of the poetic process indicate that it is and must be an ongoing process. Achieved forms and stated meanings become fossilized forms and dead meanings. Organic form leads to what has been called more recently "open form" or "composition by field"; and even more specifically it leads to the notion of a poet writing not just long poems or a long poem but a life-poem, its shape acknowledging shapelessness, its lines opening gaps, its meaning sounding the inexhaustibility and indeterminacy of meaning. Emerson's assumptions not only generated Thoreau's journals as well as his own but prefigured Whitman's *Leaves of Grass,* Pound's *Cantos,* Charles Olson's *Maximus Poems,* Robert Duncan's *Passages* and Ginsberg's notebooks in verse and prose.

Emerson could speak in strikingly modern psychological terms of "the projection of God in the unconscious" mind of man, so that the world shows "unconscious truth . . . defined in an object" and thereby brought to expression. In **"Bacchus"** the poet drinks a "remembering wine" which revives "a dazzling memory" of mythic archetypes. The poetic power is linked repeatedly with instinct, spontaneous intuition, dreams, and *"dream*-power"; and "dream delivers us to dream. . . ." Images and ideas well up from and lead back to a shared source very much like the Jungian Collective Unconscious:

> What is the aboriginal Self, on which a universal reliance may be grounded? . . . The inquiry leads us to that source, at once the essence of genius, of virtue, and of life, which we call Spontaneity or Instinct. We denote this primary wisdom as Intuition, whilst all later teachings are tuitions. In that deep force, the last fact behind which analysis cannot go, all things find their common origin. . . . We lie in the lap of immense intelligence, which makes us receivers of its truth and organs of its activity.

The conception of the poet as seer has, of course, a long history in western thought from Plato and the Greeks down to the Romantics of the nineteenth century and on into the twentieth. But the poet as prophet-seer has adapted himself in particularly vigorous and bold terms to the New World, in part because Americans saw themselves as living in more personal and intimate contact with Nature, the primitive source of inspiration, and in part because the Puritans brought to Nature a strong sense of its symbolism. Emerson came to his statement of the idea through his New England heritage—not Puritan theology but Puritan temperament; and he gave it so American a statement against American acquisitiveness that the reaction down the decades is still humming today. In fact, the Emersonian tradition is so strong and deep that Henry Miller, a writer who one might think is as far removed from Emerson as possible, speaks of the artistic process in terms which constitute a resumé of Emerson's principal contentions:

> Someone takes over and you just copy out what is being said. . . . A writer shouldn't think much. . . . I'm not very good at thinking. I

work from some deep down place; and when I write, well, I don't know just exactly what's going to happen. . . . Who writes the great books? It isn't we who sign our names. What is an artist? He's a man who has antennae, who knows how to hook up to the currents which are in the atmosphere, in the cosmos. . . . Who is original? Everything that we are doing, everything that we think, exists already, and we are intermediaries. . . . [A writer should] recognize himself as a man who was possessed of a certain faculty which he was destined to use for the service of others. He has nothing to be proud of, his name means nothing, his ego is nil, he's only an instrument in a long procession.

In fact, Emerson's sense of the primacy of inspiration and scorn for "rules and particulars" ushered the Dionysian ideal into American literature. The essay on **"The Poet"** describes him in Dionysian terms—powerful, original, unchained, filled with the god:

> there is a great public power on which he can draw, by unlocking, at all risks, his human doors, and suffering the ethereal tides to roll and circulate through him; . . . his speech is thunder, his thought is law. . . . The poet knows that he speaks adequately then only when he speaks somewhat wildly, . . . not with the intellect used as an organ, but with the intellect released from all service and suffered to take its direction from its celestial life; or as the ancients were wont to express themselves, not with intellect alone but with the intellect inebriated by nectar.

Emerson's poems are actually not nearly so wild, so drunken, so untrammelled emotionally or metrically as his theory said that poems ideally should be. He was not Whitman, much less Hart Crane, still less Charles Olson or Henry Miller or Ginsberg. He was too gentle and genteel, too fastidious and remote to be a full-blooded and abandoned Dionysian. Even the poem **"Bacchus"** allows for no misunderstanding from the very first verses: "Bring me wine, but wine which never grew / In the belly of the grape. . . ." And throughout the poem Emerson acceleratingly transcendentalizes the belly-tendencies of his Bacchus. Though sprung "from a nocturnal root," the "leaves and tendrils" of the "true" wine are "curled / Among the silver hills of heaven" and "draw everlasting dew." Through such distillation it becomes the "Wine of Wine" and the "Form of forms" and is finally so rarefied as to become one with the pure Platonic Music of the Spheres: "Wine which Music is,— / Music and Wine are one. . . . "

As Whitman would find out, Emerson was fastidious as well about dwelling on the recognition that the Spirit of Nature moves in sexual rhythms, yet, in this as in so many ways, the way for Whitman was prepared by Emerson. In however modest and unostentatious a manner, the poems move to that rhythm: "The lover watched his graceful maid" (**"Each and All"**); "And soft perfection of its plan— / Willow and violet, maiden and man" (**"May-Day"**); "She (Nature) spawneth men as mallows fresh, / Hero and maiden, flesh of her flesh" (**"Nature II"**); "Primal

chimes of sun and shade, / Of sound and echo, man and maid" (**"Woodnotes II"**); "Sex to sex, and even to odd" (**"Ode Inscribed to W. H. Channing"**). The following remarkable passage, which opens the second part of **"Merlin,"** is Emerson's most extended and explicit celebration of the sexual lifeforce to which "Song of Myself" and many subsequent poems would give loud voice:

> The rhyme of the poet
> Modulates the king's affairs;
> Balance-loving Nature
> Made all things in pairs.
> To every foot its antipode;
> Each color with its counter glowed;
> To every tone beat answering tones,
> Higher or graver;
> Flavor gladly blends with flavor;
> Leaf answers leaf upon the bough;
> And match the paired cotyledons.
> Hands to hands, and feet to feet,
> In one body grooms and brides;
> Eldest rite, two married sides
> In every mortal meet.
> Light's far furnace shines,
> Smelting balls and bars,
> Forging double stars,
> Glittering twins and trines.
> The animals are sick with love,
> Lovesick with rhyme;
> Each with all propitious Time
> Into chorus wove.

The anatomical references ("Hands to hands, and feet to feet") identify the body not just as the ground for the individual's union with his sexual complement but also as the vessel for an androgynous consciousness within the individual, which further deepens his capacity for union: "In one body grooms and brides; / Eldest rite, two married sides / In every mortal meet."

It is true that this is an uncharacteristically full-bodied moment in Emerson. He could at times see in himself the disembodied remoteness that even his friends complained of; he regretted to his journal that "the chief defect of my nature" was "the want of animal spirits" and admitted in other journal entries: "I was born cold. My bodily habit is cold. I shiver in and out . . . "; and again, "Even for those whom I really love I have not animal spirits." It is not difficult to see why he shrunk from what seemed to him the vulgarity and coarseness that Whitman came to display in some poems, and why he had only harsh reproof for those would-be Dionysians who tried to induce vision with drugs, drink, and other sensual stimulants. Since "wine, mead, narcotics, coffee, tea, opium, the fumes of sandalwood and tobacco" are "*quasi*-mechanical substitutes for the true nectar," such "counterfeit excitement and fury" can end only in "dissipation and deterioration."

Nonetheless, Emerson's advocacy of the Dionysian ideal could not have been more crucial for the course of American poetry. Emerson's informing presence made him, in fact, a chief target for twentieth-century poet-critics—Eliot, Allen Tate, Yvor Winters—who wanted to exorcise the deep, abiding influence of Romanticism. They disapproved of and dismissed Romanticism on moral and psychological as well as artistic grounds; they feared, in themselves as well as in others, that its individualism, its openness to the impuulses of experience, its sourcing of inspiration in the emotions and the unconscious led to solipsism, madness, suicide. For a critic like Winters, Emerson was particularly insidious because he made Romanticism seem sane and wholesome, and it was not enough for Winters to note that he did not "practice what he preaches." He could say "Of Poe and Whitman, the less said the better" and take that assertion as fairly self-evident; Tate agreed that the disastrous influence of both sealed Hart Crane's doom. But Winter's inverted acknowledgment of Emerson is expressed in his inveighing against Emerson "in defense of reason" with an urgent conviction that Emerson was his most dangerous adversary in America.

Emerson may not have fully practiced what he preached, but his importance lies in the fact that he did state the principles and begin the experiments. He stands, nervous and self-conscious in the role, as our teetotalling Bacchus, our New England and ministerial Pan. Now we can see that his experiments were only a point of departure for later poets, heralding Whitman's free verse, Pound's and Williams' innovations with speech rhythms and breath units and open forms, E. E. Cummings' refashioning of syntax and punctuation and typography, Charles Olson's "projective verse," Denise Levertov's organic form, the long lines and cumulative periods of Robinson Jeffers, William Everson, and Allen Ginsberg. Most of these poets, after Whitman, would not have shared with Emerson the metaphysics which was the basis for his poetics. But the metaphysical, even transcendental, impulse has remained active, even though more cautiously and circumspectly in many cases—in Pound's Platonism and his indebtedness, especially in the theory of form and language, to Ernest Fenollosa, who was himself teaching in Japan the Transcendentalist philosophy he had imbibed at Harvard; in Cummings' devotion to his father, a Unitarian minister with a strong Emersonian spirit; in Jeffers' Calvinist pantheism; in Olson's response to Carl Jung's archetypal psychology and A. N. Whitehead's process philosophy; in Duncan's fascination with myth and mysticism; in Levertov, through her father, a Jew steeped in Hasidic thought who became a Christian and an Anglican priest; in Ginsberg's Judaic, Oriental, and Blakean spirit; in Everson's fusion of Christian theology and Jungian psychology. As a result, most of these poets have viewed the poet as a special seer, and all of them, as at least a special perceiver. Their various explorations of ongoing form and emergent structure have been grounded, for all of them, in the organic yet transcendent process of nature. Along with other poets akin in spirit they comprise the distinctive strain of the American poetic tradition, and Emerson is their source, more than some of them have wished to acknowledge and more than Emerson himself could have foreseen. (pp. 149-70)

> *Albert Gelpi, "Emerson: The Paradox of Organic Form," in* Emerson: Prophecy, Metamorphosis, and Influence, *edited by David Levin, Columbia University Press, 1975, pp. 149-70.*

David Porter (essay date 1978)

[*Porter is an American educator and critic. In the following excerpt, he characterizes Emerson's poetry as defective, citing its formulaic structure and ineffective reliance on the passive voice.*]

Emerson's poetry was an art *in extremis.* Matthew Arnold announced on his American tour in 1883, the year after Emerson's death, that it was "touched with caducity." Though he praised Emerson extravagantly to the Americans for a clear and pure voice that brought a strain as new and moving and unforgettable as the strain of Newman or Carlyle or Goethe, Arnold came to a strict estimate: "in truth, one of the legitimate poets, Emerson, in my opinion, is not. His poetry is interesting, it makes one think; but it is not the poetry of one of the born poets."

The contradiction reflects a long tradition of divided judgments about Emerson. Yet his small success as a poet, by a stunning paradox, is inseparable from the brilliant invention of form that simultaneously came into being in his work. (p. 7)

Locating infelicities in specific poems constitutes the leaden chore of a century of Emerson criticism. Finding the cause of those defects, however, remains to be accomplished; it requires seeing beneath the surface awkwardnesses of individual poems to the deeper faultlines within the body of verse. From there we can establish a new perspective by which to understand how Emerson liberated his art. To know finally why his poetry has the character it has, we must see its main structural parts. The first result of this inward reading will be to see how the poetry is impoverished of life, abstracted from the reality by which its own life must finally be measured.

The hazard of abstracting, as Emerson himself recognized in the fullness of his career, is a kind of poetic forgetting: "Poppy leaves are strewn when a generalization is made . . . I can never remember the circumstances to which I owe it, so as to repeat the experiment or put myself in the conditions." Kenneth Burke [in *Transcendentalism and Its Legacy,* 1966] called it "beyonding." This is not to say the poems are without virtue. If they are passionless and abstract, they are also spare and not dismally sentimental. If generally they have a peculiar indeterminate quality, they are surprisingly interesting for their interior drama. But the majority critical opinion over the years has not been kind to Emerson's poetry. It has been judged cold and bloodless, excessively philosophical, mystical and nonsensical, egotistical, an icy fish. Early reviews called attention to the dismaying qualities. Ralph Rusk [in his *Life of Ralph Waldo Emerson,* 1949] described Emerson's contemporary reader as "a traveler suddenly set down in an arctic landscape, immensely impressed if he could properly adjust his vision, but perhaps chilled." He continued: "intellectual pallor and the brevity and irregularity of lines and meter were the faults that impressed one most in this book [*Poems,* 1847]." Caroline Sturgis, a contemporary, warned Emerson against abstractions, advising him to make sawdust pies with his daughter and hunt rattlesnakes so as to be schooled in concrete realities. Matthew Arnold, whose criticism is still among the best we have, said the poems had "no evolution" but rather tended to be series of observations. Concluding a discussion of **"The Titmouse,"** he says of Emerson: "He is not plain and concrete enough,—in other words, not poet enough,—to be able to tell us [what the titmouse actually did for him]. And a failure of this kind goes through almost all his verse, keeps him amid symbolism and allusion and the fringes of things, and, in spite of his spiritual power, deeply impairs his poetic value." More generally, Arnold said of the poetry, using Milton's terms but sounding modern and "new critical," it "is seldom either simple, or sensuous, or impassioned. In general it lacks directness; it lacks concreteness; it lacks energy. His grammar is often embarrassed; in particular, the want of clearly-marked distinction between the subject and the object of his sentence is a frequent cause of obscurity in him. A poem which shall be a plain, forcible, inevitable whole he hardly ever produces. Santayana [in his *Winds of Doctrine,* 1926] said Emerson shared with Poe and Hawthorne "a certain starved and abstract quality."

The abstract moral aim of the poetry was a matter of deliberate Platonist emphasis which Emerson declared early in an 1831 journal:

> I write the things that are
>   Not what appears;
> Of things as they are in the eye of God
>   Not in the eye of Man.

Retreating from the complicated and apparent to the abstract was the inevitable result of Emerson's enormous impatience for the clarity of large truths: "Our little circles absorb and occupy us as fully as the heavens," he said, "the only way out of it is . . . to kick the pail over, and accept the horizon instead of the pail."

Under the tyranny of such an abstracting design, lively particulars must lie stunned. In a kind of selective destruction, life-producing profusion is pressed by constant mental compaction into hard little aphorisms. One result is that Emerson's poetry creates no engaging dialect, holds few sounds of a private experience, and a reader finds it unnecessary, as it is with Whitman and Dickinson, to learn a special Emersonian poetry language. This is not to overlook how Emerson creates patches of rich detail, of contrast, of voices clearly heard, of modest liberties in prosody, and in his "runic" lines refreshing abruptnesses. But one finds no sustained inventive activity. As readers have noted, stock images dog the poetry: rubies, drops of wine, Alpine heights, stars to deck a woman's hair, and pebbles thrown in ponds. We do not trust them because they are distant from precise reality.

But there are constitutional qualities of the sort Arnold suggested that more deeply tyrannize the poems. Not simply stylistic clumsinesses, they are part of the inescapable character of Emerson's poetry. The most prominent of these properties, beginning with the general tendencies and proceeding to the specific, are linked: the presiding voice, the controlling structures, and the habits of language.

An elevated reserve in the character of Emerson's speaker and a monotonously solemn tone pervade the poetic utterances. The voice troubles us, as it did some of Emerson's

contemporaries, because it fails to alter our sense of reality, to remove barriers of reticence, to establish what seems to us important awareness, to make us strange by brute energy.

The Emersonian inertia derives in part from the passive character of the watcher-meditator who speaks in the poems. With important exceptions, it is the habitual stance of Emerson's poetic personae, appearing as early as the poem **"Good-bye,"** written when Emerson was nineteen or twenty. The poem seems to refer to his pleasurable daily return to the Roxbury countryside from his brother's school in Boston where he was teaching. It begins without originality—"Good-bye, proud world! I'm going home":

> I am going to my own hearth-stone,
> Bosomed in yon green hills alone . . .
> [Where] vulgar feet have never trod
> A spot that is sacred to thought and God.

Assertions of a like sort repeatedly convey the static condition of Emerson's observing consciousness. In *Nature,* Emerson's first major work and the program of his thoughts, he wrote that the soul "is a watcher more than a doer, and it is a doer only that it may the better watch." Elsewhere he admonished the poet to stand apart to wait:

> Sit still and Truth is near . . .
> Wait a little, you shall see
> The portraiture of things to be.

That ideal passivity never disappeared from the poetry. In his intellectual development up to the *American Scholar Address* in 1837, there is projected for *Man Thinking,* the hero of Emerson's talk, a more active role as both influential writer and teacher that he identified with Luther and Milton and that he felt himself becoming. But, for all Emerson's regard for man acting, the persistent identity of his persona is the single consciousness meditating rather than acting. Emerson admired a consciousness, as he said in the poem **"Woodnotes II,"** "Grave, chaste, contented, though retired . . . of all other men desired." In the poetry, although there are fine exceptions, little comes across of a living intensely in public view.

Part of the reason for this reclusiveness was a habit Coleridge called the "despotism of the eye." Wordsworth similarly asserted it in *The Prelude:*

> the eye was master of the heart,
> . . . in every stage of life
> The most despotic of our senses.

The visualist notion of reality, brilliantly remarked by D. H. Lawrence, produced in Emerson a highly selective subject-object distinction that abstracted experience, made the observer content with a few preferred signs of infinity, and remained insensitive to the lines of reverberation and distortion between mind and object.

This confined field of vision in the poems is crucial. The perceiving imagination, because of the eye's mediation and the mind's abstract ends, took account in reality only of those experiences that were convertible into mental and moral equations. The Platonist view was limited in Emerson's poems to things seen as part of a moral system about which it could be said they are *not this but that.* In that deliberate movement toward the moral ideal, contrary compulsions had to be annihilated. These included the concreteness of things and the coarse realities of nature, the "swinish indulgences" as Emerson called them. The correlation between vision and the narrow moralizing consciousness grows quite literal in Emerson's essay **"The Poet"**: "The sublime vision comes to the pure and simple soul in a clean and chaste body." This formula set severe limitations on the kinds of experience Emerson's imagination could perceive, and the narrow range of experience that could find its way into the poetry was a primary factor in its deprivation.

Still, Emerson's aim in the poems was not to particularize but rather to propel away from the particular to the essence. A reader of the poetry feels suspended, like Hawthorne's Coverdale: "I had never before experienced a mood that so robbed the actual world of its solidity." Where Hawthorne engaged the passionate and conflicting realities of the moral consciousness, Emerson "etherialized," as his contemporaries termed it. There was then little possibility that his poetry would take account of what Lawrence was later to call the "gruesome sort of fantasy" of nationalistic America or the "unravished local America," despite Emerson's call for such a downward vision. Lawrence's terms included, but outside of his journals Emerson's did not, "the great continent, its bitterness, its brackish quality, its vast glamour, its strange cruelty."

Rarely on the face of this withdrawn poetry of Emerson's is there apparent the theoretic activity that would anticipate the descendant poetics of twentieth-century realism. Wallace Stevens defined the ground:

> From this the poem springs: that we live in a
>   place
> That is not our own and, much more, not our-
>   selves
> And hard it is in spite of blazoned days.

Nor did there seem to be a real anticipation, as there was in 1860 by Emily Dickinson, of the bleak modern view characterized by Norman Mailer in the pathological terms the late twentieth century finds so congenial: "the modern condition may be psychically so bleak . . . so plastic . . . that studies of loneliness, silence, corruption, scatology, abortion, monstrosity, decadence, orgy, and death can give life, can give a sentiment of beauty."

From his programmatic moral vision as acted out by his persona came another constitutional depletion of the poetry: the assured declamatory voice of a man measuring his being in a world not of dense implacabilities but of pristine moral lines, a man not in a physical world of contingencies but of immanent moral possibilities. The tone inevitably drives the reader away from the experience of the actual, which is sacrificed to the need of the poetry to make stronger sense. Emerson was being faithful, of course, to a preacherly concept: "the higher use of the material world is to furnish us types or pictures to express the thoughts of the mind." The assertive voice that oppresses the verse is directly linked to the moral purpose. In **"The Problem,"** for example, another poem of curious indetermination, for all its felicities of decisive language one recoils from the weight of the rhetorical questions and lecturing tone which seem excessive for a confessional poem.

> Know'st thou what wove you woodbird's nest
> Of leaves, and feathers from her breast?
> Or how the fish outbuilt her shell,
> Painting with morn each annual cell?
> Or how the sacred pine-tree adds
> To her old leaves new myriads?
> Such and so grew these holy piles,
> Whilst love and terror laid the tiles.

This sternness, reminiscent as elsewhere of the crushing whirlwind's voice in *The Book of Job,* is relieved momentarily by a personal intrusion near the end of the poem ("I know what say the fathers wise,— / The Book itself before me lies"), but the possessing tone is public and homiletic, reflecting the frequent merging in Emerson's lines of sermon, creed, and poem.

The declamatory tone entails a structural device that may be unique to Emerson and certainly contributes to the characteristic enervation of the poetry. He said in **"Poetry and Imagination"** that poetry "must be affirmative [meaning not blindly optimistic but true to nature's harmony]. It is the piety of the intellect. 'Thus saith the Lord,' should begin the song." This moral aim induced Emerson to enlist a disembodied voice or consciousness. We encounter this curious separation of the poetic speaker almost everywhere in the poetry. Further on in **"Poetry and Imagination,"** Emerson touches on allegory: "The poet must let Humanity sit with the Muse in his head, as the charioteer sits with the hero in the Iliad." The dissociated voice is doubly drained of its power because in the customary structure of Emerson's poems even *it* is *reported* by the speaking person. In **"The Sphinx,"** it is "a poet" overheard; in **"Woodnotes II,"** a pine tree. Such a companion voice, set apart always by quotation marks, effectively distances the reader one more stage from an immediate experience within the poem. This filtering effect, curiously Emersonian, will command our attention in the discussion to come. There are notable exceptions to the ministerial cast. A reader finds that the declaiming second persona succeeds powerfully in **"Hamatreya."** "Hear what the Earth says" introduces the "Earth-Song," a bold-voiced incantation in runic lines unfettered by obtrusive meter requirements, unabashedly prosaic, intense:

> 'Mine and yours;
> Mine, not yours.
> Earth endures;
> Stars abide—
> Shine down in the old sea;
> Old are the shores;
> But where are old men?
> I who have seen much,
> Such have I never seen.'

In **"Bacchus,"** the primary voice is self-consciously learned and verges on the tendentious and decisive, a first-person imperative with its force not distorted by awkward slopes to its line-end rhymes: "Bring me wine, but wine which never grew / In the belly of the grape."

"All writings," Emerson said, "must be in a degree exoteric, written to a human *should* or *would*, instead of to the fatal *is*." That moral duty, so exclusionary for the artist, was laid early upon American poetry. Jones Very, in his 1838 essay "Epic Poetry," assumed that obligation to be the artist's as he marked, in a prescient way, the literary attention turning from outward experience to the moral battles in the interior mind. Sampson Reed formulated the coda of an age which linked poetry's moral purpose, its preoccupation with nature imagery, and its assumption of a divine ontology. "By poetry is meant," he said, "all those illustrations of truth by natural imagery, which spring from the fact that this world is the mirror of Him who made it." Emerson's version was a Platonist's equivalent: "A symbol always stimulates the intellect . . . therefore is poetry ever the best reading. The very design of imagination is to domesticate us in another, in a celestial nature." And he added this: the poet "is very well convinced that the great moments of life are those in which his own house, his own body, the tritest and nearest ways and words and things have been illuminated into prophets and teachers."

In willing bondage to these principles, but without the incisiveness of Milton's lines, Emerson's poetry was attenuated. It was art based not on aesthetic needs but on doctrine. It was art processed for ready consumption whose aim Bertolt Brecht was to call, a century later, the "fodder principle." Gertrude Stein was being Miltonic when she called art that sacrificed the reality of particular objects to a principle "pornographic." The hurtful irony as Emerson came to maturity is that, while this moralizing purpose was proudly American in character, celebrated as such, at the same time it was the generic element in the enfeeblement of American verse. American poets, Roy Harvey Pearce has said, "have defended man by showing that he at his best can make sense out of his world, no matter what its inherent confusions." The paradox in Emerson was that the price of those noble clarifications was the vitality of the art itself.

This moral commitment necessarily deflected criticism away from aesthetic concerns, and in the process some of the strengths available to the artistic imagination were neglected. Moral insight brought on aesthetic blindness. In his study of Ruskin, Roger Stein sees the closed conceptual circuit of Emerson's contemporaries with marvelous clarity: "By identifying the forms of art with the forms of nature and nature itself with Deity, the transcendentalists made the criticism of art essentially a moral venture." The impoverishment of poetry which approached sermonizing was in most hands a self-generating process. One way out was the radical innovation toward which Emerson moved. After 1836, key passages show him entertaining the redeeming view of art as intrinsically self-regarding. Here is a significant passage in **"Poetry and Imagination"**: "Poetry will never be a simple means, as when history or philosophy is rhymed, or laureate odes on state occasions are written. Itself must be its own end, or it is nothing." The division in the mind of Emerson the artist is coming into view.

Moral engagement was not confined to Emerson's age. Yeats wrote that he could see that the literary element in painting and the moral element in poetry were "the means whereby the two arts are accepted into the social order and become a part of life, and not things of the study and the exhibition." To Emerson's Platonist mind, moral concern also meant a kind of objectivity, an avoidance of the inwardness of what he regarded as the worst kind of romantic poetry. It remained to Lawrence, characteristically, to reveal the scandalous nature of this obsession with moral clarity: mentalizing everything "makes a vicious living and a spurious art . . . Everything becomes self-conscious and spurious, to the pitch of madness." Part of the counterfeit derives from the inherent solemnity of moral art. Poetry of principled order and meditation lacks saving self-deprecation and a release from gravity; it necessarily avoids the random ironies that digressive fullness and a reaching for actual experiences threaten.

The audience implied by Emerson's poetry is equally significant. To the extent that the poetry delivered sermons, it presumed an audience joined in a common moral enterprise. The audience existed not as a congregation of individuals capable of winning through to difficult judgments but rather as a homogeneous group to be reached by simple designs and admonitions. Whitman, on the contrary, was to regard his audience as individuals who could be approached one by one—"Crossing Brooklyn Ferry" is a model of the kind—and he fashioned an intimacy of expression layered with subtle activity. He invited private gestures rather than the passivity of a decorous audience. The designs of poets on their audience reveal in part their primary intentions. If Whitman prepares his audience by a kind of linguistic foreplay to receive the infusion of soul he proposes in "Crossing Brooklyn Ferry," Emerson's design is rather to persuade his audience to a collective intellectual discovery. Poe, more conspicuously musical than either, conceived his audience as mesmerizable, seeking sonorous disembodiment and flight from rational meaning.

Unlike Whitman and Dickinson, who were ahead of their audiences, laying verbal traps, contriving snares of candor outside the conventions, Emerson joined other American poets in reinforcing the audience's ideas and playing to their expectations. The construction of a moral ideal was incompatible with unprecedented experience of the noise of complexity. Poe had distinguished between *richness* in a poem—meaning suggestiveness, unexhaustible implications—and the *ideal*. They are incompatible qualities and are not to be confounded. In Emerson's poems, meaning displaced particularity, morality displaced reality, and clarity displaced body. The world was glass.

The tonal qualities Emerson addressed to this undifferentiated audience which, unlike his Lyceum audiences, he could not see, thus add their own weightiness to the poetry. The imperative mood intrudes, regularizes, limits the audience's responses. To the extent he avoided an effective particularity, he created distance, then blockage and the strict reserve of the poet as public figure. Stiffness is even notable in the Ellen poems, depending as they do on phrases drained of emotion and made sterile by the habit of a public pose. Yet Emerson's craving to make a personal cry is felt close at hand by a reader even so. It was achieved only under the terrible pressure of grief at his young wife's death in 1831. With the aid of Carl Strauch's edition of the unpublished poems, along with his invaluable discussion of them, we can see this astonishing breakout. Lines from the poem **"To Ellen,"** first printed in the Centenary Edition, evince the public role:

> If I read the page aright
> Where Hope, the soothsayer, reads our lot,
> Thyself shalt own the page was bright.
> Well that we loved, woe had we not.

The journal poem beginning "Dost thou not hear me, Ellen," written within days of Ellen's death, still moves with a public decorum:

> Dost thou not hear me, Ellen,
> Is thy ear deaf to me,
> Is thy radiant eye
> Dark that it cannot see?

Later in the same journal, a second Ellen poem holds Emerson's desolation directly to the light. Here we have "the fatal *is*"; the transforming power of natural symbol has collapsed and the attention turned inward, the language moving in blank verse so loosely in the middle lines that it is close to prose.

> Teach me I am forgotten by the dead
> And that the dead is by herself forgot,
> And I no longer would keep terms with me.
> I would not murder, steal, or fornicate,
> Nor with ambition break the peace of towns,
> But I would bury my ambition,
> The hope and action of my sovereign soul,
> In miserable ruin. Not a hope
> Should ever make a holiday for me.
> I would not be the fool of accident,
> I would not have a project seek an end
> That needed aught
> Beyond the handful of my present means.
> The sun of Duty drop from his firmament
> To be a rushlight for each petty end.
> I would not harm my fellow men
> On this low argument, *'twould harm myself.*

Emerson relies in his finished poems on syntax, aiming at the mind more than the ear. One can say of his verse what Donald Davie said of *The Prelude,* that the syntax "presents what is really going on, meditation, not argument." Syntax, especially when concentrated into epigrammatic form, gives prominence not to sensation but to logical relationship. Straightforward, inaccessible to deviation however psychologically valid, Emerson's poems are designed for the understanding rather than for the more ambiguous currents of feelings. Poetry of clarification is dutifully defined by Emerson in the essay **"The Poet."** Deliberately ascending above the teeming and distracting world, the poet insists upon an *understanding* of life and consequently upon a view from a distance. The Platonist removal plays a part in the narrow conception of the audience as well as the audience's expectations from the poetry. Emerson rhapsodizes at some length on the reader's liberation, beginning: "With what joy I begin to read a poem which I confide in as an inspiration! And now my chains are to be broken; I shall mount above these clouds and opaque airs in which I live,—opaque, though they seem transpar-

ent,—and from the heaven of truth I shall see and comprehend my relations."

Emerson reinforces the intellectual isolation in several ways: by the imperative form, by the epigrammatic reduction of experience to a strict syntactical construct, and by the habit of aphorism, incising single moral lines through complex existence. Emerson's insistence on touchstone phrases is consistent with the moral aim of his aesthetics; they are grammatically the translation of life into ideas. Even as the grammar holds technically, awkward inversions and all, the life has leaked out.

> The fiend that man harries
> Is love of the Best.
>   **("The Sphinx")**

> Who bides at home, nor looks abroad,
> Carries the eagles, and masters the sword.
>   **("Destiny")**

> For He that worketh high and wise,
>   Nor pauses in his plan,
> Will take the sun out of the skies
>   Ere freedom out of man.
>   **("Ode")**

The poetry-vision caricatures reality by reducing life to laws, language to propositions, and aesthetic development to the single trajectory of clarification. The pulpit tone, the dissociated voices, the lack of physical gesture, and the absence of a distinct dialect in the poems add up to a poetic practice that sacrifices art to meaning and experiential fullness to the goal of converting the world into idea. The full world itself is finally sacrificed to a language narrowed to the logic of propositions. Emerson's world, like his abstract audience, was inevitably the projection of the language that sought it.

Deeper than the language, restraining it, is Emerson's distinctive linear schema. Its origin and effect seem clear enough. As the poems record a rationalized, most often symbolic, experience, the activity necessarily unfolds in sequence. The encounters and thoughts of the speaker-meditator proceed to a conclusion, almost without exception to a revelation. Where Whitman muses, retraces, digresses, gathers up, echoes, kneads experience, often with a fine illusion of randomness, the poems of Emerson proceed deliberately, excluding experience and particularity all along the line. They are devices of separation in the service of a vision that imposes denouements. The syntax mirrors this, as does the prosodic awkwardness of means. Perhaps Fenollosa was right, we do not always sufficiently consider that thought is successive—but there is no escaping the successive arrangement of Emerson's poetry.

In lining up the mind to seek revelatory significance, Emerson necessarily slighted what poetry has known since Homer, what Lionel Trilling called the "exquisite particulars." The returning in poetry after Emerson to the concrete, as we see it initiated by Whitman and Dickinson, evidences the collapse of faith, however unconsciously, in those universalizing processes of mind that Emerson celebrated in his poems. His occasional excursions into particularity tend to be innocuous, rarely touching human mystery with details of the psyche or body. Catalogues sometimes constitute his specifics, as does the long one in a fragment on nature that begins

> Come search the wood for flowers,—
> Wild tea and wild pea,
> Grapevine and succory,
> Coreopsis
> And liatris,
> Flaunting in their bowers.

The flowers have no visual existence, only names, and the names are there because they rhyme or almost rhyme. We pause at the line "Nerv'd leaf of hellebore" because it stands out as a visual mark. The great peculiarity of poetic language, Winifred Nowottny has said, is its power to bridge or seem to bridge the gap between what has meaning but no particularity and what has particularity but no meaning. Emerson's structures led to meaning, with the particulars exploited for the purpose of reaching a philosophical revelation. An example in a familiar early poem is the closing passage of **"Each and All."** Despite the catalogue of forest items, their palpable being is sacrificed to the immanent revelation solemnly waiting at the end of the list. The poem marches undistractedly toward the revelation, a version of Emerson's famous eyeball experience in the final lines. Until we know more of Emerson's habitual concerns, we see only names.

> The ground-pine curled its pretty wreath,
> Running over the club-moss burrs;
> I inhaled the violet's breath;
> Around me stood the oaks and firs;
> Pine-cones and acorns lay on the ground;
> Over me soared the eternal sky,
> Full of light and of deity;
> Again I saw, again I heard,
> The rolling river, the morning bird;—
> Beauty through my senses stole;
> I yielded myself to the perfect whole.

There is no accumulated conviction, but rather only an authoritative declaration. The poem is embarrassed by its spurious revelation, a moral coin not earned but simply declared like a dividend.

Henry Adams spoke in the *Education* of wanderers who have perhaps alone "felt the world exactly as it is." The abandonment of this sort of exactitude, the relishing of irrelevance and what Ezra Pound was to call local taste, created Emerson's impoverishing abstracts. His predisposition was clear and concise in a fragment collected under the title **"The Poet":** "What parts, what gems, what colors shine,— / Ah, but I miss the grand design." Though Emerson would admonish the poet to "Hunt knowledge as the lover wooes a maid" (**"Written at Rome, 1833"**), the fleshed reality is not finally the poet's proper focus:

> [The muses] turn his heart from lovely maids,
> And make the darlings of the earth
> Swainish, coarse and nothing worth.

The paradox at the center of Emerson's poetics has been conspicuous to his readers. We hear the man of poetic imagination saying of the poet, "as everything streams and advances, as every faculty and every desire is procreant, and every perception is a destiny, there is no limit to his hope." Whitman gave verbal body to a comparable vision,

but for Emerson it remained mostly a vision haunting his own poetry, stunted as the verse was by its linear structure, impoverished by its epigrammatic language, only rarely able to grasp the possibilities of streaming life, the procreant processes and the "everyness," all that he felt swarming outside the argument of the poems. Possessing this plentitude by language, feeling man's being in it, was to be the astonishing theoretical breakthrough finally forced by his aesthetic needs as an artist.

Whereas Whitman's poems enact a coming into being, adopting their identity as they proceed, Emerson's poems stand as a remembrance, fixed in progression, insisting on significance by the finality of the argument, mechanical in their march toward a preconceived end, non-heuristic in their careful avoidance of the sudden fascinations of random attention, and unreceptive to the pressure of the language as it breeds its own meaning. We are reminded periodically that modern poetry has to do with a person *having* thoughts, not with the thoughts a person *had*. The formulation enables us to identify another characteristic of Emerson's poetry, its reportorial quality. Emerson's poems are *about* life, testimonials to an experience elsewhere than in the poem and prior to it. They are transitive poems, concerned with the revelation they record more than with the cumulative experience along the way. Wallace Stevens makes the distinction in "An Ordinary Evening in New Haven": he can conceive of monuments as littered newspapers, that is, palpable things not about events or people—a statue about George Washington, say—but objects in themselves, as newspapers, blown by the wind, are not *about* fires, theft, rape, and war, but rather pulpy flowers tumbling at the curbs. We can notice the recurrence of the figure of the poet-as-builder in Emerson's poetry. He conceived of poems as constructed after a master plan, the final shape already in the mind of the maker before he begins. "Great design belongs to a poem," he declared, "and is better than any skill of execution,—but how rare! I find it in the poems of Wordsworth,—Laodamia, and the Ode to Dion, and the plan of The Recluse. We want design, and do not forgive the bards if they have only the art of enamelling. We want an architect, and they bring us an upholsterer." He calls for substance, not surfaces, but it is clear his formulation has no place for improvisation or for finding in irrelevant particulars the vitality of the unforeseen. It was thought's tyranny.

The fact-to-truth design of Emerson's poems constitutes their characteristic structural set. It is a grammar of monumentality, of prior thought and anticipated outcome. We recognize sharp differences between poems that transfer attention from experience to concept, and poetry that is intransitive and concerned with relationships, their permutations, the discoveries available in the contemplation of balances, the irony, and finally with the possibilities of language itself as it becomes dramatically self-regarding. Emerson's poems center on images of ideas rather than bodies. In the fragment **"Transition,"** in the image of trees the movement characteristically disperses matter into concept. It is a summarizing image for Emerson, the leafless trees diffusing themselves into the air

> ever subdividing, separate
> Limbs into branches, branches into twigs,

As if they loved the element, and hasted
To dissipate their being into it.

Tension on the line that leads from fact to idea in Emerson's poems rarely develops because the success of the process rarely fails. Frost's poems, Emersonian in origin, are saved from a similar innocuousness precisely because Frost explores all the the anxieties that Emerson left out. Revelation is engagingly immanent in Frost (in "The Most of It," "Two Look at Two," "The Woodpile," even "Mending Wall"), but it is habitually denied. The man in "The Most of It" cries out for the world to signal its counter-love for him. The living creature that seems about to respond to this cry,

> Instead of proving human when it neared
> And someone else additional to him,
> As a great buck it powerfully appeared,
> Pushing the crumpled water up ahead,
> And landed pouring like a waterfall,
> And stumbled through the rocks with horny
>   tread,
> And forced the underbrush—and that was all.

The situation trembles with possibility, but the tension is never relieved. When it is, for example in "A Tuft of Flowers," the poem's strength diminishes in ratio to the cosiness of the revelation: "men work together . . . whether they work together or apart." Emerson's poems go on without interruption and the language looks ahead, excluding the hazards of the experience and dissipating vitality as the tree in its upward divisions dissolves in the airy elements.

Emerson constructed his poems according to his training under Edward T. Channing in rhetoric and oratory wherein language was conceived as the clothing of thought. "I had rather have a good symbol of my thought, or a good analogy, than the suffrage of Kant or Plato," he wrote later. His notion of thought as prior to poetry, of poetry as a "metre-making argument," flows directly from his controlling metaphor of the cosmic soul, which was the origin as well of so many of the dissociated voices that enter his poetry. The poet is "an exact reporter of the essential law. He knows that he did not make his thought,— no, his thought made him, and made the sun and the stars." Emerson's poetry is the language of that reporting. His syntactical organization of the essential law involved equations and propositions. It was an arrangement of conviction, exclusion, clarification, and of a steady reluctance to indulge in the irrelevant. It involved mental closure rather than elaboration. To be strong, Donald Davie says, poetic syntax "must bind as well as join, not only gather together but fetter too. The actual function of meaning, 'which calls for permanent contents," *must* be fulfilled. Verse may be 'strong' or it may 'aspire to the condition of music': it cannot do both." Emerson yearned for music in his verse, but he insisted on meaning. He was therefore never fully to achieve a flowing form for his own poems so that they could sweep outward to monitor an unfinished reality. Instead, Emerson's poems swallowed the world. They are converting systems, trimming the cumbersome world and shaping it to fit an idea already formed.

Thus not only was the poetry famished, to use Emerson's term, but so was the correlative world that the poetry saw. His assertive and rigidly closing poems perceived a purposeful world whose significance was the object of the poetic undertaking. The world was *exemplum* rather than reality in a state of becoming.

Reflections of this mentalizing system show in the imperatives of Emerson's poetry, early and late. In **"To Rhea,"** to which we shall return later, the rudimentary pattern of conversion stands revealed by the preferences in syntax. The not-this-but-that construction projects an obsessive sense of the two-termed mental strategy of the paradox. Illustrative lines can be picked almost at random: "Not with flatteries, but truths, / Which tarnish not, but purify"; "Thy softest pleadings seem too bold, / Thy praying lute will seem to scold; / Though thou kept the straightest road, / Yet thou errest far and broad." The poem stands essentially as a proposition that insists on a neat intellectualized displacement of selfish possession by divine generosity, of a small aspiration by a godly one, that is, of the half gods by the gods. A reader will not find a fully experienced dilemma of troublesome love and disappointment. The poem proceeds instead by terms of logical discourse: not-but, if-then, thus, and whereby. To the extent that these connectives hold the diction and direct the progression of the poem, they exclude whatever lies outside the rationalizable. In the end, the impoverishment is linked to the poem's formulaic designs and the distance they place between the reader and contingent reality. What remains is intellect holding a set of equal balances, viewing life as a proposition, not this shadow but that truth.

The doubleness in **"To Rhea"** pervades Emerson's poetry and constitutes one of the characteristic expressions of the conversion system that is their primary structure. Binary patterns appear wherever an interested reader looks. In **"To Rhea,"** phrase after phrase shows how the incessant doubles hammer along: "to the blind and deaf," "of gods or men," "his study and delight," "that creature day and night," "Adorn her as was none adorned," "Statelier forms and fairer faces." The march of equivalences is epitomized in the terminal proposition: "the god, having given all, / Is freed forever from his thrall." Duality is enforced by the regularity with which these phrasal units and line ends coincide. The poem is a toted-up column of double propositions. Moreover, the doubleness and attendant line-end correspondence are compounded by being hammered home, for better or worse, with rhymes.

This doubleness set the equation that resolved the world into clarity. Even Emerson's more supple poems are overtaken by language rigid with ideas of concord. Strong colloquial rhythm begins the **"Ode: Inscribed to W. H. Channing,"** with full-blooded, libertarian passion over Daniel Webster's support of the Fugitive Slave Act apparent in the edgy lines.

> Though loath to grieve
> The evil time's sole patriot,
> I cannot leave
> My honied thought
> For the priest's cant,
> Or statesman's rant.

> If I refuse
> My study for their politique,
> Which at the best is trick,
> The angry Muse
> Puts confusion in my brain.

The poem falls into a drumming march, however, as it looks to its conclusion after reminding the reader that "There are two laws discrete, / Not reconciled,— / Law for man, and law for thing":

> Foolish hands may mix and mar;
> Wise and sure the issues are.
> Round they roll till dark is light,
> Sex to sex, and even to odd.

The language continues on in thrall to the mind's duality and its countervision of the world as a proposition even in the bitterness of its ending:

> The Cossack eats Poland,
> Like stolen fruit;
> Her last noble is ruined,
> Her last poet mute:
> Straight, into double band
> The victors divide;
> Half for freedom strike and stand;—
> The astonished Muse finds thousands at her
> side.

In contrast to the more flexible aspects of form which a reader would expect to flow from Emerson's basic assumption of the organic circularity of the world, his major poems were, with few exceptions, linear in their structural development, logical in moral progression, and supremely intellectual in their closures. There is a strong necessity for ordered thoughts and definable emotions, and consequently a need for formal strategies. With later Emersonian poets—Williams is a good example—we cross to the other side of the divide, where *knowing* is abhorrent, forms are nonclosing, and structure itself is significant according to the shape of its progressions or, as in Pound's cantos, refractions. With the poet's conscious intention, novel forms signify in their own nonverbal way, and the poems are the richer in experience for these formal conveyances. In the strict poetics from which Emerson was to liberate himself, the poem's formal elements were conceived as packaging devices. He said of rhyme, for example, "We do not enclose watches in wooden, but in crystal cases, and rhyme is the transparent frame that allows almost the pure architecture of thought to become visible to the mental eye." The familiar emphases are here: the architectural metaphor and the abstracting consciousness. In Emerson's conception, a poem was a transfer of knowledge, where a reader is not expected to feel his life in manifold new ways but rather to locate himself intellectually.

But in attempting to fashion those ideal transparent prosodic frames. Emerson made them all the more obvious. In the end, they formed such a rigid container that his thought in turn was caricatured. No matter how adventurously he theorized on the way out of this dilemma, he was unable to accomplish the liberation in the poetry. The obtrusiveness of the prosodic maneuvers was hauled directly to his attention by Thoreau in his famous critique:

> I have a good deal of fault to find with your

"Ode to Beauty." The tune is altogether unworthy of the thoughts. You slope too quickly to the rhyme, as if that trick should be performed as soon as possible, or as if you stood over the line with a hatchet and chopped off the verses as they came out, some short and some long . . . It sounds like parody . . . Yet I love your poetry as I do little else that is near and recent, especially when you get fairly round the end of a line, and are not thrown back upon the rocks.

The conventions that constituted the prosodic boulders on which Emerson planted his feet were to his mind the literary signs of his poetry. In the prose, where his radical aesthetics took form, we see a heady repudiation of such literariness. But his evident need for those poetry signals bound Emerson to a cartoon of poetic form: conspicuous rhyme, strained sonorities, balanced ideas, cadence overpowering diction, paradox in the service of conversion, and all of the prosodic regularities that led to those moral, summing-up equations.

His mode of composition started with a prose statement of the idea to be versified. The process is of a piece with the aesthetic supposition in the idea of a meter-making argument. Edward Emerson printed the following lines as one of the "early rhythmic ventures" from which evolved **"Solution,"** a later poem that appeared in Emerson's 1867 volume. As was often true of Emerson's exploratory lines, suspended between prose and verse, they possess stark power:

> I am the Muse,
> Memory's daughter,
> I stood by Jove at the first,—
> Take me out, and no world had been
> Or chaos bare and bleak.
> If life has worth, I give it,
> And if all is taken, and I left,
> I make amends for all.
> Long I wrought
> To ripen and refine
> The stagnant, craggy lump
> To a brain
> And shoot it through
> With electric wit.
> At last the snake and dragon
> Shed their scales,
> And man was born.
> Then was Asia,
> Then was Nile,
> And at last
> On the sea-marge bleak
> Forward stepped the perfect Greek;
> That will, wit, joy might find a tongue,
> And earth grow civil, Homer sung.

The first stanza of the poem appeared refashioned this way in *May-Day and Other Pieces:*

> I am the Muse who sung alway
> By Jove, at dawn of the first day.
> Star-crowned, sole sitting, long I wrought
> To fire the stagnant earth with thought:
> On spawning slime my song prevails,
> Wolves shed their fangs, and dragons scales;
> Flushed in the sky the sweet May-morn,
> Earth smiled with flowers, and man was born.

> Then Asia yeaned her shepherd race,
> And Nile substructs her granite base,—
> Tented Tartary, columned Nile,—
> And, under vines, on rocky isle,
> Or on wind-blown sea-marge bleak,
> Forward stepped the perfect Greek:
> That wit and joy might find a tongue,
> And earth grow civil, HOMER sung.

Several strategies of expansion fill out Emerson's final version to meet the needs of meter and rhyme. Though felicitous emendations appear, much of the direct power of the original disappears in the prolixity. The blunt prosaic temper in the notebook lines holds the page halfway between spontaneous speech and verse, a condition of immense potentiality that Whitman and later artists of the quick, suggestive line were to exploit. But in Emerson's versifying process, the spare, hard words go slack. What seems to have been the original opening, "I am the Muse, / Memory's daughter, / I stood by Jove at the first," puffs out by additional words in the first two lines of the finished poem to make an extended cliché, including the illogic of "sung alway" and the redundancy of "at dawn of the first day." The most successful emendation is "spawning slime," a phrase that lay in prose in another entry in the verse-book. But Asia is expanded artificially to include a shepherd race, as is Nile; the "sea-marge bleak" is then overloaded by Emerson's felt need of cadence to produce the redundant "wind-blown sea-marge bleak." We see the constricting process inherent in Emerson's notion of language as the clothing of ideas. Impulsive thoughts thrown out in simple strong prose are actually devitalized by being enclosed in a self-conscious literary form which, as Thoreau saw, diluted the original strength Emerson intended. Not the least tyranny was his custom of thinking and therefore of composing separate line by separate line.

In the end, this dutiful laboring to display the strenuously wrought signals of "literature" diverted Emerson's poetry into narrow declamation. "Dissonance / (if you are interested) / leads to discovery," Williams was to say in *Paterson*. Emerson achieved a similar insight only when he sought in less formulaic prose a strategem for dramatizing the mind in a state of becoming. His impatience to make poems of revelation drove him to a prosodic regularity that closed off the dynamic verbal plays possible in a more spontaneous and less formal scheme. He was among the last of the old regime even as he contemplated the new consciousness demanded of poetics. The awareness flashes repeatedly in the Divinity School address, as he proclaims how the idioms of language and the figures of rhetoric usurp the place of truth. The change was to involve a liberation from the idea of closure and finish, that is, from language as monument, to the idea of poetic form as a motion of spontaneous disclosure and infinite suggestion.

Emerson's poetry held insufficient space for the lived world, and yet his imagination aspired to a redeeming liberation. The compulsion occupied the imaginative center of his life and became one of the structural necessities of much that he wrote. His libertarian aesthetic vision permeated his theology: "All who hear me," he told the divinity students, "feel that the language that describes Christ to Europe and America is not the style of friendship and enthusiasm to a good and noble heart, but is appropriated and formal." In the historically localized meanings of "friendship and enthusiasm," popular concepts that have yet to be adequately explored as cultural bases of American literature, are bundled the impulses of spontaneity, sincerity, openness, and the escape from the confines of formalism, whether in worship or literature. Emerson's aim was ultimately to escape *generic thinking*. The impediment lay in his conventional belief that truth of such a high order was properly the subject only of poetic poems.

To describe Emerson's poetry as verse in extremity seems in the light of these observations not too harsh. It is representative of poetry in America that had exhausted its initiative and lost its correspondence with reality. But this warping-away quality is the negative side of Emerson the poet and man of imagination. There would be only limited value in analyzing its impoverishment if the poetry did not display at the same time an intermittent but revealing aspect of his theory of mind from which, in a most fortunate paradox, there also arose the liberating thrust.

Though most of the poetry lacked the genuine resonance of a complex body of experience, a portion of it looked to a new authenticity. It is poetry on the border of prose, risking formlessness and chaos, calling up fuller realms of experience than it habitually did. In that poem of near excruciating self-revelation, **"The Discontented Poet,"** a work neither brought to completion nor published in Emerson's lifetime, glimpses open up of the world his poetic imagination consorted with but rarely took into the poetry. Yet Emerson had suggested in the poem **"Music,"** which was not published in his lifetime either, that even the basest of material would release its beauty under the pressure of conversion.

> in the darkest, meanest things
> There alway, alway something sings.

> in the mud and scum of things
> There alway, alway something sings.

Intimations of experience other than mentalized abstractions lurk in **"The Romany Girl"** from the *May-Day* volume:

> Go, keep your cheek's rose from the rain,
> For teeth and hair with shopmen deal;
> My swarthy tint is in the grain,
> The rocks and forest know it real.

> The wild air bloweth in our lungs,
> The keen stars twinkle in our eyes,
> The birds gave us our wily tongues,
> The panther in our dances flies.

In **"The Adirondacs,"** despite Emerson's intention toward the end to extract philosophy from the camping trip ("O world! What pictures and what harmonies are thine!"), and particularly from the news of the Atlantic cable-laying (an event calling for the sort of sustained symbol analysis that has been applied to Brooklyn Bridge), the reality of the excursion ("Hard fare, hard bed and comic misery") endures. The blank verse is firm and natural, and there is an effective deliberateness that reminds a reader of passages in *The Prelude*.

> We crossed Champlain to Keeseville with our
>   friends,
> Thence, in strong country carts, rode up the
>   forks
> Of the Ausable stream, intent to reach
> The Adirondac lakes.

But the passages of apparently artless power are lost in the general impression of strained contrivance. Again we encounter Emerson's speaker as a vaguely concerned watcher-meditator. The consciousness actualized in the poems, subservient to the despotism of the eye, selects the experiences that are convertible into mental matter. The intractable experiences are evaded: nature's mysteries, the unimagined body, whatever resists abstraction or clarification. Emerson's exclusion is deliberate Platonism, as here in a fragment:

> You shall not love me for what daily spends;
> You shall not know me in the noisy street . . .
> Nor when I'm jaded, sick, anxious or mean.
> But love me then and only, when you know
> Me for the channel of the rivers of God
> From deep ideal fontal heavens that flow.

This kind of turning to the ideal realm, at the price of the ambiguous, is sustained by the declamatory tone in the poems and the repeated voice of the moralizing imagination. In its most intellectualized form, that tone is conveyed by Emerson's habitual overheard voices, disembodied minds summoned to testify. They are the ultimate step in the mentalizing of Emerson's poetry. Otherwise to make mortal speakers deliver such thoughts would make them insufferably tendentious or put upon the poems the obligation, which Emerson's revelation-bound forms could not meet, to create adequately dramatic personae. The result is that the speaker is a reporter of spiritual voices, and the poems consequently are doubly removed from the bodied reality from which the ideas sprang. The tone presupposes an audience possessed of communal good sense and motives, willing to be preached to, and demanding little in the way of the idiosyncracies of life as lived. The designs of this epigrammatic poetry, then, are almost exclusively in the realm of meaning rather than particularity.

In structure, the poems are narrow and predictable because they are linear in disposition, projecting a field of consciousness rigorously discriminating in experience. We hear a voice that has organized experience so as to extract from it a revelation, figuratively passing from the cave to the sunlight. The formula is part of Emerson's persistent notion that the poetic idea stands prior to its language. This narrow idea of the craft enervated so much of Emerson's poetry because it took no account of the disorderly processes of the mind in the act of discovery. We find instead the habit of binary patterns—prosodic, syntactic, semantic, phonological—which create an oppressive symmetry. If there is an identifiable sound in Emerson's poetry, it involves this steady repetition of a bipolar pattern. The grammar of meaning comes too readily and is too little varied. It was Emerson arranging language to affirm "the applicability of the ideal law to this moment and the present knot of affairs." The Emersonian poem subsumed life to principle because the vision and the language in which it found its form were corelative and inextricable. One cannot say which came first.

The result is a language that is predominantly addressed to the mind and concerned more with reporting than with creating meaning as it proceeds. It is not gestic; there is a whole realm of verbal possibility outside the habitual range of Emerson's language. We miss there what I have called after Dante the element of digression: a linguistic sweep that incorporates the irrelevant, explores for meaning in new relationships, and arranges the permutations that absorb a particular world.

Wallace Stevens said that the poet lives in the world of Darwin and not in the world of Plato. The dissociation of mind from the language of factual existence was played out in Emerson's poems. It led to Arnold's judgment that the poetry of the American he so much admired for his powerful optimism is seldom sensuous, lacks concreteness and energy, and is thus seriously impaired. (pp. 7-29)

> *David Porter, in his* Emerson and Literary
> Change, *Cambridge, Mass.. Harvard Univer-*
> *sity Press, 1978, 232 p.*

Joel Porte   (essay date 1979)

[*Porte is an American educator and critic whose works include the critically acclaimed biography* Representative Man: Ralph Waldo Emerson in His Time. *In the following excerpt from that work, he discusses biblical allusions and the concept of revelation in Nature.*]

To judge by the dominant tone of his journal entries on the voyage home, Emerson's eastern journey [to Europe in 1832-1833] had brought him to a considerable boil. Like the poet whom he would later celebrate in the second series of *Essays,* Emerson was in a mood to say, "By God it is in me and must go forth of me"; prepared, that is, to see his thought "ejaculated as Logos, or Word." *Nature* was already germinating in some fashion, for as he left the coast of Ireland on the 6th of September, 1833, he wrote: "I like my book about nature & wish I knew where & how I ought to live. God will show me." Does this entry suggest that he was expecting a revelation or meditating one? Perhaps, however, the word to stress here is *like*— hinting at Emerson's nascent sense that a literary project must in some way be connected with a feeling of personal satisfaction, even pleasure. That had not been, one might say, a notable feature of the literary scene which had nurtured Emerson. Writing almost a half-century later of Hawthorne's youth, Henry James would opine that "there was no appreciable group of people in New England at that time proposing to itself to enjoy life; this was not an undertaking for which any provision had been made, or to which any encouragement was offered." The "idea of pleasure," James would insist, is necessarily connected with the life and work of an artist: "He proposes to give pleasure, and to give it he must first get it."

As Emerson's journal entry indicates, he was not at all clear on *how* he "ought" to live. Does the *ought* refer to duty or desire? Those, in fact, seem to be the terms of the debate that was taking shape on this voyage home. On

September 11, Emerson reported that he was "nihilizing as usual," but that gloomy habit appears to have been undermined by the end of the entry, when he says: "I tipple with all my heart here. May I not?" It sounds as if Emerson had picked up some dubious habits in Europe which the long sea journey—that hiatus in ordinary existence—was further encouraging. But why not "tipple," if he felt like it? Was he not free to do exactly what he pleased, even if that included occasionally acting a bit like the devil's child? . . . Wednesday's tippling was followed, perhaps penitentially (and even providentially), by a stormy Sunday which Emerson "kept . . . with Milton & a Presbyterian magazine." On Monday, puzzling, apparently, over the issue of whether it makes any sense to seek rules of conduct, or paradigms of right living, outside of oneself, Emerson hypothesized about a person who "reads in a book the praise of a wise man who could unbend & make merry & so he tosses off his glass," only to find that "round him are malicious eyes watching his guzzling & fat eating." Since he finds both the license to guzzle and criticism of that license in the world outside, clearly little help is to be looked for there. "The truth is," Emerson concludes, "you can't find any example that will suit you, nor could, if the whole family of Adam should pass in procession before you, for you are a new work of God." That lesson, to paraphrase Wallace Stevens, was probably worth crossing seas to find, and would undoubtedly inform the opening of *Nature* with its call for an "original relation to the universe": "There are new lands, new men, new thoughts. Let us demand our own works and laws and worship."

Emerson's richest and most complex journal entry during the voyage was entered on the next day, the 17th, when he was no longer in the mood to feel that malt was more efficacious than Milton in helping him justify his ways to himself:

> Milton describes himself in his letter to Diodati as enamoured of moral perfection. He did not love it more than I. That which I cannot yet declare has been my angel from childhood until now. It has separated me from men. It has watered my pillow; it has driven sleep from my bed. It has tortured me for my guilt. It has inspired me with hope. It cannot be defeated by my defeats. It cannot be questioned though all the martyrs apostatize. It is always the glory that shall be revealed; it is the "open secret" of the universe; & it is only the feebleness & dust of the observer that makes it future, the whole *is* now potentially in the bottom of his heart. It is the soul of religion. Keeping my eye on this I understand all heroism, the history of loyalty & of martyrdom & of bigotry, the heat of the methodist, the non-conformity of the dissenter, the patience of the Quaker. But what shall the hour say for distinctions such as these—this hour of southwest gales & rain dripping cabin? As the law of light is fits of easy transmission & reflection such is also the soul's law. She is only superior at intervals to pain, to fear, to temptation, only in raptures unites herself to God and Wordsworth said[:]
>
> Tis the most difficult of tasks to keep
> Heights which the soul is competent to gain.

Emerson, it seems, already knew *how* to live: namely, with an unflagging love of "moral perfection." That last phrase is difficult, suggesting as it normally does a *moralistic* concern for right conduct. But that surely is not what Emerson intends here, since the sort of passion Emerson commends he finds equally in the martyr *and* the bigot, in loyalty as well as in dissent. Perhaps a fair gloss would be to say that he longs to achieve an integrity of being consonant with the integrity of the universe (God); to live, that is, totally *toward* being in its highest manifestation. The sign that one is approaching such an integrity would be *rapture*—total pleasure in being in the world. Emerson seems to be reaching for a definition of "moral perfection" that unites the notion of one's obligation as an ethical creature with the desire for a total *creaturely* satisfaction. He has always had an inner life, he suggests, which he has never been able to "declare"—perhaps because the yearning for perfection, like the momentary attainment of it, is intrinsically ineffable. Perfection of what, one might ask? One's life? One's work? Or of some *Gestalt* that unites all things? The key term here—as indeed everywhere in Emerson—is *perfection;* and he yearns for an experience of it that will unite ethics, emotion, and expression, somewhat as he describes in this passage from an 1837 lecture, **"The Eye and Ear,"** in the "Human Culture" series:

> The doctrine of Art is that the human soul is perfectly receptive of the external Universe, and every beam of beauty which radiates from nature finds a corresponding inlet into the soul. The soul is like a circle within the circle of the world and for every point of light on the outer sphere is a point of sight on the inner. When this correspondence of the soul to nature, of the Individual to the All is perfect, then the divine loveliness passes into the Mind which way soever it turns and the Artist never rests but toils with enthusiasm to express that which he beholds, to transfer to some visible or audible object the perfection he contemplates.

Since the design of the universe is perfect, the passion for perfection in a human creature is the key to the "glory" of the whole and indeed suggests that "the whole *is* now potentially in the bottom of his heart." Writing a sort of précis of the opening pages of *Nature* in this journal entry of September 17, Emerson calls for "a religion by revelation to us" and counsels himself to "trust the perfection of the creation" despite the blowing and dripping weather. Indeed, his experience of "perfect exhilaration" in *Nature* will occur "in snow puddles . . . under a clouded sky" and will not exclude the pain and fear mentioned in the entry, since he will find himself "glad to the brink of fear." His raptures have always coexisted with tears, sleeplessness, and anguish—"hope," too, is their bed-fellow. He would later articulate the principle by saying that "Paradise is under the shadow of swords." For now, it is probably enough to say that Emerson had learned to take risks, not the least of which was a willingness to open himself to pleasure.

Indeed, though it would never be easy for him totally to abandon his "nihilizing," other lessons in the simple joy of being were multiplying as Emerson worked his way to the ecstatic expressions of *Nature.* On April 11, 1834, he spent the day in Cambridge, mostly at the Mount Auburn Cemetery:

> After much wandering & seeing many things, four snakes gliding up & down a hollow for no purpose that I could see—not to eat, not for love, but only gliding; then a whole bed of Hepatica triloba, cousins of the Anemone all blue & beautiful but constrained by niggard Nature to wear their last year's faded jacket of leaves; then a black capped titmouse who came upon a tree & when I would know his name, sang *chick a dee dee;* then a far off tree full of clamorous birds, I know not what, but you might hear them half a mile. I forsook the tombs & found a sunny hollow where the east wind could not blow & lay down against the side of a tree to most happy beholdings. At least I opened my eyes & let what would pass through them into the soul.

This afternoon odyssey through the Cambridge woods reads like a mini-allegory of Emerson's own life in this part of his career. If he felt obliged to justify his wanderings abroad (which had cost him, as Rusk says [in his *Life of Ralph Waldo Emerson,* 1949], "more than a year's salary at the Second Church at a time when he was no longer drawing a salary"), he had the example of these four sankes, "only gliding." Patience in the face of constraint was counseled by the Hepatica triloba, in "their last year's faded jacket of leaves" (but Emerson would complain angrily in *Nature* about putting "the living generation into masquerade out of [the past's] faded wardrobe.") Invited and invigorated by the noisy birds with their "floods of life," Emerson forsakes the tombs ("the sepulchres of the fathers . . . the dry bones of the past") and opens his eyes and soul to the pleasures of experience, in preview, as it were, of becoming a "transparent eye-ball" in *Nature.* Having done so, as he tells us, he "heeded no more what minute or hour our Massachusetts clocks might indicate—I saw only the noble earth on which I was born, with the great Star which warms & enlightens it." As in the previous April at Rome when he expanded in the universal sun of Pope Gregory's benediction, Emerson is fully alive to all experience. Now, however, he would read from his own Book of Revelation.

The student of Emerson's first book can hardly do better than to begin with Dr. Holmes. "It may be remembered," he writes [in his *Ralph Waldo Emerson,* 1884], "that Calvin, in his Commentary on the New Testament, stopped when he came to the book of the 'Revelation.' He found it full of difficulties which he did not care to encounter. Yet, considered only as a poem, the vision of St. John is full of noble imagery and wonderful beauty. *Nature* is the Book of Revelation of our Saint Radulphus. It has its obscurities, its extravagances, but as a poem it is noble and inspiring." Not many of us are likely to remember much about Calvin's Commentaries, but it is hard to forget Holmes's own description. Apart from the witty latinization and canonization of "Ralph," Holmes's sentence contains a useful hint about a way of approaching Emerson's sometimes difficult little treatise.

A "Revelation" (or "Apocalypse") means literally in Latin (or Greek) an *unveiling,* and this—the clarification

of vision—is Emerson's fundamental desire in *Nature.* Let us recall that in the journal entry describing that Easter service in Rome, Emerson expressed "great joy" when "the curtains [were] withdrawn from the pictures & statues." Such a gesture embodied for Emerson the essential nature, and meaning, of a religious or philosophical revelation—that which was symbolized by the idea of rebirth at Easter. What he is aiming for is stated succinctly in the final two words of his book: "perfect sight."

This notion is a central one in Emerson's writings and naturally has a long history. In his early journals, Emerson's sense of the actual powers of sight was limited ("our eyes are small, and can take in but a little at a glance"—1822), and his idea of "Revelation" was constricted within the doctrinal boundaries of his church, as when he praised William Ellery Channing, in 1823, for an eloquent sermon which "was a full view of the subject of the light of Revelation compared with Nature & to shew the insufficiency of the latter alone." Here *Revelation* carries its traditional meaning of the truth exposed in the Bible and in Christian doctrine. By 1826, Emerson had advanced far enough to write his Aunt Mary in terms that must have brought her to the brink of apoplexy: "it is one of the *feelings* of modern philosophy, that it is wrong to regard ourselves so much in a *historical* light as we do, putting Time between God & us; and that it were fitter to account every moment of the existence of the Universe as a new Creation, and *all* as a revelation proceeding each moment from the Divinity to the mind of the observer." That is fairly close to Emerson's fully unchurched position in *Nature.* "It is the office of the priest," he wrote in 1829, "to see the creation with a new eye." At such a point, the priest and the poet are hardly distinguishable. When Emerson praised Sampson Reed's *Observations on the Growth of the Mind* in 1826 (and regularly thereafter) for having the "aspect of a revelation," he undoubtedly intended the term as he himself would use it in *Nature*—with reference to the actual perfecting of vision—and might have had such a passage from Reed's book as the following in mind:

> The imagination will be refined into a chaste and sober view of unveiled nature. It will be confined within the bounds of reality. It will no longer lead the way to insanity and madness by transcending the works of creation and, as it were, wandering where God has no power to protect it; but finding a resting place in every created object, it will enter into it and explore its hidden treasures. . . . When there shall be a religion which shall see God in everything, and at all times; and the natural sciences not less than nature itself shall be regarded in connection with Him, the fire of poetry will begin to be kindled in its immortal part and will burn without consuming. The inspiration so often feigned will become real, and the mind of the poet will feel the spark which passes from God to nature. The veil will be withdrawn and beauty and innocence displayed to the eye. . . .

Setting out on his voyage westward in the fall of 1833, Emerson wrote in his journal, "The whole creation groaneth until now waiting for that which shall be revealed." Although Emerson's language (leaning, as it does, on the

New Testament) seems filled with the spirit of Apocalyptic expectation as we find it in biblical prophecy, his actual interest lay much closer to that expressed in the passage from Reed's *Observations.* As Emerson would say in the penultimate paragraph of **Nature:** "The invariable mark of wisdom is to see the miraculous in the common. What is a day? What is a year? What is summer? What is woman? What is a child? What is sleep? to our blindness, these things seem unaffecting."

In his seminal study, *Natural Supernaturalism,* M. H. Abrams has richly documented, in the total context of European Romanticism, the massive tendency, "grounded in texts of the New Testament itself, to internalize apocalypse by transferring the theater of events from the outer earth and heaven to the spirit of the single believer." Thus "Shelley's ruling figure for the advent of the renovated world is that of an instantaneous and radical alteration of sight: man's imaginative vision, suddenly liberated, penetrates to the inner forms, both of man and his world, which had been there all the time, beneath the veil." Such a formulation may be directly applied to the sixth section of *Nature,* for example, where Emerson, turning his attention to "the apocalypse of the mind," argues that "the eye of Reason" (Reason—Imagination; and let us recall Emerson's sentence of 1835: "The Imagination is Vision"), when it is "stimulated to more earnest vision," transforms surfaces so that they "become transparent" and "causes and spirits are seen through them." At the very highest reaches of his idealistic faith, Emerson insists that we can "behold unveiled the nature of Justice and Truth."

The central figure in Abrams's exposition is Wordsworth, whose apocalyptic vision, in Abrams's words, "is that of the awesome depths and height of the human mind, and of the power of that mind as in itself adequate, by consummating a holy marriage with the external universe, to create out of the world of all of us, in a quotidian and recurrent miracle, a new world which is the equivalent of paradise." This summary of the Wordsworthian vision could serve as a fairly accurate précis of Reed's *Observations on the Growth of the Mind,* which is thoroughly informed by the spirit of Wordsworth (and, indeed, the first edition in 1826 bore an epigraph from *The Excursion*), as is Emerson's own first book. It is interesting to note that the Wordsworth text upon which Abrams builds his argument, the now familiar lines from Wordsworth's "Prospectus" to *The Recluse,* is in fact quoted by Emerson in that lecture of 1837, **"The Eye and Ear,"** cited above as an illustration of Emerson's passionate desire for "perfection." Emerson writes:

> In the best moments of life, in moments of great peace we are susceptible to the beauty that fills and overflows nature. It is the song of a living poet,
>
>   Paradise and groves elysian
> Fortunate fields like those of old
> Sought in the Atlantic Main why should they be
> A history only of departed things
> Or a mere fiction of what never was?
> For the discerning intellect of man
> When wedded to this goodly Universe
> In love and holy passion, shall find these

> A simple produce of the common day.
>
> We divorce ourselves from nature. . . .

The always percipient Dr. Holmes noticed long ago that "no writer is more deeply imbued with the spirit of Wordsworth than Emerson," and went on to juxtapose Wordsworth's lines to the opening of **Nature:**

> The foregoing generations beheld God and nature face to face; we, through their eyes. Why should not we also enjoy an original relation to the universe? Why should not we have a poetry and philosophy of insight and not of tradition, and a religion by revelation to us, and not the history of theirs?

It remains to add only that the final section of **Nature,** "Prospects," which provides the *volte-face* implied in the opening sentence of the essay ("Our age is retrospective"), owes not only its title but also much of its language and imagery to Wordsworth's "Prospectus." Perhaps he and not Bronson Alcott is the "Orphic poet" whom Emerson claims at least partially to be quoting:

> A man is a god in ruins. When men are innocent, life shall be longer, and shall pass into the immortal, as gently as we awake from dreams. Now, the world would be insane and rabid, if these disorganizations should last for hundreds of years. It is kept in check by death and infancy. Infancy is the perpetual Messiah, which comes into the arms of fallen men, and pleads with them to return to paradise. . . .

> The problem of restoring to the world original and eternal beauty, is solved by the redemption of the soul. The ruin or the blank, that we see when we look at nature, is in our own eye. The axis of vision is not coincident with the axis of things, and so they appear not transparent but opake. The reason why the world lacks unity, and lies broken and in heaps, is, because man is disunited with himself. He cannot be a naturalist, until he satisfies all the demands of the spirit. Love is as much its demand, as perception. Indeed, neither can be perfect without the other. In the uttermost meaning of the words, thought is devout, and devotion is thought. Deep calls unto deep. But in actual life, the marriage is not celebrated.

In this passage, Emerson actually provides our best gloss on that "moral perfection" which he tried to illuminate in his journal entry on Milton: the glory that is here revealed—"the 'open secret' of the universe"—is simply that perception and love can, and must, unite and thereby lead us to the perfection of our moral being. When we come to look at the world with the "new eyes" that Emerson provides, we shall find "the phenomenon perfect" and have "all that Adam had." This secularized program for the redemption of the soul is Emerson's great argument in this final survey of "Prospects" where, as Holmes puts it well, Emerson "dreams of Paradise regained." Indeed, since the spirit—if not the theology—of Milton so thoroughly pervades the conclusion of Emerson's book (as it underlies Wordsworth's "Prospectus"), it is probably worth noting that book XI of *Paradise Lost* provides the model (and perhaps even some of the vocabulary) for Emerson's project here. We recall that the archangel Michael is sent down to Adam and Eve for the purpose, not only of removing them from paradise, but also of providing a preview of the history of salvation. To that end, Michael leads Adam up a mountain:

> So both ascend
> In the Visions of God: It was a Hill
> Of Paradise the highest, from whose top
> The hemisphere of Earth in clearest Ken
> Stretcht out to the amplest reach of prospect lay.

Here, Milton tells us, "Michael from Adam's eyes the Film remov'd" and proceeded to unfold the Christian vision. Such is the function that Emerson now arrogates to himself, though he has lost his belief in its theological underpinnings. In the mid-1820's Emerson noted in his journal that "Christianity . . . takes off the film that had got on the human eye" but subsequently "neglected the improvement of the intellect." Emerson surmised that "the oculist did not wish the blind man to see the sun because he only removed the film & left him no directions what to do with his eyes." Those directions Emerson himself attempted to provide in *Nature,* for as he argues in the first section of the book, "to speak truly, few adult persons can see nature. Most persons do not see the sun. At least they have a very superficial seeing."

I want to make one further point about the relationship of Emerson's vision in *Nature* to standard Christian doctrine. . . . As a beginning imaginative writer, Emerson was naturally not very far removed from the ministerial vocation in which he had been bred and which he continued fitfully to serve (for Emerson was not to abandon the pulpit definitively until early in 1839). Emerson's discourses would always, for many of his listeners and readers, carry the faint flavor of the sermon, as his manner would seem elevated and preacherly. But we can be more specific about the influence of the sermon on Emerson's literary method in at least one regard, namely, in his tendency to rely on a Bible text, or texts, to provide a point of departure (and sometimes return), though typically Emerson's use of his text would function to subvert its traditional meaning. Sometimes Bible text is quoted directly, as in the opening of "The Method of Nature" ("Where there is no vision, the people perish"; Proverbs, 29:18); often it is "submerged" or embedded in the texture of his language. In either case, it can be an important guide to Emerson's meaning or intention. We ought at least to remind ourselves that Emerson's actual audience was normally quite familiar with the Bible, and therefore could be expected to respond even to an oblique biblical reference. Emerson, however, tends to avoid recondite allusions, staying for the most part with texts that would elicit easy recognition.

Nature has at least three such texts, two in its exordium, the third in its peroration, which provide a valuable insight into the direction of Emerson's argument. The first is embedded in the second sentence of the book: "Our age is retrospective. It builds the sepulchres of the fathers." Surely there is an echo here of Christ's angry words to the lawyers in the eleventh chapter of Luke: "Woe unto you! for ye build the sepulchres of the prophets, and your fathers killed them. Truly ye bear witness that ye allow the deeds of your fathers: for they indeed killed them, and ye build their sepulchres." Emerson has, in a sense, collapsed his text by leaving out the prophets altogether, or at least insinuating that that is what his age does—building the sepulchres of the fathers and ignoring the prophets, those with direct knowledge of God. Though Emerson is not about to accuse "the fathers" of slaying prophets (he would come much closer to such a position as he himself assumed the prophetic role more explicitly at the time of the **"Divinity School Address"**), his assimilation of his own voice to that of Christ suggests that this opening paragraph of *Nature* is laced with more anger than we are normally willing to hear. In any case, we shall shortly notice that the voice of Christ, again from the gospel of Luke, explicitly surfaces at the end of Emerson's book.

The second and perhaps more significant text is not very deeply submerged in the fourth sentence of the opening: "The foregoing generations beheld God and nature face to face; we, through their eyes." Emerson's allusion is to a very familiar passage indeed from I Corinthians, chapter 13: "When I was a child, I spake as a child, I understood as a child, I thought as a child: but when I became a man, I put away childish things. For now we see through a glass, darkly: but then face to face. . . ." This text was so well known, at least in nineteenth-century America, that Mark Twain could easily expect to make humorous capital by fooling with it in his essay on Cooper ("Cooper's eye was splendidly inaccurate. Cooper seldom saw anything correctly. He saw nearly all things as through a glass eye, darkly"). And even Emerson at age sixteen was not above making his own joke at St. Paul's expense ("Been looking through a glass darkly this morning to see the Eclipse").

But Emerson's use of the text in *Nature* is serious indeed, and helps to advance his argument quite economically. For one thing, since he has been complaining strenuously about "the fathers," and particularly about being kept in what might be termed epistemological immaturity (seeing the world "through their eyes"), there is something wonderfully ironic about his depending on the authority of St. Paul to bolster his claim that he has a perfect right to put away such childish things. More importantly, however, Emerson is engaged in subverting the traditional Christian claim that full spiritual maturity, and the direct apprehension of the divine, will be attained only at the end of time, when the veil is finally removed. Notice that Emerson easily assumes that the foregoing generations have *already* beheld "God and nature face to face." Though he might be alluding to Moses, or the prophets, or to those who lived in the time of Christ, if it is the history of religion he has in mind, his lack of specificity is telling: *somebody* in the past has had an unmediated experience of God and nature. Why do we keep our heads so reverently turned to the past, he seems to be asking, if not because we believe that something has already taken place which is far more valuable than the "wool and flax" in our own fields? What has been done once, Emerson's logic clearly suggests, can surely be done again. He therefore insists on "an original relation to the universe" and demands his own "works and laws and worship." Emerson is convinced that his own eyes are adequate to any vision of the divine. As he would say in just two years, before the Divinity School at Harvard, "dare to love God without mediator or veil."

The text Emerson uses at the conclusion of *Nature* was a favorite of his and serves to culminate his quasi-religious vision in a way that picks up the Christian undertone of the essay and assimilates it to the naturalistic premise of his whole imaginative project. It is drawn from the seventeenth chapter of Luke: "And when he was demanded of the Pharisees, when the kingdom of God should come, he answered them and said, 'The kingdom of God cometh not with observation: Neither shall they say, "Lo here!" or "Lo there!" for, behold, the kingdom of God is within you.'" Emerson leans on these verses in a curious way: "The kingdom of man over nature, which cometh not with observation,—a dominion such as now is beyond his dream of God,—he shall enter without more wonder than the blind man feels who is gradually restored to perfect sight." The obvious change Emerson has made is to substitute for the kingdom of God and even greater dominion—that of man's accommodation to and eventual control of all the things outside of his spirit from which he now feels alienated, including (as Emerson told us at the outset) his own body. This ultimate kingdom of integrated being is, accordingly, the place where Emerson's version of the holy marriage described in the twenty-first chapter of the book of Revelation will be celebrated—the marriage he has called for uniting perception and love, "science with the fire of the holiest affections." Though Emerson has insisted throughout his essay on the actual cleansing of vision as the agency of this redemption, he now surprises us by associating the gradual nature of this redemption with Christ's insistence that the kingdom does not come "with observation": the visionary perfection we seek has stolen upon us unawares and lies waiting within. Once again, we remember that journal entry of September 17, 1833. The "moral perfection" which Emerson has tirelessly sought, and which he thinks of as "the glory that shall be revealed," he realizes is not *future* at all; for "it is only the feebleness & dust of the observer that makes it future, the whole *is* now potentially in the bottom of his heart."

Though few contemporary readers of Emerson's first book seem to have had a clear sense of what he was about, Carlyle's response must have been heartening: "Your little azure-coloured *Nature* gave me true satisfaction. . . . It is the true Apocalypse this when the 'open secret' becomes revealed to a man." Was Carlyle actually alluding to Emerson's apparent pretensions to rivaling, or replacing, the author of the book of Revelation? We know, at least, that Carlyle had his own view of the poet as apocalyptist, whose primary function is to help us unseal our eyes so that we might see the New Jerusalem. Great Men, Teufelsdrockh tells us [in Carlyle's *Sartor Resartus,* 1836],

> are the inspired (speaking and acting) Texts of that divine BOOK OF REVELATIONS, whereof a Chapter is completed from epoch to epoch, and by some named HISTORY; to which inspired Texts your numerous talented men, and your innumerable untalented men, are the better or worse exegetic Commentaries, and wagon-load

of too-stupid, heretical or orthodox, weekly Sermons. For my study the inspired Texts themselves!

Whether Emerson and his book indeed formed one of these inspired texts for Carlyle or just another solid heterodox sermon is not entirely clear.

But we can be more certain about Emerson's attitude toward his own work. At least by the time he came to publish his second series of *Essays* (1844), Emerson would think about "the total solitude of the critic," clearly with himself in mind, as being "the Patmos of thought." And in the same book, he would argue that there was as much need for his own existence, and work, as for that of the inspired prophet of old: "If John was perfect, why are you and I alive?" But the most interesting hint about Emerson's view of his own high function may be found in a dream entered in his journal for October, 1840:

> I dreamed that I floated at will in the great Ether, and I saw this world floating also not far off, but diminished to the size of an apple. Then an angel took it in his hand & brought it to me and said "This must thou eat." And I ate the world.

Though it might seem that Emerson was here simply symbolizing for himself his necessary recapitulation of Adam's primal sin—eating the fruit of worldly knowledge, but this time with divine sanction—other possibilities suggest themselves. His dream might also represent a figuration of the "Idealism" section of *Nature,* where man, "the immortal pupil," finds himself so dilated and deified that the whole world does indeed circulate through him, totally engulfed "in the apocalypse of the mind." In this view, Emerson's dream might be seen as a kind of rehearsal of that tremendous sense of spiritual power which had inspired his first book (and which, to judge by this later journal entry, would largely evaporate by the mid-1850's: "'Twere ridiculous for us to think of embracing the whole circle when we know we can live only while 50, 60, or 70 whirls are spun round the sun by this nimble apple we are perched upon. Can the gnat swallow the elephant?").

But the reader impressed by Emerson's prophetic and apocalyptist yearnings may hear another biblical echo behind Emerson's dream, this time from the tenth chapter of the book of Revelation:

> And the voice which I heard from heaven spake unto me again, and said, "Go and take the little book which is open in the hand of the angel which standeth upon the sea and upon the earth." And I went unto the angel, and said unto him, "Give me the little book." And he said unto me, "Take it, and eat it up; and it shall make thy belly bitter, but it shall be in thy mouth sweet as honey." And I took the little book out of the angel's hand, and ate it up; and it was in my mouth sweet as honey: and as soon as I had eaten it, my belly was bitter. And he said unto me, "Thou must prophesy again before many peoples, and nations, and tongues, and kings."

If Emerson's language and paratactic cadences really do betray the origin of his dream in this passage from the book of Revelation, his allegory suggests how heavy was the burden for him of the sort of self-defined prophecy he had undertaken to produce. Forsaking the certainties of the Eucharistic meal in favor of a bittersweet experience of the world in its complex totality, Emerson had assumed the great, and difficult, aim as an artist of bringing forth scriptures of his own that might provide, as had the Hebrew and Greek ones, "bread of life to millions." "The beauty of nature reforms itself in the mind," he writes in *Nature,* "and not for barren contemplation, but for new creation." A work of art, he insists, must be "an abstract or epitome of the world . . . the result or expression of nature, in miniature." A true scripture must pierce the "rotten diction" of trivial literature and "fasten words again to visible things" so that it becomes a revelation of the actual underpinnings of experience. Only thus can the writer/prophet help us to build a new heaven and earth of durable proportions.

The message of Saint John's parable of the little book, D. H. Lawrence tells us, is the universal one "of the destruction of the old world and creation of the new." Emerson attempted to achieve both goals in *Nature.* As he wrote to Carlyle on September 17, 1836: "I send you a little book I have just now published, as an entering wedge, I hope, for something more worthy and significant." But Carlyle, in his reply, as we have noticed, magnanimously claimed that the "little book" was sufficiently worthy to be called a "true Apocalypse": "You say it is the first chapter of something greater. I call it rather the Foundation and Ground-plan on which you may build whatsoever of great and true has been given you to build." (pp. 64-82)

Joel Porte, in his Representative Man: Ralph Waldo Emerson in His Time, *Oxford University Press, Inc., 1979, 361 p.*

B. L. Packer   (essay date 1982)

[*Packer is an American educator and critic. In the following excerpt, she explores Emerson's use of irony, asserting that the ambiguity of his essays is intended to force the reader into active interpretation rather than passive reception.*]

> Our highest insights must—and should—sound like follies and sometimes like crimes when they are heard without permission by those who are not prepared for and elected by them.
> Nietzsche, Beyond Good and Evil

Emerson once praised Landor for having "the merit of not explaining." Like most of Emerson's comments about rhetoric, this tribute celebrates the virtues of absence, the exhilarations of discontinuity. Late in life he remarked to a young admirer that the best writing is that which does not quite satisfy the reader. "A little guessing does him no harm, so I would assist him with no connections." His own refusal to provide transitions was strategic, a sacrifice of judiciousness to power. But the strategy itself reflected a deep skepticism about the capacity of language to embody truth. "Thought," he once said, "is the manna which cannot be stored."

He had not always taken so suspicious a view of his medium of expression. In his youth he had been content simply to enjoy the pleasures of rhetoric without much concern for its truth value. In college he had been so intoxicated by the ravishing pulpit eloquence of Edward Everett that (as Emerson's biographer Ralph Rusk tells us) he not only memorized particularly affecting phrases, "he could say half the sermon from which he got them on the night after he had heard it." And his college tastes were only an extension of his boyhood ones. William Henry Furness, a schoolfellow of Emerson's, thought that their boyhood days ought to be called "the era of rhetoric" because then even the youngest boy "went into ecstasies over a happy turn of expression or a brilliant figure of speech." In declamation and debate boys found a form of self-display and combativeness that their parents, teachers, and ministers actively encouraged. In James Elliot Cabot's *Memoir* there is a touching story of Emerson's pride in bringing home a college prize for declamation in hopes that his winnings—thirty dollars—would buy his mother a new shawl; he was chagrined to learn that the money had to be spent to pay the baker's bill. Even after graduation, when he had moved with his mother and brothers out into the country, his neighboring cousins could hear the Emerson boys making the woods resound with declamations and dialogues. It was in such exercises as these that Emerson perfected that rich baritone that so moved and persuaded his hearers—a voice whose power and sweetness, issuing from his ascetic-looking New England body, was so surprising that it reminded one journalist of a huge magnolia blossom lodged in the bough of an aspen tree.

Eloquence was the easiest road to success for a poor but gifted boy, whether he chose the pulpit or the political platform; it was also the surest way of reaching and influencing his fellow citizens. Foreign visitors were amazed at the apparently boundless appetite for sermons, lyceum lectures, and political debates that Americans displayed. We have lost this appetite so completely that it takes some effort of the imagination to recover it, but in Emerson's youth it was strong enough to hold out the promise of renown to any sufficiently talented speaker. Emerson himself was occasionally amused by the eagerness of his fellow citizens for oratorical entertainment. In a letter he wrote to his brother Charles he joked that he could announce a lecture on the Invisible Ox, to be *seen* at Faneuil Hall, and still be certain of an audience. As late as 1881 the American neurologist George Beard was led to adduce the well-known talent of his countrymen for oratory in support of his thesis that Americans were more highly strung than their European contemporaries (since "the masters in the oratorical art are always nervous").

With this sort of cultural background it is not surprising to find Emerson at the age of twenty-one confessing to his journal that he has inherited from his father "a passionate love for the strains of eloquence" and that he burns after that " 'aliquid immensum infinitumque' which Cicero desired." He had already determined to follow his father's profession, and though he realized that "entire success" in preaching was the lot of the few, he still "hoped to put on eloquence as a robe" and thereby "prevail over the false judgments, the rebel passions, and corrupt habits of men."

Emerson's home in Concord.

Nor is it surprising, given this notion of eloquence, that Emerson's early journals are virtually unreadable. The normal adolescent fondness for the saccharine and the overblown found little to restrain it in the prevailing literary taste of the surrounding society. Daniel Howe has remarked how far removed the "graceful sentimentality" of that taste had become from the "sparse utilitarianism" of the Puritan plain style, and adds: "In fact, could the Puritans have heard a nineteenth-century Unitarian sermon, they would probably have found its style similar to the flowery 'carnall eloquence' they detested in Anglican preachers."

Emerson's embarrassment at his own youthful excesses and his dissatisfaction with the prevailing pulpit style grew at about the same rate during the years of his young manhood. Gradually in the journals and sermons one can witness the dawning of a livelier style as Emerson begins to abandon [in Jonathan Bishop's words in *Emerson on the Soul,* 1964] the "stock properties of college rhetoric" for the pungencies of the great seventeenth-century prose masters whose works he began to study and try to imitate. The *aliquid immensum infinitumque,* he decided, was something best left to each man's youthful and private meditations; he was growing to prefer instead [in James

Russell Lowell's words in *The Nation,* 1868] the "homespun cloth-of-gold" of Donne, Jonson, Bacon, Browne. True eloquence increasingly came to seem less a thing to be put on like a robe than a thing to be gotten at by stripping away the trite, the turgid, the flowery, the insincere. He longed to attain the state of simplicity described by Sampson Reed in his "Oration on Genius," delivered at Emerson's Harvard graduation exercises. Emerson was so taken with the address that he borrowed it and made a copy; he seems to have been particularly impressed by Reed's description of that blessed poetic state where "words make one with things, and language is lost in nature." By 1831 Emerson was formulating his own maxim out of Reed's phrase: "In good writing words become one with things."

It is never entirely clear what this sort of assertion is actually supposed to mean, but what it usually suggests to native speakers of English is that good writing is writing in which words of Anglo-Saxon derivation are substituted for words derived from French and Latin, and simple nouns are preferred to poetic periphrases. That, at any rate, is what determination to achieve a "natural" or "thinglike" language has meant to every generation of linguistic reformers in English or American literary history from the Puritan opponents of "carnall eloquence" down to Pound and the Imagists.

And it was evident to Emerson's contemporaries that he saw himself as a reformer of this kind, that in his sermons and lectures he was attempting to reinvigorate language by returning it to its native roots, even if his efforts to do so obliged him to offend the reigning standards of good taste. Francis Bowen, who reviewed *Nature* for the *Christian Examiner,* thought the book marred by stylistic lapses; Emerson had gone a bit too far when he introduced aggressively "low" phrases like "pot and kettle," "huddled and lumped," and "dreams, beasts, sex" into serious philosophical discourse. But Bowen, while critical, could at least sympathize with the motives behind such offenses. He could see that the author of *Nature* was "in love with the Old Saxon idiom" and guessed that his sins against decorum stemmed not from ineptitude but from literary affectation. "He is sometimes coarse and blunt, that he may avoid the imputation of sickly refinement, and writes bathos with malice prepense, because he abhors forced dignity and unnatural elevation."

Yet the very attempt to put Reed's advice into practice, though it eventually helped Emerson achieve the pungent, aphoristic style for which he is famous, revealed the flaws in the original project. Emerson could still invoke Reed when, in one of the first letters he ever wrote to Carlyle, he expressed his puzzlement and dismay at the "grotesque teutonic apocalyptic" style of the newly published *Sartor Resartus.* "I look for the hour with impatience when the vehicle will be worthy of the spirit when the word will be as simple & so as resistless as the thought, & in short when your words will be one with things." But a year later he is no longer so sure that such perfect blending is possible:

> The aim of the author is not to tell truth—that he cannot do, but to suggest it. He has only approximated it himself, & hence his cumbrous and embarrassed speech: he uses many words, hoping that one, if not another, will bring you as near to the fact as he is.

> For language itself is young & unformed. In heaven, it will be, as Sampson Reed said, "one with things." Now, there are many things that refuse to be recorded,—perhaps the larger half. The unsaid part is the best of every discourse.

Language is related to truth, it seems, as curve to asymptote, for "heaven" in Emerson is always defined as the candid child defined the concept of infinity in mathematics: "Infinity is where things happen that don't."

By the time of *Nature* (1836) metaphors of distance—the remoteness of language from truth—give way to metaphors of active hostility: Words "cannot cover the dimensions of what is in truth. They break, chop, and impoverish it." The man who seeks to refine a statement by careful qualifications, judiciously considered objections, gets no closer to truth. He only makes the inescapable poverty of language more abject, and ends in an "Iceland of negations." Hyperbole, or a certain "violence of direction" in rhetoric, is likely to prove more effective than restraint in counteracting the downward gravitational pull that language exerts on the writer who aims at truth. "We aim above the mark to hit the mark," Emerson observes. Hence his cheerful rule for rhetoric: "omit all the negative propositions."

A style that suggests rather than tells, that refuses to defend, that combines excess with reticence, carries its dangers, as Emerson realized. "Ah, so you shall be sure to be misunderstood." Refusal to modify or explain his more shocking assertions earned him a reputation for antinomianism; omission of negative propositions, for witless optimism. Such accusations clearly hurt him—he once confessed that his greatest weakness was an excessive desire for sympathy—yet he managed to survive caricature with his sense of humor intact. In the furor following publication of the *Divinity School Address* he writes in his journal:

> How soon the sunk spirits rise again, how quick the little wounds of fortune skin over & are forgotten. I am sensitive as a leaf to impressions from abroad. And under this night's beautiful heaven I have forgotten that ever I was *reviewed.*

In the end he came to suspect that a text's susceptibility to misinterpretation was itself a mark of greatness. He quotes with approval Aristotle's paradoxical remark that his works were "published and not published." The reader picks up a book to try the author's merits; but the reader too is being tested. As Roland Barthes puts it: "The text chooses me, by a whole disposition of invisible screens, selective baffles: vocabulary, references, readability, etc.: and, lost in the midst of a text (not *behind* it, like a *deus ex machina*), there is always the other, the author." Obscurities, enigmas, lacunae—like Biblical parables—are tests of the reader's intelligence and generosity; they serve to divide the elect from the nonelect. The reader can *hear* only those texts, or portions of texts, for which he has ears. "Deep calls unto deep," Emerson notes, "& Shallow to Shallow."

A "deep" text is one that challenges the reader to intellectual activity. And Emerson's best critics have always pointed out how well his own works live up to his demand that a text must involve the reader actively. W. C. Brownell, writing in 1909 [in *American Prose Masters,* 1909], pointed out that the simple understanding of an essay by Emerson requires virtues much more strenuous than passive receptivity. "Everything means something additional. To take it in you must go beyond it. The very appreciation of an essay automatically constructs a web of thought in the weaving of which the reader shares." The ambiguities, lacunae, paradoxes, and understatements with which Emerson is so generous turn the sentences of his essays into charged terminals that the reader must take the risk of connecting; the latter's reward is a certain electric tingle. "Search for eloquence in his books and you will perchance miss it, but meanwhile you will find that it has kindled all your thoughts," writes James Russell Lowell.

It must be admitted that Emerson did everything he could to make the reader's task difficult. He deliberately rejected the carefully sloped introductions, the graceful transitions, the carefully modulated crescendos and decrescendos of the popular essayistic style. Emerson's beginnings are abrupt; his transitions, equally so. For the reader who fails to go beyond the sentences he is offered, and hence to take them in, the fragments of an Emerson essay can lie upon the page like steel filings when no magnet is present.

The connection between one sentence and another, one paragraph and another, or between anything within the essay and the world outside it, is something Emerson eliminates, something he offers the reader no assistance in forming. Self-reliance is to him first of all what it was to his Protestant ancestors: the liberty to interpret texts according to the Spirit. His scrupulous respect for the reader's liberty is what Laurence Stapleton has in mind when she entitles her chapter on Emerson in *The Elected Circle,* "Emerson and the Freedom of the Reader." There she observes that "in faithfully pursuing a writer's route to freedom, Emerson makes room for the reader. He does not wink or nod, coax or bully, scold or pontificate." Stanley Cavell makes a similar point [in *The Senses of "Walden":* *An Expanded Edition,* 1981] when he says that Emerson's prose leaves us "at liberty to discover whether he belongs to us or we to him." But it makes no effort to draw us in, to convert us. "It does not require us."

Another feature of Emerson's style that makes his work difficult to interpret is its indeterminacy of tone. Emerson's sentences can usually be read in more than one way, and only the sophisticated reader will be able to supply an imagined tone or dramatic context that makes them interesting. "I was always in favor of the solid curse as one of the most beautiful of figures," Robert Frost remarked. "It depends for variety on the tones of saying it and the situations." And he goes on to apply this observation to Emerson:

> I had a talk with John Erskine, the first time I met him, on this subject of sentences that may look tiresomely alike, short and with short words, yet turn out as calling for all sorts of ways of being said aloud or in the mind's ear, Horatio. I took Emerson's prose and verse as my illustration. Writing is unboring to the extent that it is dramatic.

That last sentence is surprising. I imagine most first-time readers of Emerson would claim that he is boring precisely because there is so little drama in his work. To a reader who has never in his life derived pleasure from a piece of oratory, nor even imagined that oratory could be pleasurable, a volume of Emerson's essays will at first seem to possess a lack of drama that can make *Walden* seem by contrast almost a gothic romance. For Emerson's essays belong to the oral, not the written, tradition. The printed text bears about the same relation to the essays as they are meant to be heard "in the mind's ear" as a score of the *Messiah* does to a performance of it.

Emerson's contemporaries were much readier than we are to respond to the text's call for dramatic renderings because they had not left wholly behind the old oral-aural world in which eloquence flourished for the print-centered, visually oriented world in which it languishes and dies. There were "voiceless" styles (or at least the ancestors of such styles) in existence even then, of course; Emerson could expect his readers to be familiar enough

with the deadpan impersonality of scientific prose to enjoy his wonderful parody of it in the opening sentences of **"Quotation and Originality":**

> Whoever looks at the insect world, at flies, aphides, gnats, and innumerable parasites, and even at the infant mammals, must have remarked the extreme content they take in suction, which constitutes the main business of their life. If we go into a library or a newsroom, we see the same function on a higher plane, performed with like ardor, with equal impatience of interruption, indicating the sweetness of the act.

But he could also count on his readers' familiarity with a whole panoply of "voiced" styles—some, indeed, in which the sense was scarcely more than an excuse for the sound. There were the cadences of the King James Bible, the well-bred fluencies of the periodical writers, the heavy sarcasm of religious and political controversialists, and the pure "pleniloquence" of the popular oratorical style. F. O. Matthiessen [in his *American Renaissance,* 1941] quotes the conclusion of Everett's "very popular and many times repeated address for Washington's birthday: '. . . the name and the memory of Washington on that gracious night will travel with the silver queen of heaven through sixty degrees of longitude, nor part company with her till she walks in her brightness through the golden gate of California, and passes serenely on to hold midnight court with her Australian stars.'" Emerson himself recalled "what fools a few sounding sentences made of me & my mates at Cambridge," and gave as an example of the kind of thing he had in mind a sentence he still remembered from a classmate's oration: "And there was a band of heroes, & round their mountain was a wreath of light, & in the midst, on the mountain top, stood Liberty, feeding her eagle."

The eagle of Liberty was probably glad of such unaccustomed repose; according to Constance Rourke [in her *American Humor,* 1931] "orators kept the bird so continuously in flight from the peak of the Alleghanies to the top of Mt. Hood that its shadow was said to have worn a trail across the basin of the Mississippi." But the existence of witticisms like this points out another important fact: the same audience that in one mood relished the pleniloquence also relished, in another, its parody in flights of pure "buncombe." (In the same way, the Augustan age in English poetry, with its worship of the ancients, was also the great age of mock-epic; and the Victorian striving after high seriousness is matched by the Victorian genius for nonsense verse.) The line between American bombast and American burlesque is very hard to draw; Rourke warns that it is "often impossible to tell one from the other without a wide context of knowledge as to the subject and the speakers. Popular declamation of the '30s and '40s has often been considered as bombast when it should be taken as comic mythology."

Irony, like buncombe, is notoriously difficult to identify with any certainty. For, as Jonathan Culler has observed, "no sentence is ironic *per se.* Sarcasm may contain internal inconsistencies which make its purport quite obvious and prevent it from being read except in one way, but for a sentence to be properly ironic it must be possible to imagine some group of readers taking it quite literally. Otherwise there is no space between apparent and assumed meaning and no space for ironic play." Culler's remarks suggest why irony provokes discomfort: it serves to divide the knowing from the innocent, the civilized from the boorish, the immature from the fully adult. In this it resembles parable, though it borrows its standards from earthly kingdoms rather than from heavenly ones. Those who can read it correctly belong to what we might call the world's elect.

The problem of recognizing irony is rendered acute when the text in question is ironic only at intervals. Emerson has many moods, but in general he adopts the stance of the Sage, a man who can give us guidance in the difficulties of living. Yet in certain crucial passages his texts seem to offer advice so radically at odds with normal standards of prudence and wisdom that they call into question the authority of the rest. If this advice is offered in all seriousness, then Emerson is either a "limb of the Devil" (as Yvor Winters calls him) or a fool. If it is offered ironically, we still must decide what kind of complacency or dishonesty the irony is meant to expose.

For an ironist usually has some discernible target, some identifiable ethical purpose. His ironies are intended, as Martin Price puts it [in his *To the Palace of Wisdom,* 1965], "to shock men into recognition; not simply recognition of values they have deserted or duties they have neglected, but of the way in which the mind constructs a coherent system as a refuge from moral cognition and an asylum from its obligation." The mind does this by rhetorical evasion, by adopting "attractive labels for unsavory mixtures." An ironist like Swift exposes this evasion by carrying it to an extreme, where the "shock of ugly confrontation is doubled by the tone of disarming plausibility." What makes Emerson baffling is that he seems to adopt Swift's technique while reversing its ethical intent. Emerson never sounds more like one of Swift's Modest Proposers than when he is urging upon us truths he professes to value most highly. This is certainly shocking, but it is harder to say what sort of recognition that shock is supposed to produce.

The problem of the misplaced Swiftian persona becomes especially acute in those rare passages in the *Essays* where Emerson pauses to answer objections to his position. Answering objections or defending assertions was something Emerson—in life or letters—usually refused to do, believing, with Blake, that "He who replies to words of Doubt/ Doth put the Light of Knowledge out." The temptation to enter the arena of disputation was naturally strongest during the furor following the *Divinity School Address,* but Emerson was able to surmount it—with a little help from the oracular wisdom of his wife:

> What said my brave Asia concerning the paragraph writers today? That "this whole practice of self justification & recrimination betwixt literary men seemed every whit as low as the quarrels of the Paddies." . . . But do you know, I asked, how many fine things I have thought of to say to these fighters? They are too good to be lost.—"Then" rejoined the queen, "there is some merit in being silent."

And he did preserve his public silence, though in the privacy of his journals he can sound as ferocious as Blake:

> And whilst I see this that you must have been shocked & must cry out at what I have said I see too that we cannot easily be reconciled for I have a great deal more to say that will shock you out of all patience.

By the time Emerson came to read selections from Blake in Gilchrist's *Life* he had long since abandoned the ambition to become the prophet of an imminent apocalypse. But he copied into his journal a proverb of Hell that appealed to him: "The tigers of wrath are wiser than the horses of instruction."

If Emerson never stoops to defend himself against external threats, still he sometimes allows a hypothetical adversary space to lodge objections in the body of an essay. And here something very curious happens. The Emerson who replies to these objections is not the vehement prophet of the journals but a mild and complaisant rationalist—who does not seem to notice that the bland evasiveness of his attempts at self-justification seem more damning than the outrageous statements they are intended to justify.

In the midst of one of his characteristic attacks on Emerson, Yvor Winters [in his *In Defense of Reason,* 1943] pauses to consider these oddly self-destructive excursions into self-defense. "Emerson," he says, "was not wholly unaware of the theoretical objections that could be made to his position, but unless we are to assume that he personally was a corrupt and vicious man, which I think we can scarcely do, we are forced to admit that he simply did not know what the objections meant." Winters cites two passages from the *Essays* as examples of this failure of comprehension. The first, from **"Self-Reliance,"** records an argument Emerson had with a "valued adviser who was wont to importune me with the dear old doctrines of the church."

> On my saying, what have I to do with the sacredness of traditions, if I live wholly from within? my friend suggested—"But these impulses may be from below, not from above." I replied, "They do not seem to me to be such; but if I am the Devil's child, I will live then from the Devil." No law can be sacred to me but that of my nature. Good and bad are but names very readily transferable to that or this; the only right is what is after my constitution, the only wrong what is against it.

Winters treats this as a perfectly serious attempt to refute a serious objection, and he disposes of it with the sneer: "Emerson appears to be ignorant of the traditional function of the Devil and of the viscera."

But the language of the paragraph in which the little debate about impulses takes place is much shiftier than Winters seems to have noticed. It begins with one of Emerson's bold declarations, meant to rouse a cowardly and conforming nation as with a Spartan fife. "Whoso would be a man must be a nonconformist. He who would gather immortal palms must not be hindered by the name of goodness, but must explore if it be goodness." So far there is little to suggest that Emerson is doing anything more than his Protestant ancestors had always claimed the right to do: judge doctrines and practices according to the inner light in each redeemed soul.

But that traditional advice is suddenly shattered by the sentences that follow. We are told that nothing is at last sacred to us but the integrity of our own minds (not souls), and then encouraged to perform a remarkable sacrament: "Absolve you to yourself, and you shall have the suffrage of the world." It is only then that Emerson pauses to consider the "dear old doctrines" of his own church—as if they were a handful of cherished mementoes or treasured family anecdotes. But this, in Emerson's view, was what organized religion, or "historical Christianity," had come to represent: a collection of traditions that had no relationship to anything in the lives of its adherents. In the *Divinity School Address* he had pointed out that "the prayers and even the dogmas of our church, are like the zodiac of Denderah, and the astronomical monuments of the Hindoos, wholly insulated from anything now extant in the life and business of the people." If the religious sentiment is to survive, it must come from "this life within life, this literal Emanuel, *God within us.*" He was well aware that his new gospel courted dangers. In a journal entry written a few months before the *Divinity School Address* he cautions himself to "beware of Antinomianism," and candidly admits that his critics are right to worry that "the loss of the old checks will sometimes be a temptation which the unripeness of the new will not countervail." But clinging blindly to the old checks was a regimen that led to certain spiritual death; it created an "automation man who is always needing directions & repairs."

Emerson's spiritual geography only makes sense if one understands that Emerson is trying to replace the old division of the world and the psyche—according to which good things were above and wicked things below—with a new division of his own—according to which good things come from within, wicked things from without. Not that *all* impulses from within are good: Emerson worries about the mind's "terrible freedom," and notes (in **"Self-Reliance"**) that "the bold sensualist will use the name of philosophy to gild his crimes." But the law of consciousness abides. No imitation of something external to the self can produce true virtue; all it can produce is the sorry substitute ridiculed by Emerson. "Men do what is called a good action, as some piece of courage or charity, much as they would pay a fine in expiation of daily non-appearance on parade. Their works are done as an apology or extenuation of their living in the world,—as invalids and the insane pay a high board."

But the trusted adviser who asks questions about impulses can think only in terms of the older divisions offered by his culture: God and the Reason above, the Devil and the passions below. Emerson does not attempt to refute this position; he merely replies: "if I am the Devil's child, I will live then from the Devil." The declaration of Byronic defiance is rendered comic chiefly by the circumstances: how could a decorous ex-minister in the town of Concord "live from the Devil" even if he wished to? At most he could do what Emerson had done: use the lecture platform to attack the derelictions of traditional Christianity, and be branded a heretic and an atheist as a result. "It is plain from all the noise that there is Atheism somewhere," he said after the *Divinity School Address.* "The only question is now, Which is the Atheist?" Your enemies will always call deviations from their own standards diabolic; the easiest thing to do is to accept the label and continue your authentic labor—the kind that is dictated from within, not from without.

It is easier to share Winters's bewilderment over the second passage he quotes, this time from **"Circles."** He does not give the full quotation, and since the sentences he omits are important ones, his reading is more than usually distorted. But the passage itself is difficult to explicate even in its unmutilated form. Emerson has been prophesying the inevitable obsolescence of all creations of the spirit. Every scientific discovery, every work of art, every religious system exists to be surpassed, he argues. All virtues are initial, none are final. No system will save us; nothing is secure but "life, transition, the energizing spirit." Emerson does not expect this doctrine to be welcomed by society. "The new statement is always hated by the old," he warns early in the essay, "and, to those dwelling in the old, comes like an abyss of skepticism." A voice of one of those dwellers suddenly rises up to question him:

> And thus, O circular philosopher, I hear some reader exclaim, you have arrived at a fine Pyrrhonism, at an equivalence and indifference of all action, and would fain teach us that *if we are true,* forsooth, our crimes may be lively stones out of which we shall construct the temple of the true God!

There is something alien in the tone of this passage; its strangely hearty mockery reminds one of Carlyle. But if this glancing parody leads us to expect a grand, jesting refutation, we are immediately disappointed. Emerson's odd reply does not seem concerned to answer the objection at all, and it is couched in his characteristically elusive rhetoric of understatement. "I am not careful to justify myself," he begins; and though the remark looks at first like a mild non sequitur, it is in fact an expression of powerful contempt, Emerson's version of the Blakean declaration that what can be made explicit to the idiot is not worth his care. The reader of **"Circles"** who accuses Emerson of teaching an equivalence and indifference of all actions is either careless or willfully stupid. "One man's justice is another's injustice; one man's beauty another's ugliness; one man's wisdom another's folly," Emerson says, but though these maxims may sound like mere variations on the proverb "one man's meat is another man's poison," they are not; since Emerson is careful to add an important qualification—"as one beholds the same objects from a higher point." If this is "thoroughgoing relativism," as Winters alleges, then so is the philosophy of St. Paul:

> For the preaching of the cross is to them that perish, foolishness; but unto us which are saved, it is the power of God.

> For it is written, I will destroy the wisdom of the wise, and will bring to nothing the understanding of the prudent.

For the wisdom of this world is foolishness with God.

Emerson urges a new faith, not an old skepticism; mere Pyrrhonism he always equated with spiritual suicide. If his gospel looks to the orthodox Christian like an abyss of skepticism—well, Emerson might have replied, Christianity too was founded on a cornerstone that the builders had rejected: "unto the Jews a stumblingblock, and unto the Greeks foolishness." But Emerson says nothing of the sort. Instead he suddenly performs a dizzying "sleight of mind," an elision so radical that it threatens to swallow up speaker and argument together, leaving only the reverberations of an oddly disembodied irony: the Tyger of Wrath as Cheshire Cat:

> I own I am gladdened by seeing the predominance of the saccharine principle throughout vegetable nature, and not less by beholding in morals that unrestrained inundation of the principle of good into every chink and hole that selfishness has left open, yea, into selfishness and sin itself; so that no evil is pure, nor hell itself without its extreme satisfactions.

If we examine the rhetorical mode of this powerful and disturbing passage, we notice that parts of it are cast in the Swiftian idiom remarked earlier. Emerson adopts the tone of the bloodless empiricist, the Royal Society "projector" who is gladdened by his observations of the saccharine principle, and who is cheered at the thought that even the damned inhabit the best of all possible hells. No wonder Winters omits these sentences; to read them straight would be to judge Emerson more than "corrupt and vicious." In **"Circles"** mere optimism, however foolish, has given way to obvious lunacy—lunacy that combines the utilitarian cheerfulness of Swift's "Digression on Madness" with the grisly complacency of his *Modest Proposal*. Not even the sourest critic is likely to take these opinions for Emerson's own.

But whose opinions are they? The journal entry upon which this passage is based is, for once, unambiguously clear:

> And thus, o circular philosopher, you have arrived at a fine Pyrrhonism, at an equivalence & indifferency of all actions & would fain teach us that *if we are true,* forsooth, our crimes may be lively stones out of which we shall construct the temple of the true God.
>
> The good Swedenborg was aware, I believe, of this wonderful predominance & excess of the saccharine principle in nature & noticed that the hells were not without their extreme satisfactions.

This is sarcasm rather than irony, but a sarcasm that is at least susceptible of explanation. Swedenborg, who at the time of *The American Scholar* had been one of Emerson's heroes, had by 1840 become one of his frequent targets of ridicule; in Emerson's account of him in *Representative Men* the Swedish visionary does in fact resemble one of Swift's creations: a cold, passionless observer of Facts, whose humorless and pedantic manner never deserts him, whether he is observing the ecstasies of heaven or the tor-

ments of hell. Worse still, Swedenborg was essentially Manichaean (as were all orthodox Christians, in Emerson's opinion) for believing in devils and permanent damnation; and he was mean, vindictive, and morbid in his preoccupation with sin. "Except Rabelais and Dean Swift," Emerson complained, "nobody ever had such science of filth and corruption."

But if the visionary was a repellent figure, the visions themselves—taken as metaphors rather than dogmas—were sometimes surprisingly poetic and imaginative. (Blake thought so too; he said that Swedenborg's writings were "False philosophy according to the letter, but true according to the spirit.") And Emerson was particularly attracted by the metaphoric truth of Swedenborg's vision of Hell: punishment there consisted in the *practice* of the same vices that had occasioned damnation in the first place. The deceitful continued to deceive, the covetous to rob, the lecherous to fornicate. These vices provide the same kind of pleasure they provide on earth, and ultimately occasion the same kind of misery.

The notion that the evil in hell are punished by the consequences of their vices, if read as an allegory of life on earth, resembles Emerson's own beloved doctrine of compensation. But what is bold and imaginative as metaphor is, if accepted as literal truth, morally indistinguishable from the doctrine it replaces. "That pure malignity can exist," Emerson argues, "is the extreme proposition of unbelief. It is not to be entertained by a rational agent; it is atheism; it is the last profanation." And the alternative to a belief in pure malignity? Emerson commends the wild humor of Burns's "Address to the Deil":

> But fare you weel, auld Nickie-Ben!
> O wad ye tak' a thought & men'

Of this sentiment Emerson observes, "If it be comical, it yet belongs to the moral sublime." To say that evil can be converted into good is not quite the same thing as saying that there is no difference between good and evil, though the distinction is likely to be lost on the orthodox, of whom Swedenborg was ultimately one.

But Swedenborg's visions can be put to other uses than the ones he intended. Like Blake in *The Marriage of Heaven and Hell*, Emerson discovers to his delight and amusement that evidence designed to support belief in eternal damnation can be cheerfully reversed to support a more generous eschatology. And this, after all, is what **"Circles."** is all about:

> There is not a piece of science but its flank may be turned tomorrow; there is not any literary reputation, not the so-called eternal names of fame, that may not be revised and condemned. The very hopes of man, the thoughts of his heart, the religion of nations, the manners and morals of mankind, are all at the mercy of a new generalization.

But of course the description I have just given of Emerson's irony fits only the 1840 journal entry, not the passage as it stands in **"Circles."** When Emerson rewrites the journal passage for inclusion in the essay, he expands it to include an explicit reference to the generosity of a vision that can joyfully await the conversion of evil to good (as Burns wishes the reclamation even of the Devil himself)—but he leaves out Swedenborg's name, and hopelessly blurs the distinction between Swedenborg's opinions and his own. He is *not* careful to justify himself: he mixes doctrines he finds offensive with beliefs he seriously supports, and he casts the whole passage into the kind of unconsciously self-destructive idiom that Augustan satire had reserved for its maddest or cruelest masks.

The passage gains in power what it loses in immediate intelligibility; indeed, its contempt for intelligibility is part of its power. Like some of the parables Jesus tells, it seems designed at once to invite misinterpretation and at the same time to radiate scorn for the misinterpreter. Emerson, like his own Uriel, simply withdraws behind a cloud, leaving it to his readers to decide whether his apparent "lapses" are the result of his incapacities or ours, whether he is unusually foolish or, on the contrary, "by knowledge grown too bright/ To hit the nerve of feebler sight."

Explaining how the strategy works is easier than guessing why it was chosen. In part, I think, Emerson had discovered that attempts to make fine distinctions were wasted effort when one's opponents were likely to condemn any revision of accepted ideas or practices with smug, undiscriminating zeal. There are only two ways of coping with resolute Philistinism—denunciation and insouciance. Emerson was sometimes tempted—particularly during the controversy following publication of the *Address*—to thunder and denounce, but he never) appears as prophet outside the privacy of his own journal, for a number of reasons. One was a laudable awareness that the prose of prophet or martyr was—in nineteenth-century Boston, at any rate—a repellent affectation. Blake's opinions might have cost him his life. What did Emerson risk? After the *Divinity School Address* he could no longer speak at Harvard, but that hardly entitled him to a martyr's crown. A journal entry for September 1838 bears the contemptuous heading "The silken persecution":

> Martyrs with thumbscrews, martyrs sawn asunder, martyrs eaten by dogs, may claim with gory stumps a crown. But the martyrs in silk stockings & barouches, martyrs with venison & champagne, in ballrooms & picture galleries, make me sick.

The second reason is harder to define. Yet we can conjecture, from the tone and content of the remarks Emerson addresses to himself in the journals of the period, that he had formulated some version of Nietzsche's warning to philosophers [in his *Beyond Good and Evil,* 1966]: "Take care, philosophers and friends, of knowledge, and beware of martyrdom, of suffering 'for the truth's sake'! Even of defending yourself." In place of defense, Nietzsche advises a mocking retreat: "Rather, go away. Flee into concealment. And have your masks and subtlety, that you may be mistaken for what you are not, or feared a little." *That you may be mistaken for what you are not*—that command (from Emerson to himself) seems to underlie those eerie and disturbing passages in which he invites the attack of hostile readers by appearing to offer them exactly the evidence they need to convict him. These passages, like the

inkblots of a Rorschach, are less important for what they contain than for the response they evoke. They ask us above all to imagine a *voice,* and the voice we imagine determines whether we think the author an ironist, a Satanist, or a fool.

Yet Emerson's lapses are not the only things that ask us to imagine a presence behind the sentences on the page, nor are hostile readers the only ones to question his self-awareness. No one who reads much of the critical literature about Emerson can fail to be struck by the number of critics who assert that Emerson *was unconscious of* some significant implication contained in, or response likely to be provoked by, his own texts. Jonathan Bishop, for instance, praises Emerson's strategy of using "metaphors of eating and nourishment for the description of mental activity," but calls the strategy "sublimely unconscious." John Lyndenberg points out [in *Critical Quarterly* 4, 1962] that the "shudder, the feeling of awe" that characterizes what he calls the Dark Tradition in American literature appears with "startling clarity" in the essay **"Experience,"** but then adds that "presumably Emerson did not intend to convey any such feeling, and possibly was not even aware that he had done so." It seems to me that what Winters and Bishop and Lyndenberg are responding to is an effect of Emerson's style, which manages to sound offhand and fortuitous even when Emerson is treating of the most serious subjects. O. W. Firkins [in his *Ralph Waldo Emerson,* 1915] had something similar in mind when he remarked that although **"Experience"** seemed to him one of the boldest essays in literature, its boldness had a rather casual air, as if a man should blow up a cathedral by way of diversion to the monotony of an evening walk.

This air of unselfconsciousness is one of the largest differences between Emerson's prose and Thoreau's. Thoreau has his paradoxes and enigmas too, but he never leaves the reader wondering who intended them, who stands behind them. Emerson's tendency from the first is to efface himself, to leave the reader no clues as to how his text is to be privately performed. If his reticence leaves room for the freedom of the reader, it also invites his distortions and mistakes. "Criticism has this defense, that, like poetry, it is the accommodation of things to the desires of the mind," he once dryly remarked, and he knew better than anyone that a strong desire of the mind was to be free of the text whose power one had been originally drawn to.

The mind does this by a curious evasive action, which gives it access to the power of a prior text without risking subjection to it. It grants the prior text its wisdom, but denies the author's intentionality. "It is remarkable . . . that we find it so hard to impute our own best sense to a dead author," Emerson observed. "The very highest praise we think of any writer, painter, sculptor, or builder is that he actually possessed the thought or feeling with which he inspired us. We hesitate at doing Spenser so great an honor as to think that he intended by his allegory the sense that we affix to it." The assertion that a text reveals a meaning its author did not consciously intend (whether of unwitting folly or oracular wisdom) is the constitutive gesture of interpretation. For it turns the text into a figure of which our explanation is the fulfillment, and hence is not the least powerful of the counterattacks we launch at the centuries who by their very existence are always conspiring "against the sanity and authority of the soul." (pp. 1-21)

> B. L. Packer, in her Emerson's Fall: A New Interpretation of the Major Essays, *Continuum, 1982, 244 p.*

Joyce W. Warren   (essay date 1984)

[*Warren is an American educator and critic. In the following excerpt, she contrasts Emerson's view of the individual man with his acceptance of his era's prevailing stereotypes regarding women.*]

Emerson's first published work, **"Nature"** (1836), established his concern with the self. He begins with an appreciation of nature, but it soon becomes apparent that his essay is not a hymn to the glories of the natural world in the tradition of the nineteenth-century nature worshippers but rather a glorification of the individual man. Emerson emphasizes that man must not make the mistake of looking at himself as only one aspect of nature. Such a view will lead him to compare himself with the grandeur of nature and consequently to regard himself as minute and insignificant. Instead, Emerson says, man should see nature as a reflection of himself: "The whole of nature is a metaphor of the human mind." Emerson's conception of man's relation to nature is vividly illustrated by a dream he recorded in his journal in 1840:

> I dreamed that I floated at will in the great Ether, and I saw this world floating also not far off, but diminished to the size of an apple. Then an angel took it in his hand and brought it to me and said, "This must thou eat." And I ate the world.

Emerson's published essays support this view of man as the center of the universe. According to him, the individual has the ability and the obligation to mold the world to his will, for man, not nature, is dominant. That Emerson means not only the extraordinary man or the poet becomes clear at the end of "Nature," where his exhortation to "build therefore your own world" is made implicitly applicable to the democratic man:

> All that Adam had, all that Caesar could, you have and can do. Adam called his house, heaven and earth; Caesar called his house Rome; you perhaps call yours, a cobbler's trade, a hundred acres of ploughed land, or a scholar's garret. Yet . . . your dominion is as great as theirs.

In his Phi Beta Kappa address the following year, Emerson refined his individualism. Although the lecture is addressed to the **"American Scholar,"** whom Emerson urges to free himself of European traditions and standards in literature, he envisions his advice being applied to the American nation as a whole. The address concludes with an exalted picture of a nation of individuals, each acting for himself and governed only by the dictates of his own nature.

Obviously, the most valuable trait for any individual is self-reliance. "Trust thyself," Emerson writes in his essay **"Self-Reliance"** (1841); "Nothing is at last sacred but the integrity of your own mind." For Emerson, self-reliance meant trusting to one's self and one's own instincts independent of tradition, conventional religion, government, circumstances of birth, or even emotional entanglements.

Despite Emerson's insistence on the grandeur of the self, this philosophy in practice necessarily involves the pettiness that is inherent in any systematic refusal to learn from others. When Emerson traveled to Europe after the death of Ellen Tucker, his first wife, and after his resignation from the pulpit, he found very little of real interest to him in the intellectual life of Europe, except for Thomas Carlyle, whose self-assertion matched his own. Paris especially disappointed him, and he wrote home to his brother William of his boredom: "A lecture at the Sorbonne is far less useful to me than a lecture I write myself. . . . Je prefère mon inkstand." He felt no interest in the political, social, and economic conditions of the countries he visited, and it was during his trip home in 1833 that he formulated the concept that he was to repeat many times: "A man contains all that is needful to his government within himself. He is made a law unto himself. . . . God is in every man." One might be tempted to say that Emerson's lack of interest in Europe was owing to his recent bereavement were it not for the fact that this insularity became the prevailing attitude throughout his life. The relationship between Emerson's philosophy and the events of his life was a close one, but before we examine that relationship, we must have a clear understanding of his philosophy.

Implicit in Emerson's ideas is the provincialism and narrowness of the self-interested person. In reacting against the restrictions of Anglo-European tradition and authority, the American individualist is limited by the interests of the self. According to Emerson, the individual need not concern himself with the institutions of society because, as representatives of the outside world, they would interfere with the development of the self. In **"Self-Reliance,"** Emerson declares that "no law can be sacred to me but that of my own nature," and he insists that the individual must not rely on external conditions of society like religion, the arts, property, or government. In the **"Divinity School Address"** (1838), Emerson says that he can accept only what is in accord with himself. Other people, other traditions, however wise, can serve only to stimulate his own thinking; they can teach him nothing.

If the institutions of society are unnecessary for the individual and an infringement upon the self, literature itself is valuable only insofar as it is useful for the individual. In the Phi Beta Kappa address (1837), Emerson tells the assembled scholars that books are not necessary for knowledge because knowledge is already in one's mind. Moreover, when we read books, we see only our own thoughts. One can read nature directly, without books. In the later essay **"Nominalist and Realist,"** Emerson writes that he reads only to find his own thoughts: "What is done well I feel as if I did; what is ill done I reck not of."

For Emerson, the individual is also the key to all history. In 1839 he wrote in his journal: "There is no history; There is only Biography. . . . You can only live for yourself. . . . The new individual must work out the whole problem of science, letters, & theology for himself [,] can owe his fathers nothing." Such a claim for the powers of the individual is obviously a narrow one. The reader thinks of the rebellious adolescent, whose search for self drives him into a don't-try-to-tell-me-anything stance. As a phase of growth, perhaps, such an attitude is necessary to the development of self-awareness and individual identity. But as a permanent philosophy and way of life, it can only be insulating and self-restricting.

When Emerson says there is no history, only biography, he means not only that every man is capable of evolving the facts and truths of the world in his own person ("Of the universal mind each individual man is one more incarnation") but also that history itself is determined by individuals. In **"Self-Reliance"** he tells us that "all history resolves itself very easily into the biography of a few stout and earnest persons," and his collection of lectures, *Representative Men* (1850), explores the specific lives of some of them. The lessons to be derived from these lectures are: one should rely on one's own instincts; one should act by asserting the will; and one should not concern oneself with tradition or the opinions and concerns of others. Swedenborg, Emerson says, represents the highest form of man— the mystic—because he is able to divine what is right without relying upon his experience in this world. It is important to recognize, however, that, although Emerson ranks the mystic as the highest form of man, he does so not because mysticism per se is valuable but because mysticism makes it easier for the individual to transcend the experience of the world. Thus the mystic need not feel the qualms that might affect ordinary men concerning the essential rightness of the inner vision. The mystic *knows* he is right.

For Emerson, the strong, self-reliant individual is the ideal man, whether he is dealing in ideas or armies, real estate or railroads. In the introductory essay to *Representative Men,* he affirms that all men have the potential to be great: "There are no common men." As he declared in a speech at Dartmouth in 1838, the value for him of great men like Plato, Milton, and Shakespeare is that they show us we can be great too. And the best measure of civilization in any country, according to his essay **"Civilization"** (1862), is the strength and self-reliance of its men.

Emerson's view of the individual leaves no room for the individual's relationship to other people. His message is that the individual should insulate himself from others as much as possible. Society, Emerson says, is crippling and diminishes the individual. In his lecture on **"Literary Ethics"** (1838), Emerson told his audience of students that if they would be great, they must be solitary. More than twenty years later, he was still advising solitude. The man of genius must remain "independent of the human race," protecting himself by self-reliance: "Each must stand on his glass tripod if he would keep his electricity".

In **"Self-Reliance"** Emerson spells out very clearly what the individual's attitude must be toward other people. He must elevate himself above the demands of the world outside himself: "Friend, client, child, sickness, fear, want, charity, all knock at once at thy closet door and say,—

'come out unto us.' " But "keep thy state; come not into their confusion". Emerson makes no exceptions for close relatives: "I shun father and mother and wife and brother when my genius calls." What if the individual should cause his friends pain? Emerson's answer is clear: "I cannot sell my liberty and my power, to save their sensibility." In the essay **"Experience"** Emerson warns that other people will drown the individual if he gives them "so much as a leg or a finger" of sympathy: "The great and crescive self, rooted in absolute nature, supplants all relative existence and ruins the kingdom of mortal friendship and love."

Emerson deals with other people in the same way that he deals with everything else that is outside the individual. Other people have no existence, no substance, except as they are absorbed into or made use of by the self. In his **"Lecture on the Times"** (1841) Emerson explicitly tells his audience that nothing is real but the self: "All men, all things . . . are phantasms and unreal beside the sanctuary of the heart." **"The Transcendentalist,"** a lecture given in the same decade, asserts that the "mind is the only reality"; other people are only "reflectors." And in a later essay, **"Culture"** (1851), Emerson gives us a clue as to the function of these unreal phantasms and reflectors in the life of the transcendental self:

> I must have children, I must have events, I must have a social state and history, or my thinking and speaking want body or basis. But to give these accessories any value, I must know them as contingent and rather showy possessions, which pass for more to the people than to me.

In all of his essays and lectures Emerson never treats other people as though they had any value in their own right. They are important, he remarks in his *Society and Solitude* lectures, only because they can provide inspiration and fire the individual to performance. All acquaintances, even friends, are principally valuable for the way in which they can serve the self. The individual can absorb and use the friend's knowledge and wisdom, making it his own. In the early essay **"Nature,"** Emerson writes that a friend should be absorbed until he becomes an "object of thought." Friends are also valuable as a reflection of the self:

> In the last analysis love is only a reflection of a man's own worthiness from other men. Men have sometimes exchanged names with their friends as if they would signify that in their friends each loved his own soul.

Although at times Emerson may warn against self-love and urge concern for others, it is only to point out the importance of other people for the self. In *Representative Men* he admonishes that "we must not contend against love" or deny the existence of other people, but the reason he offers, is that other people can be useful to us: "Other men are lenses through which we read our own minds." In his journal in 1861 he wrote: "A wise man, an open mind, is as much interested in others as in himself; they are only extensions of himself." Thus, in Emerson's philosophy, everything comes back to the self. Whatever is outside the self has no function except as it is related to the self.

How does Emerson justify this total reliance on and concern with the self? The individual, he claims, has higher goals than earthly relationships to think about. Earthly love is only a training ground for higher love. In the essay **"Nature"** Emerson explains that when the individual is able to partake of the Universal Being, all earthly relationships become unimportant: "The name of the nearest friend . . . is then a trifle and a disturbance. I am the lover of uncontained and immortal beauty." Beside the infinite, all finite objects seem unimportant. This sentiment sounds very fine, but when we think about what Emerson means by the Universal Being, we see his philosophy in a new light. For Emerson, the Universal Being is within. When the individual withdraws from society to commune with Nature, what he sees is himself. Thus, when Emerson states that the individual must devote himself to higher things and cannot be distracted by trifles, what he means, ultimately, is that those higher concerns are the self. (pp. 24-31)

Given Emerson's inflated view of the self and his consequent failure to recognize the independent existence of other people, what was his view of women, the institutionalized other? It is evident from both his public and private writings that Emerson was unable to see women as individuals like himself.

Even in his own marriages, Emerson tended to think of his wife more as an abstraction than as a real person. Ellen Tucker, to whom Emerson was married for eighteen months before she died of tuberculosis in 1831, was his "beautiful angel." As Phillips Russell points out [in his *Emerson, The Wisest American,* 1929], Emerson's writing about Ellen reveals no closeness. He apparently worshipped her "from a distance; as if she were a goddess." Although Gay Wilson Allen [in his *Waldo Emerson,* 1981] is probably right that Ellen "thawed his emotions" more than anyone else, her loss cannot be the reason for his failure to commit himself to people in later years. One wonders how fully he would have been able to give himself even to Ellen had she lived. Before he met Ellen, he complained of his inability to feel: "I have not the kind affections of a pigeon." And he described himself as "ungenerous & selfish, cautious & cold." Soon after her death, he noted that now she would know the "selfishness" that he had concealed from her in life. And in later years he reproached himself that his attitude toward her had been governed too much by "coldness & prudence." Emerson referred to Ellen as "the angel who walked with me in my younger days" and thought of her as an example of the true role of woman—an angel to be revered by man and to guide him to "honor and religion." Emerson apparently loved Ellen as much as he was capable of loving anyone, but it was the love of veneration. By making a real woman into an angel, an abstraction, Emerson was able to keep himself intact.

If Ellen was his "beautiful angel," Lidian was his "good angel." A mature woman of thirty-one when she met Emerson, with a strong personality and "inexhaustible originality", [in the words of Ralph Rusk in his *Life of Ralph Waldo Emerson,* 1949], she considered herself privileged to be married to such a great man and at first believed Emerson's own estimate of himself. (She said of his Phi Beta Kappa speech that it was "God's truth—fitly spoken.") Lydia Jackson relinquished her identity when she married Emerson, not only giving up her last name but allowing him to change her first name as well. It has been suggested that Emerson made the change because he thought that the name Lidian would sound better with the surname Emerson, but his comments at the time reveal that he simply preferred the name Lidian. I believe that Emerson changed Lydia's name because he was marrying not Lydia Jackson but himself; to rename her was a way of making her a part of himself. That he chose the particular form he did, adding an *n* sound at the end, may have been a way of changing her into Ellen, the part of himself that he had lost four years before and whose name Lidian agreed to give in full to their first daughter (Emerson commented that she "magnanimously makes my gods her gods"). Lidian later rebelled against Emerson's ideas, but he never saw her as an independent being; she existed only in relation to himself. For Emerson, Lidian personified Goodness and Christian Love, and his favorite name for her was Asia, which to him meant femininity, Christianity, and all that he regarded as intuitive and static, without will or reason. (The concept of Europe he saw as masculine, active, and creative, "a land of arts, invention, trade, freedom.")

Emerson's concept of women in general was not very different from the way in which he regarded Ellen and Lidian. Just how limited that view was is apparent in his acceptance of all the contemporary stereotypes about women. He ascribed certain fixed characteristics to women as opposed to men. Man is the Head; woman, the Heart. Man is the Intellect; woman, the Affections. The purpose of marriage, he said in an 1837 lecture, is the union of intellect and affection. Moreover, man is strong; woman is weak: "A woman's strength is not masculine but is the irresistible might of weakness." Not only does Emerson maintain that women have weak wills and are capricious and unstable, but he equates femininity with defectiveness, as is apparent in his tendency to label as "effeminate" people whom he also describes as "the halt, the blind, and the invalid." That Emerson associated femininity with invalidism is not surprising, given his own experience with women. His first wife was dying of tuberculosis throughout their short marriage, and his second wife complained of chronic ill health. Even his independent friend Margaret Fuller suffered from incapacitating headaches. Since much of the female invalidism of the nineteenth century was obviously induced by cultural restrictions and conditioning, Emerson cannot be judged too harshly for accepting what seemed to be a well-substantiated fact. However, his leap from physical weakness to weakness of character is not so easily excused.

Another aspect of Emerson's man-woman dichotomy is the contrast between reason and intellect. Men are reasoning beings; women act by instinct. A few years after his marriage to Lidian, Emerson, struck by something she had said, wrote in his journal: "I, as always, venerate the oracular nature of woman. The sentiment which the man thinks he came unto gradually through the events of years, to his surprise he finds woman dwelling there in the same, as in her native home." Almost thirty years later he still considered women to be unthinking and instinctive: "Man's conclusions are reached by toil. Woman arrives at the same by sympathy." Given Emerson's high opinion of intuitive knowledge, one might interpret this view as a compliment. However, Emerson clearly associates women's intuition not with intuitive reason but with unthinking instinct. And what it reveals most of all is Emerson's failure to see women as people. If one venerates a woman, one cannot regard or treat her as a person. Moreover, to say that a woman is intuitive can also be a way of explaining how someone whom you do not consider to be very intelligent is able to make astute observations. If we think about what it means to say that women are intuitive, unreasoning creatures, we can only conclude with Emerson that they are neither very perceptive nor very intelligent. Thus when writing about Plato in his journal in 1845, Emerson commented: "Yet to women his book is Mahometan."

If women are not very intelligent, neither are they very creative. Emerson regards man as creative; woman is passive. This view of the sexes is spelled out very graphically in the sexual language Emerson uses when he attempts to explain the difference between the great man and his imitators. A great man like Luther, Montaigne, or Pascal "utters a thought or feeling in a virile manner," Emerson entered in his journal in 1859. The great man is usually followed by "any number of spiritual eunuchs and women, who talk about that thought. . . . Each of these male words . . . delight and occupy them. . . . Great bands of female souls who only receive the spermatic *aura*." That Emerson was still thinking in these terms at the age of fifty-six after having been closely connected with some of the most creative women thinkers of his time (Margaret Fuller, Harriet Martineau), after having taken a stand in support of the women's rights movement, and after having read and praised the works of leading nineteenth-century European women writers (George Sand, Madame de Stael) indicates how deeply imbedded the stereotype was in his mind. It also shows how unwilling he was to accept ideas that did not fit into his own scheme of things.

In Emerson's view of life, the best place for women was in the home. In the 1838 lecture **"The Heart,"** Emerson quotes from Felicia Hemans's poem "To Corinna at the Capitol" to illustrate this point:

> Happy, happier far than thou,
> With the laurel on thy brow,
> She who makes the humblest hearth
> Lovely but to one on earth.

In 1841, on considering the question of women testifying at trials, Emerson commented in his journal that such action would be a "misplacement of our good Angel." She should remain in the home, "that shrine of sanctity, sentiment, and solitude." Linked to this conviction that women belong in the home is the belief that, whereas man is an explorer and adventurer, woman is the keeper of civilization. Emerson's acceptance of this traditional view of women is clear from his many references to women as the

civilizers of society, the regulators of fashion, taste, and manners. Maintaining that women are constitutionally concerned with appearances, he writes in the essay **"Manners"** (1841-1842) that their function is to fill man's "vase with wine and roses to the brim," thus making his life more civilized. He also writes in **"Manners"** that fashion and manners are unimportant to the true spirit and describes fashion as "a word of narrow and often sinister meaning." Thus, despite the pleasantness of women's role, it is an insignificant one.

It should be apparent that Emerson, like most of his contemporaries, viewed women only in relation to man. The two principal functions that woman might have were "the comforter in the home and softener of man" or the goddess who inspired man to honor, morals, and religion. For her to function in the latter way, man must observe woman "reverentially" and be guided by the "bright revelations of her best nature." In either role, woman is ministering angel for man, and Emerson liked to see her as such.

Emerson must have noticed that there were women who did not fit into the category that he had assigned them, women who manifested traits that were not "feminine." Unfortunately, when Emerson did make such observations, he did not re-examine his categories. Rather, he assumed that the fault lay in the woman. He evaluated a woman's success as a woman by how faithfully she lived up to his ideal characteristics for her. For example, from his premise that affection was "the basis of the nature of Woman," he concluded that "women are charming by their submission to it." Women who did not demonstrate the characteristics Emerson admired in women he condemned as masculine. When asked to speak at a women's convention in 1855, he concluded by telling his audience of women that they should not try to act like men but should remain feminine: "A masculine woman is never strong, but a lady is."

A woman who exhibits masculine characteristics is somehow overstepping her role, but a man who contains feminine traits is a higher form of man. Thus, in **_Representative Men_** Emerson's praise of Plato is inspired partly by Plato's ability to combine in himself both the feminine principle symbolized for Emerson by Asia and the masculine principle represented by Europe. In his journal in 1842 Emerson proposed that the "highly endowed man . . . is a Man-woman and does not so much need the complement of Woman to his being." About the same time, he wrote: "Always there is this Woman as well as this man in the mind; Affection as well as Intellect." Obviously, Emerson could not conceive of a woman becoming such a Man-woman because he did not view woman as an independent being. Although he could see himself or any great man in this self-reliant role, he could see woman only in her relation to man.

The phrase from Emerson's 1840 journal that might be quoted in support of a man-woman of either sex— "Hermaphrodite, is then the symbol of the finished soul"—must be looked at in the context of the entry in which it appears. It is taken from a conversation in which others attempted to apply this principle to women. Emerson, impatient with them, criticizes as masculine the women who took part in the discussion: "Much poor talk concerning woman which at least had the effect of revealing the true sex of several of the party who usually go disguised in the form of the other sex."

Despite Emerson's emphasis on self-reliance and insistence upon high goals, then, it is clear that his philosophy was not intended to apply to women. The Transcendental Self could only be a man. In fact, one of the arguments Emerson uses for self-reliance is that a man will be better able to take care of a woman, "for how can he protect a woman, who cannot protect himself." Emerson does not expect women to have the same high goals as men. In 1842 he wrote in his journal (he later used the passage in **"Domestic Life"**) that it was a shame that so many men had low aspirations and settled too early on trifles. Of women, however, he said that it was only "reasonable" that they should settle early on love and marriage.

Emerson recognized that there were unmarried women, or women without men, but he could not consider them to be independent beings. Even they could be seen only in relation to men, as muse or goddess: "The true Virgin will raise herself by just degrees into a goddess admirable and helpful to all beholders." At one point in his journal he commented on the problem he had encountered in talking to women about his philosophy (the lady mentioned is probably Margaret Fuller, whom he had quoted two pages earlier in the journal):

> In conversing with a lady it sometimes seems a bitterness and unnecessary to insist as I decline to do, on this self-sufficiency of man. . . . We talk of courses of action. But to women my paths are shut up and the fine women I think of who have had genius and cultivation who have not been wives but muses have something tragic in their lot.

If women must be wives or muses, what then was Mary Moody Emerson, the paternal aunt with whom Emerson had corresponded since childhood and who exerted a powerful influence on his development? No one's wife, Aunt Mary was a strong-willed, independent woman upon whom Emerson's mother called from time to time to help out with her "fatherless children." She apparently was fond of her nephews and ambitious for them. However, when she disapproved of someone, she made no bones about it; Emerson and most of her relatives were afraid of her sharp tongue and caustic wit. Emerson's daughter Ellen tells of how Emerson and his mother "trembled" and marveled when Lidian answered her back. Aunt Mary obviously was no goddess, but she was Emerson's earliest muse. He called her a "sibyl" and tested out his ideas in his letters to her. Despite her irascible nature, Emerson was able to smile at her outrageous behavior. He also asserted his independence from her, both in his life and in his religion. But he respected her originality and called her a "genius" from whom any intelligent young man could learn. "By society with her," he said, "one's mind is electrified and purged." Her principal importance for Emerson was the effect that she had on him. And it was her writings that he valued, he told his brother William after her death, not her presence. Thus he was able to encompass even the formidable Mary Moody Emerson in his

philosophy by reducing her to an abstraction that was valuable only as it served the needs of the self.

How did Emerson reconcile his attitude toward women with his support of the women's rights movement? Apparently he felt able to support the call for the vote and to concede political and civil wrongs, but he could not bring himself to advocate rights that would take woman out of the home or give her autonomy as a human being. His comments reveal a fundamental inability to see woman except in her relation to man. In 1850 he wrote to Paulina W. Davis, who had asked him to take part in a convention: "I should not wish women to wish political functions, nor, if granted, assume them." Indicating that a woman is to be judged by how faithfully she lives up to man's concept of her, he continued: "I imagine that a woman whom all men would feel to be the best would decline such privileges if offered, and feel them to be rather obstacles to her legitimate influence." A woman's "legitimate influence," apparently, was the use of her feminine qualities to obtain what she wanted. Writing in his journal in 1851, he observed apropos of a women's rights convention held in Worcester that the real solution would be for all women to be healthy and beautiful. Then they would have no need to fight for their rights because all men would do their bidding. "A sound and beautiful woman," a Venus, he said, magnetizes men.

All of Emerson's ideas on women are contained in his speech to the women's rights convention in Boston in 1855. Describing women in conventional terms as unthinking, sentimental, weak, and uncreative, he told the assembled women who had come to hear the great man's wisdom that woman is the sail and the man the rudder; if women try to steer, there will be trouble. "The life of the affections is primary to woman," he admonished; she is the "Angel in the parlor," whose function is to "embellish trifles." There was no reason why women should not vote, Emerson declared, and he listed the objections that had been made: women are ignorant of affairs; they are impractical, too emotional, too idealistic. Without denying any of these stereotypes, he acknowledged only that they should not prevent women from voting. Many men are ignorant and emotional, he realized, expressing a hope that the idealism of women would counterbalance the "brutal ignorance and mere animal wants" of the "intemperate" immigrant vote.

Emerson's condescending attitude throughout the speech attempts to make womanhood appear so beautiful that no woman would be brave enough to deny it. But the implication of his words is that women *are* inferior and should trust in man's better judgment and superior knowledge to help them. Voting is a harmless exercise; votes from many different types of people cancel themselves out anyway. If woman really wants something done, her best resource, and the one best suited to her temperament and abilities, is to rely on a good man: "Woman should find in man her guardian." Emerson concluded by assuring his audience that "whatever the woman's heart is prompted to desire, the man's mind is simultaneously prompted to accomplish.

Here, then, is the "legitimate influence" of woman; she

must rely upon the good will of men and remain dependent upon them. There is no evidence that Emerson's opinion of women's rights ever changed. A speech on women written after the Civil War but apparently never delivered repeats the same arguments: women are the civilizers; they represent love and religion; and they might as well have the vote because they could not make worse choices than many men. In May 1869, in a speech before the New England Women's Suffrage Association, Emerson concluded his very general remarks with a declaration that the rights of women should not be denied. Later in the same year he sent a letter to the Essex County Women's Suffrage Association, indicating that, although he sympathized with the efforts of women, he could not really conceive of what true equality would mean.

Throughout his life, Emerson maintained the same view of women. If man is the center of the universe, woman, in her traditional role of other, is one of the feeders and reflectors of man. Man is the sun; woman the moon. Man is the subject; woman the object. (pp. 43-53)

> Joyce W. Warren, "Transcendentalism and the Self: Ralph Waldo Emerson," in her The American Narcissus: Individualism and Women in Nineteenth-Century American Fiction, *Rutgers University Press, 1984, pp. 23-53.*

Richard Bridgman　(essay date 1986)

[*Bridgman is an American educator and critic. In the following essay, he discusses* English Traits *as a reflection of Emerson's ambivalence toward both English and American society and culture.*]

Ralph Waldo Emerson found it difficult to end his 1856 work **English Traits.** The very caution of the book's title is telling. It promises not "the English character" or "the English" but only some of their "traits." Emerson's irresolution here is a mark of the subtlety of his mind, for although his role as a public spokesman seemed to oblige him to make choices, his mind rejected simple formulations. He respected much in England yet thought he perceived its limitations. He wanted to believe that America would succeed England in moral leadership, but he was all too aware of his nation's immaturity. "Great country, diminutive minds," he stated bluntly in his journal. Such opinions produced ambivalence, which in turn impeded completion of the book.

Emerson's dilemma forced him to resort to some extreme strategies. They involve what Howard Mumford Jones [in his introduction to the 1966 Belknap Press edition of **English Traits**] called "faults of construction," and they often are that, although their presence signals deeper issues that help us better understand what it meant for a citizen of an undeveloped country to visit the heart of the paternal empire.

At first glance, for example, the book would seem to open oddly, not with "Voyage to England," which is the second chapter, but rather with "First Visit to England," which describes an earlier transatlantic trip Emerson made in

A sketch of Emerson by Swedish artist Fredrika Bremer.

1832–33. Essentially, the chapter is a redaction of notes Emerson made on interviews he had had with four of Britain's chief writers: Landor, Coleridge, Carlyle, and Wordsworth. Jones found this introductory chapter "difficult to justify," and Philip Nicoloff [in his *Emerson on Race and History,* 1961] thought that it "detracted from the coherence of the book."

However curious one might think their preferential location in the book, the interviews at once establish an important impression: that the imaginative leaders of the English-speaking world no longer have anything of substance to offer an American. Emerson's meetings had been entertaining but in various ways distressing too. Landor, whom he met in Italy, was vigorously opinionated, an amusing conversationalist, with "a wonderful brain, despotic, violent and inexhaustible," but, as Emerson says, he carried "to its height the love of freak which the English delight to indulge." Coleridge, whom he next describes, proved to be egocentric and quite as opinionated as Landor, so that while a stimulating flood of strong statements emerged from him, at bottom "the visit was rather a spectacle than a conversation. . . . He was old and preoccupied, and could not bend to a new companion and think with him."

Having described visits to an expatriate and a suburbanite, Emerson next introduced the acid Scotsman, Thomas Carlyle. Again Emerson remembered having been bombarded with a series of emphatic opinions, but one can sense his reservations, even when they are not directly enunciated. "Plato [Carlyle] does not read, and he disparaged Socrates." In addition, "He took despairing or satirical views of literature at this moment." Finally, to Rydal Mount to listen to the forcefully reactionary Wordsworth, who said of Carlyle—the one member of Emerson's generation and, after their meeting, his personal friend—that he thought him "sometimes insane" and who found Goethe's *Wilhelm Meister* "like the crossing of flies in the air." Emerson found himself "surprised by the hard limits of [Wordsworth's] thought" and concluded that "off his own beat, his opinions were of no value."

The experience of these interviews had been sufficiently disillusioning at the time for Emerson to have declared in his journal, "I shall judge more justly, less timidly, of wise men forevermore. . . . they never *fill the ear*—fill the mind—." Nonetheless, this revelation had been far from liberating. Emerson returned to America in 1833 with as much ambivalence as Margaret Fuller would later. He was thinking of drowning as not unattractive. "I am glad to be on my way home yet not so glad as others & my way to the bottom I could find perchance with less regret for I think it would not hurt me[,] that is, the ducking or drowning."

As the first chapter of *English Traits* wryly establishes, a good part of Emerson's vague malaise was that the inadequacy of his culture's intellectual and imaginative leaders forced him to depend upon himself when he did not yet feel ready. "I . . . wish I knew where & how I ought to live," he told his journal ruefully. He had already rejected the guidance of the New England ecclesiastical tradition, and now his British mentors had proved to have nothing to offer him at a crucial juncture in his life. In *English Traits* Emerson was constructing his account of that crisis twenty years after the fact, although, with the same deceptive impression of casualness that Whitman displayed in compiling *Specimen Days,* he insists that he is just copying out a few notes left over from the times of his interviews. Still, we should not overlook the fact that one other person is described in this chapter, and he, the American sculptor Horatio Greenough, is deliberately treated first.

Emerson underlines the fact that Greenough was "a votary of the Greeks," who believed—unlike the vain, eccentric Britons Emerson encountered—that "art would never prosper until we left our shy jealous ways and worked in society as they." In addition, Emerson quotes from a letter Greenough had written him some time later. In it, the sculptor offered his

> theory of structure: A scientific arrangement of spaces and forms to functions and to site; an emphasis of features proportioned to their *gradated* importance in function; color and ornament to be decided and arranged and varied by strictly organic laws, having a distinct reason for each decision; the entire and immediate banishment of all make-shift and make-believe.

While no such overt assertion is made, clearly Greenough, with his conviction of the superiority of Greek social responsibility and with his commitment to the functional

and organic, is intended to stand for an American aesthetic, genuinely useful and indigenous, unlike the opinionated growls and trumpetings of the British masters who were to follow him in the chapter. Far from a formal indulgence, this prologue diplomatically gives Emerson's predecessors their due but emphatically indicates that they are no longer of active use to him.

One point should be made in connection with Emerson's analysis of the usefulness of the British tradition. It is highly selective. Save for Carlyle, Emerson remains silent about his own generation. Late in the book, he finesses the omission by simply listing the writers he met during his trip. His list is enigmatic, for no meaning is evident in the relationships produced by contiguity. "I saw," writes Emerson, "Rogers, Hallam, Macaulay, Milnes, Milman, Barry Cornwall, Dickens, Thackeray, Tennyson, Leigh Hunt, D'Israeli, Helps, Wilkinson, Bailey, Kenyon and Forster; the younger poets, Clough, Arnold and Patmore". The names precede an enumeration of "the men of science," implicitly establishing Emerson's priorities, but no other point is made by the list.

In the chapter "Literature," Emerson does make a series of brief and rather dismissive remarks about Dickens, Bulwer, Thackeray, and Macaulay. Dickens "writes London tracts," he notes. "He is a painter of English details, like Hogarth; local and temporary in his tints and style, and local in his aims." Thackeray "finds that God has made no allowance for the poor thing in his universe,—more's the pity, he thinks,—but 't is not for us to be wiser; we must renounce ideals, and accept London." As for Macaulay, "brilliant" as he is, at heart he is committed to the goodness of "material commodity."

All these deceptively casual, languidly discreet remarks finally contribute to Emerson's critique of the English and are in contrast to his own notions of where superiority is to be found. The British are devoted to the immediate, the practical. That is their strength but also their limitation. As Emerson says elsewhere in *English Traits,* "They are impatient of genius, or of minds addicted to contemplation. . . . They have a supreme eye to facts, and theirs is a logic that brings salt to soup, hammer to nail, oar to boat; the logic of cooks, carpenters, and chemists." Although the English are unusually effective in utilitarian undertakings, in higher matters, then, "they are hard of hearing and dim of sight."

If dismissing the English were all that was involved, though, *English Traits* would not have proved to be such a problematic book for Emerson to compose. On 17 December 1852, he wrote his brother William, "my English notes have now assumed the size of a pretty book, which I am eager to complete." At that point, Emerson had already been back in the United States for over four years, yet it was not until 23 June 1856 that he could inform his brother with relief that "My book is ended, at last, a week ago." The problem had not been one of phrasing his observations about the English; rather, the ultimate significance of those observations fretted him. Emerson saw plainly enough the limitations of "our old home," but he could not easily argue that those who had broken away to America were the heirs and refiners of its estate. One can feel his ambivalence in a journal entry of 1847, written not long before the trip to England that produced *English Traits.* He wrote, "The air of America seems to be loaded with imbecility, irresolution, dispersion." Then, revising that thought, he pulled back further by turning the qualified impression into a question: "Is the air of America loaded with imbecility, irresolution, dispersion?" A few pages later, he addressed the idea yet again, this time, however, having regained confidence in his condemnation. "Alas for America as I must so often say, the ungirt, the diffuse, the profuse, procumbent, one wide ground juniper, out of which no cedar, no oak will rear up a mast to the clouds! it all runs to leaves, to suckers, to tendrils, to miscellany. The air is loaded with poppy, with imbecility, with dispersion, & sloth."

Given such feelings, Emerson could not, as many of his patriotic countrymen were doing, indulge in unequivocal prophecies of coming national superiority. At one point, as he neared the end of writing *English Traits* and struggled to draw conclusions from his ideas, he entertained the notion of fashioning a hybrid as a model so that he need not be the partisan of either England or America. "I pick up some materials as I go for my chapter of the Anglo American, if I should wish to finish that." Such a synthesis never reached the book. Emerson was finally obliged to locate his position by means of hints, ironies, and paradoxes.

The central part of *English Traits* explores the nation in a series of chapters that are very like Emersonian essays; that is, each takes up the same subject but from a different angle, then turns it round, emitting flashes of insight in various aphoristic and, one must say, amused observations. The Norse, who constitute for Emerson one of the three races that formed the English, "have a singular turn for homicide; their chief end of man is to murder or to be murdered; oars, scythes, harpoons, crowbars, peatknives, and hayforks are tools valued by them all the more for their charming aptitude for assassinations." On the determining nature of climate, he writes, "No fruit ripens in England but a baked apple." Like many others in the book, this bon mot happens not to be original with Emerson, but by salting the text liberally with them, he sustains a fairly steady tone of good humor which serves to mitigate his pervasive skepticism, as when he remarks that when the Normans arrived in England, "Twenty thousand thieves landed at Hastings." But the wit also sustains a sense of superiority, of a detached observer watching some highly dubious behavior. "The logical English train a scholar as they train an engineer. Oxford is a Greek factory, as Wilton mills weave a carpet and Sheffield grinds steel." "The Anglican church is marked by the grace and good sense of its forms, by the manly grace of its clergy. The gospel it preaches is 'By taste are ye saved.'" The clergy, concerned for their material welfare, obediently do the government's bidding. "Thus a Bishop is only a surpliced merchant"; invariably "the dictates of the Holy Ghost agree with the recommendations of the Queen." Emerson admired English pragmatism, lack of cant, energy, and directness, but he also felt something was missing from what they represented. The question for him in this book was how to express his reservations while at the same time proposing a suitable alternative.

If humor was one means of offering a negative perspective, offsetting criticism with praise was another. Tennyson, therefore, "wants a subject, and climbs no mount of vision to bring its secrets to the people" (in short, for Emerson he was an Englishman). But "there is no finer ear . . . and we must be thankful for every beautiful talent." Or, after enumerating the impressive size of a series of country estates—"The Duke of Richmond has 40,000 acres at Goodwood and 300,000 at Gordon Castle"—Emerson's account begins to display thorns: "The possessions of the Earl of Lonsdale gave him eight seats in Parliament." Then: "These large domains are growing larger. The great estates are absorbing the small freeholds." Finally, although not explicitly articulated, comes Emerson's vision of the true costs and depredations of the industrial world: "All over England, scattered at short intervals among ship-yards, mills, mines, and forges, are the paradises of the nobles, where the livelong repose and refinement are heightened by the contrast with the roar of industry and necessity."

Although the English exhibit certain admirable qualities of energy, endurance, loyalty, and independence, they lack the higher vision. Like Carlyle, too many of them do not read Plato. Emerson establishes a contrast between Bacon, a climber "on the staircase of unity," and Locke, condemned as one who sees only discrepancies. Locke represents "the influx of decomposition and of prose." Such pragmatic limitations made Emerson feel that England, even at its height as an empire and as the exemplar of industrial technology, could not provide leadership for the future. But his fundamental tact, combined with a genuine uncertainty about where such inspiration might be found, made it especially hard for him to conclude *English Traits.* His ambivalence emerges in the diverse formal gestures of the last five chapters of the book, chapters that no one has found satisfactory, least of all Emerson himself, who complained that they were "weary" and "refractory." Philip Nicoloff called them "a careless miscellany" made up of "a confusion of materials." The confusion is created not by Emerson's lack of control over his materials but by his contradictory feelings. He saw English insufficiency as clearly as he felt the need for an American succession. But the limitations of his countrymen made him skeptical that they could assume power. Yet he found it difficult to accept a rudderless Anglo-American culture. All these conflicting and unresolved sentiments are present in the final chapters of *English Traits.*

Emerson's examination of the English character culminates with its literature, which he finds wanting. "I seem," he says, "to walk on a marble floor, where nothing will grow." The future of poetry might prove to be immense, but unless the English could manage "that expansiveness which is the essence of the poetic element," unless they could yield to "Oriental largeness"—and everything in Emerson's account of the English character said they could not—then direction must come from elsewhere. To be sure, Emerson never states his reservations directly, and in fact he opens the last paragraph of "Literature" by saying "I know that a retrieving power lies in the English race." Still, by failing to tie that belief to any worthy candidate, Emerson in effect nullifies his optimism.

In that context, the succeeding chapter, "The Times," takes on additional symbolic force. The contrast between literature and the newspaper is not the only consideration; the limitations of England's expanding power are also addressed. "The Thunderer" had established itself as the journal of authority—"No power in England is more felt, more feared, or more obeyed"—yet the very influence of the *Times* signifies failure to Emerson. Its circulation daily increased. It drove its rivals out of business with its technological improvements. It appeared to have the world on its knees before it. Still, it was no more than the organ of privilege. "It gives the argument, not of the majority, but of the commanding class." Subservient like the venal Church, the paper is, for Emerson, "a living index of the colossal British power." It dares not speak for "the central heart of humanity" nor become "the natural leader of British reform." Concluding the chapter in the subjunctive mode, Emerson at first appears to celebrate possibilities but in truth condemns the ramifications of the newspaper's crass ascendancy. "Would" the *Times* but assume the role of moral leadership, then would it find genius "its cordial and invincible ally" and "give to England a new millennium of beneficent power." So the chapter ends in what is at bottom a severe condemnation but one diplomatically wrapped in references to a possible world, however unrealizable, at least on that side of the Atlantic.

The placement of the next chapter, "Stonehenge," conjures up the expectation that the quotidian trivialities of journalism—that Princess Adelaide had the whooping cough—will be juxtaposed against the eternal verities of the mysterious Druidic assemblage. Interestingly enough, that is not how Emerson employs what he calls "the oldest religious monument in Britain."

Emerson visited Stonehenge with Carlyle. Together the two men formed a coalition dissatisfied with the English state. Carlyle, however, reproved Americans for dodging England because "they dislike the coldness and exclusiveness of the English" and prefer the receptivity of the French. Although Carlyle felt the English had gone dead, he still believed that Americans had much to learn from them. Americans should "manfully" stay in London, "confronting Englishmen and acquiring their culture." Emerson's response was conciliatory, but he nonetheless persisted in believing that America was now "the seat and centre of the British race." "England, an old and exhausted island, must one day be contented, like other parents, to be strong only in her children." Carlyle's reaction to Emerson's views is only hinted at in "Stonehenge": "But this was a proposition which no Englishman of whatever condition can easily entertain." In his notebook, though, Emerson wrote that Carlyle "reprimanded with severity the rebellious instincts of the native of a vast continent which made light of the British islands."

This confrontation between Emerson and Carlyle, unreported in *English Traits,* shapes the account of their visit to Stonehenge. Emerson's description emphasizes the physical simplicity of the monument. At a distance, it "looked like a group of brown dwarfs in the wide expanse," a comparison by no means derived from a sense of awe. Close up, Emerson's response remained amiable but unexcited. "It was pleasant to see that just this simplest of all simple structures—two upright stones and a lintel laid across,—had long outstood all later churches and all history." He was especially struck by the buttercups and nettles growing within the confines of the monument, and in the field surrounding it were "wild thyme, daisy, meadowsweet, goldenrod, thistle and the carpeting grass." Overhead, larks were singing. Simplicity and natural life dominated—not just daisies but thistles and nettles.

Emerson quite deliberately resists the "mysteries" of Stonehenge. After outlining theories of the stones' significance, he acknowledges that he prefers one that identifies the Druids as Phoenicians, for whom Stonehenge was "a compass-box." Concerning how the stones were placed, Emerson is pragmatically dismissive: "the like is done in all cities, every day, with no other aid than horse-power." With no further comment, the travelers leave. The balance of the chapter on Stonehenge is in fact about other visits: to Wilton Hall, where the two men observe paintings and statuary; to Salisbury and its cathedral, which disappointed Emerson; and to Winchester, whose cathedral, Emerson says, "gratified" him, "at least by the ample dimensions." He had complained that his view of the interior of Salisbury cathedral had been obstructed by the organ. "I know not why in real architecture the hunger of the eye for length of line is so rarely gratified." The general impression one derives from this chapter is that although Emerson visited several of England's major religious sites, he remained unmoved, even disappointed, and yearned for something more natural and capacious.

This assumption is verified in the account of a stopover at the home of Sir Arthur Helps. Earlier, when Emerson had declared that henceforth the center of the British race would be in America, he had had in mind "the prodigious natural advantages of that country." Now, on a rainy Sunday, Emerson was asked "whether there were any Americans?—any with an American idea,—any theory of the right future of that country?" Given the opening, Emerson, having "anticipated the objections and the fun," launched an argument. He developed it, he says, by thinking "only of the simplest and purest minds." He realized that such minds were "fanatics of a dream" who might be regarded by the present company as "ridiculous" but who nonetheless were "the only true." The nature of their utopian vision is barely enunciated by Emerson, although he does locate its core in "the law of love and justice," which he translates as "the dogma of no-government and non-resistance." Nonetheless, he admits good-naturedly that such views, lacking the practicality of mutton-chops and spinach, would strike the English as "manifest absurdity."

"Stonehenge," then, is a peculiar chapter, a mixture of the vague and the trivial, which in the end once more embodies Emerson's reservations about the range of the English character and the inertness, if not deadness, of its spiritual life. Although the rural naturalness and primitive associations of the Druidic monument did have their attractions—certainly greater attractions than the cathedrals at Salisbury and Winchester—Emerson resolutely refuses to lapse into romantic nostalgia. But if both nostalgia and pragmatic materialism are to be repudiated in the book, where is Emerson to locate his hopes?

The answer would seem obvious enough, but it proved not to be. Emerson had identified America as the present "seat and centre of the British race"; he had also specified earlier that "the American is only the continuation of the English genius into new conditions, more or less propitious." All of Emerson's reservations are contained, though, in that qualifying phrase, "more or less." He would have preferred to believe that America was still the new Jerusalem, but he knew the country too well and had too long struggled with its vaunting materialism, with its ferocious competitiveness, with its sectional divisions, and with its callous treatment of the Indian and the black to sustain that faith. Assured that Great Britain had fulfilled the limits of its destiny, he would have found it convenient to suppose, as many did, that the torch had been passed across the Atlantic. But when he reflected on the actualities, he was obliged to conclude, "The American system is more democratic, more humane; yet the American people do not yield better or more able men, or more inventions or books or benefits than the English."

This rueful perception is why, I think, Emerson had such problems bringing *English Traits* to a close. In his desperation in 1856, he avowed to his brother his intention of ending the book with "a basket of remainders." So he keeps throwing out compliments, then criticisms of his hosts. England is "the best of actual nations," but it is a "poor best." On the other hand, if it is a nation of "poor tortoises" with "no wings sprouting at their shoulders," still something "divine warms at their heart, and waits a happier hour." If this antithetical listing of strengths and limitations becomes obsessive, we can see the reason. Emerson could not resolve the oppositions. He could not arrive at a believable synthesis in his own mind, and so, quite unable to bring the book to a firm conclusion, he continued to elaborate the terms of his dilemma.

That dilemma will account for the peculiarities of the final chapter, which Howard Mumford Jones thought an "anticlimax" and which Philip Nicoloff regarded as "an expedient." Entitled "Speech at Manchester," it is precisely that. Emerson says that he has recently been looking over a newspaper account of some remarks that he had made at the Manchester Athenæum shortly after arriving on his second visit to England. He was inclined to reprint them, he says, because they express his feelings when he entered England, and because they agree "well enough with the more deliberate results of better acquaintance recorded in the foregoing pages." The exquisite backing and filling of that explanation is revelatory. The strategy resembles that he had used to complete the equally problematic *Nature.* There, he ascribed its most fervent sentences not to himself but to an unidentified "Orphic poet." Although this figure is sometimes argued to be Bronson Alcott, it is more illuminating to understand the Orphic poet as that portion of Emerson in which he could not have full confidence, to which he could subscribe only in part. In *English Traits* he could not ascribe his conclusions to an Orphic poet, but he could use the words a former self delivered at another time. Although he has changed, these sentiments will ac-

cord "well enough." Emerson will not take full responsibility for them now, even though they approximate his position. The last three paragraphs of *English Traits* are thus in quotation marks. A different, public voice speaks, one more formal and celebratory than that of the pungent commentator of the book proper.

Emerson had been well aware of the ambiguities of the occasion at the Manchester Athenæum. He begins with compliments to the intellectual influence of British minds—an influence communicated through such diverse resources as the Free-Trade League, *Punch,* Sir Archibald Alison's *History of Europe,* and *Dombey and Son.* Having offered ceremonial praise, he then remarks, "I am not here to exchange civilities with you"; rather, he says that the lure of England is "its commanding sense of right and wrong." That rectitude drew him to England. From where? Emerson's ironic self-characterization has an underlying sting to it. He was no more than "a solitary American in the woods." It was true that he had come to visit England in a "time of gloom and commercial disaster, of affliction and beggary." Still, he was confident the English would rise to the occasion, for they were never better than when under trial. "In adversity they were grand."

The rhetoric in which Emerson's impressions were being expressed now becomes even more problematically tangled with a litany of references to senescence. "And so, gentlemen, I feel in regard to this aged England, with the possessions, honors and trophies, and also with the infirmities of a thousand years gathering around her, irretrievably committed as she now is to many old customs which cannot be suddenly changed; pressed upon by the transitions of trade and new and all incalculable modes, fabrics, arts, machines and competing populations." What is England? It is "aged," it suffers "infirmities," it is locked into the conservatism of tradition. Then, lest this description seem too harsh, the speech takes yet another turn. "I see her in her old age, not decrepit, but young," Emerson proclaims. "Seeing this, I say, All hail! mother of nations, mother of heroes." Emerson rose to the public occasion. England was "truly a home to the thoughtful and generous who are born in the soil. So be it! So let it be!" A patriotic audience could wish no greater tribute than appears in those hortatory remarks.

But there is one sentence more. It is an extraordinary one, and it concludes the speech (or that portion Emerson chose to quote here); it also concludes the book. "If it be not so, if the courage of England goes with the chances of a commercial crisis, I will go back to the capes of Massachusetts and my own Indian stream, and say to my countrymen, the old race are all gone, and the elasticity and hope of mankind must henceforth remain on the Alleghany ranges, or nowhere."

"If it be not so . . . " There is a conditional affirmation of Emerson's fundamental skepticism about England's position of leadership, a skepticism enunciated at the height of her industrial and imperial power. But if not here, then where? Again, the image Emerson offers is the faintly ironic one of what the English and Europeans think of America—a place of capes, Indian streams, and mountains. It was to that primitive materiality that Emerson was to return. The future then was in America, or so one would think, were this a conventional critique. That, after all, was what Emerson has apparently been saying periodically throughout the book. America was the new center of power, or it would be. But we have also noted Emerson's repeated reservations. The conditions in America were "more or less propitious." America was "that great sloven continent," where nature lay sleeping. If England were not the solution, then America was, or might be. Or might not. In his notebook of 1852-53, Emerson recalled that many young Englishmen "look wishfully to America: I never dare say to them, Go; though I might go in their position. I observe that the idea of owning woodlands, ¢. is very attractive to the English imagination. Yet our young men find it all but impossible to live in the great continent."

That private comment helps to clarify the meaning of the closing phrase of *English Traits:* the "hope of mankind must henceforth remain on the Alleghany ranges, or nowhere." Under ordinary rhetorical conditions, the phrase "or nowhere" would merely serve to emphasize that the *only* place for mankind's hope was on the American continent. But embedded even more deeply in this conclusion was Emerson's never fully suppressed doubt about the true potentialities of mankind. It might well be that there was no place in the United States or anywhere else on this earth for those dedicated to the idealism for which he spoke. England's limitations might finally prove to be the world's. (pp. 469-85)

Richard Bridgman, "From Greenough to 'Nowhere': Emerson's 'English Traits'," in The New England Quarterly, *Vol. LIX, No. 4, December, 1986, pp. 469-85.*

Robert E. Burkholder   (essay date 1988)

[*In the following excerpt, Burkholder assesses the political implications of Emerson's "American Scholar" address, disputing Oliver Wendell Holmes's characterization of it as "our intellectual Declaration of Independence."*]

Oliver Wendell Holmes called Emerson's 1837 Phi Beta Kappa oration "our intellectual Declaration of Independence," and his characterization has become, since its first published appearance in his 1884 biography of Emerson, a sort of objective correlative for the oration itself, used by every biographer, anthologist, critic and theorist (new, or otherwise) as a way, somehow, to imply the meaning and importance of **"The American Scholar."** But what does the phrase mean? It is not unreasonable to say that "our intellectual Declaration of Independence" as a descriptor of Emerson's speech has now attained the status of a critical euphemism, a phrase that has been overused to the point of meaninglessness and useful only for the matching sections of exams in undergraduate survey courses.

The truth is that the characterization by Holmes of **"The American Scholar,"** much like the oration itself, has come to occupy a kind of acontextual limboland where meaning is compromised if not lost altogether. What Holmes said to qualify his characterization was this: "Nothing like it had been heard in the halls of Harvard since Samuel Adams supported the affirmative of the question, 'Whether it be lawful to trust the chief magistrate, if the commonwealth cannot otherwise be preserved.' " His allusion is to the 1743 Harvard commencement at which Adams, who received his master's degree at the ceremony, defended the seditious proposition that Holmes mentions in front of an aristocratic audience that, at the very least, were loyal subjects of the English king and may, in fact, have included the royal governor and his Council. Holmes' implicit contention, then, is that Emerson's Phi Beta Kappa oration was the same sort of revolutionary attack on the repressive status quo as that of Samuel Adams nearly a century before with a somewhat equivalent effect on the blue-bloods in attendance. That this is Holmes' intent is even more evident when he continues his explanation of the revolutionary character of **"The American Scholar"** by citing how upset the "grave professors and sedate clergymen" were over Emerson's breaches of the "formality of an Academic assembly," specifically what Holmes refers to as his "realism" and "domestic illustrations." Thus, to Holmes' thinking, **"The American Scholar"** is "our intellectual Declaration of Independence" principally because a few stuffed shirts were offended that Emerson would use a phrase—and this is Holmes' example, not mine—like "the meal in the firkin; the milk in the pan" to demean "so stately an occasion." For this reason, and this reason only, Holmes concludes, "No listener ever forgot that Address, and among all the noble utterances of the speaker it may be questioned if one ever contained more truth in language more like that of immediate inspiration."

Holmes' account is clearly both fanciful and melodramatic. It is the finest bit of historical fiction that one can find in all of the venerable history of Emerson studies, and it is singular in its resilience. For all the new approaches to Emerson over the past one hundred and fifty years and the alarming array of Emersons that those approaches have given us, we can still be sure of one unassailable fact: Emerson wrote "our intellectual Declaration of Independence."

Besides what common sense tells us about Holmes' outrageous characterization, how do we know he was wrong? In the first place, his description of the formality of the occasion is heightened in order to create a more fitting arena for Emerson's alleged radical assault. This, for instance, is an account by Harvard President Josiah Quincy's daughter, Maria, of the eagerness with which women sought out seats for the 1829 Phi Beta Kappa exercises:

> The moment the bolt was pushed, . . . we all rushed in. There was more strife than yesterday, but pale and trembling, we all found ourselves in our accustomed pew. It was really surprising to see the ladies leap over the tops of the pews. A number of female forms were seen rushing through our pew, and leaping over the highest side of it to those adjoining. They were headed by Mrs. Abbott Lawrence, who certainly deserved to have a degree given her for her powers of jumping.

The high jumps of Mrs. Lawrence and company seem hardly the sort of prelude one would expect to the stately academic assembly Holmes describes. Yet we can be reasonably certain that with the increasing popularity of such commencement exercises during this period, the audience for Emerson's oration was not composed exclusively of "grave professors and sedate clergymen." Presumably it contained its share of athletic females interested in the most strategic seats from which to size-up the graduates, and of others who were simply interested in the social and celebratory aspects of the occasion. We might imagine that after a speech as weighty as Emerson's, those assembled would break up into small discussion groups to consider its implications, but the truth is that the partying started almost immediately afterward.

At that celebratory dinner following Emerson's address, Charles H. Warren gave the following toast: "Mr President, I suppose all know where the orator comes from; and I suppose all know what he has said. I give you *The Spirit of Concord. It makes us all of One Mind,*" a sentiment that Emerson later said gave "the happiest turn to my old thrum." Warren's toast and Emerson's willing acceptance of its sentiment suggest another reason why Holmes' characterization of **"The American Scholar"** is unacceptable. Despite the best efforts of biographers from Holmes to Gay Wilson Allen, there is little reason to suspect that Emerson's speech was received with trepidation as an assault on the established order. Of course, it was used as a political tool by members of the New School, Cranch in the *Western Messenger* and W. H. Channing in the *Boston Quarterly Review,* to bludgeon the retrograde conservatives with evidence of growing reform-mindedness, but these are instances of Emerson's cohorts politicizing his message into very small caliber ammunition for use in the ongoing Unitarian war. One suspects that the majority of those who heard Emerson's speech reacted in much the same way as John Pierce, whom Robert E. Spiller faults for never missing one of these occasions and never understanding one either. Of **"The American Scholar"** Pierce says that "It was to me in the misty, dreamy, unintelligible style of Swedenborg, Coleridge, and Carlyle. [Emerson] professed to have method; but I could not trace it, except in his own annunciation. It was well spoken, and all seemed to attend, but how many were in my own predicament of making little of it I have no means of ascertaining." I suspect that a good many were in Pierce's predicament. In fact, it was the "misty, dreamy, unintelligible style" of **"The American Scholar"** that most upset the Jacksonian democrats at the radical weekly, the *Boston Investigator.* Significantly, they were the only group to criticize the speech publicly for its political implications, but Abner Kneeland, the leader of the Boston democrats, did not find it politically volatile. Instead, he found that its very inaccessibility tended to reinforce the status quo: "it is altogether too bombastical, metaphysical, caballistical, allegorical, rhetorical, figurative—yea, too full of every thing but plain common sense, to be useful to the common reader." So to at least one faction of Boston's political radicals, **"The American Scholar"** was simply more of the same Unitarian Whiggery, a call for reform that was empty because it was veiled in what another writer for the *Investigator* referred to in a review of another of Emerson's lectures as "the cloak of designing priests."

Yet another reason to suspect Holmes' characterization of Emerson's oration is his implicit statement that politics was somehow inappropriate to such a formal, academic occasion; that Emerson's speech, like Adams' in 1743, was unusual in its political character. Such an assumption is most handy when attempting to create a mythos of American radicalism with Emerson as a central figure, but nothing in fact could be further from the truth. As Marta Wagner demonstrates in her recent study of the first half-century of Phi Beta Kappa orations, "Phi Beta Kappa orators did take partisan stands on controversial issues." The case Wagner uses to establish her point is to a certain extent representative. In 1800, Abraham Bishop, a Yale graduate with strong Jeffersonian ties, was asked to draft an oration for the Connecticut Phi Beta Kappa's anniversary celebration. However, because his politics were suspect, the society required that he submit his speech for preliminary review. Three days before the scheduled ceremony, a clandestine meeting of the Connecticut chapter was held, apparently attended and dominated by a number of conservative members. This group rejected Bishop's speech and reprimanded him for "involving the members in that political turmoil which disgraces our country." The ceremony was, therefore, conducted without an oration. In her treatment of a variety of Phi Beta Kappa speeches, delivered from their inception at Harvard in 1782 up to Emerson's 1837 address, Wagner shows that the political intent of Bishop's rejected oration was not anomalous and that in fifty-five years of speeches at a number of colleges it is more unusual to find one that abjures politics altogether and seeks the apolitical high ground. It is in fact only common sense to suspect that an intelligent and educated human being would have a difficult time of keeping all suggestion of political partisanship out of such a speech, especially if it were delivered in highly charged political times, an apt description of the political atmosphere in this country from 1782 to the present. (pp. 37-41)

. . . . .

Two ideological levels function in **"The American Scholar."** The first is overt and conventional. It is clearly Emerson's not to the obligatory demands of the occasion, and it appears, significantly, only at the beginning and end of the oration to provide an acceptable frame for the convert and unconventional politics that Emerson wishes to advocate. Of course, I refer to those bold, nationalistic statements which suggest that the nature of Emerson's speech is that of an American literary manifesto: specifically his introductory announcement that "Our day of dependence, our long apprenticeship to the learning of other lands, draws to a close" and his perorational claim that "We have listened too long to the courtly muses of Europe." These pronouncements are among the most memorable in **"The American Scholar,"** or they have at least burned themselves into the memories of generations of readers because they underwrite the notion that Emerson's speech is principally one about literary nationalism. However, in their expression of the conventional idea of *translatio* *studii*—the classical theory of the westward movement of civilization—these memorable nationalistic phrases represent the most hackneyed thoughts in the entire oration. In them we may indeed have the expression of ideas that permit us to understand Emerson when we triangulate **"The American Scholar"** with, say, Melville's "Hawthorne and His Mosses" and Whitman's 1855 Preface. But it is, alas, not the genuine Emerson we understand in these nationalistic phrases, only the mask of conventionality, providing the folks with what they came to hear by mouthing ideas that Sacvan Bercovitch [in his *Puritan Origins of the American Self,* 1975] has traced to the first Puritan settlers of New England and Kenneth Silverman [in his *Cultural History of the American Revolution,* 1976] establishes as stock college commencement rhetoric during the Revolutionary era. It is rhetoric that one would expect to find in the oration of the conservative Whig and Unitarian James T. Austin, who in 1831 spoke on the duties of educated men, or in Parsons' 1835 address on the duties of educated men in a republic, or in any number of other orations of the 1830's and after, when it became the convention of these speeches to address the topic of the American scholar. By 1837 the concept of *translatio studii* had become such a commonplace in Phi Beta Kappa orations that it no longer carried political significance and, in Emerson's case, the very presence of this convention creates such an unsettling tension in its contrast with the unconventionality of the majority of the oration that even one allegedly as dull as John Pierce was quick to pick it up: "Toward the close, and indeed in many parts of his discourse, [Emerson] spoke severely of our dependence on British literature," Pierce observed. "Notwithstanding, I much question whether he himself would have written such an apparently incoherent and unintelligible address, had he not been familiar with the writings of [Swedenborg, Coleridge, and Carlyle]."

The tension that Pierce identifies but fails to articulate beyond the simple observation of Emerson's apparent hypocrisy is that which emerges from the conflict between Emerson's obligatory handling of the theme of American nationalism and the extent to which **"The American Scholar"** is an expression of Emerson's romantic ideology. In other words, the most substantial portions of the speech—those specifically devoted to the theoretical discussion of "The One Man" and the definition of "The Scholar"—are oddly detached from the desired practical effect of freeing American culture from the influence of Europe. The idealistic nature of the bulk of Emerson's speech rises above nationalism and disavows the need to take a specific partisan stand in relation to liberal or conservative, democrat or whig positions on the best way to lead America to its destined glory, and in that disavowal Emerson implicitly attacks the current social, political, and economic state of the nation.

In his *The Romantic Ideology,* Jerome McGann, addressing the locus of polemic in the poetry of English romantics, theorizes that "The poetic response to the age's severe political and social dislocations was to reach for solutions in the realm of ideas. The maneuver follows upon a congruent Romantic procedure, which is to define human problems in ideal and spiritual terms." To the degree to which Emerson practices this "Romantic procedure," and that is a considerable degree indeed, I find his method in **"The American Scholar"** similar to that used by Coleridge in "Kubla Khan," as described by Norman Rudich. Rudich argues that Coleridge's method is based on "mythopoeic" transformations in which specific social and historical details are transformed into symbolic forms. According to Rudich [quoted in McGann], this mechanism serves both political and aesthetic functions:

> The overthrow in men's minds of the idolatrous worship of the false gods of the State is the sacred mission of the poet. . . . This is Coleridge's flight from the political realities of his day metamorphosed into an heroic assault on the bastions of human prejudice and delusion, with the inspired poet leading the vanguard of enlightened spirits. The truth of history is that political revolutions betrayed by tyrants come and go, a bloody, repetitive succession of disappointments. The poet alone can truly lead mankind out of the infernal cycle and to the happiness of spiritual peace in harmonious reconciliation with himself and God's nature.

If we substitute Emerson's mythic "scholar" for Coleridge's "poet" and think in terms of the specific social and historical context of **"The American Scholar,"** particularly the economic turmoil at the end of Jackson's presidency and the Panic of 1837, then Rudich's description of the mechanism at work in "Kubla Khan" is an apt description of a similar process in Emerson's oration. Such a process of translation of concern for specific social and political problems into the realm of ideas is typical of much of Emerson's writing, but it is nowhere so apparent as in **"The American Scholar,"** a work whose historical context suggests a plausible rationale for the ideology expressed in it.

There are a number of typically romantic or, more accurately, typically Emersonian ploys within the address itself to convince us of the movement away from the actual into the ideal. The opening delineation of the myth of "The One Man" and the key role that myth plays in the reasoning process which permits Emerson to arrive at his conditional thesis that the scholar is "Man Thinking" is not so much a criticism of division of labor and reification as it is a comment on Emerson's own feelings of intellectual inadequacy—feelings that pervade the journal entries of the summer of 1837. The fear expressed in these entries is one all too familiar to readers of Emerson, that he had written himself out and no longer had the means to express thoughts of importance. "I sometimes fear," Emerson wrote on August 4, "that like those Savoyards who went out one day to find stock for their wooden images and discovered that they had whittled up the last of their pinetrees, so I careless of action, intent on composition, have exhausted already all my stock of experience, have fairly written it out." On August 9 he laments, "I sit and have nothing to say." What offsets this fear as it is expressed in the journal is a tendency to move from dependence upon experience to a subjective and idealized transformation of the actual. As Emerson affirms in an August 18 journal entry, the function of the scholar in society is "being a Soul among those things with which he deals. Let us look at the world as it aids his function," a sentiment that is an echo of his July 21 plea to William to provide more detailed information on the steps Emerson should take in their joint business transactions: "You write to a scholar floundering for the first time in a quagmire of business with all the dwarf brevity of a broker, as if it were enough to such a one to know a sum & date & he could foresee & transpierce all the rest. Comfort me a little by expatiating." Because dealing in the world of the actual and material does require considerable expatiation, Emerson and his scholar are more at home in the idealized sphere of Reason where a tyrannizing unity functions as law and empowers the individual with both sight and foresight impossible in the sphere of the Understanding.

This same movement away from the actual is of paramount importance in understanding Emerson's rationale for choosing his three influences upon the scholar. Nature, the past (or, more properly, books), and action seem such an unlikely threesome because action appears to be incompatible with nature and books. Both those entities suggest otherness to Emerson: nature does so as an emblem of universal spirit and books do so as a vehicle for human history. Books translate experience through the imagination of someone else, but nature (and the spirit it contains) is not accessible to the individual through similar means. Therefore, Emerson proposes a third influence which is really the scholar's means to the universal spirit in nature. Instead of action we should read (inter)action, for what Emerson really argues for is a way of getting at the universal in nature. In a confusing metaphor, he defines action as "the raw material out of which the intellect moulds her splendid products," but as he refines his idea of action it is certain that the "raw material" is experience itself and that this is only one component of action, which is a process rather than an entity. It is the process of (inter)action that allows the scholar to gather the details of experience and transform them into thought. In other words, (inter)action occurs in two stages, the first is immersion in experience and the second is conversion of that experience into thought. It is, in fact, (inter)action that assumes the role of the chain that Emerson describes in an August 19 journal entry: "Facts are disagreeable or loathsome to me so long as I have no clue to them; persons are formidable or tedious. But give me the chain that connects them to the Universal consciousness & I shall see them to be Necessary & see them to be convenient & enlarge my charity one circle more & let them in." It is not coincidental that this passage introduces a discussion of Swedenborg and the doctrine of correspondence that Emerson would later employ at the end of **"The American Scholar"** in his list of hopeful signs in the present age.

Perhaps the most persuasive evidence of Emerson's failure to confront the actual dilemmas of his age, choosing instead to criticize them obliquely by escaping into an idealistic alternative, is the list of hopeful signs of a glorious future with which he concludes the address. After returning to his myth of "The One Man" in his suggestion that materialistic and, therefore, divided men, whom he has just characterized as bugs, may be the raw material for the regeneration of mankind through "the upbuilding of a man," Emerson presents his signs of hope, signs so abstract that one should wonder if hope is not baseless.

The first of these signs constitutes another of those canonical statements that those who read **"The American Scholar"** as a literary manifesto point to as prefiguring Whitman, as it no doubt does. But it suggests considerably more. Emerson's bold announcement that "I embrace the common, I explore and sit at the feet of the familiar, the low" is, at least in part, a rejoinder to other Phi Beta Kappa orators who argued that classical learning was not only preferable but necessary in a republic. Specifically, Emerson had to have been thinking of the 1834 Phi Beta Kappa address of William Howard Gardiner on "Classical Learning and Eloquence." Gardiner's tediously long and rambling plea that Harvard take the lead in making "our youths accurate in the first rudiments of classical learning," was surely on Emerson's mind as he composed his own oration because, as Phi Beta Kappa poet in 1834, he must have had to sit stoically on the platform for the insuperable duration of Gardiner's address. Further, if we couple this hopeful sign of exploration of the low and common as a fit subject for literature with Emerson's previous contention that (inter)action is one of the duties of the scholar, it is clear that Emerson is not prescribing a sort of literary realism but the opposite of it. Since the "familiar, the low" he embraces is, as he says earlier in the address, "the raw material out of which the intellect moulds her splendid products," it becomes merely the fodder for the idealizing process and is ultimately transformed into the vocabulary of the soul. As if to underscore the process of rendering the actual abstract, Emerson contends that "Life is our dictionary."

The second sign of hope to which Emerson points is, of all things, Swedenborg's doctrine of correspondence, a sign that is really a naming of the process—the imaginative transformation of the "familiar, the low" into the matter of the soul—that is the essence of his first hopeful sign. But Emerson is ambiguous in his meaning here. Does he mean to imply that the doctrine of correspondence is so generally understood and accepted that it is likely to cause an epistemological revolution? I really doubt it. In all likelihood, Emerson is referring to the circulation of ideas expressed by Sampson Reed in his *Observations on the Growth of the Mind* and the general advocacy of those ideas by the small band of Unitarian malcontents that had been labelled "the New School" by its opponents. Clearly, he is not alluding to the widespread acceptance of organized Swedenborgianism, which did not exist in Boston until 1816 and, as late as 1828, could number only sixty-three members as formal adherents. In the hostile environment of Boston, Reed and other leaders of the New Church consciously determined not to proselytize, so at the time Emerson delivered **"The American Scholar"** the Swedenborgians were still a small nomadic sect, holding meetings in a variety of public halls and still years away from building their own place of worship.

The final hopeful sign is democracy itself, but it is democracy of a curiously Emersonian sort that does not empower the mass but the individual. As such Emerson's third sign of hope is typical of American philosophy as described by Tocqueville, who saw American philosophers as those whose goal it was "to seek by themselves and in themselves for the only reason for things, looking to results without getting entangled in the means toward them and looking through forms to the basis of things." To Tocqueville, this emphasis in American philosophy represented one of the dangers of democracy—an individualism that isolates democratic men and women from each other: "each man is narrowly shut up in himself, and from that basis makes the pretension to judge the world." It is from such individualism that Tocqueville sees egotism arising and for that reason—the separation and isolation of people from each other—he finds a similarity between the despot, who "will lightly forgive his subjects for not loving him, provided they do not love one another," and American democracy with its emphasis on self-reliance. Emerson, on the other hand, in his proclamation that "The world is nothing, the man is all" suggests, counter to Tocqueville, that only in self-reliance and the individual transformation of life into "our dictionary" of the soul can American culture and, concomitantly, American democracy itself, become established and thrive. Thus, Emerson's three signs of hope are really the same sign—the strategic retreat from the actual to the ideal, the specific to the universal—and **"The American Scholar"** might itself be appended to his list, since it, too, argues for the same sort of movement as a remedy for the chaos of the time.

. . . . .

Despite his biographers' tendency to minimize Emerson's preoccupation with his personal finances in the spring and summer of 1837, the evidence suggests that Emerson, who was forever fretting over dollars, was then even more distressed than usual over the nation's economic situation and its potential political, social, and personal ramifications. Emerson did not simply dismiss the significance of the Panic of 1837 and return to his systematic musings on the scholar but was instead so distraught over the financial crisis that his fear contributed to a return of his old lung ailment and his near incapacitation during June, a period during which he was too weak to write in his journal.

His letters to his brother William during this time are a revelation of his anxiety. New York, where William lived, was hardest hit by the suspension of specie payments by banks on May 10, and William had apparently sustained substantial losses in land speculation, a market that started to go bad when, in July 1836, Jackson issued the Specie Circular, requiring payment in gold or silver for the purchase of public land. In response to William's apparent requests for help, Emerson repeatedly pleaded a lack of capital and on April 12 even sent William a detailed statement of his financial situation to emphasize that he could be of little immediate aid. Such letters continued at fairly regular intervals through August 1837, even after Emerson was informed that he would receive an $11,674 settlement from the estate of his first wife. But how secure could Emerson feel, knowing that nearly all of his wealth, including his much anticipated inheritance from the Tucker estate, was in the form of bank stocks? Emerson's financial well-being was built on the quicksand of perhaps the most severe economic depression this country has ever seen, when banks in nearly every major city had suspended specie payments, some had closed, and many had gone out of business. His small investment in the Commercial Bank of Boston was lost when its stock became valueless, and when he wrote to William on July 10 to inform him that the Tucker estate had at last been settled, he noted that "All these stocks are now low" but added, somewhat hopefully, "I heard on Saturday, all rising."

But while he put the best possible face on his concerns about the economy in his letters to the financially troubled William, the thoughts Emerson recorded in his journal were much darker. In mid-May, just two days after the suspension of specie payments in Boston, he began a journal entry with the words, "Harder times," and this entry was followed by an unusual number of brooding entries on economy and politics that cease only when the journal entries stop altogether with the onset of his illness. "Is the world sick?" he asks, and cites "Bankruptcy in England & America" as one of the reasons for his question. On May 21, he couched his Sunday School lesson in the language of economics: "I told . . . that the misfortunes of the adult generation give a new interest to childhood as born to a new state of things, born to better fortunes," and in the same entry in which he records this, he muses on the "great scientific value" of "The black times," adding, "It is an epoch so critical a philosopher would not miss." But only a week later, on May 31, the journal stops and is not resumed until the end of June, after Emerson received the invitation to deliver the Phi Beta Kappa oration on June 22.

Even after the hiatus of nearly a month, however, his journal entries, now clearly directed toward the thoughts that would become **"The American Scholar,"** still deal with the Panic of 1837 in a way that a portion of the 21 May journal entry suggests. Addressing the "emphatic & universal calamity . . . the times bring," Emerson says in this entry that "Society has played out its last stake; it is checkmated. Young men have no hope. Adults stand like daylaborers idle in the streets. None calleth us to labor. The old wear no crown of warm light on their grey hairs. The present generation is bankrupt of principles & hope, as of property." Emerson traces this calamity to what he identifies as "the causal bankruptcy"—"the cruel oppression that the ideal should serve the actual; that the head should serve the feet"—and he finally pleads, "Let me begin anew. Let me teach the finite to know its Master. Let me ascend above my fate and work down upon the world."

"The American Scholar" thus becomes Emerson's means of teaching the "finite to know its Master," a way of countering both the real bankruptcy and despair of the financial crisis and, more important, the "causal bankruptcy" of the spirit so that he could literally arm the young men at Harvard with hope. Astutely, he realized that the economic calamities and the concomitant social and political turmoil of the spring and summer of 1837 would be so devastating to society that they would actually provide him the opportunity to teach the lesson that he prayed to be able to teach in late May. He indicates as much in this important passage late in the oration:

> If there is any period one would desire to be born in,—is it not the age of Revolution; when the old and the new stand side by side, and admit of

being compared; when the energies of all men are searched by fear and by hope; when the historic glories of the old, can be compensated by the rich possibilities of the new era? This time, like all times, is a very good one, if we but know what to do with it.

But clearly, the summer of 1837, was a better time than most for compensating the "historic glories of the old" with the "rich possibilities of the new era" that Emerson's oration envisions. Inherent in the crisis of that summer, Emerson saw the potential obliteration of accepted social, political, and economic systems. For those dislocated by the accompanying chaos of this actual and causal bankruptcy, Emerson offered the theory of "The Scholar" that in its subversive asocial and apolitical idealism—its emphasis on radical self-trust, its advocacy of the severing of cultural and familial ties, its redefinition of traditional concepts of success and democracy—serves as a potent political commentary. It is a devastating critique of the status quo, embodied in a theory that assumes the near total demise of all that was then accepted, and as such it is the sort of declaration of independence that Holmes could not have imagined. (pp. 44-53)

> *Robert E. Burkholder, "The Radical Emerson: Politics in 'The American Scholar'," in* ESQ: A Journal of the American Renaissance, *Vol. 34 nos. 1 & 2, 1st & 2nd Quarters, 1988, pp. 37-57.*

David M. Robinson   (essay date 1989)

[*In the following excerpt, Robinson explores the relationship between "will" and "acceptance" in Emerson's essays as a reflection of the theological controversy over whether salvation is attained through works or grace.*]

In an 1841 journal entry, Ralph Waldo Emerson, then the clear public leader of the Transcendentalist movement, measured himself and his contemporaries against their New England past:

> Our forefathers walked in the world and went to their graves tormented with the fear of sin and the terror of the Day of Judgment. We are happily rid of those terrors, and our torment is the utter uncertainty and perplexity of what we ought to do; the distrust of the value of what we do; and the distrust that the Necessity which we all at last believe in, is Fair.

Literary and religious historians might consider 1841 a high tide for Emerson and his movement. He began the year by sending his *Essays: First Series* to the press; he would end it in the midst of his important lecture series in Boston, "The Times." He was helping Margaret Fuller to edit the *Dial,* which was giving their "new views" a wider circulation and public attention. But as the journal entry and many more like it suggest, the apparent public successes of Transcendentalism were undercut by private struggles. Emerson's journals and essays from this period show a significant ambivalence, particularly as he tried to define the role of the will in the culture of the soul. The concept of an active or developing soul was central to Transcendentalist thinking, so the problem could not be

regarded lightly. Emerson could, at times, view this tension dialectically, seeing that moments of insight gave way necessarily to willed acts of morality, thus preparing the way for new insight. But the balance of such a dialectic was always precarious, and his journal suggests his tenuous settlements with doubt. He entitled one entry in January 1841 "The Confessional," a wry allusion to the secret sin of the optimistic Transcendentalist: skepticism. "Does Nature, my friend, never show you the wrong side of the tapestry? never come to look dingy and shabby?" Given the celebration of nature in his early work, this confession of doubt is significant. But note how the passage goes on to explain the sudden evaporation of that doubt, an event in which the individual will has no part:

> You have quite exhausted [Nature's] power to please and today you come into a new thought and lo! in an instant there stands the entire world converted suddenly into the cipher or exponent of that very thought and chanting it in full chorus from every leaf and drop of water. It has been singing that song ever since the creation in your deaf ears.

What transpires here is an experience of unity, or, as Emerson would come to call it, "ecstasy." The thought of the individual, divorced and alienated from nature, is suddenly shown to be one with it. Nature is the "cipher or exponent," that is to say, the living symbol, of human thought, and reflects that thought back to us in its every part. As he explained earlier in *Nature,* "Nature is the symbol of spirit." This is a moment in which that "correspondence" is fully realized. Moreover, the achievement of that unity is due to a transformation of the individual's perception. Nature has always sung this song of harmony—we have been deaf. But strikingly, no cause for this radical change of perception is intimated here. It remains mysterious except insofar as we can say that no individual exertion seems to have caused it. Emerson's linguistic construction confirms the essentially passive nature of the experience. We do not produce or create a new idea; we "come into a new thought." It is not our product; we are its captives.

While the passage moves from doubt to faith, though faith of mysterious origin, Emerson is also capable of moving from faith to doubt. A journal entry a few months earlier portrays the confessing Transcendentalist somewhat differently. It is entitled "the excess of direction," and this "excess" denotes the habit of the soul to generate new wants, belittling the achievements it has been driven to make. Thus, after one's discovery of a "first friend," achievement fades: the individual "finds that it was only a quasi-fulfilment, that the total inexhaustible longing is there at his heart still." From here, it is only a short step to one of the most caustic indictments of the nature of things that one is likely to find in Emerson's work:

> How contradictory and unreasonable, you say. Little careth God; he drives me forth out of my cabin as before, to love and to love. He tells me not what that is I seek,—whether choirs of beatific power, and virtue; or the value of nature shut up in a private form; or the total harmony of the Universe. From the beginning this is

promised us as the crisis and consummation of
life, but no final information is ever afforded us.

Even though the passage concerns love, it is one of the
loneliest of the journals. Even though it depicts an active,
questing, powerful soul, its ultimate conclusion is pessimism.

Bound on one side by the bafflements of the sources of
spiritual power and insight, and on the other by the chilling suspicion that even the possession of such power might
not be fulfilling (**"Circles"** is eloquent testimony to this),
Emerson faced an acute spiritual crisis. Just as his model
of self-culture seemed to be taking shape, refined through
his annual lectures of the late 1830s, its foundations of insight, will, and progress were threatened. In the early
1840s, Emerson would try that model ever more directly.

In *Essays: First Series,* a guidebook for the culture of the
soul, will and acceptance form the poles of what emerged
as one of the book's most troubling dilemmas. Most mem-
orably, the book is a hymn to strenuous and persistent effort, as the general popularity of **"Self-Reliance"** and the
critical stature of **"Circles"** suggest. In both these essays,
willed effort is at the center of the spiritual life, and Emerson's rhetorical purpose is to teach his readers to circum-
vent the various obstacles to that effort. Thus "conformity" and "consistency" are attacked as the chief hindrances
to self-trust in **"Self-Reliance,"** and the many "forms of
old age"—"rest, conservatism, appropriation, inertia"—
are exposed as the enemies of the energetic pursuit of the
new in **"Circles."** The attractiveness of this stance has
been great; it has by and large defined Emerson's place in
intellectual history. Yet within that same book is the other
Emerson who quietly affirmed in **"Spiritual Laws"** that
"our moral nature is vitiated by any interference of our
will," and reduced the wisdom of **"Compensation"** to the
maxim, "I learn to be content."

The sources of this conflict in Emerson's thinking are not
difficult to find. In the 1837 "Human Culture" lectures he
posited "a divine impulse at the core of our being" which
"impels" us to unfold our true nature. This was the basis
of his faith in self-culture. This vision affirmed human nature, finding divinity at its very core. But it also held that
divinity manifests itself as energy or "metamorphosis,"
and that growth or expansion was its evidence. Even within that vision of growth or culture, a dichotomy existed
between willed effort and passive willessness. Is the "unfolding" of the soul the product of strenuous moral effort,
or is it better conceived as a coming to oneself in a quietist
acceptance?

We might put this dilemma differently by noting that at
times in *Essays: First Series* a sense of spiritual conflict
predominates. At other moments a mood of realized spiritual achievement predominates. Such tension, though it is
here expressed in different terms, is not new to the student
of New England thought. In it, we see the theological division over the question of salvation's source in works or
grace. The Calvinist denial of the freedom of the will, and
the Arminian reaction to it, is the most notable historical
manifestation of this profound dichotomy in the New England mind. While that division did manifest itself in the
liberal and orthodox parties, it also continued to exist as

a tension in New England thinkers of both camps. Calvin-
ists, committed historically and theologically to determin-
istic assumptions, remained uneasy about the implied loss
of human freedom in their outlook. Arminians, repulsed
by that loss of freedom, continued to worry over the logic
of determinism. New England's spiritual history continued to speak through Emerson, therefore, and in him we
hear alternately the deflected voices of Puritan moral exhortation, eager to add the demands of visible sainthood
to the uneasy covenant of grace, and that of antinomian
mysticism, insisting on the direct access to the spirit which
renders the work of the world a distinctly secondary concern.

Emerson received this Puritan inheritance after it had
been filtered through the Arminian tradition in New England, which had flowered into the Unitarianism of his father's generation. William Ellery Channing had been its
most effective exponent. But his Aunt Mary Moody Emerson also kept a family legacy of orthodox Calvinism alive
for him. The liberal movement was prone to stress human
capacity, a view that ultimately stressed works as fundamental to religion. The centerpiece of Unitarian theology
thus became the doctrine of probation, which, in the
words of Emerson's ministerial predecessor at Boston's
Second Church, Henry Ware, Jr., stressed that life was a
"state of preparatory discipline." For Ware and his Unitarian associates, life was a testing ground for the cultivation of character. "In this world [the human being] is
placed in a state of trial and probation," Ware wrote, "for
the purpose of forming and bringing out his character."
Emerson's sermons are permeated with this vision of life
as a probationary state, a concept that allowed the Unitarians to reject what they perceived as the fatalism of Orthodox doctrine, while allowing them to retain the acute sense
of sin and limitation that spoke to the human condition.
It was, essentially, a theology oriented toward action.

But the Unitarians, too, were offspring of the Puritans,
even if rebellious ones. Within their stress on right action
was a strand of pietism, almost quietist or mystical in
some moments or manifestations. Daniel Walker Howe
pointed out this aspect of the "Unitarian conscience" in
1970, and thus gave scholars not only a new perspective
on Unitarianism but a new clue to the native sources of
Transcendentalism. In Channing's "Likeness to God,"
Ware's *The Formation of the Christian Character,* some of
Emerson's early sermons, and emphatically in his first
book, *Nature,* we find this pietist or devotionalist sensibility, whose stress is not on the outer world but on the spirit
within.

One anecdote regarding Emerson's double inheritance
from Unitarianism might be instructive. In December
1838, Emerson's newly discovered "saint," the mystical
poet Jones Very, paid a call on William Ellery Channing.
Very was then preaching a doctrine of "will-less existence" which had impressed many in the Transcendental
circle, including Emerson, with its spiritual intensity and
depth. Very preached an absolute surrender of the private
will to God, transforming every act into a gesture of obedience. Channing, whom many young Unitarian ministers
regarded as a kind of moral touchstone, listened attentive-

ly and sympathetically to Very's doctrine that the Spirit dictated every action, and then gently asked two direct questions. Had he come to see him that day "in obedience to the Spirit" or simply because Channing had offered him an invitation? Even more specifically, had he walked to the mantle and put his hand on it in obedience to the Spirit as well? Very answered yes to both questions, apparently preferring the possibility of ridicule to the endless chore of discriminating between will and spirit. Ridicule was of course not Channing's object. But his questions, firmly grounded in common sense and a respect for individual action, reveal his coolness about a sense of spiritual enlightenment that takes itself too seriously. Emerson's devotion to both these men is a matter of record. Such conflicting loyalties mirror his own inner conflicts.

Emerson felt an even deeper conflict when these two models of the spiritual life were paired not against each other, but against their own absence. A quietism illuminated by the inner light was sustainable, even at the cost of action. Willed, determined self-culture was fulfilling, even in the absence of visionary forgetfulness. But a quietism that courted only darkness, or a culture frustrated by the prison of constitutional restrictions, or a soul that could not be satisfied with any spiritual achievement—these possibilities were haunting. In the conflict he felt over the means of the culture of the soul, and in the further conflict over the possibility of that culture, we find those aspects of Emerson's thinking that have remained vital to a modern audience. To the age that has felt the heavy weight of creating and sustaining a self, and the heavier weight of seeing this creation as in some senses a fiction, Emerson's conflicts seem familiar.

The tensions in Emerson's thinking are apparent when one attempts to describe his intellectual position at a given moment. But "conflict" becomes less appropriate when the reader surrenders to the intellectual flow of one of the essays. It should be remembered that Emerson's style arose in good measure from the sermon form and its near relative (in his case) the lyceum lecture, a form whose highest purpose was to take the hearer up in an exemplary act of thinking. "Man Thinking" was not only the model of the scholar, but of the orator as well, and therefore of the essayist. For the reader of the essays, this means that the experience of "working through" a problem or issue is more important than isolating Emerson's opinion on that problem. The more the voice of the essays becomes internalized, the fuller this experience becomes. To analyze Emerson's philosophical position is thus to falsify somewhat the intent of the essays themselves, to violate a code of unity and process in the attempt to gain analytic distance from the workings of the essays. Only in retrospect, an inevitable retrospect perhaps, of the reading of an essay in its entirety does the question of its internal conflict become important.

To illustrate the problem, let us look in some detail at **"Self-Reliance."** Emerson brings that essay to a ringing and effective conclusion with parallel closing sentences. "Nothing can bring you peace but yourself. Nothing can bring you peace but the triumph of principles." This parallelism establishes the identity of the self with principles,

giving a final emphasis to one of the essay's chief propositions, the asserted unity of the individual self with a universal or abstract Self underlying it. Possession of the self is thus a universal rather than a private act, a confirmation of principle rather than an assertion of mere selfishness. But while this parallelism establishes the unity that is the essay's goal, it also suggests a duality woven into its entire texture. To say that "nothing can bring you peace but yourself" is to evoke quiet self-possession. To call peace a "triumph of principles" is to suggest a struggle.

Much the same dichotomy exists throughout the essay. The best-known images are those of recklessness, defiance, and irresponsibility, in which Emerson portrays the process of self-culture as a process of self-liberation. Barriers, obstacles, entanglements—these are in the nature of the world, especially the social world, and the individual must respond to them in terms of opposition, will, and action. Perhaps it is the drama of this struggle that makes these images memorable and explains the air of refreshing defiance that lingers over the whole essay.

> Your goodness must have some edge to it—else it is none. The doctrine of hatred must be preached as the counteraction of the doctrine of love when that pules and whines. I shun father and mother and wife and brother, when my genius calls me. I would write on the lintels of the door-post, *Whim.*

Such energetic self-assertion, flirting as it does with irresponsibility (and thus raising and engaging the reader, either pro or con), is the answer to the debilitating demand for social conformity. More broadly, it is the antidote for the basic dilemma of self-consciousness. Youth, even infancy, is praised for its nonconforming nonchalance. This is essential because, as Emerson puts it, "the man is, as it were, clapped into jail by his consciousness." The act of will, necessarily self-directed, is thus celebrated as an act of liberation as well, especially if its basis is in spontaneity. "What I must do, is all that concerns me, not what the people think."

This hymn to the resilient will is best incarnated in the sturdy New England provincial, an evocation of an American cultural icon worthy of Franklin. In contrast to the fine "genius" who feels ruined for not having found an office in Boston or New York immediately after his studies, "the sturdy lad from New Hampshire or Vermont . . . in turn tries all the professions, . . . *teams it, farms it, peddles,* keeps a school, preaches, edits a newspaper, goes to Congress, buys a township, and so forth, in successive years." He perfectly embodies the American rags-to-riches myth. Such a man "does not postpone his life, but lives already." He "is worth a hundred of these city dolls." As Emerson's example suggests, thought paralyzes, while action liberates.

What is easily forgotten, however, is that these images of will, strength, and defiance are built upon a foundation of trust and acceptance. Beneath the sturdy lad who seems to be creating his own identity by a vigorous attack on the world is something of a mystic who has, in the terms of the essay's second paragraph, realized that "he must take himself for better, for worse, as his portion" and decided to toil "on that plot of ground which is given him to till." In fact, it is not the call to struggle and action that we first meet in the essay, but something quite different: "Accept the place the divine Providence has found for you; the society of your contemporaries, the connexion of events." Although the essay rises to a position of defiance, it arrives there by way of acceptance. Even the exuberant, youthful defiance celebrated early in the essay, "the nonchalance of boys who are sure of a dinner," is first introduced into the essay through the praise of a different quality of youth, a simplicity of mind that is manifested in a trusting wholeness. Children lack "that divided and rebel mind," the self-conscious doubting of the adult. Only because of this fuller possession of themselves, a self-possession that even precedes conscious self-acceptance, can the child act from nature. If the essay calls on us to act with decisiveness, it does so in order that we can regain in measure this lost spontaneity, and the lost wholeness it implies. "**Self-Reliance**" thus addresses the fall of humanity as a growing self-consciousness, which must be repaired by a stricter attention to "that gleam of light which flashes across [the] mind from within." As he would later put it in "**Experience**," "It is very unhappy, but too late to be helped, the discovery we have made, that we exist. That discovery is called the Fall of Man."

This self-consciousness is a falling away from a true self, a universal Self, which stands at the basis of Emerson's philosophy. When Emerson asks, "What is the aboriginal Self on which a universal reliance may be grounded?" he answers by pointing to spontaneity and instinct, forms of a "primary wisdom" called "Intuition." Spontaneity and instinct are words suggesting action; thus when Emerson traces his way back to the aboriginal Self by this route, he emphasizes self-recovery through action. But the intuition underlying spontaneity is a form of knowledge, a natural intellectual possession. One's intuitions are given. Again, as this issue shows us, works and grace weave a complicated pattern through the essay. If in the dramatization of action the essay reaches its most climactic moments, it is constantly true that those dramatizations of will rest on a foundation of secured knowledge.

It is when we seek the origin of that knowledge that we feel the friction of the outer edges of Emerson's inquiry. "The relations of the soul to the divine spirit are so pure that it is profane to seek to interpose helps." Such an attitude protects the sanctity of intuitive knowledge by denigrating the role of the will in helping to recover such knowledge. Very little, Emerson avers, can be said about intuition. At best we have "the far off remembering of the intuition." All Emerson can do is to recommend the new and the strange, and leave these as a test for the genuine.

> When good is near you, when you have life in yourself, it is not by any known or accustomed way; you shall not discern the foot-prints of any other; you shall not see the face of man; you shall not hear any name;—the way, the thought, the good shall be wholly strange and new.

Newness, the very antithesis of custom and conformity, can only be explained as the product of self-reliance. But Emerson's metaphor of finding the new way differs from

a Whitmanian bravado that calls upon us to stride confidently down the open road. Part of the appeal of the metaphor, in fact, is that it communicates a certain sense of wandering, even groping, as part of the process of finding the new. "To talk of reliance," he notes, "is a poor external way of speaking. Speak rather of that which relies, because it works and is." The key to culture, then, is paradoxical, a reliance through work and being. Reliance suggests a borrowed or secondary existence, while working and being seem primary. As Emerson would explain, we work or exist through our act of reliance or surrender to a transcendent self. "This is the ultimate fact which we so quickly reach on this as on every topic, the resolution of all into the ever blessed ONE." Self-reliance is finally a stance of humility.

If we have followed Emerson from his sermon of acceptance through his praise of youthful disdain for restraint, this return to a quietist acceptance might seem to be the logical rounding out of the essay. But in fact this apparent synthesis comes near the middle of the essay, and it is only after the hymn to the "ever blessed ONE" that we find Emerson's most self-assertive images—the "sturdy lad from New Hampshire or Vermont" (discussed earlier), and the protesting family member whose complaint is dramatized in these terms: "O father, O mother, O wife, O brother, O friend [the modern reader will note the absence of 'O husband' from Emerson's litany], I have lived with you after appearances hitherto. Henceforward I am the truth's." This voice of direct address, suggesting a fragment of buried dialogue, gives this passage a certain power. One can see why the essay has always been regarded by university instructors as so "teachable" among Emerson's essays, tapping, as it does, reserves of adolescent rebelliousness. But the dramatic voice here also helps to underline the "newness" necessary to the stance of self-reliance. By tainting the closest, most sacred of social relationships with the possibility of debilitating conformity, Emerson warns against a facile identification of the genuine with the familiar. What is ready-to-hand in our familial ties or close friendships is not always what is spontaneous or intuitive. Always, we must absolve our actions to ourselves alone, and thus "dispense with the popular code." So the vigil never ends, nor the effort it entails. "If any one imagines that this law is lax, let him keep its commandment one day."

Read with attention to the interplay of its voices of will and acceptance, "**Self-Reliance**" shows the parameters of Emerson's spiritual world in the early 1840s. In it, he evokes both the hunger for mystical spiritual enlightenment which must be accepted as the free work of grace, and the aggressive determination of one whose spiritual culture is wholly self-generated. The success of the essay arises from Emerson's ability to make these rhetorical stances play persuasively against each other, admitting the primacy of an inner enlightenment when willfulness begins to ring hollow, and turning to determined action when a stale mysticism requires reinvigoration.

These same forces play against each other in the essay "**Spiritual Laws**," although here the case is instructively different, because in contrast to "**Self-Reliance**" the fundamental thrust of this essay is quietistic. While the prominence of willed action in **"Self-Reliance"** gradually fades into an identity with quietist surrender of self, something of the reverse occurs in **"Spiritual Laws."** Its most prominent emphasis is on an acceptance of ever-present, self-transcending laws of the spirit, which completely overshadow the working of the will. Emerson notes with disdain the way that "people represent virtue as a struggle, and take to themselves great airs upon their attainments." The facts of the case are much simpler: "Either God is there, or he is not there." Because the presence of divinity is beyond the call of will, the moral life calls for a stance of receptive openness rather than aroused aggressiveness.

Such is the lesson, Emerson argues, of the truly great individuals in human history. "We impute deep-laid, farsighted plans to Caesar and Napoleon; but the best of their power was in nature, not in them." Nature, like God, Spirit, or Self, exists in a category opposed to the individual, the will, or the self. Greatness was achieved through these great men, not by them. They succeeded by becoming "an unobstructed channel" through which "the course of thought" could flow. Although great individuals appear to operate by willed actions, the appearance is deceptive. "That which externally seemed will and immovableness, was willingness and self-annihilation." For Emerson, the definition of the moral life came to rest on the difficult distinction between "will" and "willingness."

In Emerson's praise of will-less self-growth, the metaphor of "falling" vividly illustrates the paradoxical notion of progress through surrender:

> Let us draw a lesson from nature, which always works by short ways. When the fruit is ripe, it falls. When the fruit is despatched, the leaf falls. The circuit of the waters is mere falling. The walking of man and all animals is a falling forward. All our manual labor and works of strength, as prying, splitting, digging, rowing, and so forth, are done by dint of continual falling, and the globe, earth, moon, comet, sun, star, fall forever and ever.

The irresistible pull of gravity is shown to be the physical equivalent for the spiritual law of falling forward. Through this letting go of self, we are swept along a more universal course. Even more telling is the metaphor of ripening. The image of an unconscious natural urge to fullness also carries with it the secondary sense of the giving of the self for the sustenance of others. Thus the moral life is characterized as one of a quietistic faith which finds expression in service.

Certainly the mood, if not the ultimate argument, is widely different from that of **"Self-Reliance."** But just as self-reliance comes quietly to rest on the Universal Soul, spiritual laws come finally to manifest themselves through human actions. This turn in the essay is accomplished in part through Emerson's return to the concept of spontaneity as an adequate criterion for discriminating among actions. Because "a higher law than that of our will regulates events, . . . our painful labors are unnecessary and fruitless." In contrast to laborious or willed action is the action made possible by the surrender of the will: "only in our

easy, simple, spontaneous action are we strong, and by contenting ourselves with obedience we become divine." While this action is carefully described as essentially willless, it is nevertheless action. The means may be those of surrender, but the ends are those of assertion, strength, and pragmatic result.

This emphasis on pragmatic action is enlarged when Emerson turns to the concept of choice, for choice would surely seem to signify the presence of will. *"Do not choose,"* he says, explaining that choice is commonly "a partial act." But if made whole, choice becomes the foundation for moral action. "But that which I call right or goodness, is the choice of my constitution." Such choosing is a kind of affirmation of the innate and Universal Self, a realization of it, and such a realization is signified not so much by visionary insight as by appropriate action. "That which I call heaven, and inwardly aspire after, is the state or circumstance desirable to my constitution; and the action which I in all my years tend to do, is the work for my faculties." Herein, of course, lies Emerson's modernized concept of the vocational calling: "Each man has his own vocation. The talent is the call." But in larger terms, this is a confirmation of the fact that the full possession of the universal soul within demands action or expression of some sort. Thus a thoroughly pragmatic axiom comes to summarize the lesson of the will-less acceptance of transcendent laws: "What a man does, that he has."

But the essay is not merely a hymn to doing as an end in itself. Even though Emerson can assert that " 'What has he done?' is the divine question which searches men," he is careful to insist that action must be grounded in a mental reality best understood through the metaphor of inner depth. Action is judged by its basis in thought, by the idea or motive that lies behind it, "by the depth of the sentiment from which it proceeds." Action, in the longer view, alters our lives much less profoundly than thought.

> The epochs of our life are not in the visible facts of our choice of a calling, our marriage, our acquisition of an office, and the like, but in a silent thought by the way-side as we walk; in a thought which revises our entire manner of life, and says,—"Thus hast thou done, but it were better thus."

The superficial results of the action of the self must be distinguished from the less visible but more profound thoughts of the Self. But if real life is measured by the "silent thought," it is also true that such thoughts take on their significance through their ability to "revise" life. Just as thought has bounded and answered action, action renders thought fruitful.

In his lectures "The Times" (1841-1842), Emerson pushed this tension between acceptance and action into the social sphere. His lecture **"The Conservative"** was in some respects a testing ground for the later **"Montaigne; or, The Skeptic"** in *Representative Men.* In **"The Transcendentalist"** we see a portrait even closer to self-description. Emerson assumes ironic distance from the Transcendentalist he describes, but it is finally self-directed irony.

The figure of the Transcendentalist is distilled from the

Emerson's study.

conflict between action and the ideal, sharing the political reformer's incapacity to accept the state of things, but adding to it the idealist's distrust of solutions that are material. In a tone that borders on the petulant, Emerson gives voice to the Transcendentalist's resistant posture: "I can sit in a corner and *perish,* (as you call it,) but I will not move until I have the highest command." Withered by the contempt and impatience of conservative and reformer alike, his refusal to act is a paralysis, but as Emerson passionately argues, a paralysis that is the best hope of the human spirit. "Will you not tolerate one or two solitary voices in the land, speaking for thoughts or principles not marketable or perishable?" The difficulties of the Transcendentalist suggest the precarious situation of Emerson's idealism. The searching portrait of this rebellious but paralyzed figure is veiled autobiography.

This Transcendentalist was worrisome not only to the conservative establishment, but to the political activists of the day as well. Whatever the spiritual implications of "waiting," the political ones were troubling, and Emerson remained an aloof and difficult ally for the reformers. Much of the conflict lay in the dichotomy between "materialist" and "idealist" that Emerson developed in the lecture. He argued that the Transcendentalist was only the contemporary version of the idealist, living out doctrines by no means new. "What is popularly called Transcendentalism among us, is Idealism; Idealism as it appears in 1842." He thereby claimed universal status for the Transcendentalist, linking him or her to a tradition that can be traced to classical times and beyond, a tradition so persistent because it expresses a fundamental impulse of human nature.

> His experience inclines him to behold the procession of facts you call the world, as flowing perpetually outward from an invisible, unsounded centre in himself, centre alike of him and of them, and necessitating him to regard all things as having a subjective or relative existence, relative to that aforesaid Unknown Centre of him.

Such a description sets the idealist apart from the materialist, who "takes his departure from the external world, and esteems a man as one product of that." This linking of the Transcendentalist with the ultimate source of creation, an "Unknown Centre" in himself or herself, confirms his or her identity as one version of the "Universal Man" of Emerson's philosophy. Connected to the universal mind, or moral sentiment, or now "Unknown Centre" of life and consciousness, the idealist is depicted as the figure in whom the fullest development of human capacity has been reached. "The Transcendentalist . . . believes in miracle, in the perpetual openness of the human mind to new influx of light and power; he believes in inspiration, and in ecstasy." Certainly this is the projection of an ideal, the embodiment of much for which Emerson had struggled in the 1830s. But even in this ideal portrait we can sense a shadow if we consider the resonances of the word "ecstasy." Ecstasy captures on the one hand a complete fullness, a moment's realization of unity with the larger Self of the universe. On the other hand it suggests a dangerously unstable and fleeting mystical charge.

Emerson understood the inherent tension between history and the universal and confessed "that there is no pure Transcendentalist." As he expands on this ungraspable ideal, he reveals the radical nature of the Transcendental consciousness:

> We have had many harbingers and forerunners; but of a purely spiritual life, history has yet afforded no example. I mean, we have yet no man who has leaned entirely on his character, and eaten angels' food; who, trusting to his sentiments, found life made of miracles; who, working for universal aims, found himself fed, he knew not how; clothed, sheltered, and weaponed, he knew not how, and yet it was done by his own hands.

The Biblical resonance of the passage is important ("Consider the lilies of the field . . . "), and the allusion to a "life made of miracles" echoes his declaration in the Divinity School Address that Jesus "felt that man's life was a miracle." But the suggestion of Jesus only emphasized the fact that Emerson actually denies him any special reverence or elevation. Controversial as the Divinity School Address was, and radical as Emerson's views may have seemed to many, he was careful there to afford Jesus a privileged place in the spiritual history of mankind.

> Jesus Christ belonged to the true race of prophets. He saw with open eye the mystery of the soul. Drawn by its severe harmony, ravished with its beauty, he lived in it, and had his being there. *Alone in all history,* he estimated the greatness of man. *One man* was true to what is in you and me.

Now, in 1841, he tells us that "history has yet afforded no example" of an idealist. He had offered one signpost of this movement in an 1840 journal entry that declared that "The history of Jesus is only the history of every man written large. The names he bestows on Jesus, belong to himself,—Mediator, Redeemer, Saviour." This democratizing of Jesus extends the argument of the Divinity School Address that Jesus's importance was his recognition of the potential of the individual. In **"The Transcendentalist,"**

Emerson put that potential beyond the reach even of Jesus in an attempt to emphasize its freedom from history.

The significant absence of Jesus from **"The Transcendentalist"** is the first of a number of polemical shadows that the Transcendentalist controversy cast over the address. That controversy, and Emerson's role in it, forms the first layer of autobiographical suggestion in the lecture. No emphasis on the abstract and universal figures that are the topics of this lecture series can remove the essay very far from the confessional context of Emerson's journal. Much of the lecture's rhetorical power results from Emerson's manipulation of the distance between his speaking voice and the image of the Transcendentalist that he paints. In the objective spirit of the photographer or portraitist which set his initial tone in the series, he offers much dispassionate description of Transcendentalism, including a brief technical discussion of the origin of the term "transcendental" in Kantian philosophy. These seem, however, like the formal preliminaries, which are only preparatory to the core of the argument. When Emerson discusses the Transcendentalist as most nearly in touch with that sense of the Ideal or the Better, which is the source of spiritual culture, he portrays him or her as a universal but somehow lifeless figure. It is only when he observes the social impact of the imperfect but real versions of the universal man that his portrait comes to life.

That birth occurs rhetorically when Emerson observes that the Transcendentalists "prolong their privilege of childhood" by their withdrawal from the world of action and responsibility in dedication to the ideal. If the wise child has in the past served Emerson (and the entire Romantic movement) as an image of perfected human nature, here it serves rather to emphasize the distance between youthful aspiration and adult reality. The Transcendentalists "make us feel the strange disappointment which overcasts every human youth. So many promising youths, and never a finished man!" The disappointment signals the presence of the world-weary voice that dominates an important segment of the lecture. How far we seem to be from the voice of **"Circles,"** assuring us that "Nature abhors the old, and old age seems the only disease." The dangers of a life at sea metaphorically suggest the spiritual dangers faced by the idealist; the philosophical equivalent to the question "Where are the old sailors?" is "Where are the old idealists?" It is in this admission of an inevitable defeat that Emerson sounds the funereal note for the movement only now capable of being described.

The mature distance that Emerson establishes from the Transcendentalist is thus an important sign of his changing perspective. It signals his recognition that hope of any substantial part is a complex reaction to stark limits, limits the more clearly understood with age. Even so, this voice is not final, but part of an emerging, metamorphic voice within the essay. This voice of skeptical, or disappointed, or at times bemused age is an important one, but it too has its limits.

The tone of self-accusation and the conviction of inadequacy suggest those limits to mature skepticism. If he can see in the promise of youth a source of eventual disappointment, he can also feel the disdain of youth for its failed elders. "These exacting children advertise us of our wants," he notes, and he finds most admirable their undisguised discontent. "There is no compliment, no smooth speech with them; they pay you only this one compliment, of insatiable expectation." Emerson draws the principal resonance of the essay from this confrontation of world-weary skepticism with "insatiable expectation." This forms its autobiographical core. The mature voice functions as the principle of reality in the essay, the expectant look of youth as the principle of idealism. Crucially, each sees in the other something that is oddly self-completing. After all, reality has force and finality not solely of itself but in its resistance to the unrelenting pressure of the ideal. And how else can the value of the ideal be understood apart from the fact of the real? So Emerson dramatizes his intellectual dilemma: to accommodate his increasing skepticism to an idealism that he could never wholly abandon.

That he could never wholly abandon it is suggested by the dialogue between "the world" and the stubbornly balking Transcendentalist youth who complains that he is "miserable with inaction." Emerson ought to be recognized for his understanding of one phenomenon of the modern world—that spiritual crises often manifest themselves as vocational crises. The youth is not fretting about sin and salvation here but about work. He finds none of it satisfying, and that very attitude is telling social criticism. The Transcendentalist has instead adopted the honest but unfulfilling attitude of "waiting." The response of the world is simple and cold: if you do not like the work of the world, " 'what will you do then?' " In waiting, " 'you grow old and useless.' " The youth, stung by the response, stiffens his willful refusal to work.

> Be it so: I can sit in a corner and *perish*, (as you call it,) but I will not move until I have the highest command. If no call should come for years, for centuries, then I know that the want of the universe is the attestation of faith by this my abstinence. Your virtuous projects, so called, do not cheer me. I know that which shall come will cheer me. If I cannot work, at least I need not lie.

This dramatized defiance is the tensest moment of the lecture, the intensity itself a measure of the threat the world's inescapable common sense poses to idealism. The passion of this moment is rhetorically similar to the well-known passage in **"Circles"** in which a speaker threatened by a skeptical though undeniably shrewd objector defiantly proclaims himself irresponsible to reason, and instead "an endless seeker, with no Past at my back." In **"Circles"** the defiance is expressed as experimentation, but in **"The Transcendentalist,"** as waiting. That in itself is a revealing contrast. But in both cases, the extremity of the rhetoric suggests a whistling in the dark. The "virtuous projects" that Emerson's Transcendentalist here so scornfully rejects were the very avenues of action that were a possible alternative for Emerson now. If through the figure of the Transcendentalist he enacts his rejection of action, through the shrillness of that objection he undercuts it.

As the conflict continues, the autobiographical focus of the lecture sharpens. "When I asked them concerning their private experience," the controlling voice of the lecture reports, "they answered somewhat in this wise: It is not to be denied that there must be some wide difference between my faith and other faith." And so he slides into the voice of the Transcendentalist, a transition all the easier because those words are drawn directly from private struggles that he had recorded in an 1841 journal entry. The faith described is "a certain brief experience," which comes by surprise and reveals the foolishness of daily life. But it passes, and in its passing leaves an emptiness. "My life is superficial, takes no root in the deep world; I ask, When shall I die, and be relieved of the responsibility of seeing an Universe which I do not use? I wish to exchange this flash-of-lightning faith for continuous daylight, this fever-glow for a benign climate."

This rueful admission of failure opens the theme of the "double consciousness," significant both in this lecture and in the later **"Experience."** It is a consciousness born when the brief experience of faith casts its disparaging shadow over the course of ordinary life. "To him who looks at his life from these moments of illumination" (to the Transcendentalist, in other words), his skill, his labor, the work he is given to do is stripped of value. The faith of the mystic has its cost—the experience of living itself.

Emerson had expressed this concept of the double consciousness in the summer of 1841, when he confessed that a vague sense of disappointment was "the true experience of my late years." Feeling inadequate to do the things needing to be done or to say the things needing to be said, he confessed that "I lie by, or occupy my hands with something which is only an apology for idleness until my hour comes again." If honest in refraining from false work, and humble in refusing to find in a single self the cure for the world, the price of this waiting was a chasm between his conception of life and his experience of it.

> The worst feature of our biography is that it is a sort of double consciousness, that the two lives of the Understanding and of the Soul which we lead, really show very little relation to each other, that they never meet and criticize each other, but one prevails now, all buzz and din, and the other prevails then, all infinitude and paradise, and with the progress of life the two discover no greater disposition to reconcile themselves.

Life then does not force us to surrender our faith—it forces us to bracket that faith as an ideal while it continues to demonstrate that reality proceeds as it will. That **"Experience"** was an attempt to answer this dilemma is suggested by the preliminary remarks in an early journal outline of it: "It is greatest to believe and to hope well of the world, because he who does so, quits the world of experience, and makes the world he lives in." What is most poignant here is the split between hope and experience, and the hint of escapism contained in the very attitude of hope. Here the double consciousness is stretched to its limits.

The attitude of "waiting" is therefore one that acknowledges the facts of experience without surrendering to them. It is the last gesture of faith in a world stripped of possibility. We have already noted the Transcendentalist's

defense of waiting. That dialogue is drawn from a journal entry which is preceded by a list of the new "trials of this age . . . early old age, pyrrhonism and apathy." The defiant dismissal of the accusation of Pyrrhonism in **"Circles"** was apparently short-lived. Patience, and not defiance, has now become the cardinal virtue. "Patience, then, is for us, is it not? Patience and still patience." The capacity to wait, to hold with dignity this double consciousness, was the only resource remaining for the Transcendentalist. **"Experience"** was the spiritual autobiography which fulfilled the confessional promise of **"The Transcendentalist,"** and even there, Emerson could recommend no further: "Patience and patience, we shall win at the last." (pp. 121-39)

> *David M. Robinson, "Grace and Works: Emerson's Essays in Theological Perspective," in* American Unitarianism: 1805-1865, *edited by Conrad Edick Wright, The Massachusetts Historical Society and Northeastern University Press, 1989, pp. 121-42.*

FURTHER READING

Bibliography

Burkholder, Robert E. and Myerson, Joel. *Emerson: An Annotated Secondary Bibliography.* Pittsburgh: University of Pittsburgh Press, 1985, 842 p.
   Annotated bibliography of writings on Emerson between 1816 and 1979.

Biography

Allen, Gay Wilson. *Waldo Emerson: A Biography.* New York: Viking Press, 1981, 751 p.
   Critically acclaimed biography focusing on Emerson's intellectual sources.

McAleer, John. *Ralph Waldo Emerson: Days of Encounter.* Boston: Little, Brown and Co., 1984, 748 p.
   Focuses on Emerson's interaction with family and friends.

Criticism

Ahlstrom, Sydney E. "Ralph Waldo Emerson and the American Transcendentalists." In *Nineteenth Century Religious Thought in the West,* Vol. II, edited by Ninian Smart and others, pp. 29-67. Cambridge: Cambridge University Press, 1985.
   Assesses Emerson's relationship to the Transcendentalist movement and argues that behind the apparent contradictions of Emerson's essays and journals lies a "remarkably consistent body of thought."

Barish, Evelyn. *Emerson: The Roots of Prophecy.* Princeton, N.J.: Princeton University Press, 1989, 267 p.
   Examines Emerson's early life and works.

Bishop, Jonathan. "Emerson and Christianity." *Renascence* XXXVIII, No. 3 (Spring 1986): 183-200.
   Discusses the "Divinity School Address" as documentation of Emerson's divergence from orthodox Christiani-

ty, exploring the relationship between Transcendentalism and Unitarianism.

Blasing, Mutlu Konuk. "Ralph Waldo Emerson: Essaying the Poet." In her *American Poetry: The Rhetoric of Its Forms,* pp. 67-83. New Haven, Conn.: Yale University Press, 1987.
> Provides an overview of Emerson's poetry and essays "in terms of their different yet complementary intentions."

Cady, Edwin H., and Budd, Louis J., eds. *On Emerson: The Best from "American Literature."* Durham, N.C.: Duke University Press, 1988, 282 p.
> Includes essays representing five decades of Emerson criticism in the periodical *American Literature.*

Cameron, Sharon. "Representing Grief: Emerson's 'Experience'." *Representations,* No. 15 (Summer 1986): 15-41.
> Argues that Emerson's "Experience" essay is "a powerful and systematic representation of grief."

Carafiol, Peter. "Reading Emerson: Writing History." *The Centennial Review* XXX, No. 4 (Fall 1986): 431-51.
> Offers an approach to understanding Emerson's work and Transcendentalism as "an alternative philosophy, or better perhaps, an alternative *to* metaphysical philosophy."

Cayton, Mary Kupiec. "The Making of an American Prophet: Emerson, His Audiences, and the Rise of the Culture Industry in Nineteenth-Century America." *The American Historical Review* 92, No. 3 (June 1987): 597-620.
> Examines Emerson's rise in popularity during his lifetime as a cultural phenomenon that depended as much on his audience as on his message.

————. *Emerson's Emergence: Self and Society in the Transformation of New England, 1800-1845.* Chapel Hill: University of North Carolina Press, 1989, 307 p.
> Discusses Emerson's career in the context of the social history of New England, claiming that "Emerson's task was to bring to conscious awareness new aspects of the social order and to name them for what they were."

Cheyfitz, Eric. *The Trans-Parent: Sexual Politics in the Language of Emerson.* Baltimore: Johns Hopkins University Press, 1981, 188 p.
> Examines Emerson's work, particularly *Nature,* in terms of its depiction of conflict between masculine and feminine images.

Chmaj, Betty E. "The Journey and the Mirror: Emerson and the American Arts." *Prospects* 10 (1985): 353-408.
> Analyzes the major themes of the "American Scholar" address and evaluates the essay's impact on American architecture, painting, literature, and music.

Edmundson, Mark. "Emerson and the Work of Melancholia." *Raritan* VI, No. 4 (Spring 1987): 120-36.
> Provides a Freudian analysis of Emerson's "method of self-recreation through crisis," examining his attitude toward loss and mourning as reflected in his later works.

Ellison, Julie. *Emerson's Romantic Style.* Princeton, N.J.: Princeton University Press, 1984, 257 p.
> Traces the development of Emerson's prose style as a reflection of literary Romanticism.

Hakutani, Yoshinobu. "Emerson, Whitman, and Zen Buddhism." *The Midwest Quarterly* XXXI, No. 4 (Summer 1990): 433-48.
> Compares the principles of Zen Buddhism to those of Transcendentalism as espoused by Emerson and Whitman.

Hopkins, Vivian C. *Spires of Form: A Study of Emerson's Aesthetic Theory.* 1951. Reprint. New York: Russell & Russell, 1965, 276 p.
> Offers an interpretation of Emerson's aesthetic theory in an examination of his art and literary criticism.

Hughes, Gertrude Reif. *Emerson's Demanding Optimism.* Baton Rouge: Louisiana State University Press, 1984, 182 p.
> Argues that the optimistic affirmation of individual potential is a theme consistently developed in Emerson's work.

Keating, AnnLouise. "Renaming the Dark: Emerson's Optimism and the Abyss." *ATQ* 4, No. 4 (December 1990): 305-25.
> Demonstrates ways in which Emerson's "optimistic, holistic worldview accepts both despair and faith as valid."

Kennedy, William Sloane. "Clews to Emerson's Mystic Verse." *American Transcendental Quarterly,* No. 29 (Winter 1976): 2-20.
> Reprints an essay originally published in 1903 explicating mythological, mystical, and occult elements in Emerson's poetry.

Leverenz, David. "The Politics of Emerson's Man-Making Words." *PMLA* 101, No. 1 (January 1986): 38-56.
> Evaluates the political implications of Emerson's view of his own manhood, asserting that he promoted an ideal of a "manly intellectual elite."

Marr, David. " 'The Infinitude of the Private Man': Emerson's Ideas of Nature, Culture, and Politics." In his *American Worlds Since Emerson,* pp. 40-72. Amherst: University of Massachusetts Press, 1988.
> Provides "an intellectual history of [Emerson's] idea of 'the infinitude of man' " in a study tracing Emerson's influence on American literary, intellectual, and political history.

McDermott, John J. "Spires of Influence: The Importance of Emerson for Classical American Philosophy." In his *Streams of Experience: Reflections on the History and Philosophy of American Culture,* pp. 29-43. Amherst: University of Massachusetts Press, 1986.
> Traces Emerson's influence on American philosophers William James, Josiah Royce, George Santayana, and John Dewey, and surveys their opinions of Emerson.

Mignon, Charles W. " 'Classic Art': Emerson's Pragmatic Criticism." *Studies in the American Renaissance* (1983): 203-21.
> Surveys Emerson's literary criticism of classic and contemporary authors, commenting on his "organic and deeply moral" theory of literature.

Myerson, Joel, ed. *Emerson Centenary Essays.* Carbondale: Southern Illinois University Press, 1982, 218 p.
> Includes essays by Jerome Loving, David Robinson, and Merton M. Sealts Jr., occasioned by the centenary of Emerson's death.

Packer, Barbara. "Origin and Authority: Emerson and the

Higher Criticism." In *Reconstructing American Literary History,* edited by Sacvan Bercovitch, pp. 67-92. Cambridge, Mass.: Harvard University Press, 1986.

> Considers the possible influence of German biblical scholars known as the "higher critics" on Emerson's religious beliefs and his theory of poetics.

Porter, Carolyn. "Ralph Waldo Emerson: Man as Subject Lens." In her *Seeing and Being: The Plight of the Participant Observer in Emerson, James, Adams, and Faulkner,* pp. 57-118. Middletown, Conn.: Wesleyan University Press, 1981.

> Analyzes American society during Emerson's life and discusses the essay *Nature* as demonstrating Emerson's "method for combating reification."

Railton, Stephen. " 'Assume an Identity of Sentiment': Rhetoric and Audience in Emerson's 'Divinity School Address'." *Prospects* 9 (1984): 31-47.

> Discusses the "Divinity School Address" as Emerson's attempt to challenge the assumptions of his audience and persuade them to accept his own moral insights.

Robinson, David. *Apostle of Culture: Emerson as Preacher and Lecturer.* Philadelphia: University of Pennsylvania Press, 1982, 205 p.

> Traces the development of Emerson's career as an orator, commenting on the ways in which his Unitarian background informed his works.

Scheik, William J. *The Slender Human Word: Emerson's Artistry in Prose.* Knoxville: University of Tennessee Press, 1978, 162 p.

> Analyzes Emerson's essays as prose poems structured around "hieroglyphs" or central images.

Schweitzer, Ivy. "Transcendental Sacramentals: 'The Lord's Supper' and Emerson's Doctrine of Form." *The New England Quarterly* LXI, No. 3 (September 1988): 398-418.

> Discusses the theological and philosophical implications of the sermon in which Emerson announced his resignation as a Unitarian pastor.

Sealts, Merton M., Jr. "Mulberry Leaves and Satin: Emerson's Theory of the Creative Process." *Studies in the American Renaissance* (1985): 79-94.

> Explicates Emerson's theory of creativity, focusing particularly on his 1836-37 lecture series, "The Philosophy of History."

Smith, David L. "Emerson and Deconstruction: The End(s) of Scholarship." *Soundings* LXVII, No. 4 (Winter 1984): 379-98.

> Considers parallels between Emerson's expression of skepticism and the "radical skepticism" inherent in the literary philosophy of deconstructionism.

Thurin, Erik Ingvar. *Emerson as Priest of Pan: A Study in the Metaphysics of Sex.* Lawrence: Regents Press of Kansas, 1981, 292 p.

> Discusses Emerson's views on the relations between the sexes as reflecting his "bipolaric" conception of humanity and the universe.

Van Leer, David. *Emerson's Epistemology: The Argument of the Essays.* Cambridge: Cambridge University Press, 1986, 282 p.

> Examines Emerson's major writings, particularly *Nature,* "The Divinity School Address," "Self-Reliance," and "Experience," suggesting that they possess a well-structured and unified philosophy.

Yoder, R. A. *Emerson and the Orphic Poet in America.* Berkeley and Los Angeles: University of California Press, 1978, 240 p.

> Regards Emersons views on poetry and the role of the poet as adapting and redirecting the convictions of European Romanticism.

Additional coverage of Emerson's life and career is contained in the following sources published by Gale Research: *Dictionary of Literary Biography,* Vols. 1, 59, 73; and *Nineteenth-Century Literature Criticism,* Vol. 1.

Caroline Lamb

1785-1828

English novelist and poet.

INTRODUCTION

Lamb achieved notoriety in the early nineteenth century as the author of *Glenarvon,* a roman à clef featuring a first-hand account of her scandalous extramarital affair with the poet George Gordon, Lord Byron.

Lamb was the only daughter of Lady Henrietta Spencer and Frederick Ponsonby, third Earl of Bessborough. Her early upbringing was left primarily to family servants in Italy until 1794, when she returned to London to be raised by her aunt, the Duchess of Devonshire. In 1805 she married William Lamb, who later became Lord Melbourne, and the couple had three children, only one of whom survived. Lamb met Byron in 1812 at a party at the home of her mother-in-law, Lady Melbourne; her journal entry for that evening records her often-quoted first impression of the poet as "mad, bad, and dangerous to know." Their affair began soon thereafter, and Lamb's public flaunting of Byron's affections caused a scandal. When Byron terminated the relationship a few months later, Lamb's behavior became increasingly eccentric: she masqueraded as a page in order to gain entry to Byron's home, ceremoniously burned copies of his letters to her, and stabbed herself in his presence at a party. During this time, her husband was urged by his family to seek a formal separation, but he refused.

Lamb wrote *Glenarvon* in 1816. Though she wrote the novel without her family's knowledge and published it anonymously, its authorship was immediately clear to the public, as were the thinly veiled identities of the principal characters. While the novel was a popular success, prompting three editions and an Italian translation, Lamb's characterizations and depiction of her relationship with Byron offended many of her peers; consequently, her social standing was considerably diminished. In 1819 Lamb composed and anonymously published two poems, *A New Canto* and *Gordon: A Tale,* in response to Byron's epic poem *Don Juan.* She also wrote two additional novels; however, both *Graham Hamilton,* a fictionalized depiction of the Duchess of Devonshire, and *Ada Reis,* an adventure story with exotic settings, failed to match the success of *Glenarvon.* In 1824 Lamb accidentally encountered Byron's funeral procession—an incident often cited as instrumental to her subsequent dissipation. Her abuse of alcohol and laudanum and her flirtations with other men eventually alienated her from her husband. They separated in 1825, though he allowed her to reside at his family home in Hertfordshire, where she spent the last few years of her life with her father-in-law and her son. She died in 1828.

Critical reaction to Lamb's work has centered almost exclusively on *Glenarvon.* Set in Ireland, the novel involves Calantha (Lamb), who is ignored by her husband Lord Avondale (William Lamb), and is seduced, won over, and ultimately abandoned by Glenarvon (Byron), an organizer of Irish resistance against the English government. *Glenarvon* also offers stinging criticisms of well-known members of English society, including Lady Melbourne. Byron read the novel and reportedly dismissed its characterization of him, commenting that "as for the likeness, the picture can't be good—I did not sit long enough." Lamb's motivation for publishing *Glenarvon,* and thereby risking the further disapproval of her husband and peers, has prompted varying interpretations. While it has been regarded as an attempt to punish her in-laws and Byron for what she perceived as their cruelty toward her—a motive Lamb denied in a preface to the second edition—more recent critics have suggested that Lamb's candor was intended to justify her behavior by placing the blame for the affair on her husband's inattentiveness. Other critics have maintained that Lamb sought to publicly confess her misdeeds and accept the blame for the scandal.

In an evaluation of the significance of *Glenarvon* as historical and biographical literature, David Cecil dismissed the novel as "an incoherent cross between a realistic novel of fashionable life and a fantastic tale of terror, made preposterous by every absurd device." However, Peter W. Graham has suggested that it is unique in English literature, representing a retelling of the Don Juan myth from a female point of view, and has examined the hero of Byron's *Don Juan* as a reaction to Lamb's characterization of Byron in *Glenarvon*. Other commentators, including Joseph Garver and Malcolm Kelsall, have examined the novel's political content, particularly its presentation of the attitudes of the English aristocracy toward revolution in Ireland.

Glenarvon is not widely read today, and critics generally agree that it is overly sentimental and stylistically flawed. Nevertheless, an increasing amount of critical attention in the twentieth century suggests, as Clarke Olney has noted, that when Lamb "forgoes the fustian, when she writes from her heart and from her experience, she has something to say—and she often says it well."

PRINCIPAL WORKS

Glenarvon (novel) 1816
A New Canto (poetry) 1819
Gordon: A Tale (poetry) 1821
Graham Hamilton (novel) 1822
Ada Reis (novel) 1823

David Cecil (essay date 1939)

[*Cecil was an important modern English literary critic and biographer who wrote extensively on eighteenth- and nineteenth-century authors. In addition to his distinguished studies of the lives and works of Jane Austen, Max Beerbohm, Charles Lamb, and Thomas Hardy, he wrote a critically acclaimed biography of Lamb's husband, Lord Melbourne. In the following excerpt from that work, originally published in 1939, he dismisses Glenarvon as Lamb's vain and angry reaction to her husband's desire for a formal separation.*]

[*Glenarvon*] is a deplorable production: an incoherent cross between a realistic novel of fashionable life and a fantastic tale of terror, made preposterous by every absurd device—assassins, spectres, manacled maniacs, children changed at birth—that an imagination nurtured on mock-Gothic romance could suggest. But it has its interest, as revealing the way that Caroline contrived to reshape her story so as to please her vanity. She appears as Calantha, a heroine, noble, innocent, fascinating, but too impulsive for success in a hard-hearted world. Her husband, Lord Avondale, otherwise William, in spite of the fact that he too is unusually noble-hearted, neglects her, and corrupts her morals by his cynical views. In consequence, she yields to the temptations of a depraved society and finally, though only after heroic resistance on her part, is seduced by Byron, here called Glenarvon. He is Byronism incarnate; beautiful and gifted beyond belief, but driven by the pangs of a conscience burdened with inexpiable crimes, to go about betraying and ruining people in a spirit of gloomy

desperation. Though Calantha is the love of his life, he deserts her out of pure devilry. The heartless world turns against her; she dies of a broken heart: Avondale dies shortly afterwards out of sympathy. For Glenarvon a more sensational fate is reserved. He jumps off a ship into the sea after sailing about for days, pursued by a phantom vessel manned by revengeful demons of gigantic size.

The tension of this dramatic tale is relieved by some thinly veiled satirical portraits of the Lamb family, the Devonshire family, Lady Oxford, Lady Holland, and a number of other leading social figures, notably the influential Lady Jersey. Its moral is that Caroline's misfortunes were Byron's fault, William's fault, society's fault—anyone's fault, in fact, but her own. (pp. 109-10)

> David Cecil, "Frustration," in his Melbourne: The Young Melbourne and Lord M in One Volume, The Reprint Society, 1955, pp. 108-17.

Clarke Olney (essay date 1956)

[*In the following excerpt, Olney defends* Glenarvon *as an objective and well-intentioned account of Lamb's affair with Byron.*]

In 1816, four years after [Lamb's affair with Byron] had broken off and only a few days after Byron's final departure from England, Caroline Lamb published anonymously a novel, *Glenarvon,* which had to do principally with her relationship with the poet. Its heroine, Calantha, named after the tragic heroine of John Ford's play *The Broken Heart,* is of course, Lady Caroline; Glenarvon, the desperately wicked hero, is Byron. Perhaps because of its length—some one hundred fifty thousand words—perhaps because as a novel it is so absurdly conceived and written, few modern students of Byron have taken the trouble to read it. Most have been content to assume that Lady Caroline chose this means to strike back at Byron for her betrayal and to put her own case in as favorable a light as possible. It is on such assumptions that most comments on *Glenarvon* are made. But a careful reading of the novel may lead one to somewhat different conclusions.

In the first place, it is by no means all badly written. The plotting, much of the dialogue, all of the farrago of Gothic and Byronic melodrama are shockingly amateurish and bad; but there are passages, even pages of excellence. When Caroline foregoes the fustian, when she writes from her heart and from her experience, she has something to say—and she often says it well.

There are glimpses of society and society types which are accurately observed and cleverly written. Her characterization of the Devonshire Circle (at Castle Delaval in the novel) in contrast to that at Melbourne House (Monteith) is discriminating and incisive, and when she pillories Lady Holland (as the Princess of Madagascar) and her sycophantic entourage at Holland (Barbary) House, the satire is telling.

It is in the story of the fatal love of Calantha for Glenarvon that Caroline's own version of her affair with Byron emerges. It is here that one might expect the author to gloss over her own faults at the expense of her wicked seducer. But this is precisely what she does not do. Glenarvon is pictured as depraved enough, in all conscience, but no more so than the hero of any Byron romance. And to his credit be it said that like the rattlesnake he gives ample warning before he strikes. It is not Glenarvon but Calantha who is charged with the responsibility and the blame. The course of her infatuation is told unsparingly. The wrong she does her considerate and noble husband is never condoned.

In her fictional account of actual events Lady Caroline is surprisingly objective. Of course, as the discarded mistress she cannot be expected to gaze dry-eyed upon the ruins. But for all her faults—which were chiefly of the heart—there was about Caroline Lamb a childlike candor and honesty which one feels keeps her close to the emotional if not the literal truth. The frantic unreality of the imagined portions of the story makes it possible to recognize the essential truth of her account of those events which she actually experienced. Although the guise of fiction is maintained, it wears very thin on occasions.

It is true that Lady Caroline never seems to have recognized any other Byron than the satanic, passionate, compulsion-driven hero of his own romances. Undoubtedly, for a real understanding of Lord Byron during the Years of Fame one must seek elsewhere than in the pages of *Glenarvon.* But what does emerge there is Byron as he appeared to many of the women of the time; and while Lady Caroline was perhaps his most extravagant infatuate, her picture of him in *Glenarvon* may stand as representative of the somewhat absurd figure then currently accepted as the real Lord Byron.

> That which was disgusting or terrific to man's nature, had no power over Glenarvon. He had looked upon the dying and the dead; he had seen the tear of agony without emotion; he had heard the shriek of despair, and felt the hot blood as it flowed from the heart of a murdered enemy, nor turned from the sickening sight. Even the storms of nature could not move Glenarvon . . .
>
> The rushing winds but seemed to soothe his perturbed spirit; and the calm of his brow remained unaltered in every changing scene. Yet it was the calm of hopeless despair, when passion . . . steels the heart . . . against every sentiment of mercy.
>
> Who . . . had trusted to the music of that soft voice, when it breathed forth vows of tenderness and love? . . . None—none believed or trusted in Glenarvon. Yet thousands flocked around and flattered him.

Oddly enough, Caroline's delineation of Lord Glenarvon is not on the whole especially vindictive. She spares him no accusation of diabolism and treachery, but the tone of her reproaches, more often than not, is one of regret and self-accusation, mingled at times with a kind of awed admiration. For she, like Glenarvon, felt herself fated. As one of the characters in the novel remarks: "She is in love with ruin; it stalks about in every possible shape, and in

every shape she hails it." This compulsive urge toward self-distruction, this "need of fatality" as it has been called, is one aspect of Byronism that Caroline Lamb made completely her own.

Perhaps Lady Caroline never really fell out of love with Byron or the picture she had created of him. Perhaps, as at their first meeting, "Calantha felt the power, not then alone, but evermore. She felt the empire, the charm, the peculiar charm, those features that being must have for her."

The character of William Lamb, as Lord Avondale, is sketched in loving detail; he is all nobility and indulgent tenderness. The only fault attributed to him is his unwise toleration of his wife's whimsies. He spoils Calantha; he treats her as a child, which she quite naturally resents; but he makes the tragic mistake of overestimating her ability to withstand temptations which are far beyond her undisciplined powers to resist. For the worldliness of his upbringing and the extreme latitude of his views on religion and morality have had a disastrous effect upon his naive and innocent bride. Her early principles and inhibitions have all been laughed away. She has no longer any defenses against the sinister charm of Glenarvon—nothing except an innate integrity and self-respect, and these are not enough, once her passions are aroused.

In the picture of herself as Calantha, the heroine, Caroline does not spare herself: it is no flattering portrait that she draws:

> She seemed to have a decided turn for every thing it was necessary for her to learn . . . yet never did she attain excellence, or make proficiency in any . . . With an ear the most sensible and accurate, she could neither dance nor play; with an eye acute and exact, she could not draw . . . she was bashful and unsocial in society; and with the germs of every virtue that commands esteem and praise, she was already the theme of discussion, observation and censure.

And when Lord Avondale wooed and won

> that strange uncertain being . . . he considered not . . . the qualities in which she was wholly deficient . . . discretion, prudence, firm and steady principle, obedience, humility.

It seems likely, too, that Lady Caroline created the somewhat fey character of Elinor St. Clare as a complement to Calantha, feeling perhaps that Elinor could embody aspects of the author's personality which the more lady-like Calantha could not. Elinor follows Glenarvon about "in the attire of a boy," a practice which, it will be recalled, was one of Caroline's favorite gambits in her pursuit of Byron. Too, Elinor plays wildly and beautifully on the harp and composes and sings sad, wild songs, and rides horseback magnificently, and dances madly and with abandon: and all of these were actual or wished-for accomplishments of Lady Caroline Lamb.

I have not attempted here to examine and evaluate the passages in Glenarvon which shed light upon the Byron-Lamb triangle. That, however, is a task which future biographers of Lord Byron or Lady Caroline should undertake. There does remain one further aspect of the novel to be considered: the question as to why Lady Caroline Lamb wrote and published it.

In a letter to Lord Granville, a loyal friend, Caroline described her feelings at the time she gave the manuscript to Colburn, her publisher. She had been, she said, cut and rejected by all her friends. The Lambs, she knew, despised her. Lady Melbourne and Lady Cowper—William's mother and sister—having "for four years . . . supported Lord Byron," had turned upon her, and her "wrongs, crimes, follies, even the last, were raked up from the days of infancy and brought forth to view without mercy. *To write this novel was then my sole comfort.*"

To write *Glenarvon* may indeed have been a "comfort"; but this can scarcely be accepted as her reason for publishing it. The obvious explanation would be that she was using it as a weapon to strike back at her enemies and detractors, that she desired to wound those who she felt had destroyed her. This may have been one of her motives, but I am convinced that it was not the chief one.

In the Preface to the second edition of *Glenarvon,* Caroline herself protested her innocence of any malicious or vengeful motives. And in a letter she said: "This novel may be stupid, may be unseemly for me to write, but it is assuredly anything but malevolent."

Whatever her intention may have been, the effect of the publication of *Glenarvon* was disastrous. The Lambs, a close-knit family, long since fed to the ears with the vagaries of "The Bat" or "The Little Savage" as they called her, were completely alienated. Lady Melbourne, matriarch of the family, was thoroughly disgusted. William, according to his biographer Lord David Cecil, was "utterly crushed."

Glenarvon enjoyed a success of notoriety. Three editions were published in 1816, a fourth in 1817. And it gave quietus to Lady Caroline's already precarious social standing; henceforth she was forever beyond the pale.

Granted that it was rash and foolish and ill-advised; granted that even so impulsive a person as Caroline Lamb must have foreseen at least some of the consequences—why then did she do it?

I am convinced that she intended it primarily as an act of contrition and humility; a public confession of her sin; an amende honorable to those, especially William Lamb, whom she had so cruelly wronged. It was a childish and irresponsible act—but Caroline Lamb *was* childish and irresponsible in many of the things she did. She did not blame Byron for her downfall. The fictional representations of Lady Melbourne are for the most part portrayed as kind, sympathetic, and warm-hearted—and this in spite of the fact that Caroline, by no means unintelligent, knew that William's mother was not her friend and had been serving as Byron's confidante. Had she wished to lash out at her mother-in-law, Caroline could easily have done so, for Lady Melbourne's reputation was far from invulnerable. But the Viscountess is handled with gloves.

No. In *Glenarvon* the blame is placed squarely upon Calantha, the heroine who, like her namesake in the play,

dies of a broken heart. And Calantha is the author, Lady Caroline Lamb, the rejected mistress of Lord Byron, who knew that her life had been destroyed by her own blind folly, and knowing this, inscribed as the motto of her novel two lines from the *Inferno:* "[I renew] a hopeless woe which burthens my heart, even at the very thought, before I tell thereof." (pp. 272-76)

> *Clarke Olney, " 'Glenarvon' Revisited," in* The University of Kansas City Review, *Vol. XXII, No. 4, June, 1956, pp. 271-76.*

Margot Strickland   (essay date 1974)

[*Strickland is an English actress, novelist, and biographer. In the following excerpt, she discusses the circumstances under which Lamb wrote her novels.*]

If only Caroline had contented herself with writing her novel, *Glenarvon,* and had refrained from publishing it, she might not have damned herself entirely. But she had worked herself up to a frenzy of idealistic ambition. Her delusion was not caused solely by a romantic fixation on a handsome poet; her novel was intended to be a serious indictment of a false society peopled by transparently identifiable luminaries, with Byron and herself the central figures. With it she would revenge herself on her uncaring husband, her tawdry mother-in-law and a hypocritical society which valued neither art, truth nor Caroline.

Written in a crusading spirit and at breakneck speed, it was published, mostly unrevised, a fortnight after Byron left England, by a Caroline still buoyant on the crest of a defiant wave. Therapeutic to write, it was impossible to read, written as it was in a mood of sustained daemonic frenzy. Augustus Foster wrote, 'I had not patience to get through it, it is so disordered. . . . The uncommon impudence that runs through it is to me astonishing. . . . I sadly fear a bad end for her.' But it was a certain bestseller, running to several editions, with French and German translations. The publishers were delighted and people read it avidly, identifying themselves, some with horror and others with glee. A *succès de scandale* of unedifying proportions, it ruined Caroline.

'There is nothing worse than being calumniated without the possibility of justification,' wrote Caroline, 'no situation so cruel as that of entire solitude when feverish hopes, fears and eager irritation torture the mind. From scenes . . . where events had crowded upon each other with such rapidity, the change to loneliness was insupportable.' Caroline was ostracized by an outraged society.

Caroline's only merit in Lady Melbourne's eyes was the accidental quality of her aristocratic birth, which could help to advance her husband William. Caroline's outrageous honesty was now imperilling his political career. The situation exacerbated a relationship notoriously delicate and in the Lambs' case geographically too close. Caroline's openly displayed passion for Byron and subsequent maniacal behaviour united the Lamb family in putting pressure upon William to separate legally from her. Caroline pleaded support from Lord Granville, her mother's former lover, now married to her cousin Hary-o. 'You should see my husband, who knows everything . . . and who says that he could not in honour give me up.' There had been a dreadfully unpleasant scene at Melbourne House, Caroline reminded him. 'Recollect . . . I was ordered out of the House in no gentle language: my mother was spoke to with the most barbarous roughness in my presence . . . I was *proved* mad. Mr Moore assured me I was so. . . . I appealed to a few, but my letters were not even answered. I went to Roehampton, Lady Jersey to the extreme annoyance of my father, turned her back upon me. . . . Lord Holland . . . coldly passed me by . . . I could not stand it. . . . Wm returned, a dreadful scene passed between Lord M and Mama. That night I sent the novel.'

Had Caroline been treated with greater sensitivity, the novel might never have appeared. The Lambs probably impressed upon Caroline her financial dependence upon them. Resenting this bitterly and gambling her talent alone against the forces of society, she lost her reputation, her position and, in time, her confidence. (pp. 55-6)

[In 1820] Caroline was often ill, distracting herself with wine and unsavoury company, dulling her senses with laudanum. She confined herself to the solitary pursuit of writing, to try again for the success she craved. In her second novel, **Graham Hamilton,** which she delayed publishing for two years, she made heroic efforts to discipline herself into writing well and constructing with care. Written in a mood of elegiac despair, it describes the hallucinatory effects of the drug laudanum, freely available at that time and often casually taken for an aching tooth or a slight headache. 'It was as if my imagination was struck . . . as if material objects vanished, and the perceptions of the mind became too bright and vivid for the understanding to bear. I was as if endowed for a few instants with a new sense; memory appeared to cease and futurity to open.' She suffered nightmare visions: 'It was as if a mist had enveloped me. I saw no more . . . a singing in my ears—a sickness and violent beating of the heart oppressed me. . . . I put my hand to my head—I had not power to speak . . . a vision wholly different seemed to fill the scene; everyone appeared clad in black . . . then all was terror, uproar, noise.'

But the novel, containing neither the sensational gossip of **Glenarvon,** nor a Byronic hero, failed, and Caroline suffered the discouragement of rejection in the one art she deeply cared for and in which she had laboured alone, hoping for recognition of the ability she knew she possessed. Her spark of talent, ignited by Byron and fanned by her own ambition into a consuming conflagration, wavered fatally but did not quite go out.

In 1821 Caroline wrote to her mother in Florence, 'Dearest of own Heart's blood, dearest I would you were in England. There is a strange wild story called **Ada Reis,** written they say by an American.' Caroline had somehow summoned up the energy and had confined herself to the solitude she detested and feared, to try again with a third novel, also published anonymously and also a failure. Her hopes of repeating the financial success achieved by **Glenarvon** were not fulfilled. (p. 61)

Margot Strickland, "Caroline," in her The Byron Women, *Peter Owenn Limited, London, 1974, pp. 40-66.*

From William Lamb's letter to the publisher of *Ada Reis:*

The incongruity of, and objection to, the story of **Ada Reis** can only be got over by power of writing, beauty of sentiment, striking and effective situation, etc. If Mr. Gifford thinks there is in the first two volumes anything of excellence sufficient to overbalance their manifest faults, I still hope that he will press upon Lady Caroline the absolute necessity of carefully reconsidering and revising the third volume, and particularly the conclusion of the novel. . . . I think, if it were thought that anything could be done with the novel, and that the fault of its design and structure can be got over, that I could put her in the way of writing up this part a little, and giving it something of strength, spirit, and novelty, and of making it at once more moral and more interesting. I wish you would communicate these my hasty suggestions to Mr. Gifford, and he will see the propriety of pressing Lady Caroline to take a little more time to this part of the novel. She will be guided by his authority, and her fault at present is to be too hasty and too impatient of the trouble of correcting and recasting what is faulty.

Quoted in Melbourne, *by David Cecil, The Reprint Society, 1955.*

John Clubbe (essay date 1979)

[*Clubbe is an American educator and critic who specializes in nineteenth-century English literature. In the following excerpt, he discusses Lamb's motives for writing* Glenarvon, *assessing the strengths and weaknesses of the novel and focusing particularly on revisions she made for the second edition.*]

"What—& who—the devil is 'Glenarvon'" exclaimed Byron in a letter of June 23, 1816 to John Cam Hobhouse. "I know nothing—nor ever heard of such a person." The novel had appeared in three volumes on May 9, scarcely two weeks after Byron had left England for self-chosen exile on the Continent. It bore the imprint of Henry Colburn, then beginning his career as a leading purveyor of fashionable fiction. No author's name graced the title page, but the first readers of **Glenarvon** soon perceived that some of the leading notables of the day figured (under transparent disguises) in its pages. Such notoriety assured the success of the book; talk about it spread like wildfire. By June 22, the public had called for a second edition. A third appeared within the year, a fourth in 1817. Needless to say, **Glenarvon** added to the obloquy heaped upon Byron during the spring of 1816. He had recently agreed to a separation from his wife, and rumors raced about London that his relationship with his half-sister Augusta Leigh was incestuous. When **Glenarvon** appeared, he was proceeding up the Rhine to Switzerland, writing as he went the third canto of *Childe Harold,* and unaware that further controversy raged around his name in England.

Among those Byron left behind in England no one was more distressed than William Lamb's wife. Lady Caroline had been Byron's first conquest in the great world of the Whig aristocracy to which the éclat of the first two cantos of *Childe Harold* in 1812 had gained him immediate entry. When she first saw him at a ball she turned away, noting in her journal that he was "mad—bad—and dangerous to know." Byron was twenty-four, Caroline twenty-six, but looking like a boy. They soon met again, and fell wildly in love for several months; but by October, 1812, Byron wished to terminate an affair that had grown tiresome. Yet Caroline refused to leave him alone. She deluged him with letters, to which replies became progressively rarer. Between 1813 and the spring of 1816, Caroline, her passion unabated, intruded less into Byron's life. During these years she meditated upon her relationship with him, clearly the central experience in her life, and began the narrative that became *Glenarvon.* In its settings and characters, the novel emerges out of the 1812 affair and—fictionalized, romanticized, and gothicized—recreates it.

Most critics have assumed that Caroline published *Glenarvon* as an act of revenge upon her husband's family, the Melbournes. But Caroline denied "the charge of malevolence" in the preface to the second edition. She told a correspondent, "this novel may be stupid may be unseemly for me to write may be any thing you please but is assuredly any thing but malevolent." Clarke Olney, author of one of the few articles on *Glenarvon* [*University of Kansas City Review* (June 1956)], believes that Caroline intended her novel "primarily as an act of contrition and humility; a public confession of her sin." The truth, as usual, lies somewhere in the middle. Caroline was seeking revenge, though this was not her primary motivation; she was confessing her sins publicly, though not exactly in the spirit of contrition that Olney suggests. Rather, the novel forced itself out of her: she had to write it much as Byron had to write his confessional poems. "Those who suffer deeply, will express themselves strongly," she wrote in the preface to the second edition; "those who have been cruelly attacked, will use the means of resistance, which are within their reach." During the time she worked on *Glenarvon* she lived under more than usual emotional strain: "*to write this novel was then my only comfort,*" she told her friend Lord Granville.

"In one month I wrote and sent *Glenarvon* to the press," Caroline later wrote. "It was written at night, without the knowledge of any one but a governess, Miss Walsh [Welsh]." Probably Caroline did write it secretly at night, for its appearance in print seems to have caught the Melbournes completely by surprise. But did she write it in a month? Most commentators have taken her at her word. Night after night, so the story goes, she sat dressed in page's costume composing *Glenarvon.* Yet when we consider the 150,000 words and the intricate plot of the novel, it becomes unlikely that Caroline could have written it in a month. Unpublished correspondence between her and John Murray confirms that she worked, as only "George Paston" and Peter Quennell have noted, "for two or three years" on *Glenarvon.* Though Caroline may well have revised her novel in a frenzy of activity during the early months of 1816, the correspondence to Murray indicates that it was substantially completed by June, 1815. Perhaps she conceived of *Glenarvon* as early as 1812, for in the autumn of that year her husband's family virtually exiled her to their estates in Ireland and much of the novel takes place in that country. When she heard of Byron's engagement to Annabella Milbanke in the autumn of 1814, she exclaimed to Murray, "It is the last page of my novel—all the former ones you had better destroy." In July, 1815, Caroline was in Brussels visiting her brother wounded at Waterloo. Before she left England, she told Murray, "I inclose you my drawings—& Miss Webster will send you my MSS—it is in a dreadful state I only had time to correct the 3*d* vol—which you read all the rest is merely copied from my Brouillon & terrible." In another letter she asked Murray (who was Byron's publisher) to read it and presumably to take it on; but he, not wishing to offend his most famous author, would have no part of it. "My heart is set on the Publication of my novel," she wrote him about this time, but decided that it was "still very unequal—I am going to reconsider it." Apparently she did; but we still confront the question, why did it come out when it did, shortly after Byron had left the Continent, when all the world seemed ranged against him. Caroline always claimed that she published *Glenarvon* to help Byron's cause. Perhaps in her deluded way she was sincere in her belief, but the immediate effect of publication was to blacken further the poet's already-sullied name.

To what extent do the characters in *Glenarvon* reflect contemporaries? Most readers have considered it a *roman à clef.* The most familiar key is that provided by Lady Holland:

> The outlines of few of her characters are portraits, but the *amplissage* and traits are exact. *Lady Morganet* [Margaret] is a twofold being— Dss. of Devonshire and her mother: *Lady Augusta* Lady Jersey and Lady Collier: *Sophia* Lady Granville, who had 6 years ago a passion for working fine embroidery, and she marks most *atrociously* her marriage with Lord Granville. *Lady Mandeville* is Ly. Oxford; *Buchanan* is Sir Godfrey Webster: *Glenarvon* and *Vivian* [i] are of course Lord Byron. Lady Frances Webster is sketched and some others slightly. Lady Melbourne is represented as bigotted and vulgar. . . .

And, unmentioned but obvious, the heroine—Calantha, Lady Avondale—is Caroline herself (or rather her rendering of her romantic, ideal self). Other individual portraits stud *Glenarvon.* Novels with readily identifiable characters were a specialty of Colburn, who liked to have it bruited about that his authors were famous and that the characters in their novels were real and of the nobility. *Glenarvon* must have delighted him, for he had no need to simulate when the characters were indeed based on actual personages and were readily indentifiable, as was the author of the novel. To the charge of portraiture from life Caroline defends herself somewhat weakly in the preface to the second edition: "The lineaments, with which he [the author] is most familiar, will sometimes almost involuntarily rise beneath the touch of his pencil."

Glenarvon published, its cast of characters widely known,

brought disaster upon Caroline. It ruined her social position and whatever was left of her reputation. The always critical Melbournes, together with other prominent Whig families whom she pilloried, expressed their indignation to her about a work that Lady Holland, no doubt speaking for many, termed a "strange farrago." William Lamb was so profoundly upset that, urged by his family, he took steps to arrange a separation. The English aristocracy that had turned viciously on Byron in the months before now registered their disapproval of another who had not only attacked it but who also—worse still—flaunted her transgressions against its moral code.

For a few months *Glenarvon* was on everyone's tongue. Newspapers and journals gave the book widespread publicity. Everyone sought it out for its alleged scandal and gossip about those in high life. "Your opinion of *Glenarvon* is very indulgent," Mrs. George Lamb wrote to Annabella, Lady Byron. "It has made a great noise in London, and is I think more blamed than admired." Three weeks later Augusta Leigh expressed her sentiments to Francis Hodgson: "I suppose you have heard of Lady C. L.'s extraordinary production—*Glenarvon,* a novel. The hero and heroine you may guess; the former painted in the most atrocious colours. . . . I hear this *horrid* book is supposed and believed a true delineation of *his* character." On July 10, 1816, the Duke of Wellington informed Lady Shelley that "Calantha is 'fit to be tied' " and that "all London is in arms." The day before the aged Mrs. Piozzi had written from Bath to Sir James Fellowes that "the Misses here are all reading *Glenarvon,* 'a monstrous tale of things impossible,' at least one hopes so. I have finished it at last though not comprehended it." Nor had Byron's banker friend, Douglas Kinnaird, comprehended it, for he wrote his brother, Lord Kinnaird: "Lady Caroline is much abus'd for *Glenarvon.* . . . It is unintelligible to the greater part of its readers—of which class I am one." Yet, even though *Glenarvon* left many people puzzled, it had its admirers. Shelley, in a letter to Byron of September 11, mentioned that the painter Northcote "had recommended Godwin to read *Glenarvon,* affirming that many parts of it exhibited extraordinary talent." And Edward Bulwer remembered that when he first read *Glenarvon* in school, it "made on me a deeper impression than any romance I remember, and, had its literary execution equalled the intense imagination which conceived it—I believe that it would have ranked among the few fictions which produce a permanent effect upon youth in every period of the world."

Enormous curiosity about Byron's life already existed, but no biographies had appeared. Understandably, the public eagerly scanned *Glenarvon* for clues that would reveal the mysterious author of *Childe Harold I* and *II* and the Oriental tales. Even Goethe, "though the novel bored him dreadfully . . . read it from cover to cover under the impression that he was gleaning reliable information about Byron's private life." If Goethe was befooled, small wonder that few considered *Glenarvon* as more than fictionalized biography.

Twentieth-century readers, more vocal than numerous, have not dealt kindly with the novel. (pp. 205-08)

The defects of *Glenarvon* are those of the Romantic novel

Lamb at the time of her marriage in 1805.

in general: sentimentality, shoddy construction, wooden characters, unconvincing and melodramatic scenes, a tendency to allow all encounters to slide into bathos, bad writing everywhere. The characters, except possibly Calantha and Glenarvon himself, are insufficiently introduced and awkwardly motivated. They behave in an extravagant, postured manner, untrue to the real-life models upon whom Caroline drew them. The headlong narrative of Calantha's doomed passion for Glenarvon, and the incredible pace at which crisis succeeds crisis, result in an often absurd book. Yet the defects spring from one of the virtues of *Glenarvon.* Caroline wrote the novel "from the heart," as Henry Blyth has said [*Caro, The Fatal Passion,* 1972]. "No future work was likely to have the same driving force behind it, or the same truth of feeling." For Caroline, emotional intensity and romantic enthusiasm were positive virtues in novel-writing. "In this cold & cavilling age enthusiasm is a far less natural feeling than love of ridicule & censure," she once wrote Murray. This enthusiasm she sought to convey both in her style and in her subject matter. Once she criticized Maria Edgeworth to Murray for her lack of "Genius." "She has not one single spark of it which time or opportunity could kindle—but in its place I think she has a very reasoning head much humour—& great discrimination—she paints like the Dutch school true to life—I only quarrel with her choice." Caroline's choice would be, presumably, high life, romantic blur rather than realistic detail, and Salvator Rosa-esque descriptions of nature after the manner of Mrs. Radcliffe. Though we need not make Caroline into a theorist of the novel, she had clearly given some thought to what a novel should be.

If the flaws of *Glenarvon* are legion, what of its merits? These are chiefly biographical and social—as a portrait of

Byron and as a depiction of the aristocratic Whig circles Caroline moved in. The novel does tell us something about Byron and, more usefully, about the way Caroline (and other women) viewed him. Its portrayal of Whig society may well be distorted in places, but it has the merit of having been written by someone of intelligence who knew the workings of that society. Biographers of Regency figures, such as Ethel Colburn Mayne in her account of Caroline's mother, Lady Bessborough, and Elizabeth Jenkins in her life of Caroline herself, have often found acute the rendering of personality and social scene in *Glenarvon.* "It is a mischievous book," wrote one contemporary [Charles Lemon], "but interesting as giving a true picture of the sentiment and moral sophistry of that set." *Glenarvon* succeeds best when Caroline, faithful to her admiration of Pope and Swift, indulges her talent for satire of Regency types. A virtual monologue by Lady Augusta Selwyn brilliantly captures the wit and artificial bonhomie of that gilded age. In many other passages in the novel, we discover touches of humor. Though Caroline could not spell, she had a good ear for words. Here is a conversation, not untypical in its sparkling repartee, between two minor grandees: " 'Count, you are the object of my astonishment.' 'And you, Sir, of my derision.' 'Italian, I despise you.' 'I should only feel mortified, if Sir Everard did otherwise.' 'The contempt, Sir, of the meanest, cannot be a matter of triumph.' 'It is a mark of wisdom, to be proud of the scorn of fools.' 'Passion makes me mad.' 'Sir, you were that before.' 'I shall forget myself.' 'I wish you would permit me to do so.' "

Another strength of *Glenarvon,* as of the Romantic novel in general, lies in its quality of introspective self-analysis. We read such works more for what they tell us about the author or about those depicted in its pages than for what they tell us about the art of the novel. In this regard, *Glenarvon* is akin to a poem like *Childe Harold,* for it too attempts to create a living world out of personal experience. Reading Byron's poems as they came out, Caroline modelled her work upon them and herself upon his Romantic heroes and heroines. Even the claim to have written *Glenarvon* in a month she may have made to rival Byron's vaunted feats of rapid composition. Although with both Byron and Caroline it is the ego in trauma that compels them to create, Byron's greater degree of success as a Romantic autobiographer results from his ability to plumb larger themes than his own ego.

Neither contemporary nor modern readers have noticed that the second edition of *Glenarvon* differs markedly from the first. Not only does Caroline add to the second edition a ten-page preface, but she alters significantly her major characters—Glenarvon (based on Byron), Calantha (based on herself), and Lord Avondale (based on her husband). She omits a particularly damning passage on the poet Fremore (Samuel Rogers) as well as a number of satiric observations on the Princess of Madagascar (Lady Holland). In hundreds of other changes, Caroline reveals herself a careful reviser of her work. She rewrote sentences, tightened punctuation, corrected spelling, and eliminated scores of typographical errors. Everywhere she reduced verbiage in an effort to achieve narrative clarity and to make her writing less dramatic and "gothic"

(though much sensationalism remains). Caroline did not tire of revising until after Calantha's death in the middle of the third volume, after which she made only one further major change. Those who read *Glenarvon* in the first edition, then perused the preface to the second and stopped, might justifiably consider hypocritical Caroline's insistence upon the moral purpose of her novel. Studying her revisions for the second edition, however, reveals that she was sincere in her claim "that the general tendency of the work was favourable to the interests of virtue," for she carefully revised *Glenarvon* to eliminate passages that had hurt others or shocked public taste.

In the first edition, Caroline conceives Glenarvon as being more terrifying and treacherous than any figure who ever stepped out of Byron's own pages, a prototypic Heathcliff, a Satan with an occasional touch of the angel. He is the Byronic hero gone berserk, incredible as a character though retaining interest as a projection of Caroline's response to her poet. Possibly she may wish to imply unmentionable crimes when a Count Gondimar accuses Viviani (Glenarvon in disguise), " 'You frequently allude to scenes of deeper guilt and horror, than I dare even suffer myself to imagine possible.' " Viviani parries this nicely (as would Byron in *Manfred*), " 'The heart of man is unfathomable . . . that which seems is not:—That which is, seems not.' " Glenarvon himself only makes an entrance near the end of the first volume, though the reader knows of him long before he appears. Once introduced, he will dominate the novel by his presence (or absence). Once he commits a particularly dastardly act: " 'Despair prompted me to the deed,' said Glenarvon, putting his hand to his head: 'all is not right here—madness has fallen on me.' " Few readers at this point would disagree. At the end of the novel he dies of sheer despair: "Maddening with superstitious terror, Lord Glenarvon tasted not of food or refreshment. His brain was burning. His eye, darting forward, lost not for one breathing moment sight of that terrific vision." As he sinks into Hell, Satan himself "seemed to address him: 'Hardened and impenitent sinner! the measure of your iniquity is full: the price of crime has been paid: here shall your spirit dwell for ever, and for ever.' "

Naturally enough, Calantha is smitten at first sight with this demon. The novel asserts that Byron responded fully to Caroline's passion and that his feeling for her was far stronger than his laconic letters to Lady Melbourne suggest. Although Caroline insists throughout on Glenarvon's satanism, until virtually the last page his potentiality for angelhood remains. Once, when he seems near death, Calantha traces "in that noble form, the wreck of all that is great." His visage expresses "a capability of evil," but it is also a visage not easily forgotten," either by her or by other susceptible females who find "his mind . . . superior, and his heart full of sensibility and feeling." "Sensibility and feeling," Caroline had learned from Byron, excuse grave faults. " 'I know his history, his errors,' said Calantha; 'but he feels deeply.' " To the end both author and heroine retain a dual vision of their hero as archfiend and magnetic lover. Loving Glenarvon becomes Calantha's particular form of masochism.

Glenarvon in the second edition remains a morose, passion-haunted figure, but by omitting a number of the more sensational passages Caroline tones down slightly her characterization of him as His Satanic Majesty. A new passage reflects Byron's separation from his daughter Ada and his exile from England, which had occurred between the completion of the first edition and revisions for the second: "Glenarvon . . . spoke of times long past, of scenes by all forgot, pointed with a look of despondency to his infant son!—'Who shall protect the orphan that is destitute?' he cried—'who shall restore him to the house of his fathers.' " This gesture of sympathy aside, Caroline modifies her portrait of Glenarvon, omitting such lurid descriptions as the following: "Flushed with the flow of intemperate heat, or pale with the weariness of secret woe, he vainly sought in a career of pleasure, for that happiness which his restless mind prevented him from enjoying."

Caroline is her own best psychologist. Her understanding of herself evident in the portrayal of Calantha surpasses in psychological acuity subsequent biographical accounts of her. Although *Glenarvon* may largely fail as a novel, it succeeds as a penetrating study of the heroine and her relationships with her family, in particular with William Lamb, and with Byron. Caroline's letters reveal her compulsive need to confess. *Glenarvon* she conceived as an extended confession in the form of a fictionalized autobiography; and in it she described her origins, upbringing, education (or lack of it), and her courtship and marriage to William Lamb. In a letter she said that she spoke of none of her other characters "with half the sincerity I have of Calantha," and throughout the novel she exhibits more objectivity about herself than we might expect. Wish fulfillment may predominate, but hard analysis and painful self-awareness never quite disappear. She does not gloss over Calantha's character or her faults. By naming her after the heroine in Ford's *The Broken Heart,* Caroline forewarns the reader that Calantha carries within her the burden of an unfulfilled destiny.

If Glenarvon undergoes only a minor overhaul for the second edition, Calantha submits to major modifications—in her character and background; in the nature of her relationships with Glenarvon and her husband; and in her self-justification. Although Caroline frequently expressed indifference to the opinions of her in-laws and of the world, she knew that her novel had upset the Melbournes; and she undoubtedly inserted a number of passages to mollify their feelings. In both editions, she discusses Calantha's background, but only in the second does the character become a Roman Catholic. Brought up carelessly and an auto-didact (true to what we know of Caroline's own upbringing), Calantha resides after her marriage in Monteith (Melbourne) House, home of her in-laws, where reign scepticism in religion and casualness in morality. Calantha insists that serious reading, to which she was first exposed in Monteith House, undermined her naiveté. At fifteen she had "learned nothing." Now "books of every description" caused "horror and astonishment." Her newly-acquired Roman Catholic faith forces the reader to scan more carefully subsequent paragraphs in which Calantha laments the subversion of her moral principles in the lax atmosphere of Monteith House.

Calantha's relationship with Glenarvon also undergoes total metamorphosis. The first edition clearly implies a passionate, reciprocated union involving sexual intercourse; the second deletes almost every reference suggesting physical intimacy. David Cecil [in *Melbourne*] found it impossible to tell whether the relationship between Byron and Caroline was consummated or not; but even if we did not have Byron's letters to inform us that it was, a careful reading of the first edition of *Glenarvon* (and comparison with the second) leaves no doubt as to what happens. At one point Glenarvon declares, " 'The pulse of passion beats high within her [Calantha], and pleads for the lover who dares to ask. . . . Chaste—pure! What are these terms?' " Excited descriptions of physical intimacy, all deleted from the second edition, allow Caroline to relive her passion for Byron. " 'This, this is mine,' utters Glenarvon. Saying this, he pressed her lips to his, a strange feeling thrilled to her heart as she attempted vainly to hate him, or extricate herself from his embrace"—a passage replaced in the second edition by, "if the heart be mine of what avail." Here is a later rendezvous: Glenarvon, "then clasping her nearer to his heart, 'Tell both priests and parents,' he said exultingly, 'that one kiss from the lips of those we love, is dearer than every future hope.' " Such blasphemy would have been additional reason for the deletion of the passage. Nor can an explicit avowal of intimacy such as the following remain: "At night she seldom slept; a burning fever quickened every pulse: the heart beat as if with approaching dissolution,—delirium fell upon her brain. No longer innocent, her fancy painted but visions of love; and to be his alone, was all she now wished for, or desired on earth."

Caroline rewrote chapter 75 completely in order to render platonic Calantha's guilty passion for Glenarvon. There Glenarvon presses her "to his bosom" ("hand" in the second edition) and tells her "that we are united by every tie." He continues, "but the kiss I have snatched from your lips is sweeter far for me. Oh, for another, given thus warm from the heart! It has entranced—it has made me mad." Unmercifully, he adds: "but now that fierce passions have betrayed you—now that every principle is renounced, and every feeling perverted, let us enjoy the fruits of guilt"— replaced in the second edition by "but not now; oh, not now!" No wonder that by the second edition ladies of unblemished reputation shrink from Calantha as from a " 'fallen sinner.' "

A new respect for religion accompanies, as we might expect, Calantha's conversion to Roman Catholicism. Virtually every mention of "God" in the first edition Caroline either omits in the second or replaces by "Father." In the first edition the language of religion fuses with that of passion, as it would later in the novels of George Sand, in exchanges between the lovers. "Thy words are like the joys of heaven," she tells him in the first but not in the second edition. Dropped are references implying disrespect for the deity, like this speech by Glenarvon: " 'I call your God,' said he, 'I call him now to witness, while that I breathe, I will consider you as my wife, my mistress.' " In the first edition Calantha merely dies; in the second Caroline adds a paragraph in which God forgives Calantha with pious moralizings.

Utterly unlike her in most respects is the man Calantha marries; yet whatever wrong she does her husband, she does not underestimate the extent of his love for her. Here fiction reflects autobiography almost exactly. Although William Lamb may not have been the ideal partner for Caroline, he suited her far better than did Byron. Caroline and Byron were each too mercurial, introspective, unstable of temperament, to support each other for long. Caroline's later claim that William was "delighted" with *Glenarvon* will not stand up, however; for her second edition omits passages reflecting adversely upon him as a husband and replaces them by descriptions of his fine qualities. Though she would not suppress her novel, she made every effort to mollify his hurt feelings. Calantha's relationship with Avondale, Caroline tells us in the preface, was intended to demonstrate that "no advantages, can ensure happiness and security upon earth, unless we adhere to the forms, as well as the principles of religion and morality." In light of her careful revising of Avondale's portrait for the second edition, this becomes more than a sop for the pious. Near the end of the novel, when Avondale encounters Glenarvon in an abortive duel, Caroline rewrites the episode to strengthen the impression of Avondale's nobility—though Lady Holland thought that here Caroline "insidiously censure[d]" William for not having fought a duel on her behalf. Throughout the second edition Avondale realizes that he should have guided Calantha more than he had—played Mr. Knightley, so to speak, to her Emma—and at her death he repents his folly.

The most memorable moments in *Glenarvon* occur when Caroline caricatures famous contemporaries. "The best character in it," wrote Charles Lemon to Lady Harriot Frampton, "is the Princess of Madagascar (Lady Holland), with all her Reviewers about her." In the preface to the second edition Caroline candidly admitted that "the features of the few supposed portraits are overcharged and distorted." The Princess of Madagascar "resides in an old-fashioned gothic building, called Barbary House [Holland House], three miles beyond the turnpike," surrounded by a "black hord[e] of savages . . . [who] wear collars, and chains around their necks." Caroline's bitterness at what she imagined to be Lady Holland's unjust treatment of her remains almost as virulent in the second edition as in the first: "Cold Princess! where are your boasted professions now? You taught Calantha to love you, by every petty art of which your sex is mistress. . . . You . . . flattered her into a belief that you loved her. Loved her!—it is a feeling you never felt." Caroline's final word on the Princess is a hard one: "Peace to her memory! I wish not to reproach her: a friend more false, a foe more timid yet insulting, a princess more fond of power, never before or since appeared in Europe." Neither the novel nor her portrait pleased Lady Holland. "The bonnebouche I have reserved for the last—myself," she wrote Mrs. Creevey on May 21. "Where every ridicule, folly and infirmity (my not being able from malady to move about much) is portrayed. The charge against more essential qualities is, I trust and believe, a fiction." Mrs. Creevey no doubt sympathized, but twenty years later the Creeveys were still calling her Madagascar behind her back. And those who disliked Lady Holland's imperial ways relished the portrait. Douglas Kinnaird wrote Lord Kinnaird on June 4, 1816 that "the

chapter on Barbary House appears however to redeem the book in the eyes of many persons."

Better still is Caroline's portrait of Samuel Rogers ("Tremore" in the first edition, "Fremore" in the second). Long a member of the Barbary/Holland House circle, Fremore/Rogers dances attendance upon the Princess of Madagascar. Why Caroline drew this vicious portrait of him is unknown, for during the stormy times of her liaison with Byron she had often asked him to intercede with Byron for her. But in the second edition of *Glenarvon* Caroline repents, speaks no more of Fremore as a poet, and drops this transparent description: "A poet of an emaciated and sallow complexion stood beside her [the Princess of Madagascar]; of him it was affirmed that in apparently the kindest and most engaging manner, he, at all times, said precisely that which was most unpleasant to the person he appeared to praise. This yellow hyena had, however, a heart noble, magnanimous and generous; and even his friends, could they but escape from his smile and his tongue, had no reason to complain." On the next page she omits "the *dead,* I mean sick poet" ("The *dead* poet is Mr. Ward's joke at Rogers having cheated the coroner," Lady Holland informed Mrs. Creevey). During the remainder of the chapter Caroline substitutes "Mr. Fremore" for "the sallow complexioned Poet." Anyone reading only the second edition would not be able to tell that Fremore was based on Rogers or even that he was a poet.

Byron had first learned of *Glenarvon* when Hobhouse's letter of May 26 caught up with him at the Villa Diodati outside Geneva. Hobhouse could not contain himself. "Caroline Lamb!! Glenarvon!—yes—B—who would have thought that a new Lord B. should figure in a new Atalantis? and such an atalantis!! . . . You will hardly believe it but there is not the least merit in the book in any way except in a letter beginning 'I love you no more' which I suspect to be your's." Hobhouse, who did his best to preserve whatever was left of Byron's reputation in England, never spoke of Caroline without risking apoplexy. He had heard from Augusta Leigh that a newspaper had attributed *Glenarvon* to Byron; and on May 22, he wrote Murray that "Mrs Leigh is very anxious [it] should be contradicted & has written to me to deny"—which he proceeded to do. On June 8, he must have had some satisfaction in writing to Byron that "*Glenarvon* has done nothing but render the little vicious author more odious if possible than ever."

By mid-July Byron had still not read the novel. Yet it followed him, though a thousand miles from England, everywhere he went. To his publisher he expressed his sentiments on July 22, 1816:

> Of *Glenarvon*—Madame de Stael told me (ten days ago at Cop[p]et) marvellous & grievous things—but I have seen nothing of it but the Motto—which promises amiably "For us & for our tragedy"—if such be the posy what should the ring be? "a name to all succeeding &c."—the generous moment selected for the publication is probably its kindest accompaniment—and truth to say—the time was well chosen,—I have not even a guess at the contents—except for the very vague accounts I have heard—and I know but one thing which a woman can say to the purpose

on such occasions and that she might as well for her own sake keep to herself—which by the way they very rarely can—that old reproach against their admirers of "kiss and tell" bad as it is—is surely somewhat less than———and *publish.*"

Still, even "very vague accounts" must have whetted his appetite, for on July 29, he told Samuel Rogers he had read *Glenarvon,* lent to him by Madame de Staël. His only comment was to quote Pope's *Horace Imitated:* "From furious Sappho scarce a milder fate/ [P-x'd] by her love—or libelled by her hate."

Byron's subsequent comments on the novel profess disinterest or deny any resemblance between himself and its protagonist. Understandably he found the novel unreal, and in 1817 he made no attempt to prevent the publication of an Italian translation when a word from him would have stopped it. Hobhouse confirms to Augusta Leigh on September 9, 1816, that "the novel made him rather indignant than angry—he did not discover his portrait—who would?" Claire Clairmont thought the novel had in places the resonance of life; for she told Byron on October 6, 1816, that "some of the speeches in it are yours—I am sure they are; the very impertinent way of looking in a person's face who loves you, and telling them you are very tired and wish they'd go." Madame de Staël elicited Byron's best-known comment on the novel. When asked what he thought of his portrait, he replied (not quite truthfully), "Elle aurait été plus resemblante si j'avais voulu donner plus de séances."

By the end of 1816 Byron's attitude had taken its definitive form: detached contempt for *Glenarvon,* abhorrence of its author. "It seems to me that," he wrote to Moore, "if the authoress had written the *truth,* and nothing but the truth—the whole truth—the romance would not only have been more romantic, but more entertaining." In 1820 he lent Teresa Guiccioli his copy of the novel and had much to answer for. "Your little head is heated now by

that dammed novel," he exclaimed, "the author of which has been—in every country and at all times—my evil Genius." Canto II of *Don Juan* (1819) had included the line, "Some play the devil, and then write a novel," which provoked Caroline as it was intended to. She was, as on everything else, of two minds about the poem. To Murray she wrote, "you cannot think how clever I think *Don Juan* is, in my heart" *and* that the poem was "neither witty, nor in very good taste." Her own production had been neither, but that, perhaps, was another matter. (pp. 208-15)

John Clubbe, "Glenarvon Revised—and Revisited," in The Wordsworth Circle, *Vol. X, No. 2, April, 1979, pp. 205-17.*

Joseph Garver (essay date 1980)

[*In the following excerpt, Garver examines* Glenarvon *as a reflection of the political and cultural orientation of its author.*]

Hitherto this crude but impassioned novel [*Glenarvon*] has been of interest only as a *roman à clef.* However, it is worth re-examining not only for its appropriation of Anglo-Irish literary myth but also in view of its authorship and readership in ruling-class circles.

Among other Gothic novels of Irish setting *Glenarvon* is perhaps most extreme in its unreality of detail, its blurring of scene. Lady Morgan, though much occupied with the "wild and savage sublimity" of Irish scenery, was usually careful, in keeping with her semi-documentary intention, to supply topographical signposts. Maturin, except for the Wicklow scenes of *Melmoth,* usually settled for such a vague designation as "a castle in the wild, western extremities of Ireland". But the setting of *Glenarvon* is mythical in its vagueness, a landscape of snowy peaks and cavernous defiles, sheltered valleys and swift rivers, castles and ruins, all in an Ossianic climate of storm and gloom or dazzling brightness. In this Ireland, of which not even the province can be identified, the menials speak an imaginary Hiberno-English—"Oh musha! there be strange things heard in these here old houses: one must not always believe all one hears"—while the nobles express themselves in the lofty idiom of sensibility. Scenes are often phantasmagoric, complementing the excesses of passion or feeling that continually threaten the characters.

This unreality is naive rather than studied, arising not only from "those struggles of passion when the soul trembles on the verge of the unlawful and the unhallowed", but also from a complete acceptance of myth. In *Glenarvon* the transformation or distortion of Ireland into a metaphor is total, verisimilitude not being lost but never being sought, as fantasies, such as the familiar one of hereditary doom, hold the stage in Ascendancy trappings. Now the handling of this hereditary theme in literature is not necessarily fantastic or Gothic, as [Maria Edgeworth's] *Castle Rackrent* shows; similarly, in *The MacDermots of Ballycloran* (1847), Anthony Trollope's doomed heroine "walked as if all the blood of the old Irish Princes was in her veins", yet "her shoes were seldom clean, often slipshod, usually in holes". In effect, novels such as the latter two deflate myth to its social or historical basis, reversing

---

Elizabeth Jenkins on *Glenarvon:*

It is usual to refer to *Glenarvon* as a book unreadable except that it contains what is meant for a portrait of Byron; but a reviewer of modern novels who never had to read anything worse would think himself lucky. Judged as a novel it is not a competent piece of work, and it does, in places, verge upon idiocy. But not upon the vapid idiocy of the modern Society young lady's novel; it is true that, like her successors, Lady Caroline's aim is to tell the reader about herself; but, unlike theirs, her confidences are not concerned with details of her own maquillage, hairdressing, and underclothes, the conversations of girl friends, and the compliments paid to her, either by Oxford poets in a meadow or by young men of the Corps Diplomatique in an aroma of gardenias and white kid gloves. To compare her novel with one of the modern type is only to see, in striking perspective, to what a different order of intelligence she belonged.

Elizabeth Jenkins, in her Lady Caroline Lamb, *Little, Brown, and Company, 1932.*

---

the process of *Glenarvon,* where, in any event, an ancient line in decay, as in the novels of Maturin and Le Fanu, can only be demonic.

The plot of *Glenarvon* defies summary though hardly more extravantly encumbered than that of [Charles Maturin's] *The Milesian Chief,* to which it owes much. In fact such plots were then common. The story of *Glenarvon* centres on two neighbouring "big houses", Castle Delaval, prosperous seat of the Duke of Altamonte, and Belfont Abbey, seat of the earldom of Glenarvon. The latter "exhibited a melancholy picture of neglect and oppression", as its last rightful lord, a Jacobite, had fallen at Culloden, while its youthful heir, Clarence de Ruthven, called Glenarvon, "had never yet appeared to petition for his attainted titled and forfeited estates." Delaval is also involved in dynastic difficulty, for the Duke, except for his beautiful daughter Calantha, is childless. He proposes therefore to affiance her to his sister Margaret's son. However, when the Duchess bears a son after all, Margaret, whose "depraved imagination" is fascinated by "vice and malignity", suborns the "young enthusiast" Count Viviani to murder her unwelcome nephew, offering her favours as reward. The infatuated Italian, himself "enveloped" in "deep melancholy" and "dark mystery", reluctantly complies, only to be repulsed with horror when he claims his reward. He disappears vowing vengeance.

This is merely the background to the story proper of *Glenarvon,* which is told from the viewpoint of the hyperaesthetic, "enthusiastic" Calantha. Having fallen in love with the Earl of Avondale, she threatens madness if forced to wed her cousin and thus defeats Margaret's ambitions. Yet she succumbs to hysteria at the wedding with Avondale, "and it was with shrieks of despair she was torn from her father's bosom". Avondale foolishly encourages his wife's "excess of sensibility", and introduces her to those new philosophical works "which have unfortunately been traced by the hand of unrestrained enquiry, and daring speculation". Thus subverted both in heart and mind, Calantha is a potential prey "for the spoiler", a part which Viviani, attracted by her reputation for sensibility, promises to play.

Time in *Glenarvon* is as vague as place, but the catastrophe of the devoted Calantha's life comes "in the time of the Irish Rebellion" of 1797-8, about eight years after the murder of her infant brother. The young Glenarvon, preceded by rumours of his intrigues, now defiantly appears at his ancestral demesne, "to disseminate his wicked doctrines amongst an innocent but weak people", as a United Irish organizer. Reputedly commanding an underground army, he is worshipped by the peasantry and followed even by many hitherto respectable ladies, like Bacchantes, "their hair dishevelled, their heads ornamented with green cockades", "singing in chorus the song of liberty". Among them is the "lovely recluse" of the Glenaa convent, Elinor St. Clare, a racier Wild Irish Girl, now serving as Glenarvon's camp mistress and lieutenant commander. In her enslavement by "uncontrolled passions" and "imagination, wild and lawless", Calantha fearfully senses a prefiguration of her own fate. Later, on an improbable tourist excursion to Belfont Abbey, Calantha, amidst "its secret mysteries and recesses", is lured by strange music into the presence of a pale young flautist. Obliviously, his

> eye beamed into life as it threw up its dark ardent gaze, with a look nearly of inspiration, while the proud curl of the upper lip expressed haughtiness and bitter contempt; yet, even mixed with these fierce characteristic feelings, an air of melancholy and dejection shaded over and softened every harsher expression. . . . [Calantha] could have knelt and prayed to heaven . . . to bless the fallen angel in whose presence she at that moment stood, to give peace to that soul, upon which was plainly stamped the heavenly image of sensibility and genius.

This "singular being" is, of course, Glenarvon; and this encounter begins the fatal infatuation. Oddly enough, Glenarvon, despite his reputation, is lionized and becomes a favoured guest at Delaval, where the affair with Calantha proceeds openly. But his character is enveloped in "impenetrable mystery"; and his fascination of Calantha, like that of the serpent for the dove, partakes of the "spirit of evil". He delights alike in the raging of the elements and that of a chained madman, and variously reveals to Calantha that he is tortured by a "horrid secret", that he is dedicated to "the freedom of Ireland, and the deathless renown of such as supported her fallen rights", and that he cannot live if not preferred, even before God, by Calantha. In his secret cavern, "standing amidst the grotesque and ferocious rabble, like some *Being* from a higher world", Glenarvon promises "vengeance on the detested government of England!" or death "defending the rights of man—the independence of Ireland".

Yet for all the impassioned rhetoric expended between the two lovers—once they exchange pledges in a "rite accounted infamous amongst christians"—their affair is never consummated. A plan for elopement comes to nothing; Calantha's one flight ends in her being returned home by Glenarvon himself; and their passion runs hot and cold as in the Regency sport of adulterous flirtation. But while Glenarvon's "capability of evil" is prodigious because "his passions were all subject to his controul", Calantha is victimized both by him and by her own feelings. Finally, he cynically and contemptuously deserts her for an heiress. Meanwhile Avondale, who has been away during the height of the affair, returns to inform Calantha of his decision to separate from her. He sets off again; but Calantha with her youngest child desperately pursues and overtakes him, to die in his arms in an ecstasy of penitence.

The novel then precipitantly concludes. Glenarvon treacherously stabs Avondale when he demands satisfaction. No less treacherously he deserts the United Irishmen in return for the restoration of his estates and a command in the Royal Navy. The Duke of Altamonte learns mysteriously that his son had not really been murdered but had been kidnapped, Viviani substituting the body of another murdered child, and is now concealed at Belfont Abbey. Viviani himself reappears, stabs Margaret on the spot where the innocent child had been murdered to appease her, and as further expiation prepares to leap with the Belfont heir into the chasm convenient to Belfont. The Duke arrives to stop him, but when stripped of his cloak Viviani proves to be only another identity of Glenarvon. Pleading insanity, he is released to join his command in the fleet, which is directed to intercept a French invasion of Ireland. Meanwhile Elinor, alternately execrating and glorifying Glenarvon, leads his betrayed followers in a rising. They fire Belfont as she prophesies the doom of its line; then, as its "blazing turrets" fall, she spurs her blindfolded steed into the chasm. Afterwards the insurgents are slaughtered by the yeomanry. But an even worse retribution is reserved for Glenarvon. At sea he is pursued by the ghosts of Calantha, Avondale, and others of his many victims; and after displaying "more than his usual bravery" in battle, he leaps from his frigate in despair as a phantom ship, bearing a re-enactment of the first of his crimes in dumb show, appears. He is pulled from the sea dying by his men while a terrible voice as from a gulf beneath pronounces his perdition.

Thus, like many bad novels, *Glenarvon* is grandiose in conception, absurd and incoherent in execution, acquiring additional interest, however, in contemporary literary context. Glenarvon's horrific end, "immured in darkness", with the hellish voice exulting, "you did not controul the fiend in your bosom . . . [and] he now has mastered you, and brought you here", recalls the gloating doom of Lewis's *The Monk* (1796). Making the leader of rebellion a hereditary noble imitates *The Milesian Chief;* but Glenarvon's hereditary Jacobitism, especially with the mention of Culloden, was probably inspired by [Sir Walter Scott's] *Waverley.* However, in its peculiar mingling of stylistic preciosity and a frenetic moralism fascinated by the satanic outrage of female purity, *Glenarvon* most strikingly recalls the Gothic novelette *St. Irvyne* (1811) by Shelley, who, like Glenarvon, exposed the injustices of Ireland in pamphlets: "Poor Eloise de St. Irvyne! many, many are in thy situation; but few have a heart so full of sensibility and excellence for the demoniac malice of man to deform, and then glut itself with hellish pleasure."

But the most meaningful context of *Glenarvon* is the autobiographical, not in the narrow sense of the *roman à clef* but in the broader sense of the author's cultural orientation. Like Trollope's *The MacDermots, Glenarvon* is hardly in the category of Anglo-Irish fiction, for though Lady Caroline Lamb, *née* Ponsonby (1785-1828), only daughter of the third earl of Bessborough, was the scion of a great Anglo-Irish family, her personal background and outlook were English; and her only experience of Ireland was a few months' exile, in the autumn of 1812, at the Ponsonby seat, Bessborough, near Carrick-on-Suir, Co. Kilkenny, which was probably the model for Castle Delaval. Yet few authors could have been in a better position to comprehend the Anglo-Irish situation. Besides her own family, which included a powerful cadet branch at Bishopscourt, Co. Kildare, she was intimately connected with two other great families involved in Ireland, the Melbournes and the Devonshires whose residence Lismore Castle, Co. Waterford, disappointed her Gothic expectations. Her husband was heir to the Irish viscountcy of Melbourne, seated at Kilmore, Co. Cavan; and he pursued a Parliamentary interest which was eventually to bring him the Irish secretaryship and of course, ultimately, the premiership. Her brothers were members for Ireland; and her cousin George Ponsonby, though a leader of opposition to the Union, became Lord Chancellor of Ireland in 1806. A typical Ascendancy seat, Bessborough, originally Castle Kildalton, had been granted to Sir John Ponsonby by Cromwell on the attainder of its thirteenth-century Norman founders, the Daltons. In 1689 it was Williamite; in 1744 rebuilt in the flowering of Georgian architecture; after 1800 a symbol of absentee power; in 1923 burnt by the Republicans. There Lady Caroline would have seen The White Lady's Tree which, in legend, the last Dalton heiress, hopelessly mad after her desertion by Sir John Ponsonby, had haunted.

At the age of twelve, Lady Caroline Ponsonby, according to her own account, frustrated the design of her maternal uncle-in-law, the Duke of Devonshire, to betroth her to his son, by falling in love with "a friend of Charles Fox—a friend of liberty", the brilliant young Whig William Lamb, future Lord Melbourne. Despite her debilitating nervousness she and Lamb were married in 1805. By 1809, however, while Lamb advanced in the House of Commons, his young wife was growing restless and, unsettled by the worldly books to which he introduced her, already beginning to engage in the flirtations then fashionable so long as certain proprieties were observed.

The stage was thus set for the notorious affair with Byron, who, aged about twenty-four, having just published *Childe Harold,* was the lion of the 1812 season. Although he professed to detest delicate or high-strung women, he was soon reciprocating the excesses of Lady Caroline, whom he met in March of that year, regaling her with confessions not only of love but of personal and ancestral depravity. Newstead Abbey, near Nottingham, the seat of his barony, seems to have inspired Belfont Abbey, in *Glenarvon,* with its "large dreary apartment hung with tapestry [where] John de Ruthven drank hot blood from the skull of his enemy and died". And, as in *Glenarvon,* the affair was more rhetorical than criminal in the legal sense. However, it was not crime but notoriety that was objectionable; and after Caroline's embarrassing flight from Melbourne House when Byron's help had to be asked to recapture her, she was packed off to Bessborough. While in Ireland she received his studiously cruel valedictory letter, later printed as Glenarvon's. Following the rupture, however, her behaviour—including attempted suicide in Byron's presence at a ball—became so outrageous that the long-suffering Lamb finally agreed in 1816 to his family's demand for a separation. But while this was being drawn up, *Glenarvon* was also being drafted, secretly and in feverish haste. It was a *succès de scandale,* going through three editions in as many weeks; and it put its anonymous but only too well known author permanently outside the social pale, especially as it recognizably caricatured figures of society other than the central triangle. Yet, on the very day Lamb was to sign the order of separation, Caroline somehow obtained his forgiveness—she later confided to Lady Morgan that it was his "delight" with *Glenarvon* which effected the reconciliation—and separation was delayed until 1825.

In this context *Glenarvon* reads as metaphoric autobiography, as an "objective correlative" of raging but unconsummated Romantic passion. It remains "an incoherent cross between a realistic novel of fashionable life and a fantastic tale of terror" [David Cecil, *Melbourne*], because, unfortunately, this passion was unconsummated in art as well as life. Its author could not resolve an often ludicrous confusion of literal and metaphoric meaning, making Glenarvon a quick change artist between roles of Regency dandy and demonic rebel. She could neither control Gothic sensibility by a grasp of its distinction from sanity—as does Jane Austen in *Northanger Abbey* (1818) and even Mrs. Radcliffe in *Udolpho*—nor dare to give it its head, as does Maturin in *Melmoth*. In the latter sense Lady Caroline, who later feared she would be shut away, was not quite mad enough. But perhaps her authorship and personality, both hysterical, demonstrate a significant historical or social fact; that "the delicacies of a strong sensibility" [Austen, *Sense and Sensibility*] were not merely a figment and that "spirits that are 'finely touched' " [Lady Morgan, *Memoirs*] really inhabited *salon* and mansionhouse.

But despite her Romantic euphoria and upbringing in a great Whig centre, Devonshire House, where Rousseau was discussed and her aunt the Duchess posed with the Phrygian cap, the author of *Glenarvon* was no longer "a friend of liberty". The impulsion "to enforce the danger of too entire liberty either of conduct, or of opinion", which complements the Gothicism of *Glenarvon*, is the novel's ultimate autobiographical significance. As a United Irish leader, Glenarvon, like his "ferocious rabble", is a figment of that imagination of revolutionary conspiracy which began to characterize Gothic fiction after the French Revolution. Like Miss Edgeworth in *Ennui*, Maturin in *The Milesian Chief*, and Lady Morgan in *Florence Macarthy* (1816), (though the context is ironic in the latter), Lady Caroline found Ireland the appropriate setting for the disimprisonment, by villains, fanatics, or fiends, of that demonic potential of "liberty" which so obsessed Burke's last writings. As a vestige of the commoner Gothic setting, various characters in *Glenarvon* are Italianate; but Glenarvon's murderous *alter ego*, the "enthusiast" Viviani (for Glenarvon is his own *Doppelgänger*), illustrates also that sinister dualism supposedly represented by such monstrous liberators as Robespierre and Napoleon. The character of Glenarvon is not so much a malicious caricature of Byron as a hysterical projection of Byronism.

Although Gothic novels were usually moralistic or didactic, the intrusive anti-Jacobinism of *Glenarvon*, the obsession with "licentious democrats" and "rebellious libertines", partakes of the author's personal revulsion against the "enthusiasm" and sensibility which she believed to have ruined her life but which she could never really escape since they were inherent in herself, a psychological fact which perhaps explains her suicidal hysteria. But this hysterical revulsion may also be placed in the larger context of a Whig reaction against "liberty" which was evident even before Fox's death in 1806. Lamb, for example, whose student declamation, "The Progressive Improvements of Mankind" (1798), was quoted in Parliament by Fox himself, and who, as aspiring statesman, opposed war with France, later became obsessed with a fear of revolution and became an enforcer of "coercion" in England as well as Ireland. Facing rebellion in its manifold forms of

whiteboys, luddites, ribbonmen, rick-burners, and chartists, Lamb, at Whitehall, might well have exclaimed, like Avondale confronted with his riotous tenantry: "Fickle, senseless beings! . . . These are the creatures we would take to govern us: this is the voice of the people: these are the rights of man".

Gothic Ireland, at least in *Glenarvon*, was the nightmare of sensibility, dreamed in the sleep of reason. (pp. 219-27)

> *Joseph Garver, "Gothic Ireland: Lady Caroline Lamb's 'Glenarvon',' " in Irish University Review, Vol. 10, No. 2, Autumn, 1980, pp. 213-28.*

Malcolm Kelsall   (essay date 1981)

[*Kelsall is an English educator and critic. In the following essay, he discusses the revolutionary politics of the title character in* Glenarvon.]

My subject is the politics of *Glenarvon*. I shall place Caroline Lamb's novel briefly in the context of romantic novels on the Irish problem, and describe in detail her treatment of the revolution of 1798. The leader of the insurgents is the eponymous villain: Lady Caroline's version of the Byronic hero. What is the political ambiance of this figure? Where does he stand in relation to the philosophical radicalism propagated by Godwin, and by Shelley, especially in the *Address to the Irish People* (1812)? How may he be related to the divide between the old and the new Whigs analysed by Burke? In what way would he be judged according to the principles of contemporary political parties?

These questions concerning the Byronic hero raise issues far wider than this novel. As Lady Caroline was well aware, the rising of '98 was directly inspired by the revolution in France; and the discontent in Ireland, *mutatis mutandis*, might be paralleled in England in 1816. As a colonists' rising against imperialism the Irish patriots might seek authority from America; in 1824 the real Lord Byron died in another colonial conflict in Greece. Both the Byronic hero and Byron as hero demand to be considered in this broader context. A short paper can do no more than acknowledge this. But *Glenarvon* is the epicentre of its author's imaginative conception of such events. The literary reaction to political Byronism which the work represents issues from the very heartland of Whig society; the author was to be a correspondent of Godwin's; the original of her villain became a friend of Shelley; and William Lamb, by an appropriate irony, was appointed Secretary of State for Ireland in Canning's administration.

It may be objected that this is to give too much weight to a novel which has hitherto been regarded as merely the distressed outpourings of diseased sexuality. On the contrary, the very spontaneity of Lady Caroline's portrayal of Whig society and of Byronism enhances the value of the insights which the work offers. As if with the clarity of a Freudian dream it reveals the inherent contradictions of the Whig ideology in which she was reared and the utility of the Byronic myth in providing a scapegoat for the failure of her society to find a solution to the Irish problem.

The Irish situation is described in the novel thus:

> The whole kingdom, indeed, was in a state of ferment and disorder. Complaints were made, redress was claimed, and the people were everywhere mutinous and discontented. Even the few of their own countrymen, who possessed the power, refused to attend to the grievances and burthens of which the nation generally complained, and sold themselves for hire, to the English government. Numerous absentees had drawn great part of the money out of the country; oppressive taxes were continued; land was let and sub-let to bankers and stewards of estates, to the utter ruin of their tenants; and all this caused the greatest discontent.

It is a familiar story—associated particularly with the names of Edgeworth and Carleton in the novel in the nineteenth century. The romantic school of writers to which Lady Caroline belongs were more inclined to approach the subject by symbolic evocation: the poetry of Ossian, the heroic associations of the landscape and ruins of Ireland, the song of the harp, the wearing of the green, the wild rose which blooms in the little green place. Typically these writers approach the sufferings of Ireland from a social position both above and outside, trailing clouds of aristocratic and Ascendancy glory past or present. It is a pattern reflected in life as well as literature, and may still be traced in the culminative events of Easter 1916. The paternalism of this outlook may be clearly seen in Maturin's *The Milesian Chief* (1812) where it is argued that the Irish mob is too wild and ignorant to merit present support, and that only a long period of indoctrination and education from a benevolent Ascendancy class could aid the peasantry. A characteristic movement from the natural Irish scene to the sophistication of English society from which alone redress can be obtained may be seen in Lady Morgan's *O'Donnel: A National Tale* (1814). Equally representative, and true to the Irish situation, is the conversion to romantic Irish nationalism of the hero of Maturin's *The Wild Irish Boy* (1808) by his reading of Ossian in the Lake District, where his mind is enraptured by a vision of an untaught yet noble people "proud, irritable, impetuous, indolent and superstitious" who demand him as their preserver. An irrational worship for an irrecoverable past is a *leitmotiv* for Mortimer, the profligate Ascendancy hero of Lady Morgan's *The Wild Irish Girl* (1806). How much of this fiction Lady Caroline had read is unknown, but *Glenarvon* is imbued with such attitudes.

Hence the Ossianic opening of the novel where Elinor is carried by the aged seer, her father, to the topmost heights of Inis Tara where, in the wizard's glen, "the spirits of departed heroes and countrymen, freed from the bonds of mortality, were ascending in solemn grandeur" while the song of the Banshees "mourning for the sorrows of their country, broke upon the silence of the night." The lamentable vision is prophetic of the evils which will befall Ireland because of revolution. The nation is invoked by Lady Caroline in a visionary rather than a socio-political spirit and there is no account of the oppression which has provoked the troubles to come. Mountain, abbey and glen combine in a landscape of the picturesque imagination framing the seer Camioli as he breaks into lament while

Self-portrait of Lamb with her two-year-old son Augustus.

carrying Elinor for protection to the Abbess of Glenaa: "Woe to the house of Glenarvon."

Glenarvon in this fiction will be symbolically presented as an embodiment of the perversions of Irish rebellion, as seen by the Whig nobility, while Elinor will come to represent Erin herself riding in nationalistic dress "To perdition, . . . and they that wish to follow must ride apace." So she is described as she gallops by later wearing "The hat and plume of sacred green, the emerald clasp, the gift of Glenarvon". The evil of the rebel leader, the perverted fate of the Irish people, a romantic cry of nostalgic misery, which communicates, none the less, a frisson of melancholy pleasure, such are the motifs Lady Caroline evokes.

The elements of political description tend to be subsumed in the heady mixture of Satanism and sexuality with which Glenarvon is endowed. He is destructive to women, and at the end is literally carried away by the powers of darkness in a frenzy of madness. Yet here and there the novel offers straightfoward analysis of the evils of revolution, and even Satanism and sexuality are not without their political implications. Lady Caroline clearly spells out the social threat which Glenarvon represents in her description of the reformative movements in Ireland:

> Whilst . . . the more moderate with sincerity imagined, that they were up holding the cause of liberty and religion; the more violent, who had emancipated their minds from every restraint of prejudice or principle, did not conceal that the equalization of property, and the destruction of rank and titles was their real object. The revolutionary spirit was fast spreading, and since the appearance of Glenarvon at Belfont, the whole of the country around was in a state of actual rebellion.

The argument for the equalization of property and the destruction of rank suggests the philosophical radicalism of

Godwin and Shelley more than anything we might associate with the historical Byron, but it was with the Byronic myth and the Byronic hero that Lady Caroline was more concerned: a violent force emancipated from "every restraint of . . . principle" which, as soon as it appears, induces rebellion.

Glenarvon's role is ostensibly Satanic as the evil genius of insurrection, but one recalls that even the mild and abstract Godwin saw Milton's fallen angel as possessing qualities which would have been beneficial and illustrious in another situation. Satan disdained "to be subdued by despotic power," for he saw "no sufficient reason for that extreme inequality of rank and power which the Creator assumed", but he was seduced through his hatred of tyranny by aims too personal, the philosopher argues. Likewise, with Glenarvon it is difficult at times to disentangle the valid from the perverse in his demonic characterisation:

> "Irishmen," said Glenarvon, throwing his dark mantle off, and standing amidst the grotesque and ferocious rabble, like some God from a higher world—"Irishmen, our country shall soon be free:—you are about to be avenged. That vile government, which has so long, and so cruelly oppressed you, shall soon be no more! The national flag—the sacred green—shall fly over the ruins of despotism; and that fair capital, which has too long witnessed the debauchery, the plots, the crimes of your tyrants, shall soon be the citadel of triumphant patriotism and virtue. Even if we fail, let us die defending the rights of man—the independence of Ireland."

The fallen angel—like some God from a higher world—is speaking the language of Tom Paine. The whole of this long speech, moreover, has an authentic patriot ring, and rightly so, because the liberal sympathy of Lady Caroline, like that of her fellow Irish novelists, was genuinely stirred by the ills of the people. When Glenarvon, taking his farewell of Ireland, wished "may better hearts support her rights" he is for once speaking an honest sentiment to which many a breast would respond.

The evil of Glenarvon, like that of Satan in Godwin's description, in part lies in the junction of rebellion with pride. "Glenarvon and Ireland for ever," he cries, betraying his ambition, and thus the cause, at the same instant. He is fascinated with "the romantic splendour of ideal liberty" yet is praised as "the deliverer of his country", "their Lord . . . their King". This *libido dominandi* debauches the political aim just as, in the role of lover, Glenarvon debauches both the women in the novel. The type might readily be derived from Byronic heroes like Lara and the Giaour, but might be found outside fiction as well. It was Edmund Burke who observed of the new revolutionary Whigs: "often the desire and design of a tyrannic domination lurks in the claim of an extravagant liberty."

The motif of sexual domination is linked to the Satanic politics. When Glenarvon courts Calantha he presents her with a ring: "an emerald with a harp engraved upon it— the armorial bearing of Ireland"—a gift, he says untruthfully, meant "merely politically". Calantha is fatally attracted by one whose "countenance lighted with the ray

of enthusiasm" for "the freedom of Ireland, and the deathless renown of such as supported her fallen rights", and, trying to disengage herself she falls into the Gaelic cant of the hour: "I will walk no more with you to Inis Tara:— the harp sounds mournfully on those high cliffs:—I wish no more to hear it." The passage parallels Elinor's similar lament in the persona of Ireland to the harp for the departure of her false lover: "He is gone . . . the leader of the brave". Part of the seductive appeal of Glenarvon lies in his political enthusiasm, but his abandonment of those he loves, and his destruction of them is a manifestation of the dangerous propensities of his ideology. Self-gratification and personal dominance leading to disaster are the personal and sexual consequences of revolution's principles.

The fullest example of this is in the depiction of Elinor. Consider her death where, as the spirit of Erin, she cries:

> "The dream of life is past; the song of the wild harper has ceased; famine war, and slavery, shall encompass my country,
>
> But yet all its fond recollections suppressing, One last dying wish this sad bosom shall draw: O, Erin, an exile bequeaths thee his blessing; Land of my forefathers; Erin go brah."
>
> As she sung the last strain of the song, which the sons of freedom had learned, she tore the green mantle from her breast, and throwing it around the head of her steed, so that he could not perceive any external object, she pressed the spurs into his sides and galloped in haste to the edge of the cliff, from which she beheld, like a sheet of fire reddening the heavens, the blazing turrents of Belfont.

The blazing house is Glenarvon's home, set on fire by the very revolutionaries he had inspired. This fulfills, structurally, the Ossianic prophecy with which the novel began. It also serves as a clear warning to an insurrectionist and an aristocrat of the kind of ills which he will bring down on his own head by a violent attack on the basis of society. The icon of the galloping horse blindfolded with nationalist green could not be clearer as Elinor rides to destruction. It is Glenarvon who is the cause: sexually and politically.

The neatness of this structural pattern is disturbed by the extended development of Calantha in the novel. Glenarvon has two major lovers, and though Calantha is linked with Irish motifs, she is not given the clear symbolic role of Elinor. *Glenarvon* is too diffuse to be categorised as a programmatic work, and the autobiographical elements sometimes dominate the fiction. Yet the myths with which Lady Caroline chose to involve her own life, since they are conventionally romantic, are far from merely personal, but are manifestations of the *Zeitgeist*. The individual case becomes representational as in Calantha, Lady Caroline shows the corruption of natural innocence by the sophistication of Whig society and by the Byronic spirit.

To explore this theme in all its ramifications would be a distraction from the political issue, but it will be readily seen that the foundations of education are not without political consequences, and the society which opens Calantha to corruption by Byronism is also part of the dominant forces of the political world to which Ireland (and England) had to look for reform.

Calantha's upbringing, as described by Lady Margaret, seems to be something after the manner of Rousseau: "the system which nature dictates and every feeling of the heart willingly accedes to", which is compared, favourably, with the upbringing of conventional "paragons of propriety" who are no more than "sober minded steady automations." It is exactly the distinction which politically concerned Burke when he considered whether "it is more safe to live under the jurisdiction of severe but steady reason, than under the empire of indulgent, but capricious passion." Calantha, reared according to Lady Margaret's "indulgent" doctrines is passionate in feeling, wild in her wishes, a lover of solitude, one without self-control or the power to "disguise" her feelings, "uncivilized and savage". Lady Caroline again uses the image of the unbridled horse—literally manifest in the fate of Elinor—to indicate the state of Calantha's mind:

> The steed that never has felt the curb, as it flies lightly and wildly proud of its liberty among its native hills and valleys, may toss its head and plunge as it snuffs the air and rejoices in its existence, while the tame and goaded hack trots along the beaten road, starting from the lash under which it trembles and stumbling and falling, if not constantly upheld . . . Nor curb, nor rein have ever fettered the pupil of nature—the proud, the daring votress of liberty and love. What though she quit the common path, if honour and praise accompany her steps, and crown her with success.

This is both a proleptic image and an ambiguous one. The invocation of "liberty" among "native hills" is the very stuff of the revolutionary attitudes of Glenarvon. This theme of liberty is joined with love, just as Calantha's political affiliations are to be interwoven with her sexual passion for the seductive Glenarvon. "Honour and praise" are the self-gratulatory aristocratic goals to be won, and in what better cause than that of liberty? The opposed image of the "goaded hack" is far from attractive, and though rebellion will be shown both to be wrong and destructive, the regular pathway of propriety does not attract. Calantha, obviously, is a spirit open to penetration by Byronism. The passage occurs after Calantha has been introduced to Whig society. The devastating satiric portrayal by Lady Caroline of things as they are has often been examined. Two elements particularly relate to the political theme: the bigotry and prejudice of party spirit as shown by Lady Monteith's circle; the satiric turn of society's mind which merely plays with ideas in a spirit of caustic liberality. The corruption of Calantha's innocence is described:

> Her reason by degrees became convinced by the arguments which she continually heard; and all that was spoken at random, she treasured up as truth: even whilst vehemently contending and disputing in defence of her favourite tenets, she became of another opinion. So dangerous is a little knowledge—so unstable is violence. Her soul's immortal hopes seemed to be shaken by the unguarded jests of the profane, . . . she read till she confounded truth and falsehood, nor knew any longer what to believe—she heard folly censured till she took it to be criminal; but crime she saw tolerated if well concealed.

One would like to know what books Calantha read, what spurious arguments tossed off in debate, perverted her mind, what profane jests sullied her imagination. Might one guess that a certain strain of continental sentimentalism mixed with ideas of political justice and the rights of man coloured her reading, that a certain blending of political and sexual liberty was involved in conversation? Much which convinced this wild and savage child of nature did not convince its promulgators. The society Lady Caroline describes is rotten with intellectual and moral hypocrisy— what Byron called "cant" moral and political: "crime she saw tolerated if well concealed."

On the one hand the evil of revolution, on the other the corruptions of the only party with a reformist policy—one may credit Lady Caroline with a sharper eye for political dialectic than, for instance, Godwin in *Caleb Williams*. The novel offers, however, an ideal in the figure of the noble Avondale: Ascendancy, Protestant, patriotic, rational, and hence, presumably, concerned for the welfare of his tenantry and beloved by them. Lady Caroline yields to crude political propaganda when the revolution of '98 breaks out and the rebels ambush Avondale in his English military costume—"Sure he's one of the butchers sent to destroy us. We'll have no masters, no lords." Their true master indignantly replies: "Had I no commission, no title to defend, still as a man, free and independent, I would protect the laws and rights of my insulted country". This rejoinder, and the rebels' recognition of Avondale, produces the following *volte face:*

> "Long life to your honour!" exclaimed one and all; and in a moment the enthusiasm in his favour was as great, as general, as had been at first the execration and violence against him. The attachment they bore to their lord was still strong. "Fickle, senseless beings!" he said with bitter contempt, as he heard their loyal cry. "These are the creatures we would take to govern us: this is the voice of the people: these are the rights of man."—"Sure but you'll pity us, and forgive us; and you'll be our king again, and live amongst us; and the young master's just gone to the mansion; and didn't we draw him into his own courts? and ain't we returning to our cabins after seeing the dear creature safe: and, for all the world, didn't we indade take ye for one of the murderers in the uniform, come to kill us, and make us slaves? Long life to your honour!"

The political opposition is between "the rights of man" and a Burkean social conception of "the laws and rights of my . . . country." The fictional argument is that the common people, when not misled by opportunistic demogogues, recognise their natural leaders. One may parallel from real life Lord Albemarle after Peterloo: "Nothing can save the country, nothing can prevent revolution, anarchy, and bloodshed, but the union of men of character, talent and respectability throughout the kingdom." These events in the novel reach their climax when the rebels invade the duke's park only to be dispersed by three notes from a distant bugle (*Fidelio* reversed?), and end by calling for the true heir of Delaval who, it is falsely rumoured, has been murdered by Glenarvon. The symbolic structuring is manifest, especially since Avondale and Glenarvon are alternative forms of the same name. The two men fight a duel, without result, in which Glenarvon admits that he only pretended to the virtues which Avondale truly possesses. Once again Lady Caroline's sense of the dialectic of events is strong, and her resolution is socially conservative.

Avondale stands for legitimacy. His defensive attitude to the rights of his country and class would place him, in Burke's analysis, as an old rather than a new Whig, though when faced with the dangers of radicalism the division between Whig and Tory at this time tends to disappear (so William Lamb votes with the government for the use of spies and informers). In the "race between anarchy and despotism"—Graham's phrase—we may credit Avondale with the desire to serve the interests of his class and tenantry by minimal reform. Glenarvon's language, on the other hand, is new Whig, its philosophical origins in the enlightenment, the closest contemporary similarities being to writers like Godwin, Paine and Shelley. None the less, the revolutionary strain of Byronism which the figure represents is manifestly not philosophically radical. Godwin generally abhorred violence. Shelley's *Address to the Irish People* and his *Proposals for an Association of Philanthropists* pertinently analyse the ills of the Irish condition, concluding: "England has made her poor, and the poverty of a rich nation will make its people very desperate and wicked", but his manifest distrust of the "warmth" of the Irish character, and his fears of the wilful and vicious tyranny which revolution will produce, is exactly parallel to Lady Caroline's views. Nourish a revisionary hope with a change of monarchy; rely on the superior ranks of society for reform; meantime form philosophical debating societies to encourage a rational reform of human nature: such are Shelley's proposals for solving the Irish question. A cynic might suggest that such philosophical radicalism, by infinitely putting off reform, enables the established order to enjoy all the complacent pleasure of describing the beauty of virtue without ever threatening the privileges of their own class by action. Or put another way: philosophical London will despatch a printing press for the welfare of revolutionary Greece, whereas Byron demanded rockets.

How far the Satanic element in Glenarvon is a fair representation of political Byronism is an open question. Theoretically it should be possible to distinguish between the politics of Byron's poetry and the interpretation post-Napoleonic Europe put upon it, but in practice the quest for scholarly objectivity may be spurious when we are dealing with an art often symbolical in mode and psychologically obscure. The reason why Lady Caroline uses Byronism in the way she does, however, is probably easier to describe. Glenarvon, I have suggested, is the classic figure of the scapegoat. He is created to salve the guilty conscience of liberal society. A reformative movement, intellectually sceptical in its radical wing, faced with the manifest ills of Irish (and English) society, was only too aware

of the likelihood of the dispossessed to break an ancient "contract" imposed on them by force of arms. The right of resistance was a fundamental tenet of the oligarchs of 1688. Yet such a right could not be permitted by the oligarchy outside their own ranks since it would substitute class revolution for reform. It is a classic dilemma. Hence the Byronic hero who is both the product of a liberal society, yet who is execrated by it as an expression of a collective sense of guilt. He embodies both the fundamental human feeling that revolution is necessary to change the evil of things, and the practical fear of the disastrous consequences of insurrection. So Byron, far away in Greece and safely dead was to be idolised as a hero of nineteenth-century liberalism, but the same policies pursued at home in Ireland produce the Satanic image of Glenarvon. His heirs are John O'Leary, the bomber, Connolly and Pearse, urban guerrillas; revolutionary heroes or subversive terrorists, depending on one's historical perspective. (pp. 4-6, 9-10, 13-16)

> *Malcolm Kelsall, "The Byronic Hero and Revolution in Ireland: The Politics of 'Glenarvon'," in* The Byron Journal, *No. 9, 1981, pp. 4-6, 9-10, 13-16, 19.*

Peter W. Graham   (essay date 1990)

[*Graham is an American educator and critic. In the following excerpt, he offers a comparison of Lamb's works, particularly* Glenarvon, *with Byron's epic poem* Don Juan.]

Glenarvon does not feature a young Spaniard traveling in England and observing English life from a Continental perspective, nor does it contain so many attitudes and opinions so surprisingly similar to those voiced in *Don Juan*. What *Glenarvon* does offer Byron, I would suggest, is an English version of the Don Juan myth told (almost uniquely in its history) from the female point of view. This shifted point of view widens the scope of a legend that in most of its versions centers rather narrowly on the character of Don Juan. In *Glenarvon*, Lady Caroline shows herself fascinated with the seducer's qualities—but she gives prominence to the nature, feelings, and motivations of the seduced. Doing so results, I think, in a portrayal that Byron took seriously enough to refute, however dismissive his comments on Lady Caroline's production may have been. As a number of readers have noticed in different ways, one of the most surprising differences between Byron's Don Juan and others is the transformation of an irresistible man into an unresisting one—a good-natured and innately obliging fellow made the romantic toy of a parade of powerful women. I see this reversal of convention as Byron's rebuttal of *Glenarvon*, a work where the male title character actively, treacherously, compulsively seduces almost every female crossing his path in the story; but it also seems that *Don Juan*'s recognition of women as potent, complex beings could be a lesson learned from *Glenarvon*, an intermittent empathy across gender lines that is yet another variety of the poem's cosmopolitanism.

From the moment of its publication in 1816, *Glenarvon* has been a work known and read less for its literary merits than for its not-so-thickly veiled portrayal of Lady Caroline, Byron, and their romantic relationship. When after a few months Byron's attention turned to other women, including her confidante Lady Oxford and her husband's cousin Annabella Milbanke, Lady Caroline made numerous private and public efforts to reclaim him through scenes enacted with varying degrees of outrageousness. She turned up at his lodgings in page-boy attire, ran away from home, made an apparent attempt to stab herself at Lady Heathcote's ball. But having "played the devil," as Byron puts it in *Don Juan,* her final gambit was to "write a novel." The work she produced is occasionally dazzling, far from polished, deeply flawed. Despite its defects, though, *Glenarvon* warrants serious consideration, in part because its very flaws and excesses are testimony to how talent can be thwarted, how barriers of personality, gender, class, and education can keep a mind from achieving its full potential, in part because its view of the relations between men and women can be seen as providing Byron crucial ideas to refute and reflect in *Don Juan.* In this essay, I shall be thinking about *Glenarvon* both as a semi-adequate expression of one sensibility (Lady Caroline's) and as an entirely effective catalyst for another (Byron's). Besides showing something interesting about the two writers and *Don Juan,* this examination of *Glenarvon* will, I hope, have relevance as a case study of how circumstance can lame talent, how talent can struggle against circumstance, and how literary texts can be a forum for sustained conversation where author-reader replies to reader-author. (pp. 90-2)

When Byron ended their connection, the unstable Lady Caroline went into a period of emotional turmoil that spawned *Glenarvon,* with its often hysterical but sometimes dead-accurate portraits of herself, her husband, Byron, and the Great World in which their melodrama took place. Excluded by the final, unforgivable indiscretion of publication from the circles into which she had been born, she sank into a sad and dissipated middle age during which she wrote two other, less controversial novels, *Graham Hamilton* (1822) and *Ada Reis* (1823). She died at Melbourne House in 1828.

As is exemplified in "Shakespeare's Sister," that marvelous exercise in historical supposition Virginia Woolf includes in *A Room of One's Own,* women of talent and energy have at different times and in different ways been kept from effectively exerting their powers. Tillie Olsen voices the recognition, which she goes on to amplify and probe in *Silences,* her study of thwarted creativity, this way: "Where the gifted among women (*and men*) have remained mute, or have never attained full capacity, it is because of circumstances, inner or outer, which oppose the needs of creation."

England under the Prince Regent was not so uncongenial a place for the development of female creativity as England under Elizabeth had been. Women were writing—writing, publishing, and being read, as the careers of Lady Caroline's contemporaries and near-contemporaries Jane Austen, Fanny Burney, Maria Edgworth, Ann Radcliffe, and Mary Shelley attest. Lady Caroline herself was able to write, publish, and be read, for better or worse—witness

Glenarvon and her other two novels. Nonetheless, a writer can be muted without being reduced to complete and literal wordlessness. It is thus worth asking if and how Lady Caroline's writing was restrained by her gender, class, and education. It is worth considering *Glenarvon* as an upper-class woman's attempt to do what a ruling-class man (her husband the politician or her lover the poet) or a woman who had been brought up differently might do—to achieve personal, even public success rather than merely promote the achievement of others. It is worth asking if chronic frustration of talent might not have given rise to the famous fits of temper and temperament Lady Caroline suffered—for in any case, her mental sufferings take palpable form in *Glenarvon,* whose very defects and inconsistencies bespeak a naturally powerful but undisciplined mind.

But if the questions are worth asking, the answers do not seem simple. Lady Caroline Lamb was both lucky and unlucky—in some ways society's victim, but not just a victim. Growing up without much formal education was a handicap (one she shared with most women and men of her time) but not an insurmountable one, given that she passed her days in houses where books were present and ideas cherished, where the likes of Charles James Fox and Richard Brinsley Sheridan were regular fixtures. Furthermore, her first years of marriage, like Mary Shelley's, were filled with intellectual adventures. William, entertaining, unpedantic, and six years the senior, liked teaching; Caroline, quick and enthusiastic, liked learning; and their days as she describes them resemble an agreeable tutorial:

> Wm. and I get up about ten or half after or later (if late at night)—have our breakfast—talk a little—read Newton on the Prophecies with the Bible, having finished Sherlock—then I hear him his part [William was then acting Captain Absolute in amateur theatricals], he goes to eat and walk—I finish dressing and take a drive or a little walk—then come upstairs where Wm. meets me and we read Hume with Shakespeare till the dressing bell.

William was not eccentric in appreciating and cultivating his wife's mind. Unlike certain other circles and classes, the aristocratic Whigs among whom Lady Caroline lived valued learning and intelligence in women. She even had examples of female literary achievement in her family—she was a descendant of Sarah duchess of Marlborough, and in the nearer past her aunt Devonshire somehow, amid busy days of gaming, love, and friendship, found time to have written better-than-passable poetry and a novel, *The Sylph.* Most important of all, with money, leisure, and a squadron of servants, Lady Caroline had absolutely no need to be the "angel in the house" Virginia Woolf had to kill in herself or the "essential angel," that more mundane provider of daily family necessities that Tillie Olsen sees as impeding or killing many a woman's talent.

Privileged though she may have been in many ways, Lady Caroline appears to have been hobbled in certain other regards. The laissez faire of Devonshire House may have gone far toward developing her individuality, but nothing could have been less likely to teach her the self-discipline a writer needs; and she had no reason to feel any of the externally imposed disciplines that sometimes can substitute for the inner sort. Her upbringing and station provided Lady Caroline with most sorts of confidence but not the kind necessary for taking on serious work in a major genre—a confidence that would come more easily to men of her class, whose early educations centered on memorizing the classics and composing in limitation of the classical masters. We shall soon go into the possible reasons why she wrote *Glenarvon;* but whatever her reasons, she chose to write the book as a roman à clef, a form that seldom gains high esteem. Of course, basing a first novel on direct personal experience is quite ordinary; but Lady Caroline chose to highlight the personal source of her fiction. In doing so she may have been taking a small and relatively easy step toward ultimate success in a greater and more challenging genre. She may have been condemning herself to a kind of failure, shutting off the possibility of major achievement by working in a minor vein. In any case, this choice of form is consistent with her ways of displaying her talent in the years before *Glenarvon.* Though Byron's letters speak of her great gift for poetry, and Regency memorialists pay high tribute to her abilities as a painter, Lady Caroline limited herself to working in forms generally considered "small." She produced songs, occasional verses, charades, beautifully detailed miniature paintings less than an inch square—all socially acceptable outlets for feminine talents.

Though her choice of literary ends may have been conventional, her means were exotic. When Lady Caroline wrote *Glenarvon* (at night, in secret, so she claimed) she allegedly put on male attire—a page boy's costume. When she presented her manuscript to a copyist, she chose to dress her companion, Miss Welsh, as the society lady and to present herself (and the manuscript's author) as a fourteen-year-old serving boy, William Ormonde. These impersonations are blatantly suggestive, but determining exactly what they signify is difficult. There are simply too many possible meanings. Did Lady Caroline, anticipating by a quarter of a century the habit of George Sand (another female novelist who took fictional revenge on her famous lovers), cast off womanly circumscriptions and assume masculine power by changing clothes? Was she escaping from the complexities of maturity by retreating into childhood? Was she overcoming upper-class restraints, a possibility not to be discounted in someone who grew up in the aftermath of the French Revolution, perhaps the first time mob attire became modish? Was she indulging a characteristically aristocratic taste for fancy dress? All these responses, some conventional and some subversive for a person of her sex and station, seem worth arguing. All of them imply at least a measure of dissatisfaction with her situation and its constraints. But during the period of *Glenarvon's* composition another possibility is equally plausible. Lady Caroline's pageboy disguise may have been an exercise in nostalgia for the happier days of her love affair, a period during which she had learned that the livery she enjoyed wearing possessed the extra advantage of presenting her elfin charm in the way it would appeal most strongly to Byron.

David Cecil [in *Melbourne*] characterizes *Glenarvon* as "a deplorable production, an incoherent cross between a realistic novel of fashionable life and a fantastic tale of terror, made preposterous by every absurd device." On strictly literary grounds, this assessment is plausible, and everyone who writes on Lady Caroline Lamb more or less echoes the verdict. At the core of *Glenarvon* is the education—which is to say the ruin—of Calantha, a noble, innocent, idealistic, impulsive beauty too fine to thrive in a hard world. Calantha marries young, as Lady Caroline did. Her husband, Lord Avondale, though warm-hearted, wise, and tolerant as was William Lamb, corrupts Calantha's morals by introducing her too abruptly to mundane realities, then abandoning her rudderless on the high seas of high society, where, after some struggle, she succumbs to Glenarvon, a Byronic seducer of unrivaled charisma, intelligence, gloom, and guilt. Loving Calantha deeply, Glenarvon nonetheless deserts her cruelly and callously. The world despises her. She dies of heartbreak. The men who survive her meet in a duel. In the first edition, Glenarvon injures his adversary with provocation; Avondale rides away with a flesh wound and a bruised ego, and when he dies it is from sadness. In the second edition, the scene culminates with Glenarvon plunging a dagger into Avondale's heart (which, metaphorically speaking, he has already done in seducing Calantha) and departing a murderer in fact. Glenarvon dies theatrically—self-starved, half drowned, pursued by real or imagined demons. Superadded to this melodrama are other Gothic excesses: maniacs, murderers, wicked Italians, babies switched in the cradle, revolutionaries, ghosts, an anchoress-poet turned harlot. Contrasting the extravagantly lurid scenes of the novel (all of which are set in Ireland, where Caroline had been sent for her sins in September of 1812) are sparkling and believable portraits of London society, with its grandeurs, *longeurs,* hypocrisies, and absurdities, in chapters acclaimed even by the novel's harshest detractors.

It is hard to do anything but go along with critical consensus and condemn *Glenarvon* if we take it as a whole and judge it as a novel. That is how its author wanted it judged, ultimately. She signaled as much by publishing it, a process requiring some persistence on her part, and by somewhat carefully and sometimes effectively revising the published work between first and second editions—reducing verbiage, correcting errors, toning down the incredible Gothicisms, cutting offensive passages, refining and altering her chief characters, stressing the work's moral efficacy. But *Glenarvon* is a much more interesting work if we see it less narrowly, as something more than a novel. Indeed, its earliest readers purchased, perused, and condemned it not for fictions but for supposed truths—truths about Whig society, about the author and her husband, most especially about Byron. How true those truths may be is an unsettled matter. As John Galt's memorable phrase puts it, Lady Caroline was renowned for "acuteness blended with phrensy and talent"; and she once spoke of truth as "what one believes at the moment," thus sounding like a sophisticated postmodernist rather than a naive Regency writer. Byron repeatedly claimed that *Glenarvon's* mendacity was one of the reasons for its literary weakness: "It seems to me that, if the authoress had written the *truth,* and nothing but the truth—the whole truth—the romance would not only have been more *romantic,* but more entertaining." If we consider *Glenarvon* in terms of its blend of facts and fictions, conscious and subconscious ones, if we think about why it came to be written and what powerful feelings lie underneath, or sometimes burst through, the flawed surface of narrative, the book becomes a document of more meaning to its author, of more potential value to Byron and other readers. Let us begin with the circumstances of composition—themselves a muddle of truth telling and theatrical dissembling.

Why did Lady Caroline write and publish *Glenarvon?* For revenge, according to the most widely held belief—revenge against all who had wronged her, the Melbournes, Lady Holland, Lady Oxford, Byron. For personal repentance and the public good, as respectively asserted by Clark Olney [*University of Kansas City Review* 22 (1956)] and Lady Caroline herself in the moralizing preface to the second edition. For a mixture of these reasons, says John Clubbe [*Wordsworth Circle* 10 (1979)], who recognizes that "the novel forced itself out of her: she had to write it much as Byron had to write his confessional poems."

Glenarvon does indeed seem to have "forced itself out." We might see the expressive process as a kind of childbirth, Lady Caroline's "illegitimate" novel as the love child that resulted from her romance with Byron. From the start his attraction for her had been a literary one. The fact is acknowledged in her obituary, a composition attributed to William Lamb: "The world is very lenient to the mistresses of poets, and perhaps not without justice, for their attachments have something of excuse . . . they arise from imagination, not depravity." Lady Caroline, like the rest of fashionable London, first knew of Byron as the young traveler-poet who had written and presumably posed for *Childe Harold*. She fell in love with that potent Byronic fiction, a mask self-created but thrust on him by his admirers. The charms or deficiencies of the real man mattered little: warned by Samuel Rogers that the lionized poet had a club foot and a habit of nail-biting, the lady already in love with an idea replied, "If he is as ugly as Aesop, I must see him."

Writing *Glenarvon* seems to be the product of a confessional impulse Lady Caroline shared with or derived from Byron—that and her attempt to emulate, or maybe even surpass, him. The act is comparable to the creation of *Frankenstein* a year or two later, Mary Shelley's making a "Modern Prometheus" out of parts derived from her two poet-heroes and replying in her novel to their Promethean poems. Similarly, Lady Caroline's fiction combines bits of Lord Byron with pieces of the Byronic hero in a tale with more guilt and mystification than can be found in *Childe Harold* and all the Oriental tales combined. Her need to resemble the writer she loved (and the lover she had lost) extended beyond the matters of subject and tone to manner of composition. "In one month I wrote and sent *Glenarvon* to the press," was Lady Caroline's claim concerning the gestation of her literary progeny, a generally accepted but demonstrably false statement. Her correspondence with John Murray proves that the task cost her two or three years of labor that left the book "substantially completed" in June 1815. A need to be like Byron can best account for Lady Caroline's feeling that her novel should

be taken for an extemporaneous effusion in the Byron line—though spontaneity was something of a pose with him also. Publishing the results of her so-called month of composition barely two weeks after Byron's April 1816 flight from England seems like nothing so much as another act of emulation. Hobhouse and others saw Lady Caroline's ill- or well-timed novel as attacking Byron's character when it was most vulnerable; she unconvincingly but perhaps sincerely spoke of *Glenarvon* as her defense of Byron. But whatever its effect on him, the book clearly caused her to share his banishment. Publishing *Glenarvon*—flaunting the literary consequences of her infidelity before the world—may have been her Byronic gesture of self-exile, a deliberate if imperfectly calculated act she would come to regret.

Childbirth is not the only metaphor that comes readily to mind as suitable for characterizing the production of *Glenarvon.* Another apt comparison is one that Byron rejects as too tired to be worth pursuing in the English cantos of *Don Juan:* the volcano. "Poor thing! How frequently, by me and others, / It hath been stirred up till its smoke quite smothers," the narrator says as he hunts for figurative speech to convey the repressed passion of Lady Adeline Amundeville, modeled in part on Lady Caroline. Earlier, Byron himself [in a letter] uses the image both to speak of Lady Caroline ("—Then your heart—my poor Caro, what a little volcano! that pours *lava* through your veins, & yet I cannot wish it a bit colder") and, in a famous phrase, to describe poetry ("it is the lava of the imagination whose eruption prevents an earth-quake"). Hélène Cixous, in "The Laugh of the Medusa," resorts to the volcano as she describes feminine writing in general. Her words, however, are a particularly apt representation of what *Glenarvon* is—and, matters of gender aside, of what *Don Juan* does: "A feminine text cannot fail to be more than subversive. It is volcanic; as it is written it brings about an upheaval of the old property crust, carrier of masculine investments; there's no other way." This eruption, as Cixous puts it, serves "to smash everything, to shatter the framework of institutions, to blow up the law, to break up the 'truth' with laughter."

Glenarvon's eruption contains little that is intentionally laughter producing; but it seems to have followed Cixous's model rather than Byron's in causing rather than preventing an earthquake. The upheaval *Glenarvon* brought about in Whig drawing rooms, at Almack's, Brooks's, and other haunts of the Regency powers and exquisites, came chiefly because Lady Caroline did what Cixous claims to be necessary in the second sentence of her essay: "Woman must write her self." Lady Caroline continuously hints that in Calantha she is writing her self—and the concluding sentence of one of Calantha's many self-abasements forthrightly erases the distinction between author and protagonist. " 'Yet when they read my history—' " says the heroine, conscious for the moment of her fictional status, " 'if amidst the severity of justice which such a narrative must excite, some feelings of forgiveness and pity should arise, perhaps the prayer of one, who has suffered much, may ascend for them, and the thanks of a broken heart be accepted in return.' "

Lady Caroline's "writing her self" gives *Glenarvon* some of its best and worst features. Unwilling or unable to get beyond her own story, she offers something intense and undirected. Her view of the truth may not always have resembled other people's visions, but in *Glenarvon* (the first edition, that is) she stays true to what she saw in her upbringing, marriage, experience of society, and romance with Byron. The feelings and events presented are not edited in such a way as to fit them into the world as it is generally understood or into the realistic novel as it is generally constructed. The perspective is an eccentric one. Faithfulness to this singular view of things obliges *Glenarvon* to contain characters the common reader will find hypocritical, overblown, self-indulgent—effusions that to the ordinary ear sound incredibly naive and sentimental—incidents that are downright absurd. The problem, however, is not that *Glenarvon* fails to reflect "real life" but that life as experienced by Lady Caroline and embodied in *Glenarvon* has little in common with what most readers (even in her own day and of her own class) would find real. Sincerely recording her own congenital insincerity, foolishly publishing a transcript of her own folly, Lady Caroline makes a good confession but a bad novel. This mixed thing is perfectly characterized by a further Cixous phrase: *Glenarvon* is above all "the chaosmos of the 'personal.'"

How so? One place to begin might be with names and their role in characterization. Two or three possible conventions for creating and naming characters seem to be the rule in fiction. The distinctions become clear when we look at two novels published during the same year as *Glenarvon,* Jane Austen's *Emma* and Thomas Love Peacock's *Headlong Hall.* An author aiming at lifelike characters would typically operate as Jane Austen does and provide names that may be subject to interpretation, playful or serious, but that nevertheless would pass muster in the real world. "Emma Woodhouse" and "George Knightley" may be names we can read for meaning, but they are also utterly believable. The writer whose fiction makes no pretenses of reality would be more likely to choose, as Peacock does, incredible names ("Patrick O'Prism," "Philomela Poppyseed") or to undercut credible names by explicitly announcing their significance in the literary game being played (as Peacock's playfully erudite footnotes do for "Foster," "Escot," and "Jenkinson"). Lady Caroline goes by neither Austen's rules nor Peacock's. *Glenarvon* does aim at transcribing a version of reality in its characters—that is the first objective of roman à clef. But *Glenarvon*'s names announce that they are laden with meaning in loud if not always intelligible tones. The heroine, to begin where we should, is called "Lady Calantha Delaval." The number of syllables matches word for word with "Lady Caroline Ponsonby"—but how much richer Lady Caroline's fictionalized name is than her actual one! "Calantha" announces through its reference to the heroine of Ford's *The Broken Heart* just what is in store for the protagonist—and if the reader misses the allusion, Lady Augusta Selwyn, one of the novel's best-drawn characters, facetiously spells the matter out: "'Come, tell me truly, is not your heart in torture? and, like your namesake Calantha, while lightly dancing the gayest in the ring, has not the shaft already been struck, and shall you not die ere you attain the goal?'" After thinking about the volcanic na-

ture of Lady Caroline Lamb and her fiction, one sees the surname "Delaval" as something more than an attractively aristocratic combination of syllables. The letters of "Delaval" are "lava" enclosed—a detail especially intriguing in light of the title that accompanies the name, for Calantha's father is duke of Altamonte. The sounds of "Delaval" are close to, though not identical with, "devil." This heroine's name explains in various sorts of shorthand what sort of person she will show herself to be in the course of the novel and signals the loftiness and the intense, potentially destructive sensibility she is said to possess in the first lengthy description of her nature:

> Her feelings indeed swelled with a tide too powerful for the unequal resistance of her understanding:—her motives appeared the very best, but the actions which resulted from them were absurd and exaggerated. Thoughts, swift as lightening, hurried through her brain:—projects, seducing, but visionary crowded upon her view: without a curb she followed the impulse of her feelings; and those feelings varied with every varying interest and impression. . . .

> . . . All that was base or mean, she, from her soul, despised; a fearless spirit raised her, as she fondly imagined, above the vulgar herd; self confident, she scarcely deigned to bow the knee before her God; and man, as she had read of him in history, appeared too weak, too trivial to inspire either alarm or admiration.

> It was thus, with bright prospects, strong love of virtue, high ideas of honour, that she entered upon life.

Lady Caroline's background, character, and story may be Calantha's—but Calantha does not suffice to express her complexities. Her less ladylike attributes and her unfulfilled impulses are projected into other characters. One is Zerbellini, a child who turns out to be Calantha's abducted brother and who is sent as a page to Castle Delaval by Glenarvon's alter ego, Viviani. As a boy, a changeling, a servant, an embodied connection between Glenarvon and Calantha, Zerbellini plays a number of roles Lady Caroline acted, or fancied the idea of acting, in her real drama with Byron. A more extreme vision of Lady Caroline as she might have been had her actions corresponded fully to her inclinations is presented in Elinor St. Clare, a character whose behavior and qualities Calantha explicitly compares with her own at a number of crucial points in the novel. This beautiful and wild young creature, who like Lady Caroline (and Calantha) is raised by an aunt, expresses her author's vital energy, notably absent from the ethereal though passionate Calantha, and takes Lady Caroline's capacity for outrageous action several steps farther. "St. Clare," as she is typically styled, has Lady Caroline's fierce idealism, her talent for poetry and music, her tastes for riding, dressing in male attire, and political activism. Although she has been raised in a convent and betrothed to Christ rather than married to an earthly lord, St. Clare shows none of Calantha's scruples in yielding to Glenarvon. While Calantha continues to feel social constraints and keeps on with her old life after becoming fascinated with Glenarvon, St. Clare boldly renounces her old ties for the new, engrossing, disgraceful one—unlike Lady Caroline or Calantha, she goes off with the fatal object of her passions. The demands of the nineteenth-century novel being what they are, each of Lady Caroline's fictive shadows pays for her error—but the ways are different and the differences illuminating. While Calantha, torn apart by conflicting demands and emotions, dies of a broken heart and nervous exhaustion in the middle of volume 3 (rather a serious structural problem if the novel were merely roman à clef), St. Clare endures to the denouement and perishes grandly: having kept the faith with her band of Irish revolutionaries, fought like a man in battle, and burned the turncoat Glenarvon's ancestral home, she makes an equestrian leap from cliff to sea and dies theatrically, a Sappho on horseback.

"St. Clare," like "Calantha Delaval," is a name that calls out to be explicated—it is impossible not to recognize its suggestions of holiness and purity, appropriate connotations as the book begins, ironic ones later on—and also demands to be connected with other names. Within the novel St. Clare is echoed in Glenarvon's Christian name, Clarence, in what he calls his illegitimate child by Alice MacAllain, Clare of Costolly, and in Clarendon, the surname of the poet who has enraptured Calantha's society friends, a man "gifted with every kind of merit," including "an open ingenuous countenance, expressive eyes, and a strong and powerful mind." Moving from fiction to the world of fact, one finds affinities between *Glenarvon's* St. Clare and Clare of Assisi, "Sister Moon" to St. Francis's "Brother Sun" and, like her fictional namesake, a woman whose love for a charismatic man (though a saint rather than a seducer) inspired her to join and lead a cause. It is less obvious but equally interesting that Calantha's course, like Lady Caroline's own, parallels and then at key points inverts the life of St. Clare of Rimini, who married young and lived scandalously until her conversion at the age of thirty-four, after which time she devoted herself to penance, prayer, and good works. It is also worth observing that earl of Clare was the title belonging to one of Byron's Harrow favorites, the object of an idealized schoolboy affection that Byron characterized in a letter to Mary Shelley as his only true friendship with a member of his own sex: "I do not know the *male* human being, except Lord Clare, the friend of my infancy, for whom I feel any thing

Lady Melbourne's Brocket Hall, where Lamb lived after separating from her husband.

that deserves the name." And of course one of the small but remarkable coincidences of Byron's life was that in April of 1816, as he prepared to leave England and Lady Caroline awaited the publication of her novel, another Clare, this one female, self-named, persistent, and finally detested, entered his life: Mary Godwin's stepsister Mary Jane (Clara, Clare, or Claire) Clairmont.

These variants of *Clare* with their connections and repetitions seem fraught with significance—but the intricacy of whatever pattern there may be thwarts the recognition for which that pattern seems to call. Is the choice of *Clare* arbitrary? Doubtful, considering its repetition. Is the repetition a clumsy inadvertence? If so, Lady Caroline probably would have made changes for the second edition. A sign of links between characters? Almost certainly in the case of Clarence Lord Glenarvon and his bastard son; it is less certain but more interesting to speculate that St. Clare and Clarence indicate a deliberate connection of the book's two boldest renegades, an authorial awareness of the spiritual likeness between herself and Byron. Does Lady Caroline mean for us to see connections between her fiction and the saints' lives? Very likely, especially in light of her having added explicit references to Calantha's Catholicism to the second edition. Are the variations on *Clare* a bridge between Lady Caroline's Byronic fiction and the facts of Byron's life? Perhaps. The prophetic allusion to Claire Clairmont is of course happenstance, but Byron may well have spoken to Lady Caroline, or to someone she knew, of his regard for Lord Clare. What purpose, if any, would allusion to this friendship serve? Confronting the chaosmos of the personal, one cannot be certain. The full meaning of *Clare* is far from clear—it seems to have risen less out of simple intention than out of the free play of wit as Schlegel understands it when he says that "A witty idea is a disintegration of spiritual substances which, before being suddenly separated, must have been thoroughly mixed. The imagination must first be satiated with all sorts of life before one can electrify it."

Doubling and repetition work toward a more intelligible effect in Avondale and Glenarvon, the titles assigned to the novel's representatives of sinned-against William Lamb and sinning Byron. Among the surprising features of *Glenarvon's* first edition is that these two lords, who in terms of both literary convention and real life ought to appear as opposites, are in certain ways the same man: part hero, part villain. Their titles, compound words consisting of reversed near-equivalents (*Glen* is synonymous with *dale; arvon* corresponds to *Avon*), exactly represent their kinship with one another and topographically suggest their shared antithetical relation to the daughter of Alta-*monte*. However wicked Lady Caroline intended the one to seem and however admirable she wished to show the other as being, Glenarvon and Avondale respond to and affect Calantha in comparable ways: both men love and lower her.

Avondale, the good and noble husband, is nevertheless a free-thinker, a man of the world. In educating Calantha, he begins her corruption:

> Eager to oppose and conquer those opinions in his wife, which savoured as he thought of bigot-

ry and prudish reserve, he tore the veil at once from her eyes, and opened hastily her wondering mind to a world before unknown. He foresaw not the peril to which he exposed her:—he heeded not the rapid progress of her thoughts—the boundless views of an over-heated imagination. At first she shrunk with pain and horror, from every feeling which to her mind appeared less chaste, less pure, than those to which she had long been accustomed; but when her principles, or rather her prejudices, yielded to the power of love, she broke from a restraint too rigid, into a liberty the most dangerous from its novelty, its wildness and uncertainty.

The debasement Avondale brings upon Calantha is only theoretical—thanks to him she experiences not firsthand sin and guilt but "books of every description," more precisely characterized in the second edition as "the works of Historians, Philosophers, and Metaphysicians." This progressive corruption of innocence, however, is just what Glenarvon vows to continue in the sphere of practice when, disguised as the Italian Viviani, he first encounters Calantha at a London ball: " 'Let me see her, and I will sing to her till the chaste veil of every modest feeling is thrown aside, and thoughts of fire dart into her bosom, and loosen every principle within.' " For the time, this is all just talk. But when he arrives in his own person back in Ireland, Glenarvon proceeds to do what he has promised. The second of the novel's three volumes is chiefly devoted to his insidious but irresistible destruction of Calantha's principles. His villainy is entirely intentional, and he insists on making Calantha fully conscious of her progressive debauchery: " 'Remember when a word or look were regarded by you as a crime,' " Glenarvon remarks when he has lured Calantha approximately halfway from her position as respectable matron to the infernal marriage vows that represent her ultimate corruption, " '—how you shuddered at the bare idea of guilt. Now you can hear its language with interest: it has lost its horror: Ah soon it shall be the only language your heart will like.' "

According to common sense and the usual rubrics of fiction, the choice of parallel names for hero and villain would seem an awkward confusion; and presenting a husband's and a seducer's moral effects on the heroine as comparable would be yet more of a defect—a serious lapse from orthodox understanding of those roles. But a powerful if subconscious point is being made. Stressing the similarities between the "best" man in the novel and the "worst" one demonstrates Lady Caroline's adherence to the truths of her heart. She does not use her book as an opportunity to make Byron seem worse than he was—the crimes ascribed to Glenarvon are melodramatically incredible ones, and his charm and potential goodness remain evident to the last. Nor does she excuse William from what she perceived as his part in her downfall, much as she loved him and grateful as she was for his loyalty when the world had turned against her. A further consequence of this linkage is to generalize the corruption of Calantha, to make it resonate as a sort of archetypal act: what men, even truly loving men, do to women—and, as Byron demonstrates in *Don Juan,* what women also do to men.

The mythic proportions of this act are clearer because Glenarvon's debasement of Calantha is not a unique event, just as Don Juan's falling for the more experienced Julia is but the first instance of what we come to see as his life's pattern. In the course of the novel Glenarvon seduces virtually every important female character, or at least charms each one to the point where seduction would be possible should he choose it. [In] volume 1, Glenarvon makes his debut as a Don Juan by pursuing and acquiring the "most beautiful woman in Florence," whose outraged husband revenges the insult to his honor by killing the lady. From there, Glenarvon's list of mistresses known to the reader expands to include Lady Margaret Buchanan, Alice MacAllain, Elinor St. Clare, Calantha, and Lady Mandeville. The women attracted to Glenarvon though not debauched by him include Calantha's cousins, Lady Augusta Selwyn, and the heiress Miss Monmouth.

In *Glenarvon* the function of man seems to be stealing, staining, and breaking feminine hearts—but nonetheless, the novel lets men off more lightly than it does the author's own sex. The real victims of Lady Caroline's pen are not William Lamb or Byron. Avondale's offenses are slight and more than counterbalanced by his love and virtues. Glenarvon's assorted wickednesses are either improbable or trivial and, like Avondale's, offset by what is fine in him. For believable villainy—treachery, heartlessness, cruelty, and selfishness as they are generally understood to manifest themselves—we must turn to *Glenarvon*'s gallery of women. In Caroline's portraits of the great ladies of Whig society we find sharper outlines and less ambivalence, we sense how formidable Lady Caroline's powers of observation and understanding could be, we feel the force of Elizabeth Jenkins's assertion [in *Lady Caroline Lamb*] that "Lady Caroline had the gifts of a novelist without being able to write a novel." Thanks to these gifts, even the portraits of the women she sets out to denounce retain the excellences that brought worldly success to their originals. The false Lady Mandeville, who professes friendship even as she steals Glenarvon from Calantha, is Lady Oxford to the life—the ripe beauty and winning amiability of that countess being transcribed along with her classical pedantry and notorious promiscuity. Lady Margaret Buchanan, whose hard wisdom, amorality, ambition, and attractiveness to the much younger Glenarvon make her resemble nothing so much as an extrapolation from Lady Melbourne, is the blackest English character in the story. Like many a British novelist of her day, Lady Caroline reserves the novel's darkest deed for a foreigner, the Italian La Crusca; but Lady Margaret plans that wicked act, the abduction and murder of her infant nephew to permit her son's succession to the dukedom, and she perseveres in subsequent treachery to her immediate family. Yet she is permitted heroic grandeur and the courage of extraordinary aspirations, for herself and for Calantha, of whom she says to the more conventional aunt, Mrs. Seymour, "I wish her not only to be virtuous; I will acknowledge it,—I wish her to be distinguished and great." The other feminine portraits—Calantha's cousins (in real life the daughters of the Devonshires, Lady Georgiana and Lady Harriet Spencer), Lady Augusta Selwyn (diversely identified but perhaps likeliest to be Lady Cahir), and the most famous and brilliant of them all, the comic apotheosis of

Lady Holland as the Princess of Madagascar, dominatrix to her reviewer-slaves at Barbary House—demonstrate that Lady Caroline could achieve, if not sustain, the blend of selectivity and truth to life that makes for successful satire.

As for the depiction of Calantha herself, one cannot fairly accuse Lady Caroline of self-indulgence. Instead, she is [according to Clubbe] "her own best psychologist," as her biographers implicitly acknowledge by relying on *Glenarvon* to supplement primary sources of information on her life. Insight and candor characterize the following representative passage, an assessment of Calantha's character in London society:

> Calantha was esteemed generous; yet indifference for what others valued, and thoughtless profusion were the only qualities she possessed. It is true that the sufferings of others melted a young and ardent heart into the performance of many actions which would never have occurred to those of a colder and more prudent nature. But was there any self-denial practised; and was not she, who bestowed, possessed of every luxury and comfort, her varying and fanciful caprices could desire! Never did she resist the smallest impulse or temptation. If to give had been a crime, she had committed it; for it gave her pain to refuse, and she knew not how to deprive herself of any gratification.

For Lady Caroline as she wrote *Glenarvon,* one of these indispensable gratifications was self-expression, a process that poured forth much that is powerful and promising. But only occasionally did she go beyond self-expression to shape the truths that had emerged into that more or less "made" thing fiction is generally seen to be.

As Byron was beginning *Don Juan, Glenarvon* would have been useful enought as a reminder that though confession and literature may be related, they are not identical: that eruption of the personal, however fascinating, is not enough. But the novel had more to offer than a negative example. The character of Glenarvon is a "half-real hero" like Don Juan, if in quite a different way. Both the truths and the myths that comprise Lady Caroline's *homme fatal* can be seen as calling for refutation, even if Byron could not dignify her publication with a direct reply. Don Juan and the Byronic narrator both serve as such a refutation, one that resembles Lady Caroline's portrait in its shifting proportions of fact and fancy. Glenarvon's relationships with women in particular demanded a response—for Byron was very far from seeing himself as the Byronic seducer *Glenarvon* depicts. Apart from Glenarvon's predations, though, Lady Caroline's comments on love, marriage, and the differences between men and women in the Great World are much in the vein of Byron's observations on these topics in *Don Juan.* If Byron found her opinions worth echoing and deliberately echoed them, he was a cosmopolite in realms beyond nationality. Even if the resemblances between his pronouncements and Lady Caroline's show nothing more than a shared position, we must reassess popular conceptions of them both, must recognize the good sense coexisting with her absurdities and the sensitivity behind his cynicism.

Byron told Madame de Staël, Thomas Moore, and others that Glenarvon could not be a good portrait because he had not sat long enough for a likeness to be caught; but in fact Lady Caroline captured some of his salient features and combined them with the Byronic legend to striking effect. Glenarvon's story is not Byron's, but many specific details, sometimes combined or applied in new ways, do come from Byron's life and legend. Glenarvon's appearance and manner are Byron's as they were generally perceived by those who read him into *Childe Harold* and the Oriental tales:

> It was one of those faces which, having once beheld, we never afterwards forget. It seemed as if the soul of passion had been stamped and printed upon every feature. The eye beamed into life as it threw up its dark ardent gaze, with a look nearly of inspiration, while the proud curl of the upper lip expressed haughtiness and bitter contempt; yet, even mixed with these fierce characteristic feelings, an air of melancholy and dejection shaded and softened every harsher expression. Such a countenance spoke to the heart.

Like the public image of "Byron," a mask or misconception half revealing and half revising the man behind it, Glenarvon resembles without being identical to Byron the man. The son of a mother "of doubtful character" (Mrs. Byron's character was unimpugned, but her temper and mental balance were questionable), Glenarvon inherits a ruinous abbey from a disreputable grandfather (as opposed to Byron's succeeding his great-uncle, the "Wicked Lord"). He rents the estate during his minority to a lord whose name is de Ruthven (Lord Grey de Ruthyn leased Newstead Abbey) and spends his youth in traveling widely (mostly in Italy rather than Byron's Greece and Turkey). Lady Caroline draws in Byron's fondness for monk's robes, his skull cup (associated with drinking blood, not wine, in the novel), and his love of Mediterranean climes. From *Childe Harold* and the Oriental romances she takes the Byronic sense of a guilty secret and a soul "scorched with living fire"; uncannily anticipating Byron's Swiss and Italian years, she associates Glenarvon with storms and boats. She shrewdly and accurately captures Byron's special blend of liberal politics and conservative social attitudes. Glenarvon is an aristocrat keen on his hereditary privileges, but also a charismatic revolutionary, inflaming Irish radicals of the country round his estate:

> whilst many of those who had adopted the same language had voluntarily thrown off their titles, and divided their property amongst their partizans, he made a formal claim for the titles his grandfather had forfeited; and though he had received no positive assurance that his claim would be considered, he called himself by that name alone, and insisted upon his followers addressing him in no other manner.

Lady Caroline's presenting her Byronic hero as a revolutionary is a stroke of fiction that might at first seem downright prophetic, for Byron's involvement with the cause of liberty in Italy and Greece was still years ahead. But her affair with Byron had taken place during the short period when he had involved himself in parliamentary politics, speaking for the sort of Whig views Lady Caroline's childhood hero Fox had represented, a young lord defending his provincial populace (Nottingham frame-breakers, not Irish tenantry) from repressive Tory policies. It was resourceful and apt that Lady Caroline should make her promising revolutionary a part of the continuing conflict that she would have seen at first hand during her 1812 stay in Ireland. It is interesting that she should have resolved the contradiction in her hero's nature in favor of his aristocratic side. Regaining his title and lands, engaging himself to an English heiress who like Annabella Milbanke found reclaiming a handsome genius "a task too delightful to be rejected," taking command of an English ship, Glenarvon sails in league with Lord Avondale's uncle and betrays his former comrades in revolution.

Similarly, the passionate progress of Calantha's involvement with Glenarvon closely follows the pattern of Lady Caroline's romance with Byron, though details are often rearranged. Calantha and Glenarvon first meet at a ball (Glenarvon, however, is in double disguise as Viviani masquing as a monk). Glenarvon, like Byron, notices his lady's exquisite talent and pleasure in dancing—but in wanting to partner her in this expression of "the animal spirits of youth" he is the exact opposite of Byron, who during their liaison prohibited Lady Caroline's waltzing. Editing out Byron's limp and imagining him as a potential dancing partner signal Lady Caroline's strong impulse to idealize her lover and their love—and perhaps a concurrent urge to revenge herself on him by publicly repairing the flaw. The most successfully dramatic real gestures of their courtship also appear in the fictional one. Three examples are Calantha's recognition that the face of this fallen angel is her destiny, Glenarvon's presenting a rose to the lady who values, as he claims, "all that is new or rare . . . for a moment," and Glenarvon's grudging avowal of Avondale's excellences in the Shakespearean comparison "He is as superior to me as Hyperion to a satyr." The circumstances of Glenarvon's announcing "I am no longer your lover" and advising his cast-off mistress to "correct your vanity, which is ridiculous; exert your absurd caprices upon others; and leave me in peace" exactly match Byron's informing Lady Caroline of his new liaison in a letter dispatched from Lady Oxford's Armidian bower—and the words of dismissal are generally believed to have been Byron's, though only phrases of the published piece are to be found in his extant correspondence, and those phrases are in separate letters. Art, in *Glenarvon,* thus consists of rearrangement rather than invention—and in chronicling the "fatal passion," Lady Caroline's rearrangement is limited to details. The pace and tone of the literary affair are if anything too faithful to the torturous and incredible real one—the result of this fidelity being that volumes 2 and 3 (the parts of the book given over to the liaison) are nearly unendurable.

Because *Glenarvon* is in its odd way a truth-telling book and because no biographies or memoirs of Byron had yet appeared, the vast and curious readership beyond Byron's circle of personal acquaintance would have had no reason not to accept Lady Caroline's portrait as an accurate one. Accordingly, Byron may have wished more strongly than he would admit for a public way of setting the record straight and detaching himself from Lady Caroline's cre-

ation. *Don Juan,* with its teasing, self-conscious air of half-real confession, would offer just such an opportunity. (pp. 92-111)

The publication of *Don Juan* (serial as it was) did not comprise the last act in Byron's and Lady Caroline's drama, nor did it offer the last word in the literary conversation that has been considered here. Even after her fall from grace through offenses in life and literature alike, Lady Caroline had not learned discretion. Her reaction to *Don Juan* resembled that mixture of amusement, awareness of brilliance, and acknowledgment of impropriety voiced by Hobhouse, Moore, and other such men of the world rather than the revulsion deemed appropriate to such respectable females as would admit to being readers. She told John Murray, "you cannot think how clever I think 'Don Juan' is, in my heart," though, qualifying that praise, she conceded the poem to be "neither witty, nor in very good taste." Like some other readers with poetical talents of their own, she was in fact so taken with Byron's accomplishment that she apparently had to emulate it—in two anonymous effusions, *A New Canto* (to *Don Juan*) and *Gordon: A Tale.* The latter, two cantos' worth of critical comment on *Don Juan,* effectively demonstrates how tedious ottava rima can be when it lacks the beautifully modulated variety of tone and topic found in *Don Juan.* The first of *Gordon's* cantos, amplifying the sense of Lady Caroline's letter to Murray and taking much the same line as was taken by Hobhouse and company, recognizes the poet's genius and deplores the immoral ends it achieves. The second canto, rather more dramatic if less coherent, offers an argument between the (male) narrator and a demonic visitor on the merits of Byron's poem and concludes with the view of hell *Don Juan* promises to display in its "canto twelfth." *Gordon's* final poetic gesture, to serve Byron just as he served Southey in *Don Juan,* stands as clear proof that it is generally wiser not to try reenacting a trick superbly executed by someone else:

> "This was" the author's "earliest scrape, but whether
> "I shall proceed with his adventures, is
> "Dependent on the public altogether,
> "We'll see, however, what they say to this."
> To *see* what people *say* is awkward rather,
> At least in my view, if not so in his.
> "The first four rhymes are" Byron's "every line,
> "For God's sake, reader! Take them not for mine."

Gordon can be seen or said to exhibit some of *Glenarvon's* worst features rather than a selection of *Don Juan's* best ones, but *A New Canto* is a far more impressive achievement. Where *Gordon* discusses, the *New Canto* impersonates. Instead of vying with Byron by attempting an ottava rima review of *Don Juan,* Lady Caroline "becomes" him and "continues" *Don Juan,* a venture made easier by temperamental mobility, the acuteness obsession can confer, and the superb ear that served her well in the society conversation of *Glenarvon* and in the lines she wrote for music. Through the act of poetic impersonation she implicitly reveals a shrewd and profound understanding of *Don Juan* and Byron alike. A good indication of Lady Caroline's perceptiveness is her sometimes uncanny way of anticipating, in this response to the first two cantos of *Don Juan,* some of the themes, images, and preoccupations that would later become important in Byron's poem.

Like **Gordon**, *A New Canto* takes as a point of departure Byron's promise that his twelfth canto will show "The very place where wicked people go"—but here the form this revelation takes is not a glimpse into hell but the coming of the apocalypse to London and the world beyond it, a fiery catastrophe not unlike the one Byron will imagine destroying, à la Cuvier, the Regency world he has known. Lady Caroline's apocalypse enlarges—and redirects the heat of—the carefully staged Brocket bonfire at which she burned facsimiles of Byron's letters and love gifts while white-clad village girls chanted verses of her devising. In *A New Canto* the verses punish, through the assumed voice and vision of Byron, the canting English public that had condemned the "immorality" of both *Glenarvon* and *Don Juan.* It is a vigorous and perhaps intensely gratifying fantasy, this business of Lady Caroline becoming one with Byron: in the imagined role of Caroline-as-Byron she can at once enjoy the active satisfaction of dealing out vengeance herself and the more passive one of being avenged by the poet she still loved too well. She can both worship and mock at Byron's shrine.

Writing as Byron empowered Lady Caroline in a way that her page-boy disguise could not. Even as it represses her Devonshire House lisp, the narrative strategy of *A New Canto* frees her pent-up strength and passion. Caroline-as-Byron frankly and vigorously relishes the global damnation that awaits flagrant and hypocritical sinners alike. As the *New Canto* begins, there is no time or place for moralizing or sentimentalizing: the end of the world is a one-performance-only extravaganza to be witnessed in the spirit with which Byron had observed a public guillotining at Venice, "as one should see every thing once—with attention."

Caroline-as-Byron chooses as the fittest place from which to view the apocalypse St. Paul's, the edifice that, in ways we have already seen, epitomizes London and England in *Letters from England* and *Don Juan:*

> When doomsday comes, St. Paul's will be on
>   fire—
> I should not wonder if we live to see it—
> Of us, proof pickles, Heaven must rather tire,
> And want a reckoning—if so, so be it—
> Only about the Cupola, or higher,
> If there's a place unoccupied, give me it—
> To catch, before I touch my sinner's salary,
> The first grand crackle in the whispering gallery.
>
> The ball comes tumbling in a lively crash,
> And splits the pavement up, and shakes the
>   shops,
> Teeth chatter, china dances, spreads the flash,
> The omnium falls, the Bank of England stops;
> Loyal and radical, discreet and rash,
> Each on his knees in tribulation flops;
> The Regent raves (Moore chuckling at his pain)
> And sends about for Ministers in vain.
>
> The roaring streamers flap, red flakes are shot
> This way and that, the town is a volcano—
> And yells are heard, like those provoked by Lot,

> Some, of the Smithfield sort, and some *soprano;*
> Some holy water seek, the font is hot,
> And fizzing in a tea-kettle *piano.*
> Now bring your magistrates, with yeomen
>   back'd,
> Bawls Belial, and read the Riot-Act!—

"Fair maids and ugly men," "the dainty and the shabby," "high dames" and "the wander'ng beggar" are caught up in this natural event more democratic than anything the most radical reform bill could legislate. The spectacle grows increasingly cosmopolitan. "There'll be at Petersburgh a sudden thaw"; Norway's Baltic copper mines "Swell, heave, and rumble with their boiling ore, / Like some griped giant's motion peristaltic"; and "The Turkish infidel may now restore / His wives to liberty, and ere to Hell he go, / Roll in the bottom of the Archipelago!" Freed by poetic impersonation from the various constraints on her talent, Lady Caroline here becomes in art the "little volcano" she was so notably capable of being in life. The lava of emotion and imagination, to return to that metaphor shared by Byron and Cixous, bursts through the crust of multiple conventions, sparing only the prose of impersonation. Caroline-as-Byron is free to savor the "Delicious chaos" that bewilders and appalls more conventional souls, free to write as Byron might and in fact, in later cantos, would. If, as Margot Strickland has suggested [in *The Byron Women*], Lady Caroline was, without knowing it, "a captive Celtic woman artist, struggling to free herself from oppressive Anglo-Saxon male domination," it is no small irony that speaking in the voice of the half-English, half-Scots lord she had loved with self-enslaving intensity should ultimately prove her successful means of self-expression.

Once all things and people, from St. Paul's and the Peak of Derbyshire to Alexander's Winter Palace, from Napoleon to an unnamed "bright beauty" with raven tresses to the "rank elders, fearful of denials" who "pick Susannahs up in Seven dials," have been consigned to incendiary damnation, the narrator's anger seems to cool.

> Perhaps the thing may take another turn,
> And one smart shock may split the world in two,
> And I in Italy, you soon may learn,
> On t'other half am reeling far from you.

Starting in this fashion, the last ten stanzas of the poem offer a more modest cataclysm, one where Caroline-as-Byron presents the everlasting separation between Lady Caroline and Byron in the grand platonic image of sundered halves, a world cracked apart at "Some wicked capital, for instance Paris." In this second vision, the narrator soothes those "poor nervous souls" earlier affrighted by the inflammatory muse. We see "spotless spirits, snowy white" rising serenely from the ruined world. As is the case with George III in Byron's *Vision of Judgment,* personal virtues do purchase salvation—but not for the narrator, burdened with "never quench'd desire, / Still quench'd, still kindling, every thought devout / Lost in the changeful torment." This "changeful torment" is perhaps the dark side of mobility shared by Lady Caroline and Byron, and also, it is implied, by the audience addressed: "Return we to our heaven, our fire and smoke."

And there amid the fire and smoke we find the blazing author of *Don Juan* (Byron as Caroline-as-Byron reads him) requiring and despising the fame that has proved to be his hell on earth:

> Mad world! for fame we rant, call names, and
>   fight—
> I scorn it heartily, yet love to dazzle it,
> Dark intellects by day, as shops by night,
> All with a bright, new speculative gas lit.
> Wars the blue vapour with the oil-fed light,
> Hot sputter Blackwood, Jeffrey, Giffard, Haz-
>   litt—
> The Muse runs madder, and, as mine may tell,
> Like a loose comet, mingles Heaven and Hell.
> You shall have more of her another time,
> Since gulled you will be with our flights poetic,
> Our eight, and ten, and twenty feet sublime,
> Our maudlin, hey-down-derrified pathetic.
> For my part, though I'm doomed to write in
>   rhyme,
> To read it would be worse than an emetic—
> But something must be done to cure the spleen,
> And keep my name in capitals, like Kean.

The *Don Juan* echoes (of cantos written) and prophecies (of cantos yet to come) are complex and multiple here. Among other things we see, in forms more blatantly self-mocking than Byron himself would choose, *Don Juan*'s double-minded attitude toward fame and "flights poetic." The language conveying that ambivalence is also typical of *Don Juan,* as is the self-swallowing conclusion, an utterance blending celebrity with indigestion and neatly reprising the sense of the words opening *A New Canto,* "I'm sick of fame—I'm gorged with it." The reflexive metrical comments and attacks on critics have already appeared in *Don Juan*—the images of gaslight, lamps burning blue, and Heaven mingled with Hell are yet to come, in the English cantos. The varied affinities between these heated lines and *Don Juan* demonstrate both Lady Caroline's accurate reading of Byron and her intense identification with him— the latter implied throughout but finally announced, in the telltale pronoun shift from "my" to "our" for the first half of the final stanza.

Impersonation was from childhood a particular forte of Lady Caroline, so it seems highly fitting that one of her replies to *Don Juan* should be long-distance ventriloquism in ottava rima. Equally daring and appropriate to her dramatic nature was a visual reply, her enacting Don Juan surrounded by a throng of devils at an Almack's masquerade. This bit of bravado inspired Byron to tell his and Caroline's correspondent Murray, "What you say of Lady Caroline Lamb's Juan at the Masquerade don't surprise me—I only wonder that She went so far as 'the *Theatre*' for '*the Devils*' having them so much more natural at home." Gestures of this sort guaranteed that Lady Caroline, like Byron, would gain the goal acknowledged by Caroline-as-Byron in the last line of the *New Canto.* Lady Caroline Lamb's name, like Lord Byron's and Edmund Kean's, has been kept in capitals. And the victory was more than typographical; it was cosmopolitan. Just as the still-infatuated Lady Caroline "kept" BYRON in the Brit-

ish "capital" he had left behind, so her sayings and doings, most especially ***Glenarvon,*** kept CARO LAMB with him, in the capitals and provincial towns of his exile. (pp. 118-24)

> *Peter W. Graham, "A Don, Two Lords, and a Lady," in his* Don Juan and Regency England, *University Press of Virginia, 1990, pp. 89-124.*

FURTHER READING

Airlie, Mabell, Countess of. *In Whig Society, 1775-1818.* London: Hodder and Stoughton, 1921, 205 p.

> Contains biographical information on Lamb and her contemporaries as well as a brief discussion of *Glenarvon* as "a strange medley. . . . [containing] some pretty writing and melodious verses."

"Lady Caroline Lamb." *The Annual Biography and Obituary of 1828* 13 (1828): 51-7.

> Obituary tribute—alleged by some to have been written by Lamb's husband—claiming that *Glenarvon* was "the first testimony that had been given, in the form of a novel, of the dangers of a life of fashion. . . . "

Blyth, Henry. *Caro, the Fatal Passion: The Life of Lady Caroline Lamb.* London: Rupert Hart-Davis, 1972, 260 p.
> Biographical and critical study of Lamb.

Chew, Samuel C. "Byron in Fiction." In his *Byron in England: His Fame and After-Fame,* pp. 141-68. 1924. Reprint. New York: Russell & Russell, 1965.

> Includes a brief assessment of *Glenarvon,* calling it "the product of hysteria" but conceding that the novel has "some occasional imaginative interest."

Kelly, Gary. "Amelia Opie, Lady Caroline Lamb, and Maria Edgeworth: Official and Unofficial Ideology." *Ariel* 12, No. 4 (October 1981): 3-24.

> Discusses the relation of the individual to family and society as expressed in *Glenarvon* and in works by Opie and Edgeworth.

Paston, George [pseudonym of Emily Morse Symonds], and Quennell, Peter. "Lady Caroline Lamb." In their *"To Lord Byron": Feminine Profiles Based upon Unpublished Letters, 1807-1824,* pp. 40-90. New York: Charles Scribner's Sons, 1939.

> Details Lamb's involvement with Byron, drawing largely upon her own letters and those of her contemporaries.

Soderholm, James. "Lady Caroline Lamb: Byron's Miniature Writ Large." *Keats-Shelly Journal* XL (1991): 24-46.

> Examines the circumstances surrounding Lamb's forgery of a letter in Byron's handwriting in order to obtain a portrait of him, focusing on Byron's reaction to the incident.

John Henry Newman

1801-1890

English theologian, historian, essayist, autobiographer, novelist, editor, and poet.

INTRODUCTION

A prominent nineteenth-century religious figure, Newman is best known for his spiritual autobiography *Apologia pro Vita Sua,* a passionate defense of his conversion from Anglicanism to Roman Catholicism that has been hailed as a masterpiece of English prose. The *Apologia,* which has prompted frequent comparisons to St. Augustine's *Confessions,* epitomizes the argumentative skill, psychological acuity, and rhetorical brilliance that distinguish many of the author's finest writings—among them his *Essay on the Development of Christian Doctrine, Discourses on the Scope and Nature of University Education,* and *Essay in Aid of a Grammar of Assent.* These works invariably reflect Newman's primary concern: to defend religious faith and the authority of church institutions in an age of increasing liberalism and disbelief.

Newman was the eldest of six children born to a London banker. Raised in the Anglican faith, he delighted in reading the Bible and contemplating spiritual matters. He resolved at an early age to remain celibate and to consecrate his life to ministerial work. However, Newman was also drawn to the literature of religious skepticism during these early years, fascinated by the plausibility of arguments refuting Bible accounts and religious dogma. One of Newman's early schoolmasters introduced him to Calvinism, and he subscribed to the tenets of this religion for nearly a decade. He entered Trinity College at Oxford in 1817, graduating with a Bachelor's degree before the age of twenty. In 1822, Newman was awarded a fellowship at Oxford's Oriel College, where he met the prominent English logician and theologian Richard Whately. Whately and others at Oriel influenced Newman's gradual reacceptance of Anglican dogma, stressing the importance of the church in directing Bible interpretation and the significance of tradition in fostering religious feeling.

Newman was ordained a deacon in the Anglican church in 1824 and was appointed to its priesthood the following year. He became vicar of St. Mary's—Oxford University's church—in 1828; there he delivered what are considered his most memorable and influential sermons, some of which were published later in the collection *Sermons, Chiefly on the Theory of Religious Belief, Preached Before the University of Oxford.* Among his associates during these years were Richard Hurrell Froude and John Keble. Froude argued against the Protestant rejection of traditional rites and practices and corresponding insistence upon the Bible as the sole source of dogma; Keble urged complete separation of church and state. Under their in-

fluence Newman became convinced of the dangers of private interpretation of scripture and of secular interference in church matters. Together Newman and these men—disturbed at what they perceived as liberal compromises and increasing governmental influence within the Church of England—initiated the Oxford Movement, a call for the reformation of the Anglican church. Newman's contributions to a series of *Tracts for the Times,* published during an eight-year period beginning in 1833, forcefully expressed the concerns of the group, drawing the attention and assistance of the prominent theologian and Hebrew scholar E. B. Pusey in the process. As the decade progressed, however, Newman became increasingly disillusioned with the Anglican church, questioning whether it was not merely another sect attempting to supplant the time-honored and widely held authority of Roman Catholicism. *Tract 90,* the last and most controversial of the *Tracts for the Times,* consisted of Newman's "Remarks on Certain Passages in the Thirty-Nine Articles." His suggestion that the views propounded in these fundamental Anglican principles were more nearly Catholic than Protestant sparked widespread indignation against him. Newman left Oxford early in 1842, retiring to a parish in the nearby town of Littlemore. He preached his last Anglican sermon, the highly regarded "Parting of Friends," the following year, and began work in seclusion on his *Essay on the Development of Christian Doctrine.*

Newman's conversion to Catholicism late in 1845 was followed by a period of study and training in Rome; he was ordained a priest early in 1847. During the next fifteen years Newman published lectures, sermons, a collection of poetry, and two novels; many of these works addressed not only prominent issues of the day but also the phenomenon of religious conversion. However, Newman had yet to defend publically his own conversion to Roman Catholicism—despite his critics' insinuations that his Oxford Movement efforts had been largely an unethical attempt to subvert the Anglican Church. Late in 1863, the Anglican clergyman Charles Kingsley, a well-known novelist, professor of history at Cambridge, and chaplain to the Queen, attacked Newman's integrity and, in a vague allusion to his celibacy, Newman's masculinity, contending: "Truth for its own sake, had never been a virtue with the Roman clergy. Father Newman informs us that it need not, and on the whole ought not to be; that cunning is the weapon which Heaven has given to the Saints wherewith to withstand the brute male force of the wicked world which marries and is given in marriage." Newman objected, and a dispute ensued between the two that was carried out in a series of published letters and pamphlets. Newman considered this a providential opportunity to explain himself; his *Apologia pro Vita Sua* was issued in a series of installments during a two-month period early in 1864 and was an immense success. Following another decade of prolific literary activity—during which the author completed his theoretical study on the relation of faith and reason, *Essay in Aid of a Grammar of Assent*—Newman was honored by both Oxford University and the Roman Catholic church. In 1877, he was elected the first honorary fellow of Trinity College; two years later he was appointed a cardinal by Pope Leo XIII. His health began to fail shortly thereafter, and Newman lived the remainder of his life in retirement until his death in 1890.

The Oxford Movement—variously known as the Tractarian Movement or, acknowledging its most well-known adherent, Puseyism—provided in its *Tracts* a forum for the expression of Newman's concept of the Anglican church as a *via media,* or middle road, between the perceived excesses of Protestantism and the corruption of Roman Catholicism. In these writings, Newman viewed the Church of England not as a sect created in the sixteenth century but rather as the ancient Catholic church refined of its later doctrinal impurities. Newman's first book-length study, *The Arians of the Fourth Century,* a product of his investigations into the history of the Christian church, examined early religious conflicts regarding the conception of the Trinity. Newman considered this teaching an elementary and essential Christian truth, and admired the role of the Catholic church in rejecting the discordant claims of Arius and his followers. His study of this episode heightened Newman's fear of undirected interpretation of scripture and strengthened his conviction of the need for an authoritative, universal church. But he and his Oxford Movement colleagues were largely thwarted in their efforts to prompt reform in the Church of England. New-

man resigned his place in the Movement following church censure of his *Tract 90,* and meditated on his only real objection to Roman Catholicism: its additions to the teachings and practices of the primitive church. His *Essay on the Development of Christian Doctrine* expounded his conclusion that these additions were positive, logical developments of early Christian thought.

Following his conversion to Roman Catholicism Newman continued to defend the claims of religious faith and, now, the authority of the Catholic church. His acclaimed series of *Discourses on the Scope and Nature of University Education* championed theology as an important branch of human knowledge and an essential part of a university's curriculum, providing what is considered a seminal vindication of the liberal arts ideal of knowledge "as its own end" in the process. Another of the works of these later years, Newman's *Essay in Aid of a Grammar of Assent,* returned to arguments presented in his Oxford University *Sermons* on the relation of faith and reason, offering a theoretical treatise on the psychology of religious belief. His imaginative works of this period were—like his *Apologia*—largely drawn from his own experience. Newman's two novels, *Loss and Gain* and *Callista,* are, according to Joseph Ellis Baker, essentially argumentative conversion stories "largely devoted to presenting Catholic doctrines and portraying Catholic practices." Each of these works reveals the author's sympathetic understanding of the arduous process of religious conversion. Similarly, Newman's dramatic monologue *The Dream of Gerontius* details another sort of "spiritual journey": its protagonist, paralleling the author's movement toward the Roman Catholic church, proceeds from death through judgment and purgatory before entering the eternal bliss of life in heaven.

Newman's insight into human psychology, his ability to anticipate many of the doubts and contentions of his audience in matters of faith and logic, enabled him to defend Christian orthodoxy against the prevailing liberalism and skepticism of his day with an eloquence that has been admired by numerous commentators. His graceful and impassioned use of colloquial English created what is acknowledged to be a lucid and, according to C. F. Harrold, "eminently readable" quality in his sermons and other writings. Joseph J. Reilly has compared him with the "prophets" Thomas Carlyle, John Ruskin, and Matthew Arnold. According to Reilly, these prominent social critics were primarily concerned with "a man's obligations to others," whereas "a fourth great Victorian, the peer of these as a master of prose and their superior in intellect, was primarily concerned with man's obligation to God. This fourth prophet," continues Reilly, "was Newman."

PRINCIPAL WORKS

St. Bartholomew's Eve: A Tale of the Sixteenth Century in Two Cantos [with John William Bowden] (poetry) 1818
The Arians of the Fourth Century: Their Doctrine, Temper, and Conduct (history) 1833

Tracts for the Times, by Members of the University of Oxford (prose) 1833-41

Parochial and Plain Sermons. 8 vols. (sermons) 1834-43

Lyra Apostolica [with John William Bowden, Richard Hurrell Froude, John Keble, Robert Isaac Wilberforce, and Isaac Williams] (poetry) 1836

Lectures on the Prophetical Office of the Church, Viewed Relatively to Romanism and Popular Protestantism (lectures) 1837

Lectures on Justification (lectures) 1838

The Tamworth Reading Room: Letters on an Address Delivered by Sir Robert Peel, Bart. M.P., on the Establishment of a Reading Room at Tamworth (essays) 1841

An Essay on the Miracles Recorded in the Ecclesiastical History of the Early Ages (prose) 1843

Sermons Bearing on Subjects of the Day (sermons) 1843

Sermons, Chiefly on the Theory of Religious Belief, Preached Before the University of Oxford (sermons) 1843

An Essay on the Development of Christian Doctrine (prose) 1845

Loss and Gain (novel) 1848

Discourses Addressed to Mixed Congregations (sermons) 1849

Lectures on Certain Difficulties Felt by Anglicans in Submitting to the Catholic Church (lectures) 1850

Lectures on the Present Position of Catholics in England (lectures) 1851

†*Discourses on the Scope and Nature of University Education* (prose) 1852

Callista: A Sketch of the Third Century (novel) 1856

Sermons Preached on Various Occasions (sermons) 1857

†*Lectures and Essays on University Subjects* (prose) 1859

Apologia pro Vita Sua: Being a Reply to a Pamphlet Entitled "What, Then, Does Dr. Newman Mean?" (autobiography) 1864; also published as *History of My Religious Opinions,* 1865

The Dream of Gerontius (poetry) 1866

Verses on Various Occasions (poetry) 1868

An Essay in Aid of a Grammar of Assent (prose) 1870

Essays Critical and Historical. 2 vols. (essays) 1871

Discussions and Arguments on Various Subjects (prose) 1872

Historical Sketches. 3 vols. (history) 1872-73

Tracts Theological and Ecclesiastical (prose) 1874

A Letter Addressed to His Grace the Duke of Norfolk on Occasion of Mr. Gladstone's Recent Expostulation (letter) 1875

The Via Media of the Anglican Church, Illustrated in Lectures, Letters, and Tracts Written between 1830 and 1841. 2 vols. (prose) 1877

Letters and Correspondence of John Henry Newman During His Life in the English Church, with a Brief Autobiography. 2 vols. [edited by Anne Mozley] (letters, memoirs) 1891

Works of John Henry Newman. 41 vols. (novels, poetry, history, essays, sermons, letters) 1908-18

*Of the *Tracts,* Newman wrote or co-wrote nos. 1, 2, 3, 6, 7, 8, 10, 11, 15, 19, 20, 21, 31, 33, 34, 38, 41, 45, 47, 71, 73, 74, 75, 76, 79, 82, 83, 85, 88, and 90.

†These works were published together in 1873 as *The Idea of a University Defined and Illustrated.*

Fraser's Magazine (essay date 1846)

[*In the following excerpt, the critic presents a negative assessment of Newman's* Essay on the Development of Christian Doctrine, *questioning the sincerity of the author's conversion to Roman Catholicism.*]

[*An Essay on the Development of Christian Doctrine*] is a very elaborate, studied work, full of research, bearing proofs of long preparation; the result of matured thought; the conclusions of a course of reasoning which can now be traced back in Mr. Newman's writings to several years since, during which, we now know from authority, he has been meditating his recent step. It is not the questioning—the anxious, wavering questioning of an undecided mind; but the formal proof of a long-weighed conclusion. And during all this time where has Mr. Newman been? In what name, and in what authority, has he been teaching the children of the English church, if not by his voice in the pulpit, at least by private communication, and by his previously published works? His sermons have been read as those of a minister of the Church, even those which contained the germs of the poison which he is now openly administering to the Church. His reasonings have been listened to, have been permitted to find access to minds, from which they would have been anxiously excluded under the present title.

These comments. . .come from no semi-Dissenter, with whom St. Paul's and the Weigh House are equally sacred, and Binney and Barrow co-efficient authorities. On the contrary, they are the sentiments of one of the representatives of that large body in the Church of England, who think that her orders are apostolical, and that her Halls and Beveridges knew something of the Fathers; who, with Hooker, can revere her majestic polity; and with Horsley, refuse to be scared by the bugbear of purgatory; who, with the greatest men of the brightest times, believe nothing to be holy which is not honest; and scorn to acknowledge any devotion to be profitable or sincere which grows only in the dark, and is fed only by deception. Mr. Newman would have us to believe that his conversion rushed upon him with an irresistible impetus, while he was descending these inclined planes of developement. But no, we are wrong. It was not until type had imparted to his arguments that clear symmetry, by which they are recommended to the general reader, that the blaze of conviction burst full upon his eyes. Not by his own, but his printer's proofs, was the change to be effected. "When he had got some way in the printing, he recognised in himself a conviction of the truth of the conclusion, to which the discussion leads, so clear as to supersede further deliberation."

Can this statement be received for a moment? Is it credible? Is it possible? Every understanding is undoubtedly open to new accessions of light; and one eye perceives some defects in a book, that another is unconscious of. Montaigne was accustomed to say that he read in Livy what another could not, and that Plutarch read there what he did not. In like manner, Bolingbroke confessed of himself, that he had read at fifty what he never could find in the same book at twenty-five. This we can easily comprehend; for not only does the intellectual eye-sight reflect its own colours upon the object, but its vigour and penetration vary with conditions of the moral health. But Mr. Newman comes within neither exemption. If the theory of developement made him a Romanist, it would have made him one in its working. No; the solution of the mystery is to be sought and found in the book itself. The author has furnished the key to the problem. At the end of the introduction the inquirer will find this sentence,

> It would be the work of a life to apply the theory of developements so carefully to the writings of the fathers and the history of controversies and councils, as thereby to vindicate the reasonableness of every decree of Rome; much less can such an undertaking be imagined by one who IN THE MIDDLE OF HIS DAYS IS BEGINNING LIFE AGAIN.

We entreat our readers to mark these words. Where do they occur? Not in the preface, not in the postscript, not even at the close of the volume, where the faint ray of Roman Catholic sunrise may be supposed to have broken upon the pilgrim, then ascending, after so wearisome a journey, into the sweet garden and paradisiacal atmosphere of indulgences and image-worship. In none of those positions will this declaration be discovered. It stands in the beginning of the *Essay,* and that essay, which the writer commenced and finished according to his own assurance, while belonging to the Church of England. There can be no mistake here; the meaning of the passage is distinct and positive. To become a Romanist is literally to begin life again; to begin it with a desecrated Baptism, and an inheritance of imposture. What shall we say, then, to Mr. Newman's assertion, that

> his first act on his own conversion was to offer his Work for revision to the proper authorities; but the offer was declined, on the ground that it was written, and partly printed, before he was a Catholic, and that it would come before the reader in a more persuasive form, if he read it as the author wrote it?

We repeat,—what shall we say? What can we say, but that the author has been committing a fraud upon his reader, and perhaps upon himself? When he wrote the first page of this essay on developement, he was as much an alien from the English communion as he is at the present moment. He held, indeed, nothing of hers, except her Fellowship. He may not have been a Romanist, but only a sceptic. "Possibly," writes Bishop Taylor in his inscription of the *Great Exemplar* to Hatton,

> two or three weak or interested, fantastic and easy understandings, pass from church to church upon grounds as weak as those for which

formerly they did dissent; and the same arguments are good, or bad, as exterior accidents, or interior appetites, shall determine.

In attributing this fantastic temperament to Mr. Newman, we are not unsupported by the highest authority in that splendid city which he has so long troubled and infected. Bishop Wilberforce was not afraid to denounce him, even in the cathedral of Christ Church, as having been borne upon the wings of an unbounded scepticism into the bosom of an unfathomable superstition. Mr. Newman does not hesitate to confess, that between Popery and infidelity is the only choice; drawn gradually to the grassy margin of the precipice, he may have felt the impulse, so common to those who gaze down into an abyss, to plunge into it; but, scared back again by the appalling darkness beneath, he caught at Romanism. Will it hold him? We doubt it. For what Romanism is it, which this unhappy person has grasped in his plunge, and now seeks to recommend openly to the hopeful youth of England? Is it that Romanism which strikes out its roots into the early seed-land of Christendom; and whose boughs have truly sheltered some of the noblest spirits who fought, or perished, for patriotism or virtue? Is it the system of faith that sweetened the temper of Fisher, or endears to the affection of all time the beautiful piety of More? which woke the eloquence of Bossuet, and wasted the bloom from the cheek of Pascal? It is none of these. It is German infidelity communicated in the music and perfume of St. Peter's;—it is Strauss in the garment and rope of the Franciscan. It is a system which offers no insurmountable difficulty to the producer, because, in the words of Horsley, it is a system of his own making.

These complaints are uttered in no bitterness of controversy. We write them with sorrow and pain, though the vehemence of Pascal might well be pardoned, when Escobar is alive again. We know how admirably it has been said by Donne, that when God gave a flaming sword to cherubims in Paradise, they guarded the place, but the sword killed none, wounded none; and that, in like manner, God gives to his servants zeal to guard their station and integrity of religion, but not to wound or deface any man. May we never forget the allegory and its lesson! Let every available apology be tendered for one, who manifests so little disposition to apologise for himself. No eye becomes dim or confused at once. It is the result of continued derangement of the constitution. So may Mr. Newman have weakened the intellectual eyesight, not only by the disordered functions of the moral frame, but by protracted labours in the dark mines and heavy air of papal theology. Nay, we will even give him the advantage of Johnson's remark on Burnet, and think that he has not told falsehoods with intention; but that prejudice, or scepticism, deterred him from recognising the truth when he saw it. That he will adhere to his theory for a season, now that he has launched it, is naturally to be expected. The French essayist had looked into the heart, when he said, *"Toute opinion est assez forte pour se faire épouser au prix de la vie."*

It was one of the many forcible sayings of Atterbury to his most celebrated friend, that he hated to see a book gravely written, and in all the forms of argumentation, that proves nothing and says nothing,—the only object of which is to occasion a general distrust of our own faculties, to unsettle our conclusions and bewilder our vision, until the reader is driven to doubt whether it be possible, in any case, to distinguish truth from falsehood, the good from the evil, the beautiful from the coarse; whether, in fact, the Lutheran be more a Christian than the Arian, Cæsar a braver soldier than Horace, or Pope a nobler poet than Pomfret. Now, of Mr. Newman's essay, in whatever degree the other objections of Atterbury may be able to attach themselves, it cannot, with the slightest show of justice, be affirmed, that it says nothing. Throughout 450 very closely printed pages, the learning and ingenuity of the writer are kept in constant motion; and cloud after cloud of sophism is subjected to the embrace of a genius, singularly vigorous, lively, and productive. That the offspring inherit some of the unsubstantial elements of their creation, will excite surprise in none who reflect upon their composition.

And, perhaps, of all the subjects which the author endeavours to demolish, not one engages so much of his attention as that religious designation which is known as *Protestant*. Almost from the very first page of the book, the attack upon Protestantism begins. Whatever be historical Christianity, we are assured that it is not the religion of Protestants. Again, the Protestant is said to be compelled to allow, that if such a system as he would introduce, "ever existed in early times, it has been clean swept away as if by a deluge, suddenly, silently, and without memorial; by a deluge coming in at night, and utterly soaking, rotting, heaving up, and hurrying off every vestige of what it found in the Church." This is only a weak specimen of the hard things which Protestantism has to submit to in the course of 400 pages. It is quite melancholy to see how naked and defenceless the objector turns it out, to brave the hail, and wind, and snow; with not a shed to shelter its penury and starvation, amid all the sumptuous architecture of developement. Now, we wish it to be distinctly understood, that in using the word Protestant, we are not identifying ourselves with those well-meaning, but not particularly well-informed gentlemen, who deliver historical mistakes, with such vehement seriousness, to a tumult of bonnets, or drive over the May streams of Exeter Hall, before a hurricane of pocket-handkerchiefs. We understand the word in the sense in which Bishop Taylor understood it, when he affirmed of the Church of England, that "Catholic is her name, and Protestant her surname;" when, in the preface to his excellent devotions at Golden Grove, he said, "Let us secure that our young men be good Christians, it is easy to make them good Protestants." In the sense in which the late admirable Mr. Davison employed the word, when remarking of Taylor, that he had an absolute and independent grasp "of Protestant principles;" in the sense in which Bishop Hall accepted it, when he summoned believers in general to have no peace with Rome; in the sense of our Articles and our Liturgy. Catholic is our name, and Protestant our surname; we acknowledge the Homilies and the Prayer-Book, not the Evangelical Alliance and Dr. Leifchild. And of the faith of this Catholic Protestant Church, the famous rule of Vincentius furnishes a concise and a just interpretation; it holds what *has been held always, every where, and by all.* Mr. Newman, of course, attacking the rule, because it confirms the English Church, and overthrows the Roman. He accordingly finds insur-

mountable difficulties in rendering it available. He formerly professed a different opinion. He could once describe it as being not of a mathematical, or demonstrative, but of a moral character; and, therefore, requiring practical judgment and good sense to apply it. He was plain and forcible then, he is mystical and weak now. The rule of Vincentius, like every canon in literature, in science, or in art, demands judgment in its employment. Will the most admirable telescope *act* upon the landscape or the planet, if the proper elevation or depression be not obtained? Could Herschell discover a star, if Hume directed the glass?

When Goldsmith presumed on one occasion to differ from Johnson, he was interrupted by this vehement objurgation, "Nay, sir, why should not you think what every body else thinks?" Goldsmith was unconsciously silenced by the rule of Vincentius. Literary history swarms with illustrations. Virgil has been elevated to the throne of Latin poetry by the acclamation of criticism; yet Scaliger considered him inferior to Lucan. Among descriptive poets, Thomson has been regarded as the most attractive, yet he only excited the scorn of Walpole. *Lycidas* is the delight of every poetical heart; yet Johnson thought death in a surfeit of bad taste—a reasonable retribution for a repeated perusal. What then? Is not the *Æneid*, after all, the most precious of Latin poems? and are not the *Seasons* delightful transcripts of nature? and is not Milton's Elegy worthy to be bound up with *Paradise Lost?* Certainly; each and all deserve their fame. The rule of Vincentius binds them together. *Always, every where, and by all,* their grace, and fancy, and truthfulness, have been acknowledged; and the corrupt taste of Scaliger, the contempt of Walpole, and the prejudices of Johnson, no more weaken the universal and potential reputation of the authors, than the election of a member of parliament is affected, by the indignant opposition of those voters who expected to be bribed; or the sermon of the preacher is shorn of its eloquence by the disapproval of the beadle, who received notice in the morning to relinquish his hat.

Now, in despite of all the vehement arguments, with which the Roman besiegers seek to beat down this admirable breast-work of Catholic-Protestantism, we entertain no doubt whatever of its capacity of resistance and permanence. Of those great central doctrines which our Church holds and teaches, we affirm, without hesitation, that they have been held always, every where, and by all. Remembering Mr. Newman's own caution, that this rule is not demonstrative or mathematical, but moral, and therefore requiring discrimination and good sense in its application, we trace up to immediate contact with the Apostles and earliest missionaries of the Faith, our orders of ministers, our discipline and unity, our form of worship, our doctrines and creeds. We prove that the English, like the primitive, is a Trinitarian Church. The corrupted Nature of man, the new life of Regeneration, its communication in Baptism, sacramental Grace, justification by Faith, the omnipotence of the Cross, the sanctification by the Spirit;—these are central doctrines, and orbs of glory diffusing light and warmth over the entire system of the Gospel, which our Church teaches; and not only teaches, but follows back through the fathers of the first and second centuries, and asserts to have had from the beginning an universal admission; to have been received *always, every where, and by all.* And we consider the rule of Vincentius, thus applied, to be no more mutilated by heresy here, or scepticism there, than we admit the genius of Virgil to be humbled by the preference of Scaliger, or the music of Milton to be jarred out of tune by the growl of Johnson.

But it does not answer the Romanising mission of Mr. Newman to admit the completeness of Revelation.

> As to Christianity, considering the unsystematic character of its inspired documents, and the all but silence of contemporary history, if we attempt to determine its one original profession, undertaking, or announcement, we shall be reduced to those eclectic and arbitrary decisions which have in all ages been so common.

Gibbon seems to be a favourite with this writer; and if we rightly remember, he calls him our only Church historian; but really this sneer at the Gospel is almost too plain. The philosopher of Lausanne would have shaped it into a more harmonious sentence of mystery. Of course it will startle ordinary Christians, to be told that the one original profession, undertaking, or announcement of their holy Faith, cannot be ascertained from any direct or internal testimony. The Bible is to be a blank, until it has been illuminated into a missal; the form of godliness is a mutilation and a wreck, until it has been moulded into symmetry by the artistical handicraft of Councils; the Cross and Expiation, the Resurrection and Beautification, the Life of Probation, and the Season of Judgment;—nothing is clear; every thing is confused. Religion is lifeless, the Gospel is a chaos; and our single method of interpreting the Epistle of St. Peter is by the paraphrase of his Successor; and the Vatican contains the only serviceable key to the cypher of St. John.

But if that numerous class who, unfavoured by the visions of Mr. Newman, are called by him "ordinary Christians," continue to inquire how it is that inspired documents, such as the Holy Scriptures, do not at once determine a doctrine without further trouble, their scruples are thus removed:—

> They were intended to create an idea, and that idea is not in the sacred text, but in the mind of the reader, and the question is, whether that idea is communicated to him, in its completeness and minute accuracy, on its first apprehension, or expands in his heart and intellect, and comes to perfection in the course of time. Nor could it be maintained, without extravagance, that the letter of the New Testament, or of any assignable number of books, comprises a delineation of all possible forms which a divine message will assume when submitted to a multitude of minds.

Now we say nothing here of the frame of thought that could venture to classify Christianity among the fine arts, and try its Author by the rules of criticism. The impiety is not ours, we have only to expose its fraud. Of the gradual growth and expansion of religious truths on a mind disposed by God's grace to receive, and by God's blessing to mature them, no person will presume to express a doubt. Nay, rather every tongue will join in proclaiming the joyful reality. In hours of loneliness and suffering, in vigils of

sickness or sorrow, in the desolation of distant lands and amid the abandonment or ruin of whatever is dear and precious to the heart—oh! then it is that the promises of the Gospel, and the consolations of Faith, and the hopes of Apostles, return upon the heart with light, and bloom, and fragrancy, and strength, of which it had hitherto been unconscious. Every declaration of a Prophet, every recollection of an Evangelist, every song of a Psalmist, seems to expand and brighten into new revelations of loveliness, of joyfulness, and of gratitude. Before the earnest, lingering, believing eye of the lowly and sincere disciple, every jewel in the breastplate of Righteousness appears to give an answer in hues of lustre, beauty, and fulness, never revealed before.

If you call these clearer views of truth by the name of *developements,* we shall not litigate the question. (pp. 254-59)

Such a theory of developement all men must acknowledge. What, in truth, is the fruit of learned investigation and hallowed meditation during a period of 1500 years—the gold of the fathers, the costly wisdom of English eloquence in the sixteenth and seventeenth centuries, the sagacious scrutiny of criticism, ancient and modern—what is it all, but the exposition of Scripture truth? Thus Pearson's illustration of the Creed and Paley's history of St. Paul are both developements, and they are so because they bring prominently out into the gaze of men facts and doctrines which really do exist, and require only combination and induction to give them irresistible force and impression. It is quite different with the pretended developements of Popery. When these are not corruptions, they are certainly inventions; when they are not distortions of the tree, they are grafts into it. The worship of the Virgin Mary is not only unsanctioned by every passage of the New Testament, but the impious probability of such an event seems never to have presented itself to the minds of the Evangelists. It was, however, very important to discover some scriptural countenance for the key-stone of the Romish superstition. Accordingly, Mr. Newman assumed the *cultus* to be a true development of an incident at the marriage at Cana. In his latest work he takes this for granted; his ingenious proof of it had been previously given in the sermons on subjects of the day, in which the members of a Protestant university were taught, by a clergyman of a Protestant Church, to perceive *"the present influence and power of the mother of God."* But hear the interpretation. "Observe, He said to His mother, 'What have I to do with thee? Mine hour is not come.' Perhaps this implies, that *when* His hour was come, *then* He would have to do with her again as before; and such really seems to be the meaning of the passage." And such daring travestie of the inspired narrative was suffered to pass without rebuke in the home of sound learning and religious education, where Hammond meditated and Usher preached!

But Mr. Newman shall state, in his own words, the nature of this developing theory, which is to accomplish what erudition and eloquence have hitherto failed in performing, and shew that Romanism is in harmony with Revelation. His essay is directed, as we are told, towards the solution—

Of the difficulty which lies in the way of using the testimony of our most natural informant concerning the doctrine and worship of Christianity; viz., the history of 1800 years. The view on which it is written has at all times, perhaps, been implicitly adopted by theologians, and, I believe, has been recently illustrated by several distinguished writers of the Continent, such as De Maistre and Möhler; viz., that the increase and expansion of the Christian Creed Ritual, and the variations that have attended the process in the case of individual writers and churches, are the necessary attendants on any philosophy or polity which takes possession of the intellect and heart, and has had any wide or extended dominion; that, from the nature of the human mind, time is necessary for the full comprehension and perfection of great ideas; and that the highest and most wonderful truths, though communicated to the world once for all by inspired teachers, would not be comprehended all at once by the recipients, but, as received and transmitted by minds not inspired and through media which were human, have required only the longer time and deeper thought for their full elucidation. This may be called the *Theory of Developements.*

Now in this exposition of a theory there is little, at the first glance, to censure in the general spirit and tendency, or, more properly speaking, in the abstract signification of it. The assertion that the constitution of the mind demands periods of time for the full comprehension and perfection of great ideas, is so obviously in accordance with all experience, that, instead of a novelty, it is only a truism. The history of Genius is a commentary on the maxim. Our eyes travel back to the rising of the star by the luminous path it has kindled during its journey into our horizon. We are sometimes tempted to estimate the influence of Shakespeare among his contemporaries by the splendour which his poetry sheds upon ourselves. But it should be remembered, that this clear and brilliant atmosphere of opinion, in which we now contemplate his beauty, has been produced by the gradual influence of his own vital energy and heat, transfused by slow degrees and effluxes of radiance into the cold and colourless mists by which his genius was for a long time enveloped. The same remark would be true of Milton. It was only after many pauses, with long intervals of gloom, that the darkness finally rolled away from his Garden, and the bloom of his Paradise was felt upon the breeze. Reynolds, by continued meditation absorbing into his own perception the divine graces of Raffaelle, is a corresponding example in art. With reference, therefore, to the intellectual application of the theory, we do not complain of its author; but when we find it employed upon Religion, when we are assured that every peculiarity of Romanism so far from being an accretion, a distortion, or even a supplement, is only a developement, we are entitled to ask for some certain means of distinguishing such a transformation when we see it. And Mr. Newman has provided tests for that purpose, of which we will specify one or two of the most important. The first is supplied by the analogy of physical growth, it being necessary that the *developed* form should correspond in parts and proportions to the *rudimental*—the adult to the infant. The wing of the bird becomes stronger, but it never changes into a fin; unity of type is, therefore, the most "obvious characteristic of a faithful developement." But the author had no sooner made this admission, than he perceived its fatal consequences to his own argument, and immediately prepared to ward them off. A developement may admit of *variation.* "The fledged bird differs from its rudimental form in the egg; the butterfly is the developement, but not, in any sense, the image of the grub." This expedient of variation is worked with rare subtlety and talent, but the gulf cannot be crossed upon it. The torrent will soon bear away the bridge. Ingenuity may build it up again, with new artifices of support; but it cannot stand; and if Romanism has no other means of keeping up a direct intercourse with the primitive ages of faith, she must be contented to put out to sea again, and endeavour to reach the harbour through all the perils and difficulties of tradition and infallibility.

But we are informed that a true developement may be described as one conservative of the course of the developement that preceded it, "which is that developement, and something besides—an addition which illustrates, and not obscures, corroborates, not corrects, the body of thought from which it proceeds." And this of Romanism! And men, "ordinary Christians," and in the possession only of those ordinary gifts of understanding known as common sense, are to receive the invocation of saints as the conservative developement of the doctrine of Mediation, purgatory of Baptism, and celibacy of the Sacraments. They have no choice. "You must accept the whole or reject the whole; reduction does but enfeeble, and amputation mutilate."

Let us for a moment make a familiar application of one of these tests, and see how a developement may be conservative of the thing developed. It may be truly said that the rich light of an autumnal evening, filling the woods with many-coloured shadows, is a diffusion of the ray that gilded the boughs in the morning; and the tree, with its gnarled trunk, and massy umbrage, and far-spreading gloom, is the natural growth and expansion of the sapling that a century before cast a reflection of a span's width over the warm grass, as it swayed to and fro in the breeze of summer; and the river, flowing in a broad surface of crystal to the distant sea, is truly the confluence of many streams all kindred of the same lone spring far up in the green retirements of pastoral hills; and the autumnal twilight of evening, the glimmering branches of the tree, and the majestic tide of the river, are so many enlargements of original types, each conservative of the nature of its original, only imparting to it a wider diffusion and an enlarged energy, and therefore coming under the definition of Developement. But take the contrary view, and suppose the purple flush, that called up the lark to matins, to disappear in storm and rain; the tree to be interlaced, encumbered, and choked by parasitical plants, and mouldering into decay by the corrosion of insects; and the river to be not only discoloured by the soil through which it has flowed, but rendered impure by artificial springs, designedly set running into its current. Is not the character of each altogether altered? The peculiarity of a developement is gone, and that of a corruption appears in its place. The beautiful light is not recognised in the vapour and tempest, nor the tree in its distortion and rottenness, nor the mountain-spring in the discoloured and infected river.

And if our test be applied to the faith which Romanism produces as that which was once delivered to the saints, we think that it will be found not less demonstrative. For, once more taking up those examples which we have submitted to its agency, let the ray of sunrise behind the hills represent the early gleam of the spiritual Day-Spring, slowly ascending over the dark mountains; and let the mellower and fuller light of Evangelic and Apostolic message and commentary be the illumination that filled the dark recesses of Paganism with beauty; and let the tree, spreading into verdant amplitude, indicate that growth of Gospel-doctrine which was to cover the human race with the shadow of its boughs; and let the river become the emblem of that sacramental stream of Grace on which the Holy Spirit moves, quickening and sanctifying the waters for the restoration and cure of wounded souls. Under each of these aspects we recognise the lineaments of the primitive type; each is conservative of its original. The scattered beams have converged into orbs and melted into atmosphere; the seed is lost in the tree, that yet retains all the properties of vigour, and fruitfulness, and beauty, which that germ of vegetation at first communicated; and the river is equally clear, only with a fuller current and a deeper channel.

But examine the same objects in the interpretation of Romanism, prove them by the same test, measure them by the same standard, resolve them into the same elements. What is the result? You perceive the Day-Spring, indeed, but the spiritual is contrasted with the artificial light; you have the sun with the farthing candle flaring up at it; you have the tree of sacred truth, but trained into distortion, choked and decaying, flaunting with streamers, and offering in its leaves no blessed healing for the nations; you have the stream of sacramental grace, but no longer preserving the purity of its source, no longer the "river of water of life, clear as crystal, proceeding out of the throne of God." Mr. Newman's own definition is completely fulfilled; and if "the corruption of an idea is that state of a developement which undoes its previous advances," then is Romanism, in all its intricate multiplicity of ritual and doctrines, only one vast corruption of the perfect and luminous idea of Christianity. Nor should we lose any advantage by accepting the more amplified definition which the writer furnishes a little further on, and admitting that "every developement is to be considered a corruption, which *obscures* or *prejudices* its essential idea, or which *disturbs the laws of developement* which constitute its organisation, or which *reverses its course of developement.*"

It is needless to specify any more of Mr. Newman's tests. And is it by these, or such as these, that the purity of Romish gold and Romish jewels is to be ascertained and established? If it be, is there any well-informed and honest member of that Communion who will abide by the result? If supplications to the Virgin as a mediator, almost as a deity, do not *prejudice* the essential idea of the one Intercessor, and disturb the whole organisation of Christianity—if the belief in the *atoning* influence of penance do not

altogether *reverse* the course of developement in the universal Satisfaction of the Cross—if the setting a premium upon sin in the dispensation of indulgences and the sale of absolution, be not, in the strictest sense of the word, an *undoing* of the previous advances of that idea of Christianity which confronts every crime with the stern eye of a judgment to come—If each and all of these instances be not a prejudice, a reversing, and an undoing of the original truth, then, indeed, has the holy sun of Scripture risen and shone in vain; then in vain has the eyesight been healed by spiritual ointment. The whole landscape of divine history swims and wavers; the nerve of vision is diseased; and, instead of accurately distinguishing objects, we are only able, by looking up, to see *men, as trees, walking.*

But there is another argument which it is now the practice to urge upon the ear with every artifice of vehemence and persuasion, and that is, the unity and harmony of Popery. We might appeal to every visitor of foreign climes to state the effect of this unity and harmony upon his own feelings. When that accomplished person, whose epitaph, in Richmond Church, records him to have been the chosen friend of one of our dearest poets, was at length enabled to make his long-desired journey to France, his road led him to Amiens. It was a lovely summer morning when he rose to survey the magnificent cathedral of that city. But what a scene met his eye! He found, as he said, a thousand different kinds of devotion going forward at the same time at different altars and in different chapels, little bells of various tones perpetually tinkling,—in short, he declared that the Boulevards subsequently put him very much in mind of it, and that the exterior of French life was the aptest emblem of their religious interiors. Both were alike picturesque, changeable, showy, and superficial. And this beholder was no common idler—ignorant or irreligious; but a Christian and a gentleman, a clergyman and a scholar. Who has not felt the same sensations? Who has not sighed over the developements of Christianity?

These difficulties have not affected the expounder of this new theory, and no passages of his book are more instinct with life, or more glowing with eloquence, than those in which he weaves all the hypothetical beauties of Romanism into one crowning panegyric. The following is a happy example:—

> If there be a form of Christianity now in the world which is accused of gross superstition, of borrowing its rites and customs from the heathen, and of ascribing to forms and ceremonies an occult virtue,—a religion which is considered to burden and enslave the mind by its requisitions, to address itself to the weak-minded and ignorant, to be supported by sophistry and imposture, and to contradict reason and exalt mere irrational faith,—a religion which impresses on the serious mind very distressing views of the guilt and consequences of sin, sets upon the minute acts of the day one by one their definite value for praise or blame, and thus casts a grave shadow over the future,—a religion which holds up to admiration the surrender of wealth, and disables serious persons from enjoying it if they would,—a religion, the doctrines of which, be they good or bad, are to the generality of men

unknown; which is considered to bear on its very surface signs of folly and falsehood so distinct, that a glance suffices to judge of it, and careful examination is preposterous; which is felt to be so simply bad that it may be calumniated at hazard and at pleasure, it being nothing but absurdity to stand upon the accurate distribution of its guilt among its particular acts, or painfully to determine how far this or that story is literally true, what must be allowed in candour, or what is improbable, or what cuts two ways, or what is not proved, or what may be plausibly defended,—a religion such that men look at a convert to it, with a feeling which no other sect raises, except Judaism, Socialism, or Mormonism; with curiosity, fear, suspicion, disgust, as the case may be; as if something strange had befallen him; as if he had had an initiation into a dreadful mystery, and had come into communion with dreadful influences; as if he were now one of a confederacy which claimed him, absorbed him, stripped him of his personality, reduced him to a mere instrument or organ of the whole,—a religion which men hate, as proselytising, anti-social, revolutionary; as dividing families, separating chief friends, corrupting the maxims of government, making a mock at law, dissolving the empire, the enemy of human nature, and a 'conspirator against its rites and privileges,'—a religion which they consider the champion and instrument of darkness, and a pollution calling down upon the land the anger of Heaven,—a religion which they associate with intrigue and conspiracy, which they speak about in whispers, which they detect by anticipation in whatever goes wrong, and to which they impute whatever is unaccountable,—a religion, the very name of which they cast out as evil, and use simply as a bad epithet, and which, from the impulse of self-preservation, they would persecute if they could; if there be such a religion now in the world, it is not unlike Christianity as that same world viewed it, when first it came forth from its Divine Author.

We shall not analyse the veracity of these statements, but rather give our own delineation of that system which they profess to recommend. Did we say our own? Nay, rather, the delineation of history itself, drawn in its bold and vivid outline and attitude, and bright with its lasting colours. Look, then, we ask our readers, upon *this* picture, as well as on *that;* hang them together, as two vast antitheses upon canvass.

If there be a religion which has almost elevated a creature to the throne of the Creator, and withdrawn the Cross of the Redeemer behind the picture of Mary; if it violate the injunction of St. Paul, to "do all in the name of the Lord Jesus, giving thanks to God and the Father by Him," by substituting for the name of Jesus the name of his mother; if it mutilate the grandeur of the Intercessor, by the invocation of saints; if it blaspheme the Divine Presence, by affirming that He contracts his glory to dwell in the Elements; if it cherish idolatry by image-worship, and desecrate the Lord of Heaven by a familiarity so dreadful, that, more than a century since, a scoffer beheld a representation of Him over the altar of a chapel, in a full-bottomed

wig, well powdered; if it replace the Atonement by penance, and repentance by Purgatory; if it make the word of God to be of none effect by tradition, and expound, not the gloss by the Gospel, but the Gospel by the gloss; if it proclaim the infallibility of a ruler, and bracket the council-chamber of Trent with the upper room of the Apostles; if it uphold the sanctity of relics and the fitness of falsehood; if it encourage persecution, and preach with the fagot; if it has been ever animated by an imperial heart, and looked upon conversion and conquest as convertible terms; if it has stooped only to rise, and worn the horsehair only to make sure of the purple; if it has cast over all this variety of superstition and error, the splendour of enthusiasm and the allurements of poetry; if it has combined the noblest achievements with the basest designs; if it has helped to decorate and to defile the world, to illuminate and to darken it; if it created a Bonner and a Fénélon; if it has fostered Raffaelle, and imprisoned Galileo; if it erected St. Peter's, and invented the Inquisition; if it elicited all the wonders of genius to emblazon its home, and paid for them by the traffic in Indulgences; if it kept the torch of Virgil burning in the night of civilisation, and closes the Bible to the eyes of the weary; if it exhibits the martyr who perished in triumph, and the bandit who purchases absolution with his plunder; if there has ever been, if there be at this time, such a religion as this,—magnificent and sordid, true and false, divine and human,—it is not very unlike what Romanism may be proved to have been, as it rose from beneath the plastic hands of its successive developers, and as it has been, and continues to be now, in every stage of its disastrous, its splendid, and its tremendous career. (pp. 260-65)

It is quite clear that no system of belief, however elastic, can contain the rapidly enlarging proportions of Mr. Newman's speculation. One more spring, such as he has just made, and the Roman Catholic Directory will not hold him. He must have a red book to himself. He cannot be supposed to be blind to the imminence of his peril. He is travelling to Germany by way of Italy, and enjoying the picturesque before he settles down in the commonplace. He may take Berlin after Rome; and, perhaps, as Voltaire proffered his services to interpret Pascal, so in like manner, some aspiring Neologian may be destined to find his translator in the priest of Littlemore. For the present, he distinguishes developement from Rationalism:—

> To develope is to receive conclusions from revealed truth, to rationalise is to receive *nothing* but conclusions from received truths; to develope is positive, to rationalise is negative; the essence of developement is to extend belief, of rationalism to contract it.

If this parallel, or contrast, be not particularly lucid, we must patiently await its commentary. At all events, the Neologians have no cause to despair; nay, scepticism is looking up. The infidel's commodity rises in the market. Three hundred years, and the labours of modern writers have done much for its cause. For this we have a competent witness. "Infidelity itself," writes Mr. Newman, "is in a different, I am obliged to say, in a more hopeful position, as regards Christianity." Such a result might reasonably have been expected from recent efforts; and we cannot doubt that the new theory of composing lives of saints, after the manner of Butler or Scarron, and giving us Hudibras in a martyrology, must have proved highly effective. A great step has also been taken in the discovery, that men may pass from infidelity to Rome, and from Rome to infidelity, "from a conviction in both courses, that there is no tangible intellectual position between the two." Moreover, illustrious examples are not wanting to keep changers in countenance; they only require developing. "St. Augustine was nine years a Manichee; St. Basil for a time was in admiration of the Semi-arians; St. Sulpicius gave a momentary countenance to the Pelagians; St. Paula listened, and Malaria assented, to the Origenists."

If, therefore, this ingenious author should at a future time perceive his Romanism developing into Neology, he will only have to treat his present essay, as he has handled his former lectures on the superstition which he now professes; reverting with momentary self-reproach to his association with Dr. Wiseman and his reverence for Trent, and heaving a deeper sigh for his earlier abode among the corruptions of Protestantism, its fellowships, and its friends.

Do we write these things of a learned and an eloquent man, without feelings of poignant regret and commiseration? We do not. Such a capacity, so strengthened by exercise, so brightened by reflection, so enriched by labour, who might not honour; and for its enchantment and its obscuration, who can refuse to mourn? If his mind be viewed only on that side which intellect illuminates, it will be found to be full of beauty and light. His sermons contain thoughts that Hooker might have brooded over, and images that Augustine himself might have loved. He touches the most familiar object with a pencil, that gives life as well as colour. If he animates new ideas, he adorns old. (pp. 265-66)

> *"Mr. Newman; His Theories and Character,"* in Fraser's Magazine for Town & Country, Vol. XXXIII, No. CXCV, March, 1846, pp. 253-68.

The Spectator   (essay date 1864)

[*In the following excerpt, the critic offers a positive review of Newman's* Apologia, *commenting sympathetically on the sincerity of the author's convictions.*]

It is perhaps somewhat of a paradox to say that Dr. Newman's reply to Mr. Kingsley [*Apologia pro Vita Sua*] at once demonstrates the perfect simplicity and candour of his own nature, and yet provides more colour of excuse for Mr. Kingsley's rash charges and misapprehensions than those who judged his Anglican career either from a considerable distance or by the light of close friendship were aware. He makes it obvious that to those spectators who watched him from the middle-distance, who were neither far enough removed from him to judge him only by his writings, nor close enough to have a clear apprehension of his motives, there must have been much that was perplexing and even likely to shake the confidence in his simplicity of purpose. At the same time we not only hold to our first impression that there was absolutely no justification for Mr. Kingsley's rash accusation, but we can scarce-

ly conceive that Mr. Kingsley himself can read this apology without the profoundest personal conviction of the stedfast uprightness and true simplicity of Dr. Newman's theological career. We have reason to be glad that the charges were made, if only that they have elicited a book which so greatly enlarges our knowledge, not only of the upper currents of a wide intellect, but of the deep-sea soundings of at least as wide, though unique and singularly constituted a heart. Far as we are severed from him in almost every principle of faith, and hope, and intellectual conviction, it would be mere dulness of nature not to recognize freely the noble truthfulness and almost childlike candour of the autobiographic sketch now before us. There is no attempt to make the best of himself. Dr. Newman admits freely how blindly he groped his way for many years in the Anglican Church, and how slowly his eyes were opened to his real destiny; how friends often surprised him into momentary admissions that were not really his own; how he himself laid down in perfect confidence at one period of his career apparently fixed principles which turned out at a later period to be mere straws at which he had, as it were, caught vainly, in order to arrest his onward path towards a goal from which he recoiled almost to the last.

The impression left upon us is that all Dr. Newman's Anglican theories were really straws of this kind,—not merely untenable by him, for that is now a matter of fact,—but not even truly discovering the hidden revolution going on unconsciously in his own nature, though they registered accurately enough the points at which from time to time he had arrived. Most men, we suppose, have more or less difficulty in analyzing the true causes of their own changing convictions. It is far easier to find possible reasons for such changes than to find the actual reasons, which are indeed often beyond our reach altogether. It is a rare gift to be able to touch the true root of your own mental growth, and perhaps a rarer gift with men of genius like Dr. Newman than with more ordinary men. But certainly nothing strikes us more in this book than the wide chasm which divided Dr. Newman's tentative justifications of his successive positions in the Anglican Church from the motive powers he betrays to us, and which he ultimately perhaps recognized himself as the moving forces of his own mind. One reason, we think, why this gulf was wider in him than in most men of equal power is that the movement which he headed began with a deliberate depreciation of "private judgment." He and his friends wanted to find something safer to lean upon than that which really convinced their own minds. They thought it almost immaterial to analyze the exact sources of their own persuasion, for they wished to find some great external and objective ground more than enough to secure their own belief, to which they could point, not perhaps as really *effecting* that belief, but as justifying and verifying it on broader principles than that of any individual persuasion. It is obvious how this almost ostentatious distrust of private judgment and personal conviction would tend to multiply reasons for believing which were not the efficient causes of the writer's individual belief. And this seems to us the most remarkable intellectual feature of Dr. Newman's Anglican career. He was glad to discover a body of fact quite extraneous to the real springs of his own convictions on which to base his defence of those convictions, and of course it is not surprising that when he and his party were believing a creed for reasons more or less completely hidden from their own hearts, and justifying that creed, and demanding the belief of others for that creed on quite different formal grounds, which they thought sufficient to support it, they soon discovered that the firm body of fact on which they relied was but a moving island, which passed away from them almost as soon as they had reared their intellectual pile upon it. The grounds of our personal convictions may be insecure, and they are not always easy to detect, but they have at least this advantage, that being parts of ourselves they are much *more* likely to influence us permanently than even the most plausible grounds fetched from outside us. In one remarkable passage of this apology Dr. Newman admits how little the reasoning by which he *accounted* for his changing intellectual positions may have really represented the influences at work within him. "I felt altogether," he tells us,

> the force of the maxim of St. Ambrose, '*Non in dialecticâ complacuit Deo salvum facere populum suum,*' I had a great dislike to paper-logic. For myself, it was not logic that carried me on; as well might one say that the quicksilver in the barometer changes the weather. It is the concrete being that reasons. Pass a number of years, and I find my mind in a new place; how? the whole man moves; paper-logic is but the record of it. All the logic in the world would not have made me move faster towards Rome than I did; as well might you say that I have arrived at the end of my journey because I see the village church before me, as venture to assert that the miles over which my soul had to pass before it got to Rome could be annihilated, even though I had had some far clearer view than I then had that Rome was my ultimate destination. Great acts take time.

This is both true and fine. But with Dr. Newman the logic of his various stages of opinion scarcely even *registers,* we think, the track, though it may perhaps register the *rate,* of his advance. The true logic of conviction is the expression of that which convinces us. And we do not find much that impresses us as a real reflection of the moral constituents of his faith till after his conversion. There is a forced unnatural ring, evidently quite unperceived by himself, about his various Anglican hypotheses. They seem to us to define the stages of his mental journey only as an astronomical observation will define a ship's place at sea,—that is, merely fixing its momentary position, without giving us any hint of the actual force of steam, wind, or tide which has brought it so far and will yet take it further. To take one notable instance. After Dr. Newman had persuaded himself that the Anglican Church had been guilty of the sin of schism, that it did not possess "the note of Catholicity," and that it had no exclusive title to "the note of antiquity," he still hesitated for some years longer whether it were his duty to secede, and sustained himself during a portion of that time by drawing an analogy between the relation of the Church of England to that of Rome, and the relation of the Samaritan worship to that of Judah after the secession of the ten tribes. The Church of England was Samaria. As no divine command was given to

Samaria to be reconciled to the true Jewish Church, and a sort of worship was still permitted, so Dr. Newman thought he was justified in remaining in communion with the schismatic Church even after he had recognized it as distinctly and culpably schismatic. This was the objective fact by which he excused his reluctance to go, but it is obvious it was in no respect the intellectual ground of his hesitation, that it had nothing in fact to do with it; and as he himself tells us, before long the Samaria hypothesis simply faded away from his mind. His convictions flowed on while this artificial theory stayed behind. He looked round, and it was gone. And this seems to us the type of almost all his Anglican hypotheses. They were not within him,—they were outside him. A revolution was going on in his inmost nature of which he was little aware. He invented one hypothesis after another which simply marked his progress as we stick pins into a map to mark the progress of a campaign. And one after another, they disappeared in the wake of his progress because none of them really represented the fibres of his own belief.

It is obvious enough how misleading an impression these mere buoys on the surface of his thought must have left upon casual spectators who could see better than he could the real drift of his mind, and who took all the later signals of his temporary position as intellectual blinds, calculated, if not intended, to confuse others. Nothing could be falser. But after reading the apology we can quite understand that the reasons which Dr. Newman found for not moving faster must have greatly puzzled all but the most intimate of his friends. The true explanation was, as he says, that

---

J. Fitzjames Stephen on the *Apologia*:

[Newman's] *Apologia* is a winning, and in some ways, a touching book. It is full of courage and straightforwardness; every word that the author says of himself and his opinions bears upon it the stamp of truth. The vigour and spirit with which, in his old age, he stands up for his good name; the price which he sets upon the good opinion of the world at large; his anxiety to be freed from the most odious of all imputations on the character of a straightforward Englishman; the simple dignity with which he tells the story of his life—all these things go straight to the hearts of his readers. Almost all of us, he seems to think, are to be damned to all eternity; but with amiable inconsistency he wishes for our good opinion. He would like us to think kindly of him in hell fire. *Morituros salutat.* We have no intention to say a word inconsistent with the respect due to an old and distinguished man, who appeals so manfully to the good feeling of his countrymen; but high as Dr. Newman's personal character is, we cannot read his book without feeling that his theology is dangerous sophistry, calculated to serve no other purpose than that of drugging the minds of men who care more for peace of mind than for truth, and whose *ultima ratio* is found not in their reason, but in their fears or their fancies.

J. Fitzjames Stephen in Fraser's Magazine, *September 1864.*

"a great act takes time," and also that a fertile intellect will find all sorts of expedients, in which it will believe for a moment itself, for retarding a movement to the final result of which it looks with awe. But nothing seems to us clearer than that all his *premises* of thought were Roman Catholic from the beginning, even at the very time when he was saying honestly the hardest things he ever said of the Roman Church. Even then he felt the current sucking him in, and it was this which made him protest so eagerly against the alleged Romanizing tendencies of his school of opinion. (pp. 654-55)

> "*Dr. Newman's Apology,*" *in* The Spectator, *Vol. 37, No. 1875, June 4, 1864, pp. 654-56.*

J. A. Froude   (essay date 1870)

[*Froude was an English historian, editor, biographer, and novelist best known for his twelve-volume* History of England *(1856-1870) and for his acclaimed biography of Thomas Carlyle (1884). In the following excerpt, he analyzes Newman's* Essay in Aid of a Grammar of Assent, *praising the author's artistry but rejecting many of the premises of his argument.*]

Thirty years ago, when the tendencies Romewards of the English High Churchmen were first becoming visible, Dr. Arnold expressed his own opinion of the reasonableness of the movement in the brief sentence, 'Believe in the Pope! I would as soon believe in Jupiter.' Whether belief in Jupiter may hereafter become possible, time will show. Necromancy has been revived in spirit-rapping. We have converts to Islam among us, and England is the chosen recruiting ground of the Mormon Apostles; while [*An Essay in Aid of a Grammar of Assent*] is an attempt on the part of one of the ablest of living men, to prove that there is no reasonable standing ground between Atheism and submission to the Holy See—submission not outwardly only, or partially, or conditionally, as to an authority which has historical claims upon us, and may possibly or probably deserve our allegiance; but submission complete and entire, the unreserved resignation of our moral and spiritual intelligence. The Church of Rome, and indeed all religious dogmatic systems, are not content with insisting that there is a high probability in their favour. They call themselves infallible. They demand on our part an absolute certainty that they are right, and although they disagree among themselves and cannot all be right, and although points on which those competent to form an opinion differ, in all other things we agree to hold doubtful, they tell us that doubt is a sin, that we can be and ought to be entirely certain, that a complete and utter acquiescence which excludes the possibility of mistake, is a frame of mind at once possible and philosophically just.

It is this seeming paradox which Dr. Newman undertakes to prove. His book is composed with elaborate art, which is the more striking the more frequently we peruse it. Every line, every word tells, from the opening sentence to the last.

His object, from the beginning to the end, is to combat and overthrow the position of Locke, that reasonable assent is proportioned to evidence, and in its nature, therefore, admits of degrees.

He commences with an analysis of the elementary mental processes. He divides 'assent' into 'notional' and 'real.' He calls notional 'assent,' that which we give to general propositions, scientific, literary, or philosophical; real assent, the conclusions which we form in matters of fact, either in our sensible perceptions, or in the application of principles to details. He professes to show how, from our intellectual constitution, we are unable to rest in probabilities, and rightly or wrongly pass on to a sensation of certainty; how, notwithstanding exceptions which cannot wholly be got over, the conviction that we have hold of the truth is an evidence to us that we have hold of it in reality. Our beliefs are borne in upon our minds, we know not how, directly, indirectly, by reason, by experience, by emotion, imagination, and all the countless parts of our complicated nature. We may not be able to analyse the grounds of our faith, but the faith is none the less justifiable. And thus, after being led by the hand through an intricate series of mental phenomena, we are landed in the Catholic religion as the body of truth which completely commends itself to the undistorted intellectual perception.

The argument is extremely subtle, and often difficult to follow, but the difficulty is in the subject rather than in the treatment. Dr. Newman has watched and analysed the processes of the mind with as much care and minuteness as Ehrenberg the organisation of animalculæ. The knotted and tangled skein is disengaged and combed out till every fibre of it can be taken up separately and examined at leisure; while all along, hints are let fall from time to time, expressions, seemingly casual, illustrations, or notices of emotional peculiarities, every one of which has its purpose, and, to the careful reader, is a signpost of the road on which he is travelling.

Yet we never read a book, unless the *Ethics* of Spinoza be an exception, which is less convincing in proportion to its ability. You feel that you are in the hands of a thinker of the very highest powers; yet they are the powers rather of an intellectual conjuror than of a teacher who commands your confidence. You are astonished at the skill which is displayed, and unable to explain away the results; but you are conscious all the time that you are played with; you are perplexed but you are not attracted; and unless you bring a Catholic conclusion ready made with you to the study, you certainly will not arrive at it. For it is not a simple acknowledgment that Catholicism may perhaps be true that is required of us, or even that it is probably true, and that a reasonable person might see cause for joining the Roman communion. This is not conviction at all, nor is it related in any way to a religious frame of mind. We are expected rather to feel Catholicism to be absolutely necessary and completely true—true, not as an inference from argument, but as imposed by a spiritual command—true, in a sense which allows no possibility of error, and cannot and ought not to endure contradiction. 'The highest opinion of Protestants in religion,' he says, 'is generally speaking, assent to a probability, as even Butler has been understood or misunderstood to teach, and therefore consistent with the toleration of its contradictory.' The creed, therefore, which we are to accept is the Romanism with which we are familiar in history; persecuting from the necessity of the case, for it cannot, where it has the power, permit opposition. No heterodox opinion can be borne with, or be even heard in its own defence. 'Since mere argument,' Father Newman says elsewhere,

> is not the measure of assent, no one can be called certain of a proposition whose mind does not spontaneously and promptly reject on their first suggestion, as idle, as impertinent, as sophistical, any objections which are directed against its truth. No man is certain of a truth who can endure the thought of its contradictory existing or occurring, and that not from any set purpose or effort to reject it, but, as I have said, by the spontaneous action of the intellect. What is contradictory to it with its apparatus of argument, fades out of the mind as fast as it enters it.

We are familiar with this mode of thought, but it is not characteristic of intelligent persons. The Irish magistrate having listened to one side of a question declared himself satisfied; he had heard enough, he said, and anything further was either superfluous or perplexed his judgment. In a criminal trial, when the facts have been known and discussed beforehand, both judge and jury, from the constitution of their minds, must have formed an opinion on the merits of the case, which must have amounted often to certainty; but when the prisoner comes before them it becomes their duty to dismiss out of their minds every prepossession which they may have entertained. Instead of rejecting suggestions inconsistent with such prepossessions they are bound to welcome them, and to look for them, with the most scrupulous impartiality. The man of science is unworthy of his name if he disdains to listen to objections to a favourite theory. It is through a conviction of the inadequacy of all formulas to cover the facts of nature, it is by a constant recollection of the fallibility of the best instructed intelligence, and by an unintermittent scepticism which goes out of its way to look for difficulties, that scientific progress has been made possible. So long as Father Newman's method prevailed in Europe, every branch of practical knowledge was doomed to barrenness. Why are we to fall back upon it now, in the one department in which, according to theologians, error is most dangerous?

To give a sketch of his argument.

We entertain propositions, he tells us, in three ways—we doubt, we draw inferences, and we assent. Doubt is, of course, the opposite of certainty. Inferences being from premises to conclusions are still conditional, for our premises may be incorrect or inadequate. Assent, on the other hand, is in its nature unconditional; it means that we are quite certain, and know that we cannot be wrong.

We assent notionally when we accept a general proposition as undoubtedly true, as that the whole is greater than its part, or that the planets move in ellipses, or again, when we read a book and intellectually go along with its meaning without personally or particularly applying it. We assent really to anything which comes home in detail to our feelings or our senses, and is directly recognised as true by ourselves. Dr. Newman gives a beautiful illustration:

> Let us consider, too, how differently young and old are affected by the words of some classic author, such as Homer or Horace. Passages, which

to a boy are but rhetorical commonplaces, neither better nor worse than a hundred others which any clever writer might supply, which he gets by heart and thinks very fine, and imitates, as he thinks, successfully, in his own flowing versification, at length come home to him, when long years have passed, and he has had experience of life, and pierce him as if he had never before known them, with their sad earnestness and vivid exactness. Then he comes to understand how it is that lines, the birth of some chance morning or evening at an Ionian festival, or among the Sabine hills, have lasted generation after generation, for thousands of years, with a power over the mind, and a charm, which the current literature of his own day, with all its obvious advantages, is utterly unable to rival.

The history, the occupations, the studies of every man provide him with a multitude of assents of this kind. Proverbs become as it were realised when we feel the application of them. Opinions taken up as notions acquire the stamp of certainty, and men are only properly themselves when their thoughts thus acquire stability and they are no longer blown about by gusts of argument. Then only they learn to step out firmly with confidence and self-reliance.

Assents, Dr. Newman repeats, differ in kind from inferences. We may infer from observation the probable existence of an intelligent Creator, but we are still far from the conviction which is required for practical service, and life is not long enough for a religion built on speculative conclusions. Life is for action. We cannot wait for proof or we shall never begin to obey.

> If we insist on proof for everything we shall never come to action . . . To act we must assume, and that assumption is faith . . . . If we commence with scientific knowledge and argumentative proof, or lay any great stress upon it as the basis of personal Christianity, or attempt to make men moral or religious by libraries and museums, let us in consistency take chemists for our cooks and mineralogists for our masons.

This is perfectly true as regards individual persons. The clerk in Eastcheap, as Mr. Carlyle says, cannot be for ever verifying his ready reckoner. Yet the conclusions on which we act are nevertheless resting on producible evidence somewhere, if we cannot each of us produce it ourselves. They are the accumulations of past experience and intellectual thought, which are tested, enlarged, or modified by the practice of successive generations. We accept them confidently, not from any internal conviction that they are necessarily true, but from an inference of another kind, that if not true they would have been disproved. The believer at first hand can always give a reason for the faith that is in him. He believes, and he knows why he believes, and he can produce his reasons in a form which shall be convincing to others. The believer at second hand believes in his teacher, and can give a reason for regarding that teacher as an authority. The mason need not himself be a mineralogist, but if the master builder who employs him knows nothing of the properties of stone, his labour will be thrown away. The cook inherits the traditionary rules of his art, but if he introduces novelties in food he must either call in the chemist to advise him, or he will try his experiments at the risk of our lives.

We have not yet reached a point where we differ from Father Newman essentially; but we are already on our guard against his method. His aim is to make us acknowledge that in common things we feel a certainty disproportioned to the evidence which can be produced to justify it. It appears to us, on the contrary, that Locke's position remains unshaken; that every sound conviction which we have can be traced ultimately to experience, and that the tenacity with which we hold it is, or ought to be, proportioned to the uniformity of that experience.

From real assents in general, we pass to assents in matters of religion.

'What is a dogma of faith?' Father Newman asks,

> and what is to believe it? A dogma is a proposition. It stands for a notion or a thing, and to believe it is to give the assent of the mind to it as standing for one or the other. To give a real assent to it is an act of religion; to give a notional is a theological act. It is discerned, rested in, and appropriated as a reality by the religious imagination. It is held as a truth by the theological intellect.

The first of such dogmas or propositions contains 'belief in God.' He disclaims necessarily the intention of proving the reasonableness of this belief. He denies belief to be the result of argument, and therefore he will not argue. He proposes rather to investigate the mental process which the words 'I believe in God' imply, yet he cannot escape from the conditions of human thought, and while he will not allow belief to be an inference, he argues like anybody else that it follows irresistibly from the phenomena of our nature. Nowhere in the English language will be found the reasons for believing in a moral power as the supreme ruler of the universe, drawn out more clearly or more persuasively. There are no gratuitous assumptions—no appeals to the imagination. He lays the facts of personal experience before us: he indicates the conclusion at which they point: and when the conclusion is conceded, the obligations of obedience follow. He draws the inference though he will not allow it to be an inference. 'Inference,' he seems to say, 'has no power of persuasion and involves no duties.' Inference is but a graduated probability, and involves the toleration of an opposite opinion. But probability, as Butler says, is the guide of our lives, and may involve duties as completely as certainty. Has a child no duties to his father because it is possible, though infinitely unlikely, that his mother may have been unfaithful to her vows?

The argument itself stands thus. We regret to do injustice by compression to its singular lucidity.

'Can we,' Father Newman asks, 'give a real assent to the proposition that there is one God—not an *anima mundi* merely or an initial force, but God as the word is understood by the Theist and the Christian, a personal God, the Author and Sustainer of all things—the Moral Governor of the world?' He says that we can, and that we can be certain of it—that it is a truth which every reasonable person

is able and ought to acknowledge. He does not look for what has been called scornfully 'a clock-making Divinity.' The evidences of a contriving intellect in nature, of the adaptation of means to ends, weigh but little with him. There is no mortality in the physical constitution of things. The elements know nothing of good and evil; and we can arrive on this road only at a power adequate to the effects which we witness. The water will not rise higher than its source. The created world is finite, and can tell us nothing of an Infinite Creator. The root of religious belief lies in the conscience and in the sense of moral obligation.

> I assume, then (says Father Newman), that Conscience has a legitimate place among our mental acts; as really so, as the action of memory, of reasoning, of imagination, or as the sense of the beautiful; that, as there are objects which, when presented to the mind, cause it to feel grief, regret, joy, or desire, so there are things which excite in us its approbation or blame, and which we in consequence call right or wrong; and which, experienced in ourselves, kindle in us the specific sense of pleasure or pain, which goes by the name of a good or bad conscience. This being taken for granted, I shall attempt to show that in this special feeling, which follows on the commission of what we call right and wrong, lie the materials for the real apprehension of a Divine Sovereign and Judge.

> The feeling of conscience being, I repeat, a certain keen sensibility, pleasant or painful,—self-approval and hope, or compunction and fear,—attendant on certain of our actions, which in consequence we call right or wrong, is two-fold:—it is a moral sense, and a sense of duty; a judgment of the reason and a magisterial dictate.

Conscience, it is evident, does not furnish a rule of right conduct. It has sometimes been the sanction of crime. Sometimes it is at a loss to decide. Sometimes it gives contradictory answers. Conscience made St. Paul into a persecutor. Conscience has made kings into tyrants, and subjects into rebels. It is not a rule of right conduct, but it is a sanction of right conduct. It assures us that there is such a thing as right, and that when we know what it is we are bound to do it.

> Half the world would be puzzled to know what is meant by the moral sense, but every one knows what is meant by a good or bad conscience. Conscience is ever forcing us on by threats and by promises, that we must follow the right and avoid the wrong: so far it is one and the same in the mind of every one, whatever be its particular errors in particular minds as to the acts which it orders to be done or to be avoided. . . . It does not repose in itself like the sense of beauty. . . . It vaguely reaches forward to something beyond self, and dimly discerns a sanction higher than self for its decisions, as evidenced in that keen sense of obligation and responsibility which informs them. And hence it is that we are accustomed to speak of conscience as a voice, a term which we never should think of applying to the sense of the beautiful: and moreover a voice or the echo of a voice impera-

tive and constraining, like no other dictate in the whole of our experience.

Now what does this imply? Father Newman introduces a subtle distinction of which we hesitate to acknowledge the force. Conscience, he says, differs from the intellectual senses, from common sense, from taste, from sense of expedience, and the like, in being always 'emotional.' 'Affections are correlative with persons, and always involve the recognition of a living object towards which they are directed.' Surely there is such a thing as love of good for its own sake. But leaving refinements and looking at these phenomena as facts of experience, they seem to us to carry Father Newman's main conclusion with them. The presence of a moral sense in ourselves presumes a moral nature in the power which has called us into existence. It is impossible to conceive, as Mr. Carlyle says, 'that these high faculties should have been put into us by a Being that had none of its own.'

Father Newman continues:

> If, as is the case, we feel responsibility, are ashamed, are frightened, at transgressing the voice of conscience, this implies that there is One to whom we are responsible, before whom we are ashamed, whose claims upon us we fear. If, on doing wrong, we feel the same tearful, broken-hearted sorrow which overwhelms us on hurting a mother; if, on doing right, we enjoy the same sunny serenity of mind, the same soothing, satisfactory delight which follows on our receiving praise from a father, we certainly have within us the image of some person, to whom our love and veneration look, in whose smile we find our happiness, for whom we yearn, towards whom we direct our pleadings, in whose anger we are troubled and waste away. These feelings in us are such as require for their exciting cause an intelligent being: we are not affectionate towards a stone, nor do we feel shame before a horse or a dog; we have no remorse or compunction on breaking mere human law: yet, so it is, conscience excites all these painful emotions, confusion, foreboding, self-condemnation; and on the other hand, it sheds upon us a deep peace, a sense of security, a resignation, and a hope, which there is no sensible, no earthly object to elicit. 'The wicked flees, when no one pursueth;' then why does he flee? whence his terror? Who is it that he sees in solitude, in darkness, in the hidden chambers of his heart? If the cause of these emotions does not belong to this visible world, the Object to which his perception is directed must be Supernatural and Divine; and thus the phenomena of Conscience, as a dictate, avail to impress the imagination with the picture of a Supreme Governor, a Judge, holy, just, powerful, all-seeing, retributive, and is the creative principle of religion, as the moral sense is the principle of ethics.
>
> (pp. 561-66)

So far, with some differences which are perhaps but differences of nomenclature, we have gone heartily along with Father Newman. His book is a counterpart to Butler's *Analogy,* and as the first part of the *Analogy* has been in these bad times a support to many of us, when the formu-las of the established creeds have crumbled away, so we give cordial welcome to this addition to our stock of religious philosophy, which addresses itself to the intellect of the nineteenth century as Butler addressed that of its predecessor. But just as with Butler, when we pass from his treatment of the facts of nature to the defence of the dogmatic system of Christianity, we exchange the philosopher for the special pleader, so Father Newman at the same transition point equally ceases to convince. Assumption takes the place of reasoning. Facts are no longer looked in the face, and objections are either ignored altogether or are caricatured in order to be answered. Hitherto he has been pleading the cause of religion as it has existed in all ages and under countless varieties of form. We are now led across the morasses of technical theology. We spring from tuft to tuft and hummock to hummock. The ground shakes about us, and we are allowed no breathing time to pause, lest it give way under our feet altogether. The promised land lies before us, the land of absolute repose in the decisions of the Infallible Church. Once there we may rest for ever; and we are swung along towards it, guided, if we may use the word for an absolute surrender of reason, by the obscure emotions and half realised perceptions of what is called the imaginative intellect. We leave behind us as misleading the apparatus of faculties which conduct us successfully through ordinary life. We are told to believe, and accept it on Father Newman's authority, that we are not after all chasing a will-o'-the-wisp, and that the other side to which he points the way is really solid ground, and not a mere fog-bank.

There are two roads on which it is possible to travel, after starting from conscience and the acknowledgment of a God to whom we owe obedience. There is the theological road, and there is the road of experience and fact. To those who choose the second of these courses conscience is the sanction of right action; while experience and observation show us in what right action consists. The moral laws are inherent in nature like the laws of the material universe, and our business is to discover what they are. If we obey them, it is well with us; if we disobey them we fail, and ruin ourselves internally in our characters, and sooner or later in our external fortunes. These laws are not arbitrarily imposed from without, but are interfused in the constitution of things. Conscience insists that they must be obeyed, for they form the condition on which society holds together, and in obedience to them lies the essence of all genuine religion.

From this point of view the religious history of mankind is the history of the efforts which men have made to discover the moral law, and enforce it so far as it is known. If we are asked why the moral laws, being of so much consequence to the well-being of mankind, were not made clear from the beginning, we can but answer that we do not know. The fact has been that they have been left to human energy to discover, like the law of gravitation; our knowledge of them has been progressive, like our knowledge in every other department of nature; and religious theories exhibit the same early imperfections, and the same gradual advance as astronomy or medicine.

A second phenomenon is no less apparent on the most cur-

Oriel College and, in the background, St. Mary's, Oxford. A fellow of Oriel, Newman became vicar of St. Mary's in 1828.

sory as well as the most careful study of religious history. To obey the moral law has been always difficult; to practise particular rites, or to profess particular opinions, is comparatively easy. Religions, therefore, as their initial fervour dies away, have uniformly shown a tendency to stiffen into ceremonial or superstitious observances, or else into theological theories. Duty has been made to consist in the compliance with particular creeds, or in practices of outward devotion; and a compromise has been thus arrived at, by which men have been enabled to believe themselves religious, without parting from their private self-indulgence. Religion has had two parts: the inward moral and spiritual, the outward ritualistic, or speculative; and the division between them, and the history of their effects upon mankind, when one or the other has preponderated, is the most signal testimony to their real character, and to the relations in which they stand to each other and to the world. Where the moral element has been foremost, where men have been chiefly bent upon contending with practical evil, and making so much as they can understand of the law of God the rule of their dealings among themselves, there the religion has spread over the earth like water for the purifying the nations. Where the superstitious or theological element has been in the ascendant, where charity has been second to orthodoxy, and religion has been an affair of temples and sacrifices and devotional refinements, there as uniformly it has lost its beneficent powers, it has fraternised with the blackest and darkest of human passions, and has carried with it as its shadow, di-

vision and hatred and cruelty. The power in the universe, whatever it be, which envies human happiness, has laid hold of conscience and distracted it from its proper function. Instead of looking any more for our duties to our neighbours, we go astray, and quarrel with each other over imaginary speculative theories. We wonder at the failure of Christianity, at the small progress which it has made in comparison with the brilliancy of its rise: but if men had shown as much fanaticism in carrying into practice the Sermon on the Mount as in disputing the least of the thousand dogmatic definitions which have superseded the Gospel, we should not be now lamenting with Father Newman that 'God's control over the world is so indirect, and His action so obscure.'

The theological tendency, nevertheless, remains in possession; opinions are still looked upon as the test whether we are on the right road or the wrong; and it is in this direction and not the other that Father Newman would have us travel if our condition is to be mended.

Devotion must have its objects, he tells us; and they must be set before the mind as propositions, with which the intellect must be fed till it is saturated; the intellect in return will then guarantee that they are true by the tenacity with which it holds these propositions.

He gives an instance of what he means in the use which he prescribes for the book of Psalms. 'The exercise of the affections strengthens our apprehension of the object of them,' he says, 'and it is impossible to exaggerate the influence exerted on the religious imagination, by a book of devotions so sublime, so penetrating, so full of deep instruction, as the Psalter.' We must take it, however, as a whole, we may not enquire what part of it is authentic, or whether David, whose acts were of so mixed a character, was always divinely guided in his words. If we take the forty-second Psalm, we must take the hundred-and-ninth; and those who accept the hundred-and-ninth as the word of God, are already far on their way towards auto-da-fés and massacres of St. Bartholomew.

When the mind is thus devotionally pervaded, the Catholic theology will be developed by the theological intellect as naturally as geometrical theorems from the elementary axioms and propositions. The difficulty is with the preparation of the soil; and if we find Father Newman unpersuasive, the fault may be simply in ourselves. Persuasiveness implies agreement in first principles between the teacher and the taught. It is possible that we may be colour blind, or be without ear to follow the harmony of the theological variations. The Catholic doctrines may carry conviction only to the elect. Those who are chosen to inherit the blessing, may alone have grace to apprehend its conditions. If it be so, we are beyond help; but we claim for the present to belong to those who believe in God and in the moral laws, and to those, therefore, to whom Father Newman says that his book is addressed. In this character we have a right to speak, and when he fails to convince us, to give reasons for withholding our assent.

Having chosen his course he commences characteristically with an exulting eulogy on the Athanasian Creed. No one, he seems to admit, can understand what the creed means. 'The pure indivisible light,' he says, 'is seen only by the blessed inhabitants of Heaven.' The rays come to us on earth, 'broken into their constituent colours;' and when we attempt to combine them 'we produce only a dirty white.' Each ray, nevertheless, comes direct to us from above. It can be separately admired and adored for its particular beauty; and when intelligence fails, faith steps in. So with the million developments of theological subtlety. Simple-minded people cannot enter into these refinements; the terminology itself is unintelligible without a special and scientific education. But simple-minded men are not required to understand them. Their duty is merely to feel certain that every proposition laid down by the Church is true, and they are able to do it in virtue of a comprehensive acceptance of the authority of the Church itself. The Church says so and so, and therefore it is indisputably certain that the truth is so and so.

> The difficulty is removed by the dogma of the Church's infallibility, and of the consequent duty of 'implicit faith' in her word. The 'One Holy Catholic and Apostolic Church' is an article of the creed, and an article, which, inclusive of her infallibility, all men, high and low, can easily master and accept with a real and operative assent. It stands in the place of all abstruse propositions in a Catholic's mind, for to believe in her word is virtually to believe in them all. Even what he cannot understand, at least he can believe to be true; and he believes it to be true because he believes in the Church.

The next question of course is, how we can be certain that the Church is infallible? and to understand this we are carried back even more into the metaphysics of conviction. For the infallibility of the Church, or any truth, to produce an animating effect upon us, we must assent to it unconditionally; and Father Newman has first to prove in general, as against Locke and the inductive philosophy, that a state of undoubting assurance is itself legitimate.

'Assent,' he says, 'is a distinct act of the mind which declares that it is made up. It resembles the striking of a clock. . . . It is an intimation that argument is over, the conclusion accepted, and the possibility of error no longer entertained. Numberless propositions are, in fact, held in this way in ordinary life. Each of us, for instance, holds with undoubting certainty, the proposition that 'I shall die,' or, again, that 'England is an island.' The fact of our death is in the future, and therefore in its nature contingent. We may have never ourselves personally sailed round England. Yet, in neither case, have we any doubt, or can a person of ordinary intelligence admit that there is room for doubt.

The appeal to ordinary intelligence corresponds to the appeal at a later stage of the argument to the religious instincts of barbarous nations. Ordinary intelligence jumps hastily to conclusions. It is as often wrong as right, and the strength with which it holds a particular opinion may only be an index of want of thought. The proposition that 'I shall die' seems at the first blush as indisputable as that the whole is greater than its part. But those who accept the infallibility of St. Paul believe that, at the last trumpet, those that are alive will be caught up into the air without dying at all. The last day, they are warned, will come like a thief in the night, and they are charged to be on the watch for it. The thought, therefore, that it may come in their time will present itself not as a probability, but certainly as something not utterly impossible. Ordinary intelligence again is similarly absolutely certain that England is an island. The man of science is certain of it too, but in the sense of the word which Father Newman quarrels with. Sudden geographical changes are extremely rare; but the time has been when England was not an island, and the time may come when it will be reattached to the continent. The Channel is shallow, not much deeper anywhere than the towers of Westminster Abbey. Extensive tracts of the globe have been rapidly depressed and rapidly raised again. It is therefore possible, though very unlikely, that there may be, at some point or other in the Channel, at any moment, a sudden upheaval.

'Certainty,' Father Newman insists, 'is the same in kind wherever and by whomsoever it is experienced. The gravely and cautiously formed conclusion of the scientific investigator, and the determination of the schoolgirl that the weather is going to be fine, do not differ from each other so far as they are acts of the mind. And the schoolgirl has pro tanto an evidence in her conviction that the fact will be as she believes. Nay, rather the laborious inference hesitatingly held after patient and sceptical examination, Father Newman considers inferior in character, and likely to be less productive of fruit than assent more impulsively yielded.

In such instances of certitude, the previous labour of coming to a conclusion, and that repose of mind which I have above described as attendant on an assent to its truth, often counteracts whatever of lively sensation the fact thus concluded is in itself adapted to excite; so that what is gained in depth and exactness of belief is lost as regards freshness and vigour. Hence it is that literary or scientific men, who may have investigated some difficult point of history, philosophy, or physics, and have come to their own settled conclusion about it, having had a perfect right to form one, are far more disposed to be silent as to their convictions, and to let others alone, than partisans on either side of the question, who take it up with less thought and seriousness. And so again, in the religious world, no one seems to look for any great devotion or fervour in controversialists, writers on Christian Evidences, theologians, and the like, it being taken for granted, rightly or wrongly, that such men are too intellectual to be spiritual, and are more occupied with the truth of doctrine than with its reality. If, on the other hand, we would see what the force of simple assent can be, viewed apart from its reflex confirmation, we have but to look at the generous and uncalculating energy of faith as exemplified in the primitive Martyrs, in the youths who defied the pagan tyrant, or the maidens who were silent under his tortures. It is assent, pure and simple, which is the motive cause of great achievements; it is confidence, growing out of instincts rather than arguments, stayed upon a vivid apprehension, and animated by a transcendent logic, more concentrated in will and in deed for the very reason that it has not been subjected to any intellectual development.

Although, however, my sense of certainty is an evidence that I think myself right, there is still a bridge to be crossed between my thought and the fact. My own experience assures me too painfully of my fallibility. I have experienced equally the fallibility of others. No one can seriously maintain that a consciousness of certitude is an evidence of facts on which I can rely. Yet Father Newman clings to the belief that in some sense or other it is an evidence. 'It is characteristic of certitude,' he says,

> that its object is a truth, a truth as such, a proposition as true. There are right and wrong convictions, and certitude is a right conviction; if it is not right with a consciousness of being right, it is not certitude. Now, truth cannot change; what is once truth is always truth; and the human mind is made for truth, and so rests in truth, as it cannot rest in falsehood. When then it once becomes possessed of a truth, what is to dispossess it?

It is open to Father Newman to distinguish, if he pleases, between certitude and conviction. He may say that we may be convinced of what is false, but only certain of what is true. But this is nothing to the purpose, so long as we have no criterion to distinguish one from the other as an internal impression. Father Newman is certain that the Pope is Vicar of Christ. Luther was no less certain that the Pope was Antichrist. Father Newman believes that the substance of bread is taken away in the act of consecra-

tion. The Protestant martyrs died rather than admit that bread could cease to be bread when a priest mumbled a charm over it. Who or what is to decide between these several acts of consciousness, which was certitude and which conviction?

The Church evidently is the true *Deus ex machinâ*. The Church, in virtue of its infallibility, will resolve this and all other difficulties; and the infallibility, it seems, is somehow or other its own witness, and proves itself as Spinoza demonstrated the existence of God. 'I form a conception,' Spinoza says, 'of an absolutely perfect being. But existence is a mode of perfection; a non-existent being is an imperfect being: and therefore God's existence is involved in the Idea of Him.' Father Newman similarly appears to say that the mind is made for truth, and demands it as a natural right. Of the elementary truth that the Church is infallible it can be as sure as that Victoria is Queen of England; and this once established it has all that it requires. It is true that we have made mistakes; but *usum non tollit abusus.* That we have been often wrong does not imply that we may not be right at last. Our faculties have a correspondence with truth. They were given to us to lead us into truth, and though they fail many times they may bring us right at last. Once established in certitude we have nothing more to fear, and may defy argument thenceforth. Our past mistakes may after all have been only apparent. We have called ourselves certain, when we had only a strong presumption, an opinion, or an intellectual inference. Or again, we may fancy that we have changed our minds when in fact we have not changed our convictions but only developed them, as a Theist remains a Theist though he add to his Theism a faith in revelation; and a Protestant continues to hold the Athanasian Creed though he pass into a Catholic. St. Paul is admitted to be a difficulty; St. Paul indisputably did once hold that Christianity was an illusion: but St. Paul is got rid of by being made an exceptional person. 'His conversion, as also his after life, was miraculous.'

Any way, when once possessed of certitude, we cannot lose it. No evidence, however clear, can shake us thenceforward. 'Certitude ought to stand all trials or it is not certitude.' Its very office is to cherish and maintain its object, and its very lot and duty is to sustain such shocks in maintenance of it without being damaged by them. Father Newman takes an example, and it is an extremely significant one.

> Let us suppose we are told on an unimpeachable authority, that a man whom we saw die is now alive again and at his work, as it was his wont to be; let us suppose we actually see him and converse with him; what will become of our certitude of his death? I do not think we should give it up; how could we, when we actually saw him die? At first, indeed, we should be thrown into an astonishment and confusion so great, that the world would seem to reel round us, and we should be ready to give up the use of our senses and of our memory, of our reflective powers, and of our reason, and even to deny our power of thinking, and our existence itself. Such confidence have we in the doctrine that when life goes it never returns. Nor would our bewilderment be

less, when the first blow was over; but our reason would rally, and with our reason our certitude would come back to us. Whatever came of it, we should never cease to know and to confess to ourselves both of the contrary facts, that we saw him die, and that after dying we saw him alive again. The overpowering strangeness of our experience would have no power to shake our certitude in the facts which created it.

No better illustration could have been given of the difference between what is called in commendation 'a believing mind,' and a mind trained to careful and precise observation. In such a case as Father Newman supposes, a jury of modern physicians would indisputably conclude that the man had never been really dead, that the symptoms had been mistaken, and the phenomena of catalepsy had been confounded with the phenomena of death. If catalepsy was impossible, if the man had appeared, for instance, to lose his head on the scaffold, they would assume that there had been a substitution of persons, or that the observers had been taken in by some skilful optical trick. Father Newman may, perhaps, go further and suppose that they had themselves seen the man tied to a gun and blown to pieces beyond possibility of deception. But a man of science would reply that such a case could not occur. That men once dead do not return to life again has been revealed by an experience too uniform to allow its opposite to be entertained even as a hypothesis.

Catholic certitude involving the acceptance of miracles, the development of the subject brings up naturally the famous argument of Hume. (pp. 567-73)

'It is argued by Hume,' [Newman] says,

> against the actual occurrence of the Jewish and Christian miracles, that, whereas 'it is experience only which gives authority to human testimony, and it is the same experience which assures us of the laws of nature,' therefore, 'when these two kinds of experience are contrary' to each other, 'we are bound to subtract the one from the other;' and, in consequence, since we have no experience of a violation of natural laws, and much experience of the violation of truth, 'we may establish it as a maxim that no human testimony can have such force as to prove a miracle, and make it a just foundation for any system of religion.'

This is Hume's real argument accurately though briefly stated. How does Dr. Newman answer it?

'I will accept the general proposition,' he says,

> but I resist its application. Doubtless, it is abstractedly more likely that men should lie than that the order of nature should be infringed; but what is abstract reasoning to a question of concrete fact? To arrive at the fact of any matter, we must eschew generalities, and take things as they stand, with all their circumstances. . . . The question is not about miracles in general, or men in general, but definitely, whether these particular miracles, ascribed to the particular Peter, James, and John, are more likely to have been than not.

'More likely to have been than not' is a widely different thing from absolute certainty, and verges on the balancing of probability which elsewhere is so severely disclaimed. But after he has accepted the general proposition, how in reason can he ask what it has to do with concrete fact? What else should it have to do with? It is not an axiom of pure mathematics or a formula made up of symbols. It professes to be and it is a generalisation from concrete experience. It calls itself rightly or wrongly an expression of a universal truth, and being such, must therefore govern every particular instance which can be brought under it. Had Hume said simply that miracles were improbable, and that more evidence was required to establish them than to establish ordinary facts, the answer would have been to the purpose; but the gist of Hume's argument is that no evidence whatever can prove a miracle, and to accept the premises and to refuse its application on the plea that it is an abstract proposition, is to fly in the face of logic and common sense. Catholics, in fact, do not and cannot feel the improbability of miracles. An invisible but definite miracle is worked whenever a mass is said. In Catholic countries miracles, real or imaginary, are things of daily occurrence. Under 'particular circumstances' they are more likely to occur than not, and therefore any, even the slightest and most indirect, testimony is sufficient to make credible any given instance of miracle.

Prejudices, prepossessions, 'trifles light as air,' irregular emotions, implicit reasons, 'such as we feel, but which for some cause or other, because they are too subtle or too circuitous, we cannot put into words so as to satisfy logic,' these, and such as these in matters of religion, are genuine evidences to which, we are told, a reasonable man is expected to defer. Having once passed the line where evidence can be produced and tested, we are at the mercy of imagination, and the reader who has thus committed himself can now be led forward through the analytical labyrinth. The intellectual faculties, 'looking before and after,' are touched as it were by a torpedo. Our criteria of truth leave us. One thing seems as reasonable as another. We strike our flag and surrender. We 'consent,' as Father Newman advises us,

> to take things as they are and resign ourselves to what we find; instead of devising, which cannot be, some sufficient science of reasoning which may compel certitude in concrete conclusions, to confess that there is no ultimate test of truth besides the testimony borne to the truth by the mind itself, and that this phenomenon, perplexing as we may find it, is a normal and inevitable characteristic of the mental constitution of a being like man on a stage such as the world.

In this condition we are invited to recognise the claims of the Catholic Church upon us. 'The Catholic religion,' we are told, 'is reached by enquirers from all points of the compass, as if it mattered not where a man began so that he had an eye and heart for the truth.' Before 'the miserable deeds of the fifteenth and sixteenth centuries' 'the visible Church was the light of the world, conspicuous as the sun in the heavens. The creed was written on her forehead,' in accordance with the text, 'Who is she that looks forth at the dawn, fair as the moon, bright as the sun, terrible as an army set in array?' 'Clouds have now come over the sky, but what the Church has lost in her appeal to the imagination she has gained in philosophical cogency by the evidence of her persistent vitality. She is as vigorous in her age as in her youth, and has upon her *primâ facie* signs of divinity.'

Whether the Church has really gained in philosophical cogency by the Reformation and its consequences is a matter on which Father Newman has a right to his opinion; but others have also a right to theirs, which will probably be different. To ourselves it appears that what vitality she possesses is proportioned to the degree in which she has adopted the principles of her enemies, that so far as she retains her own she becomes every hour more powerless to act upon them. If it be vitality to have lost her hold on nine-tenths of the educated laymen in her own communion; if it be vitality to have compelled every Catholic Government to take from her the last fibre of secular and civil authority, to deprive her even of her control over education, and relegate her to the domain of mere opinion; if it be a sign of vigour that her once world-wide temporal authority is now limited to a single state, and supported there by the bayonets of a stranger, then indeed the evidence of her divinity may be said to have gained strength. In the sixteenth and seventeenth centuries the Church destroyed by sword and fire many hundreds of thousands of men and women in the effort to recover her dominion. She still professes intolerance, and Father Newman himself claims it as her right. Let her lay her hand upon one single heretic and dispose of him, as she used to do, at the stake; let but one man, now on the occasion of this brilliant Council, be publicly burnt in Rome for want of orthodoxy, and who does not know that the whole ecclesiastical fabric would be torn to pieces by the indignation of mankind?

Yet to Father Newman the position of the Church is so splendid, she is so visibly the representative of the majesty of God, that she challenges comparison with every other religious institution and has a claim in the fact of her existence to universal submission. (pp. 573-75)

> J. A. Froude, "Father Newman on 'The Grammar of Assent'," in Fraser's Magazine, Vol. 81, No. V, May, 1870, pp. 561-80.

Paul Elmer More   (essay date 1913)

[*More was an American critic who, along with Irving Babbitt, formulated the doctrines of New Humanism in the early twentieth century. The New Humanists were strict moralists who adhered to traditional conservative values in reaction to an age of scientific innovation and artistic experimentation. Regarding literature, they believed a work's support for the classical ethical norms to be of as much importance as its aesthetic qualities. More was particularly opposed to Naturalism, which he believed accentuated the animal nature of humans, and to any literature, such as Romanticism, that broke with established classical tradition. He is especially esteemed for the philosophical and literary erudition of his multivolume* Shelburne Essays *(1904-21). In the following essay, taken from that collection, More assesses New-*

man's contributions to nineteenth-century religious thought.]

Almost inevitably the romantic revival of religion in England took its rise at Oxford. From a remote age that university had stood forth again and again in a protest of the heart and the imagination against the rationalizing and utilitarian tendencies of the British character. As far back as the early years of the fourteenth century Richard Rolle of Hampole, who has been called "the true father of English literature," as a student at Oxford started a revolt against the prevailing scholasticism of Duns Scotus; and his reform is not without curious analogies with the movement that was to emanate from Oxford five centuries later. In place of the nominalism of Duns Scotus, which contains the germs of the Protestant appeal to the reason of the individual, Richard proclaimed the mystical principle of love—*universalitas mundialis creaturæ diligere diligique cupit*—and his writings in English and Latin are one long exhortation to the love of God and to the contemplative life which finds its mystical consummation in that divine emotion.

He was the father of a long line of writers and preachers who handed down the tradition of the contemplative life from his own day to Newman's, even to ours—a slender band of other-worldly men who from time to time seem merged and forgotten in the great, ruthless, practical population of England, and of whom our histories of literature speak far too little. In this he was a normal representative of one important and wholesome aspect of human nature; but there was another side to him also, that which may be called the romantic twist to the emotions and is by no means a necessary concomitant of contemplation. In his glorification of the emotions and of the contemplative love of God there was always a lurking element of self-exaltation, and his praises of the secluded life were filled with outbursts of indignation against a society which was only too willing to take him at his word and leave him to his seclusion. He is an early type of the soul that magnifies love and sympathy and at the same time clamours against its isolation in the midst of mankind. He is consumed with *ennui* and the feeling of futility; he cries out to heaven to remove him from a community of fools and worldlings among whom he languished in unregarded uselessness. Like another Carlyle he is afflicted by the very noises of society—*penales sunt mihi vociferantes et crucior quasi per incommodum quando clamor clangentium me tangit.*

This long tradition, in its aspects both of strength and of weakness, must not be forgotten when we consider the ground out of which sprang the Oxford Movement of the nineteenth century; that movement was a part of the great romantic flood that swept over Europe, and owed more to Germany than the men of Oxford were aware of, but it was still primarily English. The immediate impulse came as a reaction against the all-invading Liberal and Erastian notions of the day, and as an attempt to find a substitute within the Church of England for the fervour of Wesleyanism, and for the Evangelicalism which threatened to convert the Church into a weak imitation of Wesley's congregation. The little group of Fellows of Oriel College saw that the enthusiasm of this Evangelical revival had no tenacious anchor in that form of the religious imagination,

that still-brooding celestial love, which is almost inseparable from a humble reverence for tradition; that it was a
kind of emotional effervescence from a utilitarian rationalism and must in the end serve only to strengthen the sway
of irreligion. " 'Unstable as water, it cannot excel,' " Newman was to write of this kind of Protestantism. "It is but
the inchoate state or stage of a doctrine, and its final resolution is in Rationalism. This it has ever shown when suffered to work itself out without interruption." Newman
himself reckoned the active beginning of the propaganda
as coincident with Keble's sermon of July 14, 1833,
against the liberalizing attacks on the Church, and the
first of the Tracts that were to create such a furor was
dated September 9 of the same year. Keble himself, a Fellow of Oriel, though he may be said to have fired the first
gun in the warfare, was not one of the militant saints, and
the brunt of the battle he soon let fall on other shoulders.

Keble found his peace in the quiet ministrations of his parish at Hursley. As did Newman, he looked upon his pupil
at Oriel, Richard Hurrell Froude, brother of the historian,
as the real leader of the movement—or rather instigator,
for Froude was early carried out of active life by ill-health
and died of consumption in 1836, when still a young man.
In the first shock of his loss, it was the brilliance of his intellect that seemed to stand out as his preëminent trait. "I
never, on the whole, fell in with so gifted a person," Newman wrote in a letter the day after hearing of his friend's
death. "In variety and perfection of gifts I think he far exceeded even Keble. For myself, I cannot describe what I
owe to him as regards the intellectual principles of religion
and morals." Brilliant he no doubt was, yet, as one reads
the many testimonies of his character gathered together
in Miss Guiney's biography, it is not so much his intellect
as his audacity that impresses one. He would have been
the Rupert of the war had he lived, dashing into the ranks
of the enemy without fear and without too much circum-
spection. When others doubted, he was sure; and the most
vivid picture we have of him shows him pacing Trinity
Gardens with his hand on the shoulder of a friend, and
saying blithely, "Isaac, we must make a Row in the
world!" Dean Church speaks of his "fiery impetuosity and
the frank daring of his disrespectful vocabulary"; and
James Mozley describes him as hating "the present state
of things so excessively that any change would be a relief
to him." His own mother wrote of him in childhood that
he was "exceedingly impatient under vexatious circumstances; very much disposed to find his own amusement
in teasing and vexing others; and almost entirely incorrigible when it was necessary to reprove him." No, he was not
the intellect of the movement, and even Newman later admits in the *Apologia* that "he had no turn for theology"
and that "his power of entering into the minds of others
was not equal to his other gifts." Had he lived, he would
not have added to the gravity and lasting influence of the
movement, I think; but by his reckless indifference to the
opinion of the world he might have cut short the long hesitation of Newman between the Church of England and
Rome. He would have brought more acrimony into the
debate, but would have deprived it also of much of its profounder significance.

There were other men, important in their day, who fought
by the side of Keble and Froude and Newman, following
them at various distances. Pusey especially should not be
overlooked, whose high Tory connections brought a certain standing to the group of rebels among the Philistines
of the land. One surmises that his social position, quite as
much as his scholarship, caused the name Puseyism to be
attached to the movement in its earlier phases. Pusey was
a laborious student and plunged deep into the German literature of the day in order to combat its infidel tendencies—went so deep that he never quite emerged to the surface. In the long run Newman became the leader and representative of the group, and to-day his commanding personality and the long agony of his conversion alone retain
significance in the common memory, while the other men
are but names of history. Such is the prerogative of genius
that the whole Oxford Movement seems to us now but the
personal concern of a single soul.

John Henry Newman was born in 1801. He was, as were
also by a curious coincidence Manning and Ward, the son
of a London banker. In childhood he read much in the
Arabian Nights and was filled with odd, solitary imagin-
ings. At the age of fifteen he underwent some kind of conversion, the nature of which he has not made perfectly
clear. It was, however, attended with a dedication of himself to missionary or other religious work, and with the
conviction that he should remain a celibate through life.
More important was the strengthening within him of the
feeling, never after that to leave him, which would appear
to be the guiding sense of all deeply religious minds—the
feeling that material phenomena are unreal and that the
only realities are God and the human soul. "From a boy,"
he writes in the midst of his later struggle, "I had been led
to consider that my Maker and I, His creature, were the
two beings, luminously such, *in rerum natura*." From
boyhood, too, he could not look upon the natural world
without a strange sense of baffled illusion. Of all his letters
that I have read, none, perhaps, lets us closer to the secret
of his heart than the one written to his sister in the spring
of 1828, after returning to Oxford from a ride to Cuddes-
don:

> The country, too, is beautiful; the fresh leaves,
> the scents, the varied landscape. Yet I never felt
> so intensely the transitory nature of this world
> as when most delighted with these country
> scenes. And in riding out to-day I have been im-
> pressed more powerfully than before I had an
> idea was possible with the two lines:
>
> "Chanting with a solemn voice
> Minds us of our better choice."
>
> I could hardly believe the lines were not my own,
> and Keble had not taken them from me. I wish
> it were possible for words to put down those in-
> definite, vague, and withal subtle feelings which
> quite pierce the soul and make it sick. . . .
> What a veil and curtain this world of sense is!
> beautiful, but still a veil.

For one who can really understand the meaning of that
letter I suspect the dark places of Newman's career will
have little difficulty. He in whom these words awaken no
response had better lay down his Newman and take up his
Darwin; he will find nothing to concern him in the experi-

ence of a soul to whom, as Newman wrote in another letter, "time is nothing except as the seed of eternity."

In 1817 he went up to Oxford, entering at Trinity College. In 1822 he was elected a Fellow of Oriel, where religion was the one serious topic of the Common Room. Two years later he was ordained, and in 1828, becoming Vicar of St. Mary's, he began those sermons whose restrained eloquence held so many of the young men of Oxford spellbound. What with a less introspective mind would have been an important event was a tour of the Mediterranean taken with Hurrell Froude and his father. As a matter of fact one cannot see from his letters that the view of so many great and memorable scenes of history had much meaning for him. From Rome he wrote that he had "alas, experienced none of that largeness and expansion of mind" which he had been told he "should get from travelling." All his interest was in the journeying of his own soul, which before this had started on the long and obscure road that was to lead it to its spiritual Rome. The actual Rome of the Pope seems to have repelled and attracted him at the same time. Much that he saw there appeared to him "polytheistic, degrading, idolatrous"; but the longing in him was nevertheless increased for reunion with the ancient mother. "Oh, that Rome were not Rome!" he exclaims; "but I seem to see as clear as day that a union with her is *impossible.* She is the cruel Church asking of us impossibilities, excommunicating us for disobedience, and now watching and exulting over our approaching overthrow." At bottom one suspects that this spectacle of the visible centre of Catholicism fixed more deeply in his heart the *desiderium Romæ,* as Erasmus felt and called it, the haunting memory, the "perfume of Rome," which was really but another form of the common romantic homesickness for some place of ideal peace and loveliness where the self-tortured soul may find sympathy and healing for the coldness of this world.

In literature the chief result of the journey was the series of short poems, issued in 1834 in the *Lyra Apostolica.* Those particularly which were written after his almost fatal illness in Sicily are filled with a deep emotional realization of the other world, and belong with the best of England's religious poetry. The stanzas beginning **"Lead, Kindly Light,"** composed on shipboard while sailing from Sicily to Marseilles, express with lyric poignancy the sense of an ever-present divine Providence, but they have become too familiar for quotation. Another poem, written only a few days later at Marseilles, although the last twelve lines were added after the death of Froude, shows how close the world of spirits seemed to Newman's heart, very close yet separated by the strangeness of this earthly veil:

> Do not their souls, who 'neath the Altar wait
>   Until their second birth,
> The gift of patience need, as separate
>   From their first friends of earth?
> Not that earth's blessings are not all outshone
>   By Eden's Angel flame,
> But that earth knows not yet, the Dead has won
>   That crown, which was his aim.
> For when he left it, 't was a twilight scene
>   About his silent bier,

> A breathless struggle, faith and sight between,
>   And Hope and sacred Fear.
> Fear startled at his pains and dreary end,
>   Hope raised her chalice high,
> And the twin-sisters still his shade attend,
>   View'd in the mourner's eye.
> So day by day for him from earth ascends,
>   As steam in summer-even,
> The speechless intercession of his friends,
>   Toward the azure heaven.
> Ah! dearest, with a word he could dispel
>   All questioning, and raise
> Our hearts to rapture, whispering all was well
>   And turning prayer to praise.
> And other secrets too he could declare,
>   By patterns all divine,
> His earthly creed retouching here and there,
>   And deepening every line.
> Dearest! he longs to speak, as I to know,
>   And yet we both refrain:
> It were not good: a little doubt below,
>   And all will soon be plain.

From these personal lines the mind reverts to one of the greatest of Newman's *Parochial Sermons,* that on **"The Invisible World,"** in which, from inability to understand the lower world of animals so real to our physical senses, the preacher argues a like reality for the higher world known to our spiritual senses:

> And yet in spite of this universal world which we see, there is another world, quite as far-spreading, quite as close to us, and more wonderful; another world all around us, though we see it not, and more wonderful than the world we see, for this reason if for no other, that we do not see it. All around us are numberless objects, coming and going, watching, working, or waiting, which we see not: this is that other world, which the eyes reach not unto, but faith only. . . .

> And in that other world are the souls also of the dead. They too, when they depart hence, do not cease to exist, but they retire from this visible scene of things; or, in other words, they cease to act towards us and before us *through our senses.* . . . They remain, but without the usual means of approach towards us, and correspondence with us.

It may not be irrelevant to add that in the words of the poem, *And yet we both refrain: It were not good,* one may come close to the distinction between a vivid faith and the pseudo-science of psychical research, faith resting in profound realization of the different kinds of knowledge, pseudo-science attempting to confuse them together.

Meanwhile the religious situation had become more acute at Oxford, and on returning thither Newman plunged into the thick of the controversy. The famous series of *Tracts for the Times* was begun. The most important of these, Number 90, was written by Newman, and touches the core of the argument. Against the evangelizing and liberalizing tendency of religion at that time, Newman here proclaimed that the Church of England was essentially Catholic and had never accepted the reformed dogmas of the sixteenth century. He attempted to prove, not without some sophistry one is forced to admit, that the Thirty-nine Articles were really not intended to favour the Reformation, but were a loose compromise of contending views, and might best be interpreted as a summary of the old faith with only such verbal concessions to the radical party as the times made necessary. This was in 1841, and within a few months twelve thousand five hundred copies of the Tract had been sold. The storm that broke upon the Tractarians showed what the common sense of England perceived as the logical conclusion of their position. It saw clearly that they were tending, not towards a vague Anglican Catholicism as the Tractarians fondly believed of themselves, but towards the Catholicism of Rome; and to know all that this meant to England one must take into consideration the long history of the land, the plotting and counterplotting that followed the Reformation of Henry VIII and Elizabeth, the horrors of the Gunpowder Plot as it was conceived in the popular mind, the treacheries of Charles II, and the death struggle with the Stuart party of the eighteenth century. And essentially the common sense of England was right. The life of Newman for the next four years was a hidden tragedy in which the protagonists were his loyalty to the national tradition and his logical integrity of mind; and in the end logic with him won the day. In 1843 he resigned the Vicarage of St. Mary's, feeling that he could no longer with honesty preach in an Anglican pulpit. With a band of sympathetic comrades he retired to Littlemore, a suburb of Oxford, where he had built a Chapel of Ease on St. Mary's and converted a row of cottages into a kind of Protestant monastery. Here he set himself to the task of clarifying his own mind by analyzing the office of the church in developing, under divine guidance, the *depositum fidei* which was originally entrusted to it in the Scriptures. In this attempt to reconcile the changes of history with the everlasting immutability of truth, he began with this one assumption as certain: "Whatever history teaches, whatever it omits, whatever it says and unsays, at least the Christianity of history is not Protestantism. . . . To be deep in history is to cease to be a Protestant." Meanwhile the drama of his soul was worked out so quietly and with so little consultation with the world that the final step, however it had been seen in theory, came as a shock even to his friends. Wilfrid Ward, in his *Life of Cardinal Wiseman,* gives a vivid picture of Newman in these days:

> Those who still survive describe him as standing upright at a high desk, writing for hours together—towards the end for fourteen hours in the day—at his book [the *Essay on the Development of Christian Doctrine*]. The younger men looked in awe at their inscrutable Rector, who never spoke (unless in private to Ambrose St. John) of what was in his thoughts, and never gave them an indication that he expected them to take the great step. Day by day he seemed to grow paler, and taller, and thinner—at last almost transparent—as he stood in the light of the sun and worked at his task.

At this time Cardinal Wiseman, desiring to know how Newman stood towards the Roman Church, sent a convert, Mr. Bernard Smith, who had been Newman's curate at Littlemore, to sound him. There is a touch of humour

in the only indication that Newman gave of his position. At dinner-time he appeared and stood for a moment conspicuously in the middle of the room. He wore grey trousers, and Mr. Smith, who was acquainted with Newman's strict adherence to the clerical costume, understood that he no longer regarded himself as a priest of the Church. Shortly after this, Newman invited the Passionist Father Dominic, an Italian, to Littlemore, and on the 8th of October, 1845, he received conditional baptism. On the first day of the month following he was formally confirmed at Oscott by Cardinal Wiseman, and the great conversion was accomplished. But first, to the unfinished manuscript of his *Essay on Development* lying on his desk at Littlemore he had added this paragraph, of which it has been said that it "will be remembered as long as the English language endures":

> Such were the thoughts concerning the "Blessed Vision of Peace," of one whose long-continued petition had been that the Most Merciful would not despise the work of His own Hands, nor leave him to himself;—while yet his eyes were dim, and his breast laden, and he could but employ Reason in the things of Faith. And now, dear Reader, time is short, eternity is long. Put not from you what you have here found; regard it not as mere matter of present controversy; set not out resolved to refute it, and looking about for the best way of doing so; seduce not yourself with the imagination that it comes of disappointment, or disgust, or restlessness, or wounded feeling, or undue sensibility, or other weakness. Wrap not yourself round in the associations of years past, nor determine that to be truth which you wish to be so, nor make an idol of cherished anticipations. Time is short, eternity is long.
>
> NUNC DIMITTIS SERVUM TUUM DOMINE,
> SECUNDUM VERBUM TUUM IN PACE
> QUIA VIDERUNT OCULI MEI SALUTARE
> TUUM.

Newman's act of conversion was, undoubtedly, the most important religious event of England in the nineteenth century—so much, after all, do the struggle and destiny of a great individual soul outweigh in significance the unconscious or undeliberate movements of masses of men. Nor is the process by which he passed from Anglicanism to Romanism hard to follow. We have seen that from boyhood the one reality to him was the existence of his own soul and of God, and we have heard his confession of strange uneasiness in the presence even of the beautiful things of this world. In a passage of the *Apologia* of noble eloquence he deduces his creed quite logically from these feelings:

> Starting then with the being of a God, . . . I look out of myself into the world of men, and there I see a sight which fills me with unspeakable distress. . . . The sight of the world is nothing else than the prophet's scroll, full of "lamentations, and mourning, and woe."
>
> To consider the world in its length and breadth, its various history, the many races of man, their starts, their fortunes, their mutual alienation, their conflicts; and then their ways, habits, gov-

ernments, forms of worship; their enterprises, their aimless courses, their random achievements and acquirements, the impotent conclusion of long-standing facts, the tokens so faint and broken of a superintending design, the blind evolution of what turn out to be great powers or truths, the progress of things, as if from unreasoning elements, not towards final causes, the greatness and littleness of man, his far-reaching aims, his short duration, the curtain hung over his futurity, the disappointments of life, the defeat of good, the success of evil, physical pain, mental anguish, the prevalence and intensity of sin, the pervading idolatries, the corruptions, the dreary hopeless irreligion, that condition of the whole race, so fearfully yet exactly described in the Apostle's words, "having no hope and without God in the world,"—all this is a vision to dizzy and appal; and inflicts upon the mind the sense of a profound mystery, which is absolutely beyond human solution.

. . . And so I argue about the world;—*if* there be a God, *since* there is a God, the human race is implicated in some terrible aboriginal calamity. It is out of joint with the purposes of its Creator. This is a fact, a fact as true as the fact of its existence; and thus the doctrine of what is theologically called original sin becomes to me almost as certain as that the world exists, and as the existence of God.

In these paragraphs, which I have weakened somewhat by condensing, we have expressed, then, the basis of Newman's faith—the two realities of God and of man's fall from God, with the consequent state of the world's misery and blind ignorance. From these two supreme realities, as they seem to him, he argues that it would be perfectly natural to expect, that indeed we must expect, some clear instrument of revelation, or provision of the Creator, "for retaining in the world a knowledge of Himself, so definite and destined as to be a proof against the energy of human scepticism." This was Newman's creed when he went up to Oxford, it was his creed when he retired to Littlemore, and it was his creed when he wore the cardinal. The only difference lay in his conception of the manner in which this divine provision, or instrument of revelation, manifested itself to mankind. And his change in this respect may be expressed in a series of exclusions. To Newman it seemed that the minds of men were sharply divided, in accordance with their ways of regarding revelation, into the Roman Catholic, the Anglican, the Protestant, and the rationalistic. The last-named condition, rationalism, as it left no place for an absolute revelation, was immediately excluded by him; it was abhorrent to everything his nature craved. There remained the three forms of Christianity. But of these, Protestantism was also excluded, because he saw at once, and rightly, I think, that its certain goal was rationalism. Protestantism, as he properly used the word, differs from the Anglican and Roman creeds in looking to the Bible alone for its source of revelation, and in making the individual mind the judge of what the Bible teaches instead of subordinating the judgement of the individual to the authority of the Fathers and of the Church. Now it is clear, if the reason of the individual is to determine the meaning of revelation, that reason is the ultimate authori-

ty, and the step to rationalism is easy and inevitable. This was seen perfectly well by the controversialists of the seventeenth century, and the great bulwark of Protestantism, Chillingworth's *The Religion of Protestants a Safe Way to Salvation,* or, as one of the books of that work is entitled, *Scripture the only Rule whereby to judge of Controversies,* was a long and, it must be said, fundamentally unsuccessful attempt to rebut just such charges made against Protestantism by a certain Jesuit, Matthias Wilson, who wrote under the name of Edward Knott. History was on the side of the Jesuit, for it can be demonstrated that the deistic rationalism of the eighteenth century was a direct outcome of the Protestant rationalism of such writers as Chillingworth; and again in the nineteenth century Newman perceived that this same close kinship existed between the Protestant, or Evangelical, wing of the Church and the rationalistic and scientific tendencies of his own day.

Protestantism of the Bible was therefore excluded by Newman for a Church which claimed a direct authority outside of and supplementary to, though never subversive of, the Bible. His principal work, before his final conversion, was *The Via Media,* an endeavour to maintain the supremacy of the Anglican creed as a middle and safe way between Protestantism and Roman Catholicism. His argument, in brief, is this. He agrees with Rome in demanding some instrument of revelation outside of the individual's understanding of the Bible, some authority which can answer directly and unmistakably the many questions which

Newman as portrayed by George Richmond in 1844.

the Bible leaves obscure, and he agrees with Rome in holding that the only authority which has the divine commission to answer such questions is the Church. But he differs from Rome in defining the Church. The voice of the Church with him is in the writings of the Fathers and the decisions of the Councils up to a certain point of time. That is to say, up to and including the Council of Nicæa the Church, he thought, was united and authoritative in its interpretation and expansion of the faith, or *depositum fidei,* which was originally entrusted to it. After that date the Councils ceased to represent the whole Christian community and were subject to errors of passion and judgement. Newman at this time made much of the famous saying of St. Vincent of Lerins, *Quod semper, quod ubique, quod ab omnibus* (What has been believed always, everywhere, and by all); as a matter of fact he accepted the *ubique* and the *ab omnibus,* but rejected the *semper.* The true reformation adopted by Anglicanism was, in his view, merely a return to the ancient and universal faith of the Church by eliminating the false accretions which had been added since the Council of Nicæa and which constituted the corruptions of the Roman branch of the Church; Anglicanism was truly catholic; Romanism was sectarian.

But Newman's logical mind soon found this position as difficult to hold as that of Bible Protestantism which he had so summarily rejected. For, after all, what is the essential difference between clinging to one particular book as the sole depository of faith and accepting the books of a determined period? The Fathers and Councils must be interpreted, and selection must be made among their various sayings, by the individual reason just as in the case of the Bible. The distinction is one of magnitude only, not of kind. Against this need of interpreting the Bible or a closed set of books, Rome upheld the institution of the Church, as a living voice having divine authority to answer the questions of men as they arise and to develop the faith in accordance with the growth of human knowledge. Grant Newman's unshakable demand for a distinct verbal revelation, grant his demand for a rigidly logical and external authority, and the path would seem to be step by step to Rome.

Yet I confess I have never been able to follow him in his course without a feeling of uneasiness, and that feeling has been deepened into something like distress by reading the authoritative record of his life [Wilfrid Ward's *The Life of John Henry Cardinal Newman,* 1912]. The very plan of Mr. Ward's work is of a sort to raise disquieting questions. It gives only a single chapter to the events of Newman's life down to and including his conversion, and devotes the remainder of two bulky volumes to his experiences in the Roman Church. For this outrageous disproportion Mr. Ward is not altogether responsible. The story of the early years and conversion has already been related by Newman himself in the **Apologia,** and this has been supplemented by the two volumes of his letters edited by Miss Mozley. It was Newman's own desire that nothing should be added to those records by his present official biographer. Mr. Ward's work, therefore, should properly be read, not as a complete and independent memoir, but as a continuation of Miss Mozley's record. I am bound to say, however, that, even with this reservation, the present volumes err

somewhat in proportion. Newman was seldom at his best as a letter-writer, and a good deal of the correspondence now printed is neither necessary to an understanding of Newman's character nor entertaining in itself. For the rest, Mr. Ward's difficult task has been admirably and courageously carried through. When he himself takes the pen in hand his narrative and characterization are clear, succinct, and interesting.

But with all Mr. Ward's tact and despite his good faith as a Catholic, one cannot close these two volumes without feeling that Newman's surrender to the appeal of Rome was a pathetic mistake. It was as if the convert, by altering his direction, had suddenly brought himself face to face with a stone wall. To every plan he broached for new activity came the benumbing reply, *Non possumus.* He was hemmed in, barked at by opposition on every side, beaten down by exasperating distrust and envy. Mr. Ward tells with valiant honesty all the plans of the convert that were balked in one way or another. The difficulties that beset him as editor, as rector of the Irish Catholic University, and as promoter of a propaganda in Oxford to influence the intellectual life of England, are typical of his career. In the end, when his active years were past and he could no longer disturb those in authority, he received due recognition in the Cardinalate, and his closing days were, we like to believe, crowned with a great peace. It is true also that more than once in his bitter years, with a tone of conviction it would be dishonourable to doubt, he repudiated the suggestion of regret over his move. In his saddest moment he could write—*ex animo,* as he said—"that Protestantism is the dreariest of possible religions." He could distinguish clearly between the Church and its rulers:

> To-day is the 20th anniversary of my setting up
> the Oratory in England, and every year I have
> more to thank God for, and more cause to re-
> joice that He helped me over so great a crisis.—
> Since A.B. obliges me to say it, this I cannot
> omit to say:—I have found in the Catholic
> Church abundance of courtesy, but very little
> sympathy, among persons in high place, except
> a few—but there is a depth and a power in the
> Catholic religion, a fulness of satisfaction in its
> creed, its theology, its rites, its sacraments, its
> discipline, a freedom yet a support also, before
> which the neglect or the misapprehension about
> oneself on the part of individual living persons,
> however exalted, is as so much dust, when
> weighed in the balance. This is the true secret of
> the Church's strength, the principle of its inde-
> fectibility, and the bond of its indissoluble unity.
> It is the earnest and the beginning of the repose
> of heaven.

Yet it is true nevertheless that he resented keenly and sometimes denounced sharply not only the thwarting of his personal ambitions, but also the limitations imposed upon his intellectual and spiritual mission. He who felt himself born to be a leader of his people found himself suddenly thrust into ignoble obscurity. To his beloved Ambrose St. John he wrote, in 1857: "To the rising generation, to the sons of those who knew me, or read what I wrote fifteen or twenty years ago, I am a mere page of history. . . . It was at Oxford, and by my Parochial sermons, that I had influence—all that is past." And three years later, in the intimacy of his diary, he could exclaim: "O my God, I seem to have wasted these years that I have been a Catholic. What I wrote as a Protestant has had far greater power, force, meaning, success than my Catholic works, and this troubles me a great deal." It is not strange that his inner vision was at times perturbed, his faith almost touched. "As years go on," he records in his diary, "I have less sensible devotion and inward life." He even notes a change in his physical expression: "Till the affair of No. ninety and my going to Littlemore, I had my mouth half open, and commonly a smile on my face—and from that time onwards my mouth has been closed and contracted, and the muscles are so set now, that I cannot but look grave and forbidding." Inevitably, as this feeling of failure and loneliness deepened, he contrasted the poverty of the present with the actual power and richer promise of his Oxford career. There is a pathetic letter written in 1863 to Keble, who had started on the path with him, or even before him, but had drawn back at the edge of the precipice—a letter whose closing words are, as it were, the revelation of a great and hidden tragedy:

> I have said all this, knowing it will interest you. Never have I doubted for one moment your affection for me, never have I been hurt at your silence. I interpreted it easily—it was not the silence of others. It was not the silence of men, nor the forgetfulness of men, who can recollect about me and talk about me enough, when there is something to be said to my disparagement. You are always with me a thought of reverence and love, and there is nothing I love better than you, and Isaac, and Copeland, and many others I could name, except Him Whom I ought to love best of all and supremely. May He Himself, Who is the over-abundant compensation for all losses, give me His own Presence, and then I shall want nothing and desiderate nothing, but none *but* He *can* make up for the loss of those old familiar faces which haunt me continually.

It would be easy to exaggerate, possibly the tone of Mr. Ward's narrative tempts one to exaggerate, the sadder aspect of Newman's life in the Catholic Church. It must not be forgotten that his *Apologia,* which contains some of the most beautiful religious writing of the age, his *Idea of a University,* and other works which will not be forgotten, were written after his conversion. Yet withal it is hard to avoid the conclusion that in a purely literary way something was lost to him when he severed himself from the tradition in which his imagination and feelings were so deeply rooted. The mere physical change from the glories and haunting memories of the colleges of Oxford to the crudeness of the Oratory at Edgbaston took away one of the props of his imagination. The knowledge that he no longer belonged to the faith of the great body of his countrymen, but was regarded by them, whether rightly or wrongly, as one of a sect, deprived him of that support of sympathy which was necessary to the full unfolding of his genius. And the loss was not Newman's alone, but ours and all men's. At the close of the chapter which includes the conversion Mr. Ward quotes the beautiful words of Principal Shairp on the effect of what seemed to Anglicans an act of apostasy:

How vividly comes back the remembrance of the aching blank, the awful pause, which fell on Oxford when that voice had ceased, and we knew that we should hear it no more. It was as when, to one kneeling by night, in the silence of some vast cathedral, the great bell tolling solemnly overheard has suddenly gone still. To many, no doubt, the pause was not of long continuance. Soon they began to look this way and that for new teachers, and to rush vehemently to the opposite extremes of thought. But there were those who could not so lightly forget. All the more these withdrew into themselves. On Sunday forenoons and evenings, in the retirement of their rooms, the printed words of those marvellous sermons would thrill them till they wept "abundant and most sweet tears." Since then many voices of powerful teachers they may have heard, but none that ever penetrated the soul like his.

With no desire to intrude into the debate between Anglican and Roman, with interest centered rather upon the purely human aspect of the act, one may well feel, even to-day, something of that deep chagrin which Principal Shairp and Matthew Arnold and other contemporaries expressed. Not for Oxford controversialists alone, but for all who draw their spiritual sustenance from English literature, that event was, if not the silencing, at least the muffling, of a magic voice.

Newman, as we have seen, was led to take the fatal step by strictly logical deductions. Grant his premises, that the human mind is confined to a choice within the circle of religious authority and rationalism, and it is easy to follow him on his path to Rome. But the question remains whether this circle is indeed the boundary of man's intellectual and spiritual power. Certainly beyond the reach of rationalism, or science, to use its modern equivalent, there lies the purely sceptical habit; and there are those who will maintain that in the other direction, beyond the utmost bounds of dogma and revelation, they have discerned, more or less clearly, a realm of pure religious intuition which is reserved for the mystical eye. Now if we try to determine in what way Newman's inner circle of revelation and science is separated from the outer circle of mysticism and scepticism which he barely touched, we shall find no better mark of distinction than in the attitude of the mind, in one and the other circle, towards the unrelated details of experience. Using this criterion, we shall see that in the circle of revelation and science (philosophical science, that is, as the modern form of rationalism) the mind relaxes its grip to a certain extent on the insistent reality of details or individual moments of experience in order to preserve its belief in the universality of some supposed personal force or of some natural law; whereas in the circle of the mystic and the sceptic the mind never relaxes its grip on the individual detail for such a personal or material law. It may sound somewhat paradoxical to bring revelation and science together in such a bond, and indeed in one sense there is a real difference between the two, in so far as religion has to do with a spiritual experience while science is concerned with physical or material experience; but in their manner of dealing with these two kinds of experience they are in accord. The man to whom religion means revelation only, holds resolutely to the reality of a personal God, at once Creator and Providence, who reveals himself by the voice of authority, whether written or spoken. It makes no difference to him that creeds have changed from age to age, or that a thousand creeds exist side by side, or that this or that moment of his experience seems to contradict such a belief: his belief abides. And so with the man of science. He holds resolutely to the reality of some infallible natural cause controlling the world, which reveals itself by tradition and experiment. It makes no difference to him that the formulation of this cause has changed from age to age, or that a host of contradictory formulæ exist side by side, or that individual experiments are constantly forcing him to question his scientific belief: his belief abides. Such a definition of the scientific method may seem contrary to what is commonly held, for we are apt to think of science as the habit of mind which searches for and clings to the actual individual fact independently of presupposition or theory and regardlessly of consequence; and science in its positive form may be of that character. But the rationalistic science of which I speak, the science which really counts and which colours to-day our popular philosophies, is of quite another sort. Take as an illustration the present state of evolutionary biology: what is the actual practice of the leading biologists? They all, or nearly all, start with the presupposition that the whole animate world is developing under some evolutionary cause which has been, or can be, discovered and formulated. To one biologist this cause is the survival of the fit, to another it is Lamarckianism, or othogenesis, or mutation, or kinetogenesis, or metakinesis, or orthoplasy, or—who shall say what? I quote a strange language ignorantly. The theories differ, are indeed often diametrically opposed, but the method of theorizing is always the same. Having observed a certain number of phenomena the biologist proceeds to formulate from them his notion of the evolutionary cause. But to do this he inevitably neglects, it may be by an unconscious absorption or it may be by half dishonest closing of the eyes, all the phenomena that will not fit into his formula. Then comes a brother theorist who takes part of these neglected phenomena and builds up a different formula. The point is that this rationalistic form of science depends on an invincible belief in some universal law of nature, and on a tendency to overlook if necessary the individual phenomenon in favour of this law. The various theories "keep and pass and turn again," but the faith in theory, like the Brahma of the poem, abides unshaken:

I am the doubter and the doubt.

I cannot see that the method differs one whit from that of the dogmatist in religion: the one, maintaining his faith in an unvarying cause, and untroubled by refractory details, formulates his experience with material phenomena into a scientific hypothesis; the other, holding fast to his faith in God's revelation of himself to the human soul, expands his inner experience into a mythology, unconcerned by individual facts that cannot be reconciled to his creed. And just as these two methods agree together, so they differ in the same way from the habit of mind of the sceptic and mystic. As a confirmation of this agreement and difference you will find that the dogmatist, whose religion is confined

to revelation, and the rationalistic man of science may in the long run come together, are actually coming together today. It is a notable fact that Newman's doctrine of development is taken by the modernists as a substantial bond between revelation and evolution. Both dogmatist and scientist avert their faces from the outer ring of the mystic and the sceptic. On the other hand, it was perfectly easy for a sceptic like Sainte-Beuve to enter into the mind of a mystic such as Pascal, while Pascal himself avowed explicitly his supreme scepticism.

The genuine sceptic is very rare, but his characteristics may be known by comparing such a mind as Sainte-Beuve's with Taine's. Both men wrote much on literature, but they approached the subject in utterly different ways. Taine believed that an absolute law could be found for determining why a particular sort of writing should appear at any time. Given a complete knowledge of an author's race, environment, and epoch, his works could be analyzed as accurately as a chemist analyzes the ingredients of sugar or vitriol. This is the famous formula on which he based his *History of English Literature;* it is, as you see, the extreme application of the scientific or rationalistic method, and Taine is properly regarded as the father of scientific criticism. In his essay on Taine's *History,* Sainte-Beuve observes that such a formula, however interesting it may be, errs in leaving out of account the inexplicable and unpredictable personal equation of the writer himself. Here was the individual fact which no extent of knowledge could bring under scientific rule, but which must be held and considered in itself. And exactly here lies the distinction between the scientific and the sceptical attitude of mind—on the one side the dominating desire to correlate individual facts by means of a general cause, on the other side the grasp of the individual fact at all hazards and through all losses. Sainte-Beuve liked to think of himself as a scientific investigator, and so far as that phrase applies to laborious painstaking he is justified; but his interest clung always to the individual phenomenon and not to the general cause, and in this respect he was, I think, the most perfect example of the sceptic in modern times. Whither his scepticism led him may be known by reading the great and melancholy confession which he wrote down at the end of his long labours on the *Port-Royal.* There, too, he calls himself a servant of science and a man of truth, as indeed he was; yet he continues—

> But even that, how little it is! how limited is our view! how quickly it reaches an end! how it resembles a pale torch lighted for a moment in the midst of a vast darkness! and how he who desires most earnestly to know his subject, who is most ambitious to seize it and has most pride in depicting it, feels himself impotent and unequal to his task, on that day when, in the presence of the finished work and the result obtained, the intoxication of his energy passes away, when the final exhaustion and the inevitable distaste come over him, and when he, too, perceives that he is only a fleeting illusion in the bosom of the infinite Illusion.

That is the confession of a mind not essentially scientific but sceptical, the certain sad conclusion of one who grasps each experience as it arises, who will not relax his hold at the bidding of any command or authority or inner need, and who sees nothing in life but these unrelated experiences. And at the other extreme, beyond the believer in authority and revelation in whatsoever form, is the mystic, who, like the sceptic, keeps a firm grip on phenomena as they appear and sees in them only illusion and no ruling of Providence or of a definable law, but who, unlike the sceptic, knows within himself an infinite something, unnamed, indefinable, the one absolute reality. I scarcely know where to turn in modern times for an example of the perfect mystic. Tennyson in some of his utterances crossed the dark border, but Tennyson's mind was too much concerned also with the dominant theories of his day to afford the desired model. Certainly Newman, essentially religious as his temper was in some respects, stopped short of this last step. In my study there hang side by side the portraits of the great Cardinal and the great critic, and I often compare their faces as types of two of the master tendencies of the nineteenth century. In the firm, sinuous line of Sainte-Beuve's mouth, in the penetrating, self-contained glance of the eyes, and in the smooth capaciousness of the brow with the converging furrows of concentration over the nose, I see the supreme expression of an intelligence that saw all, and comprehended all, and retained every detail, surrendering nothing of itself; but of faith or religious submission I discover no look or mark. And then I turn to the other portrait. Cardinal Newman, as we have seen, speaks of the contraction of his features under the stress of his new life. The word, to one who examines the engraving of Timothy Cole after the painting by Ouless, does not seem quite precise. The marks of struggle are visible enough, but signs of contraction, in the sense of hardening or strengthening, I do not see. The mouth is strong, but the lines are a little relaxed; the eyes are veiled and look wistfully beyond what is immediately before them to some visionary hope; the brow is high and wrinkled transversely from the perplexity of an inner conflict. Something has gone out of this face, the contact with individual facts has been broken, and in its place has come the sweetness of self-surrender, the submissive pride of one who has given up much that he may find all—if haply he has found.

This, in the end, must be our reservation in the praise due to Newman's beautiful life, that he stopped short of the purest faith. He was born a man with deep religious needs and instincts, a man to whom the spiritual world was the absorbing reality, beside which the material world and its appearances were but as shadows gathered in a dream. But he was born also in an age when the old faith in an outer authority based on an exact and unequivocal revelation could be maintained only by doing violence to the integrity of the believer's mind. That was his dilemma, and there lay the tragedy of his choice. Two ways were open to him. On the one hand, he might have accepted manfully the sceptical demolition of the Christian mythology and the whole fabric of external religion, and on the ruins of such creeds he might have risen to that supreme insight which demands no revelation and is dependent on no authority, but is content within itself. Doing this he might possibly, by the depth of his religious nature and the eloquence of his tongue, have made himself the leader of the elect out of the long spiritual death that is likely to follow the breaking-up of the creeds. Or, if that task seemed impossible or

fraught with too great peril, he might have held to the national worship as a symbol of the religious experience of the people, and into that worship and that symbol he might have breathed the new fervour of his own faith, waiting reverently until by natural growth his people were prepared, if ever they should be prepared, to apprehend with him the invisible truth without the forms. It is written: "Blessed are they that have not seen, and yet have believed." But in the hour of need his heart failed him, and he demanded to see with his eyes and feel with his hands. He was not strong enough to hold fast to the actual discords of life and to discern his vision of peace apart from their illusory sphere, but found it necessary to warp the facts of spiritual experience so as to make them agree with a physical revelation. There is a sentence in a letter of Cardinal Wiseman which comes naturally to memory when one thinks of the agony through which the later prelate was to pass. Speaking of his own struggle as a young man in Rome, Wiseman wrote:

> I was fighting with subtle thoughts and venomous suggestions of a fiendlike infidelity which I durst not confide to any one, for there was no one that could have sympathized with me. This lasted for years; but it made me study and think, to conquer the plague—for I can hardly call it danger—both for myself and for others. . . . But during the actual struggle the simple submission of faith is the only remedy. Thoughts against faith must be treated at the time like temptations against any other virtue—put away.

There is the quick of the matter: *thoughts against faith must be treated at the time like temptations against any other virtue—put away.* The sentiment, it must be admitted, recalls a little the original metaphor of Hobbes: "For it is with the mysteries of our religion as with wholesome pills for the sick, which, swallowed whole, have the virtue to cure, but, chewed, are for the most part cast up again without effect." The same idea occurs over and over again in Newman's writings, is, in fact, the very basis of his **Grammar of Assent** and of his logical system. If we look closely into the reasoning by which he was driven step by step from Anglicanism to complete surrender to the authority of Rome, we shall see that his logic rests on an initial assumption which implies a certain lack of the highest faith and of that sceptical attitude towards our human needs upon which faith must ultimately rest. No doubt the same charge might in a way be laid against all those who from the beginning have professed a definite religious belief. Certainly this weakness, if we may so call it, is almost inextricably bound up with the Christian conception of the deity and of salvation; and one might retort that, if the religious course of Newman can be condemned as a defection from the purest insight, the same condemnation must apply to the great writers of the seventeenth century. We may admit the retort, and yet see a difference. The very fact that the central idea of a definite revelation had not yet been completely undermined permitted the men of that earlier age to accept it more naïvely, so to speak, and without so grave a surrender of their mental integrity. If the writings of such men as Henry More and the other Platonists of the seventeenth century give us a sense of freedom and enlargement which we cannot quite get from

Cardinal Newman, it is because these earlier theologians, notwithstanding their apparent dogmatism, were in reality akin to the mystics of all ages who find their peace in a faith that needs no surrender. Pascal was in a sense one of the forerunners of modern romanticism, and there is unquestionably a taint of morbidness in his practices; yet, withal, Pascal was saved by his scepticism, and beneath his apology for a fading mythology one may penetrate to the depths of the purest spiritual faith. For me, at least, there is a change in passing from these men to Newman. Say what one will, there was something in Newman's conversion of failure in duty, a betrayal of the will. In succumbing to an authority which promised to allay the anguish of his intellect, he rejected the great mission of faith, and committed what may almost be called the *gran rifiuto.* In the agony of his conversion and in his years of poignant dejection there is something of the note of modern romanticism intruding into religion. His inability to find peace without the assurance of a personal God answering to the clamour of his desires is but another aspect of that illusion of the soul which has lost its vision of the true infinite and seeks a substitute in the limitless expansion of the emotions. It has happened to me sometimes, while reflecting on Newman clothed in the cardinal and crowned with ecclesiastical honours, that, as by a trick of the imagination, I have been carried back to the vast hall to which Vathek came at the end of his journey, and that, looking intently and reverently at the sublime figure on his throne, I have "discerned through his bosom, which was transparent as crystal, his heart enveloped in flames." I have turned away in sadness and awe from the face of one who had perhaps the finest religious nature of the age, yet failed his country at her hour of greatest need.

But it would be presumptuous to end in such a strain. As we think of the many forces that were shaping the thoughts and ambitions of the century from which we have just emerged, of its dark materialism, its intellectual pride, its greed of novelty, its lust of change, its cruel egotism and blind penance of sympathy, its wandering virtues and vices, its legacy of spiritual bewilderment—as we think of all these, then let us remember also how the great convert surrendered these things and counted them as dust in the balance beside the vision of his own soul face to face with God. It may be that his seclusion in the Oratory at Edgbaston was not unrelated to the almost inevitable inability of the romantic temperament to live in harmony with society; but it sprang also from a nobler discontent. Who will be brave to assert that his prayers and penance were wasted? We of to-day need his example and may be the better for it, and life will be a little darker when his struggle and conquest are forgotten. Criticism may well stand abashed before that life. More than that, it would be uncritical not to remember that the **Oxford University Sermons,** however they may point forward to what we were bound to regard as an act of defection, contain in themselves perhaps the noblest appeals in the English tongue to the hazard of the soul. They may well stand preëminent among those witnesses to "the victory of Faith over the world's power" which their author has so passionately celebrated:

To see its triumph over the world's wisdom, we

must enter those solemn cemeteries in which are stored the relics and the monuments of ancient Faith—our libraries. Look along their shelves, and every name you read there is, in one sense or other, a trophy set up in record of the victories of Faith. How many long lives, what high aims, what single-minded devotion, what intense contemplation, what fervent prayer, what deep erudition, what untiring diligence, what toilsome conflicts has it taken to establish its supremacy! This has been the object which has given meaning to the life of Saints, and which is the subject-matter of their history. For this they have given up the comforts of earth and the charities of home, and surrendered themselves to an austere rule, nay, even to confessorship and persecution, if so be they could make some small offering, or do some casual service, or provide some additional safeguard towards the great work which was in progress.

(pp. 39-79)

Paul Elmer More, "Cardinal Newman," in his The Drift of Romanticism: Shelburne Essays, *eighth series, Houghton Mifflin Company, 1913, pp. 39-79.*

Augustine Birrell on Newman's style:

The charm of Dr. Newman's style necessarily baffles description: as well might one seek to analyse the fragrance of a flower, or to expound in words the jumping of one's heart when a beloved friend unexpectedly enters the room. It is hard to describe charm.

One can, of course, heap on words. Dr. Newman's style is pellucid, it is animated, it is varied; at times icy cold, it oftener glows with a fervent heat; it employs as its obedient and well-trained servant a vast vocabulary, and it does so always with the ease of the educated gentleman, who by a sure instinct ever avoids alike the ugly pedantry of the bookworm, the forbidding accents of the lawyer, and the stiff conceit of the man of scientific theory. Dr. Newman's sentences sometimes fall upon the ear like well-considered and final judgments, each word being weighed and counted out with dignity and precision; but at other times the demeanour and language of the judge are hastily abandoned, and, substituted for them, we encounter the impetuous torrent—the captivating rhetoric, the brilliant imagery, the frequent examples, the repetition of the same idea in different words, of the eager and accomplished advocate addressing men of like passions with himself.

Augustine Birrell, in his Collected Essays and Addresses, *Vol. II, 1923.*

Joseph Ellis Baker   (essay date 1931)

[*Baker is an American educator, editor, and critic who has written and edited several studies on English literature of the Victorian era. In the following excerpt, part of a doctoral dissertation submitted by Baker to Princeton University in 1931, he examines the style and con-*

tent of Newman's novels as expressions of the author's thought and temperament.]

John Henry Newman wrote two novels, both portraying a development of mind somewhat similar to his own,—a development which, for him, culminated in one of the most important events in the history of the Church since the Reformation, his conversion to Rome. Since fiction is freer than history, some of Newman's spiritual experiences are suggested here that are not set forth in the *Apologia*. *Loss and Gain* appeared in 1848, only three years after his conversion, and it reflects immediately the Oxford phase of the Movement. In the summer of 1847, some tale directed against the converts to the Catholic faith had been sent to Newman. "Its contents were as wantonly and preposterously fanciful, as they were injurious to those whose motives and actions it professed to represent; but a formal criticism . . . seemed . . . out of place. The suitable answer lay rather in the publication of a second tale; drawn up with a stricter regard to truth and probability, and with at least some personal knowledge of Oxford, and some perception of the various aspects of the religious phenomenon, which the work in question handled so rudely and unskilfully." The result was *Loss and Gain: The Story of a Convert*, a realistic novel of contemporary life in form largely argumentative dialogue. It is austerely barren of the pleasures of plot. Charles Reding, son of an old-fashioned clergyman of the Church of England, goes to Oxford and becomes interested in Catholicism. Suspected of being more Roman than is strictly true at the time, he is sent home from college. Because of the distractions of religious uncertainty, he fails in the examination for honours. He even postpones taking his B.A. because of conscientious difficulties in subscribing to the Articles. The conviction that Rome is the only true Church grows on him. At last, after various sects try to win him, he joins the Church of Rome.

In the early spring of the same year that *Loss and Gain* was published, Newman also began what was to become the sub-plot of *Callista: A Sketch of the Third Century*, writing then parts of chapters I, IV, and V, and sketching the character and fortunes of Juba. A year later, in a letter of February 28, 1849, he says, speaking of historical work:

> What I should like would be to bring out the ηθος of the Heathen from St. Paul's day down to St. Gregory, when under the process, or in the sight of the phenomenon, of conversion; what conversion *was* in those times, and what the position of a Christian in that world of sin, what the sophistries of philosophy viewed as realities influencing men. But besides the great difficulty of finding time, I don't think I could do it from History. I despair of finding facts enough—as if an imaginary tale could alone embody the conclusions to which existing facts *lead* [quoted in Wilfrid Ward's *The Life of John Henry Cardinal Newman*, 1912].

Evidently the general idea of what became the main plot of *Callista* was beginning to take shape in his mind. He did nothing more with this story for six years. In July, 1855, he suddenly resumed it and completed it in a few months. It appeared in 1856. Kingsley's *Hypatia*, published three years before, had offended the more Catholic party in the Church of England with its tolerance of pagan thought and its attack on monasticism among the early Christians. The purpose of Newman's novel is the opposite, that is, "to imagine and express, from a Catholic point of view, the feelings and mutual relations of Christians and heathens at the period to which it belongs." This, too, is a story of conversion, and hence its basis in the author's own experience lay in the period when he was yet an Anglican. It is something of a historical romance, something of a saint's life, something of a psychological study, and, though less so than *Loss and Gain,* something of a series of arguments. Agellius, a Christian, loves Callista, a Greek girl who works for his uncle. Though a pagan, she is interested in hearing about Christianity. Since a plague of locusts is ascribed to the presence of the Christians, a mob rises against them. In its wild fury it captures Callista at the hut of Agellius. In prison, she finally joins the Church, and becomes a martyr and saint. Her body works miracles, for instance curing of his madness Juba, brother of Agellius, who had been under the evil influence of their mother, the witch Gurta.

Although the advertisement of 1848 states specifically that *Loss and Gain* is not the history of any individual mind among the recent converts, we now know enough of Newman's life to show that he has drawn largely upon his own experience, even to many details. The hero, like the author, was retiring and over-sensitive, and in his first years at college he was much alone. Like Newman, he stood for honours and failed. Mr. [J. J. Reilly, in his *Newman as a Man of Letters,* 1925] points out that both were impatient of party men and "mere talkers," expressed a love of Gregorian music, and that "the 'Father Dominic', a Passionist born in Italy, who received Reding into the Church, was the same" in name and antecedents as he who received Newman himself. We may add that both felt from boyhood that they should remain celibate. Both delayed their entrance into the Catholic Church for a long time to be sure that they were not deluded. And Reding's estrangement from Sheffield is paralleled by Newman's from Frederic Rogers, long his most intimate friend. Like Reding and Sheffield, they had roomed on the same staircase at Oxford. On the other hand, it seems to have been an event in the life of another, a Mr. Morris, that suggested the incident in which Charles is sent home from college because of coming into conflict with his college authority over his belief in the Intercession of the Saints. Like Mr. Morris, Reding in the novel draws a distinction between Intercession and Invocation. But Reding is not Newman, and the Oxford Movement in which he is taking part has been sketched with the central figure omitted. There is a passing reference to the preaching at St. Mary's, but we miss entirely the politics, parties, combat, leadership, action of corporate bodies, and attempts to influence public opinion, which are part of the Movement. The author's gaze is turned inward upon the development of an individual soul.

As we might expect from so skillful a controversialist as Newman, his novels are largely devoted to presenting Catholic doctrines and portraying Catholic practices. That he wished some of the discussions in *Loss and Gain* to be received as serious explanations of his views is indicated by a passage in a letter written thirty-one years later: "And now I go on to the relation of the will to assent . . . as to which . . . I have not made my doctrine quite clear to you in the passage in *Loss and Gain*." He then analyzes in detail the passage in question. Sometimes Newman embodies his ideas in concrete events. Baptism suddenly produced in Callista a serenity different from anything she had ever before the power of conceiving. But more often he pushes the story aside and presents his arguments directly, putting them into the mouth of a figure who seldom exists as anything more than a mouth from which comes forth theory. Occasionally he rejects even this ghost of narrative and speaks out from the page *in propria persona*,—as when he opens a chapter [in *Loss and Gain*] by arguing that, "There is no . . . inconsistency in a person first using his private judgment [to reach Catholicism] and then denouncing its use," or when he defends dogma by saying that unless there is one center on which the mind sits men will be inconsistent, but real liberty consists in being subject to truth. Now that Newman has left the Anglican Church, it is interesting to see how he answers the thesis of his own *Tract 90,* which caused the series to be stopped: The argument is that the Articles may be given a Catholic interpretation. Charles' reply is that the English Church *might* have adopted this interpretation, but did not. Among the other subjects dealt with in the novels are the Apostolic Succession, Mass, Vestments, Confession, the Supremacy of Rome, Devotion to the Blessed Virgin.

Newman's chief opponent, Kingsley, preaching a Christianity that considered physical well-being a valuable aid to a Christian life, had prefaced *Hypatia* with an attack on asceticism. Newman takes the other side. When Callista's health is injured by the heat of the prison and she loses her former beauty, he tells us that rudiments of a diviner loveliness were taking its place. And Charles Reding says, "the idea of an apostle, unmarried, pure, in fast and nakedness, at length a martyr, is a higher idea than that of one of the old Israelites sitting under his vine and fig-tree, full of temporal goods, and surrounded by sons and grandsons." Charles says he fancied that fasting, abstinence, and celibacy might be taken as a make-up for sin. When Callista asked to be made a Christian, there was an "utter disappearance of that majesty of mien . . . a gift, so beautiful, so unsuitable to fallen man. . . . She had lost every vestige of what the world worships under the titles of proper pride and self-respect." Proud liberty of intellect is denounced. We are shown the fate of Juba, brother of the hero, who, for his free-thinking, is punished with madness, being possessed with an evil spirit. Against his will, Juba falls on his knees before an idol of Pan, laps up the blood of sacrifice, and among other horrible things spouts a chorus of Greek, a language he had never heard before. But even while yet a maniac, he has changed for the better, we are told, for his expression of pride is gone. The sign of the cross he cannot resist in spite of manifest antagonism. At last, after Callista's death, he is forced to touch the feet of her corpse. The evil spirit goes out, leaving him an idiot. Newman's direct argument for belief in miracles is much more plausible than this concrete illustration. But this part of the tale is one of the most interesting of the Catholic attacks upon the scepticism of Victorian science, and one of the strangest fruits of a strange imagination. The nineteenth century, for all its Medievalizing, seldom came nearer to producing something that might really have been written during the Middle Ages, for this incident is surrounded with no atmosphere of romantic distance. And whatever the faults of Newman as an historical novelist, we cannot accuse him of being out of sympathy with his subject. Indeed, his mind preferred to dwell in centuries earlier than the Medieval. It was to the writers of the first Christian centuries that he went for guidance. "The Fathers," he said [in his *Certain Difficulties Felt by Anglicans,* 1850], "made me a Catholic." Indeed, he himself seems to belong with the early Christians. Was not the decaying empire of pagan culture destroyed by just such penetrating dogmatism and subtle patience, sacrificing every measurable and worldly good, nay, even every liberty of the private judgment, in grim obedience to an intuition of God? I suspect that modern scepticism does not fully know the deep strength of its foe, this power of faith, that it has taken up weapons against so lightly.

The problem of the relation between an author's religious convictions and his artistic technique has been somewhat neglected by literary scholarship. We have in Newman excellent examples of this connection. His belief in miracles permits him to use, with serious intent, certain devices which, in some writers, would seem merely unreal coincidence or romantic accident. He tells us that the plague of locusts was sent from God because of the iniquity of the inhabitants of Sicca. The "natural and direct interpretation was, 'Do penance, and be converted.' " We have already mentioned how he disposes of the arguments of scepticism by delivering the sceptic to an evil spirit. But, in spite of this and other colorful materials in the historical romance, a certain tepidness of treatment keeps it from giving the delight expected. His heart was not in this sort of thing. Who was he to set himself telling of narrow escapes and love affairs, or describing the appearance of a mob or of a witch—this austere mystic? He had no interest in the externals of things. "I wish I lived as much in the unseen world," he said, "as I think I do not live in this."

> "In [Newman's] novels, action and setting are hardly more than coating for the pill. He seems to pull up his conversion-story at certain intervals, as if to say, 'Now I must stop the argument and describe the scenery or let the characters drink another cup of tea.' "
>
> —*Joseph Ellis Baker*

The plots of the two novels reflect Newman's asceticism. *Loss and Gain* is as devoid of a love story as is any biography of its author. To the conversion story of his later romance, he adds the fact that Agellius is in love with Callista. That is as far as it goes. When she, not yet a Christian, rebukes her lover for courting her instead of trying to convert her, he is shocked at his own conduct and bitterly repentant. The novel ends not in a marriage but in death. All the emotional ecstasy that would ordinarily be lavished upon sexual love is devoted to the divine. As Callista was put on the rack, "She spoke her last word, 'For Thee, my Lord and Love, for Thee! . . . Accept me, O my Love, upon this bed of pain! And come to me, O my Love, make haste and come!' " When Chione (the slave), and Agellius spoke of their Master, they blushed.

If the author does not succeed in giving us the thrill of adventure and the feeling of a colorful historical background in *Callista,* nor the political aspect of the Oxford Movement in *Loss and Gain,* it must be remembered that in both novels Newman is chiefly interested in the inner drama of a change in faith. The belief that the most important event in life is not any measurable success nor even human failure, but the attainment of a certain subjective attitude, assent, communion with the true Church, this belief makes itself manifest in the choice of incident and the management of each story, and is present in the climax. This concentration upon one character and one action gives excellent unity of structure. On the other hand, it does permit *dialogue* that is quite undramatic, that reflects merely intellectual steps along the way to conversion, not emotional reaction of man on man.

But the most important influence of Newman's religious beliefs upon his technique grows out of his conviction that the progress of a soul is ultimately not due to its surroundings nor to the individual himself, but to God. The novel of Hardy and of Zola, under the sway of "scientific" determinism, was to become a study of the influence of environment upon character. Newman in each of his novels gives us a plot based upon the opposite assumption, a picture of a character acting in a certain way *in spite of* heredity, environment, and self-interest. He considered his own conversion the result of a call, or "an election of grace." Before coming to his final decision, he had held aloof from Roman Catholics. Similarly, the hero in *Loss and Gain,* up to the time when he decides he must join their Church, does not know any Roman Catholics. It is not even the writings of the early Fathers which make Reding a Catholic, as it was in Newman's own case. In the *Apologia,* the author has told us what books caused him to doubt the validity of Anglicanism. But doubt occurs to Charles without such preparation. Charles, we are told, could not escape the destiny of being one of the elect of God. A naturalistic novel, as a study in mundane cause and effect, makes the background a part of the story, almost one of the actors, that could not be removed without breaking a link in the sequence of events. Newman's supernaturalism allows him to write without achieving that intimate fusion of setting and plot. We feel that the subjective study has been worked out first, then the frame fitted rather awkwardly around it. The social and physical world never emerges into convincing reality. In his youth, Newman had "thought life might be a dream, or I an Angel, and all this world a deception, my fellow-angels by a playful device concealing themselves from me, and deceiving me with the semblance of a material world" [*Apologia pro Vita Sua,* 1864]. In his novels, action and setting are hard-

ly more than coating for the pill. He seems to pull up his conversion-story at certain intervals, as if to say, "Now I must stop the argument and describe the scenery or let the characters drink another cup of tea."

It is interesting to compare Newman to Eliot, who, chronologically and philosophically, lies between him and the naturalists. Her position is not merely that of determinism. Protestant in her origins, she emphasizes the moral responsibility of the individual. She attempts to penetrate to the ultimate motives that cause the will to swerve from duty, and soberly analyzes the consequences of deeds. Newman, vividly conscious of being in the hand of God, shows us not the consequences of acts of will, but the stages in the path along which the soul is led by a divine power quite independent of time, place, circumstance, and personal inclination. Of course, this is not to say that Newman denies free will. It is open to the soul to decide for itself whether it will or will not follow the light which God has granted, but the important thing is the act of grace, not the act of will. Newman's chief characters do not exhibit a conflict of desire and duty. They are eager to obey if only they may learn what is right. They are full of hope, for nothing can prevent the interposition of a personal Deity, actually a *deus ex machina.* There is no real conflict, no real suspense, in these plots. From the first, we can see what is coming. And yet we miss the feeling of inevitability which an irresistible impersonal cause or Fate would give us.

In short, with the novel of psychological study, as we pass from Newman through Eliot to Hardy we pass from supernaturalism, in which a man's fate is offered him by benevolent Providence; through a form of moral Protestantism in which men owe their fate largely to their own actions, and then to Naturalism, in which fate is determined by circumstances. Hence the setting was to become more and more important. Trollope and Eliot, writing later than Newman, gave with artistic care the local color that would be perceived by the normal human consciousness, not yet the background as discovered by the mystic or scientist. But with Egdon Heath, of *The Return of the Native,* or the social milieu of Zola's *Débâcle,* the setting becomes the real center of interest. Second only to background for increasing importance is the past of the individual; in Eliot, Trollope, (and Yonge), the individual's earlier deeds; in Hardy even his heredity.

The divine influence which guides Callista is not merely conscience, but a voice from a Personality outside herself. Nevertheless, conscience is on the side of the Creator, Who has planted in us, the *Apologia* says, certain sentiments of right and wrong. Both Callista and Charles Reding seem to know what they ought to believe before they believe it, a complex psychological condition which may perhaps help us to understand Newman's own development. Callista's "was not a change which involved contrariety, but one which expanded itself in (as it were) concentric circles." Every day was the child of the preceding, yet "had she been asked . . . where was her principle and consistency, what was her logic, or whether she acted on reason, or on impulse, or on feeling, or in fancy, or in passion, she would have been reduced to silence." Hence her strange rebuke, while she is yet pagan, to her lover for not preaching Christianity to her. When she first read the Gospel, she found that here was that towards which her intellect tended, though that intellect could only approve, not originate. Charles Reding, having a notion that celibacy is better than married life, when he sees that Catholicism justifies his thoughts and explains his feeling, finds this a direct argument for Catholicism. "Conviction," says Charles, "is the eyesight of the mind, not a conclusion from premises; God works it, and His works are slow." But Charles seems to know as well as his author where he is going. And so does the reader.

The creation of characters is probably the ultimate test of an author's breadth and humanity. When Newman gives us prototypes of himself, they are real enough. But if we compare his characters, say with those of the Colloquies of Erasmus (who are also figures created for the presentation of Catholic arguments), we are tempted to conclude that Newman's sympathy was confined within the bounds of his dogma. It is not that Catholic thinking itself involves meagerness of sympathy for *la perduta gente*. Newman loved to repeat that for him there were but two beings of any consequence, God and himself. To those of his creatures who are neither Romanist nor High Anglican, he is absurdly unjust, seeming to assume that the lost soul knows at heart the truth of Catholic doctrine but through sinful stubborness refuses to admit it. Juba is not only sceptical, he is also superstitious. He uses amulets against scorpions, and stands for intellectual freedom. When a priest claims him "as one of my children" Juba winces, but says scornfully, "You are mistaken there father; speak to those who own you. I am a free man." Of these hostile portraits, the most interesting are those in which Newman, with cold scorn, angles a puppet to typify ridiculously some opinion he dislikes. In *Loss and Gain,* there is a cutting satire in designating the Evangelicals present at a tea as No. 1, No. 2, No. 3. But he makes most sport with the representatives of absurd cults who, just before Reding joins the Catholic Church, try to win him to their own religions. There is Dr. Kitchens with his book "Spiritual Elixer," of which the "operation is mild and pleasurable" and acts in a few hours. A young lady tells him that some of them are organizing a religious body. He asks their tenets.

> "Here, too," she replied, "there is much still to be done; the tenets are not fixed either, that is, they are but sketched; and we shall prize your suggestions much. Nay, you will, of course, have the opportunity, as you would have the right, to nominate any doctrine to which you may be especially inclined."

> Charles did not know how to answer to so liberal an offer.

Considered merely as a story, *Callista* shows a marked improvement over the earlier novel, for it has more plot, more suspense, more emotion, more action. On the other hand, *Loss and Gain,* dealing as it does with contemporary experience, leaves an impression of deeper sincerity. Its casual flow of argument, its England and its Oxford and its mild clerical life seem very near reality. But not on such an esthetic basis would Newman have us judge his books. The novelists of the 'forties had more serious purposes in

mind. Anne Mozley tells us that "The ethos, as Mr. Newman calls it, of a book came always foremost in his critical estimation." He writes in 1837 that he misses something in Jane Austen. "What vile creatures her parsons are! She has not a dream of the high Catholic $\eta\theta o\sigma$." And when he came to write novels himself ten years later his first concern, as I have shown, was to paint souls moved by Catholic ideals. He was using fiction to convey dramatically moral insight into values that may make character and determine conduct. Besides esthetic and ethical interest, Newman's novels have unusual historical and biographical value. He calls *Loss and Gain* "A Tale, which . . . is a more intelligible and exact representation of the thoughts, sentiments, and aspirations . . . " prevailing then at Oxford "than was to be found in the pamphlets, charges, sermons, reviews, and story-books of the day." We see what it meant to turn the back on one's family and the high wordly position of an English clergyman, to join the despised Catholics. As long as men turn to literature for serious knowledge of human character, of social history, and of the ideals that have moulded conduct, these novels will always be documents of some value. I have treated them at such length because of their earnest portrayal—with a delicate insight into rare states of mind—of a profound and very important change of belief, a Protestant's conversion to Rome, by the one who, of all men with literary power in the nineteenth century, had best knowledge of that experience. These novels are built upon that portion of Newman's life which is the central fact in the history of Romanism and of Anglo-Catholicism in modern England. (pp. 54-68)

> *Joseph Ellis Baker, "Newman as Novelist," in his* The Novel and the Oxford Movement, *Princeton University Press, 1932, pp. 54-68.*

Joseph J. Reilly   (essay date 1945)

[*In the following essay, occasioned by the centennial anniversary of Newman's conversion to Catholicism, Reilly highlights prominent features of the author's artistry, praising his lucid prose style and his penetrating insight into human psychology. This essay originally appeared in* America *in October, 1945.*]

The key to Newman as man and writer is his realization that there were "two and two only luminously self-evident beings," himself and God. To most of us, even though reasonably free from egotism, our own personal self, with its desires, sorrows, joys, and pains, is everlastingly present, often to our shame or annoyance. Though our senses fail us, our consciousness remains and incessantly returns upon itself. Each of us is to himself the one, inescapable, demonstrable reality of whose existence we never for a moment doubt. That Newman should have been as luminously aware of God as that, so intimately, indubitably, completely and constantly aware, sets him aside at once and forever.

Such certitude, coming as if with the force and convincingness of a revelation, explains many things: why his faith never wavered, why he awakened in the hearts and minds of his listeners at St. Mary's a personal conviction of the living God, why he was consumed to know the divine will and to follow its dictates.

What impressed Newman most in the England of his day was the rise of what he called "liberalism," by which he meant the sum of those influences in contemporary life that tended to undermine the bases of revealed religion. He saw in liberalism her connatural foe; hence, as an Anglican, he resisted it with all his strength and, as a Catholic, with renewed determination, more effective weapons, and a more fully ripened genius.

Herein we find the unity of his life and writings. His aim never varied. Like Wordsworth, he believed himself "a dedicated spirit" charged with a unique duty to perform "else sinning greatly," for the accomplishment of which all his endowments had been given. To this end he consecrated his life, devoting endless days to thought and study and, like Carlyle, to the agony of composition, struggling to present to the mind of his reader the conclusions at which he had arrived and to do so with a precision which left no word of his meaning to chance and with a beauty which comported with the truth he uttered.

If his aim seems narrow, it is only because we fail to understand the immense importance he attached to it. If there is no revelation, nothing supernatural about religion, if Christ is not God and God is not the supreme reality, then Arnold was right when he wrote that the life of man

> Though bearable, seems hardly worth
> This pomp of worlds, this pain of birth.

The religion of Carlyle, of Arnold, and fitfully, of Ruskin, seemed to Newman as unsubstantial as a cloud.

Regret has often been expressed that Newman seemed indifferent to social reform in the sense in which it engaged the attention of Carlyle, Ruskin, and Cardinal Manning. When Newman voluntarily went to the cholera-ridden town of Bilston in September, 1849, to help the overworked resident priest, he gave eloquent evidence of his interest in the unfortunate, and his letters of advice and consolation written to simple folk who knew him only by name are equally significant. The charge of indifference, moreover, disregards several important facts: first, that Newman's efforts were directed, as already pointed out, "to withstand and baffle the fierce energy of passion and the all-corroding, all-dissolving skepticism of the intellect in religious inquiries"; secondly, that to achieve this purpose required extraordinary gifts of patience, psychological insight, tact, scholarship, ability to recognize even the subtler protean forms which "liberalism" assumed, and mastery of the arts of clarification and persuasion; thirdly, that only one Catholic in the English-speaking world possessed the qualities and special talents needed for the task and the genius to transform them into an energizing spiritual and intellectual force.

Newman was that man. Others with different gifts might well devote them to effecting reforms in government policy, or to curing the evils begotten of the industrial revolution. To blame Newman for accepting his unique destiny is to blame Virgil for not being Caesar, or Plato for not being Euripides.

Those whose views are at variance with Newman's call him a reactionary, courteously like Arnold or derisively like Carlyle. To those who understand and sympathize with his primary aim, he was the greatest apostle of reform in the Victorian age. It was he who, as an Anglican, awoke the Anglican church to her true mission and, as a Catholic, inspired his coreligionists with a fresh confidence and a new sense of moral and intellectual energy. It was he who set before them a plan for a Catholic university in which the rightful spheres of science and letters were established and the "Science of God" vindicated as an essential part of the curriculum, and who in a series of candid and brilliant lectures won a great victory over the intolerance which had plagued them for generations. Is it too much to say that what Newman achieved by *The Idea of a University* and *The Present Position of Catholics in England* was, and still remains, a major contribution to what in the broad sense is social reform?

The term "prophet" is often applied to three great Victorian prose-masters, Carlyle, Ruskin, and Arnold. The prophet is the conscience of contemporary society, the symbol and reminder of its moral life. He speaks out of the fulness of his heart and the strength of his own mind and with the power of great convictions. He condemns the shortcomings of his day with a noble indignation and, with a sense of his mission strong upon him, points the way toward wisdom and justice as the only means of achieving the good life. He speaks as one having authority and it is to man's higher nature that he appeals and the sacred name of duty that he invokes.

Most men recognize three primary obligations, one to the individual himself, one to his fellow man, and one to God. While it is clear that Carlyle, Ruskin, and Arnold recognized these three obligations, each gave particular consideration to the one he believed to be most neglected by his generation.

First in the eyes of Carlyle and Ruskin came a man's obligations to others; in those of Arnold, his obligations to himself first, and after that to his fellows. A fourth great Victorian, the peer of these as a master of prose and their superior in intellect, was primarily concerned with man's obligation to God. This fourth prophet was Newman. The sense of an obligation to speak out, of a mission to perform, and the voice of authority which marks the true prophet are unmistakable before *Tract 90* and after October 9, 1845. There is a striking difference, however, between Newman and the others: he alone gives the impression of doubting his personal infallibility, of relying upon an authority greater than his own.

Newman's self-dedication to the cause of revealed religion made all his works in a certain sense controversial, for in asserting and defending the claims of faith he had always in mind the presence of those who questioned, doubted, or denied. As a foe of inexactness of thought and word he used to say that few arguments would occur if only (to use a legal phrase) the minds of the opponents met. This explains why he never failed to state the opposite side of the case no matter how strongly it seemed to tell against his own. He had no joy in controversy for its own sake; thus it was not his aim to breed a generation of Catholic controversialists but of Catholics whose faith was so intelligent and so strong that it could withstand "not only the hammer blows of rationalism in the 'fifties but its big guns in the 'eighties."

Despite his dedication to one great purpose and his understanding of the strength of the opposing forces, Newman was never narrow, never vehement, never ill-natured. Arnold, finding these flaws in Carlyle and Ruskin, points by contrast to Newman who has graciousness, who does not make war but persuades, who has urbanity, "the tone of the city, of the centre, the tone which always aims at a spiritual and intellectual effect, and. . . . never disjoins banter. . . . from politeness, from felicity."

It is not extravagant to say that Newman had a passion for lucidity. It sprang partly from his eagerness to convey exactly to other minds the thoughts of his own, even to the emotional and imaginative coloring that invested them and modified their meaning; partly from his instinctive distrust of, and impatience with, hazy thinking and inexplicit expression. "Mistiness is the mother of wisdom," was his ironic comment on a form of intellectual gullibility current in his time—and current still. All he learned from his studies, his personal experiences, or his association with others provided examples and analogies which he transformed into instruments of clarification rarely matched in English literature.

Among the most striking aspects of Newman's genius was his power to probe into the inner workings of men's minds. Only Browning in his century could compare with him. A case book in religious psychology could be made from his sermons alone, and increased enormously from his other writings. He knows all the temptations against faith, all the curious forms which pride assumes to corrupt us, the intoxicating sense of freedom which animates the man who casts religion aside. Newman does not stop with the individual. He has a startling insight into the workings of mob psychology and equal insight into what he calls "the popular mind." Thus he knows the right approach to an England which for nearly twenty years had believed that his conversion was tainted by intellectual dishonesty, which for generations had persecuted its Catholic citizens, and which, under the spur of Gladstone's allegations against the dogma of papal infallibility, was prepared to believe that no English Catholic could be loyal to his sovereign.

Newman's style has been universally praised for a hundred years. It is as definitely his as his personality and serves every use from the homeliest to the most sublime. He can describe the Saviour's anguish in Gethsemane in words of poignant beauty and, with no loss of dignity, the frantic efforts of a bird seeking freedom by flinging itself against a closed window. He can describe Attica, "a confined triangle," as it appears to the unimaginative eye of a traveling salesman, and a moment later he can depict in words of unforgettable loveliness what the salesman failed to see:

> the dark violet billows with their white edges down below; those graceful, fan-like jets of silver upon the rocks, which slowly rise aloft like water-spirits from the deep, then shiver, and

break, and spread, and shroud themselves, and disappear, in a soft mist of foam.

Newman's significance today is what it always has been— fundamentally spiritual and hence as changeless as the great problems with which he dealt. He teaches that duty is personal, inalienable, sacred. The current notion that it is a vague relationship between the individual and the community would be to him unthinkable. He teaches that higher education should be a process of intellectual development worth securing for its own sake; that when it brings to full flower a man's loftiest social and personal qualities it is in the best sense utilitarian; that if it is to be true to its noblest obligations there must be at the heart of it a philosophy which so deals with the universal issues of human destiny that the dignity of man and the meaning of life are made manifest. Newman was the greatest apostle of religious tolerance in English literature. He considered it an essential mark of a gentleman, an unfailing evidence of culture, one of the purest aims and essential achievements of a civilized society. Finally, he never wearies of reminding us that beyond the limitations of human insight and experience dwell those unseen realities which shall outlast the kingdoms of the world and whose splendor the mind of man has only fitfully conceived.

One last word. Let us be done with the notion that Newman was "born out of his due time," that he looked back with longing eyes to the middle ages, and that temperamentally he was of them. Nothing could be farther from the truth. Newman was a modern who saw with keener vision than any of his contemporaries the implications of the new phase of the undying war against revealed religion; a modern who scorned to ask why he was born "to set the crooked straight," but gave to the defense talents that seem to have been formed and bestowed for that special purpose; a modern, finally, whose personality flowered under stress and whose genius was quickened by the challenges of his day. It was this Newman, the true Newman, who said, "I write for the future." (pp. 65-70)

> *Joseph J. Reilly, "The Tone of the Centre," in* American Essays for the Newman Centennial, *edited by John K. Ryan and Edmond Darvil Benard, The Catholic University of America Press, 1947, pp. 65-70.*

Walter E. Houghton   (essay date 1945)

[*Houghton is an American educator and critic who has written extensively on English literature of the Victorian era. In the following excerpt, he elucidates apologetic methods used by Newman in the construction of his* Apologia.]

Newman's *Apologia* can be looked at in two ways, and these have sometimes been spoken of as though they were incompatible. Is it an autobiography? Or is it an apology? [Wilfrid Ward, in his *Life of John Henry Cardinal Newman,* 1912] referred to some readers for whom the *Apologia* belongs "to the literature of self-revelation, not to apologetic." [L. E. Gates, in his *Selections from the Prose Writings of . . . Newman,* 1895] thought people who regarded it as "frank autobiography" were quite wrong; it is "an enormously elaborate and ingenious piece of special pleading." For [C. F. Harrold, in his *A Newman Treasury,* 1943], however, "the *Apologia* is in no sense an 'apology'; it is a candid revelation of the inner and outer facts of Newman's experience." But must we, or indeed should we, choose between these assumptions?

To Newman, surely, the book was both. He spoke of it as the history of his mind, the picture of "what I am," the record of his feelings and motives, and so on. Years later, long after the controversy was over, he was ready to accept the *Apologia* as an adequate account of his life from 1833 to 1845. Yet he also insisted that "my main purpose . . . is a defence of myself "; he begged the reader to remember that "I am but vindicating myself from the charge of dishonesty"; he appealed to the British public as if to a jury and predicted that he would vanquish "not my Accuser, but my judges." Most conclusive of all is the statement in the preface to the first edition, a year after the chapters had appeared separately as pamphlets. He would like, he says, to wipe out of the volume all traces of the originating circumstances, but this is not possible because the title of *Apologia* "is too exactly borne out by its matter and structure." In the face of these remarks, we cannot disregard the influence of an apologetic motive.

And the probability is strengthened when we remember Newman's long study and use of rhetoric. In a well-known passage he described himself as a person without ideas or convictions of his own but with "rhetorical or histrionic power to represent" those he adopted from others. Anne Mozley [editor of Newman's *Letters*] noted the subtle variation of his style, even in his letters, to harmonize with the known character of each correspondent; and the same awareness of his audience appears everywhere in his published works. He shrewdly estimates the degree of resistance he must expect—and counteract—from the prejudices or preoccupations of his readers. He skillfully alters his means with every change in end. How could we expect this not to be also true in the *Apologia,* of all places?

Yet such an admission need not impugn the claim of sharp and faithful revelation. In every work of history or biography there has to be selection and emphasis. Certain materials have to be chosen, certain traits of character have to be stressed. On what principle? In Gibbon, let us say, speaking broadly, to show the formation of the historian; in Mill, to show the growth of a mind toward synthesis in an age of clashing philosophies; in Newman, to defend himself. Apology is simply one of many, and absolutely necessary, disciplines for the biographical imagination. But, it will be said, one of the most dangerous. So it is, and we shall have to inquire if Newman's picture is too favorable. But men *have* defended themselves by stating the truth. For the moment we simply ask how has Newman's desire to defend himself affected the artistic process?

Centrally, as I just said, by the selection of material. What I mean can be illustrated if we ask why Newman describes his state of mind at the start of the Movement in such detail. He suggests the answer himself when he points out that his behavior "had a mixture in it both of fierceness and of sport, . . . [which] gave offence to many." Hence it was necessary partly to acknowledge the fault and partly

to justify and palliate it by explaining his peculiar emotional bias at the time. He thus cites a series of examples which at once "apologize" and reveal. "I used irony in conversation," he says, "when matter-of-fact men would not see what I meant," which both illuminates the man and accounts for his being misjudged. Everywhere, I suggest, though often less obviously, the primary object of defence has, so to speak, been at Newman's elbow, telling him what to select and when to analyze.

The same object lies behind certain techniques already attributed to the "pure" intention of self-revelation, which is but another proof that the motives worked together and that the *Apologia* is not a combination of two things but an integrated whole. Letters and journals, quotations from books or articles, all serve both the defendant and the psychologist with first-hand contemporary evidence. "You might have letters of mine to throw light on my state of mind," he wrote to Church in April, 1864; and then added, "and this by means of contemporaneous authority." The same dual object is served by his "speaking" style. It not only gives remembrance the impact of immediacy; it has all the winning effect of simplicity, sincerity, and intimacy. No rhetorical flourishes, no pontificating, no abstruse phrasing and technical jargon, but a living voice speaking out simply and directly to every reader. And this simplicity acts as a guarantee of sincerity, a quality of the utmost importance for his rebuttal of Kingsley's charge. Newman had remarked, in the lecture on **"Literature"** [in his *Idea of a University*], that, when a man sincerely gives forth "what he has within him," his style inevitably has "the charm of an incommunicable simplicity." And many a reader must have agreed with the person who spoke of Newman's being so "absolutely himself in his power of writing" and added that this was "an example of his nature and his gift of what is called *simplicity.*" Nor should we overlook the flattering sense of intimacy which one picks up, however unconsciously, from the confidential tone, not to mention the reassuring kinship one feels with a great prelate who can speak of giving his opponents "tit for tat," of being "sore" at the Anglican divines who had "taken me in," or of having "a lounging free-and-easy way of carrying things on." In these ways we see Newman's style exemplifying his dictum that "persons influence us, voices melt us."

The impression of sincerity derived from the style merges into the more positive appreciation of Newman's candor. Every reader of an apology is suspicious, and in this case it seemed quite possible that John Bull would get not only a slick piece of special pleading, with all Newman's sins and errors whitewashed, but also a militant blast at the English Church, along with some nice Roman proselytizing. Newman was much too smart for any of that. It was all well and good, some years before, to smooth over certain difficulties in Catholic teaching for an Anglican audience of prospective converts. But now his audience was the British public and they were to judge not doctrine but a man, and a man accused of being sly, devious, and sophistical. The only possible reply was to show himself a man of remarkable candor, concerned only to state the facts and eager to see both sides of every question—in short, completely objective and impartial.

Time and again Newman disclaims any intention of preaching, or indeed even of defending his beliefs and actions beyond claiming that they were honestly reached. In the preface he announced:

> I mean to be simply personal and historical: I am not expounding Catholic doctrine, I am doing no more than explaining myself, and my opinions and actions. I wish, as far as I am able, simply to state facts, whether they are ultimately determined to be for me or against me.

And this disclaimer is astutely repeated at two crucial moments: when he first doubts the truth of Anglicanism and when he is finally converted to Rome. "Now let it be simply understood," he reminds the reader in the first case, "that I am not writing controversially, but with the one object of relating things as they happened to me." And, in the second, "Let it be recollected that I am historically relating my state of mind . . . I am not speaking theologically, nor have I any intention of going into controversy, or of defending myself." This repeated denial is reassuring.

Furthermore, the objective attitude seems confirmed by the impartial admission of errors and difficulties—in his personal conduct and thinking, in Roman Catholicism, in religious faith itself—along with impartial praise for the English Church. In such ways Newman skillfully makes himself appear calm, reasoned, fair-minded, only concerned with the bare facts, whether or not they help or hinder his cause—all of which, of course, was precisely the best possible defence. This is not to admit distortion, or

to deny it; the whole question is postponed until later. A man may really be calm, reasoned, and fair-minded, and still have to use plenty of skill to convince his judges that that is in fact his character.

Consider Newman's frequent confession of faults and mistakes, sometimes by way of accepting the truth of old charges, at least substantially (he rarely omits some qualification), but sometimes thrown in apparently gratuitously with a wonderful air of both humility and confidence, as though he were at once repentant for his sins and yet quite certain they were too few and too small to damage his cause. Of Dr. Hawkins, for example, he is sure he has often provoked him, and that "in me such provocation was unbecoming." At the opening of the Movement, he confesses, his behavior "had a mixture in it both of fierceness and of sport" which gave offence to many; "nor am I here defending it." And then he sets down blunt examples of both. In this book, written to justify his successive changes of belief, he is candid enough to admit that

> . . . persistence in a given belief is no sufficient test of its truth; but departure from it is at least a slur upon the man who has felt so certain about it. In proportion then as I had in 1832 a strong persuasion in beliefs which I have since given up, so far a sort of guilt attaches to me, not only for that vain confidence, but for my multiform conduct in consequence of it.

Even more satisfactory is his facing up to the appalling desertion and denial of the Anglican *Via Media:*

> I heard once from an eye-witness the account of

The Birmingham Oratory, founded by Newman in 1848.

a poor sailor whose legs were shattered by a ball, in the action off Algiers in 1816, and who was taken below for an operation. The surgeon and the chaplain persuaded him to have a leg off; it was done and the tourniquet applied to the wound. Then, they broke it to him that he must have the other off too. The poor fellow said, "You should have told me that, gentlemen," and deliberately unscrewed the instrument and bled to death. Would not that be the case with many friends of my own? How could I ever hope to make them believe in a second theology, when I had cheated them in the first? with what face could I publish a new edition of a dogmatic creed, and ask them to receive it as gospel? Would it not be plain to them that no certainty was to be found anywhere?

What makes this so effective is the form of expression. Are not those the very gibes which the suspicious reader would like to make? And here they are, and in an "apologia," and even in Newman's own mouth! He does not say, "I suppose the reader may wonder how I expected to make people believe in a second theology," but "how could *I* ever hope to make them believe . . . when *I* had cheated them." It was he himself, then, who first asked these embarrassing questions, fearlessly and honestly! And the word "cheated" is a masterpiece. "When I had misled them," or "misguided them," or "led them astray," or half-a-dozen other variations could hardly have been called euphemisms. But *cheated them*—how unnecessary and how wonderfully fair for Newman to state the case at its worst! Surely he must have some very ingenious excuse up his sleeve to take the sting out of that. And he has an excuse, a feeble excuse, which he saves by confessing its weakness—which in turn reflects credit on his fairness:

> Well, in my defence I could but make a lame apology; however, it was the true one, viz. that I had not read the Fathers critically enough; that in such nice points, as those which determine the angle of divergence between the two Churches, I had made considerable miscalculations.

This might well have closed the matter. But Newman hears another objection on the reader's lips and again asks the awkward question himself, and again, by doing so, produces the impression of concealing nothing. "And how came this about?" Then a fresh apology, equally feeble, and therefore again tempered with the same judicious minimizing of its force:

> And how came this about? Why, the fact was, unpleasant as it was to avow, that I had leaned too much upon the assertions of Ussher, Jeremy Taylor, or Barrow, and had been deceived by them. Valeat quantum,—it was all that *could* be said.

Much the same impression, so unexpected and so very effective in an apology, appears in his treatment of Roman Catholicism. Newman does not omit his former attacks; indeed, he reprints some savage words against the political machinations of the clergy and their methods of proselytizing. He quotes his charge of 1840 that they were "attempting to gain converts among us by unreal representations of its doctrines, plausible statements, bold assertions,

appeals to the weaknesses of human nature, to our fancies, our eccentricities, our fears, our frivolities, our false philosophies." And so through a long paragraph which could well have been omitted and surely would have been, except that its very presence here, in 1864, does credit to the man who would not suppress it—and, still more, would not retract it, for though he laments having made such insinuations, he does not deny their truth. Even apart from Roman practices, which, of course, many good Catholics condemn, Newman is honest enough to admit his difficulties. On devotions to the Virgin he remarks: "*I say frankly,* I do not fully enter into them now*" [italics added]. Later, in the fine chapter on Catholicism, he begins one paragraph, "Now I will go on *in fairness to say* what I think *is* the great trial to the Reason, when confronted with that august prerogative of the Catholic Church." And his conversion? Is it a sublime moment when the veils were lifted and the Truth at last rushed into his soul? when he came finally, in weariness and ecstasy, to rest in the divine bosom of Mother Church? That is what we expect and may well be ready to write off as the conventional unction of a Roman convert. And what do we get?

> I was not conscious to myself, on my conversion, of any difference of thought or of temper from what I had before. I was not conscious of firmer faith in the fundamental truths of revelation, or of more self-command; I had not more fervour; but it was like coming into port after a rough sea; and my happiness on that score remains to this day without interruption.

Could anything be better? The apparent effort not to make a single false claim and not to boast of the least improvement in himself. Then the reserved and measured statement.

In the same way, to the same affect, Newman candidly admits the difficulties of faith itself. He makes no easy or superior assumptions, shows no blind eye to the powerful temptations of skepticism. Voltaire's attack on immortality is dreadful but "how plausible!" The doctrine of external punishment is true but "terrible to the reason." The existence of God is, of all points of faith, "encompassed with most difficulty"; and the usual arguments in proof of a God drawn from nature and society "do not warm me or enlighten me." In fact, for Newman himself the vision of a world so full of suffering and evil, of misery and injustice, "seems simply to give the lie to that great truth." As with his confession of personal faults and errors, his recognition of the difficulties of faith could not but make him peculiarly sympathetic to the British public of the 1860's.

So far, the apologetic methods described are more negative than positive. They remove suspicious and potential hostility by presenting Newman as an honest, fair-minded human being. But, in addition, other methods seek for positive attraction by drawing out what is charming in his personality or pathetic in his story.

There is, for example, the marked strain of modesty. "I am not setting myself up," he says, "as a pattern of good sense or of anything else." He plays down his leadership of the Movement. "The true and primary author" was John Keble. And even after July, 1833, he modestly explains that "for myself, I was not the person to take the lead of a party; I never was, from first to last, more than *a* leading author of a school; nor did I ever wish to be anything else." In this connection it is significant that Newman's **"Autobiographical Memoir,"** written with no apologetic intention, reveals by contrast a strain of egotism and conceit; and the implication that he toned down the *Apologia* is borne out by parallel passages. In the account of Whately, for example, the **"Memoir"** quotes his compliment that Newman "was the clearest-headed man he knew," and reprints his praise for Newman's contribution to the *Elements of Logic.* Both are omitted from the corresponding pages in the *Apologia.* The notice of the Oriel election, barely mentioned in the latter and then only to illustrate his hero worship of Keble, appears in the **"Memoir"** replete with all the flattering details.

Not that Newman excludes all praise of himself from the *Apologia.* That too would have been a tactical error. Compliments are introduced, not too often, carefully spaced, and modestly depreciated. In a quarterly for April, 1845, was "an exceedingly kind article" in which "the writer praised me in feeling and beautiful language far above my deserts." Blanco White, after speaking "bitterly and unfairly of me" in his letters of 1833 (here omitted with the subtle implication that printing them would be as unfair to White as to Newman) changed his opinion later to high praise of "the amiable, the intellectual, the refined John Henry Newman." The praise, which is printed at length, is nicely introduced: "In 1839, when looking back, he uses terms of me, which it would be hardly modest in me to quote, were it not that what he says of me in praise is but part of a whole account of me." Writing of his conversion, he prints some sentences from a letter of Charles Marriott's, a kind of testimonial to his loyalty to the Church of England and therefore important for the defence. "I quote them," says Newman disarmingly, "for the love which I bear him, and the value that I set on his good word"— which beautifully hides his real purpose behind a compliment and completely forestalls the appearance of egotism otherwise certain to arise.

Still more winning than modesty is the impression of unselfish warmth and generosity which the last illustration suggests. Even for men with whom he was known to have quarreled there are expressions of respect, sometimes of love. He speaks of Hawkins and Whately with positive affection, and we do not question it, partly because the simplicity of style has the very air of sincerity I spoke of, partly because of the reference, without the least note of rancor, to disagreements he had with them both. Had such disagreements been omitted, then for all who knew of them—and there were many—the expression of affection, standing alone, unqualified, would have been suspect. That was the negative advantage. The positive value of admitting old differences was the implied picture of a Newman whose friendship was broad and deep and forgiving enough to survive personal frictions without cherishing the slightest ill will (the suggestion of Christian forgiveness is not to be overlooked). Incidentally, it is worth noticing that Newman spoke more harshly both of Hawkins and of himself in a private note written in 1860. There he described the state of their relations from 1829 to 1845 as

"a state of constant bickerings, of coldness, dryness, and donnishness on his part, and of provoking insubordination and petulance on mine." But, in an apologia, he could not risk expressing such rancor toward another or such damning criticism of himself.

If Newman could speak well of his enemies, it is not surprising that he could write of his friends with an ardor not the least mawkish or sentimental, and at times genuinely moving. Under the trials of 1841-45 he noted that people thought he had "much to bear externally, disappointment, slander, &c." "No," he says at once, "I have nothing to bear, but the anxiety which I feel for my friends' anxiety for me, and their perplexity." He would not confide in J. W. Bowden, his "dear and old friend." "Why should I unsettle that sweet calm tranquillity, when I had nothing to offer him instead?" And no one can forget the superb peroration with which he offers his book to his friends as a memorial of affection and gratitude:

> And to you especially, dear AMBROSE ST. JOHN; whom God gave me, when He took every one else away; who are the link between my old life and my new; who have now for twenty-one years been so devoted to me, so patient, so zealous, so tender; who have let me lean so hard upon you; who have watched me so narrowly; who have never thought of yourself, if I was in question.
>
> And in you I gather up and bear in memory those familiar affectionate companions and counsellors, who in Oxford were given to me, one after another, to be my daily solace and relief; and all those others, of great name and high example, who were my thorough friends, and showed me true attachment in times long past.

This, of course, shows Newman loved as well as loving, and elsewhere he says directly, "It was not I who sought friends, but friends who sought me. Never man had kinder or more indulgent friends than I have had." Such passages reinforce those I mentioned earlier where he allows others to praise him. Also, they show him befriended in his hour of trial. He was not suspected, rejected, attacked by everybody. No, he had a few loyal and staunch friends who knew him well and stood by him. In that way these passages make more persuasive the last and most effective appeal of all, sympathy for the innocent and pathetic victim of persecution.

This appeal is handled with great tact. Either Newman makes no direct bid for sympathy, or if he does, he counteracts any suggestion of self-pity or self-centered concern by stressing his unselfish affection for others. In the former case, he invokes a principle dear to every Englishman, the principle of fair play, which at once wins support for anyone treated unfairly, and without his having to ask for it. It is thus an ideal technique for the apologist. In the discussion of *Tract 90,* for example, Newman points out that "every creed has texts in its favour, and again texts which run counter to it." And then he continues with telling force:

> . . . how had I done worse in *Tract 90* than Anglicans, Wesleyans, and Calvinists did daily in their Sermons and their publications? how had

I done worse, than the Evangelical party in their *ex animo* reception of the Services for Baptism and Visitation of the Sick? Why was I to be dishonest and they immaculate? There was an occasion on which our Lord gave an answer, which seemed to be appropriate to my own case, when the tumult broke out against my Tract:—"He that is without sin among you, let him first cast a stone at him." I could have fancied that a sense of their own difficulties of interpretation would have persuaded the great party I have mentioned to some prudence, or at least moderation, in opposing a teacher of an opposite school. But I suppose their alarm and their anger overcame their sense of justice.

After which, what reader does not assert his *own* sense of justice—for *Newman!* The same technique is used with even greater success in the account of the petty surveillance and interference he was subjected to at Littlemore, for here he can also appeal to a second principle equally dear to the hearts of Englishmen. "Why may I not have that liberty which all others are allowed?" "Am I alone, of Englishmen, not to have the privilege to go where I will, no questions asked?" And so on, even to the sure-fire "I had thought that an Englishman's house was his castle."

Contrasted with such indirect methods for winning sympathy is the direct presentation of the "pathetic image." It has already been seen in two passages quoted earlier: that on the pain of ripping up old griefs ("See what Kingsley is putting me through"—though of course the actual implication is a good deal more oblique and delicate) and especially that on the final departure from Oxford. I have ascribed the latter to Newman's sense of the dramatic. It was equally intended (and again we see that the book is a single entity fusing apology and revelation) to end his story with the pathetic picture of a kind, affectionate man, heart-sick and lonely, leaving his old home forever. And to this is added very discreetly the image of persecution: "Trinity had never been unkind to me." But Oriel? the heads of the colleges? the Hebdomadal Board? Convocation?—every one of them, so wisely unmentioned, crowds into the reader's memory. And then the last pathetic touch: he has never seen Oxford since, except for the spires seen from the railway, with all its poignant connotations of banishment and exile. (pp. 68-84)

Perhaps the most subtle example of the pathetic image occurs in the closing paragraphs on *Tract 90.* Their very placing is skillful. Newman has just finished a full and clear statement of his case. He was not trying to Romanize the Church but simply to reassert those primitive doctrines which had once been in the English Church and which could be found, under a mass of ambiguities, in the Prayer-Book and the Articles. It was true, these doctrines were also Roman doctrines, but that was merely because Rome too had its roots in the Catholic and Apostolic Church. Now even if the reader suspects Newman's motive, he has to grant that the case is a good one. Newman might perfectly well have been doing precisely what he says he was doing—or he might not. But certainly he deserves a fair hearing. If he were not to get it, if he should be condemned without trial, persecuted, slandered—how appalling! how unjust! That is the reader's state of mind

as he reaches the conclusion, which must be quoted almost completely:

> In the universal storm of indignation with which the *Tract* was received throughout the country on its appearance, I recognize much of real religious feeling, much of honest and true principle, much of straightforward ignorant common sense. In Oxford there was genuine feeling too; but there had been a smouldering stern energetic animosity, not at all unnatural, partly rational, against its author. A false step had been made; now was the time for action. . . .
>
> I saw indeed clearly that my place in the Movement was lost; public confidence was at an end; my occupation was gone. It was simply an impossibility that I could say any thing henceforth to good effect, when I had been posted up by the marshal on the buttery hatch of every College of my University, after the manner of discommoned pastry-cooks, and when in every part of the country and every class of society, through every organ and occasion of opinion, in newspapers, in periodicals, at meetings, in pulpits, at dinner-tables, in coffee-rooms, in railway carriages, I was denounced as a traitor who had laid his train and was detected in the very act of firing it against the time-honoured Establishment. There were indeed men, besides my own immediate friends, men of name and position, who gallantly took my part, as Dr. Hook, Mr. Palmer, and Mr. Perceval: it must have been a grievous trial for themselves.

In the face of such provocation, Newman's quiet restraint is instantly admirable. And under the circumstances, how just and fair of him to recognize that there *was* "real religious feeling" and "honest and true principle" against him, as well, no doubt (the reader is now ready on his part to be broad-minded), as some ignorant common sense. Then the persecution: *this* man treated as a pastry cook, denounced as a traitor, *this* man whose case was at the worst highly debatable. And besides, a man with friends; and friends who stuck by him; and not simply personal friends but others who took his part and gallantly supported a lost cause; and they were no ordinary men, but men "of name and position." Then comes the last touch, the fine note of unselfish thoughtfulness: "it must have been a grievous trial *for themselves.*" It is irresistible. No wonder Newman won his case, hands down. For, as he knew so well, "men go by their sympathies, not by argument."

The first pamphlet (Part I) closed with a personal character sketch. As we look back on it, at this point, we can see how constantly it has been in Newman's mind, for all the methods of apology come under one or another characteristic which he ascribes to himself:

> Whatever judgment my readers may eventually form of me from these pages, I am confident that they will believe me in what I shall say in the course of them. I have no misgiving at all, that they will be ungenerous or harsh with a man who . . . has ever spoken too much rather than too little; who would have saved himself many a scrape, if he had been wise enough to hold his

tongue; who has ever been fair to the doctrines and arguments of his opponents; who has never slurred over facts and reasonings which told against himself; . . . who has never shrunk from confessing a fault when he felt that he had committed one; who has ever consulted for others more than for himself; who has given up much that he loved and prized and could have retained, but that he loved honesty better than name, and Truth better than dear friends.

"That," says Newman to the reader, "is what I really am. Read the evidence that follows and see if I don't prove it." (pp. 84-6)

> *Walter E. Houghton, in his* The Art of Newman's "Apologia," *Yale University Press, 1945, 116 p.*

Charles Frederick Harrold   (essay date 1945)

[*In the following excerpt, Harrold surveys Newman's collections of sermons, delineating the author's rhetorical strategies and commenting favorably on his literary style. Harrold also describes the manner in which Newman's early sermons anticipate many of his later writings.*]

The Victorian age, which loved oratory, from platform and pulpit alike, produced great preachers and great sermons. We of a later time find considerable difficulty in realizing with what interest the Victorians listened to the sermons of their favorite preacher, and read them when they were eventually published in a handsome and sober volume. "No right-minded Victorian," writes Amy Cruse [in her *The Victorians and Their Reading,* 1935], "thought his Sunday properly spent unless he heard at least one sermon." And no literate Victorian failed to read a sermon in times of bereavement, or in other specially serious hours. Mary Gladstone followed her father in her fondness for sermon reading, "gloating," as she said, over one preached by Canon Scott-Holland at Winchester on a Good Friday. But sermons were read on other than solemn occasions. Walter Bagehot not only took a volume of sermons with him on his honeymoon, but read a discourse by F. D. Maurice aloud to his bride. Lord and Lady Cavendish read sermons together both before and after their marriage, enjoying, for example, "two fine sermons on *The Subjection of the Creature to Vanity.*" Hearing and reading sermons—preferably long ones—was regarded not merely as a duty but as a keen intellectual pleasure and a spiritual and emotional discipline. To be sure, there were low-grade sermons not much different in their effect on readers from that of a third-rate novel; some of these George Eliot attacked in her withering article on Dr. Cumming. But in an age rich in preachers and in pulpit eloquence, the output of excellent published sermons was enormous. Sermons held the place in the public's interest that is now held by fiction.

So great was the market for sermons that successful preachers published their sermons almost as a matter of course. Even those preachers who were in no sense great, but who had won a certain amount of popularity with their own congregations and could expect at least a mod-

erate sale, were eager to see their discourses in print. Amy Cruse, who has made a study of the Victorians and their books, observes that "a congregation could offer no higher compliment to its pastor than a request that his sermon or sermons be published." Thus the Reverend John Jenkyns of Mrs. Gaskell's *Cranford* publishes, "by request," the sermon which he preached before "My Lord Judge" at the assize, and finds it necessary to go up to London to see it through the press; afterwards his portrait is painted, with his hand upon a copy of the work that has brought him local fame. For even a distinguished preacher, to achieve a published volume of sermons was the fulfillment of a soaring ambition. This is noteworthy in that Newman seems to have felt a great reluctance "against divulging to the world at large what had passed between him and his congregations" [quoted in T. Mozley's *Reminiscemces Chiefly of Oriel College and the Oxford Movement,* Vol. I, 1882]. But . . . Newman was unusual in his deep aristocratic reticence.

Of all the eloquent preachers of Newman's day, only six are regarded by one authority [L. E. Elliott-Binns, in his *Religion in the Victorian Era,* 1936] as reaching true greatness: Newman himself, then Frederick William Robertson of Brighton, Canon Liddon of St. Paul's, Charles Haddon Spurgeon of Exeter Hall and the Metropolitan Tabernacle, William Connor Magee (successively Bishop of Peterborough and Archbishop of York), and William Boyd Carpenter, Bishop of Ripon and Canon of Westminster. To these may be added Newman's friend, Dean R. W. Church of St. Paul's, Dean Stanley of Westminster, Frederick D. Maurice of Lincoln's Inn Chapel, Charles Kingsley of Eversley, Thomas Arnold of Rugby, Thomas Binney of the Weigh House Chapel, and, in the closing years of the era, Canon Scott-Holland and Bishop Charles Gore. The power and eloquence of these men have long been matters of historical record. Yet of the six greatest, Newman alone is read widely today as a master of sermon eloquence. Fashions in pulpit oratory have greatly changed since the heyday of Victorianism, and since much of preaching is personality, the Victorian master-preachers must be accepted purely on the evidence of their contemporaries, so little do their printed discourses testify to their skill. Spurgeon, Magee, and Boyd Carpenter were the greatest orators among the top-ranking six, and had to be heard rather than read for their merits to be appreciated. Robertson of Brighton, like Newman, is still read, though certainly not so widely nor with such devotion. (pp. 318-20)

[Newman's] fame as a preacher does not rest on his ability as an orator. In pulpit eloquence he was never the equal of Spurgeon or Robertson. For the most powerful and finished eloquence, we must in fact turn to France, to Bossuet, Massillon, Bourdaloue, Lacordaire. These great masters did not, like Newman, glide silently into their pulpits, and read from a manuscript in a scarcely audible voice. Newman's manner in the pulpit has been described by a contemporary writer in the *Dublin Review:*

> Action in the common sense of the word there was none. Through many of [the sermons] the preacher never moved anything but his head. His hands were literally not seen from the begin-

ning to the end. The sermon began in a calm musical voice, the key slightly rising as it went on; by-and-bye the preacher warmed with his subject, it seemed as if his very soul and body glowed with suppressed emotion. There were times when, in the midst of the most thrilling passages, he would pause, without dropping his voice, for a moment which seemed long, before he uttered with gathering force and solemnity a few weighty words.

The secret of Newman's pulpit appeal lay elsewhere than in gesture, or majestic voice, or dramatic emotion. We find that secret indicated in large part in his discourse on **"University Preaching,"** published in *The Idea of a University.* There we learn that the preacher's aim is twofold: (i) "the ministering of some definite spiritual good to those who hear him," and (ii) an intense "earnestness in pursuing it." Newman dismisses "talent, logic, learning, words, manner, voice, action" as of little importance when not serving some "definiteness of object," the "conveying to others some spiritual benefit." It was Newman's earnestness and his concentration on a single message which, even when his hands remained at his sides, caused his "very soul and body [to glow] with suppressed emotion," and gave to his voice the thrill and force noted by the writer in the *Dublin Review.* Furthermore, Newman declares in his discourse that the wise preacher will "select some distinct fact or scene, some passage in history, some truth, simple or profound, some doctrine, some principle, or some sentiment," and bring it home to others as forcefully as he has already brought it home to himself. Here is one source of the "concreteness" and singleness of effect in Newman's sermons and discourses. Here is the reason also, to some extent, for the absence of the "flowers of oratory, fine figures, [and] tuneful periods" in most of them.

Though Newman's address on **"University Preaching"** is concerned with the proper methods of reaching undergraduates, he realizes that, on the whole, "what is suitable for one audience is suitable for another; all hearers are children of Adam." Though the university preacher will concentrate, he believes, on the problems of the young, on the dangers threatening their virtue and their faith, nevertheless certain great subjects are, in his opinion, valuable above all others, as being comprehensive and permanent. Moreover, adds Newman, special dangers or probable deficiencies or the needs of his hearers should be approached *covertly,* "not showing on the surface of his discourse what he is aiming at":

> I see no advantage in a preacher professing to treat of infidelity, orthodoxy, or virtue, or the pride of reason, or riot, or sensual indulgence. To say nothing else, common-places are but blunt weapons; whereas it is particular topics that penetrate and reach their mark. Such subjects are, for instance, the improvement of time, avoiding the occasions of sin, frequenting the Sacraments, divine warnings . . . and any others, which may touch the heart and conscience, or may suggest trains of thought to the intellect, without proclaiming the main reason why they have been chosen.

In this passage, Newman is consciously or unconsciously revealing one of the sources of his pulpit irony—his habit of appearing to be considering some general subject and at the same time of being about to point to an individual hearer and saying "Thou art the man for whom these words are intended." This feature of Newman's sermons has been noted by more than one listener. It kept the congregation in a nerve-tingling suspense, and sent it inward upon itself in a passion of self-exploration, in a feverish sense of shame. Moreover, Newman's careful avoidance of commonplaces not only put sharper weapons in his hands; it brightened his sentences, and in the end gave to his printed pages the indestructibility of prose which has not rested on the subjects and emotions of a season or a decade. Finally, the "covert" approach to his audience was partly responsible for the appearance of reserve, indirection, subtlety, and refinement in his discourses. And it gave the twofold impression that Newman was extremely impersonal yet uncannily aware of one's deepest personal secrets.

Newman concludes his address by advising the preacher to prepare his sermon in writing (a few persons like Pitt may converse like a book, he says; "others must be content to write and read their writing"), and by summing up the essence of pulpit effectiveness:

> Definiteness is the life of preaching. A definite hearer, not the whole world; a definite topic, not the whole evangelical tradition; and, in like manner, a definite speaker. Nothing that is anonymous will preach; nothing that is dead and gone; nothing even which is of yesterday, however religious in itself and useful. Thought and word are one in the Eternal Logos, and must not be separate in those who are His shadows on earth. They must issue fresh and fresh, as from the preacher's mouth, so from his breast, if they are to be 'spirit and life' to the hearts of his hearers.

Turning to Newman's sermons themselves we find them distinguished for their psychological insight, their imagination, and their literary power. More specifically they are marked by a delicate realism which adjusts them to their particular audience. For example, note how tactfully, with what understanding, he enters into the minds of his youthful audience in the sermon on **"Religion a Weariness to the Natural Man,"** preached at Oxford on July 27, 1828 [collected in *Parochial and Plain Sermons,* Vol. VII]:

> 'Religion is a weariness.' . . . Alas! my brethren, is it not so? Is not religion associated in your minds with gloom . . . ? The very terms 'religion,' 'devotion,' 'piety,' 'conscientiousness,' 'mortification,' and the like you find to be inexpressibly dull and cheerless; you cannot find fault with them, indeed you would if you could; and whenever the words are explained in particulars and realized, then you do find occasion for exception and objection. But though you cannot deny the claims of religion used as a vague and general term, yet how irksome, cold, uninteresting, uninviting does it at best appear to you! how severe its voice! how forbidding its aspect! With what animation, on the contrary, do you enter into the mere pursuits of time and the world! What bright anticipations of joy and happiness flit before your eyes! How you are struck and

dazzled at the view of the prizes of this life, as they are called! How you admire the elegancies of art, the brilliance of wealth, or the force of intellect! According to your opportunities, you mix in the world, you meet and converse with persons of various conditions and pursuits, and are engaged in the numberless occurrences of daily life. You are full of news; you know what this or that person is doing, and what has befallen him; what has not happened, which was near happening, what may happen. You are full of ideas and feelings upon all that goes on around you. But from some cause or other religion has no part, no sensible influence, in your judgment of men and things. It is out of your way. Perhaps you have your pleasure parties; you readily take your share in them time after time; you pass continuous hours in society where you know that it is quite impossible even to mention the name of religion. Your heart is in scenes and places where conversation on serious subjects is strictly forbidden by the rules of the world's propriety.

This clear and emphatic recognition of his hearer's difficulties gave Newman's sermons much of their singular power. But this realism extended beyond the understanding of other men's minds; it reached into the supersensible. Most critics of Newman agree that his power of *realizing* for others the actuality of the spiritual world was the most prominent feature of his sermons. In such sermons as **"The Greatness and Littleness of Human Life"** and **"The Invisible World"** [in *Parochial and Plain Sermons,* Vol. IV], he is able to make the "glories of nature, the sun, moon, and stars, and the richness and the beauty of the earth" appear as the mere types and figures witnessing to the invisible things of God.

In his later sermons, especially in ***Discourses to Mixed Congregations,*** this exercise of his imagination manifests itself in some of the most remarkable passages in the literature of sermons, as in the sixteenth sermon on **"The Mental Sufferings of Our Lord in His Passion,"** a sermon "before which," it has been said [by R. H. Hutton in his *Cardinal Newman,* 1891], "even the richness and wealth of Jeremy Taylor's imagination looks poor in comparison." With extraordinary detail Newman realizes and conceives the various and collective sins and miseries of all humanity as pouring upon Christ in Gethsemane and being so completely absorbed as to be all but His own:

> There, then, in that most awful hour, knelt the Savior of the world, putting off the defenses of His divinity, . . . opening His arms, baring His breast, sinless as He was, to the assault of His foe,—of a foe whose breath was a pestilence, and whose embrace was an agony. There He knelt, motionless and still, while the vile and horrible fiend clad His spirit in a robe steeped in all that is hateful and heinous in human crime, which clung close round His heart, and filled His conscience, and found its way into every sense and pore of His mind, and spread over Him a moral leprosy, till He almost felt Himself to be that which He never could be . . . Are these His lips, not uttering prayer, and praise, and holy blessings, but as if defiled with oaths, and blasphemies, and doctrines of devils? . . . And His ears,

they ring with sounds of revelry and of strife; and His heart is frozen with avarice, and cruelty, and unbelief; and His very memory is laden with every sin which has been committed since the fall, in all regions of the earth, with the pride of the old giants, and the lusts of the five cities, and the obduracy of Egypt, and the ambition of Babel, and the unthankfulness and scorn of Israel . . . And adversaries such as these gather round Thee, Blessed Lord, in millions now; they come in troops more numerous than the locust or the palmer-worm, or the plagues of hail, and flies, and frogs, which were sent against Pharaoh. Of the living and of the dead and of the as yet unborn, of the lost and the saved, of Thy people and of strangers, of sinners and of Saints, all sins are there . . . It is the long history of a world, and God alone can bear the load of it. Hopes blighted, vows broken, lights quenched, warnings scorned, opportunities lost; the innocent betrayed, the young hardened, the penitent relapsing, the just overcome, the aged failing; the sophistry of misbelief, the wilfulness of passion, the obduracy of pride, the tyranny of habit, the canker of remorse, the wasting fever of care, the anguish of shame, the pining of disappointment, the sickness of despair; such cruel, such pitiable spectacles, such heartrending, revolting, detestable, maddening scenes; nay, the haggard faces, the convulsed lips, the flushed cheek, the dark brow of the willing victims of rebellion, they are all before Him now, they are upon Him and in Him. They are with Him instead of that ineffable peace which has inhabited His soul since the moment of His conception. They are upon Him; they are all but His own; He cries to His Father as if He were the criminal, not the victim; His agony takes the form of guilt and compunction. He is doing penance, He is making confession, He is exercising contrition with a reality and a virtue infinitely greater than that of all saints and penitents together; for He is the One Victim for us all, the sole Satisfaction, the real Penitent, all but the real sinner.

With the aid of the Fathers of the Church, who had analyzed the mystery of the Passion, and whose analysis and imaginative reconstruction of the scene in Gethsemane he had accepted, Newman is thus able, as it were, to enter into Christ's mind, to conceive with terrible vivacity and intensity, the vast human transgression, gathered out of all lands and all times, piling itself up in the spirit of Christ until He is "all but the real sinner." Never again did Newman allow his imagination to soar to such a height. Only in the sermon on **"The Glories of Mary for the Sake of Her Son"** did he permit himself an almost equal freedom in describing the death of the Virgin Mary. In both sermons his imaginative flight offends the Protestant's sense of history. But, judged as a feat of literary evocation, as an effort to clothe a dogma with human realism, they rank high among the world's great sermons.

United with Newman's realism is his vivid sense of the truth and the wonder of revelation. He never had the slightest difficulty in accepting as objectively real the dogmas of revealed religion. His singularly strong grasp of the reality of revelation is seen in such sermons as **"The Invisi-**

> "[A] clear and emphatic recognition of his hearer's difficulties gave Newman's sermons much of their singular power. But this realism extended beyond the understanding of other men's minds; it reached into the supersensible. Most critics of Newman agree that his power of *realizing* for others the actuality of the spiritual world was the most prominent feature of his sermons."
>
> —*C. F. Harrold*

ble World," "Faith and Sight," "Faith and Experience," "The Mysteries of Nature and of Grace," "Christ upon the Waters." For Newman, it was not the unseen world which played tricks upon the mind; it was the world of the senses: "the world overcomes us," he says, "not merely by appealing to our reason, or by exciting our passions, but *by imposing on our imagination*" [italics added; *Oxford University Sermons*]. He had little respect for "the religion of the day," which tried to reduce Christianity to the dimensions of the world, to adjust it to modern knowledge, to keep the unseen a matter of morality rather than of dogma. Hence Newman's uncompromising severity and austerity:

> Christianity, considered as a moral system, is made up of two elements, beauty and severity; whenever either is indulged in to the loss or disparagement of the other, evil ensues [*Sermons on Subjects of the Day*].

Newman shocked many of his Anglican listeners when, in a sermon on **"The Apostolical Christian,"** preached in February, 1843, he declared:

> If the truth must be spoken, what are the humble monk, and the holy nun, and other regulars, as they are called, but Christians after the very pattern given us in Scripture? . . . Who but these give up home and friends, wealth and ease, good name and liberty of will, for the kingdom of heaven? [*Sermons on Subjects of the Day*].

Most of Newman's sermons were preached to well-bred, cultivated, respectable congregations, whose emotions had long lain dormant, whose hearts were cold and complacent, whose minds were affected by modern tolerance and worldliness and liberalism. It was therefore his task to remind his listeners of the austere and threatening side of Christianity. He chose moral rather than doctrinal subjects, and treated them so skillfully that they pierced the crust of complacency and sophistication. Avoiding generalities, he aimed the arrows of his insight at the frivolities and the self-deceptions of his hearers, and discoursed on such subjects as the **"Neglect of Divine Calls and Warnings," "The Usurpations of Reason," "Secret Faults," "Unreal Words," "The Individuality of the Soul," "The Religion of the Day."**

This practice partly accounts for Newman's frequent appeal to his listener's fear, a practice commented upon by numerous critics. "A long tremor of restrained fear," says Brémond [in his *The Mystery of Newman*, translated by H. C. Corrance, 1907], "runs through the sermons at St. Mary's." Contrary to the practice of many Catholic preachers, Newman rarely seems able to end a sermon with an impression of peace and joy. What Faber calls [in his *Oxford Apostles*, 1933] "the device of fear" was probably an inheritance from Evangelicalism which he never entirely shook off. But it was also a part of Newman's *natural* approach. He tells us in his address on **"University Preaching,"** that

> He who has before his mental eye the Four Last Things [Death, Judgment, Hell, and Heaven] will have the true earnestness, the horror or the rapture, of one who witnesses a conflagration, or discerns some rich and sublime prospect of natural scenery.

The man who has constantly before his imagination the Four Last Things will be haunted by the idea of sin and punishment; one's very childhood will be "the hidden sowing-ground of sin." Such a man will be tempted to overstress "the dominion of the law." Indeed, according to Whyte, who doubtless exaggerates [in his *Newman: An Appreciation*, 1901],

> Newman's very heart of hearts never, to the day of his death, got her complete divorce, to use Paul's great word, from the dominion of the law. Newman's Maker and Law-giver and Judge was, all his days, far more self-luminous to Newman than his only Redeemer, with His sin-cleansing blood, and with His sinner-justifying righteousness . . . There is a whole shining chain of Gospel texts that Newman never touches on . . . He never preached a single sermon like John Wesley's famous St. Mary's sermon on the text, 'By grace ye are saved through faith' . . . I never take down Newman's sermons for my recovery and my comfort.

Newman does not, however, like Pusey, indulge in passages describing "The End of All Things"—"this universal burning, and this awful lurid light of a world in flames, crackling, sinking, melting, amid the deluge of the everlasting fire of God." But he does say to us, in **"The Immortality of the Soul,"** and elsewhere: "we must fear and be in sorrow, before we can rejoice," "to be at ease, is to be unsafe," "you must always fear while you hope," "you are not in a safe state—if you were now to die, you would have no hope of salvation," "fearing will secure you from what you fear" [*Parochial and Plain Sermons*, Vol. I; *Sermons on Subjects of the Day*]. Yet we must do Newman the justice of observing that for him "fear" was ordinarily more a "holy awe" at the mysterious and dreadful seriousness of man's destiny, than the mere terror of the possibility of eternal damnation which Evangelicals like Spurgeon exploited with such tremendous effect. Moreover, there are sermons, such as **"Keeping Fast and Festival"** and **"Indulgence in Religious Privileges,"** in which Newman enjoins the duty of Christian joy: "Gloom is no Christian temper . . . We must live in sunshine even when we sorrow." "Joy in all its forms," he says, was one of the chief graces of primitive Christianity. We should add, too, that listeners like J. A. Froude came away with a feeling not of fear or dread but of compassion. Of the sermons Froude [in his *Short Studies on Great Subjects,* Vol. IV, 1883] wrote:

> A tone, not of fear, but of infinite pity runs through them all, and along with it a resolution to look facts in the face, not to fly to evasive generalities about infinite mercy and benevolence . . .

Throughout all of Newman's sermons we note the union of the beauty and severity which he said were the two great features of Christianity as a moral system. But Newman's "beauty" is in itself severe—severe not only in its "passionate reserve" which Delattre so much admired [in his *La Pensée de J. H. Newman,* 1914], but also in its austere intellectuality. "The finer and the more fastidious your mind is," says Whyte, "the more you will enjoy Newman's sermons." There is no attempt to whip up one's emotions or to offer one's mind vaguely impressive ideas. Though Newman retained to the end something of the Evangelical's tendency to portray human weakness in grim and mournful colors, there is none of the "religious enthusiasm," of Romaine, Milner, or Wilberforce. Religious zeal has been transformed by the academic tradition which shaped Newman's mind and style. Yet, despite the intellectual refinement of Newman's sermons, they are for the most part strongly unintellectual, in the usual sense of that word. They are the work of a man whose theory of religious knowledge is such that he eagerly embraces every paradox as an expression of the sovereignty of faith. He sees with joy that "religious light is intellectual darkness" ["The Christian Mysteries," in *Parochial and Plain Sermons*]. For him the very "mysteriousness" of a doctrine serves as a touchstone to distinguish the hypocritical from the sincere disciple. Paradoxically, this attitude toward the intellect in matters of faith leads him to the most splendidly audacious intellectual statements of the inexpressible. Thus he achieves remarkable effects when he discusses the Incarnation, in "The Humiliation of the Eternal Son," or Christ's Passion, in "The Incarnate Son, a Sufferer and Sacrifice"; or when, as in "Peace in Believing," he expounds the doctrine of the Holy Trinity, or when, as in the remarkable sermon on "Omnipotence in Bonds," he devotes four and a half pages to a definition of God, in terms of His self-dependence.

Everywhere in the sermons there are passages memorable for their insights, dramatic contrasts, descriptive touches, exhortations. Newman's psychological insight is most strikingly seen in his gentle but merciless delineations of certain types of men—the respectably religious man, in "The Strictness of the Law of Christ"; the young man drifting away from the religion of his parents, in "Intellect, the Instrument of Religious Training"; the skeptical man, in "Faith without Sight"; the philosopher, in "The Three Offices of Christ"; the practical worldly man, in "Faith and the World." In all these delineations there is an icy pitilessness, a cold calm toward the individual yet an infinite compassion over the pathos of the world, as Newman probes and explores his listeners' hidden ugliness of soul. Sometimes there is mordant irony, scorn, or

hot indignation, as when he attacks complacency and indifference in his sermon on "The Religion of the Day." Elsewhere in the sermons we find individual passages which stand out for their vivid or apt wording: passages, for example, on the elect as constituting the true Church, in "The Visible Church for the Sake of the Elect"; on the nature of the Church, in "The Kingdom of the Saints"; on the conflict of the Church and the World, in "Faith and Experience"; on saintliness, in "Saintliness the Standard of Christian Principle" and in "St. Paul's Characteristic Gift"; on conscience as a voice within the soul witnessing to God's existence, in the sermon on "Dispositions for Faith"; on the career of Savonarola, in "The Mission of St. Philip." There are passages which anticipate certain pages in the *Apologia,* just as the passage on conscience in "Dispositions for Faith" and several of the Oxford university sermons anticipate the *Grammar of Assent.* We read, for instance, in "The Immortality of the Soul," that "To every one of us there are but two beings in the whole world, himself and God." In the sermon on "The Powers of Nature," we find pages that recall to our minds the Alexandrian Platonism which Newman discusses in the first chapter of the *Apologia.* Occasionally an aphorism startles the smooth rhythm of Newman's sentences: "Everything is plain and easy to the earnest; it is only the double-minded who find difficulties"; "Nothing is more common than for men to think that because they are familiar with words, they understand the ideas they stand for"; "Health of body and mind is a great blessing, if we can bear it"; "Nature is not inanimate; its daily toil is intelligent; its works are *duties*"; "Let it be well understood that [pain] has no sanctifying influence in itself; bad men are made worse by it." Thus Newman's sermons are marked by great variety in method and mood, even though he intentionally narrowed the scope of his subject matter. They are eminently readable, and often have the virtues of the essay, one volume of them being entitled *Discourses* rather than *Sermons.*

They are marked too by Newman's genius for the closing paragraph. Sometimes it is a simple terse reminder, as in the sermon on "God's Commandments not Grievous" [in *Parochial and Plain Sermons,* Vol. 1]:

> Any of you, my brethren, who will not take advantage of this considerate providence, if you will not turn to God now with a *warm* heart, you will hereafter be obliged to do so (if you do so at all) *with a cold heart;*—which is much harder. God keep you from this!

Very often it is an exhortation or a prayer, or a tissue of Biblical quotations, or all three in skillful combination. It is frequently couched in measured phrases, balanced or antithetical in rhythm, rising to an impressive rhetorical climax:

> After our soul's anxious travail; after the birth of the Spirit; after trial and temptation; after sorrow and pain; after daily dyings to the world; after daily risings unto holiness; at length comes that "rest which remaineth unto the people of God." After the fever of life, after wearinesses and sicknesses, fightings and despondings, languor and fretfulness, struggling and succeeding;

after all the changes and chances of this troubled, unhealthy state,—at length comes death, at length the White Throne of God, at length the Beatific Vision. [*Parochial and Plain Sermons,* Vol. VI]

The most famous close of all is, of course, that of the great sermon on **"The Parting of Friends"** [in *Sermons on Subjects of the Day*], which was Newman's farewell to the Anglican communion, a farewell expressed in the simplest of words, yet curiously moving in its mounting rhythms:

> O my brethren, O kind and affectionate hearts, O loving friends, should you know anyone whose lot it has been, by writing or by word of mouth, in some degree to help you thus to act; if he has ever told you what you knew about yourselves, or what you did not know; has read to you your wants or feelings, and comforted you by the very reading; has made you feel that there was a higher life than this daily one, and a brighter world than that you see; or encouraged you, or sobered you, or opened a way to the inquiring, or soothed the perplexed; if what he has said or done has ever made you take an interest in him, and feel well inclined towards him; remember such a one in time to come, though you hear him not, and pray for him, that in all things he may know God's will, and at all times be ready to fulfil it.

Newman's twelve volumes of sermons fall into three divisions. The first group, the *Parochial and Plain Sermons,* eight volumes, published individually between 1834 and 1843, contains sermons written or preached between January 23, 1825, and April 30, 1843. They are of great value in any analysis of Newman's mind. No reader can form an adequate impression of his personality, his art, or his message, if he leaves these sermons unread. They are exquisitely simple in the literary art with which they give body to abstract argument without seeming to do so, and with which they suddenly concentrate upon some moving illustration. Readers have sometimes found their style too austere, unadorned, even bald. And at first sight it does have this appearance. But its rhetorical art is the kind which conceals itself; the very "baldness" is the studied effect of the carefully phrased and grouped sentences, preparatory to the sudden illumination which one sentence will give to all the rest, one paragraph to the argument which has gone before. The result is the more effective because it approaches so gradually and unobtrusively. This calm, coldly chaste, Anglican style was ideally suited to Newman's purposes, the *troubling* of men into religion, the uncovering of their subtle vices and hypocrisies and self-deceptions. There is nothing topical or ephemeral in these sermons; they are concerned almost entirely with ultimate matters, though never illustrating them with the sort of experiences of which he had little personal knowledge.

However, in dealing with ultimate problems, he is never merely general. Brémond has illuminatingly contrasted Newman's methods with those of Bossuet and Massillon. The great French preachers chose such general subjects as "Justice," "Providence," "Almsgiving"; they next took a rapid survey of the subject to fix its divisions; then they covered this vast ground more slowly, in two or three stages. Newman, as we have already observed, takes just the opposite course: he deals with a particular subject; some of his titles, taken at random, are **"Contracted Views in Religion," "The Good Part of Mary," "Christian Sympathy," "Sincerity and Hypocrisy," "The Church a Home for the Lonely."** One has only to compare the sermons on "Providence" by Bossuet and Bourdaloue with Newman's on **"A Particular Providence as Revealed in the Gospel,"** to see that Newman is not interested in the idea of Providence as a dogma but in bringing home to his hearers the conviction that God beholds each one of them *individually.* And this leads to a very typical and often-quoted passage which gives one the true flavor of these Anglican sermons, so simple and concrete, so personal and direct:

> How gracious is this revelation of God's particular providence! . . . God beholds thee individually, whoever thou art. He 'calls thee by thy name.' He sees thee, and understands thee, as He made thee. He knows what is in thee, all thy peculiar feelings and thoughts . . . He sympathizes in thy hopes and thy temptations. He interests Himself in all thy anxieties and remembrances . . . He compasses thee round and bears thee in His arms . . . He looks tenderly upon thy hands and thy feet; He hears thy voice, the beating of thy heart, and thy very breathing. Thou dost not love thyself better than He loves thee. Thou canst not shrink from pain more than he dislikes thy bearing it . . . What a thought is this, a thought almost too great for our faith!

In this sermon, as in the others, Newman foregoes any temptation to set up and analyze an abstract idea, whether it be a dogma or a human type; he prefers what is specific and experienced. Instead of the theological and metaphysical approach employed by Bossuet or Lacordaire, he prefers the psychological: he probes the apathy, the indecision, the perplexities of actual men and women before him. He uses his remarkable insight into their minds to introduce them to that spiritual world which was so intensely real to him. And through it all he skillfully manages the endless resources of his seemingly simple style so that we come with a start upon a sentence or a paragraph which leaps from its quiet context, such as the following:

> What a truly wretched state is that coldness and dryness of soul, in which so many live and die, high and low, learned and unlearned. Many a great man, many a peasant, many a busy man, lives and dies with closed heart, with affections undeveloped, unexercised. You see the poor man, passing day after day, Sunday after Sunday, without a thought in his mind, to appearance almost like a stone. You see the educated man, full of thought, full of intelligence, full of action, but still with a stone heart, as cold and dead as regards his affections, as if he were the poor ignorant countryman. You see others, with warm affections, perhaps, for their families, with benevolent feelings towards their fellow-men, yet stopping there . . . Life passes, riches fly away, popularity is fickle, the senses decay, the world changes, friends die. One alone is constant; One alone is true to us; One alone can be

true; One alone can be all things to us; One alone can supply our needs; One alone can train us up to our full perfection; One alone can give a meaning to our complex and intricate nature; One alone can give us tune and harmony; One alone can form and possess us.

Or we may pause over the often-quoted passage which expresses Newman's vivid sense of the unseen:

Whenever we look abroad, we are reminded of those most gracious and holy Beings, the servants of the Holiest, who deign to minister to the heirs of salvation. Every breath of air and ray of light and heat, every beautiful prospect, is, as it were, the skirts of their garments, the waving of the robes of those whose faces see God in heaven.

The *Parochial and Plain Sermons* are marked with Newman's literal application of scriptural imagery, with the technique of fear and pity, and with his sacramental view of visible phenomena as a veil hiding the glories of the spiritual world. There are remnants of Calvinistic teaching, and the tone is generally one of mystery and awe.

The second group of sermons comprises the *Oxford University Sermons* and *Sermons on Subjects of the Day,* both volumes published in 1843. The former volume is made up of fifteen discourses delivered at various times between 1826 and 1843. Their central theme is the interrelation of faith and reason. Since they were composed primarily for a university audience, they are academic and impersonal in tone, tightly knit and closely reasoned in method. Here we find a number of memorable type-portraits: the man of the world, the "so-called philosophical Christian," the skeptic. Here, again, we find obvious anticipations of the *Grammar of Assent,* in such discourses as "The Usurpations of Reason," "Faith and Reason Contrasted as Habits of Mind," "The Nature of Faith in Relation to Reason," "Implicit and Explicit Reason," and "Wisdom as Contrasted with Faith and with Bigotry." . . . [The] final sermon gives us a preliminary sketch of the *Essay on Development.* Less frequently observed, however, is the foreshadowing of a passage of *The Idea of a University* by five pages of the sermon on wisdom contrasted with faith and bigotry, in which Newman discusses various desirable and undesirable ways of "enlarging the mind." The unity of the *Oxford University Sermons,* as a volume, is not one of its strong characteristics. Besides the sermon on development, which has nothing to do with the main theme of the volume, there are sermons on Natural and Revealed Religion, on evangelical sanctity, on justice as a principle of divine governance (directed primarily at the Benthamites), on willfullness as the sin of Saul (aimed largely at the revolutionary spirit of the early 1830's), and on "Human Responsibility as Independent of Circumstances" (aimed at the fatalistic environmentalism of the age).

Readers who find the *Grammar of Assent* intolerably technical and laborious will discover, in sermons IV and X-XIV, an easy introduction to the heart of Newman's theory. They will be protected from misunderstanding his final position regarding assent by the Preface and the footnotes which he introduced into the third edition. They will find

abundant aphorisms throughout the well-conducted argument—"It is as absurd to argue men, as to torture them, into believing," "All men have a reason, but not all men can give a reason," "Reason can but ascertain the profound difficulties of our condition, it cannot remove them." And at the end of the tenth sermon the reader will find a passage which possibly suggested the image of "ignorant armies clashing by night" in Matthew Arnold's "Dover Beach":

Controversy, at least in this age, does not lie between the hosts of heaven, Michael and his Angels on the one side, and the powers of evil on the other; but it is *a sort of night battle,* where each fights for himself, and friend and foe stand together. When men understand each other's meaning, they see, for the most part, that controversy is either superfluous or hopeless.

In the final sermon there occurs Newman's famous illustration that human nature contains within itself elements capable of expansion into infinite and eternal meanings. If God's nature is infinite, it is sometimes asked, how can a finite creature like man gain any but a hopelessly inadequate notion of Him? Newman answers by pointing to the marvels of music, with its limited number of notes:

There are seven notes in the scale; make them fourteen, yet what a slender outfit for so vast an enterprise! What science brings so much out of so little? Out of what poor elements does some great master in it create his new world! Shall we say that all this exuberant inventiveness is a mere ingenuity or trick of art, like some game or fashion of the day, without reality, without meaning? We may do so, and then perhaps we shall also account the science of theology to be a matter of words; yet, as there is a divinity in the theology of the Church which those who feel cannot communicate, so is there also in the wonderful creation of sublimity and beauty of which I am speaking. To many men the very names which the science employs are utterly incomprehensible. To speak of an 'idea' or a 'subject' seems to be fanciful or trifling, and of the views which it opens upon us to be childish extravagance; yet is it possible that that inexhaustible evolution and disposition of notes, so rich yet so simple, so intricate and yet so regulated, so various yet so majestic, should be a mere sound which is gone and perishes? Can it be that those mysterious stirrings of heart and keen emotions and strange yearnings after we know not what and awful impressions from we know not whence, should be wrought in us by what is unsubstantial and comes and goes and begins and ends in itself ? It is not so; it cannot be. No! they have escaped from some higher sphere: they are the voice of angels or the magnificat of saints, or the living laws of divine governance or the divine attributes: something are they besides themselves which we cannot compass, which we cannot utter; though mortal man, and he perhaps not otherwise distinguished above his fellows, has the gift of eliciting them.

The last of Newman's Anglican sermons were published under the title of *Sermons on Subjects of the Day* (1843).

Some of the twenty-six which make up the volume were preached as early as 1831, 1837, and 1838; all but five, however, were either written or preached between 1840 and Newman's final farewell, **"The Parting of Friends,"** in September, 1843. Though their style retains some of the chaste simplicity of the earlier sermons, these adopt a rich texture of Biblical phrase, a variety of rhythm, parallelisms, and cumulative effects which later developed into the profuse and passionate eloquence of the *Discourses to Mixed Congregations.* Many of the sermons were preached when Newman was on his "Anglican deathbed," in retirement at Littlemore. They reflect an agony of indecision. To read them, says Barry [in his *Newman,* 1905], "is to overhear the soliloquy in which every possible reason is advanced against joining the Church of Rome that could yet afford ground to one whose ideals were monastic, antiquarian, but above all, unworldly." A kind of pathos, says Hutton, "runs like a silver thread through the whole series of Oxford sermons." Newman was now painfully uncomfortable under the conditions of the Anglican Church, not only because he wanted the Church freed from all political fetters, but also because he resented the sleek complacency, the easy worldliness, the shallow piety, to which the alliance with the state had brought the Anglican clergy. For him, there could be no true church except where the ecclesiastical motive power was in the hands of men who had renounced the comforts and joys of the world for the sake of that "other world," *i.e.* in the hands of a self-denying clergy, under the moral influence of the great monastic orders. Most of these sermons show Newman's "severity" now passing into a radical otherworldliness, a frank asceticism, which shows that he is already a convert at heart to the Church of Rome. With the same skill as on other occasions, he traces the thoughts of those who take a shallowly optimistic view of the evils of the world:

> The world promises that, if we trust it, we cannot go wrong. Why? because it is so many—there are so many men in it; they must be right. This is what it seems boldly to say,—'God cannot punish so many.' So it is, we know, in human law. . . . They think that this world is too great an evil for God to punish; or rather that therefore it is not an evil, because it is a great one. They cannot compass the idea that God should allow so great an evil to exist, as the world would be, if it is evil; and therefore, since He does allow it, it is not an evil.

No passage in Newman better illustrates his unfailing and relentless power to expose inconsistent thinking.

Throughout the volume, Newman stresses the warfare between faith and the world, and between the Church and the world; he develops his mystical interpretation of Old Testament figures—Joshua and Elisha are types of Christ, the Christian Church is a continuation of the Jewish; he also develops his sense of Christianity as a supernatural order realized both in the individual and in the corporate realm of a divine society—three sermons especially show this growing institutionalism in Newman's thought, **"The Christian Church as an Imperial Power," "Sanctity the Token of the Christian Empire,"** and **"Condition of the Members of the Christian Empire."** As he relentlessly pursues his thought of the Christian empire, he finally sets before his hearers an image of an institution which can be nothing else than the Roman Church—

> a universal empire without earthly arms; temporal pretensions without temporal sanctions; a claim to rule without the power to enforce; a continual tendency to acquire with a continual exposure to be dispossessed; greatness of mind with weakness of body.

This empire will inevitably be persecuted (persecution is a token of the Church), yet it will claim a right to rule, direct, rebuke, exhort, denounce, condemn. No one in Newman's congregation thought he was describing the Anglican Church; all knew that he was envisaging an ideal, one which had found its historical approximation in that communion toward which he was tending. All knew, too, his meaning when he described the ideal Christian as being "apostolical," in a sermon which must have sounded very strange to secular-minded Anglicans.

In this volume occurs the famous sermon on **"Wisdom and Innocence,"** which so painfully impressed Charles Kingsley. Christ's followers, says Newman, were enjoined to be "wise as serpents and harmless as doves"; they were to be

Title page for the first edition of Newman's "spiritual autobiography."

God's sheep, but without the witlessness of sheep; they were to be prudent and wary "in the midst of wolves," injuring no one, yet not blurting out what might merely irritate the world without succeeding in teaching it. Newman's sermon might never have been pounced on by Kingsley if he had confessed that some churchmen have mingled a good deal too much wisdom of the serpent with too little of the harmlessness of the dove. However, the sermon as a whole leaves no impression of guile or duplicity. In one of his best closing paragraphs, Newman says:

> May He, as of old, choose 'the foolish things of the world to confound the wise, and the weak things of the world to confound the things which are mighty'! May He support us all the day long, till the shades lengthen, and the evening comes, and the busy world is hushed, and the fever of life is over, and our work is done! Then in His mercy may He give us a safe lodging, and a holy rest, and peace at the last!

But the great sermon, in some ways the very greatest of Newman's, is the final one. In preaching **"The Parting of Friends,"** Newman speaks not merely as a preacher but as a man; he takes his farewell of his parish and of his friends; he chooses the same text he had used on preaching his first sermon nineteen years before: "Man goeth forth to his work and to his labor until the evening" (Psalm civ: 23). The sermon is a tissue of Biblical diction and imagery; hardly a sentence is without its paraphrase or quotation. One result is that Newman is able to speak personally yet without embarrassment; the borrowed imagery at once protects him and intensifies the effect of his words on his congregation, which, by the end, is in tears. With simple eloquence he parallels Christ's parting from His disciples "at a feast," with his own farewell over the communion table in his chapel at Littlemore. Carrying the thought through the Old and New Testaments, he shows how similar partings took place in the lives of Jacob, Ishmael, Naomi, David, and St. Paul. By the time he reaches his closing paragraphs, he has built up a wonderfully rich texture of allusion, quotation, association, and symbol. His congregation, whose minds are already filled with Biblical image and thought, then hears him cry: "O Jerusalem, Jerusalem, which killest the prophets!" If any of them doubt the allusion, they are quickly enlightened when Newman suddenly follows with words that are now as famous, for their pathos and eloquence, as any he ever wrote:

> O mother of saints! O school of the wise! O nurse of the heroic! of whom went forth, in whom have dwelt, memorable names of old, to spread the truth abroad, or to cherish and illustrate it at home! . . . O virgin of Israel! wherefore dost thou now sit on the ground and keep silent . . . O my mother, whence is this unto thee, that thou hast good things poured upon thee and canst not keep them, and bearest children, yet darest not own them? why has thou not the skill to use their services, nor the heart to rejoice in their love? how is it that whatever is generous in purpose, and tender or deep in devotion, thy flower and thy promise, falls from thy bosom and finds no home within thine arms? Who hath put this note upon thee, to have 'a miscarrying womb, and dry

breasts,' to be strange to thine own flesh, and thine eye cruel towards thy little ones?

Only Newman could have written a sermon like this; only he, with his passionate reticence, could have so brilliantly availed himself of the shelter of scriptural phrase, so that his very rebuking of his Church could take on the mournful beauty of a religious elegy.

The *Oxford University Sermons* and the *Sermons on Subjects of the Day* may be regarded as transitional in character. Some of them are as purely Anglican as any in the *Parochial and Plain Sermons;* others are so Catholic that they might have been delivered in the Roman Church. Whoever wishes to study the growth of Newman's ideas should read chronologically the ten volumes of sermons preached during his Anglican period. There Newman will be found testing the validity and the resisting power of every new argument or theory. From year to year he moves farther and farther away from rationalistic Protestantism; his conception of religion becomes more and more intense, dogmatic, ascetic, mystical, and institutional; he lays more and more stress, as we have said, on the opposition between the world and the Church, between the natural and the supernatural, between the City of God and the city of men.

Following the two transitional volumes, Newman's third and last group of sermons appears in *Discourses to Mixed Congregations* (1849) and *Sermons Preached on Various Occasions* (1857). Newman was never very fortunate in the titles of his books; only in the titles of his sermons does he show much imagination. No one would suspect from the backstrip of the volume of 1849 that the contents were rich in eloquence and thought. These sermons were preached during the first years of Newman's Catholic ministry, when he felt the enthusiam of the convert and the freedom of the man who has found his proper sphere of action. He is no longer the perplexed Anglican; he is now the disciple of St. Philip Neri. Released from conflicting emotions, and from the self-imposed task of reconciling the apparently irreconcilable, he has developed a mature self-confidence and a vigor of style which bring out all the more vividly his own special powers as a preacher. His sermons now have a new character; they are passionate, boldly imaginative, colorful, at times consciously rhetorical. Possibly his recent seminary studies amid Italian surroundings account for some of this sudden change in Newman's style. He permits himself greater range in effects—sharper irony, exquisite pathos, sublimity, scorn, daring imagination (as in **"The Mental Sufferings of Our Lord,"** which we have already examined). He is also more direct, mercilessly pursuing his psychological probings into the hearts of his listeners, as in the sermon on **"Neglect of Divine Calls and Warnings."** He is more unsparing than ever in his delineations of worldly life, and speaks tersely in condemnation of it:

> We are not sent into this world for nothing; we are not born at random; we are not here, that we may go to bed at night, and get up in the morning, toil for our bread, eat and drink, laugh and joke, sin when we have a mind to, and reform when we are tired of sinning, rear a family and die.

In such sermons as those on the **"Glories of Mary,"** the new convert is giving free rein to what has been called the "pious impressions," with which the Catholic Fathers supplied him as interpreting and illustrating the theology of the Church. He rivals the passion of Italian and French devotion to the Virgin Mary, and even anticipates the dogma of the Immaculate Conception of the Virgin several years before it is defined. On the other hand, in such sermons as **"Nature and Grace," "Faith and Private Judgment," "Faith and Doubt,"** and **"Purity and Love,"** Newman employs a less colorful rhetoric, and engages in a tightly executed feat of distinction and definition. In **"Faith and Private Judgment,"** he sharply attacks the Protestant position; with scorn he alludes to the Protestant cast of Anglicans:

> Let them stake their eternal prospects on kings and nobles and parliaments and soldiery, let them take some mere fiction of the law, or abortion of the schools, or idol of a populace, or upstart of a crisis, or oracle of lecture-rooms, as the prophet of God.

This is hardly the language of the *Parochial and Plain Sermons.* It is in fact the language to appear shortly in certain parts of the *Difficulties of Anglicans,* and later, and more devastatingly, in the *Present Position of Catholics.*

In the *Sermons Preached on Various Occasions* (1857) Newman returns somewhat to his earlier Anglican reserve. His style is no longer the passionate rhetoric of the *Discourses to Mixed Congregations,* but is the style of a man who has found his place in English Roman Catholicism. The first eight of the fifteen sermons were delivered before the Catholic University of Ireland in 1856 and 1857, during the first year of the opening of its Church. The other seven sermons were preached on such occasions as the installation of Bishop Ullathorne, the funeral of James R. Hope-Scott, the anniversary of the Birmingham Oratory. The variety in these sermons is more limited than in the two preceding volumes; yet one notes the tight intellectuality of the sermons on **"Dispositions for Faith"** and **"Omnipotence in Bonds"**; the vivid contrasts drawn between St. Philip Neri and Savonarola in **"The Mission of St. Philip"**; the personal quality and the gentle simplicity in the sermon on Hope Scott; the searching analysis of the pharisaical "religion of mankind." But nowhere are there the flights of religious fancy which Newman permitted himself a few years earlier. Probably the most memorable single passage in the volume is that which poetically describes the conversion of England from paganism, and the rise of the Church like a solemn pageant, before which the idols of heathendom vanished like ghosts; we find it in the sermon on **"Christ upon the Waters"**:

> In a hundred years the work was done; the idols, the sacrifices, the mummeries of paganism flitted away and were not, and the pure doctrine and heavenly worship of the Cross were found in their stead. The fair form of Christianity rose up and grew and expanded like a beautiful pageant from north to south; it was majestic, it was solemn, it was bright, it was beautiful and pleasant, it was soothing to the griefs, it was indulgent to the hopes of man; it was at once a teaching and

a worship; it had a dogma, a mystery, a ritual of its own; it had an hierarchical form. A brotherhood of holy pastors, with mitre and crosier and uplifted hand, walked forth and blessed and ruled a joyful people. The crucifix headed the procession, and simple monks were there with hearts in prayer, and sweet chants resounded, and the holy Latin tongue was heard, and boys came forth in white, swinging censers, and the fragrant cloud arose, and mass was sung, and the Saints were invoked; and day after day, and in the still night, and over the woody hills and in the quiet plains, as constantly as sun and moon and stars go forth in heaven, so regular and solemn was the stately march of blessed services on earth, high festival, and gorgeous procession, and soothing dirge, and passing bell, and the familiar evening call to prayer; till he who recollected the old pagan time, would think it all unreal that he beheld and heard, and would conclude he did but see a vision, so marvelously was heaven let down upon earth, so triumphantly were chased away the fiends of darkness to their prison below.

No doubt the greatest of the sermons *On Various Occasions* is that which Newman preached at the first Synod of Oscott on the occasion of the re-establishment of the Catholic hierarchy in England. He chose for his text a verse from the Song of Songs:

> Arise, make haste, my love, my dove, my beautiful one, and come. For the winter is now past, the rain is over and gone. The flowers have appeared in our land.

This sermon, **"The Second Spring,"** even while it celebrates the triumph of his Church, is unaggressive and meek. Its spirit in the midst of victory is that of the martyr rather than of the conqueror; it speaks of the victory that is won through suffering, persecution, and renunciation, rather than through conquest and domination. "The opening [of this sermon]," one critic [J. Lewis May, in his *Cardinal Newman,* 1930] observes,

> is slow and solemn and stately, like the overture to some majestic symphony. But its splendor is not heavy or barbaric. The light shines through it, as the dawn shines through a lattice.

The theme of the sermon is the law of permanence behind the transiency of earthly things; the opening lines therefore run thus:

> We have familiar experience of the order, the constancy, the perpetual renovation of the material world which surrounds us. Frail and transitory as is every part of it, restless and migratory as are its elements, never-ceasing as are its changes, still it abides.

In addition to the usual phrasal felicity, and accumulating parallelisms, we note the remarkable number of "r's" and "l's" in these lines, resulting in a fragile sort of beauty, which is sharply rounded off by the concluding element, "still it abides." The theme now quietly continues, in undulating rhythms, and without imagery, which is to appear later in the rhetorical climax:

It is bound together by a law of permanence, it
is set up in unity; and, though it is ever dying,
it is ever coming to life again. Dissolution does
but give birth to fresh modes of organization,
and one death is the parent of a thousand lives.

Then follows a series of phrases and sentences which unite
rhythm with imagery, the abstract with the concrete:

Each hour, as it comes, is but a testimony, how
fleeting, yet how secure, how certain, is the great
whole. It is like an image on the waters, which
is ever the same, though the waters ever flow.
Change upon change—yet one change cries out
to another, like the alternate Seraphim, in praise
and in glory of their Maker. The sun sinks to rise
again; the day is swallowed up in the gloom of
the night, to be born out of it, as fresh as if it had
never been quenched. Spring passes into summer, and through summer and autumn into winter, only the more surely, by its own ultimate return, to triumph over that grave, towards which
it resolutely hastened from its first hour.

Newman now approaches the specific point which he
wishes to drive home to his elated listeners, namely, that
man and all his works are mortal; they die, and they have
no power of renovation; but through a miracle the Church
of Augustine and Anselm and St. Thomas returns after
three centuries to the land of St. Cuthbert and St. Chad
and St. Dunstan. The "second spring" has come. Great
sacrifices are to be demanded, perhaps even martyrdom.
Certainly few sermons of triumph were ever more humble
and graceful. It played no small part in allaying the fears
of non-Catholics that the restored hierarchy would be an
arrogant or aggressive force against the Anglican Establishment and the state. Reprinted as a brochure it won admirers from all quarters, and remains today the sermon
which, more than any other, keeps *Sermons on Various
Occasions* a memorable volume. (pp. 321-46)

.　.　.　.　.

One of the secrets of Newman's success as an accomplished persuader was . . . his stylistic skill in adapting
himself to the minds he was addressing. No two collections of his sermons, for example, have the same character. His Oxford University sermons, addressed to a highly
cultivated congregation, show great restraint and refinement; they are cautious, intellectual, and exploratory.
Some of the Birmingham sermons, on the other hand, are
of a popular, pictorial, almost scenic type suitable for the
presumably less fastidious audience of a mid-Victorian
commercial town. Newman paints in broader colors and
introduces dramatic effects which would have seemed out
of place at St. Mary's. In the Dublin lectures, he is formal,
precise, academic. Realizing that he is on controversial
ground, he carefully sketches his plan for his audience,
then defines and redefines his terms, anticipates objections, follows up his generalizations with convincing illustrations, turning his subject round and round, keeping a
perfect poise as he moves through its intricacies. In the
Essay on Development, Newman's method is even more
severe, though here his idiomatic language, his lucidity,
and his illustrations give this controversial work its peculiar attraction. Another secret of Newman's rhetorical

power is the sheer drudgery which went into his best
prose. He never wrote easily; in fact he seems to have
hated to write, and wrote only from a sense of duty. "The
composition of a volume," he says, "is like gestation and
childbirth." Yet he told Bellasis: "I think best when I
write" [reported in E. Bellasis's *Memorials of Mr. Ser-
geant Bellasis,* 1895]. Newman's agony in composition is
at once the mark of the craftsman and the cause of his artistic perfection. In the process of writing, Newman sacrifices all decorative impulses; he is never mannered, pretentious, or striking. Even when his prose becomes most impressive or richly imaginative, there is no effect of discontinuity; the richer passage is but a development out of his
simpler and more colloquial manner.

A third and final secret of his power lies in his breadth of
handling. In working out the design of the *Essay on Development,* or the *Difficulties of Anglicans,* or the *Grammar of Assent,* he might conceivably have restricted himself to technical details, analogies, examples, and to
straightforward argument. Instead, he occasionally
glances up from his immediate object and engages in a
searching definition, or draws up one of those general observations, from a sentence in length to several pages,
which makes some of the least promising of his essays a
delight to explore. Who would think that in an essay on
"The Theology of the Seven Epistles of St. Ignatius"
would occur the brilliant and amusing portrait of a biased
man who decides to write a book upon the Fathers? Newman shows the man taking notes from Gibbon, Mosheim,
Lardner; then dipping into the Fathers to "confirm his anticipations"; sketching off his characters, condemning or
applauding according to his preconceptions; then, finding
his time running out, drawing his work to a close and publishing, without having ever really read the Fathers. Newman's comment on this procedure [in his *Essays Critical
and Historical,* Vol. 1] is acidly reserved:

Anyhow, *he* has gained his point; he has shown
that the arguments of his adversaries admit of
question, has thrown the whole subject into the
gulf of controversy, and given a specimen of how
the age of railroads should behave towards the
age of martyrs.

This breadth of handling, this direction of individual details to a larger frame of reference, leads also to those epigrammatic sentences which sparkle in every volume. Present-day readers find some of Newman's sententious utterances very relevant, as the following: "Some races are like
children, and require a despot to nurse, and feed, and dress
them, to give them pocket money, and take them out for
airings"; "Material force is the *ultima ratio* of political society everywhere; arms alone can keep the peace" [*Discussion and Arguments,* 1872]. Everyone knows that "Calculation never made a hero," but not many have read that
"Boys are always more or less inaccurate, and too many,
or rather the majority, remain boys all their lives" [*Idea
of a University*].

Newman employed this wonderfully flexible and transparent style for one of the finest audiences any writer ever
had: the educated Victorian public. On the whole, it was
hostile to his teachings, but far from indifferent to the is-

sues which they raised. It had a deep interest in theology as well as in history and science. Newman's readers welcomed with prodigious enthusiasm his own *Apologia* and Gladstone's religious pamphlets; they read *The Origin of Species* and Lecky's *Rationalism in Europe* and innumerable three-decker novels. They were not afraid of large volumes and many of them. "It was the existence of this public," says one writer on Newman [Bertram Newman, in his *Cardinal Newman: A Biographical and Literary Study,* 1925],

> which lent to the characteristic Victorian writers a perceptible consciousness, denied to many of their successors, of being heralds of large ideas on a large stage, and it was to this consciousness that they owed at least in part the quality of impressiveness, of appeal, which distinguishes them. In this respect, if in no other, Newman is typical of the literature of his age.

(pp. 349-51)

Charles Frederick Harrold, in his John Henry Newman: An Expository and Critical Study of His Mind, Thought and Art, *Longmans, Green & Co., 1945, 472 p.*

Martin J. Svaglic (essay date 1951)

[*In the following essay, Svaglic contends that the* Apologia *is structured as "the drama of a soldier who, through defeat and submission, at last finds peace."*]

The *Apologia pro Vita Sua* is not the autobiography of Newman from 1801 to 1845. It tells us nothing of the family life, the student activities, the intellectual and artistic interests of its complex subject. Nor is it even a spiritual autobiography of those years except in a limited sense. We must turn to the *Letters and Correspondence,* with their "Autobiographical Memoir," to supplement the bare account given in the *Apologia* of Newman's conversion to Evangelical Christianity. The *Apologia* is primarily a work of rhetoric designed to persuade a body of readers or "judges," English, Protestant, and suspicious of a convert to an unpopular religion, that Newman, whom Kingsley had made a symbol of the Catholic priesthood, was a man not of dishonesty but of integrity. Newman chose autobiography as his method because of his lifelong English preference of the concrete to the abstract, his vivid realization of the rôle in persuasion of personal influence: "I am touched by my five senses, by what my eyes behold and my ears hear. . . . I gain more from the life of our Lord in the Gospels than from a treatise *de Deo*" [*Historical Sketches,* Vol. II]. "The heart is commonly reached, not through the reason, but through the imagination, by means of direct impressions, by the testimony of facts and events, by history, by description. Persons influence us, voices melt us, looks subdue us, deeds inflame us" [*Discussions and Arguments on Various Subjects*]. It was his conversion to Catholicism after a long puzzling delay, many predictions of the event, and even charges of treachery to the Church of England that had created the atmosphere of suspicion in which his character had been impugned. Therefore he would confine the autobiography principally to a brief explanation of how he arrived, to begin with, at

what so many regarded with suspicion and fear: Anglo-Catholic principles; and to a detailed one of how, having accepted them and devoted himself to propagating them, he became convinced that the principles which had led him thus far must lead him farther still, into the Catholic Church. "I am but giving a history of my opinions, and that, with the view of showing that I have come by them through intelligible processes of thought and honest external means." If that history of opinions, in spite of its limited scope, has so much of the richness and variety of great autobiography, it is because Newman held that the means by which we arrive at belief, all of which he would try to chronicle for his own life so far as that was possible, were multiform and complex.

Newman, with his extraordinary memory for personal affairs, his strong affections, and his fondness for musing on the past—that great revealer of God's providence—was peculiarly equipped to tell his story; and, as we have indicated, the scope of that story was carefully limited by his rhetorical purpose. But what kind of material was to be used, and how was it to be expressed and arranged? Newman's theories of belief and of biography, closely related, provided the answer to the first question, and his conception of life and of conversion to the second.

"It is the concrete being that reasons," Newman tells us in the *Apologia,* and the remark sums up his approach to the problem of belief, which dominates so much of his thinking from his early days as an Oxford preacher to the last years of his life, from the *University Sermons* to the *Grammar of Assent.* Since the man who assents to any given proposition is far more than a mere dialectician, an intellect in a void, the account of his reasoning (which cannot be the same as the reasoning itself) must include all the forces at work in creating his state of mind so far as they can be specified. Many of these must remain implicit; the explicit account may be syllogistic in form or may "designate particular methods of thought, according to which the mind reasons (that is, proceeds from truth to truth)" and "particular states of mind which influence its reasonings. Such methods are antecedent probability, analogy, parallel cases, testimony, and circumstantial evidences; and such states of mind are prejudice, deference to authority, party spirit, attachment to such and such principles, and the like" [*University Sermons*]. As Walter E. Houghton remarks [in his *The Art of Newman's Apologia,* 1945], this passage, written in 1840, reads like "Directions for Writing the *Apologia.*" The syllogistic method was designed for a simpler psychology than Newman's. The effect of St. Augustine's verdict, "securus iudicat orbis terrarum," for example, would be far greater on one who was deferential to authority than on one who was not. In 1841, writes a well-known historian [Esmé Wingfield-Stratford, in his *The Victorian Tragedy,* 1931], "one of those events occurred whose full horror it requires a clerical mind to appreciate. The State Churches of England and Prussia combined to set up a bishopric of Jerusalem. The idea of such communion between Christ's followers, on the scene of Christ's passion, was too much for Newman. 'It was one of the blows that broke me,' he confessed in his *Apologia.*" For the ironic "clerical mind" substitute "attachment to such and such principles" (belief in dogmatic religion, a visible church with rites and sacraments as the channels of grace, and the episcopal system, as Newman is careful to explain at the beginning of Chapter Two) and the comment, apart from its tone, is quite in harmony with Newman's thought. How did he come to hold such principles in the first place? The various "methods of thought" and "states of mind" of the first chapter supply the answer.

As we come to realize the magnitude and complexity of the task Newman set out to perform in a short space and a shorter time, we can begin to understand the expressions of difficulty which recur in the *Apologia.* As for his great "revolution of mind," he confesses:

> I feel overcome with the difficulty of satisfying myself in my account of it, and have recoiled from the attempt, till the near approach of the day, on which these lines must be given to the world, forces me to set about the task. For who can know himself, and the multitude of subtle influences which act upon him? And who can recollect, at the distance of twenty-five years, all that he once knew about his thoughts and his deeds, and that, during a portion of his life, when, even at the time, his observation, whether of himself or of the external world, was less than before or after, by very reason of the perplexity and dismay which weighed upon him. . . . It is both to head and heart an extreme trial, thus to analyze what has so long gone by, and to bring out the results of that examination.

Newman's own reticence, unusual even for an Englishman, increased the difficulty. Yet he is confident of success, for he goes on to say: "I have done various bold things in my life: this is the boldest; and, were I not sure I should after all succeed in my object, it would be madness to set about it." We can see now that far more is involved here than a rather melodramatic introduction to a chapter of crisis.

Memory alone, however, even Newman's, would be inadequate to such a task; hence the great importance of contemporary letters and documents for reliably and vividly portraying the mind in action at any given time in the past. In reading a biography, Newman said [in his *Historical Sketches,* Vol. II], he looked for "the secret heart"—"the *interior.*" And it was in the lives and letters of the ancient saints like John Chrysostom that he especially found it, for they "left behind them just that kind of literature which more than any other represents the abundance of the heart, which more than any other approaches to conversation; I mean correspondence." Thus it is that the Duke of Wellington's "despatches on campaign . . . tell us so much more about him than any panegyrical sketch." These lines were written in 1859. Five years later Newman followed his own precepts by giving us a life replete with letters and "despatches on campaign." A "silent Saint," he had written, "is the object of faith rather than of affection. If he speaks, then we have the original before us. . . . " The *Apologia* is both colloquial and dramatic in tone. The original is decidedly before us. And he impresses the reader, as Newman holds it the proper object of a "Life" to do, "with the idea of moral unity, identity,

growth, continuity, personality." As he converses with us, we are "conscious of the presence of one active principle of thought, one individual character, flowing on and into the various matters which he discusses, and the different transactions in which he mixes" [*Historical Sketches*].

That the *Apologia* is vividly dramatic in style was perhaps first pointed out, and with some regret, by the *Times* in its original review, which felt that the book lacked

> some of the graces and proper characteristics of a retrospect. It has not the calmness and serenity of a distant survey of life. . . . The writer is mentally too near the times and the controversies which he describes, and the rush of thought which carries him along is often more like a conversational explosion on the subject of an event or scene of yesterday than a recall of distant memories, and a train of feelings and relations of the past. From the freshness and vividness with which he reawakens the struggle of that occasion, it is difficult to believe that *No. 90* was not condemned last week. Everybody has, however, his own way of doing things, and if Dr. Newman's autobiography wants the calm grace of a retrospect, it has all the fire of a description of the present moment.

Precisely! For the dramatic way is indeed Newman's way and one main source of his great hold on hearer or reader. He never wrote anything truer than the remark in 1833 [recorded in his *Letters and Correspondence*], in the midst of a merciless self-analysis which events were to prove unduly severe, that "I have a vivid perception of the consequences of certain admitted principles, have a considerable intellectual capacity of drawing them out, have the refinement to admire them, *and a rhetorical or histrionic power to represent them . . .*" [italics added]. The piercing subtlety of his perceptions, his command of metaphor as well as of simple, direct speech, his sense of ironical contrasts and vivid climax—all are employed in the realization of a conception of life which rests on the "main Catholic doctrine of the warfare between the city of God and the powers of darkness."

From boyhood to old age Newman loved drama. He acted as a youth at Ealing in the plays of Terence, and in his declining years he adapted those plays for the students at his beloved Oratory school near Birmingham. He constantly saw life in dramatic terms. God's relations with the Jewish people were to him a "grand drama." The fourth century, that critical and formative period of Christianity to which above all others his mind and heart returned for inspiration, was

> [a]n eventful century, a drama in three acts, each marvellous in itself, each different from the other two! The first is the history of the Roman Empire becoming Christian; the second, that of the indefectible Church of God seeming to succumb to Arianism; the third, that of countless barbarians pouring in upon both Empire and Christendom together. And, as the great convulsions of the earth involve innumerable commotions in detail and local revolutions, and each district and neighbourhood has its own story of distress and confusion, so, in the events of the social

world, what is done in the camp or synod vibrates in every town and in every bishopric. From one end of the century to the other, the most momentous changes and the most startling vicissitudes took place; and the threshold of the Apostles was now darkened by messengers of ill, and now lit up with hope and thanksgiving.

So it was in the fourth century; so will it be to the end . . . [*Historical Sketches,* II].

And so it was in the story of his own life. Various writers like the *Times* reviewer, Bishop Samuel Wilberforce [in the *Quarterly Review* CXVI, 1864], and Lewis E. Gates [in his *Selections from the Prose Writings of John Henry Cardinal Newman,* 1895] have spoken of the dramatic quality of the *Apologia.* Walter E. Houghton has given us the first pointed analysis of the dramatic devices of the style. However, little or nothing appears to have been said about the basic structure of the work as a whole, which so heavily affects the style of the narrative and is determined by Newman's conception of life and of the nature of conversion. The editors of Newman's *Correspondence with John Keble* have likened the four chapters of the narrative proper in the *Apologia* to "four seasons of the year," not as "a piece of cheap rhetoric, but as a serviceable peg for the memory." But there is no need of apology. They are more than four stages of the year: they are four acts in the drama of Newman's conversion, carefully and skillfully planned as such.

As the protagonist of the drama, what kind of rôle does Newman play? The rôle he always admired so greatly in this world of symbols as perhaps the supreme type of the life of a Christian in the Church Militant: the soldier. It is no mere eccentricity or paradox that Newman eagerly followed the careers of his early hero Wellington, of Napoleon, and of General Gordon; or that Walter Scott was his favorite novelist; or Southey's *Thalaba* one of his best-loved poems. The despatches of the Iron Duke, J. A. Froude tells us [quoted in Wilfrid Ward's *The Life of John Henry Cardinal Newman,* 1912], drew Newman's confession that they made one "burn to have been a soldier." Froude likened Newman's face to Julius Caesar's and said Newman gave one the impression that he might have been a great general. Newman himself always preferred the society of men who exemplified the view he derived ultimately from the *Ethics* of Aristotle and the Epistles of St. Paul: that life is for action. Our Lord founded, he says [in his *Grammar of Assent*], "not merely a religion, but (what was then quite a new idea in the world) a system of religious warfare, an aggressive and militant body, a dominant Catholic Church, which aimed at the benefit of all nations by the spiritual conquest of all; and . . . this warfare, then begun by it, has gone on without cessation down to this day, and now is as living and real as ever it was. . . ."

It was not only at the start of the Oxford Movement, when he led the fight for the Catholic Church as he then conceived it, that Newman, in choosing with Hurrell Froude the motto of Achilles, sounded "the true note of the chieftain settling his own high purposes before he gathers up his closest retainers to do battle with detested and overmastering powers" [Wilberforce, in his review of the *Apologia*]. It is almost the dominant note of his life and work.

He is always the man with a mission: to spread the truth; and to spread the truth is "warfare." Long before the Oxford Movement, he had sounded the note in an awkward little poem [collected in his *Verses on Various Occasions*] for his brother's twenty-first birthday:

> Dear Frank, we both are summon'd now
>   As champions of the Lord;—
> Enroll'd am I, and shortly thou
>   Must buckle on thy sword;
> A high employ, nor lightly given,
>   To serve as messengers of heaven! . . .
> Till in the end of days we stand
> As victors in a deathless land.

Ultimately, of course, he drew this conception of life as a drama in which Christians were the warriors of the God of Revelation, from the Bible, which from childhood he knew almost entirely by heart, and especially from St. Paul, to him the "special herald and chief pattern" of grace [*Parochial and Plain Sermons*]. It was St. Paul [in his letter "To the Ephesians," contained in the *Bible*] who had warned that we (like Thalaba) "wrestle not against flesh and blood, but against principalities and powers, against the world-rulers of this darkness, against the spirits of wickedness in the high places." It was St. Paul who had flung out the ringing challenge:

> Therefore take unto you the armour of God, that you may be able to resist in the evil day, and to stand in all things perfect. Stand therefore, having your loins girt about with truth, and having on the breast-plate of justice, and your feet shod with the preparation of the gospel of peace; in all things taking the shield of faith, whereby you may be able to quench all the fiery darts of the wicked. And take unto you the helmet of salvation and the sword of the Spirit, which is the Word of God.

If the Church spreads the truth by warfare and conquest, then the man who receives or is converted to it must be a man who is conquered by truth. And this is precisely what he is for Newman: a convert to him is a man *subdued by* the word or "the force of truth." (Hence the special irony of Kingsley's charge that truth for its own sake was not a virtue with Newman.) Thus, Gregory of Neocaesarea, under the influence of Origen, was in A.D. 231 "overcome by the force of truth" [Newman, *The Arians of the Fourth Century*]. How was England converted? The "word of truth came to our ancestors in this island and subdued them to its gentle rule." As for the converts of the Oxford Movement, each of them "was lovingly subdued by the sweet mysterious influence which called him on." To prospective converts Newman says [in his *Occasional Sermons*]: "We do but wish to subdue you by appeals to your reason and to your heart; give us but a fair field. . . ." And so we are prepared to read in the Preface that the *Apologia* is the story of the process whereby the Catholic religion was able to "subdue the reason and overcome the heart, without the aid of fraud and the sophistries of the schools." In short, the *Apologia* is the drama of a soldier who, through defeat and submission, at last finds peace: a loving defeat ostensibly by his enemies but in reality by the "sweet mysterious influence which called him on."

The first chapter or first act of the drama, "History of My Religious Opinions to the Year 1833," sets the scene for the battle and supplies the inciting force. Here we find Newman gradually learning the Catholic conception of the Church from Anglican sources and then resolving to restore that conception to an establishment now weak, divided, and state-ruled, as the only possible means of preserving her from the ultimate infidelity of liberal rationalism. The Bill for the Suppression of the Irish Sees is a portent of what the Church can expect from those coming into power in the aftermath of the reforms of 1829 and 1832. *"Exoriare aliquis!"* Hamlet and Thalaba and Dido calling for vengeance all spring to his mind. "I began to think that I had a mission." Hurrell Froude and he choose for a motto the words of Achilles on returning to the battle: "You shall know the difference, now that I am back again." The chapter ends with a swiftly-paced description of his return to England (**"Lead, Kindly Light"**) just in time for Keble's sermon on "National Apostasy." He has "ever considered it the start of the religious movement of 1833"—perhaps because it was preached on July 14.

In fitting contrast, the second act begins on a quiet note: "In spite of the foregoing pages, I have no romantic story to tell." Superficially that is true—but he will make it as romantic as possible, both to keep his readers interested in the subtleties of his theological position and because his conception of life is, as we have seen, in some ways definitely romantic. "You read, my brethren," he tells us [in his *Discourses Addressed to Mixed Congregations*], "in the lives of Saints, the wonderful account of their conflicts, and their triumphs over the enemy. They are . . . like heroes of romance, so gracefully, so nobly, so royally do they bear themselves." Military imagery becomes more and more predominant. The chapter as a whole, covering the years 1833 to 1839, is the rising action: the period of confidence and strength, "in a human point of view, the happiest time of my life. I was truly at home. . . . We prospered and spread." Newman outlines his first principles, trusting like Orestes in the race to the *event,* and gives an account of how, wanting "to bring out in a substantive form a living Church of England," he published such works as the *Prophetical Office* and the *Lectures on Justification,* outlining the theory of the *Via Media.* How were the Thirty-nine Articles to be reconciled with such a view? *Tract 90* would give the answer. It is discussed in this chapter, although not published until 1841, because the speculations on which it is based arose well before that date and thus belong to the period of confidence. In the concluding pages, however, Newman does anticipate material of the next chapter by recalling the reception of *Tract 90.* Rumors of its contents had got into "the hostile camp; and not a moment was lost in proceeding to action, when I was actually fallen into the hands of the Philistines." He was "denounced as a traitor who had laid his train and was detected in the very act of firing it against the time-honoured Establishment." Echoing Othello, he tells us that "my occupation was gone."

The third act, from 1839 to 1841, is the crisis. It begins with superbly dramatic foreshadowing of "that great revolution of mind," then detains the reader for many pages of setting the mental scene. His own confident estimate of

the Movement is illustrated at length by an article from the *British Critic* of April 1839. Then the issue and status of the unavoidable controversy with Rome are analyzed, with the admission that this "will involve some dry discussion; but it is as necessary for my narrative, as plans of buildings and homesteads are at times needed in the proceedings of our law courts." The strong point of Rome is universality; but she has added to the primitive faith. England, though regrettably separated from the great body of Christians, has kept that faith. Union with Rome was a matter of expedience rather than of necessity. "As time went on, without doubting the strength of the Anglican argument from Antiquity, I felt also that it was not merely our special plea, but our only one." The *Via Media* embodied it. Yet this, he makes it clear, is still a theory, not yet a certitude.

The heart of the chapter opens with the quietly portentous remark, "The Long Vacation of 1839 began early." Then all at once, in his study, appears the first "ghost"—the analogy revealed to him by the history of the Council of Chalcedon between the position of modern Anglicans and fifth-century Monophysites. "I saw my face in that mirror, and I was a Monophysite." Then come the words of St. Augustine—"securus iudicat orbis terrarum!"—in which perhaps the greatest oracle of antiquity testifies in favor of the judgment of the universal Church. By these words, he laments, "the theory of the *Via Media* was absolutely pulverized." Nevertheless, the errors and abuses of Rome remain, and on these he now concentrates his force. Perhaps much can yet be said for the Anglican Church as a repository of Catholic truth. The whole thing needed more study, and he was becoming calm again. Meanwhile the Articles were the apparent stumbling-block: Did they exclude Catholic truth, as so many took for granted? In *Tract 90,* an "experimentum crucis," he would show that they did not; it would be like "proving cannon." In fact, though for a time the Church appeared to have stood the test, with the Tracts stopped but not condemned, it turned out to be a case of "hoisting the engineer with his own petard." Between July and November, 1841, he received the "three blows which broke" him: The ghost came a second time with the analogy of the semi-Arians; the Bishops issued formal condemnations of *Tract 90;* and at the same time, they endorsed Protestant heresy by the scheme of the Jerusalem Bishopric.

The last act, 1841 to 1845, is the resolution and denouement: the period of the dying soldier, "on my death-bed, as regards my membership with the Anglican Church," though becoming aware of the fact only by degrees. Highly complex and heavily documented, this chapter may be summarized only very crudely. There was as yet no thought of leaving Anglicanism. He retired to Littlemore, this priestly Wellington: "I called Littlemore my Torres Vedras, and thought that some day we might advance again within the Anglican Church, as we had been forced to retire." But for him the hope was to be in vain. In a theory to fit the need, since he cannot go to Rome with the view he holds of its abuses, he takes refuge in the note of sanctity and likens the Church of England to Samaria cut off from the temple, yet touched by God's grace. Meanwhile the young pro-Roman wing of the Movement drives him on remorselessly with its logic; and the Protestant foe—editors, heads of houses, even bishops—spies on him and spreads false reports of his movements. In anger and sorrow he flings back a challenge:

> [T]hey persisted: "What was I doing at Littlemore?" Doing there! have I not retreated from you? have I not given up my position and my place? am I alone, of Englishmen, not to have the privilege to go where I will, no questions asked? am I alone to be followed about by jealous prying eyes, which take note, whether I go in at a back door or at the front, and who the men are who call on me in the afternoon? Cowards! if I advanced one step, you would run away; it is not you that I fear: "Di me terrent et Jupiter hostis." It is because the Bishops still go on charging against me, though I have quite given up; it is that secret misgiving of heart which tells me that they do well, for I have neither lot nor part with them: this it is which weighs me down. I cannot walk into or out of my house, but curious eyes are upon me. Why will you not let me die in peace?

"This was the keen feeling which pierced me," he tells us, "and, I think, these are the very words in which I expressed it to myself." Newman was a born dramatist.

Meanwhile he tries to keep young men in his charge faithful to Anglicanism and holds Catholics at a distance. Gradually, however, through books provided by one of these (Dr. Russell of Maynooth) and through reflection of his own, he comes to see that devotion to the saints in the Roman Church does not interfere with the worship due solely to God; and that the principle of doctrinal development might account for what seemed on the surface unwarranted Roman additions to primitive Christianity. The way to Rome is now open to him, though he is not yet certain of his conclusions. He retracts his harsh sayings against her and resigns his living in September 1843. The liberals had beaten him in a fair field, he says; the Bishops had "seethed the kid in his mother's milk." And he concludes the account with the words Lucan applied to Pompey, beaten by the tyrant Caesar but dear to the embodiment of honor and truth, Cato: "Victrix causa diis placuit, sed victa Catoni." The remainder of the chapter, covering the two years in which opinion became conviction, treats largely of how he tried to prepare his friends for the pain he knew he would cause them. It ends in the haunting sadness of his farewell to Littlemore ("Obliviscere populum tuum et domum patris tui"), to his friends, and to his beloved Trinity College.

The minor motif of the imagery now reappears, like that of the battle ultimately Pauline in origin: faith as a journey in response to a vision, a voyage on the sea. "I realize more that we are leaving Littlemore," he writes to a friend, "and it is like going on the open sea." We hear the note in **"Lead, Kindly Light"** and other verses of the *Lyra Apostolica.* Newman elaborates it in Chapter III of the *Apologia:*

> And first, I will say, whatever comes of saying it, for I leave inferences to others, that for years I must have had something of an habitual no-

tion, though it was latent, and had never led me to distrust my own convictions, that my mind had not found its ultimate rest, and that in some sense or other I was on journey. During the same passage across the Mediterranean in which I wrote **"Lead, kindly light,"** I also wrote the verses, which are found in the *Lyra* under the head of *Providences,* beginning, "When I look back." This was in 1833; and, since I have begun this narrative, I have found a memorandum under the date of September 7, 1829, in which I speak of myself, as "now in my rooms in Oriel College, slowly advancing . . . and led on by God's hand blindly, not knowing whither he is taking me."

From St. Paul's warning against "those, who, having 'rejected a good conscience,' had 'made shipwreck of their faith' " the imagery of the sea appears to take its origin. Newman elsewhere describes the converts of the Oxford Movement in the same figure:

> He came as a spirit upon the waters; He walked to and fro Himself over that dark and troubled deep . . . hearts were stirred, and eyes were raised in hope, and feet began to move towards the Great Mother. . . . First one, and then another, sought the rest which She alone could give . . . each drawn by divine power, and against his will, for he was happy where he was. . . . One by one . . . silently, swiftly, and abundantly, they drifted in . . . [*Occasional Sermons*].

And thus it is that he brings his own story to a close: "it was like coming into port after a rough sea; and my happiness on that score remains to this day without interruption."

Now at last, in his fifth and final chapter, Newman is ready for a direct answer to some of the principal charges of Kingsley and his friends. And now, of course, it will not be easy to resist him. (pp. 138-48)

> *Martin J. Svaglic, "The Structure of Newman's 'Apologia'," in* PMLA, *Vol. LXVI, No. 2, March, 1951, pp. 138-48.*

Robert A. Colby   (essay date 1953)

[*Colby is an American educator and critic who has written extensively on nineteenth-century literature. In the following essay, he argues that the structure of the Apologia mirrors Newman's theory of "a graduated scale of assent" through which an individual arrives at certitude in matters of religious conviction.*]

It is the purpose of this paper to show that the sequence of circumstances, characters and decisions described within *The Apologia Pro Vita Sua, Being A History of His Religious Opinions* (as the 1865 text is called) follows out a unified scheme, and that shifts in diction along the way help to indicate the stages of Newman's plan. The *Apologia* contains five sections, according to Newman's revised division. These sections are chronologically arranged, marking off portions of Newman's religious experience from 1816 (the first date mentioned, although Newman alludes to his childhood in the opening pages) until 1864, the date of the first publication of the book. The years with which the respective chapters end—1833, 1839, 1841, 1845, 1864—represent the milestones on Newman's Road to Rome. He emphasizes throughout, both by the lapse of time between the first chapter and the last, and by the greater length of those chapters which cover shorter periods of time, that his conversion was not impulsive or spontaneous, but gradual and cumulative. It was based in fact on what he termed 'an *assemblage* of concurring and converging probabilities'. Newman, in addition, takes pains to establish that the progression was an interrelated series of steps and that the result was both *natural* and *inevitable*. He has so arranged the parts of his spiritual autobiography that simultaneously they cohere *logically* as the stages of attaining certitude (defined later by him [in his ***An Essay in Aid of a Grammar of Assent***] as 'a quality of mind' accompanied by 'a specific sense of intellectual satisfaction and repose'); *dramatically* as the beginning, middle and end of an action; *genetically* as the stages of a life cycle of spiritual birth, growth, decline, death and rebirth. My present consideration is with the first of these patterns, the one most thoroughly and explicitly set forth by Newman.

Newman seems to anticipate the *logical* principle of organization in Chapter I where, in describing the way in which we arrive at 'absolute certitude . . . whether as to the truths of natural theology, or as to the fact of a revelation', he refers to a 'graduated scale of assent'. In reasoning about matters non-scientific and non-demonstrable—and religious faith is one of these—Newman believed, under the influence of Bishop Butler, that 'probability is the guide to life'. Probabilities furthermore are of various strengths and degrees:

> . . . as there were probabilities which sufficed for certitude, so there were other probabilities which were legitimately adapted to create opinion; . . . it might be quite as much a matter of duty in given cases and to given persons to have about a fact an opinion of a definite strength and consistency, as in the case of greater or of more numerous probabilities it was a duty to have a certitude. . . .

In a final summation Newman divides his graduated scale of assent into seven distinct degrees. In weighing our acceptance of any testimony which has any claim upon our religious faith, it is our duty, Newman declares, to consider all the 'circumstances with which they presented themselves to us'—in short, the probabilities—

> . . . and, according to the final result of those various considerations, it was our duty to be *sure*, or to *believe*, or to *opine*, or to *surmise*, or to *tolerate*, or to *reject*, or to *denounce*. [italics added]

Newman has here outlined a range of states of mind induced by the degrees of our strength of conviction of some truth which can never be incontrovertibly demonstrated by logic. At one extreme is *certitude;* at the other is *denunciation,* its opposite. In between are states of possibility, low probability and high probability. This suggests one line of progression which Newman's history of his mind

follows, and his shifts in emphasis—events narrated, characters described, and doctrinal influences—seem to indicate it. In Chapter I (until 1833) the state of mind towards Catholicism is *denunciation* and *rejection;* in Chapter II (until 1839) the mood is predominantly *toleration* (where Newman himself says he is trying to balance the rival claims of Anglicanism and Catholicism); in Chapter III (until 1841) the condition of mind shades off gradually into what Newman variously terms *doubt, suspicion, conjecture* and *surmise* (and the balance tips towards Rome); in the long and detailed Chapter IV (until 1845) can be traced the development from *opinion* to *belief,* to being 'sure' or what Newman calls *certitude.*

In Chapter I Newman clearly indicates his original condemnation of Catholicism by the vehement negative language used wherever that Church is mentioned. The school he attended when he was a boy was 'free . . . from Catholic ideas', and 'no one had ever spoken to me on the subject of the Catholic religion'. More extremely, Newman relates how convinced he was after reading Newton's *On the Prophecies* that 'the Pope was the Antichrist predicted by Daniel, St. Paul, and St. John', a doctrine which remained, he contends, 'as a sort of false conscience' long after he had refuted the idea in his judgment. Later, in describing his conversations with Hurrell Froude, one of his fellow Tractarians who 'taught me to look with admiration towards the Church of Rome,' Newman reports: 'he could not believe . . . that I really held the Roman Church to be Antichristian. On many points he would not believe but that I agreed with him, when I did not.' The chief political event which dominates this chapter also bears out the generally denunciatory attitude. Newman was part of the Oxford opposition to Sir Robert Peel, who in 1829 introduced the Catholic Emancipation Bill.

The climax of this chapter is Newman's trip to the Mediterranean region with Hurrell Froude and his father—an episode rich in dramatic irony when contrasted with Newman's eventual destiny. The apologist here notes very carefully his *rejection* of Rome. 'I went to various coasts of the Mediterranean; parted with my friends at Rome,' he writes in one place. A little further on: 'We kept clear of Catholics throughout our tour,' and 'I saw nothing but what was external; of the hidden life of Catholics I knew nothing.'

Of the numerous personalities vividly described in Chapter I, three who are significant for this stage of Newman's religious life are Blanco White (though he is introduced rather unobtrusively), Hurrell Froude and Monsignor Wiseman. Blanco White is interesting in this connexion because when Newman met him at Oriel he had made a move directly contrary to Newman's ultimate shift—from Roman Catholicism to Anglicanism. Hurrell Froude, despite his strong pro-Catholicism, according to Newman 'was shocked by the degeneracy which he thought he saw in the Catholics of Italy'. When leaving Italy, Newman describes his restrained farewell to Wiseman, also charged with implication: 'When we took leave of Monsignore Wiseman, he had courteously expressed a wish that we might make a second visit to Rome; I said with great gravity, "We have a work to do in England." ' Newman rejected Monsignor Wiseman's invitation at his first visit to Rome, but Wiseman was destined to become the Catholic vicar in England when Newman was finally converted.

In Chapter II Newman describes the work 'we have . . . to do in England' in connexion with his prominence in the Oxford Movement. Here his tone towards Catholicism is definitely more neutral. As he himself writes of one of the tracts he contributed to the *British Critic*—number 71: 'the Tract is written as if discussing the differences of the Churches with a view to reconciliation between them'. This tract is characterized by Newman as 'controversial' rather than 'theological and didactic' and as such 'assumes as little and grants as much as possible on the points in dispute and insists on points of agreement as well as of difference'.

Newman's basic contention during this stage of his religious studies was that the core of belief of both Rome and England was essentially the same—stemming from the 'primitive' Christian Church of St. Augustine and St. Athanasius, of Antioch, Alexandria and Constantinople—and that both were in error for different reasons: Rome having engrafted modern 'accidental errors' on the ancient creed, England having cut herself off from the corporate Church. He wished to emphasize, however, that basically the Roman and Anglican Churches were not as far apart doctrinally as contemporary churchmen contended. Newman says further, ' . . . we ought to be indulgent to all that Rome taught now . . . and when we were obliged on the contrary boldly to denounce, we should do so with pain, not with exultation'. (Here is indicated Newman's shift from complete denunciation.)

This line of thought led Newman to examine the Thirty-nine Articles in which were incorporated the creed of the Anglican Church and wherein presumably he could determine precisely how Anglican doctrine differed from Catholic doctrine. He concluded as a result of this investigation that, first of all, the Articles did not condemn without qualification all 'Roman doctrine', and, secondly, the Articles were originally written not to alienate Catholics in England, but to placate them. It was only the 'dominant errors', of Rome, not the early teachings or formal decrees of the later councils, that the Articles entirely condemned, Newman contended. Newman became convinced that Henry VIII in renouncing the supremacy of the Pope was primarily concerned with strengthening his own *temporal* position in England while in sacred matters his disposition was conciliatory. Hence Newman accounts for what he discovered to be the ambiguous wording of the Articles. The Articles were designed by the divines who compiled them to make the reforms instituted by their queen, acceptable to members of all Christian faiths—Catholic and Protestant.

> . . . there was no such nice discrimination between the Catholic and the Protestant faith, no such clear recognition of formal Protestant principles and tenets, no such accurate definition of 'Roman doctrine', as is received at the present day: hence great probability accrued to my presentiment, that the Articles were tolerant, not only of what I called 'Catholic teaching', but of much that was 'Roman'.

As in the previous chapter, Newman mentions personalities as well as religious doctrines which influenced him. Early in this chapter, in which the central theme is toleration, Newman appropriately quotes John Keble's line from *The Christian Year*—'Speak *gently* of thy sister's fall.' Immediately afterwards he again mentions Hurrell Froude, this time with a different emphasis from his preceding reference: 'From the time that I knew Froude I grew less and less bitter [on the subject of Rome's fall].' It was Froude, Newman explains further, who influenced him to shift his view of the Roman Church as being 'bound up' with 'the cause of Antichrist', to the less extreme position that there was 'something "very Antichristian" or "unchristian" about her'.

It is in this chapter also that Newman introduces Edward Pusey, who was to succeed him as leader of the Oxford Movement in its earlier or doctrinal phase. Pusey, without himself turning to Roman Catholicism, wrote a treatise on the Catholic interpretation of Baptismal Regeneration (which was declared not to be a necessary part of Anglican belief in the famous Gorham Judgement of 1851), and accepted something like the Catholic doctrine of the Real Presence (for advocating which in a university sermon he was briefly suspended from preaching in 1843). Newman here seems to imply that one may be tolerant of Catholicism and yet not be converted—that the state of mind at which he had arrived was not sufficient by itself to lead him to Rome, but that subsequent developments were more crucial. Pusey is of further significance to Newman's religious progress because he wrote an Athanasian defense of orthodoxy, a type of historical investigation which he was to undertake, as described in the next chapter.

The conclusions described above were incorporated in the famous *Tract 90,* which was received with a 'sudden storm of indignation', brought upon Newman the displeasure of his Bishop for the first time in his career, and directly caused his resignation from the Oxford Movement. At this time Newman's position with regard to England and Rome was a state of *equilibrium.* He clung for some time to the theory of the *Via Media,* which he believed combined the most desirable characteristics of both the opposed Churches. Hence, this chapter is headed *My Religious Opinions from 1833 to 1839* although *Tract 90* was not published until 1841. *Tract 90* was the culmination of the investigation of The Thirty-Nine Articles. In 1839 began a new line of investigation, which upset this balance.

In the next chapter Newman describes how the balance was first tipped towards Catholicism. In the summer of 1839 he found leisure to engage in a course of reading he had long wished to undertake in early Church history, particularly in heresies and their settlements. 'For the first time a doubt came upon me of the tenableness of Anglicanism,' Newman wrote after reading and absorbing the doctrinal issues involved in the fifth century Monophysite controversy. This state of mind is the one which prevails through most of the section of the *Apologia* which deals with the years from 1839 to 1841. Newman, with his characteristic rhetorical skill, prepares the reader for this turning point in his attitude by earlier references in the chap-

Newman at about seventy years of age.

ter. The first work of his own cited in Chapter III is an article, **'The State of Religious Parties'**, which appeared in *The British Critic* for April of 1839. It has special significance for Newman for he realizes in retrospect that it contained 'the last words which I ever spoke as an Anglican to Anglicans'. In the article one of Newman's purposes was to bring together criticisms of the *Via Media* by its opponents. One in particular testifies to the disrupting influence of the movement. The writer whom Newman here quotes has contended that the *Via Media* is so splitting up the 'religious community' of England as to form two opposing factions. 'Soon,' this writer continues, 'there will be no middle ground left; and every man, and especially every clergyman, will be compelled to make his choice between the two.' Newman, in the opening of this chapter, has quoted from an anonymous opponent's pen what is in reality the theme of this portion of the *Apologia*—the abandonment of a 'middle ground'. Whereas the tone of the previous chapter had been one of reconciliation, there is a perceptible shift throughout this phase of Newman's retrospection towards contention and dispute. In fact, he anticipates that his age is about to be torn 'between contending powers, Catholic truth and Rationalism'.

Fundamentally it was the desire for a 'real' and 'distinctive' Church of England that motivated Newman's oppo-

sition to the shallowness and 'high and dry'-ness of the conventional religion of his times, and that specifically led him to his momentous study of the Fathers of the early Church. Much of his dissatisfaction with the conventional Anglicanism was caused by what he regarded as its noncommittal moderateness. The attitude of conciliation which had previously been urged by Newman in order to overcome irrational intolerance of Catholicism in this more advanced stage of theological investigation becomes for him a breeder of mere doctrinal 'mistiness'. The 'safe' Church man to him is the one who avoids controversy by reverting to vague truisms and who never enunciates any dogmatic principle without leaving place for its contradictory.

This Laodicean stalemate is just what Newman hoped to remove by a true *Via Media,* one which would be characterized not merely by moderation, but which could incorporate 'a positive Church theory erected on a definite basis'. This, Newman became convinced, was the goal of the great seventeenth century Anglican divines he admired, such as Lancelot Andrewes, Jeremy Taylor, and William Laud. When Newman embarked on his course of study of early Church history it was to *strengthen* Anglicanism, not to *undermine* it—really to make the Church of England the true rival dogmatically of the Church of Rome and an effective opponent of extreme Protestantism as embraced by the various evangelical faiths. He describes this stage of his investigations as a 'feeling about for an available *Via Media*'. That is why he can truly describe the mental reaction that resulted—so much the reverse of what he expected—as 'a shock which was to cast out of my imagination all middle courses and compromises for ever'. Newman declares quite explicitly that 'When I first turned myself to it [the study of the controversies between Rome and heretical sects] I had neither doubt on the subject, nor suspicion that doubt would ever come upon me.' And the state of mind which followed upon his reading up on the Monophysite, Donatist and Arian controversies is called by Newman specifically an 'unsettlement'.

In the study of these heresies Newman was interested not so much in the doctrines at issue as in the relative positions of the contending parties within the Church. The Monophysite heresy, for example, brought forcibly to his mind that the Church of Antiquity had been torn by dissension just as was the Modern Church and that it had its counterparts for present-day Catholicism, Anglicanism and Protestantism.

The significance of this dispute for Newman's religious development is that he now identified himself with the Monophysites, whose relationship to Rome was analogous to that of the Anglican Church to the Catholic Church. What particularly concerned Newman was that the Monophysite sect had been declared heretical by the Council. If any sect in opposition to Rome on a doctrinal question was declared heretical in the fifth century, might not any Church which stands in opposition to Rome in the nineteenth century be considered also by analogy, heretical, Newman asks himself at this point.

At this stage of his thought, Monsignor Wiseman, whose

invitation to return to Rome Newman had previously rejected, reenters Newman's consciousness with striking dramatic propriety. Towards the end of this Long Vacation of 1839, Newman's attention was directed by a friend to an article appearing in the current *Dublin Review* by Dr. Wiseman on another famous controversy—the Donatist heresy. In this instance another great Church Father, St. Augustine, declared against the schismatic party in favour of the constituted ecclesiastical authority. Augustine's ringing words *Securus judicat orbis terrarum* ('The verdict of the world is conclusive') 'struck me with a power which I never had felt from any words before,' Newman says. These words of St. Augustine, like the decision of Pope Leo, appeared to Newman with his mind for similitude to reverberate beyond the fifth century and to contain also a message for the sixteenth and the nineteenth centuries. However, Newman also recognized that analogy alone does not constitute proof nor is it sufficient to instil conviction. He is careful to state about the friend who called his attention to Wiseman's article on the Donatists that he is 'a Protestant still' (just as he pointed out in the previous chapter concerning his state of toleration that Pusey, who had previously dominated his thought, was never converted). The Primitive Church momentarily made a 'vivid impression upon my imagination', but the imagination may delude or distort, and Newman, consistent with his distrust of Private Judgement, proceeds cautiously. He is determined to reflect upon his impressions and the state of mind induced by them in order to emphasize their 'logical value' and their 'bearing upon my duty'. Reason and Conscience, for Newman, exert the necessary disciplinary controls over Imagination; for assent is the result of the 'convergence of probabilities' and as such depends upon the harmonious interaction of all the faculties, rather than the operation of any single one of them in isolation.

The language Newman uses at this point reflects bewilderment coupled with increased alertness and expectation. It also reflects the stage of *conjecture* in the scale of assent. In the previous chapter he had declared, 'we ought to be indulgent to all that Rome taught now, as to what Rome taught then, saving our protest'. Now he is ready to recognize that 'perhaps some new light was coming upon me'. Further on he remarks:

> I had a great and growing dislike, after the summer of 1839, to speak against the Roman Church herself or her formal doctrines. I was very averse to speaking against doctrines, which might possibly turn out to be true, though at the time I had no reason for thinking they were.

And a little later he finds himself beginning 'to wish for union between the Anglican Church and Rome, if, and when, it was possible'.

This line of reflexion unsettled not only Newman's mind but also began to unsettle him from his ecclesiastical office. By the end of 1840, he relates, he had reached such a state of mind that he could write to John Keble: 'For a year past a feeling has been growing on me that I ought to give up St. Mary's but I am no fit judge in the matter.' Although Keble persuaded him to retain his living for the

time being, Newman now felt a disturbing ambiguousness in his position. To his Oxford parishioners he had become known as an anti-Catholic controversialist:

> . . . the very circumstance that I have committed myself against Rome has the effect of setting to sleep people suspicious about me, which is painful now that I begin to have suspicions about myself.

This dilemma in which Newman now finds himself (and which accounts basically for his state of doubt)—*hope* for the possible union of England and Rome, coupled with *suspicion* as to the real catholicity of the Anglican Church—seems to resolve itself unhappily in the affair of the Jerusalem Bishopric which climaxes this chapter. The Archbishop of Canterbury's acceptance of the invitation by the Protestant Emperor Frederick William of Prussia to establish a branch of the British Episcopate in the Holy Land under his auspices both destroyed for Newman his hopes for unity with Rome and confirmed his suspicions about the Protestant tendency of Anglicanism. England appeared to be allying herself with Protestantism, and so Newman himself as an Anglican minister appeared to be in the position of the fifth-century Monophysites—alienated from the One Church even while professing adherence to it. His state of anxiety is further intensified: '. . . such acts as were then in progress led me to the *gravest* suspicion not that it [the Anglican Church] would soon cease to be a Church, but that, since the sixteenth century, it had never been a Church all along.' A letter to the Archbishop of Canterbury ends this section of the *Apologia* as a letter to the same dignitary had ended the previous chapter. The preceding letter had pleaded for *toleration* of the views expressed in *Tract 90,* which was an attempt at conciliation between the Anglican and Catholic viewpoints. This letter *protests against toleration* of Protestantism and expresses the trepidation Newman feels about England's veering away from the Church One, Holy, Catholic and Apostolic.

This protest serves as a transition to the beginning of the next section in which Newman becomes more firmly grounded in his opinions and the 'feeling . . . that I ought to give up St. Mary's' culminates in a positive decision.

Chapter IV, taken up with the years of Newman's retirement at Littlemore, 1841 to 1845, and ending with his crucial decision and farewell to Oxford, is, significantly, the only one of the five distinctly numbered by Newman into two sub-sections. It is also the longest of the chapters—almost twice the length of Chapter II, though it actually covers fewer years, three times the length of Chapter I, which covers the period from Newman's childhood to his joining of the Oxford Movement. Another unique characteristic of this climactic chapter is that it is the one wherein Newman is least subjected to the influence of personalities, but most solitary, self-examining and introspective.

The sub-division most obviously marks off this section of the narrative into two equal chronological periods: from Newman's extreme displeasure with the Jerusalem Bishopric to his decision to resign the living at St. Mary's in 1843; from the resignation to his reception into the Catholic Church by Father Dominic of the Passionist House at

Aston, in the year 1845. Newman makes clear also that these divisions are intended to indicate salient advances along the graduated scale of assent. A key passage is found in a letter cited by Newman early in the chapter, written to Mr. Wilkes, editor of the Evangelical organ, the *Christian Observer*. The 'Anglican principles', among which is the doctrine that a Church may be blessed even if cut off from the One, Holy, Catholic Church, are strong grounds against Rome, Newman declared to Wilkes, 'if they can be held'. But:

> For myself, I found I *could not* hold them. I left them. From the time I began to suspect their unsoundness [1841] I ceased to put them forward. When I was fairly sure of their unsoundness, I gave up my Living [1843]. When I was fully confident that the Church of Rome was the only true Church, I joined her [1845].

The first part of Chapter IV, which elucidates Newman's state of mind until 1843, reveals him in the process of becoming 'fairly sure', a state corresponding to *opinion* in the scale of assent. His position relatively to England and Rome is stated in a quotation from a letter written in March of 1842 to a young clergyman. This young clergyman is not identified, but described by Newman as one of an increasing group in England in a state of perplexity—unable to continue with their duties in the Anglican Church, veering towards Rome, but not yet converted. This condition may be felt by some, writes Newman, 'whose *despair* about our church' might suddenly develop into 'a state of conscious approximation or a *quasi-resolution* to go over'; or by others 'who feel they can with a safe conscience remain with us *while* they are allowed to *testify* in behalf of Catholicism'. Although Newman does not say so explicitly, it can be inferred that in this portion of the *Apologia* he is moving from the second state—simply *testifying* in behalf of Rome—to the first—a *quasi-resolution* to go over   since he had previously stated that his sense of duty would not allow him to remain a clergyman in the Anglican Church when he could not sincerely support her position in opposition to Rome.

This latter question was carefully argued by Newman in a letter written to his Bishop the following year when he felt called upon to clear himself of the charge of having encouraged a recently converted young clergyman to retain his living in the Anglican Church. (Interestingly, this charge prefigures the basic one levelled at Newman by Kingsley which was the immediate occasion for the *Apologia*.) The immediate cause of Newman's resignation was the actual conversion of one of his charges at Littlemore, but this incident, like so many of the incidents of the *Apologia*, precipitated a move which Newman had previously contemplated and served as its concrete justification.

Preceding the recounting of the progress of his religious thoughts and actions from 1843 to 1845 Newman states generally that during this time he came gradually to see that the Anglican Church was formally in the wrong and the Church of Rome formally in the right. The climactic nature of these last years in the movement towards certitude is made quite explicit: 'Then I had nothing more to learn; what still remained for my conversion, was, not further change of opinion, but to change opinion itself into

the clearness and firmness of intellectual conviction.' This he terms the 'last stage of my inquiry'.

In his quotations from a letter written to a friend in July of 1844 Newman shows the signs of his state of opinion shading off into the stage of belief. Here he sums up the conclusions of his reasoning on the principle of development of Christian doctrine (the subject matter of the Essay of this name which Newman published in 1845). Among the propositions Newman offers is: 'I am far more certain (according to the Fathers) that we *are* in a state of culpable separation, *than* that developments do *not* exist under the Gospel, and that the Roman developments are not the true ones.' Here Newman's certainty about the authenticity of modern Catholicism is definitely qualified, but the probabilities converge more in its favour than in the modern Anglican Church's favour. In another proposition Newman states that though certain modern Roman doctrines (such as devotion to Saints, the Supremacy of the See of Rome, the Real Presence, Invocation) are not explicitly 'drawn out' in the primitive Church, 'yet I think there is sufficient trace of them in it, to recommend and prove them *on the hypothesis* of the Church having a divine guidance, though not sufficient to prove them by itself'.

To establish that his state of mind in 1843 was still not sufficiently developed to bring him all the way to Rome, Newman again refers to associates—this time in connexion with a projected *Series of the English Saints,* of which Newman was for a brief time the general editor. This project was the first undertaken upon his resignation from St. Mary's, and Newman himself states that he did not feel he could in strict conscience undertake it while he was a beneficed clergyman of the English Church. However, Newman reminds his readers that of the writers associated with him in the Series only 'some became Catholics', while 'some remained Anglicans, and others have professed what are called free or liberal opinions'. In short, interest in and study of saints, while it may lead one to admire the Catholic Church, did not in and of itself convert one to the Church. The final step Newman had to take alone and as a result of his own convictions; he stresses the independence of mind and solitude in which he came to his ultimate decision, at a time when he both remained free of outside influences and avoided influencing others.

The portion of the *Apologia* leading up to Newman's reception into the Catholic Church is notable for brevity and understatement. Newman makes clear that here opinion changed into 'the clearness and firmness of intellectual conviction', but this stage of assent, while the most intense and the most irrevocable, is also, Newman realized, the most subjective and the most difficult to convey to others. He was later to write [in his *Grammar of Assent*], 'when assent is most intense, inference may be least distinct'. It is in Chapter V that he discusses the grounds of his beliefs in most detail, so that it serves to amplify this latter part of Chapter IV. Newman does make clear that a further two-year period beyond 1843 was necessary before he could make that change towards which he realized he was tending.

> I had one final advance of mind to accomplish,

and one final step to take. That further advance of mind was to be able honestly to say that I was *certain* of the conclusions at which I had already arrived. That further step, imperative when such certitude was attained, was my *submission* to the Catholic Church.

This submission, Newman further declares, could not possibly have been made before the two years after his resignation of his living were up 'without doubt and apprehension, that is with any true conviction of mind or certitude'.

Newman accounts also for the necessity of caution, and in so doing refers back to the opposite end of the scale of assent from which he had started—*rejection*. He realized he could not continue indefinitely in a state of quasi-resolution and partial conviction, but he had grown distrustful of his wavering mind:

> My difficulty was this: I had been deceived greatly once; how could I be sure that I was not deceived a second time? I thought myself right then; how was I to be certain that I was right now? How many years had I thought myself sure of what I now rejected?

Newman had rejected Rome at the end of Chapter I. He is now, close to the end of Chapter IV, rejecting England. *Certitude* is the only state that could quell his instability and bring him conversely to the *denunciation* of the Anglican Church. Both of these states were signalized by his formal conversion.

An indication that Newman was on his way to acceptance of modern Catholicism is made at the beginning of this second section where he describes his reading of St. Alfonso Liguori's *Sermons* and the *Exercises of St. Ignatius*. These two works helped overcome two of Newman's persistent objections to modern Catholic worship—what he called 'Mariolatry', and the devotion to saints and angels. The crucial influence, however, is brought to bear on Newman quite significantly by a work of his own authorship, the last he composed as an Anglican—the *Essay on Development of Christian Doctrine*, already alluded to. In this work Newman sought to justify superadditions of the modern Catholic Church on the creed of the early Church (the remaining obstacle to his conversion) by analogizing them variously with extensions of logical propositions, with the progression of mathematical functions, with the germination of organisms. The growing body of doctrinal principle within the Catholic Church now appeared to Newman a sign of its validity, of its dynamism, and of its maturity:

> So at the end of 1844, I came to the resolution of writing an *Essay on Doctrinal Development*, and then, if at the end of it, my convictions in favour of the Roman Church were not weaker, of taking the necessary steps for admission into her fold.

The writing of the *Essay* served to justify to Newman's *reason* what he had become convinced of in his *conscience*—that the Anglican Church was in schism and that his salvation depended upon joining the Church of Rome. As in his reading of the Monophysite controversy, Newman had feared his imagination would distort his judg-

ment, he is here concerned lest another faculty, his conscience, has disturbed his rational powers. Systematic reasoning as evidenced in his writing of the *Essay* serves as a balance for Newman's mind. 'What keeps me yet [in the Anglican Church] is what has kept me long; a fear that I am under a delusion,' he writes to a friend in this turbulent period between the end of 1844 and 8 October 1845. However, Newman observes, 'the conviction remains firm under all circumstances, in all frames of mind. And this most serious feeling is growing upon me; viz. that the reasons for which I believe . . . *must* lead me to believe more, and that not to believe more is to fall back into scepticism.' At last in October of 1845 Newman could come to this decision:

> As I advanced [on the *Essay on Development*], my difficulties so cleared away that I ceased to speak of 'the Roman Catholics' [i.e. implying that Rome contains only a part of the Church] and boldly called them Catholics [i.e. concluding that Rome is the universal Church]. Before I got to the end, I resolved to be received, and the book remains in the state in which it was then, unfinished.

The book itself remained unfinished, but the Development that Newman pondered may be said to have been completed by his reception by Father Dominic into 'the One Fold of Christ'.

Chapter IV of the *Apologia* is the longest in the whole work, signifying the great magnitude of the change which took place in Newman's mind relatively to the actual length of time involved. This highest and most serious graduation of assent because of its gravity was necessarily to be attended with the utmost caution, Newman emphasized. 'I should think lightly of that man, who, for some act of the Bishops, should all at once leave the Church,' he writes early in the chapter. 'I trust that He, who has kept me in the slow course of change hitherto, will keep me still from hasty acts, or resolves with a doubtful conscience,' he says in a letter to a friend. A proverb-like declaration of Newman's might well serve as the title for the entire chapter: 'Great acts take time'. The intricacy of reasoning involved and the mass of correspondence quoted in this chapter, slowing up the pace of the narrative as they do, magnify the period of time—quantitatively only four years—into the great span that it really was for Newman. Thus the life of the mind is superimposed upon physical chronology. It is important also that letters predominate over physical contact with acquaintances and friends more than in previous chapters, and that Newman's own meditation and reasoning rather than the persuasion and logic of others lead him to his eventual goal.

The *Apologia* then, logically considered, is organized according to the graduation of assent in Newman's mind as to theological truths, 'the concatenation of argument by which the mind ascends from its first to its final religious idea', as Newman himself expresses it. Since the final stage of assent—certitude—is reached at the end of Chapter IV, a question may be raised whether the last chapter, 'Position of My Mind Since 1845,' is necessary to complete the scheme. Chapter V is one of the most stirring, with the poignant lament on the sinful condition of man and the saddening state of the world, the acute analysis of casuistry, the touching dedication to the Priests of the Oratory. This final chapter is also invaluable for Newman's justification of the dogmatical difficulties of Catholicism, the Infallibility of the Church, and the conduct of the Catholic Priesthood. Fundamentally, however, this chapter is a most fitting culmination of the gradual advance towards certitude. 'To be certain is to know that one knows,' he had written while still in a vacillating mood. 'What inward test had I, that I should not change again, after that I had become a Catholic?' Chapter V, which shows Newman, twenty years after his conversion, declaring that 'ten thousand difficulties do not make one doubt', is a sign that the 'inward test' has been successfully passed. Newman, several years after the *Apologia,* laid down three conditions by which certitude could be distinguished from inferior grades of assent: (1) that it follow upon investigation and proof; (2) that it be accompanied by 'a specific sense of intellectual satisfaction and repose'; (3) that it be permanent. In Chapter V Newman's faith 'long sought after, tardily found . . . the fulness after many foretastes', may be said to have met to his satisfaction all three of these requirements. (pp. 140-56)

> Robert A. Colby, "The Structure of Newman's *'Apologia Pro Vita Sua'* in Relation to His Theory of Assent," in The Dublin Review, *Vol. 227, No. 460, 1953, pp. 140-56.*

Geoffrey Tillotson   (essay date 1957)

[*Tillotson was an English educator and critic who specialized in the study of eighteenth- and nineteenth-century English poetry and fiction. In the following excerpt from an essay first published in 1957, he praises Newman's artistry, insisting that the author's works be evaluated as more than occasioned responses to contemporary issues and events: they are, he argues, great literature.*]

When a great author writes mainly 'prose of thinking' there is the danger that his writing may come to belong too much to its special field and too little to literature as a whole. Pusey, let us say, was a theologian; his writings are prose of thinking; but the literary critic, for reasons I shall imply later in speaking of Newman, is quite willing to leave both him and his writings to theologians and ecclesiastical historians. With Newman, however, it must always be different. Some of his works are very much read. I recall that when books were scarce in the late war a bookseller in central London told me that, if he had had them, he could have sold two copies of the *Apologia* daily. And there can be few educated people who do not honour *The Idea of a University.* Both those books are of general interest: they are of as much interest to the secular-minded as to the religious. But if we read much further it is because we are interested in the 'ecclesiastical' matter Newman usually treats of (by 'ecclesiastical' I mean pertaining to the doctrines, character and material being of the Roman and English churches): we go to him as we go to Pusey or his modern equivalent, and should feel equally profited if his writings had been written by Pusey. This sort of reader seeks first his matter and no doubt loves it

the more because it comes to him as, say, meaning does in a sung service. Or alternatively we may read on because we like great literature, and know that Newman's writings never cease to deal with the general matters literature likes to deal with. I grant that the reader who mixes these two interests is the best sort of reader for Newman. The perfect reader is one whose mind is as like his as possible—as much that of a sensuous poet as it is that of a thinker and worshipper. The case for meeting an author with what, comparatively speaking, is identity of mind has been much discussed in recent times. It was well urged by Coleridge on behalf of George Herbert:

> G. Herbert is a true poet, but a poet *sui generis,* the merits of whose poems will never be felt without a sympathy with the mind and character of the man. To appreciate this volume [*The Temple*], it is not enough that the reader possesses a cultivated judgment, classical taste, or even poetic sensibility, unless he be likewise a *Christian,* and both a devout and a *devotional* Christian. But even this will not quite suffice. He must be an affectionate and dutiful child of the Church, and from habit, conviction and a constitutional predisposition to ceremoniousness, in piety as in manners, find her forms and ordinances aids of religion, not sources of formality; for religion is the element in which he lives, and the region in which he moves.

This desideratum applies also to readers of Newman. The ideal reader for a writer who is a great writer, and who writes mainly about the ecclesiastical, must be both a literary critic and a believer, and both of them at a high intensity. In practice we find few readers to fill this bill. Writers on Newman tend to be disproportionately one thing or the other. They proceed as by a division of labour, which is the consequence no doubt of a cleavage of ordinary human minds into species—one sort of mind deals best with a certain thing, another sort with some other thing. Among these species the ecclesiastical exists at a remove from the others. The literary critic can take on historians (say Gibbon) and politicians (say Burke) and art critics (say Ruskin) more comfortably than he can take on Newman. And the reverse is true. The ecclesiastical writer is usually far from being the literary critic. An interesting example of this separation exists in one of the best papers ever written on Newman—the late Father Henry Tristram's 'On Reading Newman' [published in *John Henry Newman: Centenary Essays,* 1945], which purports to do nothing more than give the reader a sense of whereabouts amid Newman's many writings, but does a great deal more than that. Tristram was one of the most devoted, learned and wise of Newman scholars—there is no one yet to fill the gap he has left—but I cannot help feeling that his interest in Newman's Catholicism depressed Newman for him as a writer. In that essay he makes one misvaluation, as it seems to me, which strikes at Newman's literary credentials. . . .

Everybody agrees that Newman had many dazzling gifts. He was a distinguished holder of several public offices. He was a priest and so looked up to as an example in point of piety, learning, and morality, a preacher, an instructor, a confidant and a counsellor, and his parish—to judge by his postbag—represented the whole of intellectual England. He was Fellow and Tutor of a college, the most intellectually distinguished in the Oxford of his day. He was one of the moving spirits of a great rebellion of thought. He was the centre of at least one informal and one formal fraternity. He founded and directed a school for boys. He edited magazines. He was a fashionable lecturer. He was head of a newly founded university. He became a Cardinal. And while holding all these offices he continued to be a prolific and much-read writer, unmatched for virtuosity: Polonius would have enjoyed listing the kinds—the controversial writings, tracts, poems, dialogues, essays, histories, open letters, biographies, autobiographies, lectures, treatises, novels, sermons, editorial prefacings, and annotations. In a word he was one of the supreme geniuses of nineteenth-century England. And a supremely literary genius. If we were to take upon ourselves the boldness of arranging his gifts in order of greatness, that for writing would, I think, come out near the top. There will always be a variety of views about his character and personality; as a leader of men he has had his dubious admirers; but to the literary critic he must always appear a writer among those whom it is 'vain to blame and useless to praise'. And so completely did his pen express his self, his affairs and his whole mental life—for so it seems—that his writings survive as a permanent medium for all of them in all their fullness.

He himself did not encourage people to detach his literary gift from what it served and to rank it so high. 'I am hard-hearted', he wrote in 1848, 'towards the mere literary ethos, for there is nothing I despise and detest more.' It was a thing often said in the age of Victoria. He would not have cared to be a poet as Keats had been a poet, or, much as he admired the Waverley novels, a novelist as Scott had been a novelist. He must have despised what he came to see of the movement of 'art for art's sake', which in revolt against the use, or over-use, of literature for the sake of practical matters grew strong in the latter half of the nineteenth century. Few of his writings are created without reference to contemporary affairs—the sort of contemporary affairs to which newspapers like *The Times* and the *Guardian* give their best attention. By the time he had many works to look back on he saw them as so much a part of the big public interests of their time as to fall into the category of things prompted by occasions. In the Advertisement before the *Lectures and Essays on University Subjects,* 1859, he noted (in the third person) that 'It has been the fortune of the author through life, that the Volumes which he has published have grown for the most part out of the duties which lay upon him, or the circumstances of the moment.' And again, in 1874 [quoted in Wilfrid Ward's *The Life of John Henry Cardinal Newman based on his Private Journals and Correspondence,* 1912]:

> What I have written has been for the most part what may be called official, works done in some office I held or engagement I had made—all my Sermons are such, my Lectures on the Prophetical Office, on Justification, my Essays in the *British Critic,* and translation of St. Athanasius—or has been from some especial call, or invitation, or necessity, or emergency, as my Arians, Anglican Difficulties, *Apologia* or Tales. The *Essay on Assent* is nearly the only exception. And I can-

not write without such a *stimulus.* I feel to myself going out of the way, or impertinent, and I write neither with spirit nor with point.

Many great works have been prompted by occasions and in the nineteenth century there was a higher proportion of them than in the eighteenth century and perhaps also the seventeenth century; but no nineteenth-century author wrote so high a proportion of them as Newman.

All these self-descriptions are perfectly satisfactory, but on one level only. They ignore what, if I read him rightly, has much importance—the necessity which drove him not only to write so much and to write so clearly but to write so beautifully. To judge by results, if by no other evidence, he was born to be a writer—just as Dickens was, and Thackeray, and the Brontës, and Tennyson, and Ruskin (who believed he was born to be a painter). Newman began as a born writer should—by copying the styles of the writers he admired: 'At the age of fourteen a sort of passion for writing seems to have possessed him.' And there are many boyish anticipations or buddings of his after thoughts noted down at about this date (1817). On reading these later in life, Dr. Newman is severe on his early style:

> The unpleasant style in which it is written arises from my habit as a boy, *to compose.* I seldom wrote without an eye to style, and since my taste was bad my style was bad. I wrote in style as another might write in verse, or sing instead of speaking, or dance instead of walking.

And if this is true, we must not take his insistence on occasions for more than it is worth. (pp. 239-43)

. . . . .

Nor must we take 'occasions' in too strict a sense. Many were invited. If you take orders you expect to have to deliver sermons. If you become a Fellow of an Oxford college and are also (as you had to be at that time) in orders, you may expect to be asked to preach before the University. If you become eminent in a cause, people on both sides will look to you for guidance or for 'a statement'. Many occasions Newman consciously laid himself open for. Of the rest several were potent only because he allowed them to be. The occasion for his writing *The Tamworth Reading Room* was the report of the speech delivered by a politician in his far-away constituency when opening a library for working men. The occasion for *Who's to Blame?* was less pointed still—Newman wrote it because, like the rest of England, he had read about the conduct of the Crimean War. Even the *Apologia* sprang from a *chosen* occasion—there had been many taunts against him before he chose to reply to Kingsley's. The same is true even of the novel, *Loss and Gain*—there had been many novels about religious converts before Miss Harris's *From Oxford to Rome*. And when he wrote without the sort of stimulus he had in mind, which in varying degrees we can call public, he did not step outside his usual matter—the undergraduate poem is on a religious subject, the *Dream of Gerontius* deals with a theme he had treated in the sermons, the *Grammar of Assent* follows on from the university sermons. In other words, both when he is free and when he is called, he writes on a matter one and the same. He is not a writer who wants to write on one matter but is obliged by duties to write on another. Even if his so-called occasions had not cropped up, we should have had writings, in the main, similar to those we have. Do not therefore let us take his speaking of occasions too seriously.

There was, I think, a psychological reason for his appeal to occasions. Newman subscribed to a then rather old-fashioned conception of the gentleman. We know how charming were his social manners on almost all of the thousands of recorded occasions. In his writings Matthew Arnold found the same 'delicacy' and 'urbanity'. His written words are often beautifully apologetic if he fears that there will be offence or crudity in some point or other he is driven to make. Alternative to this humility and charm there is of course fierceness and sharpness; but that comes from between the cracks. The man and writer when, as almost invariably, he lived up to his ideal for himself, was extremely polite. We can see him as wanting to write under certain conditions, one of which was the psychological or social condition of having an occasion that could be agreed to be public enough to allow him not to seem obtrusive: in the passage quoted above he speaks of his need not to feel 'impertinent'. But again we should note that his required easiness on that score is represented as a literary requirement also. Unless he felt welcome to write, the product would lack the prized literary virtues of 'spirit' and 'point'.

As final reason there was his strong need to feel assured that when he spoke he would be speaking to men. How strong that need was can be illustrated by one of the most remarkable passages he ever wrote, a passage that is one of the additions made from time to time to the manuscript account of his tour in Sicily. The particular addition was made at Littlemore in 1840, when he was taking to his 'deathbed' as an Anglican: 'The thought keeps pressing on me, while I write this, what am I writing it for? . . .'

In any man's life there must be several 'spots of time' when thoughts like these are thought, but few, if any, when they are written down. Newman provided this exception, and a hundred like it, because he was a man who found writing a solace in itself, and also because, for as profound a reason, he longed to have readers—at some near point of time for preference, but if not that, at a later. I think we can discern in much of the writing, public and private, his strong need to achieve communication. This need accounts for the clarity of everything he wrote. Of the millions of his written sentences there can be few which do not convey what they were meant to convey. But along with the need for light went the need for sweetness—or, at times, sharpness. He wished to communicate something definite and to communicate it personally. The motto he chose for his cardinalate was *cor ad cor loquitur*—heart speaks to heart. For many reasons his words had often to be written words, and as means of expression written words have notorious limitations, especially where they are speaking the matters of the heart. Communication of the most piercing kind comes usually by other even more primitive means. 'Voices melt us, looks subdue us, deeds inflame us'—that names three other powerful means. In his sermons he could rely on two of them in addition to

words, and he relied on them to some purpose, for we have many accounts of the thrilling experience of hearing and seeing him preach. His lectures, too, availed themselves of the means of words, voice and look. When writings were written only for cold print Newman used many arts to suggest the completer range of medium. His printed words carry as much personal force as any words ever have. They take on as much of tones, looks, and gestures as possible. For us who never heard his voice, the print seems to speak, and the famous face looks out from the page.

"Newman is always literary, even, all things considered, when he is most narrowly ecclesiastical."

—Geoffrey Tillotson

Newman loved the means of communication and the art of making the most of them. We are fortunate that it was so, for he might not have cared. In the **Apologia** he speaks of his 'mistrust of the reality of material phenomena' and his 'rest[ing] in the thought of two and two only supreme and luminously self-evident beings, myself and my Creator'. The words he designed for his tombstone spoke the same 'fact': 'JOHANNES HENRICUS NEWMAN / EX UMBRIS ET IMAGINIBUS / IN VERITATEM / DIE—A.S. 18[ ] / REQUIESCAT IN PACE.' Feeling the things of the world to be shadows, he might have been haunted by their insubstantiality to the point of neglecting the material a writer must use. We recall the Scotch-Calvinist gardener in [William Thackcray's novel] *The Newcomes* who handled the melons and pineapples 'provisionally, and until the end of the world'. In his writings, however, Newman handled earthly things *as if* they were real, as if he were as sure of them as he was of himself and his Creator. In his writings he seems as thoroughly at home among things as Chaucer or Shakespeare or Pope or Dickens. He speaks—if we add his unpublished to his published writings—with complete freedom: in the manuscript text of his account of the Sicilian tour he refers to piles and Epsom salts. There is nothing particularly literary in the mere possessing of this freedom, but it helps to produce the keen effects a piece of writing is the better for. Newman is constantly keen, however, not just because of his free speech but because his mind is sensuous, and therefore ready with the imagery which the sensuous mind contributes freely to thinking and feeling. He was sensitive enough as a physical organism to be sharply aware of the finger-tips of his Sicilian servant when applying vinegar to his nose, and he was agile enough of mind to connect the sensation with one stored in his memory—he writes of them as 'great bullet-tips'. Everywhere in his writings is the proof of this sensitiveness of sense and this prehensile agility of mind. It is the most obvious of the proofs that he is a poet. And it serves him very well as a philosopher. He is often dealing with abstract matter and dealing with it for the benefit of as many readers as he can gather. So that none shall turn aside because of too great an abstraction, he uses much imagery. He 'remembereth that we are dust'. His very account of thinking is as of a physical process.

Finally, it is by virtue of much of his matter that Newman stands square with our great writers. He writes often about what literature most prefers to deal with. His constant attention to the 'scope and nature' of Christianity enfolds an attention as close to quotidian affairs. He is as alert to the trivial round as Wordsworth or Hardy; as alert as Matthew Arnold to those urgent public matters of the day—e.g. cholera, mesmerism, the goldfields—which pitilessly exact from journalists their 'nutshell truths for the breakfast table'; as alert as a novelist to the personal characteristics of everybody he met. And since he is often the philosopher, there is much attention to another prime concern of literature—the nature of man. Though his hope is always to shame the nature in man and to divert his natural religion into Christianity, he does not scamp his study of all that we are by unaided nature.

Co-extensive with the consideration of all these things proceeds his untiring introspection. There were several reasons for that activity, one of which was his frank love of particulars. The nearest source of these lay in his own field of body, mind and spirit, each of which seemed to him as important as the others because making an equal contribution to a whole. In *Loss and Gain* we hear that 'a man's moral self . . . is concentrated in each moment of his life; it lives in the tips of his fingers, and the spring of his insteps'. Or there is the mixed account of his leaving Littlemore in 1846: 'I am burning and packing *pari passu* reading and disposing, passing from a metaphysical MS. to a lump of resin or a penwiper.' And in another letter written a little later: 'I quite tore myself away, and could not help kissing my bed, and mantelpiece, and other parts of the house. I have been most happy there, though in a state of suspense.' When in the *Apologia* he recalls how the Anglican Church looked to him after leaving it, he seems to be looking at it with physical as well as mental eyes:

> I have been bringing out my mind in this Volume on every subject which has come before me; and therefore I am bound to state plainly what I feel and have felt, since I was a Catholic, about the Anglican Church. I said, in a former page, that on my conversion, I was not conscious of any change in me of thought or feeling, as regards matters of doctrine; this, however, was not the case as regards some matters of fact, and, unwilling as I am to give offence to religious Anglicans, I am bound to confess that I felt a great change in my view of the Church of England. I cannot tell how soon there came on me,—but very soon,—an extreme astonishment that I had ever imagined it to be a portion of the Catholic Church. For the first time, I looked at it from without, and (as I should myself say) saw it as it was. Forthwith I could not get myself to see in it any thing else, than what I had so long fearfully suspected, from as far back as 1836,—a mere national institution. As if my eyes were suddenly opened, so I saw it—spontaneously, apart from any definite act of reason or any argument; and so I have seen it ever since. I suppose,

the main cause of this lay in the contrast which was presented to me by the Catholic Church. Then I recognized at once a reality which was quite a new thing with me. Then I was sensible that I was not making for myself a Church by an effort of thought; I needed not to make an act of faith in her; I had not painfully to force myself into a position, but my mind fell back upon itself in relaxation and in peace, and I gazed at her almost passively as a great objective fact. I looked at her;—at her rites, her ceremonial, and her precepts; and I said, "This *is* a religion;" and then, when I looked back upon the poor Anglican Church, for which I had laboured so hard, and upon all that appertained to it, and thought of our various attempts to dress it up doctrinally and esthetically, it seemed to me to be the veriest of nonentities. Vanity of vanities, all is vanity! How can I make a record of what passed within me, without seeming to be satirical?

And to take a last random instance from the mass, there is the letter of 1862 which he addressed to the *Globe* newspaper in an attempt to silence once for all the reports that he was returning to the English Church, and in which he seems to be spewing it and all its works out of his mouth:

> Therefore, in order to give them full satisfaction, if I can, I do hereby profess 'ex animo' with an absolute internal assent and consent, that Protestantism is the dreariest of possible religions; that the thought of the Anglican service makes me shiver, and the thought of the Thirty-nine Articles makes me shudder. Return to the Church of England! No! 'The net is broken and we are delivered.' I should be a consummate fool (to use a mild term) if in my old age I left 'the land flowing with milk and honey' for the city of confusion and the house of bondage.

He ejects the Anglican Church as if he has it in his system, and his life up to the secession shows us he had. That was why he was so unconscionably long a-dying as an Anglican. He drew all things into himself, so that even an external thing like a logical demonstration or a history issues from him as personal as a love letter. This unusual characteristic was soon seized on by his contemporaries: when the *Quarterly Review* began its sixty-page-long review of that book of his which had so much general interest for its own time and ours—the *Essay on the Development of Christian Doctrine*—it recognized that here was a book that was more than a book:

> Our business is with Mr. Newman's book, not with Mr. Newman himself . . . It will, however, be impossible altogether to separate the examination of his work from what Mr. Coleridge would have called the psychological study of his mind—so completely is the one the reflexion, dare we use the word, the transfiguration of one into the other.

As we should expect, he does not always rest content with the colouring his mind has given to his matter—he often lingers to describe the pigmentation and how he felt during its process. A frequent effect in his writings is that his thinking is progressing alongside a diary of the experience of the thinking for 'the whole man'. This 'whole man' contained for him the unconscious, or what we should call the subconscious. If he reproduced on paper the light in his mind, he also reproduced the darkness with which it coexisted, and he looked at the darkness as hard as at the light. Instances are everywhere in the correspondence and in the *Apologia.*

Because of all this, Newman is one of the shining demonstrations that the style is the man. His personality exists as clearly in his style as in his choice of matter—or, rather, in his choice of just that shade and aspect of his matter. And since he constantly gives us consideration of the thing as well as the thing itself, it was to be expected that he should offer an account ["**Literature,**" in his *Lectures and Essays on University Subjects,* 1859] of the personality of style. I quote it at length because it is one of the most luminous things he wrote, confirming his belief that 'simplicity . . . is the attribute of genius':

> Here then, in the first place, I observe, Gentlemen, that, Literature, from the derivation of the word, implies writing, not speaking; this, however, arises from the circumstance of the copiousness, variety, and public circulation of the matters of which it consists. What is spoken cannot outrun the range of the speaker's voice, and perishes in the uttering. When words are in demand to express a long course of thought, when they have to be conveyed to the ends of the earth, or perpetuated for the benefit of posterity, they must be written down, that is, reduced to the shape of literature; still, properly speaking, the terms, by which we denote this characteristic gift of man, belong to its exhibition by means of the voice, not of handwriting. It addresses itself, in its primary idea, to the ear, not to the eye. We call it the power of speech, we call it language, that is, the use of the tongue; and, even when we write, we still keep in mind what was its original instrument, for we use freely such terms in our books as saying, speaking, telling, talking, calling; we use the terms phraseology and diction; as if we were still addressing ourselves to the ear.

> Now I insist on this, because it shows that speech, and therefore literature, which is its permanent record, is essentially a personal work. It is not some production or result, attained by the partnership of several persons, or by machinery, or by any natural process, but in its very idea it proceeds, and must proceed, from some one given individual. Two persons cannot be the authors of the sounds which strike our ear; and, as they cannot be speaking one and the same speech, neither can they be writing one and the same lecture or discourse—which must certainly belong to some one person or other, and is the expression of that one person's ideas and feelings,—ideas and feelings personal to himself, though others may have parallel and similar ones,—proper to himself, in the same sense as his voice, his air, his countenance, his carriage, and his action, are personal. In other words, Literature expresses, not objective truth, as it is called, but subjective; not things, but thoughts.

> . . . Literature is the personal use or exercise of language. That that is so, is further proved

from the fact that one author uses it so differently from another. Language itself in its very origination would seem to be traceable to individuals. The peculiarities have given it its character. We are often able in fact to trace particular phrases or idioms to individuals; we know the history of their rise. Slang surely, as it is called, comes of, and breathes of the personal. The connection between the force of words in particular languages and the habits and sentiments of the nations speaking them, has often been pointed out. And, while the many use language, as they find it, the man of genius uses it indeed, but subjects it withal to his own purposes, and moulds it according to his own peculiarities. The throng and succession of ideas, thoughts, feelings, imaginations, aspirations, which pass within him, the abstractions, the juxtapositions, the comparisons, the discriminations, the conceptions, which are so original in him, his views of external things, his judgments upon life, manners, and history, the exercises of his wit, of his humour, of his depth, of his sagacity,—he images forth all these innumerable and incessant creations, the very pulsation and throbbing of his intellect,—he gives utterance to them all,—in a corresponding language, which is as multiform as this inward mental action itself and analogous to it, the faithful expression of his intense personality, attending on his own inward world of thought as its very shadow: so that we might as well say that one man's shadow is another's, as that the style of a really gifted mind can belong to any but himself. It follows him about *as* a shadow. His thought and feeling are personal, and so his language is personal.

Constantly exemplifying this theme, Newman is among the most fascinating writers of English. If the declared aim of his use of English was clarity, the result is not colourless transparency. Art is supposed either to hide or show itself, but there are countless degrees of the concealment and exhibition. The art of Newman's writing is never wholly hidden. It comes near to being so in the 'plain' and 'parochial' sermons, where, as I have said, it was designed to receive the added arts of the voice and general presence of the preacher. Elsewhere in his writings the art is usually less concealed. In the Tracts it is sometimes noticeably abrupt, and deliberately so—Thomas Mozley said [in his *Reminiscences chiefly of Oriel College and the Oxford Movement,* 1882] that among the Tractarians only Newman 'could write a tract', giving as explanation that only he had read enough of them himself. But, just as the variety of his art is obvious, so, by and large, it is triumphant. And, in accordance with that Newmanian law, he tells us how he made it so. . . . The thing written was expression achieved, imperfect at first and then more perfect. What guiding principle was at work is suggested in Newman's definition—one of the best we have—of style, which he called 'a thinking out into language', a process that was almost palpable for him: 'Besides re-writing, every part has to be worked out and defined as in moulding a statue.' As usual, Newman speaks his difficult matter so clearly because his experience of it has been his own, and being that, has been of extreme vividness.

In consequence of all this, the case for regarding Newman as supremely literary as well as supremely 'ecclesiastical' is inescapable. One of the points I wish to make is that Newman is always literary, even, all things considered, when he is most narrowly ecclesiastical. How well he caught himself—all the more truly because from an unusual angle—in a letter of 1850 [in *Correspondence of John Henry Newman with John Keble and Others 1839-45*]:

> You must undeceive Miss A. B. about me, though I suppose she uses words in a general sense. I have nothing of a saint about me as every one knows, and it is a severe (and salutary) mortification to be thought next door to one. I may have a high view of many things, but it is the consequence of education and a peculiar cast of intellect—but this is very different from *being* what I admire. I have no tendency to be a saint—it is a sad thing to say so. Saints are not literary men, they do not love the classics, they do not write Tales.

In quoting that I feel compunction at taking him when, comparatively, he is off his guard. So strongly does he recoil from the ascribed saintliness that he opposes to it the most secular self-description, imputing to himself the literary ethos he had said he was 'hard-hearted' against. Offered as proof of his weakness, the description is of strength in a different department. And with it goes a remark, which again one feels some compunction in overhearing—it occurs late in those sincerest of sincere documents, the letters he sent to Keble during the long period of his secession: 'My great fault is doing things in a mere literary way from the love of the work, without the thought of God's glory.' It happens that under obedience to chronology Wilfrid Ward passes directly from the letter repudiating saintliness to the **Lectures on Certain Difficulties felt by Anglicans**. . . . Merely as a matter of course he describes the lectures as 'brilliantly witty'. Yes, they are accurately that, and the ease with which he can be brilliantly witty seals him of the tribe of the Henry Jameses and Oscar Wildes as certainly as the capacity to write on ecclesiastical matters seals him of the tribe of the Puseys and W. G. Wards. And he had other gifts as literary, like that which made George Eliot find **The Present Position of Catholics** 'full of clever satire and description' [*George Eliot Letters*, Vol. i], or like that which made Pater [in his *Appreciations*, 1889] praise his **Idea of a University** as showing 'the perfect handling of a theory'. (pp. 248-58)

> *Geoffrey Tillotson, "Newman the Writer," in* Mid-Victorian Studies *by Geoffrey Tillotson and Kathleen Tillotson, The Athlone Press, 1965, pp. 239-58.*

Kenneth Rexroth   (essay date 1970)

[*Rexroth was one of the leading pioneers in the revival of jazz and poetry in the San Francisco area during the 1940s and 1950s. Largely self-educated, he became involved early in his career with such left-wing organizations as the John Reed Club, the Communist party, and the International Workers of the World. As a critic, he has been praised for his acute intelligence and wide sym-* *pathy; he has examined such varied subjects as jazz, Greek mythology, the works of D. H. Lawrence, and the cabala. In the following essay originally published in 1970, Rexroth comments on the relationship between Newman's theology and his temperament, and traces the author's influence on subsequent religious thought.*]

It would be as easy to write an essay on Newman as the leader of reaction, both political and religious, as it would be to write one claiming him as one of the fathers of Liberal Catholicism or Modernism in Great Britain.

Newman was an anomaly in so many ways. He occupied a position not unlike that Paul Tillich attributed to himself, suspended between contradictions in religion, in politics, in philosophy, in race, in family background, and not least in personal temperament. There is nothing unusual in the bare facts of his own intellectual development and his influence. He went from counterrevolution and *Restauration* to a position that could be claimed plausibly as ancestral by the first Modernists. But this is true of the Romantics generally. The medievalism of Chateaubriand becomes the socialism of William Morris. Sir Walter Scott becomes the favorite reading matter of revolutionary nationalists in Italy and the Balkans. Out of Schelling come Wagner and Nietzsche. Lamennais embodies the whole process in himself. What is consistent in Romanticism is what is consistent in Newman—anti-rationalism. Today in popular speech that term has become blurred and confused with "irrationalism" with which, in the final decadence of Romanticism, it does in fact merge. In 1830 Rationalism meant not Euclid or Aristotle or Aquinas, but Diderot, Voltaire, Condorcet, Condillac, even ironically enough, Rousseau—the whole Enlightenment lumped together.

The Romantics in their time were right. After the fall of Napoleon the *philosophes* were wrong, not for political reasons but for technological ones. Locke or Hume or Kant are philosophers, if not for all time, for a very considerable length of time, because they deal with problems that lie deep under the technological changes of ten generations. The men of the Enlightenment do not seem to us to be philosophers at all, because they accept the picture of the world provided by the tools and instruments of the eighteenth century as not just adequate, but final. This is true in medicine or astronomy. It is even more true in Biblical criticism, anthropology, comparative religion, of the subjects that bore on contemporary religious development, some of which acquired names only in the nineteenth century, and the sociology and histories of religion and ideas. In little more than two generations the simplistic picture of the world, which seemed profound on the eve of the Revolution, had become simply vulgar.

By the time of Newman's youth the secular world was well-embarked on a new scientific revolution that would eventually find the place for a sensibility such as his. In those days his opponents were too busy in practical, non-ideological activities to manage more than a kind of man-in-the-street positivism. For Newman, and all those like him, this was not enough. It's not that he could not reason, or that his reason was affronted. It's that the entire world view of the "other side" was totally irrelevant to his sensibility.

John Stuart Mill could go a long way toward understanding Newman, but to Newman, Mill belonged to another species, with a radically different nervous organization. One of the things that makes Newman so baffling is the purely personal, individual aspect of his sensibility. Thinkers who arise out of a hot spot in a highly polarized force field are usually aggressive, even violent, personalities. The metaphor is chosen to emphasize the appropriateness of the term "dynamic." Like Paul Tillich, Newman was generated at a point where contradictories and contraries cross, but unlike others so placed, Newman after youth seems to be passive, uncombative, anything but dynamic, once he has found his home in the Roman Church. Recent critics have called him a masochist, justly or not, but certainly, like masochists, his submissiveness was illusory, most of all to himself. Nothing is more domineering than indomitable submission. Geoffrey Faber is the best known of the critics who have subjected Newman and his comrades of the Oxford Movement to amateur psychoanalysis. This is another case where science and its instruments have outgrown a popular synthesis in two generations. I find his psychologizing as dated as Newman must have found Condorcet.

Nevertheless in Newman's case it is impossible to avoid personalities. That's what Newman's religion, and out of his religion, his philosophy, is—the posture of an irreducible reality—a personality—in the face of a worn-out mechanism. The story of the Oxford Movement has been told countless times, and almost always the tale has been centered on Newman. But Newman was the leader of the Oxford Movement not because he was its greatest theologian or Biblical critic or historian of religion, but because he was its leading personality. He was its spokesman because he spoke so well. He was in fact the only one of his colleagues who did not write abominably. Newman was the master of a great style. Style is the man. In the final analysis the Catholic Revival, Anglican, Roman, Russian, or French, is a matter of persons, not of doctrine or ritual or even "faith and morals." What Newman says is what Nietzsche or William Morris say, or what Blake at the very beginning says, or Kierkegaard, or Chaadayev—"There is no room for a whole person in the nineteenth century synthesis." Since there is even less in the twentieth-century synthesis, they are all still relevant.

So those critics who have either accepted and tried to trace, or who have denied, Newman's influence on Liberal Catholicism *and* Catholic Modernism have operated on a false assumption. There is nothing Liberal about Catholic Modernism. Historically it took its rise in a thoroughgoing attack on Liberal Protestantism, and specifically on Adolph Harnack. The only reason the Modernists did not attack the tradition of Lord Acton and his friends directly was that they needed all the allies they could get. The situation is analogous to those anti-Liberal movements in our time who, when they get in trouble, call on the American Civil Liberties Union to defend them from the Liberal State. The comparison is not unjust. Those who link Blake, Kierkegaard, Newman, Baudelaire with Lenin,

Mussolini, William Butler Yeats and Ezra Pound are perfectly correct. All are in revolt against the commercial industrial civilization, and in that civilization even the most humane Liberalism has its roots in the Liberalism, properly and first so-called, of the Manchester School, as those apostles of the satanic mills had their roots in the Enlightenment with its new moral and intellectual virtues that found their apotheosis in those heroic bourgeois, *le bon Franklin* and Goethe. This is the real reason why Newman is still influential. In detail much of his writing is absurd. His influence is really confined to three or four leading ideas, most especially the illative sense, the development of doctrine, the apologia to the doubting, and to his symbolic role. It's not true that "the Pope declared war on the nineteenth century with the Syllabus and the First Vatican Council." He just wanted it to be *his* nineteenth century. Newman stood against the world and the times absolutely. Yet in the end they had to make him a Cardinal. He had outlived most of his enemies. With the changing times the world was beginning to lose faith in the worldly syntheses so carefully put together, whether by Pope or Positivist.

To the Pope the doctrine of infallibility was true and proved by both logic and history. To Lord Acton and Döllinger it was false, illogical, unhistorical. To Newman it was a mystical experience. To Newman, as to Tertullian, the direct experience of Christ was primary. If that experience was incompatible with reason, so much the worse for reason. It simply showed that the world was not in that sense rational. *Sacrificium intellectus,* what Aldous Huxley with consummate irony called the *philosophia perennis,* the visionary tradition, agrees with one voice that the abandonment of the rational intellect is the first portal of illumination, the first veil of Isis. Lord Acton knew this too, but he kept it to himself behind the facade of the other *philosophia perennis,* the rationalist tradition that begins with Aristotle. Only once in a great while Acton would drop a waspish remark that was revealing only to those who already knew—"I have never in my life had an intellectual doubt."

Newman doubted every day—intellectually—and came to think of himself as the Apostle of the Doubters. This alone was enough to outrage the entire establishment from Pope to catechist. It is not permitted to doubt your reason because it is reason that supports the Magisterium. If reason can be made to support the Magisterium, Newman implies it can be made to support anything, and so reason is always inadequate. Revelation is only something that happened in history, and so submits itself to reason, says both the Magisterium and the infidel.

In Newman's day the idea that revelation was immanent in all life and time, that it was the experience of reality itself, was unheard of in the Church, except here and there by obscure scholars and contemplatives, lost in the study of forgotten medieval and patristic semi-heretics, or lost in prayer. Here lies the explanation for Newman's devotional writing so shocking to Catholic intellectuals who discover it today. He learned early from Hurrell Froude to assault and subject the intellect with absurdities and impossibilities. Bleeding and nodding statues, holy napkins and every fragment of that thirty-ton "True Cross"—

Newman accepted them all as he accepted the Holy House of Our Lady of Loreto, Patroness of Aviators.

Newman was a compulsive writer. Even in old age his output was enormous, yet when he was not sleeping or eating or playing the violin or counseling others he seems to have spent practically all of his time in prayer. There are few authentic portraits in all history so totally formed by the *"Sculpte, lime, cisèle!"* of the torch of prayer, yet his devotions are most of them the routine parochial performances you could find in a Birmingham parish of illiterate Irish working women, from his day to ours. They may shock intellectuals who go to them seeking a Liberal San Juan de la Cruz and find a more simple-minded Saint Alphonsus Liguori. They are purely disciplinary, like the rosary or *Om Mani Padme Om.* Is there any concrete evidence that Newman was really a contemplative? Very little, except the accounts of the proportion of his time he spent in prayer and meditation. His age, even, or especially, in the Church, did not give him the language or the audience. His intellectual background did not provide the tools, and finally his personality was secretive of its deepest experiences, but his entire career and everything he wrote is understandable on no other hypothesis.

Is Newman then one of the Fathers of Aggiornamento? It all depends. He is the father of one *aggiornamento,* but there are two; and the one he heralds is still largely outside the Church. If modern or Modernist Catholicism means social activism, de-mythologization, rationalization of the Gospel narrative, the liturgy in Kiwanis Club English, and sermons lifted from Norman Thomas, the ancestors of this *aggiornamento* are Newman's enemies—the elder Bishop Wilberforce, leader of the anti-slavery crusade, Charles Kingsley, founder of Muscular Christianity, and, ironically enough, the Ultramontane, but passionately rational, and tirelessly socially active, Cardinal Manning. If *aggiornamento* means a total challenge to the predatory technological society of post-capitalist Western civilization, Newman was an ancestor. At this moment when most of the progressive elements in the Church are just discovering Charles Kingsley, and are engaged in a rationalistic struggle with the rationalistic Magisterium, Newman's children are the young fellows and girls who quietly elbow their way to the front rank of peace marches, chanting Hare Krishna, who sit at the gates of army posts in the lotus posture doing *zazen,* or who have worked out detailed astrological prophecies of the fall of capitalism that supersede Marx. Before Vatican II there were large numbers of young people like this in the Church, but today the liberal and enlightened secularizers have pushed them

Newman in Rome, 1879.

aside. Where are the young Catholic Workers who once sat up all night in Greenwich Village bars arguing about St. Bonaventura and Dionysius the Areopagite, who sang Abelard and Venantius Fortunatus instead of Woody Guthrie and Pete Seeger, and marched against the atom bomb chanting *Media Vitae*?

His latter-day descendants, whether Bernard Lonergan, the young Catholic Workers, or the Dutch Bishops, would have horrified Newman and thrown him into paroxysms of penitence. He would not have believed that he had raised heretics, but that he had raised devils. Like Matteo Ricci, Newman was caught in his mission. You cannot appoint yourself Apostle to the Doubting without infecting yourself with their germs. It's the kind of inoculation that produces the disease itself in a non-virulent form by the injection of half-dead bacteria. It does no good to say that by the phrase "development of doctrine" you mean the unfolding in history of the seamless cloak given once for all to the Apostles. Your descendants will take the term literally. Newman, Keble, Pusey, but not Froude, always spoke of the Oxford Movement as apostolic. Their apologetic moved back and forth through the conciliar period, the Alexandrine, Cappadocian, and Syrian Fathers, the Apostolic Fathers, always back to the Descent of the Holy Ghost, and then forward—but to where? With such a hypertrophied notion of the Sacrament of Orders, Newman finally could make no sense of the House of Bishops of the Established Church. He had to find an absolute authority, because he had to believe that Holy Orders was not just a sacrament conferring an indelible grace, but an absolute one. With the body and blood of Christ it is all or nothing. If the body and blood of omniscience, omnipotence, eternity, infinity, flows through the dual flame symbolized by the cloven bishop's mitre—with it flows infallibility. All the terms of what is communicated in Holy Communion imply it, either the collective infallibility of the Council of Apostles or the guaranteed infallibility of their chairman's successor. The white and gold thread of the Papacy must go back clear through the unfolding, seamless robe to "Feed my sheep. Feed my lambs," because it obviously did not go back through the collective Anglican Episcopacy.

There is only one answer for Newman to the technique of systematic doubt, and that is infallibility. His descendants would find systematic doubt in itself as a foundation for faith. They would say, "In the sub-Apostolic period, where you are seeking evidences for infallible authority, there is no evidence for belief in the Trinity, much less for the primacy of Peter's descendants, or even evidence that anyone believed he had any descendants as such." It is significant that doctrinally Newman chose to agitate himself with the finest-drawn definitions of the conciliar period, Monothelitism and semi-Pelagianism. Newman, as he said of himself, was shaped early by Gibbon. Where Gibbon said in a sarcastic footnote that when the Pope read the Athanasian Creed, he threw up, Newman clutched it to his breast like the arrow of St. Theresa. Pascal, Kierkegaard, Newman—doubt, the instrument of ecstasy. Later generations would simply accept doubt as the normal environment of the soul, just as the most spiritually developed amongst them would accept the habitude of illumi-

nation as birds accept air, and fish, water. Eventually the mystic consciousness that Newman kept so carefully hidden would come to recognize doubt and illumination as two faces of the same coin, on one: the owl of Athena, on the other: In God We Trust.

Here is the source of Newman's "illative" sense. Illumination precedes thought. Vision precedes knowing. There is, in the actual fact, no epistemological problem. When the words "actual fact" are used in their etymological sense, they produce nothing resembling the process described by all the fathers of the epistemological dilemma, from Aristotle to Locke, Hume and Kant. In Newman's guide to the doubting, the illative sense sometimes sounds like a childish or even vulgar and sentimental conception, but it subverts the entire structure of epistemology, so carefully founded on tiny blocks of blue and green, salt and sour, loud and quiet, soft and hard, foetid and perfumed. His is the epistemology of mysticism. In the heyday of scholastic rationalism it was the epistemology of the Victorines and behind them of Arabo-Jewish mysticism, as it would later be the epistemology of the post-nominalist mystics, of Wilhelm Meister, Henry Suso, and Nicholas Cusanus. Here was the source of authority, not the Chair of Peter. Newman could never be content with it. He lived in England in the nineteenth century under Queen Victoria. His most fundamental experiences were socially disgraceful. There was nothing in his intellectual environment to provide him with the means to understand, much less express, his position at the center of the X which marks the spot where all contradictions and contraries cross. The time would come when his Catholic followers would read the Diamond Sutra with comprehension, but it was a hundred years away, a hundred years even from the old, gentle, gracious man refined by all the fires of prayer, who would soon be made a prince of the Church, a courtier of that Papal State at last reduced to a walled palace.

We must realize that always for Newman, poverty, chastity, and obedience were not only great virtues but they were very close to being sacraments—and most especially obedience. Newman carried over into the Roman Church his Anglican ultra-Episcopalianism. This explains his seemingly perverse masochism in crises like the Irish university, the translation of the Bible, the Oxford chaplaincy. Bishops were channels of grace. Submission was a door into prayer, but it's a strange grace the act of obedience confers, for its distinguishing virtue is *contemptu mundi*—not in the final analysis very complementary to its "matter," a bunch of politically motivated Irish-American bishops, for example.

Had Newman remained an Anglican, he too would probably have ended up a highly skilled political bishop. Certainly his role in the Oxford Movement was primarily that of publicist and political boss, or of course, he might have dribbled himself away, an ill-tempered neurotic, like Kierkegaard, blasted in quarrels with fools. Rome made a saint of him because it enabled his techniques of achieving sanctity.

Newman's Copernican revolution was not faith founded on skepticism, as in Tertullian, or de Maistre, but the shifting of the grounds of apologetic to ultimately purely psychological evidence, an immanent and continuous, rather than sudden, pentecostal Evangelicanism. Newman's opponents could not understand what he was doing but they could feel it. In those years there may have been no profound intellectual activity in the Roman Catholic Church in England except Newman's, but there was enough intelligence and experience, both in Westminster and in the Vatican, to recognize the gravity of the threat. Newman, far more than Pascal, is the religious empiricist par excellence. Pascal leads to Kierkegaard and thence to Barth and thence through Scheler to secular existentialism. Newman, as has been remarked countless times, and each time angrily denied, leads to Father Tyrrell. Father Tyrrell leads to Evelyn Underhill, who leads to—where? Aldous Huxley? Alan Watts? Simon L. Frank?

The rock of Newman's epistemology is purely and simply experiential—the fact of dialogue—the echo of the Word of the Person speaking to me is the essential principle and sanction of the Christian life, and of the Church—from *I and Thou* to Mounier, to Father Perrin. Newman's apologetic was like the hormones that kill weeds by overstimulating their growth. What was so important in the nineteenth century was the resistance he generated. Now that the resistance is almost impotent, what remains of Newman's apologetic is the sacramental life, the apostolic life, Pentecost. The progression, skepticism, empiricism, experientialism, existentialism falls away as only a patina of polysyllables. What remains is the sacramentalization of the world and the divinization of man. This was the Patristic progression as it must have been in real life, lived day by day, the apostolic progression in the actual lives of the Apostles. What was going on underground in Newman's apologetic was the same development that was going on in Russian Orthodox theology or philosophy. The Magisterium was at least philosophically astute enough to strike this new growth at its roots. To a theology of doubt it answers, "No doubt about it!" To the illative sense, a quiver full of quotations from St. Thomas on *De Anima;* to the development of doctrine, the flat statement that the brothers of the Son of Miriamne the Mother of the Lord believed in her immaculate conception and stood with faces uplifted while she rose bodily from the tomb fluttering into the clouds. Charges such as this can only be answered with obedience considered as a sacrament. *Contemptu mundi.* (pp. 258-68)

> *Kenneth Rexroth, "Some Notes on Newman,"*
> *in his* The Elastic Retort: Essays in Literature
> and Ideas, *The Seabury, 1973, pp. 258-68.*

Linda H. Peterson   (essay date 1986)

[*Peterson is an American educator and critic specializing in the study of nineteenth-century literature. In the following excerpt, she maintains that Newman's* Apologia *is a spiritual autobiography consciously modeled on previous Catholic and Protestant autobiographical writings.*]

When John Henry Newman revised the *Apologia pro vita sua* in 1865 for publication as a book, he replaced the original parts I and II of his text, "Mr. Kingsley's Method of Disputation" and "True Mode of Meeting Mr. Kingsley," with a brief summary of the events that had occasioned the work. In his original response to Kingsley, published serially from 21 April to 2 June 1864, Newman had begun by confronting the charges against him, referring directly to the accusation that he had denied truth to be a virtue for its own sake and refuting as well the implicit charge that he had acted with deceit during his years as an Anglican priest. In his revision, however, he chose to omit specific details of the controversy and emphasize instead his intellectual and spiritual development. "He [Kingsley] asks what I *mean*," Newman generalized, "not about my words, not about my arguments, not about my actions, as his ultimate point, but about that living intelligence, by which I write, and argue, and act." Accordingly, Newman decided that the *Apologia* should give the "true key" to his life, in order to "show what I am, that it may be seen what I am not"; "I mean to be simply personal and historical: I am not expounding Catholic doctrine."

Given this emphasis upon the "personal" and "historical" nature of the account, this desire to interpret a "living intelligence" to a public audience, one could hardly ask for a more explicit declaration of autobiographical intention. The [1865] alteration of the title, moreover, from the original *Apologia pro vita sua* to the *History of My Religious Opinions* suggests an attempt to make the work's intention as a spiritual autobiography clear, the combination of "history" and "religious opinions" signaling two fundamental elements of the genre. Yet in critical discussions of the *Apologia* the misconception still lingers that, in some fundamental way, the work is not a true autobiography. This assumption may be stated explicitly, as in Robert A. Colby's comment [in his "The Poetical Structure of Newman's *Apologia pro vita sua,*" *Journal of Religion* 33 (1953)] that the *Apologia* is generically a "fusion of theological disputation, epic, and biography" or in Martin A. Svaglic's ["The Structure of Newman's *Apologia,*" *PMLA* 66 (1951)] that the work, lacking details of Newman's family life, student activities, and intellectual interests, is thus neither "the autobiography of Newman from 1801 to 1845," nor "even a spiritual autobiography of those years except in a limited sense." More frequently, the assumption remains implicit, nonetheless controlling critical analyses of the work that rely on the terminology of other literary genres, including the epic, the drama, or the novel.

The circumstances under which the *Apologia* was published certainly add to the suspicion that the work is not an autobiography in the usual sense: rather than the calm, retrospective account of the traditional autobiographer, Newman's work was dashed off in seven weekly installments to counter a public attack. Yet despite the generic misconceptions of its readers, and despite the circumstantial evidence of publication, the *Apologia* is a classic example of the spiritual autobiography—indeed, the culminating English example. Newman's motivation for composing the work, and hence his rationale for handling his materials, are characteristic of autobiography as a genre; as he states in the 1865 preface, he intends not only to "draw out, as far as may be, the history of my mind," but also to "give the true key to my whole life." More important, the works to which Newman responds consciously as he shapes his personal history are models of the spiritual autobiography in not one tradition, but two: the first, a Protestant tradition that informs English autobiography generally; the other, an Augustinian and Catholic tradition that Newman re-introduced to the Victorians.

Newman's goal as autobiographer is to negotiate successfully between these two traditions. And he uses the conventions of both to shape his argument, as well as to define the specific problem he faced as a Catholic autobiographer writing within an English generic tradition that was inseparable from its Protestant theological origins and that imposed its conventions upon his process of self-composition and self-interpretation.

When Newman wrote the *Apologia,* the dominant form of self-writing in England was the spiritual autobiography, descended . . . from accounts such as John Bunyan's *Grace Abounding to the Chief of Sinners* and continued by Methodists and evangelicals such as George Whitefield, John Newton, William Cowper, and Thomas Scott. Newman was familiar with this tradition of spiritual autobiography, particularly in its evangelical manifestations. In the opening pages of the *Apologia,* he refers to Thomas Scott as "the writer who made a deeper impression on my mind than any other, and the man to whom (humanly speaking) I almost owe my soul," and he cites Scott's autobiography, *The Force of Truth,* not simply as a book he possessed, but as a book he "had been possessed of " since his boyhood. Moreover, in an autobiographical memoir written in 1874 to supplement the *Apologia,* and thus to supply the details of his evangelical phase at Oxford ["**Autobiographical Memoir,**" in *Autobiographical Writings,* edited by Henry Tristram, 1957], Newman refers specifically to Scott's *The Force of Truth,* Beveridge's *Private Thoughts,* and Doddridge's *The Rise and Progress of Religion in the Soul* as crucial influences. These seminal works of English evangelical thought, he notes, "had sheltered and protected him in his most dangerous years" and "brought him on in habits of devotion till the time came when he was to dedicate himself to the Christian ministry."

If Newman was familiar with the standard works of English Protestant spiritual autobiography, he also knew intimately the pattern of conversion they represented. In the supplementary memoir of 1874, Newman tells of a private memorandum written years before, in 1821, in which he used these standard autobiographies, along with scriptural texts, to draw up "an account of the evangelical process of conversion." His description of the stages in the process—"conviction of sin, terror, despair, news of the free and full salvation, apprehension of Christ, sense of pardon, assurance of salvation, joy and peace, and so on to final perseverance"—reads like an outline for a classic spiritual autobiography. Indeed, it might have been taken directly from Philip Doddridge's *The Rise and Progress* which, although not an autobiographical work per se, attempts to describe the stages in a Christian's journey from sin to salvation.

Although Newman was familiar with this tradition of spiritual autobiography, he was not experimentally knowledgeable (to use an evangelical phrase) of the intense, often violent process of conversion it described. In a footnote to the private memorandum, he observed that his own experience had not been characteristically evangelical: "I speak of conversion with great diffidence, being obliged to adopt the language of books. For my feelings, as far as I remember, were so far different from any account I have ever read, that I dare not go by what may be an individual case." Five years later, he noted more emphatically on the same memorandum: "I wrote *juxta praescriptum.* In the matter in question, viz. conversion, my own feelings were *not* violent, but a returning to, a renewing of, principles, under the power of the Holy Spirit, which I had already felt, and in a measure acted on, when young." Finally, when he wrote the autobiographical memoir in 1874, thirty years after his conversion to Catholicism and ten years after the publication of the *Apologia,* he stressed again that he "had ever been wanting in those special evangelical experiences, which, like the grip of the hand or other prescribed signs of a secret society, are the sure token of a member." The added footnotes suggest the power which "the language of books," the written tradition of spiritual autobiography, had upon Newman's way of thinking and writing about his life. He felt compelled to record three times that the evangelical pattern of experience did not represent his own, a denial of "experimental knowledge" that could scarcely have been more insistent.

Newman in fact exaggerates the exclusivity of the pattern. In the preface to *The Rise and Progress,* Philip Doddridge states quite clearly that the dramatic process frequently described in spiritual autobiographies is not the only possible form of conversion. The renewing of principles acquired in youth, which Newman describes as his own experience, resembles an alternative Doddridge explicitly suggests:

> I would by no means be thought to insinuate, that every one who is brought to that happy resolution, arrives at it through those particular steps, or feels agitations of mind equal in degree to those I have described. . . . God is pleased sometimes to begin the work of his grace on the heart almost from the first dawning of reason, and to carry it on by such gentle and insensible degrees that very excellent persons, who have made the most eminent attainments in the divine life, have been unable to recount any remarkable history of their conversion.

But to cite Doddridge as counterevidence is to miss Newman's motive, for it was more than a lack of personal experience that prevented Newman from writing an autobiography in the standard English mode. His Catholic theology inclined him against using literary forms, however popular, that held the stain of Protestant dogma, and the English spiritual autobiography certainly had been shaped, if not stained, by its Protestant theological origins.

The *Apologia* does nevertheless respond to the dominant tradition of English autobiography, both by imitating and diverging from it. Newman's model in the first two chapters is, I suggest, Thomas Scott's *The Force of Truth,* the autobiography of the writer who, according to Newman's testimony in the opening pages of the *Apologia,* "followed truth wherever it led him" and thus "planted deep in my mind that fundamental truth of religion." Scott's emphasis upon truth and truth-seeking appealed in a crucial way to Newman, who had been accused of condoning falsehood in theological teaching and thus might be suspected of practicing falsehood in his autobiography. Kingsley's attack, as Newman realized, had attempted "to cut the ground from under my feet;—to poison by anticipation the public mind against me, John Henry Newman, and to infuse into the imagination of my readers, suspicion and mistrust of everything that I may say in reply to him." But equally important was Scott's variation on the pattern of conversion. Rhetorically, Newman needed a model that his readers would recognize as a legitimate form of spiritual autobiography, but not one they would associate with the common evangelical pattern of conversion.

Scott's autobiography, *The Force of Truth,* is a modest, carefully documented account of conversion from Socinianism to evangelical Christianity. Unlike the autobiographies of Bunyan and later of Cowper, Newton, and Whitefield, all painfully introspective tales that dwell upon conviction of sin and despair of salvation, this is an eminently rational work. Scott stresses his wrestling with biblical and ecclesiastical texts, not with angelic messengers or demonic voices. "I never was taught any thing," he insists, "by impulses, impressions, visions, dreams, or revelations; except so far as the work of the Spirit, in enlightening the understanding for the reception of those truths contained in the Holy Scriptures, is sometimes styled revelation." Instead . . . Scott presents his conversion as the outcome of extensive reading in the Anglican divines, begun in 1775 to shore up his defenses of Socinianism and continued until 1777, when the old theology he had "proposed to repair, was pulled down to the ground, and the foundation of the new building of God laid aright."

Scott organizes his account in terms of books read and doctrines derived. An episode typically begins with a statement of what he read ("In January, 1777, I met with a very high commendation of Mr. Hooker's works"); includes a doctrine or passage that troubled him ("I had no sooner read this passage, than I acquired such an insight into the strictness and spirituality of the divine law, . . . that my whole life appeared to be one continued series of transgressions"); and concludes with an alteration he made in his religious beliefs ("Thus was I effectually convinced, that if ever I was saved, it must be in some way of unmerited mercy and grace"). Typically, too, Scott insists upon the orthodoxy of the doctrine he has discovered. Conscious of the prejudice of Churchmen against Methodists and Dissenters, he is careful to point out that he avoided sources not purely Anglican: "Had I at this time met with such passages in the writings of Dissenters, or any of those modern publications, which under the brand of methodistical publications, are condemned without reading, or perused with invincible prejudice, I should not have thought them worth regard, but should have rejected them as wild enthusiasm. But I knew that Hooker was deemed perfectly orthodox."

Given this extreme (inter)textuality, it seems odd that *The Force of Truth* should have become one of the most popular conversion narratives of the late eighteenth and early

nineteenth centuries: the book is literally a debate among theological texts. But the conversion of Socinians to a more orthodox understanding of Christian tenets, especially the doctrine of the Trinity, was a major preoccupation of evangelicals, and Scott himself, as the author of an influential commentary on the Bible, exerted a special attraction in evangelical circles like those Newman mixed with during his early days at Oxford. When Newman wrote the *Apologia,* however, *The Force of Truth* was attractive not only for its author's sake, but for the solution it provided to the problem of generic form. Scott's model allowed Newman to write within the English autobiographical tradition without acquiescing, in narrative pattern, to radical Protestant notions of conversion.

In the first two chapters of the *Apologia,* Newman makes his account almost exclusively a series of encounters with theological texts. Like Scott, Newman chronicles the sources of his beliefs in "The History of My Religious Opinions to the Year 1833," beginning with those he acquired from evangelical associates or writers: the need for conversion and "a definite Creed" from the Rev. Walter Mayers, one of his masters at Ealing; an informed belief in the Holy Trinity from the essays of Thomas Scott and Jones of Nayland; the doctrine of the final perseverance from the works of William Romaine; and a zealous anti-Romanism from Joseph Milner's *History of the Church of Christ.* He continues with the more general Anglican tenets that he learned at Oxford from tutors and friends: that of baptismal regeneration from Richard Whately, of tradition from Dr. Hawkins, of apostolical succession from the Reverend William James, of analogy and probability from Butler's *The Analogy of Religion,* and so on throughout the first chapter. "I am all along engaged," Newman writes in explanation of his method, "with matters of belief and opinion, and am introducing others into my narrative, not for their own sake, or because I love or have loved them, so much as because, and so far as, they have influenced my theological views."

Newman's emphasis on the sources of his religious opinions, to the omission of details of family and student life, has led some literary critics to exclude the *Apologia* from the canon of English autobiography. But it is precisely the work's omission of secular concerns and its consistent attention to the development of Newman's theological beliefs that provide the most conclusive evidence of its generic intention. In *Grace Abounding,* for instance, Bunyan mentions his wife and her father only to explain his familiarity with *The Plain Man's Pathway to Heaven* and *The Practice of Piety.* Similarly, John Newton [in *An Authentic Narrative*] tells of his courtship and its effect upon his life only to satisfy the queries of one of his patrons. Scott, Newman's immediate model, mentions his "increasing family" and his lack of "private fortune" in an appendix, but only to argue that his situation in life rendered a conversion to evangelicalism for personal gain improbable. The generic precedent, in other words, inclined against the mention of personal details superfluous to the development of the autobiographer's soul or intellect.

Just as Newman's method of constructing his autobiography follows Scott's model, the motives informing the method are Scott's as well: he intends to demonstrate that his religious opinions derive exclusively from orthodox Anglican theology. To *The Force of Truth* Scott had appended some "Observations on the Foregoing Narrative," in which he argued the validity of his conversion to evangelical Christianity on the grounds that, first, as a Socinian, he was "a most unlikely person to embrace this [evangelical] system of doctrine" and that, further, he had changed his religious beliefs "without any teaching from the persons, to whose sentiments I have now acceded." Like other evangelicals, Scott believed that anyone who disinterestedly studied the Scriptures and Anglican theology would adopt, sooner or later, the evangelical position. Newman uses the same sort of argument implicitly throughout the *Apologia* to counter the prejudices of his anti-Catholic readers, on whom the allusions to Scott's autobiography and its principle of truth would not be lost. Late in his account, Newman explicitly repeats the point made in Scott's "Observations": "My opinions in religion were not gained, as the world [has] said, from Roman sources, but were, on the contrary, the birth of my own mind and of the circumstances in which I had been placed." This combination of a divinely endowed mind and divinely ordained circumstances is Newman's adaptation of Scott's argument and, indeed, a revision of the evangelical formula for conversion.

"[Despite] the generic misconceptions of its readers, and despite the circumstantial evidence of publication, the *Apologia* is a classic example of the spiritual autobiography—indeed, the culminating English example."

—*Linda H. Peterson*

Whether or not contemporary readers of the *Apologia* recognized the allusions to *The Force of Truth,* the deliberate repetition of Scott's method and argument suggests that Newman himself felt the need to engage the dominant English tradition of autobiography and shape it to his own ends. Newman records, as we have seen, that he "had been possessed of" Scott's essays and autobiography "from a boy." This way of phrasing the matter suggests that Scott's work had somehow possessed the young Newman—possessed, if not his very self, at least his self-conception.

In the autobiographical tradition, prior works of the genre do somehow possess each new autobiographer's self: they determine how he views his experience, how he understands the self, how he orders the contours of his personal history. Yet if the autobiographer cannot escape the power of the generic conventions to shape his self-conception, it is equally impossible to imagine an autobiography (that is, a history of an individual self) that merely repeats the conventions. In order to write an autobiography, the auto-

biographer must in some way violate the generic tradition or deviate from it—and, in so doing, discover the self.

For Newman the violation of generic predecessors is a self-conscious literary act, one that extends to autobiography a technique he had used before in arguing against evangelical critics. Newman explains it this way:

> "Two can play at that," was often in my mouth, when men of Protestant sentiments appealed to the Articles, Homilies, or Reformers; in the sense that, if they had a right to speak loud, I had the liberty to speak out as well as they, and had the means, by the same or parallel appeals, of giving them tit for tat. . . . I aimed at bringing into effect the promise contained in the motto to the Lyra, "They shall know the difference now."

Newman calls his means in religious controversy "by the same or parallel appeals," and it describes as well his use of *The Force of Truth.* Even as he adopts Scott's model to present his own history, his method is tit for tat: a repetition of its major structural patterns (what the repetition of the consonantal *t's* in Newman's metaphor suggests), but with the intended effect of difference (what the variation between the vocalic *i* and *a* creates). The models and methods of the evangelicals are, in Newman's hands, to be turned to different ends.

Newman creates this difference in the *Apologia* by maintaining Scott's narrative structure, while replacing Scott's fundamental principle of interpretation with one of his own. In the closing "Observations," Scott had designated the crucial factor in his conversion as "the great influence which the study of Scriptures had in producing [the] change." Men were too apt, he complained, to borrow their "schemes of divinity from other authors" or to think they possessed sufficient proof of their doctrines if they could "produce the sanction of some great name." Given his conversion to evangelicalism, Scott is thoroughly predictable in the principle he enunciates: evangelicals believed the Bible, not any ecclesiastical interpretation, to be the ultimate authority in matters of faith and practice. In contrast, Newman makes his principle as thoroughly Catholic as Scott's is Protestant. In the final exposition of his religious beliefs, "Position of My Mind since 1845," Newman assigns to the Church "the means of maintaining religious truth in this anarchical world": its judgment "must be extended even to Scripture, though Scripture be divine." The Bible itself, he allows in acknowledgment of testimonies like Scott's, "may be accidentally the means of the conversion of individuals," but by attempting to ground religious interpretation solely in the Bible, Protestants make it "answer a purpose for which it was never intended."

Newman's divergence from Scott may seem to be merely the doctrinal divergence of a Catholic from an evangelical Protestant. But it involves much more than a rejection of an evangelical tenet that Newman had earlier held. The "purpose for which it was never intended" includes a purpose to which English evangelicals put the biblical text in the writing of spiritual autobiography; their commitment to the Bible as the authority in matters of interpretation directly influenced the form and method of the autobiographies they composed. In diverging from Scott in principle, then, Newman had also to diverge in autobiographical method.

In writing spiritual autobiography, English Protestants from Bunyan through Newton, Cowper, and Scott had depended upon the hermeneutic method of biblical typology. Bunyan justified the publication of *Grace Abounding . . .* by treating the wanderings of the Israelites as prefigurative of his own experiences and Moses' record of these events as prefigurative also. His use of scriptural texts had been necessary for his own autobiographical act: as Sacvan Bercovitch has observed [in his *The Puritan Origins of the American Self,* 1975] for American Puritan writers, without the biblical model the writing of autobiography would have been impossible, its goal being not to proclaim the self but, as for Bunyan, to efface it, to "dissolve [it] into the timeless pattern of spiritual biography." Bunyan's use of the Exodus had, in turn, a profound effect upon the tradition of spiritual autobiography that followed. As history made literary classics of *Grace Abounding* and *The Pilgrim's Progress,* and as the latter became what might be called a prospectus for anyman's autobiography, subsequent autobiographers came to follow the narrative patterns and system of interpretation that Bunyan had introduced.

A generation after Bunyan, the Quaker Alice Hayes described her spiritual experiences just as Bunyan had—as a repetition of "the Mistery [of] what Israel of old passed through, while in Egypt's land, and by the Red Sea; and their Travels through the Deeps with their coming up on the Banks of Deliverance" [*A Legacy, or Widow's Mite, Left by Alice Hayes, to Her Children and Others,* 1723]. Nearly a century later, John Newton began his *Authentic Narrative* with "reflections upon that promise made to the Israelites in Deuteronomy viii,2": "Thou shalt remember all the way, by which the Lord thy God led thee through this wilderness." Like Hayes, Newton interpreted this text "in a spiritual sense," as "addressed to all who are passing through the wilderness of this world to a heavenly Canaan," and like Bunyan, he used it and a variety of other biblical types to interpret his spiritual predicament. While enumerating the disasters he faced on board a foundering slave ship, for instance, Newton viewed himself not only as an Israelite, but as a Jonah, reproached by the captain as "the cause of the present calamity." And Newton's sometimes mad contemporary Alexander Cruden interpreted his life using an even greater variety of types, ranging from Joseph (whose life he believed was "emblematical and typical" of his own) to Alexander the Great (after whom he titled his autobiography, *The Adventures of Alexander the Corrector*).

The possibilities for such acts of self-interpretation were numerous, limited only by loosely defined principles of typological hermeneutics and by the interpreter's imagination. It was probably the excessiveness of the evangelical imagination, displayed so frequently in spiritual accounts like Cruden's, that made Newman shun typology as his mode of interpretation in the *Apologia*—that and its cause, the Protestant dependence on private judgment and

on what was known in matters of biblical interpretation as "the inspiration of the Holy Spirit."

Newman did not object to typological interpretation in itself. As an Anglican priest, he had used biblical typology in his *Plain and Parochial Sermons,* applying types to both individual experiences and historical events. As a Catholic autobiographer, he might legitimately have continued a method that had originated in Patristic hermeneutics, one that even Augustine had used in the *Confessions.* In the nineteenth century, however, typology was so intricately bound to the tradition of the evangelical conversion narrative that Newman could not have used it without seeming to acquiesce in the theology with which it was associated. Newman had once spoken of his evangelical years at Oxford as "a type of Protestantism": "zeal, earnestness, resolution, without a guide; effort without a result." They were "a pattern instance of private judgment and its characteristics." Surely he had no desire to propagate in the *Apologia* a pattern of private interpretation he had rejected as insufficient for his life.

Biblical allusions, then, because of their associations with evangelical spiritual autobiography, do not dominate the text of the *Apologia,* and those that do appear are not typological in intention. When Newman compares his indecision before his conversion to Catholicism with the uncertainty Samuel felt "before 'he knew the word of the Lord,' " he uses the Old Testament character to explain a psychological state, not to establish a typological link between the prophet's life and his own. So, too, when he discusses the difficulty of keeping young disciples under control and remarks that "a mixed multitude went out of Egypt with the Israelites," he intends to illustrate his predicament as leader, not to provide a pattern for the history of the Oxford Movement. Such biblical allusions (and they are few) focus upon the audience's understanding, not the autobiographer's, and in this focus they resemble Newman's allusions to classical myths or historical events. When Newman echoes Achilles' words on returning to battle, "You shall know the difference, now that I am back again," or repeats Dido's cry on her funeral pyre, "Exoriare aliquis!" he is using a classical echo to explain a predicament or to illustrate a state of mind, here his emotional state on the return from his Sicilian journey. These allusions, like the biblical ones, do not represent a mode of self-scrutiny or a method of autobiographical interpretation. To put it another way, the purpose of both kinds of allusions is primarily rhetorical, not hermeneutic: they involve neither a systematic approach to interpretation nor a self-conscious stance toward the interpretive act.

The most telling evidence of Newman's rejection of evangelical patterns of autobiography, however, is the absence of a specific set of allusions: allusions to the Exodus, the biblical type fundamental to the genre. Newman had used the Exodus frequently in the verse of the *Lyra Apostolica,* especially in his best-known autobiographical poem, **"Lead, Kindly Light."** In the *Apologia,* however, he does not cast his account as a spiritual pilgrimage, despite the fact that he wandered for years before finding his peace in the Catholic church. Quite distinctly, he avoids allusions to exile, exodus, or wilderness wandering, and substitutes an alternative method of interpretation. Newman bases this new hermeneutic on the analogy of ecclesiastical history rather than on the more characteristically evangelical correlations of biblical typology.

Because the argument of the *Apologia* depends upon the Anglican origin of his religious knowledge, Newman links his hermeneutic method to standard Anglican divines. In chapter I, he points out that he learned from Bishop Bull "to consider that Antiquity was the true exponent of the doctrines of Christianity" and this belief, coupled with the principle of analogy that he learned from Butler, prepares for the view of ecclesiastical history that eventually leads to Rome. In chapter I, too, Newman emphasizes the "doctrine of Tradition": both Hawkins and Froude taught him, he notes, to view Tradition as the teacher and Scripture as the verifier of truth. Moreover, as Newman describes his participation in the Tractarian Movement, he again points out that he found his arguments in the writings of the early Church: "my stronghold was Antiquity."

Newman was, of course, as deeply influenced by Catholic sources, including Augustine, as he was by the Anglican divines he cites. But whether the influences were Anglican or Roman Catholic, the effect on the course of his life is well known. It was in reading a segment of early Church history, the fifth-century controversy between the Monophysites of Alexandria and the Chalcedonian Catholics, that Newman came to understand the impossibility of holding the Anglican position of the *Via Media*. In that fifth-century controversy, he found the doctrinal and ecclesiastical issues of the sixteenth and nineteenth centuries foreshadowed: "I saw my face in that mirror, and I was a Monophysite. The Church of the *Via Media* was in the position of the Oriental communion; Rome was, where she now is; and the Protestants were the Eutychians."

Not all readers of the *Apologia* can understand how Newman reached the conclusion he did or, to continue his metaphor, how he received anything but an extremely distorted reflection from the mirror of church history. As Henry Chadwick has explained [in his *The Early Church*, 1967], both the Roman Chalcedonians and the African Monophysites adhered to legitimate doctrines, both positing reasonable definitions of the nature of Christ and both articulating formulae about the union of the human and divine (the Chalcedonian, "in two natures," and the Monophysite, "out of two natures" or sometimes "one nature of the incarnate Word") that were "fully orthodox in intention and fact." But this is to ignore Newman's perspective. For if his face and not our own reflects from the mirror of history, that is as it should be in the *Apologia.* For Newman, the essential issue was not one of doctrine, but of attitude and action. In the refusal of the African Church to honor the decree of the Council of Chaldedon, in its acquittal of the heretic Eutyches, and in its defiance of Leo, the Bishop of Rome—in all these acts, Newman found parallels to the acts of the Anglican Church in the modern period.

In the middle chapters of the *Apologia,* then, Newman introduces a new hermeneutic principle, one derived from Anglican and Patristic sources and formulated specifically for the autobiographical situation he feels compelled to understand. According to the interpretation this principle

generates, it is the Anglican Church, not the Roman, that has fostered heresy and dissension, and his own participation in the Anglican-Roman controversy, however well-intentioned, has contributed to the dissension:

> What was the use of continuing the controversy, or defending my position, if, after all, I was forging arguments for Arius or Eutyches, and turning devil's advocate against the much-enduring Athanasius and the majestic Leo? Be my soul with the Saints! and shall I lift up my hand against them? Sooner may my right hand forget her cunning, and wither outright, as his who once stretched it out against a prophet of God!

The basis of self-interpretation here is ecclesiastical rather than biblical. Newman equates himself with religious sects, the Arians and Eutychians: "I was forging arguments" and "turning devil's advocate." The biblical parallels—from Psalm 137, which laments Israel's exile in Babylon, and I Kings 13, which narrates Jereboam's paralysis for opposing God's prophet—become secondary, following as rhetorical emphasis, as elaboration and verification of the truth that Tradition has authoritatively taught.

By replacing biblical with what might be termed "ecclesiastical hermeneutics," Newman moves the *Apologia* away from the tradition of Bunyan and nearer that of Augustine. This movement will not be complete—nor, indeed, even figurally obvious—until the opening lines of chapter IV in which Newman invokes the Augustinian topos of the medical crisis. Before he can turn to a specifically Augustinian topos, however, Newman must undergo a generic crisis. For the movement from one tradition to another represents a matter of both uneasiness and desire—the uneasiness of a convert from Protestantism about an autobiographical method tainted by old patterns, the desire of an advocate of Catholicism for an account thoroughly orthodox in principle and method.

The uneasiness appears as Newman draws the analogy between Christendom in the fifth and nineteenth centuries. He admits surprise (even in retrospect) that the Monophysite controversy should have instigated his conversion:

> Of all passages of history, since history has been, who would have thought of going to the sayings and doings of old Eutyches, that *delirus senex,* as (I think) Petavius calls him, and to the enormities of the unprincipled Dioscorus, in order to be converted to Rome!

In this admission Newman virtually undermines the validity of his self-interpretation by drawing attention to inconsistencies within the original analogy: not only is Eutyches, the prefiguration of Protestantism, a "crazy old man," but Dioscorus, the man whose position is analogous to his own, is a leader "unprincipled" in the extreme—the very charge the *Apologia* seeks to refute. And if the analogy creates uneasiness, Newman seems doubly uneasy as he insists that he is not writing "controversially," but is merely telling his story, narrating the events "with the one object of relating things as they happened to me in the course of my conversion." With this statement he tries to deny that he has made any interpretation at all, at least any for which he is accountable. He claims his object to be narration—something controlled by chronology, not by autobiographical intention.

Why should Newman write with such uneasiness? In one sense, his response typifies the uneasiness of all spiritual autobiographers who formulate interpretations upon which their souls depend. As Bunyan searches for an appropriate type in *Grace Abounding,* for instance, he runs through the list of possible Old Testament precursors not once, but twice, each time trying desperately to find one who, like himself, having sinned greatly after receiving God's grace, has yet been forgiven. In his *Memoir* William Cowper, too, is riddled with guilt about faulty interpretations he has made in the past; central to his account, as the sin that led to attempted suicide, is a failure in hermeneutics, a failure to believe in the possibility of providential interpretation. Some of Newman's uneasiness is of this general sort. Newman admits that "on occasion," when he reached new interpretations of ecclesiastical material, he felt "a positive doubt" whether "the suggestion did not come from below," the same fearful thought that plagues Bunyan and Cowper.

If Newman's uneasiness is typical of the genre, however, it is also particular to the *Apologia*—that is, to the *Apologia* as a Catholic autobiography in the English tradition. Protestant autobiographers had extended typological hermeneutics, after all, to correlate the events of biblical history with episodes in their own lives, and Newman perhaps feared that his method would simply seem a modification of theirs, one that drew on post-biblical history rather than on biblical narrative. As Martin J. Svaglic has pointed out ["Why Newman wrote the *Apologia,*" in David J. DeLaura's edition of the *Apologia,* 1968], among the readers whom Newman felt he must reach were "his fellow Catholics," so many of whom "had begun to have doubts about him." It is one thing for Newman to declare that it does not matter to him "if any Catholic says . . . that I have been converted in a wrong way, I cannot help that now." It is another for him to demonstrate, as he composes his autobiography with a new hermeneutic method, that it does not matter. What he needs as a Catholic autobiographer is a validation of his method.

This validation Newman finds in the Augustinian sentence, "Securus judicat orbis terrarum." The words themselves derive from the *Contra epistolam Parmeniani* (III.iv.24), a minor polemical work in which Augustine urges the Donatists, a separatist sect, to rejoin their Catholic brethren and create a unified Christian community in Africa: "The world judges with assurance that they are not good men who, in whatever part of the world, separate themselves from the rest of the world." But Newman's immediate source is an 1839 essay in the *Dublin Review,* in which Nicholas Wiseman quotes Augustine in order to argue against contemporary Anglican claims of apostolical succession. According to Wiseman, it does not matter whether the case between contemporary Catholics and Protestants is precisely the same or "so simple as that of Donatists and the Catholics of their times." Augustine's words represent "an axiom," "a golden sentence," for the Church in all ages.

Newman calls these words "palmary," associating them with a key Catholic principle of interpretation and then with Augustinian autobiography itself, and his motives suggest a desire for assurance that his uneasiness has provoked. Obviously, Newman calls the words "palmary" because he finds in them a superior interpretation of the Donatist and Anglican controversies—and of his own situation in 1839. But he also calls them "palmary," I suspect, because they remove the necessity of self-interpretation altogether. "Securus judicat orbis terrarum": with their initial stress upon "securus," the words signal Newman's primary need for assurance, for certain judgment, for reliable interpretation. The Augustinian principle avoids the ambiguity of historical circumstances and the uneasiness of the interpreter, ecclesiastical or autobiographical, who must understand them. The simplicity appeals. Newman concludes that the words "decided ecclesiastical questions *on a simpler rule* than than of Antiquity; nay, St. Augustine himself was one of the prime oracles of Antiquity. . . . What a light was hereby thrown upon every controversy in the Church!"

In this principle, articulated by the great Catholic divine of antiquity and repeated by a leading English Catholic of the nineteenth century, Newman finds validation for his use of ecclesiastical history in the *Apologia.* He recalls that Augustine's words struck him "with a power which I never had felt from any words before." They were "like the 'Tolle, lege,—Tolle, lege,' of the child, which converted St. Augustine himself." The allusion to the unprecedented power of the Augustinian sentence revokes the power that Scott's text once had over Newman: he is no longer "possessed of" *The Force of Truth.* And the association of the Augustinian principle with the *Confessions* itself is crucial, for it supplies the autobiographical authority that Newman otherwise lacks. In this passage Newman effectively transfers the *Apologia* from an English Protestant tradition to a Catholic literary form, distinct from that tradition and chronologically prior to it. By the end of the third chapter he has prepared the way for an Augustinian version of the spiritual autobiography.

Augustine's *Confessions* has frequently been cited as a seminal work in the tradition of spiritual autobiography, but in the English tradition before Newman its formal influence was, in fact, negligible. English autobiographers might have read the *Confessions* in the original Latin or in a seventeenth-century translation by Tobias Matthew or William Watts, but they made little attempt, as Karl J. Weintraub has argued [in his *The Value of the Individual: Self and Circumstance in Autobiography,* 1978], to imitate its figural motifs or larger formal structure. It was Newman who re-introduced the *Confessions* to the English reading public through the editions of the Church Fathers he sponsored, and it was Newman, too, who through the *Apologia* reminded English autobiographers of the Augustinian figures and form they might use as alternatives to Bunyanesque patterns. Newman's version of an Augustinian autobiography takes shape in chapters IV and V through a repetition of two characteristic Augustinian figures—the deathbed motif of chapter IV and the elegiac closure of chapter V—and, more generally, through an adaptation of the multiple forms of confession that organize Augustine's work and inform Newman's final statement of faith.

Chapter IV of the *Apologia* opens with Newman, as he puts it, "on my death-bed, as regards my membership with the Anglican Church." This scene repeats the *Confessions,* book VI, which begins with Augustine bodily in Milan, under the tutelage of St. Ambrose, but spiritually still in Africa, in a state of "grievous peril, through despair of ever finding truth." To describe this state, Augustine introduces two figures: that of a dead man on his bier and that of a sick man on his deathbed. My mother "bewailed me as one dead," he begins, "carrying me forth upon the bier of her thoughts, that Thou mightest say to the son of the window, Young man, I say unto thee, Arise." A few sentences later, the figure alters: "she anticipated most confidently that I should pass from sickness unto health, after the access, as it were, or a sharper fit, which physicians call 'the crisis.' " The figures originate in Luke 7:11-18, where Christ comes upon a funeral procession from the city of Nain and raises a dead man, "the only son of his mother," from his bier. For Augustine, the biblical account of a bodily resurrection has come to stand for the spiritual regeneration of all Christians and, here, of himself as autobiographer. Augustine the protagonist may seem to be on his deathbed-cum-bier, but Augustine the autobiographer knows that his state is one of crisis-cum-conversion.

For Newman, the figures of deathbed and bier provide a crucial strategy: they reveal and they avoid. The figures explain why his actions seemed so erratic during the period 1841-45, wavering between Anglicanism and Roman Catholicism and going in both directions (and no direction) at once: "A death-bed has scarcely a history; it is a tedious decline, with seasons of rallying and seasons of falling back; . . . it is a season when doors are closed and curtains drawn, and when the sick man neither cares nor is able to record the stages of his malady. I was in these circumstances, except so far as I was not allowed to die in peace." But the figures also avoid the stain of evangelicalism, the language of the Protestant conversion experience. As images of disease and debilitation, they provide an alternative to the trope of wandering in the wilderness, and except for them, Newman's account might sound at this point like countless other evangelical conversion narratives. Instead of "seasons of rallying and seasons of falling back," the text might have read, for example, "periods of forging ahead and periods of losing my way"—as, indeed, out of habit, I used the more traditional spatial metaphor of wandering, adopting it implicitly in the phrase "going in both directions (and in no direction) at once."

The figures of deathbed and bier are crucial in another way: they allow Newman to interpret his Anglican past with both truth and tact. As Newman understood very well, the moment of "crisis" described in the *Confessions* was the moment of transition from Manicheanism to Roman Catholicism. As a Manichee, Augustine had been a heretic; as neither Manichee nor Catholic, his state was one of spiritual death. Once rescued from death, Augustine recognized the errors of the Manichean doctrines and the soundness of Catholic teaching; "with joy I blushed,"

he confesses, "at having so many years barked not against the Catholic faith, but against the fictions of carnal imaginations." By adopting the Augustinian figures, Newman passes judgment on his defense of the *Via Media* and on many of the doctrines he held previously, recognizing them in retrospect as heresy, as a source of spiritual death. But of course the word *heresy* is never invoked.

What follows in chapter IV of the *Apologia* is modeled on books VI and VII of *Confessions.* For Newman, as for Augustine, the transition from death to life involves a recognition of error and a confession of Catholic truth. The first half of the chapter (1841-43) describes the recognition, with the shattering of the *Via Media* as a tenable system. Like Augustine in book VI, Newman cannot yet embrace Roman Catholicism; he quotes a letter in which he had explained to a Catholic acquaintance, "That my *sympathies* have grown towards the religion of Rome I do not deny; that my *reasons* for *shunning* her communion have lessened or altered it would be difficult perhaps to prove." The second half of the chapter (1843-45) makes the confession, beginning with a formal retraction "of all the hard things which I had said against the Church of Rome." Again like Augustine, who had condemned the Catholic faith for what were in fact his own misconceptions, Newman traces the steps that led him to accept all the Church's teachings, including those on the Blessed Virgin and the saints that had initially been a stumbling block: "this I know full well now, and did not know then, that the Catholic Church allows no image of any sort, material or immaterial, no dogmatic symbol, no rite, no sacrament, no Saint, not even the Blessed Virgin herself, to come between the soul and its Creator. It is face to face, 'solus cum solo,' in all matters between man and his God." With this confession, the dead man has been raised from his bier, an Augustinian pattern has replaced a Protestant one, and Newman is free to complete his autobiography in a Catholic mode.

This completion involves a second repetition of the *Confessions* in the elegiac inscription that closes the *Apologia.* Instead of concluding with a Pisgah vision, the traditional form of closure in Bunyanesque autobiography, Newman writes what he calls a "memorial of affection and gratitude" to his brother priests of the Birmingham Oratory. Just as Augustine's text in book IX creates a substitute for the burial market that his mother, who died in Ostia, was never to have in her Numidian homeland, so the text of the *Apologia* carves the priests' names on the page in upper-case letters and their deeds beneath them in epitaphic clauses:

> AMBROSE ST. JOHN, HENRY AUSTIN MILLS,
> HENRY BITTLESTON, EDWARD CASWALL,
> WILLIAM PAINE NEVILLE, and HENRY IGNA-
>   TIUS DUDLEY RYDER [:]
> who have been so faithful to me;
> who have been so sensitive of my needs;
> who have been so indulgent of my failings;
> who have carried me through so many trials;
> who have grudged no sacrifice, if I asked for it;
> who have been so cheerful under discourage-
>   ments of my causing;
> who have done so many good works, and let me
>   have the credit of them;

        —with whom I have lived so long, with whom
            I hope to die.

Newman intends to pay tribute to the priests as examples of Christian charity, just as Augustine commends his mother as an example of Christian piety, but the choice of the elegiac here has a more complex Augustinian purpose, redemptive as well as nostalgic and rhetorical. Augustine closes book IX of the *Confessions,* the biographical account of his mother, with a hope that his readers might in prayer "remember my parents in this transitory light, my brethren under Thee our Father in our Catholic Mother, and my fellow-citizens in that eternal Jerusalem which Thy pilgrim people sigheth after from their Exodus, even unto their return thither." Newman closes the *Apologia* with a similar prayer for redemption and reunion: "And I earnestly pray for this whole company, with a hope against hope, that all of us, who once were so united, and so happy in our union, may even now be brought at length, by the Power of the Divine Will, into One Fold and under One Shepherd." The biblical metaphor has been altered, once again to mute what might be mistaken for Protestant overtones, but paradoxically even this alteration demonstrates Newman's commitment to Augustinian autobiography. The traditional Protestant form of closure concerns itself with the redemption of the individual soul; the Augustinian form recalls the communion of saints.

Despite the similarity of the prayers, however, Newman's closure is curiously different from its original, and the choice of *living* priests for the subjects of elegy signals the problem. In the *Confessions* Augustine appropriately gives life through words to the woman who gave him life through flesh. His elegy pays tribute to a woman now dead who, as he so clearly states, "brought me forth, both in the flesh, that I might be born to this temporal light, and in heart, that I might be born to Light eternal."

Newman can write no such tribute to his mother—nor to father, brother, or sister. His mother had died before his conversion to Roman Catholicism, but that was not, of course, the obstacle. Had she lived, his conversion might very well have caused an irreconcilable breach, as it did with his sisters. More to the point, had his mother lived, Newman might never have converted. Issac Williams, his curate at St. Mary's and author of a memoir supplementary to the *Apologia,* suggests [in his *Autobiography of Issac Williams . . . As Throwing Further Light on the History of the Oxford Movement,* 1892] that Newman's mother corrected "that want of balance and repose in the soul, which [was] the malady of both brothers"; once she died, her sons lost this balance, Francis taking the direction of theological rationalism and John Henry, the direction of Roman Catholicism.

If Williams is correct about the maternal influence, then the elegy that closes Newman's autobiography may be not only a conscious tribute, but also an unconscious series of substitutions. It substitutes first a memorial to his "dearest brothers of this House" for the elegy to his mother that he could not write. In this substitution, Newman consciously brings to fruition a notion introduced in the preface—that he, like Abraham, had "left 'my kindred and my father's house' for a Church from which I once turned

Cardinal Newman. Photograph by Lewis Barraud.

away with dread"—and reiterated throughout the *Apologia* in a complex of metaphors involving the loss of home, family, and friends. He substitutes as well Ambrose St. John, "the link between my old life and my new," for the many links, both temporal and spiritual, that Augustine had to commemorate in book IX: his friend Alypius, his son Adeodatus, as well as his mother Monica, all of whom were "fellow-citizens in that eternal Jerusalem." Most significantly, Newman's elegy substitutes an apparent object of loss for the real object of loss. For it is not his brother priests (who are, after all, still alive) whom Newman mourns in this elegiac passage. Rather, it is the loss of his mother—absent from him now, perhaps absent eternally—that gives the elegiac closure of the *Apologia* its power.

If the repetition of Augustinian figures allows Newman to bring the *Apologia* within a Catholic tradition, the repetition of a larger Augustinian form explains the final chapter, "Position of My Mind since 1845," and provides Newman with a means of reconciling a disjunction within the form of the English autobiography itself. In a seminal work on the genre [*English Autobiography: Its Emergence, Materials, and Form,* 1954], Wayne Shumaker has observed that the English autobiography, particularly in the Victorian period, is a "mixed mode": it combines exposition and narration—or, to describe it negatively, it represents something in between, a combination or an alternation of modes. Following Shumaker, most literary historians have viewed the development of the genre as a process of purification: as the autobiography becomes self-conscious and self-assured, it moves away from exposition and toward narration; it moves closer, that is, to the novel. These versions of literary history assume that the most important characteristic of the genre is its factuality and the most important development, its blurring of the boundary between fact and fiction.

Newman, however, was a keener historian of the genre and a more perceptive interpreter of the disjunction between narration and exposition. He understood the genre to be essentially hermeneutic, a category that supersedes the label of fiction or non-fiction. He recognized, too, that the primary concern of autobiographers had traditionally been to find an adequate hermeneutic method. Thus, the expository element was not dross to be refined, but the legitimate articulation of principles that had governed the autobiographer's interpretation of narrative all along.

This relation of narrative to exposition, of narrative to theology and philosophy, is most clear in the arrangement of the *Confessions,* and it is Augustine's clarity of generic intention and form that Newman brings to the final chapter of the *Apologia.* Augustine's narrative ends with book IX when, hearing the *tolle lege* of the young child, he decides to abandon his professorship of rhetoric and seek baptism at the hand of Ambrose. After the account of his conversion, the mode of the *Confessions* shifts radically, from the narrative of books I-IX to the exposition of X-XIII. John C. Cooper [in his "Why Did Augustine Write Books XI-XIII of the *Confessions?*" *Augustinian Studies* 2 (1971)] has explained this shift in terms of the two meanings of the word *confessions:* Augustine engages in *confessio peccati* in the narrative of his life from birth to spiritual conversion; he shifts to *confessio fidei* in the personal reflections of book X and in the theological exposition of Genesis in books XI-XIII.

Although Cooper mentions only the common ecclesiastical distinction, he might also have cited evidence from the *Confessions* itself. In book VII, Augustine anticipates the distinct forms that his work will embody as he considers the value of past experience:

> Upon these [false books] Thou therefore willedst that I should fall, before I studied Thy Scriptures, that it might be imprinted on my memory how I was affected by them; and that afterwards when my spirits were tamed through Thy books, and my wounds touched by Thy healing fingers, I might discern and distinguish between *presumption* and *confession;* between those who saw whither they were to go, yet saw not the way, and the way that leadeth not to behold only but to dwell in the beatific country.

The key distinction, as my emphasis suggests, is between presumption and confession. It would be presumptuous for anyone to write an exposition of doctrine, to make a *confessio fidei,* before undergoing personal experiences that teach the truth of Christian doctrine. Such an exposition would be mere presumption or assumption, a state-

ment made before the fact or without the facts. For Augustine, in other words, experiential confession comes first; doctrinal confession, second. Hence the arrangement of the *Confessions,* with the narrative books preceding the expository.

Newman observes this Augustinian arrangement in the *Apologia* by detailing the process of his conversion in chapters I-IV and then systematically setting forth his theological beliefs in the "Position of My Mind since 1845." The first line of the final chapter announces the cessation of narrative: "From the time I became a Catholic, of course I have no further *history* of my religious opinions to *narrate*" (italics mine). Like Pusey's translation of the *Confessions,* which introduces books XI-XIII with the headnote, "Augustine breaks off the history of the mode whereby God led him to holy Orders, in order to 'confess' God's mercies," Newman's self-announcement signals a breaking off. He concludes the historical narrative in order to begin a confession of the "Creed of the Church."

That Newman includes an explicit defense of Catholics who hold the creed against Protestants who charge deceit and hypocrisy in no way lessens the Augustinian impact. One obstacle to faith prior to Augustine's conversion, an obstacle implanted and then nurtured by the Manichees, was the Church's teaching on creation. Augustine's exposition of Genesis I in books XI-XIII represents, in this context, a confession of faith and a renunciation of former heresy, as well as a direct defense of Catholic doctrine against its contemporary critics. If Newman's defense in chapter V addresses accusations of deceit and dishonesty, it is because they were, like the Manichean perversions of the fourth century, the pressing issues of his day. Just as the narrative of chapters I-IV answers charges of personal dishonesty, the exposition of the creed answers the more general Protestant charge that the Catholic church sanctions—and even encourages—deceit.

Newman's transition from narration to exposition at the end of the *Apologia* thus recognizes the formal mixture that had traditionally marked autobiography as a genre. More important, it represents an attempt to make the theological implications of narrative absolutely clear. At the conclusion of *Grace Abounding,* Bunyan had appended a list of "seven abominations in my heart" and seven good things that "the Wisdom of God doth order"— fourteen theological truths that his experience had taught him. Thomas Scott, too, had added his "Observations," some of which, like the influence of prayer or the study of Scripture, made doctrinal assumptions. But neither Bunyan nor Scott was self-conscious as an autobiographer about the relation between the narrative he was presenting and the theology he espoused; indeed, Scott seems to assume that he has told his story "straight," uninfluenced by his theology. With the *Apologia,* the autobiography becomes self-conscious as a genre: it realizes its hermeneutic intention. By formally distinguishing between the two modes of autobiography, Newman paradoxically re-integrates them and, in the re-integration, reflects upon the hermeneutic enterprise on which both narrative and theology depend. (pp. 93-119)

Linda H. Peterson, "Newman's 'Apologia pro

vita sua': The Dilemma of the Catholic Autobiographer," in her Victorian Autobiography: The Tradition of Self-Interpretation, *Yale University Press, 1986, pp. 93-119.*

Roger Sharrock   (essay date 1990)

[*Sharrock was an English educator and critic best known for compiling a complete edition of the works of seventeenth-century British author John Bunyan. Sharrock's interests also extended to Romantic poetry, and he edited works by William Wordsworth and John Keats. In the following essay, he surveys Newman's poetry.*]

Newman's poems form a subsidiary and comparatively small part of his total work. The title of *Verses on Various Occasions* (1868), the volume in which they were first collected, seems an adequate acknowledgement of the manner in which for the most part they are attached to passing moods and to particular events. Even his most substantial poetic work *The Dream of Gerontius* was occasioned by an illness which led him to contemplate the onset of death. Yet, after all, most of the great prose works of Newman, the *Apologia* and *The Idea of a University* among them, were in the same way connected with particular occasions. The poems share with the prose the quality of presenting the encounter of a powerful mind with individual problems, personal or public, so that the treatment of reality and God is never abstract but arises freshly out of actual incidents and the demands of certain moments in the life of an intellectual man of action. For this reason, and because his verse is, after a fashion, less considered, less serious than his prose, an enquirer into this neglected branch of his work may at least hope to uncover some inadvertent betrayals of the hidden springs of his mental life. It is of the nature of autobiography that we should not look for these in the *Apologia;* honesty as the world sees it is a seamless garment of integrity and is not inclined to inner revelation or self-betrayal. Newman wrote his poems more loosely than his prose, partly in deference to the Romantic doctrine of spontaneity, partly in accordance with the contemporary view of verse as every educated man's plaything. So it is in the poems that we might be able to trace, as it were, the dream-work of his imagination upon the contents of his thought. This essay may show whether the hope is to be fulfilled.

There are two kinds of difficulty which stand between today's reader and Newman. I think they apply to Christian as well as to non-Christian readers, though perhaps to the former rather differently and rather less acutely. The first difficulty applies to his works in general; the second is a special problem associated with the poems.

The first obstacle is that created by Newman's opposition to liberalism, and still more by its nature and passion. For it is the sheer passion of dogmatic adherence which cuts Newman off from our own age. Even in a period when, in the *Spectator* and elsewhere, a variety of intellectual conservatism is moderately fashionable, his stance of *Athanasius contra mundum* teaches us that, at least in England, liberalism has won the battle of intellectual manners. It was to the age of Basil and Athanasius that he felt instinc-

tively drawn. 'I had fierce thoughts against the Liberals', he writes at the period of the bill for the suppression of the Irish sees. His fierceness is that of the Newman who said, after reading the *Despatches* of the Duke of Wellington, 'It makes on burn to have been a soldier' [*The Letters and Diaries of John Henry Newman,* edited by Charles Stephen Dessain, et al., 1961-72]. An aspect of fierceness is that terrifying Oxford aloofness or coldness he shows at times, as in his rejection of Mgr. Talbot's invitation to preach in Rome ('Birmingham people have souls; and I have neither taste nor talent for the sort of work which you cut out for me. And I beg to decline your offer.'). Certainly this uncompromising quality is also to be found in other Victorian figures, like Gladstone; it was an age which saw moral and spiritual issues in black and white, and that marks the difference from our relativism and eirenicism, even when the issues seem to be still with us, or to come round again. The recent controversy on authority in the Church of England, both preceding and following the *Crockford's* Preface (1987), echoed, but with how muffled a sound, the old Tractarian debates.

This distancing of Newman is thus a matter of personal and period style, but it is reinforced by more material factors. One of these is the narrowness of range of his interest in the thought and literature of his own day; all that new growth of speculative philosophy and historical method in Germany, of which Matthew Arnold was so much aware, was totally occluded from his gaze. The interesting attempt by some recent writers to place Newman as the successor of Coleridge and a vital participator in a 'common tradition' linking *Aids to Reflection* with modern theology, is relevant here. There are important parallels between the two; but to claim Newman for a tradition of seeing like Coleridge the essential unity of the religious and the literary symbol is to ignore the hard dogmatism of his mental style and its resistance to synthesis. He speaks sharply of Coleridge 'looking at the Church, sacraments, doctrines &c., rather as symbols of a philosophy than as truths—as the mere accidental types of principles.' In the light of this remark we can imagine what he would have made of Coleridge's highly metaphysical rendering of the Trinity into an ingeniously balanced pattern of ideas.

The sceptical thread running through all his thought is the most effective means we have to align Newman on the interpretative horizon of the modern reader. The common tradition here can be followed from Pascal's wager through Newman to twentieth-century converts like T. S. Eliot and Graham Greene. They are united with Newman in their realistic and practical acceptance of orthodoxy: 'If the Church would be vigorous and influential it must be decided and plainspoken in its doctrine' [*The Arians of the Fourth Century*]. They are linked by their imaginative and practical recognition of the 'vast aboriginal calamity' under which mankind labours. But in Newman's case this recognition which saw beyond the confidence of a century of progress did not result in the production of imaginative work, as it did for Baudelaire, Eliot, and Greene. *Loss and Gain* and *Callista* are far removed from *The Waste Land* and *The Power and the Glory; Callista* even might be said to resemble the saint's life read by the mother to her little boy in *The Power and the Glory. Loss and Gain* is an elegy over a certain moment of Oxford culture and to say that is to accept the gulf that time has fixed.

The other obstacle, which especially applies to the poetry, is more immediate and palpable, less a matter of taste. It shows in the stiltedness of diction and the commonplace and unexciting movement of most of the lyric metres. Like many minor writers of the second quarter of the century, the period following after the great Romantics, Newman is content to behave in verse as if nothing had happened and to make do with a late eighteenth-century vocabulary and phraseology. If he is at times Wordsworthian, he is mildly Wordsworthian.

> There is a spirit ranging through
>   The earth, the stream, the air;
> Ten thousand shapes, garbs ever new,
>   That restless One doth wear;
> In colour, scent, and taste, and sound
>   The energy of life is found.

The logical upshot of this poem **'Nature and Art'** is the superiority of the former to the latter; it is a doubtful position for a poet of talent. The poet goes to 'Where iron rule, stern precedent / Mistreat the graceful day', presumably to his new office as tutorial fellow of Oriel; the conflict is finally resolved since he will carry memories of his rural retreat into his new life, 'an Ulcombe of the heart'. This may seem a too easy resolution to finish a poem, but what is really significant here is the glimpse of a strain in Newman which consistently rejects the active business of life in favour of an inner spiritual quietness. It is thus with a great effort, and as it were against nature, that he sets himself to the campaigning of the Oxford Movement. Newman must surely have been influenced by Keble's lectures in the chair of poetry; and Keble is at his most interesting and suggestive when he outlines an intimate kinship between poetry and religion:

> since it is clear, or at least a probable hypothesis, that in the highest of all interests, on which alone depends the final happiness of the race of man, poetry was providentially destined to prepare the way for Revealed Truth itself, and to guide and shape men's minds for reception of still nobler teaching, it is consistent to see the same principle at work in what I may call less important departments of its influence [Keble, *Lectures on Poetry*].

But his expression of the idea is usually more tepid than this, and it is further diluted by a tendency to view poetry as a form of relief for overcharged feelings, a palliative for violent emotions anaesthetizing in its function:

> Let us therefore deem the glorious art of Poetry a kind of medicine divinely bestowed upon man: which gives healing relief to secret mental emotion, yet without detriment to modest reserve: and, while giving scope to enthusiasm, yet rules it with order and due control.

This is far removed from the lofty conception of the relation of the poet and the Christian believer set out by Wordsworth in the Preface in 1815 which Keble must have known: there it is the dynamic power of poetry over

the human spirit which associates it with sacramental religion.

As G. B. Tennyson has noted [in his *Victorian Devotional Poetry: The Tractarian Mode,* 1981], in many of his short lyrics Newman leans more to a Wordsworthian programme than to that of Keble. He claims a more active and less merely therapeutic role for poetry. The greater number of these poems were included in **_Lyra Apostolica_** (1836) where they greatly outnumber those of Keble, Isaac Williams, and the other contributors. In that volume they sketch out a militant programme for the new Tractarian movement. In the best of these poems Newman sounds a different kind of Wordsworthian note, the rallying trumpet-call of the sonnets on national liberty and independence. **'Progress of Unbelief'** is a comment on that national apostasy denounced by Keble in the sermon which is usually taken as inaugurating the Oxford Movement.

> Truth after truth, of various scent and hue,
> Fades, and in fading stirs the angels' grief.

In **'Protestantism'** it is prophesied that a personified Wrath from heaven will make to suffer the Church which has betrayed the charge of the Holy Spirit. The mark of this crusade, which was to result in the Tracts and twelve years' disruption in the Church of England, is its dedicated severity; the poem **'Zeal and Love'** declares that charity is only reached after 'Hatred of sin, and Zeal, and Fear', and then it must appear as a form of self-denial. The dedication is a highly personal one: it is the psychological history of the disciplining of a sensitive spirit to a cause, rather than mere advocacy, that gives these poems their interest and intensity. The sense of calling is anticipated in an early poem to his brother Francis, **'To F. W. N.'** (1826). But it is most present in the large group of poems written on his Mediterranean tour with Hurrell Froude in 1832-3. If these are read as a group, a kind of progression in resoluteness may be traced. Sometimes the tone is one of intimate personal confession as in **'Sensitiveness',** where he condemns his own gentle and shrinking personality for hindering him from speaking out on previous occasions; now all will be different, uncompromising: 'Such dread of sin was indolence'. A number of poems salute major figures of the Old Testament, Isaac, Moses, Melchisedek, Joseph, and Jeremiah, but always with a sense of immediate empathy and kinship which enables Newman to greet them almost as collaborators in the present struggle. There follow poems in the same vein on St Paul; again the concern is personal and immediate. Paul is of aid to the exile brooding on the crisis in England because he can teach how the claims of zeal and patience may be reconciled; and the passionate wish for association with the saint,

> I dream'd that, with a passionate complaint
>   I wish'd me born amid God's deeds of might:

is answered with superb assurance when a voice proclaims, 'St Paul is at thy side.'

This assured voice speaks with most eloquence in **'The Pillar of the Cloud',** Newman's most famous short poem. Its reputation has inevitably caused it to be included in hymn books. But the determination it expresses is too personal and introspective to make it suitable for congregational use. The best characteristics of Newman's religious lyrics are here, simplicity, intense feeling, but also an authoritative firmness which leaves no doubt that he knows the way he is going: the mode of address to God is presumably an optative but it has a commanding imperative ring about it. The second stanza, 'I was not ever thus . . .' was condemned outright by one writer on Newman's literary work as constituting a complete departure from the initial thought to which a return is only made in the third and final stanza. However, any difficulty is removed if this poem is read as one among the whole series of the Sicilian voyage, a crucial stage in the unified account of the progress and disciplining of an individual soul for the great contest in store for it (as with the faults overcome which are recounted in **'Sensitiveness'**). At any point in the progress the subject can look backwards or forwards to earlier or later stages. It is all part of a complex ascetic exercise, the preparation of a spiritual Achilles for that moment when he shall re-enter on the scene and be able to say, 'You shall know the difference now that I am back.'

The delicate yet resolved spirit that endures this discipline is, to begin with, strangely remote from the life with which it now must grapple:

> Then what this world to thee, my heart?
> Its gifts nor feed thee nor can bless.
> Thou hast no owner's part
> In all its fleetingness.
>
> The flame, the storm, the quaking ground,
> Earth's joy, earth's terror, nought is thine;
> Thou must but hear the sound
> Of the still voice divine.

Even when the spirit can aspire to see itself as one of 'a chosen few', a company of saints, with his fellows he is marked off from the world, living a secret life shut away from the noise of history:

> Hid are the saints of God—
> Uncertified by high angelic sign;
> Nor raiment soft nor empire's golden rod
> Marks them divine.
> Theirs but the unbought air, earth's parent sod,
> And the sun's smile benign;—
> Christ rears his throne within the secret heart,
> From the haughty world apart.

This sense of the uniqueness and separateness of the individual soul owes something to Newman's early Calvinist training; but it is a feature that remains part of him. **'Substance and Shadow'** is a sonnet embodying his rejection of the 'mechanical philosophy' of the last age, still current in the ideas and programmes of the utilitarians. The octave dwells on the folly of creating idols out of the limited evidence of sense-experience, but it is in the sestet, which carries a more decisive turn of thought than is usual in Newman's sonnets, that the real emphasis of the argument lies:

> Know thy dread gift,—a creature, yet a cause:
> Each mind is its own centre, and it draws
> Home to itself, and moulds in its thought's span
> All outward things.

It is in moments like this when the rhetoric of his poetry

plays around the core of his deepest thought that the imperatives and assertions which constitute the grammar of these poems are at their most powerful: they have the weight of solemn personal directives in a diary of the soul. The chastening scepticism of Newman which rejects 'viewiness' and abstraction is not so much a scepticism about human knowledge conceived in terms of the capability of a single Cartesian mind as an acceptance that real knowledge must be filtered through a myriad individual perceptions.

It has been suggested that Newman's contribution to **Lyra Apostolica** can best be appreciated when read as parts of an integrated whole, a record of faith and self-discipline written on his memorable tour, on the voyage out, in the Adriatic, in Malta and Sicily, or becalmed in the Strait of Bonifacio; when incorporated into **Lyra Apostolica** they appeared suitably enough in the later editions of that work on pages designed like those of a devotional book with red and black lines and Gothic type for headings. But one cannot help but be dismayed by signs of the low esteem in which Newman held the art of poetry; in receiving and adapting Keble's aesthetic, which associated poetry with religion, it is as if while he was prepared to accept a Church speaking through poetry, in liturgy and symbol, he was not ready to elevate poetry in a corresponding manner; he only adhered to a half of the high Romantic compact. If he does not shrink from the claims of the aesthetic he certainly rations them. In **'The Pilgrim'** he positively vows not to indulge in natural beauty, turning his face away from the loved scenes of the Devon countryside. He passes through the scenery of the Dart as one who 'durst not love' it and who keeps his vow of nonattachment inviolate, 'prizing his pilgrim-lot'. There is evidence that he viewed the writing of verse as a form of relaxation; though he revised in later editions there is no parallel to the artistic care he lavished on the prose works. A letter of 1833 suggests that the dress of verse might be a fitting receptacle for ideas for which the writer might not desire to claim full responsibility. The steady flow of poems on the Mediterranean journey may have been partly due to an effort to relieve the tedium of a long voyage. But once Newman got into the vein there is no doubt that a serious part of his mind became engaged by the contemplation of a distant England under the sway of liberalism; nor that the ensuing series gained a momentum of its own and developed into a minor **Apologia,** a review of the writer's spiritual fitness together with his weaknesses and his aspirations.

What remains bewildering is the width of the gap between the conventional rhetoric of most of these poems and the exceptional mind behind them. Newman's poetic practice is at odds with his eloquent exposition in **The Idea of a University** of the essential unity of personal thought and a personal language in the greatest writers. The passage looks back to the Romantic concept of the unified imagination; but it also anticipates structuralist and poststructuralist concern with the primacy of the forms of language in the literary work. Indeed it might be said that Newman's analysis of literary language takes into account the actual discourse of an individual's *parole* while Saussure, having made the distinction between *parole* and *langue,* concentrated solely on the synchronic language of the latter and the distinction of its signs. Newman insists on the element of distinguishable personality by which *parole* is informed. If there is so little cultivation of a personal idiom in his verse it may be due to humility. At its best the verse rises above conventional diction into a sturdy neutral plainness. This is marked in some of the sonnets, in the straightforward meditation of **'Angelic Guidance'**, the plain assertion of **'Substance and Shadow'**; it is of course there in the powerfully reiterated 'Lead thou me on' of **'The Pillar of the Cloud'**. In many poems what looks at first like a logical progression can be seen more exactly as a movement associated with the technique of meditative prayer. Thus in the two stanzas of **'The Power of Prayer',** there is in the first the statement that any faithful soul may obtain grace for itself by prayer; by a natural association there follows in the second stanza the thought that the prayer of the truly heavenward mind is for the relief of others, for 'gifts on the world to shower', and that this is far harder to obtain. The alternating shorter lines create a halting, slowed down rhythm imitative of the slow progression of the habit of prayer.

Brevity, a biblical plainness, a sort of businesslike spirituality, guide these poems of the voyage, and a few later ones such as **'The Two Worlds'**. As Meriol Trevor has said [in his *Newman: The Pillar of the Cloud,* 1962], they are 'stark as bits of stone in a field'; but their kind of objective strength, so different from the gently flowing rill of Keble's verse, has not often been remarked because it is presented without any ostentation and restrained by natural speech forms.

Newman's metrical practice is on the whole unremarkable, though varied and capable, ranging through common metre, ballad stanza, the sonnet, and various other stanzas. There are however exceptions in two poems of much more interest which he describes as 'tragic choruses': **'The Elements'** and **'Judaism'**. In these, clearly looking towards the choruses of Aeschylus and Sophocles, Newman does catch at a Greek austerity and gnomic concentration in tune with his own verse habits. The choric model enhances his disciplined plainness; at the same time he avails himself, if somewhat sparingly, of the freer movement of Greek choric verse:

> Man is permitted much
> To scan and learn
> In Nature's frame;
> Till he well-nigh can tame
> Brute mischiefs and can touch
> Invisible things, and turn
> All warring ills to purposes of good.
> Thus, as a god below,
> He can control,
> And harmonize, what seems amiss to flow
> As sever'd from the whole
> And dimly understood.
>
> But o'er the elements
> One hand alone
> One hand has sway.
> What influence day by day
> In straiter belt prevents
> The impious Ocean, thrown
> Alternate o'er the ever-sounding shore?

> Or who has eye to trace
> How the Plague came?
> Forerun the doublings of the Tempest's race?
> Or the Air's weight and flame
> On a set scale explore?

In these verses Newman, speaking in the accents of natural religion, achieves an effective compromise with an Aeschylean spirit of $\sigma\omega\phi\rho\sigma\sigma\upsilon\nu\eta$: man must know his own feebleness, since he is 'Encompass'd all his hours by fearfullest powers / Inflexible to him'; the conclusion is that God holds the keys 'of either home', this world and that to come. The second stanza is crucial for our reading today since it creates a strong doubt whether this sort of humanist criticism of scientific claims is not now after a century and a half wholly outmoded. What exactly does he mean by 'the Air's weight and flame'? There had been quantitative investigation of the elements in the atmosphere by Dalton and Gay-Lussac within his own lifetime. The ignorance on one side of the division of the two cultures seems blatantly obvious here: only thirty years later Pasteur, with his germ theory of disease, was to establish 'how the Plague came'. If he had said in this stanza that even in an advanced stage of human science and technology the ravages of infectious disease and tempest might not be entirely resisted, he would still be persuasive. But his abrupt rejection here of the very possibility of further human knowledge is unwarranted dogmatism; it is on a part with his claim elsewhere that theology and the Bible furnish a knowledge as exact as that of physical science. The story of the Ark must simply be accepted as a truth of revelation. It is curious to find Newman underwriting the literalism of Arnold's contestant Bishop Colenso. His more judicious voice speaks elsewhere in *The Idea of a University* when he prefers to dwell on the harmlessly neutral role of the special sciences in the eye of faith.

The experimental choric verse of **'The Elements'** may be compared to that of Arnold in *The Strayed Reveller* and a few other poems. Arnold too was aspiring to an objective voice and recalling the integral steadiness of Sophocles; however his free verse has a looser movement than Newman's lines because of his study of the same form in Goethe and Heine. To invoke Arnold is to notice a more fundamental difference of point of view on the history of human culture. Within the frame of his perennial humanism Arnold can find room for the fact of nineteenth-century scientific progress.

When he collected his poems in 1868 Newman wrote to R. H. Hutton:

> If I had my way I should give myself up to verse-making; it is nearly the only kind of composition which is not a trouble to me, but I have never had time. As to my prose volumes, I have scarcely written any one without an external stimulus.

Yet the two great poetic efforts of his life were each associated with external pressures. Behind the group of lyrics written on the Mediterranean journey was the intense nervous stimulus of convalescence from his dangerous fever in Sicily; and over all those poems hung the challenge of the religious crisis at home. Thirty years later he wrote *The Dream of Gerontius* with great rapidity in January and February 1865. He had lately emerged from the strains of the controversy with Kingsley and *Apologia pro Vita Sua* had been published in the previous year. He had at that time a vivid sense of impending death. This took the form of a particular concern about sudden paralysis. It is as if he contemplated the attack on the vital powers which would most threaten his intense and all-absorbing sense of identity. The period of the Kingsley controversy came at the end of the saddest and most frustrating year of Newman's life. The Achilli libel suit, the *Rambler* affair, and the opposition of Manning, all conspired to make him feel neglected and useless. Then the reception of the *Apologia* brought relief and exhilaration. Thus there were external factors at work in both his chief poetic epochs. At each time his sensitive spirit was oriented outwards to public debate; at each time he was convalescent from sickness and under the threat of death. The short poems and the longer dramatic one each communicate a sense of the precious uniqueness of the individual soul and the corresponding weight of its moral responsibility.

The composition of *The Dream of Gerontius* took about three weeks. Newman records, 'I wrote on till it was finished on small bits of paper, and I could no more write anything else by willing it than I could fly.' The poem was published in the Jesuit periodical *The Month* in the April and May issues of 1865. Its immediate popularity with a readership far wider than the Roman Catholic public again links it with the literary activity of 1833. Gordon at Khartoum read and reread his underlined copy of *Gerontius* which after his death came into Newman's hands. **'The Pillar of the Cloud'** likewise exerted a universal appeal.

English poetry in the mid-century schooled itself to contemplate the last things. There was *In Memoriam* and Philip John Bailey's *Festus*. In the use of blank verse for the psychological analysis of exceptional mental states Newman, surprisingly, recalls the Browning of *Paracelsus*. The poem begins at the moment before death. Consciousness of identity brings as its corollary fear of the destruction of that identity:

> I can no more; for now it comes again,
> That sense of ruin, which is worse than pain,
> That masterful negation and collapse
> Of all that makes me man; as though I bent
> Over the dizzy brink
> Of some sheer infinite descent;
> Or worse, as though
> Down, down for ever I was falling through
> The solid framework of created things,
> And needs must sink and sink
> Into the vast abyss.

The whole work is an extraordinary feat. Colourless, pure, austere, it exhibits more daring in its metrical and sound effects than most of Newman's verse. The lines given to the Assistants at the moment of Gerontius's death have a calypso dip and lilt about them.

> Rescue him, O Lord, in this his evil hour,
> As of old so many by Thy gracious power:
> (Amen)
> Enoch and Elias from the common doom;
> (Amen)

Noe from the waters in a saving home; (Amen)
Abraham from th' abounding guilt of Heathenesse; (Amen)
Job from all his multiform and fell distress;
(Amen)
Isaac, when his father's knife was raised to slay;
(Amen)
Lot from burning Sodom on its judgment-day;
(Amen)
Moses from the land of bondage and despair;
(Amen)
Daniel from the hungry lions in their lair;
(Amen)

From the first it was apparent that the work invited a musical setting. The personal meditation of the soul is firmly supported in a liturgical framework: the priest utters the prayers for the dying by the bedside, 'Proficiscere, anima Christiana, de hoc mundo', and later the Angelic choirs chant hymns of praise. But the first hymn, **'Firmly I believe and truly'**, a concise summary of the dogma of the Incarnation, is spoken by Gerontius, the English lines merging into the Latin Office hymn:

> Sanctus fortis, Sanctus Deus,
> De profundis oro te,
> Miserere, Judex meus,
> Mortis in discrimine.

Most extraordinary, here and elsewhere, is the absence of any false note, the avoidance of all sentimentality or local indulgence which might come to be dated. There are few long Victorian poems which do not at some point date themselves in this way or invite untoward mirth. The part of *Gerontius* which contemporary and later critics have been least happy about is the speeches assigned to the Demons immediately after Gerontius's death. These have an animal vulgarity: the Demons jeer at human intellectual pretentions, at 'the mind bold and independent, the purpose free', and at the saint who is a stinking bag of bones before his death; Gerontius cannot see them but hears their scoffing which breaks out in jerky dissonant lines. Critics of their dissonance are essentially making a protest against indecorum. But to demand more dignity and a better tune for the devil is a Romantic, Byronic illusion. Marlowe in the comic parts of *Faustus* and C. S. Lewis in *The Screwtape Letters* have demonstrated that the demonic is a burlesque activity mimicking and playing upon human weaknesses. The Demons are ridiculous and disgusting even when they are presenting the most deadly temptation—the thought that the saint, like Eliot's Becket, may be doing the right thing for the wrong reason.

Gerontius awakens to the first moments of death and the company of his good Angel. There is imagination of a state beyond temporal understanding which is yet necessarily rendered by analogy with experience in time; the levels of experience are finely discriminated in tentative questions.

> Hitherto
> All has been darkness since I left the earth;
> Shall I remain thus sight-bereft all through
> My penance-time? If so, how comes it then
> That I have hearing still, and taste, and touch,
> Yet not a glimmer of that princely sense
> Which binds ideas in one and makes them live?

This discrimination, and the subsequent halt, in extreme adoration and fear, at a point short of the presence of God, are far more strangely moving than any attempt to paint a paradise in words. The difficult idea that the soul, freed from the controlling framework of time and space, has its own thought as a mode of organization is conveyed by the Angel in a luminous scholastic statement, free from jargon:

> Nor touch, nor taste, nor hearing has thou now;
> Thou livest in a world of signs and types,
> The presentation of most holy truths,
> Living and strong, which now encompass thee.
> A disembodied soul, thou hast by right
> No converse with aught else beside thyself;
> But, lest so stern a solitude should load
> And break thy being, in mercy are vouchsafed
> Some lower measures of perception,
> Which seems to thee, as though through channels brought,
> Through ear, or nerves, or palate, which are gone.
> And thou art wrapp'd and swathed around in dreams,
> Dreams that are true, yet enigmatical;
> For the belongings of thy present state,
> Save through such symbols, come not home to thee.

The soul now lives 'in a world of signs and types', wrapped round by dreams which are truth-telling. It is a world familiar to literary critics of the last generation, the realm of the poetic symbol in which meaning and sensuous effect are perfectly joined; the dream or 'sign' is the concrete universal adumbrated by Kant and Hegel and defined by W. K. Wimsatt. Yet, as has been noted earlier, in the prose writings Newman is ambivalent in his attitude towards the Romantic unifying symbol and distrustful of the speculative philosophy of Coleridge who detected such symbols both in works of the secular poetic imagination and in the Bible, and therefore proceeded to view the reception of divine truth as another exercise of the synthetic imagination. If there is a paradox here it may be resolved by attempting to take the perspective of the soul on the threshold of the beatific vision. Beyond the frontiers of life the nature of theological orthodoxy and its defence can be seen as purely instrumental. Truth is now mediated directly but it must still be spoken of in that language of concrete particulars which the soul has heard on earth.

The feeling, the passion for holiness, is not poured out loosely, but conforms to the measured edifice of belief which sustains the ascent of the soul. The five choirs of Angelicals present in their hymns this tiered structure in which theological truth has become pure fact: successively they sing the Incarnation, Man, the Fall, and the Redemption. The fusion of intense feeling, doctrinal precision, and metrical control is assured (perhaps especially in the fifth hymn).

As the soul prepares for the vision of God before entering purgatory it listens to the choirs of Angelicals. Between the songs of the second and third choirs the soul responds with a metaphor which alludes, gently and remotely, to the Romantic tradition of natural religion which is now superseded by revealed truth:

> The sound is like the rushing of the wind—
> The summer wind—among the lofty pines;
> Swelling and dying, echoing round about,
> Now here, now distant, wild and beautiful;
> While, scatter'd from the branches it has stirr'd,
> Descend ecstatic odours.

There are many instances of the Romantic poets employing the image of the Aeolian harp stirred by the wind to render inspiration, natural genius, and the working of the creative imagination. Keats [in his *The Fall of Hyperion*] likens the words of Thea to the fallen Saturn to this natural magic:

> As when upon a trancèd summer night,
> Forests, branch-charmèd by the earnest stars,
> Dream, and so dream all night, without a noise,
> Save from one gradual solitary gust,
> Swelling upon the silence; dying off;
> As if the ebbing air had but one wave.

Here there is no harp, only the natural magic of trees in the wind. Coleridge in *The Aeolian Harp* traces out the full image of a harp designed to catch the wind and indulges in the speculation whether 'all of animated nature' may be a vehicle for divinity in this manner. The image of the breathing life of the wind as adapted by Newman has archaic origins in most Indo-European languages. It has always been able to function in either direction of the naturalism/supernaturalism polarity. In Greek the word $\pi\nu\epsilon\upsilon\mu\alpha$ served for both 'breath' and 'spirit', and the usage is similar in Hebrew. What is brought into play is a fundamental semantic resource for describing life, physical or spiritual. The life of being is everything in the House of Judgment now described. The Angel has already informed Gerontius that 'a million-million-millionth part' of a moment could not suffice to describe the minuteness of the interval between death and the soul's recognition of its new state; in keeping with this rejection of any scheme based on human time, and in line with Newman's austere refusal of metaphor, the House of Judgment is wholly immaterial; it is composed of living Being:

> The very pavement is made up of life.

Symbol of a sort has allowed Gerontius to communicate in this state because, though as a disembodied soul

> thou hast by right
> No converse with aught else beside thyself

such a sublime solipsism would impose too stern a solitude 'and break thy being'.

With all its simplicity and restraint the measured account of fundamental Christian belief in the hymns might seem too much a mere balancing of the books if there were not in this world where the categories are living being a living dynamic act on the part of Gerontius. This comes in the rush of sympathy by which he enters completely into Christ's sacrifice and sufferings:

> Thou wilt be sick with love, and yearn for Him,
> And feel as though thou couldst but pity Him.

This act leads on naturally to the soul's prostrating itself at the feet of the Saviour. The pain of purgatory is embraced both necessarily and voluntarily. It is to be remarked here how, in spite of a few phrases like 'sick with love', 'scorch'd and shrivell'd', the language absolutely abstains from that ecstatic Counter-Reformation rhetoric in which other Catholic poets, Crashaw for instance, have indulged themselves. This avoidance of the local, of the narrowly cultural, might have freed the poem for infinity at the expense of ultimate human impoverishment. Is not Newman throwing aside every device by which language lives and has its being? Is he not likely to fail in thus reducing time and space and material richness to a pale Platonic Form of Forms? The form of his heaven cannot even permit him to dwell much on the human side of Christ's nature, vital for the soul though that link is in the total scene. It is only a partial answer to say that much is accomplished by grace and sweetness of diction and by the tact which steers deftly between mild archaism and natural word order. The formal problem is that of depicting a state where depiction is ruled out beforehand; in which there are no points of reference except one, God, who cannot be approached directly. By skirting these impossibilities Newman clears a space in this ecstatic world which is a true standing outside of all recognizable experience. He has abstained from the effort to evoke paradise by any more charged and colourful imagery; but he does succeed in finding a substitute for the suspension of temporal succession in the eternal state. Fallen human nerves demand a point to look forward to beyond whatever is the present stage of things; thought is unimaginable that is not entangled with hope or fear or expectation. The total freedom of heaven from linear time and the riddenness of space in the world is unimaginable. So Newman's poem allows the strangeness of its vision to be mediated to the reader by certain points of expectation which have been retained. There is a before and after for the soul's vision of God; then there is the expectation of purgatory. When the Angel commits the soul to purgatory at the end it is a stage, or a series of stages, and thus the graspable notion of a period of probation, an ascesis, familiar from the saint's period of probation on earth, is retained.

The poem begins as a kind of personal commentary on the Office for the Dead; it ends in a similar manner by returning to its biblical and liturgical sources. The Angel's last speech, committing the soul to a 'night of trial' which will be brief, is preceded by a prose version of Psalm 90. It is a measure of Newman's achievement and its assured serenity that it can mingle its rhythms unostentatiously with biblical texts. The serenity is not impersonal and there is a sense in which *The Dream of Gerontius* completes the *Apologia.* It follows on from it chronologically in Newman's writing career, but it also embodies the completion of this particular Christian soul's journey—from the particularity of Oxford and Birmingham to this purely spiritual ascent.

And yet in the process Gerontius has become a simpler, less subtle man than Newman. There is a sense in which no literary work can be described as finished or enjoying a full existence until it has achieved perfect understanding and possession by a public: it must come to terms with its society. This was accomplished for *The Dream of Gerontius* in and after 1900 when Elgar's musical setting brought the work into the minds of English concert audiences as

a satisfying amalgam of aesthetic and religious emotion. To be liable to this the austerity of the text had left certain points of entry; there are, for instance, the warm tenderness of the lines following on 'Take me away and in the lowest deep / There let me be . . . '. The frontier of the personality of Gerontius as thrown out by Newman had to be extended to permit a more typical, a more identifiable man; but the potentiality for this extension had to be there in the first place, in the seed of that individuality generalized by death which the text proclaims:

> Look here: I imagine Gerontius to be a man like us, not a priest or a saint but a *sinner,* a repentant one of course but still no end of a *worldly* man in his life, and now brought to book. Therefore I've not filled *his* part with church tunes and rubbish, but a good, healthy, full-blooded romantic, remembered worldliness, so to speak. It is, I imagine, much more difficult to tear one's self away from a well-to-do world than from a cloister. [Edward Elgar, letter to A. J. Jaeger (1900) quoted in Basil Main, *Elgar: His Life and Words,* 1932]

(pp. 43-61)

Roger Sharrock, "Newman's Poetry," in Newman after a Hundred Years, *edited by Ian Ker and Alan G. Hill, Oxford at the Clarendon Press, 1990, pp. 43-62.*

FURTHER READING

Biography

Trevor, Meriol. *Newman: The Pillar of the Cloud* and *Newman: Light in Winter.* London: Macmillan & Co., 1962.
    Definitive, two-volume study of Newman's life.

Ward, Wilfrid. *The Life of John Henry Cardinal Newman: Based on His Private Journals and Correspondence.* 1912. Reprint. London: Longmans, Green, and Co., 1927, 1187 p.
    Standard biography based on Newman's letters and other documents.

Criticism

Beer, John. "Newman and the Romantic Sensibility." In *The English Mind: Studies in the English Moralists Presented to Basil Willey,* edited by Hugh Sykes Davies and George Watson, pp. 193-218. Cambridge: University Press, 1964.
    Examines the influence of nineteenth-century Romanticism on Newman's thought and art.

Blehl, Vincent Ferrer, and Connolly, Francis X., eds. *Newman's "Apologia": A Classic Reconsidered.* New York: Harcourt, Brace, & World, 1964, 182 p.
    Collection of essays that includes studies by Martin J. Svaglic and William E. Buckler.

Capps, Donald. "Newman's Illness in Sicily: The Reformer as Biographer." In *The Biographical Process: Studies in the History and Psychology of Religion,* edited by Frank E. Reynolds and Donald Capps, pp. 201-18. The Hague: Mouton & Co., 1976.

> Study that proposes to both examine Newman's illness in Sicily "in light of its influence on his [subsequent] biographical study of saints and, conversely, consider the biographies for what they reveal concerning his own self-reflections as prompted by this event."

Chadwick, Owen. *Newman.* Oxford: Oxford University Press, 1983, 83 p.

> Elucidates Newman's thoughts on religious faith, higher education, and Roman Catholic dogma. Chadwick maintains that "the aims to which Newman dedicated his life" were all aspects of the "single task of preserving the force of apostolic Christianity in a world which looked to be about to reject religion as behind the times."

Epstein, Harry. "The Relevance of Newman's *Apologia* to its Modern Reader." *Southern Humanities Review* X, No. 3 (Summer 1976): 205-20.

> Finds in Newman's *Apologia* an "exploration of the self" which has "far-ranging implications for all those disciplines whose object is the study of man."

Hazen, James F. "Newman on 'Toleration'." In *History and Humanities: Essays in Honor of Wilbur S. Shepperson,* edited by Francis X. Hartigan, pp. 253-69. Reno: University of Nevada Press, 1989.

> Discusses Newman's theology, addressing his tolerance of opposing or unorthodox views.

Holloway, John. "Newman." In his *The Victorian Sage: Studies in Argument,* pp. 158-201. London: Macmillan & Co., 1953.

> Seminal study of Newman's method. Holloway writes that Newman "had a comprehensive doctrine about the world, man's place in it, and how he ought to live." In the author's writings, Holloway adds, "a variety of techniques—metaphor and analogy, discussions of meaning, carefully chosen examples—steadily tend to make the controversial non-controversial, so that we are not coerced by any 'smart syllogism' into accepting Newman's conclusions in the abstract, but brought imperceptibly to a living understanding of his creed."

Houghton, Walter E. "The Issue Between Kingsley and Newman." In *Victorian Literature: Selected Essays,* edited by Robert O. Preyer, pp. 13-36. New York: Harper & Row, 1966.

> Argues that the 1864 "clash between Kingsley and Newman is the fundamental clash, both then and now, between Protestant Liberalism and Christian Orthodoxy."

Inge, William Ralph. "Cardinal Newman." In his *Outspoken Essays,* pp. 172-204. London: Longmans, Green, and Co., 1920.

> Sketches Newman's life and career, commenting on his religious thought. Inge contends that "there was something in the composition of his mind which prevented him from being either a complete Catholic or a complete Protestant."

Lapati, Americo D. *John Henry Newman.* New York: Twayne Publishers, 1972, 161 p.

> Biographical and critical overview with a selected bibiography of primary and secondary sources on Newman.

Levine, George. "Newman: Non-Fiction as Art." *Style* 3, No. 3 (Fall 1969): 209-25.

> Analyzes stylistic aspects of the *Apologia* "to suggest how such analysis can lead one back to the major concerns of the book and can illuminate the way in which the technique becomes 'the medium of felt experience.' "

Maurice, F. D. "Dr. Newman's *Grammar of Assent.*" *The Contemporary Review* XIV (May 1870): 151-72.

> Elucidates the theoretical framework of the *Grammar of Assent,* questioning the propositions on which Newman's theory is based.

Pick, John. "Newman the Poet." *Renascence* VIII, No. 3 (Spring 1956): 127-35.

> Assesses the strengths and weaknesses of Newman's poetry. Pick concludes that the enduring value of the author's work in this genre is its contribution to "the formation of one of England's greatest prose styles."

Rickett, Arthur. "Cardinal Newman." In his *Personal Forces in Modern Literature,* pp. 3-24. 1906. Reprint. Freeport, N.Y.: Books for Libraries Press, 1968.

> Examines aspects of Newman's temperament—notably his "power of sensitive sympathy" and his sincerity—as they relate to the thought and artistry expressed in his works.

Ryan, John K. "Newman as Poet." *Thought* XX, No. 79 (December 1945): 645-56.

> Comments favorably on many features of Newman's poetry but adds that the author's work in this genre is often of a "derivative character" marked by a concomitant "lack of spontaneity and passion."

Ryan, Michael. "A Grammatology of Assent: Cardinal Newman's *Apologia pro vita sua.*" In *Approaches to Victorian Autobiography,* edited by George P. Landow, pp. 128-57. Athens: Ohio University Press, 1979.

> Maintains that Newman's theory of assent "finds its most powerful expression" in the *Apologia,* where it serves as the "grounds for [his] self-defense."

Stephen, Leslie. "Newman's Theory of Belief." In his *An Agnostic's Apology and Other Essays,* pp. 168-241. New York: G. P. Putnam's Sons, 1893.

> Analyzes Newman's theology as outlined in both his *Essay on the Development of Christian Doctrine* and his *Essay in Aid of a Grammar of Assent.* Stephen asserts that Newman will "comfortably appeal to history so long as it testifies to the life of a creed, and contemptuously reject its testimony when it exhibits the creed as ossifying or decaying."

Svaglic, Martin J. "The Revision of Newman's *Apologia.*" *Modern Philology* L, No. 1 (August 1952): 43-9.

> Traces the evolution of the *Apologia,* commenting on the significance of various revisions introduced in later editions of the work.

——. "John Henry Newman: The Victorian Experience." In *The Victorian Experience: The Prose Writers,* edited by Richard A. Levine, pp. 47-82. Athens: Ohio University Press, 1982.

> Appreciative discussion of Newman's thought. Svaglic writes: "Many Victorians who had no inclination to abandon their Christianity but wished at the same time to retain their rationality and openness to the modern

world found an embodiment of this ideal in John Henry Newman."

Thirlwall, John C. "John Henry Newman: His Poetry and Conversion." *The Dublin Review* 242, No. 515 (Spring 1968): 75-88.

    Examines Newman's poetry for its relation to his evolving views of Catholicism. Thirlwall adds that Newman's verse "started and ended with an examination of the state of his own soul."

Tillotson, Geoffrey. "Newman's Essay on Poetry: An Exposition and Comment." In his *Criticism and the Nineteenth Century,* pp. 147-87. London: The Athlone Press, 1951.

    Asserts that "the intellectual range and powers of Newman as a young don are nowhere concentrated more splendidly than in his essay on poetry."

Weatherby, Harold L. *Cardinal Newman in His Age: His Place in English Theology and Literature.* Nashville: Vanderbilt University Press, 1973, 296 p.

    Contends that Newman accepted the "subjectivism, individualism, and relativism which constitute the lineaments of modern thought" and determined these philosophies "capable of synthesis with Catholic dogma." In so doing, Weatherby adds, Newman "prepared for the revolution in Catholic teaching, in both the Roman and Anglican communions, which is so prominent a factor

in the theology and literature of the twentieth century. . . ."

Weaver, Mary Jo, ed. *Newman and the Modernists.* Lanham, Md.: University Press of America, 1985, 223 p.

    Collection of essays purporting to "display and interpret the various faces of Newman as drawn by the Modernists and their antagonists."

Wheeler, Michael. "Newman, *The Dream of Gerontius.*" In his *Death and Future Life in Victorian Literature and Theology,* pp. 305-39. Cambridge: Cambridge University Press, 1990.

    Explication of *The Dream of Gerontius,* followed by an analysis of Edward Elgar's 1900 oratorio based on the poem. Wheeler describes *The Dream* as one of the "best known and most frequently discussed literary work[s] on the subject of death and the future life to be published during the Victorian Age."

[Wilberforce, Samuel]. Review of *Apologia pro Vita suâ. The Quarterly Review* 116, No. 232 (October 1864): 528-73.

    Comments on Newman's career, his relationships with many of his contemporaries, and his theology. Wilberforce highly esteems the *Apologia,* claiming: "There is in these pages an absolute revealing of the hidden life in its acting, and its processes, which at times is almost startling, which is everywhere of the deepest interest."

Additional coverage of Newman's life and career is contained in the following sources published by Gale Research: *Dictionary of Literary Biography,* Vols. 18, 32, 55.

William Wordsworth

The Prelude

English poet, critic, essayist, and dramatist.

The following entry presents criticism of Wordsworth's poem *The Prelude; or, Growth of a Poet's Mind* (1850). For additional discussion of *The Prelude* and Wordsworth's complete career, see *NCLC,* Volume 12.

INTRODUCTION

The first known poetic autobiography, *The Prelude; or, Growth of a Poet's Mind* is an epic poem widely regarded as one of the principal literary representations of the Romantic sensibility. In plain diction easily accessible to the common reader, the poem relates Wordsworth's childhood and adult experiences, focusing particularly on his interaction with nature. Critics agree, however, that the most significant theme and unifying force of *The Prelude* is the poet's depiction of the role of the imagination in the creative process. Promoting the primacy of subjectivity, *The Prelude* fulfills the Romantic credo and stands as the definitive achievement of one of the most influential poets of the nineteenth century.

Encouraged by the poet Samuel Taylor Coleridge, Wordsworth began composing an epic philosophical poem entitled *The Recluse; or, Views on Man, Nature, and on Human Life* in 1798. Soon overwhelmed by doubts about his ability to complete such an ambitious work, he felt compelled to examine his motives and abilities; *The Prelude* was the result of this self-evaluation. Wordsworth intended the autobiographical poem to serve as an introduction to *The Recluse.* However, *The Recluse* was never completed, and *The Prelude* far exceeded Wordsworth's expectations in length, scope, and significance. Admitting that "it was a thing unprecedented in literary history, that a man should talk so much about himself," Wordsworth maintained that he was motivated not by conceit but by self-doubt. The poem was neither titled nor published during his life, because he felt that only the completion of *The Recluse*—the poem that he hoped would place him among Edmund Spenser and John Milton as one of the greatest English poets—would justify the intense self-scrutiny of *The Prelude.* Shortly after his death in 1850, *The Prelude* was published with the title given to it by his wife, Mary Wordsworth.

The Prelude exists in three versions dated 1799, 1805, and 1850. The 1799 version of less than a thousand lines is divided into two sections on the poet's childhood and adolescence, examining his interaction with nature in order to express its importance in the development of the creative process. In the 1805 *Prelude,* Wordsworth added discussions of his travels in France, his endorsement of Godwinian rationalist philosophy, and his spiritual crisis of 1796, during which he was troubled by the conflict between his patriotism as an Englishman and his approval of the French Revolution. Although *The Prelude* was essentially

complete at this time, Wordsworth returned to the poem frequently over the next thirty-five years; critics note that the 1850 version, which is the result of three full-scale reworkings of the poem in 1828, 1832, and 1839, contains significant structural and stylistic changes. Many critics have found that while Wordsworth made the language more exact, he sacrificed the freshness and spontaneity of the early versions. In the words of Russell Noyes, "revision often . . . replaced the living fact with an intellectual statement about it." Critics generally agree that the most significant change in the 1850 *Prelude* is the prominence of conventional Christian precepts, which replaced the radical nature worship of the 1805 version. In an introduction to a 1926 edition of *The Prelude,* Ernest de Selincourt noted this drastic change, citing the revision: "I worshipped then among the depths of things / As my soul bade me . . . / I felt and nothing else" to "Worshipping then among the depths of things / As piety ordained . . . / I felt, observed, and pondered." Such revisions, critics observe, effectively disguise Wordsworth's earlier pantheism and rejection of religious convention.

Nevertheless, most critics consider the 1850 *Prelude* the definitive version. Consisting of nearly nine thousand lines of blank verse, the poem generally realizes Wordsworth's goal to use in poetry "the language really used by men," and features elements of epic, autobiography, and political history. In relating Wordsworth's artistic development, spiritual crisis, and recovery, the poem recalls the steps through which his creative powers matured. In the opening section, the poet describes his unconscious union with nature during childhood and his growing awareness of nature's power, maintaining that a spiritual devotion to nature awakens and informs the poet's faculties. The middle books include descriptions of his years at Cambridge University, two separate episodes of living in London, and his experience in France during the Revolution. Wordsworth also recounts his acceptance of Godwin's philosophy, which caused him to examine nature intellectually and lose the easy communion of his youth. In the last books, Wordsworth's imaginative power is restored when he dedicates his life to celebrating the nobility of humanity and the beauty of nature. The narrative is interspersed with reflective commentary on the poet's experiences. Although some critics maintain that the epic character of the poem is disrupted by these sections, others suggest that they enhance the work. Critics note that because Wordsworth was less concerned with providing an accurate account of events than with capturing the process by which his mind absorbed and shaped experiences, *The Prelude* is not a factual rendering but an idealization of the poet's development.

The Prelude was highly regarded among those with whom Wordsworth shared the work-in-progress. Coleridge and Thomas De Quincey responded enthusiastically to a private reading of the 1805 manuscript. Praising the Romantic sensibility it expressed, Coleridge described *The Prelude* in his poem "To William Wordsworth" as "Of Truth profound a sweet continuous Song / Not learnt, but native, her own natural notes!" Victorian critics, however, regarded *The Prelude* as lacking a meaningful message for their age and faulted the poem's didacticism, claiming that its subject was suitable for prose but not for poetry. Matthew Arnold's influential 1879 essay on Wordsworth characterized him simply as a "nature poet."

A lecture delivered by A. C. Bradley in 1903 marked a turning point in Wordsworth scholarship; Bradley's analysis of *The Prelude* drew attention to Wordsworth's importance as a philosophical poet capable of capturing "visionary feeling." Twentieth-century interpretations of *The Prelude* emphasize its importance as autobiography, focusing on Wordsworth's depiction of his obligations as a poet. R. D. Havens's influential study, *The Mind of a Poet,* argues that Wordsworth intended to generalize his personal experience, suggesting that the poet's priority was not to present his own development but rather to characterize incidents that influenced his generation. Similarly, other critics have noted the poem's importance as a historical record, interpreting Wordsworth's support for the French Revolution, and subsequent efforts to come to terms with its failure, as representative of the Romantic response to the social upheaval. Critics today generally agree that *The Prelude* was significant in establishing the maturation of the artist as an acceptable literary subject, maintaining that *The Prelude* is among the most influential works in English literature.

Samuel Taylor Coleridge   (poem date 1807)

[*An English poet and critic, Coleridge was central to the English Romantic movement and is considered one of the greatest literary critics in the English language. Besides his poetry, his most important contributions include his formulation of Romantic theory, his introduction of the ideas of the German Romantics to England, and his Shakespearean criticism, which overthrew the last remnants of the Neoclassical approach to Shakespeare and focused on Shakespeare as a masterful portrayer of human character. In the following poem, composed shortly after a reading of* The Prelude *in 1807, he offers his response to the poem.*]

O Friend! O Teacher! God's great Gift to me!
Into my heart have I receiv'd that Lay
More than historic, that prophetic Lay
Wherein (high theme by Thee first sung aright)
Of the Foundations and the Building-up
Of thy own Spirit, thou hast lov'd to tell
What may be told to th' understanding mind
Revealable; and what within the mind
May rise enkindled. Theme as hard as high!
Of Smiles spontaneous, and mysterious Fear;
(The First-born they of Reason, and Twin-birth)
Of Tides obedient to external Force,
And Currents self-determin'd, as might seem,
Or by interior Power: of Moments aweful.
Now in thy hidden Life; and now abroad,
Mid festive Crowds, *thy* Brows too garlanded,
A Brother of the Feast: of Fancies fair,
Hyblæan Murmurs of poetic Thought,
Industrious in its Joy, by lilied Streams
Native or outland, Lakes and famous Hills!
Of more than Fancy, of the Hope of Man
Amid the tremor of a Realm aglow—
Where France in all her Towns lay vibrating,
Ev'n as a Bark becalm'd on sultry seas
Beneath the voice from Heaven, the bursting Crash
Of Heaven's immediate thunder! when no Cloud
Is visible, or Shadow on the Main!
Ah! soon night roll'd on night, and every Cloud
Open'd its eye of Fire: and Hope aloft
Now flutter'd, and now toss'd upon the Storm
Floating! Of Hope afflicted, and struck down,
Thence summon'd homeward—homeward to thy Heart,
Oft from the Watch-tower of Man's absolute Self,
With Light unwaning on her eyes, to look
Far on—herself a Glory to behold,
The Angel of the Vision! Then (last strain!)
Of *Duty,* chosen Laws controlling choice,
Virtue and Love! An Orphic Tale indeed,
A Tale divine of high and passionate Thoughts
To their own music chaunted!

    Ah great Bard!
Ere yet that last Swell dying aw'd the Air,

With stedfast ken I view'd thee in the Choir
Of ever-enduring Men. The truly Great
Have all one Age, and from one visible space
Shed influence: for they, both power and act,
Are permanent, and Time is not with them,
Save as it worketh for them, they in it.
Nor less a sacred Roll, than those of old,
And to be plac'd, as they, with gradual fame
Among the Archives of mankind, thy Work
Makes audible a linked Song of Truth.
Of Truth profound a sweet continuous Song
Not learnt, but native, her own natural notes!
Dear shall it be to every human Heart.
To me how more than dearest! Me, on whom
Comfort from Thee and utterance of thy Love
Came with such heights and depths of Harmony
Such sense of Wings uplifting, that the Storm
Scatter'd and whirl'd me, till my Thoughts be-
came
A bodily Tumult! and thy faithful Hopes,
Thy Hopes of me, dear Friend! by me unfelt
Were troubles to me, almost as a Voice
Familiar once and more than musical
To one cast forth, whose hope had seem'd to die,
A Wanderer with a worn-out heart,
Mid Strangers pining with untended Wounds!

O Friend! too well thou know'st, of what sad
years
The long suppression had benumm'd my soul,
That even as Life returns upon the Drown'd,
Th' unusual Joy awoke a throng of Pains—
Keen Pangs of LOVE, awakening, as a Babe,
Turbulent, with an outcry in the Heart:
And Fears self-will'd, that shunn'd the eye of
Hope,
And Hope, that would not know itself from
Fear:
Sense of pass'd Youth, and Manhood come in
vain;
And Genius given, and Knowledge won in vain;
And all, which I had cull'd in Wood-walks wild,
And all, which patient Toil had rear'd, and all
Commune with Thee had open'd out, but Flow-
ers
Strew'd on my Corse, and borne upon my Bier,
In the same Coffin, for the self-same Grave!

—That way no more! and ill beseems it me,
Who came a Welcomer in Herald's Guise
Singing of Glory and Futurity,
To wander back on such unhealthful Road
Plucking the Poisons of Self-harm! and ill
Such Intertwine beseems triumphal wreaths
Strew'd before thy Advancing! Thou too,
Friend!
O injure not the memory of that Hour
Of thy communion with my nobler mind
By pity or grief, already felt too long!
Nor let my words import more blame than
needs.
The Tumult rose and ceas'd: for Peace is nigh
Where Wisdom's Voice has found a list'ning
Heart.
Amid the howl of more than wintry Storms,
The Halcyon hears the voice of vernal Hours,
Already on the wing!

Eve following eve,

Dear tranquil Time, when the sweet sense of
Home
Becomes most sweet! hours for their own sake
hail'd,
And more desir'd, more precious, for thy song!
In silence list'ning, like a devout Child,
My soul lay passive, by thy various strain
Driven as in surges now, beneath the stars,
With momentary Stars of my own Birth,
Fair constellated Foam still darting off
Into the darkness! now a tranquil Sea
Outspread and bright, yet swelling to the Moon!

And when O Friend! my Comforter! my Guide!
Strong in thyself and powerful to give strength!
Thy long sustained Lay finally clos'd
And thy deep Voice had ceas'd—(yet thou thy-
self
Wert still before mine eyes, and round us both
That happy Vision of beloved Faces!
All, whom I deepliest love, in one room all!),
Scarce conscious and yet conscious of it's Close,
I sate, my Being blended in one Thought,
(Thought was it? or aspiration? or Resolve?)
Absorb'd, yet hanging still upon the sound:
And when I rose, I found myself in Prayer!

(pp. 542-45)

Samuel Taylor Coleridge, "To William Wordsworth," in "The Prelude: 1799, 1805, 1850" by William Wordsworth: Authoritative Texts, Context and Reception, Recent Critical Essays, Jonathan Wordsworth, M. H. Abrams, and Stephen Gill, eds., W. W. Norton & Company, Inc., 1979, pp. 542-45.

Thomas De Quincey   (essay date 1839)

[*An English critic and essayist, De Quincey is best known for his* Confessions of an English Opium Eater *(1822), in which he chronicled his addiction to opium. De Quincey contributed reviews to a number of London journals and earned a reputation as an insightful if occasionally verbose literary critic. In the following excerpt, from a three-part essay on Wordsworth originally published in 1839, he recalls Wordsworth's reading of* The Prelude.]

About the year 1810, by way of expressing an interest in *The Friend,* which Coleridge was just at that time publishing in weekly numbers, Wordsworth allowed Coleridge to print an extract from the poem on his own life, descriptive of the games celebrated upon the ice of Esthwaite by all who were able to skate: the mimic chases of hare and hounds, pursued long after the last orange gleam of light had died away from the western horizon—oftentimes far into the night—a circumstance which does not speak much for the discipline of the schools—or rather, perhaps, *does* speak much for the advantages of a situation so pure, and free from the usual perils of a town, as this primitive village of Hawkshead. Wordsworth, in this descriptive passage—which I wish that I had at this moment the means of citing, in order to amplify my account of his earliest tyrocinium—speaks of himself as frequently wheeling aside from his joyous companions to cut across the image of a star; and thus already, in the midst of sportiveness, and by a movement of sportiveness, half unconsciously to himself expressing the growing necessity of retirement to his habits of thought. At another period of the year, when the golden summer allowed the students a long season of early play before the studies of the day began, he describes himself as roaming, hand-in-hand, with one companion, along the banks of Esthwaite Water, chanting, with one voice, the verses of Goldsmith and of Gray—verses which, at the time of recording the fact, he had come to look upon as either in parts false in the principles of their composition, or, at any rate, as wofully below the tone of high poetic passion; but which, at that time of life, when the profounder feelings were as yet only germinating, filled them with an enthusiasm which he describes as brighter than the dreams of fever or of wine. . . .

Wordsworth was a profound admirer of the sublimer mathematics; at least of the higher geometry. The secret of this admiration for geometry lay in the antagonism between this world of bodiless abstraction and the world of passion. And here I may mention appropriately, and I hope without any breach of confidence, that, in a great philosophic poem of Wordsworth's, which is still in MS., and will remain in MS. until after his death, there is, at the opening of one of the books, a dream, which reaches the very *ne plus ultra* of sublimity in my opinion, expressly framed to illustrate the eternity and the independence of all social modes or fashions of existence, conceded to these two hemispheres, as it were, that compose the total world of human power—mathematics on the one hand, poetry on the other.

> The one that held acquaintance with the stars
> ———undisturbed by space or time;
> The other that was a god—yea, many gods—
> Had voices more than all the winds, and was
> A joy, a consolation, and a hope.

I scarcely know whether I am entitled to quote—as my memory (though not refreshed by a sight of the poem for more than twenty years) would well enable me to do—any long extract; but thus much I may allowably say, as it cannot in any way affect Mr Wordsworth's interests, that the form of the dream is as follows; and, by the way, even this form is not arbitrary; but, with exquisite skill in the art of composition, is made to arise out of the situation in which the poet had previously found himself, and is faintly prefigured in the elements of that situation. He had been reading *Don Quixote* by the seaside; and, oppressed by the heat of the sun, he had fallen asleep whilst gazing on the barren sands before him. He dreams that, walking in some sandy wilderness of Africa, some endless Zaarrah, he sees, at a distance

> An Arab of the desert, lance in rest,
> Mounted upon a dromedary.

The Arab rides forward to meet him; and the dreamer perceives, in the countenance of the rider, the agitation of fear, and that he often looks behind him in a troubled way, whilst in his hand he holds two books—one of which is Euclid's *Elements;* the other, which is a book and yet not a book, seeming, in fact, a shell as well as a book, sometimes neither, and yet both at once. The Arab directs him to apply his ear; upon which—

"In an unknown tongue, which yet I understood," the dreamer says that he heard

> A wild prophetic blast of harmony,
> An ode, as if in passion utter'd, that foretold
> Destruction to the people of this earth
> By deluge near at hand.

The Arab, with grave countenance, assures him that it is even so; that all was true which had been said; and that he himself was riding upon a divine mission, having it in charge

> To bury those two books;
> The one that held acquaintance with the stars,
> &c.—

that is, in effect, to secure the two great interests of poetry and mathematics from sharing in the watery ruin. As he talks, suddenly the dreamer perceives that the Arab's

> ———countenance grew more disturb'd,

and that his eye was often reverted; upon which the dreaming poet also looks along the desert in the same direction; and in the far horizon he descries

> ———a glittering light.

What is it? he asks of the Arab rider. "It is," said he, "the waters of the earth," that even then were travelling on their awful errand. Upon which, the poet sees this apostle of the desert riding off,

> With the fleet waters of the world in chase of
> him.

(pp. 545-47)

> *Thomas De Quincey, "William Wordsworth,"
> in* "The Prelude: 1799, 1805, 1850" *by William Wordsworth: Authoritative Texts, Context and Reception, Recent Critical Essays, Jonathan Wordsworth, M. H. Abrams, and Stephen Gill, eds., W. W. Norton & Company, Inc., 1979, pp. 545-47.*

The Eclectic Review (essay date 1850)

[*In the following excerpt, the reviewer praises Wordsworth's poetic achievement in* The Prelude.]

For well nigh thirty-four years the public curiosity has been excited by the knowledge that there existed in MS. an unfinished poem, of very high pretensions, and extraordinary magnitude, from the pen of the late—is he to be the last?—poet-laureate of Britain. At the tidings, Lord Jeffrey made himself very merry, and sought for a powerful calculus to compute the supposed magnitude of the poem. De Quincey, on the other hand, had read it, and, both in his writings and conversation, was in the habit of alluding to, quoting, and panegyrizing it as more than equal to Wordsworth's other achievements. All of it that is publishable, or shall ever be published, now lies before us; and we approach it with curiously-mingled emotions—mingled, because although a fragment, it is so vast, and in parts so finished, and because it may be regarded as at once an early production of his genius, and its latest legacy to the world. It seems a large fossil relic—imperfect and magnificent—newly dug up, and with the fresh earth and the old dim subsoil meeting and mingling around it.

The Prelude is the first *regular versified* autobiography we remember in our language. Passages, indeed, and parts of the lives of celebrated men, have been at times represented in verse, but in general a veil of fiction has been dropt over the real facts, as in the case of Dcn Juan; and in all the revelation made has resembled rather an escapade or a partial confession than a systematic and slowly-consolidated life. The mere circumstances, too, of life, have been more regarded than the inner current of life itself. We class the *Prelude* at once with *Sartor Resartus*—although the latter wants the poetic *form*—as the two most interesting and faithful records of the individual experience of men of genius which exist.

And yet, how different the two men, and the two sets of experience. Sartor resembles the unfilled and yawning crescent moon, Wordsworth the rounded harvest orb: Sartor's cry is 'Give, give!' Wordsworth's, 'I have found it, I have found it!' Sartor cannot, amid a universe of work, find a task fit for him to do, and yet can much less be utterly idle; while to Wordsworth, basking in the sun, or loitering near an evening stream, is sufficient and satisfactory work. To Sartor, Nature is a divine tormentor—her works at once inspire and agonize him; Wordsworth loves her with the passion of a perpetual honeymoon. Both are intensely self-conscious; but Sartor's is the consciousness of disease, Wordsworth's of high health standing before a mirror. Both have 'a demon,' but Sartor's is exceedingly fierce, dwelling among the tombs—Wordsworth's a mild eremite, loving the rocks and the woods. Sartor's experience has been frightfully peculiar, and Wordsworth's peculiarly felicitous. Both have passed through the valley of the shadow of death; but the one has found it as Christian found it, dark and noisy,—the other has passed it, with Faithful, by daylight. Sartor is more of a representative man than Wordsworth, for many have had part at least of his sad experiences, whereas Wordsworth's soul dwells apart: his joys and sorrows, his virtues and his sins, are alike his own, and he can circulate his being as soon as them. Sartor is a brother-man in fury and fever—Wordsworth seems a cherub, almost chillingly pure, and whose very warmth is borrowed from another sun than ours. We love and fear Sartor with almost equal intensity—Wordsworth we respect and wonder at with a great admiration.

Compare their different biographies. Sartor's is brief and abrupt, as a confession; the author seems hurrying away from the memory of his woe—Wordsworth lingers over his past self, like a lover over the history of his courtship. Sartor is a reminiscence of Prometheus—the *Prelude,* an account of the education of Pan. The agonies of Sartor are connected chiefly with his own individual history, shadowing that of innumerable individuals besides—those of Wordsworth, with the fate of nations, and the world at large. Sartor craves, but cannot find a creed—belief seems to flow in Wordsworth's blood; to see is to believe with him. The lives of both are fragments, but Sartor seems to shut his so abruptly, because he dare not disclose all his struggles; and Wordsworth, because he dares not reveal all

his peculiar and incommunicable joys. To use Sartor's own words, applied to the poet before us, we may inscribe upon Wordsworth's grave, 'Here lies a man who did what he intended;' while over Sartor's, disappointed ages may say, 'Here lies a man whose intentions were noble, and his powers gigantic, but who from lack of proper correspondence between them did little or nothing, said much, but only told the world his own sad story.'

To the *Prelude* and to its author we find in the current literature of the day not a few objections urged. The sun has now set, and not a few birds of darkness are abroad, screaming at the luminary they dared not face. It is said, for instance, that his place is not fixed or permanent—that his writings are fragmentary—that his originality is all of manner—that he is too metaphysical—that to sympathize with his poetry we must be facsimiles of himself—and that he has added nothing to the great stock of literature, save an able analysis of his own idiosyncrasy.

To some of those charges, the poet himself has long ago pleaded guilty. He speaks of himself, as

> Retired in summer shade,
> To pipe a simple song to thinking hearts;

and as gathering

> The harvest of a quiet eye,
> *That broods and sleeps on its own heart.*

He has found his mission in the task of faithfully and fully registering his own experiences, recording his own impressions, and painting his own image—feeling that these are so peculiar as to be worth everlasting transmission—and that they are so peculiar *because* they reflect nature, in a manner in which it was never reflected before. He loves to draw his own eye, not merely because it is bright, nor because it is *his,* but because the works of God are mirrored on it, at an angle and in colours altogether singular. His writings are all confessions of his passionate love to the material universe, and of the strange relation in which material objects stand to his mind. And if men pardon the egotism of Montaigne and Rousseau, for the sake of the frank and full disclosure their writings give of two curious and anomalous structures of mind and morale; much more should the innocent shrift of a pure and peculiar spirit like Wordsworth's, whose sole sin lies in loving nature too well, be accepted, nay, welcomed with gladness by every lover of poetry, nature, and man.

Or if the word confessions be deemed too strong, let us call them apologies. Why, it might have been asked, hast thou, endowed as thou art with such rare qualities, retired from the public world, and allowed far meaner spirits to gain a cheap and easy triumph, retired to govern colewort, loiter by streams, and slumber in noontide valleys? To this, Wordsworth has replied, by proving in his works the might of the enchantment which drew him apart—the power of the voice which came to him, saying, 'Come hither, and I will show thee a thing,'—the glory of the mystery which was revealed to him in solitude, and the perfection of that peace which there descended upon his spirit. 'I aspire not to rule over men, care not for the gewgaws of fashion or the vulgar prizes of power, I covet not even the popularity of authorship, or the buzz of reputation; I wish to dwell in another element, to lead a lonely life, to keep myself unspotted from the world, to cultivate that intimacy with nature which she has begun, by shedding on me some of her choicest gifts; and thus to build up for myself an enduring monument, which shall be crowned with fame.' It is the very story of his own 'good Lord Clifford.' On him, the rusty armour of his fathers called in vain. Possessed of a warrior's power and valour, he had a shepherd's quiet and gentle spirit, and preferred to the bustle and the laurels of the battlefield—

> The silence that is in the starry sky,
> The sleep that is among the lonely hills.

Surely, the hero and his poet both must be reckoned by the wise to have 'chosen the better part.'

We grant, then, to Wordsworth's detractors, that his eye was introverted, that he studied himself more profoundly than aught else but nature—that his genius was neither epic, nor lyric, nor dramatic—that he did not 'look abroad into universality'—that he is monotonous—and that to sympathize fully with his strains, requires a certain share both of his powers and of their peculiar training. But all this we look at as only a needful statement of his limitations; and we pity those who produce it for any other purpose. Future ages will be thankful that a formation so peculiar, has been so carefully preserved. The 'moods' of such a mind will be ranked with the dramas, lyrics, and epics of inferior poets. His monotony will be compared to that of the ocean surges, which break now on the shore to the same tune as they did the eve before the deluge. His obscurities will appear jet black ornaments. His fragments will be valued as if they were bits of the ark. Men will remember, too, that many of the poems of contemporary writers, which are apparently more finished, are really more fragmentary than his. What comparison between his **"Eclipse in Italy"** and "Lalla Rookh," his **"Laodamia"** and the "Lady of the Lake"? His purely silly or absurd poems will, like the drunken form of the patriarch Noah, be covered under a mantle of grave oblivion;—even Peter Bell shall be decently interred. And a similar oblivion, we trust, awaits the attacks which have been made upon his growing and monumental renown, from the light piercing Pythonic shafts of Jeffrey, to the blunt arrows which we notice from some quarters of late, directed against his glorious sepulchre.

It has been said, that his place is not fixed, while that of all his contemporary poets is. It takes a long time to fix the place of a great original poet. It is not easy calculating the distance of a star. Milton's place was not fixed till a century after his death—Waller's was immediately. So the age has already, if we mistake not, fixed the place of Moore, and Scott, and Rogers, as versifiers true and of a first, and poets of a second rank—of Campbell, as the most elegant of popular poets—and of Byron, as the most passionate and English of modern bards. But Keats, Shelley, and Wordsworth, as partaking so much of the infinite, and being prophets after their manner, it is handing down for full appreciation to the future, which, in all likelihood, shall rank them immediately, though at a distance, below Chaucer, Spenser, Milton, and Shakspere.

Each great poet passes through a fourfold state in regard to the world. First, his peculiar qualities are ignored; secondly, they are acknowledged; thirdly, they are appreciated; and fourthly, they are canonized. Wordsworth has only as yet reached the second stage. His merits are generally acknowledged, but generally appreciated they are not, nor are soon likely to be. Moore, Rogers, and their like, have already received their full meed of appreciation, and apotheosis for them—there is none.

'Wordsworth,' says one of the scribes referred to, 'must always be found to be an unnatural writer.—His works are as wide of nature as an allegory.—His sentiments, compared to those in Gray's "Elegy" are "slight." ' Indeed! The sternest adherer to the truth of nature, who, were Nature a book lost, could almost supply another copy, 'known to every star and every wind that blows,' free alike by birth and education, and life-long residence, of that city, the builder and maker of which is God, an unnatural writer, and his works wide of nature!! Let us next hear of the narrowness of Shakspere and the coldness of Byron. And HIS thought who says—

> To me the meanest flower that blows can give
> Thoughts which do often lie too deep for tears.

'Slight!' *Our* thought of the writer of such malignant nonsense is, we do assure him, far from being slight. We have a strong conviction that he is very nearly related to an intimate friend of Peter *Bell's.*

Enough, however, of such puny detractors. Let us return to the **Prelude** itself. It is a scroll of power and magic, unrolling slowly, not like that

> Banner bright which was unfurled
> Before him suddenly,

of which he elsewhere speaks. The tale it tells is such as one happy spirit might recount to another in the groves of Elysium, where the afternoon never darkens into the twilight. 'Have patience with me and I will *tell* thee all,' is the spirit of the story. Lingeringly does he walk down the deserted halls of the past, and converse with the pictures which he sees suspended there. The book reads like a long soliloquy. It contains no stirring adventures, few incidents of much interest, no passages of early love. His courtship and marriage are passed by in silence; the whole romance of the life is reflected from the beautiful country where his youth and manhood were passed, or arises from the recital of his own day-dreams, or profounder meditations upon man and nature, society and books.

In reading the **Prelude,** we should never forget that his object is not to weave an artful and amusing story, but sternly and elaborately to trace the 'growth of a poet's mind.' This is a metaphysical more than a biographical purpose. He leads us accordingly, not so much from incident to incident, as from thought to thought, along the salient points of his mental history. Skiddaw, Cambridge, Paris, London, the Alps, are but milestones marking his progress onwards, from the measured turbulence of his youth, to the calm 'philosophic mind' brought him by the 'years' of his manhood. No object, however august, is here described solely for its intrinsic charms, or made awkwardly to outstand from the main current of the story. Were Ossa an excrescence, he would treat it as if it were a wart—were a wart a point of interest, he would dilate on it as if it were an Ossa. His strong personal feeling bends in all that is needful to his purpose, and rejects all that is extraneous. The sun seems but the day-lamp of *his* valley—the moon couches in the leaves of the tall ash seen through *his* window—Jupiter is his 'own beloved star'—Orion, the Seven, and Sirius, when he returns from college, 'appear in their *old haunts,*' over his glittering southern crags, or resting on some particular mountain-top dear to him; and the great road to London and the world is but the footpath to his imagination, which delights most to walk along it when midnight and she can pace it undisturbed and together.

The book is thus a record of 'moods of his own mind,' selected from a life composed of little else, upon the principle of showing how, succeeding and supplanting each other, they move 'Hyperion-like on high.' Very lofty mountains are jagged, torn, and precipitous; loftier ones still are rounded off on their summits into the smoothest of contours. Thus Wordsworth shows himself rising gradually into the measure and the stature of supernal unity and peace.

The chapters of the poem might have been very properly entitled, 'Moods in Boyhood,' 'Moods in Cambridge,' 'Moods among my Books,' 'Moods among the Alps,' 'Moods in France,' &c. Characters, indeed, rush occasionally across those moods. Now it is his humble 'dame'—now it is his amiable sister—now it is a friend of youth, departed—and now the 'rapt one with the Godlike forehead,' the wondrous Coleridge; but they come like shadows, and like shadows depart, nor does their presence prevail for more than a moment to burst the web of the great soliloquy. Indeed, whether with them or without them, among mountains or men, with his faithful terrier, and talking to himself by the wayside, or pacing the Palais Royale, Wordsworth is equally and always alone.

Equally alone, but not equally at home, is the poet among the crowd. He has here depicted his impressions of London, but they seem to us somewhat vague and somewhat commonplace. That ocean of man—now up in one furious surge—now heaving in million minute waves—and now sunk in dream-haunted repose (who shall write a poem, or make a painting on the 'Dreams of London?') has not the same interest to Wordsworth's eye as his Cumberland ocean of mountains. With his 'little boat' he proudly skims the one, but his movements through the other are perplexed and chartless. 'The quenchless poetry mankind' is not the true source of his inspiration, or the fittest subject for his song. A silent morning in London he has admirably pictured—London become a desert he would have painted better still; but of the actual noonday, or evening city, he has neither given a powerful general sketch, nor marked out from it any striking individualities. How differently would the peasant bard of Scotland have described a visit to the metropolis. In one burning hour, and one burning page, he could have limned London to the life in its sorrows and mirth, virtue and vice, mean miseries and giant follies; and all men had still been screaming with laughter, or bursting into tears, over a pendant to the 'Twa Dogs,' or a supplement to his 'Address to the King.' Because he

would have laid his strong hot hand upon this ocean's mane, whereas Wordsworth has only pointed to it daintily from afar, as if with one of those 'silver wands' with which he fills the hands of the 'saints in heaven.'

With Paris, possessed as it was for a time by the unity of a demon, wallowing in blood, and foaming in blasphemy, Wordsworth has more poetic sympathy, and his descriptions of it, of France, of the disappointment of his hopes, and of his joy at the fall of Robespierre, rank with the finest passages in the poem. Hear his exulting pæan over the doom of the enemy of men and mothers:—

> Great was my transport, deep my gratitude
> To everlasting justice, by this fiat
> Made manifest. "Come now, ye golden times,"
> Said I, forthpouring on those open sands
> A hymn of triumph: "as the morning comes
> From out the bosom of the night, come ye.
> Thus far our trust is verified; behold!
> They who with clumsy desperation brought
> A river of blood, and preached that nothing else
> Could cleanse the Augean stable, by the might
> Of their own helper have been swept away,
> Their madness stands declared and visible;
> Elsewhere will safety now be sought, and earth
> March firmly toward righteousness and peace."
> Then schemes I framed more calmly, when and how
> The maddening factions might be tranquillized,
> And how, through hardships manifold and long,
> The glorious renovation would proceed.
> Thus interrupted by uneasy bursts
> Of exultation, I pursued my way
> Along that very shore which I had skimmed
> In former days; when, spurring from the vale
> Of Nightshade, and St. Mary's mouldering fane
> And the stone abbot, after circuit made
> In wantonness of heart, a joyous band
> Of schoolboys hasting to their distant home
> Along the margin of the moonlight sea—
> We beat with thundering hoofs the level sand.

Perhaps the finest chapter in the *Prelude* is that on books; at least it strikes us more, because we had expected less from it than from the rest. Books have had less share in Wordsworth's culture than in that of any great modern author. His sermons have been stones, fields his books, mountains his ancient manuscripts. To authors, books are either guides or they are law-givers, or they are sources of inspiration, or they are the avenues of mere amusement. Wordsworth has seldom submitted to their guidance, never yielded implicitly to their laws, and rarely condescended to lie down that they might tickle him into good humour, or soothe him into repose. For inspiration even, he has generally repaired to more ancient and awful fountains—to the ocean, the sky, the wells of eternal light we call the stars, or to the deep tranquil waters of his own spirit. Two classes of books alone does he seem much to relish. These are, first the old undisputed masterpieces—

> From Homer the great Thunderer, from the voice
> That roars along the bed of Jewish song,
> And that more varied and elaborate,
> Those trumpet-tones of harmony that shake
> Our shores in England.

The second class is composed of the simple ballads and story-books of childhood, such as 'Chevy Chase,' the 'Children in the Wood,' and the 'Arabian Nights.'

And here we see the great paradox of his genius, as well as of his taste. He emulates Milton on the one hand, and a nursery rhymster on the other. He affects extremes. He now tries to write a *Gil Morris,* and anon to add another book to the *Paradise Lost.* And to this at least he has attained, that passages of his more adventurous style cope worthily with all but Milton's highest flights, and that many of his smaller poems, with much of the simplicity and pathos of the elder ballad, unite a depth of thought and a delicacy of sentiment to which it had no pretensions.

In this chapter on books occurs (next perhaps to his description of the Grecian Mythology) the noblest of all his blank-verse passages. It is his dream of the 'Arab seated on a Dromedary,' and riding off to hide Euclid's Elements and the Shell of the Bard,

> With the fleet waters of a drowning world
> In chase of him.

The conception of this is sublime in a very high degree, and the execution is not inferior. Never were the dim horror—the motley confusion—the wild wave-like fluctuation—the unearthly scenery of a poet's or giant's dream more faithfully represented. As in Kubla Khan, we fancy that the words have arisen *like images* before the slumbering eye, so entirely is the 'dream *one.*'

In contemplating the *Prelude* as a whole, we feel that all our formerly-expressed notions of his poetry are confirmed. The slow motion, as of a fleet leaving the harbour—the cumbrous manner in which he relates little things—the clumsiness of the connecting links in the history—the deliberate dallyings with his subject, till he has accumulated strength and breath for a great effort—the superb and elaborate architecture of particular passages—the profundity of certain individual thoughts, and the weight and strength of particular lines, which seem to lie on his page *salted in glory,* and cast a lustre all around them—the sympathy with the lowlier passages of human life, and the simpler forms of nature—his profound natural piety and almost superhuman purity, are all found written large in the *Prelude.* We find, too, in it, what we may call his peculiar differentia as an artist, which seems to be his *uniform subordination of the materials of art to art itself.* Other poets worship the materials which they transmute into song, and cannot work except on a certain set of materials, which they deem poetical. Wordsworth can extract poety from anything in the heaven above, the earth below, or the waters under the earth. His eye anoints every object it encounters. He bends and broods over things, till they tell him all the mystery and beauty which are in their hearts. Like the bee, he is equally at home in the lofty lime and in the bosom of the lowly cowslip. Flowers and stars, queen-lilies and queens, bubbles and thunder-clouds, leech-gatherers and heroes, are alike to him, because all seem to be contemplated by him from a height which diminishes their gradations of difference, and because all are seen by him, to use an expression of Coleridge, not by moonlight, sunlight, or starlight, but just by the fairy glory which is around his own head. (pp. 550-59)

"Wordsworth's 'Growth of a Poet's Mind'," in The Eclectic Review, *n.s. Vol. XXVIII, November, 1850, pp. 550-62.*

A. C. Bradley on the mystic aspect of Wordsworth's poetry:

[Not] a little of Wordsworth's poetry either approaches or actually enters the province of the sublime. His strongest natural inclination tended there. He himself speaks of his temperament as 'stern,' and tells us that

> to the very going-out of youth
> [He] too exclusively esteemed *that* love,
> And sought *that* beauty, which, as Milton says,
> Hath terror in it.

This disposition is easily traced in the imaginative impressions of his childhood as he describes them in the *Prelude.* His fixed habit of looking

> with feelings of fraternal love
> Upon the unassuming things that hold
> A silent station in this beauteous world,

was only formed, it would seem, under his sister's influence, after his recovery from the crisis that followed the ruin of his towering hopes in the French Revolution. It was a part of his endeavour to find something of the distant ideal in life's familiar face. And though this attitude of sympathy and humility did become habitual, the first bent towards grandeur, austerity, sublimity, retained its force. It is evident in the political poems, and in all those pictures of life which depict the unconquerable power of affection, passion, resolution, patience, or faith. . . .

However much Wordsworth was the poet of small and humble things, and the poet who saw his ideal realised, not in Utopia, but here and now before his eyes, he was, quite as much, what some would call a mystic.

A. C. Bradley, in his Oxford Lectures on Poetry, *Macmillan, 1909.*

Solomon Francis Gingerich   (essay date 1924)

[*In the following excerpt, Gingerich compares* The Prelude *with Wordsworth's earlier poems to show the development of his philosophy.*]

Wordsworth was always primarily a poet and an artist. But he was also in a true sense a psychological and a philosophical poet, which fact or facts are necessary to grasp in order to understand the true import of his work. He not only "attended with care to the reports of the senses" and showed remarkable "ability to observe with accuracy things as they are in themselves," but also sedulously traced in his poems "the primary laws of our nature," attempting to show the action and reaction of mind upon its environment. Always strongly introspective, he revealed the workings of his own mind, or with rare insight transferred some of his own mental processes to those of his characters, giving them a verisimilitude to life. He was throughout his career profoundly interested in the growth of the mind, to which the long poem *The Prelude* is devoted.

Not only did he consider deeply the origin and nature of human knowledge, but it was almost habitual with him to contemplate a given object in its largest and ultimate relations. He viewed social problems, political issues, incidents of every-day life, and external nature, in the light of moral and spiritual principles. Even when dealing with an ordinary landscape or a simple story, his mind reached outward to a horizon that is infinite and penetrated inward to a world that is spiritual. By virtue of this interpenetrating energy of mind, which perceived the ideal in the real, the spiritual in the sensuous, and which reverently applied ultimate moral principles with transforming effect to many phases of life, Wordsworth's poetry may be said to embody a religious philosophy.

The spiritual growth of Wordsworth was steady and continuous. His outlook from any two points of his life more than a few years apart was not the same; he had undergone a change. He was constantly testing his past experiences by new truth or by new experiences, and thus he put into practice his deep belief in growth. The development in his philosophy of life was strikingly similar to that of Coleridge, although he was not so radically necessitarian in his youth nor so extremely transcendental in his mature years. The changes in him were also far more subtle than in Coleridge. Due, however, to a certain simplicity in his art and to his genuine sincerity, his poems accurately register the subtle changes; so that if one looks at the poems closely from a chronological point of view one can trace the story of the inner life of the poet. (pp. 91-2)

The first two books of *The Prelude* were written by 1800 and contain a few passages of still earlier composition. But the remaining twelve books were composed in 1804 and 1805, though also containing some passages of little earlier date. The poem is a spiritual autobiography, recounting the inner life of the author from childhood to maturity. It selects only such incidents as, in the memory of the poet, had a significant bearing upon his inner spiritual development. As such it is both authentic and final, save that, by an inevitable human limitation, it is colored by the philosophy of the poet at the time of composing. That is, the *feelings* the poet had had at any given time are rendered with absolute certainty, but the language and philosophic implications are contemporaneous with the period of composition. Book Thirteen, for instance, which gives an account of how Wordsworth came to select the characters for the poems of the *Lyrical Ballads,* renders with integrity the religious feeling of reverence and awe with which he then approached the divinity in lowly human beings, yet the presentation is touched with his transcendental conceptions of the time he gave the account.

The first two books especially, harmonizing in spirit with the poems of 1799 and 1800, are more strongly naturalistic than the later books. Here the Powers of Nature are all-sufficing to build up the human soul. Diety is conceived as impersonal and pervasive, co-equal with Nature—"the Uncreated," "Thou Soul that are the Eternity of Thought," etc. It is striking that, though occurring fre-

quently throughout the remainder of the poem, the word "God" occurs but once, and that purely incidentally, in the whole of the first two books. But early in Book Three the poet speaks of Deity as "the God who sees into the heart," which suggests the Diety's emergence as a personal Being from the vast order of Nature, and which indicates a new religious attitude. The change is not abrupt, but subtle; yet change it is, and important.

Indeed, the inward meaning of the latter twelve books of *The Prelude* is strikingly similar to that of the . . . [earlier poems]. Often it is drawn out more specifically in longer and more prosiac passages; but sometimes it is rendered with as much or greater imaginative and spiritual insight than in the shorter poems. As in **"Intimations of Immortality"** so in *The Prelude* the poet glorifies the inward reality that takes its rise in childhood intuitions and bases his faith in man's greatness and immortality upon it. This is a recurring theme and holds a surprisingly large place in the poem. It was Wordsworth's dearest wish to prove beyond a doubt the continuity of our personal identity through all the vicissitudes of life, the reality of an inviolable inward nature that passeth understanding. By strict logic the following passages belong to the first and second books, but by what they imply they belong where they are. In Book Five the poet says:

> Our simple childhood, sits upon a throne
> That hath more power than all the elements.
> I guess not what this tells of Being past,
> Nor what it augurs of the life to come;—
> (lines 508-511)

which is repeated in Book Twelve:

> Oh! mystery of man, from what a depth
> Proceed thy honours. I am lost, but see
> In simple childhood something of the base
> On which thy greatness stands; but this I feel,
> That from thyself it comes, that thou must give,
> Else never canst receive.
> (lines 272-7)

Again as in the **"Intimations of Immortality"** the poet considers the mind as existing in a world of wider compass than that which contains the phenomena of sensation and as of no ascertainable beginning so in *The Prelude* he believes thought to be of a mysterious origin, other than that of sensation, and of an imperishable character:

> Hard task, vain hope, to analyze the mind,
> If each most obvious and particular thought,
> Not in a mystical and idle sense,
> But in the words of Reason deeply weighed,
> Hath no beginning.
> (Book II, lines 228-232)

In short, this passage, and much else in the remainder of *The Prelude* and some things in the **"Intimations of Immortality,"** are in flat contradiction to the fundamental naturalistic and associational assumption that "all mental states are derived from sensation." Thought, not having a beginning, is prior to sensation; mental growth is rooted, not in sensation, but in self-consciousness. Wordsworth's purpose was to get behind sensation—to find out what it means, how we may interpret it at all. We must postulate an active mind, a self-consciousness, prior to sensation, in order that it may at all yield any meaning. Not denying necessarily the psychological method of association Wordsworth subverts its fundamental philosophical tenet; and this happens midway in the great years of his work. If we read him mainly in the light of **"Lines Above Tintern Abbey"** he is of course essentially naturalistic. But if we read him in the light of the great Political Sonnets and of the **"Intimations of Immortality"** and all that goes with it and comes after it he is essentially transcendental and human; that is, he is more deeply interested, as he has often told us, in the human mind, its self-contained and constituent energies, its active, transcendental powers, than in external Nature and sensation and the language of the sense. This change in him accounts in large measure for the differences of critics in interpreting him. Those who lay stress on the earlier poems, as does Leguois, find him mainly a poet of Nature and a believer in Rousseauistic Naturalism; those who emphasize the weightier matter of the later poems find him mainly transcendental, as does Bradley. A reading of his poems in strict chronological order, with an open mind as to the important new influences that entered into Wordsworth's growth, should go far to harmonize opposing views of critics and should clear up many of the difficulties of Wordsworth interpretation.

As in the **"Ode to Duty"** so in *The Prelude* the poet finds that

> A gracious spirit o'er this earth presides,
> And o'er the heart of man.
> > (Book v, lines 491-2)

Like **"Elegiac Stanzas,"** *The Prelude* recounts the sad experiences that had humanized the poet's soul and had, in each case, left him with more strength to combat the weaknesses of mortal flesh. Examples of this are the remarkable episode at the close of Book Twelve which tells of his father's death when the poet was a lad of thirteen, and the account, in Books Nine, Ten, and Eleven, of his deepening experiences with the French Revolution which found him a buoyant youth and left him "a meditative, oft a suffering, man." (Bk. xiv, 1, 143). Like **"The Happy Warrior"** this poem accentuates the transcendental power of the human mind embodied in heroic deeds.

However, *The Prelude* is not merely a poem containing passages parallel to the shorter poems written at the same time but makes a distinctive contribution to the poet's thought. In the early books Wordsworth traces back into childhood just as far as he can the birth, the awakening, of his imaginative and moral sense. He presses hard toward the very origin of "those first-born affinities that fit our new existence to existing things" (Bk. i, 1, 555). He finds this awakening very early indeed in some unusual moments of experience, such as when by stealth, as a mere child, he rowed a boat of an evening on the lake, or when at night he watched a storm from beneath a rock among the mountains. He ascribes the awakening to some divine ministry of Nature, working by some mysterious active agencies through his sensations. But in the later books, wherever he touches on the subject, he ascribes the origin of man's greatness not to a naturalistic but to a transcen-

dental source, as for instance in the passages just quoted from books Five and Twelve, especially the lines—

> But this I feel
> That from thyself it comes, that thou must give,
> Else never canst receive;—

which suggests a subjective origin. The immortal soul has power to thaw "the deepest sleep that time can lay upon her" (Bk. iv, 1, 167), is not amenable to time, is transcendental.

Again, in *The Prelude* the poet sets forth certain doctrines about the imagination, the feelings, and the reason. The three following passages taken in the order in which they appear in the poem reveal certain interrelations of the terms:

> But all the meditations of mankind,
> Yea, all the adamantine holds of truth
> By reason built, or passion, which itself
> Is highest reason in a soul sublime.
> > (Book v, lines 38-41)

> Imagination—here the Power so called
> Through sad incompetence of human speech,
> That awful Power rose from the mind's abyss.
> > (Book vi, lines 592-4)

> This spiritual Love acts not nor can exist
> Without Imagination, which, in truth,
> Is but another name for absolute power
> And clearest insight, amplitude of mind,
> And Reason in her most exalted mood.
> This faculty hath been the feeding source
> Of our long labour.
> > (Book xiv, lines 188-194)

Love cannot exist without imagination, imagination is reason in her most exalted mood, and passion also is reason in a soul sublime. It may seem absurd to identify these terms in such a way. But Wordsworth is aiming to set forth an entity, a Power, a central energy, the ultimate reality in the human mind, and there is no word that can adequately describe it. He confesses to the sad incompetence of human speech, and the best he can do is to vary the descriptive words. Yet the originality and everlasting freshness and beauty of *The Prelude* is in large measure due to the fact that he breaks through formal language and formal terms and formal psychologies, including the psychology of the Associationists, in his utmost effort to set forth his own intense vision of the inmost nature of our being— its origin, its growth, its continuity of existence, its immortality. He often falters at this almost more than human task. "How awful is the might of human souls," he exclaims in Book Three, and admits that the "high argument" in the main "lies far hidden from the reach of words." He takes courage however when he remembers that the reality he is describing reveals itself in the great moments of life: "There's not a man that lives who hath not known his godlike hours" (Bk. III, 1, 191). The record of these rare but supreme moments, which reassure the poet of man's high destiny, is the heart of *The Prelude.* And the poet has his reward:

> But to my conscious soul I now can say—
> "I recognize thy glory": in such strength
> Of usurpation, when the light of sense

Goes out, but with a flash that has revealed
The invisible world;—
(Book VI, lines 598-602)

which is a transcendent experience.

The importance of the principle of transcendence seems
to have grown in Wordsworth's mind as he was writing
The Prelude, it being more marked in the later books.
From many instances that abound a few must suffice. In
Book Five the poet inquires:

Oh! why hath not the Mind
Some element to stamp her image on
In nature somewhat nearer to her own?
Why, gifted with such powers to send abroad
Her spirit, must it lodge in shrines so frail?
(lines 45-49)

There is such a disparity between what constitutes man
and what constitutes nature that man, who must needs use
a stone or a shell or something that nature supplies when
he wishes to make a record of himself, finds that he cannot
at all do his gifted powers justice. In Book Eight the poet
exalts man as a transcendental Being, who is

Both in perception and discernment, first
In every capability of rapture,
Through the divine effect of power and love;
As, more than anything we know, instinct
With godhead, and, by reason and by will,
Acknowledging dependency sublime.
(lines 489-494)

The godhead in man is even more emphatically asserted
in Book Ten but is at the same time conceived to be dependent on the "Power Supreme" whom the poet represents
as

Making man what he is, creature divine,
In single or in social eminence,
Above the rest raised infinite ascents
When reason that enables him to be
Is not sequestered.
(lines 424-8)

This transcendental might of the mind, that "dread
watch-tower of man's absolute self," is perhaps nowhere
in Wordsworth more powerfully set forth than in the last
book of **The Prelude.** After a marvellous description of a
midnight view from the top of Snowdown, in which he beheld (he says)

The Moon hung naked in a firmament
Of azure without cloud, and at my feet
Rested a silent sea of hoary mist,—

There appeared to him, from out of that vision, "the type
of a majestic intellect":

There I beheld the emblem of a mind
That feeds upon infinity, that broods
Over the dark abyss, intent to hear
Its voices issuing forth to silent light
In one continuous stream; a mind sustained
By recognitions of transcendent power,
In sense conducting to ideal form,
In soul of more than mortal privilege.
(lines 70-77)

The power that, amid circumstances awful and sublime,
Nature exerts on "the face of outward things" is the express

Resemblance of that glorious faculty
That higher minds bear with them as their own.
. . . In a world of life they live
By sensible impression not enthralled,
But by their quickening impulse made more
  prompt
To hold fit converse with the spiritual world,
And with the generations of mankind
Spread over time, past, present, and to come,
Age after age, till Time shall be no more.
Such minds are truly from the Deity,
For they are Powers; and hence the highest bliss
That flesh can know is theirs—the consciousness
Of Whom they are, habitually infused
Through every image and through every
  thought,
And all affections by communion raised
From earth to heaven, from human to divine;
Hence endless occupation for the Soul,
Whether discursive or intuitive;
Hence cheerfulness for acts of daily life,
Emotions which best foresight need not fear,
Most worthy then of trust when most intense.
(lines 89-123)

In Book Twelve he again says that

The mind is lord and master—outward sense
The obedient servant of her will.
(lines 222-3)

Such minds must find their permanent home in an order
of existence that extends beyond Nature:

Our destiny, our being's heart and home
Is with infinitude, and only there;
With hope it is, hope that can never die,
Effort, and expectation, and desire,
And something evermore about to be.
(Book VI, lines 603-7)

Thus in **The Prelude** Wordsworth traverses the same
ground and with the same underlying purpose as in the
shorter poems that synchronize with it. This homogeneity
attests once more to the integrity of his mind. Rare are the
poets who have revealed their whole minds so fully, who
are so frank and yet so dignified and even reserved. Rarer
still is the poet who, if he be as profoundly self-revealing
as Wordsworth, manifests such little deviation out of his
true orbit, such a wide scanning of man and Nature and
ultimate truth from a deep-seated center of his own being.
(pp. 155-64)

Solomon Francis Gingerich, "Wordsworth," in
his Essays in the Romantic Poets, The Mac-
millan Company, 1924, pp. 91-194.

Ernest de Selincourt   (essay date 1926)

[*In the following excerpt, Selincourt surveys the development of structure and content in revisions of* The Prelude.]

It was in the early months of 1798 that Wordsworth conceived the idea of writing a history of the growth of his

own mind. Partly on the suggestion of Coleridge, and spurred on by his enthusiastic encouragement, he had determined to compose a great philosophic poem to be entitled *The Recluse, or Views on Man, Nature, and Society.* It seems probable that a rough draft of those lines afterwards printed as the *Prospectus to the Excursion* was struck off in the first heat of this resolve. He had already written '**The Ruined Cottage**' and other verse which would naturally find its place in his comprehensive scheme; 'for', he wrote, 'I know not anything which will not come within the scope of my plan'. In the eager confidence with which he embarked on the enterprise he anticipated its completion in less than two years; but the 'paramount impulse not to be withstood' soon gave way to doubt. Has he the strength to assume so awful a burthen? Would it not be wiser to await those 'mellower years' that 'bring a riper mind'? Are his misgivings justly founded, or are they mere timidity and laziness, a subtle form of selfishness cloaked in 'humility and modest awe'? The answer can only be found by taking stock of himself and examining how far Nature and Education have qualified him for his task. And so he wrote *The Prelude.*

It is clear that in its initial stages Wordsworth regarded his spiritual autobiography as an integral part of *The Recluse,* and not as a separate poem preparatory to it. More than a year later, in October 1799, Coleridge refers to it as *The Recluse,* and it seems likely that until the early months of 1800, when '**Home in Grasmere**' was written to form the introductory book of his great poem, the history of his early life was not viewed as an independent work. Even then it was given no definite title. Wordsworth refers to it as 'a poem on my own earlier life'. Dorothy calls it 'the poem to C.' or 'the poem on his own earlier life'. Coleridge, as late as February 1804, still speaks of it as *The Recluse,* and in *The Friend* (1808-9) refers to it as 'an unpublished Poem on the Growth and Revolutions of an Individual Mind'. Only on publication after the poet's death did it receive, from Mrs. Wordsworth, the name by which it is known to-day.

Its independence of the larger poem followed naturally from its growth under his hand to a length he had not foreseen. It is possible that even in the five books which, as late as March 1804, were to complete the poem, he had already exceeded his original conception of it. This shorter *Prelude* would have taken his history no further than his first Long Vacation, and its culminating episode was to be the consecration of his life to poetry upon the heights above Hawkshead (IV. 320-45). But though this was, perhaps, the great moment of his life, he realized that to stop there would not fulfil his purpose. The experiences of the next six years,—his hopes and his despair for the Revolution in France, his life in London and in the country, homeless, and without means of livelihood, his sudden glad release from the bondage of circumstance, his settling at Racedown with Dorothy and his friendship with Coleridge,— had all 'borne a part, and that a needful one', in making him the poet that he was. And eight more books were added.

But in writing thus fully of himself he encroached inevitably upon his first design. *The Recluse,* 'as having for its

principal subject the sensations and opinions of a poet living in retirement', was itself essentially autobiographical—even in *The Excursion,* which was intended to be dramatic, not only the hero but also the Solitary and the Vicar were thinly veiled portraits of their author,—and much of the poetry he wished to write would, in fact, be equally well suited to either work. There can be no doubt that the wealth of *The Prelude* impoverished *The Recluse.* But this cannot be regretted. The ambitious design of *The Recluse* demanded a philosophic unity which Coleridge, indeed, might confidently anticipate, but which it was not in Wordsworth to supply; from the first it was doomed to failure. In *The Prelude,* which had a unity springing directly from the poet's own mind and personality, Wordsworth produced a masterpiece.

As it stands *The Prelude* has not merely a unity of design; it has something of epic structure. It opens with an outburst of joy that after years of anxiety the poet is at last free to devote his life to its true vocation: its 'last word of personal concern' records his gratitude for the gift which brought him that freedom. Within this frame he places the history of his life from the seedtime of infancy to those days when, chaunting alternate songs with Coleridge as they roamed the Quantock hills together, he was first fully conscious that his genius was bearing fruit. Books I-IV

Manuscript title page of The Prelude.

lead up, through an account of his early life, to the first great climax, his poetic consecration; after which there is a pause in the narrative, whilst he reviews, in Book V, his early debt to literature. Books VI and VII resume his life's history, and carry it down to the moment before the second great climax—the awakening of his passionate interest in man (Book IX). But before this, the narrative pauses once more, whilst in Book VIII he gives a philosophic retrospect of his whole period of preparation. Book X leads up to and records the catastrophe—the destruction of his hopes for man in so far as they were identified with the French Revolution, and his consequent despair of mind: Books XI-XIII give the reconciliation, his recovery from despair, the rebuilding of his hopes for man upon a sounder basis and, as a consequence, his entrance into his poetic heritage.

Wordsworth was in evident agreement with Milton on the true nature of the epic subject. Both of them repudiated military exploits, 'hitherto the only argument heroic deemed', in the desire to bring within its confines a more spiritual conflict. Only the pedant will dissent from their conception; and those who regard the mind of Wordsworth as both great in itself and essentially representative of the highest, the imaginative type of mind, will recognize its adventures as a fit theme for epic treatment. But Wordsworth himself, though he claimed this dignity for *The Recluse,* where his theme was the 'mind of man', was humbler in his comments on *The Prelude.* He admitted, indeed, that 'it was a thing unprecedented in literary history that a man should talk so much about himself'. 'It is not self-conceit', he wrote truly, 'that has induced me to do this, but real humility. I began the work because I was unprepared to treat any more arduous subject, and diffident of my own powers. Here, at least, I hoped that to a certain degree I should be sure of succeeding, as I had nothing to do but describe what I had felt and thought; therefore could not easily be bewildered. This might certainly have been done in narrower compass by a man of more address; but I have done my best.' Yet, in truth, Wordsworth was never more eloquent than when he spoke of himself, and his best in *The Prelude* has never been rivalled in its own kind.

. . . . .

For the task before him Wordsworth was well equipped by his wide knowledge of the literature of the past. The servant-maid at Rydal Mount, who told a visitor that her master's study was in the fields, touched unquestionably upon the main source of his inspiration, but her pretty epigram did not comprise the whole truth of the matter; and the poet who spoke of books as 'Powers only less than Nature's self, which is the breath of God', was not likely to neglect them. Yet the superficial critic has always tended to underrate their influence upon him. *The Prelude* foresaw this error, but gave some countenance to it; for the section entitled 'Books' takes us no further than his school-days, and is rather a general discourse on the value of imaginative literature than a detailed account of his actual reading. Yet it tells us, at least, that as a boy he read voraciously; and no habit acquired in childhood is easily discarded. As a matter of fact he retained the habit till his

middle age, and only gave it up when his eyes declined their office. At Cambridge 'many books were skimmed, devoured, or studiously perused',—in Greek and Latin, Italian, French and Spanish, as well as in his mother tongue,—and not poetry alone, but history also. There is evidence that when he settled at Racedown he not only read widely, but was convinced that success in his art could not be acquired otherwise. In his search for a metaphysical basis to his theory of life he studied the philosophers of the eighteenth century: De Quincey bore witness later to his extensive knowledge of ancient history. He had at all times a passion for the literature of travel, and insisted on its value in widening his outlook and enriching his experience. 'If ', he wrote to a friend in March 1798, 'you could collect for me any books of travels, you would render me an essential service, as without much of such reading my present labours cannot be brought to a conclusion'; and the pages of *The Prelude* are studded with simile, metaphor, and allusion drawn from the narratives of famous navigators, and explorers of unknown continents. But naturally his chief reading was in English poetry. Few poets could equal Wordsworth in a knowledge of their forerunners. Of his intimacy with the minor poets of the eighteenth century **'The Evening Walk'** and *Descriptive Sketches* bore painful witness: in *The Prelude* he was to show his true ancestry. 'When I began', he says, 'to give myself up to the profession of a poet for life, I was impressed with a conviction that there were four poets whom I must have continually before me as examples—Chaucer, Shakespeare, Spenser and Milton. These I must study, and equal *if I could:* I need not think of the rest.' He was true to his conviction. The quintessence of Spenser's charm he could distil into two perfect lines:

> Sweet Spenser, moving through his clouded heaven
> With the moon's beauty and the moon's soft pace,

and the fragrance of Spenser is recalled on several pages of *The Prelude.* The poem abounds in reminiscence of Shakespearian scene and phrasing. Of Milton there is still more. It was his avowed ambition to be the Milton of his age; nor, as Keats recognized, was that ambition ill-founded. He had the same lofty conception of his art, the same passionate devotion to it, and like Milton, though in his own way, he strove 'to justify the ways of God to man'. Throughout *The Prelude* there are signs of devout Miltonic study. Not only does the style of the poem in its more eloquent passages take on a distinctly Miltonic manner, but constantly, in places when they would least be expected, Miltonic echoes can be heard. That Wordsworth himself was probably unconscious of them is only a proof of the completeness with which he had absorbed his master, so that Milton's phrase and cadence had become a natural and inseparable element in his own speech.

This study of the supreme artists was supported by prolonged meditation on both the principles and the technical minutiae of his art. He chose the metre for his poem with a full consciousness of its pitfalls. It is significant to find copied into the notebook that contains the earliest fragments of *The Prelude* the warnings which Dr. Johnson had uttered on the peculiar dangers incident to the writing of blank verse. From the contorted and unnatural phrasing of the ***Descriptive Sketches*** he was already in revolt. ***The Prelude*** was not written, like some of ***The Lyrical Ballads,*** to illustrate a theory of poetic diction; yet it demonstrates clearly enough that 'a selection from the real language of men in a state of vivid sensation is adapted to the purposes of poetic pleasure',—at least when the man Wordsworth is addressing his closest friend. For its language is selected from the whole of his experience, and the style to which he moulds it rises with the character and the intensity of the emotion it has to express. And with Coleridge he had not only discussed the cardinal points of poetry, but had argued upon matters of form and style. His main conclusions, despite occasional overstatement, the natural reaction from the false ideals of his youth, kept him, as Coleridge himself admitted, in the great tradition. The epithets 'simple' and 'natural', commonly applied to Wordsworth's poetry, alike for praise and blame, suggest a general ignorance of the intense study and careful artistry that lay behind it. But the popular view is in itself a tribute to the powerful originality of his mind and manner. His style is Wordsworthian as truly as Milton's is Miltonic. (pp. xxv-xxxi)

. . . . .

Some time before ***The Prelude*** was finished Wordsworth had given up all ideas of immediate publication. His high hopes in the poetic future that lay before him, and the spiritual history on which those hopes were founded, might indeed be confided to the friend who was his second self, but could not, without arrogance, be proclaimed to the world before he had given some solid earnest of their fulfilment. 'This poem', he wrote to De Quincey (March 6, 1804), 'will not be published these many years, and never during my lifetime, till I have finished a larger and more important work to which it is tributary.' Moreover, he was himself dissatisfied with it. 'When I looked back upon it', he wrote only a fortnight after its completion, 'it seemed to have a dead weight about it—the reality so far short of the expectation. It was the first long labour that I had finished, and the doubt whether I should ever live to write ***The Recluse*** and the sense which I had of this poem being so far below what I had seemed capable of executing depressed me much.' Nearly ten years later, as a first instalment of ***The Recluse,*** he published ***The Excursion,*** and there can be no doubt that his depression sank deeper, even as it was more fully justified. ***The Prelude*** had at least won the enthusiastic praise of Coleridge, but Coleridge made it quite clear that he was disappointed with ***The Excursion;*** and as Wordsworth read his friend's cool and measured commendation of this later work, and recalled the glowing tribute accorded to the earlier:

> an Orphic song indeed,
> To its own music chanted!

he had little heart to continue his great task. How soon the scheme of ***The Recluse*** was definitely abandoned we do not know; but its abandonment would only strengthen his resolve that ***The Prelude*** should remain in manuscript till after his death.

But ***The Prelude*** was not laid aside and forgotten. Though he thought it inferior to what it might have been, he was

fully conscious of its worth. The vital intimacy of its theme, which, doubtless, had made him peculiarly sensitive to its shortcomings, made him all the more anxious to perfect it. His resolve that the poem was to appear posthumously did not lessen his interest, for he knew that the destiny of all his writings lay with posterity, not with his immediate public; it only gave him a larger leisure in which to review it. For thirty-five years he continually went back to ***The Prelude,*** retouching and revising. The poem which appeared in 1850 differed in many respects from that which he read to Coleridge in 1806. From the MSS., . . . we are able to note the nature and the extent of the alterations introduced into the text; and a fresh light is thrown, not only upon the changes which came over the poet's mind, but also upon his principles and methods as an artist. (pp. xli-xlii)

Writing in 1816 of some minor pieces which he had just composed he calls them 'effusions rather than compositions, though in justice to myself I must say that upon the correction of the style I have bestowed, as I always do, great labour'. 'The composition of verse', he wrote later, 'is infinitely more an art than men are prepared to believe, and absolute success in it depends on innumerable *minutiae*. . . . Milton speaks of pouring "easy his unpremeditated verse". It would be harsh, untrue, and odious to say there is anything like cant in this, but it is not *true* to the letter, and tends to mislead.' He might have added that his own description of poetry as 'the spontaneous overflow of powerful feelings' was liable to the same misconstruction. For experience had taught him that this 'spontaneous overflow' was no more than the raw material of art. It was easy enough to give those feelings a loose impressionistic language adequate to record them for himself. But such language was not poetry: it had not really expressed them, and could not transmit them to others. The poet, Wordsworth knew well, was a craftsman, who must toil with unremitting patience at every detail of his work, till it has gained a clearer outline, a fuller substance: not otherwise could it acquire that organic power which is the sure touchstone of art:

> The vital spirit of a perfect form.

The labour that Wordsworth bestowed on revision was at least equal to that of first composition, and was pursued when less scrupulous artists would have been well content to leave their work untouched. To Coleridge in 1798 **'The Ruined Cottage'** was 'superior to anything in our language which at all resembles it', yet three years later Wordsworth is found wearing himself out in trying to make it better. The slightness of the difference between many passages found in the rough notebooks, where they were jotted down in the hurry of immediate inspiration . . . affords ample proof that Wordsworth was postponing correction rather than that he was satisfied with his work as it stood. It is reasonable, therefore, to suppose that had he prepared it for press in 1805 he would have introduced into the text many of those changes which made their first appearance at a much later date. (pp. xlii-xliv)

. . . . .

To the student of the poet's mind the first version of ***The***

Prelude is chiefly valuable because it presents us with the history of his spiritual growth as he saw it when his powers were still at their height, and when he was writing those poems on which his greatness rests most securely. No man is the same at seventy years of age as he was at thirty-five, and Wordsworth, perhaps, changed more than most of us; for though, like others, he descended into the vale of years, he descended from far more glorious heights. The Wordsworth who, when the conversation turned upon Orleans, could say to his wife 'I wonder how I came to stay there so long, and at a period so exciting', was either a very different man from his younger self, or he had a keener sense of humour than is usually allowed him. When he wrote *The Prelude* he was gifted with a penetrative imagination that none of our poets, save Shakespeare, can surpass; but even then the gift came to him fitfully:

> I see by glimpses now, as age comes on
> May scarcely see at all.

The pathetic prophecy was fulfilled; as age came on, his sight was dimmed; and not only did he see less, but he tended to lose complete confidence in his earlier vision. He still towered above his fellows. As late as 1841 he could impress John Stuart Mill with the 'extensive range of his thoughts and the expansiveness of his feelings'. But compared with what he had once been he was narrow, and he was timid; and many of the later changes in the text of *The Prelude* are criticisms directed by a man of seventy winters against his own past.

It is not to be expected that he would find much to alter in his reminiscences of childhood; nor had he written anything of Cambridge that would seriously disquiet his more prudent age. He knew the darker side to the picture, for he told De Quincey that 'the manners of the young men were very frantic and dissolute at that time'; but to this he barely alludes in *The Prelude.* For there 'his tale was of himself', and the 'baser pleasures of the place' were 'by him unshared, and only now and then observed'. There could hardly be stronger testimony to the soundness of his early education and the strength of his character than that he could pass unscathed through the Cambridge of his day:

> For me, I grieve not; happy is the man,
> Who only misses what I miss'd, who falls
> No lower than I fell.

The University had, in fact, little of academic worth to offer him; but the very apathy of those in authority, and the barren curriculum which they prescribed, had justified him in indulging his incorrigible passion for liberty. He had re-echoed in his heart the comment passed on Cambridge by his latest poetic predecessor—'If these are the profits of the place, give me the amusements of it'; but looking back from a maturer manhood, he saw little in this to regret. If his reading had been desultory, it had been far wider than is generally supposed. At Cambridge, too, he had learnt one of the supporting truths of his life, 'the spiritual presences of absent things'. Moreover he never ceased to recognize that he 'was not for that hour, or for that place'. But when he revised the book he made some slight concessions to the susceptibilities of his Alma Mater. He retained his attack on compulsory College

chapel, but compensated for it by inserting here and there a few phrases which give the book a more religious flavour. He now defends his own idleness with less defiance, and exonerates his University from some of her responsibility for it. The later omission of lines, such as

> Why should I grieve? I was a chosen son . . .
> I was a Freeman, in the purest sense
> Was free, and to majestic ends was strong,

and the inclusion of others—

> Yet why take refuge in that plea? the fault
> This, I repeat, was mine, mine be the blame.

sufficiently indicate a change of tone, befitting one who had sons of undergraduate age, and whose brother was Master of Trinity.

. . . . .

From the first he was uncertain how he should deal with those fateful years that followed his departure from Cambridge. His original intention was to leave them out of *The Prelude* altogether, and reserve all reflections upon the French Revolution for more dispassionate and impersonal treatment in *The Recluse;* and when he saw that to follow this course would leave the history of his mind's growth incomplete, he seems to have hesitated as to the amount of detail he should introduce. After recounting his return to England, the narrative, up to this point clear and consecutive, becomes involved and wavering; he goes backwards and forwards, so that the progress of events is not easy to trace. The order in which Books VII and IX were written suggests, at least, that at one time the book devoted to London was to follow and not precede the account of his residence in France; had it done so it must have included not merely the first impressions of an eager, bewildered stranger 'in the vast metropolis', but some details of those exciting months when, with his revolutionary ardour at its height, he was associating with the English radical leaders; and also of that later time when, in the bitter mood of disenchantment, he clung to such straws of hope as he could clutch from the abstract principles of Godwin. There is no part of his life of which we know so little as that which intervened between his departure from France and his settlement at Racedown; there is none of which we would fain know more. His references to it in later years were often vague and misleading; but even when he wrote *The Prelude* he felt no inclination to say more of it than was barely necessary to explain his recovery and release from it.

Critics who approach Wordsworth with a strong revolutionary bias have sometimes expected that the first version of *The Prelude* would reveal a poet far more after their own heart than they have found in the version of 1850. They forget that in the year 1804 he was already heart and soul with his own country in her struggle with Napoleon, convinced that the cause of true liberty depended on her ultimate triumph. Then, as later, in speaking of his Revolutionary ardour, 'juvenile errors' were his theme (X. 54). The words with which in 1821 he met the charge of apostasy express a conviction that he held as firmly when he wrote *The Prelude:* 'You have been deluded by places and persons, while I have stuck to principles. I abandoned

France and her rulers when they abandoned Liberty, gave themselves up to tyranny, and endeavoured to enslave the world.' In point of fact his renunciation of France preceded the full blossoming of his poetic genius. All later political changes came gradually, insensibly to himself. He never regretted his enthusiasm for the Revolution in its early days of promise, and retained to the last that democratic idealism, inherent in his nature, which had first attracted him to it. Nor was he ever in theory the solid Tory that he became in practice. There was always, he said, something of the Chartist in him. But with the passage of years, as he himself admitted, he lost courage; and his revision of *The Prelude* shows clear signs of his growing conservatism.

Book IX, which relates his conversion, under the inspired guidance of Beaupuy, to the cause of France, he could leave almost untouched: he revised more drastically those books which recorded a sympathy with the Revolution that seemed less justifiable. As time passed, he grew more severe upon France, more indulgent to English foreign policy, more apologetic for himself. *The Prelude* records how the September massacres, though they appalled him, did not damp his ardour; for he was buoyed up by the faith that one great man might still save France from the Jacobins and restore her to her ideals. 'Enflamed with hope', the phrase with which he describes this faith in 1804, gives probably a truer impression of his emotion at the time than the more sober 'Cheered with this hope' which later he substituted for it. Moreover, in 1804 he could still endorse it in the pregnant words

> Creed which ten shameful years have not annulled.

The removal of this line from his text not only points to a loss of faith, it removes the implication that his own country bore her part in the shame which those years brought forth. The originally bare account of his reluctant return homewards was elaborated into a passionately patriotic tribute to Albion's sacred shores, which was hardly his sentiment at the time of which it was written. To the motives which he had given for the French declaration of a republic (September 1792) he now added others that were less worthy, and were quite foreign to his thoughts either then or in 1804; and though he admitted later, to no less stalwart a Tory than Lord Lonsdale, that he had 'disapproved of the war against France at its commencement, thinking, which was, perhaps, an error, that it might have been avoided' (note the 'perhaps', he is not sure of it even in 1821); he could not leave unmitigated the terms in which . . . he had denounced it. In 1804 he had attributed it to 'the unhappy counsel of a few weak men', and laid greater stress on the extent of English sympathy with the Revolutionary cause, whilst his condemnation of the government for their persecution of the English radicals, severe, indeed, in the final text, was before at once more passionate and more contemptuous:

> Our Shepherds (this say merely) at that time
> Thirsted to make the guardian Crook of Law
> A tool of Murder; they who ruled the State,
> Though with such awful proof before their eyes
> That he who would sow death, reaps death, or worse,

> And can reap nothing better, child-like long'd
> To imitate, not wise enough to avoid,
> Giants in their impiety alone,
> But, in their weapons and their warfare base
> As vermin working out of reach, they leagu'd
> Their strength perfidiously, to undermine
> Justice, and make an end of Liberty.
> (X. 646-57.)

This is strong language to use against an English cabinet, and we cannot be surprised that it was modified upon revision.

But more significant, perhaps, is the introduction into Book VII, some time after 1820, of an enthusiastic tribute to Burke. There is no trace of this eulogy in the original text. Burke's oratory would, doubtless, have stirred the poet on his visits to London in either 1791 or 1793, but it would have stirred him to very different emotions from those which inspired the added lines. It is possible that even in 1804 he might have written them, but their insertion in the account of his early impressions of London, when he had lately returned from a holiday across a Europe which

> was thrilled with joy,
> France standing on the top of golden hours,
> And human nature seeming born again,

creates a misleading impression as to the state of his mind in that period of which the book professes to be the record.

. . . . .

But most to be regretted are those alterations in the text which have obscured the statement of that religious faith which is reflected in all the poet's greatest work. When Wordsworth wrote *The Prelude* he had in nothing swerved from the faith that inspired the **'Lines composed a few miles above Tintern Abbey'**. This faith need only be referred to here in the barest outline. Starting from a fervid belief in the inherent goodness of human nature, Wordsworth attributes the growth of the whole moral and intellectual being,—from infancy through the stages of childhood and adolescence, to maturity,—to impressions made upon the senses, bound together, reacting on one another, and ever growing in fullness and intensity by means of the law of association. The philosophical parentage of this conception is unmistakable; it is the direct offspring of the sensationalism of the eighteenth century, and in particular of David Hartley [in the words of Coleridge from his *Religious Musings*,],

> he of mortal kind
> Wisest, he first who marked the ideal tribes
> Up the fine fibres of the sentient brain,

but it is Hartley transcendentalized by Coleridge, and at once modified and exalted by Wordsworth's own mystical experience. For to him there was always this great paradox, that though it is simply by the proper exercise of eye and ear that man reaches his full moral and intellectual stature, so that he can recognize

> In Nature and the language of the sense
> The anchor of my purest thoughts, the nurse,
> The guide, the guardian of my heart, and soul
> Of all my moral being,

yet revelation flashes upon him when 'the light of sense goes out'; and 'laid asleep in body', he becomes deeply conscious of the presence of God within him. In the highest mood of ecstasy this consciousness of complete oneness with God is so overwhelming, that his other attributes as man seem to fall from him, and he knows only that

> one interior life
> In which all beings live with God, themselves
> Are God, existing in the mighty whole,
> As indistinguishable as the cloudless east
> Is from the cloudless west, when all
> The hemisphere is one cerulean blue,

How far this intense mystical experience is compatible with Christianity let theologians determine. Coleridge, whether, like a bee that draws its food from many different flowers, he took his nourishment from the Neo-Platonists, or Hartley, or Spinoza, or, as later, from the German metaphysicians, always contrived to give his honey some Christian flavour; and Wordsworth himself strayed no further from orthodoxy than Coleridge had done in *Religious Musings* and *The Eolian Harp*. When Coleridge described his friend as a semi-atheist he was not objecting to his positive faith, but rather reflecting on what he regarded as its incompleteness. Certainly at this time Wordsworth's faith was in no way tinged with dogmatic Christianity. It is doubtful whether ever, except in those dark years of scepticism when he had wholly lost his bearings, he would have regarded himself as an opponent to Christianity: but Christianity had no special message for him. With Coleridge's attempt to fuse philosophy and religion he was wholly unconcerned. His philosophy, as far as he was a philosopher, *was* his religion; he never examined its logical implications, and any analysis that seemed to disturb its integrity he would have set down to 'that false secondary power by which we multiply distinctions', appealing against it to the tribunal of his own deepest experience. His faith was a passionate intuition of God present in the Universe and in the mind of man; his philosophy no more than the struggle of his reason to account for it. And to the end of his life this intuition remained the living centre of his creed; something

> Which neither listlessness nor mad endeavour,
> Nor all that is at enmity with joy,
> Can utterly abolish or destroy.

He always resented that cruder orthodoxy 'which considers the Supreme Being as bearing the same relation to the Universe as a watchmaker bears to a watch'. The Temple in which he worshipped most devoutly was still one not made with hands, the Bible in which he read the deepest lessons was still 'the Bible of the Universe, as it speaks to the ear of the intelligent, and as it lies open to the eyes of the humble-minded'. But later the vision grew dim, and though at times it was 'by miracle restored', it was no longer sufficient to meet his needs. Gradually, therefore, he turned more consciously to the Christian faith. This change was the almost inevitable outcome of his experience of life. The Wordsworth of 1798-1804 was the exultant champion of 'man's unconquerable mind': 'dignity', 'majesty', 'sovereignty' are words again and again applied to the human mind in the early *Prelude,* and again and again qualified in the later texts. Inspired by a passionate

sense of the spiritual greatness of man, he forgot man's natural weakness. But the inevitable yoke brought by the years taught him the need of humility. We may resent the intrusion into a passage which in magnificent verse eulogizes man as 'of all visible natures crown' (VIII. 630-9) of what seems the unnecessary reminder that he is 'born of dust and kindred to the worm'. But the inserted phrase tells something that was essential to Wordsworth's later thought. Christian meekness had come to have a real meaning for him, and the more so because, of all the Christian virtues, it was for him the hardest to achieve.

Moreover, he felt a deep sense of responsibility as a teacher, and he had good reason to know that he was misunderstood. Both **'Lines composed . . . above Tintern Abbey'** and the **'Ode: Intimations of Immortality'** had proved a stumbling-block to many. He was accused, even by readers of *The Excursion,* of not distinguishing 'Nature as the work of God and God himself', and he felt it incumbent on him to remove from *The Prelude* all that might be interpreted as giving support to the heresy, and to bring that poem into accord with the later modifications of his faith. He took pains to relate, as far as possible, his naturalistic religion to a definitely Christian dogma. He toned down passages that savoured too much of independence. He inserted lines here and there which might lull asleep the watchful eye of the heresy hunter. Sometimes these are merely what might be called pietistic embroidery, in no way affecting the argument, but creating, by the use of conventional phraseology, a familiar atmosphere of edification. In this spirit he adds a reference to matins and vespers [I. 45], includes among possible themes for poetic treatment 'Christian meekness hallowing youthful loves' [I. 185], changes the simple phrase 'as were a joy to hear of' into the more elaborate

> To which the silver wands of saints in Heaven
> Might point with rapturous joy,
>
>   [X. 485-6.]

qualifies a statement that seems to him overbold with the line

> So, with devout humility be it said,
>
>   [X. 447.]

and adds, as a reason for the respect due for man as man, that he is

> Here placed to be the inheritor of Heaven.
>   [VIII. 336.]

These are small matters in themselves, but they give a new colour to his work, and are foreign to its original spirit.

He is, throughout, careful, by a small change in word or phrase, or the addition of a sentence, to cover up the traces of his early pantheism. Thus

> A soul divine which we participate,
> A deathless spirit
>
>   (V. 16-17.)

becomes

> As might appear to the eye of fleeting time,
> A deathless spirit,

and

> God and nature's single sovereignty
> 　　　　　　　　　(IX. 237.)

becomes

> Presences of God's mysterious power
> Made manifest in Nature's sovereignty.

Most noticeable is his relapse from that religion of joy which springs from feeling, the reward of 'glad hearts without reproach or blot', to a less spontaneous, a disciplined emotion. The spirit of the early *Prelude* is that of one who, with God and nature communing,

> saw one life and felt that it was joy.
> 　　　　　　　　　(II. 430.)

But even to this simple utterance he adds the gloss

> Communing in this sort through earth and heaven
> With every form of creature, as it looked
> Towards the Uncreated with a countenance
> Of adoration, with an eye of love.

Nothing could be more significant than the change of

> I worshipped then among the depths of things
> As my soul bade me . . .
> I felt and nothing else
> 　　　　　　　　　(XI. 234-8.)

to

> Worshipping then among the depths of things
> As piety ordained . . .
> I felt, observed, and pondered.

(Of 'natural piety', indeed, the original *Prelude* is full: of what is ordinarily called piety there is nothing.)

In the same way

> The feeling of life endless, the great thought
> By which we live, Infinity and God
> 　　　　　　　　　(XIII. 183-4.)

becomes later

> Faith in life endless, the sustaining thought
> Of human Being, Eternity and God.

The highest achievement of that Power which he has learnt to reverence in Nature was . . . that it 'lifts the being into magnanimity', i.e. to that greatness of soul which raises us above our petty selves to realize the 'Godhead that is ours, as natural beings in the strength of nature'. In the later version this same power

> Trains to meekness and exalts by humble faith.

And so, that imaginative rapture, that is 'balanced by a Reason which indeed is reason' (XIII. 264-5), is later presented as

> balanced by pathetic truth, by trust
> In hopeful reason, leaning on the stay
> Of Providence,

and its lasting inspiration, 'sanctified by reason and by truth' (*ib.* 443-4), is later

sanctified by reason, blest by faith.

By changes such as these, the last Book in particular, which is the philosophical conclusion of the whole matter, leaves a totally different impression from that created by the earlier text. The ideas he has introduced are from the brain that wrote the *Ecclesiastical Sonnets,* they were entirely alien to his thought and feeling, not only in that youth and early manhood of which *The Prelude* recounts the history, but in that maturer period when it was written; and they have no rightful place in the poem. Whether he ought to have felt them, or wished, when he was reviewing his work, that he had felt them, is another matter. The essential point for us to realize is that their intrusion has falsified our estimate of the authentic Wordsworth, the poet of the years 1798-1805.

The first signs of the change which dictated this revision are seen in the very months during which he was completing the poem—in the **'Ode to Duty'**, where he renounces his reliance on the genial sense of youth

> When love is an unerring light
> And joy its own security,—

in the second half of the **'Immortal Ode'**, written, as the **'Ode to Duty'**, under the immediate influence of his brother's death. But though prostration with grief at that loss suspended for a time his work upon *The Prelude,* he completed it in the spirit in which it had been begun, with no sign of wavering from his early faith. In the first version of *The Prelude* he wrote nothing that he might not have felt on that eventful day when he revisited Tintern Abbey; and of 'that serene and blessed mood' to which the lines then written give utterance, Wordsworth is the inspired interpreter.

The revised *Prelude* represents another, less independent creed. The position into which he had now withdrawn was not for him a false position. He was sincere, now as ever. But if he was conscious of a change, as it is abundantly clear that he was, he would surely have done better to leave as it stood what he had first written for Coleridge, and, instead of disguising his former faith, to have expounded in a book of *The Recluse,* or elsewhere, the reasons that led him to move from it, and the manner in which it could be reconciled with the tenets of an historic Church. In truth that compromise, which provided so secure a haven for his later years, was worthy of a finer exposition than he was ever able to give it. It may have brought him peace, but it never stirred him to that rapture of which great art is born. When his poetry was commended for the purity of its morals he insisted that he, on the other hand, valued it according to the power of the mind which it presupposed in the writer and excited in the hearer. That work of his which most triumphantly stands this test belongs to the years 1798-1807; and of the vital source and hiding-places of its power the original *Prelude* is the frankest and most direct confession. (pp. li-lxii)

Ernest de Selincourt, in an introduction to The Prelude; or, Growth of a Poet's Mind *by William Wordsworth, edited by Ernest de Selincourt, Oxford at the Clarendon Press, 1926, pp. xv-lxii.*

Raymond Dexter Havens   (essay date 1941)

[*In the following excerpt, Havens discusses* The Prelude *as an autobiography, stressing in particular Wordsworth's refashioning of his past experience.*]

The Prelude is an autobiography, of a kind; yet it is by no means a narrative of the first twenty-seven years of its author's life. It is not chronologically arranged, it omits much, covers some periods twice, and dwells at length on occasions when nothing happened. For example, Wordsworth mentions his parents and his brothers but once and incidentally and tells practically nothing of his first nine years; yet he describes in detail his chance encounter with a solitary soldier and his waiting for the horses which were to take him home for the holidays. He has much to say about education and children's stories but almost nothing concerning study or adult reading. The one college subject on which he dilates, mathematics, is the one he neglected most; concerning Italian, in which he was interested and proficient, he is silent. To his first year at Cambridge he devoted an entire book but to the remaining three only a few lines, most of which are concerned with a single tree. His first and last college vacations he describes at length; but of his earliest visit to Wales, which continued three or four months, he makes no mention. Even the account of his last vacation, in the Alps, deals with only five incidents in the first half of the trip and is silent about the rest.

Moreover, *The Prelude* exhibits a simplification of facts such as biographers are supposed not to practice. The picture of the first year at Cambridge probably includes aspects and developments that came in the two and a half years which followed, just as the 917 lines in Books VII and VIII which are supposed to be devoted to the three and a half months of his earliest residence in London really cover impressions received on later and more extended visits. When he went to France Wordsworth stayed at Orleans, at Blois, then again at Orleans; yet *The Prelude* speaks only of a single town or city on the Loire. As Annette enters the story here, some have seen in this simplification of the facts a deliberate attempt at concealment, although no sinister motive has been suggested for the fusing, in the picture of the boy of Winander, of the poet himself and a lad who died in childhood. Furthermore, the growth of the conviction that his field was to be "the actual world of our familiar days" is pictured as more steady and unwavering than it really was. Such simplifications were presumably made in order that the essential truth might be presented clearly. The complete story of almost any man's development is far more complicated than he or any one else knows or, if he knew, could relate briefly.

Then too, Wordsworth was an artist, far more of an artist than is commonly realized. "He was a severe critic on himself, and would not leave a line or an expression with which he was dissatisfied until he had brought it to what he liked. He thought this due to the gift of poetry and the character of the poet. Carelessness in the finish of composition he seemed to look on almost as an offence" [Justice Coleridge, *Memoirs*]. He remarked to his nephew: "I have bestowed great pains on my *style,* full as much as any of my contemporaries have done on theirs. I yield to none in *love for my art.*" To the astronomer W. R. Hamilton, who

attempted versifying, he wrote: "The logical faculty has infinitely more to do with poetry than the young and the inexperienced, whether writer or critic, ever dreams of," and "The composition of verse is infinitely more of an art than men are prepared to believe; and absolute success in it depends upon innumerable minutiae." *The Prelude* was conceived as a significant piece of art, as "a Work that shall endure," a kind of philosophic epic, and he had strong convictions as to the dignity of such a work, as to how it should be constructed, and as to what it should and should not include. It should not, for example, be partisan, go to extremes, or be as frank and passionate as private conversation. Thus in speaking of the time, after he turned from the Revolution, when he was lost in analysis and doubt, he expressed a wish to deal with the subject in

> some dramatic tale, endued with shapes
> Livelier, and flinging out less guarded words
> Than suit the work we fashion.

The work he was fashioning was to be of such breadth and general significance as to exclude the merely personal:

> whatever else there be
> Of power or pleasure, sown or fostered thus,
> Peculiar to myself, let that remain
> Where it lies hidden.
> > (v. A 194-7)

> But this is passion over-near ourselves,
> Reality too close and too intense,
> And intermixed with something, in my mind,
> Of scorn and condemnation personal,
> That would profane the sanctity of verse.
> > (xi. 57-61)

As Aubrey de Vere remarked: "There was in his being a region of tumult as well as a higher region of calm, though it was almost wholly in the latter that his poetry lived. It turned aside from mere *personal* excitements." And when a friend expressed the wish that he print his poems in the order of their composition he manifested a "feeling akin to indignation. . . . He said that such proceeding would indicate on the part of a poet an amount of egotism, placing interest in himself above interest in the subjects treated by him, which could not belong to a true poet caring for the elements of poetry in their right proportion." "At the head of the first class [of poets]," he remarked, "I would place Homer and Shakspeare, . . . [who do not bring] their own individuality before the reader. . . . you never find *themselves.* At the head of the second class, those whom you can trace individually in all they write, I would place Spenser and Milton."

Clearly it is difficult to write an autobiography which does not bring one's own individuality before the reader; yet for a work of its kind *The Prelude* is singularly impersonal. This will be more obvious if it is compared with Rousseau's *Confessions* or with the poet's own Autobiographical Memoranda, which is devoted almost exclusively to facts not mentioned in *The Prelude.* The most English of poets, Wordsworth has the English reserve; Byron boasts of swimming the Hellespont but Wordsworth, although he has an admirable description of skating, gives no hint of his life-long delight in this sport. Nor does he reveal, as many autobiographers have done, whether he is fond of children, or clothes, or dogs, or fruit, or wine, or reading in bed, or a hundred other things. Few persons or places are named and few dates given. Jones, his companion on the Swiss trip and the ascent of Snowdon, is referred to as "a youthful friend"; Cockermouth, Hawkshead, Penrith, Patterdale, Cartmel, and other places very dear to him are not mentioned in the final text, although some of them were named in earlier versions—he showed a marked tendency to eliminate the personal in revision. Neither the village nor the school of Hawkshead, which furnish the background for a third of the poem, are described, and nothing is said of Anne Tyson's cottage although the ash that stood near it received five lines.

These three motives,—the avoidance of the merely personal, the sense of form and artistic effectiveness, and simplification in the interest of clarity,—were jointly responsible for one aspect of Wordsworth's plan which is commonly overlooked. For *The Prelude* is not so much an account of its author's development as of the development of certain traits in him and the influence of certain forces on him. Thus I and II deal with the growth of his love of Nature; III and parts of IV and VI treat mainly of Cambridge and its influence; V, of books and early education; VII, of London and the effect of city life; VIII, of the growth of a lofty conception of man; IX, X, XI, and part of VI, of the French Revolution and its results; XII, XIII, and XIV, of the imagination. Within each subject the method is usually chronological but there is no attempt to make clear where the individual, William Wordsworth, in his totality, stood at any one time. What he was as a schoolboy, for example, is revealed chiefly in the first two books; but there are further hints in IV, and we must turn to V for his early reading and education, to VII for his boyish feeling about London, to VIII for the growth in childhood of his lofty conception of man and of his fancy, to IX for the democracy learned at Hawkshead, to XII for his attitude towards nature while there and for his watching for the horses which were to take him home for the holidays, to XIV for the independence and endurance learned at school and for his early pre-occupation with "*that* beauty, which . . . Hath terror in it." This is not all, even on this one period, but it is enough to show, not that Wordsworth arranged his material badly—quite the contrary,—but that he presented it according to subjects and did not attempt to give in one place his complete development at a certain period. A simpler illustration may be found in IX-XI, which deal exclusively with the Revolution and (except in the story of Vaudracour and Julia) give no hint of the attention devoted at this time to love and to poetry. Similarly in the description of the time when he "felt the sentiment of Being spread O'er all," there is no hint of the resulting aggrandizement of man which, as we learn from a later account dealing with the growth of the love for man, was a marked feature of this period.

Furthermore, so far as *The Prelude* itself makes clear, the ascent of Snowdon might have taken place during the poet's school days instead of after his leaving the university; the growth of "wilful Fancy" described in viii. 365-475 may have come before or after nature was sought for her own sake; the love for man may have been slightly or considerably developed when the discharged soldier was en-

countered; and there may or may not have been much connection between the early versifying, the books read, and the increased love of nature. So, too, scholars have been unable to agree as to when Wordsworth lost faith in the French Revolution and when his "complete subservience to Godwin" began and ended. His recovery from the despair which terminated this period is recounted in the first part of XIII, where it is followed by a description of his wanderings on Salisbury Plain. The latter incident is told as if it were the culmination of the development already narrated, when in reality it occurred four years earlier, while his faith in the Revolution was still strong. Obviously, the general public, for whom the poem was composed, does not receive, and was not expected to receive, any clear notion of Wordsworth's biography or of the connection in time between the various aspects of his development.

In many respects, to be sure, *The Prelude* represents not what Wordsworth would but what he could do. He was dissatisfied—"it seemed to have a dead weight about it, the reality so far short of the expectation . . . the sense which I had of this poem being so far below what I seemed capable of executing, depressed me much." It "might certainly have been done in narrower compass by a man of more address, but I have done my best." If there were "redundancies" he feared they were "incurable." As Dorothy wrote later concerning his failure to go on with *The Recluse:* "but the will never governs *his* labours." If once he took hold of a subject he found it hard to let go, even though he was disappointed with the results. In consequence, London receives a disproportionate amount of space, and one would say the same of the French Revolution if the subject were not of unusual importance apart from Wordsworth and if the three books which deal with it were not unusually interesting. The discussion of the education of children is too long, and some parts of III which treat of adult education and of life at Cambridge might well have made way for descriptions of the visits to Wales or of the rest of the Swiss tour. To be sure, these matters and others like them may have been omitted for the best of reasons, that they contributed little to the poet's development; but one cannot help wondering if Wordsworth did not bring the account of his Alpine tour to a close because he thought it was already long enough, and if he would not have included his visits to Wales if he could have described them briefly and could have seen how to fit them into his scheme. One also wonders whether some episodes were not passed over because, while they stirred his imagination when they occurred, they failed to do so when he came to write.

A more baffling problem is offered by "Nutting," which was composed in Germany along with a number of the best episodes in the early books and which, according to the Fenwick note, was "intended as part of a poem on my own life, but struck out as not being wanted there." Why it was not wanted is a mystery, since it is greater poetry and is more directly connected with the imagination and with the growth of the poet's mind than hundreds of passages that were retained. Since it is not found in any of the early manuscripts of *The Prelude* there is a bare possibility that it was misplaced and, for a time, overlooked. But if so, why was it not worked into *The Prelude* on revision? This question raises another, larger one: why were no incidents, except the visit to the Chartreuse, added on any of the numerous revisions of the poem? It is almost incredible that Wordsworth told every significant happening in his early life, that in the thirty-three years during which he worked over the poem he never thought of an aspect of his youth or an event in it that might well have been included. What seems more likely is that after 1805 he came, at least so far as *The Prelude* was concerned, to distrust his creative powers. Artists often have this feeling and wisely refuse to touch a work which they see to be faulty. Wordsworth was quite willing to revise the phraseology of the poem but not to make any structural change.

As to the part the warmer emotions, friendship as well as love, play in adolescence and in early manhood there are only a few hints, but this is what the reticence of the period and of the author's temperament would lead us to expect. Possibly such emotions did not minister to the growth of his imagination, but they feed the imagination of most men and the poem is thinner and narrower by their exclusion. One other omission, which would seem to be of some importance, we know of from the lines in which he says that Burns

> showed my youth
> How Verse may build a princely throne
> On humble truth.
>
> **("At the Grave of Burns,"** 34-6)

Now *The Prelude* describes at length how its author came to make verse "deal boldly with substantial things" but it does not mention Burns. Did Wordsworth forget or did he decide that the story was already longer and more complicated than it should be and this was one of the things that must be passed over?

For in concluding the poem he confessed, "Much hath been omitted, as need was," and referred specifically to books, fancy, nature, and human nature. In the case of books we are perhaps able to see what happened—how, in V, he wandered from books in general to humble works which delight cottagers and children, thence to the freedom children should have in selecting their reading, then to the general subject of freedom in education with the boy of Winander presumably as an illustration, then back to the *Arabian Nights,* a defense of romances, and a description of his early enthusiasm for poetry. Clearly V, although entitled "Books," is in great part devoted to other subjects; and further reading reveals many comments on books which are not in V. A more unfortunate result is that Wordsworth never comes to grips with this important theme. On the other hand, as a discussion of the education of children V is inadequate since it has nothing about the development of the emotions, the religious instincts, and the imagination; these and other important aspects of the subject are treated in earlier and later books. Equally desultory is VIII, "Retrospect," with its picture of the Helvellyn Fair, of Gehol's matchless gardens, of the idyllic life of shepherds in old time, and the story of Michael and the lost sheep. Then, too, in the books devoted to Cambridge, London, and the French Revolution, Wordsworth tends to describe places, conditions, and movements rather than

to show how he was influenced by them. In treating London he so far forgets his purpose as to write,

> More lofty themes,
> Such as at least do wear a prouder face,
> Solicit our regard; but when I think
> Of these, I feel the imaginative power
> Languish within me.
>
> (vii. 465-9)

What he should have said is that he was not writing a description of London but an account of the development of his imagination, and as the more lofty themes failed to touch his imagination they had no place in his work.

Inspiration is seldom systematic or orderly and Wordsworth's certainly was not; when he tried to harness Pegasus he produced *The Excursion* and *Ecclesiastical Sonnets.* On the other hand, he took fire at a number of incidents apparently of little importance in his development or otherwise and incorporated them in his poem: card-playing at Hawkshead, drinking in the college room Milton had occupied, hearing of the death of Robespierre, and wondering at the schoolmate who had visited London,—not to mention Anne Tyson in her Sunday best, and the dog that guarded his walks when he composed verse. No one wishes these passages removed, but in view of them, of the extended treatment of matters that contributed little to making the poet, and of the omission of incidents that did have influence, one cannot say that *The Prelude* is concerned exclusively with the growth of a poet's mind. (pp. 270-77)

It seems likely . . . that *The Prelude* is as unprejudiced an account of his development as Wordsworth was able to give, and more honest as well as much more vivid than most men could compose. This is not to deny that, like all human productions, it is colored by its author's interests, desires, beliefs, prejudices, and sufferings; that it presents his youth in part as he wished to see it, and passes lightly over some things on which he disliked to dwell; that it simplifies his history and, ignoring losses, pictures his later development as a steady progress. It is not to overlook the fact that, as a great work of art, *The Prelude* is a selection, intensification, and so a misrepresentation of everyday reality. And, finally, it is not to forget that, as W. H. Hudson writes [in *Far Away and Long Ago,* 1918]:

> It is difficult, impossible I am told, for any one
> to recall his boyhood exactly as it was. It could
> not have been what it seems to the adult mind,
> since we cannot escape from what we are, how-
> ever great our detachment may be; and in going
> back we must take our present selves with us.

But most criticism of the truth of the poem has been based on a misconception of its purpose, on the assumption that it was intended to be an autobiography. . . . *The Prelude,* although by no means a miracle of architectonics, since it does not follow any one purpose throughout, since it omits things that seem important and narrates in detail incidents that appear irrelevant, is, however, more closely integrated than is generally believed, inasmuch as it usually passes over merely personal matters as well as purely intellectual or technical developments and in the main keeps to its theme, the growth of the poet's imagination. It seems likely that this unity of purpose is not, except in the last three books, the result of deliberate planning. Wordsworth wrote about what moved him most, incidents and scenes to which he "oft repaired, and thence would drink, As at a fountain." Not until later did he reflect that in these passages of life

> We have had deepest feeling that the mind
> Is lord and master, and that outward sense
> Is but the obedient servant of her will.
>
> (xii. A 270-3)

The poem is the more convincing because of this spontaneity, because the episodes are usually not fitted into the argument, because it reveals that a great creative artist in surveying his past without any thesis to prove finds that what is significant in it has been made so by the transforming power of the imagination. (pp. 286-87)

> *Raymond Dexter Havens, in his* The Mind of a Poet: The Study of Wordsworth's Thought with Particular Reference to "The Prelude," *The Johns Hopkins Press, 1941, 670 p.*

An excerpt from Wordsworth's letter to Sir George Beaumont dated 1 May 1805

I turned my thoughts again to the poem on my own life, and you will be glad to hear that I have added three hundred lines to it in the course of last week. Two books more will conclude it. It will not be much less than nine thousand lines,—not hundred but thousand lines long,—an alarming length! and a thing unprecedented in literary history that a man should talk so much about himself. It is not self-conceit, as you know well, that has induced me to do this, but real humility. I began the work because I was unprepared to treat any more arduous subject, and diffident of my own powers. Here, at least, I hoped that to a certain degree I should be sure of succeeding, as I had nothing to do but describe what I had felt and thought; therefore could not easily be bewildered. This might certainly have been done in narrower compass by a man of more address; but I have done my best.

Quoted by Arthur Beatty, in his William Wordsworth: His Doctrine and Art in Their Historical Relations, *University of Wisconsin Press, 1960.*

Mark Van Doren   (essay date 1946)

[*Van Doren was one of the most prolific American literary scholars of the twentieth century. His work includes poetry (his* Collected Poems 1922-1938 *won the Pulitzer Prize in 1940), fiction, drama, criticism, and social commentary. Van Doren's criticism is aimed at the general reader, rather than the scholar or specialist, and is noted for its lively perception and wide interest. Like his poetry and fiction, his criticism consistently examines the inner, idealistic life of the individual. In the following excerpt, Van Doren finds Wordsworth's ambitions for* The Prelude *pretentious and considers the work ineffective.*]

"I want a subject." Thus Wordsworth would, or could, or

should have begun his poem in fourteen books about himself. He did not so begin because he thought he had a subject—the only one in sight. Wordsworth created modern poetry when he decided that the man who writes is more important than the men and the things he writes about. Wordsworth had special reasons for deciding this: he did not know men, and the fountain of things had dried up. The world was a barren place, producing no further mythologies. The poet stood alone, and without a lyre. If poetry was to live again, he must make it live from nothing. He must make the dry bones sound.

Milton, searching for a subject, had found one that needed loads of ornament before it could seem substantial. Wordsworth, searching in the same fashion, found none at all; and ornament for him was not in order. He was honest, and furthermore there was no art of poetry extant, no set of pleasures with which he could play. The least sportive of poets—this certainly he was—could not be expected to go forth with a fowling-piece like Lord Byron's and litter the waste land with carcasses of crows. If he was anything he was a philosophical poet. Indeed he would have to be one, for only such a man could build poetry again. Intuition had departed; the rules for it must be rediscovered. If the world was to bloom once more with living truth, poetry must work the ground. Truth in the fortunate ages had been something for poetry to express. Now it was something for poetry to find.

But what is poetry? Wordsworth had first to answer that simple question. At least it is simple before it is asked. The greatest poets never asked it; they simply went to work. Wordsworth, having no work to do until he had produced a definition, devoted his life to the discovery that poetry is the art of finding truth—general truth, as distinguished from the particular truths of science. It is an unsatisfactory answer, being circular, but so have all subsequent answers proved unsatisfactory. For Wordsworth started an interminable series of attempts on the part of poets to say what they thought they were doing. It is as if a secret had been lost. It had been, apparently, and still is. If we do not know what poetry is we shall never get anywhere by arguing its definition; and, worst of all, we shall not get poetry. It was a happier thing when it could be taken for granted—even laughed at, as Shakespeare laughed at it. For then it had natural work to do. It could contemplate the actions of men. Modern poetry contemplates itself, and makes grand claims for what it is. But poetry that is sure of itself makes no such claims. It wastes no strength on schools, manifestoes, and experiments; or upon lamentations about the times, the ugly, unpropitious times which threaten to make poetry impossible.

Wordsworth wondered whether poetry had become impossible, and if not, by what superhuman efforts it might be restored. This is what he discussed with Coleridge during the long walks and talks they had at the turn of their century. Wordsworth emerged from those talks, and from meditations of his own, with notions which have become classic. Genuine poetry is ahead of its time; it is destined to a bitter struggle against misunderstanding—a struggle which it will win with the help of an original audience which is small but faithful. For only a few living persons can know at first the purity of its author's feeling. That is what matters. "The feeling gives importance to the action and the situation, and not the action and situation to the feeling."

Which is true, but Wordsworth takes it to the point where it means that the subject need be nothing at all compared with the nature of the man who treats it. Homer could have treated Troy without the distinction it deserved, but it deserved distinction, and he seems never to have doubted this, any more than Dante doubted the deep import of the universe his poem dared to enter. It was there before his poem was. But for Wordsworth there is no universe until he makes one with his poetry. All the power there can be is in his feelings. No meaning exists until his own "organic sensibility" has created it. The test of a poem is the character of its author. He must be like other men— "poets do not write for poets alone"—and yet he must be different too. Wordsworth would like to see this difference as a difference merely of degree, but every thought he has forces him to describe a difference in kind. The knowledge of which poetry is the "breath and finer spirit" is a special knowledge, and only special persons possess it. Poets are exalted men; they organize, ennoble, and educate the emotions of other men.

Which again is true. We learn from Shakespeare. But it was not the intention of Shakespeare to teach us—not the intention, nor the promise. With Wordsworth it is all promise. We never get beyond his proof that he will teach us if we listen—never, at least, in his masterpiece *The Prelude*. The business of *The Prelude* is to prove that Wordsworth is a poet; for he is ambitious to do great work, and he must first be sure he has the calling. The great work is to be a long poem to which this one is but preliminary. Hence its subtitle: *Growth of a Poet's Mind*. In 1814, when he published a fragment of the great work to be—a fragment, called *The Excursion,* which few have read or ever will—he explained how it was:

> Several years ago, when the author retired to his native mountains with the hope of being enabled to construct a literary work that might live, it was a reasonable thing that he should take a review of his own mind, and examine how far nature and education had qualified him for such employment. As subsidiary to this preparation, he undertook to record, in verse, the origin and progress of his own powers, as far as he was acquainted with them. That work, addressed to a dear friend, most distinguished for his knowledge and genius, and to whom the author's intellect is deeply indebted, has been long finished; and the result of the investigation which gave [...] philosophical poem, containing views of Man, Nature, and Society; and to be entitled *The Recluse;* as having for its principal subject the sensations and opinions of a poet living in retirement. The preparatory poem is biographical, and conducts the history of the author's mind to the point when he was emboldened to hope that his faculties were sufficiently matured for entering upon the arduous labor which he had proposed to himself.

Perhaps no more amazing statement was ever made by a poet about himself. If it is not amazing, then we have forgotten how Shakespeare, for one, came to his maturity— not by retiring to take an inventory of his powers, as yet unsuspected, but by staying in London and writing *Henry VI* and a dozen other plays in the course of which he developed those powers. That is the way of the apprentice, of the poet for whom there is an art that he will master if he can. For Wordsworth there was no art unless he dug it out of himself. He never climbed out of the excavation.

For the paramount fact in Wordsworth's biography is the fact that he did not finish his great work. He had almost half a century to do it in, but *The Recluse* as he planned it does not exist. He was too much interested in the preparation. *The Prelude* he kept always by him, revising it toward some perfection that he felt yet never found. It saw the light only when he was dead, and when the hope had died in him that he might serve Calliope as Homer, Shakespeare, Spenser, and Milton had. The preliminaries absorbed him: the preliminaries of defining what a poet is, and of deciding whether he was one. His only subject could be himself, for the only world he had was within his mind.

The world of poetry had gone, and with it every other world. Wordsworth then must live his poetry; he must be unique or nothing; he must make a mythology out of his faculties, a god out of his mind; he must cultivate a temperament from which wisdom once again might flow like waters from a long-forgotten spring. And all this in the absence of aid from the poor society around him. *The Prelude* is Wordsworth's announcement that he was successful—at discovering the power. The poem did not follow.

The Prelude has a special setting in its author's life. Like most modern poets, Wordsworth draws us into his biography; he lives not so much in his works as for them, or rather they live for him. They keep him going, and we must learn what they meant to him before we shall know what they can possibly mean to us. *The Prelude* is Wordsworth's answer to the French Revolution, which in its first stages he accepted but which as time went on he wanted to reject—and did not know how except by substituting for its public program of reconstruction by reason a private program of resurrection by feeling. The French Revolution had made him by 1792 the most miserable of men: sick of its excesses, but also guilty because he could not completely comprehend his desire to escape it. With all the discussion it brought in its wake it was not for him. He tried in London to maintain his original ardor, he tried to keep up with each new turn of thought, he tried to hold [...] spired, but he grew weary and bewildered; and because he was bewildered he blamed himself—until, set free by the legacy of a friend to wander into the West Country and meet Coleridge, he realized with a rush that within his very self, his obscure and personal self, he had the makings of a religion—a "natural" religion—which might displace the revolution whose science he had not mastered. *The Prelude* begins at this point of rapture, this point of a scarcely articulate joy over being suddenly set free "from the vast city where I long had pined, a discontented so-journer."

> The earth is all before me. With a heart
> Joyous, nor scared at its own liberty,
> I look about; and should the chosen guide
> Be nothing better than a wandering cloud,
> I cannot miss my way. I breathe again!
> Trances of thought and mountings of the mind
> Come fast upon me: it is shaken off,
> That burthen of my own unnatural self,
> The heavy weight of many a weary day
> Not mine, and such as were not made for me.

The "dear friend" to whom he addresses the poem—Coleridge, of course—is asked to believe what we as readers must believe through fourteen books if the poem is to be successful with us: that in a single blessed moment, a mystical moment which quieted the earth and all men's voices on it, Wordsworth slipped into the heart of truth. It was

>   a day
> With silver clouds, and sunshine on the grass,
> And in the sheltered and the sheltering grove
> A perfect stillness.

It was such a day as only Wordsworth could create, and anyone may envy him because he had it. But it does not follow that we shall find comprehensible the demonstration he goes on to provide of a past which had produced this present—a past which we are to understand as having been ordained to make him now the priest of a simpler and better life than revolutions and new laws will ever manage.

Wordsworth goes on to show how his life to date has prepared him to feel as poets feel, and therefore to teach all men how they should feel. It is important to him that he should show this beyond the shadow of a doubt. For there must be no mistake, he is indeed ordained. Without his knowing it, but no less certainly for that, Nature had been educating him all the while. The universe had conspired to make him its one philosopher of feeling. His favorite word is "thus." We are not to assume that he merely hopes or fancies. He knows. And we must know—that the man he now is was always there, in the boy who played, a dedicated spirit, among those native mountains. The demonstration must be perfect.

But there is no demonstration. There is a series of pictures recovered from the past, and these are among the most beautiful objects poetry possesses; they are the reason *The Prelude* deserves talking about. And, alternating with them, there is a series of statements concerning what they meant and mean, there is a connecting tissue of proof, a web of words designed to convince us—and convince Wordsworth—that the man he now is has been "restored," after nightmares of reason and revolution, from the youth he once was. It is the statements that do not stand. *The Prelude* proves nothing except that Wordsworth remembered certain moments. They were worth remembering, and the poetry that preserves them is sure to live. But the intercalary verses do not live. They have been thought to do so, but such thought thins with the passage of time, which nothing fools forever. *The Prelude* is not autobiography. It is apologetics.

The first book establishes the pattern, which never again is quite so clear although it is discernible throughout. A vignette is given us—clouds lift from one of memory's peaks—and then, while another vignette is preparing, we hear Wordsworth's voice exhorting us to comprehend what he thinks he comprehends, namely, that the Spirit of the Universe sat brooding over all such scenes. As for the scenes—of springes to catch woodcocks, of the little boat, of skating, of games, of water off the sands of Westmoreland—nothing in poetry could be better than the easy vigor, the effortless sublimity, with which Wordsworth's verse renders their reality, their fact.

>   Ere I had told
> Ten birthdays, when among the mountain slopes
> Frost, and the breath of frosty wind, had
>   snapped
> The last autumnal crocus, 'twas my joy
> With store of springes o'er my shoulder hung
> To range the open heights where woodcocks run
> Along the smooth green turf.

Who could doubt that this is the way it was? The movement of the words is the movement of the boy, as again is the case when he finds a boat one summer evening, tied to a willow tree, and steps into it to steal a ride.

>   It was an act of stealth
> And troubled pleasure, nor without the voice
> Of mountain echoes did my boat move on. . . .
> She was an elfin pinnace; lustily
> I dipped my oars into the silent lake,
> And, as I rose upon the stroke, my boat
> Went heaving through the water like a swan.

Or as when he and his companions hiss along the polished ice:

> So through the darkness and the cold we flew,
> And not a voice was idle; with the din
> Smitten, the precipices rang aloud;
> The leafless trees and every icy crag
> Tinkled like iron; while far distant hills
> Into the tumult sent an alien sound
> Of melancholy not unnoticed, while the stars
> Eastward were sparkling clear, and in the west
> The orange sky of evening died away.
> Not seldom from the uproar I retired
> Into a silent bay, or sportively
> Glanced sideway, leaving the tumultuous
>   throng,
> To cut across the reflex of a star
> That fled, and, flying still before me, gleamed
> Upon the glassy plain; and oftentimes,
> When we had given our bodies to the wind,
> And all the shadowy banks on either side
> Came sweeping through the darkness, spinning
>   still
> The rapid line of motion, then at once
> Have I, reclining back upon my heels,
> Stopped short; yet still the solitary cliffs
> Wheeled by me—even as if the earth had rolled
> With visible motion her diurnal round!

But the voice of the prophet is a different matter. The dissertations which intervene, the proofs which press their way into the dead spaces between fact and fact, come with a dull, cotton sound.

Dust as we are, the immortal spirit grows
Like harmony in music; there is a dark
Inscrutable workmanship that reconciles
Discordant elements, makes them cling together
In one society. How strange, that all
The terrors, pains, and early miseries,
Regrets, vexations, lassitudes interfused
Within my mind, should e'er have borne a part,
And that a needful part, in making up
The calm existence that is mine when I
Am worthy of myself! Praise to the end! . . .

Wisdom and Spirit of the universe!
Thou Soul that art the eternity of thought,
That givest to forms and images a breath
And everlasting motion, not in vain
By day or starlight thus from my first dawn
Of childhood didst thou intertwine for me
The passions that build up our human soul. . . .

Ye Presences of Nature in the sky
And on the earth! Ye Visions of the hills!
And Souls of lonely places! can I think
A vulgar hope was yours when ye employed
Such ministry, when ye, through many a year
Haunting me thus among my boyish sports,
In caves and trees, upon the woods and hills,
Impressed, upon all forms, the characters
Of danger or desire; and thus did make
The surface of the universal earth,
With triumph and delight, with hope and fear,
Work like a sea? . . .

        Even then
I held unconscious intercourse with beauty
Old as creation, drinking in a pure
Organic pleasure. . . .

For they are not proofs. They are Wordsworth filling in with metaphor, and a confused metaphor at that. What he wants to believe is that Nature taught him more than man, revolutionary man, will ever teach anybody; and that the lesson was continuous. He does not know that it was continuous, or even that it *was.* All the more reason, then, to ransack his vocabulary in search of terms which will seem to do the work of demonstration. He finds too many terms, and he pours them forth in too exigent a profusion. They do not mix. A reader of *The Prelude* may be impressed by its tendentious passages, and think them vaguely august or grand. They are, but the emphasis is on "vaguely." Another reader will not be satisfied so soon. He will be embarrassed by the capital letters, the exclamation marks; and he will be suspicious of the rhetorical questions—suspicious that even Wordsworth does not know their answers.

Above all, however, the careful reader of *The Prelude,* the reader who insists upon understanding the words he sees, will be baffled in such passages by the abstractions that fight for his attention. It will be clear to him that Wordsworth is set on saying he was somehow taught by something; but sooner or later it will be plain that the how and the what are misty matters whereon this language throws no light. There is a darkness, rather, of symbols that tangle with one another and choke their own art. Interfuse, intertwine, intercourse—Wordsworth has a fatal weakness for the prefix. Reconcile, build up, minister, inform, impress,

create, and grow—he cannot decide which verb it is that best will name the process of his teaching. There was a oneness, surely, between Nature and himself in those good days, but how shall it be referred to—as union, as affinity, as connection, as association, as correspondence, as linkage, as impregnation, or as what? The terms pour together into a mixture too rich for reason and too dark for sense. The intercourse, furthermore, is "unconscious," and the workmanship is "inscrutable." The activity asserted is never seen.

There was no such activity. *The Prelude* is the work of an honest poet, and in its pictures it is the work of a very brilliant one, but at its core it is unintelligible. Wordsworth undoubtedly meant the preposterous prose of his concluding lines to Coleridge:

And now, O Friend! this history is brought
To its appointed close: the discipline
And consummation of a Poet's mind,
In everything that stood most prominent,
Have faithfully been pictured; we have reached
The time (our guiding object from the first)
When we may, not presumptuously, I hope,
Suppose my powers so far confirmed, and such
My knowledge, as to make me capable
Of building up a Work that shall endure.

But there has been no history, and the discipline has been too passive to be worthy of such a name. The most that Wordsworth now possesses is a faculty which he calls imagination. Imagination is what he will see the truth with—not such truth as shines in his vignettes and will shine forever there, but the truth that lies behind things, the "essences" and "forms" with which his mind is so infatuated. He says he has learned

That Poets, even as Prophets, each with each
Connected in a mighty scheme of truth,
Have each his own peculiar faculty,
Heaven's gift, a sense that fits him to perceive
Objects unseen before.

With his own peculiar faculty he will go forth in the world and see into the souls of men—

Souls that appear to have no depth at all
To careless eyes.

And he will take most pleasure in scrutinizing rustic countenances:

Nature for all conditions wants not power
To consecrate, if we have eyes to see,
The outside of her creatures, and to breathe
Grandeur upon the very humblest face
Of human life.

For man—or Man—is still his subject. Man is the creature he must save. And he can do this best by telling the world henceforth how noble are "the simplicities of cottage life," where shepherds sit in the shade with dogs and never once suspect how important they appear to the poet—or the Poet—who beholds them.

How little they, they and their doings, seem,
And yet how great!

The condescension seems not to bother Wordsworth, or

the vanity. Having found his mind, he must give it work to do though the heavens fall. No poet ever knew less about people, but no poet has been so sure that he was wise concerning Man.

At its center, then, *The Prelude* yields little or nothing. It is barren of sense in the end, and so as poetry it was doomed from the start. The business of poetry is to tell men what they already know, not to convince them that what they have seen so far is vulgar illusion. The greatest poets have seen what was there to see. Wordsworth, insisting on more, finds less. His imagination, boasting of its power to deal with what is "really" there, suggests that nothing is there at all for men of sense to see. Such men withhold the final word of praise from such poetry as *The Prelude* is. And they are right. Its author promised to use the "language really used by men," but he did not keep that promise in what was for him the thinking heart of *The Prelude.*

It is a psychological, not a philosophical, poem, and as such it was bound to be obscure. It is not a poem that says things, it is a poem whose author is getting ready to say things. The world waited, and they were not said. *The Recluse* was never written. Nor could it have been written in the longest of eternities. If *The Prelude* proves anything it proves just that. For it has proved that a poet exists. The miracle having happened, nothing more is needed. The further miracle of poems about men and the actions of men, of poems with other subjects than their authors, of poems like Homer's and Shakespeare's, or even like Virgil's and Milton's, is not to be thought of yet. Poetry is possible. That, ye Ministers and Presences, is enough for now.

If *The Prelude* is a work of fancy after all—a work in which sensory magic has saved from oblivion a few moments out of one man's life—the blow to Wordsworth's shade must be very bitter. For he despised fancy as he despised fact. And he would not have liked to think that his little pictures were all he had to give us. He had a gospel to give, and used these pictures only to point its truth. But the truth is in them—so accidentally remembered, so immediately loved, and so sharply fixed in words. Between them there is only that semblance of truth, that rootless and useless wisdom, which in all times discredits poetry. In all times, including ours. (pp. 303-19)

> *Mark Van Doren, "The Prelude," in his* The Noble Voice: A Study of Ten Great Poems, *Henry Holt and Company, 1946, pp. 303-20.*

Herbert Read   (essay date 1957)

[*Read was a prolific English poet, critic, and novelist. In the following essay, he praises Wordsworth's vision in* The Prelude.]

One wintry evening, a hundred and forty years ago, a party of friends, deeply attached to each other, was gathered round the fire at a farmhouse near Coleorton, in Leicestershire. There were present William Wordsworth and his family, his sister Dorothy, his wife's sister, Sarah Hutchinson, Coleridge, and Coleridge's son, Hartley. To

this group Wordsworth read, for the first time, his great poem on "the growth of an individual mind", as he then described it. Everyone present was deeply moved . . . Coleridge so much so that he retired to his room and in the middle of the night composed those lines beginning:

> O Friend! O Teacher! God's great gift to me!
> Into my heart have I received that Lay
> More than historic, that prophetic Lay
> Wherein (high theme by thee first sung aright)
> Of the foundations and the building up
> Of a Human Spirit thou hast dared to tell
> What may be told, to the understanding mind
> Revealable . . .

They had listened to

> An Orphic song indeed,
> A song divine of high and passionate thoughts
> To their own music chaunted!

and when it was finished—when, said Coleridge addressing Wordsworth in this poem, when

> Thy long sustained Song finally closed,
> And thy deep voice had ceased—yet thou thyself
> Wert still before my eyes, and round us both
> That happy vision of beloved faces—
> Scarce conscious, and yet conscious of its close
> I sate, my being blended in one thought
> (Thought was it? or aspiration? or resolve?)
> Absorbed, yet hanging still upon the sound—
> And when I rose, I found myself in prayer.

The poem which Wordsworth read to his friends in January, 1807, was not to be published until the year of the poet's death, 1850, and it was then given the title *The Prelude or Growth of a Poet's Mind; an Autobiographical Poem.* It is said that Mrs. Wordsworth invented the title *The Prelude,* and as a title it is appropriate enough, considering the poem's origin, and the place it occupies in Wordsworth's work. Nine years before that first recitation of *The Prelude,* Wordsworth and Coleridge had discussed the possibility of Wordsworth composing a great philosophical poem, to be called *The Recluse, or Views on Man, Nature, and Society.* Coleridge suggested that Wordsworth "should assume the station of a man in mental repose, one whose principles were made up, and so prepared to deliver upon authority a system of philosophy. He was to treat man as man—a subject of eye, ear, touch, and taste, in contact with external nature, and informing the senses from the mind, and not compounding a mind out of the senses; then he was to describe the pastoral and other states of society, assuming something of the Juvenalian spirit as he approached the high civilization of cities and towns, and opening a melancholy picture of the present state of degeneracy and vice; thence he was to infer and reveal the proof of, and necessity for, the whole state of man and society being subject to, and illustrative of, a redemptive process in operation, showing how this idea reconciled all the anomalies, and promised future glory and restoration".

That grandiose conception was never to be realized. We have, as part of it, *The Prelude,* a poem of twelve Books and 7,883 lines, *The Excursion,* nine Books and 8,850 lines, and a noble fragment of 107 lines of *The Recluse* itself, which Wordsworth printed in his Preface to the first edition of *The Excursion,* "as a kind of Prospectus of the design and scope of the whole poem". In that same Preface he refers to the unpublished *Prelude* in these terms:

> Several years ago, when the Author retired to his native mountains, with the hope of being able to construct a literary Work that might live, it was a reasonable thing that he should take a review of his own mind, and examine how far Nature and Education had qualified him for such employment. As subsidiary to this preparation, he undertook to record in verse, the origin and progress of his own powers, as far as he was acquainted with them. That Work, addressed to a dear Friend, most distinguished for his knowledge and genius, and to whom the Author's Intellect is deeply indebted, has been long finished; and the result of the investigation which gave rise to it was a determination to compose a philosophical poem, containing views of Man, Nature, and Society; and to be entitled, *The Recluse,* as having for its principal subject the sensations and opinions of a poet living in retirement. The preparatory poem is biographical, and conducts the history of the Author's mind to the point when he was emboldened to hope that his faculties were sufficiently matured for entering upon the arduous labour which he had proposed to himself; and the two Works have the same kind of relation to each other, if he may so express himself, as the ante-chapel has to the body of a gothic church.

Admittedly, all this sounds a little pompous, even portentous. But we shall never understand Wordsworth, much less sympathize with him, unless we realize that he regarded himself as "a dedicated Spirit". At the conclusion of one of the most magnificent passages in *The Prelude,* in which he had recalled "one particular hour" of his youth, a moment of unreflective ecstasy, he breaks off to address Coleridge in these words:

> Ah! need I say, dear Friend, that to the brim
> My heart was full; I made no vows, but vows
> Were then made for me; bond unknown to me
> Was given, that I should be, else sinning greatly,
> A dedicated Spirit. On I walk'd
> In blessedness, which even yet remains.

No great poet has ever taken himself so seriously as Wordsworth. His whole life reveals an obstinate, at times a selfish determination to fulfil his poetic destiny. It was perhaps this very determination, involving as it did seclusion and a limitation of experience, which explains Wordsworth's failure to achieve his great plan. Poetry depends, to an extent not always appreciated by poets themselves, on the maintenance of normal contacts, on the daily stimulus of unanticipated events. *The Recluse* was not the happiest title for a poem on man, nature and society, nor was "retirement" of the prolonged kind which actually occurred the right condition. We must realize that when he set out on his great self-imposed task, Wordsworth hoped to complete the whole of the great philosophical poem he envisaged in less than two years. In the Advertisement which precedes the 1850 edition of *The Prelude* it is stated that this part of the plan "was commenced in the begin-

ning of the year 1799, and completed in the summer of 1805". That statement is not quite accurate. Professor Garrod has proved that the Preamble to the poem was written in September, 1795. The first draft of *The Prelude* as a whole was complete by 1806; *The Excursion* was not published until 1814; and as late as 1824 Dorothy writes as though *The Recluse* were still to be regarded as "work in progress", though she says that her brother "seems to feel the task so weighty that he shrinks from beginning with it". But Professor de Selincourt was probably right in suspecting that by this time Wordsworth himself knew that he would never go on with *The Recluse.* What had been conceived as a two-years' task had petered out after nearly thirty years of slow, frustrated effort.

It was "*comparatively* with the *former* poem", that is to say, with *The Prelude,* that *The Excursion* disappointed Coleridge's expectations, and in his letter to Wordsworth about *The Excursion* (written reluctantly nine months after that poem had been published) Coleridge conjectured that its inferiority "might have been occasioned by the influence of self-established convictions having given to certain thoughts and expressions a depth and force which they had not for readers in general". Later critics did not seek any such subtle explanations: a few passages excepted, which were of earlier composition, they found the poem desperately dull. But it is only against the achievement of *The Prelude* that this judgment becomes of critical interest. I do not wish to engage in a defence of *The Excursion,* which stands in relation to *The Prelude* very much as *Paradise Regained* stands to *Paradise Lost.* The failure is one of organic continuity. The later poem was, as Coleridge said, "to have sprung up as the tree" from "the ground plot and roots" which had been prepared in *The Prelude,* and as far as there was the same sap in both, they should have formed one complete whole, each revealing, for its distinct purpose, "the vital spirit of a perfect form". Well, let us admit that *The Excursion* has no organic power of this kind: let us return to the groundwork of *The Prelude,* to that "Orphic song" which Coleridge could praise without reservations, and which remains, a hundred and fifty years after its conception, a poem unique in kind and unsurpassed in its particular brand of eloquence.

The poem is unique, not in its form, but in its subject-matter. In form it is an epic, like *Paradise Lost,* but the subject is the poet's own mind—not the poet himself, as eponymous hero, but the poet as dedicated spirit—as a spirit dedicated to a task for which, without scrupulous self-examination and self-assessment, he might not deem himself sufficiently disciplined, sufficiently worthy. Wordsworth admitted that "it was a thing unprecedented in literary history, that a man should talk so much about himself", but he added, in perfect sincerity, that it was not self-conceit that induced him to do this, but real humility. He began the work, he said, because he was unprepared to treat any more arduous subject, and diffident of his own powers. At the same time he confesses, in the first Book of *The Prelude,* that when in this way he makes "rigorous inquisition" of himself, "the report is often cheering": for, he continues,

> I neither seem
> To lack that first great gift, the vital soul,
> Nor general Truths, which are themselves a sort
> Of Elements and Agents, Under-powers,
> Subordinate helpers of the living mind.
> Nor am I naked in external things,
> Forms, images, nor numerous other aids
> Of less regard, though won perhaps with toil,
> And needful to build up a Poet's praise.

This is self-confident enough, but a little later he confesses that when it comes to his "last and favourite aspiration",

> some philosophic song
> Of truth that cherishes our daily life

that then

> from this awful burthern I full soon
> Take refuge and beguile myself with trust
> That mellower years will bring a riper mind
> And clearer insight.

Already, in 1805, he had made a very shrewd analysis of his powers and capacities, of the psychological inhibitions that would defeat his greater purpose:

> Thus from day to day
> I live, a mockery of the brotherhood
> Of vice and virtue, with no skill to part
> Vague longing that is bred by want of power,
> From paramount impulse not to be withstood,
> A timorous capacity from prudence;
> From circumspection, infinite delay.
> Humility and modest awe themselves
> Betray me, serving often for a cloak
> To a more subtle selfishness, that now
> Doth lock my functions up in blank reserve,
> Now dupes me by an over-anxious eye
> That with intrusive restlessness beats off
> Simplicity and self-presented truth.

Wordsworth must undoubtedly be described as an egoist—romantic artists commonly are. But do not let us make the mistake of assuming that he was naïve. He is as subtle as Shakespeare in his psychological penetration, and like Shakespeare he was, as Coleridge pointed out, always the *spectator ab extra*—the merciless, objective analyst. From this point of view, the poetic work that comes nearest to *The Prelude* is *Hamlet.*

I should now perhaps say something about the structure of *The Prelude.* It is in narrative form, divided into books which represent various stages in the growth of the poet's mind. But the narrative is interspersed with reflective passages which sometimes, as in the case of Book VIII (entitled *Retrospect*) and Book XIV (*The Conclusion*), extend over the greater part of that section. The epic character of the poem is undoubtedly diluted by such philosophic musings. Various versions of the poem survive. These were collected and collated by the late Ernest de Selincourt, the greatest Wordsworthian scholar of our time, and his edition of *The Prelude* makes a comparison of the texts very easy. The conclusion that Professor de Selincourt came to after a careful study of the two main texts was that from a poetic or technical point of view, the final version, all things considered, is undoubtedly the better one. "Weak phrases are strengthened and its whole tex-

ture is more closely knit," he says, and he adds: "The 1805 text . . . leaves often the impression of a man writing rapidly, thinking aloud or talking to his friend without waiting to shape his thought into the most concise and telling form, satisfied for the moment if he can put it into metre by inverting the prose order of the words."

If our schools and universities were to take an interest in the writing of poetry (they generally confine themselves to its history and classification) then a study of the evolution of the text of *The Prelude* would be of incomparable value. There is no document in the whole of our literature which has so much to teach the practising poet. Take, for example, the use of the verb "to be" as an auxiliary. The auxiliary is always to be avoided in poetry because it produces a softening or dimming of the statement made. 'The gentleness of heaven *is on* the sea' was the original reading of a line in one of Wordsworth's best-known sonnets ("It is a beauteous evening, calm and free"). Wordsworth later altered this line to read: "The gentleness of heaven *broods o'er* the sea", and there is an obvious gain in vividness. In the same way, in *The Prelude,* to make use of an example given by de Selincourt, the description of the morning of Wordsworth's poetic dedication originally ran:

> Magnificent
> The morning was, in memorable pomp,
> More glorious than I ever had beheld.
> The Sea was laughing at a distance; all
> The solid Mountains were as bright as clouds.

"Many a poet," observes de Selincourt, "would have rested satisfied with those lines as they stood, but no one can miss the gain in strength and vividness effected by the simple changes:

> Magnificent
> The morning rose, in memorable pomp,
> Glorious as e'er I had beheld—in front
> The sea lay laughing at a distance; near,
> The solid mountains shone, bright as the clouds.

The difference is simple—the substitution, for "was" and "were", of the active verbs "rose", "lay" and "shone".

In this way, and in the revision of many other details of composition, the whole text of *The Prelude* was cleaned up between 1805 and 1850, and we cannot but agree with de Selincourt that "the cumulative effect of such changes, each one perhaps trifling in itself, cannot easily be overestimated". Not all the changes, even of diction, are for the better—there is a tendency to substitute abstract and grandiloquent phrases for simple words—thus "thought and quietness" becomes "meditative peace" and even a "woman" is dignified as a "female". Other changes are due to a shift in intention—the original version was addressed directly to Coleridge and had some of the intimacy of a confession made to a friend; the final version, though it does not abandon this device, is much more circumspect and discreet. On balance, we have to conclude with Professor de Selincourt that the ideal text of *The Prelude* would follow no single manuscript, and we must each construct, from the material supplied by de Selincourt, our ideal text.

The Prelude is written in blank verse, the unrhymed metre

that Shakespeare habitually used, and Milton in his great epics. It is usual to compare Wordsworth's diction with Milton's, and there are a few passages of striking similarity. But in general Wordsworth's diction bears little resemblance either to the rich imaginative texture of Shakespeare's verse, or to the baroque pomp of Milton's. We must remember that Wordsworth's declared intention was to use in his poetry "a selection of the real language of men in a state of vivid sensation". Coleridge, with his usual perspicacity, found a parallel in "well-languaged Daniel".

Samuel Daniel is still, as he was in Coleridge's day, a "causelessly neglected poet", but we know that Wordsworth admired him greatly. His contemporaries thought him prosaic, and most succeeding critics have agreed with them. Coleridge thought his style and language "just such as any very pure and manly writer of the present-day—Wordsworth, for example—would use; it seems quite modern in comparison with the style of Shakespeare". He further characterized this style as "the neutral ground of prose and verse . . . common to both", but such a neutral style is not negligible. On the contrary, Daniel's diction, wrote Coleridge in *Biographia Literaria,* "bears no mark of time, no distinction of age, which has been, and as long as our language shall last, will be so far the language of the today and for ever, as that it is more intelligible to us, than the transitory fashions of our own particular age". As an example of this neutral style in Wordsworth, Coleridge gave the famous description of skating from the first book of *The Prelude:*

> So through the darkness and the cold we flew,
> And not a voice was idle; with the din
> Smitten, the precipices rang aloud;
> The leafless trees and every icy crag
> Tinkled like iron; while far distant hills
> Into the tumult sent an alien sound
> Of melancholy not unnoticed, while the stars
> Eastward were sparkling clear, and in the west
> The orange sky of evening died away.

That is the neutral style—no "multitudinous seas incarnadine": no Hallelujahs from the Empyrean rung, but simple words in natural order, creating, we do not know why, a *curiosa felicitas,* a subtle beauty beyond analysis.

Coleridge distinguished several other virtues in Wordsworth's poetic diction: I will only mention one further one—what he called "meditative pathos—a union of deep and subtle thought with sensibility; a sympathy with man as man; the sympathy indeed of a contemplator, rather than a fellow-sufferer or co-mate . . . but a contemplator, from whose view no difference of rank conceals the sameness of the nature; no injuries of wind or weather, or toil, or even of ignorance, wholly disguise the human face divine". In this mind and philosophic pathos", Coleridge continues, "Wordsworth appears to me without a compeer. Such he *is:* so he *writes.*" This meditative pathos pervades the whole poem, but a specific instance of it will be found in the story of Vaudracour and Julia.

The philosophy which emerges from this great exercise in self-examination is a philosophy—or rather, a philosophic faith—that has some relevance to our present quandary and incessant heart-searchings. Coleridge once—it was in

their early days—characterized Wordsworth as a "semi-atheist", and in spiritual matters he did indeed question some of the complacent assumptions of his contemporaries. But the more we ponder that faith of his, and contrast it with nihilism on the one hand and intolerant dogma on the other, the more appealing and satisfying it becomes. Wordsworth has also been called a pantheist; that, too, is a misleading label. He was essentially a humanist—not a sceptical humanist like Montaigne, but a pious humanist, like Spinoza or Erasmus. The poet, he said,

> hath stood
> By Nature's side among the men of old
> And so shall stand for ever.

And Nature was valued by the poet because it has the power to "consecrate", "to breathe Grandeur upon the very humblest face of human life".

This faith is so clearly expressed in the two concluding books of *The Prelude* that it is difficult to understand how so many misconceptions of Wordsworth's philosophical position could have arisen. It is true that the poem is not all plain sailing—no poet has written 8,000 lines without lapses into flatness or obscurity. I doubt if Wordsworth is ever hopelessly obscure, but he could be dull. When he attempts the description of scenes for which he has no innate sympathy—as in the account of his residence in London—he can be painfully stilted, and at times grotesque. But the style is the man himself, a man, like most of us, of imperfect sympathies. I do not think we can say with Coleridge that Wordsworth does to *all* thoughts and *all* objects

> add that gleam,
> The light that never was, on sea or land,
> The consecration, and the poet's dream.

But he added that light to the widest, the most entrancing landscape in English literature. He did not people that landscape with the vivid figures of a Shakespeare, nor shake its shores with Milton's "trumpet-tones of harmony". Wordsworth is by no means devoid of imaginative sympathy, and he had a perfect comprehension of the simple folk of his native fells. But the characteristic figure in his landscape is a Solitary, a Wanderer, a man for whom every common sight has significance, who from a fund of natural wisdom can communicate perfect understanding. The best description of such a figure is his own, in *The Excursion:*

> Early had he learned
> To reverence the volume that displays
> The mystery, the life which cannot die;
> But in the mountains did he *feel* his faith.
> All things, responsive to the writing, there
> Breathed immortality, revolving life,
> And greatness still revolving; infinite:
> There littleness was not; the least of things
> Seemed infinite; and there his spirit shaped
> Her prospects, nor did he believe—he *saw.*

A spirit that *sees,* a faith that is *felt*—Wordsworth's uniqueness as a poet lies in his affirmation of this correspondency between subject and object, between existence and transcendence, between the many and the one, between Man and God. It is a faith that inspired him to write some of the greatest poetry in our language, poetry that has lost none of its significance with the passing of a hundred years. (pp. 215-27)

Herbert Read, "The Prelude," in his The Tenth Muse: Essays in Criticism, *1957. Reprint by Horizon Press, 1958, pp. 215-27.*

R. A. Foakes   (essay date 1958)

[*In the following excerpt, Foakes traces the theme of the romantic journey in* The Prelude, *particularly as it represents Wordsworth's intellectual development.*]

The Prelude is an unfinished poem in the sense that *Prometheus Unbound* is incomplete. It has a superficial resemblance to an epic in twelve books, and owes something in diction, structure, and perhaps in the religious colouring of its theme, to Milton's *Paradise Lost,* so that it has become common to speak of its 'epic structure'. But **The Prelude** spills over into thirteen books, fourteen in the final version, and lacks that architectonic quality of *Paradise Lost,* the steady drive through a series of balanced episodes towards a predetermined conclusion, which is made to seem inevitable by the organization of the theme. Wordsworth wrote it casually, in fits and starts, and intended it to be the 'ante-chapel' to a larger work, **The Recluse,** which was never finished. It meanders loosely along, confesses to intervals between spells of writing,

> Five years are vanish'd since I first pour'd out
> Saluted by that animating breeze
> Which met me issuing from the City's Walls,
> A glad preamble to this Verse . . . ,
>
> (VII. 1-4)

confesses also to a change of plan in the middle,

> as this work was taking in my thoughts
> Proportions that seem'd larger than had first
> Been meditated.
>
> (V. 633-5)

The addition of another book to *Paradise Lost* would ruin the poem's shape, but it would make little difference to **The Prelude** if Wordsworth had added another hundred or two hundred lines, especially perhaps at those places where, as he occasionally admits.

> My drift hath scarcely,
> I fear, been obvious.
>
> (V. 291-2)

Indeed, he seems to have had difficulty at times in restraining himself from that anecdotal extravagance which mars the tale of Vaudracour and Julia; so in Book VI the account of his travels by Lake Como is broken off abruptly:

> But here I must break off, and quit at once,
> Though loth, the record of these wanderings,
> A theme which may seduce me else beyond
> All reasonable bounds.
>
> (VI. 658-61)

The real principle of structure in the poem is a journey as an image of development; it is a voyage in time and in space, of indefinite duration, and as on other long journeys, there are breaks, for refreshment, as it were, in a story or a piece of descriptive writing, for meditation on a particular prospect or theme, and for looking back to see the shape of what has gone before. All these may be relevant to the main thread of development, and the journey is still there to be continued after a pause. In an ultimate sense, it is the voyage of life, and the end of it is death, or some kind of defeat of death; the life-in-death of the ancient mariner or Keats's knight, or the triumphant vision of Wordsworth absorbed into

> The feeling of life endless, the great thought
> By which we live, Infinity and God.
>
> (XIII. 183-4)

The progress of the poem, as Wordsworth was well aware, is meandering, like life itself; he compares it to the course of a river:

> As oftentimes a River, it might seem,
> Yielding in part to old remembrances,
> Part sway'd by fear to tread an onward road
> That leads direct to the devouring sea
> Turns, and will measure back his course, far
>   back,
> Towards the very regions which he cross'd
> In his first outset; so have we long time
> Made motions retrograde, in like pursuit
> Detain'd. But now we start afresh; I feel
> An impulse to precipitate my Verse.
> Fair greetings to this shapeless eagerness,
> Whene'er it comes . . .
>
> (IX. 1-12)

Not the poem, but life itself leads to the 'devouring sea' of death, and this image of the river, with its application both to the structure of the poem and its main theme, indicates a conception of **The Prelude** which Wordsworth had from the beginning, as a progress towards the culmination of life:

> A Traveller I am,
> And all my Tale is of myself; even so,
> So be it, if the pure in heart delight
> To follow me.
>
> (III. 196-8)

This is one of the main thematic elements of the poem from the first book, in which it seemed to the poet that 'The road lies plain before me' (I. 668), to the last, in which he wrote, 'the termination of my course Is nearer now, much nearer' (XIII. 372-3).

The image of the journey operates on several planes, the simplest being the many descriptions of journeys which actually formed part of the poet's life, as for instance the journey to Cambridge (Book III), the return on vacation (Book IV), the travels over the Alps and into Italy (Book VI), into France (Book IX) and the final excusion into Wales (Book XIII). These are not simply literal accounts of travels, but mark a progress in time, in the development of the poet's imagination, and so interact with and pass into metaphors and similes of journeys, that they also come to act as images of impression. So, for instance, in Book III, the description of the poet's arrival in Cambridge, and his roaming 'through the motley spectacle' (II. 29ff) there, is set off against the account a little later of his escape from the city to walk alone in the fields (II.

97ff); the experience of Cambridge taught him to know himself and his powers, and the literal journey passes into and fortifies a figurative journey:

> it is enough
> To notice that I was ascending now
> To such community with highest truth.
>
> A track pursuing not untrod before,
> From deep analogies by thought supplied,
> Or consciousnesses not to be subdued,
> To every natural form, rock, fruit or flower,
> Even the loose stones that cover the high-way,
> I gave a moral life . . .
>
> (III. 118-26)

The track pursued by the poet seems to be at once the literal 'high-way' of his wanderings, and the course along which his mind developed on the ascent to truth. The same double implication is often apparent, as later in this book when he says 'now into a populous Plain We must descend' (II. 195-6), for this is literally true, connecting with the opening description of his arriving on the 'flat plains of Huntingdon' as the coach approached Cambridge, but is also an image of his giving himself up to social pleasures, neglecting his studies, and rejecting those who worked hard,

> Willingly did I part from these, and turn
> Out of their track, to travel with the shoal
> Of more unthinking Natures.
>
> (III. 517-19)

This interrelation of the overtly figurative and the apparently literal image of a journey operates throughout the poem, and culminates in the ascent of Snowdon described in the last book, which is at the same time an ascent to a spiritual conquest. Perhaps the most striking example of the fusion of the two comes in Book VI, where, as the poet *wrote* of crossing the Alps, he was seized by an imaginative vision:

> And all the answers which the Man
>   return'd . . .
> Ended in this; that we had crossed the Alps.
>
> Imagination! lifting up itself
> Before the eye and progress of my Song
> Like an unfather'd vapour; here that Power,
> In all the might of its endowments, came
> Athwart me; I was lost as in a cloud,
> Halted, without a struggle to break through.
>
> (VI. 521-30)

It is easy to read this passage without noticing that the vision does not belong to the moment of crossing the mountains, but to the moment of writing, for the image of the journey is carried on in the words and phrases 'progress', 'came Athwart me', 'lost', 'Halted', 'break through', and the associations of mountains are continued in the images of the vapour and the cloud; in addition, the attainment of the highest point on his road out of Switzerland, the summit of the mountains, is appropriate to the vision inasmuch as mountains are associated with aspiration, and to reach a summit is an achievement of danger and difficulty, or at least of effort and strain. So here the literal becomes figurative, and the actual journey over the Alps becomes

identified with the progress of the song and the achievement of the vision.

The journeys described in **The Prelude** thus contribute to that figurative journey which is the poem's main theme, and what the poet said about his travels in Switzerland and Italy applies in some measure to them all:

> whate'er
> I saw, or heard, or felt, was but a stream
> That flow'd into a kindred stream, a gale
> That help'd me forwards, did administer
> To grandeur and to tenderness, to the one
> Directly, but to tender thoughts by means
> Less often instantaneous in effect;
> Conducted me to these along a path
> Which in the main was more circuitous.
>
> (VI. 672-80)

The travels described in the poem relate to the spiritual journey which shapes it, and gives to it the character of a pilgrimage; so Wordsworth addresses Coleridge,

> O Friend, for whom
> I travel in these dim uncertain ways
> Thou wilt assist me as a pilgrim gone
> In quest of highest truth.
>
> (XI. 390-3)

In this aspect, the journey of Wordsworth is similar in many ways to that of the ancient mariner: he travels from his home, the happy landscape of his boyhood, through a desert of the spirit, like the barren waste where the mariner is forced to linger, to a rediscovery of the power of nature working in himself, and of his powers as a poet, and he returns home, to nature, changed by his experience. The journey begins in the valleys and hills of the Lake District, where as a boy he was subjected to the influence of the natural scene, and the first books describe

> The way I travell'd when I first began
> To love the woods and fields.
>
> (II.4-5)

In the valleys of peace and mountains of aspiration he found a sense of identification with a larger unity, and grew 'Foster'd alike by beauty and by fear' to feel himself 'an agent of the one great mind',

> I saw one life, and felt that it was joy.
>
> (II. 430)

A kind of stagnation came when he left school, home and the natural world for Cambridge, the university and city, where he felt a desolation of soul, as if he were rotting on a dead sea,

> Rotted as by a charm, my life became
> A floating island, an amphibious thing
> Unsound, of spongy texture, yet withal,
> Not wanting a fair face of water-weeds
> And pleasant flowers.
>
> (III. 339-43)

Yet this was only a 'first transit' from

> the smooth delights,
> And wild outlandish walks of simple youth,
> To something that resembled an approach
> Towards mortal business; to a privileg'd world

Within a world, a midway residence . . .

(III. 550-4)

and except for the interlude of 'transcendent peace' on his first vacation in the Lake District, where, on a walk in the mountains overlooking the sea, the poet became a 'dedicated spirit', the next books trace the poet's growing experience. His yielding to the 'vague heartless chace Of trivial pleasures' taught him the value of his own bringing-up, of the combination of book-learning and nature's lore, in contrast to the childhood of Coleridge, spent in the city,

Debarr'd from Nature's living images,
Compelled to be a life unto itself.

(VI. 313-14)

Wordsworth's own experience of the city follows, in his description of life in London, where after leaving Cambridge, he lived 'Single in the wide waste', and

pitch'd my vagrant tent,
A casual Reveller and at large, among
The unfenc'd regions of society.

(VII. 60-62)

The central books of *The Prelude* deal with the poet's passage through these desert regions, through

the years
That bear us forward to distress and guilt,
Pain and abasement.

(VII. 403-5)

Although he was fortunate in starting his journey with his 'face towards the truth',

Happy in this, that I with nature walk'd,
Not having a too early intercourse
With the deformities of crowded life,

(VIII. 462-4)

so that his experience of the labyrinth of London, where 'the imaginative Power' languished and slept, did not destroy his faith in man, yet those 'deformities' were to bring a devastating shock to him. Books IX and X take him to France, where Wordsworth's early rejoicing in the success of the Revolution was soon modified, first by the intervention of Britain,

No shock
Given to my moral nature had I known
Down to that very moment; neither lapse
Nor turn of sentiment that might be nam'd
A revolution, save at this one time,
All else was progress on the self-same path
On which with a diversity of pace
I had been travelling; this a stride at once
Into another region.

(X. 234-42)

Then the atrocities of the Reign of Terror brought 'a sense Of treachery and desertion', culminating in his loss of 'all feeling of conviction', his faith in nature and in man. The last books describe the final stages of the journey, the return to England beginning a process of restoration in the peace of the world, where

Nature's self, by human love
Assisted, through the weary labyrinth
Conducted me again to open day.

(X. 922-4)

This restoration is completed in the great vision on the top of Snowdon described in Book XIII, with a renewed assertion of faith in man and nature, and in immortality, made more profound and valuable because it has been tested and earned by the poet's own suffering.

Something of the basic shape of the poem is indicated in this outline of Wordsworth's journey of development, a shape deliberately contrived by a rearrangement of events to form a fictitious sequence: the ascent of Snowdon which the poet probably made in 1791, before the visit to France recorded in Book IX, becomes the appropriate symbolic climax and termination of a progress of the imagination, the spirit. It is a progress in which the boy's simple and solitary love of nature and self-identification with the natural scene, 'I saw one life, and felt that it was joy', is modified by life in cities, by contact with human love, suffering and evil (a process described in Book VIII, a retrospective view of the poet's growth of attachment to 'the good and ill of human life'); this more sober faith, after finding an object of attachment in the French Revolution, collapses in the succeeding Reign of Terror, so that the imaginative faculty itself seems to die; and the progress ends with the regeneration of the imagination in a grander vision of love and unity. It is a progress from a simple faith through suffering and despair to a more profound and satisfying vision of man's relation to the universe, a journey of death and regeneration like that of Coleridge's ancient mariner.

So far the character of the journey as one taking place in space and time, as a voyage of life, a pilgrimage of the spirit in quest of truth, and a development of the imagination, has been noted. It has also a character in terms of descent and ascent. It begins among the mountains, symbols of the poet's aspiration and faith,

if in this time
Of dereliction and dismay, I yet
Despair not of our nature; but retain
A more than Roman confidence, a faith
That fails not, in all sorrow my support,
The blessing of my life, the gift is yours,
Ye mountains! thine, O Nature!

(II. 456-62)

But soon there is a descent to the plains of Cambridge, which sucks the poet in like a whirlpool, with 'an eddy's force', and his sufferings, his acquisition of experience, take place on the lower levels of the plains, the sea, the desert, and the city, which shares the quality of these. For the city is a waste where all are 'melted and reduced to one identity' in a kind of 'blank confusion', and at one point Wordsworth's entry into it is compared to a passage into 'some Vault of Earth', a subterranean cave (VIII. 71 1ff). In this suffering he learns

That transmigration could be undergone,
A fall of being suffer'd, and of hope
By creature that appear'd to have received
Entire conviction what a great ascent
Had been accomplish'd, what high faculties
It had been call'd to.

(X. 600-5)

After this descent 'Through times of honour, and through

times of shame' (X.943) there comes an ascent finally to 'highest truth', which also culminates in the poet's vision on the top of Snowdon, as he is restored again to the mountains. These various aspects of the journey and modes of Wordsworth's progress are all finally caught up in a passage in the last book, where he says of the imagination,

> This faculty hath been the moving soul
> Of our long labour: we have traced the stream
> From darkness, and the very place of birth
> In its blind cavern, whence is faintly heard
> The sound of waters; follow'd it to light
> And open day, accompanied its course
> Among the ways of Nature, afterwards
> Lost sight of it bewilder'd and engulph'd,
> Then given it greeting, as it rose once more
> With strength, reflecting in its solemn breast
> The works of man and face of human life,
> And lastly, from its progress have we drawn
> The feeling of life endless, the great thought
> By which we live, Infinity and God.
>
> (XIII. 171-84)

All the various aspects of Wordsworth's development on this journey, the basic image of *The Prelude,* are expressed in terms of images of impression, drawn chiefly from the natural world. In particular, mountains, winds or breezes, the sun, the moon and light generally (as in the passage just quoted), are associated with aspiration, with the achievement of the vision, with the work of the imagination. The valleys among the mountains seem to represent havens of peace; islands, places where a temporary pause is made for rest and refreshment of the soul, or places of complete stagnation; and rivers are types of the progress of the soul on its meandering path. The desert, the city and the sea are forms of the wilderness through which the human spirit has to pass, enduring suffering and loss, in gaining that experience which enriches the final assertion. All these relate to the journey, and the various images interact in the poem's total effect.

This interrelation may be illustrated by a more detailed examination of the use of one of these images. The image of the sea is interesting, and is directly established in a relationship to the image of the journey in a passage of recapitulation towards the end:

> This History, my Friend, hath chiefly told
> Of intellectual power, from stage to stage
> Advancing, hand in hand with love and joy,
> And of imagination teaching truth
> Until that natural graciousness of mind
> Gave way to over-pressure from the times
> And their disastrous issues. What avail'd,
> When Spells forbade the Voyager to land,
> The fragrance which did ever and anon
> Give notice of the Shore, from arbours breathed
> Of blessed sentiment and fearless love?
> What did such sweet remembrances avail,
> Perfidious then, as seem'd, what serv'd they then?
> My business was upon the barren sea,
> My errand was to sail to other coasts.
>
> (XI. 42-56)

The poet's 'business' in the central books of the poem has

been to sail a 'barren sea', a voyage through a wilderness of spiritual desolation, which has to be endured before the shore can be reached. The sea is a vast medium of the spiritual voyage the poet has made, and, like most of the main images, it enters in the opening lines, celebrating Wordsworth's escape from the 'prison' of the city to the country, and his new liberty

> Enough that I am free; for months to come
> May dedicate myself to chosen tasks;
> May quit the tiresome sea and dwell on shore.
>
> (I. 33-35)

The rest of the poem recounts the journey over that sea.

In the first two books, which describe his childhood, spent in the safe valleys of the Lake District, the sea is chiefly an emblem of might and sometimes terror. Splitting ice makes a sound like the noise of wolves 'When they are howling round the Bothnic main' (I. 570), and when the power of nature most disturbs the boy, it seems to make the earth's surface

> With triumph, and delight, and hope, and fear,
> Work like a sea.
>
> (I. 500-1)

The repose of the inland valleys is unaffected by the sea wind, 'Though wind of roughest temper' (II. 116); and at the height of his joy in nature, when he feels one life in all things, the sea is included with a 'yea' which indicates his respect for it,

> all that glides
> Beneath the wave, yea, in the wave itself
> And mighty depth of waters.
>
> (II. 426-8)

There are other, gentler, references to the sea in these books, but the dominant impression is perhaps that at this period of childhood the sea represents a strange, vast, and unexperienced power.

The first sense that he has launched out on the sea comes in Book III, the story of his leaving home for the first time to study at Cambridge, which sucked him in as with 'an eddy's force' (III. 11). Here his life became a 'floating island', luxuriant but rotting; he had been attracted by the fame of the town and university, but found life trivial there, and he warns against its siren-like appeal:

> If the Mariner,
> When at reluctant distance he hath pass'd
> Some fair enticing Island, did but know
> What fate might have been his, could he have brought
> His Bark to land upon the wished-for spot,
> Good cause full often would be his to bless
> The belt of churlish Surf that scared him thence.
>
> (III. 496-502)

From this book on, the sea appears as an image of an experience of life which the poet has to endure. In a long simile in Book IV he compares his progress in the poem to that of a traveller in a slow-moving boat on 'the surface of past time'. Book V begins with the account of a dream in which the sea, the waters of the deep, seem to pursue an Arab as he escapes across a wilderness carrying his precious

Be little profitted, would see, and ask
Where is the obligation to enforce?
And to acknowledged law rebellious, still
As selfish passion urged, would act amiss,
The dupe of folly, or the slave of crime.
       Depressed, *bewildered* ~~confounded~~ thus I did not walk
With scoffers, seeking light and gay revenge
From indiscriminate laughter, nor sate down
In reconcilement with an utter waste
Of Intellect; such sloth I could not brook
(Too well I loved in that my spring of life
Pains-taking thoughts and truth their dear reward)
But *turned* to abstract science, and there sought
Work for the reasoning faculty enthroned

Thanks to The bounteous Giver of all Good!
That the beloved woman in whose sight
Those days were passed, now speaking in a voice
Of sudden admonition like a brook
That does but cross a lonely road, and now
Seen, heard, and felt, and caught at every turn,
Companion never lost thro' many a league,

Manuscript from Book XI *of* The Prelude.

burden of a stone, symbolizing geometric truth, and a shell, symbolizing poetry; the dreamer, who had expected that the Arab would be a guide to 'lead him through the desert', sees him at last

> riding o'er the Desert sands
> With the fleet waters of the drowning world
> In chase of him, whereat I wak'd in terror,
> And saw the Sea before me . . .
>
> (V. 135-9)

The sea here represents that necessary involvement in the life of the world from which it is impossible to preserve inviolate truth and poetry; but Wordsworth felt tempted to try, felt that he might emulate the Arab,

> Could share that Maniac's anxiousness, could go
> Upon like errand.
>
> (V. 160-1)

There is another long image in the next book which relates to this; in it he illustrates the attraction the 'independent world' of mathematics exerts over his mind by the tale of a mariner, who, cast by shipwreck on an uninhabited island, finds that he can console himself and 'almost Forget' his misery in the study of geometry. This passage (VI. 160ff) also looks forward to the time when Wordsworth was, as it were, shipwrecked in the sea of life, and sought in mathematics his relief (X. 890ff.)

Meanwhile the journey has to be continued, as in a ship on a fair sea (VI. 435), through the Alps into Italy, during the period of his residence in London and then his stay in France, a time culminating in the desolation of the Terror after the French Revolution. Even this had its 'bright spots':

> as the desert hath green spots, the sea
> Small islands in the midst of stormy waves,
> So that disastrous period did not want
> Such sprinklings of all human excellence,
> As were a joy to hear of.
>
> (X. 441-5)

But eventually the depravity of the times led to the poet's yielding 'up moral questions in despair', to the decay of his imaginative power; recovery from this critical stage of his development came on his return to England, whence he could look back on the time when his 'business was upon the barren sea'. His business there had been to learn the importance of living

> Not in Utopia, subterranean Fields,
> Or some secreted Island, Heaven knows where,
> But in the very world which is the world
> Of all of us, the place in which, in the end,
> We find our happiness, or not at all.
>
> (X. 724-8)

So Wordsworth's journey, now almost over, has been invested, through the sea imagery, with

> something of the grandeur which invests
> The Mariner who sails the roaring sea
> Through storm and darkness.
>
> (XII. 153-5)

Much of the grandeur and meaning of the final vision are created by the image Wordsworth employs: the triumph of the imagination is represented by his ascent of Snowdon, which is also an ascent of the soul to a spiritual height on the mountain, overlooking at last the terrible sea, the sea of experience through which he has voyaged. This is the true end of that journey through the depths which is the heart of the poem, and the mountain is an image of his own mind in contact with the infinite, the sea an image of what has been overcome:

> on the shore
> I found myself of a huge sea of mist
> Which, meek and silent, rested at my feet:
> A hundred hills their dusky backs upheaved
> All over this still Ocean, and beyond
> Far, far beyond, the vapours shot themselves,
> In headlands, tongues, and promontory shapes,
> Into the Sea, the real Sea, that seem'd
> To dwindle, and give up its majesty,
> Usurp'd upon as far as sight could reach.
>
> (XIII. 42-51)

The peculiar strength of this climactic image resides in the double recession of the sea, conquered and tamed beneath the 'meek' sea of mist, removed in depth and distance far from the poet, who seems to stand infinitely high above it. On this great scene the moon shines, an emblem perhaps of that light which the poet has at last attained; and a little way off the shore a chasm in the mist brings to his ears the noise of the sea,

> the roar of waters, torrents, streams
> Innumerable, roaring with one voice . . .
> . . . in that breach
> Through which the homeless voice of waters rose,
> That dark deep thoroughfare had Nature lodg'd
> The Soul, the Imagination of the whole.
>
> (XIII. 58-65)

For the poet has completed his journey over the sea, has reached home, gained the shore, with a sense of lofty security; the 'blue chasm' links the conquered sea, the mountain and the moon as symbols not only of the poet's journey of the spirit, but also again of his ascent to triumph.

These images of impression in **The Prelude** fortify and give body to the statements of the vision, of the assertion of the poet, which are necessarily vague, and are recorded largely in a vocabulary of value-words, whose function is to act as counters, as equivalents for what cannot be described, and so to work on our feelings. But for these to be effective, our feelings have to be wrought into a state in which we are prepared to accept the assertion they make, and the images of impression have to lend solidity and force to them, or they become mere empty rhetoric. In **The Prelude**, image and assertion reinforce each other fully, so that the great visionary passages are convincing. There is a complete sympathy between the value-words and the imagery, as is well illustrated by a passage cited earlier, describing the vision which came to the poet as he was writing about crossing the Alps:

> Imagination! lifting up itself
> Before the eye and progress of my Song
> Like an unfather'd vapour; here that Power,
> In all the might of its endowments, came

Athwart me; I was lost as in a cloud,
Halted, without a struggle to break through.
And now recovering, to my Soul I say
I recognize thy glory; in such strength
Of usurpation, in such visitings
Of awful promise, when the light of sense
Goes out in flashes that have shewn to us
The invisible world, doth Greatness make
  abode,
There harbours whether we be young or old.
Our destiny, our nature, and our home
Is with infinitude, and only there;
With hope it is, hope that can never die,
Effort, and expectation, and desire,
And something ever more about to be.
                        (VI. 525-42)

As noted earlier, the account of crossing the mountains is carried over into the imagery of this passage, so that an experience which defies direct description, except in such vague terms as 'visitings of awful promise', is given a specific character and value: the physical effort of gaining the summit is transferred to the achievement of the vision. The other images in the passage, of light—the light of sense extinguished in 'flashes' of a greater illumination—of harbour and home, all carry pleasant and valuable associations. The last two continue the idea of a journey from the account of the mountain-crossing, and suggest a culmination generally desired, in a place of welcome rest and security. So the images support the assertion, and the value-words, like 'glory', 'strength', 'promise', 'Greatness', 'infinitude', 'expectation', 'desire', 'hope', are given a focus, and in turn guide us to an appreciation of Wordsworth's experience here as something noble, important and valuable.

The repetition of value-words in different contexts of image and description also increases their effectiveness and lends them an aura of meaning. One prominent word of this kind is *power*. The 'objects great and fair' that afford a symbolic framework for the poem are often referred to as *powers*, so that this word becomes a means by which the natural world and the imagination, the symbols and the assertion, are integrated. The creative impulse is commonly described as a power, often with a capital 'P', as indicating the imagination; the intellect on the other hand is

that false secondary power, by which,
In weakness, we create distinctions.
                        (II. 221-2)

The elements of the natural world are also called powers, like that of the imagination. Wordsworth begins the poem with an account of the first manifestation of his creative sensibility in childhood, when 'a plastic power Abode within me' (II.381), and in adolescence, when he felt that he was a chosen son endowed with 'holy powers' (III. 83). In the context of these and other uses of the word *power,* it becomes clear what he means when, for instance, he says

      Of Genius, Power,
Creation and Divinity itself
I have been speaking, for my theme has been
What pass'd within me.
                        (III. 171-4)

The power is that of the imagination and of the natural world, whose

      lovely forms
Had also left less space within my mind,
Which, wrought upon instinctively, had found
A freshness in those objects of its love,
A winning power, beyond all other power.
                        (III. 366-70)

Further aids to the development of the supreme imaginative Power are general truths, called 'Under-Powers, Subordinate helpers of the living mind' (I.163), and books, which receive Wordsworth's highest praise as

      Powers
For ever to be hallowed; only less,
For what we may become, and what we need,
Than Nature's self, which is the breath of God.
                        (V. 219-22)

Books, like the forms of nature, foster the imagination in men, and both should be studied in order to acquire 'Knowledge not purchas'd with the loss of power', the poetic power that attends on nature:

      Visionary Power
Attends upon the motions of the winds
Embodied in the mystery of words.
                        (V. 619-21)

The poet's experience on the sea of life in London and France caused his imaginative Power to languish at first, but also brought about an enlargement of his sympathies, so that although he lacked his

early converse with the works of God
Among all regions; chiefly where appear
Most obviously simplicity and power,
                        (VII. 718-20)

he gained enormously in other respects. He learned to love the 'Human Kind', to think of man as having at least the opportunity of becoming 'a Power Or Genius, under Nature, under God, Presiding'. He learned to distinguish the true poetic power from the 'adulterate Power', the fancy; and he sought a full expansion of his poetic faculties:

      I sought not then
Knowledge; but crav'd for power, and power I
  found
In all things.
                        (VIII. 753-5)

So he found even in the wilderness of London objects which engaged his sensibility, while he remained conscious that the strength of his imagination was due to

      subservience from the first
To God and Nature's single sovereignty,
Familiar presences of awful Power.
                        (IX. 236-8)

The middle books describe the impairing of his imagination and the last books its restoration; only through this experience did he learn the value and quality of the power he possessed:

I had been taught to reverence a Power
That is the very quality and shape
And image of right reason, that matures

Her processes by steadfast laws, gives birth
To no impatient or fallacious hopes,
No heat of passion or excessive zeal,
No vain conceits, provokes to no quick turns
Of self-applauding intellect, but lifts
The Being into magnanimity.

                                        (XII. 24-32)

He hoped that his poem might embody his relationship
with nature, might reveal the hiding-places of his power,
and recreate for the reader the workings of the creative
imagination, 'might become A power like one of Nature's'. The great vision from Snowdon in Book XIII is a
recognition of the brotherhood of the power of nature and
the power of the imagination; as he looked from the mountain at the forms of the scene before him, he felt that

        The Power which these
Acknowledge when thus moved, which Nature
        thus
Thrusts forth upon the senses, is the express
Resemblance, in the fulness of its strength
Made visible, a genuine Counterpart
And Brother of the glorious faculty
Which higher minds bear with them as their
        own.

                                        (XIII. 84-90)

So the poem ends, having 'tracked the main essential
Power, Imagination, up her way sublime', with this fine
affirmation. The *power* which the forms of nature exert on
the senses is identified as the 'express resemblance' of the
power of the imagination, and this word, defined and enriched in meaning through repeated association with imagery, has become a means of making the strong assertion
of this passage acceptable, of identifying image and assertion. The value-words and the assertions of the poem rest

---

An excerpt from Christopher Wordsworth, Jr.'s *Memoirs of William Wordsworth*:

Its title, *The Prelude,* had not been fixed on by the author
himself: the Poem remained anonymous till his death. The
present title has been prefixed to it at the suggestion of [his
wife Mary,] the beloved partner of his life, and the best interpreter of his thoughts, from considerations of its tentative and preliminary character. Obviously it would have
been desirable to mark its relation to *The Recluse* by some
analogous appellation; but this could not easily be done, at
the same time that its other essential characteristics were indicated, Besides, the appearance of this poem, *after* the author's death, might tend to lead some readers into an opinion that it was his *final* production, instead of being, as it
really is, one of his *earlier* works. They were to be guarded
against this supposition. Hence a name has been adopted,
which may serve to keep the true nature and position of the
poem constantly before the eye of the reader; and *THE PRE-
LUDE* will now be perused and estimated with the feelings
properly due to its preparatory character, and to the period
at which it was composed.

Christopher Wordsworth, Jr., in his Memoirs of William
Wordsworth, *1851. Reprinted in* The Prelude *by William
Wordsworth, edited by Jonathan Wordsworth, M. H.
Abrams, and Stephen Gill, Norton, 1979.*

---

on the images of impression, and it is these which endow
the abstractions with life. The nearest way for Wordsworth to embody his theme was in terms of a voyage involving seas, rivers and islands, mountains, valleys and deserts, the sun, moon and the winds, and other natural phenomena, which act as counterparts of the imaginative faculty or symbols of its growth through experience; these interact with the value-words to establish the grandeur of
Wordsworth's imaginative achievement. (pp. 59-79)

> *R. A. Foakes, "The Unfinished Journey:
> Wordsworth's 'The Prelude'," in his* The Ro-
> mantic Assertion: A Study in the Language of
> Nineteenth Century Poetry, *Yale University
> Press, 1958, pp. 51-79.*

Herbert Lindenberger   (essay date 1963)

[*In the following excerpt, Lindenberger suggests that
Wordsworth uses "spots of time" to communicate his
emotional reactions to past experiences.*]

        . . . There's not a man
That lives who hath not had his godlike hours
                                        (III, 191-192)

It is characteristic of Wordsworth's retrospective method
[in *The Prelude*] that the reader always remains aware of
two points of time, the bleak, quiet present, in which the
poet sits writing to Coleridge and meditating upon the epic
task imposed by his ambition to create a poem on "Nature, Man, and Society," and the deep well of the personal
past to which he returns again and again so that he

        might fetch
Invigorating thoughts from former years,
Might fix the wavering balance of my mind,
And haply meet reproaches, too, whose power
May spur me on, in manhood now mature,
To honorable toil.

                                        (I, 648-653)

This past, the quest for which in fact is the substance of
The Prelude, is not re-created in and for itself, but only
within the perspective of the present, through which alone
it derives meaning. Wordsworth's method, one might say,
is the antithesis of that of the historical novelist, who seeks
to immerse his readers so fully in the re-created past that,
if he succeeds, they lose sight of any reality outside this
past. Wordsworth's past, no matter how vivid and "invigorating" it may be, never aims toward an autonomy of this
sort; moreover, through the influence that the past exerts
upon the present, and through his much-repeated desire
to find nourishment in the past, he constantly engages in
a two-way movement, back and forth, between present
and past.

The characteristic form which Wordsworth developed to
probe into the past is the "spot of time," a term he coined
to describe two childhood incidents narrated in Book XI.
The "spot of time" is defined in terms of its salutary effects
upon him:

        There are in our existence spots of time,
        Which with distinct pre-eminence retain
        A vivifying Virtue, whence . . .

our minds
Are nourished and invisibly repair'd. . . .
                                    (XI, 258-265)

But the "spot of time" can also be viewed as a literary form—one peculiar to *The Prelude* as it is not, for instance, to *The Excursion* or, for that matter, to the contemplative poetry of the preceding century. At its simplest level the "spot" is the record of a concrete past event used to illustrate some more general statements about the past. Take, for example, the passage in which Wordsworth recaptures his moment of self-dedication to poetry:

> The memory of one particular hour
> Doth here rise up against me. In a throng,
> A festal company of Maids and Youths,
> Old Men, and Matrons staid, promiscuous rout,
> A medley of all tempers, I had pass'd
> The night in dancing, gaiety and mirth;
> With din of instruments, and shuffling feet,
> And glancing forms, and tapers glittering,
> And unaim'd prattle flying up and down,
> Spirits upon the stretch, and here and there
> Slight shocks of young love-liking interspers'd,
> That mounted up like joy into the head,
> And tingled through the veins. Ere we retired,
> The cock had crow'd, the sky was bright with
>   day.
> Two miles I had to walk along the fields
> Before I reached my home. Magnificent
> The morning was, a memorable pomp,
> More glorious than I ever had beheld.
> The Sea was laughing at a distance; all
> The solid Mountains were as bright as clouds,
> Grain-tinctured, drench'd in empyrean light;
> And, in the meadows and the lower grounds,
> Was all the sweetness of a common dawn,
> Dews, vapours, and the melody of birds,
> And Labourers going forth into the fields.
> —Ah! need I say, dear Friend, that to the brim
> My heart was full; I made no vows, but vows
> Were then made for me; bond unknown to me
> Was given, that I should be, else sinning greatly,
> A dedicated Spirit. On I walk'd
> In blessedness, which even yet remains.
>   (IV, 315-345)

On one level, at least, one could view this memory as a sort of anecdote, called forth in the poet's mind by association and framed on each side by general commentary about the course of his life. At bottom, however, the passage strives to accomplish more than it at first pretends, for the anecdote itself must create the transition from the offhanded introductory remark ("The memory of one particular hour / Doth here rise up against me") to the culminating statement ("On I walk'd / In blessedness, which even yet remains"). By the end of the passage, with its celebration of the ability of the past to project its powers into the present, Wordsworth has shifted context from casual reminiscence to religious vision.

In its whole rhetorical development the passage is typical of innumerable other "spots of time" scattered throughout *The Prelude*. Like the episode about the stolen boat in Book I ("One evening . . . I went alone into a Shepherd's Boat") it starts out by describing a tangible world of more or less ordinary things, in this instance a public celebra-

tion that occurs at regular intervals, almost like a ritual, to break the monotony of country routine. But its ritual quality ("a *festal* company") seems strictly secular in nature and only later in the description does the reader even become aware of the emotional effect it has upon Wordsworth ("Slight shocks of young love-liking . . . / That mounted up like joy into the head / And tingled through the veins"). The passion released here still remains essentially physical, though it points forward to the spiritual vision encompassed in the images of the sea and mountains, above all in the phrase "empyrean light." By the end of the passage everything that passes through the poet's view—fields, birds, laborers going off to their daily routine—all are endowed with a religious aura. The passage progresses, one might say, from "trivial pleasures" to "deeper passions" (both of these phrases are drawn from an introductory passage to this "spot of time"—ll. 305, 310); from a world of transitory things to intimations of a more eternal realm (which includes even the "Labourers going forth," who, in contrast to the dancers, are tied to the recurring cycle of nature); from the language of prose ("the memory of one particular hour") through a landscape appropriate to the short lyric ("and shuffling feet, / And glancing forms, and tapers glittering") to the Miltonic grandeur of the later lines ("Magnificent / The morning was, a memorable pomp"). In time the passage moves from a sense of great distance between Wordsworth's present state and the event he is depicting ("I *had pass'd* / The night in dancing") to a gradual apprehension of the oneness of past and present ("On I walk'd / In blessedness, which even yet remains"); moreover, what was trivial in the past—the surface gaiety of the dance—still retains its great distance in time, while the visionary experience of that night remains within him to dissolve the boundaries which the conceptualizing mind has created between present and past.

"In Wordsworth's most excited mood we have rather the reflexion of the flame than the authentic and derivative fire itself. Its heat and glare pass to us through some less pervious and colder lens."

Thus complained the *Gentleman's Magazine* in 1850, in a review of the newly published *Prelude*. The "fire itself," so conspicuously lacking in Wordsworth's poem, was amply to be found in Shelley's work, the reviewer assured his readers. To a mid-Victorian audience, accustomed as it was to a more heightened and direct expression of emotion than Wordsworth was willing to give, *The Prelude* must have seemed a relatively tame poem, too much akin, perhaps, to the contemplative verse of the eighteenth century to thrill the reader with the impassioned sweep he so much admired in *Prometheus Unbound*.

That "less pervious and colder lens" to which the reviewer objects might be described as Wordsworth's habit of approaching the more intense areas of his experience only by first insisting on their great distance in time. One might, in fact, speak of the "spot of time" as a distancing device, a way of portraying emotion by refracting it through experiences far distant from the present. The invariably prosaic openings of the "spots":

> When summer came

It was the pastime of our afternoons . . .

> Upon a small
> And rocky Island near, a fragment stood
> (Itself like a sea rock) of what had been
> A Romish Chapel . . .

> One Christmas-time,
> The day before the Holidays began . . .
> (II, 55-56; X, 518-521; XI, 345-346)

serve as a sort of lens through which the feelings about to be uncovered may be refracted and brought into open view. It is as though the poet were too reticent to release emotions directly, as though the distancing in time and the casualness of tone could make a deeply personal experience less overtly and embarrassingly personal; in our own age, indeed, the Victorian demand for the "flame itself" seems considerably more antiquated than Wordsworth's attempt to objectify feelings by refraction, a process which has something in common with such modern attempts to impersonalize emotions as we have come to characterize by the terms *persona, mask,* and *objective correlative.* Wordsworth, in fact, is sometimes at pains to separate his past self, which it is the object of the poem to explore, from the present self which speaks directly to the reader:

> So wide appears
> The vacancy between me and those days,
> Which yet have such self-presence in my mind
> That, sometimes, when I think of them, I seem
> Two consciousnesses, conscious of myself
> And of some other Being.
> (II, 28-33)

But if the spot of time in one sense serves to set emotion at an appropriately classical distance, in another sense it works to reawaken and set free long-since-forgotten feelings which, in turn, give new life and energy to the present. Or, to put it another way, the restrained classicism that characterizes the spot of time as a literary technique is counterbalanced through the claims which the spot of time makes for the meaningfulness of powerful feelings.

The ability of the retrospective process to help give vitality to the present through exploration of the past is at its most conspicuous, perhaps, in that spot of time in Book XI in which the poet describes his childhood visit to the scene where a murderer had once been executed. What is extraordinary about the passage is that Wordsworth does not explore merely a single past event, but that he moves through several separate points of time, each recalling the next by association and each, as it were, gathering up energy from the last. The passage starts out in the same casual way as the other spots of time:

> At a time
> When scarcely (I was then not six years old)
> My hand could hold a bridle, with proud hopes
> I mounted, and we rode towards the hills:
> We were a pair of Horsemen; honest James
> Was with me, my encourager and guide.
> We had not travell'd long, ere some mischance
> Disjoin'd me from my Comrade, and, through fear
> Dismounting, down the rough and stony Moor
> I led my Horse, and stumbling on, at length
> Came to a bottom, where in former times

A Murderer had been hung in iron chains.
> The Gibbet-mast was moulder'd down, the bones
> And iron case were gone; but on the turf,
> Hard by, soon after that fell deed was wrought
> Some unknown hand had carved the Murderer's name.
> (279-294)

Thus far, we have no reason to expect anything more than straightforward narrative, something on the order of "**Michael.**" The fussy preciseness with which Wordsworth interjects his age ("I was then not six years old"), the introduction of "honest James" as though he were already quite familiar to the reader, the painstakingness with which each of the poet's movements is recorded—all point to a prime concern with the things of this world. Only in the light of what follows would one look back on these details and speculate on more symbolic meanings: that the journey into the hills and into past time is as much a spiritual as a physical journey; and, moreover, that the story of the execution is weighted with some symbolic meaning (witness the "unknown hand," the "moulder'd" gibbet-mast, the phrase "in former times," whose plural form suggests a vast world of the past and points forward to the "times long past" a few lines later). The underlying significance of the incident becomes more evident in the lines that follow:

> The monumental writing was engraven
> In times long past, and still, from year to year,
> By superstition of the neighborhood,
> The grass is clear'd away; and to this hour
> The letters are all fresh and visible.
> Faltering, and ignorant where I was, at length
> I chanced to espy those characters inscribed
> On the green sod: forthwith I left the spot
> And, reascending the bare Common, saw
> A naked Pool that lay beneath the hills,
> The Beacon on the summit, and more near,
> A Girl who bore a Pitcher on her head
> And seem'd with difficult steps to force her way
> Against the blowing wind. It was, in truth,
> An ordinary sight; but I should need
> Colours and words that are unknown to man
> To paint the visionary dreariness
> Which, while I look'd all round for my lost Guide,
> Did at that time invest the naked Pool,
> The Beacon on the lonely Eminence,
> The Woman, and her garments vex'd and toss'd
> By the strong wind.
> (295-316)

Thus far we are aware of three separate points of time: the present, from which Wordsworth looks back to his childhood and from which, in turn, a new perspective is introduced upon far earlier times. The "monumental" quality of the carved letters; the ritual of clearing away the grass (in citing local superstitions Wordsworth anticipates a device employed by novelists like Hawthorne to hint at deeper meanings which they neither wish to verify nor make too explicit); the ever-lasting "freshness" of the letters (contrasting with the "moulder'd gibbet-mast," as if to indicate the vitality latent in the seemingly dead past)—all, by the very intensity they call forth, prepare the ground (literally even) for the vision that follows. At this point the poet confronts the letters directly and, as though instinctively gathering up the energies latent within the scene, begins a new "journey," upward, to a point from which he can view the three objects—the pool, the beacon, the girl—which form the center of the vision. Yet these objects, awesome as they seem to the poet, are presented on a naturalistic level—an "ordinary sight," as Wordsworth at first puts it—and are not drawn from any recognizable tradition of symbols. If one encountered such images in the work of a conscious symbolist such as Blake or Shelley one would feel impelled to seek out a symbolic meaning for each of them. But in the present context the three images seem less significant for the individual meanings which we can assign to them than for the total effect which they produce. Through the animating medium of the wind they are fused together into a single momentous vision, which in its bleakness and fierceness seems to suggest the precariousness of human endeavor in the face of larger forces (the girl balancing the pitcher on her head is still another of Wordsworth's figures of endurance, like Margaret in **"The Ruined Cottage"**). Beyond that, the wind, with all the brute power which it symbolizes, sets into motion a new, even more intense movement of thought. As though having gathered something of its power within himself, Wordsworth moves forward once more to the present time in order to contemplate the past vision in still fuller perspective. Once again, in the final lines quoted, the three objects reappear, but the tone with which they are listed is more formal, almost declamatory, as if to indicate the far greater intensity with which they are now charged in his mind.

Thus far the incident is complete as it was first written, probably in 1798. But Wordsworth added still a new perspective in time in 1804, during the later stages of the poem's composition:

> When, in a blessed season
> With those two dear Ones, to my heart so dear,
> When in the blessed time of early love,
> Long afterwards, I roam'd about
> In daily presence of this very scene,
> Upon the naked pool and dreary crags,
> And on the melancholy Beacon, fell
> The spirit of pleasure and youth's golden gleam;
> And think ye not with radiance more divine
> From these remembrances, and from the power
> They left behind? So feeling comes in aid
> Of feeling, and diversity of strength
> Attends us, if but once we have been strong.
> Oh! mystery of Man, from what a depth
> Proceed thy honours! I am lost, but see
> In simple childhood something of the base
> On which thy greatness stands, but this I feel,
> That from thyself it is that thou must give
> Else never canst receive. The days gone by
> Come back upon me from the dawn almost
> Of life: the hiding-places of my power
> Seem open; I approach, and then they close;
> I see by glimpses now; when age comes on,
> May scarcely see at all, and I would give,
> While yet we may, as far as words can give,
> A substance and a life to what I feel:
> I would enshrine the spirit of the past
> For future restoration.

(316-343)

In its final development the memory of this dreary scene is refracted through still another memory, this one benign with "the spirit of pleasure and youth's golden gleam." To put it another way, the memory of early love works to transform the "visionary dreariness" of the earlier memory into a more benign, though no less forceful power. If I may take up once more the metaphor with which I started, the energies latent in Wordsworth's memories are like rays of light that pass through a prism and reveal constantly new possibilities of color to the observing eye. But analogies will go only a short way to illuminate a process which remains so largely implicit in the text. Wordsworth himself describes the process with deliberate imprecision: "So feeling comes in aid / Of feeling. . . ." Thus, while reflecting in 1798 upon the meaning of his earliest memories, he cites a particular incident which occurred when he was six; reflection upon this incident, in turn, opens up a more distant and impersonal past, the time of the murderer's execution ("Times long past"); and this memory, in turn, recalls another, much later personal memory, from his eighteenth or nineteenth year. But if this process, on one level, consists of a simple, though non-chronological, line of mental associations, on another level it takes the form of a mysterious and complex transfer of power, both backward and forward, from one period of time to another: the memory of young love, though recalled by the frightening earlier childhood memory, sets this earlier memory into a new, more benign perspective and thus transforms it, while the combined effect of these memories will project into the future—a future well beyond the time of writing—to comfort the aging poet and, beyond that, through the "substance" and "life" with which they have been endowed in his poetry, to exert their effect upon readers in an even more distant future. And yet the whole process—down to the climactic statement, "Oh! mystery of Man, from what a depth / Proceed thy honours!"—seems to follow so naturally from the incident narrated offhandedly at the beginning that the reader is scarcely aware of the complexity of the thought structure into which he has been led.

In a discussion of another spot of time—the one directly following, of the poet waiting in the storm at Christmastime for the horses to fetch him home—A. C. Bradley long ago remarked [in his *Oxford Lectures on Poetry*, 1909], "Everything here is natural, but everything is apocalyptic. And we happen to know why. Wordsworth is describing the scene in the light of memory." The writer who sets out to recapture the past can thus do two things simultaneously: on the pretext of telling the reader something about himself he can uncover an objective, tangible world and at the same time he can cast a mythical aura about it. He can reveal it in all its concrete fullness and he can use it as a symbol of still another world behind it. He can be both realist and symbolist at once. (pp. 143-54)

What separates *The Prelude* at once from the poems of personal or pseudo-personal reminiscence of the late eighteenth century is the fact that the individual memories and the poet's discursive comments upon them are no longer scattered about, tied to one another only by association, but rather that Wordsworth has worked out a new rhetorical form, a new genre, in fact, to fuse together concrete perception and a statement of its significance, and beyond that to make poetry assert and celebrate at the same time that it describes and analyzes. Earl R. Wasserman, in his recent attempt to define the essential difference between eighteenth- and nineteenth-century poetry [*The Subtler Language,* 1959], described the task of the romantic poets in the following terms:

> Largely deprived of *topoi* rich in publicly accessible values and cut off from the older conceptions of world-orders, they [the poets of the early nineteenth century] were compelled to cultivate fresh values in the objects of experience and to organize these values into a special structure within the poem so as to avail themselves of the expressive powers of a revivified vocabulary and a new syntactical system. It is, therefore, not merely in the overt statements, often disarmingly simple, but especially in the inner subtleties of their language—in the recurrences and transformations of images, in what superficially might seem only a convenient and otherwise purposeless turn of phrase, for example—that we must seek the articulation of a modern poem's fullest meaning.

The spot of time, one might say, is that "special structure" which Wordsworth organized out of the objects of his personal experience—a structure, moreover, which articulates its meanings not primarily through traditional figures of speech appealing to an outward frame of reference, but by creating its own rhetoric—for instance, through the use of different intensities of tone at each of the three times the images of the pool, the beacon, and the girl with the pitcher appear—which in turn evolves its own inner frame of reference.

The poetic values represented by the spot of time, rooted as they are in concrete experience, have become so central a part of modern poetic tradition that, despite the obvious differences between the language of modern poetry and Wordsworth's "rhetoric of interaction," we often tend to read *The Prelude* piecemeal for its spots of time. "*The Prelude* is at the center of our experience of Wordsworth; at the center of our experience of *The Prelude* are those 'spots of time' where Wordsworth is endeavoring to express key moments in the history of his imagination"— thus begins a recent psychological interpretation of these passages [Jonathan Bishop, *English Literary History* XXVI (1959)]. To the extent that the spots of time attempt to fragmentize experience or to work toward the evocation of pure states of being—the "trances of thought and mountings of the mind" to which Wordsworth refers at the opening of the poem—they point forward to that conception of what was properly poetic which, in the century after *The Prelude,* was increasingly to claim exclusive domain over the province of poetry. If we have been inclined, perhaps, to lift the spots of time too readily out of their larger context, this is not merely a sign of their special modernity, but also . . . of the fact that we have lost the art of reading long poems. (pp. 155-56)

> Herbert Lindenberger, in his On Wordsworth's "Prelude," *Princeton University Press, 1963, 316 p.*

Brian Wilkie   (essay date 1965)

[*Wilkie is an American educator and critic. In the following excerpt, he discusses Wordsworth's reworking of epic tradition in* The Prelude, *focusing on his conception of the heroic ideal as self-fulfillment rather than self-sacrifice.*]

The best key to Wordsworth's epic creed is the passage from Book I of *The Prelude* (157-271) in which he draws up a poetic balance sheet and measures the demands of various heroic subjects against his literary powers. The many Miltonic allusions in this passage and the similarity between the problems it raises and those that Milton felt in his own search for a noble theme indicate beyond much doubt that Wordsworth was placing himself in the heroic tradition exemplified by his great mentor. What Wordsworth tells us here seems to furnish both an index to his own ideas on epic and his version of the history of epic. He begins with a general analysis of the personal endowments required of a poet with such lofty aims as his. They include "that first great gift . . . the vital soul," "general truths," "external things," including forms and images, and other aids of "less regard" but needful for the poet. (The priority of the mind and general truths to techniques, images, and other aids of "less regard" is important in Wordsworth's theory of poetry as a whole.) But all these are essentially prerequisites, even the "external" images stored in the mind and soul; the poet must objectify his inner endowments by finding "Time, place, and manners"—in short, a theme. His aim is to "summon back from lonesome banishment" some "little Band of yet remember'd names" and "make them inmates in the hearts of men / Now living, or to live in times to come." The subject, then, should be taken from the past, but not the utterly obscure past—a compromise perfectly consonant with much neoclassic theory. (Wordsworth seems most conscious of epic theory when, as here, he is still groping toward a theme.) A further implication is that the past must be linked with the present or the future in some meaningful way.

Wordsworth then lists a series of contemplated subjects for heroic treatment. The first is "some British theme, some old / Romantic tale, by Milton left unsung." Next he considers a pastoral-chivalric tale. Or, "more sternly mov'd," he would tell of Mithridates, who "became / That Odin, Father of a Race, by whom / Perish'd the Roman Empire," or of Sertorius' friends and followers, who settled in the Fortunate Isles and left there a tradition of liberty which fifteen hundred years later inspired a gallant struggle against the Europeans. Or he would tell how

> in tyrannic times some unknown Man,
> Unheard of in the Chronicles of Kings,
> Suffer'd in silence for the love of truth,

or narrate the avenging expedition of Dominique de Gourges to Florida in the sixteenth century, or Gustavus I's liberation of Sweden from Danish oppression, or Wallace's fight for Scotland and his bequeathal of his name and deeds as ghostly tokens of "independence and stern liberty" in his country.

Abandoning his list of martial themes, Wordsworth considers as another possibility "Some Tale from my own heart, more near akin / To my own passions and habitual thoughts," lofty but "with interchange of gentler things." The heroic subject, he admits, puts an unnatural strain on his powers. Lastly he mentions his favorite aspiration, a

> philosophic Song
> Of Truth that cherishes our daily life;
> With meditations passionate from deep
> Recesses in man's heart, immortal verse
> Thoughtfully fitted to the Orphean lyre.

But he draws back in fear and self-distrust before the "awful burthen" he envisages, and the passage ends with a thick cluster of Miltonic reminiscences, two of "Lycidas" and one of the sonnet "On His Blindness." Like the mourning shepherd shrinking from premature effort, Wordsworth takes refuge in the timorous hope "That mellower years will bring a riper mind / And clearer insight," and, again like the shepherd, he thinks longingly of the "vacant musing, unreprov'd neglect / Of all things, and deliberate holiday" which are the tempting alternative to stern ambition. The whole passage ends with the allusion to the "Blindness" sonnet when Wordsworth compares himself to "a false Steward who hath much received / And renders nothing back," though doubtless the Biblical influence was also direct.

Several important facts emerge from this passage. First, the epic impulse which Wordsworth feels is in part the same kind of generalized ambition to do something great that Milton expresses in much of his literary autobiography before *Paradise Lost*—in the *Vacation Exercise,* in "Elegy VI," in the *Apology for Smectymnuus,* in *The Reason of Church-Government.* Wordsworth chides himself for having

> no skill to part
> Vague longing that is bred by want of power
> From paramount impulse not to be withstood.
> (I. 240-42)

This generalized ambition is related to Wordsworth's great capacity, often illustrated in *The Prelude,* for expectations whose intensity depends in part on their vagueness; such were his expectations of Mount Blanc before its "soulless image" had "usurp'd upon a living thought / That never more could be" (VI.454-56). A more important implication of this vague longing for a great theme is the personal nature of the search. Wordsworth's problem is not merely to find an adequate theme, but, more important, to find the theme best for him. Epic, according to this view, exists first in the mind of the poet, as an undirected, potential force which must then be channeled into a particular theme, as electric power is stored in a battery before it is used to run a motor or heat an element. Yet the theme is by no means accidental, and herein Wordsworth's approach differs from Southey's, for the theme must be peculiarly right for the poet as an individual; it must be an appropriate fulfillment of his own aspirations. In any event, the search for a theme becomes an occasion for introspection and solemn self-analysis.

Secondly, Wordsworth's list of possible subjects is a catalogue of the various traditional epic subjects. He mentions the "romantic tale," the vehicle used by Spenser and

Tasso and ultimately rejected by Milton. In the Mithridates story he has a tale of empire suggestive of Virgil, though Wordsworth's story would tell of the destruction of an empire rather than its origin. Some of the themes (Gustavus, Wallace) are primarily national, as much neoclassic theory believed epic subjects should be, and possibly Wordsworth is considering Biblical material in his reference to "the Chronicles of Kings," though probably the phrase means something different. The stories of Mithridates and Sertorius are tales of wandering, like the *Odyssey* and the first half of the *Aeneid.* Even the "Tale from my own heart" and the "philosophic Song" are to be treated in a lofty way.

Thirdly, all the subjects have a spiritual significance and often they are "influential" in the light of later history, the apparent exceptions being the personal and philosophic subjects. (They are, in fact, only apparent exceptions.) Many of them have for their theme liberty, certainly a spiritual ideal for Wordsworth. Like his master Milton, Wordsworth rejects the purely martial idea of a hero. It is interesting that the only theme listed which in the early version is not moral by statement or implication is the chivalric tale, and this is expanded in later revision from the simple pastoral theme of the 1805 version to a conception of

> a song that winds
> Through ever changing scenes of votive quest
> Wrongs to redress, harmonious tribute paid
> To patient courage and unblemished truth,
> To firm devotion, zeal unquenchable,
> And Christian meekness hallowing faithful
>   loves.
> (I. 180-85)

Fourthly, there is a fairly definite progression in Wordsworth's list from subjects which most strictly confine themselves to things, manners, and other externals (like the romantic tale as briefly described in the 1805 version), through expressions of political idealism, to the most universal theme, the "philosophic Song / Of Truth." There is also a movement from those subjects most remote from modern man's experience through those, remote in time but morally or politically relevant, to those most directly bearing on contemporary life or of greatest personal significance to the poet himself. Unless the order in which the themes are mentioned is an accident, Wordsworth is implying a conception of epic as a growing rather than a static form.

Finally, the position of the pastoral theme at the head of Wordsworth's list is probably important. Renaissance convention held that the interest in pastoral poetry was an early stage in the development of the epic poet. Virgil had furnished the precedent; Spenser and Milton conformed to it. And in view of the echoes of "Lycidas" in the passage we are examining and Wordsworth's insistence later in the poem on the difference between his version of pastoral and the older, idyllic one, it is a reasonable inference that Wordsworth was recalling the pastoral-to-epic tradition. In fact, the place of pastoralism in *The Prelude* has great significance, for it symbolizes the general direction of the poet-hero's developing mind—from love of Nature to love of Man. Pastoralism is one example of Wordsworth's belief that his literary forms are not replicas of older models but rather developments of them. *The Prelude* is in part a modern pastoral, and Wordsworth, though he apparently discards the themes listed in Book I, actually uses nearly all the types there represented in his poem. There is a coloring of romance and the supernatural, description of a war for liberty, a philosophic song. A national theme is prominent—"national" in the sense which is applicable to [Robert Southey's] *Joan of Arc,* where England is not glorified but English ideals are closely scrutinized. And, of course, the autobiographical nature of the poem fulfills the promise of the "Tale from my own heart." But all these elements are finally subordinated to his main epic theme, the mind of man.

Like the great epic poets of the Renaissance, Wordsworth felt the need for a new heroic ideal. Milton, Tasso, and Camoëns had all exalted their heroes' exploits above those of antiquity. All three had made the heroic ideal Christian, and Milton in particular had pointed the way for Wordsworth by making the essential heroic attribute not deeds but a state of mind. The deepest hell is within Satan, and to Adam is revealed a "paradise within thee, happier farr." The triumphant Christ in *Paradise Regained* wins victory through the maintenance of inner integrity rather than through action.

Thus Wordsworth had ample precedent for making the heroic ideal an interior one. Yet he believed he was making a new departure, and he was right. For one thing, his method is basically different from Milton's and those of the other writers of literary epic. Wordsworth does not simply depict the heroic ideal in action; he is even more concerned with its genesis and growth in the individual hero, namely—and embarrassingly for Wordsworth—himself. The "action" of *The Prelude,* the story of Wordsworth's mental growth, is justified by the final product—the poet's mature mind. The action is purposeful and "influential," as the wanderings and struggles of Aeneas influence the growth of Rome and as the fall of Adam influences the whole later history of the world. (The analogy is not merely fanciful, nor on the other hand should it convict Wordsworth of being a megalomaniac, since his subject—the human mind—is indeed a grand one, and since Wordsworth's personal history is mainly an *exemplum* of the mind's development.) In Virgil and Milton heroism is a given quality, a means toward an end, the end being action or the adoption of a moral stance or both. But in Wordsworth heroism is the *product* of the influences and actions described in the poem. Aeneas's *pietas* helps to build the Roman Empire, and Adam, exemplifying heroism in a negative way, acts to bring "Death into the World, and all our woe." But in *The Prelude* the heroic ideal—mental equipoise, the harmony between man and his environment—is primarily an end and not a means, at least within the boundaries defined by the story of Wordsworth's early life. This last qualification is important; I shall argue presently that *The Prelude* too points toward action beyond the acquisition itself of Wordsworth's version of heroism, that the poem is not content to state an ideal of *being.* But that action is not part of the pattern of development traced in the *events* of the poem.

The emphasis on origins and development permeates much of *The Prelude,* and not merely in a narrow autobiographical sense. Wordsworth's attempt to define heroism is itself rooted in the epic poems and heroic ideal of the past. This way of thinking is probably best illustrated in Wordsworth's description of his native region as lovelier than all the beautiful paradises of fable (VIII. 119-58). As De Selincourt observes [in his introduction to *The Prelude,* 1926], the passage is based on Milton's description of Eden as surpassing all other delectable gardens. But Wordsworth's passage is not a mere echo. The allusion is to a passage in *Paradise Lost* which, like many other passages in that poem, vaunts the superiority of its subject matter over fables and traditionally heroic tales. The implication of Wordsworth's allusion, in connection with other such comparisons in *The Prelude,* is the still greater loftiness of his own theme; in other words, Wordsworth implies a kind of growth and progress in earlier epics toward his own subject, "the mind of man." Another example of this technique is the thorough discussion of the difference between the ancient pastoral life and the more vital pastoralism of the shepherds Wordsworth knew (see, for example, VIII. 182-428).

But it is not only in the function he assigns to heroism that Wordsworth differs from the traditional epic poets; the heroic ideal itself is new. Its concentration on the inner man has precedents, as we have seen, but the degree of emphasis is far greater than in previous epic writers. And there are still other innovations. Wordsworth's climactic statement of his great theme, the theme toward which Book I shows him as groping, suggests the main new elements in his heroic code:

> Of Genius, Power,
> Creation and Divinity itself
> I have been speaking, for my theme has been
> What pass'd within me. Not of outward things
> Done visibly for other minds, words, signs,
> Symbols or actions; but of my own heart
> Have I been speaking, and my youthful mind.
> O Heavens! how awful is the might of Souls,
> And what they do within themselves, while yet
> The yoke of earth is new to them, the world
> Nothing but a wide field where they were sown.
> This is, in truth, heroic argument,
> And genuine prowess . . .
> Points have we all of us within our souls,
> Where all stand single; this I feel, and make
> Breathings for incommunicable powers.
> Yet each man is a memory to himself,
> And, therefore, now that I must quit this theme,
> I am not heartless; for there's not a man
> That lives who hath not had his godlike hours,
> And knows not what majestic sway we have,
> As natural beings in the strength of nature.
>
> (III. 171-94)

There are three basic elements in the heroic ideal offered here: an emphasis on spiritual and psychological qualities ("my theme has been / What pass'd within me"), a form of egalitarianism ("there's not a man / That lives who hath not had his godlike hours"), and individualism ("Points have we all of us within our souls, / Where all stand single"). All these are fairly novel in the light of the traditional heroic pattern, especially as it exists in epic "orthodoxy"—the inner emphasis because of the enormous importance which Wordsworth gives it, the egalitarianism because it goes so far out of the way to deny that the hero is unique, the individualism because Wordsworth makes it a universal and markedly philosophical ideal.

The main emphasis in the quoted passage is on the spiritual and psychological nature of the theme. Despite the lengthy treatment of the French Revolution, the poem's values are antimartial (though, as in Southey, not strictly pacifist), and the older concept of a hero as a great warrior is nowhere in evidence, not even in Beaupuy, who is glorified mainly as a thinker. Wordsworth's antimilitarism leads him to confess with some sense of guilt that he once was led by French military victories to confound them with another victory "far higher and more difficult, / Triumphs of unambitious peace at home / And noiseless fortitude" (X. 591-93). Later he rejoices that the "wiser mood" has been re-established which sees "little worthy or sublime / In what we blazon with the pompous names / Of power and action" (XII. 45-49). His description of the pathetic separations and the domestic havoc wrought by war (IX. 273-79) is very much like Southey's in *Joan of Arc.* Southey too might, with slight modifications, have written what Wordsworth wrote in 1794: "I am a determined enemy to every species of violence. I see no connection, but what the obstinacy of pride and ignorance renders necessary, between justice and the sword, between reason and bonds." By 1802 Wordsworth had modified his views somewhat, but he still believed that "excessive admiration was paid in former times to personal prowess and military success; it is so with the latter even at the present day, but surely not nearly so much as heretofore." It is one of the more striking bits of evidence for the "lost leader" theory that in 1816 Wordsworth's views had been so transformed that he believed that "martial qualities are the natural efflorescence of a healthy state of society," and that he cites in support of this thesis the authority of Milton, among others. But it is equally significant that Wordsworth never deleted from *The Prelude* the passages I have just mentioned, for the poem always retained for him an integrity of pattern independent of his self-revelation. Even the brief temptation to join forces with the revolutionists is mainly a reaction to the French need for guidance and moral authority (X. 129-58). And, significantly, one of Dorothy's great restorative services is to "soften down" her brother's "over-sternness" (XIII. 226-27).

When in announcing his theme Wordsworth states that he rejects "outward things," "Symbols or actions," in favor of "What pass'd within me," he is not describing his poem with complete exactness, for *The Prelude* contains many pictures of the great world and of momentous events. But this passage was almost certainly written at a time when the whole poem was still intended to be only five books long and more limited in scope than it turned out to be. In the full poem Wordsworth takes pains to show the reality, indeed the practicality, of his theme. This insistence on the reality and truth of his subject is one of the things that places Wordsworth most directly in the tradition of literary epic. "What pass'd within me" is not the stuff of dreams; the "god-like hours" are part of our empire "As natural beings in the strength of nature." In his early days

of revolutionary zeal he had rejoiced that his efforts and the efforts of men like him would be exercised "Not in Utopia," but "in the very world which is the world / Of all of us" (X. 724-27), and on regaining his emotional health after his moral crisis he seeks "good in the familiar face of life," and not in "sanguine schemes" (XII. 65-67).

No statements could illustrate better than these the difference between Wordsworth's heroic standard and the standards expressed by Southey and Landor. All three poets define heroism idealistically, but Wordsworth's brand of idealism is at the more utilitarian end of the idealist's spectrum, whereas Southey and Landor preach a much simpler doctrine, bordering on escapism. The utopian ideal which helps to inform *Madoc* and the political quietism of *Gebir* are both foreign to Wordsworth's intentions in *The Prelude,* for in emphasizing psychology at the expense of martial heroism Wordsworth is not retreating from the field of human action except in what he would consider a superficial sense of the word *action,* despite his frequent praises of rural and domestic retirement. On the contrary, in exploring the mind of man he claims to be focusing on the area of human life where the most truly significant action occurs, the area which is most "substantial." It is Wordsworth's concern with the real applicability of his message which explains why *The Prelude,* if it had been published in 1805, might have been doctrinal to an age and nation in a way that was not possible for the contemporary epics of Southey and Landor. When Wordsworth, having reviewed his past life near the end of the poem, confirms his dedication to a newer, more truly heroic program, he ponders "How oft high service is perform'd within" (XII. 226). But, although one terminus of the events narrated in *The Prelude* is the poet's decision to write verse which will celebrate the inner nature of men in humble life, he declares that in this enterprise he will "Deal boldly with substantial things, in truth / And sanctity of passion" (XII. 234-35);

> it shall be my pride
> That I have dared to tread this holy ground,
> Speaking no dream but things oracular,
> Matter not lightly to be heard by those
> Who to the letter of the outward promise
> Do read the invisible soul.
>
> (XII. 250-55)

Wordsworth does not preach subjectivism; he simply believes that mental experience is entirely real and, furthermore, that the greatest practical problem of his own age is not material or institutional, but spiritual. One can readily surmise the effect this creed must have had on one of Wordsworth's disciples, the author of *Culture and Anarchy.*

Far from being neglected, external narrative has a special importance in Wordsworth's poem. It is through the action of the poem that ideas and ideals are made concrete—the ideal of true liberty, for example, through the poet's experiences with the French Revolution. Furthermore, as in Virgil, the action traces the origin, growth, and cause of the resultant—which, in *The Prelude,* is a man's mature mind. But Wordsworth's special emphasis on psychology needs external narrative not only as symbolic explanation (as in the Snowdon episode) but also as factual example.

In the Wordsworthian hero, as typified by the author himself, the inner and outer worlds are in equipoise and thus interact with each other. Hence external contingencies and action in the world are important as specific proof of the part played by the experience of external things in shaping the imagination and thought of the developing man.

The other chief ingredients in Wordsworth's heroic ideal, democratic egalitarianism and individualism, are closely dependent on each other. It had been at least half-assumed by most earlier epic poets that the hero was a great leader enjoying special gifts of Nature and Fortune. He relied on himself in all that was within human power and is distinctly contrasted with his less gifted fellows. Though Wordsworth sometimes speaks in such terms, it is in a different context, which I shall examine later; in general, Wordsworth's individualism has a more philosophic cast than in older versions of heroism. And since it is democratic, it applies to all men ("Points have we all of us within our souls, / Where all stand single"). We "stand single"—the individual is unique. But this is true of "all of us," and therefore individualism is formulated as a universal, democratic ideal.

This democratic note pervades *The Prelude;* Wordsworth denies, for example, that love requires "Retirement, leisure, language purified / By manners thoughtful and elaborate" (XII. 189-90). Yet he cannot deny the differences between men or the rarity of individuals who satisfy his heroic ideal, and the problem troubles him. The dignity of individual man—"no composition of the thought," but "the man whom we behold / With our own eyes"—is a fact of experience, but

> Why is this glorious Creature to be found
> One only in ten thousand? What one is,
> Why may not many be?
>
> (XII. 83-92)

Wordsworth's heroic ideal postulates, not a great individual hero, but a great race of individualists. The message of serious literary epic is usually a collective one in some sense, and Wordsworth's justification in turning his personal memoirs into heroic argument is his belief that, as Shelley was to put it, we have one human heart.

To be epic a poem needs more than an appropriately great subject; it must have an epic pattern as well. Although the theme of *The Excursion*—Despondency and Its Correction—has negative overtones, it is not really very different from the theme of mental discipline celebrated in *The Prelude.* But the method of *The Excursion* is discursive rather than narrative and therefore the poem could never be considered epic unless the term were unreasonably broadened, narrative method being one of the few things which epic theorists have agreed to demand of epic. *The Prelude,* however, has a standard form of epic development, a unity that is more than conceptual. The progress of the hero is essentially a mental progress, for the theme is not empire or Christian action but the mind of man. But, as much as Aeneas or Godfrey or da Gama, Wordsworth's representative hero has a mission, a vocation. The mission is a lofty one, and its way is mined with perils and surrounded by tempting and fallacious mental bypaths. Wordsworth's

progress toward the goal set for him is a task requiring heroic powers. *The Prelude* has other patterns, of course, but this standard pattern of literary epic, that of progress toward a goal, is the dominant one in the poem. Without it *The Prelude* would seriously lack unity; through it the poem becomes structurally intelligible.

Most students of Wordsworth will recognize that I am indebted to Abbie Potts for her remarks [in *Wordsworth's "Prelude": A Study of Its Literary Form,* 1953] on the epic and ordeal patterns in *The Prelude,* as well as for smaller points which have been useful to me even when I have not agreed with them. I should make it clear, however, as much in fairness to her as to myself, that in connecting the epic and ordeal patterns as closely as I do and especially in treating the ordeal as the predominant structural metaphor of the poem I am making claims which are narrower than and at the same time perhaps more far-reaching than hers.

In a way, I believe, Miss Potts's study suffers from its greatest virtue: its almost awesome comprehensiveness. She traces so many patterns in *The Prelude* that one begins to see the poem as a kind of random diary and workbook. But, though all or nearly all these patterns are present, some are more important than others. Of all the patterns, it seems to me, the governing one is that of epic mission and ordeal; indeed, one of the most impressive things about *The Prelude* is the way in which the epic-ordeal reduces these heterogeneous emphases to a satisfying artistic unity. Granted, the subordination is not perfect (though it is much more nearly so than most readers have recognized). Book VII, for example, "Residence in London," remains something of an anomaly. In the narrative structure its function is to show Wordsworth's introduction to the real world of man, as distinguished from the real but egocentric world of childhood and the human but mostly artificial world of Cambridge. We learn that the poet, during his first residence in the great city, was not yet ready for the genuine experience of love for humanity. But for the most part Book VII concerns the city itself rather than the author's experiences in it, and thus the place of the London section in the whole poem seems only vaguely articulated. The length of the description is entirely out of proportion to the importance of the poet's London experience, at least as that is revealed in *The Prelude.* Yet the patterns of mission, ordeal, and progress do account for almost every important incident in the poem and the order in which they are recounted. Without these interrelated patterns *The Prelude* would have virtually no structure, for even the autobiographical unity is defective, as has long been recognized.

Wordsworth's mission is that of poet, and a poet's function is, in the broadest sense, to "teach, / Inspire, through unadulterated ears / Pour rapture, tenderness, and hope" (XII. 237-39). He and his friend Coleridge are to be, Providence willing, "joint-labourers" in the work of man's "redemption," "Prophets of Nature" (XIII. 439-42). But just as (on the level of the poem's composition) Wordsworth's true epic theme becomes manifest only after experience and a gradual revelation, so (on the level of the poem's action) with the nature of his service. The moment when

Wordsworth becomes fully conscious of where his duty toward the world lies is preceded by a vague sense of dedication to a great but still undefined duty. At Cambridge, he tells us in messianic language, he had been disturbed by a strange sense that "I was not for that hour, / Nor for that place." But he was a "chosen Son . . . with holy powers / And faculties" both to apprehend the workings of the visible world and to change it, a man who "to majestic ends was strong" (III. 80-90). As Milton had "in the privat academies of *Italy*" felt confident for the first time that he "might perhaps leave something so written to aftertimes, as they should not willingly let it die" (a passage that Wordsworth liked to quote), so it was at Cambridge, likewise an academic setting, that Wordsworth was first encouraged to trust "that I might leave / Some monument behind me which pure hearts / Should reverence" (VI. 67-69). Describing elsewhere his life at Cambridge, the poet distinguishes characteristically between his own responsibilities and those of good but less inspired men; there for a time he forgot "the pledges interchanged / With our own inner being" and associated with a "shoal / Of more unthinking Natures; easy Minds / And pillowy" (III. 518-23). The climactic though unconscious moment of poetic dedication is one when

> I made no vows, but vows
> Were then made for me; bond unknown to me
> Was given, that I should be, else sinning greatly,
> A dedicated spirit.
>
> (IV. 341-44)

This is messianic language; it is also language applicable to the charismatic epic hero.

During the period of vague dedication Wordsworth (regarded as the hero of his poem rather than as its author) considers several vocations. The Arab of his symbolic dream in Book V, trying to preserve science and art from threatened oblivion, has often tempted the poet to forsake domestic ties and to "go / Upon like errand" (V. 160-61). In France he almost devotes his life to the Revolutionary cause, but he returns to England, as he tells us in an early addition to the original text, "Forc'd by the gracious Providence of Heaven." Had he become a partisan in France he might have perished, "A poor mistaken and bewilder'd offering," all his resolutions and hopes wasted, "A Poet only to myself, to Men / Useless" (X. 190-201). The pattern by which the hero must be guided into his true path of achievement—here, significantly, achievement useful to men—is part of the pattern of the traditional literary epic. Aeneas, Adam, Tasso's Rinaldo—all have to be made aware of their vocations through supernatural visions of the future and of their own relationship to it. In the last book of the poem Wordsworth too is to solemnize such a moment of climactic insight, of confirmation in an almost sacramental sense; throughout the poem, though, he has his autobiographical hero grope toward illumination tentatively and with dim recognitions.

The agencies by which the young Wordsworth is guided, half-consciously, toward his true mission in life constitute the epic "machinery" of the poem. But this basic term needs explanation, especially as it applies to *The Prelude*. Sometimes the word refers simply to fanciful departures from naturalism. In this sense Southey uses "machinery" in Book IX of the original version of *Joan,* where he introduces personifications of Despair, Superstition, Credulity, and similar qualities having allegorical but little narrative importance. More usually epic machinery describes a real interplay between two motivating impulses: the hero's own will and the outside forces, usually spiritual, which partly control him.

Wordsworth uses machinery in this more meaningful sense. The agencies of his machinery are, first of all, Nature, and, in a lesser degree, Books. It goes without saying that their function as machinery is mainly metaphorical. The poet's description of Books as machinery is entirely so, as to a large extent is his description of Nature, though here we encounter one of the oldest and knottiest problems in reading Wordsworth. Except in a few passages, Nature is not described as acting on the poet primarily as the instrument of a personal God. Nor, of course, did Wordsworth believe literally that Nature had a conscious plan for him; that is, he was not a pagan. But he was intensely aware of forces which guided his life independently of his conscious will. The reader may prefer to explain these forces as subconscious ones rather than as impulses from a vernal wood, but we cannot legitimately ascribe that simply naturalistic view to Wordsworth himself. We cannot strip Wordsworth's metaphor of Nature as machinery too bare unless we are willing to oversimplify his message. Like the Platonic myth in the **"Immortality Ode"** the symbolism of machinery in *The Prelude* cannot be taken literally. But, in a way that cannot be very clearly defined, Wordsworth felt it to be real.

The most striking thing about Wordsworth's relationship to Nature is its personal quality on both sides. Not only does the poet love Nature; Nature herself is pictured as having conscious intentions. She exerts an active, deliberate force on the growing poet, leading him in her own paths. This personification of Nature is partly a literary device, but what is any epic machinery but a literary device, used to emphasize man's involvement with a higher order of reality and to dramatize the limitations of his human power? One reason why *The Prelude* is such a great poem is that the idea of nature's influence, which in some of Wordsworth's lesser poems can appear banal and naïve, is here reinforced and dignified by its association with a metaphor that is not simply Wordsworth's own: the epic metaphor which shows the supernatural powers manipulating human beings in the service of a divine cause.

The metaphor which endows Nature and Books with conscious purpose is thoroughly consistent and explicit in *The Prelude.* Nature operates with a "dark / Invisible workmanship," uses "means" to an "end":

> Nature, oftentimes, when she would frame
> A favor'd Being, from his earliest dawn
> Of infancy doth open out the clouds,
> As at the touch of lightning, seeking him
> With gentlest visitation;

or she can use "Severer interventions, ministry / More palpable" (I. 351-71). The incidents of the theft of birds from a neighbor's trap and of the borrowed boat illustrate the same metaphor. After the birds were stolen the young boy hears "Low breathings coming after me, . . . steps / Almost as silent as the turf they trod" (I. 330-32). After taking the boat, he sees the menacing cliff appear "As if with voluntary power instinct," and it strides after him "like a living thing" (I. 407-12). Here Wordsworth tells us directly that he is using a metaphor and thus emphasizes the deliberateness of his choice to portray Nature as a conscious guide. But normally he uses the figure more unselfconsciously, a fact that indicates how pervasively the metaphor governed and reflected his view of his life. Fleeting illustrations in the texture of the poem are almost innumerable. "Was it for this," he asks, "That one, the fairest of all Rivers, lov'd / To blend his murmurs with my Nurse's song . . . ?" (I. 271-73); "not in vain" did the Spirit of the universe "intertwine for me / The passions that build up our human Soul" (I. 428-34). The influence of Nature helps the poet to weather "this time / Of dereliction and dismay" without losing his confidence in humanity;

> the gift is yours,
> Ye mountains! thine, O Nature! Thou hast fed
> My lofty speculations.
>
> (II. 456-63)

Life in London turns his thoughts more and more toward concern for his fellow man, but Nature is still at work: "Nature had led me on," he insists, though he often seemed "To travel independent of her help" (VIII. 864-65).

To regard Books as part of the epic machinery may seem whimsical, but although their shaping effect on Wordsworth's mind does not equal Nature's the two influences are of the same order. His mission, gradually revealed through the experience the poem relates, is a literary one, and therefore it is not surprising that literature should be an agent parallel to, if less powerful than, Nature. Only by recognizing this parallelism can one fully understand Wordsworth's hope that a work of his may "become / A power like one of Nature's" (XII. 311-12). Like Nature, Books are personified as a conscious agent, and the poet repeatedly links the two forces in a way which shows the pairing to be more than casual. He marvels at the mighty "power / Of living Nature" which could for a time keep him from books, "the best of other thoughts," so that he asks how he could even in infancy have played "an ingrate's part" (V. 166-72). (The 1850 version further points up the metaphor and the pairing with Nature by calling Books "the best of other guides / And dearest helpers"—V. 168-69). Books are "Powers / For ever to be hallowed; only less, / For what we may become . . . Than Nature's self . . . " (V. 219-22). Books of romance represent a "gracious Spirit" presiding over the earth and the human heart, one that comes "invisibly," "directing those to works of love / Who care not, know not, think not what they do"; they are "Friends" who in our childhood reconcile us to the limitations of our new human life (V. 516-47). Among the conditions of his life which led the poet to sympathize with the ideals of human equality and liberty were his lifelong tutelage to "God and Nature's single sovereignty . . . And fellowship with venerable books" (IX. 237-39). And near the end of the poem, in describing his plan to write of men in humble stations, he defines his theme as "the very heart of man" as found among those who are not "uninformed by books, good books though few, / In Nature's presence" (XII. 240-44).

Since Wordsworth's theme is (in the broadest sense) psychological, his emphasis on the debt he owes to powers outside himself—to the "machinery" of Nature and Books—is valuable in giving something of epic objectivity to what might have been the most fanciful and subjective of themes. But to stress external influence so heavily is to court another danger, that of depicting a heroic ideal which is entirely passive and therefore, of course, not heroic at all. From this danger Wordsworth saves himself by his familiar and basic belief in the reciprocating power of Imagination. The mind does not only perceive; it forms and creates. The poet seems to be distinctly aware that his emphasis on machinery, related though it is to the heroic tradition, poses a threat to the heroic pattern he is tracing in the poem, for several times he caps a passage describing his responsiveness to natural scenes with an emphatic assertion that man's greatness ultimately comes from himself, that the mind itself has an "auxiliar light" and a "plastic power" (XI. 332-34; II. 377-95), the text in both these instances emphasizing the reversal with a monitory *but*. The climactic statement of the necessity for self-reliance comes in the final book, where after naming once more the faculty of Imagination as his theme and identifying it with "intellectual Love," Wordsworth declaims in the repetitive style of the orator:

> Here must thou be, O Man!
> Strength to thyself; no Helper hast thou here;
> Here keepest thou thy individual state:
> No other can divide with thee this work,
> No secondary hand can intervene
> To fashion this ability; 'tis thine,
> The prime and vital principle is thine
> In the recesses of thy nature, far
> From any reach of outward fellowship,
> Else 'tis not thine at all.
>
> (XIII. 186-97)

Here the words "Helper" and "fellowship" do more than describe a division of powers between self and environment; they draw on the epic metaphor which sees this interplay of forces as dynamic and personal on both sides.

Thus Wordsworth's hero-self, like the hero of traditional literary epic, engages in a dialogue of action with the powers that rule his world, sometimes being impelled by his own will, sometimes by influence from above or without. But there is no question of being suspended between two conflicting forces. Wordsworth is no naturalist in the sense of the word that describes writers like Zola; in Wordsworth's universe harmony between self and environment is a realizable aspiration. His dialogue with Nature might more justly be called a dialectic; the effect of the interplay between inner and outer worlds is not hopeless conflict but synthesis. The ideal of harmonious resolution is precisely expressed in the imagery of the passage wherein Wordsworth, summing up his Alpine tour, interrupts a description of the external scene in order to extol the importance of the observer and the role played by his imagination. Here the mind is no "mean pensioner / On outward forms"; what the poet perceived with his senses "was but a stream / That flow'd into a kindred stream, a gale / That help'd me forwards," directly toward a responsiveness to grandeur, more circuitously toward "tender thoughts" (VI. 667-80). The harmonious imagery of merging streams and assisting wind is significant; Wordsworth is to re-evoke it later in the poem to illustrate the greatest threat to his imaginative progress. Incidentally, the 1850 version adds to the statement of circuitous progress the words "but not less sure / Duly to reach the point marked out by Heaven" (VI.752-53). It is easy to interpret this elaboration as symptomatic of Wordsworth's much-discussed (and, I think, much-exaggerated) tendency to bring the poem in line with Christian orthodoxy. But "to reach the point marked out by Heaven" is exactly the destined role of every hero in literary epic; Wordsworth may have been refining his epic metaphor rather than his doctrine.

The ideal of balanced harmony is stated more explicitly later in the poem, where Wordsworth describes his having come to the conviction that "outward circumstance and visible form" are subject to inner passion while meanwhile

> the forms
> Of Nature have a passion in themselves
> That intermingles with those works of man
> To which she summons him,

and that therefore the poet may go boldly among mankind "Wherever Nature leads" (XII. 287-96). Nature issues the call; the poet himself must respond with the resources of his own nature. In this harmonious dualism we have something very like the great theological dualism of grace and merit. Wordsworth seems to have thought occasionally in such terms, even in 1805, as when he ascribes such traits as his liking for geometry to "grace of Heaven and inborn tenderness" (VI. 189).

In following the pattern of literary epic which sees progress through life as mysteriously purposeful, even in its apparently trivial events, Wordsworth turns to advantage one of his most characteristic traits: optimism. In **"Tintern Abbey,"** the **"Immortality Ode," "Elegiac Stanzas,"** the **"Ode to Duty,"** and other poems Wordsworth shows his tendency to extract profit from all situations and experiences, even those involving painful loss. This is one reason why he is considered a poet of joy, yet at times the habit is irritating, since it seems to cut him off from any real appreciation of the tragic view of life. In *The Prelude,* however, with its epic pattern of purposefulness, the optimistic sense of a great guiding force and consequent belief that all is "gratulant if rightly understood" (XIII. 385) are not only sanctioned but demanded by the traditional pattern. (pp. 65-86)

> *Brian Wilkie, "Wordsworth: The Way of the Hero," in his* Romantic Poets and Epic Tradition, *The University of Wisconsin Press, 1965, pp. 59-111.*

M. H. Abrams   (essay date 1971)

[Abrams is an American educator and critic best known for his writings on English Romanticism. In the following excerpt, he analyzes the narrative structure of The Prelude, *praising Wordsworth's retrospective reordering of events.]*

In this era of constant and drastic experimentation with literary materials and forms, it is easy to overlook the radical novelty of *The Prelude* when it was completed in 1805. The poem amply justified Wordsworth's claim to have demonstrated original genius, which he defined as "the introduction of a new element into the intellectual universe" of which the "infallible sign is the widening the sphere of human sensibility."

The Prelude is a fully developed poetic equivalent of two portentous innovations in prose fiction, of which the earliest examples had appeared in Germany only a decade or so before Wordsworth began writing his poem: the *Bildungsroman* (Wordsworth called *The Prelude* a poem on "the growth of my own mind") and the *Künstlerroman* (Wordsworth also spoke of it as "a poem on my own poetical education," and it far surpassed all German examples in the detail with which his "history," as he said, was specifically "of a *Poet's* mind"). The whole poem is written as a sustained address to Coleridge—"I speak bare truth / As if alone to thee in private talk" (X, 372-3); Coleridge, however, is an auditor *in absentia,* and the solitary author often supplements this form with an interior monologue, or else carries on an extended colloquy with the landscape in which the interlocutors are "my mind" and "the speaking face of earth and heaven" (V, 11-12). The construction of *The Prelude* is radically achronological, starting not at the beginning, but at the end—during Wordsworth's walk to "the Vale that I had chosen" (I, 100), which telescopes the circumstances of two or more occasions but refers primarily to his walk to the Vale of Grasmere, that "hermitage" (I, 115) where he has taken up residence at that stage of his life with which the poem concludes. During this walk an outer breeze, "the sweet breath of Heaven," evokes within the poet "a corresponding mild creative breeze," a prophetic *spiritus* or inspiration which assures him of his poetic mission and, though it is fitful, eventually leads to his undertaking *The Prelude* itself; in the course of the poem, at times of imaginative dryness, the revivifying wind recurs in the role of a poetic leitmotif.

Wordsworth does not tell his life as a simple narrative in past time but as the present remembrance of things past, in which forms and sensations "throw back our life" (I, 660-1) and evoke the former self which coexists with the altered present self in a multiple awareness that Wordsworth calls "two consciousnesses." There is a wide "vacancy" between the I now and the I then,

> Which yet have such self-presence in my mind
> That, sometimes, when I think of them, I seem
> Two consciousnesses, conscious of myself
> And of some other Being.
>
>   (II, 27-33)

The poet is aware of the near impossibility of disengaging "the naked recollection of that time" from the intrusions of "after-meditation" (III, 644-8). In a fine and subtle figure for the interdiffusion of the two consciousnesses, he describes himself as one bending from a drifting boat on a still water, perplexed to distinguish actual objects at the bottom of the lake from surface reflections of the environing scene, from the tricks and refractions of the water currents, and from his own intrusive but inescapable image (that is, his present awareness). Thus "incumbent o'er the surface of past time" the poet, seeking the elements of continuity between his two disparate selves, conducts a persistent exploration of the nature and significance of memory, of his power to sustain freshness of sensation and his "first creative sensibility" against the deadening effect of habit and analysis, and of manifestations of the enduring and the eternal within the realm of change and time. Only intermittently does the narrative order coincide with the order of actual occurrence. Instead Wordsworth proceeds by sometimes bewildering ellipses, fusions, and as he says, "motions retrograde" in time (IX, 8).

Scholars have long been aware that it is perilous to rely on the factual validity of *The Prelude,* and in consequence Wordsworth has been charged with intellectual uncertainty, artistic ineptitude, bad memory, or even bad faith. The poem has suffered because we know so much about the process of its composition between 1798 and 1805—its evolution from a constituent part to a "tail-piece" to a "portico" of *The Recluse,* and Wordsworth's late decision to add to the beginning and end of the poem the excluded middle: his experiences in London and in France. A work is to be judged, however, as a finished and free-standing product; and in *The Prelude* as it emerged after six years of working and reworking, the major alterations and dislocations of the events of Wordsworth's life are imposed deliberately, in order that the design inherent in that life, which has become apparent only to his mature awareness, may stand revealed as a principle which was invisibly operative from the beginning. A supervising idea, in other words, controls Wordsworth's account and shapes it into a structure in which the protagonist is put forward as one who has been elected to play a special role in a providential plot. As Wordsworth said in the opening passage, which represents him after he has reached maturity: in response to the quickening outer breeze

> to the open fields I told
> A prophecy: poetic numbers came
> Spontaneously, and cloth'd in priestly robe
> My spirit, thus singled out, as it might seem,
> For holy services.
>
> (I, 59-63)

Hence in this history of a poet's mind the poet is indeed the "transitory Being," William Wordsworth, but he is also the exemplary poet-prophet who has been singled out, in a time "of hopes o'erthrown . . . of dereliction and dismay," to bring mankind tidings of comfort and joy; as Wordsworth put it in one version of the Prospectus,

> that my verse may live and be
> Even as a light hung up in heaven to chear
> Mankind in times to come.

The spaciousness of his chosen form allows Wordsworth to introduce some of the clutter and contingency of ordinary experience. In accordance with his controlling idea, however, he selects for extended treatment only those of his actions and experiences which are significant for his evolution toward an inherent end, and organizes his life around an event which he regards as the spiritual crisis not of himself only, but of his generation: that shattering of the fierce loyalties and inordinate hopes for mankind which the liberal English—and European—intellectuals had invested in the French Revolution.

> Not in my single self alone I found,
> But in the minds of all ingenuous Youth,
> Change and subversion from this hour.
>
> (X, 232-4)

The Prelude, correspondingly, is ordered in three stages. There is a process of mental development which, although at times suspended, remains a continuum; this process is violently broken by a crisis of apathy and despair; but the mind then recovers an integrity which, despite admitted losses, is represented as a level higher than the initial unity, in that the mature mind possesses powers, together with an added range, depth, and sensitivity of awareness, which are the products of the critical experiences it has undergone. The discovery of this fact resolves a central problem which has been implicit throughout *The Prelude*—the problem of how to justify the human experience of pain and loss and suffering; he is now able to recognize that his life is "in the end/ All gratulant if rightly understood" (XIII, 384-5).

The narrative is punctuated with recurrent illuminations, or "spots of time," and is climaxed by two major revelations. The first of these is Wordsworth's discovery of precisely what he has been born to be and to do. At Cambridge he had reached a stage of life, "an eminence," in which he had felt that he was "a chosen Son" (III, 82 ff., 169), and on a walk home from a dance during a summer dawn he had experienced an illumination that he should be, "else sinning greatly,/ A dedicated Spirit" (IV, 343-4); but for what chosen, or to what dedicated, had not been specified. Now, however, the recovery from the crisis of despair after his commitment to the French Revolution comprises the insight that his destiny is not one of engagement with what is blazoned "with the pompous names/ Of power and action" in "the stir/ And tumult of the world," but one of withdrawal from the world of action so that he may meditate in solitude: his role in life requires not involvement, but detachment. And that role is to be one of the "Poets, even as Prophets," each of whom is endowed with the power "to perceive/ Something unseen before," and so to write a new kind of poetry in a new poetic style. "Of these, said I, shall be my Song; of these . . . / Will I record the praises": the ordinary world of lowly, suffering men and of commonplace or trivial things transformed into "a new world . . . fit/ To be transmitted," of dignity, love, and heroic grandeur (XII, 220-379). Wordsworth's crisis, then, involved what we now call a crisis of identity, which was resolved in the discovery of "my office upon earth" (X, 921). And since the specification of this office entails the definition, in the twelfth book, of the particular innovations in poetic subjects, style, and values toward which his life had been implicitly oriented, *The Prelude* is a poem which incorporates the discovery of its own *ars poetica.*

His second revelation he achieves on a mountain top. The occasion is the ascent of Mount Snowdon, which Wordsworth, in accordance with his controlling idea, excerpts from its chronological position in his life in 1791, before the crucial experience of France, and describes in the concluding book of *The Prelude.* As he breaks through the cover of clouds the light of the moon "upon the turf/ Fell like a flash," and he sees the total scene as "the perfect image of a mighty Mind" in its free and continuously creative reciprocation with its milieu, "Willing to work and to be wrought upon" and so to "create/ A like existence" (XIII, 36-119). What has been revealed to Wordsworth in this symbolic landscape is the grand locus of *The Recluse* which he announced in the Prospectus, "The Mind of Man—/ My haunt, and the main region of my song," as well as the "high argument" of that poem, the union between the mind and the external world and the resulting "creation . . . which they with blended might/ Accomplish." The event which Wordsworth selects for the climactic revelation in *The Prelude,* then, is precisely the moment of the achievement of "this Vision" by "the transitory Being" whose life he had, in the Prospectus, undertaken to describe as an integral part of *The Recluse.*

In the course of *The Prelude* Wordsworth repeatedly drops the clue that his work has been designed to round back to its point of departure. "Not with these began/ Our Song, and not with these our Song must end," he had cried after the crisis of France, invoking the "breezes and soft airs" that had blown in the "glad preamble" to his poem (XI, 1 ff. and VII, 1 ff.). As he nears the end of the song, he says that his self-discovery constitutes a religious conclusion ("The rapture of the Hallelujah sent/ From all that breathes and is") which is at the same time, as he had planned from the outset, an artistic beginning:

> And now, O Friend; this history is brought
> To its appointed close: the discipline
> And consummation of the Poet's mind.

>   . . . we have reach'd
> The time (which was our object from the first)
> When we may, not presumptuously, I hope,
> Suppose my powers so far confirmed, and such
> My knowledge, as to make me capable
> Of building up a work that should endure.
>   (XIII, 261-78)

That work, of course, is *The Recluse,* for which *The Prelude* was designed to serve as "portico . . . part of the same building." *The Prelude,* then, is an involuted poem which is about its own genesis—a prelude to itself. Its structural end is its own beginning; and its temporal beginning, as I have pointed out, is Wordsworth's entrance upon the stage of his life at which it ends. The conclusion goes on to specify the circular shape of the whole. Wordsworth there asks Coleridge to "Call back to mind/ The mood in which this Poem was begun." At that time,

>   I rose
> As if on wings, and saw beneath me stretch'd
> Vast prospect of the world which I had been
> And was; and hence this Song, which like a lark
> I have protracted. . . .
>   (XIII, 370-81)

This song, describing the prospect of his life which had been made visible to him at the opening of *The Prelude,*

is *The Prelude* whose composition he is even now concluding. (pp. 74-80)

M. H. Abrams, "Wordsworth's 'Prelude' and the Crisis-Autobiography," in his Natural Supernaturalism: Tradition and Revolution in Romantic Literature, *1971. Reprint by W. W. Norton & Company, 1973, pp. 71-140.*

Jim Springer Borck   (essay date 1973)

[*In the following essay, Borck suggests that Wordsworth's revisions of the 1805 Prelude reflect his awareness of the instability of language and the difficulties inherent in recounting childhood experiences.*]

Attempting to define further what he means by the pejorative term "Poetic Diction," Wordsworth in the 1802 Appendix to his **"Preface to the *Lyrical Ballads*"** falls back upon an eighteenth century critical commonplace. The theory is bluntly and openly stated: the poetry of his present age is staggering under a burden of artificially imposed rhetorical niceties. The poetry of an unsophisticated society was not so burdened. "The first Poets," Wordsworth says, spoke a natural, unaffected language designed to be immediately understood:

> This circumstance, however, was disregarded by their successors; they found that they could please by easier means: they became proud of modes of expression which they had themselves invented, and which were uttered only by themselves. In process of time metre became a symbol of promise of this unusual language, and whoever took upon him to write in metre, according as he possessed more or less of true poetic genius, introduced less or more of this adulterated phraseology into his compositions, and the true and the false were inseparably interwoven until, the taste of men becoming gradually perverted, this language was received as natural language: and at length, by the influence of books upon men, did to a certain degree really become so. Abuses of this kind were imported from one nation to another, and with the progress of refinement this diction became daily more and more corrupt, thrusting out of sight the plain humanities of nature by a motley masquerade of tricks, quaintnesses, hieroglyphics, and enigmas.

Wordsworth uses this notion of interference to explain away the numerous objections to the tautologies, repetitions, and overly simple language critics find in his poetry. But further, underlying any statement about the past art of poetry is his unwavering belief that the present capacities of the art are inadequate: "now every man must know that an attempt is rarely made to communicate impassioned feelings without something of an accompanying consciousness of the inadequateness of our own power, of the deficiencies of language."

This sense of physical and mental grappling causes him to conclude at the end of his *Essay on Epitaphs* that language is an exceptionally unstable medium of communication. Moreover, language's transformations reflect more than instability; in process of human time they exemplify denudation and destruction: "Language, if it do not uphold, and feed, and leave in quiet, like the power of gravitation or the air we breathe, is a counter-spirit, unremittingly and noiselessly at work, to subvert to lay waste, to vitiate, and to dissolve." Language's ability to be a "counter-spirit," then, causes problems in Wordsworth's own conception of how the words, syntax, and symbols in his poetry work. Though this notion of progressive imprecision can perhaps be used to discuss various aspects of Wordsworth's poetic usage—like the relative conventionality of Wordsworth's later career—a more immediate and a more correct understanding of this theory is to be seen in Wordsworth's confessions of his loss of linguistic ability in the 1805 and the 1850 *Prelude,* for in these poems he specifically investigates the inadequacy of his poetic power and the deficiencies of his language. Further, the differences between the 1805 and the 1850 *Prelude* indicate Wordsworth is conscious that language does in fact unremittingly "dissolve" in time that original and inarticulate union the poet senses during the moment of creative power. Therefore, the problems caused by language's instability eventually force Wordsworth to write his poetry with definitions of language that indicate transformation and loss, symbols which cannot by their nature be explicit, and a syntax that is heavily conditional.

In Book Eleven of the 1805 *Prelude,* Wordsworth reflects that

> There are in our existence spots of time,
> Which with distinct pre-eminence retain
> A vivifying Virtue, whence, depressed
> By false opinion and contentious thought,
> Or aught of heavier or more deadly weight,
> In trivial occupations, and the round
> Of ordinary intercourse, our minds
> Are nourished and invisibly repair'd.

These spots of time lurk in periods of "degradation," when we are depressed and "fallen." Despite the hope expressed in these lines for nourishment and repair, the passage which follows is one that heavily qualifies and ultimately limits the promissory forms of "vivifying Virtue"; his example of a spot of time begins with the gibbet-mast scene (279-304). Wordsworth remembers a time from his childhood when he stumbled "Faltering, and ignorant" over broken ground to encounter a murderer's name engraved near the mouldered remains of a gallows. Through mischance, fear, and physical location, Wordsworth has been depressed; he is mentally and physically prepared for the spot of time; he is lost, having been separated from his companion, and in his fear he has dismounted from his horse and crept down to a "bottom."

In the bottom Wordsworth discovers one object. The man-made structure of execution, the gallows, has disappeared by the passage of a period of lengthy time; it has "moulder'd," causing the spot to be marked by a group of letters which seem incredibly enduring. The "iron chains" have gone, but "hard by," carved in monumental writing is a group of letters still "all fresh and visible," created "in times long past," and periodically cleansed from "year to year." This memorial of destruction and oppression becomes an object of inspiration and identification. The aura of fear begun in line 285 is augmented in these

lines by the occult nature of Wordsworth's surroundings. Other than the six-year-old boy, there are no humans about. The letters seem not attended by any human agent but by the "superstition of the neighborhood." Wordsworth admits he is lost, floundering about psychically and spatially: "down the rough and stony Moor"; "stumbling on, at length"; "Faltering, and ignorant where I was, at length." His sentences are jumbled, broken by parenthetical and prepositional phrases, interrupted by commas and words indicating hiatus. Yet when, by chance, he "espys" the memorial letters, he immediately knows where he is and where he is to go. The structures of man, whose purpose is to snuff out life, are transitory; curiously, the objects of destruction have created the vehicle of inspiration, the "monumental letters." And though he seizes upon the engraved letters as an enduring artifact, the letters are not spoken; the word is not heard. It too is silent, contributing to his solitude.

Wordsworth leaves the "spot" (the reference to line 258 seems to be intentional) to reascend the bare common. "Reascending" is an important gerund, for it indicates he is now treading a path he has been on previously, continuing an upward motion he has been diverted from. Once he has seen the characters on the stone and reascended the "Common," "Common" being the noun referring to the phrase "An ordinary sight" of line 309, the landscape changes as he changes his perspective. No longer looking down at the ground to the stones, he now sees past the ground, "beneath the hills," past "A naked Pool," to "The Beacon on the summit, and more near,/ A Girl who bore a Pitcher on her head." Again Wordsworth confesses his inarticulateness and he is unable to represent the implications of the scene he sees. His sentence (lines 309-316) is incomplete in its reference; Wordsworth does not say what "the visionary dreariness" invests the pool, the beacon, and the girl with. Likewise, he uses exceedingly complex grammar in the next sentence to gloss over problems in symbolic reference. Lines 316-326 are basically multiple and paratactic in nature, and, introduced by two conditional temporal clauses, they form the transition from the first person "I" of lines 312 and 319 to the direct address "ye" of line 324. Being paratactic, that is with "The spirit of pleasure and youth's golden gleam [fell]" being parallel and subordinate in meaning to "When . . . I roam'd about," the cumulative effect of the continuous "and" conjunctions is heightened; thus the transitive form leads firmly to the conclusive conjunction "so" of line 326 and the inclusive pronouns "we . . . us" in the aphoristic expression of lines 326-328. Once the transition is complete, a transition also involving his shift from the past of his boyhood to the present of his address, Wordsworth can directly address mankind as a whole. However, the address states not what he "knows" of the mystery of man, but what he "feels."

> Oh! mystery of Man, from what a depth
> Proceed thy honours! I am lost, but see
> In simple childhood something of the base
> On which thy greatness stands, but this I feel,
> That from thyself it is that thou must give,
> Else never canst receive. The days gone by
> Come back upon me from the dawn almost
> Of life: the hiding-places of my power

Seem open; I approach, and then they close;
I see by glimpses now; when age comes on,
May scarcely see at all, and I would give,
While yet we may, as far as words can give,
A substance and a life to what I feel:
I would enshrine the spirit of the past
For future restoration.

(329-343)

His view, then, is here quite nostalgic. It is almost from the dawn of life that the hiding places of his power "seem open"; from the spirit of the past comes future restoration "if but once we have been strong." But the vision is now, when he approaches it in adulthood, blocked. His attempts to give substance and life to what he feels are severely limited by the expressive modes he is able to muster. Therefore, "now," as far as his language will permit him, he would like to create an enduring memorial like that which marks the mouldered ruins of the gibbet. Though it can be created only by poetry conditional in tense, frequently stopped by periods, commas, and semicolons, he "would give . . . as far as words can give." It is a curious admission for a poet to make—that he can not formulate representational forms—and it is an admission Wordsworth makes frequently. And further, in this spot of time, a single glance when he was a boy at the memorial carvings caused him to turn immediately from the limits imposed by the written words to the unlimited visionary prospect of the beacon and the naked pool; now, as an adult, he must resort to grammatical devices to suggest what he knew as a boy. As an adult, Wordsworth cannot recreate that original, engraven, and enduring form; words entangle, create inadequate suppositional propositions, and bind.

As I have suggested, Wordsworth's frank confessions of inarticulateness initially rely heavily upon nostalgia. For example, in Book Three of **The Prelude** he tells Coleridge that when he was a child he had a world of fruitfulness and this past world mocks his recent studies at Cambridge. Hence he is turning away from the university in order to recall "the glory of my youth . . . Genius, power, Creation and Divinity," glories created in the poet while the "yoke of the earth is new." But his hope is qualified; Wordsworth concludes his statement of purpose by saying that which he seeks "lies far hidden from the reach of words." His eye, which looks for shades of difference "as they lie hid in all exterior forms," is ultimately unable to decide upon the proper expressive forms. That time when his thoughts were "deep quiet and majestic" is, as the verb tense indicates, past, and now his mind's simplicity is impaired by the "treasonable growth of indecisive judgments" and an unhappy substitution of "empty noise and superficial pastimes" (III. 121-217).

Yet nostalgia is really just the emotion which expresses Wordsworth's longing for his past creative age; an emotion is not, of course, the reason for his longing. There is, I think, a specific reason. Geoffrey Hartman's very suggestive book [*The Unmediated Vision: An Interpretation of Wordsworth, Hopkins, Rilke, and Valéry,* 1954] ascribes the limitations Wordsworth has to a self-imposed curb; Wordsworth is afraid that the "apocalyptic" nature of his imagination might destroy the natural forms he must

A portrait of Wordsworth by Henry William Pickersgill, 1832.

work with. Hartman's thesis is logically presented, but it evades the issue that Wordsworth raises. Wordsworth says his written word, the vehicle of his poetic thought, is "now" inadequate, and he, the adult poet, cannot specifically delineate his original response to the external object that caused the moment of creative consciousness. It is because the adult poet cannot recreate the exact forms that nurtured his youthful poetic grace that Wordsworth cannot decipher the shades of meaning "as they lie hid in all exterior forms." Likewise, after the adult poet defines the nourishing aspects of the spots of time, he recalls his stumbling as a child across a murderer's name chiseled in stone; but the adult poet does not tell us what the inscription is.

More linguistically oriented critics see Wordsworth's stumblings as a common and human inability to translate poetic perception of an ultimate reality into communicable language. But this critical view overlooks the Wordsworthian insistence upon the "once." "Once we have been strong" Wordsworth repeatedly asserts, an assertion I think important to the interpretation of his poetry.

The idea of an orphic being, a primitive singer-poet, a figure existing without the imposition of the modern limitations of language and therefore more closely attuned to the processes of nature, is a common one in the eighteenth and nineteenth centuries. Collins' "Ode on the Popular Superstitions of the Highlands of Scotland" (1794), Gray's "The Bard" (1757), and Macpherson's Ossianic books (1760-1765) are only three examples of the eighteenth century's preoccupation with the primitive singer figure. In the nineteenth century Coleridge, Byron, and Scott are similarly fascinated by, for example, the image of [in the words of Gray] "a venerable figure seated on the summit of an inaccessible rock, who [speaks] with a voice more than human." But more immediately relevant to an investigation of Wordsworth are the critical theories which state that language has drifted away from its initial representational function, that somehow men are unable to express themselves as they could when language was first created or in its infancy. Because they are now unable to express themselves, the created experience as it is described is not the same as the original; their fictional forms cannot support reality, and the metaphoric universe they have constructed and live in "now" is not quite as it should be. Words, instead of steadying and supporting the foundations of rational thought, imperil and obstruct the orderly flow of thinking and its linguistic representations.

Lord Monboddo, who cites lengthy examples of his linguistic theory in the Amerindian languages says [in *Of the Origin and Progress of Language,* 1774-1809] that

> it is evident that the name with which he [the primitive man] marks any thing must denote, beside the qualities common to the species, some that belong only to individuals. Thus he will not denote a bear by a name signifying only that species of animal, but he will use a word signifying a *great bear,* or a *small bear,* a *strong bear,* or a *weak bear,* or any other quality of the individual bear that affects his senses or imagination most. . . . Thus it appears, that at first there would be no name of any substance considered abstractly by itself . . . but the word expressing any such substance would always denote a something more than the substance itself.

But, as language develops, it becomes cumbersome and unwieldy: "the natural progress [of language] is from what is easy to what is more difficult." Lord Kames is himself more concerned with the effect writing has on the development of language, but his conclusions [in *Sketches of the History of Man,* 1774] are the same as Lord Monboddo's:

> The following part of the progress [of language] is equally obvious. People acquainted with no written compositions but what were in verse [here Kames is speaking of primitive man], composed in verse their laws, their religious ceremonies, and every memorable transaction that was intended to be preserved in memory by writing. But when subjects of writing multiplied and became more and more involved, when people began to reason, to teach, and to harangue, they were obliged to descend to humble prose: for to confine a writer or speaker to verse in handling subjects of that nature, would be a burden insupportable.

Words create tremendous difficulties for the eighteenth-century linguist, for the linguists conclude that words are unable to maintain a consistently meaningful and notional stability. As Dr. Johnson says in the Preface to his *Dictionary,* because many words have an "exuberance of signification," frequently "the original sense is often driven out by use of their metaphorical acceptation." The labor of

compiling a dictionary was much more complicated than he had expected; in investigating every word of popular usage "it was requisite to mark the progress of its meaning, and show by what gradations of intermediate sense it has passed from its primitive to its remote and accidental signification." And this task proves to be impossible, for the variety of meanings ultimately swamps the poet and scholar in complexity:

> When I had thus enquired into the original of words, I resolved to show likewise my attention to things; to pierce deep into every science, to enquire the nature of every substance of which I inserted the name, to limit every idea by a definition strictly logical, and exhibit every production of art or nature in an accurate description, that my book might be in place of all other dictionaries whether appelative or technical. But these were the dreams of a poet doomed at last to wake a lexicographer.

The task of a person who wrestles with a word is finally to place limits upon both the depth of his research and the variety of that word's meanings. This limitation, however, creates the aura of poignancy these Johnsonian sentences have; though the desire "to enquire the nature of every substance of which I inserted the name" is the desire of a poet, the poetic act is stifled because the materials a dreamer has to work with are the heavy latinate substantives of lexicography. Words here, even in the thought of a learned man who battled against primitivism and pseudepigrapha, evidence a translation away from their original meanings.

John Horne Tooke, whose works Wordsworth knew, makes similar statements. Tooke consistently argues in *The Diversions of Purley* that contemporary English has grave difficulty in expressing ideas, especially abstract ideas. For example, the word "right" can be used as a substantive, an adjective, and an adverb; it also has, Tooke reckons, "between thirty and forty meanings." These equivocal uses and meanings hardly fulfill what Tooke considers to be the primary duty of any language: "the first aim of language was to *communicate* our thoughts." The "inventions of all ages" have confused the original meanings through a looseness of application, a looseness caused by an inadequate grasp of grammar. Therefore he can state with certitude: "it is true that almost all of the *Complex Terms* . . . which we have adopted from other languages, might be, and many of them were, better expressed in the Anglosaxon." Tooke states the issue I think Wordsworth raises in **The Prelude,** that mankind has lost a linguistic ability he once possessed when he existed in a less complex world. And the Romantics recognized Tooke as stating this loss; the central sentence in Hazlitt's laudatory essay, "The Late Mr. Horne Tooke," says approvingly: "Mr. Tooke . . . saw language stripped of the clothing of habit or sentiment, or the disguises of doting pedantry, naked in its cradle and in its primitive state."

The eighteenth-century notion that modern forms of language interfere with the expression of thought has strong support in our own nostalgic decades. Otto Jespersen's conclusion to his *Language, Its Nature, Development and Origin* states:

In primitive picture-writing, each sign meant a whole sentence or even more—the image of a situation or of an incident being given as a whole; this developed into an ideographic writing of each word by itself; this system was succeeded by syllabic methods, which had in their turn to give place to alphabetic writing. . . . Just as here the advance is due to a further analysis of language, smaller and smaller units of speech being progressively represented by single signs, in an exactly similar way, though not quite so unmistakably the history of language shows us a progressive tendency towards analyzing into smaller and smaller units that which in the earlier states was taken as an inseparable whole.

Jespersen's statements concur with those expressed by James Harris, Paul Mallet, Charles Gildon, Thomas Astlc, and a host of others in the eighteenth century.

This critical theory is, I think, influential for Wordsworth and the other Romantics, for it frequently causes them to express a form of poetic impotence. In Wordsworth, though, the passage of time has the most marked effect upon the form of his poetry. For example, though the two versions of the gibbet-scene (the 1805 and the 1850) are almost identical, what changes Wordsworth does make in the later text support my thesis—that the farther away in time he gets from the original experience in childhood, the less sure of himself he becomes when he recreates it. In the 1850 edition (Book Twelve, ll.234-248), Wordsworth's flash of poetic recognition after stumbling across the monumental carvings is less clearly presented than in the 1805 *Prelude,* for the changes he introduces actually delay the recognition process. That is, the faintness, ignorance, and faltering occur before Wordsworth sees the letters in the 1805; however, in the 1850 version, after seeing the letters, he still remains "Faltering and faint, and ignorant of the road." The awareness that came to him with one word when he was six is even less immediate than it was in the 1805 retelling.

Again, what substantial changes Wordsworth makes in the 1805 *Prelude* are those which further qualify and make more precise the loss of articulative power that occurs in the passage of time, and the poem's progressive linguistic decay is also seen in other comparisons of the two versions. For example, in Book Two Wordsworth primarily discusses the methods by which a poet gives to his expressions of adult duty and truth "the eagerness of infantine desire" (II. 26). Yet Wordsworth states that it is a "Hard task" to describe such a state of eagerness if "each most obvious and particular thought . . . in the words of reason . . . Hath no beginning" (II. 232-237). Nonetheless, he attempts a description in the "Bless'd the infant Babe" passage, for in this attempt and with his best conjectures he "would trace the progress of our being" (II. 237-239). When he concludes his initial account of the child (II. 239-264), Wordsworth states "Emphatically such a Being lives,/ An inmate of this *active* universe," a being who works in participatory alliance with the objects it perceives. In 1850, however, Wordsworth alters the text so as to make clearer the increased qualification he feels about the empathy of the "Blest . . . Babe." The introductory hesitation found in the 1805 version is further under-

scored; it is now not only a "Hard task" to analyze this early state of infantine desire, it is also a "vain hope" (II. 228). Wordsworth capitalizes the descriptive noun "Reason" (II. 231). And, in this later description of the infant state before the intrusion of language, Wordsworth removes the fourteen lines describing how the infant had fused "all the elements/ And parts of the same object" which were otherwise "detach'd/ And loth to coalesce" (1805, II. 244-257). Perhaps then it is no surprise that in 1850 Wordsworth deitalicizes the adjective "active" in the 1805 affirmation that "Emphatically such a Being lives,/ An inmate of this *active* universe" and inserts two qualifying appositive phrases ("Frail creature as he is, helpless as Frail") between the two lines.

The same pattern is also seen in the changes Wordsworth makes in the boat-stealing episode of Book One. Wordsworth writes that as a boy he once took a small skiff from the shores of Patterdale one summer evening, "surely" led by Nature; yet, as he struck across Ullswater, "a huge Cliff . . . Rose up between me and the stars, and still,/ With measur'd motion, like a living thing,/ Strode after me." The frightened boy returned the boat to its mooring-place, and, after he had seen "That spectacle," Wordsworth states "in my thoughts/ There was a darkness, call it solitude,/ Or blank desertion" (I. 372-422). Accordingly, in 1850 Wordsworth modifies this passage to reflect the progressive qualification and removal the spectacle undergoes in his remembrance of it. In the later *Prelude,* he deletes the specific references to "the shores of Patterdale" and "the Village Inn" from which he had wandered; the "small Skiff" becomes a "little boat," and that Nature which once led him, "surely," is now a minor parenthetical aside—"(led by her)." Further, the "huge Cliff" of lines 406 and 409 becomes the "huge peak" (378) and the "grim shape" (381). And the accumulative intensification of the lines which describe the cliff stalking the boy is abruptly broken by a series of appositional prepositional phrases:

> I struck and struck again,
> And growing still in stature the grim shape
> Towered up between me and the stars, and still,
> For so it seemed, with purpose of its own
> And measured motion like a living thing,
> Strode after me.
>
>   (I. 380-385)

Thus, though in the 1805 telling there "was" a darkness "in" his thoughts after his experience, in 1850 the darkness "hung . . . o'er" his thoughts (I. 420-421; I. 393-394).

Therefore the Romantics' failure is not so much a conceptual lacking—as some of our contemporary critics will have it—but is, perhaps, a failure of their expressive medium, a failure exhibited in their nostalgic longings and in their method of composition. It can be for this reason that the usual nature of their revisions for their longer poems involves a form of addition to the text; Keats's *Hyperion* fragments, Byron's *Don Juan,* Shelley's *The Triumph of Life* all show a curious inability to conclude. And Wordsworth, in effect, adds an extra book to the 1850 *Prelude,* though this extra book is essentially created by his dividing Book Ten to make Books Ten and Eleven. In *The Pre-*

lude, then, and in *The Excursion* and *The Recluse,* Wordsworth, removed from his "first childhood," feels compelled to define and redefine. But his definitions as given in the language of his poetry are failures because his words cannot create the original inseparable whole he knew as a child. Instead, his words are somehow non-ideographic, non-representational. The source of his poetry, and its visionary articulation, is like the name graven at the foot of the gallows. It cannot be semantically presented; it can only be periodically cleansed. (pp. 605-16)

Jim Springer Borck, "Wordsworth's 'The Prelude' and the Failure of Language," in Studies in English Literature, 1500-1900, *Vol. XIII, No. 4, Autumn, 1973, pp. 605-16.*

An excerpt from *The Prelude* (1850)

One summer evening . . . I found
A little boat tied to a willow tree
Within a rocky cave, its usual home.
Straight I unloosed her chain, and stepping in
Pushed from the shore. It was an act of stealth
And troubled pleasure, nor without the voice
Of mountain-echoes did my boat move on;
Leaving behind her still, on either side,
Small circles glittering idly in the moon,
Until they melted all into one track
Of sparkling light. But now, like one who rows,
Proud of his skill, to reach a chosen point
With an unswerving line, I fixed my view
Upon the summit of a craggy ridge,
The horizon's utmost boundary; far above
Was nothing but the stars and the grey sky.
She was an elfin pinnace; lustily
I dipped my oars into the silent lake,
And, as I rose upon the stroke, my boat
Went heaving through the water like a swan;
When, from behind that craggy steep till then
The horizon's bound, a huge peak, black and huge,
As if with voluntary power instinct
Upreared its head. I struck and struck again,
And growing still in stature the grim shape
Towered up between me and the stars, and still,
For so it seemed, with purpose of its own
And measured motion like a living thing,
Strode after me. With trembling oars I turned,
And through the silent water stole my way
Back to the covert of the willow tree;
There in her mooring-place I left my bark,—
And through the meadows homeward went, in grave
And serious mood; but after I had seen
That spectacle, for many days, my brain
Worked with a dim and undetermined sense
Of unknown modes of being; o'er my thoughts
There hung a darkness, call it solitude
Or blank desertion. No familiar shapes
Remained, no pleasant images of trees,
Of sea or sky, no colours of green fields;
But huge and mighty forms, that do not live
Like living men, moved slowly through the mind
By day, and were a trouble to my dreams.

William Wordsworth, in his The Prelude, *edited by Ernest de Selincourt, Clarendon Press, 1926.*

John T. Ogden   (essay date 1975)

[*In the following excerpt, Ogden suggests that Wordsworth organized and unified* The Prelude *through a pattern of excursion and return.*]

Wordsworth himself provides the simplest and most direct account of how the imagination operates in a structured manner. The mind receives a particularly deep and powerful impression if, first, "the attention is energetically braced up to an act of steady observation, or of steady expectation"; next, "this intense condition of vigilance should suddenly relax"; and then, a beautiful or impressive object, or collection of objects, happen to fall upon the eye. He explained this process to De Quincey late one night as they were waiting for the carrier to bring the latest news of the war in Spain. He had just put his ear to the ground, straining to hear the sound of wheels. When he raised his head, "in final abandonment of hope," a bright star "fell suddenly upon my eye, and penetrated my capacity of apprehension with a pathos and a sense of the Infinite."

The star is made particularly vivid by the circumstances: it exists in an aesthetic and heavenly realm in contrast to the practical and earthly realm of the carrier; and it exists as light, not as sound, as Wordsworth had expected. The shifts in his body and mind correspond to these contrasts—from bending down to rising up, from hearing to sight, from expectation to surprise, and from "abandonment of hope" to a sense of fulfillment in which eye, mind, and heart all participate. The imaginative act, then, proceeds through three different stages—from expectation through an interruption that is called in one instance relaxation, in another "abandonment of hope," to an interpenetration of mind and object. A fourth stage, manifested in the very act of explanation, displays the poet's recognition of what has happened and satisfaction in that occurrence. (pp. 290-91)

The structure of imaginative experience finds its fullest manisfestation in *The Prelude.* All the "spots of time" embody this structure, though in various ways and degrees of completeness and complexity. **"There Was a Boy,"** incorporated into *The Prelude* as one of these "spots" (V, 364-97), is one of the most impressive instances. In the boat-stealing episode from Book I, Wordsworth is first engaged in a fanciful race, only to be shocked by the appearance of a huge peak moving towards him. At this point he stood frightfully alone, with nature opposed to him. Then the scene slipped into his mind and coalesced with the workings of his brain (I, 357-400). On another occasion, waiting to come home for Christmas vacation, he stood expectantly on a hillside, looking for the horses that would carry him and his brothers home. He fancifully thinks of himself as "scout-like," with a sheep and a hawthorn as his "companions." That Christmas his father died, leaving him an orphan. Afterwards, the scene often returned to him as a "fountain" from which he would "drink" (XII,

287-335). During another vacation later in his youth, he spent a night "in dancing, gaiety, and mirth"; afterwards, returning home alone, he encountered a magnificent sunrise that filled his heart and left him in a state of "thankful blessedness, which yet survives" (IV, 309-38). There are over twenty such "spots of time" in *The Prelude,* each of which moves from the mind's engagement, to its separation, to an unexpected synthesis with the scene, and finally to a resolution.

In the "spots of time" from Wordsworth's childhood and youth, the later stages in the structure of imaginative experience are undeveloped but implicitly or potentially present. Just as sensation anticipates intellection (I, 549-53), so the early stages in imaginative experience anticipate the later ones. For example, the Boy of Winander never gains the self-consciousness that completes the structure, but the foundation for the self-consciousness is laid in the third stage—in what I mentioned above as the psychological affirmation of the boy's existence. Similarly, after witnessing a maginificent sunrise in his nineteenth year, Wordsworth experiences only a fullness of heart and a "thankful blessedness"; the bond of dedication that arises from the experience remains unknown to him until a later time, when the experience ripens in his memory.

"Spots of time" from the still earlier period of childhood appear even less developed. The second stage—separation, alienation, or loss—predominates in these episodes. In the third stage, internal feelings coalesce with external accidents, but without the child's awareness of his part in the coalescence, so that he experiences not a merging of inner and outer, but a vivid embodiment of the second stage. The fourth stage, self-consciousness, is also implicitly present but not fully recognized until later recollection revives the experience. "The terrors, pains, and early miseries" of childhood evolve into the adult poet's "calm existence" (I, 344-50).

From these examples it may be seen that the structure of imaginative experience governs the over-all development of human life as well as the individual moments of experience. The infant is fully engaged in his world (II, 241-44). He lives in unconscious harmony with nature. But in childhood, with the development of consciousness and the dawning of memory, he first encounters bewilderment and feels alienated (e.g., I, 315-17). As he passes from childhood to youth, the synthesis of mind and world becomes predominant (e.g., II, 170-74, 350-52, 394-418). In adulthood he gains a fully matured self-consciousness. The experience of youth is highly subjective, so that he sees "A prospect in the mind" (II, 352); in adulthood, however, experience gains an objective orientation: from Mount Snowdon Wordsworth sees a mind in the prospect (XIV, 66-67, 70).

Between the single event and the development of a lifetime the structure of imaginative experience may be seen unfolding in various intermediate spans of experience. Wordsworth's first summer vacation from Cambridge (Book IV), for example, begins with a lively attentiveness and somewhat fanciful mood, enters into a period of discouragement over "that heartless chase/ Of trivial pleasures," but then concludes with two influential and pro-

found spots of time—the one when the glory of nature left him with unknown vows, the other when an old, discharged soldier provided his view of nature with an appropriate human center. Broader spans of development are evident in the way that Cambridge, London, and France present Wordsworth with obstacles to imagination that ultimately serve to stimulate its activity. His experience with each of these places begins in a mood that is attentive though light-hearted, even fanciful, but it soon shifts into the second stage, which predominates. In each case imagination sleeps (III, 260, 332-34; VII, 468-69; XII, 147). His mood soon becomes troubled by the emptiness, vanity, and perversion that he encounters. His language becomes consciously artificial and satirical to accord with the situation, and his bitterness and frustration increase until, in the case of France, he falls into despair. Each of these experiences, however, prepares Wordsworth for a succeeding stage of illumination and fulfillment. Cambridge is followed by summer vacation, where he gains a human-heartedness to his love (IV, 233). After his stay in London, he attains a new perspective that elevates his view of human nature (VIII, 644-75). The disaster of the French Revolution forces him into the realization that political reform depends upon moral reform, which in turn depends upon a reform of sensibility, which he as a poet can hope to effect.

Regardless of the span of time involved—whether a moment, several months, several years, or thirty-five years—the structure of imaginative experience involves the same sequence of four stages. Because the structure exists in time, it becomes realized—that is, made real, and brought to one's awareness—by means of memory. "Spots of time" are scattered like seeds through one's past. While the total structure is contained in the seed, it reveals itself only as the seed grows in memory. As a "spot of time" develops, it may alter its character drastically. Getting lost near a gibbet was terrifying to the five-year-old; however, the memory of it adds sublimity to the youth's pleasure, and to the mature poet it becomes a renovating revelation of how the mind is lord and master over outward sense (XII, 208-69).

Memory plays its most powerful role in the "spot of time" of crossing the Alps (VI, 557-640). In the original event, the lofty expectation turns into disappointment when the two travelers learn that they have overlooked the point of crossing, but the disappointment is recompensed shortly afterwards by an apocalyptic scene in the Simplon Pass. In memory, however, imagination intrudes at the point of Wordsworth's disappointment and reveals to him that man's glory exists in the expectation itself, not in the object of expectation. The original compensatory scene, spectacular though it is, was apparently insufficient to answer to the depths of his initial expectation and disappointment. He had been looking outside himself for a glory whose source is within. The revelation bursts upon him with a most surprising and powerful flash, and then subsides to the still powerful but calmer, beneficent image of the fertilizing Nile.

Memory itself, as the above episode shows, is governed by the structure of imaginative experience. After the original event has engaged the mind in the outside world, the experience lies dormant (I, 586-96), though during this time it may be germinating in the unconscious. Then it reappears unexpectedly in memory, catching the poet by surprise and prompting him to reinvest it with an imaginative power similar to the imaginative power of the original event. More than a memory, it becomes a present experience in the mind of the poet, leading to renewed strength, consolation, and gratitude.

The process of recollection (as it may be distinguished from the faculty of memory) is also based on the same structure. As the poet tries to recapture the past, he may recollect an earlier event, but without satisfying his original desire. The dissatisfaction grows into a state of mind in which he feels lost (VI, 596; XII, 273), for he sees no way to attain his original goal, and he is disoriented between the present place and time and the past place and time. In the midst of his confusion, a sudden recognition breaks through the mental barrier and satisfies his desire in an unexpected way. The fulfilling memory or satisfying recognition is not accessible to the poet's conscious and voluntary efforts but must come of itself (XII, 277-80). Because these sources of strength are not always accessible, Wordsworth will "enshrine" them in poetry (XII, 281-86), the written poem thus becoming the fourth and final stage in the structure of imaginative experience.

Poetic composition, which Wordsworth allies with recollection, is itself based on the structure of imaginative experience. Wordsworth's explanation falls into the four stages that I have outlined. First, "poetry . . . takes its origin from emotion recollected in tranquillity." Secondly, "by a species of re-action, the tranquillity gradually disappears." Thirdly, "an emotion, kindred to that which was before the subject of contemplation, is gradually produced, and does itself actually exist in the mind." This emotion swells into "the spontaneous overflow of powerful feelings" which, finally, becomes the poem. While composition begins in tranquillity, it rises to an excitement that may be as intense as, or even more intense than, the original experience was.

The process of poetic composition is fully displayed in *The Prelude,* the organization of which is based on the structure of imaginative experience not only in the tale that the narrator is telling of his past life but also in the act of poetic composition that he is dramatizing. Beginning with a joyous celebration at the initiation of his career as a poet, Wordsworth delights in the expectation of what lies before him. But soon his hopes meet impediments, and his ambitions become an awful burden. He is confused, anxious, rootless, baffled, and plagued (I, 234-69). Selfishness cloaked by humility "Locks every function up in blank reserve" (I, 246). As a poet, he is "lost;/ Halted without an effort to break through" (VI, 596-97), as Wordsworth describes a different but analogous situation. In his despair he asks, "Was it for this"—for this vain perplexity, this sense of futility and uselessness—that Nature gave him such a glorious childhood? His expression of despair suddenly turns into a hymn of joy, praise, and thanksgiving. The theme for which he has been searching in vain quite

unexpectedly presents itself, captures his mind, and elevates his mood.

The imaginative act of poetic composition repeats itself throughout the poem, so that we see the poem growing and its themes evolving during the course of the poem. The theme of his own childhood, which seemed to present itself fortuitously, is taken up as something manageable (I, 641-45), in contrast to the epic themes considered in the Introduction of the poem; but soon Wordsworth comes to realize that his theme is indeed "heroic argument" (III, 184). What at first appears to him as an "infirmity"—his "love of days/ Disowned by memory" (I, 614-15)—turns out to be an aspect of his major strength, his retention of "creative sensibility" (II, 360). The significance of "spots of time" is partially understood from the beginning (I, 621-26), but only toward the end of the poem is the idea fully realized (XII, 208-25), thus making explicit what has been happening throughout the poem. Similarly, imagination is displayed pre-eminently in the early books but referred to only indirectly and obscurely as "a dark/ Inscrutable workmanship" (I, 341-42), "a superadded soul" (II, 328). "A plastic power" (II, 362), and "an auxiliar light" (II, 368). Halfway through the poem "Imagination" bursts forth directly, but even then Wordsworth uses the word only with apology (VI, 592-93). By the end of the poem he can state that imagination has been his theme (XIV, 206). The poem itself has been a process of working out its own identity and bringing about a recognition of what it is.

The poem is thus the culmination of the structure of imaginative experience. It both represents and manifests that structure, and it develops most fully the fourth stage, which draws together elements of the earlier three stages in a way that harmonizes, rectifies, and completes them. The poem is the poet's expression of gratitude, and the tribute which he renders in return for all he has recieved. The poem perfects his self-consciousness (XIV, 113-18), and fulfills his original high aspiration for "some philosophic song/ Of Truth that cherishes our daily life" (I, 227-30).

The four-stage structure of imaginative experience thus governs both the momentary experience and the experience of a lifetime; it governs the primary experience as well as the reflected and poetized experience. The four stages of the single "spot of time" are a miniature version of the four ages of man's life. The "spot of time" is the individual cell of experience, and it has the same basic structure as the whole body of experience that makes up the total life of a man. These correspondencies give *The Prelude* its intricacy, intensity, and organic unity. They bind together past and present, and make the poem an integral part of the poet's life.

The structure of imaginative experience in Wordsworth's poetry is highly original but not so novel as it may appear. It may be understood as a variant of the conventional plot-structure of most drama and narrative, which moves from introduction to complication to climax to resolution. Even more to the point is the way that it reflects a universal structure of experience, as seen for example in such diverse areas as religious conversion, secular love, problem solving, or Gestalt perception. The holy man was at first attached to this world, fell into despair, encountered divine revelation, and now is filled with blessed assurance of his redemption. The lover begins in dalliance, meets with resistance, receives his lady's favor in ecstasy, and subsides into a grateful and gratified calm. Problem solving goes through stages of hypothesis, experiment, discovery, and application or publication. Perception, in terms of Gestalt theory, progresses from contacting the environment, to complications that heighten consciousness, to spontaneous recognition of the Gestalt, to evaluation of the experience. Different as these areas of experience are, they proceed through similar psychological stages. The similarities suggest a universal law by which the human mind operates. Such a law is what Wordsworth desired to represent in his poetry, as he told Lady Beaumont, and as he stated in the **"Preface to *Lyrical Ballads*."** Imagination itself, as Wordsworth conceived it, is "governed by certain fixed laws."

While Wordsworth's structure of imaginative experience may thus appear traditional in its general outlines, its value derives from its origins within the individual mind. Wordsworth formulated this structure by means of memory and introspection: such structuring of the mind is what "I have remarked, from my earliest days," he told De Quincey. Writing **"There Was a Boy,"** he was "Guided by one of my own primary consciousnesses." Thus, poetic structure need not depend on rhetorical conventions outside the poem but may derive from the psychological dimensions represented within the poem, so that the poem will, in Coleridge's words, "contain in itself the reason why it is so, and not otherwise." Finally, the structure is re-created by the reader as he imaginatively grasps the poem. The value of the structure comes not from knowing it in the abstract form that I have presented, but from the act of realizing it, which is itself a re-enactment of this structure. (pp. 293-97)

John T. Ogden, "The Structure of Imaginative Experience in Wordsworth's 'Prelude'," in The Wordsworth Circle, *Vol. VI, No. 4, Autumn, 1975, pp. 290-98.*

Charles I. Patterson, Jr.   (essay date 1977)

[*In the following essay, Patterson examines three aspects of prophecy in* The Prelude, *focusing on Wordsworth's transcendentalism.*]

Among those who have called Wordsworth prophet are Herbert Lindenberger, who says [in *On Wordsworth's "Prelude"*, 1963] that **The Prelude** "wavers between personal history and prophetic utterance"; William Kerrigan, who says [in *The Prophetic Milton*, 1974] that Milton "inspired the prophetic voices of Blake, Wordsworth, and Shelley"; Abbie F. Potts [in *Wordsworth's "Prelude"*, 1953] and Brian Wilkie [in *Romantic Poets and Epic Tradition*, 1964], who point out a Miltonic fall-and-redemption theme in the poem; and M. H. Abrams, who also stressing Miltonic influences, but no fall, discusses [in *Natural Supernaturalism*, 1971] the secularization of the redemption in **The Prelude,** relating it to current interest

in the recovery of a lost paradise. However, no one has yet traced the prophetic element in full throughout the whole poem. It is my purpose to do so herein with emphasis upon three aspects of prophecy.

First, Wordsworth recurringly proclaims himself prophet in the sense of *vates,* discerning truths fundamental to humanity; and at the end he claims the gift of prophetic foreteller that man must cling to these truths in order to prevail and endure. There is, however, a significant difference between Wordsworth and other prophetic poets, including the ancient Hebrews. Milton transmits the basic ideas of Christianity and Shelley expresses Platonic thought—sources external to the poets themselves. Blake's sources, however, are primarily within, and similarly, Wordsworth's sources are within, centered in what he calls "the universal heart." But Wordsworth is reticent, not loud-voiced; his insights are given quietly though he has the intense purposiveness necessary to prophecy, as well as the symbolism and indistinctness characteristic of it. Also, he continually likens himself to ancient prophets and acknowledges an absolute God beyond the spirit of nature, though not strictly the Judaic-Christian God at times.

Secondly, the prophetic element in the poem throws emphasis upon Wordsworth's humanism and transcendentalism, which have higher intellectual standing, rather than upon his Romantic naturalism and sentimentalism, which have less intellectual respectability. The main substance of his prophecy is the vastness of what is within the human consciousness, including the unconscious, which can be constitutive of man's world. Wordsworth believed that nature's power and the mind's power were two modes of one energy—the "one life within us and abroad"—as Coleridge called it and Wordsworth stated at length in **"Tintern Abbey"** and again in *The Prelude* as the "spirit of God's works / . . . in Nature or in Man / . . . separate or conjoined" (IV, 351-53). R. D. Havens compares this energy to the third member of the trinity, the Holy Spirit considered as a force rather than a person. As *The Prelude* progresses, nature becomes less and less the *source* of truth, but becomes the *agent* by means of which the mind discovers truth within itself and becomes in part an external emblem of that inward truth. Here Wordsworth fulfills another requisite of prophecy—the coalescence of past, present and future into the eternal.

Third, the prophetic message in the poem develops by gradual accrual; it is not given in one sudden Apocalypse, *i.e.,* one completed prophetic vision or revelation of events which will end the present world order and immediately replace it by a perfected one. I cannot agree with Geoffrey Hartman's assertion [in *Wordsworth's Poetry, 1791-1814,* 1965] that Wordsworth deliberately drew back from the threshold of Apocalypse. Rather, I think, Wordsworth simply tells us honestly *as much as he saw,* and *no more,* each time insight came. In these recurring Apocalyptical experiences, transcendental intuition replaces the customary supernatural revelation, while external nature and the structure of mind supplant the customary supernatural machinery. Apocalyptic vision, an unveiling of hidden truth, need not be sudden and complete and need not employ supernatural framework in the Biblical sense. The skepticism of The Enlightenment had cast severe doubt upon religious supernaturalism, and Wordsworth was writing for a modern audience. But his accruing insights are nonetheless Apocalyptic, for they cumulatively unveil truths hidden from the sensory eye, and they are projected in a grand scaffolding analogous to the supernatural visions of ancient prophets in scope and majesty, but made up of spectacles in external nature linked to the inner structure of the mind. Wordsworth became prophetic *while writing the poem,* not while living the events it records. I am dealing only with the poet and prophecy as represented in the poem.

I shall trace the gradual accrual of Wordsworth's prophecy, its transcendental and humanistic emphases, and his claim to prophetic authority in crucial passages in the order of their occurrence. Early in Book I, having alluded to lost Eden (I, 10-14), he designates himself prophet with a priestly office:

> To the open fields I told
> A prophecy: poetic numbers came
> Spontaneously to clothe in priestly robe
> A renovated spirit singled out,
> Such hope was mine, for holy services.
>
> (I, 50-54)

Glimpses of an order of things different from worldly came to him early. When he heard in storm winds "the ghostly language of the ancient earth," he would "drink the visionary power," deeming such moods "kindred to our purer mind / and intellectual life" (II, 307-22), that is, kindred to that portion of our thought life deeper than the empirical, which is dominated by sensory cognition of things, and beyond the rational, which is dominated by fixed methods. At times, he said, "bodily eyes / Were utterly forgotten, and what I saw / appeared like something in myself, a dream, / A prospect in the mind" (II, 349-52). At college he believed himself "endowed with holy powers / And faculties" (III, 88-89) and able to see "things viewed / By poets in old time, and higher up / By . . . earth's first inhabitants" (III, 153-55). Outwardly, he "looked for universal things" (III, 109), and everywhere saw traces "Of that first paradise whence man was driven" (III, 112). Wordsworth saw sufficient evidences of the Edenic remaining on earth to indicate that we could regain it by activating what is within us; and he called the vale of Esthwaite "the paradise / Where I was born" (VIII, 99-110). "Turning the mind in upon herself" (III, 116), he intuitively perceived a transcendent deity beyond the spirit of nature, "That tolerates the indignities of Time / And from the centre of Eternity" rules over all (III, 118-24). "I was mounting now / To . . . community with highest truth," he said, (III, 125-26). Like this deity, he too had "independent solaces" that "mitigate the injurious sway of place / Or circumstance" (III, 101-09). He declared, "I had a world about me—'twas my own; / I made it, for it only lived to me / And to the God who sees into the heart" (III, 144-46). . . . "Some called it madness—so indeed it was, / . . . If prophecy be madness" (III, 149-53). The heart's knowings are supra-rational, and prophets often seem mad to people who do not yet understand their message.

His first extended inward vision occurs in Book IV, during the first summer vacation, after a day of "consummate happiness" and "perfect joy of heart" amid familiar scenes (IV, 135-40):

> Gently did my soul
> Put off her veil, and, self-transmuted, stood
> Naked as in the presence of her God. . . .
> —Of that external scene which round me lay,
> Little, in this abstraction did I see;
> Remembered less; but I had inward hopes
> And swellings of the spirit, was rapt and
>   soothed,
> *Conversed with promises,* had glimmering views
> How life pervades the undecaying mind;
> How the immortal soul with God-like power
> Informs, creates, and thaws the deepest sleep
> That time can lay upon her.
>
> (IV, 150-67, italics added)

That he means this as a prophetic vision is indicated by the metaphor of his soul's putting off her veil, as Moses did when talking with God after receiving the Commandments, and by his conversing "with promises," which is reminiscent of Hebrew prophets like Isaiah and Ezekial who received promises and covenants from God. It is noteworthy, though, that Wordsworth says that his soul stood *as if* in the presence of her God, not *in the presence.* The experience is *not* a vision of the glory of God *external to himself* and mankind but is an intense awareness of the human mind's remarkable powers to "inform" and "create," thereby largely *to make* man's world. Soon after, he experiences his prophet-like dedication to poetry while returning home at dawn after a night of revelry, again, among scenes familiar since boyhood:

> My heart was full; I made no vows, but vows
> Were then made for me; bond unknown to me
> Was given, that I should be, else sinning greatly,
> A dedicated spirit.
>
> (IV, 334-37)

Another incident that contributes to Wordsworth's growing prophetic vision is a dream that results from his reading in *Don Quixote* and musing upon Euclid's elements of geometry (V, 65-66), which Wordsworth called something "created out of pure intelligence" (IV, 167), a symbol "for finite natures of the one / Supreme Existence," (IV, 132-39). After his reading and musing, Wordsworth fell asleep and dreamed (V, 70-139) that in a sandy wilderness an Arab on a camel rode up holding under one arm a stone, which seemed also a book of Euclid's geometry (as the Arab said it was) and in the other hand a shell, which seemed also a book of prophetic poetry. The Arab called it "something of more worth" than the stone and asked the poet to hold it to his ear, whereupon he heard "in an unknown tongue, / which yet [he] understood, . . . a loud prophetic blast of harmony; / An Ode, in passion uttered, which foretold / Destruction to the children of the earth / By deluge now at hand" (V, 94-98). Like the great prophets Wordsworth is clothing his prophecy in symbols; for this shell-horn suggests the trumpets of the last judgment. Like St. John, Wordsworth is hearing a horn of prophecy, not from an angel of Jehovah but from his own consciousness; and as poet-prophet he is calling his people to preserve god-like powers within them when industrial growth was threatening to extinguish these powers. As the dream ends, the Arab, now appearing as Don Quixote himself, gallops off just ahead of what Wordsworth terms "the waters of the deep / Gathering upon us" (V, 130-131), the poet following him. The Arab then proclaims that he will bury both of his symbolic *"books"* (the stone-geometry and the shell-horn prophecy), an action which suggests that the enduring truths in geometry, symbol for men of Godhead, "the one Supreme Existence" (IV, 132-38), and those in prophetic poetry, symbol of the Godlike in man (V, 553-77, 591-97), may be the only means of man's resuscitation and reëmergence above the flood. After Wordsworth wakes from this dream of Don Quixote, he comments: "I . . . felt / Reverence was due to a being thus employed; / And thought that, in the blind and awful lair / Of *such madness, reason* did lie couched. . . . I could share / That maniac's fond anxiety, and go / Upon like errand" (V, 149-60, italics added). Wordsworth concludes Book V asserting that the "works / Of mighty poets" nurture the power of Apocalyptic vision in man:

> There, even forms and substances are circum-
> fused
> By that transparent veil with light divine,
> And . . .
> Present themselves as objects recognized,
> In flashes, and with glory not their own.
>
> (V, 598-605)

This recognition of the mind's power to transform objects is fitting preparation for the climactic Alps-crossing episode which follows in Book VI, a powerful dramatization of the supremacy of mind over external nature. On the day in 1790 when Wordsworth and Robert Jones intended to cross the continental divide at the Simplon Pass, they set out in the morning filled with anticipations of arriving at the summit. But they quickly became lost, crossed the continental divide without realizing just when, and upon finding their trail again saw that it led steadily downward. Suddenly, Wordsworth realized that his whole conscious being was still yearning upward in defiance of this sensory evidence that they had already crossed the divide. He burst forth in a rhapsody concerning the mind's power to rise above the sensory:

> To my conscious soul I now can say—
> "I recognize thy glory:" in such strength
> Of usurpation, when the light of sense
> Goes out, but with a flash that has revealed
> The invisible world, doth greatness make abode,
> There harbours; whether we be young or old,
> Our destiny, our being's heart and home
> Is with infinitude and only there.
>
> (VI, 598-605)

That he intends this "usurpation" of the senses by the total mind, *i.e.,* by the imagination, as an Apocalyptic vision of prophetic truth is indicated by what he says during "The melancholy slackening that ensued" (VI, 617). Having just perceived inwardly the powerful constituency of mind in experience, he now turns his supercharged consciousness outward and perceived the parallel energy at the heart of nature at the point where both these energies conjoin in the "one life":

> The immeasurable height
> Of woods decaying, never to be decayed, . . .

The unfettered clouds and region of the
  Heavens, . . .
Were all like workings of one mind, the features
Of the same face, blossoms upon one tree;
Characters of the great Apocalypse,
The types and symbols of Eternity,
Of first, and last, the midst, and without end.

(VI, 624-40)

The effective images here for the unity of all life ("workings of one mind," "features of the same face," and "blossoms upon one tree") are reëmphasized by the ensuing coalescence of past, present, and future into the Eternal, an emblem of which is constituted by the total scene thus viewed and modified by this human consciousness. Since nature serves here as objective correlative of both God and the human mind, God and man are united, as is foretold in Biblical Apocalyptical writings; but they are united *without being equated,* just as God and nature are united here without being equated, for God's power made the scene and man's mind made the scene into the emblem of both by seeing it thus. The far-reaching significance of Wordsworth's inclusion of a transcendent deity above the spirit of nature in the poem has not been sufficiently taken into account, even though this deity does not perform *in action presented directly* to the reader (and we should remember Milton's difficulties with the matter). This deity still functions in important ways, "fill[ing] / The veins that branch through every frame of life" and "Making man what he is, *creature divine*" (X, 420-24), with free will and with the concomitant duty to work out his own salvation with divine aid, similar to Milton's concept of man in *Paradise Lost.*

This perception underlies and in part explains what immediately follows in Books seven and eight—man's power to withstand ignominy and debasement in the City of London without being completely overborne by them. Wordsworth proclaims that a sense of what in the great city was being endured and suffered gave him an exalted view of human nature (VIII, 625-45) and a "sublime idea" of man made up from elements of past, present, and future. He says that he discerned in the city "more than elsewhere / Is possible, *the unity of man*" (VIII, 667-68), and that nothing could overthrow his "trust / In what we may become" (VIII, 649-50).

From here on there are continual affirmations of man's God-like potential and of Wordsworth's own role as prophet of that truth. For example, during his adherence to the French Revolution in the hope that it would bring back the lost earthly paradise, he states, "But as the ancient prophets, borne aloft / In vision, . . . / So, did a portion of that spirit fall / On me" (X, 437-49). He represents himself as struggling to oppose false prophecies of the time—the Benthamite utilitarian theory of morals and the shallow conceptions of man voiced by theorists of the Revolution like Godwin, Helvétius, and D'Holbach (XI, 223-320). Sorely disappointed in these underlying ideologies and in French military conquests of other nations, Wordsworth foresaw the impending failure of the Revolution and foretold it in the image of the traditional epic scales held aloft:

> Now mounted up,

Openly in the eye of earth and heaven,
The scale of liberty. I read her doom,
With anger vexed, with disappointment sore.
                                        (XI, 209-13).

That is, conquest and inadequate ideology weighed heavier in the balance, and liberty lighter, signifying that the latter was losing out. Wordsworth did not easily bear "the shame / Of a false prophet" (XI, 214-15) and still tried hard to make sense of the Revolution and remain loyal. But again, "a veil had been / Uplifted" (XI, 266-67), and he saw during the writing of the poem that he had been a false prophet indeed. Looking back, he then perceived fully the inadequacies of the Revolution and his own mistake in going along with it. Just before voicing his recantation, he suggests that his conversation to the Revolution had been that of a man betrayed, for he mentions "errors into which I fell, betrayed / By present objects, and by reasonings false / From their beginnings" (XI, 287-93). He states that he had been "dispensing truth" and "diffusing / Prophetic sympathies of genial faith" until deflected by "overpressure from the times / And their disastrous issues" (XII, 46-52), echoed near the end in the reference to his "lapse and hesitating choice" and to "whatsoever falls my better mind . . . / May have sustained" (XIV, 137, 147-49). In retrospect he lends to that conversion the aura of a fall somewhat like that of Adam in *Paradise Lost,* but here a lapse from the *recta ratio* of high idealism in favor of the contemporary empirical and rational theories of human betterment, which later he had to renounce because they had omitted the mystery, spirit, and complexity of man. Once he compares himself to Adam directly, "Yet in Paradise / Though fallen from bliss" (VIII, 659-60). In a letter Coleridge, who called *The Prelude* "that prophetic lay," mentions that Wordsworth intended to incorporate a "fall" somewhere within *The Recluse.* He evidently decided to put it here in the prefatory poem, and he represents it as something of a "Fortunate Fall," a *Felix Culpa,* which resulted ultimately in putting him on the right road after the mental bankruptcy (XI, 301-307) that came over him at full realization of his error, just as Adam had looked back and viewed his fall in *Paradise Lost* (XII, 469-78). For Wordsworth now proclaims that "Nature's self / *By all varieties of human love* / Assisted, led me back through opening day / To those sweet counsels between head and heart / Whence grew that genuine knowledge, fraught with peace" (XI, 350-54, italics added), that is, led him back to a unified consciousness with the imaginative inclusiveness to perceive the deeper truths of mankind. "Nature's self" had already been designated "the breath of God" (V, 221) in both the 1805 and 1850 texts and the "spirit of God's works / . . . in Nature or in man" (IV, 351-52), the one energy with two modes coming from the Godhead. His sister Dorothy, Coleridge, and Mary Hutchinson (his wife) loomed large among these "varieties of human love" that assisted in his redemption; but in view of his recurring emphasis upon the capacity of lowly people for unselfish love and sacrifice (XIII, 44-119, 166-85, 224-41), the dalesmen of Westmoreland and humble men everywhere, like the solicitous father in London looking at his sick child "with love unutterable" (VII, 598-618), constitute another "variety" of this human love that helped to heal the fallen prophet and that he later placed

at the very center of his vision of earthly paradise (XIV, 112). As he says in *The Recluse* (lines 811-15), "By words / Which speak of nothing more than what we are, / Would I arouse the sensual from their sleep / Of Death, and win the vacant and the vain to noble raptures." In "what we are" he sees the love potential that can bring about the wedding of man's mind to the universe in the regained paradise; but the union will not be an equal one—mind germinated by this love will be the dominant partner, somewhat resembling Christ's marriage with the world.

Having recovered, Wordsworth becomes again in his redemption a "creative soul" with prophetic insights, voiced especially in the famous "spots of time" (XII, 208-25). Truthfully he can say, "Long time in search of knowledge did I range / The field of human life, . . . / the dawn beginning now / To reappear" (XIII, 16-19). He proclaims, "I . . . tread this holy ground / Speaking no dream, but things oracular" (XIII, 252-53). . . . "Poets, even as Prophets / Have each his own peculiar faculty,/ . . . to perceive / Objects unseen before"; [and he] "The humblest, . . . dares to hope / [that] a work of his / *Proceeding from a source of untaught things* . . . may become / A power like one of Nature's" (XIII, 301-12, italics added). This "source of untaught things" is evidently the one energy with its two modes, coming from Godhead itself, which if transmitted through his mind into his poem would give it a power to mold and shape men like that power in nature which molds and shapes her species. He says he has now gained "clear sight / of a *new world* . . . that was fit / To be transmitted, and to other eyes / Made visible; as ruled by those fixed laws / . . . Which do both give it being and maintain / A balance, an ennobling interchange / Of action from without, and from within" (XIII, 369-76), a reëmphasis of the one divine energy with its two modes operating in man and in nature.

But Wordsworth as prophet emphasizes more strongly the mode of the one energy that operates in the consciousness of man. For example, in the "spots of time" passage he proclaims, "The mind is lord and master—outward sense / The obedient servant of her will" (XII, 222-23); and of man's "greatness" he says, "From thyself it comes, . . . thou must give, / Else never canst receive" (XII, 276-77). He sees a powerful emblem of man's ability to endure hardship, and yet prevail, in a scene of "visionary dreariness" in the highlands where an executed murderer's name had been carved in the turf and where now a girl with a pitcher of water on her head forces her way homeward against gusts of wind that toss her garments and impede her progress (XII, 235-71), hauntingly suggesting that the spiritual water in her effort is more salutary than its symbol, the physical water in her pitcher. Then he recalls another tempestuous day after his father had died when a single sheep, a blasted hawthorn, and the bleak sound of the wind became for him another emblem of human hardihood that remained ever after in memory, so that on stormy nights he would from it "drink / As at a fountain" (XII, 297-326).

Wordsworth's gradually accruing Apocalyptic vision of the mind's power to create and to constitute is concluded by his account in Book XIV of a nocturnal hike up Mount Snowdon by the sea in Wales presented in the grand manner of a prophetic revelation of profound significance:

> The moon hung naked in a firmament
> Of azure without cloud, and at my feet
> Rested a silent sea of hoary mist. . . .
> . . . The solid vapours stretched, . . .
> Into the main Atlantic, that appeared
> To dwindle, and give up his majesty,
> Usurped upon far as the sight could reach.
> Not so the ethereal vault; encroachment none
> Was there, nor loss. . . . [near by]
> Mounted the roar of waters, torrents, streams.
> (XIV, 40-59)

This scene with its accompanying sounds, he says,

> Appeared to me the type
> Of a majestic intellect, . . .
> There I beheld the emblem of a mind
> That feeds upon infinity, . . .
> The power . . . which Nature thus
> To bodily sense exhibits, is the express
> Resemblance of that glorious faculty
> That higher minds bear with them as their
>   own. . . .
> They from their native selves can send abroad
> Kindred mutations; for themselves create
> A like existence. . . .
> (XIV, 66-95)

Well had he marveled in *The Recluse* at how external nature and mind were suited to each other (lines 815-21). Not only does the external scene here suggest the three mental faculties (reason, understanding, and senses), but also the process in nature that brought together that complex spectacle is called an emblem of the imagination, the "glorious faculty" that puts together and completes the apprehensions of the other three; achieves a coalescence of past, present, and future; and creates "a like existence." "Such minds are truly from the deity," he says *in both texts* (XIV, 112). Then follows an affirmation of intellectual and spiritual love, co-partner of imagination, which is here called "Reason in her most exalted mood" (XIV, 168-209), but "Centring all in love" (XIV, 38). Wordsworth is too realistic to contend, as Milton does in *Paradise Lost*, that this love will overcome the "real evil" which he acknowledges in *The Recluse* (lines 361-406); but this love, by energizing man's mind and impelling its wedding with the universe, can enable man to cope with evil and to get the better of it sufficiently often to justify its existence in a world created and ruled by the benevolent deity that Wordsworth affirms in both texts of *The Prelude.* Near the end of *The Recluse* Wordsworth sums up the functions of this love while denying that paradise is either a departed thing or a fiction apart.

> For the discerning intellect of Man,
> When wedded to his goodly universe
> *In love and holy passion,* shall find these [paradises]
> A simple produce of the common day.
> (lines 800-808, italics added)

In the concluding lines of *The Prelude* Wordsworth again designates himself a prophet and foretells that if men "by

nations sink together" and "fall back to old idolatry," the truths he has unveiled will lift them up again, as if he believes that recurring fall and redemption constitute the very systole and diastole of spiritual progress in this world. Here his emphasis upon the imaginative mind's constituency in experience and supremacy over matter is attributed directly to the mind's relationship with the transcendent deity. *Nature* is now used as a term for that "highest truth" (III, 126) which he had been seeking, and Divine Providence is ruler over all. I quote now from the earlier text of 1805, as he proclaims himself and Coleridge:

> Joint-labourers in a work . . .
> Of their redemption, surely yet to come.
> Prophets of Nature, we to them will speak
> A lasting inspiration, sanctified
> By reason and by truth. . . . [We shall],
> Instruct them how the mind of man becomes
> A thousand times more beautiful than the earth
> On which he dwells, above this Frame of
>   things . . .
> In beauty exalted, as it is itself
> Of substance and of fabric more divine.
> (XIII, 441-54, 1805 text)

The word *substance* in the last line (*quality* in the 1850 text) drives home this final assertion of the mind's connection with the divine.

In sum, Wordsworth sustains throughout the poem the representation of himself as a developing poet-prophet and his message as an accruing revelation of the power of man's consciousness, with tacit divine aid though not divine intervention, to redeem itself and to remake the world more nearly in accord with the deep truth that lies within the depths of that human consciousness. Neither this power nor this truth comes *to* man *from* nature, though the same power operates in nature as well as in man. The so-called "subjectivity" of his doctrine should not be allowed to obscure its universality, which he stresses in the prophetic strain in *The Prelude,* in some of the shorter poems, and in *The Excursion,* where he shows the spiritualizing value of our traditional culture. The widespread notion that all this constitutes the "bad" poet in Wordsworth is untenable, as is the kindred idea that the "real" Wordsworth is the "high priest of nature." In *The Prelude* (XIII, 240-45), he affirms, "My theme / No other than the very heart of man" nurtured by "religious faith" and "good books. . . . / In Nature's presence"; in *The Recluse* (lines 793-94) he proclaims "the Mind of Man— / My haunt, and the main region of my song." His prophetic role and his prophecy in *The Prelude* help to bear out the truth of these claims. He shows that though conditioned differently our minds are structured similarly, and in that fact lies our best hope of making the world better. The absence of clumsy supernatural machinery goes far to make his message palatable. He is a prophet of the possibility of an earthly paradise, not of its inevitability. Viewed in this light he is far from sentimental; in fact, he is toughminded, somewhat like William Blake in his own age and Arnold Toynbee in ours. His ideas in *The Prelude* may be apprehended without our seeing them in the matrix of prophecy; but seeing them thus puts them in the perspective which he evidently intended and suggests that he is primarily a humanistic poet in the tradition of Milton, as do the echoes of *Paradise Lost* in its structure and texture. (pp. 385-95)

Charles I. Patterson, Jr., "Prophecy and the Prophetic Poet in 'The Prelude'," in The Southern Humanities Review, *Vol. 11, No. 4, Fall, 1977, pp. 385-96.*

John Holloway   (essay date 1977)

[*Holloway is an English poet and critic. In the following excerpt, he interprets* The Prelude *as a quest for knowledge.*]

[*The Prelude*] may be seen from three different points of view, each as it were more inward than the last. It may be seen simply as a biography of external events in the poet's life: his childhood, years at the university, visits to London, travels on the Continent. More significantly, it may be seen as an apologia: in fact, this side of the poem is surprisingly, almost disquietingly prominent. Wordsworth seems almost unduly anxious to excuse his idleness at Cambridge and to engage in what is known nowadays as an 'auto-critique' in respect of (to continue in the same language) his formalist errors in the period of the early French Revolution. Possibly this note of self-extenuation, which runs through the work, stems from a sense of guilt and failure having more to do with Annette Vallon and the confused and helpless sonnet **'On Calais Sands'** than with any political issue.

Third and most important, the poem invites reading as a spiritual autobiography, a 'pilgrimage', in its own words, towards 'highest truth'. This strand of the poem's meaning takes the form of meditation and recollection, but at the same time the sense of a quest is present too, in part directly, in part through metaphor. It is a quest for knowledge of ultimates, and it is pursued with as high a sense of calling as Milton shows in his own epic:

> Be mine to follow with no timid step
> Where knowledge leads me: it shall be my pride
> That I have dared to tread this holy ground,
> Speaking no dream, but things oracular . . .
>
> (XII.249)

Life for Wordsworth is a progress not an accident. 'I would trace / The progress of our being', he says early in the poem (II. 238). A significant passage in Book II depicts the transition from life as accident to life as an ordained and imposed searching after a higher reality:

> Thus, day by day,
> Subjected to the discipline of love . . .
>
> (250)

(an indication, of course, of how gentle and psychically creative is that subjection and imposition)—

> His organs and recipient faculties
> Are quickened, are more vigorous, his mind
>   spreads,
> Tenacious of the forms which it receives.

From the child's mother, in the first instance, there comes:

> A virtue which irradiates and exalts
> All objects through all intercourse of sense.
>
> (259)

Under this creative influence, life becomes not a vagary merely, but what is ordained by a superior call to the individual:

> No outcast he, bewildered and depressed:
> Along his infant veins are interfused
> The gravitation and the filial bond
> Of Nature that connect him with the world.
> Emphatically such a Being lives,
> An inmate of this *active* universe;

(That is to say, there is an activity which works upon him from outside, and which at the same time renders him active from within):

> From nature largely he receives; nor so
> Is satisfied, but largely gives again . . .
> Even as an agent of the one great Mind,
>   . . . Such, verily, is the first
> Poetic spirit of our human life.
>
> (272)

The upshot of this passage is to bring out how Wordsworth sees growing up as transition to activity which, for all that it is activity, is also one with the 'wise passivity' of early childhood.

A later passage introduces the vocabulary characteristic of this poetic mode as a whole:

> . . . from the firm habitual *quest*
> Of feeding pleasures, from that eager zeal,
> Those yearnings which had every day been
>   mine . . .
>
> (IV.278)

The search of life had been for 'feeding' pleasures in the sense that they nourished what was other than themselves. They ministered to spiritual progress rather than merely enjoyment. It is interesting to see how exactly the passage quoted justifies the word 'quest': something more ambitious, more dedicated than a search merely. It is the word 'zeal' which makes clear that 'firm' in the passage above does not qualify 'habitual' only, or even chiefly. It is not doing duty just for 'firmly'; in the end, it is the quest itself which is 'firm'. The firmness is doubtless in part a matter of habit; but more than that, it is one of deep desire ('yearning') and of zeal. Custom is reinforced by a major movement of the mind.

The Prelude cannot be seen as recounting any quest in a literal sense. At that level, it is a meditative autobiography, and the travels it records were those normal enough for a young man in Wordsworth's social position. All the same, this does not bring out how the incidents and phases of the poem are treated. Recurrently, the idea of a journey enters the climactic Books of the poem (XI-XIII in the 1805 edition) *as metaphor;* this is true of Wordsworth's phase of aberration, and one of the metaphors he uses must by now be strikingly reminiscent:

> My business was *upon the barren sea,*
> My errand was to *sail* to other coasts.
>
> (XI.55)

> Yet was I often greedy in the chase,
> And roamed from hill to hill, from rock to rock,

Still craving combinations of new forms,
New pleasures, wider empires from the
    sight . . .

(XI.190)

Once again the metaphors delimit precisely: the *hunter* (he who is engaged in a 'chase') has a goal which means that his course, his 'errand', is determined from something outside himself—but at a fuller level of analysis, it is determined rather from within, and by choice and dedication.

The quest, the ordained journey, enters the poem also as metaphor for what Wordsworth does when he follows the narrow but saving line of rightness:

. . . O Friend, for whom
I *travel* in these dim uncertain ways;
Thou wilt assist me as a *pilgrim* gone
In search of highest truth.

(XI.390)

The search after insight is a recurrent idea:

Long time *in search of knowledge* desperate,
I was *benighted* heart and mind;

(XII.20)

Disposes her [i.e. the mind] . . .
To seek in man, and in the frame of life,
Social and individual, what there is
Desirable, affecting, good or fair
Of kindred permanence . . .

(XII.37)

sanguine schemes,
Ambitious virtues, pleased me less; I sought
For good in the familiar face of life . . .

(XII.65)

Moreover, although Wordsworth's 'search for good' is not a literal, physical quest, the idea of a quest or journey is present, literally, through much of the poem. Here is an example: the lines

A favourite pleasure hath it been with me,
From time of earliest youth, to walk alone
Along the public way . . .

(IV.363)

open one of the best-known passages in the Book describing Wordsworth's 'summer vacation' from Cambridge, and we soon find that the 'walk' has more of the quest in it, of a response to some kind of summons, than appeared at first:

While thus I wandered, step by step *led on,*
It chanced a sudden turning of the road
Presented to my view an uncouth shape
So near . . .

(400)

The tall, desolate soldier is himself a walker on the 'public way'. In Book V comes the incident in which the dreamer meets the Arab who will be 'a guide / To lead him through the desert' (82). The Arab *pursues his journey* in what seems like deep absorption of mind:

On he passed
Not heeding me . . .

(117)

In Book VI, Wordsworth writes 'my poem *leads* me' (334) to 'wanderings of my own'. While at Cambridge, he and a fellow student

staff in hand, on foot pursued our way
Towards the distant Alps . . .

(341)

They sound like pilgrims, and as they go through Switzerland that is what Wordsworth calls them, in a passage which emphasizes how the pilgrimage is one in search of major truth:

we could not choose but read
A frequent lesson of sound tenderness,
The universal reason of mankind,
The truth of young and old. Nor, side by side
Pacing, two brother *pilgrims* . . .

(474)

The celebrated moment of semi-mystical illumination that Wordsworth experienced as he descended the Alps on the Italian side is not the outcome of a quest for illumination, in the literal sense; but it is closely bound up with pursuit of the pilgrim journey. In fact, it is almost as if the poet has a sense of this. The two travellers lose their way. Then they find it again. Having re-discovered their fore-ordained route, they pursue it in a mood of solemnity and dedication:

Downwards we hurried fast,
And entered with the road which we had missed
Into a narrow chasm. The brook and road
Were fellow-travellers in this gloomy pass,
And with them did we journey several hours
At a slow step.

(VI.551)

The passage which follows (ll.556-72) is a celebrated one. It depicts the details of what this dedicated journey spread out before the travellers. Its intricate syntax and periodic structure ought not to be overlooked, and it is from these details that Wordsworth makes emerge his moment of vision. As the structure of the sentence at last unfolds itself, the long catalogue of impressions prove to be:

. . . *all* like workings of one mind, the features
Of the same face, blossoms upon one tree . . .

(VI.568)

The pilgrim journey is precisely what transforms life to a higher power of itself.

Much later, in the resolution of the poem, the idea of the road re-appears:

I love a public road: few sights there are
That please me more . . .

(XII.145)

Wordsworth goes on to speak of the fundamental illuminative power, and movement towards the open, transforming kind of knowledge, that the idea seemed to him always to have:

. . . such object hath had power
O'er my imagination since the dawn
Of childhood, when its disappearing line . . .
Was *like a guide into eternity,*
At least to *things unknown and without bound.*

As he grew up, the power of the idea realized itself for him:

> When I began to enquire
> To watch and question those I met, and held
> Familiar talk with them, *the lonely roads*
> *Were schools to me* in which I daily read
> With most delight the passions of mankind,
> There saw into the depth of human souls . . .
>
> (XII.161)

'School' emphasizes the idea of learning and knowledge, but the passage quoted last but one makes clear ('a guide . . . to things unknown and without bound') that the knowledge is a new knowledge, a searching-out of the mysterious and open-ended. The visionary nature of the whole experience shows in a later passage. Wordsworth says (XII.305 ff.), that he has hoped to write a poem which 'Proceeding from the depth of untaught things', might be 'A power like one of Nature's': be, in other words, revelatory at a radical, primal level. Then he goes on to recount an occasion when those hopes became uniquely strong. He was a traveller on Salisbury Plain, going over the Downs with not track to guide him, or

> along the bare white roads
> Lengthening in solitude their dreary line . . .
>
> (XII.316)

The precise nature of the image should be noted. The road is long and empty ('bare'), there are no distractions and there are no alternative routes (the road before him is 'lengthening in solitude'). The atmosphere of the walk is melancholy and solemn. These things are what make up the structure of a journey which is a quest. Wordsworth indicates the psychic consequences of such journeying:

> . . . While through those vestiges of ancient
> times,
> I range, and by the solitude o'ercome,
> I *had a reverie and saw the past* . . .
>
> (XII.318)

Influenced by the sight of Stonehenge and perhaps some of the other prehistoric monuments of the Plain, Wordsworth's vision in this setting is of Stone Age times; but the essential point is that here, once again, the image of the road and of the ordained journey, the quest, leads forward into a sense of visionary, preternatural insight.

Wordsworth's poem thus proves to have a distinctive structure. It is not the poem it seems. It by no means simply recounts, and meditates upon, such various experiences as made up the first thirty or so years of the poet's life. Underlying these experiences, or often as a literally constituent part of them, is an idea which seems to be sleeping throughout the whole poem, and at the same time constantly to start into life in it. Nor is this just the idea of the road as 'image'. It is more structured and dynamic than that. It is the idea of a journey which is solemn, which is ordained, and which at the same time is the route to knowledge and self-mastery. In other words, the idea of the quest. Wordsworth's poem assimilates, and deeply, covertly embodies, a structure which proves to be more explicitly utilized elsewhere.

The quest for knowledge and self-mastery may lead men to remote and strange places. It can also lead them home: quest turns out to be Odyssey. The inter-action between the two conceptions is of much interest for poetry between Wordsworth's time and the present; and in view of how the quest-poem seems to owe something to the European explorations of the seventeenth and eighteenth centuries, it is of interest in trying to comprehend the whole development of Western European culture over that period. Looked at more and more closely, *The Prelude* came to seem more and more like a quest-poem, though indirectly so; but there comes a point when we realize, because Wordsworth realizes, that this poem's quest is an Odyssey:

> Shall I avow that I had hope to see,
> I mean that future times would surely see,
> The man to come, parted, as by a gulph,
> From him who had been . . .
>
> (XI.57)

This 'seeing' would be the product of a quest for knowledge which led forward into unknown regions. Everyone knows how in the end, the poem recognizes that idea as the central and irremediable aberration. It is 'life's familiar face . . .' (1850, XII.62), the goal of Odysseus, which is the true goal of the enquiring spirit.

The point is confirmed by the *local* in which *The Prelude* is written. The opening of the first book describes Wordsworth making a journey, freely chosen by himself, back to the known and familiar places of his childhood; and it stresses how he has hopes that this very fact will release his major poetic powers. The poem, which opens with an echo of the closing lines of *Paradise Lost:* 'The earth is all

---

An excerpt from a letter to Sir George Beaumont, dated 3 June 1805

I have the pleasure to say, that I have finished [*The Prelude*] about a fortnight ago. I had looked forward to the day as a most happy one; and I was indeed grateful to God for giving me life to complete the work, such as it is. But it was not a happy day for me; I was dejected on many accounts: when I looked back upon the performance, it seemed to have a dead weight about it—the reality so far short of the expectation. It was the first long labour that I had finished; and the doubt whether I should ever live to write *The Recluse,* and the sense which I had of this poem being so far below what I seemed capable of executing depressed me much; above all, many heavy thoughts of my poor departed brother hung upon me, the joy which I should have had in showing him the manuscript, and a thousand other vain fancies and dreams. I have spoken of this, because it was a state of feeling new to me, the occasion being new. This work may be considered as a sort of portico to *The Recluse,* part of the same building, which I hope to be able, ere long to begin with in earnest; if I am permitted to bring it to a conclusion, and to write, further, a narrative poem of the epic kind, I shall consider the task of my life as over.

Quoted in Letters of Literary Men: The Nineteenth Century, *edited by Frank Arthur Mumby, George Routledge & Sons, 1906.*

before me . . .' (I.15), comes to rest in the 'house and fields' (83) which the poet can see in his mind's eye before he reaches them, and which will be the 'hermitage' (115) where the poem will come to fruition. This is Wordsworth's idea, in *The Prelude,* of (to quote Milton's lines again) ' . . . where to choose'. (pp. 94-102)

> *John Holloway, "The Odyssey and the Quest," in his* The Proud Knowledge: Poetry, Insight and the Self, 1620-1920, *Routledge & Kegan Paul, 1977, pp. 88-131.*

Paul Jay   (essay date 1984)

[*In the following excerpt, Jay discusses the meaning behind Wordsworth's autobiographical search for origins in* The Prelude.]

A brief over-view of the aims and the structure of Wordsworth's poem will begin to reveal the "serious paradox" generated by [the search for an authoritative and powerful *poetic* language]. As a poem that is searching for origins, *The Prelude* seeks to both enact the poet's return to the beginning, the source, of his poetic power and to reanimate an "original" lost poetic language. This can be seen clearly in Wordsworth's essay, **"Poetic Diction,"** which more than anything else outlines the larger boundaries of his poetic quest in *The Prelude.* The following passage, for example, goes a long way toward making explicit what Wordsworth's autobiographical search for origins is all about:

> The earliest poets of all nations generally wrote from passion excited by real events; they wrote naturally, and as men: feeling powerfully as they did, their language was daring, and figurative. In succeeding times, Poets, and Men ambitious of the fame of Poets, perceiving the influence of such language, and desirous of producing the same effect without being animated by the same passion, set themselves to a mechanical adoption of these figures of speech, and made use of them, sometimes with propriety, but much more frequently applied them to feelings and thoughts with which they had no natural connection whatsoever. A language was thus insensibly produced, differing materially from the real language of men in *any situation.* The Reader or Hearer of this distorted language found himself in a perturbed and unusual state of mind . . . he had no instinctive and infallible perception of the true to make him reject the false . . . the Poet spake to him in the character of a man to be looked up to, a man of genius and authority. Thus, from a variety of other causes, this distorted language was received with admiration; and Poets, it is probable, who had before contented themselves for the most part with misapplying only expressions which at first had been dictated by real passion, carried the abuse still further, and introduced phrases composed apparently in the spirit of the original figurative language of passion, yet altogether of their own invention, and characterized by various degrees of wanton deviation from good sense and Nature . . . This was the great temptation . . . which followed

> [the first poets]. . . . But the first Poets, as I have said, spake a language which, though unusual, was still the language of men.

This essay on diction actually constitutes a mythical genealogy of the development of poetic language and poetic power. As such, it is Wordsworth's own creative rendering of what amounts to a mythic history of his own craft, a rendering that authorizes and valorizes the nature of his own preoccupations as a poet—especially as they are presented in *The Prelude.* Here the transposed structure of a Christian return surfaces as the poet's desire that poets and their poetry return to the privileged language of the "earliest," impassioned poets. Wordsworth's view reflects a Christian pattern of "natural" creation, fall, and redemption: the first poets wrote in a "natural" language that subsequently fell into "distortion," "insensibility," and "mechanicalness"; this fall requires that poetic language be redeemed by a poet like Wordsworth, who wrote in his **"Preface to *Lyrical Ballads"*** that "The principal object . . . proposed in these Poems was to choose incidents and situations from common life, and to relate or describe them, throughout, as far as was possible in a selection of language really used by men . . . tracing . . . the primary laws of our nature."

The language of "common" life, the poet emphasizes, was chosen because in it "our elementary feelings co-exist in a state of greater simplicity," and "in that condition the passions of men are incorporated with the beautiful and permanent forms of nature." Since "all good poetry is the spontaneous overflow of powerful feelings," the poet chose to "adopt the very language of men . . . figure[s] of speech . . . prompted by passion." By achieving such a poetry, Wordsworth feels he can unite himself with those he deems the "first poets." Thus at *The Prelude*'s "appointed close" Wordsworth writes that he has "faithfully pictured" the "discipline / And consummation of the Poet's mind" (13:263-66), asserting that he can now stand as an "original" poet, a branch on the genealogical tree sketched out in his essay, where "Poets, even as Prophets," stand "each with each / Connected in a mighty scheme of truth" (12:301-2). As we will see below, this enabling function is an important goal of Wordsworth's poem.

While Wordsworth's ideas about the origins of poetry are generally informed by various "primitivist" theories current during the eighteenth century, they have their closest analogue in Vico's cyclical view of history. Vico wrote that the "master key" of his *New Science,* whose cyclical theory of history postulated an original age of the Gods, followed by the Age of Heroes, the Age of Men, and a *ricorso* to repeat the cycle, was his "discovery" that "the early gentile people . . . were poets who spoke in poetic characters." Vico's three ages correspond to three languages; an early "mute language of signs," the "poetic language" of "heroic" man, and finally a "human" language worked out by agreement among people. In Vico's schema the first spoken language was the language of the poets, a language "formed by feelings of passion" in the "imagination." Since these "theological poets" were the first "wise men," Vico posits their "poetic wisdom" as the "first wisdom of the gentile world," a wisdom that "must have begun with metaphysics not rational and abstract . . . but felt and imagined as that of these first men . . . all robust sense and vigorous imagination." Vico's "first poets" correspond to Wordsworth's "earliest poets," who wrote in the "excitement" of "passion," while Wordsworth's vision of the earliest poets' language falling into the "mechanistic" language of "ornamentation" duplicates the fall of poetic language into the "vulgar," the "rational," and the "abstract" in Vico's. Vico's *ricorso* is implicit, moreover, in Wordsworth's attempt to return to the connected scheme of poets reaching back to the first Prophet-Bards.

Wordsworth's hope of achieving a Vichian return to the sources of an "original" poetic language is echoed by the cyclical growth of his mind depicted in *The Prelude.* That is, the historical *ricorso* that Wordsworth seeks for poetry is duplicated by the personal *ricorso* outlined in *The Prelude*'s structure, which depicts a boy's "original," "natural" power, his loss of that power in the growing rationality of his manhood, and his return to the original sources of his power in the reanimation of a proper poetic language. The young poet who is to "redeem" the work of the "earliest poets" must himself first experience the askesis of his own *ricorso.*

This is why, in looking back over the course of his development as a poet, Wordsworth sees a cyclical pattern in the flux of his past experience. He presents his earliest relationship to language as a "natural" one that must somehow be recaptured. That relationship came to the poet in moments when, he writes:

> I would stand,
> Beneath some rock, listening to sounds that are
> The ghostly language of the ancient earth,
> Or make their dim abode in distant winds.
> Thence did I drink the visionary power.
> [2:326-30]

By the time the young Wordsworth reached Cambridge, the stark contrast between college and rural life made him realize that "I was not for that hour, / Nor for that place" (3:80-81). Writing that he was a "chosen Son" who had come to Cambridge with "holy powers," the poet asserts that since he could "apprehend all passions" (3:81-85) he "was ascending . . . To . . . community with highest truth" (119-20). Because of his "powers and habits" (106) of mind "all / That [he] beheld respired with inward meaning" (129). In these lines, he likens his "steady moods of thoughtfulness, matur'd / To inspiration" (149) to the prophetic, visionary powers of "Poets in old time, and higher up / By the first men, earth's first inhabitants" (152-153). In retrospect, Wordsworth writes that this point in his development was an "eminence," the "glory" of his youth; a time, in short, when he had the "Genius" and "Power" to "create like Divinity itself" (169-72).

After depicting the growth of his mind to this "eminence," however, Wordsworth recounts the beginnings of a poetic crisis, one in which his privileged relationship to nature's "language" began to falter. He writes that he was "misled" by "words," by "the trade in classic niceties," and the "dangerous craft of picking phrases out / From languages that want the living voice" (6:124-31). Later, when the poet was "prompted" by "plain imagination" to write, he recalls that the "visible shape" of his work was influenced not by "nature's inner self " but by "works of art" and "the images of books"—a "wilfulness of fancy and conceit" (8:511-21). In Book 11, "Imagination, How Impaired and Restored," Wordsworth speaks of his "crisis" as one brought on by his attraction to "reason" and "logic," a crisis that had created such a "gulph" between himself and the great poets that he "could no more / Trust the elevation which had made me one / With the great Family that here and there / Is scatter'd through the abyss of ages past" (61-63). He writes that he was "cut off . . . / From all the sources of [his] former strength" by the influence of "syllogistic words" and by the "Charm of Logic," that he had lost touch with the "mysteries of passion" that made "One brotherhood . . . / Of poets": theirs was for him an "empire pass'd away" (82-95).

The poem is, of course, written to reach its cyclical climax in Wordsworth's return to his "former strength," a strength inherent in his renewed relationship with "Nature's presence." Concerning the "impairment" of his imaginative powers, the poet writes near the end of Book 11 that:

> I had felt
> Too forcibly, too early in my life,
> Visitings of imaginative power
> For this to last: I shook the habit off
> Entirely and for ever, and again
> In Nature's presence stood, as I stand now,
> A sensitive, and a creative soul.
> [251-57]

The strategy of the poem is embodied in this cyclical structure. Wordsworth seeks to return to the "imaginative power" of the "earliest" poets by returning in his poem to the "sources" of his own poetic power in "early life." To redeem the work of the "first" poets, he must "enshrine the spirit" of his own past "For future restoration" (11:342-43):

> From . . . remembrances, and from the power
> They left behind . . . feeling comes in aid
> Of feeling . . .
> . . . if but once we have been strong.
> [11:325-28]

The cyclical pattern inherent in this restorative return to "Nature's presence," it must be noted, does not depend upon the poet's ability to somehow actually return to the places where his lost poetic power was first experienced. It ostensibly depends, rather, on memory. Wordsworth's "renewal," as it is depicted in his poem, does not come in his actual return to nature to experience again its visitations of power, but in his creative remembering of those experiences as they lay scattered in the disorder of time. For Wordsworth, the restorative power of remembering is actually rooted in a providential *forgetting* of what he experienced, and felt, in the past. For from the memory of nature's visitations the poet "retains" only an "obscure sense / Of possible sublimity," since the mind remembers only "how she felt, but what she felt" she remembers "not" (2:335-37). Remembering the "past" thus becomes a process attended by, and at one with, poetic creation. Seeking restoration from his past, the poet inevitably faces its absence, and with that absence, he faces the gulf between his past and his present selves:

> [S]o wide appears
> The vacancy between me and those days,
> Which yet have such self-presence in my mind
> That, sometimes, when I think of it, I seem
> Two consciousnesses, conscious of myself
> And of some other Being.
>
> [2:28-33]

"Those days" have "self-presence" only because the poet can fill the "vacancy" between them and himself with a poetry that seeks to recast them as a paradise of poetic power. Since "feeling comes in aid / Of feeling *if* but once we *have been* strong," the poet must postulate this paradise in his poem in order to "remember" it. Since a central characteristic of nature's early visitations is that they are forgotten, memory becomes for the poet writing his autobiographical poem a providential remembering of something that is actually lost. The relationship between Wordsworth and nature chronicled in the first two books of *The Prelude* describes the "ministry" of nature as an "unconscious intercourse" between a "Child" and "eternal Beauty" (1:589-90): the poet writes that his mind was "impregnated," "impress'd," and "elevated," by "obscure feelings" that "were forgotten" (1:614-35). What "Nature spake to me," he writes, was "doom'd to sleep / Until maturer seasons call'd them forth" (1:615, 622-23). The poet writes that he conceives of what nature "spoke" to him in its visitations only as "rememberable things" (1:616).

When Wordsworth circles back in his poem to the restoration of his poetic powers that followed the "impairment" of his imagination, declaring that he stands "Once more in Nature's presence, thus restored," (11:393-94) he does not, significantly, recount the "story" of this restoration, since, in fact, it exists in no single story. Instead, he remembers a series of experiences—past visitations of nature's power—out of their chronological order, all of which *pre-date* the crisis outlined in Book 11. In the final three books of the poem, restoration is not situated in any identifiable past event but is in fact generated in the very moments of the poem's composition. Only after he recollects his famous "spots of time," his experiences on the Plain of Sarum, and his ascension of Mt. Snowden into the narrative that constitutes the final three books of *The Prelude,* can the poet declare himself "restored" (13:262-71). Since restoration attends the activity of remembering what has been lost, its achievement in the poem can only present itself as coincident with this remembering, coincident, that is, with its writing: the experience of remembering depicted *in* the story of the poem form a series of moments that must necessarily extend into the very activity of its writing. Even in the earlier books, "restoration" is represented as a repeated experience, which in the poem becomes diffused into the very texture of the poet's existence. *The Prelude* begins, for example, with Wordsworth singing the "praises" of the restorative feelings he experienced while returning from London to Racedown in 1795, which he conflates with similar feelings attending his return to Grasmere in 1799, after having spent time with Coleridge. However, in Book 4 the poet writes that "restoration came" in 1788 when during his summer vacation

he "convers'd . . . with God-like power" (146-56). Again, in 1804, while *composing* Book 7, Wordsworth writes that his "strength" had been "stopp'd for years," and that he "resume[s] with chearful hope" the "Poet's task" because he had been "fit(ted)" with his strength the night before (1-56). By Book 11, though, the poet laments *as he writes* that he is "lost" again (330). This is why he returns to his "spots of time," and why he goes on in the remaining books to "remember" the other visitations with which he concludes his poem.

Wordsworth, then, in seeking to restore his creative powers by returning to his own past to rewrite it, weds the need for a Vichian *ricorso* to what Hegel identified as man's need to "produce himself" in the "practical activity" of art. The poet's "reduplication" of himself in *The Prelude* is enacted in a retrospective journey whose topography is inward knowledge. The contents of Wordsworth's art, which are to become "spiritualized" in their "passage" through his mind, are the recollected contents of his own past. In composing his poem, Wordsworth hopes that "speaking" of what has passed within him will enable him to reenvision his past as the development of Divine "Genius" and "Power":

> Of Genius, Power,
> Creation and Divinity itself
> I have been speaking, for my theme has been
> What pass'd within me.
>
> [3:171-74]

Since the spiritual value in art, according to Hegel, is produced in the creative process by the passage of material through the mind, Wordsworth's ability to transcend his loss of power hinges upon the mediating power of his own poem and the passage of his past through it. What "pass'd within" the poet must pass within him once more in the composition of his autobiographical poem, so that the process of his "reduplication" in it will help further the growth of the poet's mind and the restoration of his imaginative powers. Wordsworth's journey back to wholeness and poetic power is coincident with the activity of composing his poem. His narrative seeks to extend his past restoration(s) in the same way that Augustine's seeks to extend his past conversion—in and by the activity of writing.

Written at the beginning of the Romantic period, though, Wordsworth's text, as Hartman reminds us, is linked to the autonomous and individual, so that in the end it becomes "as problematic as the individual himself." Though he is "a pilgrim gone / In quest of highest truth," in writing his poem he has had to "travel in . . . dim uncertain ways" (11:391-93). This dimness and uncertainty specify the kind of "places" where his power resides. The poet's journey is seen to take place in the half-light of his own inner self:

> The days gone by
> Come back upon me from the dawn almost
> Of life: the hiding-places of my power
> Seem open; I approach, and then they close;
> I see by glimpses now; when age comes on,
> May scarcely see at all, and I would give,
> While yet we may, as far as words can give,
> A substance and a life to what I feel:
>
> [11:334-41]

Wordsworth's poem exemplifies the paradox Hartman identifies as central to Romantic poetry: the entire weight of having to transcend the purely autonomous and individual must be born by the poet personally, so that the problem of subjectivity itself becomes particularly acute in the poem. The "wide vacancy" between the author of the poem and its subject makes of them *two* consciousnesses, and the freedom of poetic creation has for its other side the abyss of endless figuration. This is why both the poet and the poem turn in upon themselves. The burden of overcoming the loss and the absence felt by Wordsworth at the beginning of *The Prelude* must be shared by both his past *and* his poem, since the two merge in a single present—the time of the poem's composition.

The poem's insistent self-consciousness is a measure of the tension generated by such a burden. In the middle of Book 2, Wordsworth interrupts his retrospective story to complain that it is a

> Hard task to analyse a soul, in which,
> Not only general habits and desires,
> But each most obvious and particular thought,
> Not in a mystical and idle sense,
> But in the words of reason deeply weigh'd,
> Hath no beginning.
>
> [2:232-37]

Here is another aspect of Wordsworth's serious paradox: in the act of composing a poem that seeks to return to the "beginning," he has come to realize that there may in fact be none. The seriousness of this paradox arises in part from Wordsworth's attempt to return to his own beginnings in writing *The Prelude* and at the same time to make his beginning as an original poet. He writes at the poem's conclusion in 1805 that

> . . . we have reach'd
> The time (which was our object from the first)
> When we may, not presumptuously, I hope,
> Suppose my powers so far confirm'd, and such
> My knowledge, as to make me capable
> Of building up a work that should endure.
>
> [13:266-71]

A key component of Wordsworth's "hard task" of self-analysis is his hope that the activity of composing a poem about his past will *prepare* him to become an "original poet" in the sense outlined in the essay on poetic diction. Thus Wordsworth asserts to his friend George Beaumont, "I began [*The Prelude*] because I was unprepared to treat any more arduous subject, and diffident of my own powers."

The surely unintended double meaning of Wordsworth's phrase about "treating" a "subject" in his poem serves to emphasize its similarity to the psychoanalytic process, for the "I" in his poem is being "treated" analytically as certainly as his past is being treated as subject matter. Here we can supplement our earlier discussion of the general relationship between autobiographical self-analysis and the "talking cure" by noting the self-reflexive text's potential function as a tool for the analyst's own analysis of *himself*. Freud insists on the preparatory necessity of self-analysis for the analyst as surely as Wordsworth insists on it for the poet. Referring to the analyst as someone who must

learn to "practice a particular art," Freud asks rhetorically in "Analysis Terminable and Interminable," "But where and how is the poor wretch to acquire the ideal qualifications which he will need in his profession? The answer is, in an analysis of himself, with which his preparation for his future activity begins." While the poet/analyst's qualifications are earned in the preparation of his self-analytical poem, the poem shares the problematic experienced by the analyst: the interminability of analysis (which Freud viewed as at best a mixed blessing). Wordsworth's composition of *The Prelude* was . . . a literally interminable experience. Composing it represented an arduous spiritual journey comparable with Augustine's. At the same time, however, it stands as a text exemplary of the serious paradoxes inherent in literary self-representation from the Romantic period on. (pp. 46-59)

> *Paul Jay, "The Wavering Balance: Wordsworth's Journey through 'The Prelude',"* in his Being in the Text: Self-Representation from Wordsworth to Roland Barthes, *Cornell University Press, 1984, pp. 39-72.*

Richard Gravil   (essay date 1989)

[*In the following essay, Gravil examines Wordsworth's convictions concerning the French Revolution as represented in* The Prelude.]

> I have said that poetry is the spontaneous overflow of powerful feelings; it takes its origin from emotion recollected in tranquillity; the emotion is contemplated till by a species of reaction the tranquillity gradually disappears, and an emotion, kindred to that which was before the subject of contemplation, is gradually produced and does itself actually exist in the mind.
>
> **"Preface to *Lyrical Ballads*"**

> A tranquillising spirit presses now
> On my corporeal frame, so wide appears
> The vacancy between me and those days
> Which yet have such self-presence in my mind,
> That, musing on them, often do I seem
> Two consciousnesses, conscious of myself
> And of some other Being.
>
> (*The Prelude,* II. 27)

There is—on the face of it—no doubt that the three revolutionary books of the 1850 text of *The Prelude* are intended to present a spectacle of woe, an illustration of human ignorance and guilt. They constitute a confession that Wordsworth (like Coleridge, the poem's addressee, who is now recuperating in the Mediterranean) has been capable of being parted from his better self. He too has experienced nightmares of incrimination, and periods 'Of sickliness, disjoining, joining things / Without the light of knowledge' (VIII.436-37). He has been taught to 'tame the pride of intellect'. Wordsworth presents himself as 'lured' into France (IX.34), over-confident in his capacity to understand the course of history, and 'enchanted' by revolutionary illusions. Man, he comes to feel, is mocked by possession of the 'lordly attributes of will and choice', having in himself no guide to good and evil (XI.306-20).

Yet no one who reads *The Prelude* attentively can fail to

notice that Wordsworth's presentment of his earlier self has a candour which contrasts strikingly with Coleridge's lack of it in *Biographia Literaria.* Wordsworth is so bold to look on painful things that it becomes harder, the more familiar one becomes with the procedure of his account, to avoid the impression that while one of Wordsworth's consciousnesses is concerned to present himself as prey to delusions, another is anxious to present Coleridge with an image of one whose loyalty to the revolution—well after the Great Terror of 1794, and by implication right up to the Coronation of Napoleon in 1804—is, as a form of natural piety, a matter of self-congratulation.

The manner of Wordsworth's self-presentation was well debated in *The Critical Quarterly* in 1976/77 by George Watson, John Beer and David Ellis. Since then it has been more minutely examined by Michael Friedman [in *The Making of a Tory Humanist,* 1979] and James Chandler [in *Wordsworth's Second Nature: A Study of the Poetry and the Politics,* 1984]. The present essay agrees substantially with each of these contributions. I accept, with George Watson, that Wordsworth intends his account as a warning against allowing oneself to be seduced into political malignancy by the ardour of undisciplined benevolence. I accept with David Ellis that the rhetoric of **The Prelude** none the less sometimes works harder to enforce than to

criticize the classical argument for political terror. I accept with Chandler that Wordsworth is quite clearly arguing in Burkean terms, even in the 1805 text, that 'upstart Theory'—whether French or Godwinian—is counter-humanist.

I am not here concerned with the arguments of Chandler and Friedman, that Wordsworth's politics is—even in **Lyrical Ballads**—that of a convert to Burke, or that he is by this date (ensconced in Grasmere) well on the way to becoming a 'tory humanist'. My concern is rather with what is created in the rhetorical structure of Books IX, X, and XI: and initially, at least, with the way in which **The Prelude** embodies within its critique of the ardour of undisciplined benevolence, a more powerful argument against those who were not, at the time, capable of such 'indiscipline'.

As one reads **The Prelude** it becomes very hard to escape the impression that as Wordsworth recollects, in tranquillity, the year of the terror, 'an emotion, kindred to that which was before the subject of contemplation, is gradually produced and does itself actually exist in the mind' so that the persona who addresses us from the midst of these events is a revolutionary persona, and if not a 'Terrorist', then certainly, in the phrase implausibly used of Coleridge

Rydal Mount, where Wordsworth resided from 1813 until his death.

by John Thelwall, a 'man of blood'. In Book IV, Wordsworth's subject is the rediscovery of a true self beneath the Cambridge patina so recently interposed between the world and himself. In Book II, more famously, Wordsworth finds such 'self-presence' of the past that 'often do I seem / Two consciousnesses, conscious of myself and of some other Being'. What creates the difficulty for the reader of the revolutionary triad is the 'self-presence', alongside the autobiographer, of a Robespierrean *alter ego* who is capable of thrusting aside whatever attempts Wordsworth may make to sustain a tone of apologetics. This *alter ego* is related of course to those other manifestations of Wordsworth's revolutionary persona, the Solitary of *The Excursion* and Oswald in *The Borderers,* in whose mouths Wordsworth places many of his own best lines.

The recollected revolutionary self is younger, and more self-confident, than the writer. He may of course be more Satanic, but he may also be, as Wordsworth twice recognizes, 'a child of nature' (XI.168), for youth maintains 'Communion more direct and intimate / With Nature,— hence, ofttimes with reason too—/ Than age or manhood even' (XI.29). One of Wordsworth's major themes is that of loyalty to the self or recovery of a self which has become 'bedimmed and changed / Both as a clouded and a waning moon' (XI.344). It would be perverse to argue that *The Prelude* consciously entertains any doubt as to which is the 'true self', for that self is explicitly associated with the feelings of my earlier [i.e. pre-revolutionary] life (*1805*, x.924—not in *1850*), yet the possibility constantly presents itself that the self of 1792/93, the imaginative self, which usurps, by a species of reaction, upon the recollecting poet, may be in some sense 'truer' than the one it has left behind.

. . . . .

The problems begin as early as Book VI. Wordsworth's excursion through France and the Alps with Robert Jones is 'chartered' (an interesting term, given its status in the revolution debate) by Nature. Nature being sovereign in his mind, her 'mighty forms . . . had given a charter to irregular hopes'. Logically one would suppose the forms alluded to to be the Alps, but tropically, and in context (VI. 333-41) they turn out to be a trinity of personifications—namely those of

> Europe . . . thrilled with joy,
> France standing on the top of golden hours,
> And human nature seeming born again.

There is little doubt that in *The Prelude* the devil has all the best images, even if these images must be read with the caution called for when reading Satan's rhetoric in *Paradise Lost.* Wordsworth presents himself as beset, and ensures that the reader is beset, with countless cases of seeming. Implicit in the fairground figure of France standing on the top of golden hours is a prefiguring of subsequent decline. The 'seeming' of 'seeming born again' is read to begin with as meaning merely 'as if': only later does one understand it to signify deception. The Wordsworth who tells us later that 'I had approached, like other youths, the shield / Of human nature from the golden side' expects us to recall the mediaeval fable of knights in combat over the true colour of a shield which was in reality silver on one side and gold on the other. But even if we do, chivalry is chivalry and silver is silver. We may think him mistaken, but we will hardly think him culpable. Each of these images is designed to tell the truth twice: the truth of enthusiasm and the truth of disenchantment.

The millennial 'born again' image is followed, in any case, by an extended picture of rejoiced humanity. This passage, with its wondering record of 'How bright a face is worn when joy of one / Is joy for tens of millions', its register of 'benevolence and blessedness / Spread like a fragrance everywhere', of 'amity and glee' and continuous dance, is vivid enough to remain as a reminder of a contrary state of the human soul depicted in London in Book VII. The long dance-like traverse of regenerated France (VI.342-408) is Wordsworth's most Blakean vision of human possibility. It much surpasses the glimpse of 'Helvellyn fair' which, as the opening of Book VIII (ll. 1-69) is more often noted as the contrary to unregenerate St. Bartholomew's (VII. 675-730).

Wordsworth's architectonics are much underrated, perhaps because they are so understated. In what might be called the second quatrain of the fourteen-book structure (the first quatrain having to do with the building of Wordsworth's own selfhood), Book V concerns itself with the culture man creates, and with the culture of man, including his ways of imagining other ways of being. Books VI, VII, and VIII appear to be designed to follow this theoretical introduction by counterpointing three successive visions of actual human life. 'Human nature seeming born again' (VI.341) is contrasted in Book VII with Londoners 'melted and reduced / To one identity' (VII.726). In Book VIII the central figure is a Cumbrian shepherd 'wedded to his life / Of hope and hazard', whose feet 'Crush out a livelier fragrance from the flowers / Of lowly thyme'. This third vision of human possibility refers back, not surprisingly, to the patriarchal Swiss ('to hardship born and compassed round with / Danger' (VI.509-10). More surprisingly perhaps it also refers forward, though only in the more carefully articulated *1850* text, to Book IX's introduction of Michel Beaupuy as a man whose nature 'Did breathe its sweetness out most sensibly, / As aromatic flowers on Alpine turf, / When foot hath crushed them'.

The introduction of Beaupuy is, however, contextualized by two strains echoed from Book VIII, and this conjunction creates a remarkable ambivalence. Shepherdlike he may be, in ll. 294-98, but in 298-302 he appears as a character wandering in perfect faith through a realm of Romance. Might Beaupuy, like Wordsworth in Book VIII, be guilty of excessive exercise of 'that first poetic faculty / Of plain Imagination and severe' and consequently of 'wilfulness of fancy and conceit'? 'From touch of this new power', Wordsworth had said of his own imagination, 'Nothing was safe' (VIII. 365–77). The phraseology is ominous, and weighty enough to be applied to that later and greater 'work / Of false imagination' (*1805*, x.848) his Godwinian new man. Beaupuy, however, is not presented, as Coleridge is in Book VIII, as one 'in endless dreams / Of sickliness, disjoining, joining, things / Without the light of knowledge' (l. 435). Wordsworth and Beaupuy be-

held a 'living confirmation' of their theories and their aspirations, and

> saw in rudest men,
> Self-sacrifice the firmest; generous love,
> And continence of mind, and sense of right,
> Uppermost in the midst of fiercest strife.
>   (IX.386)

They were steadied in their speculations by having real and solid forms about them.

The most striking 'form' of this book, the hunger-bitten girl of Blois, licenses Wordsworth's most positive enunciation of a political manifesto. The girl is employed, as every reader of *The Prelude* knows, as a mobile object to which a heifer can be conveniently tethered, an emblem of the utmost human degradation. What Wordsworth tethers to her, within the same long sentence, is first the unsurprising hope that 'poverty / Abject as this would in a little time / Be found no more' and then a striking series of constitutional demands. The 'heartless' girl releases in him a hope to see

> All institutes for ever blotted out
> That legalized exclusion, empty pomp
> Abolished, sensual state and cruel power
> Whether by edict of the one or few;
> And finally, as sum and crown of all,
> Should see the people having a strong hand
> In framing their own laws; . . .

What we have here is, in effect, a recollected Rousseauistic preview of the politics of the *Letter to the Bishop of Llandaff.*

Wordsworth's tale up to this point in Book IX projects a young man only slowly deciding upon his stance and sympathies. Lured (IX. 34) into a 'theatre, whose stage was filled / And busy with an action far advanced' (IX. 94) he was 'unprepared with needful knowledge'. The National Synod, and the Bastille, are tourist attractions, like but less powerful than 'the painted Magdalen of le Brun' (IX. 42-80). Only by a species of reaction to Royalist feeling and opinion does he discover that 'The soil of common life, was, at that time, / Too hot to tread on'. His political science, before Beaupuy, amounts to a feeling that 'the best ruled not, and feeling that they ought to rule', a position rooted in his schooltime experience of 'ancient homeliness' in Lakeland's admittedly untypical 'nook'. The events of France seem to have happened 'rather late than soon'. Identifying with the French in their desire to share in such ancient homeliness as Cumbrians enjoy, and with the 'bravest youth of France' enlisting in defence of their revolution, he thunderously concludes that no one could resist their cause

> Who was not lost, abandoned, selfish, proud,
> Mean, miserable, wilfully depraved,
> Hater perverse of equity and truth.

There is, then, little in Book IX except its frame, to suggest that this is a cautionary tale. The framing should be noted, however. Book IX began with an ominous image: that of the poet fearing to press on for fear of the 'ravenous', or in *1805* 'devouring', sea that lies in wait (IX. 4). It ends, in *1805,* with the narrative of Vaudracour and Julia as an oblique instance of impatience, illegitimacy and untethered mind.

. . . . .

In October 1792 the fierce metropolis finds Wordsworth—now bound for England—by no means as indifferent to late events as he had been the previous year. The account given in the first paragraph of Book X, of the historical state of play, leaves one in no doubt which side Wordsworth is on. The revolutionary state has a high and fearless soul, and is a republic in body as well as in name. The late and lamentable crimes are past, and 'the plains of liberty' seems a suitable periphrasis for French soil. In daylight, however, the Carousel is no more affecting than was the Bastille a year before: he seems still unable to unlock the meaning of Parisian stones. Only at night, in his lonely garret room, does the carnage of the previous month, in the September Massacres, seem close enough to touch. Or rather, for this is Wordsworth's most manufactured 'spot', the events can be made to yield a 'substantial dread' by one willing to work and to be wrought upon by apocalyptic incantations and tragic fictions and appropriate echoes of Shakespeare. The brilliant, if over-literary, vision ends by grafting Burke's 'swinish multitude' onto Blake's revolutionary tigers to produce a sense of Paris as a place 'Defenceless as a wood where tigers roam' (IX. 93).

One's suspicion that this dread is somewhat factitious, a product of Burke's intoxicating bowl, is reinforced by its slight effect on Wordsworth's daytime consciousness. True, he attributes to himself foresight of widening terror, but the immediate consequence is that he toys with the idea of summoning an international brigade to descend on France 'from the four quarters of the winds' to compel her to be free. In such a cause he would have been prepared to offer 'Service however dangerous'. When he reflects that

> A spirit thoroughly faithful to itself,
> Is for Society's unreasoning herd
> A domineering instinct
>   (x. 167)

it is not entirely clear whether he sees himself as the needful bellwether, or is merely expressing willingness, as an insignificant stranger, to serve some other 'paramount mind'.

At home in England, Wordsworth presents himself as no woolly-minded liberal but a strident revolutionary—more Stalinist than Hegelian—indifferent to the outcome of Clarkson's campaign against the slave-trade not because slavery isn't a rotten business, but because it is fatuous to concern oneself with pruning a tree which is on the point of being felled.

> for I brought with me the faith
> That if France prospered, good men would not
>   long
> Pay fruitless worship to humanity,
> And this most rotten branch of human shame.
> Object, so seemed it, of superfluous pains,
> Would fall together with its parent tree.
>   (x. 257)

This systemic metaphor should caution one against any

reading of Wordsworth's convictions at this date based upon a compendium of good causes: the 1805 text expresses derision for disappointed campaigners awaiting the next fashionable 'caravan', just as the 1850 introduces a barbed reference to English liberals experiencing 'a novel heat of virtuous feeling'. Unless the metaphor is loosely chosen, slavery is here envisioned as part of a shameful system of exploitation, based upon division, ownership, and the failure to recognize the good of humanity as an end in itself. Wordsworth's relative indifference to it as a single issue indicates a confidence in the imminent fall of all social organizations based upon any but '*equity* and justice'. 'Such was my then belief', (*1805* continues), 'that there was one, / And only one, solicitude for all'.

There follows 'the conflict of sensations without name' brought about by the declaration of war between Britain and France. Britain's rulers could not see that to test old-fashioned 'patriotic love' at the very moment when the volcano of revolution was bringing to birth a new and higher loyalty, to human freedom itself, was akin to deifying John the Baptist and spurning the Christ. The implication of this outrageous analogy is that responsibility for the crucifixion of humanity that follows must be laid at the door of English idolaters. Should we miss that implication it does not matter, because Wordsworth's account of the Great Terror begins, at line 331, by arraigning Pitt for provoking it.

Nothing in *The Prelude,* in either text, exculpates Pitt. There were of course men in France who 'for their desperate ends had plucked up mercy by the roots', but only Pitt's goad could have created the coalition of temperaments necessary to the instigation and the continuance of revolutionary terror. In describing the terror, which began in June 1794, Wordsworth uses the oddest of his exculpatory tropes: the guillotine whirls like a windmill, with a kind of macabre innocence. The infant revolution, we are invited to conclude, exemplifies like any other infant the recurring Wordsworthian theme of 'the might of souls . . . while yet the yoke of earth is new to them' (III. 180), and the desirable 'eagerness of infantine desire'. One of Wordsworth's selves parenthetically questions the image, but does not censor it:

> Domestic carnage now filled the whole year
> With feast-days; old men from the chimney nook,
> The maiden from the bosom of her love,
> The mother from the cradle of her babe,
> The warrior from the field—all perished, all—
> Friends, enemies, of all parties, ages, ranks,
> Head after head, and never heads enough
> For those that bade them fall. They found their joy,
> They made it proudly, eager as a child,
> (If light desires of innocent little ones
> May with such heinous appetites be compared),
> Pleased in some open field to exercise
> A toy that mimics with revolving wings
> The motion of a windmill; though the air
> Do of itself blow fresh, and make the vanes
> Spin in his eyesight, *that* contents him not,
> But, with the plaything at arm's length, he sets
> His front against the blast, and runs amain,

> That it may whirl the faster.

(x. 356)

The edict which released the worst phase of the Terror was passed on 10 June 1794. Two days before that, on 8 June 1794, Wordsworth told Mathews (with whom he was planning a somewhat Fabian organ of reform to be called *The Philanthropist*) that he 'recoiled from the bare idea of a revolution'. He described himself as 'a determined enemy to every species of violence'. Ten years later *The Prelude* certainly expresses in these lines a horror of violence, but Wordsworth seems equally capable of finding images expressive of something which is not merely horror, but a kind of dreadful fascination. Either Wordsworth the philanthropist was not, in fact, as 'determined' an enemy to 'every species of violence' as he pretended, or Wordsworth the poet has become aware, whether in writing *The Prelude* or at some point in between, that the rage for destruction is something he had shared.

A second 'childhood' image is introduced at line 391, dignified by its association with both Classical and English myth: 'The Herculean Commonwealth had put forth her arms and throttled with an infant godhead's might / The snakes about her cradle'. Part of its function is to prepare for the curious usage of the terms 'treachery' and 'desertion' in the nightmare passage which follows: Wordsworth presents himself as tortured 'through months, through years, long after the last beat / Of those atrocities' (well into the Racedown period, that is) by nightmares of imprisonment, nightmares in which he appears to plead before unjust tribunals 'with a voice / Labouring, a brain confounded, and a sense, / Death-like, of treacherous desertion, felt / In the last place of refuge—my own soul'. The ambiguity is of the sharpest order: would it be more treacherous to plead against the victims of the terror, or on their behalf ? The function of the 'Herculean Commonwealth' image, and the repeated child motif, is to give weight to the less expected sense, that the treachery is to the infant commonwealth, the rough beast that born-again human nature turns out to be.

Can human nature in its 'dog-day' aspect be worshipped as physical nature had been worshipped in its tumultuous states? The answer to that strange question (if that is what the paragraph x. 416-36 means) appears to be yes. Wordsworth identifies with those (briefly alluded to at x. 340) who see the terror as part of the wrath of providence, a sublime retribution: he experiences 'daring sympathies with power', sympathies whose 'dread vibration is to this hour prolonged' (x. 457-60—the final phrase in *1850* only). The devouring sea, threatened at the beginning of Book IX, is now (x. 470-80) understood as a 'deluge' of ancient guilt, spreading its loathsome charge, to fertilize (if one may extrapolate the image as Wordsworth does elsewhere) the plains of liberty.

That being so, it is hard to see why Robespierre, prime strangler of the snakes about the cradle of the commonwealth, and lancer of the boils of ancient guilt, should come in for such rhetorical vengeance as he receives at Wordsworth's hands in x. 481-603. If those of the Poole circle in 1794 could view Robespierre as 'a ministering angel of mercy, sent to slay thousands that he might save millions' why should Wordsworth react so differently? That he did rejoice so immoderately one may doubt. But even as an instance of editorial self-exculpation, a distancing, it is quite out of character with the rest of the account. The extent of Wordsworth's alleged glee is puzzling. The reference to Robespierre as 'chief regent' of 'this foul Tribe of Moloch' might be understood as an ironic adoption of fiercely anti-Jacobin sentiments except that no irony seems to be present. Or we might see Robespierre as having given too many hostages to Tory propagandists and having fuelled counter-revolutionary zeal. But there is a further consideration. Robespierre appears as having incarnated Wordsworth's own revolutionary self, a self which was far closer to the reality of the 'angel of death' so lightly spoken of in Nether Stowey, and which the poet of 1805 is relieved to lay to rest.

The letter to Mathews already quoted contains—presumably by coincidence—the very image Coleridge would use in 1795 to describe Robespierre. Wordsworth in June 1794 can see himself as one who 'in [his] ardour to attain the goal, [does] not forget the nature of the ground where the race is to be run': Coleridge sees Robespierre as one whose eagerness to reach the 'grand and beautiful' prospect ahead of him, caused him to 'neglect the foulness of the road'. Whether or not Wordsworth has Robespierre in mind, in choosing his image, it is clear that he does not choose to present himself to Mathews as one who has already been seduced into excessive hatred, or undisciplined benevolence, or discovered to what extreme consequences his conversion, by the innocent Godwin, to schemes of social engineering, could lead him.

. . . . .

The death of Robespierre is prepared for and concluded by the most complex assortment of motifs. It begins with a paragraph of recollection of the joys of Arras (Robespierre's birthplace) in 1790, and ends with a reprise of the Furness 'spot' from Wordsworth's own boyhood. It tells of a visit to the burial-place of William Taylor the wise instructor (Taylor stands in perhaps for that later tutor Michel Beaupuy, but also contrasting with him, as the one who set Wordsworth on the safer path of poetry). It includes a description of ethereal mountains observed from the Leven sands, mountains reminiscent of the 'dawn dedication' passage, and pauses to make ironic reference to the 'great sea . . . at a safe distance far retired', having momentarily suspended its ravages.

The announcement, by a passing traveller, of Robespierre's death occasions from Wordsworth a 'hymn of triumph', and (in *1805*) 'glee of spirit' and 'joy in vengeance'. It is presented as reawakening and reactivating Wordsworth's sense of himself as a power: his boyhood mastery of the horses of Furness usurps upon the fading echoes of the horsemen of apocalypse. The Wordsworth who with his boyhood associates 'beat with thundering hoofs the level sand' now sees himself, with his political associates, cleansing the Augean stables by more patient means than those of Hercules, tranquillizing the 'madding factions', and furthering 'the glorious renovation'. The shadow has passed, and its passing is recorded in a dawn image, which Wordsworth orchestrates as deliberately for humanity as

Coleridge once orchestrated a sublime sunset for Lamb in 'This Lime-Tree Bower': 'Come now, ye golden times . . . as the morning comes / From out the bosom of the night come ye'.

The reprise of 'We beat with thundering hoofs the level sand' makes so resonant a conclusion to Book x in the 1850 text that it can obscure the fact that the 'dawn' image is not yet finished with. The death of Robespierre marks in fact a rite of passage for Wordsworth's revolutionary self—all things have second birth—and he looks now (August 1794) for the republic to enjoy triumphs which will be 'Great, universal, irresistible'. Lines 19-27 of Book xi recognize that he was mistaken, but the revolutionary self is permitted an uncensored claim that what is at work, once again, is Nature's self. Wordsworth seems confident that the acquittal of Thelwall, Hardy and Tooke in the treason trials of December 1794 is a victory for Nature, Justice and Liberty over those who, in England, appeared intent on importing terror in the cause of repression.

Less clear is what happens when Wordsworth returns 'from those bitter truths' about Pitt's persecutions to continue his own history. On the face of it, Book xi lines 75-104, which review his development as a political thinker, could be dealing solely with the summer of 1792, when under Beaupuy's tutelage he was led to take 'an eager part / In arguments of civil polity'. Arguably, however, the same passage could be surveying his political development through to the end of 1794 when, with Mathews, he is striving to learn to what extent the happiness of nations depends 'Upon their laws, and fashion of the state'.

Most readers have, quite reasonably, taken the passage beginning

> Bliss was it in that dawn to be alive,
> But to be young was very Heaven!

To refer unambiguously to France's 'standing on the top of golden hours' in the period between 1790 (the walk to Como) and 1792 (the friendship with Beaupuy). The fact that the lines were separately published under the title **'Feelings of an Enthusiast upon the Commencement of the French Revolution'** appears to confirm that view, as indeed does the reflection that Wordsworth in 1794 is not thought to have known much 'bliss'.

In context however, in *The Prelude,* the antecedent dawn is that which breaks in August 1794 upon the sands of Leven. One of the most impressive features of *The Prelude,* especially in *1850,* is Wordsworth's articulation of image to image: Snowdon and Simplon are linked by usurpation of vapours, the Shepherd and Beaupuy by herbal fragrances, and so on. Could a poet who links widely separated episodes by such means *miss* the fact that the logical antecedent of 'that dawn' is the dawn of hope in 1794, a mere 134 lines before? Simply *by placing the passage where he places it,* Wordsworth invites the question whether he found in the early period of maximum political involvement following the terror, the climax of his bliss.

Moreover, the reference in this famous passage to 'Reason' seeming to assert her rights 'When most intent on making of herself a prime enchantress', seems to fit the

Godwinian period of 1794 rather better than any moment before that, as indeed does the imagery of plasticity (XI. 138) and of moulding and remoulding (XI. 150) the world one inherits. If this 'dawn' is that of 1789 or 1790 Wordsworth's description of himself as politically committed in *that* dawn is thoroughly misleading. If it is the summer of 1792, it is hard to see what the 'licence' of II. 163 refers to, or why he refers to himself as

> Not caring if the wind did now and then
> Blow keen upon an eminence that gave
> Prospect so large into futurity.

As an image for one who has come to terms with the need for political violence this has the merit of somewhat chilling understatement: as an image for one who knows of nothing worse than the fall of the Bastille, or the need to repel invaders massing upon the borders, it simply misses the mark.

What prevents one from concluding that the 'blissful dawn' is biographically as well as textually subsequent to rather than prior to the death of Robespierre is, of course, the resumption of relative chronological clarity at XI. 173. 'In the main outline, such it might be said / Was my condition, till with open war / Britain opposed the liberties of France'. This statement would certainly appear to restrict the 'blissful dawn' to a period before February 1793. Even this, however, is five months after the September Massacres. In any case the event which is blamed for clouding the blissful dawn, and bringing to an end this 'condition' of rapture is not, in the first place, Robespierre's terror but Pitt's military action against France.

No doubt Coleridge, as auditor-elect, was better equipped than we to know precisely what the landmarks were in Wordsworth's political development. For whatever reason, the frequency of Wordsworth's reference to time in Book XI does nothing to make them more distinct. 'But now', Wordsworth continues, in XI. 206, 'become oppressors in their turn, / Frenchmen had changed a war of self-defence / For one of conquest'. It is not possible to date this 'now' any earlier than May 1794, when the French began a summer of offensive military campaigns, or to know what it signifies. Dire though the news is, it makes France no worse than the autocratic powers opposing her. Wordsworth is unlikely to have sided with those fighting against France any earlier than Tom Poole (who was welcoming Napoleon's victories in May 1797), and he seems to have taken most of France's martial adventures prior to the second invasion of Switzerland in his stride. War merely prompts him to adhere 'more firmly to old tenets'.

And 'this was the time' (XI. 223) when Godwin's philosophy arrived to complete the work Pitt had begun: the stopping of the passages through which the ear converses with the heart. The poet's goaded mind takes on the mantle of Robespierre, dragging 'all precepts, judgements, maxims, creeds, / Like culprits to the bar' (XI. 295) and probing (in *1805*) 'the living body of society / Even to the heart' (*1805*. X. 875).

'Studied vagueness' understates what Wordsworth is doing with chronology throughout the first 305 lines of Book XI. They lead up to an undateable moral and intel-

lectual crisis, some time between the joint depredations of France and Godwin in 1794, and the beginnings of recovery in late 1795 under Dorothy's influence at Racedown: a crisis most probably associated with political activity during the period of residence in the great city in 1795. In any case, if one examines the images employed, even as hastily as here, one cannot but notice that something more than a haziness about dates is involved. The poetry seems designed to induce a real confusion about the sequence of events and responses, rather than merely about their intervals. Confusion has its attraction, of course, for if 'Bliss' cannot be dated, neither culpability nor apostasy can be established. But the confusion in this case seems to stem from something else: a recognition that the famous cantata to revolutionary enthusiasm seems to Wordsworth to apply with equal force to two quite separate phases in his political development, and to express two quite different states of being.

One of those states is the one which generates in the course of the narrative that striking sequence of tropes designed to rob terror of its sting: the child with his windmill, Hercules in his cradle, and the wind upon an eminence. Each figure exhibits, arguably, that use of language Wordsworth deplored in the Essays upon Epitaphs, as 'a counter-spirit, unremittingly and noiselessly at work to derange, to subvert, to lay waste, to vitiate, and to dissolve' (*Prose Works,* II, 85). More pertinently, perhaps, Wordsworth's prefatory essay to *The Borderers* directly addresses the tendency of revolutionaries to employ style to diminish atrocities. He remarks of the revolutionary mind that it will tend to 'chequer & degrade enterprises great in their atrocity by grotesque littleness of manner and fantastic obliquities' (*Prose Works,* I, 78). This is not through lack of imagination. Minds such as Oswald's possess powerful imagination, as the preface observes. The presence of powerful imagination is perhaps appropriately signified in the 'windmill' simile and the mountain-top metaphor by their common element, the correspondent breeze.

. . . . .

In Book XI. lines 224-320 Wordsworth develops his account of the intellectual crisis which ends his revolutionary career. Godwinian philosophy, the philosophy 'That promised to abstract the hopes of man / Out of his feelings', but which in fact allowed the passions to work disguised as pure reason seduces Wordsworth into the experience he dramatizes in his 'Oswald'. (Wordsworth's distrust of the reason may be Burkean, as Chandler argues, but it can also be heard as strikingly Nietzschean). What both experience is masterful personal liberty,

> Which, to the blind restraints of general laws
> Superior, magisterially adopts
> One guide, the light of circumstances, flashed
> Upon an independent intellect.

The career of 'Oswald' shows this guide to be a will o'the wisp—an abstraction operating upon a delusion—and line 248 speaks of Wordsworth's understanding as 'inflamed'. None the less, the desire that man should 'start out of his earthy, worm-like state' still appears to Wordsworth 'A noble aspiration!' To the 1805 declaration that 'yet I feel the aspiration', the 1850 text adds 'nor shall ever cease /

To feel it'. What he criticizes himself for is the desire to accomplish that transformation 'by such means as did not lie in nature'.

If the enlightenment dream of the man to come, parted as by a gulph from him who has been (XII. 59-60) is a work of 'false imagination' it is none the less justified by the upholders of 'ancient Institutions'.

> Enough, no doubt, the advocates themselves
> Of ancient Institutions had performed
> To bring disgrace upon their very names;
> Disgrace, of which, custom and written law,
> And sundry moral sentiments as props
> And emanations of those institutes,
> Too justly bore a part. *A veil had been*
> *Uplifted; why deceive ourselves? 'twas so,*
> *'Twas even so; and sorrow for the man*
> *Who either had not eyes wherewith to see,*
> *Or, seeing, hath forgotten!*
>
> (*1805*, x. 849 my italics)

Moreover it is at this point that Wordsworth describes himself as having been mentally let loose, 'let loose and goaded', a trope which combines an image earlier used of the French leaders in 1794 (goaded into Terror by Pitt's ministrations, x. 336), with one used in the *Letter to the Bishop of Llandaff* of the French people themselves: 'The animal just released from its stall will exhaust the overflow of its spirits in a round of wanton vagaries'. He thereby gratuitously associates himself with the Mountain and the People, and absolves all three.

Wordsworth's hymn of triumph at the passing of the shadow, Robespierre, one may conclude, is only partly occasioned by what he felt about the death of Robespierre himself. A major element is relief, felt at the time of writing, at the dethroning of his Godwinian self whose depredations upon the living body of society and nature's holiest places are quite clearly presented as an internalization of Robespierre's practices. Yet that self, even amid these confusing obsequies (confused by images of dawn and consecration and mingled origins at Arras and Hawkshead) asserts itself sufficiently to see the 'dawn' of Robespierre's death as the blissful dawn of its own experience.

Its continued co-presence as co-author in 1804 is responsible, one has to feel, for the fact that Wordsworth, although largely restored to his milder self, by nature and 'all varieties of human love', twice employs language of the utmost vituperation in Books X and XI. First in the reference to Pitt's verminous Tory cabinet, and its imitative bloodlust, and second in his account of the coronation of Napoleon in 1804.

> This last opprobrium *when we see the dog*
> *Returning to his vomit;* when the sun
> That rose in splendour, was alive, and moved
> In exultation among living clouds
> Hath put his function and his glory off,
> And turned into a gewgaw, a machine,
> Sets like an Opera phantom.

The sun is dead and France has killed it.

Wordsworth had been of the devil's party. In so far as to be a man of blood is to be of the devil's party, he remains

one in Book XII and XIII. It has been part of my intention to suggest that Wordsworth in *The Prelude* justifies the little terror, and partially excuses the great terror, just as he presents the character of Oswald, in *The Borderers,* as a blend of himself and Robespierre. Imagination resuscitates past selves and their loyalties.

But this explanation is too simple. It is not necessary, after all, that it should be a strictly revolutionary self that in the *1805* and *1850* texts continues to legitimate a certain connoisseurship of blood. It might also be an apocalyptic one. We see that self emerging, in fact, in the curious rhetoric of Book X where Wordsworth notes among the observers of the terror those who 'doubted not that providence had times of vengeful retribution' (x. 340), and suggests that some spirit fell on him that linked him with the ancient prophets who

> Wanted not consolations . . .
>   when they denounced
> On towns and cities, wallowing in the abyss
> Of their offences, punishment to come
>
> (x. 440)

Wordsworth's youthful and revolutionary selves were certainly more imaginative than his editorial self. The youthful imagination is unafraid of contemplating 'a world how different from this', or 'something evermore about to be'. It is pleased that a midnight storm can grow darker 'in the presence of my eye', and delights in witnessing—in the Snowdon vision—how the real sea gives up its majesty in the face of an imaginative usurpation, the sea of mist on whose shore Wordsworth finds himself. Similarly the revolutionary self is able to share the excitement of a Robespierre, or a Godwin, as they contemplate 'the man to come, parted as by a gulph from him who had been', or try to bring to birth 'a world how different from this', or drive man more rapidly along what Coleridge called the imaginative 'ascent of being'.

Most accounts of Wordsworth's imagination, however, leave out the quality of dread, which while present elsewhere emerges most clearly in the negative sublime of the Salisbury Plain spot, whose topography is associated with another of Wordsworth's literary self-projections in the 1790s, the benevolently murderous sailor of *Guilt and Sorrow.* In Book XIII lines 279-349, in a major argument too little attended to in this context, Wordsworth presents himself as wandering across Salisbury Plain in a state of confidence that he has the power to perceive things unseen before, and to create works which because they arise 'from a source of untaught things' might 'become a power like one of Nature's'. There, like his sailor in *Guilt and Sorrow,* he 'paced the bare white roads / Lengthening in solitude their dreary line'. For him, however, time fled backwards until he saw 'multitudes of men, and here and there, / A single Briton clothed in wolfskin vest' and heard 'The voice of spears':

> I called on darkness—but before the word
> Was uttered, midnight darkness seemed to take
> All objects from my sight; and lo! again

The desert visible by dismal flames;
It is the sacrificial altar, fed
With living men—how deep the groans! The
    voice
Of those that crowd the giant wicker thrills
The monumental hillocks, and the pomp
Is for both worlds, the living and the dead.

Suck wickers, according to Frazer, formed part of traditional mid-summer processions in some regions of Europe,
and particularly France and Belgium, until well into the
early years of the nineteenth century. In Brie a wicker
giant was burnt annually on Midsummer's Eve. In Paris
and elsewhere the preferred date was the nearest Sunday
to 7 July. In many areas animals—usually cats—were substituted for the human sacrifices which according to Caesar and Strabo were offered by the ancient Gauls. For contemporary cartoonists the wicker was negatively associated with the iconography of terror: Wordsworth, however,
seems able to sympathize with the sublimity of sacrifice.

While Chandler boldly deals with the early spots of time
as Burkean, in that they have to do with the discipline of
place, he has less to say about this spot, except to call it—
none too helpfully, it seems to me—'a sublime dream of
Burke's immemorial British past'. The meaning of this
reverie concerning benign druidic sacrifice may not be
welcome, but it is clear: the imaginative mind 'stands by
Nature's side among the men of old' and may indeed
'boldly take his way among mankind / Wherever nature
leads' (XIII. 296), whether it leads to contemplation of the
stars or to 'the sacrificial altar, fed / With living men' (ll.
331-32).

Imagination is geared to the sublime in so extraordinary
a degree that in 1816 Wordsworth will celebrate the
bloodshed of Waterloo as both a votive offering and a martial feat on a scale sufficient to satiate Imagination. The
'Ode: 1815' made many tremble, not least for the lines on
the deity which Wordsworth advisedly cut:

But Thy most dreaded instrument,
In working out a pure intent,
Is man arrayed for mutual slaughter,
Yea, Carnage is thy daughter

But these lines of 1816 are not, it seems to me, an aberration. They continue in a direct line from the Salisbury
Plain spot, in which Wordsworth offered his definitive
statement of what it means to be a child of nature and to
stand by Nature's side. A veil had indeed been uplifted in
the 1790s, but there was more behind it than revolutionary
sympathy. There was also the curious perception, attributed to Ovid in Geoffrey Hill's poem ('Ovid in the Third
Reich', *King Log,* 1968), that those who stand near 'the
ancient troughs of blood', though they may be damned,
'harmonise strangely with the divine love'. (pp. 127-43)

    *Richard Gravil, " 'Some Other Being': Words-
    worth in 'The Prelude'," in* The Yearbook of
    English Studies, *Vol. 19, 1989, pp. 127-43.*

FURTHER READING

Altieri, Charles. "Wordsworth's Wavering Balance: The
Thematic Rhythm of *The Prelude.*" *The Wordsworth Circle*
IV, No. 4 (Autumn 1973): 226-40.
    Suggests that Wordsworth attempts to demystify the in-
    teraction between the mind and nature in *The Prelude.*

Arac, Jonathan. "Bounding Lines: *The Prelude* and Critical
Revision." In *Post-Structuralist Readings of English Poetry,*
edited by Richard Machin and Christopher Norris, pp. 227-
47. Cambridge: Cambridge University Press, 1987.
    Analyzes Wordsworth's revisions to the original manu-
    script of *The Prelude* and surveys critics' attempts to
    recreate the original.

Brisman, Leslie. "Wordsworth: How Shall I Seek the Origin?" In his *Romantic Origins,* pp. 276-361. Ithaca, N.Y.:
Cornell University Press, 1978.
    Examines Wordsworth's reformulation of the myth of
    origins, stressing his revisions of his own past in *The Pre-
    lude.*

Chandler, James K. "Wordsworth's Reflections on the Revolution in France." In *The Golden & the Brazen World: Papers
in Literature and History, 1650-1800,* edited by John M. Wallace, pp. 140-70. Berkeley and Los Angeles: University of
California Press, 1985.
    Compares Wordsworth's reaction to the French Revolu-
    tion to that of Edmund Burke in *Reflections on the Revo-
    lution in France,* concluding that Wordsworth's attitude
    represents his generation's response to Burke's.

Cooke, Michael G. "Fruitful Failure and Incidental Cause:
The Will in *The Prelude.*" In his *The Romantic Will,* pp. 84-
117. New Haven, Conn.: Yale University Press, 1976.
    Interprets *The Prelude* as the gradual assertion of
    Wordsworth's will in his relations with the external
    world.

Dyson, A. E., and Lovelock, Julian. "The Epic of Selfhood:
Wordsworth's *The Prelude.*" In their *Masterful Images: En-
glish Poetry from Metaphysicals to Romantics,* pp. 137-74.
New York: Barnes & Noble, 1976.
    Examines the presentation of mystical experience in *The
    Prelude,* suggesting that reading the poem requires an
    understanding of Wordsworth's religious experience.

Ellis, David. "Wordsworth's Revolutionary Youth: How We
Read *The Prelude.*" *Critical Quarterly* 19, No. 4 (Winter
1977): 59-67.
    Rejects interpretations of *The Prelude* that rely upon
    biographical or historical evidence. Ellis uses only textu-
    al evidence to ascertain Wordsworth's political beliefs.

Empson, William. "Sense in *The Prelude.*" In his *The Structure of Complex Words,* pp. 289-305. Norfolk, Conn.: New
Directions, 1951.
    Analyzes Wordsworth's use of the word "sense" in *The
    Prelude,* discussing the poet's concern with the interac-
    tion between the mind and the senses.

Ferguson, Frances. "*The Prelude* and the Love of Man." In
her *Wordsworth: Language as Counter Spirit,* pp. 126-54.
New Haven, Conn.: Yale University Press, 1977.
    Discusses the relationship between language and con-
    sciousness in *The Prelude.*

French, A. L. "The 'Fair Seed-Time' in Wordsworth's *Prelude.*" *The Critical Review,* No. 17 (1974): 3-20.
> Examines the visionary passages of *The Prelude* as instances in which Wordsworth "is not rendering experience, but ruminating about it."

Hartman, Geoffrey H. "*The Prelude.*" In his *Wordsworth's Poetry: 1787-1814,* pp. 208-59. Cambridge, Mass.: Harvard University Press, 1987.
> Surveys Wordsworth's ideas about nature and humanity as reflected in *The Prelude.*

Heffernan, James A. W. "The Presence of the Absent Mother in Wordsworth's *Prelude.*" *Studies in Romanticism* 27, No. 2 (Summer 1988): 253-72.
> Interprets *The Prelude* "in light of Wordsworth's relation to his mother . . . to find the repressed memory of this woman haunting his consciousness in ways that he cannot help but express."

Horsman, E. A. "The Design of Wordsworth's *Prelude.*" In *Wordsworth's Mind and Art,* edited by A. W. Thomson, pp. 95-109. Edinburgh: Oliver and Boyd, 1969.
> Suggests that *The Prelude* is organized by a pattern of repetition signifying Wordsworth's comparisons of his past experiences.

Jacobus, Mary. "Apostrophe and Lyric Voice in *The Prelude.*" In *Lyric Poetry: Beyond New Criticism,* edited by Chaviva Hôsek and Patricia Parker, pp. 167-81. Ithaca, N.Y.: Cornell University Press, 1985.
> Examines the tension in *The Prelude* between self-assertion and immersion in nature.

Kneale, Douglas. "The Rhetoric of Imagination." *ARIEL* 15, No. 4 (October 1984): 111-27.
> Notes Wordsworth's awareness of the limitations of language in an examination of *The Prelude* as a deficient translation of the poet's "self" into language.

——. "Wordsworth's Images of Language: Voice and Letter in *The Prelude.*" *PMLA* 101, No. 3 (May 1986): 351-61.
> Studies Wordsworth's use of language in *The Prelude,* emphasizing his awareness of the differences between spoken and written words. Kneale concludes that *The Prelude* "contains its own allegory of reading" that "consists in the recurrent meeting of the poet with his own image."

Kramer, Lawrence. "Gender and Sexuality in *The Prelude:* The Question of Book Seven." *ELH* 54, No. 3 (Fall 1987): 619-37.
> Examines the characterization of Mary Johnson in Book VII of *The Prelude* suggesting that she is the externalization of Wordsworth's "gendered sexuality." Kramer also examines Wordsworth's attitude toward prostitutes, noting that they function as female counterparts to the maimed men in *The Prelude.*

Lord, George deForest. "*The Prelude:* Wordsworth's Irresolute Novel of the Self." In his *Trials of the Self: Heroic Ordeals in the Epic Tradition,* pp. 110-32. Hamden, Conn.: Shoestring Press, Archon Books, 1983.
> Describes *The Prelude* as an epic journey without a destination and suggests that the poem is characterized by "egocentric heroism" because the poet avoids the social engagement found in the traditional epic.

McConnell, Frank D. "The Sense of the Human." In his *The Confessional Imagination: A Reading of Wordsworth's "Prelude,"* pp. 59-98. Baltimore: The Johns Hopkins University Press, 1974.
> Includes a discussion of demonic elements in *The Prelude,* focusing on the boat-stealing episode in Book I.

McGavran, James Holt, Jr. "The '*Creative* Soul' of *The Prelude* and the 'Sad Incompetence of Human Speech'." *Studies in Romanticism* 16, No. 1 (Winter 1977): 35-49.
> Suggests that in *The Prelude* Wordsworth is limited by his awareness of the inadequacies of language.

Montgomery, Marion. "The Wandering Poet." In her *The Reflective Journey toward Order: Essays on Dante, Wordsworth, Eliot and Others,* pp. 198-206. Athens: University of Georgia Press, 1973.
> Regards *The Prelude* as Wordsworth's quest for "his own relation to the past or to the external world."

Morgan, Edwin. "A Prelude to *The Prelude.*" In *British Romantic Poets,* edited by Shiv K. Kumar, pp. 63-74. London: University of London Press, 1966.
> Studies *The Prelude* as a record of the poet's past and discusses how Wordsworth reacted to his past.

Nemerov, Howard. "Two Ways of the Imagination: Blake and Wordsworth." In his *New and Selected Essays,* pp. 140-60. Carbondale: Southern Illinois University Press, 1985.
> Compares *The Prelude* to William Blake's *Jerusalem* as two poems about poetic creativity.

Ogden, John T. "The Power of Distance in Wordsworth's *Prelude.*" *PMLA* 88, No. 2 (March 1973): 246-59.
> Analyzes Wordsworth's treatment of distance in *The Prelude,* focusing on the optical and psychological effects of the distance between the poet and the object of perception and temporal distance that affects Wordsworth's memory of his childhood.

Onorato, Richard J. "Imagination and Revelation." In his *The Character of the Poet: Wordsworth in "The Prelude,"* pp. 136-63. Princeton, N. J.: Princeton University Press, 1971.
> Focuses on the Mount Snowdon episode of Book XIV of *The Prelude,* concluding that the poem is mainly about the imagination.

Paulson, Ronald. "Wordsworth's *Prelude.*" In his *Representations of Revolution (1789-1820),* pp. 248-85. New Haven, Conn.: Yale University Press, 1983.
> Discusses *The Prelude* as Wordsworth's attempt not only to represent but also to come to terms with the French Revolution.

Peterfreund, Stuart. "*The Prelude:* Wordsworth's Metamorphic Epic." *Genre* XIV, No. 4 (March 1981): 441-72.
> Suggests that "for Wordsworth, the history of the individual poet . . . recapitulates the history of poetry itself, insofar as that history may be expressed in terms of the historical and developmental progression of genre."

Potts, Abbie Findlay. *Wordsworth's "Prelude": A Study of Its Literary Form.* Ithaca, N. Y.: Cornell University Press, 1953, 392 p.
> Surveys eighteenth-century influences on *The Prelude* and its importance in Wordsworth's career.

Reed, Mark I. "Chronology of *The Prelude.*" In his *Wordsworth: The Chronology of the Middle Years, 1800-1815,* pp. 628-55. Cambridge, Mass.: Harvard University Press, 1975.

A detailed examination of textual evidence documenting the chronology of Wordsworth's writing of *The Prelude.*

Sabin, Margery. " 'Love, in *The Prelude."* In her *English Romanticism and the French Tradition,* pp. 33-47. Cambridge, Mass.: Harvard University Press, 1976.

Examines Wordsworth's use of the word "love" in *The Prelude* to describe his relationship with nature, praising the poet's ability to reshape language.

Spivak, Gayatri Chakravorty. "Sex and History in *The Prelude* (1805): Books IX to XII." In *Post-Structuralist Readings of English Poetry,* edited by Richard Machin and Christopher Norris, pp. 193-226. Cambridge: Cambridge University Press, 1987.

Addresses Wordsworth's treatment of sexuality and the French Revolution in *The Prelude,* noting that "in the texts of the Great Tradition, the most remotely occluded and transparently mediating figure is woman."

Additional coverage of Wordsworth's life and career is contained in the following sources published by Gale Research: *Concise Dictionary of British Literary Biography, 1789-1832; Dictionary of Literary Biography,* **Vols. 93, 107;** *Poetry Criticism,* **Vol. 4; and** *World Literature Criticism.*

Nineteenth-Century Literature Criticism

Cumulative Indexes
Volumes 1-38

This Index Includes References to Entries in These Gale Series

Authors in the News (AITN) reprints articles from American periodicals covering authors and members of the communications media. Two volumes.

Bestsellers (BEST) furnishes information about best-selling books and their authors for the years 1989-1990.

Black Literature Criticism (BLC) provides excerpts from criticism of the most significant works of black authors of all nationalities over the past 200 years. Complete in three volumes.

Children's Literature Review (CLR) includes excerpts from reviews, criticism, and commentary on works of authors and illustrators who create books for children.

Classical and Medieval Literature Criticism (CMLC) offers criticism on the works of world authors from classical antiquity through the fourteenth century.

Contemporary Authors encompasses eight related series: *Contemporary Authors (CA)* provides biographical and bibliographical information on more than 99,000 writers of fiction, nonfiction, poetry, journalism, drama, and film. *Contemporary Authors New Revision Series (CANR)* provides updated information on active authors previously covered in *CA*. *Contemporary Authors Permanent Series (CAP)* consists of updated listings for deceased and inactive authors removed from revised volumes of *CA*. *Contemporary Authors Autobiography Series (CAAS)* presents commissioned autobiographies by leading contemporary writers. *Contemporary Authors Bibliographical Series (CABS)* contains primary and secondary bibliographies as well as bibliographical essays on major modern authors. *Black Writers (BW)* compiles selected *CA* sketches on more than 400 prominent writers. *Hispanic Writers (HW)* compiles selected *CA* sketches on twentieth-century Hispanic writers. *Major 20th-Century Writers (MTCW)* presents in four volumes selected *CA* sketches on over 1,000 of the most influential writers of this century.

Contemporary Literary Criticism (CLC) presents excerpts of criticism on the works of creative writers who are now living or who have died since 1960.

Dictionary of Literary Biography comprises five related series: *Dictionary of Literary Biography (DLB)* furnishes illustrated overviews of authors' lives and works. *Dictionary of Literary Biography Documentary Series (DLBD)* illuminates the careers of major figures through a selection of literary documents, including letters, interviews, and photographs. *Dictionary of Literary Biography Yearbook (DLBY)* summarizes the past year's literary activity and includes updated and new entries on individual authors. *Concise Dictionary of American Literary Biography (CDALB)* and *Concise Dictionary of British Literary Biography (CDBLB)* collect revised and updated sketches that were originally presented in *Dictionary of Literary Biography*.

Drama Criticism (DC) provides excerpts of criticism on the works of playwrights of all nationalities and periods of literary history.

Literature Criticism from 1400 to 1800 (LC) compiles significant passages from criticism on authors of the fifteenth through the eighteenth centuries.

Nineteenth-Century Literature Criticism (NCLC) reprints significant passages from criticism on authors who died between 1800 and 1899.

Poetry Criticism (PC) presents excerpts of criticism on the works of poets from all eras, movements, and nationalities.

Short Story Criticism (SSC) offers critical excerpts on short fiction by writers of all eras and nationalities.

Something about the Author encompasses four related series: *Something about the Author (SATA)* contains biographical sketches on authors and illustrators of juvenile and young adult literature. *Something about the Author Autobiography Series (SAAS)* presents commissioned autobiographies by prominent authors and illustrators of books for children and young adults. *Authors & Artists for Young Adults (AAYA)* provides students with profiles of their favorite creative artists. *Major Authors and Illustrators for Children and Young Adults (MAICYA)* contains in six volumes both newly written and completely updated *SATA* sketches on nearly 800 authors and illustrators for young people.

Twentieth-Century Literary Criticism (TCLC) contains critical excerpts on authors who died between 1900 and 1960.

World Literature Criticism (WLC) contains excerpts from criticism on the works of over 200 major writers from the Renaissance to the present. Complete in six volumes.

Yesterday's Authors of Books for Children (YABC) contains heavily illustrated entries on children's writers who died before 1961. Complete in two volumes.

Literary Criticism Series
Cumulative Author Index

Apuleius, (Lucius Madaurensis)
  125(?)-175(?) . . . . **CMLC 1**

Aquin, Hubert 1929-1977. . . . . **CLC 15**
  See also CA 105; DLB 53

Aragon, Louis 1897-1982. . . . . . . **CLC 3, 22**
  See also CA 69-72; 108; CANR 28;
  DLB 72; MTCW

Arany, Janos 1817-1882. . . . . **NCLC 34**

Arbuthnot, John 1667-1735 . . . . **LC 1**
  See also DLB 101

Archer, Herbert Winslow
  See Mencken, H(enry) L(ouis)

Archer, Jeffrey (Howard) 1940- . . . . **CLC 28**
  See also BEST 89:3; CA 77-80; CANR 22

Archer, Jules 1915- . . . . **CLC 12**
  See also CA 9-12R; CANR 6; SAAS 5;
  SATA 4

Archer, Lee
  See Ellison, Harlan

Arden, John 1930- . . . . **CLC 6, 13, 15**
  See also CA 13-16R; CAAS 4; CANR 31;
  DLB 13; MTCW

Arenas, Reinaldo 1943-1990 . . . . **CLC 41**
  See also CA 124; 128; 133; HW

Arendt, Hannah 1906-1975 . . . . **CLC 66**
  See also CA 17-20R; 61-64; CANR 26;
  MTCW

Aretino, Pietro 1492-1556 . . . . **LC 12**

Arguedas, Jose Maria
  1911-1969 . . . . **CLC 10, 18**
  See also CA 89-92; DLB 113; HW

Argueta, Manlio 1936- . . . . **CLC 31**
  See also CA 131; HW

Ariosto, Ludovico 1474-1533 . . . . **LC 6**

Aristides
  See Epstein, Joseph

Aristophanes
  450B.C.-385B.C. . . . . **CMLC 4; DC 2**

Arlt, Roberto (Godofredo Christophersen)
  1900-1942 . . . . **TCLC 29**
  See also CA 123; 131; HW

Armah, Ayi Kwei 1939- . . . . **CLC 5, 33**
  See also BLC 1; BW; CA 61-64; CANR 21;
  DLB 117; MTCW

Armatrading, Joan 1950- . . . . **CLC 17**
  See also CA 114

Arnette, Robert
  See Silverberg, Robert

Arnim, Achim von (Ludwig Joachim von
  Arnim) 1781-1831 . . . . **NCLC 5**
  See also DLB 90

Arnim, Bettina von 1785-1859 . . . . **NCLC 38**
  See also DLB 90

Arnold, Matthew
  1822-1888 . . . . **NCLC 6, 29; PC 5**
  See also CDBLB 1832-1890; DLB 32, 57;
  WLC

Arnold, Thomas 1795-1842 . . . . . . **NCLC 18**
  See also DLB 55

Arnow, Harriette (Louisa) Simpson
  1908-1986 . . . . **CLC 2, 7, 18**
  See also CA 9-12R; 118; CANR 14; DLB 6;
  MTCW; SATA 42, 47

Arp, Hans
  See Arp, Jean

Arp, Jean 1887-1966. . . . . **CLC 5**
  See also CA 81-84; 25-28R

Arrabal . . . . **CLC 2, 9, 18**
  See also Arrabal, Fernando

Arrabal, Fernando 1932- . . . . **CLC 58**
  See also Arrabal
  See also CA 9-12R; CANR 15

Arrick, Fran . . . . **CLC 30**

Artaud, Antonin 1896-1948 . . . . . **TCLC 3, 36**
  See also CA 104

Arthur, Ruth M(abel) 1905-1979. . . . **CLC 12**
  See also CA 9-12R; 85-88; CANR 4;
  SATA 7, 26

Artsybashev, Mikhail (Petrovich)
  1878-1927 . . . . **TCLC 31**

Arundel, Honor (Morfydd)
  1919-1973 . . . . **CLC 17**
  See also CA 21-22; 41-44R; CAP 2;
  SATA 4, 24

Asch, Sholem 1880-1957 . . . . **TCLC 3**
  See also CA 105

Ash, Shalom
  See Asch, Sholem

Ashbery, John (Lawrence)
  1927- . . . **CLC 2, 3, 4, 6, 9, 13, 15, 25, 41**
  See also CA 5-8R; CANR 9, 37; DLB 5;
  DLBY 81; MTCW

Ashdown, Clifford
  See Freeman, R(ichard) Austin

Ashe, Gordon
  See Creasey, John

Ashton-Warner, Sylvia (Constance)
  1908-1984 . . . . **CLC 19**
  See also CA 69-72; 112; CANR 29; MTCW

Asimov, Isaac
  1920-1992 . . . . **CLC 1, 3, 9, 19, 26**
  See also BEST 90:2; CA 1-4R; 137;
  CANR 2, 19, 36; CLR 12; DLB 8;
  MAICYA; MTCW; SATA 1, 26

Astley, Thea (Beatrice May)
  1925- . . . . **CLC 41**
  See also CA 65-68; CANR 11

Aston, James
  See White, T(erence) H(anbury)

Asturias, Miguel Angel
  1899-1974 . . . . **CLC 3, 8, 13**
  See also CA 25-28; 49-52; CANR 32;
  CAP 2; DLB 113; HW; MTCW

Atares, Carlos Saura
  See Saura (Atares), Carlos

Atheling, William
  See Pound, Ezra (Weston Loomis)

Atheling, William Jr.
  See Blish, James (Benjamin)

Atherton, Gertrude (Franklin Horn)
  1857-1948 . . . . **TCLC 2**
  See also CA 104; DLB 9, 78

Atherton, Lucius
  See Masters, Edgar Lee

Atkins, Jack
  See Harris, Mark

Atticus
  See Fleming, Ian (Lancaster)

Atwood, Margaret (Eleanor)
  1939- . . . . **CLC 2, 3, 4, 8, 13, 15, 25, 44;**
                                                       SSC 2
  See also BEST 89:2; CA 49-52; CANR 3,
  24, 33; DLB 53; MTCW; SATA 50; WLC

Aubigny, Pierre d'
  See Mencken, H(enry) L(ouis)

Aubin, Penelope 1685-1731(?) . . . . **LC 9**
  See also DLB 39

Auchincloss, Louis (Stanton)
  1917- . . . . **CLC 4, 6, 9, 18, 45**
  See also CA 1-4R; CANR 6, 29; DLB 2;
  DLBY 80; MTCW

Auden, W(ystan) H(ugh)
  1907-1973 . . . . . **CLC 1, 2, 3, 4, 6, 9, 11,**
                                                14, 43; PC 1
  See also CA 9-12R; 45-48; CANR 5;
  CDBLB 1914-1945; DLB 10, 20; MTCW;
  WLC

Audiberti, Jacques 1900-1965 . . . . . . **CLC 38**
  See also CA 25-28R

Auel, Jean M(arie) 1936- . . . . **CLC 31**
  See also AAYA 7; BEST 90:4; CA 103;
  CANR 21

Auerbach, Erich 1892-1957 . . . . **TCLC 43**
  See also CA 118

Augier, Emile 1820-1889 . . . . **NCLC 31**

August, John
  See De Voto, Bernard (Augustine)

Augustine, St. 354-430 . . . . **CMLC 6**

Aurelius
  See Bourne, Randolph S(illiman)

Austen, Jane
  1775-1817 . . . . **NCLC 1, 13, 19, 33**
  See also CDBLB 1789-1832; DLB 116;
  WLC

Auster, Paul 1947- . . . . **CLC 47**
  See also CA 69-72; CANR 23

Austin, Mary (Hunter)
  1868-1934 . . . . **TCLC 25**
  See also CA 109; DLB 9, 78

Autran Dourado, Waldomiro
  See Dourado, (Waldomiro Freitas) Autran

Averroes 1126-1198 . . . . **CMLC 7**
  See also DLB 115

Avison, Margaret 1918- . . . . **CLC 2, 4**
  See also CA 17-20R; DLB 53; MTCW

Ayckbourn, Alan 1939- . . . . **CLC 5, 8, 18, 33**
  See also CA 21-24R; CANR 31; DLB 13;
  MTCW

Aydy, Catherine
  See Tennant, Emma (Christina)

Ayme, Marcel (Andre) 1902-1967 . . . **CLC 11**
  See also CA 89-92; CLR 25; DLB 72

Ayrton, Michael 1921-1975 . . . . **CLC 7**
  See also CA 5-8R; 61-64; CANR 9, 21

Azorin . . . . **CLC 11**
  See also Martinez Ruiz, Jose

Azuela, Mariano 1873-1952 . . . . **TCLC 3**
  See also CA 104; 131; HW; MTCW

Baastad, Babbis Friis
  See Friis-Baastad, Babbis Ellinor

Bab
See Gilbert, W(illiam) S(chwenck)

Babbis, Eleanor
See Friis-Baastad, Babbis Ellinor

Babel, Isaac (Emanuilovich) .... TCLC 13
See also Babel, Isaak (Emmanuilovich)

Babel, Isaak (Emmanuilovich)
1894-1941(?) .... TCLC 2
See also Babel, Isaac (Emanuilovich)
See also CA 104

Babits, Mihaly 1883-1941 .... TCLC 14
See also CA 114

Babur 1483-1530 .... LC 18

Bacchelli, Riccardo 1891-1985 ..... CLC 19
See also CA 29-32R; 117

Bach, Richard (David) 1936- .... CLC 14
See also AITN 1; BEST 89:2; CA 9-12R;
CANR 18; MTCW; SATA 13

Bachman, Richard
See King, Stephen (Edwin)

Bachmann, Ingeborg 1926-1973..... CLC 69
See also CA 93-96; 45-48; DLB 85

Bacon, Francis 1561-1626 .... LC 18
See also CDBLB Before 1660

Bacovia, George .... TCLC 24
See also Vasiliu, Gheorghe

Badanes, Jerome 1937- .... CLC 59

Bagehot, Walter 1826-1877 ...... NCLC 10
See also DLB 55

Bagnold, Enid 1889-1981.......... CLC 25
See also CA 5-8R; 103; CANR 5; DLB 13;
MAICYA; SATA 1, 25

Bagrjana, Elisaveta
See Belcheva, Elisaveta

Bagryana, Elisaveta
See Belcheva, Elisaveta

Bailey, Paul 1937- .... CLC 45
See also CA 21-24R; CANR 16; DLB 14

Baillie, Joanna 1762-1851 .... NCLC 2
See also DLB 93

Bainbridge, Beryl (Margaret)
1933- .... CLC 4, 5, 8, 10, 14, 18, 22, 62
See also CA 21-24R; CANR 24; DLB 14;
MTCW

Baker, Elliott 1922- .... CLC 8
See also CA 45-48; CANR 2

Baker, Nicholson 1957- .... CLC 61
See also CA 135

Baker, Ray Stannard 1870-1946 ... TCLC 47
See also CA 118

Baker, Russell (Wayne) 1925-...... CLC 31
See also BEST 89:4; CA 57-60; CANR 11;
MTCW

Bakshi, Ralph 1938(?)- .... CLC 26
See also CA 112; 138

Bakunin, Mikhail (Alexandrovich)
1814-1876 .... NCLC 25

Baldwin, James (Arthur)
1924-1987 ..... CLC 1, 2, 3, 4, 5, 8, 13,
15, 17, 42, 50, 67; DC 1; SSC 10
See also AAYA 4; BLC 1; BW; CA 1-4R;
124; CABS 1; CANR 3, 24;
CDALB 1941-1968; DLB 2, 7, 33;
DLBY 87; MTCW; SATA 9, 54; WLC

Ballard, J(ames) G(raham)
1930- .... CLC 3, 6, 14, 36; SSC 1
See also AAYA 3; CA 5-8R; CANR 15, 39;
DLB 14; MTCW

Balmont, Konstantin (Dmitriyevich)
1867-1943 .... TCLC 11
See also CA 109

Balzac, Honore de
1799-1850 .... NCLC 5, 35; SSC 5
See also DLB 119; WLC

Bambara, Toni Cade 1939- .... CLC 19
See also AAYA 5; BLC 1; BW; CA 29-32R;
CANR 24; DLB 38; MTCW

Bamdad, A.
See Shamlu, Ahmad

Banat, D. R.
See Bradbury, Ray (Douglas)

Bancroft, Laura
See Baum, L(yman) Frank

Banim, John 1798-1842 .... NCLC 13
See also DLB 116

Banim, Michael 1796-1874 ...... NCLC 13

Banks, Iain
See Banks, Iain M(enzies)

Banks, Iain M(enzies) 1954- .... CLC 34
See also CA 123; 128

Banks, Lynne Reid .... CLC 23
See also Reid Banks, Lynne
See also AAYA 6

Banks, Russell 1940- .... CLC 37, 72
See also CA 65-68; CAAS 15; CANR 19

Banville, John 1945-.............. CLC 46
See also CA 117; 128; DLB 14

Banville, Theodore (Faullain) de
1832-1891 .... NCLC 9

Baraka, Amiri
1934- ... CLC 1, 2, 3, 5, 10, 14, 33; PC 4
See also Jones, LeRoi
See also BLC 1; BW; CA 21-24R; CABS 3;
CANR 27, 38; CDALB 1941-1968;
DLB 5, 7, 16, 38; DLBD 8; MTCW

Barbellion, W. N. P................ TCLC 24
See also Cummings, Bruce F(rederick)

Barbera, Jack 1945-.............. CLC 44
See also CA 110

Barbey d'Aurevilly, Jules Amedee
1808-1889 .... NCLC 1
See also DLB 119

Barbusse, Henri 1873-1935 .... TCLC 5
See also CA 105; DLB 65

Barclay, Bill
See Moorcock, Michael (John)

Barclay, William Ewert
See Moorcock, Michael (John)

Barea, Arturo 1897-1957 .... TCLC 14
See also CA 111

Barfoot, Joan 1946- .... CLC 18
See also CA 105

Baring, Maurice 1874-1945 .... TCLC 8
See also CA 105; DLB 34

Barker, Clive 1952- .... CLC 52
See also BEST 90:3; CA 121; 129; MTCW

Barker, George Granville
1913-1991 .... CLC 8, 48
See also CA 9-12R; 135; CANR 7, 38;
DLB 20; MTCW

Barker, Harley Granville
See Granville-Barker, Harley
See also DLB 10

Barker, Howard 1946-............ CLC 37
See also CA 102; DLB 13

Barker, Pat 1943-................ CLC 32
See also CA 117; 122

Barlow, Joel 1754-1812 .... NCLC 23
See also DLB 37

Barnard, Mary (Ethel) 1909-....... CLC 48
See also CA 21-22; CAP 2

Barnes, Djuna
1892-1982 ... CLC 3, 4, 8, 11, 29; SSC 3
See also CA 9-12R; 107; CANR 16; DLB 4,
9, 45; MTCW

Barnes, Julian 1946-.............. CLC 42
See also CA 102; CANR 19

Barnes, Peter 1931- .... CLC 5, 56
See also CA 65-68; CAAS 12; CANR 33,
34; DLB 13; MTCW

Baroja (y Nessi), Pio 1872-1956 .... TCLC 8
See also CA 104

Baron, David
See Pinter, Harold

Baron Corvo
See Rolfe, Frederick (William Serafino
Austin Lewis Mary)

Barondess, Sue K(aufman)
1926-1977 .... CLC 8
See also Kaufman, Sue
See also CA 1-4R; 69-72; CANR 1

Baron de Teive
See Pessoa, Fernando (Antonio Nogueira)

Barres, Maurice 1862-1923 .... TCLC 47

Barreto, Afonso Henrique de Lima
See Lima Barreto, Afonso Henrique de

Barrett, (Roger) Syd 1946- .... CLC 35
See also Pink Floyd

Barrett, William (Christopher)
1913- .... CLC 27
See also CA 13-16R; CANR 11

Barrie, J(ames) M(atthew)
1860-1937 .... TCLC 2
See also CA 104; 136; CDBLB 1890-1914;
CLR 16; DLB 10; MAICYA; YABC 1

Barrington, Michael
See Moorcock, Michael (John)

Barrol, Grady
See Bograd, Larry

Barry, Mike
See Malzberg, Barry N(athaniel)

Barry, Philip 1896-1949.......... TCLC 11
See also CA 109; DLB 7

Bart, Andre Schwarz
See Schwarz-Bart, Andre

Barth, John (Simmons)
1930- ...... CLC 1, 2, 3, 5, 7, 9, 10, 14,
27, 51; SSC 10
See also AITN 1, 2; CA 1-4R; CABS 1;
CANR 5, 23; DLB 2; MTCW

Barthelme, Donald
1931-1989 . . . . . **CLC 1, 2, 3, 5, 6, 8, 13, 23, 46, 59; SSC 2**
See also CA 21-24R; 129; CANR 20; DLB 2; DLBY 80, 89; MTCW; SATA 7, 62

Barthelme, Frederick 1943- . . . . **CLC 36**
See also CA 114; 122; DLBY 85

Barthes, Roland (Gerard)
1915-1980 . . . . **CLC 24**
See also CA 130; 97-100; MTCW

Barzun, Jacques (Martin) 1907- . . . . **CLC 51**
See also CA 61-64; CANR 22

Bashevis, Isaac
See Singer, Isaac Bashevis

Bashkirtseff, Marie 1859-1884 . . . **NCLC 27**

Basho
See Matsuo Basho

Bass, Kingsley B. Jr.
See Bullins, Ed

Bassani, Giorgio 1916- . . . . **CLC 9**
See also CA 65-68; CANR 33; MTCW

Bastos, Augusto (Antonio) Roa
See Roa Bastos, Augusto (Antonio)

Bataille, Georges 1897-1962 . . . . **CLC 29**
See also CA 101; 89-92

Bates, H(erbert) E(rnest)
1905-1974 . . . . **CLC 46; SSC 10**
See also CA 93-96; 45-48; CANR 34; MTCW

Bauchart
See Camus, Albert

Baudelaire, Charles
1821-1867 . . . . **NCLC 6, 29; PC 1**
See also WLC

Baudrillard, Jean 1929- . . . . **CLC 60**

Baum, L(yman) Frank 1856-1919 . . . **TCLC 7**
See also CA 108; 133; CLR 15; DLB 22; MAICYA; MTCW; SATA 18

Baum, Louis F.
See Baum, L(yman) Frank

Baumbach, Jonathan 1933- . . . . . . **CLC 6, 23**
See also CA 13-16R; CAAS 5; CANR 12; DLBY 80; MTCW

Bausch, Richard (Carl) 1945- . . . . . . **CLC 51**
See also CA 101; CAAS 14

Baxter, Charles 1947- . . . . **CLC 45**
See also CA 57-60

Baxter, James K(eir) 1926-1972 . . . . **CLC 14**
See also CA 77-80

Baxter, John
See Hunt, E(verette) Howard Jr.

Bayer, Sylvia
See Glassco, John

Beagle, Peter S(oyer) 1939- . . . . **CLC 7**
See also CA 9-12R; CANR 4; DLBY 80; SATA 60

Bean, Normal
See Burroughs, Edgar Rice

Beard, Charles A(ustin)
1874-1948 . . . . **TCLC 15**
See also CA 115; DLB 17; SATA 18

Beardsley, Aubrey 1872-1898 . . . . . **NCLC 6**

Beattie, Ann 1947- . . . **CLC 8, 13, 18, 40, 63**
See also BEST 90:2; CA 81-84; DLBY 82; MTCW

Beattie, James 1735-1803 . . . . **NCLC 25**
See also DLB 109

Beauchamp, Kathleen Mansfield 1888-1923
See Mansfield, Katherine
See also CA 104; 134

Beauvoir, Simone (Lucie Ernestine Marie Bertrand) de
1908-1986 . . . **CLC 1, 2, 4, 8, 14, 31, 44, 50, 71**
See also CA 9-12R; 118; CANR 28; DLB 72; DLBY 86; MTCW; WLC

Becker, Jurek 1937- . . . . **CLC 7, 19**
See also CA 85-88; DLB 75

Becker, Walter 1950- . . . . **CLC 26**

Beckett, Samuel (Barclay)
1906-1989 . . . . . **CLC 1, 2, 3, 4, 6, 9, 10, 11, 14, 18, 29, 57, 59**
See also CA 5-8R; 130; CANR 33; CDBLB 1945-1960; DLB 13, 15; DLBY 90; MTCW; WLC

Beckford, William 1760-1844 . . . . **NCLC 16**
See also DLB 39

Beckman, Gunnel 1910- . . . . **CLC 26**
See also CA 33-36R; CANR 15; CLR 25; MAICYA; SAAS 9; SATA 6

Becque, Henri 1837-1899 . . . . **NCLC 3**

Beddoes, Thomas Lovell
1803-1849 . . . . **NCLC 3**
See also DLB 96

Bedford, Donald F.
See Fearing, Kenneth (Flexner)

Beecher, Catharine Esther
1800-1878 . . . . **NCLC 30**
See also DLB 1

Beecher, John 1904-1980 . . . . **CLC 6**
See also AITN 1; CA 5-8R; 105, CANR 8

Beer, Johann 1655-1700 . . . . **LC 5**

Beer, Patricia 1924- . . . . **CLC 58**
See also CA 61-64; CANR 13; DLB 40

Beerbohm, Henry Maximilian
1872-1956 . . . . **TCLC 1, 24**
See also CA 104; DLB 34, 100

Begiebing, Robert J(ohn) 1946- . . . . . **CLC 70**
See also CA 122

Behan, Brendan
1923-1964 . . . . **CLC 1, 8, 11, 15**
See also CA 73-76; CANR 33; CDBLB 1945-1960; DLB 13; MTCW

Behn, Aphra 1640(?)-1689 . . . . **LC 1**
See also DLB 39, 80; WLC

Behrman, S(amuel) N(athaniel)
1893-1973 . . . . **CLC 40**
See also CA 13-16; 45-48; CAP 1; DLB 7, 44

Belasco, David 1853-1931 . . . . **TCLC 3**
See also CA 104; DLB 7

Belcheva, Elisaveta 1893- . . . . **CLC 10**

Beldone, Phil "Cheech"
See Ellison, Harlan

Beleno
See Azuela, Mariano

Belinski, Vissarion Grigoryevich
1811-1848 . . . . **NCLC 5**

Belitt, Ben 1911- . . . . **CLC 22**
See also CA 13-16R; CAAS 4; CANR 7; DLB 5

Bell, James Madison 1826-1902 . . . **TCLC 43**
See also BLC 1; BW; CA 122; 124; DLB 50

Bell, Madison (Smartt) 1957- . . . . . . **CLC 41**
See also CA 111; CANR 28

Bell, Marvin (Hartley) 1937- . . . . . **CLC 8, 31**
See also CA 21-24R; CAAS 14; DLB 5; MTCW

Bell, W. L. D.
See Mencken, H(enry) L(ouis)

Bellamy, Atwood C.
See Mencken, H(enry) L(ouis)

Bellamy, Edward 1850-1898 . . . . . . **NCLC 4**
See also DLB 12

Bellin, Edward J.
See Kuttner, Henry

Belloc, (Joseph) Hilaire (Pierre)
1870-1953 . . . . **TCLC 7, 18**
See also CA 106; DLB 19, 100; YABC 1

Belloc, Joseph Peter Rene Hilaire
See Belloc, (Joseph) Hilaire (Pierre)

Belloc, Joseph Pierre Hilaire
See Belloc, (Joseph) Hilaire (Pierre)

Belloc, M. A.
See Lowndes, Marie Adelaide (Belloc)

Bellow, Saul
1915- . . . . . **CLC 1, 2, 3, 6, 8, 10, 13, 15, 25, 33, 34, 63**
See also AITN 2; BEST 89:3; CA 5-8R; CABS 1; CANR 29; CDALB 1941-1968; DLB 2, 28; DLBD 3; DLBY 82; MTCW; WLC

Belser, Reimond Karel Maria de
1929- . . . . **CLC 14**

Bely, Andrey . . . . **TCLC 7**
See also Bugayev, Boris Nikolayevich

Benary, Margot
See Benary-Isbert, Margot

Benary-Isbert, Margot 1889-1979 . . . **CLC 12**
See also CA 5-8R; 89-92; CANR 4; CLR 12; MAICYA; SATA 2, 21

Benavente (y Martinez), Jacinto
1866-1954 . . . . **TCLC 3**
See also CA 106; 131; HW; MTCW

Benchley, Peter (Bradford)
1940- . . . . **CLC 4, 8**
See also AITN 2; CA 17-20R; CANR 12, 35; MTCW; SATA 3

Benchley, Robert (Charles)
1889-1945 . . . . **TCLC 1**
See also CA 105; DLB 11

Benedikt, Michael 1935- . . . . **CLC 4, 14**
See also CA 13-16R; CANR 7; DLB 5

Benet, Juan 1927- . . . . **CLC 28**

Benet, Stephen Vincent
1898-1943 . . . . **TCLC 7; SSC 10**
See also CA 104; DLB 4, 48, 102; YABC 1

Benet, William Rose 1886-1950 . . . **TCLC 28**
See also CA 118; DLB 45

Benford, Gregory (Albert) 1941-.... **CLC 52**
See also CA 69-72; CANR 12, 24;
DLBY 82

Benjamin, Lois
See Gould, Lois

Benjamin, Walter 1892-1940..... **TCLC 39**

Benn, Gottfried 1886-1956........ **TCLC 3**
See also CA 106; DLB 56

Bennett, Alan 1934-.............. **CLC 45**
See also CA 103; CANR 35; MTCW

Bennett, (Enoch) Arnold
1867-1931 .... **TCLC 5, 20**
See also CA 106; CDBLB 1890-1914;
DLB 10, 34, 98

Bennett, Elizabeth
See Mitchell, Margaret (Munnerlyn)

Bennett, George Harold 1930-
See Bennett, Hal
See also BW; CA 97-100

Bennett, Hal .... **CLC 5**
See also Bennett, George Harold
See also DLB 33

Bennett, Jay 1912-.............. **CLC 35**
See also CA 69-72; CANR 11; SAAS 4;
SATA 27, 41

Bennett, Louise (Simone) 1919-..... **CLC 28**
See also BLC 1; DLB 117

Benson, E(dward) F(rederic)
1867-1940 .... **TCLC 27**
See also CA 114

Benson, Jackson J. 1930-......... **CLC 34**
See also CA 25-28R; DLB 111

Benson, Sally 1900-1972 .... **CLC 17**
See also CA 19-20; 37-40R; CAP 1;
SATA 1, 27, 35

Benson, Stella 1892-1933........ **TCLC 17**
See also CA 117; DLB 36

Bentham, Jeremy 1748-1832 ..... **NCLC 38**
See also DLB 107

Bentley, E(dmund) C(lerihew)
1875-1956 .... **TCLC 12**
See also CA 108; DLB 70

Bentley, Eric (Russell) 1916-....... **CLC 24**
See also CA 5-8R; CANR 6

Beranger, Pierre Jean de
1780-1857 .... **NCLC 34**

Berger, Colonel
See Malraux, (Georges-)Andre

Berger, John (Peter) 1926- ...... **CLC 2, 19**
See also CA 81-84; DLB 14

Berger, Melvin H. 1927- .... **CLC 12**
See also CA 5-8R; CANR 4; SAAS 2;
SATA 5

Berger, Thomas (Louis)
1924- .... **CLC 3, 5, 8, 11, 18, 38**
See also CA 1-4R; CANR 5, 28; DLB 2;
DLBY 80; MTCW

Bergman, (Ernst) Ingmar
1918- .... **CLC 16, 72**
See also CA 81-84; CANR 33

Bergson, Henri 1859-1941........ **TCLC 32**

Bergstein, Eleanor 1938-.......... **CLC 4**
See also CA 53-56; CANR 5

Berkoff, Steven 1937-............. **CLC 56**
See also CA 104

Bermant, Chaim (Icyk) 1929- ...... **CLC 40**
See also CA 57-60; CANR 6, 31

Bernanos, (Paul Louis) Georges
1888-1948 .... **TCLC 3**
See also CA 104; 130; DLB 72

Bernard, April 1956- .... **CLC 59**
See also CA 131

Bernhard, Thomas
1931-1989 .... **CLC 3, 32, 61**
See also CA 85-88; 127; CANR 32;
DLB 85; MTCW

Berrigan, Daniel 1921-............. **CLC 4**
See also CA 33-36R; CAAS 1; CANR 11;
DLB 5

Berrigan, Edmund Joseph Michael Jr.
1934-1983
See Berrigan, Ted
See also CA 61-64; 110; CANR 14

Berrigan, Ted.................... **CLC 37**
See also Berrigan, Edmund Joseph Michael
Jr.
See also DLB 5

Berry, Charles Edward Anderson 1931-
See Berry, Chuck
See also CA 115

Berry, Chuck..................... **CLC 17**
See also Berry, Charles Edward Anderson

Berry, Jonas
See Ashbery, John (Lawrence)

Berry, Wendell (Erdman)
1934- .... **CLC 4, 6, 8, 27, 46**
See also AITN 1; CA 73-76; DLB 5, 6

Berryman, John
1914-1972 ..... **CLC 1, 2, 3, 4, 6, 8, 10,
13, 25, 62**
See also CA 13-16; 33-36R; CABS 2;
CANR 35; CAP 1; CDALB 1941-1968;
DLB 48; MTCW

Bertolucci, Bernardo 1940- .... **CLC 16**
See also CA 106

Bertrand, Aloysius 1807-1841 .... **NCLC 31**

Bertran de Born c. 1140-1215 ..... **CMLC 5**

Besant, Annie (Wood) 1847-1933 ... **TCLC 9**
See also CA 105

Bessie, Alvah 1904-1985........... **CLC 23**
See also CA 5-8R; 116; CANR 2; DLB 26

Bethlen, T. D.
See Silverberg, Robert

Beti, Mongo..................... **CLC 27**
See also Biyidi, Alexandre
See also BLC 1

Betjeman, John
1906-1984 .... **CLC 2, 6, 10, 34, 43**
See also CA 9-12R; 112; CANR 33;
CDBLB 1945-1960; DLB 20; DLBY 84;
MTCW

Betti, Ugo 1892-1953............. **TCLC 5**
See also CA 104

Betts, Doris (Waugh) 1932-.... **CLC 3, 6, 28**
See also CA 13-16R; CANR 9; DLBY 82

Bevan, Alistair
See Roberts, Keith (John Kingston)

Beynon, John
See Harris, John (Wyndham Parkes Lucas)
Beynon

Bialik, Chaim Nachman
1873-1934 .... **TCLC 25**

Bickerstaff, Isaac
See Swift, Jonathan

Bidart, Frank 19th cent. (?)-....... **CLC 33**

Bienek, Horst 1930-............ **CLC 7, 11**
See also CA 73-76; DLB 75

Bierce, Ambrose (Gwinett)
1842-1914(?) ..... **TCLC 1, 7, 44; SSC 9**
See also CA 104; CDALB 1865-1917;
DLB 11, 12, 23, 71, 74; WLC

Billings, Josh
See Shaw, Henry Wheeler

Billington, Rachel 1942-.......... **CLC 43**
See also AITN 2; CA 33-36R

Binyon, T(imothy) J(ohn) 1936- .... **CLC 34**
See also CA 111; CANR 28

Bioy Casares, Adolfo 1914-.... **CLC 4, 8, 13**
See also CA 29-32R; CANR 19; DLB 113;
HW; MTCW

Bird, C.
See Ellison, Harlan

Bird, Cordwainer
See Ellison, Harlan

Bird, Robert Montgomery
1806-1854 .... **NCLC 1**

Birney, (Alfred) Earle
1904- .... **CLC 1, 4, 6, 11**
See also CA 1-4R; CANR 5, 20; DLB 88;
MTCW

Bishop, Elizabeth
1911-1979 ..... **CLC 1, 4, 9, 13, 15, 32;
PC 3**
See also CA 5-8R; 89-92; CABS 2;
CANR 26; CDALB 1968-1988; DLB 5;
MTCW; SATA 24

Bishop, John 1935-............... **CLC 10**
See also CA 105

bissett, bill 1939- .... **CLC 18**
See also CA 69-72; CANR 15; DLB 53;
MTCW

Bitov, Andrei (Georgievich) 1937-... **CLC 57**

Biyidi, Alexandre 1932-
See Beti, Mongo
See also BW; CA 114; 124; MTCW

Bjarme, Brynjolf
See Ibsen, Henrik (Johan)

Bjoernson, Bjoernstjerne (Martinius)
1832-1910 .... **TCLC 7**
See also Bjornson, Bjornstjerne; Bjornson,
Bjornstjerne (Martinius)
See also CA 104

Bjornson, Bjornstjerne .... **TCLC 37**
See also Bjoernson, Bjoernstjerne
(Martinius)

Bjornson, Bjornstjerne (Martinius)... **TCLC 7**
See also Bjoernson, Bjoernstjerne
(Martinius)

Black, Robert
See Holdstock, Robert P.

Blackburn, Paul 1926-1971 . . . . . . **CLC 9, 43**
See also CA 81-84; 33-36R; CANR 34;
DLB 16; DLBY 81

Black Elk 1863-1950 . . . . **TCLC 33**

Black Hobart
See Sanders, (James) Ed(ward)

Blacklin, Malcolm
See Chambers, Aidan

Blackmore, R(ichard) D(oddridge)
1825-1900 . . . . **TCLC 27**
See also CA 120; DLB 18

Blackmur, R(ichard) P(almer)
1904-1965 . . . . **CLC 2, 24**
See also CA 11-12; 25-28R; CAP 1; DLB 63

Black Tarantula, The
See Acker, Kathy

Blackwood, Algernon (Henry)
1869-1951 . . . . **TCLC 5**
See also CA 105

Blackwood, Caroline 1931- . . . . **CLC 6, 9**
See also CA 85-88; CANR 32; DLB 14;
MTCW

Blade, Alexander
See Hamilton, Edmond; Silverberg, Robert

Blair, Eric (Arthur) 1903-1950
See Orwell, George
See also CA 104; 132; MTCW; SATA 29

Blais, Marie-Claire
1939- . . . . **CLC 2, 4, 6, 13, 22**
See also CA 21-24R; CAAS 4; CANR 38;
DLB 53; MTCW

Blaise, Clark 1940- . . . . **CLC 29**
See also AITN 2; CA 53-56; CAAS 3;
CANR 5; DLB 53

Blake, Nicholas
See Day Lewis, C(ecil)
See also DLB 77

Blake, William 1757-1827 . . . . **NCLC 13**
See also CDBLB 1789-1832; DLB 93;
MAICYA; SATA 30; WLC

Blasco Ibanez, Vicente
1867-1928 . . . . **TCLC 12**
See also CA 110; 131; HW; MTCW

Blatty, William Peter 1928- . . . . **CLC 2**
See also CA 5-8R; CANR 9

Bleeck, Oliver
See Thomas, Ross (Elmore)

Blessing, Lee 1949- . . . . **CLC 54**

Blish, James (Benjamin)
1921-1975 . . . . **CLC 14**
See also CA 1-4R; 57-60; CANR 3; DLB 8;
MTCW; SATA 66

Bliss, Reginald
See Wells, H(erbert) G(eorge)

Blixen, Karen (Christentze Dinesen)
1885-1962
See Dinesen, Isak
See also CA 25-28; CANR 22; CAP 2;
MTCW; SATA 44

Bloch, Robert (Albert) 1917- . . . . **CLC 33**
See also CA 5-8R; CANR 5; DLB 44;
SATA 12

Blok, Alexander (Alexandrovich)
1880-1921 . . . . **TCLC 5**
See also CA 104

Blom, Jan
See Breytenbach, Breyten

Bloom, Harold 1930- . . . . **CLC 24**
See also CA 13-16R; CANR 39; DLB 67

Bloomfield, Aurelius
See Bourne, Randolph S(illiman)

Blount, Roy (Alton) Jr. 1941- . . . . . . **CLC 38**
See also CA 53-56; CANR 10, 28; MTCW

Bloy, Leon 1846-1917 . . . . **TCLC 22**
See also CA 121

Blume, Judy (Sussman) 1938- . . . **CLC 12, 30**
See also AAYA 3; CA 29-32R; CANR 13,
37; CLR 2, 15; DLB 52; MAICYA;
MTCW; SATA 2, 31

Blunden, Edmund (Charles)
1896-1974 . . . . **CLC 2, 56**
See also CA 17-18; 45-48; CAP 2; DLB 20,
100; MTCW

Bly, Robert (Elwood)
1926- . . . . **CLC 1, 2, 5, 10, 15, 38**
See also CA 5-8R; DLB 5; MTCW

Bobette
See Simenon, Georges (Jacques Christian)

Boccaccio, Giovanni 1313-1375
See also SSC 10

Bochco, Steven 1943- . . . . **CLC 35**
See also CA 124; 138

Bodenheim, Maxwell 1892-1954 . . . **TCLC 44**
See also CA 110; DLB 9, 45

Bodker, Cecil 1927- . . . . **CLC 21**
See also CA 73-76; CANR 13; CLR 23;
MAICYA; SATA 14

Boell, Heinrich (Theodor)
1917-1985 . . . **CLC 2, 3, 6, 9, 11, 15, 27,
39**
See also Boll, Heinrich (Theodor)
See also CA 21-24R; 116; CANR 24;
DLB 69; DLBY 85; MTCW

Bogan, Louise 1897-1970 . . . . . **CLC 4, 39, 46**
See also CA 73-76; 25-28R; CANR 33;
DLB 45; MTCW

Bogarde, Dirk . . . . **CLC 19**
See also Van Den Bogarde, Derek Jules
Gaspard Ulric Niven
See also DLB 14

Bogosian, Eric 1953- . . . . **CLC 45**
See also CA 138

Bograd, Larry 1953- . . . . **CLC 35**
See also CA 93-96; SATA 33

Boiardo, Matteo Maria 1441-1494 . . . . **LC 6**

Boileau-Despreaux, Nicolas
1636-1711 . . . . **LC 3**

Boland, Eavan 1944- . . . . **CLC 40, 67**
See also DLB 40

Boll, Heinrich (Theodor)
1917-1985 . . . **CLC 2, 3, 6, 9, 11, 15, 27,
39, 72**
See also Boell, Heinrich (Theodor)
See also DLB 69; DLBY 85; WLC

Bolt, Robert (Oxton) 1924- . . . . **CLC 14**
See also CA 17-20R; CANR 35; DLB 13;
MTCW

Bomkauf
See Kaufman, Bob (Garnell)

Bonaventura . . . . **NCLC 35**
See also DLB 90

Bond, Edward 1934- . . . . **CLC 4, 6, 13, 23**
See also CA 25-28R; CANR 38; DLB 13;
MTCW

Bonham, Frank 1914-1989 . . . . **CLC 12**
See also AAYA 1; CA 9-12R; CANR 4, 36;
MAICYA; SAAS 3; SATA 1, 49, 62

Bonnefoy, Yves 1923- . . . . **CLC 9, 15, 58**
See also CA 85-88; CANR 33; MTCW

Bontemps, Arna(ud Wendell)
1902-1973 . . . . **CLC 1, 18**
See also BLC 1; BW; CA 1-4R; 41-44R;
CANR 4, 35; CLR 6; DLB 48, 51;
MAICYA; MTCW; SATA 2, 24, 44

Booth, Martin 1944- . . . . **CLC 13**
See also CA 93-96; CAAS 2

Booth, Philip 1925- . . . . **CLC 23**
See also CA 5-8R; CANR 5; DLBY 82

Booth, Wayne C(layson) 1921- . . . . . **CLC 24**
See also CA 1-4R; CAAS 5; CANR 3;
DLB 67

Borchert, Wolfgang 1921-1947 . . . . . **TCLC 5**
See also CA 104; DLB 69

Borges, Jorge Luis
1899-1986 . . . **CLC 1, 2, 3, 4, 6, 8, 9, 10,
13, 19, 44, 48; SSC 4**
See also CA 21-24R; CANR 19, 33;
DLB 113; DLBY 86; HW; MTCW; WLC

Borowski, Tadeusz 1922-1951 . . . . . . **TCLC 9**
See also CA 106

Borrow, George (Henry)
1803-1881 . . . . **NCLC 9**
See also DLB 21, 55

Bosschere, Jean de 1878(?)-1953 . . . **TCLC 19**
See also CA 115

Boswell, James 1740-1795 . . . . **LC 4**
See also CDBLB 1660-1789; DLB 104;
WLC

Bottoms, David 1949- . . . . **CLC 53**
See also CA 105; CANR 22; DLB 120;
DLBY 83

Boucolon, Maryse 1937-
See Conde, Maryse
See also CA 110; CANR 30

Bourget, Paul (Charles Joseph)
1852-1935 . . . . **TCLC 12**
See also CA 107

Bourjaily, Vance (Nye) 1922- . . . . **CLC 8, 62**
See also CA 1-4R; CAAS 1; CANR 2;
DLB 2

Bourne, Randolph S(illiman)
1886-1918 . . . . **TCLC 16**
See also CA 117; DLB 63

Bova, Ben(jamin William) 1932- . . . . **CLC 45**
See also CA 5-8R; CANR 11; CLR 3;
DLBY 81; MAICYA; MTCW; SATA 6,
68

Bowen, Elizabeth (Dorothea Cole)
1899-1973 . . . . . **CLC 1, 3, 6, 11, 15, 22;
SSC 3**
See also CA 17-18; 41-44R; CANR 35;
CAP 2; CDBLB 1945-1960; DLB 15;
MTCW

Bowering, George 1935-........ CLC **15, 47**
See also CA 21-24R; CAAS 16; CANR 10;
DLB 53

Bowering, Marilyn R(uthe) 1949-... CLC **32**
See also CA 101

Bowers, Edgar 1924- .... CLC **9**
See also CA 5-8R; CANR 24; DLB 5

Bowie, David.................... CLC **17**
See also Jones, David Robert

Bowles, Jane (Sydney)
1917-1973 .... CLC **3, 68**
See also CA 19-20; 41-44R; CAP 2

Bowles, Paul (Frederick)
1910- .... CLC **1, 2, 19, 53; SSC 3**
See also CA 1-4R; CAAS 1; CANR 1, 19;
DLB 5, 6; MTCW

Box, Edgar
See Vidal, Gore

Boyd, Nancy
See Millay, Edna St. Vincent

Boyd, William 1952-........ CLC **28, 53, 70**
See also CA 114; 120

Boyle, Kay 1902- .. CLC **1, 5, 19, 58; SSC 5**
See also CA 13-16R; CAAS 1; CANR 29;
DLB 4, 9, 48, 86; MTCW

Boyle, Mark
See Kienzle, William X(avier)

Boyle, Patrick 1905-1982......... CLC **19**
See also CA 127

Boyle, T. Coraghessan 1948-.... CLC **36, 55**
See also BEST 90:4; CA 120; DLBY 86

Brackenridge, Hugh Henry
1748-1816 .... NCLC **7**
See also DLB 11, 37

Bradbury, Edward P.
See Moorcock, Michael (John)

Bradbury, Malcolm (Stanley)
1932- .... CLC **32, 61**
See also CA 1-4R; CANR 1, 33; DLB 14;
MTCW

Bradbury, Ray (Douglas)
1920- .... CLC **1, 3, 10, 15, 42**
See also AITN 1, 2; CA 1-4R; CANR 2, 30;
CDALB 1968-1988; DLB 2, 8; MTCW;
SATA 11, 64; WLC

Bradford, Gamaliel 1863-1932..... TCLC **36**
See also DLB 17

Bradley, David (Henry Jr.) 1950-... CLC **23**
See also BLC 1; BW; CA 104; CANR 26;
DLB 33

Bradley, John Ed 1959-........... CLC **55**

Bradley, Marion Zimmer 1930-..... CLC **30**
See also AAYA 9; CA 57-60; CAAS 10;
CANR 7, 31; DLB 8; MTCW

Bradstreet, Anne 1612(?)-1672 .... LC **4**
See also CDALB 1640-1865; DLB 24

Bragg, Melvyn 1939- .... CLC **10**
See also BEST 89:3; CA 57-60; CANR 10;
DLB 14

Braine, John (Gerard)
1922-1986 .... CLC **1, 3, 41**
See also CA 1-4R; 120; CANR 1, 33;
CDBLB 1945-1960; DLB 15; DLBY 86;
MTCW

Brammer, William 1930(?)-1978 .... CLC **31**
See also CA 77-80

Brancati, Vitaliano 1907-1954..... TCLC **12**
See also CA 109

Brancato, Robin F(idler) 1936- ..... CLC **35**
See also AAYA 9; CA 69-72; CANR 11;
SAAS 9; SATA 23

Brand, Millen 1906-1980.......... CLC **7**
See also CA 21-24R; 97-100

Branden, Barbara .... CLC **44**

Brandes, Georg (Morris Cohen)
1842-1927 .... TCLC **10**
See also CA 105

Brandys, Kazimierz 1916- .... CLC **62**

Branley, Franklyn M(ansfield)
1915- .... CLC **21**
See also CA 33-36R; CANR 14, 39;
CLR 13; MAICYA; SATA 4, 68

Brathwaite, Edward (Kamau)
1930- .... CLC **11**
See also BW; CA 25-28R; CANR 11, 26

Brautigan, Richard (Gary)
1935-1984 ... CLC **1, 3, 5, 9, 12, 34, 42**
See also CA 53-56; 113; CANR 34; DLB 2,
5; DLBY 80, 84; MTCW; SATA 56

Braverman, Kate 1950- .... CLC **67**
See also CA 89-92

Brecht, Bertolt
1898-1956 .... TCLC **1, 6, 13, 35**
See also CA 104; 133; DLB 56; MTCW;
WLC

Brecht, Eugen Berthold Friedrich
See Brecht, Bertolt

Bremer, Fredrika 1801-1865 ..... NCLC **11**

Brennan, Christopher John
1870-1932 .... TCLC **17**
See also CA 117

Brennan, Maeve 1917-............. CLC **5**
See also CA 81-84

Brentano, Clemens (Maria)
1778-1842 .... NCLC **1**

Brent of Bin Bin
See Franklin, (Stella Maraia Sarah) Miles

Brenton, Howard 1942-........... CLC **31**
See also CA 69-72; CANR 33; DLB 13;
MTCW

Breslin, James 1930-
See Breslin, Jimmy
See also CA 73-76; CANR 31; MTCW

Breslin, Jimmy .... CLC **4, 43**
See also Breslin, James
See also AITN 1

Bresson, Robert 1907-............ CLC **16**
See also CA 110

Breton, Andre 1896-1966... CLC **2, 9, 15, 54**
See also CA 19-20; 25-28R; CAP 2;
DLB 65; MTCW

Breytenbach, Breyten 1939(?)- .. CLC **23, 37**
See also CA 113; 129

Bridgers, Sue Ellen 1942- .... CLC **26**
See also AAYA 8; CA 65-68; CANR 11,
36; CLR 18; DLB 52; MAICYA;
SAAS 1; SATA 22

Bridges, Robert (Seymour)
1844-1930 .... TCLC **1**
See also CA 104; CDBLB 1890-1914;
DLB 19, 98

Bridie, James.................... TCLC **3**
See also Mavor, Osborne Henry
See also DLB 10

Brin, David 1950-................ CLC **34**
See also CA 102; CANR 24; SATA 65

Brink, Andre (Philippus)
1935- .... CLC **18, 36**
See also CA 104; CANR 39; MTCW

Brinsmead, H(esba) F(ay) 1922-.... CLC **21**
See also CA 21-24R; CANR 10; MAICYA;
SAAS 5; SATA 18

Brittain, Vera (Mary)
1893(?)-1970 .... CLC **23**
See also CA 13-16; 25-28R; CAP 1; MTCW

Broch, Hermann 1886-1951...... TCLC **20**
See also CA 117; DLB 85

Brock, Rose
See Hansen, Joseph

Brodkey, Harold 1930-........... CLC **56**
See also CA 111

Brodsky, Iosif Alexandrovich 1940-
See Brodsky, Joseph
See also AITN 1; CA 41-44R; CANR 37;
MTCW

Brodsky, Joseph .... CLC **4, 6, 13, 36, 50**
See also Brodsky, Iosif Alexandrovich

Brodsky, Michael Mark 1948- ..... CLC **19**
See also CA 102; CANR 18

Bromell, Henry 1947-............. CLC **5**
See also CA 53-56; CANR 9

Bromfield, Louis (Brucker)
1896-1956 .... TCLC **11**
See also CA 107; DLB 4, 9, 86

Broner, E(sther) M(asserman)
1930- .... CLC **19**
See also CA 17-20R; CANR 8, 25; DLB 28

Bronk, William 1918-............. CLC **10**
See also CA 89-92; CANR 23

Bronstein, Lev Davidovich
See Trotsky, Leon

Bronte, Anne 1820-1849.......... NCLC **4**
See also DLB 21

Bronte, Charlotte
1816-1855 .... NCLC **3, 8, 33**
See also CDBLB 1832-1890; DLB 21; WLC

Bronte, (Jane) Emily
1818-1848 .... NCLC **16, 35**
See also CDBLB 1832-1890; DLB 21, 32;
WLC

Brooke, Frances 1724-1789 .... LC **6**
See also DLB 39, 99

Brooke, Henry 1703(?)-1783 .... LC **1**
See also DLB 39

Brooke, Rupert (Chawner)
1887-1915 .... TCLC **2, 7**
See also CA 104; 132; CDBLB 1914-1945;
DLB 19; MTCW; WLC

Brooke-Haven, P.
See Wodehouse, P(elham) G(renville)

Brooke-Rose, Christine 1926- . . . . . . **CLC 40**
See also CA 13-16R; DLB 14

Brookner, Anita 1928- . . . . . . **CLC 32, 34, 51**
See also CA 114; 120; CANR 37; DLBY 87;
MTCW

Brooks, Cleanth 1906- . . . . **CLC 24**
See also CA 17-20R; CANR 33, 35;
DLB 63; MTCW

Brooks, George
See Baum, L(yman) Frank

Brooks, Gwendolyn
1917- . . . . **CLC 1, 2, 4, 5, 15, 49**
See also AITN 1; BLC 1; BW; CA 1-4R;
CANR 1, 27; CDALB 1941-1968;
CLR 27; DLB 5, 76; MTCW; SATA 6;
WLC

Brooks, Mel . . . . **CLC 12**
See also Kaminsky, Melvin
See also DLB 26

Brooks, Peter 1938- . . . . **CLC 34**
See also CA 45-48; CANR 1

Brooks, Van Wyck 1886-1963 . . . . . . **CLC 29**
See also CA 1-4R; CANR 6; DLB 45, 63,
103

Brophy, Brigid (Antonia)
1929- . . . . **CLC 6, 11, 29**
See also CA 5-8R; CAAS 4; CANR 25;
DLB 14; MTCW

Brosman, Catharine Savage 1934- . . . . **CLC 9**
See also CA 61-64; CANR 21

Brother Antoninus
See Everson, William (Oliver)

Broughton, T(homas) Alan 1936- . . . **CLC 19**
See also CA 45-48; CANR 2, 23

Broumas, Olga 1949- . . . . **CLC 10**
See also CA 85-88; CANR 20

Brown, Charles Brockden
1771-1810 . . . . **NCLC 22**
See also CDALB 1640-1865; DLB 37, 59,
73

Brown, Christy 1932-1981 . . . . **CLC 63**
See also CA 105; 104; DLB 14

Brown, Claude 1937- . . . . **CLC 30**
See also AAYA 7; BLC 1; BW; CA 73-76

Brown, Dee (Alexander) 1908- . . **CLC 18, 47**
See also CA 13-16R; CAAS 6; CANR 11;
DLBY 80; MTCW; SATA 5

Brown, George
See Wertmueller, Lina

Brown, George Douglas
1869-1902 . . . . **TCLC 28**

Brown, George Mackay 1921- . . . . **CLC 5, 48**
See also CA 21-24R; CAAS 6; CANR 12,
37; DLB 14, 27; MTCW; SATA 35

Brown, Moses
See Barrett, William (Christopher)

Brown, Rita Mae 1944- . . . . **CLC 18, 43**
See also CA 45-48; CANR 2, 11, 35;
MTCW

Brown, Roderick (Langmere) Haig-
See Haig-Brown, Roderick (Langmere)

Brown, Rosellen 1939- . . . . **CLC 32**
See also CA 77-80; CAAS 10; CANR 14

Brown, Sterling Allen
1901-1989 . . . . **CLC 1, 23, 59**
See also BLC 1; BW; CA 85-88; 127;
CANR 26; DLB 48, 51, 63; MTCW

Brown, Will
See Ainsworth, William Harrison

Brown, William Wells
1813-1884 . . . . **NCLC 2; DC 1**
See also BLC 1; DLB 3, 50

Browne, (Clyde) Jackson 1948(?)- . . . **CLC 21**
See also CA 120

Browning, Elizabeth Barrett
1806-1861 . . . . **NCLC 1, 16**
See also CDBLB 1832-1890; DLB 32; WLC

Browning, Robert
1812-1889 . . . . **NCLC 19; PC 2**
See also CDBLB 1832-1890; DLB 32;
YABC 1

Browning, Tod 1882-1962 . . . . **CLC 16**
See also CA 117

Bruccoli, Matthew J(oseph) 1931- . . **CLC 34**
See also CA 9-12R; CANR 7; DLB 103

Bruce, Lenny . . . . **CLC 21**
See also Schneider, Leonard Alfred

Bruin, John
See Brutus, Dennis

Brulls, Christian
See Simenon, Georges (Jacques Christian)

Brunner, John (Kilian Houston)
1934- . . . . **CLC 8, 10**
See also CA 1-4R; CAAS 8; CANR 2, 37;
MTCW

Brutus, Dennis 1924- . . . . **CLC 43**
See also BLC 1; BW; CA 49-52; CAAS 14;
CANR 2, 27; DLB 117

Bryan, C(ourtlandt) D(ixon) B(arnes)
1936- . . . . **CLC 29**
See also CA 73-76; CANR 13

Bryan, Michael
See Moore, Brian

Bryant, William Cullen
1794-1878 . . . . **NCLC 6**
See also CDALB 1640-1865; DLB 3, 43, 59

Bryusov, Valery Yakovlevich
1873-1924 . . . . **TCLC 10**
See also CA 107

Buchan, John 1875-1940 . . . . **TCLC 41**
See also CA 108; DLB 34, 70; YABC 2

Buchanan, George 1506-1582 . . . . **LC 4**

Buchheim, Lothar-Guenther 1918- . . . **CLC 6**
See also CA 85-88

Buchner, (Karl) Georg
1813-1837 . . . . **NCLC 26**

Buchwald, Art(hur) 1925- . . . . **CLC 33**
See also AITN 1; CA 5-8R; CANR 21;
MTCW; SATA 10

Buck, Pearl S(ydenstricker)
1892-1973 . . . . **CLC 7, 11, 18**
See also AITN 1; CA 1-4R; 41-44R;
CANR 1, 34; DLB 9, 102; MTCW;
SATA 1, 25

Buckler, Ernest 1908-1984 . . . . **CLC 13**
See also CA 11-12; 114; CAP 1; DLB 68;
SATA 47

Buckley, Vincent (Thomas)
1925-1988 . . . . **CLC 57**
See also CA 101

Buckley, William F(rank) Jr.
1925- . . . . **CLC 7, 18, 37**
See also AITN 1; CA 1-4R; CANR 1, 24;
DLBY 80; MTCW

Buechner, (Carl) Frederick
1926- . . . . **CLC 2, 4, 6, 9**
See also CA 13-16R; CANR 11, 39;
DLBY 80; MTCW

Buell, John (Edward) 1927- . . . . **CLC 10**
See also CA 1-4R; DLB 53

Buero Vallejo, Antonio 1916- . . . **CLC 15, 46**
See also CA 106; CANR 24; HW; MTCW

Bugayev, Boris Nikolayevich 1880-1934
See Bely, Andrey
See also CA 104

Bukowski, Charles 1920- . . . . **CLC 2, 5, 9, 41**
See also CA 17-20R; DLB 5; MTCW

Bulgakov, Mikhail (Afanas'evich)
1891-1940 . . . . **TCLC 2, 16**
See also CA 105

Bullins, Ed 1935- . . . . **CLC 1, 5, 7**
See also BLC 1; BW; CA 49-52; CAAS 16;
CANR 24; DLB 7, 38; MTCW

Bulwer-Lytton, Edward (George Earle Lytton)
1803-1873 . . . . **NCLC 1**
See also DLB 21

Bunin, Ivan Alexeyevich
1870-1953 . . . . **TCLC 6; SSC 5**
See also CA 104

Bunting, Basil 1900-1985 . . . . **CLC 10, 39, 47**
See also CA 53-56; 115; CANR 7; DLB 20

Bunuel, Luis 1900-1983 . . . . **CLC 16**
See also CA 101; 110; CANR 32; HW

Bunyan, John 1628-1688 . . . . **LC 4**
See also CDBLB 1660-1789; DLB 39; WLC

Burford, Eleanor
See Hibbert, Eleanor Burford

Burgess, Anthony
. . **CLC 1, 2, 4, 5, 8, 10, 13, 15, 22, 40, 62**
See also Wilson, John (Anthony) Burgess
See also AITN 1; CDBLB 1960 to Present;
DLB 14

Burke, Edmund 1729(?)-1797 . . . . **LC 7**
See also DLB 104; WLC

Burke, Kenneth (Duva) 1897- . . . . **CLC 2, 24**
See also CA 5-8R; CANR 39; DLB 45, 63;
MTCW

Burke, Leda
See Garnett, David

Burke, Ralph
See Silverberg, Robert

Burney, Fanny 1752-1840 . . . . **NCLC 12**
See also DLB 39

Burns, Robert 1759-1796 . . . . **LC 3**
See also CDBLB 1789-1832; DLB 109;
WLC

Burns, Tex
See L'Amour, Louis (Dearborn)

Burnshaw, Stanley 1906- . . . . . **CLC 3, 13, 44**
See also CA 9-12R; DLB 48

Chase, Mary (Coyle) 1907-1981 ...... DC 1
See also CA 77-80; 105; SATA 17, 29

Chase, Mary Ellen 1887-1973 .... CLC 2
See also CA 13-16; 41-44R; CAP 1;
SATA 10

Chase, Nicholas
See Hyde, Anthony

Chateaubriand, Francois Rene de
1768-1848 .... NCLC 3
See also DLB 119

Chatterje, Sarat Chandra 1876-1936(?)
See Chatterji, Saratchandra
See also CA 109

Chatterji, Bankim Chandra
1838-1894 .... NCLC 19

Chatterji, Saratchandra .... TCLC 13
See also Chatterje, Sarat Chandra

Chatterton, Thomas 1752-1770 ...... LC 3
See also DLB 109

Chatwin, (Charles) Bruce
1940-1989 .... CLC 28, 57, 59
See also AAYA 4; BEST 90:1; CA 85-88;
127

Chaucer, Daniel
See Ford, Ford Madox

Chaucer, Geoffrey 1340(?)-1400 ..... LC 17
See also CDBLB Before 1660

Chaviaras, Strates 1935-
See Haviaras, Stratis
See also CA 105

Chayefsky, Paddy .... CLC 23
See also Chayefsky, Sidney
See also DLB 7, 44; DLBY 81

Chayefsky, Sidney 1923-1981
See Chayefsky, Paddy
See also CA 9-12R; 104; CANR 18

Chedid, Andree 1920- .... CLC 47

Cheever, John
1912-1982 ..... CLC 3, 7, 8, 11, 15, 25,
64; SSC 1
See also CA 5-8R; 106; CABS 1; CANR 5,
27; CDALB 1941-1968; DLB 2, 102;
DLBY 80, 82; MTCW; WLC

Cheever, Susan 1943- .... CLC 18, 48
See also CA 103; CANR 27; DLBY 82

Chekhonte, Antosha
See Chekhov, Anton (Pavlovich)

Chekhov, Anton (Pavlovich)
1860-1904 ...... TCLC 3, 10, 31; SSC 2
See also CA 104; 124; WLC

Chernyshevsky, Nikolay Gavrilovich
1828-1889 .... NCLC 1

Cherry, Carolyn Janice 1942-
See Cherryh, C. J.
See also CA 65-68; CANR 10

Cherryh, C. J. .... CLC 35
See also Cherry, Carolyn Janice
See also DLBY 80

Chesnutt, Charles W(addell)
1858-1932 .... TCLC 5, 39; SSC 7
See also BLC 1; BW; CA 106; 125; DLB 12,
50, 78; MTCW

Chester, Alfred 1929(?)-1971 .... CLC 49
See also CA 33-36R

Chesterton, G(ilbert) K(eith)
1874-1936 .... TCLC 1, 6; SSC 1
See also CA 104; 132; CDBLB 1914-1945;
DLB 10, 19, 34, 70, 98; MTCW;
SATA 27

Chiang Pin-chin 1904-1986
See Ding Ling
See also CA 118

Ch'ien Chung-shu 1910- .... CLC 22
See also CA 130; MTCW

Child, L. Maria
See Child, Lydia Maria

Child, Lydia Maria 1802-1880 .... NCLC 6
See also DLB 1, 74; SATA 67

Child, Mrs.
See Child, Lydia Maria

Child, Philip 1898-1978 .... CLC 19, 68
See also CA 13-14; CAP 1; SATA 47

Childress, Alice 1920- .... CLC 12, 15
See also AAYA 8; BLC 1; BW; CA 45-48;
CANR 3, 27; CLR 14; DLB 7, 38;
MAICYA; MTCW; SATA 7, 48

Chislett, (Margaret) Anne 1943- .... CLC 34

Chitty, Thomas Willes 1926- .... CLC 11
See also Hinde, Thomas
See also CA 5-8R

Chomette, Rene Lucien 1898-1981 .. CLC 20
See also Clair, Rene
See also CA 103

Chopin, Kate .... TCLC 5, 14; SSC 8
See also Chopin, Katherine
See also CDALB 1865-1917; DLB 12, 78

Chopin, Katherine 1851-1904
See Chopin, Kate
See also CA 104; 122

Christie
See Ichikawa, Kon

Christie, Agatha (Mary Clarissa)
1890-1976 ...... CLC 1, 6, 8, 12, 39, 48
See also AAYA 9; AITN 1, 2; CA 17-20R;
61-64; CANR 10, 37; CDBLB 1914-1945;
DLB 13, 77; MTCW; SATA 36

Christie, (Ann) Philippa
See Pearce, Philippa
See also CA 5-8R; CANR 4

Christine de Pizan 1365(?)-1431(?) .... LC 9

Chubb, Elmer
See Masters, Edgar Lee

Chulkov, Mikhail Dmitrievich
1743-1792 .... LC 2

Churchill, Caryl 1938- .... CLC 31, 55
See also CA 102; CANR 22; DLB 13;
MTCW

Churchill, Charles 1731-1764 .... LC 3
See also DLB 109

Chute, Carolyn 1947- .... CLC 39
See also CA 123

Ciardi, John (Anthony)
1916-1986 .... CLC 10, 40, 44
See also CA 5-8R; 118; CAAS 2; CANR 5,
33; CLR 19; DLB 5; DLBY 86;
MAICYA; MTCW; SATA 1, 46, 65

Cicero, Marcus Tullius
106B.C.-43B.C. .... CMLC 3

Cimino, Michael 1943- .... CLC 16
See also CA 105

Cioran, E(mil) M. 1911- .... CLC 64
See also CA 25-28R

Cisneros, Sandra 1954- .... CLC 69
See also AAYA 9; CA 131; HW

Clair, Rene .... CLC 20
See also Chomette, Rene Lucien

Clampitt, Amy 1920- .... CLC 32
See also CA 110; CANR 29; DLB 105

Clancy, Thomas L. Jr. 1947-
See Clancy, Tom
See also CA 125; 131; MTCW

Clancy, Tom .... CLC 45
See also Clancy, Thomas L. Jr.
See also AAYA 9; BEST 89:1, 90:1

Clare, John 1793-1864 .... NCLC 9
See also DLB 55, 96

Clarin
See Alas (y Urena), Leopoldo (Enrique
Garcia)

Clark, (Robert) Brian 1932- .... CLC 29
See also CA 41-44R

Clark, Eleanor 1913- .... CLC 5, 19
See also CA 9-12R; DLB 6

Clark, J. P.
See Clark, John Pepper
See also DLB 117

Clark, John Pepper 1935- .... CLC 38
See also Clark, J. P.
See also BLC 1; BW; CA 65-68; CANR 16

Clark, M. R.
See Clark, Mavis Thorpe

Clark, Mavis Thorpe 1909- .... CLC 12
See also CA 57-60; CANR 8, 37; MAICYA;
SAAS 5; SATA 8

Clark, Walter Van Tilburg
1909-1971 .... CLC 28
See also CA 9-12R; 33-36R; DLB 9;
SATA 8

Clarke, Arthur C(harles)
1917- ...... CLC 1, 4, 13, 18, 35; SSC 3
See also AAYA 4; CA 1-4R; CANR 2, 28;
MAICYA; MTCW; SATA 13, 70

Clarke, Austin C(hesterfield)
1934- .... CLC 8, 53
See also BLC 1; BW; CA 25-28R;
CAAS 16; CANR 14, 32; DLB 53

Clarke, Austin 1896-1974 .... CLC 6, 9
See also CA 29-32; 49-52; CAP 2; DLB 10,
20

Clarke, Gillian 1937- .... CLC 61
See also CA 106; DLB 40

Clarke, Marcus (Andrew Hislop)
1846-1881 .... NCLC 19

Clarke, Shirley 1925- .... CLC 16

.... CLC 30
See also Headon, (Nicky) Topper; Jones,
Mick; Simonon, Paul; Strummer, Joe

Claudel, Paul (Louis Charles Marie)
1868-1955 .... TCLC 2, 10
See also CA 104

Author Index

Dillon, Eilis 1920-. . . . . **CLC 17**
See also CA 9-12R; CAAS 3; CANR 4, 38;
CLR 26; MAICYA; SATA 2

Dimont, Penelope
See Mortimer, Penelope (Ruth)

Dinesen, Isak. . . . . **CLC 10, 29; SSC 7**
See also Blixen, Karen (Christentze
Dinesen)

Ding Ling. . . . . **CLC 68**
See also Chiang Pin-chin

Disch, Thomas M(ichael) 1940-. . . **CLC 7, 36**
See also CA 21-24R; CAAS 4; CANR 17,
36; CLR 18; DLB 8; MAICYA; MTCW;
SATA 54

Disch, Tom
See Disch, Thomas M(ichael)

d'Isly, Georges
See Simenon, Georges (Jacques Christian)

Disraeli, Benjamin 1804-1881 . . . . . **NCLC 2**
See also DLB 21, 55

Ditcum, Steve
See Crumb, R(obert)

Dixon, Paige
See Corcoran, Barbara

Dixon, Stephen 1936-. . . . . **CLC 52**
See also CA 89-92; CANR 17

Doblin, Alfred . . . . **TCLC 13**
See also Doeblin, Alfred

Dobrolyubov, Nikolai Alexandrovich
1836-1861 . . . . **NCLC 5**

Dobyns, Stephen 1941-. . . . . **CLC 37**
See also CA 45-48; CANR 2, 18

Doctorow, E(dgar) L(aurence)
1931- . . . . . **CLC 6, 11, 15, 18, 37, 44, 65**
See also AITN 2; BEST 89:3; CA 45-48;
CANR 2, 33; CDALB 1968-1988; DLB 2,
28; DLBY 80; MTCW

Dodgson, Charles Lutwidge 1832-1898
See Carroll, Lewis
See also CLR 2; MAICYA; YABC 2

Doeblin, Alfred 1878-1957. . . . . . . **TCLC 13**
See also Doblin, Alfred
See also CA 110; DLB 66

Doerr, Harriet 1910- . . . . **CLC 34**
See also CA 117; 122

Domecq, H(onorio) Bustos
See Bioy Casares, Adolfo; Borges, Jorge
Luis

Domini, Rey
See Lorde, Audre (Geraldine)

Dominique
See Proust,
(Valentin-Louis-George-Eugene-)Marcel

Don, A
See Stephen, Leslie

Donaldson, Stephen R. 1947-. . . . . . . **CLC 46**
See also CA 89-92; CANR 13

Donleavy, J(ames) P(atrick)
1926- . . . . **CLC 1, 4, 6, 10, 45**
See also AITN 2; CA 9-12R; CANR 24;
DLB 6; MTCW

Donne, John 1572-1631 . . . . . . **LC 10; PC 1**
See also CDBLB Before 1660; DLB 121;
WLC

Donnell, David 1939(?)-. . . . . **CLC 34**

Donoso (Yanez), Jose
1924- . . . . **CLC 4, 8, 11, 32**
See also CA 81-84; CANR 32; DLB 113;
HW; MTCW

Donovan, John 1928-1992 . . . . **CLC 35**
See also CA 97-100; 137; CLR 3;
MAICYA; SATA 29

Don Roberto
See Cunninghame Graham, R(obert)
B(ontine)

Doolittle, Hilda
1886-1961 . . . **CLC 3, 8, 14, 31, 34; PC 5**
See also H. D.
See also CA 97-100; CANR 35; DLB 4, 45;
MTCW; WLC

Dorfman, Ariel 1942-. . . . . **CLC 48**
See also CA 124; 130; HW

Dorn, Edward (Merton) 1929-. . . **CLC 10, 18**
See also CA 93-96; DLB 5

Dorsan, Luc
See Simenon, Georges (Jacques Christian)

Dorsange, Jean
See Simenon, Georges (Jacques Christian)

Dos Passos, John (Roderigo)
1896-1970 . . . **CLC 1, 4, 8, 11, 15, 25, 34**
See also CA 1-4R; 29-32R; CANR 3;
CDALB 1929-1941; DLB 4, 9; DLBD 1;
MTCW; WLC

Dossage, Jean
See Simenon, Georges (Jacques Christian)

Dostoevsky, Fedor Mikhailovich
1821-1881 . . . . **NCLC 2, 7, 21, 33; SSC 2**
See also WLC

Doughty, Charles M(ontagu)
1843-1926 . . . . **TCLC 27**
See also CA 115; DLB 19, 57

Douglas, Gavin 1475(?)-1522. . . . . . . **LC 20**

Douglas, Keith 1920-1944 . . . . **TCLC 40**
See also DLB 27

Douglas, Leonard
See Bradbury, Ray (Douglas)

Douglas, Michael
See Crichton, (John) Michael

Douglass, Frederick 1817(?)-1895. . **NCLC 7**
See also BLC 1; CDALB 1640-1865;
DLB 1, 43, 50, 79; SATA 29; WLC

Dourado, (Waldomiro Freitas) Autran
1926- . . . . **CLC 23, 60**
See also CA 25-28R; CANR 34

Dourado, Waldomiro Autran
See Dourado, (Waldomiro Freitas) Autran

Dove, Rita (Frances) 1952- . . . . **CLC 50**
See also BW; CA 109; CANR 27; DLB 120

Dowell, Coleman 1925-1985 . . . . **CLC 60**
See also CA 25-28R; 117; CANR 10

Dowson, Ernest Christopher
1867-1900 . . . . **TCLC 4**
See also CA 105; DLB 19

Doyle, A. Conan
See Doyle, Arthur Conan

Doyle, Arthur Conan 1859-1930 . . . . **TCLC 7**
See also CA 104; 122; CDBLB 1890-1914;
DLB 18, 70; MTCW; SATA 24; WLC

Doyle, Conan
See Doyle, Arthur Conan

Doyle, John
See Graves, Robert (von Ranke)

Doyle, Sir A. Conan
See Doyle, Arthur Conan

Doyle, Sir Arthur Conan
See Doyle, Arthur Conan

Dr. A
See Asimov, Isaac; Silverstein, Alvin

Drabble, Margaret
1939- . . . . **CLC 2, 3, 5, 8, 10, 22, 53**
See also CA 13-16R; CANR 18, 35;
CDBLB 1960 to Present; DLB 14;
MTCW; SATA 48

Drapier, M. B.
See Swift, Jonathan

Drayham, James
See Mencken, H(enry) L(ouis)

Drayton, Michael 1563-1631. . . . . **LC 8**

Dreadstone, Carl
See Campbell, (John) Ramsey

Dreiser, Theodore (Herman Albert)
1871-1945 . . . . **TCLC 10, 18, 35**
See also CA 106; 132; CDALB 1865-1917;
DLB 9, 12, 102; DLBD 1; MTCW; WLC

Drexler, Rosalyn 1926- . . . . **CLC 2, 6**
See also CA 81-84

Dreyer, Carl Theodor 1889-1968. . . . **CLC 16**
See also CA 116

Drieu la Rochelle, Pierre(-Eugene)
1893-1945 . . . . **TCLC 21**
See also CA 117; DLB 72

Drop Shot
See Cable, George Washington

Droste-Hulshoff, Annette Freiin von
1797-1848 . . . . **NCLC 3**

Drummond, Walter
See Silverberg, Robert

Drummond, William Henry
1854-1907 . . . . **TCLC 25**
See also DLB 92

Drummond de Andrade, Carlos
1902-1987 . . . . **CLC 18**
See also Andrade, Carlos Drummond de
See also CA 132; 123

Drury, Allen (Stuart) 1918-. . . . . **CLC 37**
See also CA 57-60; CANR 18

Dryden, John 1631-1700 . . . . **LC 3**

Duberman, Martin 1930-. . . . . **CLC 8**
See also CA 1-4R; CANR 2

Dubie, Norman (Evans) 1945-. . . . . . **CLC 36**
See also CA 69-72; CANR 12; DLB 120

Du Bois, W(illiam) E(dward) B(urghardt)
1868-1963 . . . . **CLC 1, 2, 13, 64**
See also BLC 1; BW; CA 85-88; CANR 34;
CDALB 1865-1917; DLB 47, 50, 91;
MTCW; SATA 42; WLC

Dubus, Andre 1936-. . . . . **CLC 13, 36**
See also CA 21-24R; CANR 17

Duca Minimo
See D'Annunzio, Gabriele

Duclos, Charles Pinot 1704-1772 . . . . . **LC 1**

Eisner, Simon
  See Kornbluth, C(yril) M.

Ekeloef, (Bengt) Gunnar
  1907-1968 . . . . **CLC 27**
  See also Ekelof, (Bengt) Gunnar
  See also CA 123; 25-28R

Ekelof, (Bengt) Gunnar . . . . **CLC 27**
  See also Ekeloef, (Bengt) Gunnar

Ekwensi, C. O. D.
  See Ekwensi, Cyprian (Odiatu Duaka)

Ekwensi, Cyprian (Odiatu Duaka)
  1921- . . . . **CLC 4**
  See also BLC 1; BW; CA 29-32R;
    CANR 18; DLB 117; MTCW; SATA 66

Elaine . . . . **TCLC 18**
  See also Leverson, Ada

El Crummo
  See Crumb, R(obert)

Elia
  See Lamb, Charles

Eliade, Mircea 1907-1986 . . . . **CLC 19**
  See also CA 65-68; 119; CANR 30; MTCW

Eliot, A. D.
  See Jewett, (Theodora) Sarah Orne

Eliot, Alice
  See Jewett, (Theodora) Sarah Orne

Eliot, Dan
  See Silverberg, Robert

Eliot, George 1819-1880 . . . . **NCLC 4, 13, 23**
  See also CDBLB 1832-1890; DLB 21, 35,
    55; WLC

Eliot, John 1604-1690 . . . . **LC 5**
  See also DLB 24

Eliot, T(homas) S(tearns)
  1888-1965 . . . . **CLC 1, 2, 3, 6, 9, 10, 13,
    15, 24, 34, 41, 55, 57; PC 5**
  See also CA 5-8R; 25-28R;
    CDALB 1929-1941; DLB 7, 10, 45, 63;
    MTCW; WLC 2

Elizabeth 1866-1941 . . . . **TCLC 41**

Elkin, Stanley L(awrence)
  1930- . . . . **CLC 4, 6, 9, 14, 27, 51**
  See also CA 9-12R; CANR 8; DLB 2, 28;
    DLBY 80; MTCW

Elledge, Scott . . . . **CLC 34**

Elliott, Don
  See Silverberg, Robert

Elliott, George P(aul) 1918-1980 . . . . . **CLC 2**
  See also CA 1-4R; 97-100; CANR 2

Elliott, Janice 1931- . . . . **CLC 47**
  See also CA 13-16R; CANR 8, 29; DLB 14

Elliott, Sumner Locke 1917-1991 . . . **CLC 38**
  See also CA 5-8R; 134; CANR 2, 21

Elliott, William
  See Bradbury, Ray (Douglas)

Ellis, A. E. . . . . **CLC 7**

Ellis, Alice Thomas . . . . **CLC 40**
  See also Haycraft, Anna

Ellis, Bret Easton 1964- . . . . **CLC 39, 71**
  See also AAYA 2; CA 118; 123

Ellis, (Henry) Havelock
  1859-1939 . . . . **TCLC 14**
  See also CA 109

Ellis, Landon
  See Ellison, Harlan

Ellis, Trey 1962- . . . . **CLC 55**

Ellison, Harlan 1934- . . . . **CLC 1, 13, 42**
  See also CA 5-8R; CANR 5; DLB 8;
    MTCW

Ellison, Ralph (Waldo)
  1914- . . . . **CLC 1, 3, 11, 54**
  See also BLC 1; BW; CA 9-12R; CANR 24;
    CDALB 1941-1968; DLB 2, 76; MTCW;
    WLC

Ellmann, Lucy (Elizabeth) 1956- . . . . **CLC 61**
  See also CA 128

Ellmann, Richard (David)
  1918-1987 . . . . **CLC 50**
  See also BEST 89:2; CA 1-4R; 122;
    CANR 2, 28; DLB 103; DLBY 87;
    MTCW

Elman, Richard 1934- . . . . **CLC 19**
  See also CA 17-20R; CAAS 3

Elron
  See Hubbard, L(afayette) Ron(ald)

Eluard, Paul . . . . **TCLC 7, 41**
  See also Grindel, Eugene

Elyot, Sir Thomas 1490(?)-1546 . . . . . **LC 11**

Elytis, Odysseus 1911- . . . . **CLC 15, 49**
  See also CA 102; MTCW

Emecheta, (Florence Onye) Buchi
  1944- . . . . **CLC 14, 48**
  See also BLC 2; BW; CA 81-84; CANR 27;
    DLB 117; MTCW; SATA 66

Emerson, Ralph Waldo
  1803-1882 . . . . **NCLC 1, 38**
  See also CDALB 1640-1865; DLB 1, 59, 73;
    WLC

Eminescu, Mihail 1850-1889 . . . . . **NCLC 33**

Empson, William
  1906-1984 . . . . **CLC 3, 8, 19, 33, 34**
  See also CA 17-20R; 112; CANR 31;
    DLB 20; MTCW

Enchi Fumiko (Ueda) 1905-1986 . . . . **CLC 31**
  See also CA 129; 121

Ende, Michael (Andreas Helmuth)
  1929- . . . . **CLC 31**
  See also CA 118; 124; CANR 36; CLR 14;
    DLB 75; MAICYA; SATA 42, 61

Endo, Shusaku 1923- . . . . . **CLC 7, 14, 19, 54**
  See also CA 29-32R; CANR 21; MTCW

Engel, Marian 1933-1985 . . . . **CLC 36**
  See also CA 25-28R; CANR 12; DLB 53

Engelhardt, Frederick
  See Hubbard, L(afayette) Ron(ald)

Enright, D(ennis) J(oseph)
  1920- . . . . **CLC 4, 8, 31**
  See also CA 1-4R; CANR 1; DLB 27;
    SATA 25

Enzensberger, Hans Magnus
  1929- . . . . **CLC 43**
  See also CA 116; 119

Ephron, Nora 1941- . . . . **CLC 17, 31**
  See also AITN 2; CA 65-68; CANR 12, 39

Epsilon
  See Betjeman, John

Epstein, Daniel Mark 1948- . . . . **CLC 7**
  See also CA 49-52; CANR 2

Epstein, Jacob 1956- . . . . **CLC 19**
  See also CA 114

Epstein, Joseph 1937- . . . . **CLC 39**
  See also CA 112; 119

Epstein, Leslie 1938- . . . . **CLC 27**
  See also CA 73-76; CAAS 12; CANR 23

Equiano, Olaudah 1745(?)-1797 . . . . . . **LC 16**
  See also BLC 2; DLB 37, 50

Erasmus, Desiderius 1469(?)-1536 . . . . **LC 16**

Erdman, Paul E(mil) 1932- . . . . **CLC 25**
  See also AITN 1; CA 61-64; CANR 13

Erdrich, Louise 1954- . . . . **CLC 39, 54**
  See also BEST 89:1; CA 114; MTCW

Erenburg, Ilya (Grigoryevich)
  See Ehrenburg, Ilya (Grigoryevich)

Erickson, Stephen Michael 1950-
  See Erickson, Steve
  See also CA 129

Erickson, Steve . . . . **CLC 64**
  See also Erickson, Stephen Michael

Ericson, Walter
  See Fast, Howard (Melvin)

Eriksson, Buntel
  See Bergman, (Ernst) Ingmar

Eschenbach, Wolfram von
  See Wolfram von Eschenbach

Eseki, Bruno
  See Mphahlele, Ezekiel

Esenin, Sergei (Alexandrovich)
  1895-1925 . . . . **TCLC 4**
  See also CA 104

Eshleman, Clayton 1935- . . . . **CLC 7**
  See also CA 33-36R; CAAS 6; DLB 5

Espriella, Don Manuel Alvarez
  See Southey, Robert

Espriu, Salvador 1913-1985 . . . . **CLC 9**
  See also CA 115

Esse, James
  See Stephens, James

Esterbrook, Tom
  See Hubbard, L(afayette) Ron(ald)

Estleman, Loren D. 1952- . . . . **CLC 48**
  See also CA 85-88; CANR 27; MTCW

Evans, Mary Ann
  See Eliot, George

Evarts, Esther
  See Benson, Sally

Everett, Percival
  See Everett, Percival L.

Everett, Percival L. 1956- . . . . **CLC 57**
  See also CA 129

Everson, R(onald) G(ilmour)
  1903- . . . . **CLC 27**
  See also CA 17-20R; DLB 88

Everson, William (Oliver)
  1912- . . . . **CLC 1, 5, 14**
  See also CA 9-12R; CANR 20; DLB 5, 16;
    MTCW

Evtushenko, Evgenii Aleksandrovich
  See Yevtushenko, Yevgeny (Alexandrovich)

Ewart, Gavin (Buchanan)
1916- .... **CLC 13, 46**
See also CA 89-92; CANR 17; DLB 40;
MTCW

Ewers, Hanns Heinz 1871-1943 ... **TCLC 12**
See also CA 109

Ewing, Frederick R.
See Sturgeon, Theodore (Hamilton)

Exley, Frederick (Earl) 1929- .... **CLC 6, 11**
See also AITN 2; CA 81-84; 138; DLBY 81

Eynhardt, Guillermo
See Quiroga, Horacio (Sylvestre)

Ezekiel, Nissim 1924- .... **CLC 61**
See also CA 61-64

Ezekiel, Tish O'Dowd 1943- .... **CLC 34**
See also CA 129

Fagen, Donald 1948- .... **CLC 26**

Fainzilberg, Ilya Arnoldovich 1897-1937
See Ilf, Ilya
See also CA 120

Fair, Ronald L. 1932- .... **CLC 18**
See also BW; CA 69-72; CANR 25; DLB 33

Fairbairns, Zoe (Ann) 1948- .... **CLC 32**
See also CA 103; CANR 21

Falco, Gian
See Papini, Giovanni

Falconer, James
See Kirkup, James

Falconer, Kenneth
See Kornbluth, C(yril) M.

Falkland, Samuel
See Heijermans, Herman

Fallaci, Oriana 1930- .... **CLC 11**
See also CA 77-80; CANR 15; MTCW

Faludy, George 1913- .... **CLC 42**
See also CA 21-24R

Faludy, Gyoergy
See Faludy, George

Fanshawe, Ann .... **LC 11**

Fante, John (Thomas) 1911-1983 ... **CLC 60**
See also CA 69-72; 109; CANR 23;
DLBY 83

Farah, Nuruddin 1945- .... **CLC 53**
See also BLC 2; CA 106

Fargue, Leon-Paul 1876(?)-1947 ... **TCLC 11**
See also CA 109

Farigoule, Louis
See Romains, Jules

Farina, Richard 1936(?)-1966 .... **CLC 9**
See also CA 81-84; 25-28R

Farley, Walter (Lorimer)
1915-1989 .... **CLC 17**
See also CA 17-20R; CANR 8, 29; DLB 22;
MAICYA; SATA 2, 43

Farmer, Philip Jose 1918- .... **CLC 1, 19**
See also CA 1-4R; CANR 4, 35; DLB 8;
MTCW

Farrell, J(ames) G(ordon)
1935-1979 .... **CLC 6**
See also CA 73-76; 89-92; CANR 36;
DLB 14; MTCW

Farrell, James T(homas)
1904-1979 .... **CLC 1, 4, 8, 11, 66**
See also CA 5-8R; 89-92; CANR 9; DLB 4,
9, 86; DLBD 2; MTCW

Farren, Richard J.
See Betjeman, John

Farren, Richard M.
See Betjeman, John

Fassbinder, Rainer Werner
1946-1982 .... **CLC 20**
See also CA 93-96; 106; CANR 31

Fast, Howard (Melvin) 1914- ...... **CLC 23**
See also CA 1-4R; CANR 1, 33; DLB 9;
SATA 7

Faulcon, Robert
See Holdstock, Robert P.

Faulkner, William (Cuthbert)
1897-1962 .... **CLC 1, 3, 6, 8, 9, 11, 14,
18, 28, 52, 68; SSC 1**
See also AAYA 7; CA 81-84; CANR 33;
CDALB 1929-1941; DLB 9, 11, 44, 102;
DLBD 2; DLBY 86; MTCW; WLC

Fauset, Jessie Redmon
1884(?)-1961 .... **CLC 19, 54**
See also BLC 2; BW; CA 109; DLB 51

Faust, Irvin 1924- .... **CLC 8**
See also CA 33-36R; CANR 28; DLB 2, 28;
DLBY 80

Fawkes, Guy
See Benchley, Robert (Charles)

Fearing, Kenneth (Flexner)
1902-1961 .... **CLC 51**
See also CA 93-96; DLB 9

Fecamps, Elise
See Creasey, John

Federman, Raymond 1928- ...... **CLC 6, 47**
See also CA 17-20R; CAAS 8; CANR 10;
DLBY 80

Federspiel, J(uerg) F. 1931- .... **CLC 42**

Feiffer, Jules (Ralph) 1929- .... **CLC 2, 8, 64**
See also AAYA 3; CA 17-20R; CANR 30;
DLB 7, 44; MTCW; SATA 8, 61

Feige, Hermann Albert Otto Maximilian
See Traven, B.

Fei-Kan, Li
See Li Fei-kan

Feinberg, David B. 1956- .... **CLC 59**
See also CA 135

Feinstein, Elaine 1930- .... **CLC 36**
See also CA 69-72; CAAS 1; CANR 31;
DLB 14, 40; MTCW

Feldman, Irving (Mordecai) 1928- .... **CLC 7**
See also CA 1-4R; CANR 1

Fellini, Federico 1920- .... **CLC 16**
See also CA 65-68; CANR 33

Felsen, Henry Gregor 1916- .... **CLC 17**
See also CA 1-4R; CANR 1; SAAS 2;
SATA 1

Fenton, James Martin 1949- .... **CLC 32**
See also CA 102; DLB 40

Ferber, Edna 1887-1968 .... **CLC 18**
See also AITN 1; CA 5-8R; 25-28R; DLB 9,
28, 86; MTCW; SATA 7

Ferguson, Helen
See Kavan, Anna

Ferguson, Samuel 1810-1886 ..... **NCLC 33**
See also DLB 32

Ferling, Lawrence
See Ferlinghetti, Lawrence (Monsanto)

Ferlinghetti, Lawrence (Monsanto)
1919(?)- .... **CLC 2, 6, 10, 27; PC 1**
See also CA 5-8R; CANR 3;
CDALB 1941-1968; DLB 5, 16; MTCW

Fernandez, Vicente Garcia Huidobro
See Huidobro Fernandez, Vicente Garcia

Ferrer, Gabriel (Francisco Victor) Miro
See Miro (Ferrer), Gabriel (Francisco
Victor)

Ferrier, Susan (Edmonstone)
1782-1854 .... **NCLC 8**
See also DLB 116

Ferrigno, Robert .... **CLC 65**

Feuchtwanger, Lion 1884-1958 ..... **TCLC 3**
See also CA 104; DLB 66

Feydeau, Georges (Leon Jules Marie)
1862-1921 .... **TCLC 22**
See also CA 113

Ficino, Marsilio 1433-1499 .... **LC 12**

Fiedler, Leslie A(aron)
1917- .... **CLC 4, 13, 24**
See also CA 9-12R; CANR 7; DLB 28, 67;
MTCW

Field, Andrew 1938- .... **CLC 44**
See also CA 97-100; CANR 25

Field, Eugene 1850-1895 .... **NCLC 3**
See also DLB 23, 42; MAICYA; SATA 16

Field, Gans T.
See Wellman, Manly Wade

Field, Michael .... **TCLC 43**

Field, Peter
See Hobson, Laura Z(ametkin)

Fielding, Henry 1707-1754 .... **LC 1**
See also CDBLB 1660-1789; DLB 39, 84,
101; WLC

Fielding, Sarah 1710-1768 .... **LC 1**
See also DLB 39

Fierstein, Harvey (Forbes) 1954- ... **CLC 33**
See also CA 123; 129

Figes, Eva 1932- .... **CLC 31**
See also CA 53-56; CANR 4; DLB 14

Finch, Robert (Duer Claydon)
1900- .... **CLC 18**
See also CA 57-60; CANR 9, 24; DLB 88

Findley, Timothy 1930- .... **CLC 27**
See also CA 25-28R; CANR 12; DLB 53

Fink, William
See Mencken, H(enry) L(ouis)

Firbank, Louis 1942-
See Reed, Lou
See also CA 117

Firbank, (Arthur Annesley) Ronald
1886-1926 .... **TCLC 1**
See also CA 104; DLB 36

Fisher, Roy 1930- .... **CLC 25**
See also CA 81-84; CAAS 10; CANR 16;
DLB 40

Fisher, Rudolph   1897-1934 .... **TCLC 11**
   See also BLC 2; BW; CA 107; 124; DLB 51,
   102

Fisher, Vardis (Alvero)   1895-1968.... **CLC 7**
   See also CA 5-8R; 25-28R; DLB 9

Fiske, Tarleton
   See Bloch, Robert (Albert)

Fitch, Clarke
   See Sinclair, Upton (Beall)

Fitch, John IV
   See Cormier, Robert (Edmund)

Fitgerald, Penelope   1916- .... **CLC 61**

Fitzgerald, Captain Hugh
   See Baum, L(yman) Frank

FitzGerald, Edward   1809-1883 .... **NCLC 9**
   See also DLB 32

Fitzgerald, F(rancis) Scott (Key)
   1896-1940 .... **TCLC 1, 6, 14, 28; SSC 6**
   See also AITN 1; CA 110; 123;
      CDALB 1917-1929; DLB 4, 9, 86;
      DLBD 1; DLBY 81; MTCW; WLC

Fitzgerald, Penelope   1916- ...... **CLC 19, 51**
   See also CA 85-88; CAAS 10; DLB 14

FitzGerald, Robert D(avid)
   1902-1987 .... **CLC 19**
   See also CA 17-20R

Fitzgerald, Robert (Stuart)
   1910-1985 .... **CLC 39**
   See also CA 1-4R; 114; CANR 1; DLBY 80

Flanagan, Thomas (James Bonner)
   1923- .... **CLC 25, 52**
   See also CA 108; DLBY 80; MTCW

Flaubert, Gustave
   1821-1880 .... **NCLC 2, 10, 19**
   See also DLB 119; WLC

Flecker, (Herman) James Elroy
   1884-1915 .... **TCLC 43**
   See also CA 109; DLB 10, 19

Fleming, Ian (Lancaster)
   1908-1964 .... **CLC 3, 30**
   See also CA 5-8R; CDBLB 1945-1960;
      DLB 87; MTCW; SATA 9

Fleming, Thomas (James)   1927- .... **CLC 37**
   See also CA 5-8R; CANR 10; SATA 8

Fletcher, John Gould   1886-1950... **TCLC 35**
   See also CA 107; DLB 4, 45

Fleur, Paul
   See Pohl, Frederik

Flying Officer X
   See Bates, H(erbert) E(rnest)

Fo, Dario   1926-.................. **CLC 32**
   See also CA 116; 128; MTCW

Fogarty, Jonathan Titulescu Esq.
   See Farrell, James T(homas)

Folke, Will
   See Bloch, Robert (Albert)

Follett, Ken(neth Martin)   1949- .... **CLC 18**
   See also AAYA 6; BEST 89:4; CA 81-84;
      CANR 13, 33; DLB 87; DLBY 81;
      MTCW

~~Fontane, Theodor 1819-1898 ..... NCLC 26~~

Foote, Horton   1916-.............. **CLC 51**
   See also CA 73-76; CANR 34; DLB 26

Forbes, Esther   1891-1967.......... **CLC 12**
   See also CA 13-14; 25-28R; CAP 1;
      CLR 27; DLB 22; MAICYA; SATA 2

Forche, Carolyn (Louise)   1950-..... **CLC 25**
   See also CA 109; 117; DLB 5

Ford, Elbur
   See Hibbert, Eleanor Burford

Ford, Ford Madox
   1873-1939 .... **TCLC 1, 15, 39**
   See also CA 104; 132; CDBLB 1914-1945;
      DLB 34, 98; MTCW

Ford, John   1895-1973............. **CLC 16**
   See also CA 45-48

Ford, Richard   1944-.............. **CLC 46**
   See also CA 69-72; CANR 11

Ford, Webster
   See Masters, Edgar Lee

Foreman, Richard   1937-........... **CLC 50**
   See also CA 65-68; CANR 32

Forester, C(ecil) S(cott)
   1899-1966 .... **CLC 35**
   See also CA 73-76; 25-28R; SATA 13

Forez
   See Mauriac, Francois (Charles)

Forman, James Douglas   1932-...... **CLC 21**
   See also CA 9-12R; CANR 4, 19;
      MAICYA; SATA 8, 70

Fornes, Maria Irene   1930-...... **CLC 39, 61**
   See also CA 25-28R; CANR 28; DLB 7;
      HW; MTCW

Forrest, Leon   1937- .... **CLC 4**
   See also BW; CA 89-92; CAAS 7;
      CANR 25; DLB 33

Forster, E(dward) M(organ)
   1879-1970 .... **CLC 1, 2, 3, 4, 9, 10, 13,
                              15, 22, 45**
   See also AAYA 2; CA 13-14; 25-28R;
      CAP 1; CDBLB 1914-1945; DLB 34, 98;
      MTCW; SATA 57; WLC

Forster, John   1812-1876 .... **NCLC 11**

Forsyth, Frederick   1938-...... **CLC 2, 5, 36**
   See also BEST 89:4; CA 85-88; CANR 38;
      DLB 87; MTCW

Forten, Charlotte L. .... **TCLC 16**
   See also Grimke, Charlotte L(ottie) Forten
   See also BLC 2; DLB 50

Foscolo, Ugo   1778-1827.......... **NCLC 8**

Fosse, Bob .... **CLC 20**
   See also Fosse, Robert Louis

Fosse, Robert Louis   1927-1987
   See Fosse, Bob
   See also CA 110; 123

Foster, Stephen Collins
   1826-1864 .... **NCLC 26**

Foucault, Michel
   1926-1984 .... **CLC 31, 34, 69**
   See also CA 105; 113; CANR 34; MTCW

Fouque, Friedrich Heinrich Karl) de la Motte
   1777-1843 .... **NCLC 2**
   See also DLB 90

Fournier, Henri Alban   1886-1914
   See Alain-Fournier
   See also CA 104

Fournier, Pierre   1916-............ **CLC 11**
   See also Gascar, Pierre
   See also CA 89-92; CANR 16

Fowles, John
   1926- .... **CLC 1, 2, 3, 4, 6, 9, 10, 15, 33**
   See also CA 5-8R; CANR 25; CDBLB 1960
      to Present; DLB 14; MTCW; SATA 22

Fox, Paula   1923-................ **CLC 2, 8**
   See also AAYA 3; CA 73-76; CANR 20,
      36; CLR 1; DLB 52; MAICYA; MTCW;
      SATA 17, 60

Fox, William Price (Jr.)   1926- ..... **CLC 22**
   See also CA 17-20R; CANR 11; DLB 2;
      DLBY 81

Foxe, John   1516(?)-1587 .... **LC 14**

Frame, Janet .... **CLC 2, 3, 6, 22, 66**
   See also Clutha, Janet Paterson Frame

France, Anatole.................... **TCLC 9**
   See also Thibault, Jacques Anatole Francois

Francis, Claude   19th cent. (?)- ..... **CLC 50**

Francis, Dick   1920- .... **CLC 2, 22, 42**
   See also AAYA 5; BEST 89:3; CA 5-8R;
      CANR 9; CDBLB 1960 to Present;
      DLB 87; MTCW

Francis, Robert (Churchill)
   1901-1987 .... **CLC 15**
   See also CA 1-4R; 123; CANR 1

Frank, Anne(lies Marie)
   1929-1945 .... **TCLC 17**
   See also CA 113; 133; MTCW; SATA 42;
      WLC

Frank, Elizabeth   1945-............ **CLC 39**
   See also CA 121; 126

Franklin, Benjamin
   See Hasek, Jaroslav (Matej Frantisek)

Franklin, (Stella Maraia Sarah) Miles
   1879-1954 .... **TCLC 7**
   See also CA 104

Fraser, Antonia (Pakenham)
   1932- .... **CLC 32**
   See also CA 85-88; MTCW; SATA 32

Fraser, George MacDonald   1925-.... **CLC 7**
   See also CA 45-48; CANR 2

Fraser, Sylvia   1935-.............. **CLC 64**
   See also CA 45-48; CANR 1, 16

Frayn, Michael   1933-...... **CLC 3, 7, 31, 47**
   See also CA 5-8R; CANR 30; DLB 13, 14;
      MTCW

Fraze, Candida (Merrill)   1945-..... **CLC 50**
   See also CA 126

Frazer, J(ames) G(eorge)
   1854-1941 .... **TCLC 32**
   See also CA 118

Frazer, Robert Caine
   ~~See Creasey, John~~

Frazer, Sir James George
   See Frazer, J(ames) G(eorge)

Frazier, Ian   1951-................ **CLC 46**
   ~~See also CA 130~~

Frederic, Harold   1856-1898...... **NCLC 10**
   ~~See also DLB 12, 23~~

Frederick the Great   1712-1786 ...... **LC 14**

Fredro, Aleksander   1793-1876..... **NCLC 8**

Freeling, Nicolas 1927- .... CLC 38
See also CA 49-52; CAAS 12; CANR 1, 17;
DLB 87

Freeman, Douglas Southall
1886-1953 .... TCLC 11
See also CA 109; DLB 17

Freeman, Judith 1946- .... CLC 55

Freeman, Mary Eleanor Wilkins
1852-1930 .... TCLC 9; SSC 1
See also CA 106; DLB 12, 78

Freeman, R(ichard) Austin
1862-1943 .... TCLC 21
See also CA 113; DLB 70

French, Marilyn 1929- ...... CLC 10, 18, 60
See also CA 69-72; CANR 3, 31; MTCW

French, Paul
See Asimov, Isaac

Freneau, Philip Morin 1752-1832 .. NCLC 1
See also DLB 37, 43

Friedman, B(ernard) H(arper)
1926- .... CLC 7
See also CA 1-4R; CANR 3

Friedman, Bruce Jay 1930- .... CLC 3, 5, 56
See also CA 9-12R; CANR 25; DLB 2, 28

Friel, Brian 1929- .... CLC 5, 42, 59
See also CA 21-24R; CANR 33; DLB 13;
MTCW

Friis-Baastad, Babbis Ellinor
1921-1970 .... CLC 12
See also CA 17-20R; 134; SATA 7

Frisch, Max (Rudolf)
1911-1991 ..... CLC 3, 9, 14, 18, 32, 44
See also CA 85-88; 134; CANR 32;
DLB 69; MTCW

Fromentin, Eugene (Samuel Auguste)
1820-1876 .... NCLC 10

Frost, Robert (Lee)
1874-1963 ... CLC 1, 3, 4, 9, 10, 13, 15,
26, 34, 44; PC 1
See also CA 89-92; CANR 33;
CDALB 1917-1929; DLB 54; DLBD 7;
MTCW; SATA 14; WLC

Froy, Herald
See Waterhouse, Keith (Spencer)

Fry, Christopher 1907- .... CLC 2, 10, 14
See also CA 17-20R; CANR 9, 30; DLB 13;
MTCW; SATA 66

Frye, (Herman) Northrop
1912-1991 .... CLC 24, 70
See also CA 5-8R; 133; CANR 8, 37;
DLB 67, 68; MTCW

Fuchs, Daniel 1909- .... CLC 8, 22
See also CA 81-84; CAAS 5; DLB 9, 26, 28

Fuchs, Daniel 1934- .... CLC 34
See also CA 37-40R; CANR 14

Fuentes, Carlos
1928- ...... CLC 3, 8, 10, 13, 22, 41, 60
See also AAYA 4; AITN 2; CA 69-72;
CANR 10, 32; DLB 113; HW; MTCW;
WLC

Fuentes, Gregorio Lopez y
See Lopez y Fuentes, Gregorio

Fugard, (Harold) Athol
1932- .... CLC 5, 9, 14, 25, 40
See also CA 85-88; CANR 32; MTCW

Fugard, Sheila 1932- .... CLC 48
See also CA 125

Fuller, Charles (H. Jr.)
1939- .... CLC 25; DC 1
See also BLC 2; BW; CA 108; 112; DLB 38;
MTCW

Fuller, John (Leopold) 1937- .... CLC 62
See also CA 21-24R; CANR 9; DLB 40

Fuller, Margaret .... NCLC 5
See also Ossoli, Sarah Margaret (Fuller
marchesa d')

Fuller, Roy (Broadbent)
1912-1991 .... CLC 4, 28
See also CA 5-8R; 135; CAAS 10; DLB 15,
20

Fulton, Alice 1952- .... CLC 52
See also CA 116

Furphy, Joseph 1843-1912 .... TCLC 25

Futabatei, Shimei 1864-1909 ..... TCLC 44

Futrelle, Jacques 1875-1912 ...... TCLC 19
See also CA 113

G. B. S.
See Shaw, George Bernard

Gaboriau, Emile 1835-1873 ...... NCLC 14

Gadda, Carlo Emilio 1893-1973 .... CLC 11
See also CA 89-92

Gaddis, William
1922- .... CLC 1, 3, 6, 8, 10, 19, 43
See also CA 17-20R; CANR 21; DLB 2;
MTCW

Gaines, Ernest J(ames)
1933- .... CLC 3, 11, 18
See also AITN 1; BLC 2; BW; CA 9-12R;
CANR 6, 24; CDALB 1968-1988; DLB 2,
33; DLBY 80; MTCW

Gaitskill, Mary 1954- .... CLC 69
See also CA 128

Galdos, Benito Perez
See Perez Galdos, Benito

Gale, Zona 1874-1938 .... TCLC 7
See also CA 105; DLB 9, 78

Galeano, Eduardo (Hughes) 1940- ... CLC 72
See also CA 29-32R; CANR 13, 32; HW

Galiano, Juan Valera y Alcala
See Valera y Alcala-Galiano, Juan

Gallagher, Tess 1943- .... CLC 18, 63
See also CA 106; DLB 120

Gallant, Mavis
1922- .... CLC 7, 18, 38; SSC 5
See also CA 69-72; CANR 29; DLB 53;
MTCW

Gallant, Roy A(rthur) 1924- .... CLC 17
See also CA 5-8R; CANR 4, 29; MAICYA;
SATA 4, 68

Gallico, Paul (William) 1897-1976 ... CLC 2
See also AITN 1; CA 5-8R; 69-72;
CANR 23; DLB 9; MAICYA; SATA 13

Gallup, Ralph
See Whitemore, Hugh (John)

Galsworthy, John 1867-1933 .... TCLC 1, 45
See also CA 104; CDBLB 1890-1914;
DLB 10, 34, 98; WLC 2

Galt, John 1779-1839 .... NCLC 1
See also DLB 99, 116

Galvin, James 1951- .... CLC 38
See also CA 108; CANR 26

Gamboa, Federico 1864-1939 ..... TCLC 36

Gann, Ernest Kellogg 1910-1991 .... CLC 23
See also AITN 1; CA 1-4R; 136; CANR 1

Garcia Lorca, Federico
1898-1936 ..... TCLC 1, 7; DC 2; PC 3
See also CA 104; 131; DLB 108; HW;
MTCW; WLC

Garcia Marquez, Gabriel (Jose)
1928- ... CLC 2, 3, 8, 10, 15, 27, 47, 55;
SSC 8
See also Marquez, Gabriel (Jose) Garcia
See also AAYA 3; BEST 89:1, 90:4;
CA 33-36R; CANR 10, 28; DLB 113;
HW; MTCW; WLC

Gard, Janice
See Latham, Jean Lee

Gard, Roger Martin du
See Martin du Gard, Roger

Gardam, Jane 1928- .... CLC 43
See also CA 49-52; CANR 2, 18, 33;
CLR 12; DLB 14; MAICYA; MTCW;
SAAS 9; SATA 28, 39

Gardner, Herb .... CLC 44

Gardner, John (Champlin) Jr.
1933-1982 .... CLC 2, 3, 5, 7, 8, 10, 18,
28, 34; SSC 7
See also AITN 1; CA 65-68; 107;
CANR 33; DLB 2; DLBY 82; MTCW;
SATA 31, 40

Gardner, John (Edmund) 1926- ..... CLC 30
See also CA 103; CANR 15; MTCW

Gardner, Noel
See Kuttner, Henry

Gardons, S. S.
See Snodgrass, William D(e Witt)

Garfield, Leon 1921- .... CLC 12
See also AAYA 8; CA 17-20R; CANR 38;
CLR 21; MAICYA; SATA 1, 32

Garland, (Hannibal) Hamlin
1860-1940 .... TCLC 3
See also CA 104; DLB 12, 71, 78

Garneau, (Hector de) Saint-Denys
1912-1943 .... TCLC 13
See also CA 111; DLB 88

Garner, Alan 1934- .... CLC 17
See also CA 73-76; CANR 15; CLR 20;
MAICYA; MTCW; SATA 18, 69

Garner, Hugh 1913-1979 .... CLC 13
See also CA 69-72; CANR 31; DLB 68

Garnett, David 1892-1981 .... CLC 3
See also CA 5-8R; 103; CANR 17; DLB 34

Garos, Stephanie
See Katz, Steve

Garrett, George (Palmer)
1929- .... CLC 3, 11, 51
See also CA 1-4R; CAAS 5; CANR 1;
DLB 2, 5; DLBY 83

Garrick, David 1717-1779 .... LC 15
See also DLB 84

Garrigue, Jean 1914-1972 .... CLC 2, 8
See also CA 5-8R; 37-40R; CANR 20

Garrison, Frederick
See Sinclair, Upton (Beall)

Garth, Will
See Hamilton, Edmond; Kuttner, Henry

Garvey, Marcus (Moziah Jr.)
1887-1940 .... **TCLC 41**
See also BLC 2; BW; CA 120; 124

Gary, Romain .... **CLC 25**
See also Kacew, Romain
See also DLB 83

Gascar, Pierre .... **CLC 11**
See also Fournier, Pierre

Gascoyne, David (Emery) 1916- .... **CLC 45**
See also CA 65-68; CANR 10, 28; DLB 20;
MTCW

Gaskell, Elizabeth Cleghorn
1810-1865 .... **NCLC 5**
See also CDBLB 1832-1890; DLB 21

Gass, William H(oward)
1924- .... **CLC 1, 2, 8, 11, 15, 39**
See also CA 17-20R; CANR 30; DLB 2;
MTCW

Gasset, Jose Ortega y
See Ortega y Gasset, Jose

Gautier, Theophile 1811-1872 ..... **NCLC 1**
See also DLB 119

Gawsworth, John
See Bates, H(erbert) E(rnest)

Gaye, Marvin (Penze) 1939-1984 ... **CLC 26**
See also CA 112

Gebler, Carlo (Ernest) 1954- .... **CLC 39**
See also CA 119; 133

Gee, Maggie (Mary) 1948-......... **CLC 57**
See also CA 130

Gee, Maurice (Gough) 1931- .... **CLC 29**
See also CA 97-100; SATA 46

Gelbart, Larry (Simon) 1923- ... **CLC 21, 61**
See also CA 73-76

Gelber, Jack 1932-........... **CLC 1, 6, 14**
See also CA 1-4R; CANR 2; DLB 7

Gellhorn, Martha Ellis 1908- ... **CLC 14, 60**
See also CA 77-80; DLBY 82

Genet, Jean
1910-1986 ... **CLC 1, 2, 5, 10, 14, 44, 46**
See also CA 13-16R; CANR 18; DLB 72;
DLBY 86; MTCW

Gent, Peter 1942-................ **CLC 29**
See also AITN 1; CA 89-92; DLBY 82

George, Jean Craighead 1919-...... **CLC 35**
See also AAYA 8; CA 5-8R; CANR 25;
CLR 1; DLB 52; MAICYA; SATA 2, 68

George, Stefan (Anton)
1868-1933 .... **TCLC 2, 14**
See also CA 104

Georges, Georges Martin
See Simenon, Georges (Jacques Christian)

Gerhardi, William Alexander
See Gerhardie, William Alexander

Gerhardie, William Alexander
1895-1977 .... **CLC 5**
See also CA 25-28R; 73-76; CANR 18;
DLB 36

Gerstler, Amy 1956-.............. **CLC 70**

Gertler, T. .... **CLC 34**
See also CA 116; 121

Ghelderode, Michel de
1898-1962 .... **CLC 6, 11**
See also CA 85-88

Ghiselin, Brewster 1903- .... **CLC 23**
See also CA 13-16R; CAAS 10; CANR 13

Ghose, Zulfikar 1935-............. **CLC 42**
See also CA 65-68

Ghosh, Amitav 1956- .... **CLC 44**

Giacosa, Giuseppe 1847-1906 ...... **TCLC 7**
See also CA 104

Gibb, Lee
See Waterhouse, Keith (Spencer)

Gibbon, Lewis Grassic .... **TCLC 4**
See also Mitchell, James Leslie

Gibbons, Kaye 1960- .... **CLC 50**

Gibran, Kahlil 1883-1931....... **TCLC 1, 9**
See also CA 104

Gibson, William (Ford) 1948- ... **CLC 39, 63**
See also CA 126; 133

Gibson, William 1914-............ **CLC 23**
See also CA 9-12R; CANR 9; DLB 7;
SATA 66

Gide, Andre (Paul Guillaume)
1869-1951 .... **TCLC 5, 12, 36**
See also CA 104; 124; DLB 65; MTCW;
WLC

Gifford, Barry (Colby) 1946-....... **CLC 34**
See also CA 65-68; CANR 9, 30

Gilbert, W(illiam) S(chwenck)
1836-1911 .... **TCLC 3**
See also CA 104; SATA 36

Gilbreth, Frank B., Jr. 1911-...... **CLC 17**
See also CA 9-12R; SATA 2

Gilchrist, Ellen 1935-.......... **CLC 34, 48**
See also CA 113; 116; MTCW

Giles, Molly 1942- .... **CLC 39**
See also CA 126

Gill, Patrick
See Creasey, John

Gilliam, Terry (Vance) 1940-....... **CLC 21**
See also Monty Python
See also CA 108; 113; CANR 35

Gillian, Jerry
See Gilliam, Terry (Vance)

Gilliatt, Penelope (Ann Douglass)
1932- .... **CLC 2, 10, 13, 53**
See also AITN 2; CA 13-16R; DLB 14

Gilman, Charlotte (Anna) Perkins (Stetson)
1860-1935 .... **TCLC 9, 37**
See also CA 106

Gilmour, David 1944-............. **CLC 35**
See also Pink Floyd
See also CA 138

Gilpin, William 1724-1804....... **NCLC 30**

Gilray, J. D.
See Mencken, H(enry) L(ouis)

Gilroy, Frank D(aniel) 1925-........ **CLC 2**
See also CA 81-84; CANR 32; DLB 7

Ginsberg, Allen
1926- ..... **CLC 1, 2, 3, 4, 6, 13, 36, 69;**
PC 4
See also AITN 1; CA 1-4R; CANR 2;
CDALB 1941-1968; DLB 5, 16; MTCW;
WLC 3

Ginzburg, Natalia
1916-1991 .... **CLC 5, 11, 54, 70**
See also CA 85-88; 135; CANR 33; MTCW

Giono, Jean 1895-1970.......... **CLC 4, 11**
See also CA 45-48; 29-32R; CANR 2, 35;
DLB 72; MTCW

Giovanni, Nikki 1943- ..... **CLC 2, 4, 19, 64**
See also AITN 1; BLC 2; BW; CA 29-32R;
CAAS 6; CANR 18; CLR 6; DLB 5, 41;
MAICYA; MTCW; SATA 24

Giovene, Andrea 1904-............. **CLC 7**
See also CA 85-88

Gippius, Zinaida (Nikolayevna) 1869-1945
See Hippius, Zinaida
See also CA 106

Giraudoux, (Hippolyte) Jean
1882-1944 .... **TCLC 2, 7**
See also CA 104; DLB 65

Gironella, Jose Maria 1917- .... **CLC 11**
See also CA 101

Gissing, George (Robert)
1857-1903 .... **TCLC 3, 24, 47**
See also CA 105; DLB 18

Giurlani, Aldo
See Palazzeschi, Aldo

Gladkov, Fyodor (Vasilyevich)
1883-1958 .... **TCLC 27**

Glanville, Brian (Lester) 1931- ...... **CLC 6**
See also CA 5-8R; CAAS 9; CANR 3;
DLB 15; SATA 42

Glasgow, Ellen (Anderson Gholson)
1873(?)-1945 .... **TCLC 2, 7**
See also CA 104; DLB 9, 12

Glassco, John 1909-1981 .... **CLC 9**
See also CA 13-16R; 102; CANR 15;
DLB 68

Glasscock, Amnesia
See Steinbeck, John (Ernst)

Glasser, Ronald J. 1940(?)-........ **CLC 37**

Glassman, Joyce
See Johnson, Joyce

Glendinning, Victoria 1937-........ **CLC 50**
See also CA 120; 127

Glissant, Edouard 1928-........ **CLC 10, 68**

Gloag, Julian 1930- .... **CLC 40**
See also AITN 1; CA 65-68; CANR 10

Gluck, Louise 1943-........ **CLC 7, 22, 44**
See also Glueck, Louise
See also CA 33-36R; DLB 5

Glueck, Louise................. **CLC 7, 22**
See also Gluck, Louise
See also DLB 5

Gobineau, Joseph Arthur (Comte) de
1816-1882 .... **NCLC 17**

Godard, Jean-Luc 1930-........... **CLC 20**
See also CA 93-96

Godden, (Margaret) Rumer 1907-... **CLC 53**
See also AAYA 6; CA 5-8R; CANR 4, 27,
36; CLR 20; MAICYA; SAAS 12;
SATA 3, 36

Godoy Alcayaga, Lucila 1889-1957
See Mistral, Gabriela
See also CA 104; 131; HW; MTCW

Godwin, Gail (Kathleen)
1937- .... **CLC 5, 8, 22, 31, 69**
See also CA 29-32R; CANR 15; DLB 6;
MTCW

Godwin, William 1756-1836...... **NCLC 14**
See also CDBLB 1789-1832; DLB 39, 104

Goethe, Johann Wolfgang von
1749-1832 .... **NCLC 4, 22, 34; PC 5**
See also DLB 94; WLC 3

Gogarty, Oliver St. John
1878-1957 .... **TCLC 15**
See also CA 109; DLB 15, 19

Gogol, Nikolai (Vasilyevich)
1809-1852 ..... **NCLC 5, 15, 31; DC 1;**
SSC 4
See also WLC

Gold, Herbert 1924-....... **CLC 4, 7, 14, 42**
See also CA 9-12R; CANR 17; DLB 2;
DLBY 81

Goldbarth, Albert 1948-........ **CLC 5, 38**
See also CA 53-56; CANR 6; DLB 120

Goldberg, Anatol 1910-1982 ...... **CLC 34**
See also CA 131; 117

Goldemberg, Isaac 1945- .... **CLC 52**
See also CA 69-72; CAAS 12; CANR 11,
32; HW

Golden Silver
See Storm, Hyemeyohsts

Golding, William (Gerald)
1911- ..... **CLC 1, 2, 3, 8, 10, 17, 27, 58**
See also AAYA 5; CA 5-8R; CANR 13, 33;
CDBLB 1945-1960; DLB 15, 100;
MTCW; WLC

Goldman, Emma 1869-1940....... **TCLC 13**
See also CA 110

Goldman, William (W.) 1931- .... **CLC 1, 48**
See also CA 9-12R; CANR 29; DLB 44

Goldmann, Lucien 1913-1970 ...... **CLC 24**
See also CA 25-28; CAP 2

Goldoni, Carlo 1707-1793 .... **LC 4**

Goldsberry, Steven 1949-......... **CLC 34**
See also CA 131

Goldsmith, Oliver 1728(?)-1774....... **LC 2**

Goldsmith, Peter
See Priestley, J(ohn) B(oynton)

Gombrowicz, Witold
1904-1969 .... **CLC 4, 7, 11, 49**
See also CA 19-20; 25-28R; CAP 2

Gomez de la Serna, Ramon
1888-1963 .... **CLC 9**
See also CA 116; HW

Goncharov, Ivan Alexandrovich
1812-1891 .... **NCLC 1**

Goncourt, Edmond (Louis Antoine Huot) de
1822-1896 .... **NCLC 7**

Goncourt, Jules (Alfred Huot) de
1830-1870 .... **NCLC 7**

Gontier, Fernande 19th cent. (?)- ... **CLC 50**

Goodman, Paul 1911-1972.... **CLC 1, 2, 4, 7**
See also CA 19-20; 37-40R; CANR 34;
CAP 2; MTCW

Gordimer, Nadine
1923- .... **CLC 3, 5, 7, 10, 18, 33, 51, 70**
See also CA 5-8R; CANR 3, 28; MTCW

Gordon, Adam Lindsay
1833-1870 .... **NCLC 21**

Gordon, Caroline
1895-1981 .... **CLC 6, 13, 29**
See also CA 11-12; 103; CANR 36; CAP 1;
DLB 4, 9, 102; DLBY 81; MTCW

Gordon, Charles William 1860-1937
See Connor, Ralph
See also CA 109

Gordon, Mary (Catherine)
1949- .... **CLC 13, 22**
See also CA 102; DLB 6; DLBY 81;
MTCW

Gordon, Sol 1923-................ **CLC 26**
See also CA 53-56; CANR 4; SATA 11

Gordone, Charles 1925-.......... **CLC 1, 4**
See also BW; CA 93-96; DLB 7; MTCW

Gorenko, Anna Andreevna
See Akhmatova, Anna

Gorky, Maxim.................... TCLC 8
See also Peshkov, Alexei Maximovich
See also WLC

Goryan, Sirak
See Saroyan, William

Gosse, Edmund (William)
1849-1928 .... **TCLC 28**
See also CA 117; DLB 57

Gotlieb, Phyllis Fay (Bloom)
1926- .... **CLC 18**
See also CA 13-16R; CANR 7; DLB 88

Gottesman, S. D.
See Kornbluth, C(yril) M.; Pohl, Frederik

Gottschalk, Laura Riding
See Jackson, Laura (Riding)

Gould, Lois .... CLC 4, 10
See also CA 77-80; CANR 29; MTCW

Gourmont, Remy de 1858-1915.... **TCLC 17**
See also CA 109

Govier, Katherine 1948-.......... **CLC 51**
See also CA 101; CANR 18

Goyen, (Charles) William
1915-1983 .... **CLC 5, 8, 14, 40**
See also AITN 2; CA 5-8R; 110; CANR 6;
DLB 2; DLBY 83

Goytisolo, Juan 1931- .... **CLC 5, 10, 23**
See also CA 85-88; CANR 32; HW; MTCW

Gozzi, (Conte) Carlo 1720-1806 .. **NCLC 23**

Grabbe, Christian Dietrich
1801-1836 .... **NCLC 2**

Grace, Patricia 1937-............ **CLC 56**

Gracian y Morales, Baltasar
1601-1658 .... **LC 15**

Gracq, Julien................ CLC 11, 48
See also Poirier, Louis
See also DLB 83

Grade, Chaim 1910-1982 .... **CLC 10**
See also CA 93-96; 107

Graduate of Oxford, A
See Ruskin, John

Graham, John
See Phillips, David Graham

Graham, Jorie 1951-............. **CLC 48**
See also CA 111; DLB 120

Graham, R(obert) B(ontine) Cunninghame
See Cunninghame Graham, R(obert)
B(ontine)
See also DLB 98

Graham, Robert
See Haldeman, Joe (William)

Graham, Tom
See Lewis, (Harry) Sinclair

Graham, W(illiam) S(ydney)
1918-1986 .... **CLC 29**
See also CA 73-76; 118; DLB 20

Graham, Winston (Mawdsley)
1910- .... **CLC 23**
See also CA 49-52; CANR 2, 22; DLB 77

Granville-Barker, Harley
1877-1946 .... **TCLC 2**
See also Barker, Harley Granville
See also CA 104

Grass, Guenter (Wilhelm)
1927- .. **CLC 1, 2, 4, 6, 11, 15, 22, 32, 49**
See also CA 13-16R; CANR 20; DLB 75;
MTCW; WLC

Gratton, Thomas
See Hulme, T(homas) E(rnest)

Grau, Shirley Ann 1929- .... **CLC 4, 9**
See also CA 89-92; CANR 22; DLB 2;
MTCW

Gravel, Fern
See Hall, James Norman

Graver, Elizabeth 1964-........... **CLC 70**
See also CA 135

Graves, Richard Perceval 1945- .... **CLC 44**
See also CA 65-68; CANR 9, 26

Graves, Robert (von Ranke)
1895-1985 ... **CLC 1, 2, 6, 11, 39, 44, 45**
See also CA 5-8R; 117; CANR 5, 36;
CDBLB 1914-1945; DLB 20, 100;
DLBY 85; MTCW; SATA 45

Gray, Alasdair (James) 1934-...... **CLC 41**
See also CA 126; MTCW

Gray, Amlin 1946-................ **CLC 29**
See also CA 138

Gray, Francine du Plessix 1930-.... **CLC 22**
See also BEST 90:3; CA 61-64; CAAS 2;
CANR 11, 33; MTCW

Gray, John (Henry) 1866-1934 .... **TCLC 19**
See also CA 119

Gray, Simon (James Holliday)
1936- .... **CLC 9, 14, 36**
See also AITN 1; CA 21-24R; CAAS 3;
CANR 32; DLB 13; MTCW

Gray, Spalding 1941-............. **CLC 49**
See also CA 128

Gray, Thomas 1716-1771....... **LC 4; PC 2**
See also CDBLB 1660-1789; DLB 109;
WLC

Grayson, David
See Baker, Ray Stannard

Grayson, Richard (A.) 1951-....... **CLC 38**
See also CA 85-88; CANR 14, 31

Greeley, Andrew M(oran) 1928- .... **CLC 28**
See also CA 5-8R; CAAS 7; CANR 7;
MTCW

Green, Brian
See Card, Orson Scott

Green, Hannah
See Greenberg, Joanne (Goldenberg)

Green, Hannah .... **CLC 3**
See also CA 73-76

Green, Henry.................. **CLC 2, 13**
See also Yorke, Henry Vincent
See also DLB 15

Green, Julian (Hartridge)
1900- .... **CLC 3, 11**
See also CA 21-24R; CANR 33; DLB 4, 72;
MTCW

Green, Julien
See Green, Julian (Hartridge)

Green, Paul (Eliot) 1894-1981...... **CLC 25**
See also AITN 1; CA 5-8R; 103; CANR 3;
DLB 7, 9; DLBY 81

Greenberg, Ivan 1908-1973
See Rahv, Philip
See also CA 85-88

Greenberg, Joanne (Goldenberg)
1932- .... **CLC 7, 30**
See also CA 5-8R; CANR 14, 32; SATA 25

Greenberg, Richard 1959(?)- .... **CLC 57**
See also CA 138

Greene, Bette 1934- .... **CLC 30**
See also AAYA 7; CA 53-56; CANR 4;
CLR 2; MAICYA; SATA 8

Greene, Gael .... **CLC 8**
See also CA 13-16R; CANR 10

Greene, Graham (Henry)
1904-1991 ... **CLC 1, 3, 6, 9, 14, 18, 27,
37, 70, 72**
See also AITN 2; CA 13-16R; 133;
CANR 35; CDBLB 1945-1960; DLB 13,
15, 77, 100; DLBY 91; MTCW;
SATA 20; WLC

Greer, Richard
See Silverberg, Robert

Greer, Richard
See Silverberg, Robert

Gregor, Arthur 1923- .... **CLC 9**
See also CA 25-28R; CAAS 10; CANR 11;
SATA 36

Gregor, Lee
See Pohl, Frederik

Gregory, Isabella Augusta (Persse)
1852-1932 .... **TCLC 1**
See also CA 104; DLB 10

Gregory, J. Dennis
See Williams, John A(lfred)

Grendon, Stephen
See Derleth, August (William)

Grenville, Kate 1950- .... **CLC 61**
See also CA 118

Grenville, Pelham
See Wodehouse, P(elham) G(renville)

Greve, Felix Paul (Berthold Friedrich)
1879-1948
See Grove, Frederick Philip
See also CA 104

Grey, Zane 1872-1939 .... **TCLC 6**
See also CA 104; 132; DLB 9; MTCW

Grieg, (Johan) Nordahl (Brun)
1902-1943 .... **TCLC 10**
See also CA 107

Grieve, C(hristopher) M(urray)
1892-1978 .... **CLC 11, 19**
See also MacDiarmid, Hugh
See also CA 5-8R; 85-88; CANR 33;
MTCW

Griffin, Gerald 1803-1840 .... **NCLC 7**

Griffin, John Howard 1920-1980.... **CLC 68**
See also AITN 1; CA 1-4R; 101; CANR 2

Griffin, Peter .... **CLC 39**

Griffiths, Trevor 1935- .... **CLC 13, 52**
See also CA 97-100; DLB 13

Grigson, Geoffrey (Edward Harvey)
1905-1985 .... **CLC 7, 39**
See also CA 25-28R; 118; CANR 20, 33;
DLB 27; MTCW

Grillparzer, Franz 1791-1872...... **NCLC 1**

Grimble, Reverend Charles James
See Eliot, T(homas) S(tearns)

Grimke, Charlotte L(ottie) Forten
1837(?)-1914
See Forten, Charlotte L.
See also BW; CA 117; 124

Grimm, Jacob Ludwig Karl
1785-1863 .... **NCLC 3**
See also DLB 90; MAICYA; SATA 22

Grimm, Wilhelm Karl 1786-1859 .. **NCLC 3**
See also DLB 90; MAICYA; SATA 22

**Grimmelshausen, Johann Jakob Christoffel
von** 1621-1676 .... **LC 6**

Grindel, Eugene 1895-1952
See Eluard, Paul
See also CA 104

Grossman, David.................. **CLC 67**
See also CA 138

Grossman, Vasily (Semenovich)
1905-1964 .... **CLC 41**
See also CA 124; 130; MTCW

Grove, Frederick Philip .... **TCLC 4**
See also Greve, Felix Paul (Berthold
Friedrich)
See also DLB 92

Grubb
See Crumb, R(obert)

Grumbach, Doris (Isaac)
1918- .... **CLC 13, 22, 64**
See also CA 5-8R; CAAS 2; CANR 9

Grundtvig, Nicolai Frederik Severin
1783-1872 .... **NCLC 1**

Grunge
See Crumb, R(obert)

Grunwald, Lisa 1959- .... **CLC 44**
See also CA 120

Guare, John 1938- .... **CLC 8, 11, 29, 67**
See also CA 73-76; CANR 21; DLB 7;
MTCW

Gudjonsson, Halldor Kiljan 1902-
See Laxness, Halldor
See also CA 103

Guenter, Erich
See Eich, Guenter

Guest, Barbara 1920- .... **CLC 34**
See also CA 25-28R; CANR 11; DLB 5

Guest, Judith (Ann) 1936-....... **CLC 8, 30**
See also AAYA 7; CA 77-80; CANR 15;
MTCW

Guild, Nicholas M. 1944-......... **CLC 33**
See also CA 93-96

Guillemin, Jacques
See Sartre, Jean-Paul

Guillen, Jorge 1893-1984.......... **CLC 11**
See also CA 89-92; 112; DLB 108; HW

Guillen (y Batista), Nicolas (Cristobal)
1902-1989 .... **CLC 48**
See also BLC 2; BW; CA 116; 125; 129;
HW

Guillevic, (Eugene) 1907-......... **CLC 33**
See also CA 93-96

Guillois
See Desnos, Robert

Guiney, Louise Imogen
1861-1920 .... **TCLC 41**
See also DLB 54

Guiraldes, Ricardo (Guillermo)
1886-1927 .... **TCLC 39**
See also CA 131; HW; MTCW

Gunn, Bill .... **CLC 5**
See also Gunn, William Harrison
See also DLB 38

Gunn, Thom(son William)
1929- .... **CLC 3, 6, 18, 32**
See also CA 17-20R; CANR 9, 33;
CDBLB 1960 to Present; DLB 27;
MTCW

Gunn, William Harrison 1934(?)-1989
See Gunn, Bill
See also AITN 1; BW; CA 13-16R; 128;
CANR 12, 25

Gunnars, Kristjana 1948-......... **CLC 69**
See also CA 113; DLB 60

Gurganus, Allan 1947-............ **CLC 70**
See also BEST 90:1; CA 135

Gurney, A(lbert) R(amsdell) Jr.
1930- .... **CLC 32, 50, 54**
See also CA 77-80; CANR 32

Gurney, Ivor (Bertie) 1890-1937... **TCLC 33**

Gurney, Peter
See Gurney, A(lbert) R(amsdell) Jr.

Gustafson, Ralph (Barker) 1909-.... **CLC 36**
See also CA 21-24R; CANR 8; DLB 88

Gut, Gom
See Simenon, Georges (Jacques Christian)

Guthrie, A(lfred) B(ertram) Jr.
1901-1991 .... **CLC 23**
See also CA 57-60; 134; CANR 24; DLB 6;
SATA 62; SATO 67

Guthrie, Isobel
See Grieve, C(hristopher) M(urray)

Guthrie, Woodrow Wilson 1912-1967
See Guthrie, Woody
See also CA 113; 93-96

Guthrie, Woody................... **CLC 35**
See also Guthrie, Woodrow Wilson

Guy, Rosa (Cuthbert) 1928-........ **CLC 26**
See also AAYA 4; BW; CA 17-20R;
CANR 14, 34; CLR 13; DLB 33;
MAICYA; SATA 14, 62

Gwendolyn
  See Bennett, (Enoch) Arnold

H. D. . . . . CLC **3, 8, 14, 31, 34; PC 5**
  See also Doolittle, Hilda

Haavikko, Paavo Juhani
      1931- . . . . CLC **18, 34**
  See also CA 106

Habbema, Koos
  See Heijermans, Herman

Hacker, Marilyn 1942- . . . . CLC **5, 9, 23, 72**
  See also CA 77-80; DLB 120

Haggard, H(enry) Rider
      1856-1925 . . . . TCLC **11**
  See also CA 108; DLB 70; SATA 16

Haig, Fenil
  See Ford, Ford Madox

Haig-Brown, Roderick (Langmere)
      1908-1976 . . . . CLC **21**
  See also CA 5-8R; 69-72; CANR 4, 38;
      DLB 88; MAICYA; SATA 12

Hailey, Arthur 1920- . . . . CLC **5**
  See also AITN 2; BEST 90:3; CA 1-4R;
      CANR 2, 36; DLB 88; DLBY 82; MTCW

Hailey, Elizabeth Forsythe 1938- . . . CLC **40**
  See also CA 93-96; CAAS 1; CANR 15

Haines, John (Meade) 1924- . . . . CLC **58**
  See also CA 17-20R; CANR 13, 34; DLB 5

Haldeman, Joe (William) 1943- . . . . . CLC **61**
  See also CA 53-56; CANR 6; DLB 8

Haley, Alex(ander Murray Palmer)
      1921-1992 . . . . CLC **8, 12**
  See also BLC 2; BW; CA 77-80; 136;
      DLB 38; MTCW

Haliburton, Thomas Chandler
      1796-1865 . . . . NCLC **15**
  See also DLB 11, 99

Hall, Donald (Andrew Jr.)
      1928- . . . . CLC **1, 13, 37, 59**
  See also CA 5-8R; CAAS 7; CANR 2;
      DLB 5; SATA 23

Hall, Frederic Sauser
  See Sauser-Hall, Frederic

Hall, James
  See Kuttner, Henry

Hall, James Norman 1887-1951 . . . TCLC **23**
  See also CA 123; SATA 21

Hall, (Marguerite) Radclyffe
      1886(?)-1943 . . . . TCLC **12**
  See also CA 110

Hall, Rodney 1935- . . . . CLC **51**
  See also CA 109

Halliday, Michael
  See Creasey, John

Halpern, Daniel 1945- . . . . CLC **14**
  See also CA 33-36R

Hamburger, Michael (Peter Leopold)
      1924- . . . . CLC **5, 14**
  See also CA 5-8R; CAAS 4; CANR 2;
      DLB 27

Hamill, Pete 1935- . . . . CLC **10**
  See also CA 25-28R; CANR 18

Hamilton, Clive
  See Lewis, C(live) S(taples)

Hamilton, Edmond 1904-1977 . . . . . . CLC **1**
  See also CA 1-4R; CANR 3; DLB 8

Hamilton, Eugene (Jacob) Lee
  See Lee-Hamilton, Eugene (Jacob)

Hamilton, Franklin
  See Silverberg, Robert

Hamilton, Gail
  See Corcoran, Barbara

Hamilton, Mollie
  See Kaye, M(ary) M(argaret)

Hamilton, (Anthony Walter) Patrick
      1904-1962 . . . . CLC **51**
  See also CA 113; DLB 10

Hamilton, Virginia 1936- . . . . CLC **26**
  See also AAYA 2; BW; CA 25-28R;
      CANR 20, 37; CLR 1, 11; DLB 33, 52;
      MAICYA; MTCW; SATA 4, 56

Hammett, (Samuel) Dashiell
      1894-1961 . . . . CLC **3, 5, 10, 19, 47**
  See also AITN 1; CA 81-84;
      CDALB 1929-1941; DLBD 6; MTCW

Hammon, Jupiter 1711(?)-1800(?) . . NCLC **5**
  See also BLC 2; DLB 31, 50

Hammond, Keith
  See Kuttner, Henry

Hamner, Earl (Henry) Jr. 1923- . . . . CLC **12**
  See also AITN 2; CA 73-76; DLB 6

Hampton, Christopher (James)
      1946- . . . . CLC **4**
  See also CA 25-28R; DLB 13; MTCW

Hamsun, Knut . . . . TCLC **2, 14**
  See also Pedersen, Knut

Handke, Peter 1942- . . CLC **5, 8, 10, 15, 38**
  See also CA 77-80; CANR 33; DLB 85;
      MTCW

Hanley, James 1901-1985 . . . CLC **3, 5, 8, 13**
  See also CA 73-76; 117; CANR 36; MTCW

Hannah, Barry 1942- . . . . CLC **23, 38**
  See also CA 108; 110; DLB 6; MTCW

Hannon, Ezra
  See Hunter, Evan

Hansberry, Lorraine (Vivian)
      1930-1965 . . . . CLC **17, 62; DC 2**
  See also BLC 2; BW; CA 109; 25-28R;
      CABS 3; CDALB 1941-1968; DLB 7, 38;
      MTCW

Hansen, Joseph 1923- . . . . CLC **38**
  See also CA 29-32R; CANR 16

Hansen, Martin A. 1909-1955 . . . . . TCLC **32**

Hanson, Kenneth O(stlin) 1922- . . . . CLC **13**
  See also CA 53-56; CANR 7

Hardwick, Elizabeth 1916- . . . . CLC **13**
  See also CA 5-8R; CANR 3, 32; DLB 6;
      MTCW

Hardy, Thomas
      1840-1928 . . . TCLC **4, 10, 18, 32; SSC 2**
  See also CA 104; 123; CDBLB 1890-1914;
      DLB 18, 19; MTCW; WLC

Hare, David 1947- . . . . CLC **29, 58**
  See also CA 97-100; CANR 39; DLB 13;
      MTCW

Harford, Henry
  See Hudson, W(illiam) H(enry)

Hargrave, Leonie
  See Disch, Thomas M(ichael)

Harlan, Louis R(udolph) 1922- . . . . . CLC **34**
  See also CA 21-24R; CANR 25

Harling, Robert 1951(?)- . . . . CLC **53**

Harmon, William (Ruth) 1938- . . . . . CLC **38**
  See also CA 33-36R; CANR 14, 32, 35;
      SATA 65

Harper, F. E. W.
  See Harper, Frances Ellen Watkins

Harper, Frances E. W.
  See Harper, Frances Ellen Watkins

Harper, Frances E. Watkins
  See Harper, Frances Ellen Watkins

Harper, Frances Ellen
  See Harper, Frances Ellen Watkins

Harper, Frances Ellen Watkins
      1825-1911 . . . . TCLC **14**
  See also BLC 2; BW; CA 111; 125; DLB 50

Harper, Michael S(teven) 1938- . . CLC **7, 22**
  See also BW; CA 33-36R; CANR 24;
      DLB 41

Harper, Mrs. F. E. W.
  See Harper, Frances Ellen Watkins

Harris, Christie (Lucy) Irwin
      1907- . . . . CLC **12**
  See also CA 5-8R; CANR 6; DLB 88;
      MAICYA; SAAS 10; SATA 6

Harris, Frank 1856(?)-1931 . . . . TCLC **24**
  See also CA 109

Harris, George Washington
      1814-1869 . . . . NCLC **23**
  See also DLB 3, 11

Harris, Joel Chandler 1848-1908 . . . TCLC **2**
  See also CA 104; 137; DLB 11, 23, 42, 78,
      91; MAICYA; YABC 1

Harris, John (Wyndham Parkes Lucas)
      Beynon 1903-1969 . . . . CLC **19**
  See also CA 102; 89-92

Harris, MacDonald
  See Heiney, Donald (William)

Harris, Mark 1922- . . . . CLC **19**
  See also CA 5-8R; CAAS 3; CANR 2;
      DLB 2; DLBY 80

Harris, (Theodore) Wilson 1921- . . . . CLC **25**
  See also BW; CA 65-68; CAAS 16;
      CANR 11, 27; DLB 117; MTCW

Harrison, Elizabeth Cavanna 1909-
  See Cavanna, Betty
  See also CA 9-12R; CANR 6, 27

Harrison, Harry (Max) 1925- . . . . . . CLC **42**
  See also CA 1-4R; CANR 5, 21; DLB 8;
      SATA 4

Harrison, James (Thomas) 1937-
  See Harrison, Jim
  See also CA 13-16R; CANR 8

Harrison, Jim . . . . CLC **6, 14, 33, 66**
  See also Harrison, James (Thomas)
  See also DLBY 82

Harrison, Kathryn 1961- . . . . CLC **70**

Harrison, Tony 1937- . . . . CLC **43**
  See also CA 65-68; DLB 40; MTCW

Harriss, Will(ard Irvin) 1922- . . . . . . CLC **34**
  See also CA 111

Holdstock, Robert P. 1948-........ **CLC 39**
See also CA 131

Holland, Isabelle 1920- .... **CLC 21**
See also CA 21-24R; CANR 10, 25;
MAICYA; SATA 8, 70

Holland, Marcus
See Caldwell, (Janet Miriam) Taylor
(Holland)

Hollander, John 1929-...... **CLC 2, 5, 8, 14**
See also CA 1-4R; CANR 1; DLB 5;
SATA 13

Hollander, Paul
See Silverberg, Robert

Holleran, Andrew 1943(?)-......... **CLC 38**

Hollinghurst, Alan 1954-.......... **CLC 55**
See also CA 114

Hollis, Jim
See Summers, Hollis (Spurgeon Jr.)

Holmes, John
See Souster, (Holmes) Raymond

Holmes, John Clellon 1926-1988.... **CLC 56**
See also CA 9-12R; 125; CANR 4; DLB 16

Holmes, Oliver Wendell
1809-1894 .... **NCLC 14**
See also CDALB 1640-1865; DLB 1;
SATA 34

Holmes, Raymond
See Souster, (Holmes) Raymond

Holt, Victoria
See Hibbert, Eleanor Burford

Holub, Miroslav 1923-............. **CLC 4**
See also CA 21-24R; CANR 10

Homer c. 8th cent. B.C.-......... **CMLC 1**

Honig, Edwin 1919-............. **CLC 33**
See also CA 5-8R; CAAS 8; CANR 4;
DLB 5

Hood, Hugh (John Blagdon)
1928-.................... **CLC 15, 28**
See also CA 49-52; CANR 1, 33; DLB 53

Hood, Thomas 1799-1845........ **NCLC 16**
See also DLB 96

Hooker, (Peter) Jeremy 1941-...... **CLC 43**
See also CA 77-80; CANR 22; DLB 40

Hope, A(lec) D(erwent) 1907-.... **CLC 3, 51**
See also CA 21-24R; CANR 33; MTCW

Hope, Brian
See Creasey, John

Hope, Christopher (David Tully)
1944-.................... **CLC 52**
See also CA 106; SATA 62

Hopkins, Gerard Manley
1844-1889 .... **NCLC 17**
See also CDBLB 1890-1914; DLB 35, 57;
WLC

Hopkins, John (Richard) 1931-...... **CLC 4**
See also CA 85-88

Hopkins, Pauline Elizabeth
1859-1930 .... **TCLC 28**
See also BLC 2; DLB 50

Horatio
See Proust,
(Valentin-Louis-George-Eugene-)Marcel

Horgan, Paul 1903- .... **CLC 9, 53**
See also CA 13-16R; CANR 9, 35;
DLB 102; DLBY 85; MTCW; SATA 13

Horn, Peter
See Kuttner, Henry

Horovitz, Israel 1939-............ **CLC 56**
See also CA 33-36R; DLB 7

Horvath, Odon von
See Horvath, Oedoen von
See also DLB 85

Horvath, Oedoen von 1901-1938... **TCLC 45**
See also Horvath, Odon von
See also CA 118

Horwitz, Julius 1920-1986........ **CLC 14**
See also CA 9-12R; 119; CANR 12

Hospital, Janette Turner 1942-..... **CLC 42**
See also CA 108

Hostos, E. M. de
See Hostos (y Bonilla), Eugenio Maria de

Hostos, Eugenio M. de
See Hostos (y Bonilla), Eugenio Maria de

Hostos, Eugenio Maria
See Hostos (y Bonilla), Eugenio Maria de

Hostos (y Bonilla), Eugenio Maria de
1839-1903 .... **TCLC 24**
See also CA 123; 131; HW

Houdini
See Lovecraft, H(oward) P(hillips)

Hougan, Carolyn 19th cent. (?)- .... **CLC 34**

Household, Geoffrey (Edward West)
1900-1988 .... **CLC 11**
See also CA 77-80; 126; DLB 87; SATA 14,
59

Housman, A(lfred) E(dward)
1859-1936 .... **TCLC 1, 10; PC 2**
See also CA 104; 125; DLB 19; MTCW

Housman, Laurence 1865-1959 ..... **TCLC 7**
See also CA 106; DLB 10; SATA 25

Howard, Elizabeth Jane 1923- ... **CLC 7, 29**
See also CA 5-8R; CANR 8

Howard, Maureen 1930- ..... **CLC 5, 14, 46**
See also CA 53-56; CANR 31; DLBY 83;
MTCW

Howard, Richard 1929-...... **CLC 7, 10, 47**
See also AITN 1; CA 85-88; CANR 25;
DLB 5

Howard, Robert Ervin 1906-1936... **TCLC 8**
See also CA 105

Howard, Warren F.
See Pohl, Frederik

Howe, Fanny 1940- .... **CLC 47**
See also CA 117; SATA 52

Howe, Julia Ward 1819-1910 ..... **TCLC 21**
See also CA 117; DLB 1

Howe, Susan 1937-............... **CLC 72**
See also DLB 120

Howe, Tina 1937-................ **CLC 48**
See also CA 109

Howell, James 1594(?)-1666 .... **LC 13**

Howells, W. D.
See Howells, William Dean

Howells, William D.
See Howells, William Dean

Howells, William Dean
1837-1920 .... **TCLC 41, 7, 17**
See also CA 104; 134; CDALB 1865-1917;
DLB 12, 64, 74, 79

Howes, Barbara 1914-............ **CLC 15**
See also CA 9-12R; CAAS 3; SATA 5

Hrabal, Bohumil 1914-......... **CLC 13, 67**
See also CA 106; CAAS 12

Hsun, Lu .... **TCLC 3**
See also Shu-Jen, Chou

Hubbard, L(afayette) Ron(ald)
1911-1986 .... **CLC 43**
See also CA 77-80; 118; CANR 22

Huch, Ricarda (Octavia)
1864-1947 .... **TCLC 13**
See also CA 111; DLB 66

Huddle, David 1942- .... **CLC 49**
See also CA 57-60

Hudson, Jeffery
See Crichton, (John) Michael

Hudson, W(illiam) H(enry)
1841-1922 .... **TCLC 29**
See also CA 115; DLB 98; SATA 35

Hueffer, Ford Madox
See Ford, Ford Madox

Hughart, Barry .... **CLC 39**
See also CA 137

Hughes, Colin
See Creasey, John

Hughes, David (John) 1930- .... **CLC 48**
See also CA 116; 129; DLB 14

Hughes, (James) Langston
1902-1967 .... **CLC 1, 5, 10, 15, 35, 44;**
PC 1; SSC 6
See also BLC 2; BW; CA 1-4R; 25-28R;
CANR 1, 34; CDALB 1929-1941;
CLR 17; DLB 4, 7, 48, 51, 86; MAICYA;
MTCW; SATA 4, 33; WLC

Hughes, Richard (Arthur Warren)
1900-1976 .... **CLC 1, 11**
See also CA 5-8R; 65-68; CANR 4;
DLB 15; MTCW; SATA 8, 25

Hughes, Ted 1930- ..... **CLC 2, 4, 9, 14, 37**
See also CA 1-4R; CANR 1, 33; CLR 3;
DLB 40; MAICYA; MTCW; SATA 27,
49

Hugo, Richard F(ranklin)
1923-1982 .... **CLC 6, 18, 32**
See also CA 49-52; 108; CANR 3; DLB 5

Hugo, Victor (Marie)
1802-1885 .... **NCLC 3, 10, 21**
See also DLB 119; SATA 47; WLC

Huidobro, Vicente
See Huidobro Fernandez, Vicente Garcia

Huidobro Fernandez, Vicente Garcia
1893-1948 .... **TCLC 31**
See also CA 131; HW

Hulme, Keri 1947- .... **CLC 39**
See also CA 125

Hulme, T(homas) E(rnest)
1883-1917 .... **TCLC 21**
See also CA 117; DLB 19

Hume, David 1711-1776............. **LC 7**
See also DLB 104

Koizumi, Yakumo
See Hearn, (Patricio) Lafcadio (Tessima Carlos)

Kolmar, Gertrud 1894-1943 . . . . . . **TCLC 40**

Konrad, George
See Konrad, Gyoergy

Konrad, Gyoergy 1933- . . . . **CLC 4, 10**
See also CA 85-88

Konwicki, Tadeusz 1926- . . . . . **CLC 8, 28, 54**
See also CA 101; CAAS 9; CANR 39;
MTCW

Kopit, Arthur (Lee) 1937- . . . . **CLC 1, 18, 33**
See also AITN 1; CA 81-84; CABS 3;
DLB 7; MTCW

Kops, Bernard 1926- . . . . **CLC 4**
See also CA 5-8R; DLB 13

Kornbluth, C(yril) M. 1923-1958. . . . **TCLC 8**
See also CA 105; DLB 8

Korolenko, V. G.
See Korolenko, Vladimir Galaktionovich

Korolenko, Vladimir
See Korolenko, Vladimir Galaktionovich

Korolenko, Vladimir G.
See Korolenko, Vladimir Galaktionovich

Korolenko, Vladimir Galaktionovich
1853-1921 . . . . **TCLC 22**
See also CA 121

Kosinski, Jerzy (Nikodem)
1933-1991 . . . **CLC 1, 2, 3, 6, 10, 15, 53, 70**
See also CA 17-20R; 134; CANR 9; DLB 2;
DLBY 82; MTCW

Kostelanetz, Richard (Cory) 1940- . . **CLC 28**
See also CA 13-16R; CAAS 8; CANR 38

Kostrowitzki, Wilhelm Apollinaris de
1880-1918
See Apollinaire, Guillaume
See also CA 104

Kotlowitz, Robert 1924- . . . . **CLC 4**
See also CA 33-36R; CANR 36

Kotzebue, August (Friedrich Ferdinand) von
1761-1819 . . . . **NCLC 25**
See also DLB 94

Kotzwinkle, William 1938- . . . **CLC 5, 14, 35**
See also CA 45-48; CANR 3; CLR 6;
MAICYA; SATA 24, 70

Kozol, Jonathan 1936- . . . . **CLC 17**
See also CA 61-64; CANR 16

Kozoll, Michael 1940(?)- . . . . **CLC 35**

Kramer, Kathryn 19th cent. (?)- . . . . **CLC 34**

Kramer, Larry 1935- . . . . **CLC 42**
See also CA 124; 126

Krasicki, Ignacy 1735-1801 . . . . **NCLC 8**

Krasinski, Zygmunt 1812-1859 . . . . **NCLC 4**

Kraus, Karl 1874-1936 . . . . **TCLC 5**
See also CA 104; DLB 118

Kreve (Mickevicius), Vincas
1882-1954 . . . . **TCLC 27**

Kristofferson, Kris 1936- . . . . **CLC 26**
See also CA 104

Krizanc, John 1956- . . . . **CLC 57**

Krleza, Miroslav 1893-1981 . . . . **CLC 8**
See also CA 97-100; 105

Kroetsch, Robert 1927- . . . . . . **CLC 5, 23, 57**
See also CA 17-20R; CANR 8, 38; DLB 53;
MTCW

Kroetz, Franz
See Kroetz, Franz Xaver

Kroetz, Franz Xaver 1946- . . . . **CLC 41**
See also CA 130

Kropotkin, Peter (Aleksieevich)
1842-1921 . . . . **TCLC 36**
See also CA 119

Krotkov, Yuri 1917- . . . . **CLC 19**
See also CA 102

Krumb
See Crumb, R(obert)

Krumgold, Joseph (Quincy)
1908-1980 . . . . **CLC 12**
See also CA 9-12R; 101; CANR 7;
MAICYA; SATA 1, 23, 48

Krumwitz
See Crumb, R(obert)

Krutch, Joseph Wood 1893-1970. . . . **CLC 24**
See also CA 1-4R; 25-28R; CANR 4;
DLB 63

Krutzch, Gus
See Eliot, T(homas) S(tearns)

Krylov, Ivan Andreevich
1768(?)-1844 . . . . **NCLC 1**

Kubin, Alfred 1877-1959 . . . . **TCLC 23**
See also CA 112; DLB 81

Kubrick, Stanley 1928- . . . . **CLC 16**
See also CA 81-84; CANR 33; DLB 26

Kumin, Maxine (Winokur)
1925- . . . . **CLC 5, 13, 28**
See also AITN 2; CA 1-4R; CAAS 8;
CANR 1, 21; DLB 5; MTCW; SATA 12

Kundera, Milan
1929- . . . . **CLC 4, 9, 19, 32, 68**
See also AAYA 2; CA 85-88; CANR 19;
MTCW

Kunitz, Stanley (Jasspon)
1905- . . . . **CLC 6, 11, 14**
See also CA 41-44R; CANR 26; DLB 48;
MTCW

Kunze, Reiner 1933- . . . . **CLC 10**
See also CA 93-96; DLB 75

Kuprin, Aleksandr Ivanovich
1870-1938 . . . . **TCLC 5**
See also CA 104

Kureishi, Hanif 1954- . . . . **CLC 64**

Kurosawa, Akira 1910- . . . . **CLC 16**
See also CA 101

Kuttner, Henry 1915-1958 . . . . **TCLC 10**
See also CA 107; DLB 8

Kuzma, Greg 1944- . . . . **CLC 7**
See also CA 33-36R

Kuzmin, Mikhail 1872(?)-1936 . . . . **TCLC 40**

Kyprianos, Iossif
See Samarakis, Antonis

La Bruyere, Jean de 1645-1696 . . . . . . **LC 17**

Laclos, Pierre Ambroise Francois Choderlos
de 1741-1803 . . . . **NCLC 4**

Lacolere, Francois
See Aragon, Louis

La Colere, Francois
See Aragon, Louis

La Deshabilleuse
See Simenon, Georges (Jacques Christian)

Lady Gregory
See Gregory, Isabella Augusta (Persse)

Lady of Quality, A
See Bagnold, Enid

La Fayette, Marie (Madelaine Pioche de la
Vergne Comtes 1634-1693 . . . . . . **LC 2**

Lafayette, Rene
See Hubbard, L(afayette) Ron(ald)

Laforgue, Jules 1860-1887 . . . . **NCLC 5**

Lagerkvist, Paer (Fabian)
1891-1974 . . . . **CLC 7, 10, 13, 54**
See also CA 85-88; 49-52; MTCW

Lagerkvist, Par
See Lagerkvist, Paer (Fabian)

Lagerloef, Selma (Ottiliana Lovisa)
1858-1940 . . . . **TCLC 4, 36**
See also Lagerlof, Selma (Ottiliana Lovisa)
See also CA 108; CLR 7; SATA 15

Lagerlof, Selma (Ottiliana Lovisa)
See Lagerloef, Selma (Ottiliana Lovisa)
See also CLR 7; SATA 15

La Guma, (Justin) Alex(ander)
1925-1985 . . . . **CLC 19**
See also BW; CA 49-52; 118; CANR 25;
DLB 117; MTCW

Laidlaw, A. K.
See Grieve, C(hristopher) M(urray)

Lainez, Manuel Mujica
See Mujica Lainez, Manuel
See also HW

Lamartine, Alphonse (Marie Louis Prat) de
1790-1869 . . . . **NCLC 11**

Lamb, Charles 1775-1834 . . . . **NCLC 10**
See also CDBLB 1789-1832; DLB 93, 107;
SATA 17; WLC

Lamb, Lady Caroline 1785-1828 . . **NCLC 38**
See also DLB 116

Lamming, George (William)
1927- . . . . **CLC 2, 4, 66**
See also BLC 2; BW; CA 85-88; CANR 26;
MTCW

L'Amour, Louis (Dearborn)
1908-1988 . . . . **CLC 25, 55**
See also AITN 2; BEST 89:2; CA 1-4R;
125; CANR 3, 25; DLBY 80; MTCW

Lampedusa, Giuseppe (Tomasi) di . . . **TCLC 13**
See also Tomasi di Lampedusa, Giuseppe

Lampman, Archibald 1861-1899 . . **NCLC 25**
See also DLB 92

Lancaster, Bruce 1896-1963 . . . . **CLC 36**
See also CA 9-10; CAP 1; SATA 9

Landau, Mark Alexandrovich
See Aldanov, Mark (Alexandrovich)

Landau-Aldanov, Mark Alexandrovich
See Aldanov, Mark (Alexandrovich)

Landis, John 1950- . . . . **CLC 26**
See also CA 112; 122

Landolfi, Tommaso 1908-1979 . . . **CLC 11, 49**
See also CA 127; 117

Landon, Letitia Elizabeth
　　1802-1838 . . . . **NCLC 15**
　　See also DLB 96

Landor, Walter Savage
　　1775-1864 . . . . **NCLC 14**
　　See also DLB 93, 107

Landwirth, Heinz 1927-
　　See Lind, Jakov
　　See also CA 9-12R; CANR 7

Lane, Patrick 1939- . . . . **CLC 25**
　　See also CA 97-100; DLB 53

Lang, Andrew 1844-1912 . . . . **TCLC 16**
　　See also CA 114; 137; DLB 98; MAICYA;
　　SATA 16

Lang, Fritz 1890-1976 . . . . **CLC 20**
　　See also CA 77-80; 69-72; CANR 30

Lange, John
　　See Crichton, (John) Michael

Langer, Elinor 1939- . . . . **CLC 34**
　　See also CA 121

Langland, William 1330(?)-1400(?) . . . **LC 19**

Langstaff, Launcelot
　　See Irving, Washington

Lanier, Sidney 1842-1881 . . . . **NCLC 6**
　　See also DLB 64; MAICYA; SATA 18

Lanyer, Aemilia 1569-1645 . . . . **LC 10**

Lao Tzu . . . . **CMLC 7**

Lapine, James (Elliot) 1949- . . . . **CLC 39**
　　See also CA 123; 130

Larbaud, Valery (Nicolas)
　　1881-1957 . . . . **TCLC 9**
　　Scc also CA 106

Lardner, Ring
　　See Lardner, Ring(gold) W(ilmer)

Lardner, Ring W. Jr.
　　See Lardner, Ring(gold) W(ilmer)

Lardner, Ring(gold) W(ilmer)
　　1885-1933 . . . . **TCLC 2, 14**
　　See also CA 104; 131; CDALB 1917-1929;
　　DLB 11, 25, 86; MTCW

Laredo, Betty
　　See Codrescu, Andrei

Larkin, Maia
　　See Wojciechowska, Maia (Teresa)

Larkin, Philip (Arthur)
　　1922-1985 . . . **CLC 3, 5, 8, 9, 13, 18, 33,
　　　　　　　　　　　　　　　　　39, 64**
　　See also CA 5-8R; 117; CANR 24;
　　CDBLB 1960 to Present; DLB 27;
　　MTCW

Larra (y Sanchez de Castro), Mariano Jose de
　　1809-1837 . . . . **NCLC 17**

Larsen, Eric 1941- . . . . **CLC 55**
　　See also CA 132

Larsen, Nella 1891-1964 . . . . **CLC 37**
　　See also BLC 2; BW; CA 125; DLB 51

Larson, Charles R(aymond) 1938- . . . **CLC 31**
　　See also CA 53-56; CANR 4

Latham, Jean Lee 1902- . . . . **CLC 12**
　　See also AITN 1; CA 5-8R; CANR 7;
　　MAICYA; SATA 2, 68

Latham, Mavis
　　See Clark, Mavis Thorpe

Lathen, Emma . . . . **CLC 2**
　　See also Hennissart, Martha; Latsis, Mary
　　J(ane)

Lathrop, Francis
　　See Leiber, Fritz (Reuter Jr.)

Latsis, Mary J(ane)
　　See Lathen, Emma
　　See also CA 85-88

Lattimore, Richmond (Alexander)
　　1906-1984 . . . . **CLC 3**
　　See also CA 1-4R; 112; CANR 1

Laughlin, James 1914- . . . . **CLC 49**
　　See also CA 21-24R; CANR 9; DLB 48

Laurence, (Jean) Margaret (Wemyss)
　　1926-1987 . . **CLC 3, 6, 13, 50, 62; SSC 7**
　　See also CA 5-8R; 121; CANR 33; DLB 53;
　　MTCW; SATA 50

Laurent, Antoine 1952- . . . . **CLC 50**

Lauscher, Hermann
　　See Hesse, Hermann

Lautreamont, Comte de
　　1846-1870 . . . . **NCLC 12**

Laverty, Donald
　　See Blish, James (Benjamin)

Lavin, Mary 1912- . . . . . . **CLC 4, 18; SSC 4**
　　See also CA 9-12R; CANR 33; DLB 15;
　　MTCW

Lavond, Paul Dennis
　　See Kornbluth, C(yril) M.; Pohl, Frederik

Lawler, Raymond Evenor 1922- . . . . **CLC 58**
　　See also CA 103

Lawrence, D(avid) H(erbert Richards)
　　1885-1930 . . . . **TCLC 2, 9, 16, 33; SSC 4**
　　See also CA 104; 121; CDBLB 1914-1945;
　　DLB 10, 19, 36, 98; MTCW; WLC

Lawrence, T(homas) E(dward)
　　1888-1935 . . . . **TCLC 18**
　　See also Dale, Colin
　　See also CA 115

Lawrence Of Arabia
　　See Lawrence, T(homas) E(dward)

Lawson, Henry (Archibald Hertzberg)
　　1867-1922 . . . . **TCLC 27**
　　See also CA 120

Laxness, Halldor . . . . **CLC 25**
　　See also Gudjonsson, Halldor Kiljan

Laye, Camara 1928-1980 . . . . **CLC 4, 38**
　　See also BLC 2; BW; CA 85-88; 97-100;
　　CANR 25; MTCW

Layton, Irving (Peter) 1912- . . . . . **CLC 2, 15**
　　See also CA 1-4R; CANR 2, 33; DLB 88;
　　MTCW

Lazarus, Emma 1849-1887 . . . . **NCLC 8**

Lazarus, Felix
　　See Cable, George Washington

Lea, Joan
　　See Neufeld, John (Arthur)

Leacock, Stephen (Butler)
　　1869-1944 . . . . **TCLC 2**
　　See also CA 104; DLB 92

Lear, Edward 1812-1888 . . . . **NCLC 3**
　　See also CLR 1; DLB 32; MAICYA;
　　SATA 18

Lear, Norman (Milton) 1922- . . . . . . **CLC 12**
　　See also CA 73-76

Leavis, F(rank) R(aymond)
　　1895-1978 . . . . **CLC 24**
　　See also CA 21-24R; 77-80; MTCW

Leavitt, David 1961- . . . . **CLC 34**
　　See also CA 116; 122

Lebowitz, Fran(ces Ann)
　　1951(?)- . . . . **CLC 11, 36**
　　See also CA 81-84; CANR 14; MTCW

le Carre, John . . . . **CLC 3, 5, 9, 15, 28**
　　See also Cornwell, David (John Moore)
　　See also BEST 89:4; CDBLB 1960 to
　　Present; DLB 87

Le Clezio, J(ean) M(arie) G(ustave)
　　1940- . . . . **CLC 31**
　　See also CA 116; 128; DLB 83

Leconte de Lisle, Charles-Marie-Rene
　　1818-1894 . . . . **NCLC 29**

Le Coq, Monsieur
　　See Simenon, Georges (Jacques Christian)

Leduc, Violette 1907-1972 . . . . **CLC 22**
　　See also CA 13-14; 33-36R; CAP 1

Ledwidge, Francis 1887(?)-1917 . . . **TCLC 23**
　　See also CA 123; DLB 20

Lee, Andrea 1953- . . . . **CLC 36**
　　See also BLC 2; BW; CA 125

Lee, Andrew
　　See Auchincloss, Louis (Stanton)

Lee, Don L. . . . . **CLC 2**
　　See also Madhubuti, Haki R.

Lee, George W(ashington)
　　1894-1976 . . . . **CLC 52**
　　See also BLC 2; BW; CA 125; DLB 51

Lee, (Nelle) Harper 1926- . . . . . . **CLC 12, 60**
　　See also CA 13-16R; CDALB 1941-1968;
　　DLB 6; MTCW; SATA 11; WLC

Lee, Julian
　　See Latham, Jean Lee

Lee, Lawrence 1903- . . . . **CLC 34**
　　See also CA 25-28R

Lee, Manfred B(ennington)
　　1905-1971 . . . . **CLC 11**
　　See also Queen, Ellery
　　See also CA 1-4R; 29-32R; CANR 2

Lee, Stan 1922- . . . . **CLC 17**
　　See also AAYA 5; CA 108; 111

Lee, Tanith 1947- . . . . **CLC 46**
　　See also CA 37-40R; SATA 8

Lee, Vernon . . . . **TCLC 5**
　　See also Paget, Violet
　　See also DLB 57

Lee, William
　　See Burroughs, William S(eward)

Lee, Willy
　　See Burroughs, William S(eward)

Lee-Hamilton, Eugene (Jacob)
　　1845-1907 . . . . **TCLC 22**
　　See also CA 117

Leet, Judith 1935- . . . . **CLC 11**

Le Fanu, Joseph Sheridan
　　1814-1873 . . . . **NCLC 9**
　　See also DLB 21, 70

Lin, Frank
See Atherton, Gertrude (Franklin Horn)

Lincoln, Abraham 1809-1865..... **NCLC 18**

Lind, Jakov .... **CLC 1, 2, 4, 27**
See also Landwirth, Heinz
See also CAAS 4

Lindsay, David 1878-1945 .... **TCLC 15**
See also CA 113

Lindsay, (Nicholas) Vachel
1879-1931 .... **TCLC 17**
See also CA 114; 135; CDALB 1865-1917;
DLB 54; SATA 40; WLC

Linke-Poot
See Doeblin, Alfred

Linney, Romulus 1930- .... **CLC 51**
See also CA 1-4R

Li Po 701-763 .... **CMLC 2**

Lipsius, Justus 1547-1606 .... **LC 16**

Lipsyte, Robert (Michael) 1938-.... **CLC 21**
See also AAYA 7; CA 17-20R; CANR 8;
CLR 23; MAICYA; SATA 5, 68

Lish, Gordon (Jay) 1934-.......... **CLC 45**
See also CA 113; 117

Lispector, Clarice 1925-1977 .... **CLC 43**
See also CA 116; DLB 113

Littell, Robert 1935(?)- .... **CLC 42**
See also CA 109; 112

Littlewit, Humphrey Gent.
See Lovecraft, H(oward) P(hillips)

Litwos
See Sienkiewicz, Henryk (Adam Alexander
Pius)

Liu E 1857-1909 .... **TCLC 15**
See also CA 115

Lively, Penelope (Margaret)
1933- .... **CLC 32, 50**
See also CA 41-44R; CANR 29; CLR 7;
DLB 14; MAICYA; MTCW; SATA 7, 60

Livesay, Dorothy (Kathleen)
1909- .... **CLC 4, 15**
See also AITN 2; CA 25-28R; CAAS 8;
CANR 36; DLB 68; MTCW

Lizardi, Jose Joaquin Fernandez de
1776-1827 .... **NCLC 30**

Llewellyn, Richard .... **CLC 7**
See also Llewellyn Lloyd, Richard Dafydd
Vivian
See also DLB 15

Llewellyn Lloyd, Richard Dafydd Vivian
1906-1983
See Llewellyn, Richard
See also CA 53-56; 111; CANR 7;
SATA 11, 37

Llosa, (Jorge) Mario (Pedro) Vargas
See Vargas Llosa, (Jorge) Mario (Pedro)

Lloyd Webber, Andrew 1948-
See Webber, Andrew Lloyd
See also AAYA 1; CA 116; SATA 56

Locke, Alain (Le Roy)
1886-1954 .... **TCLC 43**
See also BW; CA 106; 124; DLB 51

Locke, John 1632-1704 .... **LC 7**
See also DLB 101

Locke-Elliott, Sumner
See Elliott, Sumner Locke

Lockhart, John Gibson
1794-1854 .... **NCLC 6**
See also DLB 110, 116

Lodge, David (John) 1935-......... **CLC 36**
See also BEST 90:1; CA 17-20R; CANR 19;
DLB 14; MTCW

Loennbohm, Armas Eino Leopold 1878-1926
See Leino, Eino
See also CA 123

Loewinsohn, Ron(ald William)
1937- .... **CLC 52**
See also CA 25-28R

Logan, Jake
See Smith, Martin Cruz

Logan, John (Burton) 1923-1987..... **CLC 5**
See also CA 77-80; 124; DLB 5

Lo Kuan-chung 1330(?)-1400(?)...... **LC 12**

Lombard, Nap
See Johnson, Pamela Hansford

London, Jack .... **TCLC 9, 15, 39; SSC 4**
See also London, John Griffith
See also AITN 2; CDALB 1865-1917;
DLB 8, 12, 78; SATA 18; WLC

London, John Griffith 1876-1916
See London, Jack
See also CA 110; 119; MAICYA; MTCW

Long, Emmett
See Leonard, Elmore (John Jr.)

Longbaugh, Harry
See Goldman, William (W.)

Longfellow, Henry Wadsworth
1807-1882 .... **NCLC 2**
See also CDALB 1640-1865; DLB 1, 59;
SATA 19

Longley, Michael 1939-........... **CLC 29**
See also CA 102; DLB 40

Longus fl. c. 2nd cent. - .... **CMLC 7**

Longway, A. Hugh
See Lang, Andrew

Lopate, Phillip 1943- .... **CLC 29**
See also CA 97-100; DLBY 80

Lopez Portillo (y Pacheco), Jose
1920- .... **CLC 46**
See also CA 129; HW

Lopez y Fuentes, Gregorio
1897(?)-1966 .... **CLC 32**
See also CA 131; HW

Lorca, Federico Garcia
See Garcia Lorca, Federico

Lord, Bette Bao 1938- .... **CLC 23**
See also BEST 90:3; CA 107; SATA 58

Lord Auch
See Bataille, Georges

Lord Byron
See Byron, George Gordon (Noel)

Lord Dunsany .... **TCLC 2**
See also Dunsany, Edward John Moreton
Drax Plunkett

Lorde, Audre (Geraldine)
1934- .... **CLC 18, 71**
See also BLC 2; BW; CA 25-28R;
CANR 16, 26; DLB 41; MTCW

Lord Jeffrey
See Jeffrey, Francis

Lorenzo, Heberto Padilla
See Padilla (Lorenzo), Heberto

Loris
See Hofmannsthal, Hugo von

Loti, Pierre .... **TCLC 11**
See also Viaud, (Louis Marie) Julien

Louie, David Wong 1954- .... **CLC 70**

Louis, Father M.
See Merton, Thomas

Lovecraft, H(oward) P(hillips)
1890-1937 .... **TCLC 4, 22; SSC 3**
See also CA 104; 133; MTCW

Lovelace, Earl 1935-.............. **CLC 51**
See also CA 77-80; MTCW

Lowell, Amy 1874-1925 .... **TCLC 1, 8**
See also CA 104; DLB 54

Lowell, James Russell 1819-1891 .. **NCLC 2**
See also CDALB 1640-1865; DLB 1, 11, 64,
79

Lowell, Robert (Traill Spence Jr.)
1917-1977 ... **CLC 1, 2, 3, 4, 5, 8, 9, 11,
15, 37; PC 3**
See also CA 9-12R; 73-76; CABS 2;
CANR 26; DLB 5; MTCW; WLC

Lowndes, Marie Adelaide (Belloc)
1868-1947 .... **TCLC 12**
See also CA 107; DLB 70

Lowry, (Clarence) Malcolm
1909-1957 .... **TCLC 6, 40**
See also CA 105; 131; CDBLB 1945-1960;
DLB 15; MTCW

Lowry, Mina Gertrude 1882-1966
See Loy, Mina
See also CA 113

Loxsmith, John
See Brunner, John (Kilian Houston)

Loy, Mina .... **CLC 28**
See also Lowry, Mina Gertrude
See also DLB 4, 54

Loyson-Bridet
See Schwob, (Mayer Andre) Marcel

Lucas, Craig 1951-............... **CLC 64**
See also CA 137

Lucas, George 1944-.............. **CLC 16**
See also AAYA 1; CA 77-80; CANR 30;
SATA 56

Lucas, Hans
See Godard, Jean-Luc

Lucas, Victoria
See Plath, Sylvia

Ludlam, Charles 1943-1987 ..... **CLC 46, 50**
See also CA 85-88; 122

Ludlum, Robert 1927- .... **CLC 22, 43**
See also BEST 89:1, 90:3; CA 33-36R;
CANR 25; DLBY 82; MTCW

Ludwig, Ken .... **CLC 60**

Ludwig, Otto 1813-1865.......... **NCLC 4**

Lugones, Leopoldo 1874-1938 .... **TCLC 15**
See also CA 116; 131; HW

Lu Hsun 1881-1936 .... **TCLC 3**

Lukacs, George . . . . CLC 24
See also Lukacs, Gyorgy (Szegeny von)

Lukacs, Gyorgy (Szegeny von) 1885-1971
See Lukacs, George
See also CA 101; 29-32R

Luke, Peter (Ambrose Cyprian)
1919- . . . . CLC 38
See also CA 81-84; DLB 13

Lunar, Dennis
See Mungo, Raymond

Lurie, Alison 1926- . . . . CLC 4, 5, 18, 39
See also CA 1-4R; CANR 2, 17; DLB 2;
MTCW; SATA 46

Lustig, Arnost 1926- . . . . CLC 56
See also AAYA 3; CA 69-72; SATA 56

Luther, Martin 1483-1546 . . . . LC 9

Luzi, Mario 1914- . . . . CLC 13
See also CA 61-64; CANR 9

Lynch, B. Suarez
See Bioy Casares, Adolfo; Borges, Jorge
Luis

Lynch, David (K.) 1946- . . . . CLC 66
See also CA 124; 129

Lynch, James
See Andreyev, Leonid (Nikolaevich)

Lynch Davis, B.
See Bioy Casares, Adolfo; Borges, Jorge
Luis

Lyndsay, Sir David 1490-1555 . . . . LC 20

Lynn, Kenneth S(chuyler) 1923- . . . . CLC 50
See also CA 1-4R; CANR 3, 27

Lynx
See West, Rebecca

Lyons, Marcus
See Blish, James (Benjamin)

Lyre, Pinchbeck
See Sassoon, Siegfried (Lorraine)

Lytle, Andrew (Nelson) 1902- . . . . . . CLC 22
See also CA 9-12R; DLB 6

Lyttelton, George 1709-1773 . . . . LC 10

Maas, Peter 1929- . . . . CLC 29
See also CA 93-96

Macaulay, Rose 1881-1958 . . . . . TCLC 7, 44
See also CA 104; DLB 36

MaCauley, Stephen 19th cent. (?)- . . CLC 50

MacBeth, George (Mann)
1932-1992 . . . . CLC 2, 5, 9
See also CA 25-28R; 136; DLB 40; MTCW;
SATA 4; SATO 70

MacCaig, Norman (Alexander)
1910- . . . . CLC 36
See also CA 9-12R; CANR 3, 34; DLB 27

MacCarthy, (Sir Charles Otto) Desmond
1877-1952 . . . . TCLC 36

MacDiarmid, Hugh . . . . . CLC 2, 4, 11, 19, 63
See also Grieve, C(hristopher) M(urray)
See also CDBLB 1945-1960; DLB 20

MacDonald, Anson
See Heinlein, Robert A(nson)

Macdonald, Cynthia 1928- . . . . . . CLC 13, 19
See also CA 49-52; CANR 4; DLB 105

MacDonald, George 1824-1905 . . . . . TCLC 9
See also CA 106; 137; DLB 18; MAICYA;
SATA 33

Macdonald, John
See Millar, Kenneth

MacDonald, John D(ann)
1916-1986 . . . . CLC 3, 27, 44
See also CA 1-4R; 121; CANR 1, 19;
DLB 8; DLBY 86; MTCW

Macdonald, John Ross
See Millar, Kenneth

Macdonald, Ross . . . . . CLC 1, 2, 3, 14, 34, 41
See also Millar, Kenneth
See also DLBD 6

MacDougal, John
See Blish, James (Benjamin)

MacEwen, Gwendolyn (Margaret)
1941-1987 . . . . CLC 13, 55
See also CA 9-12R; 124; CANR 7, 22;
DLB 53; SATA 50, 55

Machado (y Ruiz), Antonio
1875-1939 . . . . TCLC 3
See also CA 104; DLB 108

Machado de Assis, Joaquim Maria
1839-1908 . . . . TCLC 10
See also BLC 2; CA 107

Machen, Arthur . . . . TCLC 4
See also Jones, Arthur Llewellyn
See also DLB 36

Machiavelli, Niccolo 1469-1527 . . . . . . LC 8

MacInnes, Colin 1914-1976 . . . . . . CLC 4, 23
See also CA 69-72; 65-68; CANR 21;
DLB 14; MTCW

MacInnes, Helen (Clark)
1907-1985 . . . . CLC 27, 39
See also CA 1-4R; 117; CANR 1, 28;
DLB 87; MTCW; SATA 22, 44

Mackenzie, Compton (Edward Montague)
1883-1972 . . . . CLC 18
See also CA 21-22; 37-40R; CAP 2;
DLB 34, 100

Mackintosh, Elizabeth 1896(?)-1952
See Tey, Josephine
See also CA 110

MacLaren, James
See Grieve, C(hristopher) M(urray)

Mac Laverty, Bernard 1942- . . . . CLC 31
See also CA 116; 118

MacLean, Alistair (Stuart)
1922-1987 . . . . CLC 3, 13, 50, 63
See also CA 57-60; 121; CANR 28; MTCW;
SATA 23, 50

MacLeish, Archibald
1892-1982 . . . . CLC 3, 8, 14, 68
See also CA 9-12R; 106; CANR 33; DLB 4,
7, 45; DLBY 82; MTCW

MacLennan, (John) Hugh
1907- . . . . CLC 2, 14
See also CA 5-8R; CANR 33; DLB 68;
MTCW

MacLeod, Alistair 1936- . . . . CLC 56
See also CA 123; DLB 60

MacNeice, (Frederick) Louis
1907-1963 . . . . CLC 1, 4, 10, 53
See also CA 85-88; DLB 10, 20; MTCW

MacNeill, Dand
See Fraser, George MacDonald

Macpherson, (Jean) Jay 1931- . . . . . . CLC 14
See also CA 5-8R; DLB 53

MacShane, Frank 1927- . . . . CLC 39
See also CA 9-12R; CANR 3, 33; DLB 111

Macumber, Mari
See Sandoz, Mari(e Susette)

Madach, Imre 1823-1864 . . . . NCLC 19

Madden, (Jerry) David 1933- . . . . CLC 5, 15
See also CA 1-4R; CAAS 3; CANR 4;
DLB 6; MTCW

Maddern, Al(an)
See Ellison, Harlan

Madhubuti, Haki R. 1942- . . . . CLC 6; PC 5
See also Lee, Don L.
See also BLC 2; BW; CA 73-76; CANR 24;
DLB 5, 41; DLBD 8

Madow, Pauline (Reichberg) . . . . CLC 1
See also CA 9-12R

Maepenn, Hugh
See Kuttner, Henry

Maepenn, K. H.
See Kuttner, Henry

Maeterlinck, Maurice 1862-1949 . . . TCLC 3
See also CA 104; 136; SATA 66

Maginn, William 1794-1842 . . . . . . NCLC 8
See also DLB 110

Mahapatra, Jayanta 1928- . . . . CLC 33
See also CA 73-76; CAAS 9; CANR 15, 33

Mahfouz, Naguib (Abdel Aziz Al-Sabilgi)
1911(?)-
See Mahfuz, Najib
See also BEST 89:2; CA 128; MTCW

Mahfuz, Najib . . . . CLC 52, 55
See also Mahfouz, Naguib (Abdel Aziz
Al-Sabilgi)
See also DLBY 88

Mahon, Derek 1941- . . . . CLC 27
See also CA 113; 128; DLB 40

Mailer, Norman
1923- . . . . . . CLC 1, 2, 3, 4, 5, 8, 11, 14,
28, 39
See also AITN 2; CA 9-12R; CABS 1;
CANR 28; CDALB 1968-1988; DLB 2,
16, 28; DLBD 3; DLBY 80, 83; MTCW

Maillet, Antonine 1929- . . . . CLC 54
See also CA 115; 120; DLB 60

Mais, Roger 1905-1955 . . . . TCLC 8
See also BW; CA 105; 124; MTCW

Maitland, Sara (Louise) 1950- . . . . . . CLC 49
See also CA 69-72; CANR 13

Major, Clarence 1936- . . . . CLC 3, 19, 48
See also BLC 2; BW; CA 21-24R; CAAS 6;
CANR 13, 25; DLB 33

Major, Kevin (Gerald) 1949- . . . . CLC 26
See also CA 97-100; CANR 21, 38;
CLR 11; DLB 60; MAICYA; SATA 32

Maki, James
See Ozu, Yasujiro

Malabaila, Damiano
See Levi, Primo

Malamud, Bernard
　　1914-1986 ..... **CLC 1, 2, 3, 5, 8, 9, 11, 18, 27, 44**
　　See also CA 5-8R; 118; CABS 1; CANR 28;
　　CDALB 1941-1968; DLB 2, 28;
　　DLBY 80, 86; MTCW; WLC

Malcolm, Dan
　　See Silverberg, Robert

Malherbe, Francois de 1555-1628..... **LC 5**

Mallarme, Stephane
　　1842-1898 .... **NCLC 4; PC 4**

Mallet-Joris, Francoise 1930-...... **CLC 11**
　　See also CA 65-68; CANR 17; DLB 83

Malley, Ern
　　See McAuley, James Phillip

Mallowan, Agatha Christie
　　See Christie, Agatha (Mary Clarissa)

Maloff, Saul 1922-................ **CLC 5**
　　See also CA 33-36R

Malone, Louis
　　See MacNeice, (Frederick) Louis

Malone, Michael (Christopher)
　　1942-....................... **CLC 43**
　　See also CA 77-80; CANR 14, 32

Malory, (Sir) Thomas
　　1410(?)-1471(?)............... **LC 11**
　　See also CDBLB Before 1660; SATA 33, 59

Malouf, (George Joseph) David
　　1934-...................... **CLC 28**
　　See also CA 124

Malraux, (Georges-)Andre
　　1901-1976 ...... **CLC 1, 4, 9, 13, 15, 57**
　　See also CA 21-22; 69-72; CANR 34;
　　CAP 2; DLB 72; MTCW

Malzberg, Barry N(athaniel) 1939-... **CLC 7**
　　See also CA 61-64; CAAS 4; CANR 16;
　　DLB 8

Mamet, David (Alan)
　　1947-................CLC 9, 15, 34, 46
　　See also AAYA 3; CA 81-84; CABS 3;
　　CANR 15; DLB 7; MTCW

Mamoulian, Rouben (Zachary)
　　1897-1987 .... **CLC 16**
　　See also CA 25-28R; 124

Mandelstam, Osip (Emilievich)
　　1891(?)-1938(?) .... **TCLC 2, 6**
　　See also CA 104

Mander, (Mary) Jane 1877-1949... **TCLC 31**

Mandiargues, Andre Pieyre de....... **CLC 41**
　　See also Pieyre de Mandiargues, Andre
　　See also DLB 83

Mandrake, Ethel Belle
　　See Thurman, Wallace (Henry)

Mangan, James Clarence
　　1803-1849 .... **NCLC 27**

Maniere, J.-E.
　　See Giraudoux, (Hippolyte) Jean

Manley, (Mary) Delariviere
　　1672(?)-1724 .... **LC 1**
　　See also DLB 39, 80

Mann, Abel
　　See Creasey, John

Mann, (Luiz) Heinrich 1871-1950... **TCLC 9**
　　See also CA 106; DLB 66

Mann, (Paul) Thomas
　　1875-1955 ... **TCLC 2, 8, 14, 21, 35, 44; SSC 5**
　　See also CA 104; 128; DLB 66; MTCW;
　　WLC

Manning, Frederic 1887(?)-1935 ... **TCLC 25**
　　See also CA 124

Manning, Olivia 1915-1980...... **CLC 5, 19**
　　See also CA 5-8R; 101; CANR 29; MTCW

Mano, D. Keith 1942- .... **CLC 2, 10**
　　See also CA 25-28R; CAAS 6; CANR 26;
　　DLB 6

Mansfield, Katherine... **TCLC 2, 8, 39; SSC 9**
　　See also Beauchamp, Kathleen Mansfield
　　See also WLC

Manso, Peter 1940- .... **CLC 39**
　　See also CA 29-32R

Mantecon, Juan Jimenez
　　See Jimenez (Mantecon), Juan Ramon

Manton, Peter
　　See Creasey, John

Man Without a Spleen, A
　　See Chekhov, Anton (Pavlovich)

Manzoni, Alessandro 1785-1873 .. **NCLC 29**

Mapu, Abraham (ben Jekutiel)
　　1808-1867 .... **NCLC 18**

Mara, Sally
　　See Queneau, Raymond

Marat, Jean Paul 1743-1793........ **LC 10**

Marcel, Gabriel Honore
　　1889-1973 .... **CLC 15**
　　See also CA 102; 45-48; MTCW

Marchbanks, Samuel
　　See Davies, (William) Robertson

Marchi, Giacomo
　　See Bassani, Giorgio

Marie de France c. 12th cent. -.... **CMLC 8**

Marie de l'Incarnation 1599-1672.... **LC 10**

Mariner, Scott
　　See Pohl, Frederik

Marinetti, Filippo Tommaso
　　1876-1944 .... **TCLC 10**
　　See also CA 107; DLB 114

Marivaux, Pierre Carlet de Chamblain de
　　1688-1763 .... **LC 4**

Markandaya, Kamala .... **CLC 8, 38**
　　See also Taylor, Kamala (Purnaiya)

Markfield, Wallace 1926-........... **CLC 8**
　　See also CA 69-72; CAAS 3; DLB 2, 28

Markham, Edwin 1852-1940...... **TCLC 47**
　　See also DLB 54

Markham, Robert
　　See Amis, Kingsley (William)

Marks, J
　　See Highwater, Jamake (Mamake)

Marks-Highwater, J
　　See Highwater, Jamake (Mamake)

Markson, David M(errill) 1927-.... **CLC 67**
　　See also CA 49-52; CANR 1

Marley, Bob..................... **CLC 17**
　　See also Marley, Robert Nesta

Marley, Robert Nesta 1945-1981
　　See Marley, Bob
　　See also CA 107; 103

Marlowe, Christopher 1564-1593 ..... **DC 1**
　　See also CDBLB Before 1660; DLB 62;
　　WLC

Marmontel, Jean-Francois
　　1723-1799 .... **LC 2**

Marquand, John P(hillips)
　　1893-1960 ....**CLC 2, 10**
　　See also CA 85-88; DLB 9, 102

Marquez, Gabriel (Jose) Garcia...... **CLC 68**
　　See also Garcia Marquez, Gabriel (Jose)

Marquis, Don(ald Robert Perry)
　　1878-1937 ....**TCLC 7**
　　See also CA 104; DLB 11, 25

Marric, J. J.
　　See Creasey, John

Marrow, Bernard
　　See Moore, Brian

Marryat, Frederick 1792-1848 .... **NCLC 3**
　　See also DLB 21

Marsden, James
　　See Creasey, John

Marsh, (Edith) Ngaio
　　1899-1982 ....**CLC 7, 53**
　　See also CA 9-12R; CANR 6; DLB 77;
　　MTCW

Marshall, Garry 1934-........... **CLC 17**
　　See also AAYA 3; CA 111; SATA 60

Marshall, Paule 1929- .. **CLC 27, 72; SSC 3**
　　See also BLC 3; BW; CA 77-80; CANR 25;
　　DLB 33; MTCW

Marsten, Richard
　　See Hunter, Evan

Martha, Henry
　　See Harris, Mark

Martin, Ken
　　See Hubbard, L(afayette) Ron(ald)

Martin, Richard
　　See Creasey, John

Martin, Steve 1945-.............. **CLC 30**
　　See also CA 97-100; CANR 30; MTCW

Martin, Webber
　　See Silverberg, Robert

Martin du Gard, Roger
　　1881-1958 .... **TCLC 24**
　　See also CA 118; DLB 65

Martineau, Harriet 1802-1876.... **NCLC 26**
　　See also DLB 21, 55; YABC 2

Martines, Julia
　　See O'Faolain, Julia

Martinez, Jacinto Benavente y
　　See Benavente (y Martinez), Jacinto

Martinez Ruiz, Jose 1873-1967
　　See Azorin; Ruiz, Jose Martinez
　　See also CA 93-96; HW

Martinez Sierra, Gregorio
　　1881-1947 .... **TCLC 6**
　　See also CA 115

Martinez Sierra, Maria (de la O'LeJarraga)
　　1874-1974 .... **TCLC 6**
　　See also CA 115

Martinsen, Martin
See Follett, Ken(neth Martin)

Martinson, Harry (Edmund)
1904-1978 .... CLC 14
See also CA 77-80; CANR 34

Marut, Ret
See Traven, B.

Marut, Robert
See Traven, B.

Marvell, Andrew 1621-1678......... LC 4
See also CDBLB 1660-1789; WLC

Marx, Karl (Heinrich)
1818-1883 .... NCLC 17

Masaoka Shiki................... TCLC 18
See also Masaoka Tsunenori

Masaoka Tsunenori 1867-1902
See Masaoka Shiki
See also CA 117

Masefield, John (Edward)
1878-1967 .... CLC 11, 47
See also CA 19-20; 25-28R; CANR 33;
CAP 2; CDBLB 1890-1914; DLB 10;
MTCW; SATA 19

Maso, Carole 19th cent. (?)- .... CLC 44

Mason, Bobbie Ann
1940- .... CLC 28, 43; SSC 4
See also AAYA 5; CA 53-56; CANR 11,
31; DLBY 87; MTCW

Mason, Ernst
See Pohl, Frederik

Mason, Lee W.
See Malzberg, Barry N(athaniel)

Mason, Nick 1945-.............. CLC 35
See also Pink Floyd

Mason, Tally
See Derleth, August (William)

Mass, William
See Gibson, William

Masters, Edgar Lee
1868-1950 .... TCLC 2, 25; PC 1
See also CA 104; 133; CDALB 1865-1917;
DLB 54; MTCW

Masters, Hilary 1928-............ CLC 48
See also CA 25-28R; CANR 13

Mastrosimone, William
19th cent. (?)- .... CLC 36

Mathe, Albert
See Camus, Albert

Matheson, Richard Burton 1926- ... CLC 37
See also CA 97-100; DLB 8, 44

Mathews, Harry 1930-......... CLC 6, 52
See also CA 21-24R; CAAS 6; CANR 18

Mathias, Roland (Glyn) 1915-...... CLC 45
See also CA 97-100; CANR 19; DLB 27

Matsuo Basho 1644-1694........... PC 3

Mattheson, Rodney
See Creasey, John

Matthews, Greg 1949- .... CLC 45
See also CA 135

Matthews, William 1942-......... CLC 40
See also CA 29-32R; CANR 12; DLB 5

Matthias, John (Edward) 1941-...... CLC 9
See also CA 33-36R

Matthiessen, Peter
1927- .... CLC 5, 7, 11, 32, 64
See also AAYA 6; BEST 90:4; CA 9-12R;
CANR 21; DLB 6; MTCW; SATA 27

Maturin, Charles Robert
1780(?)-1824 .... NCLC 6

Matute (Ausejo), Ana Maria
1925- .... CLC 11
See also CA 89-92; MTCW

Maugham, W. S.
See Maugham, W(illiam) Somerset

Maugham, W(illiam) Somerset
1874-1965 .... CLC 1, 11, 15, 67; SSC 8
See also CA 5-8R; 25-28R;
CDBLB 1914-1945; DLB 10, 36, 77, 100;
MTCW; SATA 54; WLC

Maugham, William Somerset
See Maugham, W(illiam) Somerset

Maupassant, (Henri Rene Albert) Guy de
1850-1893 .... NCLC 1; SSC 1
See also WLC

Maurhut, Richard
See Traven, B.

Mauriac, Claude 1914-............. CLC 9
See also CA 89-92; DLB 83

Mauriac, Francois (Charles)
1885-1970 .... CLC 4, 9, 56
See also CA 25-28; CAP 2; DLB 65;
MTCW

Mavor, Osborne Henry 1888-1951
See Bridie, James
See also CA 104

Maxwell, William (Keepers Jr.)
1908- .... CLC 19
See also CA 93-96; DLBY 80

May, Elaine 1932- .... CLC 16
See also CA 124; DLB 44

Mayakovski, Vladimir (Vladimirovich)
1893-1930 .... TCLC 4, 18
See also CA 104

Mayhew, Henry 1812-1887 ...... NCLC 31
See also DLB 18, 55

Maynard, Joyce 1953-............ CLC 23
See also CA 111; 129

Mayne, William (James Carter)
1928- .... CLC 12
See also CA 9-12R; CANR 37; CLR 25;
MAICYA; SAAS 11; SATA 6, 68

Mayo, Jim
See L'Amour, Louis (Dearborn)

Maysles, Albert 1926- .... CLC 16
See also CA 29-32R

Maysles, David 1932-............. CLC 16

Mazer, Norma Fox 1931- .... CLC 26
See also AAYA 5; CA 69-72; CANR 12,
32; CLR 23; MAICYA; SAAS 1;
SATA 24, 67

Mazzini, Guiseppe 1805-1872 .... NCLC 34

Mazzini, Guiseppe 1805-1872 .... NCLC 34

McAuley, James Phillip
1917-1976 .... CLC 45
See also CA 97-100

McBain, Ed
See Hunter, Evan

McBrien, William Augustine
1930- .... CLC 44
See also CA 107

McCaffrey, Anne (Inez) 1926-...... CLC 17
See also AAYA 6; AITN 2; BEST 89:2;
CA 25-28R; CANR 15, 35; DLB 8;
MAICYA; MTCW; SAAS 11; SATA 8,
70

McCann, Arthur
See Campbell, John W(ood Jr.)

McCann, Edson
See Pohl, Frederik

McCarthy, Cormac 1933-........ CLC 4, 57
See also CA 13-16R; CANR 10; DLB 6

McCarthy, Mary (Therese)
1912-1989 ... CLC 1, 3, 5, 14, 24, 39, 59
See also CA 5-8R; 129; CANR 16; DLB 2;
DLBY 81; MTCW

McCartney, (James) Paul
1942- .... CLC 12, 35

McCauley, Stephen 19th cent. (?)- .. CLC 50

McClure, Michael (Thomas)
1932- .... CLC 6, 10
See also CA 21-24R; CANR 17; DLB 16

McCorkle, Jill (Collins) 1958-...... CLC 51
See also CA 121; DLBY 87

McCourt, James 1941-............. CLC 5
See also CA 57-60

McCoy, Horace (Stanley)
1897-1955 .... TCLC 28
See also CA 108; DLB 9

McCrae, John 1872-1918......... TCLC 12
See also CA 109; DLB 92

McCreigh, James
See Pohl, Frederik

McCullers, (Lula) Carson (Smith)
1917-1967 .. CLC 1, 4, 10, 12, 48; SSC 9
See also CA 5-8R; 25-28R; CABS 1, 3;
CANR 18; CDALB 1941-1968; DLB 2, 7;
MTCW; SATA 27; WLC

McCulloch, John Tyler
See Burroughs, Edgar Rice

McCullough, Colleen 1938(?)-...... CLC 27
See also CA 81-84; CANR 17; MTCW

McElroy, Joseph 1930- .... CLC 5, 47
See also CA 17-20R

McEwan, Ian (Russell) 1948- ... CLC 13, 66
See also BEST 90:4; CA 61-64; CANR 14;
DLB 14; MTCW

McFadden, David 1940-........... CLC 48
See also CA 104; DLB 60

McFarland, Dennis 1950- .... CLC 65

McGahern, John 1934-........ CLC 5, 9, 48
See also CA 17-20R; CANR 29; DLB 14;
MTCW

McGinley, Patrick (Anthony)
1937- .... CLC 41
See also CA 120; 127

McGinley, Phyllis 1905-1978 ...... CLC 14
See also CA 9-12R; 77-80; CANR 19;
DLB 11, 48; SATA 2, 24, 44

McGinniss, Joe 1942-............. CLC 32
See also AITN 2; BEST 89:2; CA 25-28R;
CANR 26

Author Index

Miller, Arthur
1915- ...... **CLC 1, 2, 6, 10, 15, 26, 47;**
DC 1
See also AITN 1; CA 1-4R; CABS 3;
CANR 2, 30; CDALB 1941-1968; DLB 7;
MTCW; WLC

Miller, Henry (Valentine)
1891-1980 ...... **CLC 1, 2, 4, 9, 14, 43**
See also CA 9-12R; 97-100; CANR 33;
CDALB 1929-1941; DLB 4, 9; DLBY 80;
MTCW; WLC

Miller, Jason 1939(?)- .... **CLC 2**
See also AITN 1; CA 73-76; DLB 7

Miller, Sue 19th cent. (?)- .... **CLC 44**
See also BEST 90:3

Miller, Walter M(ichael Jr.)
1923- .... **CLC 4, 30**
See also CA 85-88; DLB 8

Millett, Kate 1934-.............. **CLC 67**
See also AITN 1; CA 73-76; CANR 32;
MTCW

Millhauser, Steven 1943-....... **CLC 21, 54**
See also CA 110; 111; DLB 2

Millin, Sarah Gertrude 1889-1968 .. **CLC 49**
See also CA 102; 93-96

Milne, A(lan) A(lexander)
1882-1956 .... **TCLC 6**
See also CA 104; 133; CLR 1, 26; DLB 10,
77, 100; MAICYA; MTCW; YABC 1

Milner, Ron(ald) 1938-.......... **CLC 56**
See also AITN 1; BLC 3; BW; CA 73-76;
CANR 24; DLB 38; MTCW

Milosz, Czeslaw
1911- .... **CLC 5, 11, 22, 31, 56**
See also CA 81-84; CANR 23; MTCW

Milton, John 1608-1674............. **LC 9**
See also CDBLB 1660-1789; WLC

Minehaha, Cornelius
See Wedekind, (Benjamin) Frank(lin)

Miner, Valerie 1947- .... **CLC 40**
See also CA 97-100

Minimo, Duca
See D'Annunzio, Gabriele

Minot, Susan 1956- .... **CLC 44**
See also CA 134

Minus, Ed 1938-................. **CLC 39**

Miranda, Javier
See Bioy Casares, Adolfo

Miro (Ferrer), Gabriel (Francisco Victor)
1879-1930 .... **TCLC 5**
See also CA 104

Mishima, Yukio
.... **CLC 2, 4, 6, 9, 27; DC 1; SSC 4**
See also Hiraoka, Kimitake

Mistral, Gabriela................. **TCLC 2**
See also Godoy Alcayaga, Lucila

Mistry, Rohinton 1952-.......... **CLC 71**

Mitchell, Clyde
See Ellison, Harlan; Silverberg, Robert

Mitchell, James Leslie 1901-1935
See Gibbon, Lewis Grassic
See also CA 104; DLB 15

Mitchell, Joni 1943-............. **CLC 12**
See also CA 112

Mitchell, Margaret (Munnerlyn)
1900-1949 .... **TCLC 11**
See also CA 109; 125; DLB 9; MTCW

Mitchell, Peggy
See Mitchell, Margaret (Munnerlyn)

Mitchell, S(ilas) Weir 1829-1914 .. **TCLC 36**

Mitchell, W(illiam) O(rmond)
1914- .... **CLC 25**
See also CA 77-80; CANR 15; DLB 88

Mitford, Mary Russell 1787-1855.. **NCLC 4**
See also DLB 110, 116

Mitford, Nancy 1904-1973........ **CLC 44**
See also CA 9-12R

Miyamoto, Yuriko 1899-1951 ..... **TCLC 37**

Mo, Timothy (Peter) 1950(?)-...... **CLC 46**
See also CA 117; MTCW

Modarressi, Taghi (M.) 1931-...... **CLC 44**
See also CA 121; 134

Modiano, Patrick (Jean) 1945- ..... **CLC 18**
See also CA 85-88; CANR 17; DLB 83

Moerck, Paal
See Roelvaag, O(le) E(dvart)

Mofolo, Thomas (Mokopu)
1875(?)-1948 .... **TCLC 22**
See also BLC 3; CA 121

Mohr, Nicholasa 1935-............ **CLC 12**
See also AAYA 8; CA 49-52; CANR 1, 32;
CLR 22; HW; SAAS 8; SATA 8

Mojtabai, A(nn) G(race)
1938- .... **CLC 5, 9, 15, 29**
See also CA 85-88

Moliere 1622-1673 .... **LC 10**
See also WLC

Molin, Charles
See Mayne, William (James Carter)

Molnar, Ferenc 1878-1952........ **TCLC 20**
See also CA 109

Momaday, N(avarre) Scott
1934- .... **CLC 2, 19**
See also CA 25-28R; CANR 14, 34;
MTCW; SATA 30, 48

Monroe, Harriet 1860-1936....... **TCLC 12**
See also CA 109; DLB 54, 91

Monroe, Lyle
See Heinlein, Robert A(nson)

Montagu, Elizabeth 1917-........ **NCLC 7**
See also CA 9-12R

Montagu, Mary (Pierrepont) Wortley
1689-1762 .... **LC 9**
See also DLB 95, 101

Montague, John (Patrick)
1929- .... **CLC 13, 46**
See also CA 9-12R; CANR 9; DLB 40;
MTCW

Montaigne, Michel (Eyquem) de
1533-1592 .... **LC 8**
See also WLC

Montale, Eugenio 1896-1981... **CLC 7, 9, 18**
See also CA 17-20R; 104; CANR 30;
DLB 114; MTCW

Montesquieu, Charles-Louis de Secondat
1689-1755 .... **LC 7**

Montgomery, (Robert) Bruce 1921-1978
See Crispin, Edmund
See also CA 104

Montgomery, Marion H. Jr. 1925-... **CLC 7**
See also AITN 1; CA 1-4R; CANR 3;
DLB 6

Montgomery, Max
See Davenport, Guy (Mattison Jr.)

Montherlant, Henry (Milon) de
1896-1972 .... **CLC 8, 19**
See also CA 85-88; 37-40R; DLB 72;
MTCW

Monty Python .... **CLC 21**
See also Chapman, Graham; Cleese, John
(Marwood); Gilliam, Terry (Vance); Idle,
Eric; Jones, Terence Graham Parry; Palin,
Michael (Edward)
See also AAYA 7

Moodie, Susanna (Strickland)
1803-1885 .... **NCLC 14**
See also DLB 99

Mooney, Edward 1951- .... **CLC 25**
See also CA 130

Mooney, Ted
See Mooney, Edward

Moorcock, Michael (John)
1939- .... **CLC 5, 27, 58**
See also CA 45-48; CAAS 5; CANR 2, 17,
38; DLB 14; MTCW

Moore, Brian
1921- .... **CLC 1, 3, 5, 7, 8, 19, 32**
See also CA 1-4R; CANR 1, 25; MTCW

Moore, Edward
See Muir, Edwin

Moore, George Augustus
1852-1933 .... **TCLC 7**
See also CA 104; DLB 10, 18, 57

Moore, Lorrie .... **CLC 39, 45, 68**
See also Moore, Marie Lorena

Moore, Marianne (Craig)
1887-1972 ... **CLC 1, 2, 4, 8, 10, 13, 19,**
47; PC 4
See also CA 1-4R; 33-36R; CANR 3;
CDALB 1929-1941; DLB 45; DLBD 7;
MTCW; SATA 20

Moore, Marie Lorena 1957-
See Moore, Lorrie
See also CA 116; CANR 39

Moore, Thomas 1779-1852....... **NCLC 6**
See also DLB 96

Morand, Paul 1888-1976.......... **CLC 41**
See also CA 69-72; DLB 65

Morante, Elsa 1918-1985....... **CLC 8, 47**
See also CA 85-88; 117; CANR 35; MTCW

Moravia, Alberto....... **CLC 2, 7, 11, 27, 46**
See also Pincherle, Alberto

More, Hannah 1745-1833 .... **NCLC 27**
See also DLB 107, 109, 116

More, Henry 1614-1687............. **LC 9**

More, Sir Thomas 1478-1535 .... **LC 10**

Moreas, Jean.................... **TCLC 18**
See also Papadiamantopoulos, Johannes

Morgan, Berry 1919-............. **CLC 6**
See also CA 49-52; DLB 6

Morgan, Claire
See Highsmith, (Mary) Patricia

Morgan, Edwin (George) 1920- ..... **CLC 31**
See also CA 5-8R; CANR 3; DLB 27

Morgan, (George) Frederick
1922- .... **CLC 23**
See also CA 17-20R; CANR 21

Morgan, Harriet
See Mencken, H(enry) L(ouis)

Morgan, Jane
See Cooper, James Fenimore

Morgan, Janet 1945- .... **CLC 39**
See also CA 65-68

Morgan, Lady 1776(?)-1859 ...... **NCLC 29**
See also DLB 116

Morgan, Robin 1941- .... **CLC 2**
See also CA 69-72; CANR 29; MTCW

Morgan, Scott
See Kuttner, Henry

Morgan, Seth 1949(?)-1990 .... **CLC 65**
See also CA 132

Morgenstern, Christian
1871-1914 .... **TCLC 8**
See also CA 105

Morgenstern, S.
See Goldman, William (W.)

Moricz, Zsigmond 1879-1942 ..... **TCLC 33**

Morike, Eduard (Friedrich)
1804-1875 .... **NCLC 10**

Mori Ogai .... **TCLC 14**
See also Mori Rintaro

Mori Rintaro 1862-1922
See Mori Ogai
See also CA 110

Moritz, Karl Philipp 1756-1793 ...... **LC 2**
See also DLB 94

Morren, Theophil
See Hofmannsthal, Hugo von

Morris, Julian
See West, Morris L(anglo)

Morris, Steveland Judkins 1950(?)-
See Wonder, Stevie
See also CA 111

Morris, William 1834-1896 .... **NCLC 4**
See also CDBLB 1832-1890; DLB 18, 35, 57

Morris, Wright 1910- ... **CLC 1, 3, 7, 18, 37**
See also CA 9-12R; CANR 21; DLB 2;
DLBY 81; MTCW

Morrison, Chloe Anthony Wofford
See Morrison, Toni

Morrison, James Douglas 1943-1971
See Morrison, Jim
See also CA 73-76

Morrison, Jim .... **CLC 17**
See also Morrison, James Douglas

Morrison, Toni 1931- ..... **CLC 4, 10, 22, 55**
See also AAYA 1; BLC 3; BW; CA 29-32R;
CANR 27; CDALB 1968-1988; DLB 6,
33; DLBY 81; MTCW; SATA 57

Morrison, Van 1945- .... **CLC 21**
See also CA 116

Mortimer, John (Clifford)
1923- .... **CLC 28, 43**
See also CA 13-16R; CANR 21;
CDBLB 1960 to Present; DLB 13;
MTCW

Mortimer, Penelope (Ruth) 1918- .... **CLC 5**
See also CA 57-60

Morton, Anthony
See Creasey, John

Mosher, Howard Frank .... **CLC 62**

Mosley, Nicholas 1923- .... **CLC 43, 70**
See also CA 69-72; DLB 14

Moss, Howard
1922-1987 .... **CLC 7, 14, 45, 50**
See also CA 1-4R; 123; CANR 1; DLB 5

Motion, Andrew 1952- .... **CLC 47**
See also DLB 40

Motley, Willard (Francis)
1912-1965 .... **CLC 18**
See also BW; CA 117; 106; DLB 76

Mott, Michael (Charles Alston)
1930- .... **CLC 15, 34**
See also CA 5-8R; CAAS 7; CANR 7, 29

Mowat, Farley (McGill) 1921- ..... **CLC 26**
See also AAYA 1; CA 1-4R; CANR 4, 24;
CLR 20; DLB 68; MAICYA; MTCW;
SATA 3, 55

Mphahlele, Es'kia
See Mphahlele, Ezekiel

Mphahlele, Ezekiel 1919- .... **CLC 25**
See also BLC 3; BW; CA 81-84; CANR 26

Mqhayi, S(amuel) E(dward) K(rune Loliwe)
1875-1945 .... **TCLC 25**
See also BLC 3

Mr. Martin
See Burroughs, William S(eward)

Mrozek, Slawomir 1930- .... **CLC 3, 13**
See also CA 13-16R; CAAS 10; CANR 29;
MTCW

Mrs. Belloc-Lowndes
See Lowndes, Marie Adelaide (Belloc)

Mtwa, Percy 19th cent. (?)- .... **CLC 47**

Mueller, Lisel 1924- .... **CLC 13, 51**
See also CA 93-96; DLB 105

Muir, Edwin 1887-1959 .... **TCLC 2**
See also CA 104; DLB 20, 100

Muir, John 1838-1914 .... **TCLC 28**

Mujica Lainez, Manuel
1910-1984 .... **CLC 31**
See also Lainez, Manuel Mujica
See also CA 81-84; 112; CANR 32; HW

Mukherjee, Bharati 1940- .... **CLC 53**
See also BEST 89:2; CA 107; DLB 60;
MTCW

Muldoon, Paul 1951- .... **CLC 32, 72**
See also CA 113; 129; DLB 40

Mulisch, Harry 1927- .... **CLC 42**
See also CA 9-12R; CANR 6, 26

Mull, Martin 1943- .... **CLC 17**
See also CA 105

Mulock, Dinah Maria
See Craik, Dinah Maria (Mulock)

Munford, Robert 1737(?)-1783 .... **LC 5**
See also DLB 31

Mungo, Raymond 1946- .... **CLC 72**
See also CA 49-52; CANR 2

Munro, Alice
1931- .... **CLC 6, 10, 19, 50; SSC 3**
See also AITN 2; CA 33-36R; CANR 33;
DLB 53; MTCW; SATA 29

Munro, H(ector) H(ugh) 1870-1916
See Saki
See also CA 104; 130; CDBLB 1890-1914;
DLB 34; MTCW; WLC

Murasaki, Lady .... **CMLC 1**

Murdoch, (Jean) Iris
1919- ...... **CLC 1, 2, 3, 4, 6, 8, 11, 15,
22, 31, 51**
See also CA 13-16R; CANR 8;
CDBLB 1960 to Present; DLB 14;
MTCW

Murphy, Richard 1927- .... **CLC 41**
See also CA 29-32R; DLB 40

Murphy, Sylvia 1937- .... **CLC 34**
See also CA 121

Murphy, Thomas (Bernard) 1935-... **CLC 51**
See also CA 101

Murray, Les(lie) A(llan) 1938- ..... **CLC 40**
See also CA 21-24R; CANR 11, 27

Murry, J. Middleton
See Murry, John Middleton

Murry, John Middleton
1889-1957 .... **TCLC 16**
See also CA 118

Musgrave, Susan 1951- .... **CLC 13, 54**
See also CA 69-72

Musil, Robert (Edler von)
1880-1942 .... **TCLC 12**
See also CA 109; DLB 81

Musset, (Louis Charles) Alfred de
1810-1857 .... **NCLC 7**

My Brother's Brother
See Chekhov, Anton (Pavlovich)

Myers, Walter Dean 1937- .... **CLC 35**
See also AAYA 4; BLC 3; BW; CA 33-36R;
CANR 20; CLR 4, 16; DLB 33;
MAICYA; SAAS 2; SATA 27, 41, 70, 71

Myers, Walter M.
See Myers, Walter Dean

Myles, Symon
See Follett, Ken(neth Martin)

Nabokov, Vladimir (Vladimirovich)
1899-1977 .... **CLC 1, 2, 3, 6, 8, 11, 15,
23, 44, 46, 64**
See also CA 5-8R; 69-72; CANR 20;
CDALB 1941-1968; DLB 2; DLBD 3;
DLBY 80, 91; MTCW; WLC

Nagy, Laszlo 1925-1978 .... **CLC 7**
See also CA 129; 112

Naipaul, Shiva(dhar Srinivasa)
1945-1985 .... **CLC 32, 39**
See also CA 110; 112; 116; CANR 33;
DLBY 85; MTCW

Naipaul, V(idiadhar) S(urajprasad)
1932- .... **CLC 4, 7, 9, 13, 18, 37**
See also CA 1-4R; CANR 1, 33;
CDBLB 1960 to Present; DLBY 85,
MTCW

Nakos, Lilika 1899(?)- .... **CLC 29**

Narayan, R(asipuram) K(rishnaswami)
  1906- .... **CLC 7, 28, 47**
  See also CA 81-84; CANR 33; MTCW;
  SATA 62

Nash, (Frediric) Ogden 1902-1971 .. **CLC 23**
  See also CA 13-14; 29-32R; CANR 34;
  CAP 1; DLB 11; MAICYA; MTCW;
  SATA 2, 46

Nathan, Daniel
  See Dannay, Frederic

Nathan, George Jean 1882-1958 ... **TCLC 18**
  See also Hatteras, Owen
  See also CA 114

Natsume, Kinnosuke 1867-1916
  See Natsume, Soseki
  See also CA 104

Natsume, Soseki .... **TCLC 2, 10**
  See also Natsume, Kinnosuke

Natti, (Mary) Lee 1919-
  See Kingman, Lee
  See also CA 5-8R; CANR 2

Naylor, Gloria 1950- .... **CLC 28, 52**
  See also AAYA 6; BLC 3; BW; CA 107;
  CANR 27; MTCW

Neihardt, John Gneisenau
  1881-1973 .... **CLC 32**
  See also CA 13-14; CAP 1; DLB 9, 54

Nekrasov, Nikolai Alekseevich
  1821-1878 .... **NCLC 11**

Nelligan, Emile 1879-1941....... **TCLC 14**
  See also CA 114; DLB 92

Nelson, Willie 1933-.............. **CLC 17**
  See also CA 107

Nemerov, Howard (Stanley)
  1920-1991 .... **CLC 2, 6, 9, 36**
  See also CA 1-4R; 134; CABS 2; CANR 1,
  27; DLB 6; DLBY 83; MTCW

Neruda, Pablo
  1904-1973 .... **CLC 1, 2, 5, 7, 9, 28, 62;
                                        PC 4**
  See also CA 19-20; 45-48; CAP 2; HW;
  MTCW; WLC

Nerval, Gerard de 1808-1855...... **NCLC 1**

Nervo, (Jose) Amado (Ruiz de)
  1870-1919 .... **TCLC 11**
  See also CA 109; 131; HW

Nessi, Pio Baroja y
  See Baroja (y Nessi), Pio

Neufeld, John (Arthur) 1938- ...... **CLC 17**
  See also CA 25-28R; CANR 11, 37;
  MAICYA; SAAS 3; SATA 6

Neville, Emily Cheney 1919-....... **CLC 12**
  See also CA 5-8R; CANR 3, 37; MAICYA;
  SAAS 2; SATA 1

Newbound, Bernard Slade 1930-
  See Slade, Bernard
  See also CA 81-84

Newby, P(ercy) H(oward)
  1918- .... **CLC 2, 13**
  See also CA 5-8R; CANR 32; DLB 15;
  MTCW

Newlove, Donald 1928- .... **CLC 6**
  See also CA 29-32R; CANR 25

Newlove, John (Herbert) 1938-..... **CLC 14**
  See also CA 21-24R; CANR 9, 25

Newman, Charles 1938-......... **CLC 2, 8**
  See also CA 21-24R

Newman, Edwin (Harold) 1919- .... **CLC 14**
  See also AITN 1; CA 69-72; CANR 5

Newman, John Henry
  1801-1890 .... **NCLC 38**
  See also DLB 18, 32, 55

Newton, Suzanne 1936- .... **CLC 35**
  See also CA 41-44R; CANR 14; SATA 5

Nexo, Martin Andersen
  1869-1954 .... **TCLC 43**

Nezval, Vitezslav 1900-1958 ...... **TCLC 44**
  See also CA 123

Ngema, Mbongeni 1955- .... **CLC 57**

Ngugi, James T(hiong'o)........ **CLC 3, 7, 13**
  See also Ngugi wa Thiong'o

Ngugi wa Thiong'o 1938-.......... **CLC 36**
  See also Ngugi, James T(hiong'o)
  See also BLC 3; BW; CA 81-84; CANR 27;
  MTCW

Nichol, B(arrie) P(hillip)
  1944-1988 .... **CLC 18**
  See also CA 53-56; DLB 53; SATA 66

Nichols, John (Treadwell) 1940-.... **CLC 38**
  See also CA 9-12R; CAAS 2; CANR 6;
  DLBY 82

Nichols, Peter (Richard)
  1927- .... **CLC 5, 36, 65**
  See also CA 104; CANR 33; DLB 13;
  MTCW

Nicolas, F. R. E.
  See Freeling, Nicolas

Niedecker, Lorine 1903-1970.... **CLC 10, 42**
  See also CA 25-28; CAP 2; DLB 48

Nietzsche, Friedrich (Wilhelm)
  1844-1900 .... **TCLC 10, 18**
  See also CA 107; 121

Nievo, Ippolito 1831-1861 .... **NCLC 22**

Nightingale, Anne Redmon 1943-
  See Redmon, Anne
  See also CA 103

Nik.T.O.
  See Annensky, Innokenty Fyodorovich

Nin, Anais
  1903-1977 ..... **CLC 1, 4, 8, 11, 14, 60;
                                        SSC 10**
  See also AITN 2; CA 13-16R; 69-72;
  CANR 22; DLB 2, 4; MTCW

Nissenson, Hugh 1933-.......... **CLC 4, 9**
  See also CA 17-20R; CANR 27; DLB 28

Niven, Larry .... **CLC 8**
  See also Niven, Laurence Van Cott
  See also DLB 8

Niven, Laurence Van Cott 1938-
  See Niven, Larry
  See also CA 21-24R; CAAS 12; CANR 14;
  MTCW

Nixon, Agnes Eckhardt 1927-...... **CLC 21**
  See also CA 110

Nizan, Paul 1905-1940........... **TCLC 40**
  See also DLB 72

Nkosi, Lewis 1936-.............. **CLC 45**
  See also BLC 3; BW; CA 65-68; CANR 27

Nodier, (Jean) Charles (Emmanuel)
  1780-1844 .... **NCLC 19**
  See also DLB 119

Nolan, Christopher 1965-......... **CLC 58**
  See also CA 111

Norden, Charles
  See Durrell, Lawrence (George)

Nordhoff, Charles (Bernard)
  1887-1947 ....**TCLC 23**
  See also CA 108; DLB 9; SATA 23

Norman, Marsha 1947- .... **CLC 28**
  See also CA 105; CABS 3; DLBY 84

Norris, Benjamin Franklin Jr.
  1870-1902 ....**TCLC 24**
  See also Norris, Frank
  See also CA 110

Norris, Frank
  See Norris, Benjamin Franklin Jr.
  See also CDALB 1865-1917; DLB 12, 71

Norris, Leslie 1921-.............. **CLC 14**
  See also CA 11-12; CANR 14; CAP 1;
  DLB 27

North, Andrew
  See Norton, Andre

North, Captain George
  See Stevenson, Robert Louis (Balfour)

North, Milou
  See Erdrich, Louise

Northrup, B. A.
  See Hubbard, L(afayette) Ron(ald)

North Staffs
  See Hulme, T(homas) E(rnest)

Norton, Alice Mary
  See Norton, Andre
  See also MAICYA; SATA 1, 43

Norton, Andre 1912- .... **CLC 12**
  See also Norton, Alice Mary
  See also CA 1-4R; CANR 2, 31; DLB 8, 52;
  MTCW

Norway, Nevil Shute 1899-1960
  See Shute, Nevil
  See also CA 102; 93-96

Norwid, Cyprian Kamil
  1821-1883 .... **NCLC 17**

Nosille, Nabrah
  See Ellison, Harlan

Nossack, Hans Erich 1901-1978..... **CLC 6**
  See also CA 93-96; 85-88; DLB 69

Nosu, Chuji
  See Ozu, Yasujiro

Nova, Craig 1945-.............. **CLC 7, 31**
  See also CA 45-48; CANR 2

Novak, Joseph
  See Kosinski, Jerzy (Nikodem)

Novalis 1772-1801 .... **NCLC 13**
  See also DLB 90

Nowlan, Alden (Albert) 1933-1983 .. **CLC 15**
  See also CA 9-12R; CANR 5; DLB 53

Noyes, Alfred 1880-1958 .... **TCLC 7**
  See also CA 104; DLB 20

Nunn, Kem 19th cent. (?)-......... **CLC 34**

Nye, Robert 1939- .... **CLC 13, 42**
  See also CA 33-36R; CANR 29; DLB 14;
  MTCW; SATA 6

Nyro, Laura 1947- . . . . CLC 17

Oates, Joyce Carol
1938- . . . . . **CLC 1, 2, 3, 6, 9, 11, 15, 19, 33, 52; SSC 6**
See also AITN 1; BEST 89:2; CA 5-8R;
CANR 25; CDALB 1968-1988; DLB 2, 5;
DLBY 81; MTCW; WLC

O'Brien, E. G.
See Clarke, Arthur C(harles)

O'Brien, Edna
1936- . . . CLC 3, 5, 8, 13, 36, 65; SSC 10
See also CA 1-4R; CANR 6; CDBLB 1960
to Present; DLB 14; MTCW

O'Brien, Fitz-James 1828-1862. . . NCLC 21
See also DLB 74

O'Brien, Flann. . . . . . . CLC 1, 4, 5, 7, 10, 47
See also O Nuallain, Brian

O'Brien, Richard 1942- . . . . CLC 17
See also CA 124

O'Brien, Tim 1946-. . . . . CLC 7, 19, 40
See also CA 85-88; DLBD 9; DLBY 80

Obstfelder, Sigbjoern 1866-1900. . . TCLC 23
See also CA 123

O'Casey, Sean
1880-1964 . . . . CLC 1, 5, 9, 11, 15
See also CA 89-92; CDBLB 1914-1945;
DLB 10; MTCW

O'Cathasaigh, Sean
See O'Casey, Sean

Ochs, Phil 1940-1976. . . . . CLC 17
See also CA 65-68

O'Connor, Edwin (Greene)
1918-1968 . . . . CLC 14
See also CA 93-96; 25-28R

O'Connor, (Mary) Flannery
1925-1964 . . . CLC 1, 2, 3, 6, 10, 13, 15, 21, 66; SSC 1
See also AAYA 7; CA 1-4R; CANR 3;
CDALB 1941-1968; DLB 2; DLBY 80;
MTCW; WLC

O'Connor, Frank. . . . . CLC 23; SSC 5
See also O'Donovan, Michael John

O'Dell, Scott 1898-1989. . . . . CLC 30
See also AAYA 3; CA 61-64; 129;
CANR 12, 30; CLR 1, 16; DLB 52;
MAICYA; SATA 12, 60

Odets, Clifford 1906-1963 . . . . CLC 2, 28
See also CA 85-88; DLB 7, 26; MTCW

O'Donnell, K. M.
See Malzberg, Barry N(athaniel)

O'Donnell, Lawrence
See Kuttner, Henry

O'Donovan, Michael John
1903-1966 . . . . CLC 14
See also O'Connor, Frank
See also CA 93-96

Oe, Kenzaburo 1935- . . . . CLC 10, 36
See also CA 97-100; CANR 36; MTCW

O'Faolain, Julia 1932- . . . . CLC 6, 19, 47
See also CA 81-84; CAAS 2; CANR 12;
DLB 14; MTCW

O'Faolain, Sean
1900-1991 . . . . CLC 1, 7, 14, 32, 70
See also CA 61-64; 134; CANR 12;
DLB 15; MTCW

O'Flaherty, Liam
1896-1984 . . . . CLC 5, 34; SSC 6
See also CA 101; 113; CANR 35; DLB 36;
DLBY 84; MTCW

Ogilvy, Gavin
See Barrie, J(ames) M(atthew)

O'Grady, Standish James
1846-1928 . . . . TCLC 5
See also CA 104

O'Grady, Timothy 1951- . . . . CLC 59
See also CA 138

O'Hara, Frank 1926-1966 . . . . . CLC 2, 5, 13
See also CA 9-12R; 25-28R; CANR 33;
DLB 5, 16; MTCW

O'Hara, John (Henry)
1905-1970 . . . . CLC 1, 2, 3, 6, 11, 42
See also CA 5-8R; 25-28R; CANR 31;
CDALB 1929-1941; DLB 9, 86; DLBD 2;
MTCW

O Hehir, Diana 1922- . . . . CLC 41
See also CA 93-96

Okigbo, Christopher (Ifenayichukwu)
1932-1967 . . . . CLC 25
See also BLC 3; BW; CA 77-80; MTCW

Olds, Sharon 1942-. . . . . CLC 32, 39
See also CA 101; CANR 18; DLB 120

Oldstyle, Jonathan
See Irving, Washington

Olesha, Yuri (Karlovich)
1899-1960 . . . . CLC 8
See also CA 85-88

Oliphant, Margaret (Oliphant Wilson)
1828-1897 . . . . NCLC 11
See also DLB 18

Oliver, Mary 1935-. . . . . CLC 19, 34
See also CA 21-24R; CANR 9; DLB 5

Olivier, Laurence (Kerr)
1907-1989 . . . . CLC 20
See also CA 111; 129

Olsen, Tillie 1913- . . . . CLC 4, 13
See also CA 1-4R; CANR 1; DLB 28;
DLBY 80; MTCW

Olson, Charles (John)
1910-1970 . . . . . CLC 1, 2, 5, 6, 9, 11, 29
See also CA 13-16; 25-28R; CABS 2;
CANR 35; CAP 1; DLB 5, 16; MTCW

Olson, Toby 1937- . . . . CLC 28
See also CA 65-68; CANR 9, 31

Olyesha, Yuri
See Olesha, Yuri (Karlovich)

Ondaatje, Michael 1943- . . . . CLC 14, 29, 51
See also CA 77-80; DLB 60

Oneal, Elizabeth 1934-
See Oneal, Zibby
See also CA 106; CANR 28; MAICYA;
SATA 30

Oneal, Zibby . . . . CLC 30
See also Oneal, Elizabeth
See also AAYA 5; CLR 13

O'Neill, Eugene (Gladstone)
1888-1953 . . . . TCLC 1, 6, 27
See also AITN 1; CA 110; 132;
CDALB 1929-1941; DLB 7; MTCW;
WLC

Onetti, Juan Carlos 1909- . . . . CLC 7, 10
See also CA 85-88; CANR 32; DLB 113;
HW; MTCW

O Nuallain, Brian 1911-1966
See O'Brien, Flann
See also CA 21-22; 25-28R; CAP 2

Oppen, George 1908-1984 . . . . CLC 7, 13, 34
See also CA 13-16R; 113; CANR 8; DLB 5

Oppenheim, E(dward) Phillips
1866-1946 . . . . TCLC 45
See also CA 111; DLB 70

Orlovitz, Gil 1918-1973 . . . . CLC 22
See also CA 77-80; 45-48; DLB 2, 5

Ortega y Gasset, Jose 1883-1955 . . . TCLC 9
See also CA 106; 130; HW; MTCW

Ortiz, Simon J(oseph) 1941- . . . . CLC 45
See also CA 134; DLB 120

Orton, Joe . . . . CLC 4, 13, 43
See also Orton, John Kingsley
See also CDBLB 1960 to Present; DLB 13

Orton, John Kingsley 1933-1967
See Orton, Joe
See also CA 85-88; CANR 35; MTCW

Orwell, George . . . . TCLC 2, 6, 15, 31
See also Blair, Eric (Arthur)
See also CDBLB 1945-1960; DLB 15, 98;
WLC

Osborne, David
See Silverberg, Robert

Osborne, George
See Silverberg, Robert

Osborne, John (James)
1929- . . . . CLC 1, 2, 5, 11, 45
See also CA 13-16R; CANR 21;
CDBLB 1945-1960; DLB 13; MTCW;
WLC

Osborne, Lawrence 1958- . . . . CLC 50

Oshima, Nagisa 1932- . . . . CLC 20
See also CA 116; 121

Oskison, John M(ilton)
1874-1947 . . . . TCLC 35

Ossoli, Sarah Margaret (Fuller marchesa d')
1810-1850
See Fuller, Margaret
See also SATA 25

Ostrovsky, Alexander
1823-1886 . . . . NCLC 30

Otero, Blas de 1916- . . . . CLC 11
See also CA 89-92

Otto, Whitney 1955-. . . . . CLC 70

Ouida . . . . TCLC 43
See also De La Ramee, (Marie) Louise
See also DLB 18

Ousmane, Sembene 1923- . . . . CLC 66
See also BLC 3; BW; CA 117; 125; MTCW

Ovid 43B.C.-18th cent. (?). . . CMLC 7; PC 2

Owen, Wilfred 1893-1918 . . . . . . TCLC 5, 27
See also CA 104; CDBLB 1914-1945;
DLB 20; WLC

Owens, Rochelle 1936-. . . . . CLC 8
See also CA 17-20R; CAAS 2; CANR 39

Oz, Amos 1939- . . . CLC 5, 8, 11, 27, 33, 54
See also CA 53-56; CANR 27; MTCW

Ozick, Cynthia 1928-...... CLC 3, 7, 28, 62
See also BEST 90:1; CA 17-20R; CANR 23;
DLB 28; DLBY 82; MTCW

Ozu, Yasujiro 1903-1963.......... CLC 16
See also CA 112

Pacheco, C.
See Pessoa, Fernando (Antonio Nogueira)

Pa Chin
See Li Fei-kan

Pack, Robert 1929-.............. CLC 13
See also CA 1-4R; CANR 3; DLB 5

Padgett, Lewis
See Kuttner, Henry

Padilla (Lorenzo), Heberto 1932-... CLC 38
See also AITN 1; CA 123; 131; HW

Page, Jimmy 1944-.............. CLC 12

Page, Louise 1955-.............. CLC 40

Page, P(atricia) K(athleen)
1916-...................... CLC 7, 18
See also CA 53-56; CANR 4, 22; DLB 68;
MTCW

Paget, Violet 1856-1935
See Lee, Vernon
See also CA 104

Paget-Lowe, Henry
See Lovecraft, H(oward) P(hillips)

Paglia, Camille 1947-............. CLC 68

Pakenham, Antonia
See Fraser, Antonia (Pakenham)

Palamas, Kostes 1859-1943....... TCLC 5
See also CA 105

Palazzeschi, Aldo 1885-1974...... CLC 11
See also CA 89-92; 53-56; DLB 114

Paley, Grace 1922-.... CLC 4, 6, 37; SSC 8
See also CA 25-28R; CANR 13; DLB 28;
MTCW

Palin, Michael (Edward) 1943-..... CLC 21
See also Monty Python
See also CA 107; CANR 35; SATA 67

Palliser, Charles 1947-............ CLC 65
See also CA 136

Palma, Ricardo 1833-1919........ TCLC 29

Pancake, Breece Dexter 1952-1979
See Pancake, Breece D'J
See also CA 123; 109

Pancake, Breece D'J.............. CLC 29
See also Pancake, Breece Dexter

Papadiamantis, Alexandros
1851-1911 .... TCLC 29

Papadiamantopoulos, Johannes 1856-1910
See Moreas, Jean
See also CA 117

Papini, Giovanni 1881-1956....... TCLC 22
See also CA 121

Paracelsus 1493-1541.............. LC 14

Parasol, Peter
See Stevens, Wallace

Parfenie, Maria
See Codrescu, Andrei

Parini, Jay (Lee) 1948-........... CLC 54
See also CA 97-100; CAAS 16; CANR 32

Park, Jordan
See Kornbluth, C(yril) M.; Pohl, Frederik

Parker, Bert
See Ellison, Harlan

Parker, Dorothy (Rothschild)
1893-1967 .... CLC 15, 68; SSC 2
See also CA 19-20; 25-28R; CAP 2;
DLB 11, 45, 86; MTCW

Parker, Robert B(rown) 1932-...... CLC 27
See also BEST 89:4; CA 49-52; CANR 1,
26; MTCW

Parkes, Lucas
See Harris, John (Wyndham Parkes Lucas)
Beynon

Parkin, Frank 1940-.............. CLC 43

Parkman, Francis Jr. 1823-1893.. NCLC 12
See also DLB 1, 30

Parks, Gordon (Alexander Buchanan)
1912- .... CLC 1, 16
See also AITN 2; BLC 3; BW; CA 41-44R;
CANR 26; DLB 33; SATA 8

Parnell, Thomas 1679-1718......... LC 3
See also DLB 94

Parra, Nicanor 1914-.............. CLC 2
See also CA 85-88; CANR 32; HW; MTCW

Parson Lot
See Kingsley, Charles

Partridge, Anthony
See Oppenheim, E(dward) Phillips

Pascoli, Giovanni 1855-1912...... TCLC 45

Pasolini, Pier Paolo
1922-1975 .... CLC 20, 37
See also CA 93-96; 61-64; MTCW

Pasquini
See Silone, Ignazio

Pastan, Linda (Olenik) 1932- ...... CLC 27
See also CA 61-64; CANR 18; DLB 5

Pasternak, Boris (Leonidovich)
1890-1960 .... CLC 7, 10, 18, 63
See also CA 127; 116; MTCW; WLC

Patchen, Kenneth 1911-1972... CLC 1, 2, 18
See also CA 1-4R; 33-36R; CANR 3, 35;
DLB 16, 48; MTCW

Pater, Walter (Horatio)
1839-1894 .... NCLC 7
See also CDBLB 1832-1890; DLB 57

Paterson, A(ndrew) B(arton)
1864-1941 .... TCLC 32

Paterson, Katherine (Womeldorf)
1932-..................... CLC 12, 30
See also AAYA 1; CA 21-24R; CANR 28;
CLR 7; DLB 52; MAICYA; MTCW;
SATA 13, 53

Patmore, Coventry Kersey Dighton
1823-1896 .... NCLC 9
See also DLB 35, 98

Paton, Alan (Stewart)
1903-1988 .... CLC 4, 10, 25, 55
See also CA 13-16; 125; CANR 22; CAP 1;
MTCW; SATA 11, 56; WLC

Paton Walsh, Gillian 1939-
See Walsh, Jill Paton
See also CANR 38; MAICYA; SAAS 3;
SATA 4

Paulding, James Kirke 1778-1860.. NCLC 2
See also DLB 3, 59, 74

Paulin, Thomas Neilson 1949-
See Paulin, Tom
See also CA 123; 128

Paulin, Tom..................... CLC 37
See also Paulin, Thomas Neilson
See also DLB 40

Paustovsky, Konstantin (Georgievich)
1892-1968 .... CLC 40
See also CA 93-96; 25-28R

Pavese, Cesare 1908-1950 .... TCLC 3
See also CA 104

Pavic, Milorad 1929-............. CLC 60
See also CA 136

Payne, Alan
See Jakes, John (William)

Paz, Gil
See Lugones, Leopoldo

Paz, Octavio
1914- ...... CLC 3, 4, 6, 10, 19, 51, 65;
PC 1
See also CA 73-76; CANR 32; DLBY 90;
HW; MTCW; WLC

Peacock, Molly 1947-............. CLC 60
See also CA 103; DLB 120

Peacock, Thomas Love
1785-1866 .... NCLC 22
See also DLB 96, 116

Peake, Mervyn 1911-1968....... CLC 7, 54
See also CA 5-8R; 25-28R; CANR 3;
DLB 15; MTCW; SATA 23

Pearce, Philippa .... CLC 21
See also Christie, (Ann) Philippa
See also CLR 9; MAICYA; SATA 1, 67

Pearl, Eric
See Elman, Richard

Pearson, T(homas) R(eid) 1956- .... CLC 39
See also CA 120; 130

Peck, John 1941-................. CLC 3
See also CA 49-52; CANR 3

Peck, Richard (Wayne) 1934-...... CLC 21
See also AAYA 1; CA 85-88; CANR 19,
38; MAICYA; SAAS 2; SATA 18, 55

Peck, Robert Newton 1928-........ CLC 17
See also AAYA 3; CA 81-84; CANR 31;
MAICYA; SAAS 1; SATA 21, 62

Peckinpah, (David) Sam(uel)
1925-1984 .... CLC 20
See also CA 109; 114

Pedersen, Knut 1859-1952
See Hamsun, Knut
See also CA 104; 119; MTCW

Peeslake, Gaffer
See Durrell, Lawrence (George)

Peguy, Charles Pierre
1873-1914 .... TCLC 10
See also CA 107

Pena, Ramon del Valle y
See Valle-Inclan, Ramon (Maria) del

Pendennis, Arthur Esquir
See Thackeray, William Makepeace

Pepys, Samuel 1633-1703.......... LC 11
See also CDBLB 1660-1789; DLB 101;
WLC

Percy, Walker
1916-1990 ... **CLC 2, 3, 6, 8, 14, 18, 47, 65**
See also CA 1-4R; 131; CANR 1, 23;
DLB 2; DLBY 80, 90; MTCW

Perec, Georges 1936-1982 .... **CLC 56**
See also DLB 83

Pereda (y Sanchez de Porrua), Jose Maria de
1833-1906 .... **TCLC 16**
See also CA 117

Pereda y Porrua, Jose Maria de
See Pereda (y Sanchez de Porrua), Jose
Maria de

Peregoy, George Weems
See Mencken, H(enry) L(ouis)

Perelman, S(idney) J(oseph)
1904-1979 ... **CLC 3, 5, 9, 15, 23, 44, 49**
See also AITN 1, 2; CA 73-76; 89-92;
CANR 18; DLB 11, 44; MTCW

Peret, Benjamin 1899-1959 .... **TCLC 20**
See also CA 117

Peretz, Isaac Loeb 1851(?)-1915... **TCLC 16**
See also CA 109

Peretz, Yitzkhok Leibush
See Peretz, Isaac Loeb

Perez Galdos, Benito 1843-1920... **TCLC 27**
See also CA 125; HW

Perrault, Charles 1628-1703 .... **LC 2**
See also MAICYA; SATA 25

Perry, Brighton
See Sherwood, Robert E(mmet)

Perse, Saint-John
See Leger, (Marie-Rene) Alexis Saint-Leger

Perse, St.-John .... **CLC 4, 11, 46**
See also Leger, (Marie-Rene) Alexis
Saint-Leger

Peseenz, Tulio F.
See Lopez y Fuentes, Gregorio

Pesetsky, Bette 1932-............. **CLC 28**
See also CA 133

Peshkov, Alexei Maximovich 1868-1936
See Gorky, Maxim
See also CA 105

Pessoa, Fernando (Antonio Nogueira)
1888-1935 .... **TCLC 27**
See also CA 125

Peterkin, Julia Mood 1880-1961.... **CLC 31**
See also CA 102; DLB 9

Peters, Joan K. 1945-............. **CLC 39**

Peters, Robert L(ouis) 1924-........ **CLC 7**
See also CA 13-16R; CAAS 8; DLB 105

Petofi, Sandor 1823-1849........ **NCLC 21**

Petrakis, Harry Mark 1923-........ **CLC 3**
See also CA 9-12R; CANR 4, 30

Petrov, Evgeny .... **TCLC 21**
See also Kataev, Evgeny Petrovich

Petry, Ann (Lane) 1908- ...... **CLC 1, 7, 18**
See also BW; CA 5-8R; CAAS 6; CANR 4;
CLR 12; DLB 76; MAICYA; MTCW;
SATA 5

Petursson, Hallgrimur 1614-1674 .... **LC 8**

Philipson, Morris H. 1926-........ **CLC 53**
See also CA 1-4R; CANR 4

Phillips, David Graham
1867-1911 .... **TCLC 44**
See also CA 108; DLB 9, 12

Phillips, Jack
See Sandburg, Carl (August)

Phillips, Jayne Anne 1952- ..... **CLC 15, 33**
See also CA 101; CANR 24; DLBY 80;
MTCW

Phillips, Richard
See Dick, Philip K(indred)

Phillips, Robert (Schaeffer) 1938-... **CLC 28**
See also CA 17-20R; CAAS 13; CANR 8;
DLB 105

Phillips, Ward
See Lovecraft, H(oward) P(hillips)

Piccolo, Lucio 1901-1969.......... **CLC 13**
See also CA 97-100; DLB 114

Pickthall, Marjorie L(owry) C(hristie)
1883-1922 .... **TCLC 21**
See also CA 107; DLB 92

Pico della Mirandola, Giovanni
1463-1494 .... **LC 15**

Piercy, Marge
1936- .... **CLC 3, 6, 14, 18, 27, 62**
See also CA 21-24R; CAAS 1; CANR 13;
DLB 120; MTCW

Piers, Robert
See Anthony, Piers

Pieyre de Mandiargues, Andre 1909-1991
See Mandiargues, Andre Pieyre de
See also CA 103; 136; CANR 22

Pilnyak, Boris .... **TCLC 23**
See also Vogau, Boris Andreyevich

Pincherle, Alberto 1907-1990... **CLC 11, 18**
See also Moravia, Alberto
See also CA 25-28R; 132; CANR 33;
MTCW

Pineda, Cecile 1942-............. **CLC 39**
See also CA 118

Pinero, Arthur Wing 1855-1934... **TCLC 32**
See also CA 110; DLB 10

Pinero, Miguel (Antonio Gomez)
1946-1988 .... **CLC 4, 55**
See also CA 61-64; 125; CANR 29; HW

Pinget, Robert 1919- .... **CLC 7, 13, 37**
See also CA 85-88; DLB 83

Pink Floyd .... **CLC 35**
See also Barrett, (Roger) Syd; Gilmour,
David; Mason, Nick; Waters, Roger;
Wright, Rick

Pinkney, Edward 1802-1828 ..... **NCLC 31**

Pinkwater, Daniel Manus 1941-.... **CLC 35**
See also Pinkwater, Manus
See also AAYA 1; CA 29-32R; CANR 12,
38; CLR 4; MAICYA; SAAS 3; SATA 46

Pinkwater, Manus
See Pinkwater, Daniel Manus
See also SATA 8

Pinsky, Robert 1940-........ **CLC 9, 19, 38**
See also CA 29-32R; CAAS 4; DLBY 82

Pinta, Harold
See Pinter, Harold

Pinter, Harold
1930- ..... **CLC 1, 3, 6, 9, 11, 15, 27, 58**
See also CA 5-8R; CANR 33; CDBLB 1960
to Present; DLB 13; MTCW; WLC

Pirandello, Luigi 1867-1936..... **TCLC 4, 29**
See also CA 104; WLC

Pirsig, Robert M(aynard) 1928- ... **CLC 4, 6**
See also CA 53-56; MTCW; SATA 39

Pisarev, Dmitry Ivanovich
1840-1868 .... **NCLC 25**

Pix, Mary (Griffith) 1666-1709....... **LC 8**
See also DLB 80

Plaidy, Jean
See Hibbert, Eleanor Burford

Plant, Robert 1948- .... **CLC 12**

Plante, David (Robert)
1940- .... **CLC 7, 23, 38**
See also CA 37-40R; CANR 12, 36;
DLBY 83; MTCW

Plath, Sylvia
1932-1963 .... **CLC 1, 2, 3, 5, 9, 11, 14,
17, 50, 51, 62; PC 1**
See also CA 19-20; CANR 34; CAP 2;
CDALB 1941-1968; DLB 5, 6; MTCW;
WLC

Plato 428(?)B.C.-348(?)B.C........ **CMLC 8**

Platonov, Andrei .... **TCLC 14**
See also Klimentov, Andrei Platonovich

Platt, Kin 1911- .... **CLC 26**
See also CA 17-20R; CANR 11; SATA 21

Plick et Plock
See Simenon, Georges (Jacques Christian)

Plimpton, George (Ames) 1927-..... **CLC 36**
See also AITN 1; CA 21-24R; CANR 32;
MTCW; SATA 10

Plomer, William Charles Franklin
1903-1973 .... **CLC 4, 8**
See also CA 21-22; CANR 34; CAP 2;
DLB 20; MTCW; SATA 24

Plowman, Piers
See Kavanagh, Patrick (Joseph)

Plum, J.
See Wodehouse, P(elham) G(renville)

Plumly, Stanley (Ross) 1939- ...... **CLC 33**
See also CA 108; 110; DLB 5

Poe, Edgar Allan
1809-1849 ... **NCLC 1, 16; PC 1; SSC 1**
See also CDALB 1640-1865; DLB 3, 59, 73,
74; SATA 23; WLC

Poet of Titchfield Street, The
See Pound, Ezra (Weston Loomis)

Pohl, Frederik 1919- .... **CLC 18**
See also CA 61-64; CAAS 1; CANR 11, 37;
DLB 8; MTCW; SATA 24

Poirier, Louis 1910-
See Gracq, Julien
See also CA 122; 126

Poitier, Sidney 1927-............. **CLC 26**
See also BW; CA 117

Polanski, Roman 1933- .... **CLC 16**
See also CA 77-80

Poliakoff, Stephen 1952-.......... **CLC 38**
See also CA 106; DLB 13

Police .... CLC 26
See also Copeland, Stewart (Armstrong);
Summers, Andrew James; Sumner,
Gordon Matthew

Pollitt, Katha 1949- .... CLC 28
See also CA 120; 122; MTCW

Pollock, Sharon 1936- .... CLC 50
See also DLB 60

Pomerance, Bernard 1940-........ CLC 13
See also CA 101

Ponge, Francis (Jean Gaston Alfred)
1899-1988 .... CLC 6, 18
See also CA 85-88; 126

Pontoppidan, Henrik 1857-1943 ... TCLC 29

Poole, Josephine .... CLC 17
See also Helyar, Jane Penelope Josephine
See also SAAS 2; SATA 5

Popa, Vasko 1922- .... CLC 19
See also CA 112

Pope, Alexander 1688-1744 .... LC 3
See also CDBLB 1660-1789; DLB 95, 101;
WLC

Porter, Connie 1960- .... CLC 70

Porter, Gene(va Grace) Stratton
1863(?)-1924 .... TCLC 21
See also CA 112

Porter, Katherine Anne
1890-1980 ..... CLC 1, 3, 7, 10, 13, 15,
27; SSC 4
See also AITN 2; CA 1-4R; 101; CANR 1;
DLB 4, 9, 102; DLBY 80; MTCW;
SATA 23, 39

Porter, Peter (Neville Frederick)
1929- .... CLC 5, 13, 33
See also CA 85-88; DLB 40

Porter, William Sydney 1862-1910
See Henry, O.
See also CA 104; 131; CDALB 1865-1917;
DLB 12, 78, 79; MTCW; YABC 2

Portillo (y Pacheco), Jose Lopez
See Lopez Portillo (y Pacheco), Jose

Post, Melville Davisson
1869-1930 .... TCLC 39
See also CA 110

Potok, Chaim 1929- .... CLC 2, 7, 14, 26
See also AITN 1, 2; CA 17-20R; CANR 19,
35; DLB 28; MTCW; SATA 33

Potter, Beatrice
See Webb, (Martha) Beatrice (Potter)
See also MAICYA

Potter, Dennis (Christopher George)
1935- .... CLC 58
See also CA 107; CANR 33; MTCW

Pound, Ezra (Weston Loomis)
1885-1972 ..... CLC 1, 2, 3, 4, 5, 7, 10,
13, 18, 34, 48, 50; PC 4
See also CA 5-8R; 37-40R;
CDALB 1917-1929; DLB 4, 45, 63;
MTCW; WLC

Povod, Reinaldo 1959-............ CLC 44
See also CA 136

Powell, Anthony (Dymoke)
1905- .... CLC 1, 3, 7, 9, 10, 31
See also CA 1-4R; CANR 1, 32;
CDBLB 1945-1960; DLB 15; MTCW

Powell, Dawn 1897-1965 .... CLC 66
See also CA 5-8R

Powell, Padgett 1952-............. CLC 34
See also CA 126

Powers, J(ames) F(arl)
1917- .... CLC 1, 4, 8, 57; SSC 4
See also CA 1-4R; CANR 2; MTCW

Powers, John J(ames) 1945-
See Powers, John R.
See also CA 69-72

Powers, John R. .... CLC 66
See also Powers, John J(ames)

Pownall, David 1938-............. CLC 10
See also CA 89-92; DLB 14

Powys, John Cowper
1872-1963 .... CLC 7, 9, 15, 46
See also CA 85-88; DLB 15; MTCW

Powys, T(heodore) F(rancis)
1875-1953 .... TCLC 9
See also CA 106; DLB 36

Prager, Emily 1952-.............. CLC 56

Pratt, Edwin John 1883-1964 ...... CLC 19
See also CA 93-96; DLB 92

Premchand...................... TCLC 21
See also Srivastava, Dhanpat Rai

Preussler, Otfried 1923-........... CLC 17
See also CA 77-80; SATA 24

Prevert, Jacques (Henri Marie)
1900-1977 .... CLC 15
See also CA 77-80; 69-72; CANR 29;
MTCW; SATA 30

Prevost, Abbe (Antoine Francois)
1697-1763 .... LC 1

Price, (Edward) Reynolds
1933- .... CLC 3, 6, 13, 43, 50, 63
See also CA 1-4R; CANR 1, 37; DLB 2

Price, Richard 1949- .... CLC 6, 12
See also CA 49-52; CANR 3; DLBY 81

Prichard, Katharine Susannah
1883-1969 .... CLC 46
See also CA 11-12; CANR 33; CAP 1;
MTCW; SATA 66

Priestley, J(ohn) B(oynton)
1894-1984 .... CLC 2, 5, 9, 34
See also CA 9-12R; 113; CANR 33;
CDBLB 1914-1945; DLB 10, 34, 77, 100;
DLBY 84; MTCW

Prince, F(rank) T(empleton) 1912- .. CLC 22
See also CA 101; DLB 20

Prince 1958(?)- .... CLC 35

Prince Kropotkin
See Kropotkin, Peter (Aleksieevich)

Prior, Matthew 1664-1721.......... LC 4
See also DLB 95

Pritchard, William H(arrison)
1932- .... CLC 34
See also CA 65-68; CANR 23; DLB 111

Pritchett, V(ictor) S(awdon)
1900- .... CLC 5, 13, 15, 41
See also CA 61-64; CANR 31; DLB 15;
MTCW

Private 19022
See Manning, Frederic

Probst, Mark 1925- .... CLC 59
See also CA 130

Prokosch, Frederic 1908-1989.... CLC 4, 48
See also CA 73-76; 128; DLB 48

Prophet, The
See Dreiser, Theodore (Herman Albert)

Prose, Francine 1947-............. CLC 45
See also CA 109; 112

Proudhon
See Cunha, Euclides (Rodrigues Pimenta) da

Proust,
(Valentin-Louis-George-Eugene-)Marcel
1871-1922 .... TCLC 7, 13, 33
See also CA 104; 120; DLB 65; MTCW;
WLC

Prowler, Harley
See Masters, Edgar Lee

Pryor, Richard (Franklin Lenox Thomas)
1940- .... CLC 26
See also CA 122

Przybyszewski, Stanislaw
1868-1927 .... TCLC 36
See also DLB 66

Pteleon
See Grieve, C(hristopher) M(urray)

Puckett, Lute
See Masters, Edgar Lee

Puig, Manuel
1932-1990 .... CLC 3, 5, 10, 28, 65
See also CA 45-48; CANR 2, 32; DLB 113;
HW; MTCW

Purdy, A(lfred) W(ellington)
1918- .... CLC 3, 6, 14, 50
See also Purdy, Al
See also CA 81-84

Purdy, Al
See Purdy, A(lfred) W(ellington)
See also DLB 88

Purdy, James (Amos)
1923- .... CLC 2, 4, 10, 28, 52
See also CA 33-36R; CAAS 1; CANR 19;
DLB 2; MTCW

Pure, Simon
See Swinnerton, Frank Arthur

Pushkin, Alexander (Sergeyevich)
1799-1837 .... NCLC 3, 27
See also SATA 61; WLC

P'u Sung-ling 1640-1715 .... LC 3

Putnam, Arthur Lee
See Alger, Horatio Jr.

Puzo, Mario 1920-......... CLC 1, 2, 6, 36
See also CA 65-68; CANR 4; DLB 6;
MTCW

Pym, Barbara (Mary Crampton)
1913-1980 .... CLC 13, 19, 37
See also CA 13-14; 97-100; CANR 13, 34;
CAP 1; DLB 14; DLBY 87; MTCW

Pynchon, Thomas (Ruggles Jr.)
1937- .. CLC 2, 3, 6, 9, 11, 18, 33, 62, 72
See also BEST 90:2; CA 17-20R; CANR 22;
DLB 2; MTCW; WLC

Qian Zhongshu
See Ch'ien Chung-shu

Qroll
See Dagerman, Stig (Halvard)

Quarrington, Paul (Lewis)　1953-....　**CLC 65**
See also CA 129

Quasimodo, Salvatore　1901-1968　...　**CLC 10**
See also CA 13-16; 25-28R; CAP 1;
DLB 114; MTCW

Queen, Ellery.................　**CLC 3, 11**
See also Dannay, Frederic; Davidson,
Avram; Lee, Manfred B(ennington);
Sturgeon, Theodore (Hamilton); Vance,
John Holbrook

Queen, Ellery Jr.
See Dannay, Frederic; Lee, Manfred
B(ennington)

Queneau, Raymond
1903-1976　...........　**CLC 2, 5, 10, 42**
See also CA 77-80; 69-72; CANR 32;
DLB 72; MTCW

Quin, Ann (Marie)　1936-1973　.......　**CLC 6**
See also CA 9-12R; 45-48; DLB 14

Quinn, Martin
See Smith, Martin Cruz

Quinn, Simon
See Smith, Martin Cruz

Quiroga, Horacio (Sylvestre)
1878-1937　..................　**TCLC 20**
See also CA 117; 131; HW; MTCW

Quoirez, Francoise　1935-...........　**CLC 9**
See Sagan, Francoise
See also CA 49-52; CANR 6, 39; MTCW

Raabe, Wilhelm　1831-1910　.......　**TCLC 45**

Rabe, David (William)　1940-...　**CLC 4, 8, 33**
See also CA 85-88; CABS 3; DLB 7

Rabelais, Francois　1483-1553　........　**LC 5**
See also WLC

Rabinovitch, Sholem　1859-1916
See Aleichem, Sholom
See also CA 104

Radcliffe, Ann (Ward)　1764-1823　..　**NCLC 6**
See also DLB 39

Radiguet, Raymond　1903-1923　....　**TCLC 29**
See also DLB 65

Radnoti, Miklos　1909-1944　.......　**TCLC 16**
See also CA 118

Rado, James　1939-...............　**CLC 17**
See also CA 105

Radvanyi, Netty　1900-1983
See Seghers, Anna
See also CA 85-88; 110

Raeburn, John (Hay)　1941-........　**CLC 34**
See also CA 57-60

Ragni, Gerome　1942-1991　.........　**CLC 17**
See also CA 105; 134

Rahv, Philip....................　**CLC 24**
See also Greenberg, Ivan

Raine, Craig　1944-　.............　**CLC 32**
See also CA 108; CANR 29; DLB 40

Raine, Kathleen (Jessie)　1908-　...　**CLC 7, 45**
See also CA 85-88; DLB 20; MTCW

Rainis, Janis　1865-1929.........　**TCLC 29**

Rakosi, Carl.....................　**CLC 47**
See also Rawley, Callman
See also CAAS 5

Raleigh, Richard
See Lovecraft, H(oward) P(hillips)

Rallentando, H. P.
See Sayers, Dorothy L(eigh)

Ramal, Walter
See de la Mare, Walter (John)

Ramon, Juan
See Jimenez (Mantecon), Juan Ramon

Ramos, Graciliano　1892-1953　.....　**TCLC 32**

Rampersad, Arnold　1941-..........　**CLC 44**
See also CA 127; 133; DLB 111

Rampling, Anne
See Rice, Anne

Ramuz, Charles-Ferdinand
1878-1947　..................　**TCLC 33**

Rand, Ayn　1905-1982.......　**CLC 3, 30, 44**
See also CA 13-16R; 105; CANR 27;
MTCW; WLC

Randall, Dudley (Felker)　1914-......　**CLC 1**
See also BLC 3; BW; CA 25-28R;
CANR 23; DLB 41

Randall, Robert
See Silverberg, Robert

Ranger, Ken
See Creasey, John

Ransom, John Crowe
1888-1974　.........　**CLC 2, 4, 5, 11, 24**
See also CA 5-8R; 49-52; CANR 6, 34;
DLB 45, 63; MTCW

Rao, Raja　1909-　..............　**CLC 25, 56**
See also CA 73-76; MTCW

Raphael, Frederic (Michael)
1931-.....................　**CLC 2, 14**
See also CA 1-4R; CANR 1; DLB 14

Ratcliffe, James P.
See Mencken, H(enry) L(ouis)

Rathbone, Julian　1935-　...........　**CLC 41**
See also CA 101; CANR 34

Rattigan, Terence (Mervyn)
1911-1977　...................　**CLC 7**
See also CA 85-88; 73-76;
CDBLB 1945-1960; DLB 13; MTCW

Ratushinskaya, Irina　1954-　........　**CLC 54**
See also CA 129

Raven, Simon (Arthur Noel)
1927-　......................　**CLC 14**
See also CA 81-84

Rawley, Callman　1903-
See Rakosi, Carl
See also CA 21-24R; CANR 12, 32

Rawlings, Marjorie Kinnan
1896-1953　..................　**TCLC 4**
See also CA 104; 137; DLB 9, 22, 102;
MAICYA; YABC 1

Ray, Satyajit　1921-..............　**CLC 16**
See also CA 114; 137

Read, Herbert Edward　1893-1968....　**CLC 4**
See also CA 85-88; 25-28R; DLB 20

Read, Piers Paul　1941-　......　**CLC 4, 10, 25**
See also CA 21-24R; CANR 38; DLB 14;
SATA 21

Reade, Charles　1814-1884　........　**NCLC 2**
See also DLB 21

Reade, Hamish
See Gray, Simon (James Holliday)

Reading, Peter　1946-　.............　**CLC 47**
See also CA 103; DLB 40

Reaney, James　1926-　.............　**CLC 13**
See also CA 41-44R; CAAS 15; DLB 68;
SATA 43

Rebreanu, Liviu　1885-1944　.......　**TCLC 28**

Rechy, John (Francisco)
1934-　.............　**CLC 1, 7, 14, 18**
See also CA 5-8R; CAAS 4; CANR 6, 32;
DLBY 82; HW

Redcam, Tom　1870-1933　.........　**TCLC 25**

Reddin, Keith....................　**CLC 67**

Redgrove, Peter (William)
1932-　....................　**CLC 6, 41**
See also CA 1-4R; CANR 3, 39; DLB 40

Redmon, Anne....................　**CLC 22**
See also Nightingale, Anne Redmon
See also DLBY 86

Reed, Eliot
See Ambler, Eric

Reed, Ishmael
1938-　.......　**CLC 2, 3, 5, 6, 13, 32, 60**
See also BLC 3; BW; CA 21-24R;
CANR 25; DLB 2, 5, 33; DLBD 8;
MTCW

Reed, John (Silas)　1887-1920　......　**TCLC 9**
See also CA 106

Reed, Lou.......................　**CLC 21**
See also Firbank, Louis

Reeve, Clara　1729-1807.........　**NCLC 19**
See also DLB 39

Reid, Christopher　1949-...........　**CLC 33**
See also DLB 40

Reid, Desmond
See Moorcock, Michael (John)

Reid Banks, Lynne　1929-
See Banks, Lynne Reid
See also CA 1-4R; CANR 6, 22, 38;
CLR 24; MAICYA; SATA 22

Reilly, William K.
See Creasey, John

Reiner, Max
See Caldwell, (Janet Miriam) Taylor
(Holland)

Reis, Ricardo
See Pessoa, Fernando (Antonio Nogueira)

Remarque, Erich Maria
1898-1970　...................　**CLC 21**
See also CA 77-80; 29-32R; DLB 56;
MTCW

Remizov, A.
See Remizov, Aleksei (Mikhailovich)

Remizov, A. M.
See Remizov, Aleksei (Mikhailovich)

Remizov, Aleksei (Mikhailovich)
1877-1957　...................　**TCLC 27**
See also CA 125; 133

Renan, Joseph Ernest
1823-1892　...................　**NCLC 26**

Renard, Jules　1864-1910　........　**TCLC 17**
See also CA 117

Renault, Mary..............　**CLC 3, 11, 17**
See also Challans, Mary
See also DLBY 83

Rendell, Ruth (Barbara) 1930- .. **CLC 28, 48**
See also Vine, Barbara
See also CA 109; CANR 32; DLB 87;
MTCW

Renoir, Jean 1894-1979 . . . . **CLC 20**
See also CA 129; 85-88

Resnais, Alain 1922-. . . . . **CLC 16**

Reverdy, Pierre 1889-1960 . . . . **CLC 53**
See also CA 97-100; 89-92

Rexroth, Kenneth
1905-1982 . . . . . . **CLC 1, 2, 6, 11, 22, 49**
See also CA 5-8R; 107; CANR 14, 34;
CDALB 1941-1968; DLB 16, 48;
DLBY 82; MTCW

Reyes, Alfonso 1889-1959 . . . . **TCLC 33**
See also CA 131; HW

Reyes y Basoalto, Ricardo Eliecer Neftali
See Neruda, Pablo

Reymont, Wladyslaw (Stanislaw)
1868(?)-1925 . . . . **TCLC 5**
See also CA 104

Reynolds, Jonathan 1942- . . . . **CLC 6, 38**
See also CA 65-68; CANR 28

Reynolds, Joshua 1723-1792 . . . . **LC 15**
See also DLB 104

Reynolds, Michael Shane 1937- . . . . **CLC 44**
See also CA 65-68; CANR 9

Reznikoff, Charles 1894-1976 . . . . **CLC 9**
See also CA 33-36; 61-64; CAP 2; DLB 28,
45

Rezzori (d'Arezzo), Gregor von
1914- . . . . **CLC 25**
See also CA 122; 136

Rhine, Richard
See Silverstein, Alvin

Rhys, Jean
1890(?)-1979 . . . . **CLC 2, 4, 6, 14, 19, 51**
See also CA 25-28R; 85-88; CANR 35;
CDBLB 1945-1960; DLB 36, 117; MTCW

Ribeiro, Darcy 1922- . . . . **CLC 34**
See also CA 33-36R

Ribeiro, Joao Ubaldo (Osorio Pimentel)
1941- . . . . **CLC 10, 67**
See also CA 81-84

Ribman, Ronald (Burt) 1932- . . . . **CLC 7**
See also CA 21-24R

Ricci, Nino 1959- . . . . **CLC 70**
See also CA 137

Rice, Anne 1941- . . . . **CLC 41**
See also AAYA 9; BEST 89:2; CA 65-68;
CANR 12, 36

Rice, Elmer (Leopold)
1892-1967 . . . . **CLC 7, 49**
See also CA 21-22; 25-28R; CAP 2; DLB 4,
7; MTCW

Rice, Tim 1944- . . . . **CLC 21**
See also CA 103

Rich, Adrienne (Cecile)
1929- . . . . . **CLC 3, 6, 7, 11, 18, 36; PC 5**
See also CA 9-12R; CANR 20; DLB 5, 67;
MTCW

Rich, Barbara
See Graves, Robert (von Ranke)

Rich, Robert
See Trumbo, Dalton

Richards, David Adams 1950- . . . . . . **CLC 59**
See also CA 93-96; DLB 53

Richards, I(vor) A(rmstrong)
1893-1979 . . . . **CLC 14, 24**
See also CA 41-44R; 89-92; CANR 34;
DLB 27

Richardson, Anne
See Roiphe, Anne Richardson

Richardson, Dorothy Miller
1873-1957 . . . . **TCLC 3**
See also CA 104; DLB 36

Richardson, Ethel Florence (Lindesay)
1870-1946
See Richardson, Henry Handel
See also CA 105

Richardson, Henry Handel. . . . . **TCLC 4**
See also Richardson, Ethel Florence
(Lindesay)

Richardson, Samuel 1689-1761 . . . . **LC 1**
See also CDBLB 1660-1789; DLB 39; WLC

Richler, Mordecai
1931- . . . . **CLC 3, 5, 9, 13, 18, 46, 70**
See also AITN 1; CA 65-68; CANR 31;
CLR 17; DLB 53; MAICYA; MTCW;
SATA 27, 44

Richter, Conrad (Michael)
1890-1968 . . . . **CLC 30**
See also CA 5-8R; 25-28R; CANR 23;
DLB 9; MTCW; SATA 3

Riddell, J. H. 1832-1906 . . . . **TCLC 40**

Riding, Laura. . . . . **CLC 3, 7**
See also Jackson, Laura (Riding)

Riefenstahl, Berta Helene Amalia 1902-
See Riefenstahl, Leni
See also CA 108

Riefenstahl, Leni. . . . . **CLC 16**
See also Riefenstahl, Berta Helene Amalia

Riffe, Ernest
See Bergman, (Ernst) Ingmar

Riley, Tex
See Creasey, John

Rilke, Rainer Maria
1875-1926 . . . . **TCLC 1, 6, 19; PC 2**
See also CA 104; 132; DLB 81; MTCW

Rimbaud, (Jean Nicolas) Arthur
1854-1891 . . . . **NCLC 4, 35; PC 3**
See also WLC

Ringmaster, The
See Mencken, H(enry) L(ouis)

Ringwood, Gwen(dolyn Margaret) Pharis
1910-1984 . . . . **CLC 48**
See also CA 112; DLB 88

Rio, Michel 19th cent. (?)-. . . . . **CLC 43**

Ritsos, Giannes
See Ritsos, Yannis

Ritsos, Yannis 1909-1990 . . . . . **CLC 6, 13, 31**
See also CA 77-80; 133; CANR 39; MTCW

Ritter, Erika 1948(?)-. . . . . **CLC 52**

Rivera, Jose Eustasio 1889-1928 . . . **TCLC 35**
See also HW

Rivers, Conrad Kent 1933-1968. . . . . . **CLC 1**
See also BW; CA 85-88; DLB 41

Rivers, Elfrida
See Bradley, Marion Zimmer

Riverside, John
See Heinlein, Robert A(nson)

Rizal, Jose 1861-1896. . . . . **NCLC 27**

Roa Bastos, Augusto (Antonio)
1917- . . . . **CLC 45**
See also CA 131; DLB 113; HW

Robbe-Grillet, Alain
1922- . . . . . . **CLC 1, 2, 4, 6, 8, 10, 14, 43**
See also CA 9-12R; CANR 33; DLB 83;
MTCW

Robbins, Harold 1916-. . . . . **CLC 5**
See also CA 73-76; CANR 26; MTCW

Robbins, Thomas Eugene 1936-
See Robbins, Tom
See also CA 81-84; CANR 29; MTCW

Robbins, Tom. . . . . **CLC 9, 32, 64**
See also Robbins, Thomas Eugene
See also BEST 90:3; DLBY 80

Robbins, Trina 1938- . . . . **CLC 21**
See also CA 128

Roberts, Charles G(eorge) D(ouglas)
1860-1943 . . . . **TCLC 8**
See also CA 105; DLB 92; SATA 29

Roberts, Kate 1891-1985 . . . . **CLC 15**
See also CA 107; 116

Roberts, Keith (John Kingston)
1935-. . . . . **CLC 14**
See also CA 25-28R

Roberts, Kenneth (Lewis)
1885-1957 . . . . **TCLC 23**
See also CA 109; DLB 9

Roberts, Michele (B.) 1949-. . . . . **CLC 48**
See also CA 115

Robertson, Ellis
See Ellison, Harlan; Silverberg, Robert

Robertson, Thomas William
1829-1871 . . . . **NCLC 35**

Robertson, Thomas William
1829-1871 . . . . **NCLC 35**

Robinson, Edwin Arlington
1869-1935 . . . . **TCLC 5; PC 1**
See also CA 104; 133; CDALB 1865-1917;
DLB 54; MTCW

Robinson, Henry Crabb
1775-1867 . . . . **NCLC 15**
See also DLB 107

Robinson, Jill 1936-. . . . . **CLC 10**
See also CA 102

Robinson, Kim Stanley 1952- . . . . . . **CLC 34**
See also CA 126

Robinson, Lloyd
See Silverberg, Robert

Robinson, Marilynne 1944-. . . . . **CLC 25**
See also CA 116

Robinson, Smokey. . . . . **CLC 21**
See also Robinson, William Jr.

Robinson, William Jr. 1940-
See Robinson, Smokey
See also CA 116

Robison, Mary 1949-. . . . . **CLC 42**
See also CA 113; 116

Roddenberry, Eugene Wesley 1921-1991
    See Roddenberry, Gene
    See also CA 110; 135; CANR 37; SATA 45

Roddenberry, Gene . . . . **CLC 17**
    See also Roddenberry, Eugene Wesley
    See also AAYA 5; SATO 69

Rodgers, Mary 1931- . . . . **CLC 12**
    See also CA 49-52; CANR 8; CLR 20;
    MAICYA; SATA 8

Rodgers, W(illiam) R(obert)
    1909-1969 . . . . **CLC 7**
    See also CA 85-88; DLB 20

Rodman, Eric
    See Silverberg, Robert

Rodman, Howard 1920(?)-1985 . . . . . **CLC 65**
    See also CA 118

Rodman, Maia
    See Wojciechowska, Maia (Teresa)

Rodriguez, Claudio 1934- . . . . **CLC 10**

Roelvaag, O(le) E(dvart)
    1876-1931 . . . . **TCLC 17**
    See also CA 117; DLB 9

Roethke, Theodore (Huebner)
    1908-1963 . . . . . . **CLC 1, 3, 8, 11, 19, 46**
    See also CA 81-84; CABS 2;
    CDALB 1941-1968; DLB 5; MTCW

Rogers, Thomas Hunton 1927- . . . . . **CLC 57**
    See also CA 89-92

Rogers, Will(iam Penn Adair)
    1879-1935 . . . . **TCLC 8**
    See also CA 105; DLB 11

Rogin, Gilbert 1929- . . . . **CLC 18**
    See also CA 65-68; CANR 15

Rohan, Koda . . . . **TCLC 22**
    See also Koda Shigeyuki

Rohmer, Eric . . . . **CLC 16**
    See also Scherer, Jean-Marie Maurice

Rohmer, Sax . . . . **TCLC 28**
    See also Ward, Arthur Henry Sarsfield
    See also DLB 70

Roiphe, Anne Richardson 1935- . . . **CLC 3, 9**
    See also CA 89-92; DLBY 80

Rolfe, Frederick (William Serafino Austin
    Lewis Mary) 1860-1913 . . . . . . **TCLC 12**
    See also CA 107; DLB 34

Rolland, Romain 1866-1944 . . . . **TCLC 23**
    See also CA 118; DLB 65

Rolvaag, O(le) E(dvart)
    See Roelvaag, O(le) E(dvart)

Romain Arnaud, Saint
    See Aragon, Louis

Romains, Jules 1885-1972 . . . . **CLC 7**
    See also CA 85-88; CANR 34; DLB 65;
    MTCW

Romero, Jose Ruben 1890-1952 . . . **TCLC 14**
    See also CA 114; 131; HW

Ronsard, Pierre de 1524-1585 . . . . **LC 6**

Rooke, Leon 1934- . . . . **CLC 25, 34**
    See also CA 25-28R; CANR 23

Roper, William 1498-1578 . . . . **LC 10**

Roquelaure, A. N.
    See Rice, Anne

Rosa, Joao Guimaraes 1908-1967 . . . **CLC 23**
    See also CA 89-92; DLB 113

Rosen, Richard (Dean) 1949- . . . . **CLC 39**
    See also CA 77-80

Rosenberg, Isaac 1890-1918 . . . . . . **TCLC 12**
    See also CA 107; DLB 20

Rosenblatt, Joe . . . . **CLC 15**
    See also Rosenblatt, Joseph

Rosenblatt, Joseph 1933-
    See Rosenblatt, Joe
    See also CA 89-92

Rosenfeld, Samuel 1896-1963
    See Tzara, Tristan
    See also CA 89-92

Rosenthal, M(acha) L(ouis) 1917- . . . **CLC 28**
    See also CA 1-4R; CAAS 6; CANR 4;
    DLB 5; SATA 59

Ross, Barnaby
    See Dannay, Frederic

Ross, Bernard L.
    See Follett, Ken(neth Martin)

Ross, J. H.
    See Lawrence, T(homas) E(dward)

Ross, (James) Sinclair 1908- . . . . **CLC 13**
    See also CA 73-76; DLB 88

Rossetti, Christina (Georgina)
    1830-1894 . . . . **NCLC 2**
    See also DLB 35; MAICYA; SATA 20;
    WLC

Rossetti, Dante Gabriel
    1828-1882 . . . . **NCLC 4**
    See also CDBLB 1832-1890; DLB 35; WLC

Rossner, Judith (Perelman)
    1935- . . . . **CLC 6, 9, 29**
    See also AITN 2; BEST 90:3; CA 17-20R;
    CANR 18; DLB 6; MTCW

Rostand, Edmond (Eugene Alexis)
    1868-1918 . . . . **TCLC 6, 37**
    See also CA 104; 126; MTCW

Roth, Henry 1906- . . . . **CLC 2, 6, 11**
    See also CA 11-12; CANR 38; CAP 1;
    DLB 28; MTCW

Roth, Joseph 1894-1939 . . . . **TCLC 33**
    See also DLB 85

Roth, Philip (Milton)
    1933- . . . . . . **CLC 1, 2, 3, 4, 6, 9, 15, 22,**
                                          31, 47, 66
    See also BEST 90:3; CA 1-4R; CANR 1, 22,
    36; CDALB 1968-1988; DLB 2, 28;
    DLBY 82; MTCW; WLC

Rothenberg, Jerome 1931- . . . . **CLC 6, 57**
    See also CA 45-48; CANR 1; DLB 5

Roumain, Jacques (Jean Baptiste)
    1907-1944 . . . . **TCLC 19**
    See also BLC 3; BW; CA 117; 125

Rourke, Constance (Mayfield)
    1885-1941 . . . . **TCLC 12**
    See also CA 107; YABC 1

Rousseau, Jean-Baptiste 1671-1741 . . . **LC 9**

Rousseau, Jean-Jacques 1712-1778 . . . **LC 14**
    See also WLC

Roussel, Raymond 1877-1933 . . . . . **TCLC 20**
    See also CA 117

Rovit, Earl (Herbert) 1927- . . . . **CLC 7**
    See also CA 5-8R; CANR 12

Rowe, Nicholas 1674-1718 . . . . **LC 8**
    See also DLB 84

Rowley, Ames Dorrance
    See Lovecraft, H(oward) P(hillips)

Rowson, Susanna Haswell
    1762(?)-1824 . . . . **NCLC 5**
    See also DLB 37

Roy, Gabrielle 1909-1983 . . . . **CLC 10, 14**
    See also CA 53-56; 110; CANR 5; DLB 68;
    MTCW

Rozewicz, Tadeusz 1921- . . . . **CLC 9, 23**
    See also CA 108; CANR 36; MTCW

Ruark, Gibbons 1941- . . . . **CLC 3**
    See also CA 33-36R; CANR 14, 31;
    DLB 120

Rubens, Bernice (Ruth) 1923- . . . **CLC 19, 31**
    See also CA 25-28R; CANR 33; DLB 14;
    MTCW

Rudkin, (James) David 1936- . . . . . . **CLC 14**
    See also CA 89-92; DLB 13

Rudnik, Raphael 1933- . . . . **CLC 7**
    See also CA 29-32R

Ruffian, M.
    See Hasek, Jaroslav (Matej Frantisek)

Ruiz, Jose Martinez . . . . **CLC 11**
    See also Martinez Ruiz, Jose

Rukeyser, Muriel
    1913-1980 . . . . **CLC 6, 10, 15, 27**
    See also CA 5-8R; 93-96; CANR 26;
    DLB 48; MTCW; SATA 22

Rule, Jane (Vance) 1931- . . . . **CLC 27**
    See also CA 25-28R; CANR 12; DLB 60

Rulfo, Juan 1918-1986 . . . . **CLC 8**
    See also CA 85-88; 118; CANR 26;
    DLB 113; HW; MTCW

Runyon, (Alfred) Damon
    1884(?)-1946 . . . . **TCLC 10**
    See also CA 107; DLB 11, 86

Rush, Norman 1933- . . . . **CLC 44**
    See also CA 121; 126

Rushdie, (Ahmed) Salman
    1947- . . . . **CLC 23, 31, 55**
    See also BEST 89:3; CA 108; 111;
    CANR 33; MTCW

Rushforth, Peter (Scott) 1945- . . . . . **CLC 19**
    See also CA 101

Ruskin, John 1819-1900 . . . . **TCLC 20**
    See also CA 114; 129; CDBLB 1832-1890;
    DLB 55; SATA 24

Russ, Joanna 1937- . . . . **CLC 15**
    See also CA 25-28R; CANR 11, 31; DLB 8;
    MTCW

Russell, George William 1867-1935
    See A. E.
    See also CA 104; CDBLB 1890-1914

Russell, (Henry) Ken(neth Alfred)
    1927- . . . . **CLC 16**
    See also CA 105

Russell, Willy 1947- . . . . **CLC 60**

Rutherford, Mark . . . . **TCLC 25**
    See also White, William Hale
    See also DLB 18

Savage, Catharine
  See Brosman, Catharine Savage

Savage, Thomas 1915-............ **CLC 40**
  See also CA 126; 132; CAAS 15

Savan, Glenn .... **CLC 50**

Saven, Glenn 19th cent. (?)-........ **CLC 50**

Sayers, Dorothy L(eigh)
  1893-1957 .... **TCLC 2, 15**
  See also CA 104; 119; CDBLB 1914-1945;
    DLB 10, 36, 77, 100; MTCW

Sayers, Valerie 1952-............. **CLC 50**
  See also CA 134

Sayles, John Thomas 1950-.... **CLC 7, 10, 14**
  See also CA 57-60; DLB 44

Scammell, Michael .... **CLC 34**

Scannell, Vernon 1922- .... **CLC 49**
  See also CA 5-8R; CANR 8, 24; DLB 27;
    SATA 59

Scarlett, Susan
  See Streatfeild, (Mary) Noel

Schaeffer, Susan Fromberg
  1941-.................. **CLC 6, 11, 22**
  See also CA 49-52; CANR 18; DLB 28;
    MTCW; SATA 22

Schary, Jill
  See Robinson, Jill

Schell, Jonathan 1943-............ **CLC 35**
  See also CA 73-76; CANR 12

Schelling, Friedrich Wilhelm Joseph von
  1775-1854 .... **NCLC 30**
  See also DLB 90

Scherer, Jean-Marie Maurice 1920-
  See Rohmer, Eric
  See also CA 110

Schevill, James (Erwin) 1920-....... **CLC 7**
  See also CA 5-8R; CAAS 12

Schisgal, Murray (Joseph) 1926-..... **CLC 6**
  See also CA 21-24R

Schlee, Ann 1934-................ **CLC 35**
  See also CA 101; CANR 29; SATA 36, 44

Schlegel, August Wilhelm von
  1767-1845 .... **NCLC 15**
  See also DLB 94

Schlegel, Johann Elias (von)
  1719(?)-1749 .... **LC 5**

Schmidt, Arno (Otto) 1914-1979.... **CLC 56**
  See also CA 128; 109; DLB 69

Schmitz, Aron Hector 1861-1928
  See Svevo, Italo
  See also CA 104; 122; MTCW

Schnackenberg, Gjertrud 1953-..... **CLC 40**
  See also CA 116; DLB 120

Schneider, Leonard Alfred 1925-1966
  See Bruce, Lenny
  See also CA 89-92

Schnitzler, Arthur 1862-1931 ...... **TCLC 4**
  See also CA 104; DLB 81, 118

Schor, Sandra (M.) 1932(?)-1990 ... **CLC 65**
  See also CA 132

Schorer, Mark 1908-1977 .... **CLC 9**
  See also CA 5-8R; 73-76; CANR 7;
    DLB 103

Schrader, Paul Joseph 1946-....... **CLC 26**
  See also CA 37-40R; DLB 44

Schreiner, Olive (Emilie Albertina)
  1855-1920 .... **TCLC 9**
  See also CA 105; DLB 18

Schulberg, Budd (Wilson)
  1914-.................... **CLC 7, 48**
  See also CA 25-28R; CANR 19; DLB 6, 26,
    28; DLBY 81

Schulz, Bruno 1892-1942......... **TCLC 5**
  See also CA 115; 123

Schulz, Charles M(onroe) 1922-.... **CLC 12**
  See also CA 9-12R; CANR 6; SATA 10

Schuyler, James Marcus
  1923-1991 .... **CLC 5, 23**
  See also CA 101; 134; DLB 5

Schwartz, Delmore (David)
  1913-1966 .... **CLC 2, 4, 10, 45**
  See also CA 17-18; 25-28R; CANR 35;
    CAP 2; DLB 28, 48; MTCW

Schwartz, Ernst
  See Ozu, Yasujiro

Schwartz, John Burnham 1965- .... **CLC 59**
  See also CA 132

Schwartz, Lynne Sharon 1939-..... **CLC 31**
  See also CA 103

Schwartz, Muriel A.
  See Eliot, T(homas) S(tearns)

Schwarz-Bart, Andre 1928-....... **CLC 2, 4**
  See also CA 89-92

Schwarz-Bart, Simone 1938-........ **CLC 7**
  See also CA 97-100

Schwob, (Mayer Andre) Marcel
  1867-1905 .... **TCLC 20**
  See also CA 117

Sciascia, Leonardo
  1921-1989 .... **CLC 8, 9, 41**
  See also CA 85-88; 130; CANR 35; MTCW

Scoppettone, Sandra 1936-........ **CLC 26**
  See also CA 5-8R; SATA 9

Scorsese, Martin 1942- .... **CLC 20**
  See also CA 110; 114

Scotland, Jay
  See Jakes, John (William)

Scott, Duncan Campbell
  1862-1947 .... **TCLC 6**
  See also CA 104; DLB 92

Scott, Evelyn 1893-1963........... **CLC 43**
  See also CA 104; 112; DLB 9, 48

Scott, F(rancis) R(eginald)
  1899-1985 .... **CLC 22**
  See also CA 101; 114; DLB 88

Scott, Frank
  See Scott, F(rancis) R(eginald)

Scott, Joanna 1900- .... **CLC 50**
  See also CA 126

Scott, Paul (Mark) 1920-1978.... **CLC 9, 60**
  See also CA 81-84; 77-80; CANR 33;
    DLB 14; MTCW

Scott, Walter 1771-1832......... **NCLC 15**
  See also CDBLB 1789-1832; DLB 93, 107,
    116; WLC; YABC 2

Scribe, (Augustin) Eugene
  1791-1861 .... **NCLC 16**

Scrum, R.
  See Crumb, R(obert)

Scudery, Madeleine de 1607-1701..... **LC 2**

Scum
  See Crumb, R(obert)

Scumbag, Little Bobby
  See Crumb, R(obert)

Seabrook, John
  See Hubbard, L(afayette) Ron(ald)

Sealy, I. Allan 1951- .... **CLC 55**

Search, Alexander
  See Pessoa, Fernando (Antonio Nogueira)

Sebastian, Lee
  See Silverberg, Robert

Sebastian Owl
  See Thompson, Hunter S(tockton)

Sebestyen, Ouida 1924-........... **CLC 30**
  See also AAYA 8; CA 107; CLR 17;
    MAICYA; SAAS 10; SATA 39

Sedges, John
  See Buck, Pearl S(ydenstricker)

Sedgwick, Catharine Maria
  1789-1867 .... **NCLC 19**
  See also DLB 1, 74

Seelye, John 1931-................ **CLC 7**

Seferiades, Giorgos Stylianou 1900-1971
  See Seferis, George
  See also CA 5-8R; 33-36R; CANR 5, 36;
    MTCW

Seferis, George .... **CLC 5, 11**
  See also Seferiades, Giorgos Stylianou

Segal, Erich (Wolf) 1937- .... **CLC 3, 10**
  See also BEST 89:1; CA 25-28R; CANR 20,
    36; DLBY 86; MTCW

Seger, Bob 1945-................. **CLC 35**

Seghers, Anna .... **CLC 7**
  See also Radvanyi, Netty
  See also DLB 69

Seidel, Frederick (Lewis) 1936-..... **CLC 18**
  See also CA 13-16R; CANR 8; DLBY 84

Seifert, Jaroslav 1901-1986..... **CLC 34, 44**
  See also CA 127; MTCW

Sei Shonagon c. 966-1017(?) ...... **CMLC 6**

Selby, Hubert Jr. 1928-......**CLC 1, 2, 4, 8**
  See also CA 13-16R; CANR 33; DLB 2

Sembene, Ousmane
  See Ousmane, Sembene

Senancour, Etienne Pivert de
  1770-1846 .... **NCLC 16**
  See also DLB 119

Sender, Ramon (Jose) 1902-1982 .... **CLC 8**
  See also CA 5-8R; 105; CANR 8; HW;
    MTCW

Seneca, Lucius Annaeus
  4B.C.-65.................... **CMLC 6**

Senghor, Leopold Sedar 1906-...... **CLC 54**
  See also BLC 3; BW; CA 116; 125; MTCW

Serling, (Edward) Rod(man)
  1924-1975 .... **CLC 30**
  See also AITN 1; CA 65-68; 57-60; DLB 26

Serna, Ramon Gomez de la
  See Gomez de la Serna, Ramon

Serpieres
See Guillevic, (Eugene)

Service, Robert
See Service, Robert W(illiam)
See also DLB 92

Service, Robert W(illiam)
1874(?)-1958 . . . . TCLC 15
See also Service, Robert
See also CA 115; SATA 20; WLC

Seth, Vikram 1952- . . . . CLC 43
See also CA 121; 127; DLB 120

Seton, Cynthia Propper
1926-1982 . . . . CLC 27
See also CA 5-8R; 108; CANR 7

Seton, Ernest (Evan) Thompson
1860-1946 . . . . TCLC 31
See also CA 109; DLB 92; SATA 18

Seton-Thompson, Ernest
See Seton, Ernest (Evan) Thompson

Settle, Mary Lee 1918- . . . . CLC 19, 61
See also CA 89-92; CAAS 1; DLB 6

Seuphor, Michel
See Arp, Jean

Sevine, Marquise de Marie de
Rabutin-Chantal 1626-1696 . . . . . LC 11

Sevine, Marquise de Marie de
Rabutin-Chantal 1626-1696 . . . . . LC 11

Sexton, Anne (Harvey)
1928-1974 . . . CLC 2, 4, 6, 8, 10, 15, 53;
PC 2
See also CA 1-4R; 53-56; CABS 2;
CANR 3, 36; CDALB 1941-1968; DLB 5;
MTCW; SATA 10; WLC

Shaara, Michael (Joseph Jr.)
1929-1988 . . . . CLC 15
See also AITN 1; CA 102; DLBY 83

Shackleton, C. C.
See Aldiss, Brian W(ilson)

Shacochis, Bob . . . . CLC 39
See also Shacochis, Robert G.

Shacochis, Robert G. 1951-
See Shacochis, Bob
See also CA 119; 124

Shaffer, Anthony (Joshua) 1926- . . . . CLC 19
See also CA 110; 116; DLB 13

Shaffer, Peter (Levin)
1926- . . . . CLC 5, 14, 18, 37, 60
See also CA 25-28R; CANR 25;
CDBLB 1960 to Present; DLB 13;
MTCW

Shakey, Bernard
See Young, Neil

Shalamov, Varlam (Tikhonovich)
1907(?)-1982 . . . . CLC 18
See also CA 129; 105

Shamlu, Ahmad 1925- . . . . CLC 10

Shammas, Anton 1951- . . . . CLC 55

Shange, Ntozake 1948- . . . . CLC 8, 25, 38
See also AAYA 9; BLC 3; BW; CA 85-88;
CABS 3; CANR 27; DLB 38; MTCW

Shapcott, Thomas William 1935- . . . CLC 38
See also CA 69-72

Shapiro, Karl (Jay) 1913- . . CLC 4, 8, 15, 53
See also CA 1-4R; CAAS 6; CANR 1, 36;
DLB 48; MTCW

Sharp, William 1855-1905 . . . . TCLC 39

Sharpe, Thomas Ridley 1928-
See Sharpe, Tom
See also CA 114; 122

Sharpe, Tom . . . . CLC 36
See also Sharpe, Thomas Ridley
See also DLB 14

Shaw, Bernard . . . . TCLC 45
See also Shaw, George Bernard

Shaw, G. Bernard
See Shaw, George Bernard

Shaw, George Bernard
1856-1950 . . . . TCLC 3, 9, 21
See also Shaw, Bernard
See also CA 104; 128; CDBLB 1914-1945;
DLB 10, 57; MTCW; WLC

Shaw, Henry Wheeler
1818-1885 . . . . NCLC 15
See also DLB 11

Shaw, Irwin 1913-1984 . . . . . . CLC 7, 23, 34
See also AITN 1; CA 13-16R; 112;
CANR 21; CDALB 1941-1968; DLB 6,
102; DLBY 84; MTCW

Shaw, Robert 1927-1978 . . . . CLC 5
See also AITN 1; CA 1-4R; 81-84;
CANR 4; DLB 13, 14

Shaw, T. E.
See Lawrence, T(homas) E(dward)

Shawn, Wallace 1943- . . . . CLC 41
See also CA 112

Sheed, Wilfrid (John Joseph)
1930- . . . . CLC 2, 4, 10, 53
See also CA 65-68; CANR 30; DLB 6;
MTCW

Sheldon, Alice Hastings Bradley
1915(?)-1987
See Tiptree, James Jr.
See also CA 108; 122; CANR 34; MTCW

Sheldon, John
See Bloch, Robert (Albert)

Shelley, Mary Wollstonecraft (Godwin)
1797-1851 . . . . NCLC 14
See also CDBLB 1789-1832; DLB 110, 116;
SATA 29; WLC

Shelley, Percy Bysshe
1792-1822 . . . . NCLC 18
See also CDBLB 1789-1832; DLB 96, 110;
WLC

Shepard, Jim 1956- . . . . CLC 36
See also CA 137

Shepard, Lucius 19th cent. (?)- . . . . . CLC 34
See also CA 128

Shepard, Sam
1943- . . . . CLC 4, 6, 17, 34, 41, 44
See also AAYA 1; CA 69-72; CABS 3;
CANR 22; DLB 7; MTCW

Shepherd, Michael
See Ludlum, Robert

Sherburne, Zoa (Morin) 1912- . . . . . . CLC 30
See also CA 1-4R; CANR 3, 37; MAICYA;
SATA 3

Sheridan, Frances 1724-1766 . . . . LC 7
See also DLB 39, 84

Sheridan, Richard Brinsley
1751-1816 . . . . NCLC 5; DC 1
See also CDBLB 1660-1789; DLB 89; WLC

Sherman, Jonathan Marc . . . . CLC 55

Sherman, Martin 1941(?)- . . . . CLC 19
See also CA 116; 123

Sherwin, Judith Johnson 1936- . . . CLC 7, 15
See also CA 25-28R; CANR 34

Sherwood, Robert E(mmet)
1896-1955 . . . . TCLC 3
See also CA 104; DLB 7, 26

Shiel, M(atthew) P(hipps)
1865-1947 . . . . TCLC 8
See also CA 106

Shiga, Naoya 1883-1971 . . . . CLC 33
See also CA 101; 33-36R

Shimazaki Haruki 1872-1943
See Shimazaki Toson
See also CA 105; 134

Shimazaki Toson . . . . TCLC 5
See also Shimazaki Haruki

Sholokhov, Mikhail (Aleksandrovich)
1905-1984 . . . . CLC 7, 15
See also CA 101; 112; MTCW; SATA 36

Shone, Patric
See Hanley, James

Shreve, Susan Richards 1939- . . . . . . CLC 23
See also CA 49-52; CAAS 5; CANR 5, 38;
MAICYA; SATA 41, 46

Shue, Larry 1946-1985 . . . . CLC 52
See also CA 117

Shu-Jen, Chou 1881-1936
See Hsun, Lu
See also CA 104

Shulman, Alix Kates 1932- . . . . CLC 2, 10
See also CA 29-32R; SATA 7

Shuster, Joe 1914- . . . . CLC 21

Shute, Nevil . . . . CLC 30
See also Norway, Nevil Shute

Shuttle, Penelope (Diane) 1947- . . . . . CLC 7
See also CA 93-96; CANR 39; DLB 14, 40

Sidney, Mary 1561-1621 . . . . LC 19

Sidney, Sir Philip 1554-1586 . . . . LC 19
See also CDBLB Before 1660

Siegel, Jerome 1914- . . . . CLC 21
See also CA 116

Siegel, Jerry
See Siegel, Jerome

Sienkiewicz, Henryk (Adam Alexander Pius)
1846-1916 . . . . TCLC 3
See also CA 104; 134

Sierra, Gregorio Martinez
See Martinez Sierra, Gregorio

Sierra, Maria (de la O'LeJarraga) Martinez
See Martinez Sierra, Maria (de la
O'LeJarraga)

Sigal, Clancy 1926- . . . . CLC 7
See also CA 1-4R

Sigourney, Lydia Howard (Huntley)
1791-1865 . . . . NCLC 21
See also DLB 1, 42, 73

Stairs, Gordon
   See Austin, Mary (Hunter)

Stannard, Martin................**CLC 44**

Stanton, Maura 1946- ....**CLC 9**
   See also CA 89-92; CANR 15; DLB 120

Stanton, Schuyler
   See Baum, L(yman) Frank

Stapledon, (William) Olaf
      1886-1950 ....**TCLC 22**
   See also CA 111; DLB 15

Starbuck, George (Edwin) 1931- .....**CLC 53**
   See also CA 21-24R; CANR 23

Stark, Richard
   See Westlake, Donald E(dwin)

Staunton, Schuyler
   See Baum, L(yman) Frank

Stead, Christina (Ellen)
      1902-1983 ....**CLC 2, 5, 8, 32**
   See also CA 13-16R; 109; CANR 33;
   MTCW

Steele, Richard 1672-1729.........**LC 18**
   See also CDBLB 1660-1789; DLB 84, 101

Steele, Timothy (Reid) 1948-.......**CLC 45**
   See also CA 93-96; CANR 16; DLB 120

Steffens, (Joseph) Lincoln
      1866-1936 ....**TCLC 20**
   See also CA 117

Stegner, Wallace (Earle) 1909- ...**CLC 9, 49**
   See also AITN 1; BEST 90:3; CA 1-4R;
   CAAS 9; CANR 1, 21; DLB 9; MTCW

Stein, Gertrude 1874-1946... **TCLC 1, 6, 28**
   See also CA 104; 132; CDALB 1917-1929;
   DLB 4, 54, 86; MTCW; WLC

Steinbeck, John (Ernst)
      1902-1968 ... **CLC 1, 5, 9, 13, 21, 34, 45**
   See also CA 1-4R; 25-28R; CANR 1, 35;
   CDALB 1929-1941; DLB 7, 9; DLBD 2;
   MTCW; SATA 9; WLC

Steinem, Gloria 1934-..............**CLC 63**
   See also CA 53-56; CANR 28; MTCW

Steiner, George 1929-..............**CLC 24**
   See also CA 73-76; CANR 31; DLB 67;
   MTCW; SATA 62

Steiner, Rudolf 1861-1925........**TCLC 13**
   See also CA 107

Stendhal 1783-1842.............**NCLC 23**
   See also DLB 119; WLC

Stephen, Leslie 1832-1904........**TCLC 23**
   See also CA 123; DLB 57

Stephen, Sir Leslie
   See Stephen, Leslie

Stephen, Virginia
   See Woolf, (Adeline) Virginia

Stephens, James 1882(?) 1950......**TCLC 4**
   See also CA 104; DLB 19

Stephens, Reed
   See Donaldson, Stephen R.

Steptoe, Lydia
   See Barnes, Djuna

Sterchi, Beat 1949-..............**CLC 65**

Sterling, Brett
   See Bradbury, Ray (Douglas); Hamilton,
   Edmond

Sterling, Bruce 1954-.............**CLC 72**
   See also CA 119

Sterling, George 1869-1926.......**TCLC 20**
   See also CA 117; DLB 54

Stern, Gerald 1925- ....**CLC 40**
   See also CA 81-84; CANR 28; DLB 105

Stern, Richard (Gustave) 1928-... **CLC 4, 39**
   See also CA 1-4R; CANR 1, 25; DLBY 87

Sternberg, Josef von 1894-1969.....**CLC 20**
   See also CA 81-84

Sterne, Laurence 1713-1768.........**LC 2**
   See also CDBLB 1660-1789; DLB 39; WLC

Sternheim, (William Adolf) Carl
      1878-1942 ....**TCLC 8**
   See also CA 105; DLB 56, 118

Stevens, Mark 1951- ....**CLC 34**
   See also CA 122

Stevens, Wallace
      1879-1955 ....**TCLC 3, 12, 45**
   See also CA 104; 124; CDALB 1929-1941;
   DLB 54; MTCW; WLC

Stevenson, Anne (Katharine)
      1933- ....**CLC 7, 33**
   See also CA 17-20R; CAAS 9; CANR 9, 33;
   DLB 40; MTCW

Stevenson, Robert Louis (Balfour)
      1850-1894 ....**NCLC 5, 14**
   See also CDBLB 1890-1914; CLR 10, 11;
   DLB 18, 57; MAICYA; WLC; YABC 2

Stewart, J(ohn) I(nnes) M(ackintosh)
      1906- ....**CLC 7, 14, 32**
   See also CA 85-88; CAAS 3; MTCW

Stewart, Mary (Florence Elinor)
      1916- ....**CLC 7, 35**
   See also CA 1-4R; CANR 1; SATA 12

Stewart, Mary Rainbow
   See Stewart, Mary (Florence Elinor)

Still, James 1906-................**CLC 49**
   See also CA 65-68; CANR 10, 26; DLB 9;
   SATA 29

Sting
   See Sumner, Gordon Matthew

Stirling, Arthur
   See Sinclair, Upton (Beall)

Stitt, Milan 1941-................**CLC 29**
   See also CA 69-72

Stockton, Francis Richard 1834-1902
   See Stockton, Frank R.
   See also CA 108; 137; MAICYA; SATA 44

Stockton, Frank R................**TCLC 47**
   See also Stockton, Francis Richard
   See also DLB 42, 74; SATA 32

Stoddard, Charles
   See Kuttner, Henry

Stoker, Abraham 1847-1912
   See Stoker, Bram
   See also CA 105; SATA 29

Stoker, Bram....................**TCLC 8**
   See also Stoker, Abraham
   See also CDBLB 1890-1914; DLB 36, 70;
   WLC

Stolz, Mary (Slattery) 1920-.......**CLC 12**
   See also AAYA 8; AITN 1; CA 5-8R;
   CANR 13; MAICYA; SAAS 3;
   SATA 10, 70, 71

Stone, Irving 1903-1989............**CLC 7**
   See also AITN 1; CA 1-4R; 129; CAAS 3;
   CANR 1, 23; MTCW; SATA 3; SATO 64

Stone, Robert (Anthony)
      1937- ....**CLC 5, 23, 42**
   See also CA 85-88; CANR 23; MTCW

Stone, Zachary
   See Follett, Ken(neth Martin)

Stoppard, Tom
      1937- ... **CLC 1, 3, 4, 5, 8, 15, 29, 34, 63**
   See also CA 81-84; CANR 39;
   CDBLB 1960 to Present; DLB 13;
   DLBY 85; MTCW; WLC

Storey, David (Malcolm)
      1933- ....**CLC 2, 4, 5, 8**
   See also CA 81-84; CANR 36; DLB 13, 14;
   MTCW

Storm, Hyemeyohsts 1935-.........**CLC 3**
   See also CA 81-84

Storm, (Hans) Theodor (Woldsen)
      1817-1888 ....**NCLC 1**

Storni, Alfonsina 1892-1938 ....**TCLC 5**
   See also CA 104; 131; HW

Stout, Rex (Todhunter) 1886-1975 ... **CLC 3**
   See also AITN 2; CA 61-64

Stow, (Julian) Randolph 1935- .. **CLC 23, 48**
   See also CA 13-16R; CANR 33; MTCW

Stowe, Harriet (Elizabeth) Beecher
      1811-1896 ....**NCLC 3**
   See also CDALB 1865-1917; DLB 1, 12, 42,
   74; MAICYA; WLC; YABC 1

Strachey, (Giles) Lytton
      1880-1932 ....**TCLC 12**
   See also CA 110

Strand, Mark 1934-......**CLC 6, 18, 41, 71**
   See also CA 21-24R; DLB 5; SATA 41

Straub, Peter (Francis) 1943- ......**CLC 28**
   See also BEST 89:1; CA 85-88; CANR 28;
   DLBY 84; MTCW

Strauss, Botho 1944- ....**CLC 22**

Streatfeild, (Mary) Noel
      1895(?)-1986 ....**CLC 21**
   See also CA 81-84; 120; CANR 31;
   CLR 17; MAICYA; SATA 20, 48

Stribling, T(homas) S(igismund)
      1881-1965 ....**CLC 23**
   See also CA 107; DLB 9

Strindberg, (Johan) August
      1849-1912 ....**TCLC 1, 8, 21, 47**
   See also CA 104; 135; WLC

Stringer, Arthur 1874-1950.......**TCLC 37**
   See also DLB 92

Stringer, David
   See Roberts, Keith (John Kingston)

Strugatskii, Arkadii (Natanovich)
      1925-1991 ....**CLC 27**
   See also CA 106; 135

Strugatskii, Boris (Natanovich)
      1933- ....**CLC 27**
   See also CA 106

Strummer, Joe 1953(?)- ....**CLC 30**
   See also The Clash

Stuart, Don A.
   See Campbell, John W(ood Jr.)

Washington, Alex
  See Harris, Mark

Washington, Booker T(aliaferro)
  1856-1915 .... **TCLC 10**
  See also BLC 3; BW; CA 114; 125;
  SATA 28

Wassermann, (Karl) Jakob
  1873-1934 .... **TCLC 6**
  See also CA 104; DLB 66

Wasserstein, Wendy 1950-...... **CLC 32, 59**
  See also CA 121; 129; CABS 3

Waterhouse, Keith (Spencer)
  1929-........................ **CLC 47**
  See also CA 5-8R; CANR 38; DLB 13, 15;
  MTCW

Waters, Roger 1944-.............. **CLC 35**
  See also Pink Floyd

Watkins, Frances Ellen
  See Harper, Frances Ellen Watkins

Watkins, Gerrold
  See Malzberg, Barry N(athaniel)

Watkins, Paul 1964-.............. **CLC 55**
  See also CA 132

Watkins, Vernon Phillips
  1906-1967 .... **CLC 43**
  See also CA 9-10; 25-28R; CAP 1; DLB 20

Watson, Irving S.
  See Mencken, H(enry) L(ouis)

Watson, John H.
  See Farmer, Philip Jose

Watson, Richard F.
  See Silverberg, Robert

Waugh, Auberon (Alexander) 1939-.. **CLC 7**
  See also CA 45-48; CANR 6, 22; DLB 14

Waugh, Evelyn (Arthur St. John)
  1903-1966 ... **CLC 1, 3, 8, 13, 19, 27, 44**
  See also CA 85-88; 25-28R; CANR 22;
  CDBLB 1914-1945; DLB 15; MTCW;
  WLC

Waugh, Harriet 1944- .... **CLC 6**
  See also CA 85-88; CANR 22

Ways, C. R.
  See Blount, Roy (Alton) Jr.

Waystaff, Simon
  See Swift, Jonathan

Webb, (Martha) Beatrice (Potter)
  1858-1943 .... **TCLC 22**
  See also Potter, Beatrice
  See also CA 117

Webb, Charles (Richard) 1939-...... **CLC 7**
  See also CA 25-28R

Webb, James H(enry) Jr. 1946- .... **CLC 22**
  See also CA 81-84

Webb, Mary (Gladys Meredith)
  1881-1927 .... **TCLC 24**
  See also CA 123; DLB 34

Webb, Mrs. Sidney
  See Webb, (Martha) Beatrice (Potter)

Webb, Phyllis 1927-.............. **CLC 18**
  See also CA 104; CANR 23; DLB 53

Webb, Sidney (James)
  1859-1947 .... **TCLC 22**
  See also CA 117

Webber, Andrew Lloyd.............. **CLC 21**
  See also Lloyd Webber, Andrew

Weber, Lenora Mattingly
  1895-1971 .... **CLC 12**
  See also CA 19-20; 29-32R; CAP 1;
  SATA 2, 26

Webster, John 1579(?)-1634(?) .... **DC 2**
  See also CDBLB Before 1660; DLB 58;
  WLC

Webster, Noah 1758-1843 .... **NCLC 30**

Wedekind, (Benjamin) Frank(lin)
  1864-1918 .... **TCLC 7**
  See also CA 104; DLB 118

Weidman, Jerome 1913-.......... **CLC 7**
  See also AITN 2; CA 1-4R; CANR 1;
  DLB 28

Weil, Simone (Adolphine)
  1909-1943 .... **TCLC 23**
  See also CA 117

Weinstein, Nathan
  See West, Nathanael

Weinstein, Nathan von Wallenstein
  See West, Nathanael

Weir, Peter (Lindsay) 1944- .... **CLC 20**
  See also CA 113; 123

Weiss, Peter (Ulrich)
  1916-1982 .... **CLC 3, 15, 51**
  See also CA 45-48; 106; CANR 3; DLB 69

Weiss, Theodore (Russell)
  1916- .... **CLC 3, 8, 14**
  See also CA 9-12R; CAAS 2; DLB 5

Welch, (Maurice) Denton
  1915-1948 .... **TCLC 22**
  See also CA 121

Welch, James 1940-........ **CLC 6, 14, 52**
  See also CA 85-88

Weldon, Fay
  1933(?)-....... **CLC 6, 9, 11, 19, 36, 59**
  See also CA 21-24R; CANR 16;
  CDBLB 1960 to Present; DLB 14;
  MTCW

Wellek, Rene 1903- .... **CLC 28**
  See also CA 5-8R; CAAS 7; CANR 8;
  DLB 63

Weller, Michael 1942-......... **CLC 10, 53**
  See also CA 85-88

Weller, Paul 1958-.............. **CLC 26**

Wellershoff, Dieter 1925-.......... **CLC 46**
  See also CA 89-92; CANR 16, 37

Welles, (George) Orson
  1915-1985 .... **CLC 20**
  See also CA 93-96; 117

Wellman, Mac 1945- .... **CLC 65**

Wellman, Manly Wade 1903-1986 .. **CLC 49**
  See also CA 1-4R; 118; CANR 6, 16;
  SATA 6, 47

Wells, Carolyn 1869(?)-1942 ...... **TCLC 35**
  See also CA 113; DLB 11

Wells, H(erbert) G(eorge)
  1866-1946 ..... **TCLC 6, 12, 19; SSC 6**
  See also CA 110; 121; CDBLB 1914-1945;
  DLB 34, 70; MTCW; SATA 20; WLC

Wells, Rosemary 1943-............ **CLC 12**
  See also CA 85-88; CLR 16; MAICYA;
  SAAS 1; SATA 18, 69

Welty, Eudora
  1909- .... **CLC 1, 2, 5, 14, 22, 33; SSC 1**
  See also CA 9-12R; CABS 1; CANR 32;
  CDALB 1941-1968; DLB 2, 102;
  DLBY 87; MTCW; WLC

Wen I-to 1899-1946 .... **TCLC 28**

Wentworth, Robert
  See Hamilton, Edmond

Werfel, Franz (V.) 1890-1945 ...... **TCLC 8**
  See also CA 104; DLB 81

Wergeland, Henrik Arnold
  1808-1845 .... **NCLC 5**

Wersba, Barbara 1932-............ **CLC 30**
  See also AAYA 2; CA 29-32R; CANR 16,
  38; CLR 3; DLB 52; MAICYA; SAAS 2;
  SATA 1, 58

Wertmueller, Lina 1928- .... **CLC 16**
  See also CA 97-100; CANR 39

Wescott, Glenway 1901-1987....... **CLC 13**
  See also CA 13-16R; 121; CANR 23;
  DLB 4, 9, 102

Wesker, Arnold 1932- .... **CLC 3, 5, 42**
  See also CA 1-4R; CAAS 7; CANR 1, 33;
  CDBLB 1960 to Present; DLB 13;
  MTCW

Wesley, Richard (Errol) 1945-....... **CLC 7**
  See also BW; CA 57-60; DLB 38

Wessel, Johan Herman 1742-1785 .... **LC 7**

West, Anthony (Panther)
  1914-1987 .... **CLC 50**
  See also CA 45-48; 124; CANR 3, 19;
  DLB 15

West, C. P.
  See Wodehouse, P(elham) G(renville)

West, (Mary) Jessamyn
  1902-1984 .... **CLC 7, 17**
  See also CA 9-12R; 112; CANR 27; DLB 6;
  DLBY 84; MTCW; SATA 37

West, Morris L(anglo) 1916-..... **CLC 6, 33**
  See also CA 5-8R; CANR 24; MTCW

West, Nathanael
  1903-1940 .... **TCLC 1, 14, 44**
  See also CA 104; 125; CDALB 1929-1941;
  DLB 4, 9, 28; MTCW

West, Paul 1930- .... **CLC 7, 14**
  See also CA 13-16R; CAAS 7; CANR 22;
  DLB 14

West, Rebecca 1892-1983 .. **CLC 7, 9, 31, 50**
  See also CA 5-8R; 109; CANR 19; DLB 36;
  DLBY 83; MTCW

Westall, Robert (Atkinson) 1929-... **CLC 17**
  See also CA 69-72; CANR 18; CLR 13;
  MAICYA; SAAS 2; SATA 23, 69

Westlake, Donald E(dwin)
  1933- .... **CLC 7, 33**
  See also CA 17-20R; CAAS 13; CANR 16

Westmacott, Mary
  See Christie, Agatha (Mary Clarissa)

Weston, Allen
  See Norton, Andre

Wetcheek, J. L.
  See Feuchtwanger, Lion

Wetering, Janwillem van de
See van de Wetering, Janwillem

Wetherell, Elizabeth
See Warner, Susan (Bogert)

Whalen, Philip 1923- . . . . CLC 6, 29
See also CA 9-12R; CANR 5, 39; DLB 16

Wharton, Edith (Newbold Jones)
1862-1937 . . . . TCLC 3, 9, 27; SSC 6
See also CA 104; 132; CDALB 1865-1917;
DLB 4, 9, 12, 78; MTCW; WLC

Wharton, James
See Mencken, H(enry) L(ouis)

Wharton, William (a pseudonym)
. . . . CLC 18, 37
See also CA 93-96; DLBY 80

Wheatley (Peters), Phillis
1754(?)-1784 . . . . LC 3; PC 3
See also BLC 3; CDALB 1640-1865;
DLB 31, 50; WLC

Wheelock, John Hall 1886-1978 . . . . CLC 14
See also CA 13-16R; 77-80; CANR 14;
DLB 45

White, E(lwyn) B(rooks)
1899-1985 . . . . CLC 10, 34, 39
See also AITN 2; CA 13-16R; 116;
CANR 16, 37; CLR 1, 21; DLB 11, 22;
MAICYA; MTCW; SATA 2, 29, 44

White, Edmund (Valentine III)
1940- . . . . CLC 27
See also AAYA 7; CA 45-48; CANR 3, 19,
36; MTCW

White, Patrick (Victor Martindale)
1912-1990 . . CLC 3, 4, 5, 7, 9, 18, 65, 69
See also CA 81-84; 132; MTCW

White, Phyllis Dorothy James 1920-
See James, P. D.
See also CA 21-24R; CANR 17; MTCW

White, T(erence) H(anbury)
1906-1964 . . . . CLC 30
See also CA 73-76; CANR 37; MAICYA;
SATA 12

White, Terence de Vere 1912- . . . . . . CLC 49
See also CA 49-52; CANR 3

White, Walter
See White, Walter F(rancis)
See also BLC 3

White, Walter F(rancis)
1893-1955 . . . . TCLC 15
See also White, Walter
See also CA 115; 124; DLB 51

White, William Hale 1831-1913
See Rutherford, Mark
See also CA 121

Whitehead, E(dward) A(nthony)
1933- . . . . CLC 5
See also CA 65-68

Whitemore, Hugh (John) 1936- . . . . . CLC 37
See also CA 132

Whitman, Sarah Helen (Power)
1803-1878 . . . . NCLC 19
See also DLB 1

Whitman, Walt(er)
1819-1892 . . . . NCLC 4, 31; PC 3
See also CDALB 1640-1865; DLB 3, 64;
SATA 20; WLC

Whitney, Phyllis A(yame) 1903- . . . . CLC 42
See also AITN 2; BEST 90:3; CA 1-4R;
CANR 3, 25, 38; MAICYA; SATA 1, 30

Whittemore, (Edward) Reed (Jr.)
1919- . . . . CLC 4
See also CA 9-12R; CAAS 8; CANR 4;
DLB 5

Whittier, John Greenleaf
1807-1892 . . . . NCLC 8
See also CDALB 1640-1865; DLB 1

Whittlebot, Hernia
See Coward, Noel (Peirce)

Wicker, Thomas Grey 1926-
See Wicker, Tom
See also CA 65-68; CANR 21

Wicker, Tom . . . . CLC 7
See also Wicker, Thomas Grey

Wideman, John Edgar
1941- . . . . CLC 5, 34, 36, 67
See also BLC 3; BW; CA 85-88; CANR 14;
DLB 33

Wiebe, Rudy (H.) 1934- . . . . . . CLC 6, 11, 14
See also CA 37-40R; DLB 60

Wieland, Christoph Martin
1733-1813 . . . . NCLC 17
See also DLB 97

Wieners, John 1934- . . . . CLC 7
See also CA 13-16R; DLB 16

Wiesel, Elie(zer) 1928- . . . . . CLC 3, 5, 11, 37
See also AAYA 7; AITN 1; CA 5-8R;
CAAS 4; CANR 8; DLB 83; DLBY 87;
MTCW; SATA 56

Wiggins, Marianne 1947- . . . . CLC 57
See also BEST 89:3; CA 130

Wight, James Alfred 1916-
See Herriot, James
See also CA 77-80; SATA 44, 55

Wilbur, Richard (Purdy)
1921- . . . . CLC 3, 6, 9, 14, 53
See also CA 1-4R; CABS 2; CANR 2, 29;
DLB 5; MTCW; SATA 9

Wild, Peter 1940- . . . . CLC 14
See also CA 37-40R; DLB 5

Wilde, Oscar (Fingal O'Flahertie Wills)
1854(?)-1900 . . . . . . TCLC 1, 8, 23, 41
See also CA 104; 119; CDBLB 1890-1914;
DLB 10, 19, 34, 57; SATA 24; WLC

Wilder, Billy . . . . CLC 20
See also Wilder, Samuel
See also DLB 26

Wilder, Samuel 1906-
See Wilder, Billy
See also CA 89-92

Wilder, Thornton (Niven)
1897-1975 . . . . . CLC 1, 5, 6, 10, 15, 35;
DC 1
See also AITN 2; CA 13-16R; 61-64;
DLB 4, 7, 9; MTCW; WLC

Wiley, Richard 1944- . . . . CLC 44
See also CA 121; 129

Wilhelm, Kate . . . . CLC 7
See also Wilhelm, Katie Gertrude
See also CAAS 5; DLB 8

Wilhelm, Katie Gertrude 1928-
See Wilhelm, Kate
See also CA 37-40R; CANR 17, 36; MTCW

Wilkins, Mary
See Freeman, Mary Eleanor Wilkins

Willard, Nancy 1936- . . . . CLC 7, 37
See also CA 89-92; CANR 10, 39; CLR 5;
DLB 5, 52; MAICYA; MTCW;
SATA 30, 37, 71

Williams, C(harles) K(enneth)
1936- . . . . CLC 33, 56
See also CA 37-40R; DLB 5

Williams, Charles
See Collier, James L(incoln)

Williams, Charles (Walter Stansby)
1886-1945 . . . . TCLC 1, 11
See also CA 104; DLB 100

Williams, (George) Emlyn
1905-1987 . . . . CLC 15
See also CA 104; 123; CANR 36; DLB 10,
77; MTCW

Williams, Hugo 1942- . . . . CLC 42
See also CA 17-20R; DLB 40

Williams, J. Walker
See Wodehouse, P(elham) G(renville)

Williams, John A(lfred) 1925- . . . . CLC 5, 13
See also BLC 3; BW; CA 53-56; CAAS 3;
CANR 6, 26; DLB 2, 33

Williams, Jonathan (Chamberlain)
1929- . . . . CLC 13
See also CA 9-12R; CAAS 12; CANR 8;
DLB 5

Williams, Joy 1944- . . . . CLC 31
See also CA 41-44R; CANR 22

Williams, Norman 1952- . . . . CLC 39
See also CA 118

Williams, Tennessee
1911-1983 . . . . CLC 1, 2, 5, 7, 8, 11, 15,
19, 30, 39, 45, 71
See also AITN 1, 2; CA 5-8R; 108;
CABS 3; CANR 31; CDALB 1941-1968;
DLB 7; DLBD 4; DLBY 83; MTCW;
WLC

Williams, Thomas (Alonzo)
1926-1990 . . . . CLC 14
See also CA 1-4R; 132; CANR 2

Williams, William C.
See Williams, William Carlos

Williams, William Carlos
1883-1963 . . . CLC 1, 2, 5, 9, 13, 22, 42,
67
See also CA 89-92; CANR 34;
CDALB 1917-1929; DLB 4, 16, 54, 86;
MTCW

Williamson, David Keith 1942- . . . . . CLC 56
See also CA 103

Williamson, Jack . . . . CLC 29
See also Williamson, John Stewart
See also CAAS 8; DLB 8

Williamson, John Stewart 1908-
See Williamson, Jack
See also CA 17-20R; CANR 23

Willie, Frederick
See Lovecraft, H(oward) P(hillips)

Willingham, Calder (Baynard Jr.)
1922- .... CLC 5, 51
See also CA 5-8R; CANR 3; DLB 2, 44;
MTCW

Willis, Charles
See Clarke, Arthur C(harles)

Willy
See Colette, (Sidonie-Gabrielle)

Willy, Colette
See Colette, (Sidonie-Gabrielle)

Wilson, A(ndrew) N(orman)   1950- .. CLC 33
See also CA 112; 122; DLB 14

Wilson, Angus (Frank Johnstone)
1913-1991 .... CLC 2, 3, 5, 25, 34
See also CA 5-8R; 134; CANR 21; DLB 15;
MTCW

Wilson, August
1945- .... CLC 39, 50, 63; DC 2
See also BLC 3; BW; CA 115; 122; MTCW

Wilson, Brian   1942- .... CLC 12

Wilson, Colin   1931- .... CLC 3, 14
See also CA 1-4R; CAAS 5; CANR 1, 22,
33; DLB 14; MTCW

Wilson, Dirk
See Pohl, Frederik

Wilson, Edmund
1895-1972 .... CLC 1, 2, 3, 8, 24
See also CA 1-4R; 37-40R; CANR 1;
DLB 63; MTCW

Wilson, Ethel Davis (Bryant)
1888(?)-1980 .... CLC 13
See also CA 102; DLB 68; MTCW

Wilson, John (Anthony) Burgess
1917- .... CLC 8, 10, 13
See also Burgess, Anthony
See also CA 1-4R; CANR 2; MTCW

Wilson, John   1785-1854 .... NCLC 5

Wilson, Lanford   1937- .... CLC 7, 14, 36
See also CA 17-20R; CABS 3; DLB 7

Wilson, Robert M.   1944- .... CLC 7, 9
See also CA 49-52; CANR 2; MTCW

Wilson, Robert McLiam   1964- ..... CLC 59
See also CA 132

Wilson, Sloan   1920- .... CLC 32
See also CA 1-4R; CANR 1

Wilson, Snoo   1948-............... CLC 33
See also CA 69-72

Wilson, William S(mith)   1932- ..... CLC 49
See also CA 81-84

Winchilsea, Anne (Kingsmill) Finch Counte
1661-1720 .... LC 3

Windham, Basil
See Wodehouse, P(elham) G(renville)

Wingrove, David (John)   1954-...... CLC 68
See also CA 133

Winters, Janet Lewis .... CLC 41
See also Lewis, Janet
See also DLBY 87

Winters, (Arthur) Yvor
1900-1968 .... CLC 4, 8, 32
See also CA 11-12; 25-28R; CAP 1;
DLB 48; MTCW

Winterson, Jeanette   1959-......... CLC 64
See also CA 136

Wiseman, Frederick   1930-........ CLC 20

Wister, Owen   1860-1938 .... TCLC 21
See also CA 108; DLB 9, 78; SATA 62

Witkacy
See Witkiewicz, Stanislaw Ignacy

Witkiewicz, Stanislaw Ignacy
1885-1939 .... TCLC 8
See also CA 105

Wittig, Monique   1935(?)-.......... CLC 22
See also CA 116; 135; DLB 83

Wittlin, Jozef   1896-1976 .... CLC 25
See also CA 49-52; 65-68; CANR 3

Wodehouse, P(elham) G(renville)
1881-1975 ... CLC 1, 2, 5, 10, 22; SSC 2
See also AITN 2; CA 45-48; 57-60;
CANR 3, 33; CDBLB 1914-1945;
DLB 34; MTCW; SATA 22

Woiwode, L.
See Woiwode, Larry (Alfred)

Woiwode, Larry (Alfred)   1941-... CLC 6, 10
See also CA 73-76; CANR 16; DLB 6

Wojciechowska, Maia (Teresa)
1927- .... CLC 26
See also AAYA 8; CA 9-12R; CANR 4;
CLR 1; MAICYA; SAAS 1; SATA 1, 28

Wolf, Christa   1929- .... CLC 14, 29, 58
See also CA 85-88; DLB 75; MTCW

Wolfe, Gene (Rodman)   1931-....... CLC 25
See also CA 57-60; CAAS 9; CANR 6, 32;
DLB 8

Wolfe, George C.   1954- .... CLC 49

Wolfe, Thomas (Clayton)
1900-1938 .... TCLC 4, 13, 29
See also CA 104; 132; CDALB 1929-1941;
DLB 9, 102; DLBD 2; DLBY 85;
MTCW; WLC

Wolfe, Thomas Kennerly Jr.   1930-
See Wolfe, Tom
See also CA 13-16R; CANR 9, 33; MTCW

Wolfe, Tom .... CLC 1, 2, 9, 15, 35, 51
See also Wolfe, Thomas Kennerly Jr.
See also AAYA 8; AITN 2; BEST 89:1

Wolff, Geoffrey (Ansell)   1937- ..... CLC 41
See also CA 29-32R; CANR 29

Wolff, Sonia
See Levitin, Sonia (Wolff)

Wolff, Tobias (Jonathan Ansell)
1945- .... CLC 39, 64
See also BEST 90:2; CA 114; 117

Wolfram von Eschenbach
c. 1170-c. 1220 .... CMLC 5

Wolitzer, Hilma   1930-............ CLC 17
See also CA 65-68; CANR 18; SATA 31

Wollstonecraft, Mary   1759-1797 ...... LC 5
See also CDBLB 1789-1832; DLB 39, 104

Wonder, Stevie .... CLC 12
See also Morris, Steveland Judkins

Wong, Jade Snow   1922-............ CLC 17
See also CA 109

Woodcott, Keith
See Brunner, John (Kilian Houston)

Woodruff, Robert W.
See Mencken, H(enry) L(ouis)

Woolf, (Adeline) Virginia
1882-1941 .... TCLC 1, 5, 20, 43; SSC 7
See also CA 104; 130; CDBLB 1914-1945;
DLB 36, 100; MTCW; WLC

Woollcott, Alexander (Humphreys)
1887-1943 .... TCLC 5
See also CA 105; DLB 29

Wordsworth, Dorothy
1771-1855 .... NCLC 25
See also DLB 107

Wordsworth, William
1770-1850 .... NCLC 12, 38; PC 4
See also CDBLB 1789-1832; DLB 93, 107;
WLC

Wouk, Herman   1915-......... CLC 1, 9, 38
See also CA 5-8R; CANR 6, 33; DLBY 82;
MTCW

Wright, Charles (Penzel Jr.)
1935- .... CLC 6, 13, 28
See also CA 29-32R; CAAS 7; CANR 23,
36; DLBY 82; MTCW

Wright, Charles Stevenson   1932- ... CLC 49
See also BLC 3; BW; CA 9-12R; CANR 26;
DLB 33

Wright, Jack R.
See Harris, Mark

Wright, James (Arlington)
1927-1980 .... CLC 3, 5, 10, 28
See also AITN 2; CA 49-52; 97-100;
CANR 4, 34; DLB 5; MTCW

Wright, Judith (Arandell)
1915- .... CLC 11, 53
See also CA 13-16R; CANR 31; MTCW;
SATA 14

Wright, L(aurali) R. .... CLC 44
See also CA 138

Wright, Richard B(ruce)   1937- ...... CLC 6
See also CA 85-88; DLB 53

Wright, Richard (Nathaniel)
1908-1960 ... CLC 1, 3, 4, 9, 14, 21, 48;
                                       SSC 2
See also AAYA 5; BLC 3; BW; CA 108;
CDALB 1929-1941; DLB 76, 102;
DLBD 2; MTCW; WLC

Wright, Rick   1945-............... CLC 35
See also Pink Floyd

Wright, Rowland
See Wells, Carolyn

Wright, Stephen   1946-............. CLC 33

Wright, Willard Huntington   1888-1939
See Van Dine, S. S.
See also CA 115

Wright, William   1930-............ CLC 44
See also CA 53-56; CANR 7, 23

Wu Ch'eng-en   1500(?)-1582(?)........ LC 7

Wu Ching-tzu   1701-1754 .... LC 2

Wurlitzer, Rudolph   1938(?)- ... CLC 2, 4, 15
See also CA 85-88

Wycherley, William   1641-1715 .... LC 8
See also CDBLB 1660-1789; DLB 80

Wylie, Elinor (Morton Hoyt)
1885-1928 .... TCLC 8
See also CA 105; DLB 9, 45

Wylie, Philip (Gordon)   1902-1971... CLC 43
See also CA 21-22; 33-36R; CAP 2; DLB 9

Wyndham, John
See Harris, John (Wyndham Parkes Lucas) Beynon

Wyss, Johann David Von
1743-1818 .... NCLC 10
See also MAICYA; SATA 27, 29

Yakumo Koizumi
See Hearn, (Patricio) Lafcadio (Tessima Carlos)

Yanez, Jose Donoso
See Donoso (Yanez), Jose

Yanovsky, Basile S.
See Yanovsky, V(assily) S(emenovich)

Yanovsky, V(assily) S(emenovich)
1906-1989 .... CLC 2, 18
See also CA 97-100; 129

Yates, Richard 1926- .... CLC 7, 8, 23
See also CA 5-8R; CANR 10; DLB 2; DLBY 81

Yeats, W. B.
See Yeats, William Butler

Yeats, William Butler
1865-1939 .... TCLC 1, 11, 18, 31
See also CA 104; 127; CDBLB 1890-1914; DLB 10, 19, 98; MTCW; WLC

Yehoshua, Abraham B. 1936- ... CLC 13, 31
See also CA 33-36R

Yep, Laurence Michael 1948- ...... CLC 35
See also AAYA 5; CA 49-52; CANR 1; CLR 3, 17; DLB 52; MAICYA; SATA 7, 69

Yerby, Frank G(arvin)
1916-1991 .... CLC 1, 7, 22
See also BLC 3; BW; CA 9-12R; 136; CANR 16; DLB 76; MTCW

Yesenin, Sergei Alexandrovich
See Esenin, Sergei (Alexandrovich)

Yevtushenko, Yevgeny (Alexandrovich)
1933- .... CLC 1, 3, 13, 26, 51
See also CA 81-84; CANR 33; MTCW

Yezierska, Anzia 1885(?)-1970 ..... CLC 46
See also CA 126; 89-92; DLB 28; MTCW

Yglesias, Helen 1915- .... CLC 7, 22
See also CA 37-40R; CANR 15; MTCW

Yokomitsu Riichi 1898-1947 ...... TCLC 47

York, Jeremy
See Creasey, John

York, Simon
See Heinlein, Robert A(nson)

Yorke, Henry Vincent 1905-1974 ... CLC 13
See Green, Henry
See also CA 85-88; 49-52

Young, Al(bert James) 1939- .... CLC 19
See also BLC 3; BW; CA 29-32R; CANR 26; DLB 33

Young, Andrew (John) 1885-1971 .... CLC 5
See also CA 5-8R; CANR 7, 29

Young, Collier
See Bloch, Robert (Albert)

Young, Edward 1683-1765 .... LC 3
See also DLB 95

Young, Neil 1945- .... CLC 17
See also CA 110

Yourcenar, Marguerite
1903-1987 .... CLC 19, 38, 50
See also CA 69-72; CANR 23; DLB 72; DLBY 88; MTCW

Yurick, Sol 1925- .... CLC 6
See also CA 13-16R; CANR 25

Zamiatin, Yevgenii
See Zamyatin, Evgeny Ivanovich

Zamyatin, Evgeny Ivanovich
1884-1937 .... TCLC 8, 37
See also CA 105

Zangwill, Israel 1864-1926 .... TCLC 16
See also CA 109; DLB 10

Zappa, Francis Vincent Jr. 1940-
See Zappa, Frank
See also CA 108

Zappa, Frank .... CLC 17
See also Zappa, Francis Vincent Jr.

Zaturenska, Marya 1902-1982 .... CLC 6, 11
See also CA 13-16R; 105; CANR 22

Zelazny, Roger (Joseph) 1937- ..... CLC 21
See also AAYA 7; CA 21-24R; CANR 26; DLB 8; MTCW; SATA 39, 57

Zhdanov, Andrei A(lexandrovich)
1896-1948 .... TCLC 18
See also CA 117

Zhukovsky, Vasily 1783-1852 .... NCLC 35

Ziegenhagen, Eric .... CLC 55

Zimmer, Jill Schary
See Robinson, Jill

Zimmerman, Robert
See Dylan, Bob

Zindel, Paul 1936- .... CLC 6, 26
See also AAYA 2; CA 73-76; CANR 31; CLR 3; DLB 7, 52; MAICYA; MTCW; SATA 16, 58

Zinov'Ev, A. A.
See Zinoviev, Alexander (Aleksandrovich)

Zinoviev, Alexander (Aleksandrovich)
1922- .... CLC 19
See also CA 116; 133; CAAS 10

Zoilus
See Lovecraft, H(oward) P(hillips)

Zola, Emile 1840-1902 ... TCLC 1, 6, 21, 41
See also CA 104; WLC

Zoline, Pamela 1941- .... CLC 62

Zorrilla y Moral, Jose 1817-1893 .. NCLC 6

Zoshchenko, Mikhail (Mikhailovich)
1895-1958 .... TCLC 15
See also CA 115

Zuckmayer, Carl 1896-1977 .... CLC 18
See also CA 69-72; DLB 56

Zuk, Georges
See Skelton, Robin

Zukofsky, Louis
1904-1978 .... CLC 1, 2, 4, 7, 11, 18
See also CA 9-12R; 77-80; CANR 39; DLB 5; MTCW

Zweig, Paul 1935-1984 .... CLC 34, 42
See also CA 85-88; 113

Zweig, Stefan 1881-1942 .... TCLC 17
See also CA 112; DLB 81, 118

Literary Criticism Series
Cumulative Topic Index

This index lists all topic entries in the Gale Literary Criticism Series *Contemporary Literary Criticism, Literature Criticism from 1400 to 1800, Nineteenth-Century Literature Criticism,* and *Twentieth-Century Literary Criticism.*

Topic Index

Topic Index

NCLC Cumulative Nationality Index

Nationality Index

NCLC 38

ISBN 0-8103-9191-0